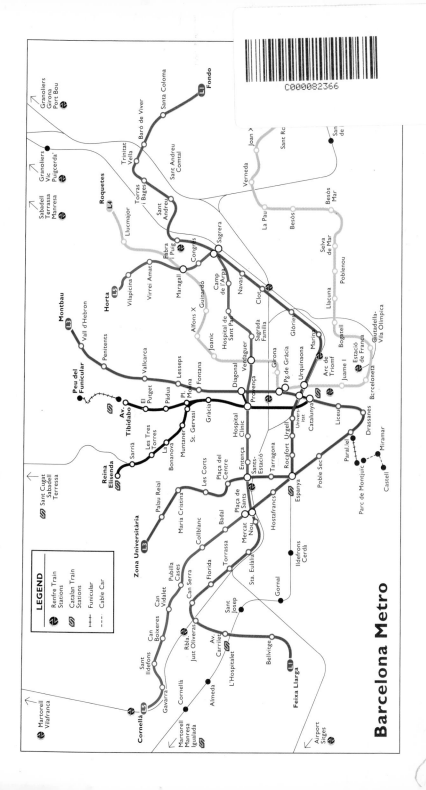

Barcelona Metro

Madrid Metro

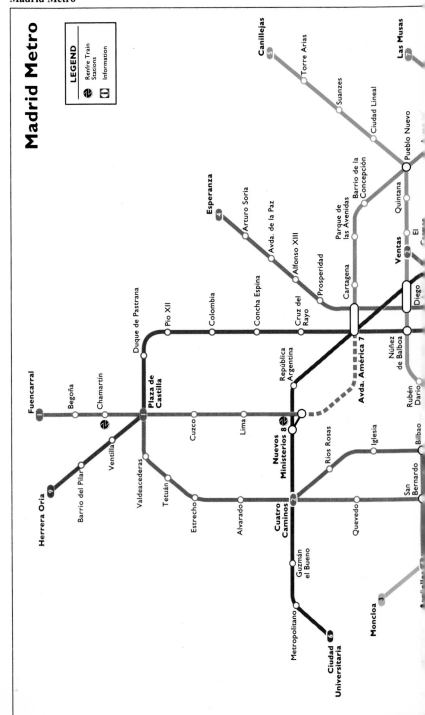

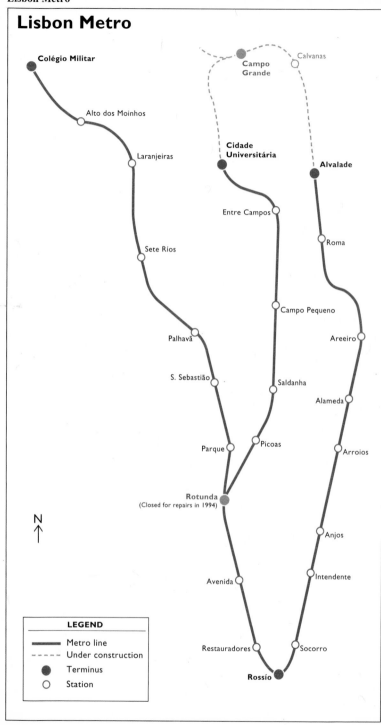

Let's Go

SPAIN & PORTUGAL

is the best book for anyone traveling on a budget. Here's why:

▧ No other guidebook has as many budget listings.

In Spain and Portugal we list over 6,000 budget travel bargains. We tell you the cheapest way to get around, and where to get an inexpensive and satisfying meal once you've arrived. We give hundreds of money-saving tips that anyone can use, plus invaluable advice on discounts and deals for students, children, families, and senior travelers.

▧ Let's Go researchers have to make it on their own.

Our Harvard-Radcliffe researcher-writers travel on budgets as tight as your own—no expense accounts, no free hotel rooms.

▧ Let's Go is completely revised each year.

We don't just update the prices, we go back to the place. If a charming café has become an overpriced tourist trap, we'll replace the listing with a new and better one.

▧ No other guidebook includes all this:

Honest, engaging coverage of both the cities and the countryside; up-to-the-minute prices, directions, addresses, phone numbers, and opening hours; in-depth essays on local culture, history, and politics; comprehensive listings on transportation between and within regions and cities; straight advice on work and study, budget accommodations, sights, nightlife, and food; detailed city and regional maps; and much more.

▧ Let's Go is for anyone who wants to see Spain and Portugal on a budget.

Books by Let's Go, Inc.

EUROPE

Let's Go: Europe

Let's Go: Austria & Switzerland

Let's Go: Britain & Ireland

Let's Go: Eastern Europe

Let's Go: France

Let's Go: Germany

Let's Go: Greece & Turkey

Let's Go: Ireland

Let's Go: Italy

Let's Go: London

Let's Go: Paris

Let's Go: Rome

Let's Go: Spain & Portugal

NORTH & CENTRAL AMERICA

Let's Go: USA & Canada

Let's Go: Alaska & The Pacific Northwest

Let's Go: California

Let's Go: New York City

Let's Go: Washington, D.C.

Let's Go: Mexico

MIDDLE EAST & ASIA

Let's Go: Israel & Egypt

Let's Go: Thailand

Let's Go

The Budget Guide to

SPAIN &
PORTUGAL
1995

María Colbert
Editor

Yael Schenker
Associate Editor

Manuel Francisco Cachán
Assistant Editor

Written by
Let's Go, Inc.
A subsidiary of
Harvard Student Agencies, Inc.

MACMILLAN

HELPING LET'S GO

If you have suggestions or corrections, or just want to share your discoveries, drop us a line. We read every piece of correspondence, whether a 10-page e-mail letter, a velveteen Elvis postcard, or, as in one case, a collage. All suggestions are passed along to our researcher-writers. Please note that mail received after May 5, 1995 will probably be too late for the 1996 book, but will be retained for the following edition.

Address mail to:

Let's Go: Spain & Portugal
Let's Go, Inc.
I Story Street
Cambridge, MA 02138
USA

Or send e-mail to:
letsgo@delphi.com

In addition to the invaluable travel advice our readers share with us, many are kind enough to offer their services as researchers or editors. Unfortunately, the charter of Let's Go, Inc. and Harvard Student Agencies, Inc. enables us to employ only currently enrolled Harvard-Radcliffe students.

Published in Great Britain 1995 by Macmillan, Cavaye Place, London SW10 9PG.

10 9 8 7 6 5 4 3 2 1

Maps by David Lindroth, copyright © 1995, 1994, 1993, 1992, 1991, 1990, 1989, 1986 by St. Martin's Press, Inc.

Published in the United States of America by St. Martin's Press, Inc.

ISBN: 0 333 62229 4

Let's Go: **Spain & Portugal** is written by the Publishing Division of Let's Go, Inc., 1 Story Street, Cambridge, MA 02138.

Let's Go® is a registered trademark of Let's Go, Inc. Printed in the U.S.A. on recycled paper with biodegradable soy ink.

About Let's Go

Back in 1960, a few students at Harvard University got together to produce a 20-page pamphlet offering a collection of tips on budget travel in Europe. For three years, Harvard Student Agencies, a student-run nonprofit corporation, had been doing a brisk business booking charter flights to Europe; this modest, mimeographed packet was offered to passengers as an extra. The following year, students traveling to Europe researched the first full-fledged edition of *Let's Go: Europe*, a pocket-sized book featuring advice on shoestring travel, irreverent write-ups of sights, and a decidedly youthful slant.

Throughout the 60s, the guides reflected the times: one section of the 1968 *Let's Go: Europe* talked about "Street Singing in Europe on No Dollars a Day." During the 70s, *Let's Go* gradually became a large-scale operation, adding regional European guides and expanding coverage into North Africa and Asia. The 80s saw the arrival of *Let's Go: USA & Canada* and *Let's Go: Mexico*, as well as regional North American guides; in the 90s we introduced five in-depth city guides to Paris, London, Rome, New York City, and Washington, DC. And as the budget travel world expands, so do we; the first edition of *Let's Go: Thailand* hit the shelves last year, and this year's edition adds coverage of Malaysia, Singapore, Tokyo, and Hong Kong.

This year we're proud to announce the birth of *Let's Go: Eastern Europe*—the most comprehensive guide to this renascent region, with more practical information and insider tips than any other. *Let's Go: Eastern Europe* brings our total number of titles, with their spirit of adventure and reputation for honesty, accuracy, and editorial integrity, to 21.

We've seen a lot in 35 years. *Let's Go: Europe* is now the world's #1 best selling international guide, translated into seven languages. And our guides are still researched, written, and produced entirely by students who know first-hand how to see the world on the cheap.

Every spring, we recruit over 100 researchers and 50 editors to write our books anew. Come summertime, after several months of training, researchers hit the road for seven weeks of exploration, from Bangkok to Budapest, Anchorage to Ankara. With pen and notebook in hand, a few changes of underwear stuffed in our backpacks, and a budget as tight as yours, we visit every *pensione*, *palapa*, pizzeria, café, club, campground, or castle we can find to make sure you'll get the most out of *your* trip.

We've put the best of our discoveries into the book you're now holding. A brand-new edition of each guide hits the shelves every year, only months after it is researched, so you know you're getting the most reliable, up-to-date, and comprehensive information available. The budget travel world is constantly changing, and where other guides quickly become obsolete, our annual research keeps you abreast of the very latest travel insights. And even as you read this, work on next year's editions is well underway.

At *Let's Go*, we think of budget travel not only as a means of cutting down on costs, but as a way of breaking down a few walls as well. Living cheap and simple on the road brings you closer to the real people and places you've been saving up to visit. This book will ease your anxieties and answer your questions about the basics—to help *you* get off the beaten track and explore. We encourage you to put *Let's Go* away now and then and strike out on your own. As any seasoned traveler will tell you, the best discoveries are often those you make yourself. If you find something worth sharing, drop us a line. We're at Let's Go, Inc., 1 Story Street, Cambridge, MA, 02138, USA (e-mail: letsgo@delphi.com).

Happy travels!

Don't forget to write.

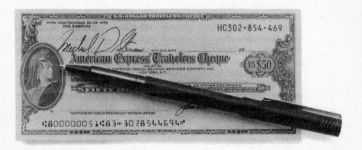

Now that you've said, "Let's go," it's time to say
"Let's get American Express® Travelers Cheques." If they are lost or
stolen, you can get a fast and full refund virtually anywhere you
travel. So before you leave be sure and write.

Contents

x ■ CONTENTS

Maps

Acknowledgments

Con pan y vino se anda el camino. Gracias to our RWs, your dedication and sense of humor kept us truckin'. To all our timely connections in Spain—Carmen and Pablo Sala, Angeles Goicoa—thanks for being there when we couldn't be. To Brad Epps—the most dedicated of professors—thank you for introducing us, and sharing your knowledge of all things Iberian. Sean's wit, humor, and insight were invaluable to our Morocco section. The Bosserts were the best of hosts, here and in Portugal. Thank you for your outstanding generosity. Alexis saved our lives (and our computer files) more than once; her expertise and level-headedness kept us sane. Thank you to *nuestras familias*—Ana Colbert's keen eye was especially priceless.

To all those francophiles—Natalie, Livy, Liz, Miranda—*merci* to *vous*. Your consistent cheer and enviable acuity made us never want to leave the office. Thank you for pulling through to the end. Joe and the Mullin family, your Portuguese perspective perked up Portugal. Manny, *mil gracias por tu paciencia simpática y tu ayuda.* Stylish Declan and Anna were sharp in work and in play; it was our pleasure working with you. Thank you Cina for your journal, Alp for your spontaneous prosaic graces, Seth for your editing, Matt and Sam for your visits. To Nadim, for all the long-distance attention. To Jimmy, Enrique, David, Phoebe, and Hilary—thanks for your familial cheer. *Un montón de gracias a todos.* **MC and YS**

Thanks Maria and Yael for letting me work with you. Thanks to those who got me here: God, Mami y Papi, Tía Sara, la familia. Thanks also: Mirta Lopez, Gil, Sandrita, Jamie, Kristi, Miguel, Rudy, Natán. *A Cuba: ¡Serás Libre! (y pronto)* **MFC**

■ Staff

Editor	María Colbert
Associate Editor	Yael Schenker
Assistant Editor	Manuel Francisco Cachán
Managing Editor	Joseph E. Mullin III
Publishing Director	Pete Keith
Production Manager	Alexis G. Averbuck
Production Assistant	Elizabeth J. Stein
Financial Manager	Matt Heid
Assistant General Manager	Anne E. Chisholm
Sales Group Manager	Sherice R. Guillory
Sales Department Coordinator	Andrea N. Taylor
Sales Group Representatives	Eli K. Aheto
	Timur Okay Harry Hiçyılmaz
	Arzhang Kamerei
	Hollister Jane Leopold
	David L. Yuan
President	Lucienne D. Lester
General Manager	Richard M. Olken

Researcher-Writers

Sonia Batra *Portugal*
We asked for a model researcher, and the powers that be delivered. Sonia covered Portugal with thoroughness and efficiency, mastering the language before she left and sending back picture-perfect copy batches. Her confidence in dealing with sticky situations left us impressed with her savvy and diplomacy, her research left us assured and delighted with her R-W skills.

Daniela Bleichmar *Andalucía*
Darling of Seville, Daniela charmed her way across southern Spain, downing cupfuls of *tinto de verano* to survive the heat and loosen her pen. Sharp and gregarious, Daniela convinced the locals to reveal their best-kept secrets. Her skill in discovering popular hang-outs was unparalleled, and will be much appreciated by those who follow in her foot steps.

David Joerg *Cataluña, Valencia, Murcia, Islas Baleares*
We forwarded pounds and pounds of Dave's mail to Spain; he promptly sent back pages of racy copy, candid evaluations of previous researchers, and a few burlesque postcards. Discriminating in his choice of destinations, David island-hopped with style. His critical RW eye deftly reduced each locale to concise, original images, penned by a competent hand.

Christopher Kagay *Morocco*
Reflective and precise, Chris braved bedbugs and hustlers to discover Morocco's sundry beauties. He thought of everything, and his superb copy reflected tireless efforts to include multiple perspectives. Chris's dedication and engagement never flagged—last minute faxes and bits of advice ensured the most up-to-date, accurate Moroccan coverage.

Daryna McKeand *Andalucía*
Spunky and outgoing, Daryna took off for the sunny south at a moment's notice, and bounced back into the office with a mile-high pile of information and brochures. She volunteered for every task, no matter tedious, showering us with stories, pictures, and key pieces of information. The coverage of Andalucía benefitted from her pop culture expertise and her loyalty to *Let's Go*.

Gabriel Piedrahita *País Vasco, La Rioja, Navarra, Aragón, Costa Brava, Catalan Pyrenees, Soria*
Indefatigable, meticulous, and independent, Gabriel wrote reams of romantic prose on northern Spain. Fighting the battle against cynicism, he thoughtfully and eloquently expanded his itinerary. Despite a demanding schedule, Gabriel delivered flawless research, and still found time to dash through the streets of Pamplona, one step ahead of the bulls.

Kurt Schumacher *Galicia, Asturias, Cantabria, Castilla y León, northern Portugal*
As long as the sun was shining, the sea was blue, his girlfriend still loved him, and Jimmy Buffet was still alive (phew!), Kurt was happy as a clam. Always flexible and upbeat, Kurt met the challenges of a provincial itinerary with a positive outlook and a clear head. His lucidity and smile transformed undiscovered sights on the northern coast into appealing, well-documented *Let's Go* destinations.

Erica Werner *Madrid, Castilla la Mancha, Castilla y León, Extremadura*
Half researcher, half art critic, Erica lost herself in the halls of the Prado, and delved deep into Spain's artistic and mythical splendors. She conquered the heat and the frustrations of feisty ATMs to produce the neatest illustrated copy *Let's Go* has ever seen. With a vocabulary more expansive than the confines of our dictionary, Erica hammed up the sights of central Spain with quirky stories and intelligent research.

How To Use This Book

Let's Go blurs the distinction between doing and teaching: our researchers know first-hand what it's like to arrive into a town wanting only a bed and getting only bureaucracy; how it feels to crave a real meal while anticipating yet another bread and fruit run. These are people for whom finding convenient accommodations, inexpensive food, funky new sights, and interesting aspects of old ones is a mission.

In the section **Planning Your Trip** we guide you through the gobs of tasks—from obtaining a passport to packing—that need to get done before you go. In **Getting There,** we exhaust the possibilities for cheap travel to Spain and Portugal. We also have **Essentials** sections at the beginning of each country's coverage. They provide information about getting around, accommodations, food and drink, communications, and money. Addresses of your home country's embassy and consulates are included. Next comes **Life and Times,** accounts of each country's history and culture. At the back of the book in the **Appendices** are flip-to references for translations of Castilian, Catalan, Galician, and Portuguese words and more country-specific practical information. Appendices include phone codes, clothing sizes, festivals and holiday lists, climate information, and more.

For each town we cover, the **Orientation and Practical Information** section describes the town's accessibility from other points in the country and the layout of the town, as well as addresses and phone numbers of relevant places (such as tourist offices) and people (such as police). For larger cities, *Let's Go* also provides a map and information about airports, student travel and American Express offices, hospitals, bookstores, laundromats, and resources for travelers with special needs. **Accommodations, Food, Sights,** and **Entertainment** are self-explanatory.

Let's Go: Spain & Portugal divides Iberia into 22 regions. The chapters on Spain are arranged geographically in two clockwise spirals, a tight one around Madrid and a larger one moving from the Castillas northwest to Galicia and round the periphery. Portugal's scheme takes the reader from Lisboa north through Estremadura, along the coast to the northern frontier, then south to the Algarve. This method closely reflects the peninsula's transportation network. Morocco begins with Tangier, the point of entry from Europe, then swings southwest through the northern cities and down to the tip of the desert.

A NOTE TO OUR READERS

The information for this book is gathered by *Let's Go*'s researchers during the late spring and summer months. Each listing is derived from the assigned researcher's opinion based upon his or her visit at a particular time. The opinions are expressed in a candid and forthright manner. Other travelers might disagree. Those traveling at a different time may have different experiences since prices, dates, hours, and conditions are always subject to change. You are urged to check beforehand to avoid inconvenience and surprises. Travel always involves a certain degree of risk, especially in low-cost areas. When traveling, especially on a budget, you should always take particular care to ensure your safety.

Fortunately, when you travel on Rail Europe, there are some sights you'll miss.

No goofy hats. No big sunglasses. No plaid shirts with striped shorts. Instead, on Rail Europe, you'll experience Europe the way Europeans do. You'll enjoy scenic countryside no one else can show you. And meet unique and interesting people. In short, you'll explore Europe the way it was meant to be explored. When it comes to visiting 33 European countries, get real. Go Rail Europe. Because traveling any other way could end up showing you some pretty dreadful sights. To learn more, call your travel agent or 1-800-4-EURAIL. (1-800-438-7245)

Rail Europe

Europe. To the trained eye.

■ ESSENTIALS

PLANNING YOUR TRIP

■■■ WHEN TO GO

Traveling during the **off-season** (or "low season," *temporada baja*) has various advantages, such as sparser crowds, lower prices for accommodations and transportation, and more vacant rooms. Since off-season coincides with the academic year, the university towns spring to life. However, some small and tourist-oriented (e.g, seaside) towns virtually shut down in off-season; tourist offices and sights maintain shorter hours and some restaurants close. Overcast skies and cold temperatures in certain regions may make traveling unpleasant.

High season (*temporada alta*) in Spain and Portugal is summer (roughly June-Sept.) for coastal and interior regions. For mountainous ski resorts, winter is high season. In many places, high season includes **Semana Santa** (Holy Week, starting the Sunday before Easter Sunday) and festival days, too. In August most of Europe goes on holiday, leaving behind scores of closed restaurants, lodgings, and offices.

■■■ DOCUMENTS & FORMALITIES

Apply early for travel documents to save yourself needless headaches. Some agencies have backlogs.

PASSPORTS

You must have a valid passport to enter and leave Spain, Portugal, and Morocco. (Generally, Morocco does not enforce the Arab League ban on allowing people whose passports bear an Israeli stamp into the country. You should have no problems, but you can apply for a new passport if you're concerned.) Carry your passport with you at all times. In all three countries (Spain, Portugal, and Morocco), the police have the right to see it on demand.

Before you leave, you should photocopy your entire passport. Keep the copy, as well as an extra proof of citizenship (expired passport or a birth certificate) and maybe even a spare set of passport photos, in a separate part of your baggage. It's also wise to leave a copy with a relative or friend back home. While a copy doesn't serve as a substitute for a valid passport, it expedites the process of replacing one.

If you lose your passport while traveling, notify the local police and the nearest consulate of your home government immediately. Your consulate will be able to issue you a new passport or temporary traveling papers.

U.S. citizens may apply for a passport, valid for 10 years (5yr. if under 18), at any federal or state courthouse or post office authorized to accept passport applications, or at a U.S. Passport Agency (Boston, Chicago, Honolulu, Houston, Los Angeles, Miami, New Orleans, New York, Philadelphia, San Francisco, Seattle, Stamford, CT, and Washington, DC). Parents must apply in person for children under 13. You must apply in person if it is your first passport, if you're under 18, or if your current passport is more than 12 years old or was issued before your 18th birthday. The fee is US$65 (US$55 if the passport is a renewal, US$40 if the applicant is under 18). For information, call the U.S. Passport Information's 24-hr. recording (tel. (202) 647-0518), contact the Passport Agency nearest you, or ask at the post office. If your passport is lost or stolen in the U.S., report it in writing

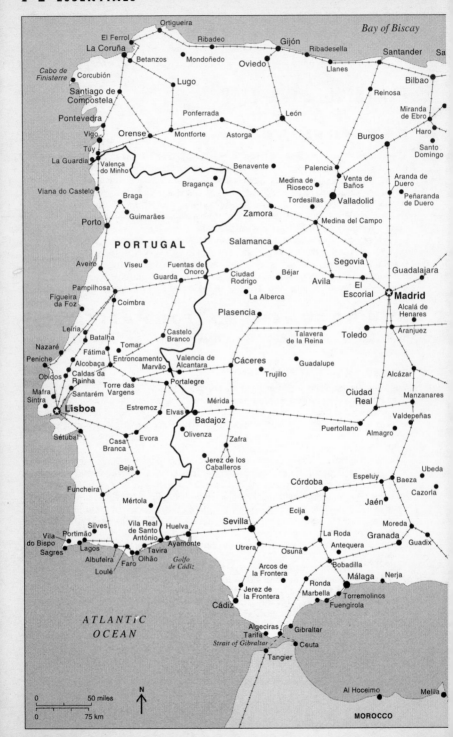

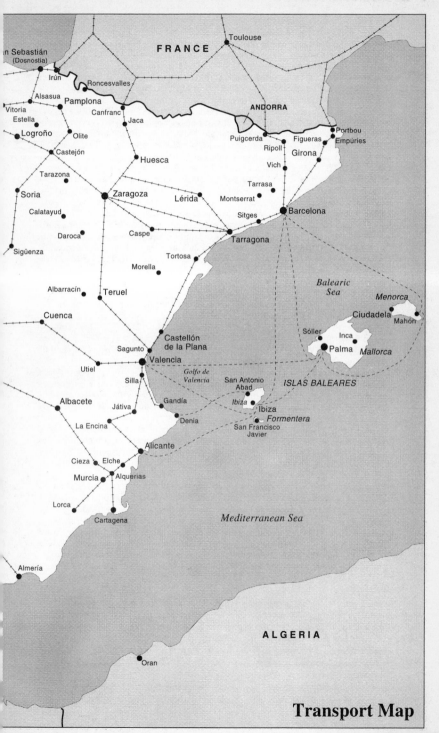

Transport Map

to **Passport Services**, 1111 19th St., NW, Department of State, Washington, DC 20522-1705, or to the nearest passport agency.

Canadian citizens can pick up an application form in English or French for a five-year, non-renewable passport at all passport offices, post offices, and most travel agencies. Canadian citizens may apply in person at one of 28 regional Passport Offices across Canada; citizens residing abroad should contact the nearest Canadian embassy or consulate for an application form and instructions. To apply by mail, send a completed application with appropriate documentation and the CDN$35 fee to Passport Office, Foreign Affairs, Ottawa, Ont. K1A 0G3. Processing time is approximately five days for in-person applications, three weeks for mailed ones. For more information, call the 24-hr. information number (tel. (800) 567-6868) from Canada only, or refer to the booklet *Bon Voyage, But...*, available free from any passport office or from Info-Export (BPTE), Foreign Affairs, Ottawa, Ont. K1A 0G2.

British citizens can obtain either a Full British Passport or a British Visitor's Passport. For a Full British Passport, valid for ten years, apply in person or by mail to one of six passport office (London, Newport, Liverpool, Peterborough, Glasgow, Belfast). Application forms are also available from main post offices. The fee is £18. The one-year British Visitor's Passport covers travel to some western European countries and Bermuda only. It is not valid for the purpose of employment, nor for a visit of longer than three months in any one country. Applicants must be residents of the U.K., the Channel Islands, or the Isle of Man. The Visitor's Passport may be obtained for £12 at main post offices in England, Scotland, and Wales, and from passport offices in Northern Ireland, the Channel Islands, and the Isle of Man.

Irish citizens can apply for a passport by mail to either the Department of Foreign Affairs, Passport Office, Setanta Centre, Molesworth St., Dublin 2 (tel. (01) 671 16 33) or the Passport Office, 1A South Mall, Cork (tel. (021) 27 25 25). You can obtain an application form at a local Garda station or passport office. Passports cost £45 and are valid for ten years. Citizens younger than 18 and older than 65 can request a 3-year passport (£10).

Australian citizens must apply for a passport in person at a local post office, a passport office, or an Australian diplomatic mission overseas. An appointment may be necessary. Passport offices are located in Adelaide, Brisbane, Canberra, Darwin, Hobart, Melbourne, Newcastle, Perth and Sydney. Application fees are adjusted every three months.

New Zealand passport applicants must contact their local Link Centre, travel agency, or New Zealand Representative for an application form, which they must complete and mail to the New Zealand Passport Office, Documents of National Identity Division, Department of Internal Affairs, P.O. Box 10-526, Wellington (tel. (04) 474 81 00). Citizens applying from overseas should send the passport application to the nearest embassy, high commission, or consulate that is authorized to issue passports. The application fee is NZ$80 for an application submitted in New Zealand and NZ$130 for one submitted overseas (under age 16: NZ$40; NZ$65).

South African citizens can apply for a passport at any Department of Home Affairs Office. Two photos, either a birth certificate or an identity book, and the R38-00 fee must accompany a completed application. For further information, contact the nearest Department of Home Affairs Office.

VISAS

A visa is a stamp in your passport by a foreign government allowing you to stay in their country for a specified period of time. **American** and **Canadian citizens** need only a passport to remain in Spain for 90, Portugal for 60, and Morocco for 90 days. **British citizens** may remain in Spain, Portugal, and Morocco for 90 days. **New Zealand citizens** may remain in Spain for 30, Portugal for 60, and Morocco for 90 days. **Australian citizens** may remain in Portugal for 60 days, Morocco for 90 days, and require a visa for entry to Spain.

If you want to stay for longer, apply for a visa at the country's embassy or consulate in your home country well before your departure (see Useful Addresses: Embassies and Consulates for addresses). Unless you're a student, extending your stay once abroad is more difficult. You must contact the country's immigration officials or local police well before your time is up, although in Portugal you may apply to the *Serviço de Estrangeiros* seven days prior to your original date of expiration. You must show sound proof of financial resources.

For more **information,** send for the U.S. government pamphlet *Foreign Entry Requirements* (Item 356A, US$0.50). Mail a check for US$0.50 to R Woods, Consumer Information Center, Pueblo, CO 81009 (tel. (719) 948-4000). If you don't want to deal with federal bureaucracy, contact **Center for International Business and Travel (CIBT),** 25 West 43rd St., Suite 1420, New York, NY 10036 (tel. (800) 925-2428 or (212) 575-2811 from NYC). This organization secures visas for travel to and from all possible countries. The service charge varies; the average cost for a U.S. citizen is US$15-20 per visa.

CUSTOMS

Don't be alarmed by customs procedures. Customs officials may snoop through your most personal possessions both when you enter and leave Spain, Portugal, or Morocco and upon return home. The rules for importing and exporting are exceedingly complicated.

Imports

First, there's an **allowance** on what you can bring into a country. Anything exceeding the allowance must be **declared** and is charged a **duty.** All three countries permit up to 200 cigarettes and one still and one movie camera, with 10 rolls of film per camera. Note that it's illegal to import Moroccan *dirhams*.

Before leaving home you should make a list of the serial number, model, make, and/or description of any expensive items, especially foreign-made ones, that you're bringing into the country. (Canadian citizens should do this on the Y-38 forms provided by the customs offices.) Have your list stamped by a customs official prior to departure in order to prove that you really did buy that valuable Spanish belt at Macy's, not in Madrid.

Exports

On leaving a country, you must **declare** all articles acquired abroad; keep receipts for everything that you bought. Note that items bought at duty-free shops are *not* exempt from duty when you return home. However, only the truly profligate budget traveler will exceed the maximum allowances and be compelled to deal closely with customs officials.

Also note that it's illegal to export **Moroccan dirhams.** On leaving Morocco, you may convert 50% of the *dirhams* in your possession (100% if you've been in the country less than 48hrs.) by presenting exchange slips (to prove they were purchased at the official rate) to an authorized bank at your point of departure. Save your receipts as proof each time you change money, and try not to end up with too many extra *dirhams*.

U.S. citizens returning home must declare all merchandise acquired abroad, so it's wise to keep sales slips handy in carry-on luggage. The first $400 worth of merchandise intended for personal or household use may be entered duty-free. This personal exemption is good once every 30 days, provided you have been out of the country for at least 48hrs., and may include: 100 cigars, 200 cigarettes, and 1 liter (33.8 fl. oz.) alcoholic beverages. (You must be 21 or older to import alcoholic beverages.) The next $1000 worth of merchandise is subject to a flat 10% duty rate. For more information about U.S. Customs procedures, request the booklet *Know Before You Go* from the U.S. Customs Service, Box 7407, Washington, DC 20044 (tel. (202) 927-6724). Foreign nationals living in the U.S. should request a copy of *Customs Hints for Visitors (Nonresidents)* from the same address, as somewhat different regulations may apply.

TOP 5 Ways to Save Money While Traveling

5. Ship yourself in a crate marked "Livestock." Remember to poke holes in the crate.

4. Board a train dressed as Elvis and sneer and say "The King rides for free."

3. Ask if you can walk through the Channel Tunnel.

2. Board the plane dressed as an airline pilot, nod to the flight attendants, and hide in the rest room until the plane lands.

1. Bring a balloon to the airline ticket counter, kneel, breathe in the helium, and ask for the kiddie fare.

But if you're serious about saving money while you're traveling abroad, just get an ISIC--the International Student Identity Card. Discounts for students on international airfares, hotels and motels, car rentals, international phone calls, financial services, and more.

International Student Identity Card
Carte Internationale d'Etudiant/Carnet Internacional de estudiante

Family name/Nom de famille/Apellido
GRAHAM
First name/Prénom/Nombre
DONNA
Born/Né le/Nacido
10/29/70   Date of Issue
              7/5/94
Nationality/Nationalité/Nacionalidad
USA
Studies at/Etablissement/Estab. de Enseñanza
U OREGON
STUDENT

Canadian citizens who remain abroad for at least one week may bring back up to CDN$300 worth of goods duty-free once every calendar year; goods that exceed this allowance will be taxed at 12%. Citizens over the legal age (which varies by province) may import in person (not through the mail) up to 200 cigarettes, 50 cigars, 400g loose tobacco, 1.14 liters wine or alcohol, and 355ml beer; the value of these products is included in the CDN$300 allowance. For more information, write to Canadian Customs, 2265 St. Laurent Blvd., Ottawa, Ont. K1G 4K3 (tel. (613) 993-0534, from within Canada (800) 461-9999).

British citizens or visitors arriving in the U.K. from outside the EU must declare any goods in excess of the following allowances: (1) 200 cigarettes, or 100 cigarillos, or 50 cigars, or 250g tobacco; (2) 2 liters still table wine; (3) 1 liter strong liquor (over 22% vol.), or 2 liters fortified or sparkling wine or other liquor, or 2 liters additional still table wine allowance; (4) 60cc/ml perfume; (5) 250cc/ml toilet water; and (6) £136 worth of all other goods. You must be over 17 to import liquor or tobacco. These allowances also apply to duty-free purchases within the EU, except for the last category, other goods, which then has an allowance of £71. Goods obtained duty and tax paid for personal use within the EU do not require any further customs duty. For information, contact Her Majesty's Customs and Excise, Custom House, Heathrow Airport North, Hounslow, Middlesex, TW6 2LA (tel. (0181) 910 37 44; fax (0181) 910 37 65).

Irish citizens and visitors to Ireland must declare everything in excess of the following allowances for goods obtained outside the EU or duty and tax free in the EU: (1) 200 cigarettes, or 100 cigarillos, or 50 cigars, or 250g tobacco; (2) 1 liter alcoholic drinks over 22% vol., or 2 liters alcoholic drinks under 22% vol.; (3) 2 liters still wine; (4) 50g perfume; (5) ¼ liter toilet water; (6) IR£34 other goods per adult traveler (IR£17 per traveler under 15 years of age). Travelers under 17 are not entitled to any allowance for tobacco or alcoholic products. Goods obtained duty and tax paid for personal use in another EU country will not be subject to additional customs duty. For more information, contact The Revenue Commissioners, Dublin Castle (tel. (01) 679-2777; fax (01) 671-2021) or The Collector of Customs and Excise, The Custom House, Dublin 1.

Australian citizens and visitors may bring an unlimited amount of Australian and/ or foreign cash into Australia; however, amounts of A$5000 or more, or equivalent in foreign currency, must be reported. Each traveler over age 18 may bring back 1 liter of liquor and 250 cigarettes or 250g of tobacco products into Australia duty/tax free. In addition, a duty/tax free allowance of A$400 (under 18, A$200) is available for other goods intended as gifts. For further information, contact the Australian Customs Service, 5 Constitution Ave., Canberra, ACT 2601 (tel. (6) 275 62 55; fax (6) 275 69 89).

New Zealand citizens may bring home up to NZ$700 worth of goods duty-free for personal use or unsolicited gifts. The concession is 200 cigarettes (1 carton), 250g tobacco, or 50 cigars, or a combination of all three not to exceed 250g. You may also import 4.5 liters beer or wine and 1.125 liters liquor. Only travelers over 17 may import tobacco or alcoholic beverages. For more information, consult *New Zealand Customs Guide for Travelers,* available from customs offices, or contact New Zealand Customs, 50 Anzac Avenue, Box 29, Aukland (tel. (09) 377 35 20; fax 309 29 78).

South African citizens may import duty-free: 400 cigarettes, 50 cigars, 250g tobacco, 2 liters wine, 1 liter spirits, 250ml toilet water, 50ml perfume, and other items up to a value of R500. Amounts exceeding this limit are fully dutiable. You may not export or import South African bank notes in excess of R500. For more information, request the pamphlet *South African Customs Information* from The Commissioner for Customs and Excise, Private Bag X47, Pretoria, 0001. South Africans in the U.S. should contact the South African Mission to the IMF/ World Bank, 3201 New Mexico Ave. #380, NW, Washington, DC 20016 (tel. (202) 364-8320/1; fax 364-6008).

STUDENT AND YOUTH IDENTIFICATION

The **International Student Identity Card (ISIC),** put out by the **International Student Travel Confederation (ISTC),** is the most widely accepted form of student identification. Card holders qualify for student discounts on airfare and admission to sights and museums. The ISIC also provides medical/accident insurance (see Insurance below) and a toll-free, 24-hr. Traveler's Assistance Hotline, whose multilingual staff can provide help in medical, legal, and financial emergencies overseas. ISTC also offers an **International Teacher Identity Card (ITIC)** with similar benefits.

In **Spain** and **Portugal,** students with identification are entitled to free or discounted admission to museums and monuments.

The **Go 25 Card,** put out by the **Federation of International Youth Travel Organizations,** can be obtained by anyone under the age of 26, and offers a range of discounts on transportation and admissions worldwide.

Refer to Useful Addresses: Travel Services for a list off organizations which issue ISIC, ITIC and Go 25 cards.

HOSTELLING ORGANIZATIONS

Hostelling International (HI) is a worldwide federation of youth hostels (more than 5000 total). A one-year HI membership allows you to stay at youth hostels all over Spain, Portugal, and Morocco at unbeatable prices. Those over 25 pay only slightly more money for a bed. Obtaining a membership card before you leave home will save you time and trouble, and may be cheaper depending on currency exchange rates. HI cards are rarely sold on the spot at youth hostels, and only in Spain are they commonly sold at TIVE travel agencies; so you may want to have one before you arrive. HI now offers an **International Booking Network** which allows travelers to make confirmed reservations at any one of almost 200 hostels for US$2 (in addition to the regular overnight fee). To make a reservation, call **HI-AYH** (listed below). For more details on youth hostels, see Essentials: Accommodations for each country.

HI cards are available from some travel agencies (see Useful Addresses: Travel Services), and from the following organizations:

Hostelling International (HI), Headquarters at 9 Guessens Rd., Welwyn Garden City, Herts AL8 6QW, England (tel. (01707) 33 24 87).

American Youth Hostels (HI-AYH), 733 15th St. NW, Suite 840, Washington, DC 20005 (tel. (202) 783-6161; fax (202) 783-6171). HI-AYH membership cards: US$25, renewals US$20, under 18 US$10, over 54 US$15, family cards US$35.

Canadian Hostelling Association (HI-Canada), 400-205 Catherine St., Ottawa, Ont. K2P 1C3 (tel. (613) 237-7884; fax (613) 237-7868). One-year membership fee: CDN$26.75, under 18 CDN$12.84. Two-year: CDN$37.45.

Youth Hostels Association of England and Wales (YHA), Trevelyan House, 8 St. Stephen's Hill, St. Albans, Herts AL1 2DY (tel. (727) 85 52 15); or 14 Southampton St., Covent Garden, London WC2E 7HY (tel. (0171) 836 10 36). Membership fees: adult £9, under 18 £3, 2-day introductory membership £3.

An Óige (Irish Youth Hostel Association), 61 Mountjoy St., Dublin 7, Ireland (tel. (01) 830 45 55; fax (01) 830 58 08). One-year membership fee is £7.50, under 18 £4, family £15.

Australian Youth Hostels Association (AYHA), Level 3, 10 Mallett St., Camperdown, New South Wales, 2050 Australia (tel. (02) 565 16 99; fax (02) 565 13 25). Fee: AUD$40, renewal AUD$24. Under 18: fee and renewal both AUD$12.

Youth Hostels Association of New Zealand (YHANZ), P.O. Box 436, 173 Gloucester St., Christchurch 1, New Zealand (tel. (03) 379 99 70; fax (03) 365 44 76). Annual membership fees: adult NZD$34, youth (15-17) NZD$12, under 15 free. Lower rates for 2-3 year memberships. Life membership NZD$240. New Zealand memberships are not renewable overseas.

INTERNATIONAL DRIVING PERMIT AND INSURANCE CERTIFICATE

An **International Driving Permit (IDP)** is officially required to drive in Spain, Portugal, and Morocco. The permit smooths out difficulties with foreign police officers and is an additional piece of identification. However, the IDP isn't required at most car rental agencies, so you can choose to risk driving without one.

Permits are available on the spot from any branch office of the **American Automobile Association (AAA),** or by mail from their main office, 1000 AAA Drive (mail stop 28), Heathrow, FL 32746-5080 (tel. (407) 444-4245; fax (407) 444-7823). Applicants must be 18 or over and possess a valid U.S. driver's license. Permits are valid for one year and cost US$10.

In Canada, citizens 18 or older with valid Canadian driver's licenses can purchase a permit from any branch office of the **Canadian Automobile Association (CAA).** Their main office is at: CAA Toronto, 60 Commerce Valley Dr. East, Thornhill, Ont. L3T 7P9 (tel. (905) 771-3000; fax (905) 771-3046). CAA club membership is not required for purchase. Fee: CDN$10.

Standard insurance is covered by most credit cards. If you rent, lease, or borrow a car, you'll need a **green card** or **International Insurance Certificate,** to *prove* that you have liability insurance. Get it through the car **rental agency;** most of them include coverage in their prices. If you lease a car, get a green card through the dealer. Some travel agents offer the card, and it's available at the border. If you have auto insurance that applies abroad, you'll still need a green card to certify this to foreign officials. Inquire at the Foreign Motoring Services division of AAA or CAA (see addresses above).

■ ■ ■ MONEY

The information in this book was researched in the summer of 1994. Since then, prices may have risen by as much as 5-15%. The exchange rates listed were compiled in early September. Since rates fluctuate considerably, check them before you go. For information on banking hours, Value-Added Tax (VAT), and tipping in Spain, Portugal, and Morocco, see Essentials: More Money for each country.

CURRENCY AND EXCHANGE

In Spain the unit of currency is the *peseta* (pta); in Portugal, the *escudo* ($); in Morocco, the *dirham* (dh).

Before leaving home, buy about US$100 in the currency of the first country you'll visit to save time and money at the airport—the poor exchange rate at home banks still beats airport rates.

Once there, shop around at **banks** for the best rates. Commission charges sometimes outweigh a good exchange rate. Conversion charges are usually calculated by bulk sum rather than percentage, so it's preferable to convert infrequently and in large amounts. On the other hand, don't convert more than is safe to carry around. For typical banking hours in Spain, Portugal, and Morocco, see the Essentials: More Money for each country.

In Portugal, banks in larger cities often have high-tech **automatic exchange machines.** Like ATMs, these machines provide 24-hour service. Simply insert American bills, and *escudos* pop out. In Spain, machines are also common.

TRAVELER'S CHECKS

Traveler's checks are the safest way to carry money, can be replaced if lost or stolen, and may save you money (since commission charges are nonexistent or lower than for currency exchange). Most banks and several agencies sell checks, usually at face value plus a 1% commission.

Although some low-cost establishments may not accept traveler's checks as payment, you can exchange them for currency at American Express offices and most banks. Be sure to have your passport with you whenever you plan to use your checks. If you bring checks, you need bring almost no cash from your home country (but it's still useful to have a bit for emergencies). The major brands of checks (such as American Express, Visa, Thomas Cook/MasterCard) are recognized across Spain and Portugal. In Morocco most banks recognize major checks, but many smaller hotels and restaurants only accept American Express.

MONEY

MONEY

If your checks are lost or stolen, expect red tape and delays. To expedite the refund process, keep your check receipts in a safe place separate from your checks. Also leave the check numbers with a loved one at home. To help identify which checks are missing, record check numbers before you go and tick them off every time you cash some. When you buy your checks, ask for a list of refund centers. Most importantly, keep a separate stash of cash or checks for emergencies.

American Express (tel. (800) 221-7282 in the U.S. and Canada; (0800) 52 13 13 in the U.K.; (1800) 62 60 00 in Ireland; (008) 25 19 02 in Australia (except Sydney); (612) 886 06 89 collect in Sydney; (0800) 44 10 68 in New Zealand; (801) 964-6665 collect from elsewhere). Checks in 9 currencies. Small fee for check purchases is waved for U.S. Platinum Card and AAA members. "Cheques for Two" allows two people traveling together to sign for one set of checks. Most AmEx offices cash their own checks commission-free. The *American Express Traveler's Companion* (free for customers) lists all AmEx offices and travel services. Be sure to request this booklet far in advance, as it is in high demand. AmEx also offers a **Global Assist Hotline** (in the U.S. (800) 554-2639; from elsewhere call collect (202) 783-7474) for emergency medical, legal, and financial services.

Barclay's Bank sells Visa traveler's checks in US$, CDN$, British£, and German marks; 1-3% commission is charged. For information call (800) 221-2426 (collect if calling from outside the U.S.). To report lost or stolen checks, call Visa at (800) 227-6811 in the U.S. or Canada; (0171) 937 80 91 in the U.K.; or (212) 858-8500 collect from elsewhere. Barclay's banks cash Visa checks commission-free.

Citicorp sells Visa checks in US$, British£, AUD$, German marks, and Japanese yen with 1-2% commission. For information or to report lost checks, call (800) 645-6556 in the US; (0171) 982 40 40 in the U.K.; or (813) 623-1709 collect from elsewhere. Check-holders are automatically enrolled for 45 days in Citicorp's **Travel Assist Hotline** (800) 523-1199, which provides travelers with English-speaking doctor, lawyer, and interpreter referrals, as well as check refund assistance.

MasterCard International (tel. (800) 223-9920 or (609) 987-7300 collect in the U.S., Canada, or Mexico; (44) 733 50 29 95 collect from elsewhere). Offers checks in 11 currencies. Available from participating banks (look for MasterCard logo in window) at 1-2% commission. Also available from **Thomas Cook** (tel. same as MasterCard) at potentially lower commissions.

CREDIT CARDS

Although many smaller establishments will not accept them, major credit cards— **American Express, Mastercard,** and **Visa**, the most welcomed internationally—can still be useful. Look for their logo at restaurants and lodgings. In Europe, MasterCard is called Eurocard, while Visa is Carte Bleue; however, their logos are the same.

Major credit cards can also extract instant cash in local currency from banks and ATMs (albeit with hefty interest charges). Credit cards are invaluable in case of an emergency, when an unexpected bill or the loss of traveler's checks may leave you temporarily without other resources. An array of other services is offered, depending completely on the card issuer. Some cards allow you to cash personal checks.

In Spain, **Visa** is far more widely accepted than **MasterCard.** Both are issued by individual banks, each of which determine their card's membership fees and benefits. **American Express** (tel. (800) 528-4800) is especially useful, since branch offices throughout the world offer a variety of services. Membership fee US$55 per year. Personal checks up to US$1000 (US$5000 with Gold Card) cashed every 21 days while abroad and mail held at AmEx offices for cardholders. Purchase Protection Plan insures most purchases for 90 days against theft or accidental damage (up to US$1000). Special benefits for student cardholders include vouchers for discount airfares within the continental U.S. (See Traveler's Checks for additional services.)

ATMS

Most ATMs (automatic teller machines) in Europe belong to the **Cirrus** network (tel. (800) 4-CIRRUS). ATMs accept either major credit cards or "cash cards" from your local bank. Cirrus charges $5 for each international cash-card transaction, but often offers better exchange rates for withdrawals in local currency than either banks or traveler's checks. In Europe 4-digits personal identification numbers (PINS) are standard, so have yours changed before you leave home if necessary. If your credit card has no PIN, have your bank or credit card company assign you one. Memorize your PIN numerically, as many ATM keypads abroad do not have letters.

SENDING MONEY ABROAD

The easiest way to get money from home is through the **American Express personal check service** (see Credit Cards). Outside AmEx offices, cashing a check in a foreign currency takes weeks to clear and incurs a substantial fee. You can access accounts back home through ATMs with several of the major **credit cards.**

Otherwise, money can be **wired** abroad through American Express or Western Union. AmEx offers a **Moneygram Service** (tel. (800) 543-4080 in the U.S., (800) 933-3278 in Canada). This service wires money to Spain or Portugal in 10 minutes (unfortunately there is no service to Morocco). The charge is US$45 to send US$500; US$70 to send US$1000. The money is disbursed in AmEx traveler's checks (in US$). Go to an AmEx office or call the above number for information on the nearest locations for sending and receiving money. **Western Union** wires money to major cities in Spain in 15 minutes (no service to Portugal or Morocco). Call for procedures and a list of locations (tel. (800) 325-6000 in the U.S., Canada, or Mexico; (448) 174 13639 (the London office); or (0800) 83 38 33 from Europe). The charge is US$29 to send US$250; US$40 to send US$500; and US$50 to send US$1000.

The least expensive but often cumbersome route is to **cable** money from bank to bank. Both sender and receiver must have accounts at the respective banks. The sender must give exact information, including passport number and the recipient bank name and address. Send through an international bank that has an office in your home country; local banks are slower. Transfer takes from one day to a week; the fee is usually a flat US$20-30.

In life or death emergencies, U.S. citizens can have money sent to them abroad through the **State Department's Citizens Emergency Center,** Dept. of State, 2201 C St. NW, Washington, DC 20520 (tel. (202) 647-5225; after business hours call (202) 647-4000). They will send a modest amount of money to the nearest consular office. The quickest way is to cable the money to the State Department through Western Union; or to bring cash, certified check, bank draft, or money order to the State Department.

■■■ INSURANCE

Beware of unnecessary coverage—your current policies might well extend to many travel-related accidents. **Medical insurance** (especially university policies) often cover costs incurred abroad, although **Medicare's** foreign travel coverage is limited to Canada and Mexico. **Canadians** are protected by their home province's health insurance plan up to 90 days after leaving the country; check with the provincial Ministry of Health or Health Plan Headquarters. **EU citizens** are covered for emergency medical treatment throughout the EU by holding an E111 form, available from their local national health authority. Your **homeowners' insurance** (or your family's coverage) often covers theft during travel and loss of documents (passport, plane ticket, railpass, etc.) up to about US$500.

ISIC and **ITIC cards** provide US$3000 worth of accident and illness insurance plus US$100 per day for up to 60 days of hospitalization. **CIEE** offers an inexpensive **Trip-Safe** plan for cardholders, with options covering medical treatment and hospitalization, accidents, baggage loss, and charter flights missed due to illness. If you're ineligible for these cards, Trip-Safe extends coverage of the insurance you have. **AmEx cardholders** receive car rental and flight insurance on purchases made with the card.

File insurance claims upon return home. Keep all relevant documents (such as police reports, doctor's statements, receipts). Check the time limit on filing to make sure that you'll be returning home in time to secure reimbursement. The following firms offer insurance programs; almost all cover trip cancellation and medical expenses in some form.

Access America, Inc., 6600 W. Broad St., P.O. Box 11188, Richmond, VA 23230 (tel. (800) 294-8300; fax (804) 673-1491). 24-hr. hotline. Covers trip cancellation/interruption, on-the-spot hospital admittance costs, emergency medical evacuation, sickness, and baggage loss.

ARM Coverage, Inc./Carefree Travel Insurance, 100 Garden City Plaza, P.O. Box 9366, Garden City, N.Y. 11530-9366 (tel. (800) 323-3149 or (516) 294-0220; fax (516) 294-1821). 24-hr. hotline. Offers 2 comprehensive insurance packages.

Travel Assistance International, by Worldwide Assistance Services, Inc., 1133 15th St. NW, Suite 400, Washington, DC 20005-2710 (tel. (800) 821-2828; fax (202) 331-1530). Short-term and long-term plans available. 24-hr. emergency multilingual assistance hotline and worldwide local presence. Provides on-the-spot medical coverage and unlimited medical evacuation insurance.

Travel Guard International, 1145 Clark St., Stevens Point, WI 54481 (tel. (800) 826-1300 or (715) 345-0505; fax (715) 345-0525). 24-hr. emergency hotline. Offer "Travel Guard Gold" packages for medical expenses, baggage and travel documents, travel delay, baggage delay, emergency assistance, and trip cancellation/interruption. Basic package ($19), Deluxe ($39), and Comprehensive (9% of total trip cost).

■■■ PACKING

Pack light. Set out everything you think you'll need, eliminate half, and take more money. You can buy anything you need in Europe.

LUGGAGE

Decide what kind of luggage is best suited for your trip.

Backpack: Ideal if you're planning to hike over a lot of ground or camp. **Internal-frame** packs are flexible and mold to your back. They are also more manageable on crowded trains, and are less likely to get caught and mangled in airline baggage conveyors. An excellent choice is a conversion pack, an internal-frame pack which converts easily into a suitcase. **External-frame** packs are more cumbersome, and don't travel as well. Quality packs cost US$200-300. Beware of suspiciously cheap prices; this is one area where it does not pay to economize.

Light suitcase, carry-on/overnight bag, or large shoulder bag: Best suited for people who plan to stay in cities and large towns and don't want to stand out as budget tourists.

Daypack or bookbag: Bring a smaller bag in addition to a larger pack or suitcase. Make sure it's big enough to hold lunch, camera, water bottle, and *Let's Go*. Frees you up from your larger pack, which you can store in a locker or leave in a hotel. Get one with secure zippers and closures.

Moneybelt or neck pouch: Invaluable for guarding money, passport, railpass, etc. (see Safety).

CLOTHING AND FOOTWEAR

Bring few, but comfortable clothes which can be layered for maximum versatility. Keep accessories to a minimum.

In general: Climate should determine your wardrobe. Dark colors show less dirt, but light colors will be cooler when summer temperatures skyrocket. Loose garments in natural fibers and cotton blends are the coolest choices; synthetics trap heat. Bring non-wrinkling, quick-drying clothes that you can wash in a sink, as laundromats are very expensive and may be hard to find. Cotton pants are cooler,

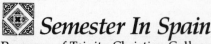

more comfortable, and faster-drying than jeans. For women, a long skirt is cooler, and less tourist-looking than pants or shorts.

Conservative clothes: Dress codes are extremely important for both men and women. Running shorts, cut-offs, tank and tube tops, and T-shirts mark the tourist. Bare shoulders and bare knees are considered immodest, especially in the countryside. Churches, synagogues, and other places of worship often refuse admission to visitors who have not bothered to cover up. (Also, see Specific Concerns: Women Travelers.)

Walking shoes: A must, whether you're in the city or the country. Sturdy, rubber-soled shoes made for walking (not for tennis, basketball, or running) will serve you best. For alpine forays, a good pair of **hiking boots** is essential, and a double pair of socks—thin polypropylene for a lining and light wool outside—will keep your feet dry and comfortable. Always break in and waterproof your shoes and/or hiking boots before you go to avoid agonizing blisters and soggy feet.

Don't forget: Raingear and a light sweater or jacket, even in summer. Gloves and thermal underwear are handy, perhaps necessary, in winter.

MISCELLANEOUS

You'll find the following miscellaneous items valuable.

umbrella	Ziploc bags (for damp clothes, soap, food, pens)
petite alarm clock	waterproof matches
sun hat	moleskin (for blisters)
needle and thread	safety pins
sunglasses	a personal stereo (Walkman) with headphones
pocketknife	notebook and pens
plastic water bottle	pocket English-language phrasebook
small flashlight	string (makeshift clothesline and lashing material)
towel	

An all-purpose **first-aid kit** includes: bandages, aspirin, medications for motion sickness and diarrhea, mild antiseptic soap, antibiotic ointment such as Bacitracin, mosquito repellent, an antihistamine, sunscreen, and lip balm.

Stores in Europe stock most **toiletries.** Still, a **cold-water soap** always comes in handy (what could be more *a propos* than all-natural Dr. Bronner's Castile Soap, sold at camping stores, usable for anything from washing clothes, bathing, and shampooing to brushing your teeth). **Tampons** and **contact-lens fluids** tend to be expensive, so bring some. Don't expect to find your preferred brand of **condoms** (see Health below).

If planning to stay in youth hostels, make the requisite **sleepsack** yourself (instead of paying the hostel's linen charge). Fold a full size sheet in half the long way, then sew it closed along the open long side and one of the short sides.

If you must bring electrical appliances you'll need a **converter.** North American current runs at 110 volts AC, while in Europe most outlets are 220 volts AC. Also, as European outlets are made for 2 round prongs, you'll need an **adapter.** Converters and adapters are sold at many hardware stores. If you don't feel like going to the hardware store, order a converter (about US$20) or the free pamphlet *Foreign Electricity is No Deep Dark Secret* by mail; write to the Franzus, Murtha Industrial Park, P.O. Box 142, Railroad Ave., Beacon Falls, CT 06403 (tel. (203) 723-6664; fax (203) 723-6666).

Film is expensive in Europe, so you'll probably want to buy it before you leave home. Airport security X-rays generally don't affect film with an ASA below 1000, but skeptical travelers should pack theirs in a lead-lined pouch, sold at camera stores. Although developing is inexpensive and fast in Spain, the use of non-standard chemicals sometimes does weird things; try to wait to develop your pictures until you get home.

English-language books, whether novels or *Let's Go,* are expensive overseas and don't exist in smaller towns. The entire *Let's Go* series is quite elusive in Spain, Portugal, and Morocco. If you're planning to travel to more countries it's wise to buy the guides back home (we're not pulling your leg; we don't work on commission). In our Orientation and Practical Information listings for each town, we'll tell you where English-language books are sold.

CAMPING EQUIPMENT

Purchase equipment before you leave. If you intend to do a lot of hiking or biking, you should have a **frame backpack** (see Luggage above).

Most of the better sleeping bags—down (lightweight and warm) or synthetic (cheaper, heavier, more durable, lower maintenance, and warmer when wet)—are rated according to the lowest outdoor temperature at which they will keep you warm. Lowest prices for good sleeping bags: US$65-80 for a summer synthetic; US$135-180 for a three-season synthetic; US$170-225 for a three-season down bag, and US$270-550 for a down bag you can use in the winter. Sleeping bag pads range from US$15-30, while air mattresses go for about US$25-50.

The best **tents** are free-standing, with their own frames and suspension systems. They set up quickly and require no staking (though staking will keep you from blowing away). Be sure your tent has a rain fly. Good two-person tents start at about US$135; US$200 fetches a four-person. You can, however, often find last year's version for about half the price.

Other camping basics include a battery-operated **lantern** (*never* gas) and a simple plastic **groundcloth** to protect the tent floor. **Campstoves** come in all sizes, weights and fuel types (US$30-85). A water bottle, Swiss army knife, insect repellent, and waterproof matches are other small, essential items.

The following **organizations** provide camping services and/or supplies.

Campmor, P.O. Box 700, Saddle River, NJ 07458-0700 (tel. (800) 526-4784; fax (201) 447-5559). Monstrous selection of backpacking and travel equipment at low prices.

Family Campers & RVers, 4804 Transit Rd., Bldg. 2, Depew, NY 14043 (tel. (716) 668-6242). Sells the **International Camping Carnet** (US$30, includes membership in FCRV and 10 issues of *Camping Today!*). The carnet—required at some European campgrounds, but usually available for on-the-spot purchase—entitles you to a discount at some campgrounds and may often be substituted for your passport as a security deposit.

L.L. Bean, Casco St., Freeport, ME 04033 (tel. (800) 878-2104, outside U.S. and Canada (207) 865-3111; fax (207) 878-2104). Open 24 hours a day, 365 days a year. Supplies its own equipment and national-brand merchandise, all available through mail order.

Recreational Equipment, Inc. (REI), P.O. Box 1700, Sumner, WA 98352-0001 (tel. (800) 426-4840). Stocks a wide range of the latest in camping gear and holds great seasonal sales. Publishes *Europa Camping and Caravanning* (US$20), an annually updated catalog of campsites in Europe.

■ ■ ■ HEALTH

See Packing: Miscellaneous above for a suggested compact **first-aid kit.**

If you'll be taking any **medication** while traveling, obtain a full supply before you leave, since matching your prescription with a foreign equivalent can be a total nightmare. Always carry up-to-date prescriptions (including the medication's trade name, manufacturer, chemical name, and dosage) and a statement from your doctor. If you use **birth control pills,** definitely stock up. If you wear **glasses** or **contact lenses,** take an extra pair along. It's also wise to leave a copy of your prescription with someone at home so you can have a new pair sent if disaster strikes. Contact wearers should pack plenty of lens solution, as it may be difficult to find in Europe. Pack all medications and prescriptions in your carry-on bag.

All travelers should be concerned about **AIDS,** transmitted through the exchange of body fluids with an infected individual who is HIV-positive. For information on HIV and AIDS, call the United States' Center for Disease Control's **AIDS Hotline** (tel. (800) 342-2437). The World Health Organization maintains an international AIDS statistics number (tel. (202) 861-4346) and provides written information on AIDS internationally. In Europe, call +41 (22) 791 46 73 (Switzerland) or write to the World Health Organization, attn: Global Program on AIDS, 20 Avenue Appia, 1211 Geneva 27, Switzerland.

Condoms are in stores under the name of *preservativo* in Spain and Portugal, and are often over-the-counter, usually in pharmacies. However, you may feel more comfortable using your favorite brand from home. Bring some with you.

Consult your doctor regarding hepatitis, cholera, and typhoid **shots** as well as malaria pills. In Morocco, watch any open sores, scratches, cuts, or mosquito bites: heat and iffy sanitation conditions increase the likelihood of infection.

Food poisoning can spoil your trip. In Spain you can pretty well do as you would in your home country. In some areas of Portugal and throughout Morocco, street vendors sell aged or otherwise fishy food; avoid unpeeled fruits and vegetables, particularly hard-to-wash leafy greens. Drink plenty of bottled fluids.

Unfortunate as it may be, traveling and **diarrhea** often go hand-in-hand. Most stomachs have at least some trouble adjusting to new cuisine, but if symptoms persist for more than a few days, consult a physician immediately. Unyielding diarrhea can signify dysentery or another parasitic condition which could haunt your gastro-intestinal tract for a long time after you've returned home.

In Morocco, drinking **water** from the village pump is a serious risk; rely on bottled or boiled water. Insist on breaking the plastic seal on the bottle yourself before paying to make sure you're not getting tap water. Remember: if you can't drink the water, you can't suck the ice. For information on **diabetic travelers,** see Specific Concerns: Diabetic below.

Overexposure to **sun** is always dangerous. In summer, residents of Spain, Portugal, and Morocco frequently restrict their activities during the hottest parts of the day. Follow their example and drink plenty of liquids to avoid unnecessary fatigue, sunburn, and heat stroke. Soothe a case of **prickly heat** (strange rash) by bathing frequently, dusting with talcum powder, and keeping cool. Wear a sun hat, sunglasses, and SPF 30 **sunscreen.**

The **United States Centers for Disease Control (CDC)** is an excellent source of general information on health for travelers around the world, and maintains an international traveler's hotline (tel. (404) 332-4559). The CDC publishes the booklet *Health Information for International Travelers* (pub. #HHS-CDC 90-8280, US$6), an annual global rundown of disease, immunization, and general health advice. Request the booklet by writing to the Superintendent of Documents, U.S. Govt. Printing Office, Washington, DC 20402.

In remote areas you may have difficulty finding emergency medical care. The **International Association for Medical Assistance to Travelers (IAMAT)** is a non-profit organization that provides medical care to travelers. Membership is free. IAMAT offers a membership ID card, an international directory of IAMAT physicians who have agreed to treat members for a set fee schedule, and a series of detailed brochures and charts on immunization requirements, various tropical diseases, and climate and sanitation. Contact IAMAT in the U.S. at 417 Center St., Lewiston, NY 14092 (tel. (716) 754-4883); in Canada at 40 Regal Rd., Guelph, Ont. N1K 1B5 (tel. (519) 836-0102) or 1287 St. Clair Ave. West, Toronto, M6E 1B8 (tel. (416) 652-0137); in New Zealand at P.O. Box 5049, Christchurch 5 (tel. (03) 352 90 53; fax (03) 352 46 30).

American, Canadian, and British embassies and consulates, and AmEx offices can also help find English-speaking doctors. Full payment in cash before check-out (sometimes before treatment) is virtually the rule at most European hospitals.

■■■ SAFETY

The **emergency police number** is: 091 in Spain, 115 in Portugal, and 19 in Morocco. Memorize it.

No place is absolutely safe, and naive, hapless tourists are particularly vulnerable to crime. To avoid falling prey to thieves and hustlers, always look like you know what's up. In general, the less you flaunt your income or foreign status, the less vulnerable you'll be to sticky fingers or large, blunt objects. Keep money and valuables in a **moneybelt** or **neck pouch** or stuffed in your bra or pinned to your underclothes. On the cutting edge of theft-proof bodywear is the **leg pouch.** Thieves can easily slip into your moneybelt on a crowded bus, but it's much harder to get into your pants.

In major cities, watch out for thieves who are fast and professional. Remember that **pickpockets** come in all shapes and sizes and are in on some unbelievable rackets. Pros can unzip a bag in just a few seconds, and have been known to slit open backpacks and purses with razor blades while their victims are spacing out. Wear your bag with the opening against your body. Threading a safety pin or keyring through both zippers on a pack makes it difficult to open quickly and prevents it from slipping open accidentally.

Never leave valuables unattended, even during the day. If you plan to sleep outside or don't want to carry everything with you, store your gear at a train or bus station. (See Appendix: Luggage Storage.)

Overnight **trains** are favorite hangouts for petty criminals. Always steer clear of empty train compartments, particularly at night. Size potential berth-mates up carefully and avoid fishy ones. If you have a compartment on a train and you are sure the train won't be stopping, sleep with the window open; berths have been known to be gassed and burgled. In a couchette, try to reserve a top bunk when you buy your ticket; the awkward height may deter thieves. Don't check luggage on trains, especially if switching trains en route.

Make photocopies of all **important documents,** including your passport, identification, credit cards, and traveler's check serial numbers. Keep one set in your luggage and leave another set with friends at home. Although copies won't substitute for lost or stolen documents, they'll expedite replacements.

In **Morocco,** solo travelers may be singled out for harassment. Firmly saying *imshi* (go away) will sometimes stop hecklers. Don't tolerate any prolonged harassment, even if it means protesting loudly; passers-by will generally come to your assistance if you yell. Invitations to a home-cooked Moroccan meal or friendly directions to a bargain rug dealer are possible lures into a huge scam. (See Morocco Essentials: Additional Concerns: Hustlers and Guides.)

For more information, see Specific Concerns: **Women Travelers** below.

■ ■ ■ SPECIFIC CONCERNS

DIABETIC

People with diabetes should consult the *Ticket to Safe Travel*, a booklet put out by the **American Diabetes Association,** 1660 Duke St., Alexandria, VA 22314 (tel. (800) 232-3472). The ADA can also give you a wallet-size ID card with information on diabetes.

DIETS

Halal

For halal food, look under "halal" in the yellow pages of phone books, where shops and restaurants (if they exist) will be listed. In large cities, try the Muslim quarters.

Kosher

The prospects aren't so good in Spain, Portugal, and Morocco. For **information** about kosher food abroad, consult *The Jewish Travel Guide* (US$11.95, postage US$1.75), which lists kosher restaurants, synagogues, and other Jewish institutions in over 80 countries. Write to **Sepher-Hermon Press, Inc.,** 1265 46th St., Brooklyn, NY 11219 (tel. (718) 972-9010). In the U.K., order it from **Jewish Chronicle Publications,** 25 Furnival St., London EC4A 1JT, United Kingdom (tel. +44 (0171) 405 92 52; fax +44 (0171) 831 51 88).

Vegetarian

Vegetarians will have no trouble if cooking for themselves in Spain, Portugal, or Morocco. Virtually every town has a local **market,** with a wide selection of fresh and inexpensive produce (under each city see Food for addresses and hours). Requests for vegetarian entrees in restaurants and private homes, however, may provoke raised eyebrows and skeptical looks. Asking for two first courses *(primer platos)* is often a good option, as the main dish *(segundo plato)* will invariably contain meat. *Let's Go* lists several vegetarian restaurants in larger cities and tourist resorts. Call (800) 435-9610 to order the *Vegetarian Times* or the *European Vegetarian Guide to Restaurants and Hotels*. For more information, contact the **Vegetarian Society of the U.K.,** Parkdale, Dunham Rd., Altringham, Cheshire WA14 4QG, England (tel. 44 (61) 928 07 93). The VSUK offers copies of the *International Vegetarian Travel Guide* (last published in 1991) for £3, as well as several other titles.

DRUGS

Don't buy drugs and never carry drugs across borders. The horror stories about drug busts in Europe and North Africa are grounded in fact. Every year, hundreds of travelers are arrested in foreign countries for illegal possession, use, and trafficking of drugs. About forty percent of those arrested are charged with possession of a tiny amount of marijuana (as little as a single seed). Some countries—Morocco—are especially severe in their treatment of those arrested on dope-related charges.

Although plenty of locals may be using hashish, this openness is an illusion. In **Morocco** dealers often work for the police. In one racket, a drug dealer sells to a foreign visitor, heads straight for the police, describes the patron in detail, collects a fee for information, and gets the goods back when the buyer is arrested.

Your government is completely powerless in the judicial system of a foreign country. Consular officers can only visit a prisoner, provide a list of attorneys, and inform family and friends. Once you leave your home country, you are not covered by its laws. The legal codes in some countries, including Morocco, provide for guilt by association; *you* may be charged if your companions are found in possession of illegal drugs. This is scary stuff—the burden of proof usually lies on the accused to prove her or his innocence, and many countries will not give you the benefits of jury trial, bail, or parole.

For more **information** on the subject of drugs overseas, send for the free pamphlet *Travel Warning on Drugs Abroad* from the Bureau of Consular Affairs, Public Affairs #5807, Dept. of State, Washington, DC 20520 (tel. (202) 647-1488). Enclose a stamped, self-addressed envelope.

GAY AND LESBIAN TRAVELERS

In Spain and Portugal, the legal minimum age for sexual intercourse is 18. Some consider the gay scene in **Spain** the most open in Europe; in the major cities (Madrid, Barcelona) people are quite tolerant. Sitges, Ibiza, and Cádiz also have thriving gay communities. The semi-monthly magazine *Entiendes...?*, with articles in Spanish about gay issues, and a comprehensive list of gay services, groups, and activities, plus a personals section, is available in some bookstores.

Portugal is more conservative. Gay people should exercise discretion, especially in less urban areas. In **Morocco,** both civil and Islamic law prohibit the practice of homosexuality.

Under each major city in *Let's Go,* see Orientation and Practical Information: Gay and Lesbian Services for bookstores, hotlines, and information specific to individual cities. Also, check kiosks and bookstores in each city you visit for local publications and services.

Are You Two...Together? (US$18). A travel guide filled with anecdotes and handy tips for gays and lesbians traveling in Europe. Available in bookstores, or contact Giovanni's Room or Renaissance House.

Ferrari Publications, P.O. Box 37887, Phoenix, AZ 85069 (tel. (602) 863-2408). Publishes *Places of Interest* (US$16), *Places for Women* (US$13), *Places for Men* (US$15), and *Inn Places: USA and Worldwide Gay Accommodations* (US$14.95). Available in bookstores, or by mail order (postage US$3.50 for the first item, $0.50 for each additional item).

Gay's The Word, 66 Marchmont St., London WC1N 1AB, England (tel. 44 (0171) 278 76 54). A gay and lesbian bookstore which also sells videos, jewelry, and postcards. Mail order service available. Open Mon.-Fri. 11am-7pm, Sat. 10am-6pm, Sun. and holidays 2-6pm.

Giovanni's Room, 345 S. 12th St., Philadelphia, PA 19107 (tel. (215) 923-2960; fax (215) 923-0813). Bookstore with an enormous range of international gay, lesbian, and feminist literature, including many of the publications listed here. Big mail order business; call or write for a free catalog.

Odysseus Guide, USA and International (US$21). A good accommodations guide. Available in bookstores, or contact Giovanni's Room or Renaissance House.

Renaissance House, P.O. Box 533, Village Station, New York, NY 10014 (tel. (212) 674-0120; fax (212) 420-1126). A comprehensive gay bookstore which carries many of the titles listed in this section. Send self-addressed, stamped envelope for a free mail-order catalog.

Spartacus International Gay Guide (US$29.95). Published by Bruno Gmünder. One of the oldest and most popular guides for gay men. Lists bars, restaurants, hotels, bookstores, and hotlines worldwide. Available in the U.S. from Giovanni's Room and from Renaissance House.

Women Going Places (US$14). Annually revised international guide for lesbians (and all women) lists women-owned and -operated enterprises, local lesbian, feminist, and gay info numbers, bookstores, restaurants, hotels, and meeting places. Published by Inland Book Company. Available in bookstores.

SENIOR TRAVELERS

In **Spain,** only Spanish seniors (over 60) receive a discount on train fares with RENFE's *Tarjeta Dorada* (Gold Card). However, museum and monument admissions in Spain are discounted for seniors (over 60) of any nationality. **Portugal** offers similar transportation discounts to Portuguese seniors (over 65). Sights in Portugal are discounted for all seniors (over 65).

In many cases, student discounts are available to senior citizens as well. An **HI card** is US$15 if you're over 54. (See Documents and Formalities: Hostelling Organizations above.) Always ask if there are discounts for seniors. The following organizations and publications provide information on services and discounts for senior travelers.

American Association of Retired Persons (AARP), 601 E St. NW, Washington, DC 20049 (tel. (202) 434-2277). Membership open to anyone over 49. Annual fee: US$8 per couple. Benefits include the AARP Travel Experience from American Express (tel. (800) 927-0111), the AARP Motoring Plan from Amoco (tel. (800) 334-3300), and discounts on lodging, car rental, and sight-seeing companies.

Bureau of Consular Affairs, Superintendent of Documents, U.S. Government Printing Office, Washington, DC 20402 (tel. (202) 783-3238). Publishes *Travel Tips for Older Americans* (US$1) with health, safety and travel info for seniors.

Elderhostel, 75 Federal St., 3rd fl., Boston, MA 02110-1941 (tel. (617) 426-8056). Weeklong residential academic programs, focusing on varied subjects, at colleges in over 47 countries. Must be over 59 to enroll, and may bring a spouse.

Gateway Books, 2023 Clemens Rd., Oakland, CA 94602 (tel. (510) 530-0299, for credit card orders (800) 669-0773; fax (510) 530-0497). Publishes *Get Up and Go: A Guide for the Mature Traveler* (US$10.95) and *Adventures Abroad* (US$12.95), which offer general hints for the budget-conscious senior traveler.

National Council of Senior Citizens, 1331 F St. NW, Washington, DC 20004 (tel. (202) 347-8800). Annual (US$12), three-year (US$30), or lifetime (US$150) membership provides discounts on hotels, car rentals, and travel agents; supplemental Medicare insurance (if over age 65); and a mail-order prescription drug service.

Pilot Books, 103 Cooper St., Babylon, NY 11702 (tel. (516) 422-2225). Publishes *The International Health Guide for Senior Citizen Travelers* (US$4.95) and *The Senior Citizens' Guide to Budget Travel in Europe* (US$5.95). Postage for each book US$1.

TRAVELERS WITH CHILDREN

Avoid hassles by booking rooms ahead and planning sight-seeing stops that your children will enjoy. *Take your Kids to Europe,* by Cynthia Harriman (US$13.95), an excellent budget guide geared toward family travel, is published by **Mason Grant Publications,** P.O. Box 6547, Portsmouth, NH 03802 (tel. (603) 436-1608; fax (603) 427-0015). Also check out *Travel with Children* (US$10.95, postage US$1.50), available from **Lonely Planet Publications,** Embarcadero West, 155 Philbert St., Suite 251, Oakland, CA 94607 (tel. (800) 275-8555 or (510) 893-8555; fax (510) 893-8563); also P.O. Box 617, Hawthorn, Victoria 3122, Australia. *Backpacking with Babies and Small Children* (US$10.95) is available from **Wilderness Press,** 2440 Bancroft Way, Berkeley, CA 94704 (tel. (800) 443-7227 or (510) 843-8080).

TRAVELERS WITH DISABILITIES

Accessibility varies widely. Guidebooks and brochures don't have accurate information about ramps, door widths, and elevator dimensions. The best method is to directly ask restaurants, hotels, railways, and airlines about their facilities. Rail is usually the most convenient form of travel. Call **Rail Europe** (tel. (800) 848-7245 or (800) 438-7245) for information on discounted rail travel.

The customary six-month quarantine on all animals, including **guide dogs,** is a serious pain in the butt. Spain and Morocco require an international health and inoculation certificate for pets; for Spain, this document must be certified at the Spanish consulate, and then signed by the Federal Veterinarian, who can be found at your local chapter of the USDA Animal and Plant Health Inspection Services, Veterinary Services. The following organizations provide more information.

American Foundation for the Blind, 15 W. 16th St., New York, NY 10011 (tel. (212) 620-2147). Open Mon.-Fri. 9am-2pm. Info, travel books, and ID cards (US$10) for the blind. ID cards and AFB catalogs can also be ordered by phone (Product Center tel. (800) 829-0500).

Directions Unlimited, 720 North Bedford Rd., Bedford Hills, NY 10507 (tel. (800) 533-5343 or (914) 241-1700; fax (914) 241-0243). Specializes in arranging individual and group vacations, tours, and cruises for those with physical disabilities.

The Guided Tour, Elkins Park House, Suite 114B, 7900 Old York Road, Elkins Park, PA 19117-2339 (tel. (215) 782-1370). Year-round travel programs for adults with developmental and physical challenges. Call or write for free brochure.

Mobility International, USA (MIUSA), P.O. Box 10767, Eugene, OR 97440 (voice and TDD tel. (503) 343-1284; fax (503) 343-6812); and 228 Borough High St., London SE1 1JX, United Kingdom (tel. 44 (0171) 403 56 88). Annual membership (US$20), newsletter (US$10). Information on travel programs, international work camps, organized tours, accommodations, and access guides for those with physical disabilities. Contacts in over 30 countries. Sells *A World of Options: A Guide to International Educational Exchange, Community Service and Travel for Persons with Disabilities* (US$14, non-members US$16).

Travel Information Service, Moss Rehabilitation Hospital, 1200 W. Tabor Road, Philadelphia, PA 19141 (tel. (215) 456-9603). Telephone information on international travel accessibility and other concerns for travelers with disabilities.

Twin Peaks Press, P.O. Box 129, Vancouver, WA 98666-0129 (tel. (206) 694-2462, orders only (MC and Visa) tel. (800) 637-2256; fax (206) 696-3210). Publishes *Travel for the Disabled* (US$19.95), *Directory for Travel Agencies of the Disabled* (US$19.95), *Wheelchair Vagabond* (US$14.95), and *Directory of Accessible Van Rentals* (US$9.95). Postage US$2 for the first book, US$1 for each additional book.

WOMEN TRAVELERS

Women traveling alone—particularly those who look foreign—often must deal with unwarranted harassment. You've probably heard it all before, but here it is again: a litany of **precautions.** Walk as if you know where you are going, avoid eye contact (sunglasses are indispensable), meet all advances and catcalls with silence, and, if still troubled, walk or stand near older women or couples until you feel safe. Ask for directions from women or couples rather than men. Keep spare change handy for telephones and emergency bus and taxi fares. If someone starts following you, tell a policeman if possible; tell anyone, and you'll often frighten your pursuer away. Alternatively, walk to the police station. In any situation that becomes threatening, don't hesitate to call for help. Memorize the **emergency police number** (091 for Spain; 115 for Portugal; 19 for Morocco).

Unfortunately, wearing tighter or more revealing **clothes** means more annoying hassle from macho pigs in the streets. Below-the-knee hemlines or pants reduce harassment. Furthermore, obviously American garb (sweatshirts, college t-shirts, sneakers, hiking shorts) tends to draw hecklers.

Budget **accommodations** sometimes mean more risk than savings. Avoid dives and the city outskirts in favor of university dorms or youth hostels. Centrally located accommodations are usually safest to return to after dark.

For more **information,** consult the *Handbook for Women Travelers* (£8.99) by Maggie and Gemma Moss, available from **Piatkus Books,** 5 Windmill St., London W1P 1HF, England (tel. (0171) 631 07 10). Also check out *A Journey of One's Own* (Eighth Mountain Press, US$14.95) by Thalia Zepatos. Includes an excellent bibliography of other books and resources.

In **Morocco,** where Islamic culture requires women to be veiled and secluded even in their own homes, women traveling alone or with other women may be discriminated against, threatened, or hissed at. Strolling arm in arm with another woman, a common European and North African practice, can lessen the risk of harassment or violence. Particularly in the larger inland cities, expect other, subtler forms of discrimination, such as being refused a room in a hotel that isn't full; proprietors would rather not be responsible for your well-being. Many bars refuse to admit women. Again, the best response to most harassment is none at all; any reply may be interpreted as encouragement. Finally, see the general information listed under Safety (above).

■■■ ALTERNATIVES TO TOURISM

STUDY

Foreign study in **Spain** is available through U.S. university programs, U.S. youth organizations (such as Academic Year Abroad), Spanish universities, and language centers for foreign students. If your language skills are good, you can enroll directly in a Spanish university. The best resources for foreign study programs are colleges; research your options at a school nearby.

All universities in **Portugal** are open to foreign students. Contact individual institutions for specifics. Foreigners can enter language-study programs at the **University of Lisboa's** Faculdade de Lingua e Cultura, Cidade Universitária, 1699 Lisboa CODEX (tel. (01) 793 33 56); the **University of Coimbra's** Faculdade de Artes, Largo da Porta Ferrea, 3049 Coimbra CODEX (tel. (039) 255 51/52/53); and the **Univer-**

ALTERNATIVES TO TOURISM

sity of the Minho's Instituto de Letras e Ciências Humanas, Campus do Gualtar, 4719 Braga CODEX (tel. (053) 67 63 76).

For more **information** on study abroad, contact the following organizations.

Council on International Educational Exchange (CIEE). For address, phone number, and more details see Useful Addresses: Travel Services below. A good place to start. Heaps of info on study abroad.

American Field Service Intercultural Programs, 220 E. 42nd St., 3rd fl., New York, NY 10017 (tel. (800) 237-4636 or (212) 949-4242). Summer, semester, and year-long homestay exchange programs for high schoolers in over 55 countries.

American Institute for Foreign Study (AIFS), College Division, 102 Greenwich Ave., Greenwich, CT 06830 (tel. (800) 727-2437). Study abroad programs at universities in Australia, Austria, France, Germany, Italy, Japan, Mexico, Russia, Spain, and U.K. For high school traveling programs, call (800) 888-ACIS (888-2247).

Education Office of Spain, 150 Fifth Ave., #918, New York, NY 10011 (tel. (212) 741-5144/5145). 1350 Connecticut Ave. NW, #1050, Washington, DC 20036 (tel. (202) 452-0005). Much information on study in Spain.

Eurocentre, 101 N. Union St., #300, Alexandria, VA 22314 (tel. (800) 648-4809 or (703) 684-1494; fax (703) 684-1495). Coordinates language programs and homestays in France, Germany, Italy, Japan, Russia, Spain, U.K., and U.S. Minimum age for most programs is 16.

Institute of International Education Books (IIE Books), 809 United Nations Plaza, New York, NY 10017-3580 (tel. (212) 984-5412; fax (212) 984-5358). Offers free pamphlet *Basic Facts on Foreign Study,* and several annually-updated, extensive reference books on study abroad. *Academic Year Abroad* (US$42.95) and *Vacation Study Abroad* (US$36.95) detail over 3600 programs offered by U.S. colleges and universities overseas. Also sells books by the Central Bureau for Educational Visits and Exchanges (see Work and Volunteering below). Postage US$4 per book.

School for International Training (SIT), College Semester Abroad Admissions, Kipling Rd., P.O. Box 676, Brattleboro, VT 05302 (tel. (800) 336-1616 or (802) 258-3279). Part of **World Learning,** SIT conducts college semester-abroad programs around the world. Limited scholarships; U.S. federal financial aid will apply to the program.

WORK AND VOLUNTEERING

The employment situation in Spain, Portugal, and Morocco is grim for citizens and worse for foreigners. Getting a **work visa** is extremely difficult. Jobs in restaurants and bars are good sources of under-the-table income. In rural areas, you might try working on farms.

Teaching English is another source of official and unofficial employment in Spain and Portugal, and probably the only one in Morocco. Some English-language schools arrange work permits for employees. Inquire at language and private schools. Try posting signs in markets and on message boards stating that you're a native speaker; scan the classified of local papers, where residents advertise for language instruction. The U.S. State Dept. **Office of Overseas Schools** (Rm. 245 SA-29, Dept. of State, Washington, DC 20522-2902 (tel. (703) 875-7800) maintains a list of elementary and secondary schools abroad, and agencies that arrange placement for teaching abroad. Call or write for a free copy.

Summer positions as **tour group leaders** are available with **World Learning,** Summer Abroad Leadership, Kipling Rd., P.O. Box 676, Brattleboro, VT 05302 (tel. (800) 345-2929 or (802) 257-7751). Applicants must be at least 24, fluent in the language, and have previous in-country experience.

International work camps allow volunteers to live and work together on two- to four-week community projects. Room and board are spartan.

For **information** on these and other work options, look up some of the following sources.

Addison Wesley, Order Department, Jacob Way, Reading, MA 01867 (tel. (800) 358-4566). Publishes the general guide *International Jobs: Where They Are, How to Get Them,* by Eric Kocher (US$14.95).

Archaeological Institute of America, 675 Commonwealth Ave., Boston, MA 02215 (tel. (617) 353-9361; fax (617) 353-6550). Publishes the *Archaeological Fieldwork Opportunities Bulletin,* which can be purchased from Kendall/Hunt Publishing, 4500 Westmark Dr., Dubuque, IA 52002 (tel. (800) 228-0810). The Archaeological Institute does not distribute the bulletin, but they may have further information on work opportunities.

Central Bureau for Educational Visits and Exchanges, Seymour Mews House, Seymour Mews, London W1H 9PE, England (tel. (0171) 486 51 01; fax (0171) 935 57 41). Publishes *Working Holidays 1995, Volunteer Work,* and *Teach Abroad,* as well as *Study Holidays* and *Home from Home* with information on international study, homestays and exchanges. All books £8.99 including postage. Several Bureau publications also sold (albeit at higher prices) by IIE (see Study above).

CIEE, International Work Camp Dept., 205 E. 42nd St., New York, NY 10017 (tel. (212) 661-1414, ext. 1139). Operates international summer work camps (US$165 participation fee), including hundreds of locations in Spain and Morocco. Volunteers must be over age 18 and have conversational language skills. Also sells assorted guides about work and volunteer programs abroad (see Useful Addresses: Travel Services for titles and prices).

Interexchange Program, 161 Sixth Ave., New York, NY 10013 (tel. (212) 924-0446). Provides information on work programs and au pair positions in Europe.

International Association for the Exchange of Students for Technical Experience (IAESTE), c/o AIPT, #250, 10400 Little Patuxent Parkway, Columbia, MD 21044 (tel. (410) 997-2200). Internship exchange programs for science, engineering, math, architecture, and agriculture students who have completed at least two years of college. Applications (US$75) due Dec. 10 for summer placement.

International Schools Services (ISS), P.O. Box 5910, Princeton, NJ 08543 (tel. (609) 452-0990). Their Educational Staffing Dept. coordinates placement of teachers in international and American schools. Publishes free booklet *Your Brochure to Teaching and Administrative Opportunities Abroad*. Free newsletter *Newslinks* with information chiefly for teachers and school administrators.

Peterson's Guides, 202 Carnegie Center, Princeton, NJ 08543 (tel. (800) 338-3282 or (609) 243-9111). Distributes *The Directory of Overseas Summer Jobs* (US$14.95) and the *ISS Directory of Overseas Schools* (US$34.95). Also publishes *Work Your Way Around the World* (US$17.95). Order directly from Peterson's (postage US$5.75 for the first book, US$1 for each additional book), or request from any good bookstore.

Tagus Turismo Juvenil. Paid and volunteer work in Portugal (see Useful Addresses: Travel Services).

Volunteers for Peace Inc. (VFP), 43 Tiffany Rd., Belmont, VT 05730 (tel. (802) 259-2759; fax (802) 259-2922). Coordinates workcamps in 40 countries. Publishes the *International Workcamp Directory* (US$10 postpaid, deductible from future program fees), and a free newsletter. Placement is quick; reservations are generally confirmed within 3 days. Most volunteers register between mid-April and mid-May. Fee for most workcamps (US$150); camps open to 16- 18-year-olds (US$175).

World Trade Academy Press, 50 E. 42nd St., New York, NY 10017 (tel. (212) 697-4999). Publishes *Looking for Employment in Foreign Countries* (US$16.50) with advice on federal, commercial, and volunteer jobs abroad, and resumes and interviews.

■■■ USEFUL ADDRESSES

The organizations and publications listed below can help you put your travel ideas together.

TOURIST OFFICES

National tourist offices are valuable sources of information, but often don't answer faxes. Make your inquiries as specific as possible. For information on tourist offices in Spain, Portugal, and Morocco, turn to Essentials: Tourist Offices for each country.

Tourist Office of Spain

U.S.: 665 Fifth Ave., **New York,** NY 10022 (tel. (212) 759-8822; fax (212) 658-1061). 845 N. Michigan Ave., **Chicago,** IL 60611 (tel. (312) 642-1992; fax (312) 642-9817). San Vicente Plaza Bldg., 8383 Wilshire Blvd., #960, **Beverly Hills,** CA 90211 (tel. (213) 658-7188; fax (213) 658-1061).

Canada: 102 Bloor St. W., 14th fl., **Toronto,** Ont. M5S 1M8 (tel. (416) 961-3131; fax (416) 961-1992).

U.K.: 57-58 St. James St., **London** SW1A ILD (tel. (0171) 499 11 69 or (0171) 499 09 01; fax (0171) 629 42 57).

Australia: 203 Castlereagh St., #21A, **Sydney South,** NSW 2000 (tel. (2) 264 79 66; fax (2) 267 51 11).

Portuguese National Tourist Office

U.S.: 590 Fifth Ave., 4th fl., **New York,** NY 10036-4704 (tel. (212) 354-4403; fax (212) 764-6137). Portuguese Trade & Tourism Office, 1900 L St. NW, Suite 310, **Washington, DC** 20036 (tel. (202) 331-8222; fax (202) 331-8236).

Canada: Portuguese Trade & Tourism Commission, 60 Bloor St. W., Suite 1005, **Toronto,** Ont. M4W 3B8 (tel. (416) 921-7376; fax (416) 921-1353). 500 Sherbrooke St. W, Suite 940, **Montréal,** Que. H3A 3C6 (tel. (514) 282-1264; fax (514) 499-1450).

U.K.: Portuguese Trade & Tourism Office, 22/25A Sackville St., **London** W1X 1DE (tel. (0171) 494 14 41; fax (0171) 494 18 68).

Ireland: Portuguese Trade & Tourism Office, Portuguese Embassy, Knocksinna, Foxrock, **Dublin** 18 (tel./fax +353 (1) 289 68 52).

South Africa: Diamond Corner, 8th fl., 68 Eloff St., P.O. Box 70, 2000 **Johannesburg** (+27 (11) 337 47 75 or 337 47 82; fax +27 (11) 337 16 13).

Moroccan National Tourist Office

U.S.: 20 E. 46th St., #1201, **New York,** NY 11017 (tel. (212) 557-2520; fax (212) 949-8148). P.O. Box 22662, Moroccan Pavilion, Epcot Center, **Lake Buena Vista,** FL 32830 (tel. (407) 827-5337).

Canada: 2001 rue Université, #1460, **Montréal,** Que. H3A 2A6 (tel. (514) 842-8111; fax (514) 842-5316; telex 055-62191).

U.K.: 205 Regent St., **London** W1R 7DE (tel. (0171) 437 00 73; fax (0171) 734 81 72).

Australia: 11 West St., **North Sydney,** NSW 2060 (tel. 957 67 17 or 922 49 99; fax 923 10 53).

EMBASSIES AND GENERAL CONSULATES

Note that you should direct questions concerning visas and passports to consulates, not embassies (whose function is solely diplomatic). For addresses of your home country's embassies and consulates in Spain, Portugal, and Morocco, turn to Essentials: Embassies and Consulates for each country.

Embassy and Consulate of Spain

U.S.: Embassy, 2375 Pennsylvania Ave., NW, Washington, DC 20037-1736 (tel. (202) 452-0100; fax (202) 328-3212). **Consulate,** 150 E. 58th St., 30th fl., New York, NY 10155 (tel. (212) 355-4080; fax (212) 644-3751).

Canada: Embassy, 350 Sparks St., #802, Ottawa, Ont. KIR 758 (tel. (613) 237-2193; fax (613) 236-1502).

U.K.: Embassy, 24 Belgrave Sq., London SW1X 8QA (tel. (0171) 235 55 55; fax (0171) 259 53 92). **Consulate,** 22 Manchester Sq., London SW1X 8QA (tel. (0171) 581 59 21).

USEFUL ADDRESSES

Australia: Embassy, 15 Arkana St., Yarralumla, ACT 2600 (tel. (6) 273 35 55 or (6) 273 38 45; fax (6) 273 39 18). Mailing address: P.O. Box 9076, Deakin, ACT 2600. **Consulate,** Level 24, St. Martins Towers, 31 Market St., Sydney, NSW 2000 (tel. (2) 261 24 33 or (2) 261 24 43; fax (2) 283 16 95). Mailing address: P.O. Box E441, St. James, NSW 2000.

Embassy and Consulate of Portugal

U.S.: Embassy, 2125 Kalorama Rd. NW, Washington, DC 20008 (tel. (202) 328-8610; fax (202) 462 3726). **Consulates,** 630 Fifth Ave., Suite 378, New York, NY 10111 (tel. (212) 246-4580 or (212) 246-4582; fax (212) 246-4581). Others in Boston, Chicago, Coral Gables (FL), the Dominican Republic, Houston, Kaneohe (HI), Los Angeles, Newark, New Bedford, Philadelphia, Providence, San Francisco, San Juan (PR), and Waterbury (CT).

Canada: Embassy, 645 Island Park Dr., Ottawa, Ont. K1Y OB8 (tel. (613) 729-2270). **Consulates,** 2020 University Ave., Suite 1725, Montréal, Que. H3A 2A5 (tel. (514) 499-0621 or (514) 499-0359). 121 Richmond St. W., Suite 701, Toronto, Ont. M5H 2K1 (tel. (416) 360-8260 or (416) 360-8261). Pender Place, 700 West Pender St., Suite 904, Vancouver, B.C. V6C 1LB (tel. (604) 688-6514 or (604) 683-0015).

U.K.: Embassy, 11 Belgrave Sq., London SW1X 8PP (tel. (0171) 441 235 53 31). **Consulate,** Silver City House, 62 Brompton Road, London SW3 1BJ (tel. (0171) 441 581 87 22).

Australia: Embassy, 6 Campion St., 1st fl., Deakin ACT, 2600 Camberra (tel. (062) 85 20 84). **Consulate,** 132 Ocean St., Edgecliff, NSW 2027 (tel. (2) 326 18 44; fax (2) 327 16 07). Mailing address: G.P.O. Box 4219, Sydney, NSW 2001.

New Zealand: Embassy, 117 Arney Road, Remuera, Auckland 5 (tel. (649) 524 82 66). **Consulate,** 105-109 The Terrace, Wellington 1 (tel. (644) 72 16 77).

Embassy and Consulate of the Kingdom of Morocco

U.S.: Embassy, 1601 21st St. NW, Washington, DC 20009 (tel. (202) 462-7979). **Consulate,** 10 East 40th. St., 24th fl., New York, NY 10016 (tel. (212) 758-2625; fax (212) 779-7441).

Canada: Embassy, 38 Range Rd., Ottawa, Ont. K1N 8J4 (tel. (613) 236-7391).

U.K.: Embassy, 49 Queens Gate Garden, London SW7 5NE (tel. (0171) 581 50 01).

TRAVEL SERVICES

These organizations help with booking flights and acquiring railpasses, student ID cards, and HI memberships.

Council on International Educational Exchange (CIEE), 205 E. 42nd St., New York, NY 10017 (tel. (212) 661-1414). A private, not-for-profit organization, CIEE administers work, volunteer, academic, and professional programs around the world. They also offer identity cards (including the ISIC and the GO 25) and a range of publications, among them the useful magazine *Student Travels* (free, postage US$1) and *Going Places: The High School Student's Guide to Study, Travel, and Adventure Abroad* (US$13.95, postage US$1.50). Call or write them for further information.

Council Travel, a subsidiary of CIEE, is an agency specializing in student and budget travel. Their 41 offices across the U.S. sell charter flight tickets, guidebooks, ISIC, ITIC, and GO 25 cards, hostelling cards, and travel gear. Offices include: 729 Boylston St., Suite 201, **Boston,** MA 02116 (tel. (617) 266-1926); 1153 N. Dearborn St., 2nd fl., **Chicago,** IL 60610 (tel. (312) 951-0585); 6715 Hillcrest, **Dallas,** TX 75205 (tel. (214) 363-9941); 1093 Broxton Ave., Suite 220, **Los Angeles,** CA 90024 (tel. (310) 208-3551); 205 E. 42nd St., **New York,** NY 10017 (tel. (212) 661-1450); 530 Bush St., Ground fl., **San Francisco,** CA 94108 (tel. (415) 421-3473). Other offices in Europe include: 28A Poland St. (Oxford Circus), **London** WIV 3DB (tel. (0171) 437 77 67). (See Getting There From North America: Charter Flights for information on **Council Charter,** CIEE's air travel division.)

Educational Travel Centre (ETC), 438 N. Frances St., Madison, WI 53703 (tel. (800) 747-5551; fax (608) 256-2042). Flight information, HI/AYH cards, Eurail and regional rail passes. Write for their free pamphlet *Taking Off.*

Let's Go Travel, Harvard Student Agencies, Inc., 53-A Church St., Cambridge, MA 02138 (tel. (800) 5-LETS GO or (617) 495-9649). Railpasses, HI/AYH memberships, ISICs, International Teacher ID cards, FIYTO cards, guidebooks (including every *Let's Go*), maps, bargain flights, and a complete line of budget travel gear. All items available by mail; call or write for a catalog.

Rail Europe Inc., 230 Westchester Ave., White Plains, NY 10604 (tel. (800) 438-7245; fax (914) 682-2821). Sells all Eurail products and passes, national railpasses, and point-to-point tickets. Up-to-date information on all rail travel in Europe, including Eurostar, the English Chunnel train. For more information on Eurostar, call (800) 94-CHUNNEL.

STA Travel, 5900 Wilshire Blvd., Ste. 2110, **Los Angeles,** CA 90036 (tel. (800) 777-0112 nationwide). A student and youth travel organization with over 100 offices around the world offering discount airfares (for travelers under 26 and full-time students under 32), railpasses, accommodations, tours, insurance, and ISICs. Eleven offices in the U.S. including: 297 Newbury St., **Boston,** MA 02116 (tel. (617) 266-6014); and 48 E. 11th St., **New York,** NY 10003 (tel. (212) 477-7166). In the U.K.: 86 Old Brompton Rd., **London** SW7 3LQ and 117 Euston Rd., London NW1 2SX (tel. (0171) 937 99 21 for European travel; (0171) 937 99 71 for North American travel; (0171) 937 99 62 for long haul travel). In Australia: 222 Faraday St., **Melbourne,** VIC 3053 (tel. (3) 349 24 11). In New Zealand: 10 High St., **Auckland** (tel. (9) 398 99 95).

Tagus Turismo Juvenil, Pr. Londres, 9B, 1000 Lisboa (tel. (1) 352 55 09; fax (1) 353 27 15). R. Guedes de Azevedo, 34-36 C, 4000 Porto (tel. (2) 200 50 81; fax (2) 200 44 42). Portugal's youth travel agency. Geared mainly toward Portuguese youth, but great for booking student airline tickets. Information on workcamps and *au pair* positions, discount transportation, HI cards, student residences, camping, and study visits in Portugal. English and French spoken.

Travel CUTS, 187 College St., **Toronto,** Ont. M5T 1P7 (tel. (416) 798-CUTS; fax (416) 979-8167). Canada's national student travel bureau, with 40 offices across Canada. Also in the U.K.: 295-A Regent St., **London** W1R 7YA (tel. (0171) 637 31 61). Discount flights open to all. ISIC, FIYTO, HI hostel cards, and railpasses issued on the spot. Offers free *Student Traveler* magazine, as well as info on Student Work Abroad Program (SWAP).

PUBLICATIONS

These companies offer travel gear and accessories, travel books, guides, maps—everything except your ticket outta here.

Bon Voyage!, 2069 W. Bullard Ave., Fresno, CA 93711-1200 (tel. (800) 995-9716, from abroad (209) 447-8441). Annual mail order catalog offers an amazing range of travel products, including books, luggage, electrical converters, maps, videos, and travel accessories. All merchandise may be returned for exchange or full refund within 30 days of purchase, and prices are guaranteed (lower advertised prices will be matched and merchandise shipped free). They also search their computer database for any item not listed in the catalog. MC, Visa accepted.

Forsyth Travel Library, P.O. Box 2975, Shawnee Mission, KS 66201 (tel. (800) 367-7984; fax (913) 384-3553). Call or write for their catalog of maps, guidebooks, railpasses, timetables, and youth hostel memberships. They also have a separate catalog of travel gear, including soft luggage, converters and adapters, security items, and accessories. MC, Visa, Discover Card accepted.

Travelling Books, P.O. Box 521491, Salt Lake City, UT 84152 (tel. (801) 461-3345). Mail-order service specializing in travel guides, books, and accessories which will make the armchair traveler weep with wanderlust. Call or write for a free catalog.

Wide World Books and Maps, 1911 N. 45th St., Seattle, WA 98103 (tel. (206) 634-3453; fax (206) 634-0558). Wide selection of travel guides and literature, travel accessories, and maps. Phone, fax and mail orders welcome.

GETTING THERE

■■■ FROM NORTH AMERICA

Most major airlines maintain an incomprehensible and sometimes completely random fare structure; prices vary according to the day of the week, month of the year, amount of time spent abroad, and date of reservation. When planning your trip, try to keep your schedule and itinerary flexible.

A flight to London, Frankfurt, Amsterdam, Brussels, or Luxembourg can cost considerably less than a direct flight to Madrid or Lisboa. In fact, flying to London is usually the cheapest way across the Atlantic, though special fares to other cities (Amsterdam, Brussels) can cost even less.

Off-season fliers enjoy lower fares. Peak season rates begin on May 15 or June 1 and run until around September 15. "Midweek" (Mon.-Thurs.) flights are cheaper than weekend fares.

Usually it's less expensive to fix a return date when purchasing your ticket, even if you pay to change it later. "Open return" and one-way tickets are pricey.

Don't hesitate to comparison shop. Since commissions are smaller on cheaper flights, some agents may be less than eager to help you find the best deal. Check the travel section of the Sunday *New York Times* and other major papers for incredibly cheap (but erratic) fares. Consult **student travel agencies** such as Council Travel, Travel CUTS, and Let's Go Travel (see Useful Addresses: Travel Services). They offer special deals to students that aren't available to regular travel agents.

COMMERCIAL AIRLINES

Flying with a commercial airline is the most expensive option, but the most flexible, reliable, and comfortable one as well. Look into smaller carriers such as **Virgin Atlantic** (tel. (800) 862-8621) and **Icelandair** (tel. (800) 223-5500) that may undercut the fares of large airlines. Most airlines offer price cuts for advance purchase. If you're abnormally flexible, some airlines offer **three-day advance purchase youth fares,** available only within three days of departure; return dates are open. You must be under 25. Most airlines no longer offer standby fares, and the few that do are only in summer. Call individual companies for the latest information.

The major airlines offer viable budget options in the form of **Advanced Purchase Excursion (APEX)** fares. These provide confirmed reservations and "open-jaw" tickets, which allow you to arrive and depart from different cities. For APEX, reservations must be made 21 days in advance, with 7- to 14-day minimum and 60- to 90-day maximum stay limitations. You'll be heavily penalized for cancellation or change of reservation. For summer travel, book APEX fares early.

CHARTER FLIGHTS

Charter flights are the most economical option, especially in high season. You can book some charters up to the last minute, but most summer flights fill up months in advance. Later in the season, companies start having trouble filling their planes and either cancel flights or offer special prices. Charters allow you to mix and match arrival and departure points in Europe. Once you've made reservations, however, the flexibility ends. You must choose your departure and return dates when you book and will lose money if you cancel within 14 to 20 days of departure.

Charters are often inconvenient, inevitably delayed, and require long layovers. In addition, most companies reserve the right to cancel flights until 48 hours before departure; ask a travel agent about your charter company's reliability.

Council Charter, 205 E. 42nd St., New York, NY 10017 (tel. (800) 800-8222). Affiliated with CIEE, Council Charter is among the oldest and most reliable of charter companies. Their flights can also be booked through any **Council Travel** office in the U.S. (see Useful Addresses: Travel Services).

Travel CUTS (see Useful Addresses: Travel Services).

Unitravel, 1177 N. Warson Rd., St. Louis, MO 63132 (tel. (800) 325-2222). Discounted airfares from 125 U.S. cities to over 50 cities in Europe.

DISCOUNT CLUBS AND CONSOLIDATORS

Discount clubs and ticket consolidators proffer savings on charter flights, commercial flights, and tour packages by acting as clearinghouses for unsold tickets, available three weeks to a few days before departure. Check the travel section of the newspaper (best is the *New York Times*). Clubs generally charge yearly dues of US$30-50. Study with care their often Byzantine contracts—you may prefer not to stop over in Luxembourg for 11 hours.

Air Hitch, with two main U.S. offices at 2641 Broadway, New York, NY 10025 (tel. (212) 864-2000) and 1415 Third St., Santa Monica, CA 90410 (tel. (310) 394-0550). No membership fee. For the truly flexible. You choose a minimum 5-day date range in which you want to travel and a number of possible destinations; must be willing to accept any destination with available seats during your date range. One-way service to Europe from the East Coast US$169, from the West Coast US$229.

AirTech Unlimited, 584 Broadway, Suite 1007, New York, NY 10012 (tel. (212) 219-7000; fax (212) 219-0666). 2 rue Dussoubs, 75002 Paris, France (tel. (1) 42 36 02 34; fax (1) 42 21 14 77). Travelers choose a region (Europe, Central America, the Caribbean, and three geographical regions within the U.S.), but must be flexible about specific cities and allow a 2- 5-day window in which to travel. One-way from Northeastern U.S. to Europe US$169, from West Coast US$249, from Midwest/Southeast US$229.

Bargain Air, 655 Deep Valley Drive, #355, Rolling Hills, CA 90274 (tel. (800) 347-2345, in CA (310) 377-6349; fax (310) 877-1824).

Discount Travel International, 169 W. 81st St., New York, NY 10024 (tel. (212) 362-3636; fax (212) 362-3236). No membership fee.

Moment's Notice, 425 Madison Ave., #702, New York, NY 10017 (tel. (212) 486-0503). US$25 annual fee; worldwide service.

Travel Avenue, 10 S. Riverside Plaza, #1404, Chicago, IL 60606 (tel. (800) 333-3335). For a ticketing fee of 5-12%, depending on the number of travelers and the itinerary, Travel Avenue will search for the lowest international airfare available and then take 7% off the base price.

Worldwide Discount Travel Club, 1674 Meridian Ave., #206, Miami Beach, FL 33139 (tel. (305) 534-2082). Annual US$50 membership fee.

COURIER FLIGHTS

Intrepids who pack light might consider flying to Europe as couriers. Although they seem fishy, many courier companies are quite well established. Here's how it works: a company hires you as a courier, uses your checked luggage space for freight, and lets you bring on your own carry-on luggage. Fares vary wildly. Most companies offer single round-trip tickets leaving from New York with fixed-length (usually short) stays. Couriers must be at least 18 years old and possess a valid passport. The following are courier companies and information resources. Check the travel sections of major newspapers for more courier companies.

NOW Voyager, 74 Varick St., #307, New York, NY 10013 (tel. (212) 431-1616). The major courier service. Arranges flights all over the world; mainly from New York, although some flights are available from Houston. Registration US$50. Special last-minute deals to European capitals for as low as US$299 round-trip.

Halbart Express, 147-05 176th St., Jamaica, NY 11434 (tel. (718) 656-8279). Flies to major European cities.

Courier Travel Service, 530 Central Ave., Cedarhurst, NY 11516 (tel. (516) 374-2299). Flights from New York, San Francisco, and Dallas to major European cities US$299-399, depending on the time of year.

Thunderbird Press, 5930-10 W. Greenway Rd., #112, Glendale, AZ 85306 (tel. (800) 345-0096). Sells the *Courier Air Travel Handbook* (US$10.70), which explains the procedure for courier air travel and lists courier companies.

Travel Unlimited, P.O. Box 1058, Allston, MA 02134-1058. Distributes a comprehensive, monthly newsletter that details all possible options for courier travel. One-year subscription US$25 (abroad US$35).

■■■ FROM EUROPE

PLANE

Iberia, TAP Air, and **Royal Air Maroc** offer speedy service between Madrid, Lisboa, and Casablanca, plus other major cities. Keep in mind that flying between and within European countries is expensive and may be unnecessary—rail and bus options are always cheaper. Note that baggage limitations for intra-European flights is a low 20kg (as opposed to 70 lbs. on transatlantic flights). For more **information,** contact the following organizations.

Air Travel Advisory Bureau, Columbus House, 28 Charles Sq., London N1 6HT (tel. (0171) 636 50 00). Puts travelers in touch with the cheapest carriers out of London for free.

Council Travel, Main Office, 66 av. des Champs-Elyseés, Immeuble E, Paris 75008 (tel. 40 75 95 10). 28A Poland St., London WIV 3DB (tel (0171) 437 77 67).

STA Travel, 86 Old Brompton Rd., London SW7 3LQ, U.K. (tel. (0171) 937 99 21).

TRAIN

If you ride an overnight train in a regular coach seat, you probably won't catch many Zs. A better option is a sleeping berth in a **couchette** car. (See Safety for safety tips on trains.) For more **information,** order the ultimate in rail references, *Thomas Cook's European Timetable* (US$24.95, with accompanying map of rail lines and ferry routes US$33.96, plus US$4 for postage) or *Camp Europe by Train,* with practical recommendations and general info on train travel. Both available from Forsyth Travel Library (see Useful Addresses: Publications).

Billet International de Jeunesse

BIJ tickets are a raving bargain if you're under 26. Discounts range from 30-45%, depending on the number of countries visited and the distances covered. Tickets are valid for rail travel anywhere in Western Europe (including former East European countries), and apply to most ferry services. When you buy the ticket, you specify both destination and route, then have the option of stopping anywhere along the route for up to two months.

BIJs are sold in Europe at **Wasteels** or **Eurotrain** offices—usually in or near train stations. For international journeys departing from the U.K., France, or Germany, tickets can be purchased in the U.S. from Wasteels Travel, 7041 Grand National Dr., #207, Orlando, FL 32819 (tel. (407) 351 2537; fax (407) 363-1041).

Eurail

If you're planning much travel outside Spain, Portugal, or Morocco, consider buying a **Eurailpass.** Before you do, make sure it'll save you money. Add up the second-class fares for the major routes you plan to cover, then deduct 30% if you're eligible for BIJ tickets. Watch out for supplements; on trains that require reservations (usually any but the slowest) the railpass requires you to pay an additional fee. Even with a Eurailpass, reservations are required for trips between major cities and covering distances over 250km. Within Spain, Portugal, and Morocco, train fares are low enough to make a railpass unnecessary.

Eurailpasses are valid in 17 European countries (including Spain and Portugal, excluding Morocco and the U.K.) and entitle you passage on some ferries and reduced fares on others. If under 26, a second-class **Eurail Youthpass** ranges from

US$398 for 15 days of travel to US$768 for 2 months. The **Eurail Flexipass** allows first-class travel for a set number of days inside a longer time window; 5 days of travel within a 2-month period costs US$348, under 26 US$255. The new, complicated **Europass** offers travel in a limited number of participating European countries (France, Germany, Italy, Spain, and Switzerland) determined by the number of travel days selected; as you buy additional travel days, the number of countries in which you can travel increases.

Eurailpasses are sold *only outside of Europe*. They're available through Council Travel, Let's Go Travel, Travel CUTS, and other travel agencies (see Useful Addresses: Travel Services). A replacement can be issued only if you've bought insurance from Eurail.

Note: The **InterRail** pass (Morocco's version of Eurail) is dead.

BUS

In general, bus travel is far more comfortable in Europe than in North America. (Incidentally, buses can travel from the U.K. to Iberia via ferry.) Call the office of travel agencies, such as Council Travel, STA Travel, and Travel CUTS in the city you're departing from.

Euroline Buses, 52 Grosvenor Gardens, London SW1W 0AU (tel. (71) 730 82 35). Expresses from London to over 100 destinations, including many in Spain and Portugal.
Magic Bus, 20 Filellian St., Syntagma, Athens, Greece (tel. (1) 323 74 71). Cheap, direct service between major cities in Europe. Ask for their student discounts.
Spain-Based Companies: See Spain Essentials: Getting Around: Bus.

FERRY

The cheapest way to get to Morocco by ferry is from Algeciras, Spain. Several boat lines run between Spain and Tangier. Frequent ferries connect Málaga and the Canary Islands to Tangier.

SPAIN

US $1 = 129.87 pesetas (ptas)	100ptas = US $0.80
CDN $1 = 94.96ptas	100ptas = CDN $1.10
UK £1 = 200.58ptas	100ptas = UK £0.50
AUS $1 = 96.25ptas	100ptas = AUS $1.00
NZ $1 = 78.74ptas	100ptas = NZ $1.30
SA R1 = 36.43ptas	100ptas = SA R2.70

■ Essentials

■■■ TOURIST OFFICES

Most towns have a centrally located **Oficina de Turismo** (fondly called **Turismo**) that distributes information on sights, lodgings, and events. Turismo will give you a free map that usually includes brief descriptions of sights and useful phone numbers. Although they don't book accommodations, many a Turismo keeps lists of approved establishments or can point you to a *casa particular*. Often they'll stock maps and brochures for the whole region, if not the whole country. Larger cities tend to have a city office as well as a regional one (with regional, national, and some city info); their services and brochures don't always overlap. In smaller towns, the staff, maps, and/or brochures may not communicate in English.

Viajes TIVE, the national chain of student travel agencies, is everywhere, peddling discount travel tickets, churning out ISICs and HI cards, and dispensing transport information.

■■■ EMBASSIES AND CONSULATES

If you're seriously ill or in trouble, contact your consulate, not your embassy (whose function is solely diplomatic). Consulates provide legal advice and medical referrals and can contact relatives back home. In extreme cases, they may offer emergency financial assistance. Embassies are in Madrid; consulates (subdivisions of a country's embassy) are in other major cities. Embassies and consulates are usually open Monday through Friday (call for specific business hours).

U.S. Embassy: C. Serrano, 75, Madrid 28006 (tel. (1) 577 40 00). **Consulates:** Po. Reina Elisenda, 23, Barcelona 08034 (tel. (3) 280 22 27). Av. Lehendakári Aguirre, 11, Bilbao 48014 (tel. (4) 475 83 00). **Consular Agencies:** Po. Delicias, 7, Sevilla 41012 (tel. (95) 23 18 85). Av. Jaime III, 26, Palma de Mallorca 07012 (tel. (71) 72 26 60). Franchy y Roca, 5, Las Palmas, Canarias (tel. (28) 27 12 59). Centro Comercial Las Rampas, Fase 2, Planta 1, Locales 12G7 & 12G8, Málaga (tel. (52) 47 48 91). Paz 6, Valencia 46003 (tel. (6) 351 69 73). Cantón Grande 16-17, La Coruña 15003 (tel. (81) 21 32 33).

Canadian Embassy: Edificio Goya, C. Núñez de Balboa, 35, Madrid 28001 (tel. (1) 431 43 00; fax (1) 431 23 67). **Consulates:** Via Augusta, 125, ATICO 3A, Barcelona 08006 (tel. (3) 209 06 34). Pl. Malagueta, 3 1., Málaga 29016 (tel. (952) 22 33 46). Av. Constitución, 302, Sevilla 41001 (tel. (95) 22 94 13).

British Embassy: C. Fernando el Santo, 16, Madrid 28010 (tel. (1) 31 90 200; fax 308 10 33). **Consulates:** Marqués de la Ensenada, 16, 2nd fl., Madrid 28004 (tel. (1) 308 52 01). Av. Diagonal, 477, 13th fl., Barcelona 08036 (tel. (3) 419 90 44). Pl. Nueva 8B, Sevilla 41001 (tel. (95) 422 88 75). Alameda Urquijo, 2, 8th fl., Bil-

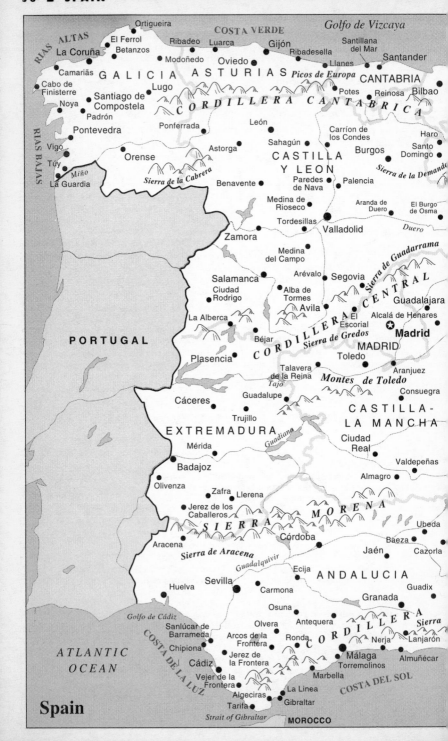

Spain

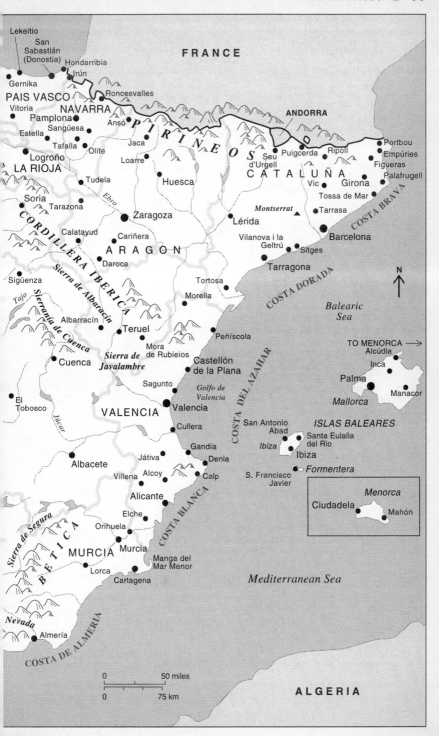

bao 48008 (tel. (4) 415 76 00). Pl. Major, 3D, Palma 07001 (tel. (71) 71 24 45). Av. Isidor Macabich, 45, Ibiza (tel. (71) 30 18 18; not a full consulate, but sends passport and visa application forms to Palma). Pl. Calvo Sotelo, 1, Alicante (tel. (96) 521 60 22). Po. Pereda, 27, Santander (tel. (942) 22 00 00). C. Reial, 33, Tarragona (tel. (977) 22 08 12). Duquesa Parcent, 8, Edificio Duquesa, Málaga (tel. (952) 221 75 71).

Irish Embassy: Claudio Coello, 73, Madrid 28001 (tel. (1) 576 35 00). **Consulates:** Torre Oeste, Gran Vía Carlos III, 94, 10-1A, Barcelona 08028 (tel. (3) 491 50 21). Galerías Santa Mónica, Av. Boliches, 15, Fuengirola, Málaga 29640 (tel. (952) 47 51 08). Pl. de Santa Cruz, 6, Sevilla 41104 (tel. (954) 421 63 61). C. San Miguel, 68A, 7th-8th fl., Palma 07002 (tel. (71) 72 25 04).

Australian Embassy: Po. Castellana, 143, Madrid 28046 (tel. (1) 579 04 28; fax (1) 570 02 04). **Consulates:** Gran Vía Carlos III, 98, Barcelona 08028 (tel. (3) 330 94 96; fax (3) 411 09 04). Federico Rubio, 14, Sevilla (tel. (5) 422 02 40; fax (5) 421 11 45).

New Zealand Embassy: Pl. Lealtad, 2, 3rd fl., Madrid 28014 (tel. (1) 523 02 26; fax (1) 523 01 71).

South African Embassy: Edificio Lista, C. Claudio Coello, 91, 6th fl., Madrid 28006 (tel. (1) 435 66 88; telefax (1) 577 74 14). **Consulate:** C. Mercedes, 31, 4th fl., Las Arenas (near Bilbao) 48930 (tel. (4) 464 11 24).

■■■ GETTING AROUND

TRAIN

Spanish trains are clean, somewhat punctual, and reasonably priced, although they don't run to some small towns. If you encounter problems, it'll be mainly at border stops, where you must change trains because of different rail gauges (although this by-product of Franco's isolationism is slowly being undone). The **Viajes TIVE** travel agencies help untangle the complex, swiftly changing world of Spanish rail.

RENFE

Spain's national railroad system is **RENFE** (**RE**d **N**acional de los **F**errocarriles **E**spañoles). Below are explanations of the numerous types of RENFE train service, ranked by convenience. Watch out for huge differences in prices; make sure you aren't cited only the most expensive. Bag on any *tranvía, semidirecto,* or *correo* train—these are ludicrously slow and are now uncommon.

AVE (*Alta Velocidad Española*): Shiny new high-speed trains that run on European gauge tracks. Although AVE trains now only dart between Madrid and Sevilla (hitting on Ciudad Real and Córdoba en route), service to Barcelona and eventually Paris is in the works. AVE soars above other trains in comfort and price, not just speed. Headsets bring movies or music to your ears, while train attendants bring newspapers, a drink, and a snack. It's like an airplane, only with human-size seats and legroom. Prices vary greatly according to time of departure. The cheapest one, the "valle," usually leaves very early in the morning; the most expensive one, "the punte," makes tracks around 2pm.

Talgo 200: *Talgo* trains that run on AVE rails. These hybrids currently service only Madrid-Cádiz, Madrid-Huelva, and Madrid-Málaga. Be warned, though: changing a Talgo 200 ticket earns you a 10% penalty.

Talgo: Generally the best choice. Elegant, low-slung trains zip passengers in air-conditioned compartments. May (or may not) be faster than *regional* (see below) but more comfortable, and costs about twice as much.

Intercity: Like a *talgo,* but not as nice or expensive. Four lines cover: Madrid-Valencia-Castellón, Madrid-Zaragoza-Barcelona, Madrid-Zaragoza-Logroño-Pamplona, and Madrid-Alicante.

Electro: Very comfortable and quick, but less so than *talgo* due to more intermediate stops.

Expreso, Estrella, and **Rápido:** The first two are usually equipped with sleeping cars. All three vary greatly in speed.

Cercanías: Commuter trains that radiate from larger cities to suburbs and nearby *pueblos,* making frequent stops and usually lacking A/C.

Regional: Similar to *cercanías,* they circulate through smaller towns.

RENFE also offers a number of discounts. Unfortunately, no youth railpass exists (not even the old *Tarjeta Joven).* Beware of **red days** (holidays), which add 10% to your fare!

Blue days: Most every day except for holidays and Friday and Saturday afternoons. On blue days, round-trip tickets are discounted 10%.

Tarjeta Turística: 3, 5, or 10 days free travel over a month (adult, 2nd class) for 15,400ptas, 24,200ptas, or 37,400ptas. More for first-class, less for children.

BIJ tickets: For international routes. Inquire at travel agencies. (For more info, see Getting There: From Europe: Train.)

Tarjeta Dorada: Only Spanish citizens or residents of at least 6 months are eligible. 40% discounts on all fares for travelers over 60.

Family Pass: Gives extra discounts to families (three or more relations) on blue days.

Buy tickets within 60 days of departure at RENFE travel offices, RENFE train stations, and authorized travel agencies. RENFE will refund 85% (75% on red days) of the ticket price for cancellation up to 15 minutes before train departure.

Unless you plan to spend every moment switching between trains, don't bother with the meticulously complete, 400+ page **Guía RENFE** (at train station bookstores, 1000ptas). This timetable doesn't list prices for any trains except AVE. It also lacks info on international routes.

FEVE and Eurail

The only other train company in Spain is **FEVE** *(Ferrocarril de Vía Estrecha),* actually a conglomeration of private companies which has short runs between northern towns not served by RENFE. Service is very slow, but dependable (kind of like a dumb, but loyal dog), and stations can be far from the center of town. FEVE can be contacted at its Madrid office, C. General Rodrigo, 6 (tel. (1) 533 70 00; open Mon.-Fri. 9am-2:30pm).

Eurail no longer sells its Spanish Rail Pass; you can either deal with RENFE's discounts or get a Eurailpass. Those with Eurailpasses must pay a small fee to make reservations on trains in Spain. (For more information, see Getting There: From Europe: Train.)

BUS

With train fares becoming more expensive and discounts being eliminated, many avant-garde budgeters have switched to bus as their preferred mode of transport. Bus routes are far more exhaustive than the rail network, are the only public transportation to isolated areas, and almost always cost less than trains. Standards of comfort are quite high, especially on longer journeys, and they are often even quicker than the corresponding train (with some glaring exceptions such as the swift, albeit pricey, Madrid-Sevilla train, which makes the trek in half the time). Particularly within a region, buses are the way to go.

Spain has no national bus line, just a multitude of private companies. This lack of centralization makes trip planning an ordeal. **Viajes TIVE** or the main information window at the bus station can help. Bus companies have worked it so that only one or two companies will serve a destination; their coverage rarely overlaps. In many cities, each bus company has its own station from which buses arrive and depart. In Madrid, most buses pass through the **Estación Sur de Autobuses** (tel. (1) 468 45 11). Note that Auto-Res/Cunisa, S.A. offers a *tarjeta joven* **(youth pass;** see details below).

Some of the major companies (all based in Madrid except Linebús) are listed below (for a list of **bus stations** in Madrid see Madrid Practical Information: Getting There By Bus). Plenty of regional companies have cities other than Madrid as their nucleus or bypass Madrid entirely.

ALSA (tel. (1) 528 28 03). Provides service between Madrid and Asturias, Galicia, and Castilla-León; and international service to Portugal, France, Italy, Switzerland, and Belgium.

Auto-Res/Cunisa, S.A. (tel. (1) 551 72 00). The workhorse of Spanish buses, though still comfortable, goes west from Madrid into southern Castilla-León and Extremadura; and from Madrid to Sevilla, Valencia, and its nearby beaches. They offer a *tarjeta joven* (youth pass, 200ptas) for those under 26, good for 10% discounts on normal fares.

Auto Transporte Julia, S.A. (tel. (1) 528 11 05). Service to Portugal, France, Italy, Switzerland, and Belgium.

Continental-Auto (tel. (1) 356 23 07). Runs to many *pueblos* of interest near Madrid, including Toledo, Guadalajara, and Alcalá de Henares.

Enatcar (tel. (1) 527 99 27 or 467 35 77). Many routes in new buses from Madrid to Andalucía (Granada, Málaga, Algeciras), Valencia (Alicante), and Cataluña (Barcelona).

Linebús (tel. (93) 265 07 00 in Barcelona, (96) 340 19 79 in Valencia). Service to France, U.K.

Samar, S.A. (tel. (1) 468 42 36). Runs south to Málaga, Granada, and Algeciras.

Sevibus, S.A. (tel. (1) 530 44 17). Between Madrid and Sevilla (including Huelva and Ayamonte) in festive-hued buses, complete with free drink and headsets for the movie or music.

PLANE

Given the substantial distances between Spanish cities, you might consider flying if you're pressed for time (or rich). **Iberia,** Spain's major national airline, flies out of hubs Madrid and Barcelona on both international and domestic routes (in Madrid tel. 587 81 56, in Barcelona tel. 301 39 93). **Aviaco,** a subsidiary of Iberia, covers only domestic routes. Prices at Aviaco and charter companies such as Air España (Palma), Aviación y Comercio (Madrid), and Euskal Air (Vitoria) are often lower than Iberia's.

Tarifas-minis are special Iberia and Aviaco fares. Available only on certain days, they cost about 60% of the normal price for round-trip, tourist-class tickets. Travelers under 24 can sometimes get an additional discount. You must buy your ticket at least three days in advance and travel round-trip (although you can take a circuitous route). There are no refunds or exchanges. Check with travel agencies such as Viajes TIVE for the latest *mini* offers.

CAR

A car brings freedom, flexibility, and handsome scenery at a cost. Spain has recently improved its highway system, so that major cities are connected by four-lane *autopistas* with plenty of service stations (although service stations still aren't common on back roads). The Spanish AAA is called the **Real Automóbil Club.**

Gas comes in super (97 octane), normal (92 octane), and diesel; an increasing number of gas stations provide unleaded. Prices are astronomical by North American standards: 110ptas per liter, or about US$3 per gallon.

Speeders beware: police can "photograph" the speed and license plate of your car, issuing you a ticket without even pulling you over. Don't cruise in the passing lane—it provokes the ire of police and fellow motorists alike. Officially you must be 18 or older and the proud owner of an **international driver's license** to drive in Spain (see Planning Your Trip: Documents and Formalities). For touring through picturesque local areas, the leaflets on *rutas turísticas*—available at tourist offices— suggest routes, but are low on practical information.

The ridesharing agency **Auto Compartido,** C. Carretas, 33, Madrid (tel./fax 522 77 72) helps match drivers and passengers for national and international destinations.

Renting a car in Spain is considerably cheaper than in many other European countries, although tax on rentals can be as much as 12%. Spain's largest national car rental company is **Atesa.** Another major rental company is **Europcar,** whose U.S. affiliate is National Car Rental. You'll find **Avis, Hertz,** and other major companies in cities and airports. Rates vary depending on whether insurance, tax, and a per km charge are included. Shop around; local companies may be cheaper. It's cheaper (for some reason) to reserve your rental in the U.S. before coming to Spain. Most companies require that you be at least 21 and have had a driver's license for at least one year. The following companies offer information on reservations.

Auto-Europe, P.O. Box 1097, Camden, ME 04843 (tel. (800) 223-5555; fax (800) 235-6321).

Avis (tel. (800) 331-1084). You must reserve while still in the U.S.

Europe By Car, Rockefeller Plaza, New York, NY 10021 (tel. (800) 223-1516 or (212) 581-3040). Student and faculty discounts.

Hertz Rent-A-Car (tel. (800) 654-3001).

Kemwel Group (tel. (800) 678-0678).

National Car Rental (tel. (800) 227-7368).

MOPED AND BICYCLE

Touring by **moped** is a breezy way to see the country. Mopeds cruise at an easy 40mph and don't use much gas. They can be extremely dangerous in rain and on rough roads or gravel, so always wear a helmet and don't pack a huge, unwieldy, unbalancing backpack. Rental agencies reside in most cities (US$20-25 per day, less in coastal areas where tourist rentals are more common).

Bicycling is a gloriously active mode of transport that allows you to see the country close up. Even experienced cyclists should think twice about pedaling through central and southern Iberia in the scorching summer (the north is cooler and less crowded). Back roads in flatlands and coastal areas are the best for bike touring; beware of more mountainous regions. Bicycles aren't permitted on toll highways.

The first thing to buy is a sturdy bike helmet, difficult to find in some areas of Spain. You'll also need a tough bike lock (the best are made by Kryptonite and cost US$35-US$50), a strong pump, and various spare parts and tools. Wise cyclists bring along a basic bike repair book and the relevant gadgetry. **Bike Nashbar,** 4112 Simon Rd., Youngstown, OH 44512 (tel. (800) 627-4227) offers excellent prices on equipment—it's generally the best deal around.

Airlines count a bicycle as your second free piece of checked luggage. As a third piece, it'll cost US$85 each way. The bike can't weigh over 70 lbs. and must be boxed (normally boxes are available at the airport). Policies vary, so call individual airlines.

A number of books about biking in Europe recommend scenic and cyclable roads. *Europe by Bike,* by Karen and Terry Whitehill (The Mountaineers Books, Seattle, WA (tel. (800) 553-4453); US$14.95), with detailed info on biking in 11 countries, is a fantastic reference for planning your trip and outfitting your bike.

HITCHHIKING

Let's Go does not recommend hitching as a means of travel; the information presented below and throughout the book is not intended to do so.

Hitchers report that Castilla and Andalucía offer little more than a long, hot wait and that hitchhiking out of Madrid—in any direction—is virtually impossible. The Mediterranean coast and the islands are supposedly more promising. Approaching people for rides at gas stations near highways and rest stops reportedly gets results.

The dangers of hitchhiking should not be underestimated. Drivers have raped, sexually assaulted, and killed passengers. If you choose to solicit a ride, avoid doing it alone. Experienced hitchers sit in the front, and never get in the back seat of a two-door car. If the driver begins to harass them, they ask firmly to be let out. In an emergency, opening the door on the road may surprise a driver enough to slow down. Pretending you're about to vomit may also help.

FERRY

Ferrying to Spain's Mediterranean and Atlantic islands is scenic, romantic, and sunny. **Transmediterránea** is the major player between the Islas Baleares (Balearic Islands) and the Islas Canarias (Canary Islands); also investigate smaller companies such as **Flebasa.** Don't forget to ask about discount fares. During high season, make reservations and expect overcrowding. Buy your ticket at least an hour prior to departure to avoid paying a surcharge on board.

Couchettes are good deals on overnight trips. A *silla,* the least expensive option, is a deck chair. A *butaca,* good for sleeping and sunning alike, is more akin to an airplane seat.

■■■ ACCOMMODATIONS

Note: Accommodations prices listed throughout *Let's Go* are not set in stone and should not be used as proof (i.e. *don't* shove *Let's Go* under a hostel owner's nose if you're quoted a price higher than the one we list). Due to inflation, prices will inevitably go up.

YOUTH HOSTELS

The **Red Española de Albergues Juveniles (REAJ),** the Spanish Hostelling International (HI) affiliate, runs about 100 youth hostels year-round and over 140 in summer. A bargain bed costs from 650-1500ptas per night, depending on location and the (relative) poshness of the facilities. Rates are slightly higher for guests 26 or older. **Pensión completa** (full board: a bed and two meals) and **pensión media** (half board: a bed and one meal) are sometimes offered. Hostels are typically some distance away from the town center. Early curfews are common and enforced lockouts may cramp your style. As they're often brimming with school groups, don't expect much privacy. To reserve a bed in high-season (July and August), obtain an **International Booking Voucher** from REAJ (or your home country's HI affiliate) and send it to the desired hostel four to eight weeks in advance of your stay.

To stay in a hostel, an **HI card** (1800ptas) is almost always required. Rarely sold on the spot, they're easily found at Viajes TIVE, other travel agencies, and REAJ offices. Also mandatory is a **sleepsack,** so either bring your own or rent one from the hostel—in listings we'll write "Sheets 200ptas." (To make a cheap sleepsack, see Planning Your Trip: Packing.) Youth hostels are not to be confused with posh *albergues nacionales,* ritzy government-run establishments in out-of-the-way places.

For **information** such as hostel addresses, contact REAJ, C. José Ortega y Gasset, 71, Apartado 208, Madrid 28006 (tel. (1) 347 76 29 or 347 76 30; fax (1) 401 81 60). (See also Planning Your Trip: Documents and Formalities: Hostelling Organizations.)

PENSIONES AND HOSTALES

Accommodations have many an alias in Spain; each name indicates a specific type of establishment. All legally registered establishments must display a blue plaque identifying their category. The outlaws (terms no longer registered with Turismo, hence not required to fulfill its standards) are *fondas* and *casas de huéspedes.* Many cities are swamped in high-season (see Accommodations sections under specific cities); make reservations or start searching for lodgings early in the day.

Cheapest and barest are **casas de huéspedes** and **hospedajes.** The terms are mostly equivalent, though the latter is more common in the north, the former in the south. **Pensiones** and **fondas** are one step up. **Hostales** have sinks in their bedrooms, whereas **hostal-residencias** verge on hotel poshness. *Hostales* are rated by the government on a two-star system; even one-star places in this category are usually very comfortable. Note that *pensiones, casas de huéspedes,* and *casas* are basically boarding houses, often lacking heat, having curfews, and fonder of long-term guests *(estables)*. The highest-priced accommodations are **hoteles** (which must have a bathroom in each room), often beyond the reach of budget travelers. Many establishments are family-run, and make up their own rules. When in doubt, ask.

"**Full bath**" or "**bath**" refers to a shower and toilet, while "**shower**" means just a shower stall. Most rooms that *Let's Go* lists have winter heating, as it can get cold in Spain (particularly the mountainous north).

Before handing over your passport, ask to see a room and verify the price, which proprietors are required by law to post prominently in every room and by the main entrance. Minimum and maximum prices are fixed according to the facilities, but don't expect these to correspond exactly to low and high seasons. Prices can be undercut, but not legally exceeded. Haggling for prices in small inns is still acceptable. Single rooms are sometimes hard to come by, so solo travelers should be prepared to pay for a double.

If you run into trouble when it's time to pay, ask for the **libro de reclamaciones** (complaint book), which by law must be produced on demand. The argument will usually end immediately, since all complaints must be forwarded to the authorities within 48 hours and hotel-keepers are penalized for overcharging. As many tourist offices keep lists of accommodations, report any problems to them; tourist officials may offer to call the establishment for you to resolve disputes.

CAMPING

Campgrounds are the cheapest genre of accommodations for groups of two or more people. They either charge separate per person, per tent, and per car fees, or charge for a *parcela*—a small plot of land which includes space for car and tent—plus a possible additional per person fee. Prices can add up for lone travelers, and even for pairs. The government regulates campgrounds on a three-class system, rating and pricing them by the quality of amenities. All campgrounds must post fees within view of the entrance and are required by law to provide sinks, showers, and toilets. The ritzier ones may have a playground, grocery store, cafe/restaurant, post office, car wash, and pool. In high-season, make reservations and arrive early. Information on official camping areas is available from most tourist offices, which also stock the **Guía de campings,** a fat guide to all official campgrounds in Spain.

ALTERNATIVE ACCOMMODATIONS

In some regions tourist authorities are aggressively promoting alternate types of accommodations to help deal with insufficient accommodations in larger cities and to bolster tourism in rural areas.

Casas particulares (private residences): May be the only choice in less touristed towns. Some tourist offices keep lists of residences, though in many places past troubles have led them to withhold information on the subject. Restaurant proprietors and bartenders often supply names and directions.

Casas rurales (rural cottages) and **casas rústicas** (farmhouses): Referred to in official publications as *agroturismo*. Most popular in the Basque Country and Navarra. Overnight rates range from 1000 to 3500ptas.

Refugios: Rustic huts in the mountains. You usually have to walk to them. Write to the Federación Española de Deportes de Montaña y Escalada, Alberto Aguilera, 3, 28015 Madrid (tel. (1) 445 13 82; fax (1) 445 14 38) for more information and the address of the autonomic federation in your mountain of choice.

Colegios mayores (state university student dorms): Open to travelers in summer; the Consulate General of Spain (see Planning Your Trip: Useful Addresses: Embassies and Consulates) has more information. Private universities also rent out rooms in their **residencias** (dorms). Ask local tourist offices for more information.

Monasteries—Benedictine and Cistercian—and **Convents:** Peaceful lodgings in somewhat rural settings. Where else can you enjoy Gregorian chants and austere Romanesque and Gothic architecture? Silence, prayer, and seclusion are the rule. Lodgings are usually single-sex and visitors are expected to respect the ways of the Order. Several monasteries refuse to charge, instead suggesting a donation (about 1500ptas). Both the national and local tourist offices keep lists with directions, telephone numbers, rules, and suggested donations. Reservations generally must be made well in advance.

Paradores Nacionales: The pride of the Spanish tourist industry. Castles, palaces, convents, and historic buildings that have been converted into luxurious hotels. At least 12,000ptas for a double, if not more.

■■■ FOOD AND DRINK

The Spanish prize fresh ingredients and sauces that don't overpower a dish. Each region has developed its own gorgeous repertoire of dishes based on indigenous produce, meats, and fish (often in combination). While the most well known Spanish dishes—*paella, gazpacho,* and *tortilla española*—are from Valencia, Andalucía, and Castilla respectively, the most sophisticated and varied cuisines on the peninsula were developed in the País Vasco, Navarra, Cataluña, and Galicia.

TYPICAL FARE

Coastal areas prepare their catches distinctively and deliciously. The Basques are undisputed masters of *bacalao* (cod), *chipirones en su tinta* (squid in its own ink), *sopa de pescado* (fish soup), and mouthwatering *angulas a la bilbaína* (baby eels in garlic). Along an earthier vein, their *pimientos del piquillo* (roasted red peppers) are heavenly whether *rellenos* (stuffed) or alone with bread. Galicians drool over *empanadas* (pies) filled with uncommonly good *bonito* (tuna), *pulpo* (octopus), *mejillones* (mussels), and *santiaguiños* (spider crabs). Cataluña is the home of *zarzuela*, a seafood and tomato bouillabaisse, and its own version of *langosta* (lobster). Cataluña is also famed for its juxtapositions of sweet and sour flavors, as in *oca con peras* (goose with pears). A simpler but no less delicious specialty are *torradas*, hearty toast spread with crushed tomato and sometimes topped with *butifarra* (sausage), ham, or other more substantial fare. Menorcan mayonnaise was the precursor of Miracle Whip (and named for the capital Mahón). Chefs of the Islas Baleares stir up a variety of fish stews, while Andalusians are masters of the light touch in fried fish. Mallorca's *ensaimada*, angel's hair pastry smothered in powdered sugar, sweetens up breakfast throughout the mainland.

Valencia's menu makes innovative use of rice; its *paella*, the saffron-seasoned dish made with meat, fish, poultry, vegetables, or snails, is an international celebrity (there are over 200 varieties throughout the region). In the north, Asturias warms to *fabada* (bean stew) and finishes it off with *queso cabrales* (blue cheese). Landlocked Castilla churns out dense *cocido* (stew) of meats, sausage, and chick-peas, as well as *chorizo,* an ugly but savory little sausage seasoned with paprika and garlic. For pork lovers, impossibly tender (such that it can be sliced with a plate) *cochinillo asado al horno* (roast suckling pig) is a glutton's delight. Culinary adventurers shouldn't miss Navarra's quirky *perdiz con chocolate* (partridge in chocolate). Grilled meats and fish are described as *"a la parrilla,"* while roasted meats are *"asados."*

Spain's greatest contribution to civilization is available throughout the country: *jamón serrano/jamón del país* (the best of which comes from pigs fed only acorns) is cured ham, stronger and more flavorful than regular ham, which the Spanish call *jamón york* or *jamón dulce*. It is served in exquisitely simple dishes, as an appetizer—as in *melón con jamón* (canteloupe and ham)—or as a full meal.

Two delightful English-language **reference books** on Spanish foods and wines are Penelope Casas's *The Foods and Wines of Spain* and *Tapas*. Campsa, the petro-chemicals company, publishes an excellent, regularly updated guide to Spanish res-taurants called *Guía Campsa*. Also see our **Glossary of Food and Restaurant Terms** in the back of the book.

MEALS AND DINING HOURS

Spaniards start their day with a continental breakfast of coffee or thick, liquid choc-olate and *bollos* (rolls) or *churros* (lightly fried fritters). *Café solo* means black cof-fee; add a splash of milk and it's *café cortado*. *Café con leche* (coffee with milk) is what most people quaff at breakfast.

As in most of Europe, dinner ("lunch" to Americans) is served at midday, between 2 and 3pm. The midday meal traditionally consists of several courses: an *entremesa* (appetizer) of soup, salad, or another starter; a main course of meat or fish; and a dessert of fruit and *queso* (cheese), or perhaps a sweet. Often you must order the vegetable separately. In family-style restaurants, servers may automatically set out a lettuce and tomato salad before a group of diners.

Supper at home is light and devoured around 8pm. Supper out begins any time after 9pm, usually at 10pm, and is a light, three-course meal.

RESTAURANTS

Some restaurants are "open" from 8am until 1 or 2am, but most serve meals from 1 or 2pm to 4pm only, and in the evening from 8 until 11pm or midnight. Eating at the bar is always cheaper than at tables. Usually the check isn't brought to your table unless you request it. You can leave the proper amount on the table or pay at the register.

Each city's tourist office rates its *restaurantes* with a row of forks, five forks indi-cating luxury. *Cafeterías* are rated by a row of up to three cups. All *cafeterías* and one- and two-fork establishments are in the budget range. Prices for a full meal range from about 800ptas in the cheapest bar-restaurants to perhaps 1800ptas in a four-forker.

Dining options are three: **Platos combinados** (combination platters) include a main course and side dishes on a single plate, plus bread and sometimes beverage. **Menú del día**—two or three dishes, bread, wine/beer/mineral water, and dessert—costs roughly 800-1500ptas. Generally, you choose one dish from Group A and one from Group B. Spanish workers, from blue-collars to CEOs, usually settle into a favorite restaurant, ordering the *menú* every day at lunch. The food ranges from decent to superb, and the dishes are the most typically Spanish—you'll be full when the dust clears. *Lentejas* (lentils), *cocido* (stew with chick-peas), *ensalada* (salad), *sopa* (soup), *paella, pollo* (chicken) in all its forms, seafood, and *patatas* (potatoes) often turn up on menus. **A la carta** is a written menu from which you order sepa-rate entrees. A full meal ordered in this fashion can run twice as much, or more, than the *menú*.

TAPAS

Devoured in bars, **tapas** (named for the *tapa* or sausage slice that used to be placed atop a wine glass to keep flies out) are ever so conducive to convivial good spirits. Seek out these varied delights in *tascas* that specialize in given varieties (in many bars, regrettably, they're not made on the premises). A *tasca*, often also called a **tab-erna,** is a bar or pub that serves *tapas* at a counter or a few tables in back. *Tabernas* are generally open noon to 4pm and 8pm 'til midnight or 2am. **Mesones** are *taber-nas* that primarily serve at tables, though some have bars for standing. Those who don't speak Spanish can indicate their *tapa* of choice by pointing at the array on (or behind) the counter. Some *tapas* terms:

Tapas are regular appetizer-like servings.
Pinchos are *tapas* in the País Vasco.

Raciones may be equal to an entree in size.
Bocadillos are *tapas* served as a sandwich on a hunk of thick bread—often a viable substitute for lunch.

Your fork may find its way into the following: *pimientos rellenos* (stuffed peppers), *champiñones al ajillo* (mushrooms in garlic sauce), *jamón serrano* (smoked ham), *atún* or *bonito* (tuna), *merluza* (hake), *calamares fritos* (fried squid), *chorizo* (spicy sausage), *gambas* (shrimp), *boquerones* (smelts), *ternera* (veal), *lomo* (pork), *judías verdes* (green beans), and *lenguado* (sole).

DRINKS

Wash down your *tapas* with a draft beer (request *cerveza del país* for uniformly excellent Spanish beer), a glass of wine (**vino** *blanco* is white, *vino tinto* red, *vino rosado* (rosé), or sherry *(jerez)*. The *vino de la casa* (house wine) makes an economical, often delicious, choice.

Perhaps the most famous of Spanish wines is **jerez** (sherry), which hails—and takes its name—from Jerez de la Frontera in Andalucía. Tipple the dry *fino* and *amontillado* as aperitifs, or finish off a rich supper with the sweet *oloroso* and *dulce*. The *manzanilla* produced in Sanlúcar (near Cádiz) has a slightly salty aftertaste, which some ascribe to the salt-impregnated soil of this coastal area.

The region around Córdoba presses the delicious dry wines Montilla and Morilas. La Rioja's vintages, Castilla's Valle del Duero (e.g., Vega Sicilia, strictly for Prime Ministers) labels, and Cataluña's whites and *cavas* (champagnes) are world-famous. But even Lord Peter Wimsey would deem local wines and liqueurs uniformly fine. You might down some Tenerife from the Islas Canarias or the full-bodied reds from Cariñena near Zaragoza. Also for swigging are the fresh young Ribeiro and more delicate Albariño from Galicia, the muscatel of Málaga, and **sidra** (alcoholic cider) from Asturias and País Vasco (see San Sebastián: Food). Spanish **sangría,** a red-wine punch, stirs in sliced peaches and oranges, seltzer, and sugar; a dash of brandy supplies the kick. A lighter option is *tinto de verano,* a cold summer drink of red wine and carbonated mineral water.

A **caña** is a normal-sized draft beer, a **tubo** a large (served in a tall cylindrical glass), a **corto** (or a **zurito** in the Basque country) a teeny-tiny one. The blanket term for beer is **cerveza**. A **chato** is a small glass of wine. A mixed drink in a wine glass is generically called a **bica** or **copa.** A refreshing blend of beer and *gaseosa* (sweetened seltzer, resembling 7-Up) is called a **clara.** In entertainment listings, look under the *Ir de Copas* heading for late-night places to drink.

Spain whips up numerous non-alcoholic quenchers, most notably **horchata de chufa** (a cooling orgeat made from pressed almonds) and the crushed-ice **granizados.** Toast your shady spot on a *terraza* (outdoor café) with *blanco y negro* (white and black, i.e., ice cream and coffee float). Or a *leche manchada* (stained milk), steamed milk with a dash of coffee. The Spanish take on *batidos* (milkshakes) is wickedly creamy.

■■■ COMMUNICATIONS

MAIL

The most reliable way to send a message is actually via telegram (see below); the least is by surface mail, which may take over two months. Mail sent from small towns takes longer than from major cities. Stamps are sold at post offices, hotels, and tobacconists. (Identify tobacconists by the brown sign with yellow lettering and an icon of a tobacco leaf; they always have postal scales.)

Air mail: *Por avión.* Takes 7-10 business days to reach the U.S. and Canada; faster to the U.K. and Ireland; slower to Australia and New Zealand. Postage for a letter 91ptas.

Surface mail: *Por barco.* Takes one month or more, packages two to three months. Considerably less expensive than air mail.

Postcards: *Postales.* Take even longer than letters. Postage 91ptas.

Registered or express mail: *Registrado* or *certificado.* The most reliable way to send a letter or parcel home. Takes 4-7 business days. Postage for a letter 500ptas.

Overnight mail: *Postal Expres.* Recipient must sign upon receipt. Spain's equivalent of Federal Express. Promises overnight national delivery but inevitably takes 2-3 business days; promises 2-4 day international delivery but usually takes 5-7 days. It is best to go private with companies like DHL, UPS, or the Spanish company SEUR. Look under *mensajerías* in the yellow pages. Postage 4300-5500ptas.

General Delivery mail: *Lista de Correos.* Letters or packages held for pick-up. Letters should be addressed as follows: LAST NAME, First Name; Lista de Correos; City Name; Postal Code; COUNTRY; AIR MAIL. When you pick it up, always ask for mail under both your first and last name to make sure it hasn't been misfiled. You can have mail forwarded to another Lista de Correos address if you must leave town while expecting mail. Usually no charge for pick-up.

American Express: Mail (no packages) for cardholders may be sent to some AmEx offices, where it'll be held. This service may be less reliable than Lista de Correos. A directory of which offices hold mail can be had from any AmEx office, or contact their main office at American Express Tower C, Royal Financial Center, 200 Vesey St., New York, NY 10285 (tel. (800) 528-4800). Will keep mail for one to three months after receipt.

TELEGRAPH

A telegram *(telegrama)* is the most reliable means of communication. Telegraph offices are inside **post offices.** Costs 145ptas per word.

FAX

Most Spanish **post offices** have fax services. Some photocopy shops and some telephone offices *(Telefónica)* also offer fax service, but they charge more than the post office (whose rates are regulated by the government), and faxes can only be sent, not received. The word for fax is the same in Spanish.

Throughout Spain, the price at post offices is standardized. (Prices not including IVA.) To send to North America: 1460ptas for the first page, 1225ptas each additional page. To receive: 360ptas for the first page, 215ptas each additional page.

TELEPHONE

Country Code: 34.
Local Operator: 003.
National Police Emergency: 091.
Municipal Police Emergency: 092.
Guardia Civil: 062.

Phone booths are marked by signs that say *Teléfono público* or *Locutorio.* Most bars also have pay phones. Local calls cost 25ptas. A three-minute call to anywhere in Spain is 100ptas. An international connection is 500ptas. **Phonecards** in 1000 and 2000pta denominations are more convenient than feeding coin after coin into a pay phone; they're sold at tobacconists (although, mysteriously, they're often sold out).

Direct-dialing from a phone booth is the cheapest way to make international calls. It can take up to 30 seconds after you dial to make the connection. You can call the operator beforehand to get an idea of how much your call will be. Then dial 07, **wait for the high-pitched dial tone,** then it's: country code + city code + phone number. Handy calling cards let you make calls even when you don't have a pocket full of coins, but their rates are higher. The country code for U.S. is (1).

AT&T calling card: Two services offered: USADirect for calling from overseas to the U.S. and AT&T World Connect for calling between two countries other than the U.S. Callers must have an AT&T card. To call the U.S., dial 900 99 00 11 for an English-speaking AT&T operator, then give the operator the number you want to reach and your calling card number. In Spain, you can use your AT&T calling card to use the "Dedicated Phone Line" at the Madrid airport and the Madrid Colón *Telefónica.* This allows you to contact a U.S. operator directly and be charged at U.S. rates.

MCI calling card: WorldPhone allows callers to access MCI service and bill calls to their calling cards. To call the U.S., dial 900 99 00 14, then give the operator the number you want and your calling card number. The system isn't perfect, so you may have to press a special button in the phone booth rather than dialing the number above.

Collect calls *(cobro revertido)* are billed according to pricier person-to-person *(persona a persona)* rates but may still be cheaper than calls from hotels. Amaze your friends by making collect calls from a non-public phone! (1) Dial 005. (2) State the number and your name. (3) Hang up the phone. (4) The phone magically rings when your call has been accepted.

Telefónica is a central phone office, for local, non-local, and international calls, where you take a number and then sit down in comfort. The doting staff does the legwork—service you'll be paying extra for. Offices are generally crowded. Some are open 24hrs. Visa credit cards are accepted.

Overseas Access is a telephone service offered by EurAide, P.O. Box 2375, Naperville, IL 60567 (tel. (708) 420-2343). Between May 2 and Octoberfest, European travelers can have phone messages collected for them at a "home base" in Munich. They can then call and retrieve their messages at any time. Particularly useful for travelers without a set itinerary. The cost is US$15 per week or US$40 per month, plus US$15 registration fee.

■■■ MORE MONEY

The smallest denomination of paper currency is 1000ptas. Coins come in 1, 2, 5, the rare 10, 25, 50, 100, 200, and 500ptas. Be aware that coins of the same denomination (i.e. 5 or 25 ptas) may have a number of very different looking coins. Sometimes coins of different value are more similar in appearance to one another than to those of corresponding value. The slang term for 5ptas is *"un duro."*

In summer, **banking hours** are Monday through Friday 9am-2pm; in winter, banks are also open Saturday 9am-1pm. The odd bank is open in the afternoon as well. Banks charge a minimum of 500-750ptas for currency exchange. Ubiquitous **ATMs,** in most Spanish cities, allow access to your bank account back home at a great exchange rate—though often for an additional fee. Look for Cirrus or appropriate symbols.

EL CORTE INGLÉS

This Spanish department store chain exchanges currency at competitive rates. (In Madrid: 1% commission, 250pta min. charge on cash; 2% commission, 500pta min. charge on traveler's checks. Open Mon.-Sat. 10am-9pm, Sun. noon-8pm.) You can make all purchases in US dollars or in traveler's checks, though they'll charge you 0.4% commission for checks and give you your change in *pesetas.* Located in the heart of larger cities close to subway or bus stops, El Corte Inglés also gives out free, excellent, indexed street maps. This multi-purpose retailing giant offers many conveniences to the traveler: pay phones, English-language novels and guidebooks, interpreters, a beauty salon, eateries, a bargain floor, sometimes supermarkets, and its very own travel agency. They've got it all. Watch for storewide sales in July and August.

VALUE-ADDED TAX (VAT)

The Value-Added Tax (VAT; in Spain **IVA**) is a sales tax levied on all goods and services in the European Union, at a rate that depends on the item. Stores, restaurants, and lodgings include IVA in posted prices, unless otherwise noted. In Spain the basic rate is 6-10%. Ask at stores and tourist offices about IVA refunds—a rare possibility with many restrictions (e.g., you must have made a single purchase of 15,000ptas or more). The tax on accommodations and other "services" is not refundable. Prices quoted in *Let's Go* include VAT except where noted.

TIPPING

Most restaurants add a service charge to your bill. It's customary to round off the sum to the next highest unit of currency and leave the change as a tip. In Spain you should generally tip 5-10%, more if the service is exceptional. Everyone else deserves a tip too: bar people 25ptas, train or airport porters 100-150ptas per bag, taxi drivers 10% of the meter fare (if they're nice), hotel porters 100-150ptas, parking lot attendants 15-25ptas, cloakroom attendants 25-100ptas, shoeshiners 25ptas, washroom attendants 25ptas, and hotel chambermaids 65-100ptas per day (optional).

■■■ LIFE AND TIMES

LANGUAGE(S)

Woody Allen once quipped that the Russian Revolution started when people realized that the Czar and the Tsar were the same person. Unfortunately, the five official languages in Spain differ far more than cosmetically from one another, although some spelling replacements can be of superficial use to Castilian speakers. The languages are **Castilian** (Spanish), **Catalan, Galician, Valencian,** and **Basque.** Castilian is universally spoken. Catalan, never having lost its prestige among the elite classes, is spoken in all of Cataluña, and has given birth through a number of permutations to Valencian, the regional language of the eastern region Valencia, and Mallorquin, the dialect of the Balearic Islands. Galician—related to Portuguese—is the language of the once-Celtic northwest corner. Although more prevalent in the countryside than in the cities, Galician is now spreading among the young, as is Basque, formerly confined to the rural citizens of País Vasco and northern Navarra.

All five languages have long-established standardized grammars and, except Basque, have ancient literary traditions. They're being saved from death by regional television broadcasts, native film industries, strong political associations, and extensive schooling.

City and provincial names in this text are listed in Castilian first, followed by the regional language in parentheses, where appropriate. Information within cities (i.e. street names or plaza names), on the other hand, is listed in the regional language in order to facilitate the use of street maps and street signs. Generally when traveling throughout Spain, Castilian names will suffice and are more universally understood. However, it is wise within the specific regions to excercise caution and politeness, and respect the language of choice.

Although Spanish is pronounced differently from country to country in Latin America, the Castilian spoken in Spain differs most in the pronunciation of "c" before "e" or "i." **Note: Let's Go provides a glossary and pronunciation guide in the back of the book for all terms used recurrently throughout the text.**

HISTORY AND POLITICS

This Just In...

On June 6, 1993, Felipe Gonzalez's socialists narrowly escaped defeat at the hands of the conservative Popular Party. Spain's economy has flagged recently, after a boom fueled both by massive foreign investment when Spain was integrated into the European Union and by heavy public spending to prepare the 1992 Expo and Olympic games. Unglamorous Popular Party leaders came close enough to victory to warn the Spanish government that voters—accustomed from 1986-1990 to Europe's largest growth rate at a frenetic 5% per year—are feeling the pinch.

Spain is still growing faster than most other European countries, but then again it was poorer to start with. In many respects, such as infrastructure, social service provision, environmental protection, and, notably of late, employment rate, Spain lags behind its EU cohorts. Some go so far as to say that "catching up" with Europe is Spain's unhealthy obsession: massive national improvement projects (such as the high-speed train between Madrid and Sevilla meant to induce oohs and aahs during the Expo) drain resources and are not guarantors of future revenue. The increasingly cynical populace is left to wonder when it will receive dividends from the big toys, and, fueled by the corruption scandals that have plagued the government, has put the pressure on González and his PSOE compatriots.

The post-Franco years have, not surprisingly, witnessed progressive social change. To the relief of many couples, divorce was finally legalized in 1981. Women are voting more, and currently comprise more than 50% of University students. The usual bag of social indicators highlight the modernization: church-going is at an all-time low (note that no major political party in Spain is religiously affiliated), drug use and petty crime are up. A particularly Spanish, or rather anti-Spanish, phenomenon has also accompanied the last eighteen years: regionalism. Cataluña's insistence that the Olympics were in the country of Cataluña, the June 1993 bombing of Madrid by Basque terrorists, and the vandalizing of Castilian signs in Galicia all illustrate the centrifugal forces unleashed by the loosening of Franco's stern centralism. However, the violent regionalists are very much the minority, and the majority of the population seems to be satisfied with the degree of autonomy its regions have already gained in the 1979 accords. By the early 1980s, many regions had control over all but their foreign relations. Most are pleased with the process—Parliamentary Democracy— if not always the substance of the central government, and see little point in pursuing unrealistic separatist politics.

And who could forget culture: a gifted generation of new artists and filmmakers—Almodóvar springs immediately to mind—is turning out innovative and laudable works. The government is happy to be in on the cultural-revival act, and in 1993 it purchased the 775-piece Thyssen collection for 350 million dollars, the largest in the world save Queen Elizabeth's.

Way Back

Spain was colonized by a succession of civilizations—Basque (here to this day), Tartesian, Iberian, Celtic, Greek, Phoenician, and Carthaginian—long before the Romans stomped in (the 2nd century BC). The **Romans** left their language, architecture, direct roads, and their techniques for the irrigation and care of grapes, olives, and wheat. A slew of Germanic tribes, including the Swabians (in Galicia) and the Vandals, swept over the peninsula, but only the **Visigoths** established a hold after converting to Christianity. Their influence has been exaggerated by the Orthodox Right (nicknamed the *godos* or Goths), who apotheosized their reign as a period of Christian purity and national unity (hence the predilection in the Middle Ages and among some sectors today for Visigothic names such as Guzmán and Gonzalo).

The Moors and the Reconquista

Following the unification of Arabs and their rides to victory in the Middle East and northern Africa, a small force of Arabs, Berbers, and Syrians invaded Spain in 711. Perhaps even welcomed by a portion of the badly divided Visigoths, the Arabs encountered no effective resistance, and the peninsula fell under the sovereignty of Damascus, generating a period of Muslim civilization and culture which reached its pinnacle in the 10th century. Under the Caliphate of Córdoba and its ruler Abderramán III, Spain was the wealthiest and most cultivated country in the world. Abderramán's successor, the ruthless dictator Almanazor, who is said to have had 40 poets in his retinue, snuffed out all opposition within his court and undertook a series of military campaigns that climaxed with the destruction of Santiago de Compostela, a Christian holy city, in 997.

The **Reconquista** (the Christian conquest and expulsion of the Moors) was not continuous: there were many periods of peaceful coexistence between the Moors and Christians. Rather, the turning point came when Almanazar died, leaving a power vacuum in Córdoba. The Caliphate holdings shattered into petty states called *taifas*. From that moment on, the Christians had the upper hand, first under the leadership of the Kingdom of León, followed by that of the tough Castilians. Christian policy was official (though not always de facto) toleration of Muslims and Jews, a policy that fostered a syncretic culture whose style of art is called **Mudejar.**

The Jews

In 1369 Enrique de Trastámara defeated his half-brother Pedro el Cruel (a legendary Richard III type) at Montiel, inaugurating the Trastámara dynasty that was to spawn Isabel la Católica. Always a bit precarious, toleration was substituted by Christian rigidity à la 14th-century France. The pogroms of 1391 started soon after, when thousands of Jews were massacred and many more converted. If a Jew converted, he or she was labeled a *converso,* and could still be persecuted and tortured. On the other hand, *converso*s could rise to the highest ranks of political, ecclesiastical, and intellectual institutions and hook up with the Christian aristocratic and merchant classes. The Catholic saint and author Teresa of Avila (1515-1582), for example, was the daughter of a *converso,* as was Luis de Santángel, the secretary of Isabel, and a big promoter of Columbus. The conversion of such a great number of Jews led to a paradoxical situation in which a "tainted" upper class desperately sought to deny its Semitic heritage by devising false genealogies, among other tactics. As a result, *Converso* culture is neither entirely Jewish nor Christian.

The Catholic Monarchs

In 1469, the marriage of **Fernando** de Aragón and **Isabel** de Castilla (a.k.a. Ferdinand and Isabella) joined Iberia's two mightiest Christian kingdoms. By 1492, the unstoppable duo had captured Granada (the last Moorish stronghold) and had shipped off Columbus, among others, to "explore" the New World. The couple's strong leadership would make the Spanish Empire the most powerful in the world by the next century. Following Christian Europe's example, the Catholic Monarchs introduced the evil **Inquisition.** Unlike the Italian Inquisition, the Spanish version was deployed to strengthen the authority of both newly-unified Spain and the Church.

The expulsion (or forced conversion) of the Jews in 1492 was remarkable because it was late by European standards (postdating England's and France's by two centuries) and because of the sheer numbers of native Jews that were kicked out. Such a drastic policy was all the more shocking given the fairly tolerant tradition of religious *convivencia* (coexistence) that had lasted until then.

The Hapsburgs and the Golden Age

The daughter of Fernando and Isabel, Juana La Loca (the Mad), married Felipe el Hermoso (the Fair), scion of the powerful Hapsburg dynasty. Ms. Crazy and Mr. Handsome spawned **Carlos I** (also called Charles V, 1516-1556), who reigned supreme over an immense empire—what is today the Netherlands, Belgium, part of Germany, Austria, Spain, and the colonies in the Americas. As the last Holy Roman Emperor, Carlos embroiled Spain in a war with France; as a cultured absolutist monarch and art patron of superb taste, he nabbed Titian as his court painter. The austere but grand emperor was a trend-setter too; he introduced to Spain the Hapsburg fashion of wearing all black—the first time in history black clothing was hip. (The fashion spread to the Netherlands as well and would last through three generations.)

But trouble was a-brewing in the Netherlands (then called the Low Countries and Flanders). After Carlos I died, his son **Felipe II** (Philip II, 1556-1598) was left holding the bag—a bag full of rebellious colonies. This stick-in-the-mud ruler was even more of a paper-pusher and fanatic Catholic than his father, controlling the country with an iron fist and jumpstarting the Inquisition. He even managed to snag Portugal when the king died in 1580. One year later the Dutch, led by Amsterdam, declared their independence from Spain. Poor greedy Felipe began a war with the Protestants, then provoked yet another with England (a country of non-Catholics) soon after. The latter ground to a halt when the Spanish Armada was creamed by Sir Francis Drake in 1588. Felipe retreated to his grim, newly built palace (El Escorial) and blubbered in his somber quarters when nobody was watching.

Felipe III (1598-1621) was a spoiled playboy who was having too much fun to bother running a big, centralized nation, so he let his adviser, the Duque de Lerma (Duke of Lerma) pull the strings. The ace puppetmaster was loathed by the rest of the court (and still is by historians). Inconveniently, the **Thirty Years' War** (1618-1648) broke out all over Europe, and defending Catholicism sapped Spain's resources. Charming Felipe expelled a total of almost 300,000 Moors during his reign.

Mustached wall-flower **Felipe IV** (1621-1665) held the country together through his long, tumultuous reign. Fighting with the Dutch had its ups (the successful siege of Breda, commemorated in the Velázquez painting) and its downs (the final independence of the Netherlands and truce-signing in 1848). In the early years, the Conde Duque de Olivares (Count-Duke Olivares), yet another scheming, ambitious advisor, manipulated impressionable young Felipe. Eventually the king's somber blood came to the fore, and he carried out his duties free of undue influence. Emulating his great-grandfather Carlos I, he was a discerning patron of art (painter Diego Velázquez, playwrights Lope de Vega and Calderón de la Barca) and architecture (the Buen Retiro in Madrid), and donned the very plainest black garb (all made of the most luxurious fabrics, of course). War with France ended with the marital union of his daughter and Louis XIV. His successor **Carlos II,** called the *"hechizado"* (the bewitched), was the product of generations of inbreeding, and was both epileptic and impotent. Upon his death at a young age, the country fell into disarray and a war of succession. Ironically, in an economically and culturally bankrupt Spain, once-thriving Castilla was the region most deeply wounded by the Golden Age.

The Bourbons and the Nineteenth Century

The 1713 Treaty of Utrecht seated **Felipe V,** a Bourbon grandson of Louis XIV, on the Spanish throne. The king built extravagant palaces like mad (to ape Versailles in France) and cultivated a flamboyant, decadent court of debauchery. Despite his example, the Bourbons who followed Felipe were able administrators who began to regain control of the Spanish-American trade lost to northern Europeans. They were also great patrons and entrepreneurs, responsible for scores of new canals, roads, and resettlement schemes, as well as for agricultural reform and encouragement of industry, the sciences, and the arts (through centralized academies). **Carlos III** goes down in history as Madrid's all-time best mayor for his radical transformation of the capital. Spain's standing in the world had recovered sufficiently that it could team up with France to secure the U.S.'s independence from Britain, chiefly through a succession of victories engineered in the southern states by Captain Gálvez. The next monarch, **Carlos IV,** is best known as the corrupt, ugly guy depicted in countless portraits by Goya.

This recovery period was shattered by the Napoleonic occupation and the subsequent restoration of arch-reactionary **Fernando VII,** supported by Wellington in his bid to revoke the highly progressive Constitución de Cádiz of 1812. As a result of Fernando's ineptitude, and partly inspired by the Liberal ideas embodied in that constitution, most of Spain's Latin American empire finally threw off the yoke during the first quarter of the 19th century. Parliamentary Liberalism was restored in 1833 upon Fernando VII's death and dominated Spanish politics with brief interruptions until the advent of Primo de Rivera's mild dictatorship in the 1920s.

The 19th century was a period of rapid industrialization and some regions, particularly Cataluña, prospered. A case in point is Cataluña's *Renaixença* (Renaissance), which produced the **Modernista** movement in architecture and design, led by the brilliantly creative Antoni Gaudí. However, most of Spain remained indigent and agricultural throughout the 19th century.

Recent History

In April 1931, **King Alfonso XIII** left Spain in ignominy and the Second Republic was born. Republican Liberals and Socialists established safeguards for farmers and industrial workers, granted women's suffrage and religious liberty, and chipped away at the influence of the military. The national euphoria of the Republic's first days faded fast. The 1933 elections broke the Republican-Socialist coalition and gave increased power to rightist and Catholic parties in the parliamentary *Cortes*. Military dissatisfaction and the rise of the Fascist *Falange* further polarized national politics. By 1936, the Radicals, Anarchists, Socialists, and Republicans had formed a loosely federated alliance to win the next elections. But then **Generalísimo Francisco Franco** grabbed command of the Spanish army and, aided by militarist uprisings inside Spain, plunged the nation into Civil War.

The three-year **Civil War** ignited worldwide ideological passions. Germany and Italy dumped masses of troops, supplies, and munitions straight into Franco's lap. Although Franco enjoyed popular support in Andalucía, Galicia, Navarra, and parts of Castilla, the Republicans controlled all major populations and industrial centers. The Soviet Union, via COMINTERN, atypically called for a **Popular Front** of Communists, Socialists, and other left sympathizers to stave off the threat of Fascism. However, the coalition was abandoned by the West and had only the International Brigade for outside support. The aid from the Soviet Union waned as Stalin, disgruntled by the Spanish left's insistence on ideological autonomy, and increasingly convinced that he would actually benefit from an alliance with Hitler, lost interest in the Spanish cause. It's remarkable that the anti-Franco resistance held out for even three years, proof in itself that many Spaniards rejected Fascism. 600,000 lives were lost to bombing, executions, combat, starvation, and disease.

Brain-drain followed on the heels of Franco's victory, as leading scientists, artists, and intellectuals emigrated en masse from totalitarian Spain. Worker dissatisfaction, student unrest, regional discontent, and international isolation characterized the first decades of the Franco dictatorship. A number of anarchist and nationalist groups, most notably the separatist Basque ETA, resisted the dictatorship through violent terrorist acts. As Franco aged, he attempted to smooth international relations by joining NATO and encouraging tourism, but the "national tragedy" did not officially end until Franco's death in 1975.

King Juan Carlos, grandson of Alfonso XIII and a Franco protege, sensed the national mood and undid much of Franco's damage. In 1978, under centrist premier Adolfo Suárez, the Spanish adopted a new constitution in a national referendum that led to the restoration of parliamentary government and regional autonomy.

Charismatic **Felipe González** led the PSOE (Spanish Socialist Worker's Party) to victory in the 1982 elections. González opened the Spanish economy and hobnobbed with mainstream politicians, overseeing Spain's integration into the EU in 1986. Despite his support for continued membership in NATO (he had originally promised to withdraw if he won) and unpopular economic policies, González was reelected in 1986 and continued a program of massive public investment. Inflation has been tamed and unemployment somewhat reduced; Spain's long stretch of startling economic growth has catapulted its economy to the front ranks of the industrialized world. Despite a recent tailing off in this growth and a strong challenge from the rejuvenated, more conservative Popular Party, González was once again reelected in 1993.

Revelations about massive corruption—most notably of the former head of the Guardia Civil (national police)—led to a resounding socialist defeat in the 1994 European parliamentary elections at the hands of the Popular Party. Although Felipe González continues to preside over a socialist government, the negative attention has also triggered losses in regional elections in the president's homeland and traditional socialist stronghold, Andalucía.

ART

Spanish painting first flowered in the Golden Age, at the height of the Spanish empire (roughly 1492-1650). Toledo's adopted Cretan and maestro of mannerism **El Greco** (1541-1614) used elongated figures to create atmospheres of boundless space. His most famous work, *The Burial of Count Orgaz,* stands proudly alone in Toledo's Santo Tomé. Court painter and Baroque artist extraordinare **Diego Velázquez** (1599-1660) created hermeneutic conundrums and slews of royal portraits. His joint treatise on brilliant optical realism, perspective, and ambiguity, *Las meninas,* can be found in Madrid's Prado; the artist himself can be found just to the left of the little girl. Velázquez's contemporaries created religious work for all tastes: **Francisco de Zurbarán** (1598-1664) a mystical austerity, **José Ribera** (1591-1652) a crude realism, and **Bartolomé Murillo** (1617-1682) a bland sentimentalism.

During the Neo-Classicist years, noted genius and libertarian **Francisco Goya** (1746-1828) used brush and canvas both to upstage his French contemporaries and to publicize his political views. Funded by the court, Goya mocked his corrupt patrons in *The Family of Charles IV* (Prado, Madrid), in which the royal family looks slightly less attractive than the Munster Family. Also in the Prado, *El tres de mayo de 1808,* one of Goya's most striking and well-known political paintings, comments on Napoleon's invasion of Spain. The Prado houses an entire room of Goya's Black Paintings, nightmarish visions such as *Bobabilicón.*

Spanish artists (often working in France) rebounded from centuries of mediocrity in the early twentieth century. **Pablo Picasso** (1881-1973) inaugurated his "Blue Period" while in Barcelona, and later co-pioneered Cubism, in which he shows an object from all angles in space. His 1937 *Guernica* portrays the horrible bombing of that title farming village during the Spanish Civil War. Save one silent hour to stare at it. Catalan **Joan Miró** (1904-1983) explored playful, colorful abstract compositions. Fellow Catalan and mustached person **Salvador Dalí** (1904-1991) was a major player in Surrealism, and proudly depicted, among other things, melted clocks. His wild autobiography (a precursor of the Warhol Diaries) is titled *Diary of a Genius.*

Antoni Tàpies, Antonio Saura and the hyperrealist **Antonio Lopez** have bridged the artistic scene to our day, as have sculptors **Chillida** and **Oteiza.** Since Franco's death in 1975, a new generation of Spanish artists—mere lads and lasses during the dictator's reign—has thrived. With the opening of new museums of modern art in Madrid, Barcelona, Valencia, Sevilla, and soon in Bilbao, Spanish painters and sculptors have, for the first time in a long time, been given a national forum for their creativity. Many of today's artists seem far more interested in message than in form. Some of these pre-balding upstarts include **Miquel Barceló,** (whose big, dense portraits look like swarms of black flies), abstract artist **José María Sicilia,** and sculptor **Susana Solano.** These works are so special in part because the artists have been unable to express themselves for so long; not only does a great deal of pent up emotion translate into a great deal of art, but today's Spanish artists, fresh on the scene, do not suffer from the cultural fatigue which mars the works of some of their European contemporaries.

ARCHITECTURE

Scattered **Roman ruins**—aqueducts, temples, and theaters—lie principally in Tarragona, Segovia, and Mérida. Since the **Moors'** religion banned representations of humans and animals, they channeled their brilliance into spectacular buildings and ornately patterned surfaces (such as the Alhambra in Granada and the Mesquita in Córdoba). Islamic and Christian influences melded in the **Spanish Romanesque** style, whose heavy stone monasteries and churches, such as Salamanca's *catedral,* proliferated in the 11th and 12th centuries.

Christians under Muslim rule created the **Mozarabic** fad. But after the Reconquista, it was Muslims who developed the truly novel **Mudejar** style, combining the Gothic and the Islamic in the Alcazars at Sevilla and Segovia. Toledo, center of Spain's Jewish culture, boasts some of the oldest **synagogues** in the world.

The embarrassing riches of the New World funded the **Plateresque** ("in the manner of a silversmith") movement, a flash variant of Gothic—unrestrained gold and silver and intricate ornamentation adorned every surface in Plateresque Salamanca. Influenced by the Italians, Jaén's Andrés de Vandelvira pioneered the **Spanish Renaissance** style, as seen in fundamentalist Felipe II's El Escorial. The pendulum swung back to opulence in 17th- and 18th-century Baroque, in Spain taking the form of the compressed ornament, shells, and garlands of the **Churrigueresque** style (named after José Benito Churriguera, though he was not a major architect of this overwrought style). Flamboyant examples include the altar of Toledo's cathedral.

In the late 19th and early 20th centuries, Catalan **Modernista** burst on the scene at Barcelona, led by quirky genius **Antonio Gaudí, Luis Domènich i Montaner,** and **José Puig y Caldafalch.** Modernista buildings take the notion of freedom seriously, swooping wildly about with voluptuous curves and unexpected textures. The new style took some inspiration from Mudejar relics, but relied heavily on the inspiration of organic natural forms and human imagination. The tradition of outstanding architects continues with such trendsetters as **Josep María Sert, Ricardo Bofill,** and **Rafael Moneo.**

LITERATURE

Spain's first important literary works appeared during the later Middle Ages, roughly during the years 1000-1500. The most significant work of this time period—as well as Spain's eldest surviving work—is the 12th-century *Cantar de Mío Cid* (Song of My Cid), a sober yet suggestive epic poem which chronicles national hero El Cid's life and military battles, from his exile from Castilla to his return to grace at the king's court. The period ended with *La Celestina,* a soap opera dialogue novel about a young man who uses an old, dishonest go-between to win over a girl's heart.

La Celestina is a precursor to the **picaresque novel** *(Lazarillo de Tormes, Guzmán de Alfarache)*, a rags-to-riches, Horatio Alger-esque story about a poor boy *(pícaro)* who, overcoming incredible odds, manages to become wealthy. This literary form is one of many which surfaced during Spain's **Golden Age,** roughly the 16th and 17th centuries, the era of the nation's greatest cultural (including literary) growth. Poetry thrived, and the sonnets and **romances** of **Garcilaso de la Vega** are still considered some of the most perfect ever written in Castilian. Along with friend **Joan Boscán,** Garcilaso is credited with having introduced the 'Italian' style (Petrarchan love conventions, etc.) to Iberia. **Sta. Teresa of Avila** and **San Juan de la Cruz** introduced **mysticism.** Much quality drama was also penned, including the works of **Calderón de la Barca** and **Lope de Vega,** who single-handedly knocked off more than 2000 plays. Both promoted the neo-platonic view of love in their works, claiming that if a person falls in love with another, his or her life will change both drastically and forever. **Miguel de Cervantes'** two-part *Don Quixote de la Mancha*—often considered the world's first novel—is perhaps the most famous work of Spanish literature, telling the hilarious tale of the hapless, marble-missing don and his sidekick, Sancho Panza, who, believing that they are *caballeros* (knights), try to save the world.

The 19th century produced such contrasts as the acerbic journalistic prose of **Larra,** foremost critic of Spanish society; **Zorrilla's** romantic *Don Juan Tenorio,* where the most popular of the Don Juanes dies and goes to heaven; and the classic great novel *La Regenta,* by **Leopoldo Alas "Clarín,"** about a tormented provincial town heroine à la Anna Karenina.

Modern literature begins with the **Generación del '98,** a group led by **Miguel de Unamuno** (essayist and professor at Salamanca) and cultural critic **José Ortega y Gasset.** Reacting to Spain's embarrassing defeat in the Spanish-American War (1898), these nationalistic authors used primarily the essay and novel forms to argue that the individual must regenerate spiritually and ideologically before the society can do the same. They were followed by the **Generación del 1927,** a group of experimental and renovating lyric poets, who yield from surrealistic and vanguard poetry to a deeply felt humanism, include Pedro Salinas, **Frederico García Lorca** (assassinated at the start of the Civil War), **Rafael Alberti,** and **Vicente Aleixandre.** In the 20th century, the Nobel Committee has honored playwright and essayist **Jacinto Benavente y Martínez,** poet **Vicente Aleixandre,** and novelist **Camilo José Cela** (author of *La Familia de Pascal Duarte*). Women writers, such as **Mercè Rodoreda** and **Carmen Martín Gaite,** have also made great strides during the past century.

READING MATTER

Bullfighting

Bullfighting as we know it (on foot) started in the seventeenth century, to the partial dismay of the Church, who feared the risks involved made the activity tantamount to suicidal (ergo sinful). Although anti-bullfighting arguments have persisted and evolved (in the Age of Reason they bemoaned the irrational use of land to raise bulls; now animal rights activists chain themselves to ring entrance gates), the fascination with the "spectacle" or the "rite" (it's not considered a sport) prevails. The activity has been analyzed as everything from a mythical to a psycho-sexual to a Nationalist phenomenon. The recent bullfighting renaissance has been accompanied by a couple of books by English-speakers on the subject. Bruce Shoenfeld's *The Last Serious Thing* examines the minutiae of the activity with vignettes such as "The Ticket Line" and "News of a Goring," as well as an interesting bullfighting defense in "Defending the Faith." Timothy Mitchell's *Blood Sport: A History of Spanish Bullfighting* rightfully criticizes the outsiders' tendency to judge bullfighting out of its historical context and proceeds to delineate one. Of course, we would be negligent not to plug Ernest Hemingway's famous account of bullfighting (and machismo) in *The Sun Also Rises* and *Death in the Afternoon*.

History

H.V. Livermore's *The Origins of Spain and Portugal* is a good one-volume history reaching back to the pre-Roman era. In *The Structure of Spanish History,* Américo Castro opened the door to a reevaluation of the Jewish part in Spanish culture. For a delightful survey of the Catholic Monarchs' and Hapsburg eras, read J. H. Elliott's *Imperial Spain 1469-1714.* Raymond Carr has documented the modern era well in *Spain, 1808-1939,* as has Pablo Fusi in *Spain: Dictatorship to Democracy.*

Art and Architecture

The best bibliographies and accounts of political, architectural, and art history are in *The Blue Guide*—especially learned and reliable since it's written by specialists. The standard work on Spanish architecture is Bernard Bevan's *History of Spanish Architecture. Palace For a King,* by J. H. Elliott and Christopher Brown, is a page-turner about the building of Felipe IV's Buen Retiro in Madrid. Fred Licht's collection of essays, *Goya,* is a must-read for fans of that artist. Robert Hughes' *Barcelona* (1992) traces nearly 2000 years of the city's architectural, cultural, and political history, from Barcelona's roots in the 1st century AD through the death of Gaudí in 1926.

Literature

A good survey of Spanish literature (in 8 volumes) is *A Literary History of Spain,* by R.O. Jones. Gerald Brenan's *The Literature of the Spanish People* is a comprehensive, opinionated history. N.D. Shergold's *History of the Spanish Stage* is a splendidly documented backstage account of Spain's brilliant Golden Age (16th-17th century) drama.

City Guides

The best architecture guides to Madrid are Guerra de La Vega's excellent, multi-volume illustrated series and the Madrid Colegio de Arquitectos' two-volume *Guía* (in

Spanish). Francisco Azorín's *Leyendas y Anécdotas del Viejo Madrid* outlines an entertaining, story-filled walking tour of the capital city. *Michael's Guide to Madrid* also sketches out walking tours of the capital (in English). The *Insight City Guide* series has an excellent volume on Barcelona written by long-term residents.

Other

In good bookstore travel sections you'll find books devoted to specialized aspects of travel in Spain. Ever since Washington Irving took up residence in Granada and wrote *Tales of the Alhambra,* American and British authors have been inspired by Spanish landscapes. The undisputed classics on Spain are 20th-century Bloomsbury-Circle-expatriate Gerald Brenan's *The Face of Spain, The Spanish Labyrinth,* and *South from Granada.* For good fiction and a taste of authentic Mallorcan flavor, try Robert Graves' Mallorcan stories in his *Collected Works.*

■■■ THE MEDIA

FOR VISITORS ONLY

Spain's tourist industry is superbly organized; national and regional governments publish excellent **brochures** and **pamphlets** on highly specialized subjects (e.g., snow sports, gastronomy, and festivals), usually in English as well as Spanish.

Lookout magazine contains classifieds and regular features on taxes, work permits, and sundry practical matters. It's published in English on the Costa del Sol (and available at newsstands in larger cities). Their publishing house also has a full line of books on the foods and wines of Spain, gardening, etc.

The Spanish Ministerio del Interior and national tourist office distribute a pamphlet called *Living in Spain,* which explains foreigners' rights and responsibilities, regulations governing residence and work, and special services available.

NEWSPAPERS AND MAGAZINES

ABC is the oldest national daily paper and has a somewhat conservative bent. *El País* has perhaps the largest readership and is the most professional of the bunch. *El Mundo* is a left-wing, younger rag. Barcelona's *La Vanguardia* is the regional newspaper of largest audience. *La Voz de Galicia* enjoys large readership particularly in Spain's northwest. *Diario 16* is critical but more moderate than *El Mundo.* The same publishers put out a popular newsweekly *Cambio 16,* with *Tiempo* as its main competitor.

Magazines called *revistas del corazón* (magazines of the heart) are tremendously popular in Spain. *Hola* is the most popular, followed by *Semana.*

TELEVISION

The state-run channels are called TVE1 and La2. The private national stations are Tele5 and Antena3. Every region has its own local autonomous network, broadcast in the region's language. In Madrid, for example, the local channel is TeleMadrid (TM3). News is on at 3 and 8:30pm on most stations. Programming includes well-dubbed American movies, sports (including bullfights), steamy Latin American *telenovelas* or *culebrones* (soaps/mini-series), *concursos* (game shows), and kitschy three-hour variety-show extravaganzas. Newspapers publish listings and schedules.

Canal Plus is Spain's HBO equivalent. It appears scrambled unless you pay for it, although once in a while it mysteriously unscrambles, to lure viewers to sign up.

Madrid

With broad, leafy boulevards, grandiose Renaissance and neoclassical monuments, endless museums, and a passion for nightlife, Spain's First City of 3 million dazzles and bewilders a steady stream of visitors from quieter corners of the world. Madrid combines the worldliness of New York, the glamour of Paris, the edginess of Chicago, the haphazardness of Mexico City, and the quirky intensity of L.A. into a fascinating, ceaselessly booming whole. Home to the frenetic characters in Almodóvar's films, Madrid nourishes an avant-garde social and political scene made famous by Spain's rich crop of contemporary authors and artists. Bright lights and a perpetual stream of automobile and pedestrian traffic blur the distinction between 4pm and 4am. Infinitely energized *madrileños* crowd bars and discos until the wee hours of the morning, often topping off a night of revelry with a traditional breakfast of *churros y chocolate.*

Trapped smack in the hot, dry Castilian plain, Madrid remains well-connected with the rest of the country. The sea is nowhere near the city, but a flotilla of overnight refrigerated transport ensure some of the freshest seafood in Europe. Even the Manzanares, what Lope de Vega called a wanna-be river, is sufficient excuse to build Renaissance and Baroque bridges worthy of the Guadalquivir or even the Seine. Although Madrid is as modern as any city, restrained building heights preclude the hyper-urban quality that skyscrapers evince. The scenery can change every couple of blocks: wide thoroughfares, modern office buildings, and luxury hotels border on older, narrow streets crowded with small shops and *pensiones;* bustling international shopping boulevards lead to quiet plazas and outdoor markets. Lush public parks provide some respite from the often oppressive summer heat.

Although it witnessed the coronation of Fernando and Isabel, Madrid was of no great importance until Hapsburg Felipe II moved the Spanish court here permanently in 1561—an unlikely choice of capital considering the city's distance from vital ports and rivers. Yet from that moment on, the city became the seat of wealth, culture, and imperial glory, watching over Spain's 16th- and 17th-century Golden Age of literature (Lope de Vega, Cervates), art (Velázquez, Zurbarán, El Greco), and architecture. Today's Madrid owes much of its neoclassical flair, from the Palacio Real in the west to the Museo del Prado in the east, to the 18th-century urban renewal of Bourbon Felipe V.

Passionately hostile to Franco's nationalists, the center was the last city to fall save for Valencia in the Spanish Civil War. Since then Madrid has kept up a furious pace. The capital of contemporary Spanish cultural life, surpassing Barcelona as the country's manufacturing and financial center, the city is anything but a museum piece. Despite Spain's recent economic recession, and a series of embarrassing government scandals, Madrid retains an unusual energy and vitality which make it a fitting symbol of Spain's newfound place as a leading European country.

■■■ ORIENTATION

The "Kilometro 0" marker on the sidewalk in front of the police station signals the epicenter of Madrid at **Puerta del Sol,** an intersection of eight streets. Sol is *the* transportation hub of the city: below ground, three Metro lines (blue #1, red #2, yellow #3) converge and transport people to within walking distance of any point in the city; above ground, buses and taxis swarm. Moreover, from Sol, most sights, museums, restaurants, *hostales,* and nightclubs are under a half-hour's walk away. Sol itself is packed with restaurants, *cafeterías, hostales,* shops, banks, *casas de cambio,* and services of all kinds.

Four major streets conduct traffic in and out of Sol. With your back to the clock tower on the **police station** (a good landmark):

1) The street leading traffic out of Sol (on the far left) is **Calle del Arenal.** C. Arenal runs into **Calle de Bailén** at its other end (in front of the Plaza de Oriente and Palacio Real). A right turn on Bailén leads to **Plaza de España,** with **Parque del Oeste** to the left and a view over the **Casa del Campo** beyond it (½hr.). **Paseo del Pintor Rosales** and its many *terrazas* border the park, the western edge of Madrid's *centro* (city center).

2) The street leading traffic into Sol is **Calle Mayor** (on the near left). Down this street is the **Plaza Mayor,** where the municipal tourist office is located (far left side). C. Mayor ends at C. Bailén, across from the **Catedral de Ntra. Sra. de la Almudena** (next to the **Palacio Real**), consecrated during the papal visit of June 1993. A left onto C. Bailén moves away from the big building scene over a *viaducto* into **La Latina,** Madrid's oldest neighborhood (on the left after crossing the bridge; 20min.).

3) At Sol, the continuation of C. Mayor emerges from the other side of the intersection, now called **Carrera San Jerónimo** (on your near right). **Plaza Canalejas** is just down the street; **Calle Príncipe** leads from the right of the plaza to **Plaza Santa Ana** and a zone of quality restaurants, bars, and *terrazas.* Continuing downhill with C. San Jerónimo, you come to the **Plaza de las Cortes,** home to Madrid's American Express office. C. San Jerónimo ends at the wide **Paseo del Prado,** across from the **Museo del Prado** (20min.).

4) The last of the big four avenues is **Calle Alcalá** (on your far right), which lets traffic into the intersection. Down this street are "bank palaces," including the imposing Banco de España at the foot of the slope, ending at **Plaza Cibeles** and Po. Prado. Take the pedestrian underpass to reach the **Palacio de Comunicaciones** (post office palace) on the other side of Po. Prado. Beyond the post office is **Plaza de la Independencia** and the **Parque del Retiro** (½hr.). **Calle Serrano,** lined with chic designer stores, leads out from the other side of the plaza, stretching north to form the western border of the posh, residential neighborhood **Salamanca.**

South of Sol, reached by **Calle de Carretas,** is **Calle de Atocha,** which runs downhill to train-filled **Estación de Atocha.** South of C. Atocha lies the neighborhood **Arganzuela.**

North of Sol, and bounded by **Gran Vía,** is a major shopping zone; El Corte Inglés (see Practical Information) and many other shops, *cafeterías,* bars, and hotels fill this area. **Calle Montera,** the one street with car traffic amidst these pedestrian thoroughfares, leads from Sol to the massive Gran Vía and the eponymous Metro stop. To the left, Gran Vía runs by **Plaza de Callao** and heads downhill to Pl. España (20min.). Past Pl. España, the Gran Vía becomes C. Princesa, stretching uphill through the residential **Argüelles** and collegiate **Moncloa** neighborhoods. Even farther north is the **Ciudad Universitaria** (1-1½hr.).

One of the most important roads—in both traffic volume and tourist interest— leading off the Gran Vía to the north is **Calle Fuencarral.** *Hostales* and shops abound on this narrow street. It also forms the eastern border of **Malasaña,** once a lively middle-class neighborhood which has recently fallen somewhat into disrepute but remains a popular place to get down at night. Parallel to C. Fuencarral is C. Hortaleza, which heads into the working-class neighborhood **Chueca,** full of restaurants, nightclubs, and *hostales,* and a site of the city's increasingly open gay scene. North of these two zones, Madrid becomes more modern, gentrified, and residential.

If Puerta del Sol is the heart of Madrid, then the single long avenue named in turn **Paseo Prado, Recoletos,** and **Castellana** is its spine. This *paseo* extends the length of the city, from historical and cultural sights northwards into various financial and business centers, government ministries, skyscrapers, and the Estadio Santiago Bernabéu.

Madrid is extremely safe compared to other major European cities, but the Puerta del Sol, Plaza 2 de Mayo in Malasaña, Plaza de Chueca, and Pl. España are particularly intimidating late at night. Generally, avoid the parks and quiet residential areas after dark. Watch out for thieves and pickpockets in the Metro and on crowded city streets, and be wary of opportunists whose clever scams are often targeted at tour-

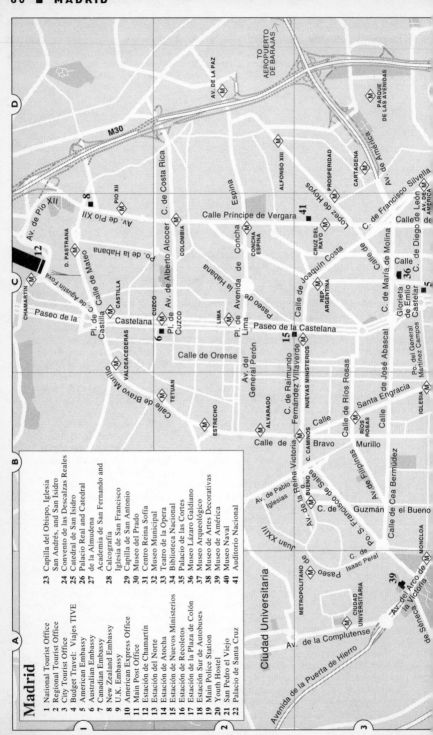

Madrid

1 National Tourist Office
2 Regional Tourist Office
3 City Tourist Office
4 Budget Travel: Viajes TIVE
5 American Embassy
6 Australian Embassy
7 Canadian Embassy
8 New Zealand Embassy
9 U.K. Embassy
10 American Express Office
11 Main Post Office
12 Estación de Chamartín
13 Estación del Norte
14 Estación de Atocha
15 Estación de Nuevos Ministerios
16 Estación de Recoletos
17 Estación de la Plaza de Colón
18 Estación Sur de Autobuses
19 Main Police Station
20 Youth Hostel
21 San Pedro el Viejo
22 Palacio de Santa Cruz

23 Capilla del Obispo, Iglesia
   San Andrés, and San Isidro
24 Convento de las Descalzas Reales
25 Catedral de San Isidro
26 Palacio Real and Catedral
   de la Almudena
27 Academia de San Fernando and
   Calcografía
28 Iglesia de San Francisco
29 Capilla de San Antonio
30 Museo del Prado
31 Centro Reina Sofía
32 Museo Municipal
33 Teatro de la Opera
34 Biblioteca Nacional
35 Palacio de las Cortes
36 Museo Lázaro Galdiano
37 Museo Arqueológico
38 Museo de Artes Decorativas
39 Museo de América
40 Museo Naval
41 Auditorio Nacional

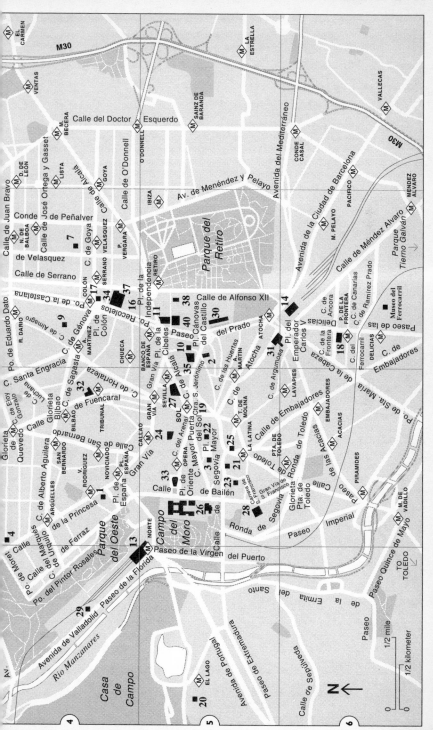

ists. The preeminence of the con artist, particularly around Madrid's *centro*, is a tradition which dates far back in Madrid's cultural history.

■■■ PRACTICAL INFORMATION

GETTING THERE

By Plane

All flights land at the **Aeropuerto Internacional de Barajas,** in the town of the same name a half-hour by car northeast of Madrid. The simplest and cheapest way to get into town is the **Bus-Aeropuerto** (look for EMT signs just outside the doors), which stops every 15 minutes outside the national and international terminals (300ptas).

The bus from the airport stops underground beneath the Jardines del Descubrimiento in **Plaza de Colón,** which is on Paseo de Recoletos. Exit from the side of the park with the noisy waterfall and you'll be on Paseo de Recoletos. The Colón Metro station (on the brown line #4) is directly across the street. To get to Puerta del Sol, switch at Metro: Bilbao to line #1, and ride three stops. On foot, walk left down Paseo de Recoletos to the next plaza, Plaza de la Cibeles; turn right down Calle de Alcalá, and bear left at the next fork (20 min.).

A fleet of taxis waits at the airport. The ride to Puerta del Sol costs 2000-2500ptas, depending on the number of bags and traffic. Some drivers claim not to know the address to which they're asked to drive, or claim it's in a dangerous area and refuse to go there. They may also try to take the naive to an expensive conspiring hotel. Don't be their dupe—insist firmly on being taken to your destination or a nearby landmark. Fares from the airport to downtown Madrid should be no more than 3000ptas.

In the airport, a branch of the regional tourist office (see Tourist Office below) in the international arrivals area has maps and other basics. (Open Mon.-Fri. 8am-8pm, Sat. 8am-1pm.) In the airport and the Bus-Aeropuerto stop in Pl. Colón, branches of the Brújula accommodations service (see Accommodations Service below) can find visitors places to stay immediately.

Iberia: C. Goya, 29 (tel. 587 81 56). Open Mon.-Fri. 9:30am-2pm and 4-7pm. For international reservations call 329 43 53; for domestic call 411 10 11. 24 hr.

American Airlines: C. Pedro Texeira, 8 (tel. 597 20 68 and toll-free 900 05 56). **Metro:** Lima. Open Mon.-Fri. 9am-5:30pm. For reservations, call Mon.-Fri. 9am-6:30pm, Sat. 9am-3pm.

TWA: Pl. Colón, Torres de Jerez (tel. 310 37 60). Metro: Colón. Open Mon.-Fri. 9am-5:30pm. For reservations, call 310 30 94 Mon.-Fri. 9am-5:30pm, Sat 8am-3pm.

By Train

Two *largo recorrido* (long distance) and two intermediate stations connect Madrid to the rest of the world. (No trains originate from Recoletos or Nuevos Ministerios, the intermediate stops.) In addition to those listed below, RENFE short-distance tickets can be purchased and trains boarded at the following Metro stations: Embajadores, Méndez Alvaro, Laguna, Aluche, and Norte (access via extension from Metro: Opera). For general railway information, call 429 02 02. **RENFE Main Office:** C. Alcalá, 44 (tel. 563 02 02), where Gran Vía hits C. Alcalá. Metro: Banco de España. A useful, well-organized place. Purchase national and international tickets here, for departure from the Chamartín station. Handy schedules, RENFE and AVE (Alta Velocidad Española) tickets also available. Open Mon.-Fri. 9:30am-8pm.

Estación Chamartín: Agustín de Foxá (tel. 323 21 21). Metro: Chamartín, line #8 (1 stop from Pl. Castilla stop on blue line #1). Bus #5 runs to and from Sol (45min.); the stop is just beyond the lockers. Chamartín services towns throughout Spain (La Coruña, Albacete, Alicante, Avila, Barcelona, Bilbao, Cádiz, Carta-gena, Córdoba, Irún, León, Lugo, Málaga, Oviedo, Orense, Salamanca, Santander, Segovia, Sevilla, Soria, Valladolid, Zamora, Zaragoza), Portugal, and France (with connections at the French border). In addition to these *largo recorrido* destina-tions, all *cercanías* trains can be boarded here (see *cercanías* below). Chamartín has a tourist office, currency exchange, accommodations service, post office, tele-phones, car rental, lockers, bookstores, *cafeterías,* and police—not to mention the astrology booth at the ticket window, and the roller-disco-bowl-a-rama right beyond the lockers. Ticket windows open 6:45am-11:35pm.

Estación Atocha: Av. Ciudad de Barcelona (tel. 527 31 60). Metro: Atocha-Renfe (on blue line #1). Newly-renovated Atocha has expanded its service from small towns in Castilla-La Mancha, Andalucía, and Extremadura to include Valencia, Granada, Córdoba, Cuenca, Ciudad Real, Badajoz, Mérida, Almería, Cádiz, Toledo, and Salamanca. Frequent trains to El Escorial. Also AVE service to Sevilla via Cór-doba (tel. 534 05 05). Service to Portugal. Art galleries, boutiques, restaurants, and cafés ease the wait. Ticket windows open 6:30am-11:30pm.

Estación de Recoletos: Po. de Recoletos, 4 (tel. 232 15 15). Metro: Colón. Entrance is in the middle of a split road with a tree-lined promenade in the center. Intermediate stop only. Trains every 5-10min.

Estación Nuevos Ministerios: C. Raimundo Fernández Villaverde, on the corner with Po. Castellana. Metro: Nuevos Ministerios. Trains every 5-10min.

Cercanías (commuter train) fares are based on a zone layout á la London's Under-ground. Self-explanatory, easy-to-use automatic ticket machines are in all stations. Chamartín, Atocha, and the intermediate stations Recoletos and Nuevos Ministerios are all in the center zone. To get from one station to another, the fare is 100ptas. *Cercanías* trains are slow and make many stops. While some are modern and com-fortable, others lack A/C and can be unpleasant in summer. In contrast, regional or **regional-expres** trains cost only a little more and get there twice as fast. For instance, the *cercanía* fare to Avila is 620ptas, while the *regional-expres* is only 710ptas.

By Bus

Numerous private companies, each with its own station and set of destinations, serve Madrid (see Spain Essentials: Getting Around: Bus for a list of major compa-nies). Buses depart from and arrive back to each station, usually passing through the big, central **Estación Sur de Autobuses,** C. Canarias, E-16 (tel. 468 22 00 or 468 45 11) en route. Part of the Palos de la Frontera Metro station (yellow line, #3), the Est-ación Sur is convenient for services and transport into the center of Madrid, though not all city buses pass through here. Call between 7am and 11pm to make sure your destination is covered. An amazing computerized ticket information service, on the left near entrance, provides info in English.

Estación Auto Res: Pl. Conde de Casal, 6 (tel. 551 72 00). Metro: Conde de Casal. To Salamanca (8:30am, 10:30am, 1:30pm, 3pm, 4:30pm, 5:30pm, 8pm (except Sat.), 10pm; 3¼hr. Express service: 8am, 10am, 12:30pm, 2:30pm, 4pm, 5pm, 6pm, 7:30pm, 9pm, 11pm; 2½hr.). To Cuenca (6:45am (except Sat.), 8am, noon, 2:30pm, 4:30pm, 8pm, 10pm (except Sat.); 2½hr.).

Estación Empresa Alacuher: Paseo Moret (tel. 376 01 04). Metro: Moncloa. To El Pardo (every 15min. from 6:30am-1am; 20min.).

Estación Empresa Continental Auto: C. Avenida de América, 34 (tel. 356 23 07). Metro: Avenida de América. To Alcalá de Henares (every 15-20min. from 6:15am-11pm, 40 min., same return schedule). To Guadalajara (every hr. from 8am-2pm, every ½hr. from 2-10pm; 1hr.).

Estación Empresa Larrea: Paseo de la Florida, 11 (tel. 547 52 61 or 530 48 00). Metro: Norte (via extension from Metro: Opera). To Avila (10am, 2:30pm, 8pm; 2hr.). To Puerto de Navacerrada, Puerto Cotos, Valdesqui (Mon.-Fri. 9:30am, Sat. 8am, 9:30am, 3pm; 1¼hr.).

Estación Empresa Ruíz: Rda. Atocha, 12 (tel. 468 08 50). Metro: Atocha. Ticket office open 8am-1pm and 3:15-7:30pm.

Estación Herranz: C. Fernández de los Ríos (tel. 543 81 67 or 543 36 45), a little booth half a block from the corner of C. Isaac Peral. Metro: Moncloa. To El Escorial (about every hr., 1hr., 335ptas). Continuing from El Escorial to Valle de los Caídos (leaves 3:15pm, returns to El Escorial 5:30pm, 20min.). Return buses to Madrid from El Escorial, every hour until 9pm. In El Escorial call 890 41 00.

Estación La Sepulvedana: Po. de la Florida, 11 (tel. 547 52 61 or 530 48 00). Metro: Norte (via extension from Metro: Opera). To Avila (3 per day, 2hr.) and Segovia (hourly until 10:15pm, 1½hr.).

By Rideshare and Thumb

Auto Compartido, C. Carretas, 33, 3rd. fl. (tel. and fax 522 77 72), off Puerta del Sol. Metro: Sol. They arrange shared journeys to destinations inside and outside Spain. Also check the message boards at HI hostels, the TIVE travel agency, and English language bookstores (see below Other) for rideshare offers.

Hitchhikers use national highways which emanate from Madrid to travel all over Spain. However, neither popular nor safe, hitchiking is not a recommendable means of travel. The following routes start in Madrid: N-I (north) for Burgos and Irún; N-II (northeast) for Zaragoza and Barcelona; N-III (east) for Cuenca and Valencia; N-IV (south) for Aranjuez, Alicante, and Andalucía; N-V (west) for Badajoz; N-VI (northwest) for Avila, Sierra de Guadarrama, Segovia, Salamanca, and Galicia; E-4 (west) for Extremadura and Portugal; 401 (southeast) for Toledo.

GETTING AROUND

Maps

Both the *Plano de Madrid* and the *Plano de los Transportes,* free at city tourist offices, are good maps of the city center, but do not include street indexes. For a comprehensive map with street index, try the Falk map or the Chequepoint map, both about 800ptas at newspaper kiosks. Small one-page maps of Madrid are free at most hostels, or at any Corte Inglés (see Other below).

Metro

Madrid is blessed with a fabulous Metro which puts almost every other big-city subway system to shame. Trains are clean and run frequently; only on Sundays and late at night is a wait more than five minutes. Cheery green timers hang above the platforms to tell how long it's been since the last one departed. Wall maps of the Metro, and of surrounding neighborhoods, abound in every station, as do signs with information on fares and schedules. The free, compact *Plano del Metro* (available at any ticket booth) is easier to use than the unwieldy *Plano de los Transportes*.

Ten lines connect 120 stations throughout Madrid. The various lines are referred to by color and number. An individual Metro ride costs 125ptas, but most experienced riders opt for the *billete de diez* (ticket of 10 rides) at 600ptas, or for a monthly pass. Youth passes are also available. For more details, call 552 49 00 (general Metro information line) or ask at any ticket booth. Make sure to hold on to your ticket or pass until you leave the Metro—riding without a receipt carries a fat 5000pta fine.

Trains run 6am-1:30am, not late enough (in Madrid time) to be deserted. Crime in the Metro stations is fairly rare, and women usually feel safe traveling alone. Do watch out for pickpocketing attempts in crowded cars—thieves may drop a handful of change or shove a passenger, and grab wallets in the ensuing confusion. Ride in the first car where the conductor sits (always at the far left end of the platform) if you feel uncomfortable. Avoid empty cars at night. Some stations, particularly those that handle two or more lines, have long tunnels and series of escalators; exercise caution here and stick with people. The Chueca, Gran Vía, Sol, Tirso de Molina, La Latina, and Plaza de España stations surface in areas which are somewhat intimidating after midnight. On the whole, the Metro is clean, efficient, and generally worry-free.

Bus

The extensive city bus system (150 routes) can be frustrating to novices. Finding the route you want and its corresponding stops is easy enough with the *Plano de los Transportes*, but getting off is trickier since stops are often not visibly marked.

The fare is 125ptas and a 10-ride *bonobus* pass, sold at newsstands and tobacco shops, costs 600ptas. Buses run from 6am until midnight. Between midnight and 3am, 11 nocturnal buses travel from Sol and Pl. Cibeles to the outskirts every half-hour; after that, every hour until 5am. Nocturnal buses (numbered N1-N11) are indicated on a special section on the Plano. There are N stops all along the marked routes, not just in Sol and Pl. Cibeles. For information on buses call Empresa Municipal de Transportes (EMT) at 401 31 00 or 555 72 96. Functionaries of the different bus routes are not always well-informed about other routes.

Taxi

Zillions of taxis zip around Madrid at all hours of the day and night. If, by some freak chance, one does not appear when you need it, or if you want to summon one to your door, call 445 90 08 or 447 51 80. A green *libre* sign in the window or a lit green light indicates availability. Taxis are affordable for groups of two to four people, and particularly useful late at night when only nocturnal buses run.

The base fare is 200ptas, plus 50-75ptas per km. Common supplements include: to or from the airport (300ptas); to bus and train stations (125ptas); luggage charge (50ptas per bag); on Sundays and holidays (150ptas); at night (11pm-6am, 150ptas). The fare from the city center to the airport is about 2000ptas (cheaper from Pl. Colón, more from Sol or Pl. España). To Estación Chamartín from Pl. Colón costs about 800ptas.

You can request an estimate before entering the cab, but generally taxi drivers do not cheat passengers; make sure, however, that the driver actually turns on the meter. Also, beware of requesting hostel, restaurant, or club recommendations as taxi drivers sometimes have deals going with the owners of such establishments. If you have a complaint or think you've been overcharged, demand a *recibo oficial* (official receipt) and *hoja de reclamaciones* (complaint form), which the driver is required to supply. Take down the license number, route taken, and fare charged. Drop off the forms and information at the City Hall, Pl. Villa, 4 (tel. 447 07 15 or 447 07 14) to possibly get a refund.

To request taxi service for the the handicapped, call 547 82 00, 547 85 00, or 547 86 00; the rates for this service are identical to those of other taxis.

Car Rental

Don't do it unless you're planning to zoom out of the city. Traffic in Madrid is congested and parking a nightmare. Tobacco shops sell parking permits. To find out if your car has been towed or merely stolen, call 457 08 15; for information on road conditions 535 22 22; for RACE (the autoclub) 593 33 33.

You must be over 21 and have an International Driver's License and major credit card (or leave a deposit equal to the estimated rental fee). Gas isn't included in the price, and averages to about 100ptas per liter. If renting for less than a week, you may be charged per kilometer.

Atesa: C. Orense, 83 (tel. 571 32 94). Metro: Tetuán. C. Francisco leads to C. Orense. Medium-sized car 1700ptas per day, IVA and insurance included; 5500ptas for a week. Open Mon.-Fri. 8:30am-1:30pm and 4:30-8pm, Sat. 9am-1pm. Also at the airport (tel. 305 86 60). Open daily 7am-midnight.

Autos Bravo: C. Toledo, 136 (tel. 474 80 75). Metro: Puerta de Toledo. Medium-sized car 5000ptas per day plus 50ptas per km; if renting for more than a week 10,000ptas per day, no per km charge. 20,000ptas deposit. Open Mon.-Fri. 8:30am-1:30pm and 4-8pm, Sat.-Sun. 9am-1pm.

Autos Viaducto: C. Segovia, 26 (tel. 548 48 48). Medium-sized car 1100ptas per day plus 17ptas per km. Minimum charge of 100km per day. Insurance and IVA not included. 20,000ptas deposit. Also at C. Martín de los Heros, 23 (tel. 541 55 41) and Arda. Mediterráneo, 4 (tel. 433 12 33 or 552 10 44). Open Mon.-Fri. 9am-1:30pm and 4-7:30pm.

Moped Rental

Popular with Madrid's young residents, mopeds are swift and easy to park. A lock and helmet are needed. Try **Motocicletas Antonio Castro,** C. Conde Duque, 13 (tel. 542 06 57), at Santa Cruz de Marcenado. Metro: San Bernardo. A 49cc Vespino costs 3300ptas per day (8am-8pm) plus 13% IVA; 36,000ptas for a week. Prices include mileage and insurance but not gas; the deposit is a minimum of 10,000ptas, depending on the model you rent. Renters must be at least 18 and have a driver's license and passport. (Open Mon.-Fri. 8am-1:30pm and 5-8pm.)

TOURIST INFORMATION

Tourist Offices

The staff at the following locations are generally helpful and speak English.

Municipal: Pl. Mayor, 3 (tel. 366 54 77 or 588 16 36; fax 366 54 77). Metro: Sol. Inside the Plaza Mayor. Hands out city and transportation maps, as well as *En Madrid*, a monthly activities guide. Open Mon.-Fri. 10am-8pm, Sat. 10am-2pm.

Regional/Provincial Office of the Comunidad de Madrid: C. Princesa, 1, Torre de España (tel. 541 23 25), entrance faces Pl. España. Metro: Pl. España. Brochures, transport info, and maps for towns in the Comunidad. Also has brochures about towns, campsites, highways, daytrips, and *paradores* throughout Spain. Open Mon.-Fri. 9am-7pm, Sat. 9:30am-1:30pm. A **second office** is at C. Duque Medinaceli, 2 (tel. 429 49 51, 429 31 71, or 429 37 05), just off Pl. Cortes. Metro: Sol. Open Mon.-Fri. 9am-7pm, Sat. 9am-1:30pm. Other offices at **Estación Chamartín** (tel. 315 99 76; open Mon.-Fri. 8am-8pm, Sat. 9am-1pm) and the **airport,** in the international arrivals area (tel. 305 86 56; same hrs. as Chamartín).

TOURS

Read the fine print before signing up if you don't want to pay an arm and a leg to take a walk around the block. Of the following, the first two are geared towards tourists, and given in English.

Pullmantur, Pl. Oriente, 8 (tel. 241 18 05). Metro: Opera. Several tours of Madrid, averaging around 3500ptas. Also excursions to outlying areas. Prices include transportation and admission to museums and monuments.

Trapsatur, San Bernardo, 23 (tel. 542 66 66). Metro: Santo Domingo. Same deal as above.

Descubre Madrid: run by the Patronato Municipal de Turismo, C. Mayor, 69 (tel. 588 29 00), under the arch and the first door on the right. Open Mon.-Fri. 9am-3pm. These guided walking and bus tours, designed primarily for residents, are excellent and cheaper than those prepared for tourists. Drawbacks: they're given only in Spanish, and you have to sign up 2 months in advance. Over 60 tours each season (March-July and Sept.-Jan.) cover topics ranging from masterpieces in the Prado to medieval archaeology to music. Bilingual tours can sometimes be arranged in advance for groups. Walking tours average 400ptas; bus tours 800ptas. Package deals available. Discounts for students under 25 and seniors.

BUDGET TRAVEL

Viajes TIVE: C. Fernando el Católico, 88 (tel. 543 02 08 or 543 74 12; fax 544 00 62). Metro: Moncloa. Branch office at José Ortega y Gasset, 71 (tel. 347 77 78). Metro: Lista. A *Let's Go* dream organization. Sponsored and run by the Comunidad de Madrid, so no commissions are added. Some English spoken. Discount airfares and ticket sales. Organized group excursions and language classes. Thriving message board with rides, cheap tickets, and apartment sharing notices. General lodgings and student residence infomation. BIJ train tickets. InterRail pass for

1 month of train travel (under 26) 45,670ptas. ISIC 500ptas. FIYTO (under 26, good for RENFE discounts) 500ptas. HI cards 300ptas. Both offices open Mon.-Fri. 9am-2pm, Sat. 9am-noon. Arrive early.

Comunidad de Madrid, Dirección General de Juventud: C. Alcalá, 31 (tel. 580 42 16 or 580 42 42). Metro: Banco de España. Same type of documentation as TIVE, though no tickets sold here.

Viajes Araque/Eurojoven: Pl. España, Edificio España, 15th fl., (tel. 541 39 11). Metro: Pl. España. Discounted airfare information.

Viajes Lanzani: Gran Vía, 88 (tel. 541 54 95). Metro: Gran Vía. Information on discount and student airfare, bus, and train tickets. Also discounted tours and excursion packages, language courses, and accommodations information.

EMBASSIES AND CONSULATES

See Spain Essentials: Embassies and Consulates.

MONEY

For currency exchange, American Express has the best rates for traveler's checks. Banks (1-2% commission, 500ptas min. charge), El Corte Inglés (see Other: El Corte Inglés), and even four- and five-star hotels offer exchange services for varying rates. Those places open on weekends and as late as 2am, such as Exact Change, Cambios-Uno, and Chequepoint, are not a good deal for cashing traveler's checks: no commission and small (250-300ptas) minimum charges, but poor rates. On the other hand, for small-denomination bills (for instance, US$20 or US$50) they may be the best option. Many are at Sol and on the Gran Vía.

Additionally, most of the plentiful automatic teller machines in Madrid accept bank cards with one or more of the Cirrus, Star, and NYCE logos. Be forewarned: use only the first four digits of your PIN code. Also, Spanish machines operate only with numbers, not letters—so if your PIN code is your cat's name, be sure you know its numerical translation.

American Express: Pl. Cortes, 2, Madrid 28014 (tel. 322 54 24). Metro: Sevilla. The office has "Agencia de Viajes" written in big letters on the windows. In addition to currency exchange (1% cash and 2% traveler's check commission; no commission on AmEx traveler's checks; no min. charge), they'll hold mail and help send and receive wired money. In an emergency, AmEx cashes personal checks up to US$1000 for cardholders only. Express Cash machine. To report or cancel lost traveler's checks, call 24-hr., toll-free (900) 99 44 26. Open Mon.-Fri. 9am-5:30pm, Sat. 9am-noon.

COMMUNICATIONS

Post Office: Palacio de Comunicaciones, Pl. Cibeles (tel. 396 24 43). Metro: Banco de España. An enormous palace on the far side of the plaza from the Metro. **Information** desk open Mon.-Fri. 8am-10pm or call this very useful info line (tel. 537 64 94). Open for **stamp purchase** and **certified mail** Mon.-Fri. 8am-10pm, Sat. 8:30am-2pm, Sun. 9:30am-1pm. Open for *Lista de Correos* Mon.-Fri. 8am-9:30pm, Sat. 8:30am-2pm. Open for **telegrams** 24-hr. Telegram assistance available Mon.-Fri. 8am-10pm (at window 27) and 10pm-12am (through Door H), Sat. 10am-8pm (at window 27) and 8-10pm (through door H), Sun. 8am-10pm (through door H). To send telegrams by phone, call 522 20 00. Open for **postal exprés** Mon.-Fri. 8am-5pm, Sat. 8:30am-2pm (through door K). Open for sending **packages** Mon.-Fri. 8am-9pm, Sat. 8:30am-1:30pm (through door N). Open for **telex, fax,** and **phone** service Mon.-Fri. 8am-midnight, Sat.-Sun. 8am-10pm. English and French spoken at information desk. **Postal Code:** 28070.

Telephones: Telefónica, Gran Vía, 30, at C. Valverde. Metro: Gran Vía. Direct-dial lines to the U.S. (phone #9, long lines in the evening). Almodóvar used to work here. Open Mon.-Sat. 9am-midnight, Sun. 10am-midnight. The **Palacio de Comunicaciones** (above) is somewhat quieter, but unlike Telefónica, has no place to sit while placing a call. Enter door H, next to the gold mailboxes on Po. Prado. Calls over 500ptas can be charged to a credit card. Open Mon.-Fri. 8am-midnight,

Sat.-Sun. and holidays 8am-10pm. Long-distance calls may also be placed at **Po. Recolectos, 43,** off Pl. Colón. Open same hours as Gran Vía office. **Telephone Code:** 91.

EMERGENCY, HEALTH, AND HELP

General Information Line: tel. 010. Run by the Ayuntamiento, they'll tell you anything about Madrid, from the address of the nearest police station to a zoo's hours. Spanish only. **Information:** tel. 003 (the Madrid equivalent of 411).

Emergency: tel. 091 (national police), 092 (local police).

Police: C. Luna, 29 (tel. 521 12 36). Metro: Callao. From Gran Vía walk down C. Arenal. This station has forms in English. To report crimes committed in the Metro, go to the office in the Sol station (tel. 521 09 11). Open 8am-11pm.

Fire: tel. 080.

Ambulance: tel. 061 or **Red Cross** (tel. 522 22 22, 734 47 94, or 735 01 95), or **Municipal Ambulance Service** (tel. 588 44 00).

Hospital: Most are in the north and east ends of the city. Prompt appointments are hard to obtain (emergency rooms are best option for immediate attention), but public hospitals here treat patients whether or not they pay in advance. If your Spanish is poor, try the **Anglo-American Medical Unit,** Conde de Aranda, 1, 1st fl. (tel. 435 18 23), to the left. Metro: Serrano. Doctors, dentists, optometrists. Run partly by British and Americans. Regular personnel on duty 9am-8pm, but assistance is available at all hours. *Not* an emergency clinic. Embassies and consulates also keep lists of English-speaking doctors in private practice. **Hospital Clínico San Carlos,** Pl. Cristo Rey (tel. 544 17 05). Metro: Moncloa. **Hospital General Gregorio Marañón,** C. Dr. Esquerdo, 46 (tel. 586 80 00). Metro: O'Donnell. **Hospital Santa Cristina,** C. O'Donnell, 59 (tel. 573 62 00). Metro: O'Donnell. Run by *Insalud,* Spain's National Health Institute.

Emergency Clinic: Ciudad Sanitaria La Paz, P. de la Castellana, 261 (tel. 734 26 00). Metro: Begoña or Chamartín. **Hospital Provincial,** Ibiza, 45 (tel. 586 80 00). Metro: O'Donnell. **Equipo Quirúrgico Municipal No I,** C. Montera, 22 (tel. 401 80 50). Metro: Manuel Becerra. **Hospital Ramón y Cajal,** Ctra. de Colmenar, km. 9100 (tel. 729 00 00). Metro: Begoña.

Late-Night Pharmacy: For information (tel. 098), or check *Farmacias de Guardia* listings in local papers to find pharmacies open after 8pm. Lists of the nearest on-duty pharmacy are also posted in all pharmacy windows. Contraceptive products sold over the counter in most Spanish pharmacies and at **Profilácticos,** C. Fuencarral, 10.

Alcohólicos Anónimos, C. Juan Bravo, 40, 2nd fl. (tel. 309 19 47 or crisis line in Spanish 532 30 30). Metro: Núñez de Balboa. Meetings in English Mon.-Fri. 8-9:15pm, Sat. 6-7:15pm, Sun 7-8:15pm. All meetings closed except on Tue. and Fri.

Crisis Lines: Poison Control (tel. 593 03 02 or 562 04 20). **AIDS Information Hotline** (tel. 445 23 28). **Illicit drug addiction** (430 60 77). **Women's Medical Issues Hotline** (tel. 730 49 01). English here is poor. Open Mon.-Fri. 3:30-6:30pm. **Malos Tratos a Mujeres** (women's helpline tel. 593 45 23). **Sociedad Sexológica de Madrid** (tel. 522 25 10) for information and advice on sexual matters. **English-Language Helpline** (tel. 559 13 93) for practical information and confidentiality from trained volunteers 7-11pm. Answering machine other hours. **Guardia Civil** (tel. 062 or 533 11 00). **Protección Civil** (tel. 537 17 00). **Highway accidents** (tel. 457 77 00).

Rape hotline: tel. 574 01 10.

OTHER

El Corte Inglés: C. Preciados, 3 (tel. 532 18 00). Metro: Sol. C. Goya, 76 (tel. 577 71 71). Metro: Goya. C. Princesa, 42 (tel. 542 48 00). Metro: Argüelles. C. Raimundo Fernández Villaverde, 79 (tel. 556 23 00). Metro: Nuevos Ministerios. Good city **map. Currency exchange:** 1% commission on cash (250pta min. charge); 2% commission on traveler's checks (500pta min. charge); mediocre rates. Haircutting, cafeteria and restaurant, **telephones,** some books in English. Excellent **supermarket.** Open Mon.-Sat. 10am-9pm, Sun. noon-8pm.

Luggage Storage: Estaciones de Chamartín and Atocha. Automatic lockers for backpacks 300ptas per day, for large packs and suitcases 500ptas per day. Open 7:30am-11:30pm. Lockers may be opened only once with each payment. **Estación Sur de Autobuses.** Bags checked (80ptas per bag per day).

Lost Property: At the Ayuntamiento, Pl. Legazpi, 7 (tel. 588 43 46). Metro: Legazpi. Also at **Almacén de Objetos Perdidos,** C. Santa Engracia, 120 (tel. 441 02 11). Metro: Ríos Rosas. The latter holds lost items 2yrs. For objects lost on the **Metro,** check at Cuatro Caminos Station (tel. 552 49 00).

Message Boards: All three of the bookstores listed below have excellent, full message boards with info about language *intercambios*, jobs for native English speakers, apartment sharing, etc. **TIVE** travel agency (see Budget Travel above) also has a board brimful with cheap travel tickets and ridesharing offers. At **Albergue Juvenil Santa Cruz (HI)** (see Accommodations below), the same types of notices but less of them.

English Bookstores: Librería Turner, C. Genova, 3 (tel. 319 09 26). Metro: Colón. Brand-new editions (and thus more expensive than the same books at home) of the classics and new releases in English, French, German, and Spanish. Also books on tape and a respectable sci-fi collection. Open Mon.-Fri. 10am-8pm, Sat. 10am-2pm. **Booksellers,** C. José Abascal, 48 (tel. 442 79 59 or 442 81 04). Metro: Iglesia. From the Metro station, walk down C. Santa Engracia for five blocks, and take a right on C. José Abascal. A vast array of new books in English, plus lots of American and English magazines. Open Mon.-Fri. 9:30am-2pm and 5-8pm, Sat. 10am-2pm. **English Editions,** Pl. San Amaro, 5 (tel. 571 03 21). Metro: Estrecho. In the tiny Pl. San Amaro, off C. General Perón. Used novels bought and sold—excellent selection. Also a quirky little mini-mart featuring English and American specialties such as Skippy peanut butter, Bisquik, and Meat Pies. Open Mon.-Thurs. noon-7pm, Fri. noon-8pm, Sat. 11am-2pm.

Library: Bibliotecas Populares, for information call 445 98 45. The one at Metro: Cuatro Caminos (C. Raimundo Fernández Villaverde, 8, one block from the station) is small and crowded; the bigger, nicer branch is at Metro: Puerta de Toledo. Both have English-language magazines. If you bring your passport and two ID-size photos, they'll issue a card on the spot, free. Open Mon.-Fri. 8:30am-8:45pm, Sat. 9am-1:45pm; for card issuance Mon.-Fri. 8:30am-8:45pm, Sat. 9am-1pm. **Biblioteca Nacional,** C. Serrano, next to the Museo Arqueológico. Metro: Serrano. Not open for reading or browsing, although it is sometimes possible to obtain a daypass. Otherwise, limited to scholars doing doctorate and post-doctorate research. To use the facilities, bring letters of recommendation and a project proposal.

English-Language Periodicals: International edition dailies and weeklies available at kiosks on the Gran Vía, Paseos Prado, Recoletos, and Castellana, and around Puerta del Sol. If you're dying for the Sunday New York Times, go to the store inside the VIPS restaurant chain—but be prepared to spend a pretty penny.

Women's Services: Librería de Mujeres, C. San Cristóbal, 17 (tel. 521 70 43), near Pl. Mayor. Metro: Sol. The motto of this pleasant shop—which sells, along with books by or about women, various knick-knacks and cosmetic items—is "Los libros no muerden, el feminismo tampoco" (Books don't bite, neither does feminism). Information about concerts, readings, lectures, political activities, and movie screenings. Open Mon.-Fri. 10am-2pm and 5-8pm, Sat. 10am-2pm. **Women's Groups,** C. Barquillo, 44, 1st fl. (tel. 419 36 89). For information, call after 8pm.

Gay and Lesbian Services: The Colectivo de Gais y Lesbianas de Madrid (COGAM), C. Carretas, 12, 3rd fl. (tel. and fax 522 45 17), very close to Puerta del Sol. Metro: Sol. Provides a wide range of services and activities of interest to gays, lesbians, bisexuals, transsexuals, and others. Reception hours Mon.-Fri. 5-9pm. Free screenings of gay-interest movies, COGAM youth group (25 and under), and HIV-positive support group. Free counseling Mon.-Thurs. 7-9pm. COGAM library, specializing in gay-theme books and publications, open daily 7-9pm. COGAM also publishes the semi-monthly *Entiendes...?*, a magazine in Spanish about gay issues, as well as a comprehensive list, the "Pink and Black Pages," of gay services, groups, activities, and personals. (Magazine available at many kiosks and in **Berkana Librería Gai y Lesbiana** and **Librería El Galeón.) GAI-**

INFORM, a gay information line (tel. 523 00 70; Mon.-Fri. 5-9pm), provides information in Spanish about gay associations, leisure-time activities, and health issues. The same number has info on **Brujulai,** COGAM's weekend excursion group. **Colectivo de Feministas Lesbianas de Madrid (CFLM)** responds to tel. 319 36 89. **Lesbianas Sin Duda (LSD)** (Lesbians without a doubt) meets Wed. 8pm in the FAI building on C. Hortaleza, 19, 1st fl. Metro: Antón Martín or Gran Vía.

Cultural Center: Washington Irving Center, C. Marqués Villamagna, 8 (tel. 435 70 95). Metro: Serrano. From the station, walk up C. Serrano, and turn left on C. Marqués Villamagna. Good selection of U.S. magazines and books. Anyone over 16 can check out the books for up to 2 weeks by filling out a simple application form; allow about a week for processing. Occasional photography exhibit. Library open Mon.-Fri. 2-6pm.

Youth Organization: Instituto de la Juventud, C. José Ortega y Gasset, 71 (tel. 401 13 00). Metro: Núñez de Balboa or Lista.

Religious Services: Our Lady of Mercy English-Speaking Parish, C. Alfonso XIII, 165, on the corner of P. de la Habana (tel. 533 20 32 am, 554 28 60 pm). Mass in English 10:30am, religious classes for children and coffee for adults 11:30am-12:15pm. **Immanuel Baptist Church,** C. Hernández de Tejada, 4 (tel. 407 43 47). Services in English. Morning worship 11am; evening worship 7pm. **The Community Church of Madrid,** C. Bravo Murillo, 85 (tel. 838 55 57). Metro: Cuatro Caminos. At the Colegio El Porvenir. Protestant, interdenominational services in English, Sun. 10am. **British Embassy Church of St. George,** C. Núñez de Balboa, 43 (tel. 576 51 09; call 8am-4pm). Metro: Velázquez. Services Sun. 8:30am, 10am, and 11:15am; Fri. 10:30am. **North American Catholic Church,** Av. Alfonso XIII, 165 (tel. 519 87 07). Metro: Puente de Vallecas, off Av. Peña Prieta. **Sinagoga Beth Yaacov,** C. Balmes, 3 (tel. 445 98 43 or 445 98 35), near Pl. Sorolla. Metro: Iglesia. Also small chapel, two social halls, room for Sun. classes, mikvah, library, and facilities for kosher catering. Kosher restaurant can be reserved if called ahead. **Centro Islámico,** C. Alonso Cano, 3 (tel. 326 04 80). Metro: Iglesia.

Laundromat: Lavandería Donoso Cortés, C. Donoso Cortés, 17 (tel. 446 96 90). Metro: Quevedo. From the station, walk down C. Bravo Murillo to C. Donoso Cortés. Self-service: wash 550ptas, dryer 25ptas for five min., detergent 60ptas., iron 50ptas. Dry cleaning 1200ptas for 4kg. Open Mon.-Fri. 9am-7pm, Sat. 8:30am-1pm. **Lavomatique,** C. León at C. Cervantes, near Pl. Santa Ana. Metro: Sol. Walk down C. San Jerónimo, turn right down C. Ventura de la Vega, which turns into C. Leon after C. Prado. Self service: wash 500ptas, dryer 25ptas for five min. Open daily 9am-2pm and 4:30-8pm. **Tintorerías Arenal,** C. Donados, 1 (tel. 541 11 15), off C. Arenal. Metro: Opera, Sol, or Callao. Dry cleaning (pants 600ptas, blouse 850ptas). Also full-service laundry (about 100ptas per 5kg). Overnight service. Open Mon.-Sat. 9am-1:45pm and 4:30-8pm.

Toilets: Public ones at any El Corte Inglés, Galerías Preciados, or McDonald's.

PUBLICATIONS ABOUT MADRID

Newspapers frequently have a section on local news; check the *Cartelera* section in *El País* for a good summary of entertainment options. *En Madrid* is a monthly calendar of events available free at the municipal tourist office. *Guía del Ocio* (100ptas) is a weekly entertainment paper with listings of concerts, exhibits, cinema, restaurants, bars, clubs, sports, and TV. The *guía* comes out on Thurs. or Fri. for the week beginning the following Mon., and is available at any news kiosk. *The Broadsheet*, a free, monthly publication in English geared toward long-term residents of Madrid has information about services, activities, and job opportunities for English-speakers. Available at bookstores listed above.

■■■ ACCOMMODATIONS AND CAMPING

Though demand for rooms rises dramatically in summer, Madrid has more *hostales* than you could shake a stick at. Expect to pay between 1700ptas and 2700ptas per person for a typical *hostal* room, a bit more for a two-star *hostal*, and slightly less for a bed in a *pensión*. The once-common practice of raising prices for the high season (*temporada alta*, May-Oct.) and lowering them for the low season (*temporada baja*, Nov.-April) is now pretty much out the window—with a few noted exceptions—due to Spain's troubled tourist industry and managers' consequent fears of losing guests. None of the establishments listed below has a *temporada alta*. It's never a bad idea to try to bargain down the price of your room, especially if you are sharing with two or more friends or staying more than a few days.

ACCOMMODATIONS SERVICE

Viajes Brújula: Torre de Madrid, 6th fl. (tel. 559 97 04 or 559 97 05; fax 548 46 24), at Pl. España (in a huge building with signs for Alitalia and Kuwait Airlines on the ground floor). For 225ptas and the cost of any long-distance phone call involved, they make reservations for anywhere in Spain. You provide location and price range, they plug them into their magic computer. You must go in person. After they've reserved a room, you leave a deposit with them—about 1/3 of the room price—which is subtracted from the price you pay once at the hotel. Since it's a private company, they charge a commission from the hotel or *hostal*, so prices may be slightly higher. Not every establishment is signed up with Brújula (no youth hostels). Nevertheless, it's a good deal and convenient to have a bed secured when you've just arrived in town. They also arrange (expensive) guided tours of Madrid through the three major tour companies. English spoken. Open July-Sept. Mon.-Fri. 9am-7pm, Sat. 9am-2pm; Oct.-June Mon.-Fri. 9am-2pm and 4-7pm, Sat. 9am-2pm. Branch offices located at: Estación Atocha (tel. 539 11 73; open 8am-midnight); Estación Chamartín (tel. 315 78 94; open 7:15am-11:30pm); and the airport bus terminal in Pl. Colón (tel. 575 96 80; open 8am-10pm).

YOUTH HOSTELS

Madrid's two HI youth hostels lack central locations and privacy, but charge reasonable fees and serve meals for a modest price. Security has improved at both thanks to new lockers. Both hostels fill quickly, even in winter. An HI card is required and can be purchased for 1800ptas at either hostel. Both have a three-day maximum stay and require written reservations 15 days in advance.

Albergue Juvenil Santa Cruz de Marcenado (HI), C. Santa Cruz de Marcenado, 28 (tel. 547 45 32). Metro: Argüelles. Walk down C. Princesa, turn left on C. Serrano Jover, and right on C. Santa Cruz de Marcenado. Modern, recently renovated facilities located near the student district. 75 firm beds in airy rooms. Message board. English spoken. Reception open 9am-10:30pm. Strict curfew 1:30am. 650ptas, over 26 800ptas. Tiny breakfast included. *Pensión completa* 1450ptas, over 26 1700ptas. *Pensión media* 1050ptas, over 26 1300ptas.

Albergue Juvenil Richard Schirrman (HI), Casa de Campo (tel. 463 56 99). Metro: El Lago. Turn left (downhill) upon leaving the station, left at the paved road which runs parallel to the Metro tracks, and look for signs for the hostel, which is on the left. On the outskirts of the city, in an enormous park, close to a lake and municipal swimming pool. Don't even contemplate walking alone through the unlit, densely wooded park at night. 130 bunk beds. Bar with TV, library, basketball court, laundry facilities (500ptas per load). English spoken. Each austere 8-person room has a bath. Same bed and meal prices as above.

HOSTALES AND PENSIONES

The actual differences between two-star *hostales*, one-star *hostales*, and *pensiones* in Madrid are often minimal. A room in a one- or two-star *hostal* has at least these basics: bed, closet space, desk with chair, sink and towel, window, light fixture, and lock on the door. Winter heating is standard; air-conditioning is not. *Hostales* we list may or may not have: showers or full baths in the rooms, showers in a communal bathroom included in the price of your room, private telephones, and private TVs. Only a select few offer breakfast, laundry service, or accept credit cards. Most places accept reservations, though nowhere are they required. As a rule in Madrid, especially in competitive central zones, *hostales* are well-kept and comfortable places in which to stay. Usually owners are accustomed to opening the doors, albeit groggily, at all hours, or provide sets of keys for guests. However, before club-hopping until the wee hours, ask about specific rules; late-night lockouts or confrontations with irate owners are no fun.

Pensiones are like boarding houses: they often dish out home-cooked meals, as well as curfews, and tend to prefer longer-term guests (*estables*). The same goes for *casas de huéspedes* or simply *casas*. In Madrid, many lack winter heating.

BETWEEN PUERTA DEL SOL AND PALACIO REAL

This centrally located quarter is the oldest and one of the most popular in Madrid. Tourists swarm in this historic area of narrow streets, potted-flower balconies, and decaying facades. Stray several blocks from the Puerta del Sol to find better deals.

Hostal-Residencia Miño, C. Arenal, 16, 2nd fl. (tel. 531 50 79 or 531 97 89). Metro: Opera or Sol. A melting pot of rooms ranging from large with hardwood floors and balconies to tight quarters with vinyl underfoot. Some rooms overlook busy C. Arenal, others a quiet alley. Singles 2200ptas, with shower 2900ptas. Doubles with shower 3900ptas, with bath 4500ptas. Triples 6000ptas.

Hostal Santa Cruz, Pl. Santa Cruz, 6, 2nd fl. (tel. 522 24 41). Metro: Sol. In the lovely and atmospheric—though extraordinarily touristy—Pl. Santa Cruz, next to the Plaza Mayor. Stately high ceilings and a palatial lounge. Reservations accepted by fax (same as tel. number). Tiny singles without sink 1700ptas, good-sized with sink 2400ptas, with shower 2800ptas. Doubles 3600ptas, with bath 4400ptas. Triples 4400ptas, with bath 5500ptas.

Hostal-Residencia Jeyma, C. Arenal 24, 3rd fl. (tel. 541 63 29). Metro: Opera. Venerable *dueña* with several cats. Rustic decor. Nothing cheaper or quieter than these singles anywhere within a light year of Puerta del Sol. Singles 1300ptas, doubles 2600ptas.

Hostal-Residencia Rober, C. Arenal, 26, 5th fl. (tel. 541 91 75). Metro: Opera. Possibly the only locale in Madrid, except the banks, where smoking is strictly prohibited. Enormous communal bathroom and wall-to-wall, industrial-type carpeting in all rooms. Singles 3000ptas, with bath 3800ptas. Doubles with bath 4800ptas. Triples with bath 6000ptas.

Hostal-Residencia María del Mar, C. Marqués Viudo de Pontejo, 7, 2nd and 3rd fl. (tel. 531 90 64), reached via C. Correo from the Puerta del Sol. Metro: Sol. 40 recently renovated rooms with shining tile floors and blond, shapely furniture. Lounge with TV. No smoking permitted in common areas. Singles 1600ptas. Doubles 2800ptas, with bath (and bigger room) 5000ptas.

Hostal-Residencia Paz, C. Flora, 4, 1st fl. (tel. 547 30 47), on a quiet street parallel to C. Arenal, reached via C. Donados or C. Hileras. Metro: Sol or Opera. Lovely, spotless rooms with windows overlooking a tree-filled courtyard. Ten recently renovated rooms have quality beds. Singles 2300ptas. Doubles 3400ptas, with shower 4000ptas. Triples with shower 4800ptas. Reservations encouraged.

Hostal La Macarena, C. Cava de San Miguel, 8, 2nd fl. (tel. 365 92 21 or 366 61 11; fax 364 27 57), off of C. Mayor, west of Pl. Mayor. Metro: Sol or Opera. A hotspot for *madrileño* youth, the spectacular Cava de San Miguel is dotted with bars and cafés built into caves. A disturbingly life-like plastic dog and a cluttered, homey lounge greet you as you enter the *hostal*. All rooms with full bath. Singles 3500ptas. Doubles 5500ptas. Triples 7000ptas. Quads 8000ptas.

Hostal Alicante, C. Arenal, 16, 2nd fl. (tel. 531 51 78). Metro: Opera or Sol. Central location and gregarious lounge compensate in part for quiet dark rooms. Singles 2400ptas, with shower 2800ptas. Doubles with shower 4000ptas, with bath 4400ptas. Triples with bath 5700ptas.

Hostal Montalvo, Zaragoza, 6, 3rd fl. (tel. 365 59 10), between Pl. Mayor and Pl. Santa Cruz. Metro: Sol. A creepy staircase leads to this *hostal* with a split personality: an old half with antique-looking furniture and vertiginous balconies, and a new with carpeted floors and impersonal comfort. Very quiet. TV lounge. Singles

2500ptas, with bath 3500ptas. Doubles 3500ptas, with bath 4800ptas, with double bed and bath 4500ptas. Prices are negotiable for stays of more than two days.

Hostal Soledad, C. San Cristobal, 11, 2nd fl. (tel. 521 22 10), off C. Mayor near Pl. Santa Cruz and Pl. Mayor. Metro: Sol. The manager wants only *"gente tranquila"* (quiet, well-mannered people) in her 12-room establishment; others need not apply. All rooms have balconies facing the street. Hot water 7am-midnight. Singles 1700ptas, with shower 2400ptas. Doubles 3000ptas, with shower 3500ptas, with bath 4400ptas.

Hostal-Residencia Encarnita, C. Marqués Viudo de Pontejo, 7, 4th fl. (tel. 531 90 55), above the María del Mar. Metro: Sol. Standard *hostal* charm: claustrophobic rooms, tired beds, dark halls. Coke machine in the lobby adds a cool splash of color. Singles 1500ptas. Doubles 2600ptas, with shower 2900ptas.

Hostal Amaika, C. Esparteros, 11, 3rd and 4th fl. (tel. 531 52 78), off of C. Mayor. Metro: Sol. Inside a covered shopping mall-esque area, the *hostal* building itself is beautiful. A wide, majestic staircase leads to somewhat ungainly rooms with big office desks and cute, pink-tiled baths. Singles 1700ptas, with bath 2300ptas. Doubles 2600ptas, with bath 3800ptas.

Hostal-Residencia Esparteros, C. Esparteros, 12, 4th fl. (tel. 521 09 03). No elevator in this decrepit building. An aesthetically displeasing entryway reminiscent of a hospital greets the visitor. Twelve adequate but undistinguished rooms. TV lounge. English and German spoken. Singles 1800ptas, with shower 2000ptas. Doubles with shower 3200ptas.

BETWEEN SOL AND MUSEO DEL PRADO

This area is just as historic as the neighborhood further west (see previous section). It's also central and chock full o' bars and restaurants. Although once down-at-heel, increasing gentrification has made it relatively safe.

Hostal Aguilar, C. San Jerónimo, 32, 2nd fl. (tel. 429 59 26). Metro: Sol. More than 50 big, clean rooms, all with telephone, TV, and shower. One of few *hostales* which offer quads, instead of squeezing extra beds into a double or triple. Giant, modern lounge with back-to-back couches a la airport terminal. Singles 2700ptas, with bath 3000ptas. Doubles 4100ptas, with bath 4500ptas. Triples 5500ptas, with bath 6500ptas. Quads 7500ptas, with bath 8500ptas. Reservations accepted. Visa and MC.

Hostal-Residencia Mondragón, C. San Jerónimo, 32, 4th fl. (tel. 429 68 16). Metro: Sol. In the same building as the Aguilar and several other *hostales* (Madrid Centro, San Jerónimo, and León). Spain's first motion picture was filmed in this building in 1898. Wide halls, large rooms, and a sun-splashed red-tiled terrace. Attractive reception area. Singles 1700ptas. Doubles 2400ptas, with shower 2600ptas. Triples with shower 3600ptas. Showers 100ptas. Open March-Dec.

Hostal Carreras, C. Príncipe, 18, 3rd fl. (tel. 522 00 36), off San Jerónimo, between Pl. Santa Ana and Pl. Canalejas. Metro: Antón Martín, Sol, or Sevilla. Recent renovation and expansion into the building next door make for 2 worlds at Carreras: the old (wood floors, big rooms, and weirdly-shaped communal bath) and the new (rooms off a long corridor, white-tiled floors, new furniture). Only the rooms in the annex at C. Príncipe 20 have full baths; no elevator for this part of the *hostal*. In the main section, some rooms have showers and sinks practically out on the balcony, creating an exciting, exhibitionist bathing experience. Singles 2000ptas, with bath 3500ptas. Doubles 3000ptas, with shower 3900ptas, with bath 4300ptas. Triples with shower 4500ptas.

Hostal-Residencia Regional, C. Príncipe, 18, 4th fl. (tel. 522 33 73), above Carreras. Metro: Antón Martín, Sol, or Sevilla. If you're lucky, your room will have a faux-Elizabethan chest of drawers complete with fake candles. If you're even luckier (and pay more), you'll get a frightening shower stall that looks as if it could beam you up to the Enterprise. Singles 2200ptas, with bath 4200ptas. Doubles 3200ptas, with bath 4200ptas. Triples 4500ptas, with shower 5500ptas.

Hostal Madrid Centro, C. San Jerónimo, 32, 5th fl. (tel. 429 68 13). Metro: Sol. Rooms vary from huge and bright with fireplace and charming anteroom, to smaller, poorly lit affairs. Teensy, musty lobby cluttered with odd knick-knacks.

Singles 2000ptas, with shower 2500ptas. Doubles 3000ptas, with shower 3500ptas. Triples with shower 4500ptas. Some rooms come with full bath for the price of a shower.

Hostal San Jerónimo, C. San Jerónimo, 32, 5th fl. (tel. 429 67 80), on the same floor as the Madrid Centro. Metro: Sol. A cramped, not particularly inviting *hostal*, but about as cheap as they come. Singles 1700ptas. Doubles 3000ptas. Triples 4200 ptas. Hot showers 200ptas.

Hostal León, C. San Jerónimo, 32, 4th fl. (tel. 429 67 78), on the same floor as the Mondragón. Metro: Sol. Elegant place, with fake flowers in every room and an attractive, tiled common bathroom. Hot shower included in room price. Singles 1600ptas. Doubles 3200ptas. Quads (with two double beds) 6000ptas.

Hostal Lucense, C. Núñez de Arce, 15, 2nd fl. (tel. 522 48 88), off C. Cruz, which is off San Jerónimo. Metro: Sol. The sign outside reads "Speaking Englisch," which turns out to be about right. Best for skinny people with lots of clothes—narrow rooms with immense closets. Singles 1300ptas. Doubles 2000ptas, with bath 2500ptas. Triples 3000ptas, with bath 3500ptas. Bathrooms (only in some rooms) are partitioned off with a shower curtain. If you don't have a shower in your room, you can bathe for 150ptas.

Pensión Poza, C. Núñez de Arce, 9 (tel. 522 48 71) is under the same management. The sign outside this building alleges, "We—speak English," leading one to wonder. Larger rooms than at the Lucense; same prices (see above).

Hotel Lido, C. Echegaray, 5, 2nd fl. (tel. 429 62 07), off C. San Jerónimo near Pl. Canalejas. Metro: Sol. One of four *hostales* in a rickety building surrounded by restaurants and late-night activity. Smallish rooms, some without windows; others with big, arboreous balconies. Run by an affable family who allow use of the kitchen, phone, TV, and assorted appliances. Singles 2000ptas, 35,000ptas per month. Doubles 3500ptas, 60,000ptas per month. Breakfast 350ptas.

Pensión Apolo XI, C. Espoz y Mina, 6, 3rd fl. (tel. 532 14 09), off C. San Jerónimo, a block from Puerta del Sol. Metro: Sol. A once elegant building, now in a semi-decrepit state. This 37 room *pensión* caters to groups—most rooms have 3-4 beds, and singles or pairs may wind up sharing. Brand new paint job. No elevator or winter heating. Flat rate of 1400ptas per person.

Hostal-Residencia Sud-Americana, Po. del Prado, 12, 6th fl. (tel. 429 25 64). Metro: Antón Martín or Atocha. Across from the Prado on Pl. Cánovas de Castillo. High ceilings, chandeliers, antique furniture, and polished hardwood floors lend the pleasantly scented rooms a *fin-de-siècle* elegance. Only eight rooms total—all equipped with faux-leather armchairs. Rooms facing the Po. de Prado have a great view. Singles 2100ptas. Doubles 4000ptas. Showers 400ptas.

Hostal Coruña, Po. del Prado, 12, 3rd fl. (tel. 429 25 43). Metro: Antón Martín or Atocha. Nice, breezy rooms, though less spectacular than those at the Sud-Americana above. Singles 2000ptas. Doubles 3800ptas. Triples 5000ptas.

Hostal Gonzalo, C. Cervantes, 34, 3rd fl. (tel. 429 27 14), off Pl. Cortes, near C. San Jerónimo. Metro: Antón Martín. Spacious and spic-and-span. Hallways freshly-painted in restful earth tones. Singles 2000ptas, with shower 2200ptas. Doubles with bath 4700ptas. Prices negotiable depending on length of stay.

Hostal Armesto, C. San Agustín, 6, 1st fl. (tel. 429 90 31), in front of Pl. Cortes. Metro: Antón Martín. A small establishment, with well-coordinated furniture, wallpaper, curtains, and bedspreads. Above-average quality fake art. No single rooms. Doubles with bath 5200ptas. Triples with bath 6000ptas.

THE GRAN VÍA

This broad, teeming thoroughfare is a frenetic example of Madrid's dissident pact with modernity. Grand old buildings house *cafeterías*, McDonald's, movie theaters, and floor upon floor of *hostales,* which advertise with signs high above—keep an eye out for their unprepossessing entrances as you trot along blithely at street level. Rooms on the Gran Vía are a bit more imposing on sleep and on the wallet.

Hostal Margarita, Gran Vía, 50, 5th fl. (tel. 547 35 49). Metro: Pl. España. Clean, good-sized rooms decorated with art from foreign lands. Jet-setting, English-speaking owners want to know all about you. Singles 2972ptas, with shower 3392ptas.

Doubles with shower 4240ptas, with bath 4452ptas. Triples with shower 6000ptas. Large breakfast 375ptas. Laundry service 1000ptas.

Hostal-Residencia Lamalonga, Gran Vía, 56, 2nd fl. (tel. 547 26 31 or 547 68 94). Metro: Callao. An elegant place with an air of hushed, baroque grandeur, especially in the bathrooms. All rooms have private bath. Singles 3800ptas. Doubles 5000ptas. Triples 6500ptas. Visa, MC accepted.

Hostal Lauria, Gran Vía, 50, 4th fl. (tel. 541 91 82). Metro: Pl. España. Stucco walls and light wood shutters give this *hostal* an airy, California Ranch House feel. Rooms are tastefully sparse, with big windows and pretty little bathrooms. The owner is eager to please. Singles 4000ptas. Doubles 5200ptas. Triples 7000ptas.

Hostal A. Nebrija, Gran Vía, 67, 8th fl. (stairway A) (tel. 547 73 19). Metro: Pl. España. Pleasant and spacious, with huge windows and excellent views from most rooms. All rooms with full bath. Singles 3100ptas. Doubles 4100ptas.

Hostal Excelsior, Gran Vía, 50, 2nd fl. (tel. 547 34 00, 547 34 08, or 547 34 09). Metro: Pl. España. The lobby has an odd rec-room aura, but the rooms are large and pretty, and some have balconies. All rooms with bathrooms. Singles 3390ptas. Doubles 5300ptas. Triples 7420ptas.

Hostal-Residencia Galicia, Valverde, 1, 4th fl. (tel. 522 10 13 or 522 47 70). Metro: Gran Vía. In a better world, this *hostal* would be a country manor, as witness the elegant sitting rooms and framed lithographs of the hunt. Telephones in all rooms. Singles 2500ptas. with bath 4000ptas. Doubles with bath 6000ptas. Triples with bath 7000ptas. Breakfast included.

Hostal-Residencia Malagueña, C. Preciados, 35, 4th fl. (tel. 559 52 23), between Pl. Santo Domingo and Pl. Callao. Metro: Callao. Spacious, airy rooms with high windows and decorative gas "hearths." No elevator. Singles 2000ptas. Doubles 3000ptas, with bath 3600ptas. One triple 3600ptas.

Hostal-Residencia Callao, C. Preciados, 35, 3rd fl. (tel. 542 00 67). Below the Malagueña. If your sin of choice is profligacy (it costs more) or sloth (one less flight of stairs to climb), you will prefer it to the upstairs neighbor. Singles 2500ptas, with bath 3500ptas. Doubles 3700ptas, with shower 4000ptas, with bath 4500ptas. Additional beds 2000ptas each.

Hostal-Residencia Delfina, Gran Vía, 12, 4th fl. (tel. 522 64 23 or 522 64 22). Metro: Gran Vía or Sevilla. Steel bedframes, oversized rooms, and a bit of old-fashioned charm. All rooms with bath. Singles 2800ptas. Doubles 4200ptas. Triples 6000ptas.

Hostal Los Zamoranos, Gran Vía, 12, 6th fl. (tel. 532 90 25). Metro: Gran Vía or Sevilla. Adequate but uninspiring rooms. Friendly management. Singles 1900ptas, with shower 2200ptas. Doubles 3200ptas, with shower 3400ptas. Off-season: 1600ptas; 1800ptas; 2800ptas; 2900ptas. 6% IVA not included.

Hostal-Residencia María, Miguel Moya, 4, 2nd fl (tel. 522 44 77), in the Pl. Callao. Metro: Callao. Set back from the noisome Gran Vía. Quiet rooms in pastoral colors. All rooms with bath. Singles 3000ptas. Doubles 4500ptas. Triples 6000ptas.

Hostal-Residencia Josefina, Gran Vía, 44, 7th fl. (tel. 521 81 31). Metro: Callao. Somewhat old and decrepit structure. Singles 1800ptas, with shower 2000ptas. Doubles 3000ptas. Triples 3900ptas, with bath and living room 4500ptas.

CALLE FUENCARRAL

For all its narrowness, C. Fuencarral is the main traffic pipeline to the Gran Vía for buses, taxis, commercial vehicles, scooters, and pedestrians. Jam-packed with shops, bars, and *hostales,* its buildings are continually in renovation. It may be noisier and fumier than the Gran Vía, but it's less expensive and closer to the nightlife of Malasaña and Chueca.

Hostal Palacios-Ribadavia, C. Fuencarral, 25, 2nd fl. (tel. 531 10 58 or 531 48 47). Metro: Gran Vía. A nice mom, pop, and cute-little-son operation. Renovated in 1994. All rooms have showers. Singles 2300ptas, with bath 2800ptas. Doubles 3600ptas, with bath 4200ptas. Triples 5300ptas, with bath 6000ptas. No charge for children under 10.

Hostal Medieval, C. Fuencarral, 46, 2nd fl. (tel. 522 25 49), on corner with C. Augusto Figueroa. Metro: Tribunal. Nothing remotely Dark Age-ish about the immense and sunny rooms, the plant-ridden balconies, or the neon lobby sign. The rooms are quirkily decorated with miniature paintings, plants, and fading paint. TV lounge. All rooms with shower. Singles with bath 5000ptas. Doubles 4000ptas, with bath 5000ptas. Triples 6000ptas.

Hostal-Residencia Abril, C. Fuencarral, 39, 4th fl. (tel. 531 53 38). Metro: Tribunal or Gran Vía. Cutesy prints of kitties and babies and garish mirrors amongst new-born furniture. Completely redone in 1994. Singles 1900ptas, with shower 2100ptas. Doubles 2950ptas, with shower 3300ptas, with bath 3500ptas. Triples with shower 4000ptas, with bath 4200ptas.

Hostal-Residencia Domínguez, C. Santa Brígida, 1 (tel. 532 15 47), off C. Fuencarral. Metro: Tribunal. Modern bathrooms have almost as much square footage as the spartan rooms. Dark, narrow hallways lead to windowless TV lounge with a luggage storage area. Singles 1900ptas, with shower 2100ptas. Doubles with shower 3200ptas, with bath 3500ptas.

Hostal-Residencia San José, C. Madera, 7 (tel. 532 21 28). Metro: Callao. From the station walk down Corredera Alta de San Pablo, turn right on C. Espíritu Santo, and left on C. Madera. Modest *hostal* on a quiet back street. Dark halls lit by fluorescent bulbs, rather small singles. Singles 1700ptas. Doubles 2800ptas.

ELSEWHERE

The area behind Gran Vía called **Chueca,** especially along and near C. Infantas, is about as rich in *hostales* (not to mention restaurants, bars, and nightlife) as any of the above districts. It's also less touristy—although not necessarily less pricey—and has a hipper scene.

Hostal Greco, C. Infantas, 3, 2nd fl. (tel. 522 46 32 or 522 46 31). Metro: Gran Vía or Chueca. You get lots of bang for your buck at this big, art-nouveau-ish hostal. Enormous rooms come with large bathrooms, telephones, personal safes, and emergency lights. Singles (only two of these, so you might want to call for a reservation) 3000ptas. Doubles 5000ptas. Triples 6800ptas. Visa, MC accepted.

Hostal Lorenzo, C. Infantas, 26, 3rd fl. (tel. 521 30 57 or 532 79 78). Metro: Gran Vía or Chueca. Aesthetically pleasing colonial-style rooms, some with plant-filled, glassed-in balconies. Flowers and big beds in all the rooms. Singles with shower 3000ptas, with bath 3500ptas. Doubles with bath 4800ptas. Triples with bath 6500ptas. Visa, MC accepted.

Other tourist-light zones include the mainly residential **Chamberi** (north of the boulevard formed by C. Alberto Aguilera, C. Carranza, C. Sagasta, and C. Genova) and **La Latina** (the area around the eponymous Metro stop stretching to Metro: Tirso de Molina and the Glorieta Puerta de Toledo). Near the **train station Atocha** are a handful of *hostales*, the closest down Paseo Santa María de la Cabeza. Near Chamartín train station budget lodgings are rare.

Hostal-Residencia La Montaña, C. Juan Alvárez Mendizábal, 44, 4th fl. (tel. 547 10 88). Metro: Ventura Rodríguez. One of five hostales at this address in the residential neighborhood of **Argüelles.** From the Metro station, walk down C. Luisa Fernanda; pass C. Martín de los Heroes and hit C. Juan Alvarez Mendizábal. Hilly Parque del Oeste, Pl. España, and Palacio Real are all within striking distance. Rooms are ample and sunny, quiet at night, and in much less demand. Singles 1700ptas, with shower 2100ptas. Doubles with shower 3400ptas, with bath 3700ptas. Triples with shower 5100ptas, with bath 5650ptas.

CAMPING

Tourist offices can provide information about the 13 or so campsites within 50km of Madrid. The same information is in their **Guía Oficial de Campings, España '95,** a big book which they gladly let you look through, but don't give away. Their **Mapa de Campings** lists and shows the location of every campsite in Spain. Also ask for the brochure **Hoteles, Campings, Apartamentos, España 1995,** which lists and describes hotels, campsites, and apartments in and around Madrid. For further camping information, contact the Consejería de Educación de Juventud, C. Caballero de Gracia, 32 (tel. 522 29 41 or 521 44 27). **Camping Osuna** (tel. 741 05 10; fax 320 63 65) is located on the Ajalvir-Vicálva10 road (15.5km). Take the Metro to Canillejas, then cross the pedestrian overpass, walk through the parking lot, and turn right along the freeway. Pass under two bridges (the first a freeway and the second an arch) and look for campground signs on the right (475ptas per person, per tent, and per car). **Camping Alpha** (tel. 695 80 69) hides on a shady site 12.4km down the Ctra. de Andalucía in Getafe. From the Legazpi Metro station take bus #447, which stops next to the Nissan dealership (every ½hr. until 10pm, 10min.). Ask the driver to let you off at the pedestrian overpass near the Amper building. After crossing the bridge, take an enchanting 1½km walk back toward Madrid along the edge of the busy highway. Alpha (525ptas per person and car, 550ptas per tent) has a pool. Both campgrounds can pass as autonomous cities; each has phones, hot showers, washers and dryers, safes, currency exchange, medical care, a playground, a bar, and a restaurant.

■■■ FOOD

In Madrid, it's not hard to fork it down without forking over too much of it, unless of course you're intent on elaborate fare and representatives from all the food groups at every meal. You can't walk a block without tripping over at least five *cafeterías*, where a sandwich, coffee, and dessert sell for around 500ptas. Fresh produce, however, is scarce—you may well go weeks without setting eyes on a lettuce leaf. The main food group here is ham, with pastries coming in a close second; everything else is given short shift. Vegetarians may have difficulty, as vegetarian restaurants are few and far between, and the ubiquitous *torta española* (basically a potato-pancake sandwich) grows old quickly. For a full meal at a *restaurante* or *casa,* one step up from the hegemonic *cafetería,* expect to spend at least 1000ptas, often more. Keep in mind the following essential buzz words for quicker, cheaper *madrileño* fare: *bocadillo* (200-300ptas), a sandwich on a French bread roll; *sandwich* (150-250ptas), a sandwich on sliced bread, usually grilled; *croissant* (150-250ptas), a croissant sandwich; *ración* (300-500ptas), a plate of meat, cheese, or some other finger food, served with bread; and *empanada* (150-250ptas), a puff pastry with tuna, hake, apple, and other fillings.

Excellent pastry shops and delis run amok in Madrid's streets. The sublime **Horno La Santiaguesa,** C. Mayor, 73, hawks everything from *roscones de reyes* (sweet bread for the Feast of the Epiphany) to *empanadas* to chocolate and candy. You can't go wrong at the pastry shops **Niza,** near Palacio de Justicia, or **Pastelería La Mallorquina,** on the corner of Puerta del Sol and C. Mayor. **Mallorca,** C. Velázquez, 59 (and other branches), is a renowned deli. **Juncal,** on C. (not Po.) Recoletos, satisfies the most exigent hankering for chocolate. Finally, **El Gourmet de Cuchilleros** is a gourmet store stocking all sorts of Spanish jams, honey, candy, and cheese, which make excellent gifts for that special someone. Walk through the Pl. Mayor's Arco de Cuchilleros; it's on the corner a few paces down.

Guía del Ocio lists late night eateries under *Cenar a Ultima Hora.* The orange **VIPS** (pronounced veeps) and green **BOB'S** signs that pop up all over Madrid invite patrons to these late-night restaurants. Everything from sandwiches to full dinners served. (VIPS open daily 9am-3am; BOB'S open Sun.-Thurs. 9am-1:30am, Fri.-Sat. and evenings before holidays 9am-3am.) VIPS also carries English books and magazines, records, chocolate, and canned food.

For **groceries,** try **Mercado de San Miguel,** on Pl. San Miguel, just off the northwest corner of Pl. Mayor; the discount **% Dia,** right behind the Mercado de San Miguel; or **Mercado de la Cebada,** at intersection of C. Toledo and C. San Francisco. (All open Mon.-Sat. 8am-2pm and 5:30-8pm.) Every **El Corte Inglés** has an excellent food market, usually on the ground floor. (Open Mon.-Sat. 10am-9pm, Sun. noon-8pm. See Practical Information: Other for addresses.)

In general in Madrid, a *restaurante* or *casa* is open from 1-4:30pm and 8:30pm-midnight; in the following listings, such is the case unless otherwise noted. More casual establishments such as *mesones, cafeterías, bares, cafés, terrazas,* and *tabernas* serve drinks and foodstuffs all day until midnight; some are closed on Sundays.

AROUND PUERTA DEL SOL AND PLAZA MAYOR

Choose carefully: this area is overrun by tourists. Restaurants compete to offer the most authentic local fare. Prices are fairly steep.

Casa Ciriaco, C. Mayor, 84. Metro: Sol or Opera. *Castizo* (traditional, pure) Madrid fare without pretensions. Filling bean and ham or chicken plates 1000-1200ptas. *Menú* 2100ptas; entrees about 1500ptas. Open Sept.-July Thurs.-Tues.

Madrid 1600, C. Cava de San Miguel. Metro: Sol. Another "typical" restaurant, this eensy stone-walled den has decent *cocido madrileño* (chick pea soup flavored in *chorizo* sausage). *Menú* 1500ptas. Open 1-4pm and 8pm-midnight.

Museo del Jamón, C. San Jerónimo, 6 (tel. 521 03 46), off Puerta del Sol. Metro: Sol. Five other locations throughout the city. In this charming example of Spain's love affair with pork, diners munch sandwiches and quaff beers beneath a canopy of ham—slabs of meat cover the walls, hang from the ceilings, and drip grease onto the floor. Succulent Iberian ham available in any form your piggish little heart could desire: *bocadillo* (150ptas), *chiquito* (95ptas), *croissant* (150ptas), *ración* (500ptas). Great pastries, cheeses, and *Museo del Jamón* wine. *Menú* 850ptas or 1000ptas. Open Mon.-Sat. 9am-12:30am, Sun. 10am-12:30am. Restaurant upstairs with longer menu, opens at 1pm. Visa, AmEx accepted.

Lhardy, C. San Jerónimo, 8 (tel. 521 33 85), at C. Victoria. Metro: Sol. Blue-uniformed guards mark one of Madrid's oldest restaurants, whose upstairs dining rooms remain in the original 1839 decor. A meal upstairs is a big investment; the house specialty *cocido* 3000ptas. Budget-hounds congregate in the first-floor store for cognac, sherry, and the best hors d'oeuvres in town. Prime Minister Felipe González comes here on occasion for power lunches. Also gourmet foodstuffs for sale. Open Mon.-Sat. 1-3:30pm and 9-11:30pm, Sun. 1-3:30pm. Visa, MC, AmEx accepted.

Restaurante Manacor, Pasaje de Matheú, 2. Metro: Sol. One of a few inviting restaurants with an outdoor seating area in a pedestrian byway connecting C. Victoria and C. Espoz y Mina, both off C. San Jerónimo, and right outside Puerta del Sol. Fine food; nice setting. *Menú* 850ptas.

Restaurante-Cafetería Sabatini, C. Bailén, 15 (tel. 547 92 40), opposite the Sabatini Gardens which are next to the Palacio Real. Come at sunset. Sidewalk tables face two of Madrid's most famous sights. Portly portions of *paella* (800ptas) or garlic chicken (800ptas). Open 9am-1am. Dinner served 8pm-midnight.

NEAR PLAZA SANTA ANA

Plaza Santa Ana is lovely, shady, and surprisingly less touristy than neighboring Puerta del Sol. **Calles Echegaray, Ventura de la Vega,** and **Manuel Fernández González** are the budget boulevards. Overall quality is high and prices are low.

Mesón La Caserola, C. Echegaray, off C. San Jerónimo. Metro: Sol. Bustling, crowded joint serves a solid *menú* (825ptas) to ravenous locals. Despite its proximity to Puerta del Sol, La Caserola's prices and atmosphere remain *madrileño* as opposed to *turístico*. Cozy atmosphere. Cheap *raciones* and *tapas* during off-hours; many entrees around 600ptas. Closed Mon. noon. A/C.

Restaurante Integral Artemisa, C. Ventura de la Vega, 4, off C. San Jerónimo. Metro: Sol. The leftist's dream come true: a vegetarian restaurant right next to socialist party headquarters. Decent food, though service is slow. Flavorful *potaje* (stew), pizza, purees, and salads. Many salads around 900ptas. Entrees 800-1200ptas; non-vegetarian available as well. A/C. Visa accepted.

Taberna La Quimada, on C. Echegaray, one block down from C. San Jerónimo. Metro: Sol. Romantic, dimly-lit, with burnished wood and stained-glass chandeliers. They make a mean *menú* for 1000ptas. Entrees 800-1500ptas. Across the street and down a bit is the nearly identical **Taberna La Quimada II,** under the same management. A/C.

Restaurante Tien Fu, Carrera de San Jerónimo, five minutes down from Puerta del Sol. Madrid has a surprising number of Chinese restaurants where the food is surprisingly mediocre. Entrees (500-800ptas) in a room decorated with soothing Chinese landscapes. A/C. AmEx, Visa, MC accepted.

SOUTH OF PUERTA DEL SOL

The neighborhoods south of Sol, bounded by C. Atocha and C. Toledo, are more residential and working class. No caviar or champagne here, but plenty of *menús* for around 1000ptas. A la carte is often a better bargain.

Mesón-Restaurante Abadín, C. Santa Isabel, 19. Metro: Pl. Antón Martín. Don't be put off by the display of dead fish and rabbits on ice in the window: the charming little place inside has an excellent selection of vegetable and seafood dishes. Salads and vegetable sideorders 200-500ptas, *menú* 1000ptas, seafood entrees 800-1200ptas. Visa accepted.

La Biótica, Amor de Dios, 3 (tel. 429 07 80), off C. Atocha. Metro: Alonso Martín. Totally hard-core vegetarian joint, with a little apothecary as you enter selling vitamins and herbal teas. Full a la carte meal around 1200ptas, *menú* 900ptas. 10% surcharge on all orders weekends and holidays.

El Granero de Lavapiés, C. Argumosa, 10 (tel. 467 76 11), on a lovely tree-lined street with balconied 19th-century facades in a rarely visited old neighborhood. Metro: Lavapiés. Vegetarian; some non-vegetarian fare as well. Cream of almost-anything-your-little-heart-desires soups 400-430ptas. Entrees around 700ptas: veggie burgers 775ptas, savory grilled tofu 700ptas. Open for lunch Sun.-Mon.

Bar Restaurante El Bierzo, C. Encomienda, 19 (tel. 468 54 03), on cobbled street off C. Embajadores. Metro: La Latina. Paper tablecloths, off-yellow walls, blaring TV—get the idea? No-frills dining. House specialties: *conejo al ajillo* (rabbit with garlic) and *gambas a la plancha* (fried shrimp). *Menú* 700ptas. Closed Mon.

La Terraza, off C. Bailén just past the Viaducto (tel. 366 35 78), among the trees of a slope-side park (Las Vistillas) famed for the view of the sunset. This *café-terraza* serves excellent meals at the bar and even better in its elegant *comedor*. Small list of entrees, 1000-1200ptas.

THE GRAN VÍA

McDonald's (two on Gran Vía) is the cloth out of which many *cafeterías, hamburguerías,* and *pizzarías* here have been cut. If you came to Spain to escape the Power of the Big Mac, you'll do better in another part of town.

Mesón Altamar, C. Luna, 28 (tel. 521 03 51), off C. San Bernardo, which is off Gran Vía. Metro: Santo Domingo. Fried fish amidst high seas decor. House specialty *calamares mexicanos* (Mexican squid). On Thurs. and Sun., fishy *paella. Menú* 775ptas.

Restaurante-Cafetería El Valle, C. Fuencarral, 8. Metro: Gran Vía. Local shop attendants and businessfolk take refuge midday in the cozy back room. Many a *pulpo* (octopus) dish, if that's your thing. Breakfast special 160ptas. *Menú* 875ptas.

CHUECA

The none-too-closeted gay/glam district, where scenesters crowd the chic gourmet joints and stalk the streets in platform shoes. Highest nose-ring per capita ratio of anywhere in the city. Lots of good places to wine and dine, especially the former.

Taberna Carmencita, C. San Marcos, 36, on the corner with C. Libertad. Metro: Chueca. Popular with tourists and businesspeople, this classic restaurant, founded in 1830, evokes pre-War Madrid: brass fixtures, black and white photos of bullfighters, polychrome glazed tiles, lace curtains, and iron and marble tables.

The *menú* is 1000ptas, but doesn't include appetizers, bread, wine, or 6% IVA. Excellent house wines. Entrees 700-900ptas. Visa, MC, AmEx, DC accepted.

La Carreta, Barbieri, 10 (tel. 532 70 42 or 521 60 97), off C. los Infantes. Metro: Gran Vía or Chueca. An Argentine restaurant specializing in Argentine, Uruguayan, and Chilean delights. Lots of meat dishes (of course). Try the delicious Martín Fierro dessert, named after the eponymous Argentine national novel (890ptas). Lunch *menú* 1500ptas. Entrees around 900ptas. Visa, MC, AmEx, DC accepted.

Restaurante La Vascongada, Pl. Vázquez de Mella, 10, on the edge of Chueca toward Gran Vía. Yellow sign visible from C. Infantas near the ugly parking plaza. Typical dishes of Madrid and the País Vasco (Basque country). *Menú* 700ptas. Special offer: half a chicken for 400ptas. Entrees 300-700ptas. A/C.

Nabucco, C. Hortaleza, 108 (tel. 410 06 11), a couple of blocks off Pl. Santa Bárbara. A large pizza-pasta place. Much lower prices than the upscale clientele and atmosphere suggest. Pizzas 500-800ptas, pasta dishes 600-800ptas. Visa, MC, AmEx, DC accepted.

Restaurante Zara, C. Infantes, 5, off C. Hortaleza. Metro: Gran Vía. "Typical tropical dishes"—mostly meats and rices. *Menú* 1900ptas. Meat entrees 700-1100ptas. Visa, MC, AmEx, DC accepted.

La Chocolatería-Comedor Madrid, C. Barbieri, 15 (tel. 521 00 23), four blocks from Gran Vía. Metro: Chueca. Traditional Spanish cuisine in a restaurant gone increasingly upmarket. Despite the name, not really a dessert place. Lunch *menú* 1690ptas. Entrees about 1000ptas. Open Sept.-July Mon.-Sat. 1:30-3:45pm and 9pm-1:45am, Sun. 9pm-1:45am. Bar open 6:30pm-1:45am. Closed Semana Santa.

MALASAÑA

Streets radiating from Pl. Dos de Mayo drown in a sea of *cafeterías,* bars, restaurants, and pubs. **Calle San Andrés** is most densely populated, but **Calles San Bernardo** and **Manuela Malasaña,** on the fringes of this neighborhood, shouldn't be overlooked. Many spots here are more imaginative in their cuisine and setting than the "regional specialty" clones which are legion in Madrid. Watch the colorful characters who fill the maze of tiny streets; watch them especially closely after dark.

La Granja Restaurante Vegetariano, C. San Andrés, 11 (tel. 532 87 93), off Pl. 2 de Mayo. Metro: Tribunal, Noviciado, or Bilbao. Attractive dark wood and tile interior. A vegetarian ecstasy: great food, lot's of it, and cheap. Salads and soups, vegetarian *paella, arrroz con algas* (rice with seaweed)—you name it, if it didn't walk or swim, they've got it. *Menú* 850ptas. Closed Sun. Visa accepted.

El Restaurante Vegetariano, C. Marqués de Santa Ana, 34, off Pl. Juan Pujol on the corner with C. Espíritu Santo. Metro: Tribunal. Another good bet for vegetarians, though smaller than La Granja and a wee bit pricier. Homemade bread. Quiches 775-885ptas. Soups 500ptas. Salad bar 535-735ptas. *Menú* 800ptas. Closed Mon. Visa, MC accepted.

La Gata Flora, C. 2 de Mayo, 1, and across the street at C. San Vicente Ferrer, 33 (tel. 521 20 20 or 521 27 92). Metro: Noviciado or Tribunal. Tightly packed tables and a bohemian crowd in a marvelous Italian restaurant. There's a cat in every picture. Pizzas and pastas 700-900ptas; big, verdant salads 500-675ptas. Excellent sangría 875ptas. Open 2-6pm and 8:30-midnight; Fri.-Sat. open until 1am. Visa, MC, DC accepted.

BEYOND BILBAO

The area north of Glorieta de Bilbao (Metro: Bilbao) in the V formed by **Calles Fuencarral** and **Luchana,** and including **Plaza Olavide,** is comprised of oh-so-many bars, clubs, cafés, and restaurants. Most bars and *mesones* purvey splendid, cheap *tapas* to feed the vibrant crowd of strollers that fills the streets come evening. Lunch gets pricier farther north in more gentrified territory.

Bagel: El Bocadillo Americano, C. Cardenal Cisneros, right off C. Luchana, which is off the Glorieta de Bilbao. Spain's first—and so far only—bagel shop.

These bagels will satisfy all but the most picky New York or Philadelphia bagel aficionado. Plain, garlic, onion, and cinnamon-raisin bagels for 100ptas; with cream cheese 200ptas; with lox 425ptas.

Peñasco Rodilla, C. Fuencarral, 119. Metro: Bilbao. A little of the ol' "ham-bam-thank you ma'am." The Peñasco serves up cheap and exquisite *sandwiches* (from 250ptas), *bocadillos* (from 165ptas), and hot dogs. One of several "Rodillas" in town, it's a lunch counter with an attitude: campy decorations and flashing lights everywhere you look. Great pastries. A/C.

Bar Samara, C. Cardenal Cisneros, 13. Bills itself as Egyptian, but actually offers standard, Middle Eastern staples. Hummus, babaganoush, and tahini salads 475-525ptas. Kabobs and other entrees from 1500ptas. Gets crowded after dark. A/C. Open Sun.-Thurs. until midnight, Fri.-Sat. until 1am.

ARGÜELLES AND MONCLOA

Argüelles and Moncloa are middle-class *barrios* near the Ciudad Universitaria. They're a bit out of the way for dinner, and not as attractive as other residential neighborhoods in Madrid, but full of of student-priced eateries.

Restaurante La Tuna, Fernando El Católico, 68 (tel. 243 25 24). Metro: Moncloa. Nothing spectacular, but the platefuls of wholesome fare are hearty. Meat dishes 300-600ptas, *paella* 300ptas. *Menú* 775ptas, special *menú* (two entrees instead of one) 1100ptas. Closed Mon. night.

Restaurante El Parque, Fernando el Católico, 78 (543 31 27), one bl. down from La Tuna. Metro: Moncloa. Large and unpretentious, with tiled walls and simple food. *Menú* 800ptas, entrees 400-700ptas. Long dessert menu. Closed Sun. night.

El Rey de las Tortillas, C. Andrés Mellado, 16. Metro: Argüelles. *"Come barato, bien, y rápido con nuestros famosos platos gigantes"* (eat cheaply, well, and quickly with our famous, gigantic platters) reads a sign in the window. Indeed, the servings are enormous—more cholesterol for your peseta. Combination platters 400-500ptas. One liter *sidra* (cider) 450ptas. Open Mon.-Sat. noon-4pm and 7pm-midnight.

TAPAS

Hopping from bar to bar gobbling *tapas* at the counter (see Spain: Life and Times: Food and Drink) is an active alternative to a full sit-down meal. Most *tapas* bars (a.k.a. *tascas* or *tabernas*) are open noon to 4pm and 8pm to midnight or later. Some, doubling as restaurants, cluster around **Plaza Mayor** (tourist alert!) and **Plaza Santa Ana.**

La Toscana, C. Ventura de la Vega, 22 (tel. 429 60 31). A quiet *mesón* with old architectural implements dangling from the woodwork. *Raciones* are their strong suit. Open noon-4pm and 8pm-midnight.

La Trucha, C. Fernán González, 3 (tel. 429 58 33). Cramped but cheap. Open Mon.-Sat. 12:30-4pm and 8pm-midnight.

La Chuleta, C. Echegaray, 20 (tel. 429 37 29). Spacious and modern. Savory *tortillas, calamares* (squid), and peppers. Open Sun.-Tues., Thurs. noon-1am, Fri.-Sat. noon-3am. AmEx cards and traveler's checks accepted.

La Dolores, C. Duque de Medinacelli, 4 (tel. 429 42 43), on the corner of Calles Lope de Vega and Jesús. Beer cans from every corner of the globe adorn this brightly tiled, high-ceilinged *tasca*. Extensive array of *tapas* (900-1200ptas). Open daily 11am-1am.

Viña P, Pl. Santa Ana, 3 (tel. 231 81 11). Gaze at a diorama of the *plaza de toros* as you dine on fresh seafood and mountain-cured ham. Wide price range: *pincho de salmón* 1500ptas. Visa, MC accepted.

Barranco, C. San Isidro Labrador, 14. A classic *tasca* celebrated for its shellfish and *jamón de Guijuelo* (Guijuelo cured ham).

El Anciano Rey de los Vinos, C. Bailén, 19 (tel. 248 50 52), one bl. from where C. Mayor hits C. Bailén. A bright, lofty-ceilinged bar, with a wide selection of house wines served by the glass, and cider on tap. Open 10am-3pm and 5:30-11:30pm. Closed Wed.

■■■ SIGHTS

Once the capital of the world's largest empire, Madrid is rich in cultural, artistic, architectural, and verdant treasures. The numerous tree-lined streets and lush parks fashion somewhat of a garden oasis on the calcinated plain of Castile. The municipal tourist office regularly updates its pamphlet *Madrid: Museums and Monuments,* with addresses, telephone numbers, public transport, hours, admission, and brief descriptions of Madrid's many museums (see Museums below). Consider taking one of several tours offered to acquaint visitors with Madrid (see Practical Information: Tours).

In the following pages, sights are arranged by geographical location. The grand scheme is roughly semicircular: we begin in the Medieval-Hapsburg heart of the city, and then travel successively east, north, and west, concluding with El Pardo.

FROM PLAZA MAYOR TO PUERTA DE TOLEDO

A good place to orient yourself for any walking expedition through Madrid, **Plaza Mayor** is an elegant arcaded square, topped with the Hapsburgs' black slate roofs and spindly, pagoda-like towers. The plaza was completed in 1620 for Felipe III; his statue—also from the 17th century, although not installed until 1847—graces its center. The public executions and bullfights that took place here throughout the early modern period are now but ghosts haunting the shops and cafés along the plaza's edges. During the day the plaza is often quiet—a lone statue surrounded by flocks of pigeons, empty tables, and a tourist or two. However, as soon as Madrid's unforgiving summer sun begins to set, *Madrileños* emerge from their apartments, tourists multiply, and café tables fill with lively patrons. Every Sunday morning, hundreds of collectors assemble here at the **coin and stamp market** (open 9am-2pm). Pl. Mayor explodes in boisterous festivity during the annual celebration of San Isidro. The arcades and surrounding streets house highly specialized old shops, including a renowned hat emporium. (Metro: Sol. Bus #3, 53, M-1.)

When Felipe II made Madrid capital of his empire in the 1561, most of the town huddled between Pl. Mayor and the Palacio Real, stretching north to today's Opera and south to Pl. Puerta de Moros. Only a handful of medieval buildings remain, but the labyrinthine layout is unmistakable. **Plaza de la Villa** marks the heart of what was medieval Madrid. The **Torre de los Lujanes,** a 15th-century building on the eastern side of the plaza, is the sole remnant of the once lavish residence of the Lujanes family. Note the original horseshoe-shaped Gothic door on C. Codo. The characteristically Hapsburg, 17th-century **Ayuntamiento** (or Casa de la Villa) on the plaza was both the mayor's home and the city jail. As Madrid (and its bureaucracy) grew, officials had to annex the neighboring **Casa de Cisneros**, a Plateresque house from the mid-16th century. Free guided tours (in Spanish) are offered every Monday at 5pm and start from the Oficina de Información, Pl. Villa, 5.

Southwest of Pl. Mayor on Pl. Santa Cruz, the **Palacio de Santa Cruz** exemplifies the Hapsburg style with its alternation of red brick and granite corners and black-slate towers. Ask the guard to let you eye the splendid courtyard. One block south is **Plaza de la Paja** (of the straw), the city's erstwhile main square. Here sits the imposing and highly elaborate Renaissance **Capilla del Obispo** (Bishop's Chapel), built in 1518 to hold the remains of San Isidro, Madrid's patron saint. The chapel eventually surrendered the saintly bones to its next-door neighbor, the Baroque, domed, red brick and granite **Iglesia de San Andrés** and **Capilla de San Isidro.** Inside the Iglesia de San Andrés is a magnificently carved polychrome altarpiece by Francisco Giralte, a disciple of Berruguete. An impressive set of his detailed alabaster sculptures adorns the tombs of the Vargas family. (Open for mass only.)

South of Pl. Mayor on C. Toledo looms **Iglesia de San Isidro,** a 17th-century church designed by the famed Pedro Sánchez and Francisco Bautista. The remains of San Isidro landed here after being tossed from church to church. Little is known about him except for his status as a *labrador* (peasant). His lack of learning lent him prestige: Hapsburg Madrid cultivated a heroic portrait of the "pure" *cristianos viejos* (old Christians), associating erudition with people of Jewish descent. The church was restored after the interior was burned by rioting workers in 1936. It served as the cathedral of Madrid from the late 19th century until 1993, when a new cathedral was consecrated (see "Palacio Real"). (Open for mass only. Metro: Latina. Bus #17, 23, 35, and 60.)

Weakened by plagues and political losses, Spain ended the Hapsburg era with the death of Carlos II in 1700. Felipe V, the first Spanish Bourbon, ascended the throne faced with bankruptcy, industrial stagnation, military incompetence, and widespread moral disillusionment. Undaunted, Felipe V embarked on an urban renewal program continued with zest by successors Fernando VI and Carlos III during the 18th century. The majestic **Basílica de San Francisco el Grande** (St. Francis of Assisi) at Pl. San Francisco el Grande, down C. San Francisco (5-min. walk from Pl. Mayor) is one of the most impressive results of the Bourbon plan. This Neoclassical temple wears a convex facade capped with a magnificent dome. In the somber interior, Goya's *San Bernardino of Siena Preaching* hangs among many other paintings by Goya's contemporaries. St. Francis himself allegedly built a convent on this site in the 13th century. (Open in summer Tues.-Sat. 11am-1pm and 5-8pm. Optional brief tour in Spanish. Metro: Puerta de Toledo or Latina. Bus #3, 60.)

In Pl. Puerta de Toledo (down **Gran Vía de San Francisco,** the continuation of C. Bailén), the **biblioteca pública** is a library in the round. This and some of the buildings on Gran Vía de San Francisco are of the acclaimed Madrid School, featuring pastel hues, turrets, and glass-enclosed miradors.

The broad Baroque **Puente de Toledo** arches across Río Manzanares at the end of C. Toledo, beyond the Puerta de Toledo. Sandstone carvings on one side depict San Isidro rescuing his son from a well, and on the other, his wife Santa María de la Cabeza. Renaissance **Puente de Segovia,** which fords the river from C. Segovia, was conceived by the talented designer of El Escorial. Both bridges afford gorgeous views, especially at sunset (and also fertile ground for the blossoming of Young Love).

BETWEEN SOL AND PASEO DEL PRADO

In front of the 18th-century Casa de Correos (post office, now police headquarters) in **Puerta del Sol** rests the zero-km marker. In the middle of the square, a statue of a bear hugs an arbutus tree *(madroño)*, the city's coat of arms. According to folklore, a king chased a bear to an arbutus tree in a forest clearing, which became Madrid. Puerta del Sol was the scene of one of the most resonant moments in the country's history, when citizens of Madrid rose against Napoleon's army after learning of his plan to remove the Royal Infantas. Two of Goya's paintings in the Prado, *El dos de mayo* (May 2, 1808) and *Los fusilamientos del tres de mayo* (The Execution of the Rioters: May 3, 1808), depict the gruesome episode. Every New Year's Eve citizens congregate here to swallow a dozen grapes as the clock strikes midnight.

The grand C. Alcalá leads from Sol to Po. Recoletos. Domed **Iglesia de las Calatravas,** C. Alcalá, 25, is all that remains of the huge Convento de la Concepción Real de Comendadoras. Pablo González Velázquez's Baroque altarpiece contrasts sharply with the building's stark Renaissance exterior. Artisans designed a unique ornamental cross motif now named after this church. (Open for mass only 7:30am-1pm and 6-8pm. Metro: Sevilla.) Also on C. Alcalá are the **Museo de la Real Academia de Bellas Artes de San Fernando** and the **Calcografía Real** (see Museums).

The austere, 18th-century **Real Academia de la Historia,** on the corner of C. Huertas and C. León, houses a magnificent old library. This area is Madrid's old literary quarter, where Cervantes, Góngora, Quevedo, Calderón, Moratín, and others lived. Although Golden Age playwright Lope de Vega and Miguel de Cervantes, author of *Don Quijote,* were bitter rivals, the 17th-century **Casa de Lope de Vega** is ironically located at C. Cervantes, 11 (a few blocks south of C. San Jerónimo). The great and prolific playwright spent the last 25 years of his life here. (Open Mon.-Fri. 9:30am-2:30pm, Sat. 10am-1:30pm. Admission 200ptas. Students free.)

The **Paseo del Prado** is garnished with three aqueous masterpieces. In **Fuente de Neptuno** at Pl. Cánovas del Castillo, dolphins spew torrents of water at the Roman sea god. **Fuente de Apolo** features Apollo and the four seasons. **Fuente de la Cibeles,** across from the post office, depicts the fertility goddess's triumphant arrival in a carriage drawn by lions—formerly several young men who incurred the goddess's rage and were lionized—literally—for their troubles. Myth has it that Atalanta, a fleet-footed young girl, would take as her lover only the man who could beat her in a foot race. For years and years no man was up to the challenge. Finally one cunning individual concocted a devious scheme, instructing his cohorts to scatter golden apples in Atalanta's path, thus reducing her speed as she stooped to gather them. But the goddess Cibeles, watching the prank, was overcome with wrath at the evil ways of men, turned the plotters—who protested that "she was asking for it"—into giant cats, and bade them drive her carriage. Madrid residents successfully protected this emblem of their city during Franco's Nationalist bomb raids by covering it with a pyramid made of sacks of sand. Near the southern end of Po. Prado, the **Centro de Arte Reina Sofía** preens its feathers (see Museums).

THE RETIRO AND JERÓNIMOS

Parque del Retiro, a wide expanse of greenery and pastoral delights, was originally intended to be a *buen retiro* (nice retreat) for Felipe IV. Indeed a nice retreat, the Retiro is now Madrid's top picnic and suntanning zone. Virtually deserted in the morning, the park is perfect for an early jog or daily constitutional. At nightfall (when only the north gate remains open), the Retiro's various bars and cafés come to life. Felipe IV's palace burned down in 1764; only the **Casón del Buen Retiro** and **Museo del Ejército** (see Museums) remain. Alfonso XII and his horse glare at the **Estanque Grande,** a rectangular lake in the middle of the park. Boat rentals available here (10am-sunset, 400ptas for 2 people, 100ptas for each additional person). South of the lake, the **Palacio de Cristal** hosts a variety of art shows with subjects from Bugs Bunny to Spanish portraiture. (Open Tues.-Sat. 11am-2pm and 5-8pm, Sun. 10am-2pm. Admission varies, but often free.) Many fountains punctuate the park's avenues, notably the **Fuente de la Alcachofa** (Artichoke Fountain). The northeast corner of the park swells with medieval monastery ruins and waterfalls. Carlos III moved the **Jardín Botánico** across Av. Alfonso XII onto Espalter (at the Parque del Retiro's southwestern corner, across from the main entrance to the Prado). (Garden open 10am-9pm. Admission 100ptas.)

Iglesia de San Jerónimo, built by Hieronymite monks and reendowed by the Catholic monarchs, overlooks the Museo del Prado. The industrious monks built a new monastery in a meadow *(prado)* on the outskirts of town. This church has witnessed many a joyous milestone: Fernando and Isabel were crowned and King Alfonso XIII married here. (Open 6am-1pm and 6-8pm. Bus #10, 14, 15, 19, 34, 37, and 45.)

Nearby on C. Montalbán sit the **Museo Naval, Museo de Artes Decorativas,** and **Museo Postal y Telegráfico** (see Museums). Civil War bullets permanently scarred the eastern face of the imposing Neoclassical **Puerta de Alcalá** at Pl. Independencia. Revenue from an unpopular wine tax paid for this arch honoring Carlos III in 1778.

PASEOS PRADO, RECOLETOS, AND CASTELLANA

Po. Recoletos-Prado from Estación Atocha to Pl. Colón is one of the great European ensembles of Neoclassical and revival architecture: the **Biblioteca Nacional,** the **Palacio de Buenavista** (atop a slope overlooking Pl. Cibeles), the extravagant **Palacio de Comunicaciones,** the Banco de España, the **Museo Thyssen-Bornemizsa,** the Bolsa, and the Prado line the avenue. With virtually every major museum in its immediate vicinity, this "museum mile" is the veritable cultural axis of Madrid. At night it becomes a hot spot for Madrid's elite, who flock to its elegant outdoor bars and restaurants to look languid and sip expensive drinks.

Across from Estación Atocha sits the imposing 19th-century **Ministerio de Agricultura,** with ceramic tiles and stained glass. To its east, just outside Parque Retiro
on Av. Alfonso XII, Villanueva's attractive 18th-century **Observatorio Astronómico**
reaches for the stars at the summit of a grassy slope. (Tel 227 01 07; open Mon-Fri
9am-2pm. Admission 400ptas, students free.) Between the Ministry and Observatory
sits the **Museo Etnológico,** and south of Estación Atocha the **Museo del Ferrocarril**
(see Museums). A short stroll farther south leads to the expansive Parque de Tierno
Galván, which contains a popular new **Planetario.** (Tel. 467 38 98. Admission
375ptas, children and seniors 185ptas. Metro: Méndez Alvaro.)

Just north of the Prado on Po. Prado, the **Obelisco a los Mártires del 2 de Mayo**
stands in Pl. Lealtad, stuffed with the ashes of those who died in the 1808 uprising
against Napoleon. Across from the memorial, the gracefully curved, colonnaded
Bolsa de Madrid (the city's stock exchange) generates income.

Opposite the post office on Pl. Cibeles is Palacio de Linares, a 19th-century townhouse built for Madrid nobility. Long abandoned by its former residents and proved
by a team of "scientists" to be inhabited by ghosts, it has been transformed into the
Casa de América, with a library and lecture halls for the study of Latin American
culture and politics. (Metro: Banco de España.) Casa de América sponsors frequent
art exhibitions and guest lectures, not always limited to Latin American subjects. Up
Po. Recoletos by Pl. Colón, the **Biblioteca Nacional** (entrance at #20) displays treasures from monarchs' private collections, including a first-edition copy of *Don
Quijote.* The **Museo Arqueológico Nacional** is also here (see Museums).

Jetlagged moles emerging from the ground in the **Jardines del Descubrimiento**
(Gardens of Discovery) at Pl. Colón will discover a number of huge clay boulders
inscribed with odd trivia about the New World, including Seneca's prediction of the
discovery, the names of all the mariners on board the caravels, and quotes from
Columbus's diary. Concerts, lectures, ballet, and plays entertain below the gardens
in the **Centro Cultural de la Villa** (tel. 575 60 80). On its front, facing a noisy waterfall, a large map details the dicoverer's voyages to America. A more traditional monument to Columbus stands directly above the Centro Cultural. (Metro: Colón.)

Many of the magnificent apartment buildings and mansions belonging to aristocrats before the war line **Po. Castellana** toward Pl. Emilio Castelar. Although many
were pulled down in the 60s, some of the bank and insurance buildings that
replaced the originals are boldly imaginative; the juxtaposition of new and old
money is striking. Among others, note Moneo's Bankinter at #29, the first to integrate rather than demolish a townhouse; Banco Urquijo, known as "the coffeepot";
Banca Catalana, the delicate ice cube on a cracker near the American Embassy; and
Adriática, on Pl. Emilio Castelar, whose architect Carvajal was influenced by the rev-
erence for flowing water in the Hispano-Muslim tradition. The **Instituto de Valencia
de Don Juan** and **Museo Sorolla** (see Museums) lurk on side streets.

Up the street north of Pl. Emilio Castelar, look for the **Museo Nacional de Ciencias Naturales;** the **Museo Lázaro Galdiano** is nearby on C. Serrano (see Museums).
Farther still, past Torres Picasso and Europa at Plaza de Lima, squats the **Estadio
Santiago Bernabéu** (Metro: Nuevos Ministerios or Cuzco). Fans of modern sky-
scraper architecture goosebump at the sight of the **Puerta de Europa,** a colossal
structure seen from the stadium. (Metro: Pl. Castilla. Bus #40 from C. Montera near
Gran Vía stops at Pl. Cuzco.)

NORTH OF THE GRAN VÍA

Narrow Calle Barquillo, the main throughfare of the Pl. Salesas district, is yet another
microcosm of Madrid-style architecture. **Casa de las Siete Chimeneas** (House of
Seven Chimneys, reputedly symbolic of the deadly sins), one of the oldest houses in
the city, commands the corner of C. Barquillo and C. Infantas. Built in 1577, the old
house is the eerie scene of many a ghost story. Its most famous resident was the Marqués de Esquilache, who provoked a riot in 1766 by unleashing an army of tailors on
the city: they ran around pinning up men's wide-brimmed hats and trimming their

ankle-length capes so that would-be royal assassins would have fewer places to conceal lethal little bodkins on their persons. (Metro: Banco de España.)

Near Pl. Colón on C. Bárbara de Braganza is **Iglesia de las Salesas Reales,** at Pl. Salesas. Commissioned by Bourbon King Fernando VI at the request of his wife Doña Bárbara in 1758, the Baroque-Neoclassical domed church is clad in granite, with facade sculptures by Alfonso Vergaza and dome painting by the brothers González Velázquez. The ostentatious facade and lavish interior prompted critics to pun on the queen's name: "Barbaric queen, barbaric tastes, barbaric building, barbarous expense." The royal couple is buried here. (Metro: Colón.)

Stroll past Pl. Salesas up C. Fernando VI to the **Palacio de Longoria** ("Sociedad General Autores"—writer's union—on the map) for a taste of *Modernismo* outside of Barcelona. (Metro: Tribunal or Alonso Martínez.) **Museos Romántico, Municipal,** and **de la Ciudad** are in this district (see Museums).

Pedro de Ribera, the premier early 18th-century Spanish architect, designed many buildings in the area: **Palacio Miraflores,** C. San Jerónimo, 19; **Palacio del Marqués de Ugena,** C. Príncipe, 28; **Palacio del Marqués de Perales,** C. Magdalena, 12; and the delightful hermitage on the canal called **Ermita de la Virgen del Puerto** (Po. Virgen del Puerto).

Farther west, by Plaza de España, a row of olive trees surrounds a grandiose monument to Cervantes. Next to the plaza are two of Madrid's tallest skyscrapers, the **Torre de Madrid** and the **Edificio de España.** (Café on the 26th floor open noon to early evening. Cover charge 100ptas. Metro: Pl. España.) Tucked between the two skyscrapers is crafty little **Iglesia de San Marcos,** a Neoclassical church composed of five intersecting ellipses; a Euclidean nightmare, there's not a single straight line in sight. The **Depósito de Agua** and **Museo de Cerralbo** linger near Pl. España, while **Palacio de Liria** is a bit north (see Museums).

The 19th century also witnessed the growth of several neighborhoods around the core of the city, north and northwest of the Palacio Real. Today, the area known as **Argüelles** and the zone surrounding **Calle San Bernardo** are a cluttered mixture of elegant middle-class and student housing, bohemian hangouts, and cultural activity. Heavily bombarded during the Civil War, Argüelles inspired Chilean poet Pablo Neruda, then a resident, to write his famous *España en el corazón.* Be aware that the areas around Pl. 2 de Mayo are known as Madrid's drug-dealing center. It is generally safe (because it's always busy), however caution is advised, especially at night.

THE PALACIO REAL AND ENVIRONS

With 20 square km of tapestry and the largest candelabra in Europe, the impossibly luxurious **Palacio Real** lounges at the western tip of central Madrid, overlooking the canal. Designed partly after Bernini's rejected designs for the Louvre, it was built for the first Bourbon King Felipe V to replace the burned Alcázar. His ambition was to build a palace to dwarf all others; although only a fragment was completed, it's still one of Europe's most grandiose residences. The shell took 40 years to build and interior decoration of its 2000 rooms dragged on for a century. Spanish monarchs abandoned it in the war-torn 1930s. To see the palace's collection of porcelain, tapestries, furniture, armor, and art, either stroll on your own or take a guided tour (in Spanish or English, 40min.). (Metro: Opera. Buses #4, 15, 25, 33, and 39.)

The palace's most impressive rooms include the raucously-Rococo **Salón de Gasparini** and the **Salón del Trono** (Throne Room) with Tiepolo ceiling fresco. Hundreds of ornate timepieces, collected mainly by Carlos IV, are strewn about the palace. The **Real Oficina de Farmacia** (Royal Pharmacy) features quaint crystal and china receptacles used to cut royal dope. The palace's **Biblioteca** shelves first editions of *Don Quijote* and a Bible in Romany (Gypsy language). The **Real Armería** (Armory) displays El Cid's swords, the armor of Carlos I and Felipe II, and other instruments of medieval warfare and torture. (Tel. 248 74 04; palace open, except during royal visits, Mon.-Sat. 9:30am-5:45pm, Sun. 9:30am-2pm. Admission 500ptas. Students 350ptas. Wed. free for EU citizens. Arrive early to avoid waiting.)

Beautiful gardens and parks swathe the Palacio Real. In the front across C. Bailén lies **Plaza de Oriente,** a semicircle square with statues of monarchs nearby. The sculptures were originally intended for the palace roof, but it was feared they'd fall off. On the far side of the Pl. Oriente, and with a lovely view of the palace, is the Café de Oriente (see Entertainment: Classic Cafés), a graceful and atmospheric (if a tad pricey) café with outdoor seating.

To the northwest are the serene **Jardines de Sabatini,** the park of choice for romantics (Metro: Tritones or Las Conchas). Juan Carlos opened **Campo del Moro** (facing the canal) to the public only 13 years ago; the view of the palace rising majestically on a dark green slope is straight out of a fairy tale. The **Museo de Carruajes Reales** (see Museums) is on the grounds. (Enter the *campo* on Po. Virgen del Puerto.) Directly south of the palace across a square is the recently-consecrated **Catedral de Almudena.** Madrid's two celebrated convents-turned-museums, **Convento de las Descalzas Reales** and **Convento de la Encarnación,** are also nearby (see Museums).

PARQUE DEL OESTE AND CIUDAD UNIVERSITARIA

Parque del Oeste is a large, slope-side park noteworthy for its **rosaleda** (rose garden), north of the Palacio Real. Nearby on C. Pintor Rosales stands **Templo de Debod,** the only Egyptian temple in Spain, with well-preserved hieroglyphs on the interior walls. The Egyptian government shipped the 4th-century BC temple stone by stone in appreciation of Spanish archeologists who helped rescue a series of monuments from advancing waters near the trouble-causing Aswan Dam. (Open Tues.-Fri. 10am-1pm and 4-7pm, Sat.-Sun. 10am-1pm. Admission 100ptas. Metro: Ventura Rodríguez or Plaza de España. Bus #1, 25, 33, and 39.)

The *terrazas* (outdoor cafés) along nearby **Paseo Rosales** are a perfect place to collapse in the shade of evenly spaced trees. Nearby a cable car runs down to the city's largest park, the **Casa de Campo,** with woods, a municipal pool, a zoo, and an amusement park (noon-9pm, 250ptas, round-trip 360ptas). Don't attempt to explore the park on foot; it's so large it makes Madrid's center look like a clearing in the forest. Avoid straying beyond populated areas such as the zoo and amusement park after sunset. (Amusement park open Mon.-Fri. noon-11pm, Sat. noon-1am, Sun. noon-midnight. Metro: Lago or Batán. Bus #33 or 65.)

Ermita de San Antonio de la Florida, containing Goya's pantheon, is close to Parque del Oeste on Po. Florida, near the river. Goya's frescoed dome arches above his own buried corpse—but not his skull, which was missing when the remains arrived from France. Fishy. (Tel. 542 07 22; open Tues.-Sun. 10am-2pm. Free. Metro: Norte.)

Ciudad Universitaria (University City) is quite a distance northwest of the Parque and Pl. España. A battleground in the Civil War and resistance center during Franco's rule, Spain's largest university educates over 120,000 students per year, and is second in size in the Spanish-speaking world only to Mexico City's. Mediocre **Museo Español de Arte Contemporáneo** and the **Museo de América** are in this vicintiy (see Museums). The Prime Minister's official residence, the **Palacio de Moncloa,** can be seen—but not touched—from the road through these grounds. (Metro: Moncloa.)

A prime example of Fascist Neoclassicism, the arcaded **Cuartel General del Aire** commands the perspective on the other side of Arco de la Victoria. The complex was to form part of the "Fachada del Manzanares" urban axis linking Moncloa, the Palacio de Oriente and cathedral, and the Iglesia de San Francisco. The building is clearly a ripoff of El Escorial.

EL PARDO

Built as a hunting lodge for Carlos I in 1547, **El Pardo** was subsequently enlarged by generations of Hapsburg and Bourbon royalty into the magnificent country palace that stands today—a 15-minute bus ride from the city center. Franco resided here from 1940-1975, and the palace is still the official reception site for distinguished foreign visitors who wine, dine, and politic amid gorgeous Renaissance and Neoclassical furniture, chandeliers, and works of art. Renowned for its collection of tapestries—several of which were designed by Goya—the palace also holds a little-known Velázquez depicting a deer slain by Felipe IV, and Ribera's *"Techo de los hombres ilustres"* (Ceiling of the Illustrious Men). During his stay, Franco fitted the palace with modern amenities such as TVs and air conditioning, which are cunningly camouflaged so as not to clash with the elegant decor. (Open Mon.-Sat. 9:30am-6pm, Sun. 9:30am-2pm. Compulsory 45-min. guided tour in Spanish. Admission 600ptas, students 250ptas, free Wed. for EU citizens. Catch bus #106 from Paseo de Moret, near Metro Moncloa—look for red signs and a line of green buses—15 min., 115ptas each way.) The palace's **capilla** and nearby **Casita del Príncipe,** created by Villanueva of Prado fame are free.

■■■ MUSEUMS

EL TRIÁNGULO DEL ARTE

Spain's premier museum and one of Europe's finest, the **Museo del Prado** is on Po. Prado at Pl. Cánovas del Castillo. (Metro: Banco de España or Atocha.) The Neoclassical building has sheltered the royal painting collection since the time of Fernando VII, who cared precious little for art and rather more about making an impression at home and abroad. Over 3000 paintings, many collected by Spanish monarchs between 1400 and 1700, include Spanish and foreign masterpieces, with particular strengths in the Flemish and Venetian Schools.

Innumerable hours of jostling through herds of schoolchildren cannot do justice to every canvas in the Prado. Decide beforehand what you want to see, and try not to become sidetracked by imitations and wanna-be Rubens. The museum is laid out in a fairly logical fashion and rooms are numbered, but it can be easy to lose sight of the forest for the groves of Goyas once within. Maps are pricey but helpful: the Guide to the Prado costs 1800ptas, and the abridged edition 500ptas.

The second floor houses Spanish works from the 16th and 17th centuries, most notably an unparalleled collection of works by **Diego Velázquez** (1599-1660), court painter and interior decorator to Felipe IV. The oft-imitated *Las Meninas* (The Maids of Honor)—widely considered Velázquez's ultimate masterpiece—occupies an entire wall. Velázquez is credited with radicalizing the art of portraiture with his unforgiving realism. Portraits of the royal family, especially his renderings of the foppish and fey Felipe IV, are legion.

The far-reaching influence of Velázquez's technique is evident in the work of **Francisco de Goya y Lucientes** (1746-1828), most especially in his two hilariously unflattering depictions of Carlos III, and his satirical masterpiece *La familia de Carlos IV.* In the latter work, Goya manipulates light and shadow to focus the viewer's gaze on the figure of the queen, despite the more prominent position of the king—thus manifesting contemporary popular opinion about who really was in power, without actually violating protocol. Goya's celebrated *La Maja vestida* (Clothed Maja) and *La Maja desnuda* (Nude Maja) have given rise to much gossipy speculation; some surmise that the mysteriously expressionless paintings depict the Duchess of Alba. Goya's *Cartones para tapices* (cartoons for tapestries)—so called because they were models for tapestries destined for El Escorial, not because they were meant to be humorous—depict light-hearted scenes of people cavorting in pastoral settings. Don't miss the large room devoted to Goyas' *Pinturas Negras* (Black Paintings)—works dating from the end of his life, when the artist was in poor health and living in a small country house outside Madrid, since nicknamed the *Quinta del Sordo* (the deaf man's house). Goya painted these chillingly macabre scenes on the walls of his house; years after his death they were placed on canvas and restored.

The Prado also houses many **El Grecos** (1541-1614): ubiquitous portraits of men with pointed beards and ruffs around their necks, as well as *La Trinidad* (The Trinity) and *La adoración de los pastores* (The Adoration of the Pastors). **Murillo's** (1618-1682) *Familia con pájaro pequeño* (Family with Small Bird), **Ribera's** (1591-1652) *El martirio de San Bartholomeo* (Martyrdom), and **Zurbarán's** (1598-1664) *La inmaculada* can all be found on the second floor.

The Prado has a formidable collection of Italian works, including **Titian's** (ca. 1488(90)-1576) portraits of Carlos I and Felipe II, and **Raphael's** (1483-1520) intriguing *El cardenal desconocido* (the unknown cardinal). **Tintoretto's** (1518-1594) rendition of the homicidal seductress Judith and her hapless victim Holofernes, as well as his *Washing of the Feet* and other works are here. Some minor **Botticellis** (1444-1510) and a slough of his imitators—almost exclusively paintings of people with halos—are also on display. Among the works by **Rubens**, *Un Satiro* (a satyr) stands out.

Because the Spanish Hapsburgs long ruled the Netherlands, the Flemish holdings are also top-knotch. **Van Dyck's** *Marquesa de Legunes* is here, as well as **Hieronymus Bosch's** (1450-1516) harrowing triptych, *The Garden of Earthly Delights*. In the same vein as Bosch are **Albrecht Dürer** (1471-1528) and **Peter Breughel the Elder** (1525-1569).

Among the Byzantine-esque medieval and Renaissance Spanish works, check out **Alfonso Sánchez Coello's** amusing *Las infantas Isabel Clara Eugenia y Catalina Micaela*, painted around 1500, and the two small chapels of 11th- and 12th- century paintings from the Mozarabic Church of San Baudelio de Berlanga and the Ermita de la Cruz de Maderuelo. The Spanish government swapped two New York art speculators a monastery for some of these paintings. (Tel. 420 28 36; open Tues.-Sat. 9am-7pm, Sun. 9am-2pm. Admission including the Casón del Buen Retiro (see below) 400ptas, students with ISIC and citizens of EU countries under 21 with ID free.)

MUSEO NACIONAL CENTRO DE ARTE REINA SOFÍA

A wonderful permanent collection of 20th-century art occupies only one of four floors in this pink Neoclassical building, located on C. Santa Isabel, 52, opposite Estación Atocha near the south end of Po. Prado. (Metro: Atocha.) Three additional floors contain rotating exhibits, library and archive specializing in 20th-century art (open Mon., Wed.-Fri. 10am-9pm), photography archive, music library, repertory cinema (art films in Spanish at noon and 4:30pm, 150ptas), café and gift shop. The museum is built around a gorgeous courtyard and sculpture garden.

Under glass and viewed only from a distance, Picasso's tour de force *Guernica* is the centerpiece of the Reina Sofía's permanent collection. When Germans bombed the Basque town of Guernica for the Fascists in Spain's Civil War, Picasso painted this huge colorless work of jumbled and distorted figures to denounce the bloodshed. When asked by Nazi officials whether he was responsible for this work, Picasso answered "No, you are." He gave the canvas to New York's Museum of Modern Art on condition that it return to Spain when democracy was restored. In 1981, five years after Franco's death, the *Guernica* was brought to Madrid's Casón del Buen Retiro. The move to the Reina Sofía sparked an international controversy—Picasso's *other* stipulation was that the painting hang only in the Prado, to affirm his equivalent status next to Titian and Velázquez. The masterpiece is accompanied by a fascinating array of preliminary sketches and drawings.

In other rooms of the permanent collection, the Spanish contribution to the early avant-garde, and the essential role of Spanish artists in the cubist and surrealist movements, are illustrated by the works of Miró, Julio González, Juan Gris, and Dalí, plus more Picasso. A re-encounter in the '40s with the avant-garde spirit and the increasing prominence of abstract movements are evident. Especially impressive is the exhibit of Miró's paintings from the '70s. (Tel. 467 50 62; open Mon., Wed.-Sat. 10am-9pm, Sun. 10am-2:30pm. Admission 400ptas general, students with ISIC and Spaniards free.)

MUSEO THYSSEN-BORNEMISZA

This beautiful and well-organized museum at the corner of Po. Prado and C. San Jerónimo, houses the fabulous and newly (June, 1993) purchased 775-piece Thyssen-Bornemisza collection. (Metro: Banco de España.) An 18th-century palace that has been rehabilitated by Moneo, the Thyssen is like a survey course in art history with a touch of most everything.

The array of 20th-century art on the ground floor is a wonder to behold. Almost all the great names of this century are represented: Picasso, Chagall, Max Ernst, Paul Klée, Miró, Léger, Juan Gris, Piet Mondrian, Giacometti, Kandinsky, Lichtenstein, David Hockney, Edward Hopper, Rauschenberg, Stella, Lucian Freud, Dalí, Tanguy, Georgia O'Keefe, Andrew Wyeth, Rothko, Jackson Pollock... and the list goes on and on. Among the standouts of this brilliant group are Richard Estes's *Telephone Booths* (1936), Mondrian's *New York City, New York*, and Domenico Gnoli's hilarious *Armchair*. Ben Shahn is present with two excellent pieces: *Four Piece Orchestra* (1944), and *Carnival* (1946). An impressive collection of cubist works includes several important Picassos and Braques. Hockney's coffin-shaped *In Memory of Cecchino Bracci* (1962), and Richard Lidner's striking *Moon Over Alabama* (1963) are also here.

The first floor features a great selection of impressionist, post-impressionist, fauvist, and expressionist works, as well as 17th-century Dutch paintings and still lifes, 18th-century rococo, and 19th-century romanticism and realism. A row of Toulouse-Lautrec's drawings, notorious from their days as Parisian theater posters, and Ferdinand Hodler's 1901 masterpiece *Teenager in Bergbach* are on display, as well as excellent works by Beckman, Gauguin, Cézanne, Degas, Sickert, Renoir, Pisarro, Monet, and Manet. Also on this floor are a few lesser Munchs and Derains.

The Old Masters on the second floor, including some excellent Van Eycks, and Holbein's portrait of *Henri VIII*, flesh out areas where the Prado is relatively weak. Jan de Beer's *The Birth of the Virgin* (1520) is a marvel of odd period techniques. Works by Derick Bagert stand out among the selection of 16th-century German paintings. The Titians and Tintorettos surpass those at the Prado, as do works from the early Baroque period, especially those by Caravaggio. (Tel. 420 39 44; open Tues.-Sun. 10am-7pm. No one admitted after 6:30pm. Admission 600ptas, students with ISIC and retired people 350ptas, children under 12 free.)

OTHERS

Casón del Buen Retiro, C. Alfonso XII, 28 (tel. 468 04 81), facing the Parque del Retiro. Metro: Retiro or Banco de España (see Sights: The Retiro). Once part of Felipe IV's Palacio del Buen Retiro, then a porcelain factory, the Casón del Buen Retiro was destroyed in the war against Napoleon. The rebuilt version has a superb collection of 19th-century Spanish paintings. Enter the *Sección de Arte Español del Siglo XIX* from the side. Open Tues.-Sat. 9am-6:45pm, Sun. 9am-1:45pm. Admission including the Prado 400ptas, students with ISIC and citizens of EU countries under 21 with ID free.

Convento de la Encarnación, in Pl. Encarnación (tel. 247 05 10), off C. Bailén near and east of the Palacio Real . Metro: Opera (see Sights: Palacio Real). A lovely convent, though not as impressive as the Convento de las Descalzas Reales. The fascinatingly macabre *relicuario* houses about 1500 relics of saints, including a vial of San Pantaleón's blood, believed to liquify every year on July 27. The *Exchange of Princesses on the Bidasoa,* depicting the swap weddings of French King Louis XII's sister Isabel to Felipe IV and Felipe IV's sister Anne to Louis XII, hangs here. Open Mon. and Wed. 10:30am-12:30pm and 4-5:30pm, Sun. 11am-1:30pm. Admission 600ptas, students 200ptas.

Convento de las Descalzas Reales (Convent of the Royal Barefoot Ones), Pl. Descalzas (tel. 521 27 79), between Pl. Callao and Sol. Metro: Callao or Sol (see Sights: Palacio Real). Originally a palace inhabited by the royal family of Castile, this convent was founded as such in 1559 by Juana of Austria, daughter of Carlos I. For the first few centuries of its existence, the convent was under royal patronage—widowed members of royal families commonly secluded themselves here—and thus acquired an exceptional collection of religious artwork, including tapestries, paintings, sculptures, and liturgical objects. One of 33 chapels in the upper cloister is by La Roldana, one of the few known female artists of the 17th century. The Salón de Tapices contains 10 renowned tapestries woven from cartoons by Rubens (some of which now hang in the Prado), as well as Santa Ursula's jewel-encrusted bones, and a depiction of *El viaje de Santa Ursula y las Once mil vírgenes* (The Journey of Santa Ursula and the Eleven Thousand Virgens). This museum also holds canvases by Zurbarán, Titian, and Rubens. Today the convent is still in operation, and home to 26 nuns of the Franciscan order. All visitors are taken on a guided tour conducted in Spanish (about 45min; a wait of up to 30 min. is sometimes required while enough people assemble to form a tour group). Open Tues.-Thurs. and Sat. 10:30am-12:30pm and 4-5:30pm, Fri. 10:30am-12:30pm, Sun. 11am-1:30pm. Admission 600ptas, students 200ptas. Convent's church free when mass is being given, Mon.-Sat. 8am and 7pm, Sun. 8am and noon.

Depósito de Agua, C. Santa Engracia, 125 (tel. 448 23 10, ext. 2505). Metro: Pl. España (see Sights: North of Gran Vía). This Art Deco, neo-Egyptian temple now shows temporary exhibitions of contemporary art. Open Tues.-Sat. 10am-8pm, Sun. 10am-2pm. Free.

Museo Arqueológico Nacional, C. Serrano, 13 (tel. 577 79 12). Metro: Serrano (see Sights: Along Paseos…). Travel back in time to the Middle Ages, Ancient Greece and Egypt, the Stone Age… the history of the entire world is on display in this huge museum. Astounding items from Spain's distant past include ivories from Muslim Andalucía; the suspicious *Dama de Elche,* a 4th-century Iberian masterpiece, and the hollow *Dama de Baza* (ashes of cremated bodies were deposited in this 4th-century statue, found in a tomb in the province of Granada), Romanesque and Gothic sculpture, and Celtiberian silver and gold. Open Tues.-Sat. 9:30am-8:30pm, Sun. 9:30am-2:30pm. Admission 200ptas, students free.

Museo Cerralbo, C. Ventura Rodríguez, 17 (tel. 547 36 46). Metro: Pl. España (see Sights: North of Gran Vía). Once home to the Marquis of Cerralbo XVII (1845-1922), this palatial, decadent residence-turned-museum now displays an eclectic assemblage of period furniture and ornamentation. Beautiful Venetian glass chandeliers and a so-called "mysterious" clock by Barbedienne stand out within a veritable labyrinth of marble, mirrors, and mahogany. The ballroom is an aesthetic feast, the music room holds a Louis XVI-style French piano, and the chapel houses El Greco's *The Ecstasy of Saint Francis.* Open July-Sept. Tues.-Sat. 9:30am-2:30pm, Sun. 10am-2pm. Admission 200ptas, students free.

Museo de América, Av. Reyes Católicos, 6, near Av. Puerta de Hierro and north of the C. Princesa junction (tel. 549 26 41). Metro: Moncloa (see Sights: Parque del Oeste…). Pre-Hispanic art of the Americas (mostly from Mexico and Peru). Under renovation; due to re-open in the fall of 1994.

Museo de Carruajes Reales, Po. Virgen del Puerto (tel. 559 74 04), in the Campo del Moro behind the Palacio Real. Metro: Opera (see Sights: Palacio Real). Carriage buffs alert: this former greenhouse contains the royal family's 16th- to 20th-century horse-drawn carriages. Open Mon.-Sat. 9am-6:15pm, Sun. 9am-3:15pm. Closed during official ceremonies at the Palacio Real. Admission 500ptas, students, children under 12, senior citizens, and citizens of EU countries 300ptas.

Museo de la Ciudad, Av. Príncipe de Vergara, 140 (tel. 588 65 99), near the Auditorio Nacional (see Sights: North of Gran Vía). Metro: Cruz de Rayo. This well-planned museum charts the history and development of Madrid from the 15th century to the present day. Multitudinous maps, dioramas, and photos, plus mannequins in period dress and big displays on the Metro and phone systems. Open Tues.-Fri. 10am-2pm and 4-6pm, Sat.-Sun. 10am-2pm. Free.

Museo de la Real Academia de Bellas Artes de San Fernando, C. Alcalá, 13 (tel. 522 14 91). Metro: Sol or Sevilla (see Sights: Between Puerta del Sol…). A beautiful museum with an excellent collection of Old Masters surpassed only by the Prado. The Royal Academy of San Fernando was founded in 1752 by Ferdinand VI, and served as a pedagogical institution under royal patronage until the 1960s, when the teaching facilities were transferred to the University of Madrid. Many permanent collection pieces were acquired either as educational tools or by affiliates of the academy. Masterpieces in the collection include Velázquez's portraits of Felipe IV and Mariana de Austria and Goya's *La Tirana,* a portrait of the actress María Fernández, dubbed the tyrant after her marriage to an actor who always played despots. *La primavera* (the Spring), the only work in Spain from a handful extant by Hapsburg court painter Giuseppe Milán Arcimboldo (1517-1593), depicts a man composed entirely of fruits, flowers, and plants. Notable works include the Italian Baroque collection and 17th-century canvases by Ribera, Murillo, and Zurbarán. The second floor houses a large collection of Picasso prints. Open daily July 16-Sept. 15 9am-3pm; otherwise Tues.-Fri. 9am-7pm, Sat.-Mon. 9am-3pm. Admission 200ptas, students free. The **Calcografía Real** (Royal Print and Drawing Collection) in the same building organizes excellent temporary exhibitions of works on paper. Free with museum admission.

Museo del Ejército, C. Méndez Núñez, 1 (tel. 522 89 77), just north of Casón del Buen Retiro. Metro: Retiro or Banco de España (see Sights: The Retiro). A cobbling together of military paraphernalia in a fragment of the Palacio del Buen Retiro. Plans to annex this museum to the Prado and recreate its original appearance as the Buen Retiro's Hall of Thrones (with painting cycles by Zurbarán and Velázquez) are in the works. Open Tues.-Sun. 10am-2pm. Free.

Museo del Ferrocarril, Po. Delicias, 61 (tel. 527 31 21), just south of Atocha. Metro: Delicias (see Sights: Along Paseos…). A small museum in the beautiful, old iron-and-glass station devoted to the early history of railroads in Spain. Open Tues.-Sat. 10am-5:30pm, Sun. 10am-2pm. Admission 200ptas.

Museo Español de Arte Contemporáneo, Av. Juan de Herrera, 2 (tel. 549 71 50), by Pl. Cardenal Cisneros. Metro: Moncloa (see Sights: Parque del Oeste…). Looted for and inferior to the ascendant Reina Sofía, but still holds temporary exhibits. A sculpture garden and a fountain soften the entrance of the stark modern building. Inside, two important early Dalís, some Miró, and pieces by Catalan master Isidre Nonell still hang. Open Tues.-Sat. 10am-6pm, Sun. 10am-3pm. Admission 200ptas, students free.

Museo Etnológico, Av. Alfonso XII, 68 (tel. 230 64 18), across from Estación Atocha. Metro: Atocha-Renfe (see Sights: Along Paseos…). Excellent anthropological collection, mainly drawn from Philippine and African cultures. Open Tues.-Sat. 10am-6pm, Sun. 10am-2pm. Admission 200ptas, students free.

Museo Lázaro Galdiano, C. Serrano, 122 (tel. 561 60 84). Metro: Serrano or Av. América (see Sights: Along Paseos…). The beautiful, ornate building alone makes this museum worth a visit—the ceilings are decorated with frescoes, and the walls and doorframes with elaborate woodwork. Among the riches inside are an overwhelming display of Italian Renaissance bronzes, ancient jewels, gothic reliquaries, Celtic and Visigoth brasses, and much, much more. An array of paintings includes canvases by Velázquez, Zurbarán, José de Ribera, El Greco, Mengo, Heironymos Bosch, and Goya, plus an excellent Da Vinci. Some good English stuff too—Thomas Gainsborough, Reynolds, Hopper, Constable, Turner, and T.H. Lawrence. The top floor is devoted to antique brocades and tapestries, fans, and a plethora of weaponry. Open Sept.-July Tues.-Sun. 10am-2pm. Admission 300ptas.

Museo Municipal, C. Fuencarral, 78 (tel. 522 57 32). Metro: Tribunal (see Sights: North of Gran Vía). An enormous diorama of the city as it was in 1830, a model of 17th-century Plaza Mayor, and a variety of documents trace the development of Madrid. Also an undistinguished collection of 16th- to 18th-century Spanish works, including samplings of the Velázquez school and the Baroque. Great gift shop. Open Tues.-Fri. 9:30am-8pm, Sat.-Sun. 10am-2pm. Free.

Museo Nacional de Artes Decorativas, C. Montalbán, 12 (tel. 521 34 40 or 532 64 99). Metro: Banco de España (see Sights: The Retiro). More pieces of decorative art than you could shake a stick at: Chinese bronzes and marbles, 16th-century Spanish furniture, 17th-century textiles, and a model of a Valencian kitchen. Many a precious diorama with tiny citizens going about their 18th-century business. Open Tues.-Fri. 9am-3pm, Sat.-Sun. 10am-2pm. Admission 200ptas, students under 21 free.

Museo Nacional de Ciencias Naturales (National Museum of Natural Sciences), C. José Gutiérrez Abascal, 2 (tel. 411 13 28), off Po. Castellana, next to Pl. San Juan de la Cruz. Metro: Nuevos Ministerios (see Sights: Along the Paseos…). A big museum filled with school children on field trips. Permanent geology and ecology exhibits. Open Tues.-Fri. 10am-6pm, Sat. 10am-8pm, Sun. 10am-2:30pm. Admission to permanent exhibits 300ptas, students 200ptas. Admission to temporary exhibits 400ptas, students 250ptas. Children under 8 free.

Museo Naval, C. Montalbán, 2 (tel. 521 04 19), across from the Palacio de Comunicaciones. Metro: Banco de España (see Sights: The Retiro). Maritime objects of interest even to landlubbbers, especially the many big models of ships from the olden days. A globe of the sky dating from 1693 gives a taste of 17th-century cosmology, and an enormous map charts Spanish expeditions from the 15th to 18th centuries. Also an exhibit on how to tie knots. Open Sept.-July Tues.-Sun. 10:30am-1:30pm. Free.

Museo Postal y Telegráfico, in the Palacio de Comunicaciones in Pl. Cibeles, access from C. Montalbán. Metro: Banco de España. A charming little collection of philatelic and telegraphic paraphernalia, including old post boxes, phones, telegraph machines, and of course an enormous stamp collection. Also on display are the various outfits donned by your friendly, neighborhood postperson throughout the ages. Excellent research library. Open Mon.-Fri. 10am-1:30pm and 5-7pm, Sat. 10am-1:30pm. Library open Mon.-Fri. 9:30am-2pm and 5-7pm. Free.

Museo Romántico, C. San Mateo, 13 (tel. 448 10 45 or 448 10 71). Metro: Alonso Martínez (see Sights: North of Gran Vía). Housed in a 19th-century mansion built by a disciple of Ventura Rodríguez, this museum is a time capsule of Romantic period (early 19th-century) decorative arts and painting. Open Sept.-July Tues.-Sun. 10am-3pm. Admission 200ptas.

Museo Sorolla, Po. General Martínez Campos, 37 (tel. 410 15 84). Metro: Rubén Darío or Iglesia (see Sights: Along the Paseos…). Former home and studio of Joaquín Sorolla, the acclaimed 19th-century Valencian painter. Sorolla's seaside paintings and his garden make for a refreshing break from other crowded museums. Collection includes *Paseo a orillas del mar* (Seaside Promenade) and pre-World War I society portraits. Open Sept.-July Tues.-Sun. 10am-2pm. Admission 200ptas, students free.

Museo Taurino, C. Alcalá, 237 (tel. 255 18 57), at Pl. Monumental de Las Ventas. Metro: Ventas. In a corner of Madrid's largest bullring, a remarkable collection of *trajes de luces,* capes, and posters of famous *corridas.* Open Tues.-Fri. and Sun. 9am-2pm. On bullfight days it opens 1hr. before the *lidia.* Free.

Palacio de Liria, C. Princesa, 20 (tel. 547 56 02 or 547 66 06). Metro: Ventura Rodríguez or Argüelles (see Sights: North of Gran Vía). A Neoclassical palace, the Duchess of Alba's estate is endowed with 15th- and 16th-century canvases by Titian, Rubens, and Rembrandt. Open to the public by special arrangement.

■■■ ENTERTAINMENT

Spaniards get on average one less hour of sleep than other Europeans. People in Madrid claim to need even less than that. Enormously proud of their night life (they'll tell you with a straight face that they were bored in Paris or New York), *madrileños* insist that no one goes to bed until they've killed the night—and a good part of the following morning. This is especially true in the summer: when the city sizzles by day and the stubborn sun refuses to set until at least 9pm, the fun lasts til the wee hours of the afternoon. Some clubs don't even bother opening until 4 or 5am. The only (relatively) quiet night of the week is Monday.

The weekly *Guía del Ocio* (100ptas at any newsstand) carries comprehensive entertainment listings (including clubs, restaurants, concerts, movies, and theater), as do the Friday supplement (*El Mundo's* "Metropoli," *El País's* "Guía," *Diario 16's* "Madrid") and the daily *cartelera* listings in any newspaper. The free municipal tourist office's monthly *En Madrid* is less comprehensive, but still helpful.

Pl. 2 de Mayo in Malasaña, Pl. Chueca, Pl. España, and the Gran Vía can be intimidating and sleazy. Though one should always exercise caution, Madrid is fairly safe for a city of its size. The only really fearsome places late at night are the parks.

NIGHTLIFE: CAFÉS, BARS, CLUBS, AND DISCOS

As the sun sets and bathes the streets in gold, **terrazas** (or **chiringuitos**, outdoor cafés) sprawl across sidewalks all over Madrid. In addition to our specific listings, the following neighborhoods are good places to explore.

Pl. Mayor. Flocking with tourists and pigeons, but handy for a beer or glass of wine while digesting the tourist office's brochures.

C. Bailén (by the Viaducto). Spectacular views of flaming sunsets, but if you aren't making out with someone you might feel somewhat the voyeur.

Casa del Campo. Kiosks and open-air *cafeterías* sprinkled about the greenery.

Pos. Castellana, Recoletos, and **Prado.** Fashionable and hip, hence a bit pricey. La Castellana is the trendiest, Recoletos the most sightly.

Parque del Retiro. Adorable kiosks and bars. After sundown, only the north gate stays open.

Pl. 2 de Mayo (Malasaña) and **Pl. Olavide** (Bilbao). Well-dressed young adults quaff drinks in the shade of umbrellas and trees.

Po. Pintor Rosales. Many tree-shaded *chiringuitos* frequented by university students and parkgoers.

El Viso, between Po. Castellana and C. María de Molina. A pre-war garden city within the city. Villas, walled gardens, and winding streets with *terrazas* exude a charming village-like aura.

For **clubs and discos,** life begins around 1:30am. Many discos have "afternoon" sessions (usually 7-10pm, cover 250-1000ptas) for teens; but the "night" sessions (lasting until dawn) are when to really let your hair down. Don't be surprised if at 5:30am there's still a line of people waiting to get in. Really. Cover can get as high as 2000ptas, and men may be charged up to 500ptas more than women. The *entrada* (cover) often includes a drink.

In order to facilitate bar and club hopping, *Let's Go* lists bars, clubs, and discos by neighborhood (cafés are given their own special section).

Classic Cafés

Coffee at these places is expensive (200-300ptas)—but since that's all you're getting, and given that you're expected to linger, an hour or two spent at one of these historic cafés is a most economical way to soak up a little of Madrid (and a lot of secondhand smoke).

Café Gijón, Po. Recoletos, 21 (tel. 521 54 25). Metro: Colón. On its 100th anniversary in 1988, Gijón was designated an official historic site by the *Ayuntamiento de Madrid*, making it a little easier to shell out 300ptas for a cup of coffee. (If you actually want to get something to eat, forget about sending your kids to college.) Choose between a breezy terrace and a smoky bar-restaurant. Marmoreal tables, white-uniformed waiters. Long a favorite of the literati. People bring their books to study and their friends to talk. Open 9am-1:30am.

Café Comercial, Glorieta de Bilbao, 7 (tel. 531 34 72). Metro: Bilbao. The boulevards extending from Pl. Colón to C. Princesa in Argüelles make for elegant strolling (notice the many wrought-ironed, wainscoted, chandeliered foyers with cage elevators). Traditional café with high ceilings and huge mirrors. Frequented by artists and Republican aviators alike. Anti-Franco protests started here. Frequent *tertulias* (gatherings of literati and intellectuals). A/C. Sandwiches from 150ptas. Beer 250ptas. Open 8am-1am, Fri.-Sat. until 3am.

Café de Oriente, Pl. Oriente, 2 (tel. 547 15 64). Metro: Opera. A beautiful, old-fashioned café which caters to a ritzy, older crowd. Spectacular view of the Palacio Real from the *terraza,* especially at night when the palace is spotlighted. Quite pricey (coffee on the terrace is 600ptas, entrees start at 1500ptas)—so sneak a lot of peaks at the palace for free. Open 8:30am-1:30am.

La Blanca Doble, C. Calatrava, 15. Metro: Puerta de Toledo. Specialty coffee drinks such as *jamaicano* (coffee, Tía María *licor,* brown sugar, and whipped cream) 250ptas. Sandwiches from 250ptas. Open until midnight.

Plaza Santa Ana

Plaza Santa Ana's many bars and small *terrazas* are the perfect jumping-off point for an evening of bar and club hopping. The area features a number of popular watering holes, packed with minglers, chatters, smokers, and drinkers. **Calle Huertas** is the main street, just off the plaza.

Cervecería Alemana, Pl. Santa Ana, 6 (tel. 429 70 33). A former Hemingway hangout with a slightly upscale crowd. One in a row of three *cervecerías* that all deserve exploration. Open Sun.-Fri. noon-12:30am, Sat. noon-1:30am.

No Se Lo Digas a Nadie, C. Ventura de la Vega, 7, next to Pl. Santa Ana. Metro: Antón Martín. Look for a black garage door; it's not marked on the street. Don't tell it to anybody, there are enough gyrating bodies downstairs already. Live mellow music starts around 12:15am. Drinks 500-800ptas. Open Tues.-Sat. 8:30am-1pm and 8:30pm-3am, Fri.-Sat. 8:30am-1pm and 8:30pm-4am.

La Fídula, C. Huertas, 57 (tel. 429 29 47), near Po. Prado. Metro: Antón Martín. A quiet place to listen to live classical music. Coffee 215ptas, wine 250ptas. Cover for weekend musical performances (11:30pm) 200-300ptas. Open 7pm-1:30am.

Atocha 38, C. Atocha, 38 (tel. 369 38 81). Metro: Antón Martín. Evenings: house and techno. Thurs.-Sat. nights: live salsa and (uh-oh) a laser-light show. Cover 1000ptas, includes one drink.

Viva Madrid, C. Manuel Fernández González, 7 (tel. 467 46 45), next to Pl. Santa Ana. Metro: Antón Martín. U.S. expatriate hangout. Wonderful tiles and animals carved in wood. Ink picture drawn in tribute by the poet Rafael Albertí is behind the bar. Beer and juice 400ptas, mixed drinks 700-800ptas. Open daily 8pm-3am.

Café Central, Pl. Angel, 10 (tel. 369 41 43), off Pl. Santa Ana. Metro: Antón Martín or Sol. Cover charge 900-1100ptas. Usually packed. Great live jazz 10pm-2am.

El Oso y el Madroño, C. Bolsa, 4 (tel. 522 77 96). A hand organ and old photos of Madrid. Try the potent *Licor de Madroño*, an arbutus-flavored Spanish liqueur (150ptas). Open 10am-midnight.

Malasaña

Another perennial night hotspot, but with an entirely different feel. Darker, more bohemian, and a little more sedate(d) than the Plaza Santa Ana. Heaps of small, crowded pubs, unlisted in entertainment guides.

Hippies, intellectuals, bohemians, street musicians, and junkies check each other out in the **Plaza 2 de Mayo. Calle San Vincente Ferrer,** with its tattoo parlors, secondhand clothing and leather stores, motorcycle repair shops and countless pubs, is prime Malasaña. Unless you're particularly badass, be wary here at night.

Bar Las Maravillas, Pl. 2 de Mayo, 9. One of the few places to eat late in Malasaña. Reasonably priced *tapas, bocadillos,* and *raciones.* Open Tues.-Sun. 8pm-2am.

El Puerto, C. Velarde, 13 (tel. 447 72 60). Laid-back rebels and wanna-bes drink here. Open 8am-2am.

Manuela, C. San Vicente Ferrer, 29 (tel. 531 70 37). Extremely elegant and mirrored café-bar. Live music (usually folky) begins at 11:30pm; cover for performances 300-400ptas. Open 7pm-3am.

La Tetera de la Abuela, C. Espíritu Santo, 37. "Granny's Teapot" brews together writers, actors, and students. Open Sun.-Thurs. 7:30pm-1am, Fri.-Sat. 7:30pm-2am.

El Sol de Mayo, Pl. 2 de Mayo, 4. A bar-café with a young crowd. Lame Zeppelin rip-off bands play downstairs. Beer 450ptas, mixed drinks around 600ptas. Open Sun.-Thurs. 7pm-3am, Fri.-Sat. 7pm-4am.

Vía Láctea, C. Velarde, 18 (tel. 466 78 81). This club is jam-packed and deservedly famous. The "Milky Way's" loudspeakers and slightly expensive drinks make you see stars all night. Open Tues.-Sun. 7pm-3am.

Ella's, C. San Dimas, 3, across and parallel to C. San Bernardo, on the corner of C. Palma. Just outside of Malasaña proper. A *terraza* popular with lesbians.

Bodegas el Maño, C. Jesús del Valle, 1. This enchanting *bodega* dates from 1890. Weird ancient wine casks. Stiff drinks 500-600ptas. Open 7pm-1:30am.

Bilbao

Plenty of discos and bars shake around **Glorieta de Bilbao,** especially along and between **Calles Fuencarral** and **Luchana.** The *terrazas* on **Plaza Olavide** have a mellower drink-sipping scene (drinks outside 150-250ptas).

Being frugal's no trouble in these high school and college student-filled streets. Bars and clubs—boisterous and packed year-round—tend to stay open later here than in any other neighborhood.

Club Andy Warhol's, C. Luchana, 20. Wait… Is that a Warhol print? or the person I'm dancing with? By the time you make it to this chic disco, you'll be seeing in multiples. Open 5am (yup, am)-10am, Sun. 5am-noon.

Archy, C. Marqués de Riscal, 11 (tel. 308 31 62), off C. Almagro from Pl. Alonso Martínez. Dress to kill or the fashion police at the door might laugh. *Gente guapa* (beautiful people) only; at press time *the* in place to see and be seen. Also a fancy restaurant. No cover, but drinks cost 700-900ptas. Open from noon on.

Cervecería Ratskeller's, corner of C. Luchana and C. Palafox (by the cinema Palafox). Crowds of vacationing American college students give this self-proclaimed House of Beer a Spring Break in Cancún feel. However, if that's what you go for… Open noon-3am.

Paseos Castellana, Recoletos, and Prado

The *terrazas* lining this broad avenue come alive every night around 11:30pm in July and August. Drinks can be quite pricey, reaching 500ptas for beer, 1000ptas for mixed drinks. Fashionable *terrazas de verano* in this vicinity include:

Amnesia, Po. Castellana, 93. A pretty sophisticated crowd.

Nameless place, Po. Castellana, 21. For the post-modern.

El Espejo, Po. Recoletos, 31. A petite orchestra and mixed-age clientele. Ornate and mirrored. The action usually starts around 10:30pm.

Some of Madrid's largest and loudest clubs liven up the mellower *terraza* scene in this area.

Keeper, C. Juan Bravo, 39 six blocks from Po. Castellana. Metro: Diego de León. By all accounts Madrid's biggest club, Keeper has three levels of bars and dance floors. If you're old enough to vote, this place could make you feel like a graybeard. Cover 1200ptas, includes one drink.

Cleofás, C. Goya, 7 (tel. 576 45 23 or 576 36 78), near Pl. Colón. Metro: Colón. Feeling nostalgic for the golden age of disco? This is the place for you. Open Tues.-Sat. 7:15pm-dawn, Sun. 7-11:15pm. Cover 1000ptas, includes one drink.

Chueca

Several years ago the site of a trendy, wealthy series of pubs and clubs (their husks are still open on C. Costanilla Capuchinos), Chueca is now home to a lively gay scene (mostly male). Clubs may come and go, but **C. Pelayo** is clearly the main drag.

Entiendes …?, published by Madrid's gay and lesbian coalition, COGAM (see Other: Gay and Lesbian Services), lists clubs and bars in this area. *El Mundo's* Friday supplement, "Metropoli," and the *Guía del Ocio* also note some gay and lesbian clubs. Look in El Galeón and Berkana for more guides or listings (see Books).

Pachá, C. Barceló, 11 (tel. 446 01 37), near Metro: Tribunal. Converted from an old theater, and once one of the trendiest clubs in Madrid. As Chueca's gay scene became more pronounced, Pachá's mainstream clientele scurried away. The place still fills up, however, and the crowd is not overtly gay. Open from 7pm on.

Only Man, Pl. Chueca, 1. Metro: Chueca. As the name suggests, the crowd here is entirely male. Lots of guys standing around cruising each other. By day, it's the **Café de Chueca:** lots of guys drinking coffee and cruising each other.

Bachelor, C. Reina, 2, parallel to Gran Vía. Metro: Gran Vía. Similar to the scene at Only Man, except more dancing. Beer 500ptas.

Argüelles and Moncloa

The night life here attracts students partying and socializing during the academic year until June (when exams hit) and July and August (when they leave town for vacation).

Oh! Madrid, C. Coruña, km 10 (tel. 307 87 67). Metro: Moncloa. University hangout. Head-hurting rock. No cover. Drinks 600-800ptas. Open 8pm-5am.

Zarzuela Race-Track, Av. Coruña, km 7800 (tel. 207 01 40). Buses leave from Metro: Moncloa. Hosts Nights at the Hippodrome: horse racing and betting, dancing, and a lively bar scene from dusk to dawn. Attracts a large crowd of university students. Cover charge 600ptas. Drinks 500-700ptas. July-Aug. Thurs. and Sat. 9pm-dawn; June and Sept. Sat. 9pm-dawn.

Plaza Mayor and Puerta del Sol

An easy place to start, perhaps, but high prices, tourists galore, and limited options get old quickly.

Joy Eslava, C. Arenal, 11 (tel. 266 37 33). Metro: Sol or Opera. A 3-tiered theater turned disco; 3 bars, laser lights, video screen, live entertainment. Young crowd, disco music. Cover 1500ptas, includes one drink. Open Mon.-Thurs. 11:30pm on, Fri.-Sat. 7-10:15pm and 11:30pm-5:30am.

Xenón, Pl. Callao, 3 (tel. 521 25 06 or 531 97 94). Metro: Santo Domingo. An alternative/thrasher crowd jumps up and down ferociously to house music and underground rock. Open Thurs. 11pm-5am, Fri.-Sun. 6-10:30pm and midnight-7am. Afternoon cover 600ptas, night cover 1500ptas.

La Coquette Blues Bar, C. Hileras on the corner with C. Arenal. Loud, live rock-blues in close quarters. Some seem to ignore the *"no fuméis porros"* sign (*porros* are joints). Music starts around 10:30pm. Open Tues.-Thurs. 8pm-2am.

Max, Aduana, 21 (tel. 522 98 25). Metro: Sevilla. Known as an "After Hours" club—Max opens at 4am on weekends, and stays open til 10am. Live rock 'n' roll.

Oba-Oba, C. Jacometrezo, 4 (tel. 531 06 40), off of Gran Vía. Metro: Callao or Santo Domingo. A pseudo-Brazilian/Caribbean dirty-dancing retreat. Sambas and rumbas. Tropical cocktails 700-1000ptas.

FILM AND THEATER

In summer, the city sponsors free movies and plays. The *Guía del Ocio* (100ptas at kiosks), the *Villa de Madrid* (100ptas from bus-ticket kiosks), and the entertainment supplements in all the Friday papers list these activities; they often contain discounts for commercial events, too. In July and August, the **Plaza Mayor, Plaza de Lavapiés, Plaza Villa de París,** and other meeting places host frequent plays. The **Parque del Retiro** sometimes shows free movies at 11pm.

Most *cinemas* have three showings per day at approximately 4:30pm, 7:30pm, and 10:30pm. Tickets are 500-700ptas. Wed. is usually *día del espectador:* tickets are 300-350ptas for the first showing, so show up early. Spain's flawless dubbing industry is renowned throughout the world.

The state-subsidized *filmoteca* in the renovated Art Deco **Ciné Doré,** C. Santa Isabel, 3 (tel. 369 11 25; Metro: Antón Martín), is the best for repertory cinema. It also has a bar, restaurant, and bookstore. (Tickets 200-400ptas.) The **Centro Reina Sofía** has a repertory cinema of its own. The university's **colegios mayores** sponsor film series as well (and jazz concerts, too). Subtitled films are shown in many private theaters, such as **Alphaville** and **Renoir I** and **2**—check the V.O. (for *versión original)* listings in entertainment guides. **Gran Vía** is lined with plush cinemas.

Theatergoers can also consult the well-illustrated magazines published by the state-sponsored theaters (which also sell posters of their productions for next to nothing), such as **Teatro Español, Teatro de la Comedia,** and the city's superb **Teatro María Guerrero.** Buy tickets at theater box offices or at agencies.

The theater district is bounded by Pl. Santa Ana and Pl. Colón (south to north) and Po. Prado-Recoletos and Puerta del Sol (east to west). The state-run theaters and many of the private theaters are sights in themselves.

Centro Cultural de la Villa, Pl. Colón (tel. 575 60 80). Metro: Colón or Serrano. A major performance center belonging to the city. Tickets 1500ptas, Wed. 700ptas.

Localidades Galicia, Pl. Carmen, 1 (tel. 431 27 32 or 531 91 31). Metro: Sol. Handles theater tickets, as well as those for soccer games, movies, and bullfights. Open Mon.-Fri. 10am-1pm and 4:30-7pm.

Sala Olimpia, Pl. Lavapiés (tel. 527 46 22). National troupe produces avant-garde theatrical works. Tickets 750ptas.

Teatro Alcázar, Alcalá, 20 (tel. 532 06 16). Metro: Sevilla. Private company; mostly musicals and popular or comedic works. Tickets 1500-2500ptas, reduced prices for seniors. No shows Mon.

Teatro Bellas Artes, C. Marqués de Casa Riera, 2 (tel. 532 44 37). Metro: Banco de España. Private theater devoted to staging new works.

Teatro de Cámara, C. San Cosme y San Damián, 3 (tel. 527 09 54). Metro: Atocha. Classic theater company produces canonical dramas and comedies by the likes of Gogol and Cervantes. Tickets 1000-1200ptas.

Teatro de la Comedia, C. Príncipe, 14 (tel. 521 49 31). Metro: Sevilla. The traveling *Compañía Nacional Teatro Clásico* often performs classical Spanish theater here. Tickets 500-1000ptas, reduced prices Thurs. Ticket office open 11:30am-1:30pm and 5-9pm.

Teatro Español, C. Príncipe, 25 (tel. 429 03 18; tickets and information tel. 429 62 97). Metro: Sevilla. Site of 16th-century Teatro de Príncipe, Teatro Español dates from the 18th century. A new rehearsal studio, together with a video and theater library, are planned for the site next door. Established company run by city hall regularly performs winners of the prestigious Lope de Vega award. Tickets around 1300-1700ptas, reduced prices Wed. Excellent, traditional **Café del Príncipe** within.

Teatro Estudio de Madrid, C. Cabeza, 14 (tel. 539 64 47). Metro: Tirso de Molina or Antón Martín. Amateur studio theater; avant-garde works and performance art.

Teatro La Latina, Pl. Cebada, 2 (tel. 365 28 35). Metro: Latina. A varied repertoire of works by new and established playwrights. Tickets 1600-2500ptas.

Teatro Maravillas, C. Manuela Malasaña, 6 (tel. 447 41 35). Metro: Bilbao. Popular commercial theater; mostly musicals and comedies. Tickets 600-1300ptas.

Teatro María Guerrero, C. Tamayo y Baus, 4 (tel. 310 29 49). Metro: Colón. Excellent state-supported repertory company. Tickets 400-2000ptas. Reduced price Wed. Ticket office open 11:30am-1:30pm and 5-9pm.

Teatro Nacional Clásico, C. Príncipe, 14 (tel. 521 49 31). Works by great Spanish dramatists of the past. Tickets start at 700ptas, Wed. reduced prices.

MUSIC

In summer the city sponsors free concerts, ranging from classical to jazz to bolero and salsa, at **Plazas Mayor, Lavapiés,** and **Villa de París.** Check the usual sources for information (see Entertainment: Introduction).

The **Auditorio Nacional,** C. Príncipe de Vergara, 136 (tel. 337 01 00), hosts the finest classical performances. Home to the superb Orquesta Nacional, it's equipped with a magnificent hall for symphonic music and a smaller one for chamber recitals. The **Fundación Juan March,** C. Castelló, 77 (tel. 435 42 40; Metro: Núñez de Balboa), sponsors free weekly concerts and hosts a university lecture series. The **Conservatorio Superior de Música,** recently moved into the 18th-century medical building next door to the Centro Reina Sofía, hosts free student performances, professional traveling orchestras, and celebrated soloists. **Teatro Monumental,** C. Atocha, 65 (tel. 429 12 81; Metro: Antón Martín), is home to Madrid's Orquesta Sinfónica. Reinforced concrete—a Spanish invention—was first used in its construction in the 20s; the building's acoustics are unusual.

For opera and *zarzuela,* head for the ornate **Teatro de la Zarzuela,** C. Jovellanos, 4 (tel. 429 82 25; Metro: Banco de España), modeled on La Scala. The grand, 19th-century granite **Teatro de la Opera,** on Pl. Opera, is the city's principal venue for classical ballet and the lyric genre. Ballet is also performed at the **Palacio de Gaviria,** C. Arenal, 9 (tel. 526 60 70; Metro: Sol or Opera).

For tangos, try **Cambalache,** C. San Lorenzo, 5 (tel. 410 07 01; Metro: Alonso Martínez or Tribunal). Live tangos, Argentine food, and drinks at the bar from 10pm to 5am.

Flamenco in Madrid is tourist-oriented and expensive. **Arco de Cuchilleros,** C. Cuchilleros, 7 (tel. 366 58 67; Metro: Sol), just off Pl. Mayor, features some emotive guitarists. The small seating area makes for an intimate show. (Shows 10:30pm and 12:30am. 2000ptas cover includes the show and one drink; subsequent drinks, both alcoholic and non-alcoholic, 800ptas. No dining.) More down-to-earth is **Casa Patas,** C. Cañizares, 10 (tel. 369 04 96). The flamenco starts at midnight on Fri. and Sat. nights. The cover charge varies. (Open 8:30pm-2:30am.) The **Café de Chinitas,** C. Torija, 7 (tel. 559 51 35 or 547 15 02; Metro: Santo Domingo), is about as ostentatious and flamboyant as they come. The show starts at 11:30pm; the memories last forever. Cover 1500ptas, includes one drink.

Madrid's big rock 'n' roll stadium is the **Palacio de los Deportes,** Pl. Dalí, s/n (tel. 356 22 00; Metro: Ventas). Mostly big U.S. groups (Aerosmith, for example). More alternative groups play at **Aqualung Universal,** Po. de la Ermita del Santo, 45 (tel. 470 23 62). Rock to the ilk of the Lemonheads, Nick Cave, and Arrested Development.

SHOPPING

Most Madrid stores open in the morning (approximately 9:30am-1:30 or 2pm) and early evening (approximately 5-8pm). The major department stores, such as **El Corte Inglés,** (see Practical Information: Other for details) and **Galerías Preciados** (Pl. Callao, 2; C. Goya, 85-87; and C. Serrano, 47; tel. 536 80 00 for all stores), are open from around 10am to 9pm. Recently some enterprising shops have begun to stay open on Saturday afternoons and a few, mainly big department stores, during lunch time. Many close in August, when practically everyone is away on vacation.

Clothing

From Sol to the Gran Vía, and along C. Princesa, the main department stores—El Corte Inglés and Galerías Preciados—float in a sea of smaller discount stores. Gran Vía is now a little degraded (although easier on the purse); there's a scheme afoot to restore the avenue to its pre-war splendor. It still manages scope, from chi-chi leather goods to more middlebrow women's fashion (Cortefiel, Gran Vía, 27). Budgeters with weary spirits and scraped soles shop at Los Guerrilleros (a huge store with quite low prices), Puerta del Sol, 5, diagonally across from El Corte Inglés. (Metro: Sol or Gran Vía.)

In the lovely neighborhood west of Po. Recoletos (C. Almirante and streets north to C. Génova, south to C. Alcalá, and west to C. San Bernardo), imaginative boutiques of young Spanish designers mingle with off-beat restaurants and pastry shops, cafés and bars, art galleries, and specialized bookstores. (Metro: Chueca, Colón, or Banco de España.)

The embassy quarter north of C. Génova is decidedly more haughty. Madrid's poshest shopping areas are Jerónimos and Salamanca. In the latter, couture and near-couture boutiques vogue on Calles Serrano, Príncipe de Vergara, Velázquez, Goya, Ortega y Gasset, Coello, and Alfonso XII. (Metro: Serrano or Velázquez.)

Books

Berkana Librería Gai y Lesbiana, C. La Palma, 39 (tel. and fax 532 13 93). Metro: Noviciado or Tribunal. Gay and lesbian bookstore, including curiosities and gifts (buttons, T-shirts, stationery).

Booksellers, C. José Abascal, 48 (tel. 442 79 59). Rather expensive, but a vast array of English-language books.

Casa del Libro, Gran Vía, 29. Metro: Gran Vía or Callao. A 6-story department store of books, including a selection in English. Open Mon.-Sat. 10am-9pm.

Cuesta de Moyano, along the southern border of the Jardín Botánico, 30 open-air wood stalls hawk new and used paperbacks, reference books, comics, and rare books. Metro: Atocha. Most open every day.

El Sendero Librería Esotérica, C. Villaverde, 10 (tel. 534 83 79). Metro: Cuatro Caminos. Esoteric collection of mystical/spiritual books on Buddhism, orientalism, Tarot-throwing, etc.

English Editions, Plaza de San Amaro, 5 (tel. 571 03 21), off C. General Perón. Metro: Estrecho. Used English-language novels bought and sold—excellent selection. Also a quirky little mini-mart featuring English and American specialties. Open Mon.-Thurs.

Librería Antonio Machado, C. Fernando VI. Metro: Colón or Alonso Martínez. A browser's store with an immense literature section.

Librería Crisol, C. Juan Bravo. A high-powered place with futuristic interior design; services and prices to match. Great hours. Open Mon.-Sat. 10am-10pm, Sun. 11am-6pm.

Librería de Mujeres (Women's Bookstore), C. San Cristóbal, 17 (tel. 521 70 43), near Pl. Mayor. International bookstore. Some English spoken.

Librería El Galeón, C. Sagasta, 7. Metro: Bilbao. Good prices on an eclectic collection of new and used books, including titles in English, French, German, and Italian. Carries the gay magazine and guide *Entiendes...?*

Librería Felipa, C. Libreros, off Gran Vía. The entire street is books, but only Felipa gives a 20% discount off list price. Generations of students have bought their textbooks here.

Librería Gaudí, C. Argensola, 17, and **Librería Argensola**, 20. Metro: Colón or Alonso Martínez. Two art and architecture bookstores in the neighborhood west of Po. Recoletos.

Librería Leonor Alazraki, C. Pelayo, 5 (tel. 522 72 75). Metro: Chueca. Another esoteric bookstore, featuring books on the Kabbalah, dream interpretation, divine visitation, life after death, and personal philosophy. Also crystal balls, incense, and candles.

Librería Turner, C. Génova, 3 (tel. 319 09 26). Classics, guidebooks, and the very latest—all in English, French, and German.

Other

On Sunday mornings the flea market **El Rastro** buzzes with secondhand goods, antiques, and tacky clothes. Individual side streets specialize in pets, household items, and books. (Sun. and holidays 10am-2pm. Metro: La Latina. Walking from Pl. Mayor, take C. Toledo to Pl. Cascorro, where the market begins. It ends at the bottom of C. Ribera de Curtidores.) Antiquarians lend their peculiar mustiness to Calle (not Salón or Paseo) del Prado and adjacent streets. Enormously crowded, the flea market is a den of pickpockets. Wear your backpack backwards (that is, frontwards), and be very discreet when taking out your wallet or money.

For **cassettes and CDs, Discoplay** (several branches, including one on Pl. Callao) offers a dazzlingly extensive selection. **Turner,** on C. Génova (1 bl. from Pl. Colón), sells classical recordings.

Down Gran Vía de San Francisco (the continuation of C. Bailén) in Pl. Puerta de Toledo, the city's oldest fish market has become a multi-level shopping complex. The **Mercado Puerta de Toledo,** Ronda de Toledo, 1, houses several bars, restaurants, and shops featuring Spanish fashion, ceramics, furniture, and handicrafts. The classic Spanish **cape store** Seseña has a branch here. (Gallery open Tues.-Sat. 11:30am-9pm, Sun. 11:30am-3pm. Metro: Puerta de Toledo. Buses #3, 60, C.)

SPORTS

Spanish sports fans obsess over **fútbol** (soccer). Every Sunday and some Saturdays between September and June one of two big local teams plays at home. "Real Madrid" plays at Estadio Santiago Bernebéu, Po. Castellana, 104 (tel. 457 11 12; Metro: Lima; buses #27, 40, 43). "Atlético Madrid" plays at Estadio Vicente Calderón,

C. Virgen del Puerto, 67 (tel. 366 47 07; Metro: Pirámides or Marqués de Vadillos). Tickets for seats cost 2500ptas, for standing 1000ptas. If tickets are sold out, shifty scalpers lurk by the stadium during the afternoon or evening a few days before the game. These tickets cost only 25-50% more, whereas on game day prices become astronomical. For the big games—Atlético vs. Real, either team vs. Barcelona's Barça, pennant races in April and May, summer Copas del Rey and de Europa—scalpers are the only option.

For **cycling** information and bicycle repair spin over to **Calmera Bicicletas,** C. Atocha, 98 (tel. 577 75 74; open Mon.-Fri. 9:30am-1:30pm and 4:30-8pm, Sat. 9:30am-1:30pm and 5-8pm). **Swimming** folk splash in the outdoor **Casa de Campo** pool on Av. Angel (open summer 10:30am-8pm; admission 400ptas, ages 4-13 200ptas; Metro: El Lago), and the indoor **Municipal de La Latina** pool, Pl. Cebada, 2 (open Sept.-July Mon.-Fri. 8am-6pm, Sat.-Sun. 8am-2pm, Sun. 8am-2:30pm; admission 400ptas, ages 4-13 200ptas; Metro: La Latina). Gallop over to the **Hipódromo de Madrid,** Ctra. de La Coruña, km 7800 (tel. 307 01 40), for horse-racing.

Call the **Dirección General de Deportes** (tel. 409 49 04) for further sporting information (no English spoken).

La Lidia

Bullfighters are either loved or loathed. If the crowd thinks the *matador* is a man of mettle and style, they exalt him as an emperor. If they think him a coward or a butcher, they whistle cacophonously, chant *"Vete"* (Get out!), throw their seat cushions (40ptas to rent) at him, and wait outside the ring to stone his car. Critical reviews in next morning's paper rehash the event; a bloody killing of the bull, instead of the swift death-stab, can upset the career of even the most renowned *matador.* A top *matador* may earn over three million pesetas per bullfight.

Corridas (bullfights) are held during the Festival of San Isidro and every Sunday in summer, less frequently the rest of the year. The season lasts from March to October, signalled by posters in bars and cafés (especially on C. Victoria, off C. San Jerónimo). **Plaza de las Ventas,** C. Alcalá, 237 (tel. 356 22 00), east of central Madrid, is the biggest ring in Spain. (Metro: Ventas. Bus #21, 53, or 110.) Metro or bus rides, even 1½hr. before the fight, can be asphyxiating. Ticket outlets are at C. Victoria, 3, off C. San Jerónimo east of Puerta del Sol (Metro: Sol), Pl. Carmen, 1 (tel. 531 27 32), and Pl. Toros, C. Alcalá, 237 (Metro: Ventas). A seat is 2000-20,000ptas, depending on its location either in the *sombra* (shade) or in the blistering *sol.* Tickets are usually available the Saturday before and the Sunday of the bullfight.

From mid to late May, the **Fiestas de San Isidro** bring a bullfight every day with top *toreros* (bullfighters) and fierce bulls. The festival is nationally televised, and most of those without tickets crowd into bars. **Bar-Restaurante Plata,** C. Jardines, 11 (tel. 532 48 98; Metro: Sol) has cheap *tapas* and a *loud* television. **Bar El Pavón,** C. Victoria, 8, at C. Cruz (Metro: Sol), **El Abuelo,** C. Núñez de Arce, where aficionados brandish the restaurant's famous shrimp during arguments over bullfighters, and **Bar Torre del Oro,** Pl. Mayor, 26 (tel. 566 50 16; open 10am-2pm; Metro: Sol or Opera) are all local favorites. The bar of ritzy **Hotel Wellington** on C. Velázquez is also known to have its share of *matadores* and their groupies. During the *Fiestas* it's unusual to enter a bar and *not* find the TV tuned to the bullfight.

FESTIVALS

The brochure *Las Fiestas de España,* available at tourist offices and the bigger hotels, contains historical background and general information on Spain's festivals. Madrid's **Carnaval,** inaugurated in the Middle Ages and prohibited during Franco's dictatorship, exists now as never before. The city bursts with street fiestas, dancing, and processions; the Fat Tuesday celebration culminates with the mystifying "Burial of the Sardine." In late April, the city bubbles with the quality **Festival Internacional de Teatro.** The May **Fiestas de San Isidro,** in honor of Madrid's patron saint, bring concerts, parades, and Spain's best bullfights. Throughout the summer, the city sponsors the **Veranos de la Villa,** an outstanding variety of cultural activities, including free classical music concerts, movies in open-air settings, plays, art exhibits, an international film festival, opera and *zarzuela* (Spanish operetta), ballet, and sports. In August, the neighborhoods of **San Cayetano, San Lorenzo,** and **La Paloma** celebrate their own festivities in a flurry of *madrileñismo.* When the processions, street dancing, traditional games, food, and drink are combined with home-grown hard rock and political slogans, they're a microcosm of contemporary Madrid. October's **Festivales de Otoño** (Autumn Festivals) also conjure an impressive array of music, theater, and film. On Nov. 1, **Todos los Santos** (All Saints' Day), an International Jazz Festival brings great musicians to Madrid. The **Día de la Constitución** (Day of the Constitution, or National Day) on Dec. 6 heralds the arrival of the National Company of Spanish Classical Ballet in Madrid. Tourist offices in Madrid have information on all these festivals far in advance.

COMUNIDAD DE MADRID

The Comunidad de Madrid is a self-standing administrative region, shaped like an arrowhead and pointing right at the heart of Castilla y León. Historically, Madrid and Castilla-La Mancha were known as Castilla La Nueva (New Castile), while the Castilla north of Madrid was called Castilla La Vieja (Old Castile, now part of Castilla y León).

■■■ EL ESCORIAL

The UN called it a 'World Monument.' The Spanish were even more discriminating, praising it as the 'eighth wonder of the world.' El Escorial, the object of all this sound and fury, is a fascinating, severe complex including a monastery, two palaces, a church, two pantheons, a magnificent library, and innumerable artistic treasures. Within easy striking distance of Madrid; you should arrive early in order to see it all. In the shadows of the colossus, the lively, charming small town **San Lorenzo** hosts those who need another day. Above all, *don't* come on Monday, when the whole complex and most of the town shuts down.

ORIENTATION AND PRACTICAL INFORMATION

The easiest way to get to El Escorial from Madrid, and back again, is by **bus. Autocares Herranz** runs frequently from Madrid. Buses pull right up to the kiosk outside the Moncloa Metro station (buy a ticket here), and whisk travelers to El Escorial's **Plaza Virgen de Gracia,** in the center of town, ½bl. from the **tourist office.**

El Escorial's **train** station is 2km from town, on Carretera Estación. Shuttle buses run frequently between the station and Pl. Virgen de Gracia. Once in Plaza Virgen de Gracia, turn up **Calle Floridablanca** to reach the tourist office, or walk slightly downhill to get to El Escorial complex.

> **Tourist Office:** C. Floridablanca, 10 (tel. 890 15 54), near the beginning of the street on the right. Town map (on Sun. ask for a map at the hotel next door). *La Semana del Escorial* (free) is also useful. Open Mon.-Fri. 10am-2pm and 3-4:45pm, Sat. 10am-1:45pm.
> **Post Office:** C. Juan de Toledo, 2 (tel. 890 26 90), on Pl. Virgen de Gracia. Open Mon.-Fri. 9am-2pm, Sat. 9am-1pm; for **telegrams** Mon.-Fri. 9am-8pm, Sat. 9am-1pm. **Postal Code:** 28200.
> **Telephone Code:** 91.
> **Currency Exchange:** There's about a bank a block in San Lorenzo del Escorial, all with ATMs and open weekdays 'til 1 or 2pm.
> **Trains:** Ctra. Estación (tel. 890 04 13, **RENFE** information tel. 429 02 02). To: Madrid (30 per day, the vast majority to Estación Atocha and a few to Estación Chamartín, 1hr, 640ptas round-trip); Avila (11 per day, 1 hr, 640ptas); Segovia (same as for Avila).

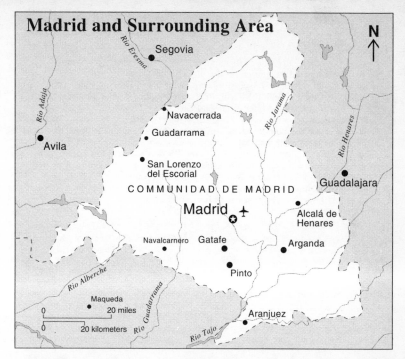

Madrid and Surrounding Area

N ↑

Segovia

Río Eresma

Río Adaja

Río Jarama

Navacerrada

Guadarrama

Río Henares

Avila

San Lorenzo
del Escorial

COMMUNIDAD DE MADRID

Guadalajara

Madrid ✈

Alcalá de
Henares

Navalcarnero Gatafe

Arganda

Río Alberche

Río Guadarrama

Pinto

Maqueda

0   20 miles

0   20 kilometers   Río

Río Tajo

Aranjuez

Buses: Pl. Virgen de Gracia. The **Herranz office,** C. Reina Victoria, 3 (tel. 890 41 22, 890 41 25 or 890 41 00), and **Bar Casino,** C. Rey, 3, sell tickets. To: Madrid (Mon.-Sat. over 40 per day, Sun. 10 per day, 1 hr., 635ptas round-trip).

Taxis: Taxis line up toward the bottom of C. Floridablanca, where a handy sign lists every likely destination in El Escorial, and how much it costs to get there. To summon one, call tel. 890 02 78 or 890 00 15.

Lost Property: Cuartel de la Guardia Civil (tel. 890 26 11), 3km down the Ctra. de Guadarrama.

General Store: C. Joaquín Costa, 4, under the black, yellow, and red CB Ahorro sign. Open Mon.-Sat. 9:30am-2pm and 6-9pm, Sun. 9:30am-2pm.

Pharmacy: San Lorenzo has several pharmacies, all with information in the window about *farmacias de guardia* (late-night pharmacies). Among them: **Fernández,** C. Rey (tel. 890 43 00) and **Villar,** C. Reina Victoria (tel. 890 41 17).

Medical Services: Hospital de la Alcadesa, C. San Pedro Regalado, 1 (tel. 890 54 44), three blocks from the monastery. Call also for **ambulance.**

Emergency: tel. 091.

Police: C. Gobernador, 2 (tel. 890 52 23).

ACCOMMODATIONS AND CAMPING

Rooms fill up quickly in July and August; the situation gets dire only during the festivals (see Entertainment below). You can reserve ahead at the youth hostel and campsite listed below, but not at the *hostales.*

Albergue Juvenil Campamiento Santa María del Buen Aire (HI) (tel. 890 36 40). Walk down Ctra. Estación just past the monastery, turn right and follow the road 1½km. 92 beds with 4-8 people per room. Sometimes full of noisy school groups, so call ahead. 650ptas, breakfast included. *Pensión completa* 1450ptas. *Pensión media* 1050ptas. Lunch 550ptas. Dinner 500ptas. Camping (electricity and bathrooms) 60ptas. Over 25: 800ptas; 1700ptas; 1300ptas; 600ptas; 550ptas;

camping same price. Reception closed Sun. Open Oct.-June. HI card required, purchasable here for 1800ptas, or at various locales in Madrid (see Madrid: Accommodations and Camping).

Hostal Vasco, Pl. Santiago, 11 (tel. 890 16 19). From the bus stop, head up C. Patriarca (perpendicular to C. Floridablanca) for 5 bl., then go left 2 bl. Charming 19th-century building with a terrace on the plaza and a lounge on each floor. Clean, spacious rooms, some with excellent views of the monastery. Singles 1900ptas. Doubles with shower 3800ptas, with full bath 4000ptas. Triples 4900ptas. Breakfast 375ptas. Lunch and dinner each 1300ptas.

Hostal Malagón, C. San Francisco, 2, 2nd fl. (tel. 890 15 76), at C. Mariano Benavente. Cute and comfy rooms with big armchairs. Singles 2300ptas. Doubles 3300ptas. Triples 4800ptas.

Hostal Cristina, C. Juan de Toledo, 6 (tel. 890 19 61). Tranquil location, next to a park and overlooking the mountain range. Garden terrace. Clean rooms with modern wood furniture, tile floors, and phones. All rooms with full bath. Doubles only (some rooms with expansive single beds) 5300ptas; off-season 5000ptas. Breakfast 350ptas. Lunch and dinner each 1600ptas. Visa, MC accepted.

Caravaning El Escorial (tel. 890 24 12), 15km away on Ctra. de Guadarrama al Escorial. 525ptas per person, per tent, per car. Electricity 350ptas.

FOOD

Appearances suggest that San Lorenzo's inhabitants and visitors have nothing better to do than sit around at sidewalk cafés all day long. Well if you can't beat 'em, join 'em. C. Floridablanca is lined with restaurants, cafés, and kiosks, as are several nearby plazas. In addition, the town is surrounded by picnic-able land. Purchase *pan, queso, y vino* at the **Mercado Público,** C. Rey, 9, two blocks off C. Floridablanca. Vendors hawk a large selection of fresh produce, deli meats, cheeses, and other staples. (Open Mon.-Wed. and Fri.-Sat. 9am-2pm and 6-9pm, Thurs. 6-9pm.) Several good *panaderías* (bakeries) are on the same street.

Cafetería-Restaurante del Arte, C. Floridablanca, 14 (tel. 890 15 20). One of the least expensive spots on this boulevard of pricey *cafeterías*. Eating outdoors in the pleasant shade ups prices about 50%. Sandwiches 335-375ptas. *Raciones* 700-1000ptas. *Platos combinados* 800ptas and up. This restaurant prides itself on its hot chocolate and fried toast (250ptas), boasting, *"Sin duda, ofrecemos el mejor chocolate con picatostes de la Sierra."* Open 8am-midnight.

La Taberna de Florida, C. Floridablanca, 30. A charming little *taberna* specializing in fondue: sign outside claims that fondue "tastes good and guarantees good humor." Fondue for two 2250ptas. Big salads 650-700ptas. Open 11am-midnight.

Taberna-Restaurante El Colmao, C. Rey, 26. Small and unpretentious, this *taberna* on the corner sells a *gran churrasco con ensalada* for two—really feeds three—for 3500ptas. *Menú* 1100ptas. Open 11am-midnight.

Mesón-Taberna La Cueva, C. San Antón, 3 (tel. 890 15 16). Built in 1768 by the same genius who designed the Prado. Stately interior, stately food. Mostly very expensive, but affordable *tortillas* (800ptas). Open 1-4pm and 9-10:30pm. For drinks and *tapas,* slip into the tavern on the 1st fl. *Copa de vino* 200ptas. Open 10:30am-2am.

SIGHTS

The entire El Escorial complex is open Tues.-Sun. 10am-1:30pm and 3:30-6:30pm; Oct. 16-April 14 10am-1:30pm and 3-6pm. Last admission to palaces, pantheons, and museums 1hr. or 30min. before closing (depending on "zone"), 15min. for the *casitas.* (Tel. 890 59 03, 890 59 04, or 866 02 38. Admission to monastery 800ptas, students 300ptas, Wed. free for EU citizens; admission to the *casitas* 150ptas.)

El Escorial—the Monastery

The **Monasterio de San Lorenzo del Escorial** was a gift from Felipe II to God, the people, and himself, commemorating his victory over the French at the battle of San Quintín in 1557. Juan Bautista de Toledo was commissioned to design the complex in 1561; when he died in 1567, Juan de Herrera inherited his mantle. Save the Panteón Real and minor additional work, the monastery was finished in a speedy 21 years, accounting for its uncommon uniformity of style.

According to tradition, Felipe oversaw much of the work from a chair-shaped rock 7km from the construction site. That stone is now known as **Silla de Felipe II** (Felipe's Chair), and the view is still regal.

The floor plan of the monastery is a subdivided rectangle; a bird's eye view shows a grill, the very device on which St. Lawrence was martyred. Considering the resources Felipe II (son of Carlos I, who had ruled the most powerful empire in the world) commanded, the building is noteworthy for its austerity, symmetry, and simplicity—in his words, "majesty without ostentation." Four massive towers pin the corners in characteristic Spanish fashion. The towers of the basilica that rise from the center are surmounted by a great dome, giving the ensemble the shape of a pyramid. At Felipe II's behest, the steep slate roofs were introduced from Flanders—the first of their kind in Spain. The delicate slate spires lend a grace to the austere structure, further mellowed by the glowing *piedra de Colmenar,* a stone hewn from nearby quarries. The monastery is at once also a palace, a church, and a pantheon (again characteristically Spanish), a prototype of what would later be called the *estilo herreriano.* Variations of this Hapsburg style of unadorned alternating granite and red brick, slate roofs, and corner towers, appear throughout Spain—particularly in Madrid and Toledo—and abroad (for example, on Paris's Place des Vosges).

To avoid the worst of the crowds, enter the Escorial by the traditional gateway on the west side of the complex (the right-hand side from C. Floridablanca), and wander through the **Patio de los Reyes** into the **basílica,** a cool and magnificent building. Marble steps lead to an altar graced by two groups of elegant sculpture by Pompeo Leoni. The figures on the left represent Carlos I and Isabel (parents of Felipe II), his daughter María, and his sisters María (Queen of Hungary) and Leonor (Queen of France). Those on the right depict Felipe II with three of his four wives and his son Carlos. The **Coro Alto** (High Choir) has a magnificent ceiling fresco of heaven filled with choirs of angels; the **cloister** shines with Titian's gigantic fresco of the Martyrdom of St. Lawrence. Pay 100ptas to illuminate the Coro Alto—an impressive sight—or wait for someone else to do it.

The Palacio Real

The Palacio Real includes the **Salón del Trono** (Throne Room) and two **dwellings** in one—Felipe II's spartan 16th-century apartments and the more luxurious 18th-century rooms of Carlos III and Carlos IV. The Bourbon half is characterized by the sumptuousness of its furniture and beautiful **tapestries** (copies of works by Goya, El Greco, and Rubens worked in intricate detail and brilliant wool yarn cover every inch of wall). The Hapsburg chambers are simple.

The long **Sala de Batallas** (Battle Room) links the two parts of the palace. A huge fresco here depicts some of Castile and Spain's greatest victories: Juan II's triumph over the Muslims in 1431 at Higueruela (note the fleeing townsfolk), Felipe II's two successful expeditions to the Azores, and the battle of San Quintín. Downstairs, in the royal chambers, observe Felipe II's very small bed, his terrible handwriting, and the view to which he woke every morning.

The Panteón Real

The astonishing **Panteón Real** (known affectionately as *el pudridero,* the rotting chamber) was another brainchild of Felipe II. Although he didn't live to see it finished, he's buried here with Carlos I and most of their royal descendants. Royal servants dumped bygone nobles in the small adjoining room so that they could dry before being stuffed into their permanent tombs (drying time varied based on climate conditions and fat content). The stairway leading to the **crypt** is elegantly adorned with black and red marble and jasper. Of the 26 gray marble sarcophagi, 23 contain the remains of Spanish monarchs, and three are still empty. Royal tradition discriminates against queens. All kings are buried here (except Felipe V and Fernando VI), but only those queens whose sons become monarchs are admitted.

The Salas Capitulares and Biblioteca

The **Salas Capitulares** (Chapter Rooms), on the far side of the complex, display an outstanding exhibition on the construction of El Escorial, with some wooden models of 16th-century machinery and the buildings themselves. Also in the Salas Capitulares is the **Pinacoteca,** which holds a collection of masterpieces by Bosch, Dürer, El Greco, Titian, Tintoretto, Velázquez, Zurbarán, Van Dyck, and others.

The **Biblioteca** (library) on the second floor holds numerous priceless books and manuscripts, despite several fires which have reduced the collection. Alfonso X's *cantigas de Santa María,* the Book of Hours of the Catholic monarchs, Saint Teresa's manuscripts and diary, the *Aureus Codex* (by German Emperor Conrad III, 1039) written in pure gold, and an 11th-century *Commentary on the Apocalypse* by Beato de Liébana are just a small selection of the choice readings.

Outringers

Commissioned by the Prince of Asturias, who later became Carlos IV, the **Casita del Príncipe** has a splendid collection of *objets d'art,* including chandeliers, lamps, rugs, furniture, clocks, tapestries, china, and engraved oranges. The French roughed up the *casita* during the Napoleonic invasions, but many rooms were redecorated by Fernando VII in the then-popular Empire style. To get to the *casita,* follow the right side of the Carretera de la Estación as far as the corner of the monastic complex, turn the corner, and take the left-hand fork (15min.).

Three km down the road to Avila lurks the **Casita del Infante,** commissioned by Gabriel de Borbón, Carlos's brother, at around the same time. Though not as sumptuous as the Casita del Príncipe, it's tranquil and has a fine view.

ENTERTAINMENT

San Lorenzo may be a small town with a big monastery, but it's got a karaoke bar—in a Chinese restaurant, no less! If the thought of tourists lip-synching to the classics within meters of royal burial grounds makes you want to run shrieking—and *not* to the tune of "Louie, Louie"—fear not: San Lorenzo is not the fossilized tourist trap one might expect. Thronging with young people, the town enjoys a vibrant night life. Older folk stroll, sit, and sip in the plazas just off **Calles Floridablanca** and **Rey,** which overflow with *cervecerías* and *cafés.* Teens and twenty-somes head a little further uphill.

Pub la Jara, C. Floridablanca, 34. A small, quiet place with a youngish clientele and a foozball machine. Strong mixed drinks. Open 6pm-3am.

Jandro's Bar, Pl. Animas. Right next door to a good *tapas* joint, **Taberna La Cueva.** A popular place for the young to build a buzz. Drinks are a tad expensive (beer 350ptas, whiskey 700ptas) and the music blares. Open 7:30pm-4am.

El Gurniato, C. Leandro Rubio, 3 (tel. 890 47 10), around the bend to the left at the end of C. Floridablanca. Happy, shiny people hold hands on the tiny terrace. Inside it's shiny and tiny as well, and filled with members of the 25-35 crowd. Open noon-3pm and 6pm-3am.

Disco-Pub Que Maz Da, C. Santiago, 11. Comfy seating plus cheap beer minus a cover charge. Open Sun.-Thurs. 8pm-midnight, Fri.-Sat. 8pm-4:30am.

Bar-Restaurante Chino Shang-Hai, on the corner of C. San Antón and C. Rey. This karaoke bar would be campy if it weren't so blissfully unselfconscious. As is, it's just tremendously tacky. Open 1-4pm and 8pm-1am.

During the **Festivals of San Lorenzo** (Aug. 10-20), parades of giant figures line the streets and fireworks fill the sky. Folk dancing contests and horse-drawn cart parades mark **Romería a la Ermita de la Virgen de Gracia,** the second Sunday in September. Ceremonies are held in the forest of Herría.

■■■ ALCALÁ DE HENARES

Alcalá (pop. 150,000) is a demure city of erstwhile greatness: the seat of a university that enjoyed fame across Europe in the 16th century, and the birthplace of Cervantes, Juan Ruiz (archpriest author of the classic medieval celebration of earthly love, *El Libro de Buen Amor)*, and Catherine of Aragón. Although the tourist attraction to square foot ratio is quite high, the town itself is charming, and a pleasant place to stroll around for a few hours.

Alcalá's center—containing most sites of interest to visitors—is shaped like an ellipse, with **Plaza de Cervantes, Puerta de Madrid, Plaza de Palacio,** and **Plaza Santos Niños** marking the four foci. Pl. Cervantes is a large square filled with rose bushes and outdoor cafés. At its southern end cluster the **Ruinas de Santa María,** ruins of a 16th-century church destroyed during the Civil War. The surviving **Capilla del Oidor,** founded by Juan II's confessor, contains white Gothic plasterworks and the fountain where Cervantes was christened. (Open Tues.-Sun. noon-2pm and 6-9pm. Free.)

Just east of Pl. Cervantes, in Pl. San Diego, sits the **Colegio Mayor de San Ildefonso,** the fulcrum of the once-illustrious university. Pioneering humanist and sharp dresser Cardinal Cisneros founded the college in 1495, thirteen years before he created the university itself. The Cardinal's printed heraldic symbol, a pair of swans, is carved on the mid-16th-century facade. Inside, the highlights are the *Paraninfo* (Great Hall) with its colorful ceiling and the 17th-century Patio Santo Tomás de Villanueva, an elegant Baroque affair. Cisneros now decays in the altar of the adjoining **Capilla de San Ildefonso,** which has a marvelous coffered ceiling. Although the whole university was transferred to Madrid in 1836, several academic departments have recently returned to Alcalá. (Open Tues.-Sat. Mandatory tours at 11am, 11:45am, 12:30pm, 1:15pm, 4pm, 4:45pm, 5:30pm, and 6:15pm. Admission 150ptas, students free.)

Down C. Mayor from Pl. Cervantes is **Casa de Cervantes,** the reconstruction *in situ* of the house where the author was born. A collection of furniture, pottery, and other artifacts fills 13 rooms. Although they're all genuine (including the map downstairs), none belonged to Cervantes or his father Rodrigo, who owned the original house. *Don Quixote* editions in every language are displayed upstairs. (Tel. 889 96 54; open Tues.-Fri. 10am-1:30pm and 4-6:30pm, Sat-Sun. 10am-1:30pm. Free.) C. Mayor leads to Pl. Santos Niños and the impressive Gothic **Iglesia Magistral de los Santos Niños Justo y Pastor** (open to visitors only during services).

Practical Information The **tourist office,** at the corner of Pl. Cervantes on Callejón de Santa María, 1, offers a list of tourist sites and a brochure entitled "Alcalá de Henares: Patrimony and History." (Tel. 889 26 94; open June 15-Sept. 15 Mon.-Fri. 9am-3pm, Sat. 11am-2pm; off-season Tues.-Sat 10am-2pm and 4-6pm, Sun. 11am-2pm.) The **post office** (tel. 889 23 34) is on Pl. Cervantes between the intersection of C. Libreros and the tourist office. (Open Mon.-Fri. 8:30am-8:30pm.) **Taxis** answer to tel. 882 21 88 and 888 10 11. The **Red Cross** (tel. 888 15 02 or 888 15 65) is at Pl. Cervantes, 12. The **police** are at tel. 888 07 16 or 888 30 10 (091 or 092 in an **emergency**). **Ambulances** respond to tel. 880 07 01 or 881 24 97.

Getting to Alcalá de Henares from Madrid is as easy as falling off a log. The **train station** (tel. 888 01 96) is located on Po. Estación. *Cercanías* run from Madrid's Atocha and back again every 15 minutes (½hr., 520ptas round-trip). The same trains continue to Guadalajara (twice the cost). To get to Pl. Cervantes from the station, turn left as you exit onto Po. Estación, walk a few blocks, and hang a left onto C. Libreros which leads straight there. The Continental-Auto **bus station** is on Av. Guadalajara, 36 (tel. 888 16 22), two blocks past C. Libreros. Buses run every 15 minutes between Madrid and Alcalá (½hr., 275ptas). To reach the city center from the bus station, turn right down Av. Guadalajara and bear left onto C. Libreros at the fork.

Accommodations and Food Because very few tourists sleep over, there are always empty beds. One of the least expensive *hostales* is **Hostal El Torero,** Puerta de Madrid, 18 (tel. 889 03 73). From Pl. Cervantes, walk down C. Libreros, which becomes C. Mayor and then C. Cifuentes. The *hostal* is through the gate, near the gas station. It's quite orange. Inside, bullfighting memorabilia clutters the public areas. (Singles with shower 2900ptas. Doubles with shower 4800ptas, with bath 6250ptas.) **Restaurante Topeca '75,** on C. Mayor ½bl. from Pl. Cervantes, is a classy place with a filling *menú* for 950ptas. Enormous jugs of *sangría* 600ptas. **Mesón Las Cuadras de Rocinante,** C. Carmen Calzado, 1, off of C. Mayor, is festooned with medieval implements and offers good, cheap fare. (Entrees 500-900ptas. Open 11am-3:30pm and 6:30pm-midnight, Fri.-Sat. 'til 1am.)

■■■ ARANJUEZ

A getaway for generations of Hapsburg and Bourbon royalty, Aranjuez's architectural and botanical splendor is somewhat mitigated by tourists and all that comes with them (i.e. vendors hawking ugly ceramic memorabilia on street corners). Yet the two rivers which converge at this town provide Aranjuez with a verdant peace which adds to the sense of noonday grandeur evoked by the royal palace.

The stately **Palacio Real** easily warrants an excursion from Madrid. A marvel in white brick, the palace was originally designed by Juan de Herrera—chief architect of El Escorial—under the aegis of Felipe II. In the years to come, both Felipe VI and Carlos III had their minions enlarge and embellish the palace to its present state of glory and ample girth. Room after opulent room display finely worked Vatican mosaic paintings in natural marble, chandeliers and mirrors from the La Granja crystal factory, Buen Retiro porcelain, Flemish tapestries, and ornate French clocks. The Oriental porcelain room with 3-D wallpaper has a dash of Rococo ceramic work; the Mozarabic smoking room has its own gaudy copy of the Alhambra. (Open Wed.-Mon. 10am-6:30pm; Oct.-May Wed.-Mon. 10am-5:30pm. Compulsory tour in Spanish. Admission 400ptas, students 275ptas, Wed. free for EU citizens.)

The Tajo (which flows all the way to Lisboa) and its tributary the Jarama water Aranjuez's beautiful gardens, in addition to providing an unpleasant touch of humidity (which can make Aranjuez seem even hotter than Madrid). River walkways run from the **Jardín de la Isla,** with its banana trees and mythological statuary, to the huge **Jardín del Príncipe,** created for the youthful amusement of Carlos IV (Goya's patron). (Gardens open 8am-8:30pm; Oct.-May 8am-6:30pm. Free.) Inside the park the **Casa del Labrador,** a mock laborer's cottage, is a treasure trove of Neoclassical decorative arts destined for courtly galas. The queen's private quarters overflow with knick-knacks such as Roman mosaics from Mérida and views of contemporary Madrid embroidered in silk. Also within Jardín del Príncipe, the **Casa de Marinos,** once the quarters of the Tajo's sailing squad, stores royal gondolas. (Casas open Tues.-Sun. 10am-6:30pm; Oct.-May Tues.-Sun. 10am-6pm. Admission to both 300ptas, students 250ptas.) Nearby is the **embarcadero** (dock) from which the royal family set sail on the swampy river. If you wish to do the same, cross the precarious footbridge to the Arboleda Bar on the far side to rent **paddleboats** (tel. 891 71 03; 350ptas per person per hr.).

Spain's second locomotive, which first ran from Madrid to Aranjuez on February 9, 1851, was dubbed the "strawberry train." Built under the reign of Isabel II, the strawberry train was all the rage in subsequent decades, carting Aranjuez strawberries to Madrid during the week and *madrileños* to Aranjuez on weekends. For the past 10 years, tourists have relived those bygone days of glory in an exact replica of that first steam train, filled with what appear to be exact replicas of its obsequious and officious porters. (May 15-Oct. Sat.-Sun. and holidays only, leaves from Madrid's Estación Atocha at 10am, returns at 8pm; round-trip fare, including admission to all sights, 2150ptas, children 1200ptas.)

ARANJUEZ

Practical Information The **tourist office** (tel. 891 04 27) is a kiosk in the Pl. Puente just across the Tajo river; from the Palacio Real turn right on Av. del Palacio and left across the bridge at the end of the street (look for signs). Provides a brochure and a map of Aranjuez. English spoken. (Open Tues.-Sun. 10am-6pm.) The **post office** (tel. 891 11 32) is at C. Peña Redonda, 3, a small street off C. Capitán Gómez, which is off C. Infantas. (Open Mon.-Fri. 8:30am-2pm; to send **telegrams** call 522 20 00.) The **Red Cross** (tel. 891 02 52) is at C. Rey, 7. A big **pharmacy** at C. Capitán Gómez, 32 (open 9am-10pm) has a list of *farmacias de guardia* in the window. The municipal **police** office (tel. 891 00 22 or 891 00 55) is at C. Stuart, 91.

The **train station** (tel. 891 02 02) is a pleasant 10-min. walk from town along tree-lined Carretera Toledo. Municipal bus N-Z also runs to and fro, with stops outside the station and on C. Stuart. Trains to: Madrid (45 *cercanías* per day to Estación Atocha, 45min., 635ptas round-trip, plus 7 *regionales* to Estación Chamartín); Toledo (3 per day, ½hr.); Valencia (1 per day, 5hr.); Segovia (1 per day, 1½hr.); Cuenca (6 per day, 2hr.); and Andalucía.

Aranjuez's **bus station** is a hole in the wall at C. Infantas, 8 (tel. 891 01 83 or 530 46 07), serviced by the ALSA bus company. (In Madrid at the Estación Sur on C. Canarias, 17; tel. 527 12 94.) Mon.-Sat. 18 buses per day travel Aranjuez to Madrid, 17 per day Madrid to Aranjuez; Sun. 5 per day go Aranjuez to Madrid, 6 per day Madrid to Aranjuez (1hr., 365ptas).

Accommodations and Food **Hostal Infantas,** Av. Infantas, 4 (tel. 891 13 41, 891 13 42, or 891 66 43), is big, unattractive, and just minutes from the traffic circle. Inside it's clean and comfortable, with TVs and phones in each of the 40 rooms. (Singles 1550ptas, with shower 2300ptas, with full bath 2500ptas. Doubles 2700ptas, with shower 4300ptas, with full bath 4700ptas. Triples 3510ptas, with shower 5500ptas, with full bath 5900ptas.) **Hostal Rusiñol,** C. San Antonio, 76 (tel. 891 01 55), off Carretera de Andalucía, on the corner with C. Stuart. Shabby in a quaint way. (Singles 1600ptas. Doubles 2350ptas, with shower 3500ptas. Triples 3500ptas, with shower 4500ptas.) They rent bicycles too: 1hr. 200ptas; ½-day 500ptas; full-day 800ptas. **Hostal Castilla,** C. Andalucía, 98 (tel. 891 26 27 or 891 61 33), glooms in medieval splendor a few blocks farther from the river than the Rusiñol. Significantly costlier than the above locales, but much more luxurious. Beautiful rooms with exposed beams and in-set windows evoke the days when knights and dragons roamed the earth. Lovely, cool courtyard. All rooms have full bath, telephone, and TV. (*Temporada alta* May 14-Oct. 15: Singles 3900ptas. Doubles 5100ptas. Triples 6350ptas. Quads 7600ptas. *Temporada media* Mar. 28-May 13: 3600ptas; 4800ptas; 5950ptas; 7100ptas. *Temporada baja* Oct. 16-Mar. 27: 3400ptas; 4500ptas; 5600ptas; 6700ptas. Breakfast 350ptas.) **Camping Soto del Castillo** (tel. 891 13 95), across the Tajo and off the highway to the right (2km from palace, watch for the signs). A beautiful site amid lush fields and near the peaceful Tajo. (530ptas per person, 665ptas per car, 560ptas per large tent. Electricity 425ptas. 10% surcharge on foreign campers. Open April-Sept.)

The town's **strawberries** and **asparagus** have been famous for centuries: nowadays, Aranjuez's strawberries are actually grown in other areas of Spain to be sold (to unsuspecting tourists) as *fresón con nata* (strawberries with cream, 300-400ptas) at kiosks and cafés throughout town. Other than this historical delicacy, Aranjuez merits no particular culinary attention, but you certainly won't go hungry: cafés and restaurants line the streets, often with tables al fresco. **La Alegría de la Huerta** (tel. 891 29 38), on Carretera Andalucía, kitty-corner from the tourist office, has an attractive inner courtyard and two large dining rooms with visions of grandeur. *Menús* 1000-3000ptas, many featuring asparagus. Excellent service. Closed Tues. Visa, MC, AmEx accepted. **Restaurante Rana Verde** (tel. 891 13 25), on the near shore of the river, satisfies those who find relief in wanton indulgence (about 3000ptas per person). The opulent *tarta al licor* (brandy-flavored cake, 600ptas) is the corker. Visa, MC, AmEx accepted.

SIERRA DE GUADARRAMA

■■■ SIERRA DE GUADARRAMA

The Sierra de Guadarrama, a pine-covered mountain range halfway between Madrid and Segovia, has the most spectacular scenery in the province of Madrid. Its dark geological shapes loom large in local imagination, as well as the local economy. *La Mujer Muerta* (The Dead Woman) rots facing the West. The *Sierra de la Maliciosa* (Mountain of the Evil Woman) schemes to the East. Between the two, the *Siete Picos* (Seven Peaks) gnash their teeth silently at the skies. Yet none of these portents of doom deter the influx of summer and winter visitors, who come to hike and ski.

EL VALLE DE LOS CAÍDOS

In a previously untouched valley of the Sierra de Guadarrama, 8km north of El Escorial, Franco built the overpowering monument of **Santa Cruz del Valle de los Caídos** (Valley of the Fallen) as a memorial to those who gave their lives in the Civil War. Naturally, the massive granite cross (150m tall and 46m wide) memorializes only those who died "serving *Dios* and *España*," i.e. the Nationalists/Fascists.

Below the monument, Franco is buried in the **basilica.** Engineers and political prisoners were forced to blast a hole in the mountain to make room for this appropriately spooky and bizarre edifice. Intimidating, tunnel-like antechambers, vaguely medieval light fixtures and tapestries, and ornaments of angels holding swords make for an eerie, fitting monument to Franco and his particular brand of fascism. Mass daily at 11am. (Open 10am-7pm; winter 10am-6pm. Admission 400ptas, free Wed. for EU citizens.)

El Valle de los Caídos is accessible only via El Escorial. Autocares Herranz (see El Escorial above) runs three **buses** daily. (They leave El Escorial at 11:15am, 1:15pm, and 3:15pm, and return at 2:15pm, 4:15pm, and 6:15pm; 15min; round-trip plus admission 620ptas.)

CERCEDILLA

Cercedilla, a picturesque town of alpine chalets, is a hub for hiking and skiing in the Sierras. Those weary of busy cities will find it a relief that this town has no monuments; the most exciting event in its history is a passing mention in Quevedo's 17th-century picaresque work, *El Buscón.* Hiking trails lead straight out of Cercedilla, and many use the town as a base for daytrips to nearby ski resorts (see below).

Cercedilla is the easiest town in the Sierras to reach by **train** as a daytrip from Madrid or Segovia. To get to town from the train station, walk uphill, take the right-hand branch at the top, and carry straight on at the train track (15-20min.). Most of the hiking action begins up the **Carretera las Dehesas,** beyond the intersection, uphill from the train station. One of the most strenuous hikes leads past the Hospital de Fuenfrías to the meadow of Navarrulaque.

Practical Information The **Agencia de Medio Ambiente,** Ctra las Dehesas, s/n (tel. 852 22 13), fulfills the function of a tourist office. About 3km up the road in a wooden chalet, it offers hiking information and sells several guidebooks and maps, including the excellent "Editorial Alpino" map of the Sierras. The free leaflet *Senderos Autoguiados* (self-guided trails) is stronger on ideas than geographical accuracy. (Open June-Nov. Mon.-Fri. 9am-6pm, Sat.-Sun. 9am-9pm.) From July 22 to Nov. free guided tours of the valley depart from the shelter across the road from the chalet at 10am and 4pm. The **post office** is halfway between the train station and the town center on C. Marquesa Casa López, 9. (Open Mon.-Fri. 9am-1pm; Oct.-May Mon.-Sat. 9am-1pm; for **telegrams** Mon.-Fri. 10am-1pm.) Cercedilla's **telephone code** is 91. Bicicletas Mariano, C. Marquesa Casa López, just past the train tracks, rents **bikes.** (½-day 800ptas, full-day 1000ptas. Open 10am-2pm and 6-9pm.) For **medical assistance,** the Centro Médico (tel. 852 30 31 or 852 31 59) is in a new and much-signposted building in the town center. In an **emergency,** dial 091. The **police** are in the Ayuntamiento, Pl. Mayor, 1 (tel. 852 02 00 or 852 04 25); call them for an **ambulance.**

The **train station** (tel. 852 00 57) is at the base of the hill on C. Emilio Serrano. Frequent service to: Madrid (over 30 per day, 1½hr., 380ptas); Segovia (10 per day, 45min., 340ptas); Los Cotos (11 per day, 45min., 125ptas, round-trip 180ptas); Puerto de Navacerrada (11 per day, ½hr., 125ptas, round-trip 180ptas). The **bus station,** Av. José Antonio, 2 (tel. 852 02 39), is across the street and to the left of the Ayuntamiento. To Guadarrama (15 per day, 20min., 100ptas).

Accommodations During late summer, ski season, and weekends year-round, vacationers pour in from Madrid, vaporizing accommodations. At other times there's plenty for all. Near Cercedilla, two capacious **HI youth hostels** offer the usual group sleeping, group meals, and 10am lockout. The **Villa Castora** (tel. 852 03 34) is closest to the train station, about 1½km up Ctra. las Dehesas on the left; it's popular with school and community groups, so try to reserve at least two days in advance. (Reception open 8am-7pm. 650ptas. *Pensión media* 1050ptas. *Pensión completa* 1450ptas. Over 26: 800ptas; 1300ptas; 1700ptas.) **Las Dehesas** (tel. 852 01 35), is closer to the hiking trails and more removed from the highway, tucked back among the trees just beyond the Agencia del Medio Ambiente on Ctra. las Dehesas. (Reception open same times and same prices as Villa Castora.) HI card, required in both to join the fun, is purchasable on the spot (1800ptas). **Camping** in general is strictly controlled throughout the Sierra de Guadarrama, and is no longer allowed within Cercedilla's town limits, which extend surprisingly far beyond the town. A list of campsites is available at the Agencia del Medio Ambiente. Reaching most of these rather remote sites requires wheels (not necessarily motorized; see bikes above).

Food Restaurant prices here are middling. **Maxcoop,** C. Docta Cañados, 2 (tel. 852 00 13), in the town center off Av. Generalísimo, is a mini-market. (Open Mon.-Sat. 9:30am-1:30pm and 5:30-9pm, Sun. 9:30am-1:30pm.) Hordes of bars peddle inexpensive *bocadillos* and *raciones* in the town proper.

PUERTO DE NAVACERRADA AND LOS COTOS

A strong magnet for outdoorsy types year-round, **Puerto de Navacerrada** offers bland skiing in the winter, and beautiful hiking terrain in the summer—backpackers use Navacerrada as a starting point to roam the peaks. A little engine leaves for Navacerrada from a separate platform of the Cercedilla station (on the left). In addition, the same *cercanía* that travels from Madrid to Cercedilla passes through Navacerrada a few stops later (1¾hr., 420ptas). The skiing season lasts from December to April; there are special areas for beginners as well as competitions for the more accomplished. For hiking in summer, exit the station, turn left at the highway, and turn left again (off the road) at the large intersection marking the pass. The dirt path leads uphill. There are many hiking routes through the pine forests; the Vía de Schmidt (or Smit) to the left leads back to Cercedilla.

Los Cotos is another popular winter resort. Nearby **Rascafría** in Los Cotos has two ski stations that are well regarded by locals, **Valdesqui** (tel. 852 04 16) and **Valcotos.** (Both open in winter roughly 10am-5pm.) For detailed information on winter sports, call the Madrid office of the Dirección General de Deportes (tel. 409 49 04). *Cercanías* run from Madrid to Los Cotos, through Cercedilla and Navacerrada (just under 2hr., 435ptas).

Castilla-La Mancha

Cervantes deliberately chose La Mancha—manxa is Arabic for parched earth—for Don Quixote's inspired adventures in order to evoke a cultural and material backwater. No need for the overworked fantasy of the Knight of the Sad Countenance to appreciate the austere beauty of this battered, windswept plateau: castles in Castilla-La Mancha (there are more than 500, and they lend the region its name) served as models for the medieval castle in Disney World. The region's strange and tumultuous history, gloomy medieval fortresses, arid plains, and awesome crags provide grist for the imagination.

In the olden days, this area was the battleground for ceaseless conflicts between the Christians and the Muslims. As Christian forces barged into Muslim Spain (Toledo was captured in 1085), La Mancha became the domain of military orders (such as Santiago, Calatrava, Montesa, and San Juan) modeled on such crusading institutions as the Knights Templar, an order of powerful warrior-monks. Later on, in the 14th and 15th centuries, it was the site of fearsome struggles between the kingdoms of Castilla and Aragón. The result of all this warring is a region which looks like the mess left over from a child's play battleground: castles, fortresses, churches, walls, and ramparts are scattered hither and yon, with a few windmills thrown in for good measure. Scored by the Tajo and the Guadiana, two great Atlantic rivers, and the smaller Júcar, which eyes the Mediterranean, La Mancha's rolling flatness is broken by the hills of the Toledo and Cuenca *Sierras,* and interrupted here and there by lakes and great stands of game-rich primeval forest.

The region is Spain's largest wine-producing area (Valdepeñas and Manzanares are common table wines), and is renowned for its abundant olive groves and excellent hunting. Stews, roast meats, and game are *manchego* staples. *Gazpacho manchego* is a hearty stew of rabbit, lamb, chicken, and pork. *Perdices escabechadas* (marinated partridges) are a specialty of Toledo, while Cuenca is known for *monteruelo* (a pâté of pig's liver and game). Perhaps Spain's most universal cheese is *manchego,* ranging from a young, creamy white to a sharp, friable *añejo* (aged).

■■■ TOLEDO

A treasury of Spanish culture and the former capital of Spain, Toledo's spectacular art, architecture, and cabalistic mysteries have attracted visitors for centuries. Cervantes described Toledo as a "rocky gravity, glory of Spain and light of her cities"; Baroque poet Góngora called it a perpetual avalanche; and Luís Buñuel, André Bretón, and their merry band of Surrealists, lured by Toledo's mystery and intrigue, had headquarters here.

Centuries of *convivencia* (co-existence of Christian, Islamic, and Hebraic cultures) have resulted in architectural syncretism (both Mudejar and Mozarabic) unequaled elsewhere in the world. With steep streets, unexpected dead ends, and a vast array of architectural styles, Toledo is at once lovely and bewildering—the more so because the city's many restaurants, shops, and *pensiones* take care to blend in with their surroundings as harmoniously as possible (don't be surprised if you find yourself ordering a beer from a docent). Surrounded on three sides by the Tajo river, Toledo is a natural fortress city. Piecemeal construction took advantage of the site's geography: Toledo's architects designed with an eye for invasion from above (in those days, nothing was more lethal than the sun's rays) and below, generating a crowded, confoundingly labyrinthine web of monuments and alleyways.

According to the purple prose in the tourist office brochure, "the streets of Toledo are like the arteries of history"—a clumsy simile, perhaps, but more than justified by the city's strange and wonderful past. In 193 BC, the Romans conquered the city and decreed the name Toletum. It was under the Visigoths, however, that

TOLEDO

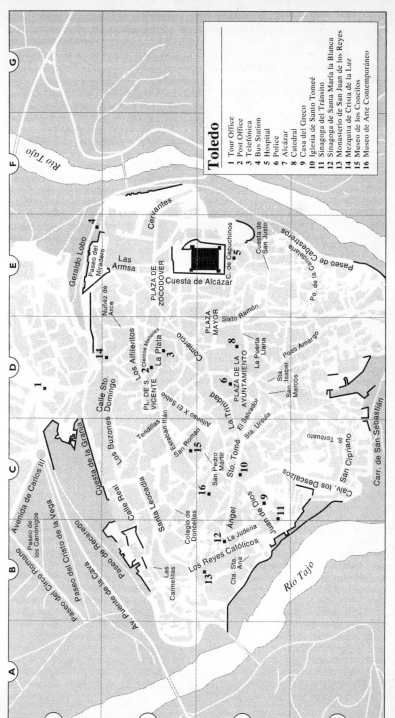

Toledo

1 Tour Office
2 Post Office
3 Telefónica
4 Bus Station
5 Police
6 Hospital
7 Alcázar
8 Catedral
9 Casa del Greco
10 Iglesia de Santo Tomeé
11 Sinagoga del Tránsito
12 Sinagoga de Santa María la Blanca
13 Monasterio de San Juan de los Reyes
14 Mezquita de Crista de la Luz
15 Museo de los Concilos
16 Museo de Arte Contemporáneo

Toledo thrived and became an important trading center, captured by the Moors in 712. The following centuries of interaction between Mozarabic Christians, Jews, and Moors sparked the economic and cultural prosperity—unweakened by the 1085 change in power when El Cid and Alfonso VI arrived—which lent Toledo its rich, multifarious quality. In tune with the achievements and happenings of the East, Toledo became the European capital for the study of natural sciences, the Bible, and languages in the Middle Ages, and its name equivalent with the notion of cultural tolerance.

Today Toledo (pop. 60,000) is famous for damascene, the ancient craft of inlaying gold filaments on a black steel background, and for its swords and knives. Many streets are cluttered with junky gift shops, selling everything from miniature suits of armor to cheesy ceramic pigs. Despite a thriving, in-your-face tourist industry—at times the city seems to have been constructed for the sole purpose of inducing you to buy that precious, damascene elephant—Toledo's wealth of culture and history surpasses its crassness. The city exerts an irresistible pull.

ORIENTATION AND PRACTICAL INFORMATION

Toledo is well connected with Madrid—several buses and trains make the 1½-hr. trip daily—but getting here from anywhere else is more difficult. To get to **Plaza de Zocodóver** in the center of town, take bus #5 or 6 (100ptas) from the stop to the right of the **train station,** or from the stop directly outside the **bus station.** Alternatively, it's not a bad walk from either station, although completely unshaded and mostly uphill (10min.). From the bus station: exit and take the first right (you'll be walking along the highway that surrounds the city). Pass through a gate after the tourist office and continue upwards to the plaza. From the train station: do *not* take the big bridge across the Tajo (although this may seem like the most obvious route). Instead, turn right out of the station and follow Po. de la Rosa to a smaller bridge called Puente de Alcántara. Cross the bridge to an eponymous stone staircase (through a set of arches); the left-hand fork after climbing the stairs leads directly to Pl. Zocodóver.

Toledo could not be more labyrinthine if it contained a real live Minotaur. Streets are well-labeled and the tourist office distributes a fairly detailed map, but it's virtually impossible not to get lost frequently. Many major sights are near or atop the central hill, which is almost exactly circular. Pl. Zocodóver and the massive Alcázar are over to the east of the circle; the cathedral is roughly in the middle, and several other sights, including the Casa del Greco and the synagogues, are southwest in the **Judería.**

Tourist Office: (tel. 22 08 43; fax 25 26 48), just outside the Puerta Nueva de Bisagra on Po. de Merchán, on the north side of town. From Pl. Zocodóver, take C. Armas, the main street leading downhill through various name changes to the gate; pass under and cross the intersection. From the RENFE station, turn right and take the busy right-hand fork; continue past the bus station, skirting the city walls until you reach the gateway. The office is across the road, outside the walls. English spoken. Up-to-date maps and information. Open Mon.-Fri. 9am-2pm and 4-6pm, Sat. 9am-3pm and 4-7pm, Sun. 9am-3pm. For a map and rudimentary info without the walk, queue up at the gray **information booth,** Pl. Zocodóver. Open Mon.-Sat. 10am-6pm, Sun. and holidays 10am-3pm. The **Regional Board of Industry and Tourism,** Pl. Santiago de los Caballeros, 5 (tel. 21 09 00 or 21 09 12; fax 21 55 64) is useful if you have questions which extend beyond the city of Toledo. English spoken. Open same hours as the tourist office.

Budget Travel: Oficina de Información Juvenil, C. Trinidad, 8 (tel. 21 20 62), by the cathedral. Student travel information, rail passes, bus and plane tickets. No English spoken. Open Mon.-Fri. 9am-2pm.

Post Office: C. Plata, 1 (tel. 22 36 11; post office info 25 10 66), off Pl. Zocodóver via C. Comercio and then C. Toledo. Open for all services, including **telegrams,** Mon-Fri. 8am-9pm, Sat. 9am-2pm. Also open Sat. 2-7pm for telegrams only. To send a telegram by phone, call 22 20 00. **Postal Code:** 45001.

Telephones: C. Plata, 20. Open Mon.-Fri. 9:30am-1:30pm and 5-9pm, Sat. 9:30am-2:30pm. Open-air pay phones—two in Pl. Zocodóver and two in Pl. San Vicente (at the end of C. Plata), as well as elsewhere throughout the city—are convenient for credit card and collect calls. All have AT&T, MCI, and Sprint USA-direct capability. **Telephone Code:** 925.

Trains: Po. Rosa, s/n (tel. 21 12 72), in a beautiful neo-Mudejar building opposite the Puente de Azarquiel. Only one line, destination Madrid Atocha (9 per day between 7am-9:30pm, 1½hr., 450ptas), passing through Aranjuez (45min., 235ptas). To get anywhere else, transfer in Madrid or Aranjuez.

Buses: (tel. 21 58 50) in the Zona Safón, 5min. from the city gate and tourist office (from Pl. Zocodóver, take C. Armas). The station is serviced by various bus companies. To: Madrid (Mon.-Sat. 6:30am-10pm, Sun. 8:30am-11:30pm, every ½hr., 1½hr., 540ptas); Cuenca (Mon.-Fri. 1 per day, 3hr., 1235ptas); Ciudad Real, for transfer to Almagro (Mon.-Fri. 1 per day, 2hr., 930ptas—from Ciudad Real, catch the bus to Almagro, ½hr., 220ptas).

Public Transportation: Buses (100ptas). #5 and 6 stop to the right of the train station and directly outside the bus station, and go straight to Pl. Zocodóver. The stop in Pl. Zocodóver is on C. Comercio.

Taxis: Call 22 16 98 to summon one. Taxis stands at Cuesta Carlos V (tel. 22 23 96), Po. de la Vega (tel. 22 16 96), and the bus station (tel. 22 16 99).

Car Rental: Avis, Po. Miradero (tel. 21 45 35), in an underground mall (Centro Comercial Miradero) downhill from Pl. Zocodóver. Open Mon.-Fri. 9:30am-1:30pm and 5-8pm, Sat. 9:30am-1:30pm.

Luggage Storage: at the train and bus stations, 300ptas per day. Open 6am-11pm.

Laundromat: Juan Pascual, C. Bolivia, 2 (tel. 22 16 03). Wash and dry 1325ptas per 5kg load. Open Mon.-Fri. 9am-1:30pm and 4-8pm.

Red Cross: tel. 22 29 00.

Medical Services: Hospital Virgen de la Salud (tel. 26 92 00), on Avenida de Barber, toward Avila highway.

Emergency: tel. 091.

Police: Municipal, Ayuntamiento, 1 (tel. 21 34 00).

ACCOMMODATIONS AND CAMPING

Toledo is chock-full of accommodations, but finding a bed during the summer, especially on weekends, can be a hassle. The tourist office provides a complete and invaluable list of hotels, *hostales,* and *pensiones,* with an address, price, and capacity for each establishment. If the time-honored go-into-the-first-*hostal*-you-see method fails you, check the cheapest *pensiones,* which don't accept phone reservations (any one-star *pensión* is a good bet).

Residencia Juvenil "San Servando" (HI), Castillo San Servando (tel. 22 45 54), uphill from the train station (15min.). Cross the street from the station, then (facing the station) walk right. Take the first right up the hill for a steep walk. A 14th-century castle. Pool, comfy TV room, and modern bathrooms. 96 rooms, each with 3 bunk beds, many with views. No toilet paper. Anyone returning alone at night should take a cab. Curfew around 11:50pm. Reserve ahead. Reception open 7:50am-11:50pm. Hot water 8:30-9:30am and 8-10pm. 775ptas, over 26 950ptas.

Pensión Descalzos, C. Descalzos, 30 (tel. 22 28 88), down the steps off Po. San Cristóbal or down the Bajada Descalzos, in the southwest corner of town. One of the few places not near the cathedral or the Alcázar. Close to the Casa del Greco and Iglesia Santo Tomé. Luxe amenities include soft toilet paper, liquid soap, and truly hot showers. Half the 14 rooms have a dramatic view of San Martín's Bridge. Rooms with bath also have music and TV. Singles 1875ptas. Doubles 3000ptas, with bath 5000ptas. Triples 6800ptas. Jan.-March 17: 1500ptas; 2500ptas; 4000ptas; 5600ptas. Continental breakfast 150ptas. Heartier breakfasts 300-500ptas. IVA not included. Visa, MC accepted.

Hostal Las Armas, C. Armas, 7 (tel. 22 16 68), just off the low end of Pl. Zocodóver. This 200-year-old house, with low ceilings, narrow twisty steps, impossible angles, and flowering patio, is like an Escher print—or a mini Toledo. The 19 rooms tend to be small and crepuscular, and those on the street can be noisy at night. Stained, faded wallpaper. Curfew 1am. Singles 1900ptas. Doubles 3000ptas. Triples 4200ptas. Prices don't include IVA. Open April-Oct.

Segovia, C. Recoletos, 2 (tel. 21 11 24), on a tiny, narrow street off C. Armas. Nine large rooms with religious theme. Cool in summer; portable heating units in winter. No singles. Doubles 1900ptas. Triples 2700ptas. Showers 200ptas.

Hostal Residencia Labrador, C. Juan Labrador, 16 (tel. 22 26 20). From Pl. Zocodóver take C. Barrio Rey. The three floors of hotel-like whitewashed rooms are rarely filled. Singles 1600ptas, with shower 2000ptas. Doubles 2300ptas, with shower 3000ptas, with bath 3200ptas. Triples with shower 3800ptas, with bath 4500ptas. Quads with bath 5500ptas. Prices don't include IVA.

Pensión Lumbreras, C. Juan Labrador, 9 (tel. 22 15 71), 2 bl. from Pl. Zocodóver, near Hostal-Residencia Labrador. Tired beds in unexceptional rooms with tourist posters. Some rooms have a view of the Toledo skyline. Singles 1400ptas. Doubles 2225ptas. One ample triple 3600ptas. Quads 4400ptas. Breakfast 200ptas.

Pensión Nuncio Viejo, C. Nuncio Viejo, 19 (tel. 22 81 78), on a street which leads off of the cathedral. Only six rooms, so you'll feel like a member of the family—like it or not. Rooms are mediocre (some don't have sinks), but your new mom is a great cook. No hot water. Singles 1400ptas. Doubles 2800ptas. Breakfast 150ptas. Lunch and dinner 500ptas each.

Camping: Camping El Greco (tel. 22 00 90), 1½km from town on the road away from Madrid (C-401), easily reached by bus #7 (from Pl. Zocodóver), which stops just up the hill and to the left. Wooded and shady 1st class site between the Tajo and an olive grove. 450ptas per person, per tent, and per car. **Circo Romano,** Av. Carlos III, 19 (tel. 22 04 42). 2nd class site. Closer but noisier, dirtier, and often in disrepair. 450ptas per person, per tent, and per car.

FOOD

As the lost tribes of Israel were blessed in their hour of need with manna from the heavens, so Toledo is blessed with a bounteous crop of restaurants, bars, and cafés (not to mention a McDonald's). It would be impossible to swing a dead cat in this city without its whiskers chancing upon a *típico* eatery of one sort or another. Restaurants catering to tourists can be a bit pricey (*menús* hover between 1200 and 1500ptas), but supply well-prepared regional specialties such as *perdiz* (fowl), *cuchifritos* (a melange of sheep, eggs, tomato, and white wine), *venado* (venison), and *carcamusas* (mystery dish).

Groceries: SPAR, C. Sixto Ramón Porro, 5, opposite the rear southeast corner of the cathedral. Open Mon.-Fri. 9am-3pm and 5-9pm, Sat. 9am-3pm. Also across from the train station. **Frutería-Pan,** C. Real Arrabal, inside the Puertas de Bisagra. Fresh fruit, basics, and water. Open same hours as SPAR. **Morning Market:** Wed.-Mon. 8:30am-2pm in the Pl. Mayor, behind the cathedral; Tues. on Po. del Carmen, across from the train station. Cheap clothing and food.

Restaurante La Cubana, Po. Rosa, 2 (tel. 22 00 88), across the river in front of Puente Viejo de Alcántara, down the road from the youth hostel. Wooded, tavern-like restaurant and outdoor *terraza* with overhanging grapevines. *Gazpacho* (390ptas) and *pollo al ajillo* (garlic chicken, 725ptas). Other dishes significantly more expensive. Open 1-4pm and 8-11pm, Fri.-Sat. until midnight.

Cafetería Fuensalida-Manila, Pl. Conde, 2 (tel. 22 20 88), in the southwest corner of town. A brick-walled, cavernous establishment underneath the Fuensalida Palace. Many salads around 500ptas. Open 8am-11pm.

SIGHTS

Toledo has a fabulous collection of museums, churches, synagogues, and mosques, as well as some that are less impressive (in the Museum of Miniatures, see El Greco's "View and Map of Toledo"—painted on a grain of rice). Within the city's fortified walls, attributed to the 7th-century King Wamba, Toledo's major sights and attractions form a belt around its fat middle. An east to west tour, beginning in Pl. Zocodóver, is mostly downhill.

El Alcázar

South and uphill from Pl. Zocodóver is the **Alcázar,** Toledo's most formidable landmark. Little remains of the original 13th-century structure; the building was largely reduced to rubble during the Civil War, as besieged Fascist troops held out against acute Republican bombardment. Posted in 19 different languages is the actual father-son telephone drama of the Moscardós: when the Republicans attacked the Alcázar, they ordered Colonel Moscardó, the man in charge, to surrender or lose his son. You can also visit the dark, windowless refuge where the five or six hundred civilians hid during the siege. The rooms above ground are now a nationalistic military museum, dedicated to the Spanish foot soldier. (Open Tues.-Sun. 9:30am-1:30pm and 4-6:30pm; winter until 5:30pm. Admission 125ptas.)

La Catedral

To the west, the grandiose **catedral,** with five naves, delicate stained glass, and endless ostentation throughout, soars from the city center. Seat of the Primate of Spain, this opulent cathedral contains an embarrassment of riches. Noteworthy pieces are the 14th-century Gothic **Virgen Blanca** (White Virgin) by the entrance and, above all, Narciso Tomés' **Transparente** (1732), a fantastically flamboyant work of the Spanish Baroque. Like Bernini's *Sta. Teresa,* this hybrid of architecture, sculpture, and painting uses much natural light. In the **Capilla Mayor** the enormous Gothic altarpiece stretches to the ceiling, covered with whimsical carved decorations. Beneath the dome is the **Capilla Mozárabe,** the only venue where the ancient Visigoth mass (in Mozarabic) is still held. The **tesoro** flaunts the Church's worldly accoutrements, including a 400-pound 16th-century gold monstrance lugged through the streets in the annual Corpus Christi procession. The **Sacristía** hoards El Grecos and two Van Dycks. In the **Sala Capitular** (chapter house), hang portraits of every archbishop of Toledo. The chains on the outside of the cathedral are from Ronda, where Christian slaves were forced to carry heavy sacks of water up 365 steps into a Moorish castle. (Cathedral open Mon.-Sat. 10:30am-1pm and 3:30-7pm, Sun. 10:30am-1:30pm and 4-7pm; Sept.-June Mon.-Sat. 10:30am-1pm and 3:30-7:30pm, Sun. 10:30-1:30pm and 4-6pm. Admission to the Sala Capitular, Capilla del Rey, tesoro, and Sacristía 350ptas.)

El Greco

Greek painter Domenico Theotocopuli (a.k.a. El Greco) lived most of his life in Toledo, churning out eerie canvases and gloomy portraits of sallow, spindly saints by the hundreds. Many of his works are displayed at various locales throughout town; the majority of his masterpieces, however, have long since been carted off to the Prado and elsewhere. Really big El Greco fans will want to visit the **Casa del Greco** (House of El Greco), at C. Levi, 3, downhill from the *Ayuntamiento* (he never actually lived here, so don't look forward to genuine bedroom slippers or anything). The rather poorly arranged museum has a copy of the *Vista y mapa de Toledo* (View and Map of Toledo) and several portraits of saints. (Open Mon.-Sat. 10am-2pm and 4-6pm, Sun. 10am-2pm. Admission 200ptas, EU citizens and students with ISIC free.) Up the hill a bit, the **Iglesia de San Tomé** houses El Greco's amazing and lugubrious *El entierro del Conde de Orgaz* (The Burial of Count Orgaz), as well as an interesting Mudejar apse. (Open Tues.-Sat. 10am-1:45pm and 3:30-6:45pm, Sun. 10am-1:45pm; off-season Tues.-Sat. 10am-1:45pm and 3:30-5:45pm, Sun. 10am-1:45pm. Admission 200ptas.)

Elsewhere

Toledo fell to Alfonso VI in 1085; thereafter followed a brilliant flowering of Jewish culture. Two synagogues, both in the **Judería** on the west side, are all that remain of what was once Spain's largest Jewish community. Samuel Halevi, treasurer to Pedro el Cruel, built the **Sinagoga del Tránsito** (1366), a simple building with wonderful Mudejar plasterwork and an *artesonado* (coffered) ceiling. Inside, the **Museo Sefardí** is stuffed with manuscripts, lids of sarcophagi, inscriptions, and amulets. (Open Tues.-Sat. 10am-2pm and 4-6pm, Sun. 10am-2pm. Admission 200ptas.) **Sinagoga de Santa María la Blanca** (1180), down the street, was the city's principal synagogue, but was later converted to a church. Now the mosque-like building makes a calm antidote to the excess of the cathedral. (Open 10am-2pm and 3:30-7pm; off-season until 6pm. Admission 200ptas.)

At the far western bulge of the city, with views of surrounding hills and the Río Tajo, stands the Franciscan **Iglesia de San Juan de los Reyes,** commissioned by Isabel and Fernando to commemorate their victory over the Portuguese in the 1476 Battle of Toro. The Plateresque monastery is a stunning mixture of Gothic and Mudejar architecture, which contrasts with the purely Gothic, light-filled cloister where Fernando and Isabel's initials are carved into the *artesonado* ceiling. The Catholic monarchs had planned the church as their burial place, but later changed their minds. (Open 10am-1:45pm and 3:30-6:45pm; off-season until 5:45pm. Admission 200ptas.)

Less touristed are the remnants of the city's Islamic past, near the Puerta del Sol off C. Real de Arrabal. Both a Muslim and a Christian house of worship at different points in its life, the striking **Mezquita del Cristo de la Luz** is the only surviving building in Toledo built before the Christian *Reconquista.* Constructed in the 10th century, its columns support arches inspired by the mosque at Córdoba. The Emirate was also responsible for the **hammams** (baths) on C. Angel.

Outside handsome Puerta Nueva de Bisagra on the road to Madrid is the 16th-century **Hospital Tavera.** Constructed under the auspices of the Cardenal de Tavera—who is buried here in a mausoleum— the building is now a private museum with five El Grecos and some Titians. The left-hand part was once the swish home of the Dukes of Lerma; a portrait of the last one (executed in the Civil War) eyes the gift shop. (Open 10:30am-1:30pm and 3:30-6pm. Admission 600ptas.)

One of the finest and least visited museums is the **Museo de Santa Cruz,** M. Cervantes, 3 (tel. 22 14 02), off Pl. Zocodóver. The huge, 15th-century Flemish *Astrolabio* tapestry of the zodiac pleases practicing astrologers. The well-preserved patio is littered with sarcophagi lids and fragments of carved stone. Down below, the basement collects the remains from archaeological digs throughout Toledo province, including elephant tusks. (Open Tues.-Sat. 10am-6:30pm, Sun. 10am-2pm, Mon. 10am-2pm and 4:30-6:30pm. Admission 200ptas, students free.)

Toledo was the seat of Visigothic rule and culture for three centuries prior to the Muslim invasion of 711. The **Museo de los Concilios y de la Cultura Visigótica** (tel. 22 78 72) on C. San Clemente, 4, is set in a 13th-century Mudejar church; the exhibits can't possibly compete with the surrounding architecture and frescoes. Delicious votive crowns of the Visigoths thrill lovers of finery. (Open Tues.-Sat. 10am-2pm and 4-6:30pm, Sun. 10am-2pm. Admission 200ptas, includes **Museo del Taller del Moro,** featuring carved woodwork and *azulejos,* near Iglesia de Santo Tomé on C. Bulas.) Nearby **Museo de Arte Contemporáneo,** C. Bulas, 15 (tel. 22 78 71), has a decent collection of contemporary Spanish art, including some good paintings by Berruete and Arredondo. (Open Tues.-Sat. 10am-2pm and 4-6:30pm, Sun. 10am-2pm. Admission 200ptas, students free.)

ENTERTAINMENT

The best area for the city's trademark gold-and-black damascene trinkets is C. San Juan de Dios, by the Iglesia de Santo Tomé. The owners of the small shops lining this street are aggressive, but willing to haggle. Quality varies. Since most nightspots cater to tourists, local nightlife tends to wander down side streets and get lost.

Calle de Santa Fe, east of Pl. Zocodóver, through the arch. Congregations of young people scarf *tapas* and gulp beer along this street.
Calle de la Sillería, west of Pl. Zocodóver. Another popular area for hedonizers.
Calle de los Alfileritos, the continuation of C. Sillería, both twenty-something crowds. Upscale bars and clubs.

Calle de la Sinagoga, north of the cathedral. Some adolescent nightlife here. Bowling and beer at the **Pub-Bolera.**

Zaida, in the Centro Comercial Miradero, downhill on C. Armas from Pl. Zocodóver. A perennial hotspot with dancing.

Corpus Christi, celebrated the eighth Sunday after Easter, is an excuse to feast. Looking like they just stepped out of an El Greco, citizens parade through the streets alongside the cathedral's weighty gold monstrance. In the middle of August, the **Fiestas de Agosto** honor the Virgen del Sagrario.

■ NEAR TOLEDO

Take care to plan around inconvenient bus departure times so you don't end up spending a night where you only wanted to stay several hours. For greater flexibility, rent a car and use Toledo as a base for excursions into this region.

Cervantes freaks come to La Mancha to follow his footsteps and those of his most famous creations, Don Quijote and the faithful Sancho Panza. Cervantes met and married Catalina de Palacios in the main church in **Esquivias** in 1584. Legend has it that he began writing his masterpiece while imprisoned in the Cueva del Medrano, in the town of **Argamasilla de Alba.** It was in **El Toboso,** 100km southeast of Toledo, that Quijote fell nobly in love with Dulcinea. A dementia worthy of the Don himself has led to the establishment of a house, the **Museo de Amor,** C. José Antonio (tel. 19 72 88), which pretends to mark the spot where Quijote first glimpsed Dulcinea. Inside are just a bunch of old housewares. (Open Tues.-Sun. 10am-2pm and 4-6:30pm. Admission 100ptas.) El Toboso is also home to the **Centro Cervantino,** which displays a fine collection of Cervantes ephemera, including translations of *Don Quixote* into 30 different languages.

A hop, skip, and a jump to the south of Toledo is the small but fierce **San Martín de Montalbán,** home to an amazing castle whose origins are shrouded in mystery and intrigue. The castle stands poised on an enormous pile of gray granite rocks, leaning out over an abysmal gorge of the River Torión. It was first a Visigoth fortress, then Arab, and later an enclave of the creepy and cabalistic Knights Templar (of *Foucault's Pendulum* fame). Legend has it that somewhere inside its ample walls lies a cache of buried treasure...

Of all Manchegan villages, tiny **Consuegra** has perhaps the most raw material for an evocation of Quijote's world. The **castle,** called the "Crestería Manchega" by locals, was a Roman, then Arab, then Christian fortress. El Cid's only son, Diego, died in the stable; you can visit his lavish tomb, near the Ayuntamiento. The castle keeps erratic hours, but the view of the surrounding plains justifies a climb anytime. Also within its diminutive circumference, Consuegra has a palace, a Franciscan convent, a Carmelite monastery, and more. Learn about it all in the **Museo de Consuegra** (tel. 48 01 85), next to the Ayuntamiento. (Hours not fixed. Admission 100ptas.) Consuegra's **post office** is at C. Florinda, 5, in the town center. (Open Mon.-Fri. 9am-2pm; off-season Mon.-Fri. 9am-2pm, Sat. 9am-1pm.) In case of **medical emergency,** dial 48 13 12. The municipal **police** station is at Pl. España, 1 (tel. 48 10 05 or 48 09 11).

Consuegra is an easy daytrip from Toledo. Samar **buses** (tel. 22 39 15) depart from Toledo's Zona Safón, just across the Puente de Azarquiel near the train station (10 per day, 510ptas). Returning to Toledo, buses take off from C. Castilla de la Mancha (7 per day). Purchase tickets from the driver when returning from Consuegra; when coming from Toledo, purchase them at the bus ticket office. Alcázar de San Juan is the primary junction for southbound trains from Madrid.

ALMAGRO

With a charming Plaza Mayor, blinding white-washed walls, and a collection of once-great churches now sinking gracefully into ruin, Almagro (pop. 8000) is one of those picturesque little towns you came to Spain to see. Although a famed, annual theater festival fills the place to overflowing during the final three weeks of July, foreign tourism during the rest of the year is confined mainly to Americans on package deals (as evidenced by the presence of three big, fancy hotels and a scarcity of budget establishments). Almagro is perfect for a daytrip (unless you come during the festival), but not the most accessible of destinations for the budget traveler—3hr. from Madrid and connected to basically nowhere else, bus and train schedules are inconvenient.

In the 13th century, tiny Almagro became the seat of the vast and powerful **Orden de Calatrava,** the oldest of the fraternities of monks-turned-soldiers that fueled the Reconquista. Built in 1519, the **Convento de la Asunción de Calatrava** attests to the order's immense power, wealth, and cabalistic machinations. (Recently closed for restoration, new hours not yet determined.)

The town's most striking attribute is the **Plaza Mayor,** whose unusual dark trim, streamlined balconies and windows, and squat proportions are due to German influence transmitted by the Fuggers, Emperor Carlos V's bankers, who portfolio-managed in Almagro. In Plaza Mayor stands the amazing **Corral de Comedias,** an open-air multilevel theater, one of only two left from the Golden Age of Spanish drama. It was here that Lope de Vega and Cervantes, competitors in theater as in all else, put on their shows in the second half of the 16th century. When the theater was restored in the early 1950s, there was great discussion as to which of these masters to honor with the inaugural performance; a compromise was reached, and the Corral reopened on May 29, 1954 with Calderón de la Barca's "La Hidalga del Valle." (Corral open July-Aug. Tues.-Sat. 10am-2pm and 6-9pm, Sun. 10am-2pm; Sept.-June Tues.-Sat. 10am-2pm and 4-7pm, Sun. 10am-2pm. Admission 100ptas.)

Directly across the plaza from the Corral, and through the arches, the new **Museo del Teatro** acts out the story of Spanish drama, focusing on costume design, stage design and technology, other theatrical arts, original manuscripts, and scores for incidental music. (Open Mon.-Fri. 10am-2pm and 6-9pm, Sat. 11am-2pm and 6-9pm, Sun. 11am-2pm. Admission 225ptas, seniors 115ptas. Sun. free.) The large and decadent **Antigua Universidad,** C. Ronda de Santo Domingo (from Pl. Mayor, walk up C. San Agustín, turn left on C. Ronda de Santo Domingo), where 17th- and 18th-century tortured, artistic types wallowed in intellectual gloom, is now a municipal office building—ah, the vicissitudes of fate.

Every year from July 6-31, Spain's most prestigious theater companies and players from around the globe descend on the town for the **Festival Internacional de Teatro Clásico de Almagro.** Daily performances of the classics—about half by international playwrights and half by Spain's own (Lope de Vega, Tirso de Molina, Calderón de la Barca, et. al.)—take place at venues throughout Almagro, including the Corral de Comedias, the Hospital de San Juan de Dios, and the Claustro de los Domínicos. The **box office** is a few doors away from the Corral at Pl. Mayor, 22. (Tel. 86 07 17; open during the festival 10am-2pm and 6-11pm. For the more popular works, purchase tickets early. Shows at 10:45pm. Tickets around 1500ptas.) Also during the festival, there are daily concerts and folkloric dances in the Pl. Mayor (9pm, free), and a series of lectures on Spanish cultural theater. Now in its 18th year, the festival is immensely popular; reservations are a must during July.

Practical Information The **tourist office** (tel. 86 07 17) is at C. Mayor de Carnicerías, 5, just off the closed end of Pl. Mayor. Look for the "Encajes de Almagro" sign—nothing else indicates that you're in the right place. (Open Mon.-Sat. 10am-2pm and 5:30-9pm, Sun. 10am-2pm.) The **post office** (tel. 86 00 52) is a few steps down the same street at #16. (Open Mon.-Fri. 9am-2pm, Sat. 9am-1pm. Open for **telegrams** Mon.-Fri. 9am-3pm, Sat. 9am-1pm; or send one by phone tel. 22 20 26 Mon.-Fri. 9am-10pm, Sat. 9am-7pm.) The **postal code** is 13004. The **telephone code** is 926. In an **emergency,** call 091. The **police** (tel. 86 00 33) guard Almagro from a building on Pl. Mayor, only a truncheon-length from the post and tourist offices.

The blissfully air-conditioned **train station** is at the end of the verdant Po. de la Estación. To get from the station to Pl. Mayor, walk down Po. de la Estación, and take a left on C. Obispo Barbado, which leads immediately to Ronda de Calatrava. At the *ejido* (with statue) turn right on C. Madre de Dios, which turns into C. Feria and leads to the plaza (15min.). Trains run to Madrid Atocha (3 per day, 2¾hr., 1590ptas; change at Aranjuez for connections to Cuenca and Toledo). **Buses** (tel. 86 08 96) stop in the *ejido*. To get to Pl. Mayor, turn right on C. Madre de Dios and follow it until it becomes C. Feria (10min.). Buses leave from the brick building (combination restaurant/bus station) at the far end of the *ejido*. Purchase tickets on the bus. To: Madrid (3 per day, 2¾hr., 1600ptas); Ciudad Real, for connection to Toledo (3 per day, ½hr., 220ptas).

Accommodations and Food   Reserve a spot at the **Hospedería Municipal de Almagro** (tel./fax 88 20 87), in the same building as the Convento de Calatrava. (Singles, doubles, triples, and quads 1850ptas per person. 1250ptas per person for a spot in the 50-bed dormitory. Prices include breakfast. Lunch and dinner 850ptas each.) Clean, cool rooms surround a begonia-filled courtyard at **Fonda Peña,** C. Piñuela, 10. Take C. San Agustín from Pl. Mayor, turn right at the end of the plaza, and take another right at Iglesia San Bartolomé El Real. (Singles 1600ptas. Doubles 2300ptas.)

Pl. Mayor is filled with restaurants, most with pleasant *terrazas,* and *menús* around 1200ptas. Follow C. Mayor de Carnicerías out of the closed side of the plaza to Plazuela de Montañes, where you can dine dirt cheap at **Sala Velo,** Plazuela Montañés, 2 (tel. 88 28 92). *Bocadillos* 300ptas, salads 200-245ptas, big pizzas 600ptas.

■■■ CUENCA

The province of Cuenca includes three distinctive terrains: mountainous La Serranía, hilly and honey-producing La Alcarria, and arid La Mancha. Self-proclaimed "city of surprises," Cuenca (pop. 40,000) is in the center of it all. Lack of space, forcing the construction of buildings close together and upward, has generated a startling vertical landscape: a city which hangs over the clifftops. New Cuenca is the site of cheap accommodations and food, as well as most offices, businesses, and homes. But the old city remains the stronghold of Cuenca's charm, with its surprisingly vertiginous and narrow alleyways, and an impressive number of fabulous museums.

ORIENTATION AND PRACTICAL INFORMATION

From the RENFE (2min.) or bus (5min.) stations, turn left until you hit the first bus shelter to catch bus #1 or 2 to **Plaza Mayor** in the old city—it's the last stop (#1 every ½hr., #2 every hr., 75ptas). On foot to Plaza Mayor, walk left from the bus shelter along **C. Fermín Caballero,** which becomes C. Cervantes, and then C. José Cobo, and then continues through Pl. Hispanidad, before turning into **C. Carretería,** the town's main drag. From here, turn right on any street (C. Fray Luís de León is the most direct) and begin trudging upwards; it's a twisty and grueling walk (15-20min.) to the plaza and the old city.

   Tourist Office: González Palencia, 2 (tel. 17 88 08), in the new city near C. Carretería. This office is more concerned with official tourism issues than with your issues; they answer questions, so long as they're in Spanish. Open Mon.-Fri. 9am-2pm and 4:30-6:30pm, Sat. 10am-1pm. You'll do better at the **Municipal Tourist Office:** C. San Pedro, 6 (tel. 23 21 19), right next to the cathedral in Plaza Mayor. Brochures, maps, hiking and excursion routes, and lots of info about goings on about town. No English spoken. Open Tues.-Sat. 9am-2pm and 4-7pm, Sun.-Mon. 9am-2pm.
   Post Office: Parque de San Julián, 18 (tel. 22 40 16; **telegrams** 22 20 00). Open Mon.-Fri. 8am-9pm, Sat. 9am-7pm. Smaller branch with fewer services next door to the RENFE station. Open Mon.-Fri. 8am-3pm, Sat. 9am-2pm. **Postal Code:** 16000.

Telephones: C. Cervantes, 2. Open Mon.-Sat. 9:30am-1:30pm and 5-10pm. A/C. **Telephone Code:** 966.

Trains: Po. del Ferrocarril, in the new city (tel. 22 07 20). To: Madrid, Estación Atocha (8 per day, 2½-3hr., 1065ptas); Aranjuez (8 per day, 2-2½hr., 835ptas); Valencia (5 per day, 2¾-3¾hr., 1150ptas). To get to Toledo, transfer in Aranjuez; to get anywhere else, transfer in Madrid.

Buses: C. Fermín Caballero, s/n (tel. 22 11 84). Down the street from the train station; look for the orange canopy. To: Madrid (10 per day, 2½hr., 1215ptas); Toledo (Mon.-Fri. at 5:30am, 3hr., 1465ptas); Valencia (1 per day, 4½hr., 1645ptas); Barcelona (1-2 per day, 7hr., 3800ptas).

Taxis: Radio-Taxi Cuenca (tel. 23 18 73). 24-hr. service. Fare from RENFE station to Pl. Mayor: 600ptas.

Car Rental: Avis (tel. 22 51 39), 2km from the train station (away from the city center). Open Mon.-Fri. 9am-1pm and 3:30-7pm, Sat. 9am-1pm.

Luggage Storage: at the train station (300ptas per day) or bus station (150ptas per day).

Red Cross: Doctor Chirino, 4 (tel. 21 19 52), in the new city.

Pharmacy: Farmacia Castellano, C. Cervantes, 18 (tel. 21 23 37). Open Mon.-Fri. 9:30am-2pm and 4:30-7:30pm, Sat. 10am-2pm. List of late-night pharmacies in the window.

Emergency: tel. 091.

Police: C. Hermanos Valdés, 4 (tel. 21 21 47), within sight of the **Municipal Police,** C. Martínez Kleiser, 4 (tel. 22 48 59).

ACCOMMODATIONS

Lots of cheap, adequate rooms collect in the new city. Rooms on the hill, with spectacular views of the old town and gorge, exact a bit more money.

Pensión Cuenca, Av. República Argentina, 8 (tel. 21 25 74). Take Hurtado de Mendoza from the train or bus station. Completely redone last year, this two-star *pensión* is the most comfortable in its price range in the new city. Full of regular lodgers during the week who vacate on weekends. Some rooms could be better ventilated. TV lounge. Singles 1400ptas, with shower 1800ptas. Doubles 2300ptas, with shower 3500ptas. Prices don't include IVA.

Hostal-Residencia Posada de San José, C. Julián Romero, 4 (tel. 21 13 00; fax 23 03 65), just up the street from the cathedral. The cheapest lodging on the hill, this former 17th-century convent flaunts sunny terraces and views of the Puente de San Pablo. Cozy bar hosts literary *tertulias* (salons) every 2nd and last Fri. of the month (open to all, 6-10:30pm). Singles 2200ptas, with shower 4000ptas. Doubles 4000ptas, with shower 6600ptas, with bath 7800ptas. Triples 5500ptas, with bath 9200ptas. One quad with bath 11,000ptas. Nov.-April: 1900ptas; 3500ptas; 3400ptas; 6000ptas; 6800ptas; 4800ptas; 8300ptas; 9500ptas. Prices do not include IVA. Breakfast 425ptas. Reserve by phone or fax two or three weeks in advance. Visa, MC, AmEx accepted.

Pensión Central, C. Alonso Chirino, 9 (tel. 21 15 11), off C. Carretería. Clean rooms with wooden floors and comfortable beds. July-Sept.: Singles 1400ptas. Doubles 2400ptas. Bargain doubles without running water 2100ptas. Triples 3175ptas. Oct.-June: 1200ptas; 2200ptas; 1900ptas; 2975ptas. IVA not included. No breakfast. Lunch and dinner 850ptas each.

Pensión La Mota, Pl. Constitución, 7, 1st fl. (tel. 22 55 67), at the end of C. Carretería. Rooms similar to those at the Cuenca, but not quite as bright; all front on a quiet courtyard. Singles 1300ptas. Doubles 2400ptas. Showers 150ptas. Prices do not include IVA.

FOOD

Cuenca's inexpensive restaurants are mediocre. Budget eateries line **Calle Cervantes** and **Calle República Argentina.** A few places still dish out *zorajo* (lamb tripe) and *el morteruelo* (a pâté dish), rare regional specialties. Get psyched over *resoli*, a typical liqueur of coffee, sugar, orange peel, and eau-de-vie. The morning **market** is held in Pl. Carros, behind the post office. **Heladería Italiana** scoops out excellent and cheap ice cream (small 85ptas); there are two within a block of each other on C. Carretería.

Groceries: Supermercado Compre Bien, C. Fermín Caballero at C. Teruel. A 2-min. walk from either station. Open 9:30am-2pm and 5-8pm. **%Día,** Av. Castilla-La Mancha at the corner of Av. República Argentina. Discount supermarket. Open Mon.-Thurs. 9:30am-2pm and 5:30-8:30pm, Fri.-Sat. 9am-2:30pm and 5:30-9pm.

Mesón-Bar Tabanqueta, Pl. Trabuco, 13 (tel. 21 12 90), at the end of C. San Pedro coming from Pl. Mayor. The hidden entrance eludes crowds. *Ensalada manchega* means chunks of tomato, egg, and tuna with olives. Simply-prepared entrees (350-600ptas). Open daily 2:30pm-2:30am; winter closed Sun.-Mon.

Restaurante Cueva del Tío Serafín, in a cave across from Hoz de Huécar and Posada Huécar, with a lair-like interior to match. Entrees 500-900ptas, beers 250ptas. Open 7:30pm-3am.

Bar-Restaurante San Miguel, at the foot of the stairs leading down toward Río Júcar from Pl. Mayor opposite the cathedral; next to Iglesia de San Pablo. Views of the Júcar. Crepuscular and cramped inside, delightful terrace outside. *Tortillas* 300ptas. Fish and meat entrees 500-1500ptas. Open 11am-1am.

SIGHTS AND ENTERTAINMENT

The **ciudad vieja** (old city) dodders beneath covered arcades set back from the steep cliffs. The 18th-century **Ayuntamiento** is built into a Baroque arch at the plaza's southern end; the **catedral,** constructed under Alfonso VIII six years after he conquered Castile (1183), dominates the other side. Under the spell of the king's English wife, Eleanor of Aquitaine, architects built what would become the only Anglo-Norman Gothic cathedral in Spain. A Spanish Renaissance facade and tower were added in the 16th and 17th centuries, only to be torn down when deemed inappropriate. A 1724 fire cut short the latest attempt to build a front, leaving the current exterior incomplete and thus reminiscent of a Hollywood set. (Open daily 8:45am-2pm and 4-7pm; winter 8:45am-2pm and 4-6pm. Free.)

The **Museo del Tesoro** houses some late medieval psalters and a great deal of gold jewelry; more impressive is the **Sala Capitular** and its positively edible ceiling. (Open Tues.-Sun. 11am-2pm and 4-6pm. Admission 200ptas.)

Down C. Obispo, the **casas colgadas** (hanging houses)—possibly summer retreats for royalty—dangle over the riverbanks as precariously today as they did six centuries ago. In his memoirs, Surrealist filmmaker Buñuel recalls a pre-war visit to Cuenca in which he spied wheeling birds beneath his toilet seat in one of these houses. The footbridge 60m above the river affords a grand view of the old houses huddling high on the cliffs, the new city spreading into the green fields beyond, and the waters rushing below. Many good hiking trails etch the hill and stone cliffs opposite the old city and footbridge. The tourist office gives out trail maps. Bring food and sturdy shoes.

Inside one of the *casas* at Pl. Ciudad de Ronda, the award-winning **Museo de Arte Abstracto Español** displays important works by the wacky and internationally known "Abstract Generation" of Spanish painters. Artist Fernando Zóbel donated his own house to the project, which now hoards canvases by himself, Canogar, Tàpies, and Chillida. (Open Tues.-Fri. 11am-2pm and 4-6pm, Sat. 11am-2pm and 4-8pm, Sun. 11am-2pm. Admission 200ptas, students 100ptas.)

Nearby on C. Obispo Valero, the **Museo Arqueológico de Cuenca** has a wide range of Roman mosaics, ceramics, coins, and other finds from local excavations, including some excellent Visigoth jewelry. (Open Tues.-Sat. 10am-2pm and 4-7pm, Sun. 10am-2pm. Admission 200ptas, EU citizens free.) Perhaps the most beautiful of the museums along this short street is the **Museo Diocesano.** Exhibits are imaginatively displayed and include Juan de Borgoña's *retablo* from local Convento de San Pablo, many colossal Flemish tapestries, and two El Grecos: the *Oración del huerto* and *Cristo con la cruz.* (Open Mon.-Fri. 11am-2pm and 4-6pm, Sat. 11am-2pm and 4-8pm, Sun. 11am-2pm. Admission 200ptas.)

Walking along **Hoz del Júcar,** or preferably **Hoz del Huécar,** the two roads that surround Cuenca's old city, is lots of fun. The side of Hoz del Huécar opposite the *casas colgadas* affords the best views of the valley. To get there, dash across (carefully) the terrifying Puente de San Pablo, whose wooden beams are beginning to wobble disconcertingly.

Nightlife in new Cuenca is basically a bar scene which extends into the wee hours. Several bars with loud music and young, snazzily-dressed crowds line small **Calle Galíndez,** off C. Fray Luís de León. For nightclubs, just off Pl. Mayor across from the cathedral, take the winding street/staircase down toward the Río Júcar.

Cuenca rings with song during the **Festival de Música Sagrada.** This famous celebration, with Spanish and international groups, occurs the week before Holy Week.

■■■ GUADALAJARA

Long, long ago Guadalajara was the capital of an enormous Muslim domain, until Alfonso VI conquered the city in 1085. During the 15th and 16th centuries, Guadalajara—then known as the Athens of La Alcarria—gloried in a brilliant renaissance under the patronage of the Mendoza family. At the beginning of the 17th century, the fates began to frown: Guadalajara slid into decadence, and was the site of a cruel war between the Bourbon Felipe and the Archduke Carlos, both aspirants to the Spanish throne. In 1808 Guadalajara was occupied by the French, whose withdrawal at the end of the war left the city in a state of abject poverty which was later exacerbated by long battles during the Civil War. Since then, this provincial capital (pop. 65,000) has recuperated economically while retaining many of its antique graces. Although the outskirts are heavily industrialized and ugly, many central areas are quite lovely, especially the cool greenery of the **Parque de la Concordia** and the charming **Plaza de Santo Domingo.** Tree-lined **Calle San Roque** is closed to traffic and a tranquil spot for a drink or a stroll.

From the train station, buses #1, 2, 4, or 5 stop at various spots close to Pl. Santo Domingo or C. Mayor. Otherwise, turn left (facing away from the station) and walk down the Paseo de la Estación, over the river, and straight uphill; Po. Estación becomes C. Madrid, and then C. Miguel Fluiters, which runs into the **Plaza de los Caídos en la Guerra Civil,** recognizable by the big white cross.

At the far end from the cross is Guadalajara's most famous sight, the **Palacio de los Duques del Infantado,** built in 1480 by Flemish architect Juan Guas and considered the finest example of Gothic civil architecture. Somber, big-chinned Felipe II married his third of four wives, Elizabeth Valois, in the palace. A placard by the door reads, "Biblioteca Pública Provincial y Archivo Histórico Provincial," which are located inside. Also inside, the **Museo Provincial de Guadalajara** has a collection of largely anonymous paintings from the 15th-17th centuries. (Open Tues.-Sat. 10:30am-2pm and 4:15-7pm, Sun. 10:30am-2pm. Admission 100ptas, free with ISIC.)

Iglesia de San Nicolás el Real, in Pl. Jardinillo, is embellished with a magnificent Rococo altar. **Iglesia de San Ginés,** on C. Virgen del Amparo, has a Gothic pantheon, where Guadalajara's once-dominant Infantado and Mendoza families mingle in post-mortem subterranean harmony. The solitary **Panteón de La Duquesa** haunts a field above the town, on Po. Francisco Aritmendi by **Parque del San Roque.** To enter this 19th-century, Byzantine-style rotunda, ask the nuns at the *portería* reception of the adjacent Convento de San Francisco; the door is in the far corner of the yard opposite the locked gate. The **tombs of the duchess** and her family are in the cavernous space below. (Open 10am-12:30pm and 4-6pm. Admission 100ptas.)

Practical Information The **tourist office** (tel. 22 06 98), in the Ayuntamiento in Pl. Mayor where C. Miguel Fluiters turns into C. Mayor, floods visitors with colorful brochures about all things Guadalajarense. (Open Mon.-Fri. 10am-2pm and 4-6pm, Sat 10am-6pm, Sun 10am-3pm.) The **post office** is at C. Teniente Figueroa, 5 (tel. 21 14 93; open Mon.-Fri. 8am-9pm, Sat. 9am-7pm). The **telephone code** is 949.

Red Cross is at Avda. Venezuela, 1 (tel. 22 22 22). The police are on Av. del Ejército (tel. 21 51 11; in an emergency call 091 or 092). Taxis leave from the train station (tel. 22 82 38) and Pl. Santo Domingo (tel. 21 22 45).

The RENFE train station (tel. 21 28 50) is on C. Francisco Aritio. Frequent service to Madrid (cercanías 45min., 400ptas); Soria (regionales at 10:21am, 3:50pm, and 7:35pm pass through Sigüenza); and Avila. Buses leave every hour for Madrid (425ptas) from the Continental-Auto bus station, at C. 2 de Mayo, 1 (tel. 88 70 94).

Accommodations and Food Hostal Arroyo, C. Gonzalo Herran, 2 (tel. 21 11 23), on the corner of C. Teniente Figueroa. Rooms are small, but clean and cheap. (Singles 1300ptas. Doubles 2500ptas.) From Pl. Santo Domingo, walk diagonally through Parque de la Concordia to reach Pensión Galicia, C. San Roque, 16 (tel. 20 00 59), upstairs from a restaurant on a pleasant street lined with trees and cafés. Talk to the people in the restaurant to reserve a room. Comfy rooms with big beds and faux-oriental throw rugs. All rooms have baths. (Singles 2800ptas. Doubles 3800ptas.) AmEx accepted. In Hotel España, C. Teniente Figueroa, 3 (tel. 21 13 03), small beds squeal; but the rooms are large and clean, and some have nice views. (Singles 2500ptas, with shower 3300ptas, with bath 3500ptas. Doubles 3500ptas, with shower 4500ptas, with bath 5000ptas. Breakfast 350ptas.) Visa accepted.

The bars here are masters of budget cuisine. Terraza San Roque, bordering Parque de San Roque, is an ideal spot for an al fresco drink (beer 150ptas) accompanied by country music. Restaurante Tropik's, Av. de Barcelona, 8 (tel. 25 38 41), is a self-service joint with a weird plastic, tropical atmosphere (omelettes 500ptas, menú 900ptas). Minaya Restaurante, in Pl. Jaranillo, on C. Mayor between Pl. Mayor and Pl. Santo Domingo, has a sumptuous menú (1000ptas) and the usual run of entrees (500-800ptas). Visa, MC, AmEx accepted. Also try the bars along C. San Roque for cheap beers and peaceful surroundings. La Tertulia and El Paseo have outside terraces.

■■■ SIGÜENZA

Sleepy Sigüenza tumbles down a gentle slope halfway between Madrid and Zaragoza; its pink stone buildings cluster around a cathedral with the attitude of a hilltop citadel. Neither the frequent presence of trains nor the Civil War damage (now rectified) has tempered the wonderful harmony of Sigüenza's architecture; unlike many Spanish towns, Sigüenza has remained outwardly untouched by modernization and industrialization.

Work on the catedral began in the mid-12th century and continued until 1495; the building ranges through Romanesque, Mudejar, and Plateresque styles. Its most renowned possession is the 15th-century Tumba del Donzel, commissioned by Isabel la Católica in memory of a favorite page who died fighting the Muslims in Granada; the young man lies happily reading a book. Across the nave, with its curvy columns typical of the Baroque, is the Capilla Mayor, housing the tomb of Archbishop Bernardo of Toledo, the first bishop of Sigüenza. Three hundred and four stone heads, each supposedly a real-life portrait, jut out of the sacristy's elaborate Renaissance ceiling. The staring faces include pious bishops, uppity soldiers, and local women. Nearby is an El Greco Anunciación. Just off the cloister, one room is hung with Flemish tapestries and houses an assortment of documents from the cathedral archives, including a 13th-century codex. (Cathedral open 11am-1:30pm and 4-7pm. No entrance during services.)

Opposite the cathedral, the small Museo de Arte Antiguo exhibits medieval and early Modern religious works. The highlight is Ribera's Jesús despojado de sus vestiduras (Jesus Dispossessed of His Garments). Zurbarán's Inmaculada niña (1644), some 15th- and 16th-century illuminated manuscripts, and a variety of 16th-century retablos are also on display. (Open 11am-2pm and 5-7:30pm; Sept.-May 11am-2pm and 4-6:30pm. Admission 200ptas.) From the lovely Plaza Mayor, a cobblestoned street leads up towards the **castillo,** a reconstruction of a 12th-century castle (now a hotel—hence the "Parador de Turismo" signs all over town).

Practical Information Covering for *turismo,* the **Ayuntamiento,** Pl. Mayor, 1 (tel. 39 08 50), hands out **maps** and answers questions. The **post office** (tel. 39 08 44) is at Pl. Hilario Yabén, 4, in the building identified on the map as the Antigua Universidad. (Open Mon.-Fri. 9am-2pm, Sat. 9am-1pm.) The **telephone code** is 949. **Taxis** can be hailed at tel. 39 14 11. In Pl. Hilario Yabén near the post office is a %Día discount **supermarket.** The **Red Cross** (tel. 39 13 33) is on Ctra. Madrid. The **police** (tel. 39 01 95), on the Carretera de Alcolea-Aranda de Duero, can be reached at tel. 091 in an **emergency.**

The **RENFE station** is on C. Alfonso VI, s/n (tel. 39 14 94). To get from the train station to the cathedral, follow C. Alfonso VI up a steep hill (and a name change to C. Humilladero); take the first left onto C. Cardenal Mendoza. Sigüenza is on the Madrid-Zaragoza train line; about 15 trains per day head in either direction. To Madrid (1½-2hr., 850-1400ptas), ticket price and journey length vary depending on whether you take an express, regular, *rápido,* or intercity train.

Accommodations and Food Although you can "do" Sigüenza in a couple of hours, it's a pleasant town in which to loiter. Accommodations are plentiful. **Hostal Veneuzano,** C. San Roque, 2 (tel. 39 03 47), near the far end of the Alameda from the train station, has comfortable, well-lit rooms. (Singles 1800ptas. Doubles 2800ptas. Triples 3800ptas.) **Hostal El Motor,** Av. Juan Carlos, 1 (tel. 39 08 27; fax 39 00 07), beyond Pl. Hilario Yabén, has carpeted rooms with TVs, telephones, and full baths. (Singles 3000ptas. Doubles 5000ptas. Breakfast 300ptas. IVA not included. A/C. Visa, MC accepted.) There's no shortage of restaurants or cafeterias either; many cluster about Pl. Mayor. Hostal El Motor's restaurant has a tasty *menú* for 1100ptas.

Castilla y León

What this central region lacks in exuberant topography (beaches are to the south and east and mountains are to the north), it makes up for in architectural prominence, historical significance, and ego. In the High Middle Ages, this Christian kingdom emerged from obscurity to lead the battle charge against Islam. The nobility grew immensely wealthy as it seized and feudalized more and more land. Well before the famous union with Aragón in 1492, it was clear that Castilla had its act together. The concept of a unified Spain—under Castilian command—took root here, and *castellano* ("Spanish") became the dominant language throughout the nation. Wealth arrived in the 16th century, due to the region's incipient textile industry, its agricultural and fishing traditions, and New World successes. However, the feudalistic land structure which had allowed the nobility to accrue so much wealth also proved hostile to intensive industrial development. Castilla y León has not been as economically successful as its more techno-happy northeastern neighbors. But—there is always culture.

Imperious León (the provinces of León, Zamora, Salamanca, Valladolid, and Palencia) has not tired of asserting that it had 24 kings before Castilla even had laws. When Spain's provinces were reorganized in the 1970s, León was lumped with Castilla, to the chagrin of many *leoneses*. The vast rippled plateau of Castilla possesses its own landlocked beauty, rough and intense. The plateau is broken only by a few mountain ranges, of which the most striking is the Sierra de Guadarrama. This area of Castilla was historically known as Castilla La Vieja, counterpart to Castilla La Nueva to the south.

A combination of farmland, primeval woods rich in game, and acres of sheer wilderness, this region's landscape is studded with splendid cathedrals, sumptuous palaces, and well-defined urban personalities. The monuments—the majestic Gothic cathedrals of Burgos and León, the slender Romanesque belfries along the Camino de Santiago in León, the intricately chased sandstone of Salamanca, and the proud city walls of Avila—have emblazoned themselves as national as well as regional images.

Castilian gastronomy favors red meats and vegetables that can be grown in relatively cold climates, such as potatoes. Beef, ham, potatoes, sausage, carrots, and garlic stewed together is called *cocido castellano. Sopa castellana* is a soup made with garlic bread, ham, and eggs. Castilians get hyperbolically excited about their lamb dishes. "This is one of those moments, dear reader," gleams one lamb enthusiast, "in which heads should be bowed before one of the greatest majesties of traditional cookery [lamb] in Castilla y León." Need we say more?

■■■ SEGOVIA

The proud old city of Segovia (pop. 55,000) rises majestically above the Castilian countryside. Long, long ago two military roads crossed here, inspiring the Romans to invade and build a mint and an aqueduct. In the early 15th century, Juan II and Enrique IV, kings of the House of Trastámara, established courts here and littered the town with new monuments. All this wealth went to Segovia's head, and a few years later headstrong local nobles and merchants did what one should not do: mess with Carlos I. This Revolt of the Comuneros (1520) was similar to many contemporaneous and later struggles in which local powerholders resisted the monarch's centralizing efforts. The city subsequently fell into decline, until the Bourbons built the Palacio de La Granja nearby.

Today, in addition to the Roman aqueduct (currently under repair for structural decay), Segovia offers amazing churches and palaces, beautiful views, twisty alleyways, and buckets of kitsch. The city has an unusually high concentration of tourists, and correspondingly high prices (about a third more than Madrid) for food and accommodations.

ORIENTATION AND PRACTICAL INFORMATION

On the far side of the Sierra de Guadarrama, 88km northwest of Madrid, Segovia is close enough for a daytrip but warrants more; it's not possible to do justice to all the sights in and near Segovia in a lightning visit.

To get to **Plaza Mayor,** the city's *centro histórico* and site of the **tourist office,** take bus 1a, 2a, or 2b from the train station, 1a or 1b from the bus station (100ptas). It's also an easy 40-min. walk from the train station, 15min. from the bus station. From the train station, turn right out of the station and walk along Po. Obispo Quesada, which soon becomes Po. Conde de Sepúlveda. Continue on Sepúlveda, take the left-hand fork onto C. Ezequiel González, and turn right onto Av. Fernández Ladreda when you see the bus station. This avenue leads past Iglesia San Millán to **Plaza Azoguejo,** near the aqueduct. Take a sharp left and follow the street to the top of the hill and the Pl. Mayor. From the bus station, cross the road onto Av. Fernández Ladreda and follow the directions above.

The city is nearly impossible to navigate without a map. The old city, high up above the newer *barrios,* is vaguely triangular in shape, with the Alcázar at its northern tip and the Pl. Mayor dead center. Running between here and Pl. Azoguejo is the busy pedestrian thoroughfare, **Calle Isabel la Católica-Calle Juan Bravo-Calle Cervantes,** where everyone and her dog promenade. The other streets radiating from Pl. Mayor are **Calle Margués de Arco, Calle Escuderos, Calle 4 de Agosto, Calle Cronista Lecea,** and **Calle Infanta Isabel.**

Tourist Office: Pl. Mayor, 10 (tel. 43 03 28), in front of the bus stop, on the south side of the plaza. Complete information on accommodations, bus, train, and sights posted in the windows. Ask for the pamphlet listing all accommodations in Segovia, with prices, addresses, and phone numbers. Helpful multilingual staff. Open Mon.-Sat. 9:30am-2pm and 5-7pm, Sun. 10am-2pm and 5-7pm. **Regional Tourist Office,** Pl. Azoguejo (tel. 44 02 05), at the foot of the steps leading to the top of the aqueduct. Less crowded than the municipal office. Stagger out the door with a pile of glossy brochures on Castilla-León. Staff can help with reservations. Open June-Sept., Holy Week, and Christmas season 10am-2pm and 4-8pm; Nov.-May Sat. 10am-2pm and 4-8pm, Sun. and holidays 10am-2pm, Mon. 4-8pm.

Post Office: Pl. Dr. Laguna, 5 (tel. 43 16 11), up C. Lecea from Pl. Mayor. Open for stamps, Lista de Correos, and **telegrams** Mon.-Sat. 8am-9pm. Buy a hot chocolate for 40ptas from the vending machine in the lobby. **Postal code:** 40006.

Telephones: C. Juan Bravo, 6. Three deluxe booths in an air-conditioned office within the shopping mall. Also a **Telefónica** in Pl. de los Huertos; from Pl. Mayor, walk down C. Cronista Lecea. Open Mon.-Fri. 10am-1pm and 5-8:45pm, Sat. 10am-1:45pm. **Telephone Code:** 921.

Trains: Po. Obispo Quesada (tel. 42 07 74). Only one line: the Segovia-Madrid *regional.* To Madrid (9 per day, 6 per day on Sun., 2hr., 600ptas). The Villalba stop halfway along the line (280ptas) is the transfer spot for El Escorial, Avila, and León, with transfer to Salamanca. Bus is often the better bet.

Buses: Estacionamiento Municipal de Autobuses, Po. Ezequile González, 10 (tel. 42 77 25), on Po. Conde de Sepúlveda at Av. Fernández Ladreda. To: Madrid (every hr. 6am-10pm, 1¾hr., 715ptas); Avila (4 per day, Sat.-Sun. 1 per day, 1hr., 520ptas); Salamanca (Mon.-Fri. 4 per day, Sat. 2 per day, 3hr., 1350ptas); Valladolid (2-4 per day, 2½hr., 920ptas); Barcelona (1 per day, 10½hr., 5375ptas); La Granja (6-10 per day, 20min., 115ptas).

Public Transportation: Transportes Urbanos de Segovia, Pl. Mayor, 8 (tel. 43 02 28). Buses 100ptas.

Taxis: Pl. Mayor (tel. 43 66 80), Pl. Oriental (tel. 42 02 58), and C. Fernández Ladreda (tel. 43 66 81). Taxis also pull up outside the train and bus stations. **Radio Taxi** (tel. 44 50 00).

Car Rental: Avis, C. José Zorrilla, 123 (tel. 42 25 84 or 42 20 32), 2 bl. from the train station.

Luggage Storage: Lockers at the **train station** (500ptas). Open 5:45am-11:30pm.
Alcoholics Anonymous: tel. 43 32 69.
Red Cross: C. Arias Dávila, 3 (tel. 43 03 11).
Medical Services: Hospital Policlínico, C. San Agustín, 13 (tel. 41 92 75). **Hospital General,** Carretería de Soria, s/n (tel. 41 90 00). Both offer emergency service. **Ambulance:** C. Santo Tomás, 7 (tel. 41 93 30).
Emergency: tel. 091 or 092.
Police: Municipal, C. Guadarrama (tel. 43 12 12). **Comisaría,** C. Avila (tel. 42 51 61).

ACCOMMODATIONS AND CAMPING

During the summer finding a *hostal* room may be nightmarish; reservations are vital. The regional tourist office helps with reservations and hands out a list of accommodations. Be prepared to pay more than 2000ptas for a decent single.

Hostal Juan Bravo, C. Juan Bravo, 12, 2nd fl. (tel. 43 55 21), right on the main thoroughfare in the old town, near Iglesia de San Martín. Bright, carpeted rooms with schmaltzy pictures are cool in summer. Some offer a view of the cathedral. A few baths are downright huge. Doubles 3200ptas, with bath 4100ptas. Triples 4400ptas, with bath 5500ptas. For quads and singles prices negotiable. Take 300ptas off for low-season. IVA not included. Visa accepted.

Hostal-Residencia Plaza, C. Cronista Lecea, 11 (tel. 46 03 03, 46 03 05, or 46 03 06). Polished brass and tasteful pictures in the public areas. Plain bedrooms with phones and (institutional) carpeting. Singles 2900ptas, with shower 4100ptas, with bath 4500ptas. Doubles 3800ptas, with shower 4500ptas, with bath 4900ptas. Nov.-Feb.: 2600ptas; 3800ptas; 4100ptas; 3400ptas; 4100ptas; 4500ptas. Prices sometimes lower than listed. Showers 350ptas. Breakfast 300ptas. Prices do not include IVA. Visa, MC accepted.

Hostal Sol Cristina, C. Obispo Quesada, 40 (tel. 42 75 13), opposite the train station. Convenient and clean. Don't expect a warm welcome or peace and quiet (the *hostal* is connected to a bar-restaurant). Doubles are brighter than singles; private baths are nicer than communal ones. Singles 2500ptas. Doubles 3600ptas, with bath 4800ptas. Quads with bath 7500ptas. Showers 350ptas. Breakfast 250ptas. Lunch or dinner 950ptas.

Pensión Aragón, Pl. Mayor, 4, 2nd fl. (tel. 43 35 27). Terrific location and cheap, but it's tough livin' baby: no sink, window, or key (the proprietor thinks it's safer with him), and very poor lighting. Throw rugs are a little luxury—but they're made of plastic. No smoking. Singles 1200ptas. Doubles 1800ptas. Triples 2300ptas. Quads 3000ptas. Hot showers 200ptas, freezing ones 100ptas.

Camping: Camping Acueducto, Ctra. Nacional, 601, km 112 (tel. 42 50 00), 2km from Segovia toward La Granja. 2nd-class site in the shadow of the Sierra de Guadarrama. 380ptas per person and per tent, children 340ptas. No hot water. Open April-Sept.

FOOD

Abundant restaurants, but watch out for high prices and unexceptional food. Steer clear of Pl. Mayor, Pl. Azoguejo, and all signs that simulate ancient, worn parchment. Segovia is famed for sublimely tender roast suckling pig (*cochinillo*) and lamb.

Segovia's morning **market,** C. Colón, off C. Cronista Lecea, displays produce, cheap clothing, and miscellaneous junk. **Fruit and vegetable stands** crowd C. Juan Bravo and its neighbors.

Groceries: Alimentación Cerezo, C. Fernández Ladreda, near Pl. Azoguejo. Open Mon.-Fri. 10am-2pm and 5-8pm. **% Día,** at C. Fernández Jimenez, 32, off C. Fernández Ladreda, and at Conde Sepúlveda, is a discount supermarket on the way from the train station. Both open Mon.-Thurs. 9:30am-2pm and 5:30-8pm, Fri.-Sat. 9am-2:30pm and 5:30-9pm. **Supermercado Super EU,** right across from the train station. Open Mon.-Fri. 9:15am-2pm and 5:30-8:30pm, Sat. 9:15am-2pm.

Restaurante-Mesón Alejandro, C. Carbitrería, the first left off C. Cronista Lecea, which is off Pl. Mayor. At the end of the (very short) street. Excellent and cheap. Delicious *paella* 590ptas. A good *menú del día* for 900ptas. Entrees 500-900ptas. Meats 900-1600ptas.

Bar-Mesón Cueva de San Esteban, C. Valdelaguila, 15, off the top of Pl. San Estéban, which is reached by C. Escuderos. Picturesque location. Stone and mortar walls, wooden pygmy footstools for seats, and reasonable *menú* (800ptas). Entrees 400ptas and up.

Restaurante-Bar Lázaro, C. Infanta Isabel, off Pl. Mayor. Not the most pleasant decor, but the food is good and there's a fish tank. *Menú* 1000ptas. Bounteous *platos combinados,* with wine or beer, 800ptas. Visa, MC accepted.

Restaurante La Oficina, C. Cronista Lecea, 10 (tel. 43 16 43), off Pl. Mayor. Founded in 1893. Carefully "typical" decor of blue *azulejos* and pictures of women in black *mantillas.* Caters to transient money-spenders. Ask specifically for the complete *menú* (1270ptas, not including wine). House specialty: *cochinillo asado* for three (3500ptas). Salads and vegetable dishes 550-1000ptas. Meat and fish entrees 1000-2000ptas. Menu in English. Open 12:30-4:30pm and 7-11:30pm. Visa, AmEx, DC accepted.

Bar El Túnel, C. Santa Columba, 3, off Pl. Azoquejo and up the stone steps overlooking the aqueduct. Add your key chain to the hundreds above the bar. Savory *platos combinados,* all with red meat, under 1000ptas. Meals served Mon.-Sat. 11am-3:30pm and 7-10:30pm.

SIGHTS

The Alcázar

The Alcázar, an archetypal late-medieval castle, juts audaciously into space at the far northern end of the old quarter. Much of its dramatic effect actually derives from an inspired reconstruction after a devastating fire in 1862. The original 11th-century fortress was gussied up by Alfonso X, becoming ever more sumptuous under successive monarchs. Isabel was crowned Queen of Castile in the Alcázar in 1474, and Felipe II married his fourth wife, Ana of Austria, here. To round off its castle duties, the Alcázar served as a prison in later centuries.

Inside, the castle is filled with trappings from its royal and bloody past: tapestries, knights in armor, thrones, cannons, and impressive sculpture and paintings. The walls of the **Sala de Reyes** are adorned with wood and gold inlay sculptures of the monarchs of Asturias, Castile, and León, and portraits of Felipe II, the Bourbon Isabel, and Ana of Austria. In the **Sala de Solio** (throne room), the inscription above the thrones "tanto monta, monta tanto" can be roughly translated "[She] mounts, as does [he]." This signifies not what your dirty mind suggests, but rather Fernando and Isabel's equal authority as sovereigns. The **Sala de Armas** holds a veritable arsenal of medieval weaponry. The **chapel** contains a beautiful 16th-century *retablo mayor* depicting scenes from the New Testament.

Climb 150 steps up a narrow, winding staircase littered with panting tourists to the top of the **torre,** where you will be rewarded with a marvelous view of Segovia and the surrounding plain. Prince Pedro, son of King Enrique IV, slipped from his nurse's arms on the balcony and fell over the ramparts to his bloody death; out of desperation the nurse leapt after him and ended her own life. (Alcázar tel. 43 01 76; open 10am-7pm; Oct.-March 10am-6pm. Admission 350ptas, seniors 250ptas.)

The Cathedral

Commissioned by Carlos I in 1525, Segovia's huge and stately cathedral towers gothically over Pl. Mayor, its spires reaching heavenward in an eternal reminder of the transience of earthly delights. With hundreds of new sights, sounds, and tactile sensations, the cathedral is more exciting than a modern-day exploratorium. A multicolored, marble-tiled **coro** is unexpectedly art deco in appearance. Lovely **chapels,** each with a cunning crucifix or saint, and some with fine frescoes, surround the cathedral's inner walls. The **museum** (tel. 43 53 25) holds an excellent collection, including Coello's 16th-century painting *La duda de Santo Tomás,* an excellent reproduction of Ribera's erotic *La caridad romana,* a remarkable Flemish triptych from the 16th century, and a series of Francisco de Solis' 17th-century paintings on marble depicting the Passion of Christ. The **Sala Capitular,** hung with well-preserved 17th-century tapestries, also displays a silver and gold chariot, and various crucifixes, chalices, and candelabras. (All open 9am-7pm; Oct.-March Mon.-Fri. 9:30am-1pm and 3-6pm, Sat. 9:30am-6pm. Cathedral free; admission to museum, cloister, and *Sala Capitular* 200ptas.)

The Aqueduct and Little Churches

The Romans built Segovia's elegant **Acueducto Romano** around 50 BC to pipe in water from the Río Frío, 18km away. Supported by 128 pillars that span 813m, the two tiers of 163 arches are constructed of great blocks of granite—without any mortar. Amazingly, the Romans' feat of engineering, restored by the Catholic Monarchs in the 15th century, was in use until just seven years ago. The most impressive view of the aqueduct is from Pl. Azoguejo (in front and to the right), where the grand structure reaches its maximum height of 28.9m. The steps on the left side of the plaza allow a diagonal view. To see the inside, continue to the top and climb over the small wooden fence. What 2000 years of turbulent history couldn't do, 20th-century pollution can—the aqueduct is now suffering from structural decay and is currently sheathed in scaffolding.

Segovia is blessed with an exceptional number of Romanesque churches from the 12th and 13th centuries, used as meeting places for guilds and brotherhoods. **San Justo,** outside the wall not far from the aqueduct, displays a powerful collection of frescoes in its main apse. **San Millán** on C. Fernández Ladreda also has a particularly fine collection of medieval frescoes, uncovered about 30 years ago under a layer of whitewash. The murals and frescoes were vivid out of necessity; in the days of mass illiteracy, they told the biblical stories. (San Millán open only during mass, daily at 8pm.) To the west, 10th-century **San Martín,** on Pl. San Martín off C. Juan Bravo, is spiced with Mozarabic touches, a beautiful Baroque *retablo,* and sepulchres pertaining to 17th-century Segovians. Thirteenth-century **San Esteban,** in the north of the city, houses a calvary from the same period. It was restored in the early 20th century. There's a splendid view of **San Andrés** from small Pl. Merced. **San Nicolás** and **San Sebastián** round out the roster of outstanding churches. When you show up at one of them you may be ambushed by a municipal employee offering free—and fascinating—tours in Spanish. (Most churches open Mon.-Sat. 11am-2pm and 4-6pm. Admission free.)

Palaces were the next architectural wave in Segovia, and proliferated in the 14th and 15th centuries. **Torreón de Lozoya,** in Pl. de San Martín off C. Juan Bravo, is a dandy. The 16th-century **Casa de los Picos,** in the southeast of the city, has an intriguing facade studded with rows of diamond-shaped stones.

Outside the Walls

Follow C. Pozo de la Nieve (on the left with your back to the Alcázar), and trot down the second stone staircase. You'll find yourself on Po. de San Juan de la Cruz, which leads, after a green ½-hr. walk, to four sights across the Eresma river. The divine numerological Knights Templar were at it again in 1208 when they built Romanesque **Iglesia de la Vera Cruz,** a suspiciously 12-sided basilica. Among its lofty vaults are two hidden chambers where clergymen secreted themselves and their valuables from robbers and highwaymen. In the same concealed rooms, the crafty Templars gathered to perform their enigmatic initiation ceremonies. (Tel. 43 14 75; open Tues.-Sun. 10:30am-1:30pm and 3:30-7pm; Oct.-March Tues.-Sun. 10:30am-1:30pm and 3:30-6pm. Admission 125ptas.)

The **Iglesia del Convento de las Carmelitas Descalzas,** with a pretty facade flanked by cypresses, is downhill from the Vera Cruz and to the right. San Juan de la Cruz, the great mystic poet, is buried here in the most grandiose of mausoleums.

The most valuable exhibit in the petite museum is his manuscript of the *Cántico espiritual.* (Tel. 43 13 49; open 10am-1:30pm and 4-7pm. Free.)

A few steps away, at the end of the park, sits the 16th-century **Santuario de la Virgen de la Fuencista,** honoring Segovia's patron saint, the virgin of la Fuencista. The church is most notable for its ornate altar. Finally, the **Monasterio del Parral,** founded by Enrique IV, lies to the east of the Vera Cruz. The monastery looks most impressive from afar, although its polychrome altarpiece calls for a close-up. (Tel. 43 12 98; open Mon.-Fri. 10am-12:30pm and 3-6:30pm. Free.)

ENTERTAINMENT

Pl. Mayor and its tributaries reign by night. Pubs crowd **Calles Infanta Isabel** and **Isabel la Católica** (nicknamed "the streets of the bars").

Café Jeyma, Pl. Mayor, 12. Extremely welcoming and popular with middle-aged and elderly locals. Beers 250ptas.

Pub Oja Blanca, Pl. Mayor, 6, next to the Hotel Victoria. Slightly more expensive and attracts a more uptown crowd. Open 9 or 10am-3am.

La Planta Baja Bar, C. Infanta Isabel, 8. A favorite haunt of teens. Loud music, billiards, and rather young company. Open 6pm-1 or 2am.

Bar Basilio, C. Herrería off C. Cronista Lecea, next to Restaurante la Oficina. A laidback place to drink. Attractive dark wood and tile decor. Old-timers pull up a seat at the bar; youngsters play pinball. Open 10am-2am.

Bar de Película, Pl. Mayor, 2 (tel. 43 09 71). Yummy hors d'oeuvres with your beer (250ptas). Patrons sit in rows on the *terraza,* all facing the street as if at the movies.

In the Pl. Mayor, loudspeakers on the rotunda spit forth a bizarre selection of tunes, ranging from Prince to *ranchera* ballads to a cheesy brass band on Sundays. In eventful July, Segovia hosts an annual **book fair** and two classical music festivals.

Near Segovia, **Zamarramala** hosts the **Fiestas de Santa Agueda** (St. Agatha) in February. For a day, women symbolically take over the town's administration, dress up in beautiful, old-fashioned costumes, and parade through the streets in memory of an abortive sneak attack on the Alcázar. The women of Zamarramala had tried to lull the castle guards with wine and song. Scandal! The town is 3km northwest.

For ski afficionados, Segovia province's ski station **La Pinilla** (winter tel. 55 03 04), is accessible via the Madrid-Burgos RENFE train (stop at Riaza) or La Castellana buses (4 per day, 380ptas). Ski rentals, lift tickets, tennis courts, and low-priced *hostales* are all available.

■ NEAR SEGOVIA

LA GRANJA DE SAN ILDEFONSO

The royal palace and grounds of **La Granja,** 11km southeast from Segovia, are the Versailles of Spain. One of four royal summer retreats (with El Pardo, El Escorial, and Aranjuez), La Granja is far and away the most extravagant. Marble everywhere, windows framed by original 250-year-old lace curtains, ceilings painted in false perspective, and lavish crystal chandeliers (made in San Ildefonso's renowned crystal factory) are just the tip of the iceberg.

In the early 18th century, Felipe V, the first Bourbon king in Spain and grandson of Louis XIV, detested the Hapsburgs' austere El Escorial and commissioned La Granja out of romantic French nostalgia for Versailles. The guided tour is mandatory but worth enduring, as the best exhibit comes last. In 1918 a fire destroyed the living quarters of the royals and their servants. The rubble was rebuilt to house one of the world's finest collections of **tapices flamencos** (Flemish tapestries). Hapsburg kings Carlos I and Felipe II covered walls with these tapestries made by artisans from the Low Countries in the 16th and 17th centuries. The domed **iglesia** flanking the palace has a red marble face and elaborate gilded woodwork. In a side chapel, bones of various saints and martyrs make an impressive display.

The cool and expansive **jardines** are surrounded by a forest with statues of children and animals. The **Cascadas Nuevas** (New Cascades) are an ensemble of sometimes illuminated pools representing the continents and the four seasons. (La Granja open Tues.-Sat. 10am-1pm and 3-5pm, Sun. 10am-2pm. Admission 500ptas, students, professors, and seniors 300ptas, Wed. EU citizens free. Fountains 300ptas, students, professors, and seniors 200ptas. Pools turned on Thurs.-Sun. at 5:30pm.)

Frequent **buses** leave Segovia's bus station for La Granja (10-13 per day, 20min., 95ptas).

PALACIO DE RIOFRÍO AND COCA

Travelers with a car might want to visit the **Palacio de Riofrío** (7km from Segovia), commissioned by Queen Isabel Farnese. The queen's failed intention was to top the grandeur of La Granja, which she had to leave when her husband (Felipe V) died. The palace was once a glorified hunting lodge, and game still roams the surrounding parkland. Inside is a **Museo de la Caza** (Museum of Hunting) and some ritzy royal apartments. No public transport serves the palace. (Open Mon. and Wed.-Sat. 10am-1pm and 3-5pm, Sun. 10am-2pm. Admission 500ptas, students, professors, and seniors 300ptas, Wed. EU citizens free.)

Coca is a slice of life in a Castilian hamlet, with a splendid castle. A Gothic monument to the power of the Fonseca family in the 15th century, **Coca Castilla** has music and passion and flamboyant fashion. Buses run to Coca from Segovia's station (Mon.-Fri. 3 per day, Sat. 1 per day, 45min., 235ptas).

■■■ AVILA

Oh, if the walls had ears, the stories Avila's serene *murallas* could tell. Sta. Teresa de Jesús and San Juan de la Cruz, famed 16th-century mystics, writers, and reformers, lived out their spiritual days here, penning mystical tracts that have recently come into vogue with the Spanish avant-garde (author Juan Goytisolo incorporates the texts of San Juan de la Cruz extensively in his writings). Sta. Teresa, founder of 17 monasteries and the Order of the Discalced Carmelites, experienced divine visitations in moments of ecstasy (described in her landmark autobiography), prompting the Counter-Reformation's appreciation of the sensuous and mysterious ways of Christ. San Juan de la Cruz was Sta. Teresa's collaborator and co-founder, and wrote *Noche oscura del alma,* in which he discusses the abnegation of the physical self and the transcendence of the soul. ("I care nothing for myself," he wrote, "what good am I to me?") Avila's 40,000 inhabitants have taken the feisty, feminist heroine Sta. Teresa as their patron saint, referring to her simply as La Santa, and naming everything from cuts of ham to driving schools after her.

Because the city sits on a rocky escarpment high above the Río Adaja valley, Avila keeps cool in the summer over the sweltering plain below. Within the classic medieval walls, carved images of bulls and hogs are mute reminders of a Celtiberian culture much older than the ancient fortifications. King Alfonso VI entrusted Raimundo de Borgoña with fortifying and repopulating Avila in 1090 in order to consolidate the kingdom of Castilla; from that moment it became one of Castilla's most important cities. Less crowded and tourist-oriented than Toledo or Cuenca, Avila's sights rival those of the best-known cities of Spain.

ORIENTATION AND PRACTICAL INFORMATION

Just west of Segovia and northwest of Madrid, Avila is a reasonable daytrip from either, although you really need a few to do it justice. The city has two central squares: **Plaza de la Victoria,** inside the city walls, and **Plaza de Santa Teresa,** just outside them. The cathedral and most of Avila's other monuments cluster between the two plazas, in the eastern half of the old city. To get to the city center from the bus station (east of the center), cross the intersection, walk down C. Duque de Alba (keeping the small park to the right), and follow the street past the Iglesia de San Pedro and the Plaza del Ejército to café-filled Pl. Santa Teresa. To reach Pl. Santa Teresa from the train station (northeast of the center), follow Av. José Antonio until it ends in a tangle of streets at Pl. Santa Ana. There you'll find C. Isaac Peral, which will lead you to C. Duque de Alba; then follow directions above (15min.). Municipal buses run from near the train station (one block in) to Pl. Victoria.

Tourist Office: Pl. Catedral, 4 (tel. 21 13 87). From Pl. Santa Teresa, walk through the main gate and turn right up winding C. Cruz Vieja, along the walls of the cathedral. The office is opposite the cathedral entrance. Open Mon.-Fri. 9:30am-2pm and 4:30-7pm, Sat. 9:30am-1:30pm and 4:30-8:30pm, Sun. 11:30am-2pm.

Post Office: Pl. Catedral, 2 (tel. 21 13 54 or 21 13 70), to the left of cathedral when facing the main entrance. Open for all services Mon.-Fri. 8am-9pm, Sat. 9am-7pm. To send **telegrams** by phone call tel. 22 20 00. **Postal Code:** 05001.

Telephones: Pl. Catedral (tel. 003), next to the post office. Open Mon.-Sat. 9am-2pm and 5-11pm, Sun. 10am-1:30pm. **Telephone Code:** 918.

Trains: Av. Portugal, 17 (tel. 22 01 88; information tel. 22 65 79; office tel. 22 07 81), at the end of Av. José Antonio on the northeast side of town. To: Madrid (20-30 per day, fewer on weekends, 2hr., 575-1050ptas); Medina del Campo, for transfer to Segovia (16 per day, 1hr., 480ptas); Salamanca (5 per day, 2hr., 580ptas); Valladolid (7 per day, 1¾hr., 1075ptas).

Buses: Av. Madrid at Av. Portugal (tel. 22 01 54), on the northeast side of town. To: Madrid (3 per day, 2hr., 835ptas); Segovia (4 per day, Sat.-Sun. 1 per day, 1hr., 520ptas); Salamanca (4 per day, Sat.-Sun. 2-3 per day, 1½hr., 875ptas). Other destinations include Valladolid, Cuenca, and Sevilla.

Taxis: Pl. Santa Teresa (tel. 21 19 59). Open 8am-10:30pm. Also at the train station (tel. 22 01 49). Open 6am-2am. From train station to Pl. Santa Teresa 350ptas plus 25ptas per piece of luggage.

Laundromat: Lavandería Mavi, C. Alférez Provisional, 9 (tel. 22 43 04), uphill from the Monasterio de San Tomás. Wash and dry 400ptas per kilo. Open Mon.-Fri. 9:30am-1:30pm and 4:30-8pm, Sat. 9:30am-1pm.

Luggage Storage: At the **train station** (300ptas) and the **bus station** (50ptas per item).

Medical Services: Red Cross (tel. 22 48 48), in Pl. Victoria. **Emergency Clinic (Seguridad Social)** (tel. 35 80 00). **Hospital Provincial** (tel. 22 16 50 or 22 16 00). **Ambulance** (tel. 12 12 20).

Emergency: tel. 091.

Police: Av. José Antonio, 3 (tel. 21 11 88).

ACCOMMODATIONS

Accommodations are plentiful and reasonably priced, though some fill in summer.

Residencia Juvenil "Duperier" (HI), Av. Juventud (tel. 21 35 48). Something of a hike from the center of town: from Pl. Sta. Teresa take Av. Alférez Provisional; cross C. Santa Fé onto Av. Juventud. Turn right into the Ciudad Deportiva complex from Av. Juventud (there's a sign); the hostel is straight down the short street in front of you. Twenty beds. Comfy and clean. Curfew 11pm. Bed 800ptas, with breakfast 900ptas. Meals 700ptas each, *pensión completa* 1800ptas, *pensión media* 1400ptas. 26 and over: 1100ptas; 1250ptas; 900ptas; 2300ptas; 1750ptas. Open July 11-30 and Aug. 8-28.

Hostal Continental, Pl. Catedral, 4 (tel. 21 15 02), next to the tourist office and in front of the cathedral. Beautiful ex-hotel in excellent location. Rooms are attractive, airy, and well-lit. Phones in all rooms. Singles 2100ptas, with bath 2300ptas. Doubles 3500ptas, with bath 3900ptas. Triples 4000ptas, with bath 4500ptas. *Temporada baja:* 1900ptas; 2100ptas; 3000ptas; 3400ptas; 3600ptas; 4000ptas. Prices don't include IVA. Visa, MC, AmEx accepted.

Hostal Santa Ana, C. Alfonso Montalvo, 2 (tel. 22 00 63), off Pl. Santa Ana, down Av. José Antonio from the train station. Efficiently run, well-kept *hostal*: sheets are snow-white, baths spic and span. Doubles 3200ptas. Triples 4500ptas. Oct.-July 14: 3000ptas; 4000ptas. Lower during winter. Showers 200ptas.

Pensión La Marquesa, Av. Portugal, 37 (tel. 21 28 86), on street leading away from bus station. A tiny, family-run *pensión* with friendly management. Small, clean rooms with the bare necessities. Singles 1600ptas. Doubles 2200ptas. Triples 2600ptas.

Hotel Reina Isabel, Av. José Antonio, 17 (tel. 22 02 00; fax 22 00 62). A possibility for doubles and triples. Luxurious, carpeted rooms, all with TV, bath, and phone. Singles 4300ptas. Doubles 6000ptas. Triples 9000ptas. Breakfast 300ptas. Visa, MC, AmEx accepted.

FOOD

Many cheap eateries cluster around **Plaza de la Victoria** and side streets. Cafés and bars in **Plaza de Sta. Teresa** are a step up pricewise, but over all dining in Avila isn't too costly (especially in comparison to Madrid).

The city won fame for its *ternera de Avila* (veal) and *mollejas* (sweetbread). The *yemas de Santa Teresa* or *yemas de Avila,* local confections made of egg yolks and honey, and *vino de Cebreros,* the smooth regional wine, are delectable. Every Friday (9am-2pm) a **mercado** in Pl. Victoria sells fruits, vegetables, meat, and other foodstuffs for cheap (plus tacky clothes and arts and crafts).

Groceries: Quiros, C. Caballeros, a few steps from Pl. Victoria, and **Alimentación Barcense,** C. Reyes Católicos, closer to the cathedral, are small bargain grocery stores. Both open Mon.-Sat. 9am-1:30pm and 4-7:30pm.

Mesón del Jamón, C. Doctor Fleming, 26 (tel. 22 84 15), off Av. Portugal. Ham however you like it: in a *bocadillo,* on a plate with some cheese, or in a big slab. Also other foods. *Menú* 1200ptas. Visa, MC, AmEx accepted.

Mesón El Rastro, Pl. Rastro, 4 (tel. 21 31 43), conveniently located at C. Cepadas and C. Caballeros at the southern wall. Large, noisy dining hall decked out like a hunting lodge. Expect to wait. Both *menús* (around 1500ptas) feature regional specialties in hearty portions. Entrees 600-1500ptas. Open 1-4pm and 9:30-11pm.

Bar/Restaurante Palomar, C. Vara del Rey (tel. 21 31 04), at C. Tomás L. de Victorias, a street to the right of the tourist office (as you face it). Pig out on *cochinillo asado* (roast suckling pig, 1500ptas). *Menú semanal* 1300ptas. *Menú* 1950ptas. Open 1:30-4:30pm and 8:30-10pm; off-season 1:30-4pm. Bar open 7:30pm-midnight.

Cafetería-Restaurante La Posada de la Fruta, C. Pedro Dávila, 8 (tel. 22 09 84), off Pl. Victoria. A big, sparce place with a long bar and a large selection of Spanish fast food. Big, yummy servings. *Bocadillos* 300-400ptas, *sandwiches* 200-400ptas, *raciones* 500-700ptas.

Restaurante El Ruedo, C. Enrique Larreta, 7 (tel. 21 31 98), between Pl. de la Catedral and Pl. Victoria. Regional specialties. *Menú* 1250ptas. Open Wed.-Sun. 1:30-4:30pm and 8pm-midnight.

SIGHTS AND ENTERTAINMENT

Avila's inner city is surrounded by the oldest and best preserved set of medieval walls of any Spanish city. Construction of the **murallas medievales** began in 1090 and most were completed the next century; this concentrated burst of activity lent the walls their unusual uniformity. Mudejar features suggest *morisco* citizens helped fortify Christian Avila. Eighty-two massive towers reinforce walls whose thickness averages 3m. The most imposing of the towers, called **Cimorro,** is actually the cathedral's bold apse. To walk on the walls, go to **Puerta del Alcázar,** at the end of C. Marqués de Sto. Domingo, on the opposite side of the walled-in section from the cathedral. (Open 11am-2pm and 5-8pm; winter 10:30am-3:30pm.)

The best view of the walls and of Avila itself is from the **Cuatro Postes,** a tiny four-pillar structure past the Río Adaja on the highway to Salamanca, 1½km northwest of the city. At this very spot, Teresa was nabbed by her uncle while she and her brother were trying to flee to the Islamic South to be martyred. Avila's walls are illuminated most summer nights from 10:30pm to midnight; Saturdays, Sundays, and holidays in off-season from 8pm to midnight; and daily from 8pm to midnight during *Las Fiestas de Santa Teresa* (Oct. 7-15) and Christmas time (Dec. 22-Jan. 7).

Inside the Walls

Some believe that the profile of the huge **catedral** looming over the watchtowers inspired Sta. Teresa's metaphor of the soul as a diamond castle. Begun in the second half of the 12th century, the oldest Spanish cathedral in the transitional Romanesque-to-Gothic style recalls the long, turbulent years of the Reconquista. Embedded in the city walls, the cathedral participated in Avila's defense system. View the **Altar de La Virgen de la Caridad,** where Sta. Teresa prostrated herself at age 12 after the death of her mother. She would later write of the experience, "I remember that when my mother died I was 12 years old, or a bit younger. As I began to understand what I had lost, I went, afflicted, to an image of Our Lady, and begged her, with many tears, to be my mother." A 14th-century baptismal font and life-sized tableaux depicting the Last Supper and the Betrayal of Christ are also on display. Behind the chancel is the alabaster **tomb** of Cardinal Alonso de Madrigal, an Avila bishop and prolific writer known as El Tostado (the Toasted) because of his dark complexion; his nickname was applied in the Golden Age to all literary wind-bags. The small **museo** has a fine collection of gold and silver work, sculptures, and paintings from the 12th to 18th centuries, including a small El Greco. (Cathedral open 8am-1pm and 3-7pm; Oct.-April 8am-1pm and 3-5pm. Free. Museum open 10am-1:30pm and 3-7pm; Oct.-April 10am-1:30pm and 3-6pm. Admission 200ptas.)

Sta. Teresa's admirers built the 17th-century **Convento de Santa Teresa** on the site of her birthplace and childhood home. Next to the convent, the small **Sala de Reliquias** holds some great Sta. Teresa relics, including her forefinger, the sole of her sandal, the cord with which she flagellated herself, and the crucifix she carried on her foundation journeys. (Convent open 9:30am-1:30pm and 3:30-9pm. Sala de Reliquios open 9:30am-1:30pm and 3:30-7:30pm. Free.)

Secular architecture is also well represented within the walled town. Spare, elegant Renaissance palaces, such as those of the Velada, Aguilar y Torre Arias, Verdugo, and Bracamonte families, and seignorial mansions, such as those built for the Oñate and the Marqués de las Navas, stand out. The **Palacio de los Polentinos,** on C. Vallespín, is fronted with a beautiful Renaissance facade. Inside seemingly weightless pillars support the upper story within a majestic blue-and-white tiled courtyard.

Casa de los Deanes, a mansion in Pl. Nalvillos with a Renaissance facade, houses Avila's splendid **Museo Provincial** (tel. 21 10 03). The museum displays lovingly restored agricultural implements, an old loom, fancy local straw hats, a bed artistically strewn with traditional costumes, a few outstanding medieval paintings, and two Baroque desks. (Open Tues.-Sat. 10am-2pm and 7-8pm, Sun. 10am-2pm. Admission 200ptas, students free.)

Outside the Walls

A short way outside the city walls, on Po. Encarnación, is the **Monasterio de la Encarnación,** where Sta. Teresa lived for 30 years—27 as a nun and three as a prioress. The mandatory guided tour unveils Sta. Teresa's tiny cell, and the small rooms called *locutorios,* where nuns peered at their guests through little barred windows. In one of these Sta. Teresa had her vision of Christ tied to a pole; in another, according to a cryptic sign, "while talking to San Juan de la Cruz they were lifted in ecstasy." Sta. Teresa confessed to San Juan de la Cruz in this monastery, and had a mystical encounter with the child Jesus on the main staircase:

Jesús: ¿Quién eres tú?
Sta. Teresa: Yo soy Santa Teresa de Avila. Y tú, ¿Quién eres?
Jesús: Yo soy Jesús de Santa Teresa.

Upstairs from the cloister, a museum features a collection of furnishings, letters, and other personal effects, plus musical instruments and elaborate trunks given to the convent by wealthier nuns as bribes to procure entrance. Teresa's reforms did away with this system of preference and imposed norms of collective property and simplicity (as exemplified by her own *celda*) for all nuns. Currently 27 nuns live in the monastery. (Open 9:30am-1:30pm and 3:30-6pm; winter 9:30am-1pm and 4-7pm. Obligatory tour in Spanish 100ptas.)

The first convent Teresa founded was the **Convento de San José,** also known as the Convento de las Madres, at C. Madres, 3, off C. Duque de Alba. Although the 1608 building is closed to visitors, the small **Museo Teresiano** exhibits the saddle she used while roaming around establishing convents, the drum she played at Christmas, and a letter written in her elegant, educated hand—not to mention one of her bones and a wonderful Zurbarán. (Open 10am-1pm and 3:30-7pm; winter 10am-1pm and 3:30-6pm. Admission 50ptas.)

Basílica de San Vicente is a large, 12th-century Romanesque and Gothic building dedicated to Vicente, Sabina, and Cristeta, three martyred saints buried beneath the church. The convent has a magnificent ensemble of Romanesque sculpture, including depictions of Jesus and ten of his apostles. (Open 10am-1pm and 4-7pm; winter 10am-1pm and 4-6pm.)

Monasterio de Santo Tomás, Pl. Granada, 1, some way from the city walls at the end of C. Jesús del Gran Poder (or of Av. de Alférez Provisional), was the summer palace of the Catholic monarchs (commissioned by Fernando and Isabel) and a frightening seat of the Inquisition. *Granada* (pomegranate) motifs recall the monarchs' triumphant 1492 capture of Granada, the last Moorish kingdom in Spain. Inside the church and in front of the *retablo* is the tomb of Prince Don Juan, Fernando and Isabel's only son, who died in 1497 at the age of 19. To the right (when facing the altar) is the **Capilla del Santo Cristo,** where Sta. Teresa came to pray and confess. Also here are the Tuscan **Cloister of the Noviciate,** the Gothic **Cloister of Silence,** and the Renaissance-Transition **Cloister of the Kings.** The **Museo de Arte Oriental** (tel. 22 04 00), in what used to be the royal bed chambers, has an uninspired collection of ancient Chinese, Japanese, and Vietnamese artifacts. (Whole complex open daily 10am-1pm and 4-7pm. Admission to the church free, to the cloisters 50ptas, to the museum 100ptas.)

Every year from October 7 to 15, the city gets a little crazy in honor of Sta. Teresa, with fairs and parades of *gigantes y cabezudos* (giant effigies). In the 2nd or 3rd week of July, the **Fiestas de Verano** (Summer Celebrations) bring exhibits, folk-singing, dancing, pop groups, fireworks, and a bullfight.

■■■ SALAMANCA

For centuries the "hand of Salamanca," the brass knocker on the doors of the city, has welcomed students, scholars, rogues, royals, and saints. Big, bustling, beautiful Salamanca (pop. 180,000) is famed for its 13th-century university—the oldest in Spain—and for its unique architectural look. Buildings here in every major architectural style are constructed in golden sandstone.

Throughout the ages, Salamanca has played a starring role in many of Spain's most significant historical vicissitudes. The city was conquered by the Arabs, taken and lost various times by the Christians, and finally captured definitively by Alfonso VI, who set about colonizing it. The university was founded in 1200 by Alfonso IX, and enjoyed the patronage of Fernando el Santo and Alfonso X el Sabio. It was dubbed by Pope Alexander IV "one of the four leading lights of the world," along with the other three great medieval centers of learning: Bologna, Paris, and Oxford. Many outstanding Spanish intellectuals have improved their minds in its halls. Nebrija, responsible for the first grammar of a modern language (1492), taught here until, disgusted by its stodgy ways, he took off to join the new humanistic university in Alcalá. Miguel de Unamuno was a professor of Greek and University Rector for many years in the early 20th century. The bulk of his philosophical and literary *obras* were written in Salamanca.

These days, the perfect balance of the active and the contemplative life is the hall-mark of the Salamantine way. In summer, a huge influx of foreign students adds a certain tang to the atmosphere, but the city in winter—especially when a thin layer of snow coats the cathedrals—is hauntingly attractive.

ORIENTATION AND PRACTICAL INFORMATION

A number of streets radiate from **Plaza Mayor.** Facing the clock and proceeding clockwise from the top left corner, they are **Calle Concejo, Calle Zamora, Calle Toro** (which leads to **Calle Azafranal), Plaza del Mercado, Plaza Poeta Iglesias** (which leads to **Calle San Pablo** and **Rua Mayor), Calle Corrillo, Calle Prior,** and **Calle Pasaje.** Most sights and a great deal of cheap food and accommodations lie south of the **Plaza Mayor.** The farther north of the plaza, the newer and more expensive the area. The **Universidad** (university) is south of the Plaza Mayor, near the **Plaza de Anaya.**

Both bus and train are 20 minutes from the town center. From the train station (northeast from the center), either catch the bus that goes to Pl. Mercado (next to Pl. Mayor) or, with your back to the station, turn left down Po. Estación to Pl. España, and walk down C. Azafranal or C. Toro (which begin directly opposite you) to Pl. Mayor. From the bus station, either catch bus #4 to Pl. Mercado or walk all the way down C. de Filiberto Villalobos, cross busy Av. Alemania, and plummet down C. Ramón y Cajal; when that reaches a dead end (just after the domed Iglesia de la Purís), jog left and immediately right up C. Prior, which runs directly to Pl. Mayor.

Tourist Office: Municipal, Pl. Mayor, 13-14 (tel. 21 83 42; fax 27 91 14). Recently remodeled office. Big and information-filled. English spoken. Open Mon.-Sat. 9am-2pm and 4:30-7pm, Sun. 10am-2pm. **Provincial,** C. Gran Vía (also called C. España), 39-41 (tel. 26 85 71). English spoken. Open Mon.-Fri. 9:30am-2pm and 4:30-7pm, Sat.-Sun. 11:30am-2pm and 4:30-8:30pm. **Information booths:** Open July-Sept. Nice students distribute maps, information, and accommodations list-ings from booths in Plaza Anaya (open Mon. 4-7pm, Tues.-Sat. 10am-1pm and 4-7pm, Sun. 10am-1pm), the train station (open Mon.-Sat. 9am-9pm, Sun. 10am-6pm), and the bus station (open Mon.-Sat. 9am-6pm, Sun. 10am-2pm).

Budget Travel: TIVE, Po. Carmelitas (also called Av. Alemania), 83 (tel. 26 77 31). Long lines; go early. Open Mon.-Fri. 9am-2pm. **Viajes Juventud,** Pl. Libertad, 4 (tel. 21 74 07 or 21 74 08; fax 21 74 08). Open Mon.-Fri. 10am-2pm and 4:30-8pm. **Viajes Zarco,** Cuesta del Carmen, 27-33 (tel. 26 94 61 or 26 91 93; fax 26 94 61; telex 225 77). Open Mon.-Fri. 9:30am-1:30pm and 4:30-8pm, Sat. 9:30am-1:30pm.

Currency Exchange: American Express, Pl. del Campillo, 4 (tel. 26 86 11; fax 26 25 83). From Pl. Mayor take C. Zamora to Pl. Ejército. Turn right on Av. Mirat and take the second right on C. Cristóbal Riesco. The office is in the small square to the left. English spoken. Check cashing, mail pick-up, money-wiring. Open Mon.-Fri. 9:30am-1:30pm and 4:30-8pm, Sat. 10am-1:30pm. For lost checks call (tel. (900) 99 44 26). 24-hr. service. **Banco de Madrid,** C. Conejos, just off Pl. Mayor, has an automatic currency exchange machine (open 24hrs.).

Post Office: Gran Vía, 25 (tel. 24 30 11). Open for stamps and information Mon.-Fri. 9am-2pm and 4-6pm, Sat. 9am-2pm; for Lista de Correos Mon.-Fri. 9am-2pm; for **telegrams** Mon.-Sat. 9am-9pm, or tel. 26 20 00. **Postal Code:** 37008.

Telephones: Pl. Peña Primera, 2 (tel. 003), off Pl. Bandos, which is off C. Zamora. Open Mon.-Sat. 9am-3pm and 4-11pm. Also in bus station (open 9am-2pm and 4-9pm). **Telephone Code:** 923.

Trains: Po. Estación Ferrocarril (tel. 22 57 42), northeast of town. **RENFE office,** Pl. Libertad, 10 (tel. 21 24 54). Open Mon.-Fri. 9am-1pm and 5-7pm. Two *regional* lines. To: Madrid (2-4 per day, 3½hr., 1250ptas), via Avila (1055ptas); Burgos (5 per day, Sat. 2 per day) via Palencia, León (3½hr., 1600ptas), and trans-fer center Valladolid. Also trains to Barcelona (2 per day, 12hr., 6135ptas).

Buses: Av. Filiberto Villalobos, 71 (tel. 23 67 17 or 23 22 66). Information open Mon.-Fri. 9am-1:30pm and 4-7pm, Sat. 9am-1:30pm. To: Avila (1-4 per day, 1-2hr., 765ptas); Ciudad Rodrigo (8 per day, Sun. 3 per day, 1hr., 670ptas); Valladolid (3-4 per day, 2hr., 835ptas); Zamora (8-19 per day, 1hr., 485ptas); Segovia (Mon.-Sat.

SALAMANCA

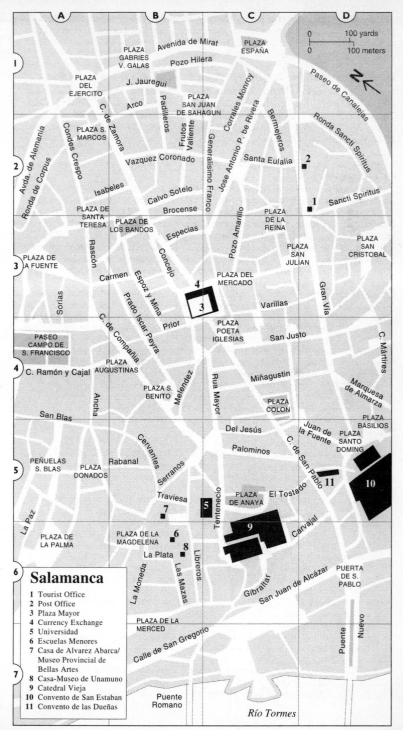

Salamanca

1 Tourist Office
2 Post Office
3 Plaza Mayor
4 Currency Exchange
5 Universidad
6 Escuelas Menores
7 Casa de Alvarez Abarca/
  Museo Provincial de
  Bellas Artes
8 Casa-Museo de Unamuno
9 Catedral Vieja
10 Convento de San Estaban
11 Convento de las Dueñas

3 per day, 2hr., 1250ptas); Madrid (frequent, 2½-3hr., 1525-1910ptas); Cáceres (3-6 per day, 4hr., 1730ptas); León (4-6 per day, 3hr., 1600ptas); Barcelona (3 per day, 11½hr., 6040ptas). Also to Cuenca, Valencia, Sevilla, and Mérida.

Taxis: tel. 26 44 44 or 25 00 00. 24-hr. service.

Car Rental: Hertz, Av. Portugal, 131 (tel. 24 31 34). Open Mon.-Fri. 9am-2pm and 4-7pm, Sat. 9am-1pm. **Avis,** Po. Canalejos, 49 (tel. 26 97 53). Open Mon.-Fri. 9am-2pm and 5-8pm, Sat. 9am-2pm. **Europcar,** C. Torres Villarroel (tel. 23 35 26).

Lost Property: Policía Municipal keeps objects a few days, then turns them over to the municipal building on C. Dr. Piñuela, next to Pl. Mayor.

English Bookstore: Cervantes, Pl. Hermanos Jerez (tel. 21 86 02), near C. Azafranal. Enormous bookstore with three entrances, all within a bl. of each other. Penguin and Wordsworth classics, plus a smattering of best-sellers. Sells the Herald Tribune (more English-language press in the Pl. Mayor kiosks). Open Mon.-Fri. 9:30am-1:30pm and 4:30-8pm, Sat. 10am-2pm. **Portonaris,** R. Mayor, 33, opposite the Casa de Conchas. Salamanca's most renowned bookstore. Penguin Classics. Open Mon.-Sat. 10am-2pm and 4:30-8pm, Sun. 10am-2pm.

Laundromat: Lavandería Soap, Av. Italia, 29 (tel. 25 32 57). From Pl. Mayor, take C. Zamora to Pl. Ejército; Av. Italia is at 10 o'clock. Self-service. 425ptas per washer and per dryer. Open Mon.-Fri. 10am-1:30pm and 4:30-8pm, Sat. 10am-1:30pm.

Swimming Pool: Las Torres, Ctra. Madrid (tel. 21 90 97), across railroad bridge. Take the Santa María and Valdelagua bus lines that stop across from the "La Riojana" on the Gran Vía (every 30min., 20min.). The cleanest and nicest of the city's 10 pools. Large afternoon crowds. Open summer 11am-8pm. Admission 500ptas, Sat.-Sun. 900ptas. **Regio,** Ctra. Madrid (tel. 20 02 50), 4km away (see Accommodations and Camping: Camping). Smaller, less crowded. Admission 425ptas.

Crisis Hotlines: Drug Addiction, tel. (900) 16 15 15. **Poison,** tel. (91) 262 04 20.

Medical Services: Hospital Clínico, Po. San Vicente, 23 (tel. 29 11 00). **Prusa España,** Edificio España, Pl. España, 4th fl. (tel. 22 14 00). Pricey private medical clinic. Fluent English, French, German, and Japanese staff. Foreign medical insurance accepted. **Ambulance:** tel. 24 09 16, 25 54 64, or 24 37 87. **Red Cross:** tel. 22 22 22.

Emergency: tel. 092. **National Police:** tel. 091. **Fire:** tel. 23 20 80.

ACCOMMODATIONS AND CAMPING

Hostales and *pensiones* abound in Salamanca, and prices tend to be quite reasonable. A tourist office brochure lists them all.

Between Plaza Mayor and the University

Many students; even more rooms. Plenty of cheap *pensiones* on side streets off Pl. Mayor, especially on **Calle Meléndez,** just south of the plaza.

Pensión Las Vegas, C. Meléndez, 13, 1st fl. (tel. 21 87 49). Pretty, clean rooms with big windows and lacy curtains. All rooms have balconies, some looking onto the street, others overlooking a flowery courtyard. Singles 1000ptas. Doubles 2000ptas, with bath 3000ptas. Triples 3000ptas, with bath 4000ptas.

Pensión Marina, C. Doctrinos, 4, 3rd fl. (tel. 21 65 69), between C. Compañía and C. Prado. On a street with several *pensiones* and bars. One of the best values in town—mammoth bedrooms, bubbly owners, and two TV lounges with over-stuffed furniture. The lone single 1600ptas. Doubles 2200ptas.

Pensión Barez, C. Meléndez, 19 (tel. 21 74 95). Owners treat you like one of the family. Sparkling clean. Balcony rooms look onto San Benito. TV lounge with table. 1100ptas per person; Oct.-May 1000ptas. Showers 125ptas.

Pensión Peña de Francia, C. San Pablo, 96 (tel. 21 66 87). Just past Iglesia de San Estéban; look for building with the blue "P" next to Churrería Graci. Don't be deterred by the external grime. Rooms are bright and furniture only a few years old. Eclectic decor; almost incandescent baths. Singles 2000ptas, with bath 2500ptas. Doubles 3000ptas, with bath 3500ptas.

Pensión Villanueva, C. San Justo, 8, 1st fl. (tel. 26 88 33). Exit Pl. Mayor via Pl. Poeta Iglesias and take the left at 5 o'clock. Large rooms with hospital-green walls.

Stays over a weekend earn kitchen privileges. Singles 1500ptas, with shower 2000ptas. Doubles with or without shower 3200ptas (first come first serve). Oct-March 14: 1300ptas; 1500ptas; 2800ptas.

North of Plaza Mayor

Prices escalate north of Pl. Mayor. The concentration of *pensiones* decreases and gives way to more expensive *hostal-residencias* near Pl. España.

Hostal Oriental, C. Azafranal, 13 (tel. 21 21 15), halfway between Pl. Mayor and Pl. España. Wimpy little singles and big hefty doubles, some jazzed up by colorful floor tiles and diminutive tables. Singles 1800ptas. Doubles 3400ptas. Showers 250ptas, but they don't always charge. Visa, MC accepted.

Hostal Carabela, Po. Canalejas, 10-12 (tel. 26 07 08), off Pl. España. Tends to be noisy, but rooms are impeccable if uninspired. Tight baths. Singles 2000ptas, with shower or bath 2600ptas. Doubles 2600ptas, with shower or bath 2900ptas. Nov.-Feb.: 1800ptas; 2300ptas; 2400ptas; 2600ptas. Showers 150ptas.

Pensión Virginia, Po. Estación, 109-115, right-hand stairway, 1st fl. (tel. 24 10 16), across from train station. Not the most attractive neighborhood. Rooms are adequate and clean, and have big windows. Singles with shower 2200ptas. Doubles 4000ptas. Breakfast 300ptas.

Camping: Regio (tel. 13 88 88; fax 13 80 44), on the Ctra. Salamanca 4km toward Madrid. A 1st-class campsite with all the amenities: nature, hot-water showers, nearby public transportation, pool, tennis courts, money changing. In a luxury tourist complex with a 4-star hotel, restaurants, *terrazas,* and bars. 425ptas per person, per tent, and per car; 375ptas for a one-person tent. Visa, MC accepted. **Don Quijote** (tel. 28 91 31), on the Ctra. Salamanca 4km toward Aldealengua. A smallish, 3rd-category campsite near the Tormes river. 325ptas per person, per tent, and per car. Open March-Oct.

FOOD

Every clique has its favorite café in **Plaza Mayor;** all serve the same moderately good food at standard, slightly inflated prices. A slew of bar-restaurants line streets between the plaza and the university, where a full meal costs no more than 1000ptas. Lots of students hang out at these little places.

Groceries: Supermercado Autoservicio, C. Zamora (tel. 21 31 91), a few bl. up from Pl. Mayor. Open Mon.-Fri. 9:45am-1:45pm and 5-8pm, Sat. 10am-2pm. Visa, MC accepted.

Restaurante El Bardo, C. Compañía, 8 (tel. 21 90 89), between the Casa de Conchas and the Clerecía. Three tiers serve excellent 3-course vegetarian and classic 2-course *menú* (800ptas) at lunch. Lively at midday; more sedate at night. *Menú de la casa* 2000ptas. Open Nov.-Sept. Tues.-Sun. 11am-4pm and 7pm-midnight. Here, and two doors down at classy **Café Alcaraván,** C. Compañía, 12, crowded message boards offer rideshares, language trades, rooms to rent, etc.

Restaurante Vegetariano El Trigal, C. Libreros, 20 (tel. 21 56 99), near the cathedral and the Patio de las Escuelas. Intimate setting, with polished wood floors and birds. Why are you not surprised it's also a yoga center? Weird fruit and vegetable juices and shakes 400-600ptas. Creative *menú* 900 or 1300ptas. *Platos combinados* 675ptas. Open 1-4pm and 8:30-11pm.

Imbis, C. Rua Mayor, 29. Good selection of *tapas.* German sausage specialty. *Platos combinados* about 700ptas. *Menú* 1000-1100ptas. Open 8am-midnight.

Bocata World Company, C. Rua Mayor, 26. Big selection of tasty, fast *bocadillos,* including some vegetarian (300-350ptas). Salads 230-245ptas.

SIGHTS

Near the Plaza Mayor

Pick a genre, any genre—they're all here (Roman, Romanesque, Gothic, Renaissance, and Baroque) and in sandstone. Nowhere is the golden glow more apparent than in the Baroque **Plaza Mayor,** a trapezoid begun in 1729 during the reign of Felipe V. Between the arches—almost 100 of them—hang medallions with bas-reliefs of famous *Españoles,* from El Cid to Franco. The **Ayuntamiento's** facade was designed by Andrés García de Quiñones. Alberto Churriguera's **Pabellón Real** is to its left.

One of Salamanca's most famous landmarks, the 15th-century **Casa de las Conchas** (House of Shells), is adorned by rows of scallop shells chiseled in sandstone. The owner of the house, a knight of the Order of Santiago, wanted to create a monument to Santiago de Compostela, the renowned pilgrimage site. Pilgrims who journeyed to Santiago wore shells like these as a token of their visit to St. James the Apostle's tomb. The building is now a public library, but the courtyard is open to tourists. (Tel. 26 93 17 or 26 93 72; open Mon.-Fri. 9am-9pm, Sat.-Sun. 10am-2pm and 4-7pm. Free.)

Across the street, the **Clerecía** (a.k.a. Real Colegio del Espíritu Santo) is a Baroque complex that until recently was used by a major Jesuit community. It consists of a church, a school, and what used to be the community's living quarters: 300 rooms in all, with 520 doors and 906 windows. Its wonderful facade can't be appreciated properly because of the narrowness of the street. In fact, a few wealthy believers once offered a large sum of money to clear the way for admiring viewers. (Tel 21 59 66; open for mass only Mon.-Sat. 1:15pm and 7:30pm, Sun. 12:30pm.)

The University

The University of Salamanca is so synonymous in Spain to the very notion of education that in order to assert the notion that even the best educations can not change scarce intelligence, this Latin adage is repeated: *"Quod natura non dat, Salamanca non praestat"* (What nature does not provide, Salamanca does not lend). The focal point of Salamanca, the **Universidad** created in 1218, is entered from the **Patio de las Escuelas,** off C. Libreros. The statue here represents Fray Luis de León, one of the most respected literati of the Golden Age, and a professor at the university along with Nebrija and Unamuno. A Hebrew scholar and a classical Spanish stylist to boot, Fray Luis was arrested by the Inquisition for translating Solomon's *Song of Songs* into Castilian, and for prefering the Hebrew version of the Bible to the Latin one. After five years of imprisonment while on trial, he returned to the university and started his first lecture with the words: *"Decíamos ayer…"* ("As we were saying yesterday… "), resuming where his last lecture had ended.

The university's **entryway** is one of the best examples of Spanish Plateresque, a style named for the filigree work of *plateros* (silversmiths). The central medallion represents King Fernando and Queen Isabel. The smallish frog carved on a skull on the right side of the facade is Salamanca's "gray eminence." It's said to represent the dankness of prison life and to bring good luck on exams. If you spot the frog without help you'll be married within the year. The walls are marked here and there by students' initials in bold red, painted upon graduation in an ink of bull's blood, olive oil, and herbs.

The old lecture halls inside are open to the public. (Don't miss the room of fossilized turtles, apparently the second most important of such collections in the world.) **Aula Fray Luis de León** has its original benches and the Fray's pulpit, with a plaque that bears Unamuno's poem on love and the students of Salamanca. The extraordinarily sumptuous **Paraninfo** (auditorium) contains Baroque tapestries and a portrait of Carlos IV attributed to Goya. Fray Luis is buried in the 18th-century **chapel.** (Tel. 29 44 00; open Mon.-Sat. 9:30am-1:30pm and 4-7:30pm, Sun. 10am-1:30pm. No one admitted less than half an hour before closing time. Admission 200ptas, seniors 100ptas, students free; Mon. mornings free.)

Also on the Patio de las Escuelas are the **Escuelas Menores,** with a smaller version of the main entryway's Plateresque facade, where *universitarios* completed preparatory studies for the Escuela Mayor. The **University Museum** is constructed on the spot where the *antigua biblioteca* (ancient library) once stood. The museum retains the library's famous ceiling, the **Cielo de Salamanca** (Sky of Salamanca), a

15th-century fresco of the zodiac, as well as robes worn by the university's rectors, professors, and chaplains. (Open Tues.-Sat. 9:30am-1:30pm and 4-6:30pm, Sun. 9:30am-1:30pm.)

The **Museo Provincial de Bellas Artes,** also known as the **Casa de los Alvarez Albarca,** occupies a beautiful 15th-century building which was once home to Alvarez Albarca, physician to the Reyes Católicos. This and the *Casa de las Conchas* are among Spain's most important examples of 15th-century architecture. The museum has a fair to good collection of painting and sculpture, mostly 17th- and 18th-century Spanish, as well as examples from the Italian, French, and Flemish schools, and a mediocre collection of modern art. The museum's most important canvases are Juan de Flandes' portrait of Saint Andrew and Luis de Morales' *Llanto por Cristo Muerto,* both from the 16th century, as well as Vascaro's ethereal *Inmaculada.* (Tel. 21 22 35; open Mon.-Fri. 9:30am-2pm and 4:30-8pm, Sat. 10am-2pm and 4:30-7:30pm, Sun. 10am-2pm. Admission 200ptas, students free.)

To the right of the principal entrance to the university is the absorbing **Casa-Museo de Unamuno.** Miguel de Unamuno was one of the primary figures of the "Generation of '98." His writings explored the relationship between faith and reason. *Abel Sánchez* is a revisionist look at the Cain and Abel story in which the murder takes the form of moral self-defense. A Fascist general in 1936 ran in on Unamuno's lecture and shouted: *"Muera la inteligencia"* ("Death to intelligence"); Miguel de Unamuno is reported to have answered: *"Vencerá pero no convencerá"* ("You may conquer but you will not convince"). Among the more charming exhibits in the philosopher-writer's house are his ruminations on his birth and his dexterous origami in the study. Note the different variations on the "nun praying" theme. (Tel. 29 44 00, ext. 1196; open Tues.-Fri. 11am-1:30pm and 4:30-6:30pm, Sat.-Sun. 10am-2pm. If the house seems closed, ring the bell and wait for the caretaker to show up. Free.)

Cathedrals and Convents

Begun in 1513 to accommodate the growing tide of believers, the spindly spires of the **catedral nueva** weren't finished until 1733. The basic structure is late Gothic, built from elegant pale stone and pierced by colorful flashes of stained glass. On the vaulting, the giltwork is luxuriant. Joaquín Churriguera fashioned the lovely cloister with its Renaissance and Baroque flourishes. The *Cristo de las batallas,* carried by El Cid in his campaigns, is kept in the **Capilla de Sagrario.** At night, dozens of storks and buzzards perch eerily on the church's spires.

The Romanesque **catedral vieja** (1140) features heavy lines—a relief from the Gothic next door. The central altarpiece narrates the story of the Virgin Mary in 53 scenes. Inside the cupola, apocalyptic angels separate the sinners from the saved. The oldest part is the **Capilla de San Martín,** with brilliantly-colored frescoes from 1242. Off to one side is the 12th-century cloister, rebuilt after the earthquake of 1755. Here, the **Capilla de Santa Bárbara,** also called the "Capilla del Título," was once the site of final exams. Prior to taking the tests, students placed their feet on the soles of a particularly wise bishop's sarcophagus, hoping to absorb his intelligence. The **Capilla de Santa Catalina** has the best gargoyles.

The **cathedral museum** features a paneled ceiling by Fernando Gallegos, Salamanca's celebrated painter, and houses the Salinas organ, named for the blind musician to whom Fray Luis dedicated an ode. (Tel. 26 74 26; both cathedrals open 10am-2pm and 4-8pm; Oct.-March 10am-1pm and 4-6pm. Closed Mon. morning and Sun. afternoon. Box office closes ½hr. before closing. Admission to old cathedral, cloister, and museum via new cathedral 200ptas. New cathedral free.)

The **Convento de San Esteban,** downhill from the cathedrals, is one of Salamanca's most dramatic monasteries. In the afternoon, its monumental facade becomes a solid mass of light depicting the stoning of St. Stephen and the crucifixion of Jesus. The beautiful **Claustro de los Reyes** (Kings' Cloister) is both Gothic and Plateresque. In the church, the huge central altarpiece, crafted in 1693 by Churriguera, is a Baroque masterpiece with intricate golden columns entwined with grapevines. (Tel. 21 50 00; open 9am-1pm and 4-7pm. Admission 150ptas.)

The nearby **Convento de las Dueñas** was formerly the Mudejar palace of a court official. The elegant cloister was a later addition, explaining why its five sides are of unequal length. With its exquisite medallions, the cloister is perhaps the most beautiful in Salamanca. (Tel. 21 54 42; open 10:30am-1pm and 4:15-7pm. Admission 100ptas. A candy shop, selling what look to be antique candies, sits inside the 1st fl.)

Elsewhere

Take a stroll down C. Rua Mayor from Pl. Mayor to find the **Puente Romano,** a 2000-year-old Roman bridge which spans the scenic Río Tormes. The bridge was part of an ancient Roman road called the Camino de la Plata (Silver Way) that wagged from Mérida, in Extremadura, to Astorga, near León. On the near end of the bridge stands the **Toro Ibérico,** a headless granite bull. The old bull figures in one of the most famous episodes of *Lazarillo de Tormes,* the prototypical 16th-century picaresque novel, when the diminutive hero finds his head unexpectedly slammed into the bull's stone ear and decides, epiphany-like, that he needs to get smart.

ENTERTAINMENT

The **Plaza Mayor** is the social center of town. Locals, students, and tourists come at all hours to sit in its cafés or *dar una vuelta* (take a stroll). At night, members of various local college or graduate school **tunas,** medieval-style student troubadour groups, often finish their rounds here. Dressed in traditional beribboned black capes, they strut around the plaza carrying guitars, mandolins, *bandurrias,* and tambourines, and serenade women. When the show's over, they make excellent drinking partners and do their best to emulate Don Juan.

Many people overflow from the plaza as far west as **San Vicente.** A lot of the student nightlife also concentrates on the **Gran Vía** and side streets, and on **Calle Bordedores.** Bars blast music ranging from reggae to vintage hard rock to *nueva canción* (modern ballads). **Calle Prior** is chock full of bars, as is **Calle Rua Mayor.** Many a charming *terraza* and fewer American tourists center in **Plaza de la Fuente,** off Av. Alemania down from Pl. Ejército.

Avoid the southwest section of town after dark unless you're accompanied by a friend or bodyguard. Salamanca's drug scene is somewhat notorious.

Café Novelty, on the northeast corner of Pl. Mayor. The oldest café in town and a meeting place for students and professors. Miguel de Unamuno was a regular.

Café El Corrillo, Pl. Mayor by C. Juan del Rey. Boasts a video jukebox and mellow clientele.

Pub Rojo y Negro, C. Espoz y Mina. Scrumptious coffee, liquor, and ice cream concoctions (250-600ptas) in an old-fashioned setting. A dance floor down below. Open until 12:30am.

El Puerto de Chus, Pl. San Julián. One of the best late-night spots, 2 bl. away from Pl. Mayor, just off the Gran Vía.

Gran Café El Pino, Av. de Alemania, 57 (tel. 21 90 98). An upscale, hard-drinking place. If you drink a Ballantine's, you'll get another free.

Café-Bar Antaño, Pl. de la Fuente, 7. Big, lively terrace; big, lively waiters; big, deadly drinks (400-600ptas).

The city's discos range from the expensive Euro variety (600-1000ptas cover) to bars with dance floors and no cover charge. All discos have evening (7-10pm) and late night (11:30pm-4am) sessions.

De Laval Genoves, C. San Justo (off Gran Vía). Built in an old submarine, a straight and gay clientele grooves under black lights.

Mezcal, Cuesta del Carmen. Live jazz nightly (at midnight and 1:30am, except in summer) in a laid-back basement.

Ambiente, an inexpensive pamphlet sold at kiosks, lists movies and special events. Posters at the **Colegio Mayor** (Palacio de Anaya) advertise university events, free films, and student theater.

In summer, the city sponsors the **Verano Cultural de Salamanca,** with silent movies, contemporary Spanish cinema, pop singers, and theater groups from Spain and abroad. On July 12, in celebration of San Juan de Sahagún, is a **corrida de toros** charity event. From September 8 to 21, the town indulges in **festivals** and **exhibitions,** most having to do with bulls. Salamanca's **Semana Santa** is also quite famous.

■ NEAR SALAMANCA

CIUDAD RODRIGO

A medieval town characterized by its fabulous masonry and its honey-colored stone (a little more golden than even Salamanca's), Ciudad Rodrigo (pop. 16,000) rises from the plains near the Portuguese border. After Count Rodrigo Gonzá!ez Girón defeated the Moors in 1100, Fernando II ordered him to repopulate this town. The walls surrounding the old city date from the medieval era, the main gateway and complex series of defensive exterior constructions from the 18th century.

The **catedral** is the town's greatest masterpiece. Originally Romanesque, the church was commissioned by Fernando II of León, who was also responsible for the city walls; the church was substantially modified, in Gothic style, in the 16th century. The **coro** was the master work of Rodrigo Alemán from 1498-1504, and includes the sculptor's signature—a carving of his head in the lower right corner. The two 16th-century organs star in a series of concerts every August.

The **claustro** alone, however, merits a trip to Ciudad Rodrigo. The left-hand triangle, as you enter, is medieval; the right-hand triangle is early modern. Biblical and mythological scenes are illustrated in fascinating stonework. At one corner, monsters devour Muslims; halfway around, at the beginning of the second side, two demons smirk as Adam and Eve receive their punishment; at the far end, two birds kiss. The cathedral's **museum** is filled with strange and thrilling old pieces, including an ancient clavichord, the ornate "ballot box" used to determine the cathedral's hierarchy, and the robes and richly embroidered slippers worn by long-dead bishops and priors. (Cathedral open 10:30am-1:30pm and 4-8pm. Free. Cloister and museum open 10:30am-1:30pm and 4-6pm. Admission 200ptas. Mandatory guided tour in Spanish.)

Few structures have appeared in Rodrigo since the days when the more ornate buildings served as palaces for noble families. The **Castillo de Enrique de Trastámara,** built in the 14th and 15th centuries by Gonzalo Arias de Genizaro, crowns the battlements and commands a terrific view of the surrounding countryside. (It is now a *parador de turismo,* a government financed luxury hotel.)

Practical Information The **tourist office,** Pl. Amayuelas, 6, is less than 1 bl. from the cathedral and 3 bl. from Pl. Mayor (tel. 46 05 61; open Mon.-Fri. 9:30am-2pm and 4:30-7pm, Sat.-Sun. 11:30am-2pm and 4:30-8:30pm). The **post office** is off Pl. Mayor at C. Dámaso Ledesma, 12 (tel. 46 01 17; open Mon.-Fri. 9am-2pm and 4-7pm, Sat. 9am-2pm). **Red Cross,** C. Gigantes, 4 (tel. 46 12 28). **Police,** Pl. Mayor, 27 (tel. 46 04 68).

Ciudad Rodrigo is most easily accessible by bus from Salamanca; trains are infrequent and the train station is 45min. from the walls of the old city. The **bus station** is at C. Campo de Toledo, s/n (tel. 46 10 09). To and from Salamanca (Mon.-Sat. 8 per day, Sun. 3 per day, 1hr., 670ptas). Turn left out of the bus station, then take the first right (heading uphill) and pass through the stone arch ahead; the tourist office is on the left.

Accommodations and Food **Pensión Madrid,** C. Madrid, 20 (tel. 46 24 67), off Pl. Mayor, has large, clean rooms. (Doubles 2500ptas. Triples with bath 6000ptas.) Cafés on the Plaza Mayor serve inexpensive *platos combinados.*

ALBA DE TORMES

Sta. Teresa left her heart in Alba de Tormes—it's in a jar in the **Museo Teresiano.** Look carefully for the horizontal wound—inflicted by an angel of the Lord with a long, fiery dart. After repeated stabbings, Sta. Teresa was left, as she writes in her memoirs, "on fire with the great love of God." The museum, in the Plazuela de Sta. Teresa, 2 bl. from Pl. Mayor, also contains relics of San Juan de la Cruz. (Open Tues.-Sat. 10am-2pm and 5-7:30pm, Sun. 10am-2pm. Admission 100ptas.) A few bl. down from the Pl. Mayor is the **Castillo de los Duques de Alba,** remnants of a 15th- to 16th-century structure, excavated in 1991 and 1993. Renaissance frescoes and an archeological exhibit of the remains are displayed. Across the street from Pl. Mayor is the **Convento de la Anunciación,** founded by Sta. Teresa in 1571. Her body found its resting place in an urn in the center of the lovely **retablo mayor.** Tiny Alba de Tormes boasts seven other churches, monasteries, and convents, and a neo-Gothic basilica.

The **tourist office** is on C. Puerta del Río (tel. 30 00 24; open Sun. only 10am-2pm and 4:30-8pm). Alba de Tormes makes an easy daytrip by **bus** from Salamanca (10-15 per day, ½hr., 170ptas). If you can't tear yourself away from Sta. Teresa's heart, stay overnight in the **Hostal América,** C. La Guía, s/n (tel. 30 00 71 or 30 03 46), a few bl. from the plaza. (Singles with shower 1700ptas. Doubles 3000ptas, with shower 3250ptas. IVA not included.)

LA ALBERCA AND THE PEÑA DE FRANCIA

Three mountain ranges to the south conceal a number of delightful small towns between the plains of Castilla y León and Extremadura. **La Alberca,** a charming, rustic village, was the first rural town in the country to be named an official National Historic-Artistic Monument (1940). Above La Alberca in the Sierra de Francia rises the province's highest peak, the **Peña de Francia** (1723m). Determined souls can scale the mountain from La Alberca. For information about La Alberca or the Peña de Francia, call La Alberca's **Ayuntamiento** (tel. 41 50 36). **Empresa V. Cosme** (tel. 30 02 71) runs buses from Salamanca to La Alberca (2 per day, Sat.-Sun. 1 per day, 1½hr., 870ptas).

■■■ ZAMORA

Set along the mighty River Duero, Zamora's moments of glory have floated in and out. In the 12th century, Sancho II died in Zamora during his attempt to subdue his errant sister Doña Urraca and consolidate his hold on the House of Castile. Although Urraca was at first excluded from her father's will in favor of her two brothers, she managed to usurp the city by threatening to sleep with every man in the kingdom.

In Zamora's shocking past, fierce warriors blazoned the city's name far and wide. Viriatus, born in this town and nicknamed the "Terror of the Romans," wore eight red streamers, one for each of his consular victories. King Fernando added an emerald one to the town's shield for the citizens' display of bravery in the Battle of Toro, 1476. One other display of courage was rewarded with suffering and not praise: Franco built a prison in Zamora for priests who spoke out against him.

Zamora of the 1990s is a rather sleepy town of 60,000. Hardly known from afar, tranquil Zamora welcomes guests with perhaps the greatest concentration of Romanesque architecture in Spain.

ORIENTATION AND PRACTICAL INFORMATION

The modern, elegant **train** and **bus stations** lounge in the northeast corner of the city, a 15- to 20-min. walk from Pl. Mayor. To get to the center from the bus station, exit and turn left onto C. Alfonso Peña; from the train station, exit and walk down C. Alfonso Peña, which quickly becomes Av. de Tres Cruces, to **Plaza Alemania;** turn left onto C. Alfonso IX, and continue on two blocks to **Calle Santa Clara,** a major pedestrian street on the right which leads directly to the **Plaza Mayor.** Many churches lie on the streets off C. Santa Clara, which becomes **Calle Ramos Carrión** (which leads to Pl. Viriato), then **Rua de los Francos,** and finally **Rua de los Notarios.** It winds its way to **Plaza de la Catedral,** the setting for Zamora's lovely **catedral,** behind which sulks the **castle.**

Tourist Office: Municipal, C. Santa Clara, 20 (tel. 53 18 45; fax 53 38 13). Busy and crowded, or at least thinks it is. Fold-out maps; English spoken. Open Mon.-Fri. 8am-3pm, Sat. 8am-2pm. **Patronato Provincial de Turismo,** Pl. Viriato, s/n (tel. 53 40 47), in the Edificio de la Diputación Provincial. Same glorious map as above, but a nicer ambience. Open Mon.-Fri. 8am-3pm.

Post Office: C. Santa Clara, 15 (tel. 51 33 71 or 51 07 67; fax 53 03 35), just past C. Benquente. Open for stamps, Lista de Correos, and **telegrams** Mon.-Fri. 8am-9pm, Sat. 9am-2pm. **Faxes** sent and received. **Postal Code:** 49070.

Telephones: Down Av. Requejo (an outward-bound continuation of C. Santa Clara) in a circular stone building in a small park. Open Mon.-Sat. 10am-1:30pm and 5-9pm. Also near tourist office on C. Santa Clara. **Telephone Code:** 988.

Trains: The station (tel. 52 19 56) is at the end of C. Alfonso Peña, 100m behind the bus station. Information open 24hrs. To: Madrid (5 per day, 4hr., *talgo* 3300ptas, *regional* 1690ptas); Valladolid (1 per day, 1½hr., 775ptas); La Coruña (3 per day, 7hr., *talgo* 4800ptas, *expres* 3500ptas); Alicante (1 *talgo* per week, Sat. 2:20pm, 6400ptas).

Buses: C. Alfonso Peña, 3 (tel. 52 12 81 or 52 12 82). To: Salamanca (11-14 per day, 1hr., 450ptas); Valladolid (7 per day, 1½hr., 710ptas); León (5 per day, 2hr., 980ptas); Madrid (8 per day, 3½hr., 1760ptas); Barcelona (2-3 per day, 12hr., 6120ptas).

Taxis: Radio Taxi (tel. 53 36 36). **Tele Taxi** (tel. 53 44 44).

Car Rental: Europcar, Av. Victor Gallego, 30 (tel. 51 24 26), past Pl. Alemania. Must be over 21 and have had license 1 yr.

Luggage Storage: The **bus station** has lockers (60ptas per bag). Open 7am-10pm. The **train station** also has lockers (300ptas). Open 24hrs. Given the short distance between the stations (2min.), the choice seems fairly clear.

Red Cross: C. Hernán Cortés, s/n (tel. 52 33 00).

Medical Services: Hospital Provincial, Campo Cascajo, s/n (tel. 52 02 00). **Ambulance:** tel. 52 73 51.

Police: Municipal (tel. 53 04 62 or 092), in Pl. Mayor. **National:** tel. 091.

ACCOMMODATIONS

For simple rooms at reasonable prices, investigate the streets off **Calle Alfonso Peña** by the train station, or off **Calle Santa Clara** near Pl. Mayor. Consider calling ahead during the *fiestas* that draw crowds in the last week of June.

Hostal de la Reina, C. de la Reina, 1, 1st fl. (tel. 53 39 39), behind Iglesia San Juan on Pl. Mayor. Huge, unadorned rooms; cramped baths. Warm, helpful owners speak English, French, Portuguese, and Italian. Garage. Singles 1500ptas, with bath 2200ptas. Doubles 2600ptas, with bath 3400ptas. Winter: 1200ptas; 2000ptas; 1900ptas; 2700ptas.

Pensión Fernando III, Pl. Fernando III, 2 (tel. 52 36 83). From the bus station, take the first right uphill off C. Alfonso Peña (2min.). Large beds in rooms that get more sun than Kokomo. Singles 1150ptas. Doubles 2130ptas. Triples 2675ptas. Oct 16-March 14: 945ptas; 2130ptas; 2545ptas. Breakfast 130ptas.

Hostal Avanda, Av. Alfonso IX (tel. 53 46 57). Modern and centrally located between Pl. Mayor and the stations. Singles 1885ptas. Doubles 2900-3300ptas.

FOOD

Restaurants and *mesones* rub elbows off **Calle Santa Clara** and around **Plaza Mayor,** particularly on **Calle los Herreros,** where an impressive 22 bars and restaurants pack 150 meters of pavement. **Mercado de Abastos,** in a domed building, purveys basics. (Open Mon.-Sat. 9am-2pm.) Roast meats, particularly *preses de ternera* (a veal dish), are regional specialties, as is *bacalao a la tranca* (cod).

Groceries: El Arbol, C. Tres Cruces, 5-10min. from bus station. Other stores line C. Tres Cruces and C. Víctor Gallego.

Restaurante Pozo, C. Ramón Alvarez, 10 (tel. 51 20 94), off the northern edge of Pl. Mayor. A popular old-fashioned restaurant of plain, filling fare—roast meats and *merluza* (hake), the house specialty. *Menú* 900ptas. Open Mon.-Sat. 2-4:30pm and 8:30pm-midnight, Sun. 2-4:30pm. Visa accepted.

Taberna la Dama, C. los Herreros, tucked 15m down. Offers quiet respite from the flurry outside. Wide selection of entrees including vegetarian options. *Menú* 1000ptas; some *bocadillos* at the bar. Open noon-4pm and 8pm-1am.

Mesón Los Abuelos, C. los Herreros, 30. A lot more kids than grandfathers at this local hangout. *Bocadillos* 275-400ptas. Open noon-2am.

SIGHTS

Zamora's foremost monument is its **catedral,** begun in 1135, whose cool Serbian-Byzantine dome sits like a bulb waiting to burst. (Open 10am-1pm and 5-8pm. Free.) Inside the cloister, the **Museo de la Catedral** holds a collection of art, documents, and the priceless 15th-century Black Tapestries. Keep an eye out for those once-trendy oversized hymnals. (Open 11am-2pm and 5-8pm; Oct.-June 9am-2pm and 4-6pm. Admission 200ptas.) Just uphill from the cathedral, a medieval castle, or what's left of it, slumbers in a pleasant garden. The rather scary walls command a fine view of the Río Duero (and not much else).

Remarkably, eight handsome **Romanesque churches** remain within the walls of the old city: San Ildefonso, Santa María de la Horta, Santo Tomé, La Magdalena, San Cipriano, San Juan, San Vicente, and Santiago del Burgo. (Open July-Sept. Tues.-Sat. 10am-1pm and 5-8pm; Nov.-June only during mass.) Each one gleams in the wake of recent restoration. If pressed for time, at least drop by the intricately carved porch of **La Magdalena.** In **Santiago de Burgo,** 12th-century masons left their signature marks on the columns of the nave.

Ruins of the mostly Roman walls are scattered about like crumbs, the most famous being the "Puerta del Traidor" (Traitor's Gate) near the castle. This is the actual site where Sancho tried to do in rebellious Urraca. El Cid was supposedly knighted in **Iglesia de Santiago de Caballeros**. Urraca wasn't.

■■■ LEÓN

The medieval *Codex Calixtinus* heaps adulation on León, calling it "the court and royal city… brimming with all kinds of felicity." Today, this city at the juncture of the Ríos Torío and Bernesga is a bustling provincial capital, and home to a magnificent cathedral—claimed by the proud Leonese to be the finest in all of Spain. León is known as *la ciudad azul* (the blue city) because of the dominant hue of the cathedral's stained-glass windows. While some iconoclasts think that it should be renamed *la ciudad dingy grey,* many pleasant parks and quiet plazas dot the otherwise urban landscape.

Historically an area of transit, León was founded in 68 AD by the Seventh Roman Legion—hence the name, a demotic corruption of *legio* (take a left the lions emblazoned everywhere postdates the naming of the city). Once a springboard for the Reconquista, León owes its continuing material comfort to the fertile agricultural hinterland and the deposits of iron and cobalt mined throughout the province.

ORIENTATION AND PRACTICAL INFORMATION

Most of León lies across the Río Bernesga from the bus and train stations. Heading east across the river from the stations, the new commercial district precedes the old city. **Avenida de Palencia** (take a left out of the bus station and right out of the train station) leads across the river to **Plaza Guzmán el Bueno,** and then becomes **Avenida de Ordoño II.** This major avenue bisects the new city and then becomes **Avenida del Generalísimo Franco** in the old town, on the other side of **Plaza de Santo Domingo.** Av. Generalísimo Franco splits the old town in two, with the **cate-**

dral in Plaza de Regla and the Basílica de San Isidoro to one side, the Ayuntamiento and **Plaza Mayor** on the other. **Plaza San Martín** is one block off of Pl. Mayor.

Tourist Office: Pl. Regla, 3 (tel. 23 70 82; fax 27 33 91), in front of the cathedral. Free city maps and regional brochures. Some English and French spoken. Open Mon.-Fri. 9am-2pm and 4:30-6:30pm, Sat. 10am-1pm.

Budget Travel: TIVE, C. Conde de Guillén, 2 (tel. 20 09 51). ISIC 500ptas. IHYF card 1800ptas. Some English spoken. Open Mon.-Fri. 9am-2pm.

Currency Exchange: Caja España, Pl. Regla, 1. Next to Tourist Office and across from cathedral. 500pta commission. Open Mon.-Fri. 8:30am-2pm.

Post Office: Jardín San Francisco (tel. 23 42 90; fax 23 47 01). From Pl. Santo Domingo, down Av. Independencia and opposite Parque San Francisco on the left. Open for stamps Mon.-Fri. 8am-9pm, Sat. 9am-2pm; for Lista de Correos Mon.-Fri. 9am-9pm, Sat. 9am-2pm; for **faxes** Mon.-Fri. 8am-9pm, Sat. 9am-7pm. **Postal Code:** 24071.

Telephones: Telefónica, C. Burgo Nuevo, 15. From Pl. Santo Domingo, take Av. Independencia and turn right onto C. Burgo Nuevo. Open Mon.-Fri. 9am-3pm and 4-11pm, Sat. 10am-2pm and 4-9pm. **Faxes** sent but not received. **Telephone Code:** 987.

Trains: RENFE, Av. Astorga, 2 (tel. 27 02 02), across the river from Pl. Guzmán el Bueno, at the bend in Av. Palencia. Information open 24hrs. Ticket office at C. Carmen, 4 (tel. 22 05 25). Open Mon.-Fri. 9:30am-2pm and 5-8pm, Sat. 10am-1:30pm. To: Astorga (11 per day, 45min., 365ptas); Palencia (10 per day, 1½hr., 1200ptas); Valladolid (10 per day, 2½hr., 1200ptas); Oviedo (7 per day, 2½hr., 850ptas); La Coruña (5 per day, 7hr., 3400ptas); Madrid (8 per day, 4½-5½hr., 1500-3900ptas). **FEVE,** Estación de Matallana, Av. Padre Isla, 48 (tel. 22 59 19), north of Pl. Santo Domingo.

Buses: Estación de Autobuses, Po. Ingeniero Saenz de Miera (tel. 21 00 00). Information open Mon.-Sat. 7:30am-9pm. To: Astorga (12 per day, 1hr., 385ptas); Valladolid (5 per day, 2hr., 950ptas); Santander (3pm, 5hr., 1975ptas); Zamora (3 per day, 2½hr., 950ptas); Salamanca (6 per day, 3½hr., 1500ptas); Madrid (7 per day, 4½hr., 3235ptas); Palencia (1:20pm, 1026ptas); Burgos (2 per day).

Taxis: Radio Taxi, tel. 24 12 11.

Car Rental: Hertz, Av. Sanjurjo, 23 (tel. 23 25 54). Must be over 21 and have had license 1 yr. Open Mon.-Fri. 9am-2pm and 4-7pm, Sat. 9am-1pm.

Luggage Storage: At the **train station** (lockers 400ptas). Open 24hrs. At the **bus station** (60ptas per bag). Open Mon.-Fri. 9-11am and 6-8pm, Sat. 9-11am.

Lost Property: At the police station.

English Bookstore: Pastor, Pl. Santo Domingo, 4 (tel. 22 58 56). Oxford and Penguin Classics. Open Mon.-Fri. 10am-1:30pm and 4:15-8pm, Sat. 10am-1:45pm.

Laundromat: Lavasec, C. Pérez Galdós, 1, off Av. Quevedo, 3 bl. from Puente San Marcos. Wash 290ptas per load, dry 100ptas per load. Open Mon.-Sat. 9:30am-2pm and 4-8pm.

Athletic Facilities: Polideportivo, Po. Ingeniero Saenz de Miera (tel. 20 05 19), turn right when exiting the bus station. Squash courts and a track. **Pool** 160ptas (open 10am-9pm). Sauna 330ptas.

Red Cross: tel. 27 00 33.

Medical Services: Hospital Provincial, C. Alvaro López Núñez, 26 (tel. 22 71 00). **Hospital General,** C. San Antonio, s/n (tel. 23 49 00). **Casa de Socorro** (tel. 25 12 10). **Ambulance** (tel. 27 00 33).

Emergency: tel. 091 or 092.

Police: Villa Benavente, 6 (tel. 20 73 12 or 091).

ACCOMMODATIONS

Budget beds aren't scarce in León, although *hostales* and *pensiones* often fill during the June *fiestas*. Look on **Avenida de Roma, Avenida de Ordoño II,** and **Avenida de la República Argentina,** which lead into the new town from Pl. Guzmán el Bueno. *Pensiones* are also scattered on the streets by the train and bus stations, but these are not as centrally located and a bit intimidating at night.

Residencia Juvenil Infanta Doña Sancha (HI), C. Corredera, 2 (tel. 20 22 01 or 20 38 11), 2 bl. past the Jardín San Francisco. A clean university dorm during the school year; open July-Aug. as a youth hostel. 800ptas per person. Groups larger than 8, 750ptas per person. *Pensión media* 1400ptas. *Pensión completa* 1800ptas. Over 26 yrs.: 1100ptas; 1000ptas; 1750ptas; 2300ptas. Breakfast 100ptas. Sheets included. Often booked solid; call ahead. 3-night max. stay.

Consejo de Europa (HI), Po. Parque, 2 (tel. 20 02 06), behind Pl. Toros. Recently renovated accommodations. 800ptas; over 26, 950ptas (prices for summer 1995 have not yet been determined). Breakfast 250ptas. Often booked; call ahead. Open July-Aug.

Hostal Oviedo, Av. Roma, 26, 2nd fl. (tel. 22 22 36). Funky iron headboards jazz up the pristine beds. Chatty proprietors offer huge rooms, many with terraces. Singles 1600ptas. Doubles 2700ptas. Triples 3500ptas. Showers 250ptas.

Hostal Europa, Av. Roma, 26 (tel. 22 22 38), downstairs from the Oviedo. Must have been a sale on iron beds, because this tremendously clean *hostal* has them too. Singles 1600ptas. Doubles 2700ptas. Showers 200ptas.

Fonda Condado, Av. República Argentina, 28 (tel. 20 61 60). Medievalish common area opens on to rooms with arches and walls covered in life-size wildlife photographs. Singles 1500ptas. Doubles 2000ptas. Showers 250ptas.

Hostal Central, Av. Ordoño II, 27 (tel. 25 18 06), on the right as you head toward the cathedral from Pl. Guzmán el Bueno. Blue floor and doors in the hallway cast an underwater glow. No singles. Doubles 2500-2800ptas. Showers 200ptas.

Hotel San Martín, Pl. Torres de Omaña, 1 (tel. 20 74 73). Take a left off Av. Generalísimo Franco onto C. Cervantes; follow for 2 bl. Located right in the old city. The huge, friendly family that lives here keeps rooms clean. Singles 1500ptas. Doubles with 1 bed 2000ptas, with 2 beds 3000ptas, with bath 4000ptas.

FOOD

Pork in all possible guises tops most menus, while roast suckling lamb is almost equally popular. 3500km of trout-fishable streams provoke the wild, avant-garde **International Trout Festival** in June. Fresh produce and eels of every size are sold at the **Mercado Municipal del Conde,** Pl. Conde, off C. General Mola (open Mon.-Sat. 9am-2pm).

Vegetable **markets** invade Pl. Mayor Wed. and Sat. Inexpensive eateries cluster by the cathedral and on the small streets off **Avenida Generalísimo Franco.** Bars and restaurants fill **Plaza San Martín,** near **Plaza Mayor.**

Groceries: Super Ama, C. Santa Nonia. Turn right off Av. Ordoño II onto Av. Independencia; Santa Nonia is 2nd right. Open Mon.-Sat. 10am-2pm and 5-8pm.

Cafetería-Restaurante Catedral, C. Mariano Domínguez Berrueta, 17 (tel. 21 59 18). On a street immediately to the right of the cathedral. Monumental portions make the *menú* a steal at 950ptas. Open Mon.-Sat. 1-4pm and 8pm-midnight.

Mesón San Martín, Pl. San Martín, 8 (tel. 25 60 55), a winding block from Pl. Mayor. House specialties include *menestra* (a vegetable and ham stew) and *pimientos rellenos* (stuffed peppers). *Menú* 850ptas. Open Mon. and Thurs. 1-4pm, Tues.-Wed. and Fri.-Sun. 1-4pm and 8-11:30pm.

Restaurante Buenos Aires, Av. Roma, 12. The Argentine mixed grille is a costly 1300ptas, but the 850pta *menú del día* starts with spaghetti bolognese and veers toward fried hake before finishing with ice cream and flan. Breakfast 125ptas.

Cafetería-Pizzeria Santa Rita, C. Juan Lorenzo Segura, 4 (tel. 22 50 22), a left turn off Av. Ordoño II. *Platos combinados* from 450ptas (ham omelet, sausage, fried potatoes). Individual pizzas from 425ptas.

SIGHTS

The 13th-century Gothic **cathedral,** *la Pulchra Leonina,* is considered by many to be the most beautiful in Spain. Its exceptionally well-preserved facade depicts everything from a smiling *Santa María la Blanca* to bug-eyed monsters munching on the damned. The real attraction, however, is the vivid stained-glass interior: windows occupy so much of the wall area that the building suffers from a lack of solid support. The sequence of windows narrates a complicated story, deciphered in the cathedral guidebook (700ptas). A splendid **museo** on the evolution of Romanesque sculpture hides beyond the vast cloister. (Museum open 9:30am-1:30pm and 4-6pm. Admission to cloister and museum 300ptas.)

Basílica de San Isidoro was dedicated in the 11th century to San Isidoro of Sevilla, whose remains were brought to León while Muslims ruled the South. The corpses of León's royal family rest in the impressive **Panteón Real,** whose ceilings are covered by vibrant tempera frescoes. Admission to the pantheon allows entrance to the treasury and library of rare books. Doña Urraca's famous chalices outshine the rest of the treasury room. A 10th-century handwritten Bible is the library's highlight. (Museum open Mon.-Sat. 10am-1:30pm and 4-6:30pm, Sun. 10am-1:30pm. Admission and tour 300ptas.) The city's **murallas romanas** are well preserved around the cathedral and San Isidoro.

Once a resting place for pilgrims en route to Santiago de Compostela, the **Monasterio San Marcos** is León's only five-star hotel with a Plateresque facade. The **museo** in the adjacent Gothic church houses objects from Roman and medieval times. (Museum open Tues.-Sat. 10am-2pm and 4-7:30pm, Sun. 10am-2pm. Admission 200ptas.)

Los Botines, in Pl. Santo Domingo, is one of the few buildings outside of Cataluña designed by *Modernista* Antonio Gaudí. The relatively restrained structure (under renovation until early 1995) displays only hints of the wild stuff to come.

ENTERTAINMENT

For the early part of the night (around 11pm-2am) the **barrio húmedo** around **Plaza San Martín** sweats with bars, discos, and techno-pop. **La Brasera,** in the corner of the square near Mesón San Martín, is an orgy of beer and chicken wings. **El Bacanal,** next door, attracts a primarily gay crowd to its Caravaggio-covered walls. **El Robote** (across the square) has mellower music and actual breathing space. After 2am, the crowds weave to **Calles Lancia** and **Conde de Guillén,** both heavily populated with discos and bars. Plenty of cool cafés line Av. Generalísimo Franco. **La Gargola** has cushy sofas and a starry-night painted ceiling. **El Gran Café,** on C. Cervantes one block off of Av. Generalísimo Franco, delivers live jazz twice nightly to its chic clientele.

Fiestas commemorating St. John and St. Peter make up a week-long celebration (June 20-29) including *la corrida de torros* (a bullfight). Highlights are the feast days of San Juan on the 24th and San Pedro on the 29th. Such notables as the King of Spain and his wife Sofía come on a yearly basis and often participate in the **International Organ Festival** at the cathedral.

■ NEAR LEÓN

ASTORGA

Whimsical Antonio Gaudí responded to a request from his friend, the bishop of Astorga, to design a new episcopal residence with the curving pillars, elaborate stained glass, and jutting turrets of a fanciful **Palacio Episcopal** (Bishop's Palace). The expense proved enormous for the poor parish, whose original residence had burned in 1886, especially since the construction dragged on for 20 years after the bishop's death. Upon its belated completion, no bishop dared occupy the fairy-tale palace.

Today the palace houses the decidedly eclectic **Museo de los Caminos,** whose ostensible purpose is to illustrate the various *caminos* (paths) that have passed through 2000-year-old Astorga. The second floor holds mediocre Renaissance art, and the third some stellar contemporary Leonese paintings, but the real treasure here is the building's elegant interior and beautiful stained-glass windows. Highlights on the second floor include Gaudí's effervescent chapel and the delightful dining room. (Open daily 10am-2pm and 4-8pm; winter 10:30am-1:30pm. Admission 200ptas.)

While in Astorga, glance at the **catedral,** opposite Gaudí's *palacio*. Though not as spectacular as León's insanely ornate 18th-century facade and beautiful *coro* are impressive. Whip through the **Museo Diocesano,** whose most intriguing possession is Alfonso III's glamorous gold and silver casket. (Cathedral open daily 9am-noon and 5-6:30pm; Oct.-May 9am-noon and 4:30-6pm. Free. At other times enter through the museum for 200ptas, or pay 325ptas for entrance into both Museo de los Caminos and the cathedral museum; open daily 11am-2pm and 4-8pm; Oct.-May 11am-2pm and 3:30-6:30pm.) Those with time to kill might also check out the unearthed Roman mosaics and ruins in Pl. San Bartolomé.

The **tourist office** is located inside the small stone church between the cathedral and the palace. (Open June-Oct. Mon.-Sat. 10am-2pm and 4-8pm.) The **post office** is on C. Alfereces. **Police** are at Pl. San Miguel (tel. 61 68 38); for **ambulances** call tel. 61 66 88; **taxis** can be reached at tel. 61 60 00. **Luggage** can be stored at the train station (400ptas).

Rooms tend to be expensive in Astorga. **Pensión García,** Bajada de Postigo, 6, has the best deals in town. (Singles 2000ptas. Doubles 3000ptas. Showers 250ptas.) Restaurants are numerous around the cathedral and on Av. Murallas, near the bus station. The posh **Restaurante Gaudí,** across from the Palacio Episcopal, offers a 900pta *menú* which changes daily. Besides the *mantecadas* (little sponge cakes) for which it is famous, Astorga is also home to the meat, bean, vegetable, and noodle stew known as *cocido maragato,* which is traditionally eaten in "reverse order" (meat to broth).

The **bus station,** Avda. Ponferrada, s/n (tel. 61 60 00), across from the Palacio Episcopal, is close to the town's sights. To get to the town center from the RENFE **train station,** Pl. Estación, s/n (tel. 61 64 44) walk uphill along C. Pedro de Castro until Pl. Obispo Alcolea; turn right here and continue to walk up. Twelve buses per day make the 45-min. journey to and from León daily (385ptas), as do thirteen trains (335ptas).

■■■ VALLADOLID

The glory days of Valladolid (pop. 300,000) were the Middle Ages, when Fernando de Aragón was crowned king of Castilla. A favorite seat of the monarchy since the 12th century, Valladolid supplanted Burgos as capital of Castilla (and newly unified Spain) after the conquest of Granada. In 1469 Fernando and Isabel were married here. Save for a brief spell under Felipe III (1601-1607), due to a whopping bribe palmed by his infamous prime minister Conde-Duque de Lerma, Valladolid lost out as capital to Madrid in 1561.

Once comparable to Florence in its wealth, political importance, and architectural treasures, Valladolid steadily declined after the capital was transferred. An industrial boom and the consequent influx of workers from the countryside, combined with unchecked construction in the 1970s, has further accelerated the old quarter's deterioration, and brought a fair crop of urban problems as well as a big-city ambience. While individual sights still evoke Valladolid's Renaissance magnificence, on the whole Valladolid is rather modern and grimy.

ORIENTATION AND PRACTICAL INFORMATION

The keystone in Castilla y León's arch, Valladolid occupies a central position halfway between León (133km) and Segovia (110km), and, at the same time, halfway between Burgos (122km) and Salamanca (114km). The bus and train stations sit on the southern edge of town. From the bus station, go left to reach the train station. From the train station, walk down C. Estación del Norte to **Plaza de Colón** (200m); follow C. Acera de Recoletos to **Plaza de Zorrilla** (and the tourist office). From here, walk down C. Santiago, a pedestrian zone, to get to **Plaza Mayor.** The **cathedral** is a 10-min. walk east from Pl. Mayor (right as you face the Ayuntamiento), as is **Plaza Universidad. Plaza de Val** is just behind Pl. Mayor, off the northeast corner.

Tourist Office: Pl. Zorilla, 3 (tel. 35 18 01). Maps, museum info, hotel listings. English spoken. Open Mon.-Fri. 9am-2pm and 4-6pm, Sat. 10am-1pm and 4:30-8:30pm, Sun. 11:30am-1pm and 4:30-8:30pm.

El Corte Inglés: Po. Zorilla, 130-32 (tel. 27 23 04 or 47 83 00). Their **map** beats the one from the tourist office. **Currency exchange:** 0.4% commission (250ptas min. charge for cash, 500ptas for traveler's checks). Novels and guidebooks in English, haircutting, cafeteria, restaurant, and **telephones.** Open Mon.-Sat. 10am-9pm.

Budget Travel: TIVE, on the 3rd fl. of the Edificio Administrativo de Use Múltiple (tel. 35 45 63). From Pl. Zorilla, take C. María de Molina to C. Doctrinos, follow Doctrinos across Puente Isabel la Católica, and then pass the parking lot. Open Mon.-Fri. 9am-2pm.

Currency Exchange: Caja Postal, in the post office on Pl. Rinconada. 1% commission (250ptas min. charge). Open Mon.-Fri. 8:30am-2pm.

Post Office: Pl. Rinconada (tel. 33 06 60; fax (983) 35 19 87), just off the far left corner of Pl. Mayor. Information open Mon.-Fri. 9am-2pm. Open for stamps and *certificado* Mon.-Fri. 8am-8pm, Sat. 9am-2pm; for Lista de Correos Mon.-Fri. 8am-9pm, Sat. 9am-2pm; for *postal exprés* and **telegrams** Mon.-Fri. 8am-9pm, Sat. 9am-2pm; for **fax** transmission and pick-up Mon.-Fri. 8am-9pm, Sat. 9am-7pm. To send telegrams by phone, call 34 20 00. **Postal Code:** 47071.

Telephones: Telefónica, Pl. Mayor, 7. You can send but not receive **faxes.** A/C and luxury. Open Mon.-Sat. 9:30am-2pm and 4:30-10pm. **Telephone Code:** 983.

Flights: Villanubla Airport, León Highway (N-601), km 13 (tel. 25 92 12). The taxi ride is 1600ptas. Daily service to Barcelona, Madrid, and Paris all year; service to the Islas Baleares in the summer. Information open 12:30-7:30pm. **Iberia,** C. Gamazo, 17 (tel. 30 06 66 or 30 26 39). Open Mon.-Fri. 9:30am-1:30pm and 4-7pm, Sat. 9:30am-1:30pm.

Trains: Estación del Norte, C. Recondo, s/n (tel. 30 35 18 or 30 75 78), at the end of Campo Grande. To: Medina del Campo (24 per day, ½hr., 240ptas); Zamora (2 per day, 40min., 775ptas); Burgos (8 per day, 2hr., 710ptas); Salamanca (9 per day, 1¾hr., 655ptas); León (11 per day, 1½hr., 950ptas); Madrid (22 per day, 4hr., 1500ptas); Santander (8 per day, 4¾hr., 1500ptas). Information (tel. 20 02 02 or 30 12 17) open 7am-11pm.

Buses: Puente Colgante, 2 (tel. 23 63 08). From the train station, turn left and follow C. Recondo which becomes C. Puente Colgante (5-min. walk). To: Medina del Campo (8 per day, ½hr., 310ptas); Zamora (7 per day, 40min., 700ptas); Burgos (6 per day, 2hr., 1030ptas); León (4 per day, 2hr., 920ptas); Segovia (6 per day, 2hr., 750ptas); Santander (3 per day, 4hr., 1165ptas); Oviedo (4 per day, 4hr., 1990ptas); Madrid (13 per day, 2½hr., 1365ptas); Barcelona (3 per day, 9hr., 5555ptas). Information open 8:30am-8:30pm.

Taxis: Agrupación de Taxistas (tel. 20 77 55). **Taxi Gran Turismo** (tel. 35 60 08).

Car Rental: Autos Castilla, C. Muro, 16 (tel. 30 18 78). Must be over 22 and have had license for at least 1 yr. Open Mon.-Fri. 8:30am-2pm and 4-8pm, Sat. 8:30am-2pm.

Luggage Storage: Estación del Norte has lockers. Counters are available at the ticket window (300ptas). Baggage check at the **bus station** (50ptas per bag). Open 9am-10pm.

Lost Property: in the **Ayuntamiento** in Pl. Mayor (tel. 35 04 99). Open Mon.-Fri. 9am-2pm.

English Bookstore: Librería Lara, C. Fuente Dorada, 17 (tel. 30 03 66). About 40 Penguin titles and 40 Grafton and Oxford titles. Open Mon.-Fri. 10am-1:30pm and 5-8pm, Sat. 10am-2pm.

Swimming Pool: Piscinas Deportivas, next to the river off Po. Isabel la Católica, near Puente del Poniente. Outdoors. Admission 290ptas. Open June-Sept. 11am-8:30pm. Also swimming in the **river** nearby.

Crisis Lines: AIDS hotline (tel. 33 93 35). **Women's information line** (tel. 30 08 93). **De la Esperanza** (tel. 30 70 77) and **Voces Amigas** (tel. 33 46 35 or 33 19 13) for depression. Limited English.

Red Cross: tel. 22 22 22.

Late-Night Pharmacy: Check *El Norte de Castilla* or *El Mundo de Valladolid* (local papers, 100ptas) for listing.

Hospitals: Hospital Clínico Universitario, Av. Ramón y Cajal, s/n (tel. 25 40 00). **Hospital Pío del Río Hortega,** C. Santa Teresa, s/n (tel. 42 04 00 or 35 48 04 from 9pm-7am). Some doctors speak English.

Emergency: tel. 092 (local **police**) or 091 (national police).

ACCOMMODATIONS

The distant youth hostel is a student dorm and open to travelers during the summer. Cheap lodgings (all with winter heating) are abundant in Valladolid. The streets off the right side of **Acera de Recoletos** near train station—though a little dark and scary—and those near the cathedral and behind Pl. Mayor at **Plaza del Val** are packed with cheap *pensiones* and *hostales*.

Albergue Juvenil Río Esgueve (HI), Camino Cementerio (tel. 25 15 50). Take bus #1 or 8 from Pl. Mayor and get off at the last stop before the tiny river Esgueva on C. Madre de Dios (every 10min., 10min., 80ptas). True trekkers follow C. Ferrari from Pl. Mayor to Bajada Libertad, which becomes C. Angustia, and turn right onto C. San Martín, two bl. before Pl. San Pablo. C. San Martín becomes C. de Chancilleria, then C. Madre de Dios, and finally Camino del Cementerio (30-min. walk). 3-day max. stay. 800ptas. Lunch or dinner 650ptas. *Pensión completa* 1650ptas. Over 26: 1000ptas; 800ptas; 2250ptas. Open July-Aug.

Hostal El Val, Pl. Val, 6 (tel. 37 57 52), a short distance beyond the right-hand corner of Pl. Mayor as you face the Ayuntamiento. A Valley Girl would be pleased to the max: clean rooms with sink or bath and TV rooms with couches. Singles 1500ptas. Doubles 2500ptas, with bath fit for a queen 3500ptas. Oct.-March (except Semana Santa): 2000ptas; 3000ptas.

Pensión Dos Rosas, C. Perú, 11, 2nd fl. (tel. 20 74 39). From the train station, walk up Av. Acera Recoletos and turn right on C. Perú. Sunny rooms with scrubbed wood floors; especially spacious doubles. A fantastic bargain only 2 bl. from Pl. Zorilla. Portable heaters in winter. Singles 1150ptas. Doubles 2100ptas. Triples 2850ptas. Hot water costs 175ptas extra.

Pensión Dani, C. Perú, 11, 1st fl. (tel. 30 02 49), downstairs from Dos Rosas. Newly renovated and painted. Very clean rooms with cutesy floral bedspreads and modern baths. Singles 1300ptas. Large doubles 2300ptas. Prices here include hot-water showers.

FOOD

Stiff competition keeps prices down and makes many elegant restaurants accessible to budget diners. Restaurants are plentiful between **Plaza Mayor** and **Plaza Val.** Explore **Plaza de la Universidad,** near the cathedral, for *tapas*. The **Mercado del Val** on C. Sandoval, in Pl. Val, handles vegetables, meat, and fruit. (Open Mon.-Sat. 9am-3pm.)

Groceries: Simago, C. Santiago, 13, 8 bl. from Pl. Zorrilla. Open Mon.-Sat. 9:30am-8:30pm.

Café-Bar Los Condes, C. Gamazo, 17 (tel. 29 14 21), two minutes from Pl. Colón. Classy restaurant with seemingly infinite choices on its *menú del día* (1000ptas). Open 9am-1am.

Restaurante Covadonga, C. Zapico, 1 (tel. 33 07 98), up the street from Pl. Val. Busy yet elegant. *Menú* with bread, wine, and dessert (895ptas). Lots of meat and fresh veggies. Open Aug.-June Mon.-Sat. 1-4pm and 9-11pm, Sun. 1-4pm.

Antigua Cervecería, C. Arzobispo Gondásegui, 2, on the left corner of Pl. Portugalete as you face the cathedral. *Tapas* bar with strange hybrid of American and Spanish quick eats. *Bocadillos* 200-250ptas. French fries 250ptas. Crown jewel of the bunch is *hamburguesa vavi* (bacon cheeseburger, 130ptas). Open Mon.-Fri. noon-midnight, Sat.-Sun. noon-1:30am.

Restaurant El Val, Pl. Rinconada, 10 (tel. 35 37 93). From Pl. Mayor, up C. Jesús and to the right. On the first floor of building with huge wood doors. Warm *come-*

dor resembles a bar mitzvah reception room. *Menú* 750ptas. *Lentejas* 240ptas. Roasty good ½-chicken 325ptas. Open Sept.-July Tues.-Sun. 10am-4pm and 9-11pm.

Tele Pizza, C. Puente Colgante, 49 (tel. 27 50 50). Follow Po. Zorrilla 2 bl. past the park. They deliver, or you can eat there. Small pizza 650ptas; 80ptas per each additional topping; 900ptas min. for delivery. Open Sun.-Thurs. 1-4pm and 6:30pm-midnight, Fri.-Sat. 1-4pm and 6:30pm-1am.

SIGHTS

Glory slipped through the fingers of Valladolid. The **catedral,** in Pl. Universidad, should have been four times larger, and there is something poignant about this monumental incomplete fragment. Designed by Juan de Herrera (responsible for El Escorial) in 1580, its interior is cold and severe, with light streaming through the windows set in colossal white stone arches. (100ptas to illuminate the main altar for 15 seconds; side altar 25ptas.) The **Museo Diocesano** inside is worth a look for its jewelry, wooden polychrome statues of John the Baptist, and a model of the basilica's original design. (Open Tues.-Fri. 10am-1:30pm and 4:30-7pm, Sat.-Sun. 10am-2pm. Cathedral free, museum 200ptas. Cathedral often closes early afternoon.) Behind the cathedral, the Romanesque tower of **Santa María la Antigua** caps a mainly Gothic underpinning.

Religious treasures, most made of wood, are displayed at the **Museo Nacional de Escultura** in the **Colegio de San Gregorio** (tel. 25 03 75). The *colegio* is some minutes beyond the cathedral, near Pl. San Pablo, just off C. Angustias. (Open Tues.-Sat. 10am-2pm and 4-6pm, Sun. 10am-2pm. Admission 200ptas, students free.) The **patio's** interwoven masonry is hypnotizing.

Spain's best collection of Asian art is tucked away in the **Museo Oriental,** in the basement of the **Real Colegio Padres Agustinos Filipinos,** Po. Filipinos, 7 (tel. 30 68 00) near the train station, south of the Campo Grande. During four centuries of missionary work, Jesuits accumulated this collection of largely Chinese and Philippine works. The highlight is a 15-inch ship crafted from cloves. (Open Mon.-Sat. 4-7pm, Sun. 10am-1pm. Admission 200ptas, groups of students and seniors 150ptas.)

The discoverer of America and the creator of Don Quixote both came here to die. Plush **Casa de Colón,** on C. Colón (tel. 29 13 53), is now part research library and part museum. (Open Mon.-Sat. 11am-1pm and 4-6pm, Sun. 11am-1pm. Shorter hours in winter. Free.) From the looks of the **Casa de Cervantes,** off C. Castro, you might conclude that the writer died of boredom. There's an amusing collection of old books and furniture, but the medieval bed-warmer is the real highlight. (Open Tues.-Sat. 10am-3:30pm, Sun. 10am-3pm. Admission 200ptas.)

ENTERTAINMENT

Valladolid's cafés and bars are lively, though nothing to write home about. Fun-seekers migrate from bars near the university in the early evening to **Plaza Cantarranas,** two blocks east, later on; or spend long evenings in one of the ubiquitous *terrazas.* Valladolid is also big on movies. **Cine Casablanca,** C. Platerías, 1, shows them with English subtitles. The city holds a highly regarded **Festival Internacional de Cine** in late-October and early-November. Schedules unavailable until festival.

Semana Santa (Holy Week) in Valladolid ranks with Sevilla's as one of Spain's most fascinating religious festivals. It is distinguished by its solemnity and austerity, enriched by the rituals of *cofradías* (brotherhoods) and religious orders. Sept. 16-23 marks the **Fiesta Mayor** celebrations, featuring bullfights, carnivals, and parades.

■ NEAR VALLADOLID: TORDESILLAS

The birthplace of Isabel la Católica, 29km from Valladolid, Tordesillas boasts a number of mueums, a monastery with a Mudejar patio, Arab baths, and a rich history. The 1494 **Treaty of Tordesillas,** written by Isabel and Fernando and Juan II of Portugal, divided the world between Spain and Portugal, in the name of God. Tordesillas is also the site of the imprisonment of Juana la Loca (the Mad). After she wandered about with the body of her dead husband and king, handsome Felipe, Juana's own son had her locked up in this very town.

■■■ PALENCIA

A sole neon sign in Palencia stands out, almost as if to call attention to the surrounding provincialism by its very uniqueness—people and cows cross paths here with surprising frequency. Palencia established Spain's first university in 1208 (which moved to Salamanca in 1239), and later, in 1321, constructed its crowning glory, the Santa Iglesia Catedral de San Antolín, called *la bella desconocida* (the unknown beauty).

Although some parts of Palencia are fairly dull, sights here and in nearby towns offer refreshing calm compared to Spain's more popular tourist areas. For those who wish to take in a concentration of Spanish architecture without the hype of heavy tourism, Palencia and its satellite *pueblos* house some of the country's most important Romanesque and Visigothic monuments.

ORIENTATION AND PRACTICAL INFORMATION

Palencia has length but is short on width. **Calle Mayor,** the main pedestrian artery and shopping zone, runs through the old city. **Los Jardinillos** is a park at the north end of C. Mayor, in front of the train and bus stations. C. Mayor begins at **Plaza León,** a traffic rotary adjacent to the park. The **tourist office** is a 10-min. walk at the south end of C. Mayor, on the left before Av. José Antonio Primo de Rivera where the pedestrian zone ends. Thereafter C. Mayor becomes **Avenida República Argentina** and then **Avenida de Valladolid.** To reach the **cathedral,** take the first right off C. Mayor after leaving Pl. León for three blocks.

Tourist Office: C. Mayor, 105 (tel. 74 00 68; fax 70 08 22). Free maps, posters, and all sorts of nifty information on Palencia and environs. Friendly and helpful staff speaks some English and French. Poster at entrance displays extremely useful information. Open Mon.-Fri. 9am-2pm and 4-6pm, Sat. 10am-1pm.

Currency Exchange: Banco Central Hispanoamericano, C. Mayor, 21 (tel. 74 98 22), on the corner with Boca Plaza. 1% commission (min. charge 250ptas for cash, 500ptas for traveler's checks). Open Mon.-Fri. 8:30am-2pm; Sept.-June Mon.-Fri. 8:30am-4:30pm.

Post Office: Pl. León, 1 (tel. 74 21 80). Sends and receives **faxes** (fax 74 22 60). Open for stamps, **telegrams,** and *certificado* Mon.-Fri. 8am-9pm, Sat. 9am-7pm; for Lista de Correos Mon.-Fri. 8am-9pm, Sat. 9am-2pm. **Postal Code:** 34070.

Telephones: Telefónica, Patio de Castaño, off C. Mayor, to the right. You can send (but not receive) **faxes.** Open Mon.-Sat. 10am-2pm and 4-9pm. **Telephone Code:** 988.

Trains: at Jardinillos (tel. 74 30 19). Information (tel. 20 02 02) open 24hrs. To: Madrid (12 per day, 4hr., 1800-3000ptas); Barcelona (3 per day, 8hr., 5400ptas); Santander (8 per day, 4hr., 1200-1400ptas); Valladolid (24 per day, 45min., 315ptas); Burgos (4 per day, 45min., 450-1250ptas); León (10 per day, 1¼hr., 710-1550ptas).

Buses: (tel. 74 32 22), at Jardinillos to the right of the train station. To get to Pl. León and C. Mayor, exit the station and turn right; then turn left on Av. Dr. Simón Nieto, which hits Pl. León. Information open 9:30am-8pm. To: Madrid (4 per day, 3½hr., 1640ptas); Barcelona (2 per day, 7½hr., 4455ptas); Vitoria (1 per day, 4hr., 2500ptas); Valladolid (12 per day, 45min., 370ptas); Burgos (3 per day, 1½hr., 640ptas); León (1 per day, 2hr., 860ptas); Santander (4 per day, 4hr., 960ptas).

Taxis: tel. 74 39 19 or 74 21 26.

Car Rental: Avis, Av. Casado del Alisal, 43 (tel. 74 11 76). From the train station turn left and it's up Casado del Alisal on the left. Must be over 22 and have had a license for at least 1 yr. Open Mon.-Fri. 9am-1:30pm and 4-8pm, Sat. 9am-1:30pm.

Luggage Storage: The **train station** has lockers (300ptas per day).

English Bookstore: Librería Alfar, C. Tintes, s/n (tel. 72 65 40), off Av. República Argentina to the right. Classy bookstore with about 2 shelves of Penguins. Open Mon.-Fri. 10am-2pm and 5-8:30pm; winter 10am-1:30pm and 4-8pm.
Red Cross: tel. 22 22 22.
Late-Night Pharmacy: check *El Norte de Castilla* (local paper, 150ptas) under *de guardia* listings.
Hospital: Hospital Provincial "San Telmo," Av. San Telmo (tel. 72 82 00). **Hospital Río Carrión,** Carretera de Villamuriel, s/n (tel. 72 29 00 or 72 29 84). **Ambulance:** tel. 72 22 40.
Emergency: local **police** (tel. 092) or national police (tel. 091).

ACCOMMODATIONS

The **Victorio Macho** (tel. 72 04 62) and **Escuela Castilla** (tel. 72 14 75) youth hostels are open only in the summer and have eight and ten spaces respectively. Call ahead to check for unlikely availability; Bus B from Jardinillos (every 12min., 70ptas) avoids a hike to either. Plenty of reasonably priced *hostales* with clean, if plain, rooms on side streets running from **Calle Mayor** toward the **Río Carrión**.

Pensión el Hotelito, C. General Amor, 5 (tel. 74 69 13). From Pl. León take C. Mayor to C. General Franco, turn right, then left onto C. General Amor. Offers spacious rooms with wooden beds and ocean motif decorations. Singles 1800-2000ptas. Doubles 3000ptas, with bath 3500ptas. Triples 4000ptas, with bath 4500ptas. No running water in rooms without bath.

El Salón, Av. República Argentina, 10 (tel. 72 64 42). A little far, but worth the walk. Polished furniture, chandeliers, and an endearing bathroom floral motif embellish the spotless interior and spacious rooms. Singles 1800ptas. Doubles 3000ptas. Triples 4000ptas. Dec.-June 1: 1000ptas; 2500ptas; 3500ptas.

Hostal Tres de Noviembre, C. Mancornador, 18 (tel. 74 16 47 am, 70 30 35 pm). From C. Mayor turn right on Av. José Antonio Primo de Rivera, then right again on C. Mancornador. A modern *pensión* with firm mattresses and plain, airy rooms. Sketches of old Palencia decorate the walls. Singles 1300ptas. Doubles 2600ptas.

El Edén Camping (tel. 88 01 85), 2 bl. from the central Café España in Carrión de los Condes, hugging the river. Follow the signs. Three buses per day connect Palencia to Carrión (30min., 295ptas). 300ptas per person, 300-400ptas per tent, 300ptas per car. Children 250ptas. Electricity 250ptas.

FOOD

Palencia's **market** off Pl. Mayor (open 9am-2pm) pleases most hungry travelers. Numerous restaurants and *tapas* bars—most of similar price and quality—line the streets just off **Calle Mayor**.

Groceries: Simago, C. Menéndez y Pelayo at the corner of C. Pedro Moreno, across the street from Telefónica. Down C. Mayor from Pl. León and right on C. Patio de Castaño. Open Mon.-Sat. 9:30am-9pm.

Taberna Plaza Mayor, Pl. Mayor, s/n. Specialties are written on the tiled wall behind the bar. *Menú* 1000ptas. *Tapas* bar downstairs has huge selection; quiet upstairs dining for full meals. Open 7:30am-1am.

El Chaval de Lorenzo, C. José Antonio Primo de Rivera, 3 (tel. 75 12 25). Turn left at the south end of C. Mayor past the tourist office. Students play pool and cards or watch TV on the big screen. Choice array of *tapas: champiñones al ajillo* (mushrooms in garlic sauce, 100ptas) and *tortilla* are among the staples, along with *bocadillos* (250-350ptas). *Raciones* 200ptas and up. Open 10am-1am.

Restaurante Skarlotas, C. Mancornador, 1 (tel. 74 16 47). Follow directions for Hostal Tres de Noviembre (above)—same owner. Friendly barman serves up cheap and tasty *tapas*. Sit down *menú* (700ptas) choices are limited. Open Sat.-Thurs.

PALENCIA

SIGHTS

Palencia's biggest attraction is the 14th-century Gothic cathedral, **Santa Iglesia de San Antolín** (tel. 70 13 47), in which 14-year-old Catherine of Lancaster married 10-year-old Enrique III in 1388. A statue of the virgin under a gravity-defying halo greets penitents in the **Plaza de la Inmaculada Concepción.** The **Museum** has stellar works, including El Greco's famed *San Sebastián,* spectacular 16th-century Flemish tapestries, a caricature of Carlos I, and medieval hymnals bound in the skin of unborn calves. The orgy of medieval religiosity ends way, way down a stone staircase at the musty, spooky **Cripta de San Antolín,** a 7th-century sepulchre. (Cathedral open Mon.-Sat. 8:30am-1pm and 4-6:30pm, Sun. 8:45am-2pm. Museum open Mon.-Sat. 9:30am-1pm and 4-6pm. Sometimes irregular hours. 200ptas.)

More religious artifacts repose in the **Iglesia de Santa Clara,** the resting place for a Jesus with a mummy-like corpus, blackened fingernails, decomposed toes, and gaping mouth. (Open 8:30am-8pm.) A favorite of El Cid fans, **Iglesia de San Miguel,** on C. General Moia, between the bridges, is the site of his marriage to Doña Jimena.

Every year for two weeks in July and August, Palencia province hosts an international classical music festival.

■ NEAR PALENCIA

Palencia is close to some of the oldest examples of Romanesque architecture in Spain. It takes some effort to reach these outlying towns by train or bus.

CARRIÓN DE LOS CONDES

Forty km north of Palencia on the **Camino de Santiago** (Road to Compostela), tiny Carrión (pop. 1000) offers a few incredible sights and its own riverside beauty. The **Iglesia de Santa María** (tel. 88 00 72) is a 12th-century temple with a morbid portal: the south side depicts the legendary annual tribute of 100 Carrión maidens to Moorish conquerors. (Open 8am-2pm and 5-8pm; open for mass 8:30am, holidays 10:30am and noon.)

On the far side of the Río Carrión looms the secularized **Monasterio de San Zoilo** (tel. 88 00 49 or 88 00 50). Faces of saints and popes stare down from the ornate arches of the Renaissance cloister, which is only partially open to the public. The tombs of the notorious Infantes de Carrión of the *Cantar del Mío Cid,* who married El Cid's daughters, beat them and then abandoned them in the middle of nowhere, are situated near the exit. (Open Tues.-Sun. 10am-1pm and 4-7pm.)

Carrión's hidden treasure is the **Convento de Santa Clara,** also known as Las Clarisas. The *repostería* (pastry shop) bakes delicious cookies. Since the nuns are cloistered, all transactions are expedited by a revolving cabinet while they peer out from behind two iron gratings. The convent has recently inaugurated a **museo;** ring the bell and ask for Sr. Antonio (50ptas). The whimsically eclectic collection includes shepherds' nutcrackers, a statue of baby Jesus with a toothache, and 14th-century fabric from bishops' frocks. (Tel. 88 01 34; open Tues.-Sun. 10:30am-2pm and 4:30-8:30pm; off-season Tues.-Sun. 11am-2pm and 4-7pm.)

Carrión's **tourist office** (not a government office; hours vary) is in a wood-frame hut across the street from **Café-Bar España,** where the bus drops off. **Hostal La Corte,** C. Santa María, 34 (tel. 88 01 38), provides luxurious, spotless, and spacious doubles (3000ptas). For **camping,** see Palencia: Accommodations. Three **buses** per day (tel. 74 32 22) carry day (or ½-day) trippers from Palencia to Carrión (295ptas).

BAÑOS DE CERRATO

The perfectly preserved Visigothic **Basílica de San Juan de Baños,** built in 661 AD, lures visitors south to Baños de Cerrato. Visigothic King Recesvinto left two marks here: an inscription above the altar, and the impression of his royal extremities on the floor. The caretaker of the oldest Christian temple in Spain and his impossibly large keys reside at C. San Juan de Baños. Sr. Patricio unlocks the doors, sells postcards, and reveals all the basilica's deep, dark secrets. It's most impressive from the inside, where six cool marble columns stretch up to the ceiling. (Tel. 77 00 69; open Tues.-Sun. 9am-1pm and 5-7pm.) Take the train 9km from Palencia to **Ventas de Baños** (15 per day, 10min., 150ptas), an ugly industrial town. Turn left at the station entrance and keep walking; Baños de Cerrato is visible 2km down the road and the basilica is on the far side.

■■■ BURGOS

Although the smokestacks and industrial buildings initially disappoint travelers who enter Burgos (pop. 160,000) by train or bus, a short walk across the Río Arlanzón rewards visitors with a cheerful city rich in tradition. The *Cabeza de Castilla* (Head of Castile) in the Middle Ages, Burgos rose to prominence as capital of the province, and then of the kingdom of Castile, before losing out to Valladolid in 1492 as the residence permanent court of newly unified Spain. Burgos retains some influence, however, as the headquarters for the powerful *Mesta* guild of shepherds, and as a crossroads for pilgrims journeying to Santiago.

Burgos's huge renowned Gothic cathedral looks down on a lively city. Belying its politically conservative reputation, Burgos pulsates with the music and dancing of an energetic youth culture as soon as night falls.

ORIENTATION AND PRACTICAL INFORMATION

Burgos lies about 240km north of Madrid on the main route between Madrid and the French border. The Río Arlanzón divides the city into north and south sides. The train and bus stations are on the south side, while the **cathedral** and all other sights of interest are located on the north side. From the train station, follow **Avenida Conde de Guadalhorce** across the river, and take the first right onto **Avenida del Generalísimo Franco,** which turns into **Paseo del Espolón** farther down. The cathedral is just beyond this tree-lined street; at the end of the street stands a large statue of El Cid. A short walk up this street leads to **Plaza de España.** Look here for signs to the tourist office, which is located in **Plaza de Alonso Martínez.** The **Plaza José Antonio** (or **Plaza Mayor**) is between the cathedral and the tourist office, slightly east of the former.

Tourist Office: Pl. Alonso Martínez, 7 (tel. 20 31 25). From Pl. José Antonio, take Laín Calvo for 3 bl. The office, located across from the official-looking Capitanía General building, offers a variety of multilingual brochures and maps, and even has a computer which will take you on a video tour of the region. Some English spoken. Open Mon.-Fri. 9am-2pm and 4:30-6:30pm, Sat. 10am-1:30pm.

Budget Travel: Viajes TIVE (tel. 20 98 81). From Pl. España, take C. San Lesmes to Pl. San Juan, which is on your left. Unmarked door on the first floor of the Casa de Cultura. Student IDs (500ptas) and HI cards (1800ptas). Some English spoken. Open Mon.-Fri. 9am-2pm.

Currency Exchange: Citibank, Pl. Rey, 4, located across from side entrance to the cathedral. High exchange rate, but won't change American Express traveler's checks. Open Mon.-Fri. 8:30am-2pm.

Post Office: Pl. Conde de Castro, 1 (tel. 26 27 50), across the river from Pl. Primo de Rivera where El Cid points the way. Open for stamps, Lista de Correos, and **telegrams** Mon.-Fri. 8am-9pm, Sat. 9am-2pm. **Postal Code:** 09000.

Telephones: Telefónica shut down last year. Look for phone booths in the major plazas and many bars.

Trains: At the end of Av. Conde Guadalhorce, across the river from Pl. Castilla (tel. 20 35 60). A 10-min. walk southwest of the city center, or 500pta taxi ride. Information open 7am-11pm. **RENFE,** C. Moneda, 21 (tel. 20 91 31). Open Mon.-Fri. 9am-1pm and 4-7pm, Sat. 9am-1pm. To: Palencia (7 per day, 1hr., 400-1100ptas); Valladolid (13 per day, 1½hr., 1200ptas); San Sebastián (11 per day, 3hr., 1900ptas); Logroño (3 per day, 2hr., 1500ptas); León (5 per day, 2hr., 1600ptas); Bilbao (5 per day, 3hr., 1500ptas); Madrid (8 per day, 3½hr., 1400-2700ptas); Barcelona (4 per day, 8hr., 5200ptas); Santiago (1 per day, 7hr., 4500ptas); La Coruña (4 per day, 8hr., 4500ptas). Prices vary widely depending on day or time of travel.

Buses: C. Miranda, 4 (tel. 20 55 65), just off Pl. Vega. (Pl. Vega is on the south side of river, equidistant from train station and statue of El Cid, which is on the north side.) Each bus company has its own ticket window, its own routes, and— alas!— its own schedule. To: Madrid (10 per day, 3hr., 1720ptas); Barcelona (4 per day, 7hr., 4455ptas); Bilbao (4 per day, 2hr., 1350ptas); Palencia (3 per day, 1½hr., 700ptas); Valladolid (2 per day, 1½hr., 1030ptas); Santander (1 per day, 3hr., 1280ptas); León (1 per day, 2hr. 1655ptas); Vitoria (9 per day, 1½hr., 825ptas).

Taxis: Radio Taxi (tel. 27 77 77).

Car Rentals: Hertz, Av. Madrid, 10 (tel. 20 16 75), straight down from Pl. Vega and around the corner from the bus station. Must be 21 or over with credit card, 25 or over without. Smallest car with unlimited mileage is 4995ptas per day. Cheaper for longer rentals. Open Mon.-Fri. 9am-2pm and 4-7pm, Sat. 9am-1pm. **Avis,** Av. Generalísimo Franco, 5 (tel. 20 58 13). Same rates and restrictions as Hertz, but offers special weekend rates (Fri.-Sun. 8750ptas plus tax, unlimited mileage). Open Mon.-Fri. 8:30am-1:30pm and 4-8pm, Sat 8:30am-1:30pm.

Hitchhiking: To Madrid, hitchers walk south along C. Madrid from Pl. Vega until highway N-1; to Santander, hitchers walk north on Av. General Vigón, but remember we don't recommend it.

Luggage Storage: At the **train station** (tel. 20 33 60; lockers 300ptas). At the **bus station** you can check your bag (100ptas per bag). Open Mon.-Fri. 9am-8pm, Sat. 9am-6pm.

Bookstore: Librería Luz y Vida, C. Laín Calvo, 38 (tel. 20 35 56). A moderate and eclectic selection of English fiction. Open Mon.-Fri. 10am-2pm and 5-8pm, Sat. 9:30am-1pm.

Athletic Facilities: Gimnasio Sport Tres, C. San Agustín, 9 (tel. 27 62 63). Walk up C. Madrid, cross the train tracks, and turn right at the bunch of trees. Membership (500ptas) includes tae kwon do, karate, aerobics classes, and use of the weight room. Open Mon.-Fri. 9am-2pm and 4-10pm, Sat. 10am-1pm and 5:30-8:30pm. **El Plantío** (tel. 22 00 01), to the east along the river, by the Plaza de Toros (bullring), is a swimming pool. Open June 15-Sept. 200ptas.

Crisis Hotlines: Don't count on English being spoken. **SOS Droga** (tel. 26 36 00) for drug addiction. **Alcoholics Anonymous** (tel. 23 65 52). **Teléfono de Esperanza** (tel. 20 42 22) for depression and suicidal thoughts.

Red Cross: tel. 22 22 22.

Late-Night Pharmacy: Check the listings in *El Diario de Burgos* (local paper, 90ptas) or the sign posted in every pharmacy.

Medical Services: Casa de Socorro, Conde de Vallellano, 4 (tel. 26 14 10), at C. Ramón y Cajal near the post office.

Ambulance: tel. 22 22 22.

Emergency: tel. 091 (police), or 092.

ACCOMMODATIONS AND CAMPING

Head to the neighborhood around **Plaza Vega,** near the bus and train stations, or to the streets near **Plaza Alonso Martínez** on the north side. **Calle San Juan** and adjoining streets are dotted with reasonably priced *hostales*. Reservations are crucial for the last week of June and the first week of July (feast days of St. Paul and St. Peter) and are advisable through August. The "Fuentes Blancas" bus (from El Cid statue, 65ptas) voyages to **Camping Fuentes Blancas,** 3½km outside Burgos. (Open April-Sept. 450ptas per person, per tent, and per car.)

Around Plaza Alonso Martínez

Hostal Hidalgo, C. Almirante Bonifaz, 14 (tel. 20 34 81), one bl. from Pl. Alonso Martínez, off C. San Juan, just past Galerías Preciados. A dark, spooky stairway leads to a warm and friendly *hostal*. Rooms have high ceilings and hardwood floors. Singles 1800ptas. Doubles 3200-3400ptas.

Pensión Peña, C. Puebla, 18 (tel. 20 63 23). From Pl. España, take C. San Lesmes; C. Puebla is the 3rd right. The ABCs of budget travel: affordable, basic, and clean. Singles 1000-1500ptas. Doubles 2000-2200ptas. Showers 220ptas.

Hostal Joma, C. San Juan, 26 (tel. 20 33 50). From El Cid's statue, walk up C. Santander past Pl. Calvo Sotelo and turn right on C. San Juan. Quiet and cheap, but many rooms go to long-term boarders. Owner serves up cookies and coffee for breakfast in the small dining room. Singles 1300-1500ptas. Doubles 1800-2200ptas. Showers 200ptas. Breakfast 225ptas.

Hostal Victoria, C. San Juan, 3 (tel. 20 15 42), a little north of Hostal Joma. Local students fill the rooms from October through June. Singles 2000ptas. Doubles 2800ptas. Triples 4000ptas.

Hostal-Restaurante Castellano, C. Laín Calvo, 48 (tel. 20 50 40). Centrally located near the tourist office and only 2 bl. up from Pl. José Antonio. Find a partner: only doubles have windows. If your "we" must remain royal, then enjoy the singles' regal decorations such as wine-colored bedspreads, green velvet chairs, and the stately garden. Singles 2000ptas. Doubles 4000ptas. Triples 6000ptas. Shower included. Closed Dec. 20-Feb. 2.

Around Plaza de la Vega (near stations)

Pensión Ansa, C. Miranda, 9 (tel. 20 47 67), across the street from the bus station. The petunias in the windows brighten already sparkling rooms. Singles 2000ptas. Doubles 3400ptas. Triples 4500ptas. Showers included.

Hostal Niza, C. General Mola, 12 (tel. 26 19 17). From Pl. Vega, follow C. Madrid and take the 2nd left onto General Mola; the *hostal* is at the end of the block. Large rooms, some with balconies. Elevator. Singles 2500ptas. Doubles 3000ptas. Triples 4525ptas. Showers 250ptas.

FOOD

Let's Go does not recommend vegetarians stay too long... landlocked Burgos specializes in meat, meat, and more meat. Try *picadillo de cerdo* (minced pork), *cordero asado* (roast lamb), or, for a taste of everything, *olla podrida,* a stew in which sausage, beans, pork, cured beef, and bacon mingle as one. Sausage straight up is another specialty, especially *morcilla* (blood pudding). Locals covet *sopa burgalesa,* prepared with lamb and crawfish tails. Burgos's own *queso de Burgos* (cheese) is delicious by itself or with honey. Polish off a meal with *yemas de Burgos,* the unique sickly-sweet sugared egg yolks.

Burgos has two markets, **Mercado Norte** near Pl. España and the smaller **Mercado de Abastos,** on C. Miranda near the bus station. Markets open Mon.-Sat. 7am-3pm. Mercado Norte stays open later on Fri. (5:30-8pm). Head to C. San Lorenzo at night for *tapas*-munching heaven.

Groceries: Alimentación Pardo Simancas, C. San Lorenzo, 21. Open Mon.-Fri. 9am-2pm and 5-8pm, Sat. 9am-2pm. **Casa Ojeda,** on C. Vitoria, is a posh *charcutería,* selling all kinds of meats, cheeses, sweets, and prepared foods. **Health food store: Los Tilso,** C. General Yagüe, 6, 1 bl. from Pl. España. Open Mon.-Fri. 10am-2pm and 5-8pm, Sat. 10am-2pm.

Restaurante Sotillano, C. Avellanos, 5 (tel. 20 61 88), off Pl. Alonso Martínez. Waiter/chef of this bargain hunter's dream stuffs patrons with a 1000pta *menú,* a scrumptious feast of local specialties. Open 11:30am-5pm and 8pm-midnight.

Mesón Arlanza, C. Fernán González, 44 (tel. 26 01 48), uphill from the cathedral. Delicious *paella* and sauteed trout serve as one of several 850pta *menús del día.* Friendly staff prepares the meal to your specifications. Open Sun.-Thurs. 10am-1am, Fri.-Sat. 10am-3am. Closed Tues. afternoons in winter.

Restaurante de Angel, C. Fernán González, 36 (tel. 20 86 08), uphill from the cathedral. Heavenly dining room, lit with skylights and odd lamps in the shape of medieval towers. *Menú del día* 900ptas. *Filete de vaca* (beef), *cordero* (lamb), and *ternera* (veal) feature prominently on the menu. Open 1:30-3:30pm and 8:30-11:30pm. Closed Wed. and the last two weeks of Sept. and Feb.

Mesón de los Herreros, C. San Lorenzo, 20, between Pl. Mayor and Pl. Alonso Martínez. *Tapas*-o-rama. The *cojonudo* (spicy sausage with egg and pimento) is a specialty as are *patatas bravas* (french fries in spicy orange sauce, 100ptas). *Raciones* 300-800ptas. Only the brave eat *morritos* (pig nose, 350ptas), *patas de* *cordero* (lamb feet, 550ptas), and pick the *sesos* (lamb brains). Open Mon.-Sat. 9:30am-3:30pm and 6pm-12:30am, Sun. 11am-3:30pm and 6pm-midnight.

Restaurante La Flor, C. Avellanos, 9 (tel. 26 60 52), off Pl. Alonso Martínez. The light, airy *comedor* is just past the bar. Light blue walls and TV humming overhead. A feast. *Platos combinados* 600-750ptas. *Menú* with *pollo asado con ajo* (a house specialty), bread, wine, and dessert (1000ptas). Open 1-4pm and 8-11pm; closed Thurs. in winter.

La Cabaña Arandina, on the corner of C. Sommeria and C. Diego Porcelos, between the cathedral and Pl. José Antonio. Locals and pilgrims (including the occasional nun) crowd around the three-sided bar for tasty stuffed peppers (175ptas), *boquerones* (anchovies, 175ptas), and crayfish in saffron sauce (575ptas). *Bocadillos* from 100ptas, heartbreakingly tiny beers 50ptas.

Cafetería Don Diego, C. Diego Porcelo, directly behind the cathedral. Behind the wood facade and lace curtains, they serve filling *platos combinados* (750-850ptas). Open Mon.-Thurs. 9am-12:30am, Fri.-Sat. 9am-2am.

SIGHTS

Cathedral and Nearby

The magnificent Gothic **cathedral** (tel. 20 47 12) dominates the city. A powerful group of 13th-century gentlemen sheep farmers (the *Mesta*) funded its construction with their extraordinary merino wool. Two towers flank the main facade, a fantastic concoction of intricately detailed windows and quirky sculpture crowned by openwork spires from the 15th century. The north facade and the *Puerta del Sacramental* are 13th-century Gothic; the Puerta de la Pellejería was added in the 16th century. The interior is equally ostentatious and impressive. In the **Capilla Mayor,** at the east end, El Cid's bones and those of his wife Jimena comingle in marmoreal serenity. Sunlight pours through an eight-point glass skylight set into the **cimborrio** (dome) above the late Gothic **Capilla de Condestable.** Exceptions to the stony-faced architecture include the main Gothic crossing (more glass than stone) and the early 16th-century **Escalera Dorada** (Gilded Staircase) in the northern transept. Before leaving the cathedral, look for the fly catcher high up near the main door in the central aisle. As it strikes the hours, the strange creature opens its mouth in imitation of the crowds gawking below. Befriend the sacristan, and he may show you *The Painting al la Magdalena* by Leonardo da Vinci which is tucked behind a wooden cabinet in the gift shop. (Open daily 9:30am-1pm and 4-7pm. Admission to sacristy and museum 350ptas, students 100ptas.)

The cathedral's dwarfish neighbor, the **Iglesia de San Nicolás,** cowers across the Pl. Santa María and up the steps. The elaborately carved *retablo* is the highlight of the unfinished interior. (Open in summer 9am-2pm and 4-8pm, Sun. 9am-2pm and 5-6pm; winter Mon. all day, Tues.-Fri. 6:30-7:30pm, Sat. 9:30am-2pm and 5-7pm, Sun. 9am-2pm and 5-6pm. Free.)

The ruins of a **Medieval Castle** dominate a hilltop rising to the side of the cathedral. From C. San Esteban, follow the paved road up for about 15 minutes, through fields of wildflowers. At the top there are spectacular views of the surrounding countryside and the roof of the cathedral. Alternatively, take the route up C. Murallas, where the stations of the cross mark appropriate sites to request assistance.

Elsewhere

Burgos is the city of legendary hero El Cid; the **estatua del Cid** in Pl. General Primo de Rivera is Burgos's most venerated landmark after the cathedral. Rodrigo Díaz de Vivar (Cid comes from the Arabic for Lord) won his fame through bold exploits in battle against Moors, and is generally thought to be the most famous Castilian of all time. The medieval poem celebrating his life, *El Cantar de Mío Cid,* is considered the first great work in the Castilian language. Burgos tradition compels its youth to climb the statue and fondle the testicles of El Cid's horse, thus ensuring their own strength, courage, and fame.

Just up C. Santander on the other side of the statue and on the right, the restored **Casa del Cordón** glows in the sunshine. Here Columbus met with Fernando and Isabel after his second trip to America. Felipe el Hermoso (the Handsome) died here after an exhausting game of *pelota* (jai-alai), provoking the madness of his wife Juana la Loca (the Mad) who later dragged his corpse through the streets (for more story see Near Valladolid: Tordesillas).

Renovations of the **Monasterio de San Juan** (now called **Museo de Pintura Marceliano Santa María,** tel. 20 56 87) left the remaining walls of a destroyed church untouched while fully recovering and enclosing the cloister. Rich landscape scenes and portraits by Marceliano Santa María, a 20th-century local artist, hang within. To reach the monastery, follow C. Vitoria away from the statue of El Cid and take the second left. (Open Tues.-Sat. 10am-2pm and 5-8pm, Sun. 10am-2pm. Admission 25ptas; students free.) The **Museo de Burgos**, C. Calera, 25 (tel. 26 58 75), holds an impressive archaeological museum—with everything from prehistoric jawbones to Celtic-Iberian razors to Roman glasswork—and a painting collection in one 15th-century building. The museum also holds some stunning medieval pieces, including the Gothic tomb of Juan de Padilla, and an 11th-century Moorish ivory casket. (Open Mon.-Sat. 10am-2pm and 5-7:30pm, Sun. 10am-2pm; winter Tues.-Sat. 10am-2pm and 4:30-7pm. Admission 200ptas, free with student ID.) One km west of Burgos, the **Museo-Monasterio de las Huelgas Reales** (tel. 20 16 30) was a summer palace of Castilian kings and later an elite convent for Cistercian nuns, led by an abbess who was rumored to be only slightly less regal than the queen herself. A small band of nuns still camps out here. The church, in which several Castilian kings were knighted, takes the form of a Latin cross. Some classic Islamic motifs such as the peacock tail and stars are still visible in the Gothic cloister's badly damaged ceiling. The **Museo de Telas** (Textile Museum) keeps the entire wardrobe of Fernando de Cerda (1225-1275), son of Alfonso el Sabio, including billowing silver-threaded smocks and elaborately embroidered shirts. The only way to visit the museum and the monastery is with a tour in Spanish, valuable even if you don't understand a word. (Open Tues.-Sat. 10:30am-2pm and 4-6:30pm, Sun. and holidays 10:30am-3pm. Admission 400ptas, free Wed.) To get here, take the "Barrio del Pilar" bus from El Cid's statue in Pl. Primo de Rivera (65ptas) to the "Museo" stop.

The **Cartuja de Miraflores** is a Carthusian monastery that houses the ornate tombs of King Juan II of Castile, Queen Isabel of Portugal, and their son Don Alfonso. Debate rages as to whether Alfonso's early death was caused by scheming noblemen or a bad cold. His sister Isabel benefited from his demise: she eventually ascended to the throne and married Fernando. (Open Mon.-Sat. 10:15am-3pm and 4-6pm, Sun. and holidays 11:20am-12:30pm, 1-3pm, and 4-6pm. Open for mass Mon.-Sat. 9am, Sun. and holidays 7:30am and 10:15am. Free.) To get here, take the "Fuentes Blancas" bus (4 per day at 9:30am, 12:30pm, 4:15pm, and 7:15pm from the statue of El Cid; 65ptas) or walk 3km east along the Po. Quinta.

ENTERTAINMENT

Burgos really outdoes itself with a nightlife which rivals that of the big cities. Students congregate in the zone next to the cathedral and **Plaza Huerto del Rey,** known by the young as **Las Llanas.** Most bars don't start to fill up until after 10pm, but **Olivers,** an Irish pub, plays loud rock for the students who begin to crowd its cozy sofas in the early evening. An even larger student crowd attacks **Calle San Juan** and enjoys the spoils at the neon **Picoco** and in **La Faberna Pahl,** with its *sevillanas,* a popular form of flamenco that incites lustful dancing. The elegant and relatively tranquil cafés along Po. Espolón draw a slightly older crowd. **La Trastienda,** just off the Paseo at the corner of C. Eduardo Martínez de Campo, 4, attracts a hip crowd who drink beer, smoke cigarettes, and listen to early Ella Fitzgerald among the café's artistically placed antiques (draft beer 125ptas).

Nightlife switches into higher gear from June 23 to July 8, when Burgos honors its patron saints Peter and Paul with concerts, parades, fireworks, bullfights, and dances. The day after Corpus Christi, citizens parade through town with the *Pendón de las Navas,* a banner captured from the Moors in 1212.

■ NEAR BURGOS

ABADÍA DE SANTO DOMINGO DE SILOS

Located amid rolling hills 60km north of Burgos, idyllic **Santo Domingo de Silos** (tel. (947) 38 07 68) is home to the first group of chanting monks ever to hit number one on pop charts around the world. Long recognized around Burgos, the Benedictine monks of the **Abadía** (Abbey) here have recently gained international stardom, and now rival the Beastie Boys for the attention of European and American youth. They chant vespers every night at 7pm, complete mass at 9am (noon on holidays). (Abbey open Mon.-Sat. 10am-1pm and 4:30-6pm, Sun. and holidays 4:30-6pm. Admission 150ptas.) Silos is also renowned for its Romanesque **cloister**—look for the parade of stylized, hieratic, symmetrically paired harpies, monster gazelles, and other sculptured quadrupeds filing past on the capitals of the east gallery. In the 18th century, the original 11th-century Romanesque basilica was replaced by a grand, restrained Baroque church. Rooms are a cinch to find in this friendly small town of 200 people. **Hostal Cruces** and **Mesón Asador** have the cheapest rates and good restaurants. The owners suggest short hikes in the hills where grazing sheep sometimes block the path. A **bus** leaves the Burgos station (Mon.-Thurs. at 5:30pm, Fri. at 6:30pm, Sat. at 2pm; 565ptas) for the monastery and returns at 8:30am every morning. Because of the monastery's hours, this worthwhile daytrip really requires a two-night stay.

SAN PEDRO DE CARDEÑA

El Cid left Jimena in the Cistercian monastery of San Pedro de Cardeña (tel. 29 00 33), 10km east of Burgos, when he went into exile. Monks offer tours which include the lookout where Jimena kept watch for her beloved and the coffer presented by El Cid to the Jews who lent him money. The hero himself was buried here until 1921. (Monastery open April-Oct. Tues.-Sat. 10am-1:30pm and 4-6pm, Sun. 10:30am-3pm; Nov.-March Tues.-Sat. 10am-1:30pm and 3:30-5:30pm, Sun. 10:30am-3pm. Mass at 7am. Admission 100ptas.) The **Mesón del Canto,** across from the monastery, welcomes those who make the trip with cold beer and reasonably-priced meals. To get here, take the "Fuentes Blancas" bus (see Camping) and then walk the additional 6½km. To return, walk back to Fuentes Blancas and wait for the bus at 9:45am, 12:45pm, 4:30pm, and 7:30pm.

■■■ SORIA

In a description of how a Sorian noble might spend his days, Romantic great Gustavo Adolfo Bécquer captures a certain essence of this city: "Perhaps he is in the monastery's cloister, sitting on the edge of a tomb trying to catch pieces of dead souls' conversations; or at the bridge, watching the river's waves rush one by one below its arches; or crouched in a rock's cleft, lost in counting the stars in the skies or in following a passing cloud. Anywhere he might be, except where people are." While enjoying Soria need not entail such isolation, this compact provincial capital in the midst of gently rolling green and amber hills certainly lends itself to flights of fantasy and pathos.

Modern development hasn't bypassed Soria (pop. 30,000), but the city has retained its slow and salubrious pace. Black-bereted pensioners tote bundles of bread past reddish Romanesque churches, and Soria's inhabitants religiously observe the *paseo,* strolling and chatting with friends every evening through the city's splendid park and tidy cobbled streets. Soria receives few foreign visitors. Come to relax, and leave all "must dos" and "must sees" behind at the bus station.

ORIENTATION AND PRACTICAL INFORMATION

The bus station is a 10-min. walk northwest of the city center. From the traffic circle outside the station, signs on Av. Valladolid point the way to the *centro ciudad.* Persist for about five bl., then bear right at the traffic light onto **Paseo Espolón,** which borders the park of the same name. Where the park comes to a halt you'll see the central **Plaza Mariano Granados** right in front of you. To get here from the train station (south of the center), turn left onto Carretera de Madrid and follow the signs to *centro ciudad.* Follow C. Almazán until it forks; take Av. Mariano Vicen on the left for four bl., and stay left on C. Alfonso VIII at the next fork for two bl. until you reach Pl. Mariano Granados (15min.). From the side of the *plaza* opposite the park, C. Marques de Vadillo leads to **Calle El Collado,** which cuts through the old quarter past **Plaza San Esteban** to **Plaza Mayor.**

Tourist Office: Pl. Ramón y Cajal, s/n (tel. 21 20 52). Cross Pl. Mariano Granados from the entrance past the sculpted column; a small glass hut set back from the street. Ask for the *Ruta de los poetas* map and the *Guía,* which has basic information on the province of Soria. Open Mon.-Fri. 10am-2:30pm and 4:30-7pm, Sat.-Sun. 11:30am-2pm and 4:30-8:30pm.

Budget Travel: TIVE, C. Campo, 5 (tel. 22 31 11), up the hill from Pl. Mariano Granados at the corner of C. Mesta. ISIC 500ptas. HI cards 1800ptas. Open Mon.-Fri. 8am-3pm; Oct.-June also Mon. 5-8pm.

Post Office: C. Sagunto, s/n (tel. 22 41 14), an immediate left as you enter Pl. Mariano Granados from Po. Espolón, then a first left. Open for **telegrams** (tel. 22 20 00) and stamps Mon.-Fri. 8am-9pm, Sat. 9am-7pm. For Lista de Correos Mon.-Fri. 8am-9pm, Sat. 9am-2pm. **Postal Code:** 42070.

Telephones: C. Aduana Vieja, 2, left off C. Collado at Pl. San Esteban. **Fax** sending service. Open Mon.-Fri. 9am-2pm and 5-10pm, Sat. 10am-2pm; Oct. 16-May 14 Mon.-Fri. 10am-2pm and 5-9pm, Sat. 10am-2pm. **Telephone Code:** 975.

Trains: Estación El Cañuelo (info tel. 23 02 02). Bus shuttles between station and Pl. Mariano Granados, 20min. before each departure. Information booth open 7am-1pm and 4-8:30pm. To: Pamplona (1 per day, 3hr., 1000ptas); Olite (1 per day, 2¼hr., 890ptas); Alcalá de Henares (2-3 per day, 2¾hr., 1225ptas); Madrid (2-3 per day, 3hr., 1380ptas).

Buses: Av. Valladolid, s/n (tel. 22 51 60), at Av. Gaya Nuño. Shuttle bus from Pl. Mariano Granados every ½hr., 9:30am-2:30pm. Information open 6:30am-9pm. When bus companies are listed without a phone number, call the station for information. **Therpresa** (tel. 22 20 60) to Tarazona (4-5 per day, 1hr., 470ptas) and Zaragoza (4-5 per day, 2hr., 970ptas). **Gonzalo Ruiz** (tel. 22 43 55) to El Burgo de Osma (Mon.-Sat. 2 per day, 50min., 400ptas). **La Serrana** to Burgos (2-4 per day, 3hr., 1100ptas). **Linecar** (tel. 22 51 55) to Zaragoza (2-3 per day, 2hr., 960ptas) and Valladolid (2-4 per day, 3hr., 1275ptas). **CONDA** (tel. 22 44 01) to Pamplona (4-5 per day, 2hr., 1340ptas). **Continental Auto** (tel. 22 44 01) to Garray (see Near Soria); Madrid (Mon.-Sat. 4-5 per day, Sun. 1 at per day, 2½hr., 1565ptas) and Logroño (4-6 per day, 1¾hr., 770ptas). **RENFE-Iñigo** to Salamanca (2-3 per day, 5hr., 2420ptas) and Barcelona (2-3 per day, 6hr., 3650ptas).

Taxis: tel. 21 30 34 or 22 17 14. Line up on C. Marques de Vadillo. To the ruins of Numancia (1200ptas each way).

Car Rental: Avis, Av. Mariano Vicén, 1 (tel. 22 84 61). Left from tourist office into Pl. Los Jurados, then follow Av. Navarra until it meets Av. Mariano Vicén. Opel Corsa Swing 5600-6500ptas per day (depending on degree of coverage). Must be 21. Open Mon.-Fri. 9am-1pm and 4-5pm, Sat. 10am-1pm.

Luggage Storage: Bags checked at the **bus station** information booth (75ptas first day, 25ptas per day after that). Open 7am-10pm.

Swimming Pool: Pabellón Polideportivo San Andrés, E.C. Geólogo Palacios, s/n (tel. 22 35 37). From Residencia Juvenil Antonio Machado onto Po. San Andrés and left after 1 bl. Open June-Sept. 11am-8:30pm. Admission 200ptas.

24-hr. Pharmacy: Check the door of any pharmacy, call the police, or consult the local newspapers *Soria 7 Días* or *Diario Soria.*

Medical Services: Hospital General, Ctra. Logroño (tel. 22 08 50). **Ambulatorio (National Health Clinic),** tel. 22 15 50. **Ambulance:** tel. 23 00 00. **Red Cross:** tel. 21 26 40, **emergency** tel. 22 22 22.
Emergency: tel. 091 or 092.
Police: National Police, C. Nicolás Rabal, 11 (tel. 091). **Municipal Police** (tel. 21 18 62). **Guardia Civil** (tel. 22 03 50).

ACCOMMODATIONS AND CAMPING

Don't count on any bargains. Affordable *pensiones* can be found in the streets around **Plazas Olivo** and **del Salvador,** both near Pl. Mariano Granados. Reservations are necessary during the *fiestas* in the last week of June, and they're a good idea mid-July through mid-Sept.

Residencia Juvenil Juan Antonio Gaya Nuño (HI), Po. San Francisco, 1 (tel. 22 14 66). From Pl. Mariano Granados take C. Nicolás Rabal, the 2nd left on C. Santa Luisa de Marillac, then the next right. A modern college dorm disguised as a hostel July-Aug. Mostly doubles and quads. Joined in Aug. by **Residencia Juvenil Antonio Machado (HI),** Pl. José Antonio, 1 (tel. 22 17 89) another seasonal hostel. Continue down Po. San Francisco, turn right on C. Diego Laínez, immediate left on C. Nicolás Rabal, and then left again on reaching Pl. José Antonio. Both can fill with youth groups in the blink of an eye. Members only. 11pm curfew. 800ptas, over 26 1100ptas. Breakfast 100ptas, over 26 150ptas.
Casa Diocesana Pío XII, C. San Juan, 5 (tel. 21 21 76). From Pl. San Esteban bear right onto C. El Collado, then take the first right; enter through iron gates under "Residencias" sign. Large rooms with baths. Popular, modern retreat. Singles 2250ptas. Doubles 3000ptas. Sept.-mid-June: 1900ptas; 2650ptas.
Pensión el Sol, C. Ferial, 8 (tel. 22 72 02), an immediate left when entering Pl. Mariano Granados from Po. Espolón. Simple, clean rooms a hop, skip, and a jump from all the action. Singles 1300ptas. Doubles 2550ptas. Showers 150ptas.
Camping: Camping Fuente la Teja (tel. 22 29 67), 1½km from town on Ctra. Madrid (km233). Swimming pool. 350ptas per person and per car, 400ptas per tent. Open March 15-Sept.

FOOD

Such specialties as *sopa castellana* (soup with bread, garlic, egg, *chorizo,* and ham) and *migas pastoriles* (shepherds' bread crumbs; i.e., bread with garlic and *chorizo)* are especially delectable here. The region's bread and butter are celebrated throughout Spain. **Calle M. Vincente y Tutor** is spiced with bars and inexpensive restaurants. Merchants sell fresh produce, meat, and fish at the **market** on C. Estudios, a left from C. Collado. (Open Mon.-Sat. 9am-3pm.)

Supermarket: Autoservicio Muñoz, C. Collado, 36. Open Mon.-Fri. 9:30am-2pm and 4:30-8:30pm, Sat. 9am-3pm and (sometimes) 6-8pm.
Bar Restaurante Palafox, C. M. Vicente y Tutor, 5 (tel. 22 00 76). Take C. Ferial off Pl. Mariano Granados and hang the second left. Relaxed. Functional decor spiced up by a TV. Fair 2-course *menú* 750ptas. Entrees 400-1500ptas. Open 1-4:30pm and 9-11:30pm. Visa, MC accepted.
La Pizzería, C. Aguirre, 8 (tel. 23 12 16). The serene, modern *comedor* contrasts with the lively bar and exterior tables. A delectable respite from heavy local specialties. Fresh pastas (600ptas) and pizzas (625-875ptas; 600ptas by the bar). Open 1:30-4pm and 8:30pm-midnight. Closed Sun. MC, Visa accepted.
Cafetería Restaurante Josán, Pl. Ramón Benito Aceña, 2 (tel. 22 72 51), left on the way to the phone center from Pl. Mariano Granados. Brightly lit dining room and commendable *(menú* 1200ptas). Entrees 600-1700ptas. Open daily 1-4pm and 9pm-midnight. Visa, MC accepted.
Nueva York, C. Collado, 14 (tel. 22 68 84), 1 bl. past Pl. San Esteban. No hot dogs, bagels, or big apples here, but you'll want to be a part of breakfast (served until 12:30pm) of coffee, fresh orange juice, and choice of pastry (220-240ptas). Open 8am-10pm; winter 8am-9:30pm.

SIGHTS AND ENTERTAINMENT

The **Río Duero** shapes a lazy arc around Soria, which the great 20th-century poet Antonio Machado likened to a drawn bow. The melancholy elms, poplars, and oaks bordering the river inspired him to compose a collection of deep thoughts on Castilla's landscape. Gustavo Adolfo Bécquer made Soria his home for a time (a plaque on Pl. Ramón Benito Aceña marks the spot), and many of his 19th-century *Leyendas* are set in the hills along the Duero. To find the river, from Pl. Mariano Granados walk past Nueva York and straight down C. Zapatería. Halfway down the hill, C. Zapatería changes its name to C. Real. Follow this to Pl. San Pedro. The **Concatedral de San Pedro** will be on the left; the bridge lies just ahead. The far side of the river is the place to take in Soria's becoming profile of churches, convents, and monasteries. (Unless otherwise noted, open daily 10am-2pm and 5-9pm; Oct.-June Tues.-Sat. 10am-2pm and 4-7pm, Sun. 10am-2pm.)

Iglesia de Santo Domingo has a 12th-century Romanesque facade and remarkable sculpture.

San Juan de Rabanera is smaller and perhaps more beautiful than the Santo Domingo. Otherwise typically Romanesque, this church plays nonconformist with its cruciform shape and Byzantine touches. Its tympanum was salvaged from the ruins of the Iglesia de San Nicolás.

Convento de las Carmelitas, Pl. Fuente de Cabrejos, off C. Zapatería, was founded by Sta. Teresa de Avila in the 16th century. The square is a favorite hangout for Soria's elderly. Open for mass only.

Concatedral de San Pedro, with a fine Plateresque door, is a late Gothic church. . Cloister afternoon hours 5-7pm. Admission 50ptas.

Monasterio San Juan de Duero, in a peaceful setting across the river, is more original than any of the above. Built by the ubiquitous Templars. Its beautiful cloister is partially in ruins, but the Arab arches are still here. To reach the monastery, follow the signs after crossing the bridge. Admission 200ptas for foreigners, EU citizens under 21 free.

Ermita de San Saturio, 1km downstream, clings dangerously to rocky riverside slopes riddled with caves. The monks who built it decided to integrate the caves into their *ermita*; hence rooms and chambers are partly monk-made, partly geological givens. To reach the frescoed chapel at the top, follow a series of climbing passages that wind in and out of the limestone caves. Note the window from which a young child fell in 1772, landing on his knees unharmed, according to the monks, thanks to the intervention of the *Santo*.

Regarding secular architecture, the **Palacio de los Condes de Gómara** houses government offices behind a 16th-century Renaissance facade and a handsome tower. Seven statues out front honor Soria's greats, including a visionary nun killed in the Inquisition for heresy. The **Museo Numantino,** Po. Espolón, 8 (tel. 22 13 97), displays an excellent collection of elephant pelvises, not to mention Stone, Bronze, and Iron Age artifacts and Roman relics. The third floor features a super exhibit on the ruins of nearby Numancia, along with others illustrating the region's history. (Wheelchair accessible from Pl. Rey Sabio. Open Tues.-Sat. 10am-2pm and 5-9pm, Sun. 10am-2pm; Oct.-April Tues.-Sat. 9:30am-7:30pm, Sun. 10am-2pm. Admission 200ptas; use the same ticket for San Juan de Duero Monastery.)

Come evening, *everybody* in Soria heads for the old town. Early evening finds them in the area between C. Collado and Pl. San Clemente, affectionately known as **El Tubo Estrecho.** Then it's on to the bars, cafés, and outside seating of **Plaza Ramón Benito Aceña.** Late-night hedonism takes place at the disco/bars grouped around the intersection of **Rota de Calatañazer** and **Calle Cardenal Frías.**

The five-day **Fiesta de San Juan** kicks off the first Wednesday after June 23.

■NEAR SORIA

RUINS OF NUMANCIA

Nineteenth-century archeologists uncovered the ruins of Numancia, a hilltop settlement 8km north of Soria dating back more than 4000 years. The two key periods represented at the site are Celtiberian and Roman. The Celtiberians had settled by the 3rd century BC and tenaciously resisted the Romans. It took 10 years of the Numantian Wars and the direction of General P. Cornelio Escipión, called in after his victory at Carthage, to dislodge them. Escipión erected a system of walls 9km long, 3m wide, and 2½m thick to encircle the town and starve its residents. High on his victory, he saved 50 survivors as trophies, sold the rest into slavery, burned the city, and divided its lands among his allies. Numancia, however, lived on as a metaphor for patriotic heroism in Golden Age and Neoclassical tragedies.

The ruins, though battered, are still worth a visit. Check out the foundations of the Roman houses and the underground wells. (Ruins open Mon.-Sat. 10am-2pm and 5-9pm; Oct.-June Tues.-Sat. 10am-2pm and 4-7pm, Sun. 10am-2pm. Admission 200ptas.)

Getting there can be a problem for the carless. **Buses** runs to Garray (1km from the ruins, Mon.-Fri. at 1:30pm and 3:15pm, Sat. at 1:30pm, 10min., 65-70ptas). Unfortunately this means you arrive 30min. to 3½hrs. before afternoon opening time. A **taxi** to the ruins costs about 1200ptas each way. Getting back from Numancia is even tougher; the buses don't return until the next day. The trek along the highway back to Soria takes two hours. On a brighter note, taxis in Soria can be called from Garray.

EL BURGO DE OSMA

El Burgo de Osma (pop. 5000) has a handful of beautiful buildings amid a slew of ugly ones; two of the more attractive are **Hospital San Agustín** and the **Casas Consistoriales** on Pl. Mayor. In fulfillment of a vow, the Cluniac monk Don Pedro de Osma erected the magnificent 13th-century Gothic **catedral** on the site of an earlier one. Most of the work is Gothic, save for some Renaissance elements within and the Baroque belfry and chapels. The cathedral's two **museos** have an important collection of codices, including a richly illuminated Beato de Liébana commentary on the Apocalypse and a 12th-century charter thought to be one of the earliest examples of usage of the written Castilian vernacular. (Open 10am-1pm and 4-7pm; Oct.-May 10am-1pm and 3:30-6pm. Guided tour in Spanish 150ptas, solo travelers 200ptas.)

A **tourist office** operates from early-July to early-September in the Ayuntamiento/ Casa Consistorial on Pl. Mayor. Some English, better French spoken. (Open Tues. 5-8pm, Wed.-Sun. 10am-2pm and 5-8pm.) The Ayuntamiento shares its phone with the **municipal police** (tel. 34 01 07). If you ask nicely, either will get a tourist official for you on the phone. The **post office** is at C. Francisco Federico (tel. 34 00 25); the **postal code** is 42300. The **telephone code** is 975. The **Red Cross** respond at tel. 34 01 51, the **ambulatorio** at tel. 34 12 11, and the **Guardia Civil** at tel. 34 00 74.

C. Universidad is lined with affordable beds. The **Hostal Residencia La Perdiz** (tel. 34 03 09), C. Universidad, 33, on the edge of town, has frumpy rooms with baths overlooking a gas station. (Singles 2500ptas. Doubles 4000ptas.) From June to September, **Camping La Pedriza** on Ctra. El Burgo-Retortillo (tel. 34 08 06) is open for campers. (350ptas per person and per car, 400ptas per tent.)

Buses (tel. 34 10 24) run to and from Soria (Mon.-Sat. 2 per day, 50min., 400ptas).

Galicia (Galiza)

No, my fair lady, the rain in Spain is *not* mainly in the plains—it's right here in the far northwest. Galicia looks and feels like no other region in Spain: frequently veiled by a misty drizzle, its ferny woods, plunging valleys, and slate-roofed fishing villages sit beside long white beaches. The scent of eucalyptus permeates the countryside. Rivers wind through hills, gradually widening into the famous *rías* (inlets or estuaries) that empty into the Cantabrian Sea and Atlantic Ocean. A rest stop on the Celts' journey to Ireland around 900 BC, this region has always been atypical. Ancient Celtic *castros* (fortress-villages), Celtic inscriptions, *dólmenes* (funerary chambers), and the regional instrument *gaita* (bagpipes) testify to Galicia's Celtiberian past, as does lingering lore about witches, fountain fairies, and buried treasure beneath the *castros*.

Near-impenetrable mountain barriers kept the region historically isolated from the rest of Spain. Until Columbus's voyage, Cabo Finisterre was regarded as the end of the world. The Romans halfheartedly tossed off an occasional settlement here long after they had colonized the Iberian coast. The Moors could barely pay attention to Galicia long enough to destroy Santiago, and were gone by 1000 AD. Unfortunately, political peace has not translated into economic prosperity for this poor region. The minuscule size of farm plots, while precluding the rise of inequitable land structures à la Andalucía, discouraged the proliferation of agricultural technology or large-scale production. The net (the fishing ports of Vigo and La Coruña are among the most important in Europe) and the plow remain Galicia's economic mainstays. National and regional governments are trying (in part to encourage the new tourist popularity of the region) to upgrade Galicia's roads, which aren't always adequate. Bus connections are infrequent and hitchhiking difficult. Rail service by RENFE is reliable but limited to the major cities, while clanking FEVE does its thing in the rural areas.

Galicians speak *gallego,* a language related to Portuguese and Castilian. It differs from Castilian mainly by replacing "La" and "El" with "A" and "O;" from Portuguese, by replacing "J" with "X." Although the regionalism here does not make headlines as do its eastern Basque and Catalan counterparts, heated discussion of Galician Nationalism penetrates politics and daily life.

Regional cuisine features *caldo gallego* (a vegetable broth), *pulpo a la gallega* (marinated octopus), *vieiras* (scallops, the pilgrim's trophy), and the *empanada* (turnover/pasty stuffed with tomato and tuna, among other fillings). *Tetilla* is a creamy, tangy cheese. A sublimely dense almond pie named for Santiago, *torta compostelana,* has escaped to conquer dessert menus all over Spain. The area's Ribeiro wine is tart and slightly cloudy.

■■■ SANTIAGO DE COMPOSTELA

Embraced by the Ríos Tambre and Ulla, Santiago was founded in 813, when, according to legend, Bishop Teodomiro informed Asturian King Alfonso II of the miraculous discovery of a tomb containing the remains of the Apostle St. James, the man responsible for bringing the word of Christ into Spain. In his Spanish incarnation, the gruesomely named St. James the Moorslayer (Santiago Matamoros) rallied the peninsula's Christians and occasionally appeared on a white charger to lead them into battle. The Christians attributed their victory at Clavijo (844) to the intervention of the saint. Cordoban dictator Almanzor razed the city in 997; it was entirely rebuilt two centuries later. The rest of the town's name derives from *campo stellae,* Latin for "field of the star"—the star which guided to discover the tomb.

Santiago thus became one of Christianity's three holy cities and, like Rome and Jerusalem, the destination of pilgrimages. The clever Benedictine monks built monasteries to host the pilgrims on the way, giving rise for the first time in European history to a large-scale travel industry. By the 12th century, the pilgrims' route became one of the most traveled in Europe (for more information, see Sights: El Camino de Santiago). UNESCO has designated Santiago a world heritage site. At any hour of the day or night, the granite streets surrounding Santiago's famous cathedral are filled with musicians, street-walkers, and smiling nuns, all just celebrating the fact that they're there.

ORIENTATION AND PRACTICAL INFORMATION

Street names in Santiago can be confusing, as the use of Galician and Castilian is not always coordinated between street signs and maps. Yet since the two languages are similar, it's not hopeless: *Calle* in Castilian becomes *Rúa* in Galician, and *del* becomes *do.* The **cathedral** marks the center of the old city, which sits higher than the new city. Three main streets lead directly to the cathedral from the south side (train station side) of town: **Rúa do Franco** (Calle del Franco), **Rúa do Vilar** (Calle del Vilar), and **Rúa Nova** (Calle Nueva).

From the train station, turn right at the top of the stairs and take C. Hórreo to **Praza de Galiza** (do *not* take Avenida de Lugo), then one more block to **Entrecalles,** from which three cathedral-bound streets spring. From the bus station, take bus #10 to Pr. Galiza (every 10-15min., 35ptas).

Tourist Office: R. Vilar, 43 (tel. 58 40 81), in the old town under the arches of a colonnade. English and French spoken. Useful pamphlets with unindexed maps of Santiago and Galicia. Bus schedules and accommodations information. Open Mon.-Fri. 9am-2pm and 4-7pm, Sat. 10am-1:30pm. Also a **branch** in Pr. Galiza; same hours, same services.

Budget Travel: TIVE, Plazuela del Matadero, s/n (tel. 57 24 26), turn right up R. Fonte Santo Antonio from Pr. Galiza. Train, bus, and plane tickets for international destinations. ISIC 500ptas. HI card 1800ptas. Open Mon.-Fri. 9am-2pm.

American Express: Ultratur Viajes, Av. Figueroa, 6 (tel. 58 70 00). Open Mon.-Fri. 9am-2pm and 4:30-7pm, Sat. 9am-2pm.

Currency Exchange: Banco Hispano Americano, R. Vilar, 30 (tel. 58 16 12). 1% commission (500ptas min. charge). Open Mon.-Fri. 9am-2pm. Many banks on Pr. Galiza.

Post Office: Travesa de Fonseca (tel. 58 12 52; fax 56 32 88), on the corner of R. Franco. Open for stamps and Lista de Correos Mon.-Fri. 8am-9pm, Sat. 9am-2pm; for **telegrams** Mon.-Fri. 8am-9pm, Sat. 9am-7pm; for **faxes** Mon.-Fri 8am-9pm, Sat. 9am-7pm. **Postal Code:** 15080.

Telephones: C. Bautizados, 13, in the old town off Pr. Toral. Open Mon.-Fri. 10am-11:30pm, Sat. 10am-8pm, Sun. 11am-3pm and 5-9:30pm. **Telephone Code:** 981.

Flights: Aeropuerto Lavacolla (tel. 59 74 00), 10km away on road to Lugo. A bus connects it to Santiago, stopping at the bus station, the train station, and C. General Pardiñas, 26 (8 per day, 110ptas). National connections and direct flights to London, Paris, Zürich, Amsterdam, and Frankfurt. Information open 24hrs. **Iberia,** C. General Pardiñas, 36 (tel. 57 20 24). Open Mon.-Fri. 9:30am-2pm and 4-7:30pm, Sat 10am-1pm.

Trains: R. General Franco (tel. 52 02 02). Information open Mon.-Sat. 7am-9pm, Sun. 7am-1pm. To: La Coruña (15 per day, 1hr., 400-460ptas); Vigo (12 per day, 2hr., 600ptas); Pontevedra (12 per day, 1½hr., 420ptas); Madrid (2 per day, 8hr., 4000-6000ptas).

Buses: Estación Central de Autobuses, C. San Cayetano (tel. 58 77 00). Nothing central about it: ½-hr. walk from downtown. #10 bus leaves every 15min. for center (35ptas). Information open 8am-10pm. **ALSA** (tel. 58 64 53). To: Madrid (2 per day, 8-9hr., 5090ptas); San Sebastián (1 per day, 6hr., 3120ptas); Bilbao (2 per day, 9½hr., 5320ptas). **Castromil** (tel. 58 97 00). To: La Coruña (17 per day, 1½hr., 715ptas); El Ferrol (6 per day, 2hr., 835ptas); Pontevedra (15 per day, 1½hr., 540ptas); Noya (11 per day, 1hr., 375ptas); Muros (11 per day, 2hr., 675ptas); Vigo (15 per day, 2½hr., 835ptas). **Finisterre** (tel. 58 73 16). To: Camariñas (2 per day, 2hr., 955ptas); Finisterre (2 per day, 2½hr., 1185ptas). **Empresa**

Santiago de Compostela

1 Tourism Office
2 Post Office
3 Hospital General de Galicia
4 Palacio de Gelmírez
5 Monasterio de San Martín Pinario
6 Monasterio de San Pelayo
7 Ayuntamiento
8 Plaza de la Fonseca
9 Plaza de la Inmaculada
10 Plaza de las Platerías
11 Plaza San Martín
12 Plaza Cervantes
13 Plaza de San Miguel
14 Plaza de Feijoo
15 Plaza del Mercado
16 Buses to the Bus Station

Freire (tel. 58 81 11). To Lugo (7 per day, 725ptas). Also, buses to Amsterdam, Paris, Hamburg, and Zürich.

Public Transportation: (tel. 58 18 15). Blue buses travel through all parts of the city and beyond. #6 goes to the train station, #9 to the campgrounds, #10 to the bus station (begins service at 6am). 70ptas. Buses begin running between 7-8am, end around 10:30pm.

Taxis: tel. 59 84 88 or 58 24 50.

Car Rental: Autotur, C. General Pardiñas, 3 (tel. 58 64 96), 2 bl. from Pr. Galiza in the new town. Must be at least 21 and have had license 1 yr. Open Mon.-Fri. 9am-2pm and 4-8pm, Sat. 10am-1:30pm.

Luggage Storage: At the train station (lockers 400ptas). Open 7:30am-11pm. At the bus station (75ptas per bag). Open 8am-10pm.

English Bookstore: Librería Galicia, Pr. Universidad, 2 bl. east of R. Nova. Excellent selection. Open Mon.-Fri. 10am-2pm and 4-7:30pm, Sat. 10am-1pm.

Religious Services: Pilgrim's Mass in the cathedral daily at 9:30am, noon—with *botafumeiro* (incense burner on steroids)—5pm, and 7pm. Sun. schedule slightly different.

Laundromat: Lava-Express, C. República El Salvador, 21 (tel. 59 00 95), in the new town at the corner with C. Alfredo Brañas. Self-service wash and dry 550ptas per 4kg load. Full same-day service 750ptas per load. Open Mon.-Fri. 9:30am-2pm and 4-8:30pm, Sat. 10am-2pm.

Swimming Pool: Piscina Municipal, Tras. Santa Isabel, s/n (tel. 58 60 39), to the left off C. Galeras, west of the old town. Adults 380ptas, children 230ptas. Open Mon.-Fri. 4-10pm, Sat. 5-8pm.

Drug Crisis Line: UMA Drogodependencia (tel. 58 86 56).

Late-Night Pharmacy: Bescansa, Pr. Toural, 10 (tel. 58 59 40), 1 bl. up toward the cathedral from Pr. Galiza. For 24-hr. pharmacies, check the signs posted in any pharmacy window.

Medical Assistance: Hospital Xeral, C. Galeras (tel. 54 00 00). **Ambulance:** tel. 59 36 56. **Red Cross:** C. San Cayetano (tel. 58 54 54).

Emergency: Policía Municipal (tel. 092).

Guardia Civil: tel. 58 22 66 or 58 16 11.

ACCOMMODATIONS AND CAMPING

Finding a room in Santiago is not difficult. *Hospedajes* and *pensiones* seem to multiply around **Rúa do Vilar** and **Calle Raíña** (a small street between R. Vilar and R. Franco), and hand-drawn *"habitaciones"* signs are everywhere else. Citizens linger about the stations offering rooms in their homes, but these lodgings vary vastly in quality and price. Legitimate pilgrims can stay in the many Albergues de Peregrinos for free. Inquire at the tourist office.

Hospedaje Santa Cruz, R. Vilar, 42, 2nd fl. (tel. 58 28 15). Right where all the action is. Rooms in shades of tan have big windows overlooking the most popular street in Santiago. Bathrooms are less than spotless, but passable. Singles 2000ptas. Doubles 2500ptas. Winter: 1500ptas; 2000ptas.

Hospedaje Viño, Pr. Mazarelos, 7 (tel. 58 51 85). At Pr. Galiza, take a right onto R. Fonte San Antonio and turn left through a purple-flowered archway. Look for the green door alongside the eponymous bar. Spotless rooms overlook a peaceful plaza. Singles 1000-1500ptas. Doubles 2000-2500ptas.

Hospedaje Ramos, C. Raíña, 18, 2nd fl. (tel. 58 18 59). Simple but comfortable and clean. Rooms with private baths are nicer and a far better deal (though public bath is spotless). Try to get one with a view of the cathedral, but don't despair if you fail; you'll still be serenaded by the *tuna* (see Entertainment, not Food) that performs nightly in the square below. Singles 1300ptas, with bath 1500ptas. Doubles 3000ptas, with bath 3500ptas.

Hospedaje Recarey, Patio de Madres, 15, 3rd fl. (tel. 58 81 94), a right off R. Fonte San Antonio, 2 bl. from Pr. Galiza. On a quiet street overlooking a convent. Flower bedspreads clash with the mod chairs, but rooms are spacious and sparkling clean. Singles 1500-2000ptas. Doubles 2500ptas, with bath 3500-4000ptas.

Hopedaje Sofía, C. Cardenal Paya, 16 (tel. 58 51 50). A few bl. from Pr. Galiza, near the Facultad de Historia. Immense rooms, some with sofas and/or bookcases. Clean bathrooms. Singles 1800ptas. Doubles 3000ptas. Prices lower in winter.

Hostal-Residencia La Senra, R. Senra (a.k.a. C. General Mola), 13, 2nd fl. (tel. 50 04 48), right in front of Pr. Galiza. Pastel bedspreads and enormous billowing curtains. Vaguely institutional rooms rival some of the cathedral's chapels in size. Doubles 3000ptas. Triples 4000ptas, with bath 5000ptas.

Camping: Camping As Cancelas, R. 25 de Xullo, 35 (tel. 58 02 66), 2km from cathedral on the northern edge of town. Take bus #6 or 9. Souvenirs, laundry, supermarket, and pool make this the Club Med of camping. 495ptas per person, 525ptas per car and per tent. Electricity 400ptas. **Camping Santiago** (tel. 88 80 02), about 6km from town on the road to La Coruña, next door to the Guardia Civil. 460ptas per person, 450ptas per tent, 485ptas per car. Electricity 400ptas. Open June 20-Sept. 25.

FOOD

Santiago is a budget diner's dream. Bars and cafeterias line the streets of the old town, proffering a shocking variety of finned and hoofed *raciones,* often the best alternative to expensive *menús.* Most restaurants in the old town lie south of the cathedral, notably on **Rúa do Vilar, Rúa Franco,** and **Calle Raíña;** for fewer tourists try the streets radiating out from Pr. Roxa in the new city. *Empanadas, pulpo a la gallega,* and the breast-shaped cheese *tetilla* are specialties (see Galicia Intro). *Tarta de Santiago,* an almond cake emblazoned with a stylized cross, is the way to end a meal.

Produce carts, meat stalls, and everything else from flowers to baby clothes for pilgrim tots line the streets of the open **market,** which stretches from Pr. San Felix to Convento de San Agustín, north of the cathedral. (Open Mon.-Sat. 7:30am-2pm.)

Supermarket: Supermercados Lorenzo Froiz, Pr. Toural, s/n, 1 bl. up from Pr. Galiza. Open Mon.-Fri. 9:15am-3pm and 4:30-9pm, Sat. 9am-3pm and 5-9pm.

Casa Manolo, R. Traviesa, 27 (tel. 58 29 50), near the market and Pr. San Augustín. Come early or be prepared to stand in line. 650pta *menú* offers twenty choices for each course! Bread, wine, and flan included. Menus in English and German to help you decide. Open Tues.-Sun. 1-4pm and 8pm-midnight.

Restaurante-Bar Los Caracoles, C. Raíña, 14 (tel. 56 14 98). Quiet dining room in back offers a refreshing change from dark, noisy bars and *mesones. Menú del día* 800ptas. Entrees 400-1200ptas. Open 1-4pm and 7pm-midnight.

Café-Bar El Metro, R. Nova, 12. Snag a table beneath the archway outside. *Menú del día* (850ptas) with seafood, roasted meats, and *paella.* Entrees 350-600ptas. Open 1-5pm and 8pm-midnight. Closed Christmas week and Semana Santa.

Bar Coruña, C. Raíña, 17 (tel. 58 39 68). Spazzy *jamones* dangle from the ceiling. The Coruña is known as *"el rey del bocadillo"*—that is, just about anything slapped between two slices of bread, from anchovies (185ptas) to *tortillas* (140ptas). Open 9:30am-midnight.

Cervecería Dakar, R. Franco, 13. An amiable and active bar. Elegant and spacious with wood panelling. Rich *batidos* (milkshakes, 250ptas) of nutmeg and delicious liqueurs—5 flavors. Students spread their papers all over tables. Open Fri.-Wed. 8am-midnight, closed the last 2 weeks of Sept.

Casa Parades, C. Carretas, 1 (tel. 58 59 20), off the west corner of Pr. Obradoiro. *Menú del día* (795ptas) and *menú de la casa* (995ptas) served in a *comedor* with pink tablecloths and local paintings. Open noon-4pm and 7pm-midnight.

Café-Bar Os Bigotes, C. Raíña, 7. Garlic hangs in front of the wine rack. Standing room only in this bar. *Empanadas* 175ptas. *Bocadillos* 130-175ptas. *Mejillones,* the city's least expensive, 300ptas. Open Wed.-Mon. 9am-1am.

Mesón Candilexas, C. Cardenal Paya, 13. Eight tables, and they're nearly always full. Stairs lead down to a wood-panelled dining room, where a *menú* of *ensaladilla* and *merluza* comes to only 600ptas. Entrees 350-1500ptas.

SIGHTS

The entire old town has been designated a national monument; feast your art-historian heart out on every door and square. The **catedral's** kernel is an admirable Romanesque Latin cross with ambulatory and radiating chapels. The cathedral has four facades, each a masterpiece from a different period. Four separate entrances open onto different plazas: Platerías, Quintana, Obradoiro, and Azabaxería. From the southern **Praza de Platerías,** enter the cathedral by way of a Romanesque-arched set of double doors, crusted over with columns and an assortment of icons in various stages of undress. This is the oldest facade; its portico is adorned with robust granite figures and includes a profusion of rounded arches, statues, and bas-relief details.

The **Torro do Reloxio** (clock tower) adds a Gothic, craggy touch. The clock tower, Pórtico Real, and Porta Santa face onto the **Praza da Quintana,** to the west of the cathedral. Crowning the door is a 17th-century rendering of Santiago in *mufti.* To the north, the **Azabaxería** facade combines Romanesque and Neoclassical styles in a headache-inducing blend of Doric columns, Ionic columns, and a smattering of those ubiquitous religious icons. Consecrated in 1211, the cathedral later acquired Gothic chapels in the apse and transept, a 15th-century dome, a 16th-century cloister, and the Baroque facade called the **Obradoiro,** whose two exquisitely ornate towers soar above the city. The shrine's international clout is made evident by the 18th-century stone flowers representing the world over. The Obradoiro facade faces **Praza da Obradoiro** (to the west), where camera-snappers, souvenir hawkers and (watch out!) *tunas* (young men dressed in medieval garb strumming lutes, see Entertainment) coexist in a Baroque frenzy of faith, travel, and tourism. Encased in this facade, the **Pórtico de la Gloria** by Maestro Mateo, is considered the crowning achievement of Spanish Romanesque sculpture. This unusual 12th century amalgamation of sculptures—angels, prophets, saints, sinners, demons, monsters—form a compendium of Christian theology. Unlike most Romanesque rigid statues, those in the *Pórtico* smile, whisper, lean, and talk to each other, inspiring Galician author Rosalia del Castro to proclaim: "It looks as if their lips are moving... might they be alive?" The *catedral* includes a life-like bust of the sculptor Mateo—unusual for the Middle Ages when artists were rarely known or recognized. It is believed that by knocking your head three times against his, some of his talent will rub off.

Inside the cathedral, the organ pipes protruding from stone arches along the central aisle are designed to resemble trumpet horns over the heads of the congregation. Santiago's revered remains lie beneath the high altar in a silver coffer, while his bejeweled bust sits above. His bones were hidden from the English in the 16th century and misplaced until somebody finally dug up his holy remains three centuries later. The identity was confirmed when a shard of skull, brought from Italy, fit perfectly into the hole in the skeleton's head. The **botafumeiro** is an enormous silver incense burner swung from end to end in the transept during high mass and major liturgical ceremonies. The **museo** and **claustros** impress with gorgeous and intricately-detailed 16th-century tapestries. The museum also houses manuscripts from the *Códice Calixtino* and Romanesque remains dug up during one of the many archaeological excavations here. The early 12th-century *Códice,* a series of manuscripts in five volumes on the tories of the apostles, includes all sorts of traveling practical information for pilgrims, a la *Let's Go.* (Museum open 10am-1:30pm and 4-7pm, holidays 10:30am-1:30pm. Admission to museum and cloisters 300ptas.)

Across Pr. Obradoiro, facing the cathedral, the long, majestic facade of the former **Pazo de Raxoi** (Royal Palace) shines with gold-accented balconies and monumental columns in vigorous neoclassical style. The bas-relief within of the Battle of Clavijo is a remarkable work in the same style. It's now home to the Ayuntamiento and the office of the president of the Xunta de Galiza. Also in Pr. Obradoiro, stands the 15th-century Renaissance **Hospital Real,** now Hotel dos Reyes Católicos, a ritzy *parador.* The *parador* still upholds the building's ancient tradition of feeding 10 pilgrims per day (in the employees' dining hall). The hotel's doorway is a carved masterpiece;

ask the concierge for permission to see its four courtyards, the chapel, and sculpture. (Open 10am-2pm and 4-7pm.)

Back on the other side of the cathedral in Pr. Quintana, the **Mosteiro de San Pelayo** surpasses the usual supply of relics with a striking statue of Mary holding Jesus and clubbing a demon. (Open Mon.-Sat. 10am-1pm and 4-7pm, Sun. 10am-2pm. Admission 150ptas.)

Off Pr. Platerias, residential architecture holds its own in Baroque **Casa del Deán** and **Casa del Cabildo.** Farther from the cathedral area near Pr. Camino, both the **Museo do Pobo Galego** (tel. 58 36 20) and the **Museo Municipal** exhibit interesting tidbits of Galician culture in the Gothic **Monasterio de Santo Domingo.** (Open Mon.-Sat. 10am-1pm and 4-7pm. Free.) West of the old town, the city wove a neoclassical **universidad** into its otherwise Romanesque and Baroque warp. Located one km from the cathedral, the 15th-century **Colexiata de Santa María do Sar** has a disintegrating Romanesque cloister that started crumbling in the 12th century and just never stopped. Inside, pillars leaning at frighteningly unlikely angles give the impression that the whole is about to collapse into a picturesque pile of rubble. (Open Mon.-Sat. 10am-1pm and 4-6:30pm. Admission 50ptas.)

Squeezed between the old city and the new, the **Caballeira de Santa Susana** is a lovely place in which to stave off monument overdose. Its manicured gardens and eucalyptus-lined walkways open onto gorgeous views of the cathedral on one side and rolling farmland on the other.

El Camino de Santiago

Since the 12th century, voluminous numbers have followed the **Camino de Santiago,** many as true believers, others as a stipulation to inheritance, an alternative to prison, or a lucrative adventure, hoping to make money from all that faith, hope, and charity. The Camino was the vehicle for the introduction in Spain of Romanesque art, provençal lyric, epic, legend, and music. Pilgrims, easily identified by their crook-necked staffs and scallop shell necklaces, still follow the superhighway (Crta. 120) and back roads which lead to Santiago. Tourist offices all over Spain provide information on how and where to join the Camino on foot, bike, or horse— the only vehicles the true *romero* is allowed. The most common route, La Ruta Francesa, leads from **Roncesvalles,** Navarra, to Santiago. Guides list numerous *refugíos* (shelters) where pilgrims can stay for free, and get a stamp which certifies them as legitimate. On foot, calculating about 30km per day, the Camino takes 25 to 30 days. Though surprisingly few Americans join the pilgrims, in part comprised of pockets of students from all over Europe), guru Shirley MacLaine walked in 1994 from Roncesvalles to Santiago, surprising locals and fellow *romeros* along the way with her huge backpack.

1993 was a Holy Year in Santiago (the next one is 1999; the years fall on a pattern of eleven, five, and six) because the Feast of St. James fell on a Sunday, and an estimated 5 million tourists added their forces to the 30,000 university students already here, overwhelming Santiago's population of 100,000. All those visitors, many of whom trekked through the Pyrenees or faced the vagaries of Galician bus travel to get here, make for a decidedly festive atmosphere.

ENTERTAINMENT

Two years ago, the city proudly unveiled an **auditorio** (concert hall), which schedules everything from Ray Charles concerts to performances by the Turkish National Orchestra (check for information at the tourist office and in newspaper entertainment sections). The **Teatro Principal** on R. Nova lines up a similarly eclectic mix; puppet shows, ballets, and Shakespeare all go up there. (Tickets available at the box office 12:30-2pm and 6pm-showtime.) Santiago's **fiestas** occur July 18 to 31.

At night, various student singing troupes called **tunas** dress in medieval garb and sing ribald songs and an occasional serenade in the streets of the old city. Dating from the Middle Ages, the *tunas* traditionally performed as a way of feeding themselves while at school; today they offer females lots of flirtatious, if unrequested, attention. Think of them as frat boys with lutes. Many *tunas,* however, are quite respectable, and in any event this thoroughly Spanish form of entertainment is free.

At night, crowds flood the city's cellars. Bars on R. Nova, R. Vilar, and R. Franco are packed all night. (All clubs open roughly 11pm-4am, with action starting well after midnight; women generally free, men 400-600ptas.)

Modus Vivendi, Pr. Feixoo, 5min. east of cathedral. An eclectic dungeon strikes a balance between Galician bagpipes and David Bowie. Outdoor dance floor.

Poison, near Pr. Cervantes. Students sip refreshing local wines in large glasses.

Araguaney, C. Montero Rios, 25, a few bl. west of Pr. Galiza in Hotel Araguaney complex. Slick neon interior and Euro house music.

Discoteca Black, C. Rosalia de Castro, inside Hotel Peregrino. Popular club for all age groups.

RÍAS BAJAS (RÍAS BAIXAS)

Protected coves lure *gallegos* to the Rías Bajas (Low Estuaries) for surfing and weekend visits. Tourism is gradually eclipsing fishing as the main local industry; foreigners now join Spanish visitors in search of seductive beach towns and quiet fishing ports. Charming stone villages and Celtic ruins speckle the countryside. Public transportation between towns is often sparse in this area; either rent a car or plan your itinerary carefully.

■■■ VIGO

The major port city of the Ría de Vigo, sprawling Vigo's (pop. 300,000) greatest virtue is its well-developed service economy. The city is noisy and polluted, but ferries, buses, and trains shuttle visitors efficiently to the nearby Ría de Vigo and Río Miño, while a network of hotels and shops pamper tourists between excursions. Several nearby towns are close and convenient for day trips. And Vigo itself is not totally devoid of charm: the *casco antigo* (old quarter) has a certain appeal, and the wide boulevards and elegant cafés near the water are soothing places to while away an evening.

ORIENTATION AND PRACTICAL INFORMATION

The **Gran Vía** is the main thoroughfare, stretching south to north from Pr. América, through **Praza de España,** ending at the perpendicular **Rúa Príncipe Urzáiz.** The train station lies just off R. Urzáiz in Pr. Estación. R. Urzáiz becomes **Calle Colón,** and continues to near the port. **As Avenidas** is the main street along the water, just north of **Praza de Compostela.**

Tourist Office: As Avenidas, s/n (tel. 43 05 77). Take a right onto R. Urzáiz (up the hill from the train station), then right again as it becomes C. Colón to its port end; As Avenidas is to the left. From the bus station, turn right onto Alcalde Gregorio Espino, and follow uphill to Pr. España. At the rotary, take the second street on the right, Gran Vía, and follow until it intersects R. Urzáiz. Take a left, then follow instructions above. Alternately, catch a red Vitrasa bus at the bus station (#L27, L23, or R7 to the city center; 100ptas). The office is in the gray circular building across from the Estación Marítima. Wide selection of brochures and maps. English spoken. Open Mon.-Fri. 9am-2pm and 4:30-6:30pm, Sat. 10am-12:30pm.

El Corte Inglés: Gran Vía, 25-27 (tel. 41 51 11). Walking downhill on R. Urzáiz, turn left onto Gran Vía. As always, they have good **maps. Currency exchange:** 250ptas min. charge for cash, 500ptas for traveler's checks—same as the banks. They also offer novels and guidebooks in English, haircutting, cafeteria and restaurant, and **telephones.** Open Mon.-Sat. 10am-9pm.

Budget Travel: Viajes TIVE, C. Uruguay, 15, 2nd fl. (tel. 22 61 17 or 43 59 44). From R. Urzáiz, turn right onto C. Cervantes; C. Uruguay is the 3rd left. ISIC 500ptas. HI card 1800ptas. Some English spoken. Open Mon.-Fri. 9am-2pm.

Currency Exchange: see **El Corte Inglés** above.

Post Office: Pr. Compostela, 3 (tel. 21 70 09 or 43 40 09; fax 37 47 26). From C. Colón, turn left onto Pr. Compostela. Open for stamps, Lista de Correos, and **telegrams** Mon.-Fri. 8am-9pm, Sat. 9am-2pm; for **faxes** Mon.-Fri. 9am-9pm. **Postal Code:** 36200.

Telephones: Telefónica, R. Urzáiz, 3, near the intersection with C. Colón. **Faxes** sent but not received. Open Mon.-Sat. 9am-9pm. Also phones outside Estación Marítima. **Telephone Code:** 986.

Flights: Aeropuerto de Vigo, Av. Aeroporto, s/n (tel. 48 74 09). Daily flights to Madrid, Barcelona, Bilbao, and Valencia. **Iberia's** office is at Marqués de Valladares, 17 (tel. 22 70 05). A **bus** runs regularly from the Estación Marítima to the airport, stopping also at the train and bus stations (100ptas).

Trains: RENFE, Pr. Estación, s/n (tel. 43 11 14), down the stairs from R. Urzáiz. Information open 10am-11pm. To: Pontevedra (16 per day, 35min., 195ptas); Túy (4 per day, 45min., 270ptas); Santiago de Compostela (10 per day, 2hr., 600ptas); La Coruña (9 per day, 3hr., 1075ptas); Valladolid (1 per day, change at Medina del Campo, 3800ptas); Madrid (2 per day, 8-9hr., 4500-6500ptas); Valença do Minho, Portugal (4 per day, 1hr., 300ptas); Porto, Portugal (3 per day, 2½hr., 1500ptas).

Buses: Estación de Autobuses, Av. Madrid, s/n (tel. 37 34 11). On the corner with R. Alcalde Gregorio Espino. **Castromil** (tel. 27 81 12). To: Santiago de Compostela (17 per day, every hr. on the ½hr., 2hr., 835ptas); La Coruña (9 per day, 2½hr., 1500ptas); Pontevedra (15 per day, 45min., 265ptas). **ATSA** (tel. 60 00 22). To: Túy (every ½hr., 45min., 280ptas); La Guardia (every ½hr., 1hr., 525ptas); Bayona (every ½hr., ½hr., 215ptas, last bus back leaves at 9pm); Pontevedra (every ½hr., 40min., 275ptas). For ATSA buses, go straight downstairs to gates and buy tickets when boarding. **Travel Bus** (tel. 37 78 78). To: Madrid (7 per day, 9hr., 3190ptas). **Galicia Euskadi** (tel. 26 13 23). To: Bilbao (3 per day, 6hr., 3655ptas). **Vibasa** (tel. 26 13 23). To: Barcelona (2 per day at 7am and 2pm, 14hr., 6335ptas).

Ferries: Estación Marítima de Ría, As Avenidas, s/n (tel. 43 90 69), just past the nautical club. Ferries to Cangas (every hr. 6:30am-9pm, Sun. 8:30am-9pm, 20min., round-trip 330ptas) and Moaña (every hr., ½hr., round-trip 375ptas; same schedule). Service to Islas Cíes June-Sept. only (5 per day, round-trip 1250ptas).

Public Transportation: Red **Vitrasa** buses (tel. 29 16 00) run to every corner of the city (100ptas).

Taxis: Radio Taxi (tel. 47 00 00).

Car Rental: Atesa, C. Urzáiz, 84 (tel. 41 80 76). Must be 21 and have had license 1 yr. Open Mon.-Fri. 8:30am-1:30pm and 4-8pm, Sat. 9am-1pm. **Avis,** C. Uruguay, 12 (tel. 43 59 11). Must be 23 and have had license 1 yr. Open Mon.-Fri. 9am-1:15pm and 4-7pm, Sat. 9am-noon.

Luggage Storage: At the **train station** (lockers 300ptas). Open 7am-9:45pm. At the **bus station** (60ptas per bag). Open Mon.-Fri. 9:30am-1:30pm and 3-7pm, Sat. 9am-2pm. The train station is infinitely more central.

English Bookstore: Librería Cervantes, R. Policarpio Sanz, 27 (tel. 43 94 08), off C. Colón. Modest miscellany of novels in English. Open Mon.-Fri. 9:30am-1:30pm and 4:30-8pm, Sat. 9:30am-1:30pm.

Laundromat: Vicus Autoservicio, C. Ecuador, 43 (tel. 43 03 03), south of and parallel to R. Urzáiz. 400ptas per 4kg load to wash, 100ptas to dry. Open Mon.-Sat. 9am-8pm.

Red Cross: tel. 22 22 22.

24-Hour Pharmacy: Check *Farmacias de Guardia* listings in *Faro de Vigo* (local paper, 90ptas) or the sign posted in all pharmacy windows.

Hospitals: Hospital Xeral, C. Pizarro, 32 (tel. 81 60 00). **Hospital Municipal,** C. Camelias, 109 (tel. 41 12 44). **Ambulance** (tel. 41 64 29 or 22 60 31). **Emergency:** tel. 092. **Casa de Socorro** (tel. 43 25 09).

Police: Policia Municipa, Pr. Rèi (tel. 43 22 11).

ACCOMMODATIONS

Budgeters take advantage of Vigo's inexpensive rooms, using the city as a base from which to explore surrounding areas. **Calle Alfonso XIII** (immediately to the right upon exiting the train station) looks like a Las Vegas, not of casinos, but of affordable *hostales*. The streets around the **port** (particularly **Calle Carral**) and **Calle Urzáiz** are also awash with reasonable accommodations.

Hostal-Residencia Madrid, C. Alfonso XIII, 63 (tel. 22 55 23). Doubles big enough to hold an olympic pool and sunny enough to get a tan. Prices may be flexible. Singles 1500ptas. Doubles 1600-2800ptas. Showers included.

Hostal-Residencia Orensano, C. Lepanto, 9 (43 51 12), 1 bl. from train station. Plain, simple, and cheap. Rooms are clean but on the small side. Singles 1000-1200ptas. Doubles 2000-2500ptas.

Hostal Ría de Vigo, C. Cervantes, 14 (tel. 43 72 40), a left off C. Alfonso XIII. Simple, spacious, and squeaky clean. All rooms have bath. Singles 1800ptas. Doubles with one bed 2000-2500ptas, with two beds 2500-3500ptas.

Hostal Savoy, C. Carral, 20 (tel. 43 25 41), 1 bl. up the street from the Estación Marítima. Classy rooms with wood floors, muted color schemes, and free-standing showers only inches from the beds. Singles 1700-2000ptas. Doubles 2800-3500ptas.

FOOD

The **Gran Vía** and **Calle Venezuela** are brimming with shiny, bright *cafeterías* and outdoor *terrazas*. Side streets off **Calle Urzáiz** are equally rewarding and tend to be a bit cheaper. Streets leading away from the port hide dens of seafood iniquity.

Groceries: Exo-Ama, C. Alcalde Vásquez Varela, 3, perpendicular to C. Urzáiz (tel. 40 39 44), a left turn, then a right, after exiting the train station. Open Mon.-Fri. 9am-2pm and 5-8:30pm, Sat. 9am-2pm.

Cafetería Lido, Gran Vía, 3 (tel. 41 09 18), near R. Urzáiz. Elegant, long wood bar with tables in back and out front. A glass case of rich desserts. Veggie sandwich 275ptas. *Platos combinados* from 400ptas. Open daily 7:30am-2am.

Mesón Don Sancho, C. García Olloqui, 1. At the end of Pr. Compostela, and 1 bl. up from the Estación Marítima. A popular place to make a meal of delicious *tapas*. Fresh grilled shrimp 450ptas, clams steamed in wine and garlic 500ptas, meatballs 40ptas each. Open daily 11am-midnight.

Cafetería Cariba, C. Ecuador, 73, right behind El Corte Inglés. Cavernous preppy (pink and green) interior and tranquilizing music soothe the soul as the array of *bocadillos* and *raciones* soothe the stomach. *Terraza* outside, A/C inside. *Platos combinados* offer it all (500-700ptas). Open 7am-1am.

ENTERTAINMENT

Starting in the late afternoon, students pack the streets of the *casco antigo*, which becomes progressively sleazier as the night wears on. In honor of its notorious past as a center for witches (good and bad), Vigo hosts *Expomagia* in mid-June, a celebration of all things occult. Tantric yogis and practitioners of *umbanda* (a Brazilian cult with practices similar to voodoo) offer demonstrations and sell their wares down at the port.

■ NEAR VIGO

The Vigo estuary has a particularly wide entrance—as if, as the tourist brochure so eloquently states, "it were about to swallow up a big piece of ocean." The big fat mouth and its lively port explain why the towns of this *ría* have grown like mad in the past half century. Cangas, Bayona, Túy, and La Guardia are all easy day trips from Vigo.

The Río Miño marks a quiet and, after Maastricht, altogether porous national border. Running southwest from Lugo, the Río Miño empties into the Atlantic Ocean, about 25km further west. One lone bridge, bearing trains, automobiles, and pedestrians, spans the river between Túy in Galicia and Valença do Minho in Portugal.

CANGAS

A 20-minute ferry ride across the Ría de Vigo, Cangas (pop. 5000) is hardly an unspoiled paradise—but it does retain a small-town feeling and its white **beach** offers plenty of respite from the urban bustle of Vigo. Where the ferry drops visitors, the **turismo** welcomes them in a small light-blue shack behind the ticket office. (Open Mon.-Sat. 9am-2pm and 4:30-6:30pm.) The **post office** is at C. Pablo Iglesias, 24. (Open Mon.-Sat. 9am-9pm.) Inexpensive lodging is scarce—spend the night in Vigo. **Hostal Belén** (tel. 30 00 15), on C. Antonio Nores, is central and about the cheapest. (Doubles 4000ptas; mid-Sept.-June 3000ptas.) **Camping Cangas** (tel. 30 47 26), on Playa de Limens, has beach-front sites for tent-pitching. (450ptas per person and per car. Open May-Sept. 9.) The municipal **market** is to the right of the ferry, at the corner of Av. 25 de Vulio and Paseo do Caslelo. **Mesón O Batel,** half a block behind the market in Pr. Constitución, is popular with locals. *(Platos combinados* about 500ptas.) Simple, cheap *cafeterías* lie scattered along Av. Ourense, behind the path to the beach. **Ferries** travel from Vigo to Cangas and back again (every ½hr., 20min., round-trip 330ptas). La Unión **buses** (tel. 30 01 22) run from Cangas to Pontevedra several times per day. Look for the blue "Parada" sign on C. Montero Ríos, near the beach, or in the lot by the ferry.

BAYONA (BAIONA)

21km southwest of Vigo, snug in its own mini-estuary, Bayona was the first European town to receive word from the New World when La Pinta returned to its port in March 1493. Now a seductive beach town, Bayona (pop. 10,000) boasts one *parador nacional* and a handful of churches. A stroll along the stone walls of the 16th-century **castillo**-*cum*-hotel—the *parador* that was once the castle of the Condes de Gondomar—provides the most breathtaking sea views in the area. Admission to the grounds is a worthwhile 100ptas; rose bushes, pine trees, and riotous flowers spill out onto spectacular views of the port and ocean. From the bus stop on C. Angel Eldouayan, walk uphill to the right. **Turismo,** on Pr. Pedro de Castro, at the end of C. Ventura Misa and behind the 1493 commemorative monolith, is open Mon.-Sat. 9:30am-1:30pm. The **post office** at C. Ciudad de Vigo, 3 (tel. 35 63 50), is open Mon.-Sat. 9am-9pm. Budget accommodations, unfortunately, don't live up to *parador* splendor. **Hospedaje Kin,** C. Ventura Misa, 27 (tel. 35 72 15), provides more modest lodging. (Singles 1600ptas. Doubles 2800ptas, with bath 3700ptas.) **Camping Bayona Playa** (tel. 35 00 35) is open June-Sept. (570ptas per person, 460ptas per tent, 580ptas per car.) For *comida,* check out **Calle Ventura Misa,** which is lined with *mesones* and *cafeterías.* At **El Túnel,** C. Ventura Misa, 21 (tel. 35 51 09), local families devour table-long trays of shellfish. (Fresh grilled sardines 500ptas, fried baby squid *(chipirones)* 500ptas. Open daily 1-4pm and 8:30pm-midnight.) **Buses** run from Vigo (every ½hr., 45min.-1¼hr. depending on traffic, 215ptas). Those coming for the **beach** would do better to get off at Praia América, about 4km before Bayona.

TÚY (TUI)

The small border town of Túy (pop. 16,000), while charming, offers tourists little more than the opportunity to walk into Portugal. The 1km stroll to Valença do Minho, across a metal planked walkway over the Río Miño, is the stuff of which *National Geographic* and PBS documentaries are made. While the narrow bridge may be nerve-wracking to some, the landscape of rolling hills, farmlands, and tree-lined river banks is tranquil and beautiful. Túy's small **catedral** is a mix of Gothic and Romanesque, reflecting the town's Portuguese, Spanish, and Galician roots. Look inside for the relics of San Telmo, the patron saint of sailors.

    Turismo, Puente Tripes, s/n (tel. 60 17 89), is in the wood building behind the old city, on the road leading to Portugal. (Open Mon.-Fri. 9am-2pm and 4:30-

6:30pm, Sat. 10am-12:30pm.) For the **Red Cross,** call tel. 60 16 84. The **police,** next to the cathedral, answer at tel. 60 04 13. The **post office** (tel. 60 02 20) is at C. Martínez Padín.

For pleasant accommodations, **Habitaciones Otilia,** Generalísimo, 8, 2nd fl. (tel. 60 10 62), behind C. Calvo Sotelo en route to the cathedral, has snugly beds topped by quilted bedspreads. With surrealistically tilting floors and moldy wallpaper, it's appealingly spooky. (Doubles 2000ptas.) **Hostal Generosa,** C. Calvo Sotelo, 37 (tel. 60 00 55), has large rooms and similar prices. (Doubles 2200-2400ptas.) If it's Thursday, stroll down the Paseo Calvo Sotelo to the weekly **market,** which has been around since 1679. **Restaurante Galicia,** C. Augusto Gonzales Besada, 8, one bl. off C. Calvo Sotelo (tel. 60 00 01), is slightly pricey, but comes complete with mirrored walls and a slick-haired waiter. Serves a delicious and filling *pollo al gilllo* (600ptas) and a fabulous *sopa de marisco* (250ptas). (Open Mon.-Sat. 1-4pm and 8-11pm.) Through windows carved out of its medieval stone walls, **Bar el Formo,** C. Entiehornos, 11, provides twinkling views of Portugal, along with beer and sandwiches (275ptas). (Open Mon.-Sat. 7pm-1am.)

The ATSA (tel. 60 00 22) **bus** from Vigo stops on C. Calvo Sotelo opposite the Iglesia de San Francisco, and returns to Vigo from the other side of the street (every ½hr., 45min., 270ptas). Three **trains** (tel. 60 08 13) per day run from Vigo to Túy, then cross the border to Valença and Viana do Castelo, Portugal. They stop for 15min. on both sides for customs and passport control. The train stations in each town are nowhere near the border or the center of town; taking the bus or walking across makes more sense.

LA GUARDIA (A GUARDIA)

Perched between the mouth of the Miño and the Atlantic Ocean, La Guardia (pop. 6500) relies on an active fishing industry and 250,000 annual tourists, who invade its small beach and big mountain. The bus stops at the corner of C. Domínguez Fontela and C. Concepción Arenal. Take C. Domínguez Fontela to the central C. José Antonio and turn right to climb the majestic **Monte Santa Tecla.** Bear right onto C. Rosalía de Castro to start the 6km mountain ascent. At the checkpoint 300m from the end of C. Rosalía de Castro, hikers pay 50ptas to sweat their way to the peak, to see remains of an old *castro* (celtic village), with it's circular stone houses covered by *pallazos* (thatched roofs). Near the top is a chapel dedicated to Santa Tecla, the patron saint of headaches and heart disease.

La Guardia's **tourist office** at Pr. España, 1 (tel. 61 00 00), in the Ayuntamiento, hands out a brochure (multilingual, atrociously translated) but no maps.

The one hotel on the mountain, **Hotel Pazo Santa Tecla** (tel. 61 00 02), takes advantage of its spectacular location with terraces which overlook the valley. (Singles with bath 3200ptas. Doubles with bath 4600ptas. Off-season: 2750ptas; 4200ptas. Breakfast 350ptas. Open Semana Santa-Oct.) In La Guardia proper, **Hostal Martírrey,** C. José Antonio, 8 (tel. 61 03 49), welcomes guests in a room that looks like something out of a Bogart flick, then leads them to their own spacious and beautiful rooms. (Singles 1300-1700ptas. Doubles 2300-3000ptas, with bath 3300-3700ptas. Breakfast 250ptas; lunch and dinner 1100ptas each.) Although the **market** is right on C. Concepción Arenal, those hungry for seafood should try **Bar Bodegón Puerto Guardés,** C. Calvo Sotelo, 1 (tel. 61 16 47), right in the port, where loud-talking fisherfolk come in for fresh grilled salmon (with salad and potatoes, 400ptas) and terrific fried *calamares* (400ptas). La Guardia hosts a **lobster festival** in the third week of June, as well as the mysterious "Burial of the Swordfish" during Carnival. Pilgrimages and folk festivals mark the Feria de Monte de Sta. Tecla the second week of August.

Buses run to Túy (45min., 280ptas) on their way to Vigo (every ½hr., 1½hr., 515ptas). They leave from Pr. Avelino Vincente, just off C. José Antonio.

■■■ RÍA DE PONTEVEDRA: PONTEVEDRA

With its fine transportation network and a supply of inexpensive accommodations, Pontevedra makes an excellent jumping-off point for tours of the Rías Bajas, Ría de Pontevedra, and Ría de Arousa. 50km south of Santiago, this city of 70,000 also merits a visit in its own right for its evocative arcades, granite walkways, and seigneurial houses.

ORIENTATION AND PRACTICAL INFORMATION

The center of town is the **Praza Peregrina,** from which two main streets—**Calle Peregrina** and **Calle Michelena**—radiate out in opposite directions. **Praza Galiza** is a 5-min. walk south of Pr. Peregrina. The **train** and **bus stations,** located across from each other, lie about 1km away from town. To get to the center, turn right upon exiting the train station, or right then immediately left from the bus station, and walk straight until intersecting C. Peregrina. Turn right—the main square is 4 bl. up.

Tourist Office: C. General Mola, 3 (tel. 85 08 14), 1 bl. from Pr. Peregrina, a left off C. Michelena. Tons of slick brochures and maps. Some English spoken. Open Mon.-Fri. 9am-2pm and 5-7pm, Sat. 10am-12:30pm.

Currency Exchange: Banco Central Hispanoamerica, C. Michelena, 1 (tel. 85 38 12). Acceptable rates, typical 500pta commission. Open Mon.-Fri. 8:30am-2:30pm; Oct.-May also Sat. 8:30am-1pm.

Post Office: C. Olivia, s/n (tel. 85 16 77), a pedestrian street off Pr. Peregrina. Open for stamps and Lista de Correos Mon.-Fri. 8am-9pm, Sat. 8am-2pm. **Postal Code:** 36001.

Telephones: Telefónica, C. Alondiga, 1, just behind the Ayuntamiento in Pr. España. (Closed for renovations.) **Telephone Code:** 986.

Trains: C. Alféreces Provisionales, s/n (tel. 85 13 13). A sizable walk from town. Taxis to the center cost about 275ptas. Information open 7:30am-1:30pm and 3:30-9:30pm. To: Madrid (1 per day, 11hr., 4900-5400ptas); Santiago (12 per day, 1½hr., 400ptas); La Coruña (8 per day, 3hr., 850ptas); Vigo (16 per day, 45 min., 190ptas).

Buses: C. Alféreces Provisionales, s/n (tel. 85 24 08 or 85 25 30). Information open Mon.-Sat. 8:30am-9pm. Service is more frequent than by rail. To: Santiago (every hr., 1hr., 550ptas); La Coruña (10 per day, 2¼hr., 1300ptas); Cambados (9 per day, 1hr., 450ptas); Sanxenxo (every ½hr., ½hr., 205ptas); El Grove and La Toja (every ½hr., 1hr., 360ptas); Madrid (8 per day, 8hr., 3065ptas).

Taxis: tel. 85 12 89 or 85 12 85.

Car Rental: Avis, C. Peregina, 47 (tel. 85 20 25). Rates around 8000ptas per day, unlimited mileage, less for longer periods of time. You must be at least 23 and have had license 1 yr. Open Mon.-Fri. 9am-1:30pm and 4-7pm, Sat. 9am-1pm.

Luggage Storage: Lockers at the train station cost 300ptas; at the bus station, 70ptas per bag. Open 8am-8pm.

English Bookstore: Librería Michelena, C. Michelena, 22 (tel. 85 87 46). Astounding selection of classics and contemporary works in Spanish and English. Open 9am-2pm and 4-6pm.

Red Cross: C. Padre Gaile, s/n (tel. 85 20 77).

Hospital: Hospital Provincial, C. Doctor Loureiro Crespo, 2 (tel. 85 55 00).

Ambulance: División Azul (tel. 85 27 99).

Police: C. Joaquín Costa, 19 (tel. 85 38 00 or 091).

ACCOMMODATIONS AND FOOD

Rooms, although generally inexpensive, are not terribly easy to find—calling ahead may be a good idea. **Calles Michelena** and **Peregrina,** and the area around **Praza Galiza,** are lightly dotted with *fondas* and *pensiones.* Like most towns in Galicia, Pontevedra prides itself on its seafood. In the evening, locals crowd tiny bars on **Calle Figueroa** to munch on an endless variety of fishy tapas, washed down with the local Albariño wine.

Pensión La Cueva, C. Andrés Mellado, 7 (tel. 85 12 71), right in Pr. Galiza. Huge rooms where Chinese art clashes with plaid lumberjack bedspreads. Very clean and very cheap. Look for the owner in the bar downstairs. Singles 900ptas. Doubles 1500-2000ptas.

Pensión Fortes, C. Sagasta, 11 (tel. 85 12 62), off C. Peregrina, a few bl. south of the main square. Gorgeous rooms accented with dark wood furniture, varnished floors, crisp white linens, and some with geraniums. Kind owners keep everything spotless, and may tell you about the oxcarts it took to build the place 40 years ago. Singles 1100-1600ptas. Doubles 2600ptas.

Bar Estrella, C. Figueroa, 3, off Pr. Peregrina. All kinds of *raciones* (300-900ptas), though seafood is the more popular fare. Open Fri.-Wed. 11am-3pm and 7pm-midnight.

Bodegón Picota, C. Peregrina, 4 (tel. 85 59 17). An intriguing alternative to the café-bar scene. Their motto, "Fresh Food, Curiously Selected," explains their menu: asparagus soup 385ptas, cheese plates 345ptas, barbecued ribs 950ptas, and mango pie 400ptas. Open 1-4pm and 8pm-midnight.

SIGHTS

Pontevedra's old town is built almost entirely from granite; in the evening its arcades and stone walls give off a luminescent glow. Commissioned by the Sailors' Guild in the 16th century, the **Basílica Menor de Sta. Maria** has a golden Plateresque door that's floodlit at night, and wax figures (men, pigs, arms) left as ex-votos in the chapels. 18th-century **Basílica de la Peregrina** takes its round shape from the scallop shell associated with Santiago; the church houses Pontevedra's patron saint, the Virgin Mary, disguised as a pilgrim. The **Museo Provincial** in Pr. Leña holds an intriguing archaeological collection of Roman hatchets and glass work, as well as an eclectic inventory of unrelated exhibits. (Tel. 85 14 55; open Mon.-Sat. 10am-2:15pm and 5-8:45pm, Sun. 11am-1pm; winter Tues.-Sun. 9am-1pm and 5-7pm.) To imagine what an open-air Gothic cathedral would look like, tour the ruins of the **Santo Domingo Convent,** resting in a corner of Pr. España.

■■■ RÍA DE AROUSA

Frequent bus service runs through this area from Pontevedra to Vilagarcía de Arousa, the commercial center of central Galicia (45min., 250ptas), making the following towns perfect for day trips from Pontevedra.

EL GROVE AND LA TOJA

Many Europeans vacation at rocky-shored **El Grove** (O Grove, pop. 10,725), 32km west of Pontevedra, and the nearby island of **La Toja** (A Toxa). The tour of El Grove itself is short on beaches but long on cheap *pensiones* and seafood restaurants. Sun and surf seekers should try the long stretches of powdery sand at nearby **La Lazada** and **Praia do Foxes,** which can be reached from town by taking the Unión **bus** that leaves regularly for Pontevedra from the end of the waterfront promenade.

Across the ridge from El Grove, La Toja lures the wealthy with a casino, expensive housing development, and slightly less appealing beaches. La Toja's two claims to fame are a seashell-covered church, and the popular black soap (Magno) which is produced here. Iron oxide—not dye—tints the soap ebony. Hotels on La Toja cater to the casino crowd; staying across the *ría* in El Grove (or back in Pontevedra) is economically more feasible. The cheapest is **Hostal La Concha,** C. Teniente Dominguez, 35 (tel. 73 00 60), with its airy rooms, water views, and shiny bathrooms. (2600-4000ptas. Closes in winter if there are no guests; call first.) Camp near the gorgeous La Canzada beach at **Camping Muiñeira** (tel. 73 12 40; 450ptas per person, per tent, and per car). Buses run from Pontevedra to El Grove and La Toja (every ½hr., 1hr., 360ptas).

CAMBADOS

26km from Pontevedra, Cambados (pop. 13,000) needs only one thing—a beach. A pretty harbor and the remains of some Roman hill forts hardly draw the sun-worshipping masses that descend on El Grove. To compensate, Cambados throws a **fiesta** in the streets virtually every night in midsummer, beginning with the July celebration of Sta. Mariña, and culminating the first Friday in August with the official tasting of the previous year's local Albariño, a light, fruity wine. The **Pazo de Fefiñanes** is an attractive 16th-century palace turned bodega. Rooms couldn't be easier to find. Try **Hostal Pazos,** C. Curros Enriquez, 1 (tel. 54 28 10), with marble-floored, shiny rooms. (Doubles 3775ptas; Sept.-June 2100-3300ptas.) **Buses** run frequently from Pontevedra (9 per day, 1hr., 450ptas).

■ ■ ■ RÍA DE MUROS Y NOYA

The northernmost of the Rías Bajas, this *ría* isn't much touristed. Frequent Castromil buses make these towns easy day trip material.

MUROS

The only unnatural substance you'll encounter in Muros is the medication for the bus ride. Sitting pretty 65km west of Santiago, on the north side of the *ría,* the town of 3200 inhabitants combines exquisite mountain views with the warmth and friendliness of a fishing village. Stone houses, winding, hilly streets, and a collection of chapels tell the story of a lively little town high in the mountains of Galicia.

Muros has served as a leper hospital and a pit stop for pilgrims en route to Cabo Finisterre. The town's church, the **Colexiata do Santa María,** sports Romanesque and Gothic vestiges, thanks to Lope de Mendoza's refurbishing job in 1400. The **Paseo Marítimo,** along the port where the bus stops, crackles with action in summer.

The **Ayuntamiento,** at the right end of the street as you face the water, stocks maps and brochures. (Open Mon.-Fri. 8:30am-2:30pm.) For **taxis,** call tel. 82 62 27. The **municipal police** hide out in the Casa do Concello building with the Ayuntamiento (tel. 82 72 76). For **medical assistance,** call tel. 82 72 50, and for an **ambulance,** tel. 82 68 91 or 76 33 89.

Hostal Ría de Muros, located right where the bus stops on R. Castelao, 53 (tel. 82 60 56), offers huge rooms with huge baths and tremendous views of the port, *ría,* and mountains. (Doubles with bath 4000ptas; Sept.-May 3000ptas.) Up the street, the friendly owners of **Hospedaje A Vianda,** R. Castelao, 47 (tel. 82 63 22), are refugees from Newark, New Jersey, and welcome visitors to airy rooms, some with views, for 2500-3500ptas. Downstairs they serve up *raciones* of scallops (450ptas) and a 1000pta *menú.* More restaurants line R. Castelao. Prices range greatly, but the cuisine is constant: seafood. Fishing continues to be the lifeblood of Muros' economy. On Friday mornings, you can buy all the beachwear you forgot to pack, for very low prices, at the **outdoor market** in the streets behind R. Castelao.

Castromil **buses** run from Santiago (every hr., 2hr., 675ptas.) Transportes Finisterre buses (tel. 82 69 83) provide service between Muros and nearby towns. They pass the **Playa San Francisco,** 3km away, on their way to Cée (about every 2hr., 10min., 40ptas). Catch them in front of Banco Pastor on R. Castelao.

Near Muros

4km from Muros, little **Louro's** isolated beaches hug an untamed forest. Some say these are the most virgin of beaches in the Rías Bajas. **Camping A Bouga** (tel. 82 60 25) makes the trip a great wilderness escapade. (435ptas per adult, per tent, and per car. Electricity 375ptas. Open May 15-Sept. 15.)

NOYA (NOIA)

Nicknamed "the little Compostela" for the density of its monuments, Noya may actually be better known for its braided straw hats with black bands. Gothic arcades and 15th-century stone houses surround this town's many small squares. 14th-century **Igrexa de Santa María** is juxtaposed with 16th-century **Igrexa de San Francisco** and the **Ayuntamiento**. The Galician Gothic facade of the **Igrexa de San Martín** is comprised of numerous statues. **Hostal Sol y Mar,** Avda. San Lorenzo, s/n (tel. 82 09 00), has pretty rooms with views and sinks. (Doubles 2500-3000ptas, with bath 3500ptas.) The Castromil **bus** (tel. 58 90 90 from Santiago, tel. 82 05 19 from Noya) which runs from Santiago to Muros stops in Noya (every hr. 8am-8pm, 1hr., 400ptas).

O CASTRO DE BAROÑA

One of the coast's hidden treasures, **O Castro de Baroña** was originally an ancient Celtic fortress (inhabited until the 5th century). The circular foundations of the houses remain here, protected by defensive walls on the narrow isthmus. Thank the Romans for the lighthouse and tourist inertia for the paucity of daytrippers along this long expanse of soft, sandy beach.

Café-Bar O Castro (tel. 85 30 76), through the woods on the main road, has spotless rooms upstairs. (Singles 1700ptas. Doubles 2200ptas. Bargain for stays longer than one night. *Menú* 750ptas. *Ración* of *empanada* 300ptas.) The nearest town is **Porto do Son,** which has a virtually empty beach itself.

RÍAS DE LA COSTA DE LA MUERTE (RÍAS DA COSTA DA MORTE)

Although the appellation "Coast of Death" refers to the number of shipwrecks that have occurred along the rocky coastline, it could just as well apply to the tragedy bred by exquisite gourmet tastes. Each year several fishers lose their lives attempting to extract the most expensive and sought after seafood *percebes* (barnicles) from the sharp rocks that jut out along the coast. The beaches here are arguably the cleanest, emptiest, and loveliest in Spain. If Galicia is the forgotten corner of Spain, then the small *rías* of the Costa de la Muerte are the forgotten corner of Galicia.

The greatest challenge is finding quick transportation to these remote Elysian fields. Fortunately, both Cabo Finisterre and Camariñas can be reached by bus from Santiago and La Coruña. Bus service to the smaller towns and isolated beaches is infrequent or nonexistent. There is no evidence of trains. The roads are tortuous and sometimes poorly paved. Road signs are vague, and soupy mists tend to settle in during the morning.

The local population reveals its isolation; fields are still plowed by oxen, and women carry homegrown produce to market in baskets on their heads. Campgrounds along the coast tend to be overpriced and dirty; some fail to offer even the basic amenities.

CABO FINISTERRE (CABO FISTERRA)

No, you haven't died and gone to heaven—you've just reached the end of the world. The coastal **faro** (lighthouse), a 4km walk from town (45min.), permits stunning views of cliffs dropping sharply to the water below. To the left spreads the Ría de Corcubión, across which spread the attractive beaches of Sardineiro and Langosteira. To the right shimmers the unforgiving landscape of the open sea, where rocky, jagged mountains meet the crashing waves of the Atlantic. Straight ahead stands the lighthouse that guided ships toward land, though many were destroyed by the whirlpools, rocks, and fatally strong currents. Such hazards have also kept the region from becoming another Club Med; hidden turquoise beaches such as **Praia de Corbeiro** seduce the more intrepid traveler.

Finisterre (from the Latin *finis terrae* or end of the earth) is an unassuming fishing village (pop. 3000) best known for its geographical location. Still, its gorgeous beaches attract thousands of visitors—including Spain's Nobel Prize winning novelist Camilo José Cela—every summer. The rocky promontory over Finisterre's harbor was once a sacred hill for Roman legionnaires and then for Celtic settlers. Locals hid in the cliff's cool caves to escape the Viking raids. Nearby, **Ezaro** is a typical beach town with the added allure of magnificent waterfalls and a picturesque lagoon 1km up the river behind Finisterre.

Besides the glorious views from the lighthouse on Cabo Finisterre, there's not a whole lot to see. The **Capilla de Santa María das Areas** contains a painting of the "Christ of the Golden Beard," rumored to have been thrown overboard by a British ship and miraculously found by a local fisherman.

The Casa do Concello, C. Santa Catalina (tel. 74 00 01), hands out some nice stickers, but only the barest minimum of **tourist information.** (Open Mon.-Fri. 8:30am-2:30pm, Sat. 9am-1pm; Oct.-May Mon.-Fri. 9am-2pm and 5-7pm, Sat. 9am-2pm.) The **postal code** is 15004; **telephone code** 981. Next door, the Casa del Mar Clínica (tel. 74 02 52) offers **medical assistance.** In a **medical emergency,** call 74 52 83.

Although Finisterre is a feasible day trip from Santiago, **Hospedaje López,** C. Carrasqueira, 4 (tel. 74 04 49), provides cheap, immaculate, light-filled rooms, some with views of the ocean, and a bit of Disney cheer. Head uphill, away from the main statue at the port, then turn right onto C. Carrasqueira and walk for 5 minutes. (Singles 1500ptas. Doubles 3000ptas. Triples 3000-3500ptas. Call first in winter, as they may be closed.) Many a plump lobster waves hello from the mirrored tanks at the entrance to **Hostal Cabo Finisterre,** C. Santa Catalina, s/n (tel. 74 00 00), 50m uphill from the statue at the port. The spic-and-span rooms all come with bath and telephone. (Singles 1500ptas. Doubles 3000ptas. Triples 4000ptas.) For organized camping and more temperate water, head to the opposite side of the isthmus connecting Finisterre with the mainland. **Camping Ruta Finisterre** (tel. 74 63 02) is on Ctra. Coruña, east of Finisterre on the Playa del Estorde in Cée. (425ptas per person, per tent, and per car. Open April and June15-Sept. 15.)

Supermercados El Cruce, C. Coruña (continuation of C. Santa Catalina, heading east), stocks the basics. (Open Mon.-Sat. 9am-2:30pm and 5-9pm.) Although most restaurants along the dock are rather overpriced, **Restaurante O Centalo** (tel. 74 04 52) serves a 1000pta *menú* and a large variety of *raciones* (325-700ptas). (Open 10am-midnight.)

Three Finisterre **buses** make the trip from Santiago daily, and two return (2½hr., 1135ptas). Buses often require transfer in Vimianzo, but there is never a wait. If you plan to see Finisterre as a day trip from Santiago, check return times carefully, as the last bus may leave in mid-afternoon.

CAMARIÑAS

With shades of Penelope, who wove and wove as her husband Odysseus sailed the seas, the women in Camariñas (pop. 3250, north of Cabo Finisterre on the other side of the *ría*) sit on their doorsteps making the intricate, expensive, and delicate *encaje de bolsillos* lace, an activity introduced by the Celts. The difference, of course, is that these women are not waiting for their own sea-faring husbands; rather, they are keeping this whitewashed town afloat economically. The *palilleiras* (lace-makers) are the beach town's secret weapon; they are honored by a statue in the town square.

To the left of the port, the **faro** (lighthouse) looms about 5km (1hr. walk) up a mountain road adorned with shepherds, roosters, and an occasional farmer. Towards Ctra. General, the main highway, rest **Area da Vila** and **Lingunde,** two virtually untouched beaches, approachable only via a sandy, rocky cliffhanger of a path (off the road to the lighthouse). If you value your car and/or your life, stick to the phenomenal view from above. Many a watery tragedy has struck here; the wreck of the British ship *The Serpent* is commemorated by a tombstone for the sailors who died when the ship approached Camariñas one cold, rainy night in 1890. Only three men of over 300 survived.

Across the *ría* from Camariñas, on a rocky point in **Muxía**, a collection of historic model ships hangs from the ceiling of **Igrexa de Nossa Señora da Barca** (Our Lady of the Ship). The rocks in front of the church supposedly hum when innocent people walk by. (They didn't hum for us...)

Behind the statue of the *palilleira* stands the **Casa Consistorial** (tel. 73 60 00 or 73 60 25), purveyor of tourist tips. (Open Mon.-Fri. 8am-2:30pm, Sat. 9am-2pm.) Right on C. Miguel Freijo on the water is Caixa Galicia for **currency exchange.** (Open Mon.-Fri. 8:30am-2pm.) The **postal code** is 15002. The **telephone code** is 981. Up on C. Generalísimo Franco, 5, sits the **Guardia Civil** (tel. 73 62 62; if closed tel. 66 86 01 or 062; open 9am-2pm and 5-8pm).

There's no room shortage here. **Hostal La Marina,** Cantón Miguel Freijo, 4 (tel. 73 60 30), offers large rooms, many with views of the water. (Singles 1900ptas. Doubles 3000ptas, with bath 3500ptas.) **Hostal Plaza,** C. Real, 12 (tel. 73 61 03), has ridiculously clean rooms, a sitting room with TV, and pink wonderland bathrooms. (Singles 2000ptas. Doubles 3000ptas, with bath 4000ptas. Off-season: 1500ptas; 2500ptas; 3500ptas.)

Restaurants serving fresh seafood line C. Miguel Freijo along the docks. **Supermercados Más y Más,** on Pr. Insuela by the statue of the *palilleira,* sells picnic fixings. (Open Mon.-Fri. 9am-2pm and 4:30-8:30pm.) **La Marina's** restaurant downstairs serves a filling *menú* (750ptas).

Transportes Finisterre **buses** (tel. 74 51 71) run three times a day from Santiago (2hr., 955ptas), returning twice. They also travel twice daily from La Coruña. Camariñas can technically be reached from Finisterre, but you might have to wait for hours in the tiny town of Vimianzo for a transfer.

ELSEWHERE

The minor coastal road passes isolated beaches such as **Praia Traba** on its way to the Ría de Laxe-Corme. At **Laxe** on the western side of the *ría,* a vast, open stretch of sand separates a Geological Institute at one end from the fishing fleet at the other.

On the other side of the *ría,* **Corme** is famous for its delicious *percebes* (barnacles), which are pried off of rocks in treacherous waters. Try them or whatever else is swimming in the tanks at **O Biscoiteiro,** C. Remedios (tel. 73 83 76). They bake their own tart bread and cook fresh, bountiful entrees (600-900ptas). Locals insist that many citizens of Corme descend from mermaids.

51km from La Coruña, **Malpica** has its own small peninsula further north. The site of excellent seafood restaurants, Malpica also offers a pleasant beach and local pottery. For bus information, call tel. 72 04 02. The town's **Concello,** R. Emilio González, 1 (tel. 72 00 01), has brochures on the area. Any beach here will do, but the mayor prefers **Praia de Barizo,** 7km away. Join the seagulls on the **Illas Sisargas,** three green rocks off the cape. No boats head that way, but fishers sometimes schlepp tourists there. At **Restaurante San Francisco,** on R. Eduardo Podal and overlooking the rocks, the beaming owner serves fresh fish cooked to order.

■■■ LA CORUÑA (A CORUÑA)

While the newer parts of La Coruña are gray and mundane, recent massive efforts by the city have made *la ciudad vieja* (the old city) and port areas much more attractive to visitors. Sailboats line the northern end of the port, and gardens and parks hide within the old city. Many of the La Coruña's 250,000 residents while away afternoons at pleasant waterfront cafés along the brand new Paseo Marítimo. An excellent base for exploring the Rías Altas, La Coruña's stellar nightlife, historic old town, and attractive beaches make it easy to overlook the tankers in the harbor and the dingier parts of town.

ORIENTATION AND PRACTICAL INFORMATION

Avenida de la Marina leads past the tourist office into the lovely *ciudad vieja* (old city), whose shaded streets and old stone buildings fill the southern tip of the peninsula overlooking the port. **Praia del Orzán** (boogie and surfboard heaven) and **Praia de Riazor** are about a 10-min. walk northwest from the tourist office on the other side of the peninsula's neck. The **bus** and **train stations** are a 45-min. walk from the old city. Take bus #1 or 1A, which run straight to the tourist office (90ptas). If you insist on walking, find Av. Primo de Rivera and follow it through five name changes until it reaches the port. Turn left and walk (with the water on your right) until you reach the **tourist office**, on **Dársena de la Marina. Praza de María Pita** is one bl. from the port.

Tourist Office: Dársena de la Marina (tel. 22 18 22), on the south side of the isthmus connecting the peninsula and the mainland, near the waterfront. Full of tips on trips to the Rías Altas. Slick brochures on Galicia and the rest of Spain. Open Mon.-Fri. 9am-2pm and 4-6pm, Sat. 10:30am-1pm.

El Corte Inglés: C. Ramón y Cajal, 57-59 (tel. 29 00 11). A sharp right from the bus station exit. **Currency exchange:** 1% commission (500pta min. charge on cash, 250pta on traveler's checks). Also a **map,** novels and guidebooks in English, haircutting, cafeteria, restaurant, and **telephones.** Open Mon.-Sat. 10am-9pm.

Consulate: See Spain Essentials: Embassies and Consulates.

American Express Travel: Viajes Amado, C. Compostela, 1 (tel. 22 99 72). Open Mon.-Fri. 9:30am-1:30pm and 4:30-7:30pm, Sat. 9:45am-1:30pm. All the usual AmEx services.

Post Office: C. Alcalde Manuel Casas (tel. 22 19 56; fax 29 51 63), just past Teatro Colón on Av. Marina. Open for stamps and Lista de Correos Mon.-Fri. 8am-9pm, Sat. 9am-2pm; for **telegrams** and **faxes** Mon.-Fri. 8am-9pm, Sat. 9am-7pm. **Postal Code:** 15000.

Telephones: C. Alcalde Canuto Berea, 4, off C. Real. Open Mon.-Sat. 9am-11pm. Also at C. San Andrés, 90. Open Mon.-Sat. 9am-3pm and 4:30-10:30pm. Phone banks all over the city. **Telephone Code:** 981.

Flights: Aeropuerto de Alvedro (tel. 23 22 40), 9km south of the city. Served only by Aviaco. **Iberia,** Pr. Galiza, 6 (tel. 29 38 55). Open Mon.-Fri. 9:30am-2pm and 4-7pm, Sat. 10am-1pm.

Trains: Pr. San Cristóbal, s/n (tel 15 02 02). Buses #1 and 1A (85ptas) run from here to the tourist office and the *marina.* Information open 7am-11pm. To: Santiago (13 per day, 1¼hr., 460ptas); Vigo (8 per day, 3hr., 1100ptas); El Ferrol (3 per day, 1¾hr., 450ptas); Betanzos (3 per day, ½hr., 270ptas); Madrid (3 per day, *talgo* 8½hr., 7500ptas; *expreso* 11hr., 5300ptas); Barcelona (1 per day, 17hr., 7500ptas). **RENFE,** C. Fonseca, 3 (tel. 22 19 48), just up from Pr. Lugo.

Buses: C. Caballeros (tel. 23 96 44), across Av. Alcalde Molina from the train station. Bus #1 (85ptas) runs from here to the tourist office. Buses serve the Rías Altas and surrounding area. **ALSA-Intercar** (tel. 23 70 44). To: Madrid (4 per day, 8½hr., 4520ptas); Santiago (every hr., 1hr., 590ptas); Oviedo (3 per day, 5hr., 2620ptas); San Sebastián (1 per day, 14hr., 5890ptas). **IASA** (tel. 23 90 01). To: Betanzos (frequent, 45min., 215ptas); Vivero (with stops at O Barqueiro, Ortigueira, El Ferrol, Vicedo, Betanzos; 4 per day, 4hr., 1400ptas); Ribadeo (2 per day, 3hr., 1175ptas); El Ferrol, with transfer to Cedeira (every hr., 1¾hr., 610ptas). Other companies have routes to Vigo, Camariñas, and other destinations.

Public Transportation: Red buses run by **Compañía de Tranvías de la Coruña** (tel. 25 01 00; about 7am-11:30pm; 85ptas). Bus stops post full itineraries of the buses that stop there.

Taxis: Radio Taxi (tel. 24 33 33 or 24 33 77). **Tele Taxi** (tel. 28 77 77).

Car Rental: Useful for exploring the Rías Altas. **Autos Brea,** Av. Fernández Latorre, 110 (tel. 23 86 45). From the bus station turn right, then a sharp left before El Corte Inglés. Must be at least 21 and have had license 1 yr. Open Mon.-Fri. 9am-1pm and 4-7pm, Sat. 9am-2pm. **Avis,** Pr. Vigo, 5 (tel. 12 12 01), under the awnings. From Av. Linares Rivas, turn left onto Marcial de Adalid. Must be at least

23 and have had license 1 yr. Open Mon.-Fri. 9am-1:15pm and 4-7pm, Sat. 9am-12:45pm.

Luggage Storage: At the **train station** (lockers 300ptas). Open 6:30am-1:30am. At the **bus station** (75ptas per checked bag). Open 8am-10pm.

Lost Property: At the **guardia municipal** (see below).

English Bookstore: Librería Colón, C. Real, 24 (tel. 22 22 06), a few bl. from the tourist office. Shakespeare meets Tom Clancy and Danielle Steele. Open Mon.-Fri. 10am-1:30pm and 5-8:30pm, Sat. 10:30am-2pm.

Laundromat: Lavandería Glu Glu, C. Alcalde Marchesi, 4 (tel. 28 28 04), off Pr. Cuatro Caminos. Wash and dry self-serve 700ptas per 5kg load. Full service 800ptas per load. Open Mon.-Sat. 9:30am-9pm.

Red Cross: C. Curros Enríquez, s/n **(ambulance** tel. 20 59 75; urgent care tel. 22 22 22).

Late-Night Pharmacy: Check listings in *La Voz de Galicia* (90ptas) or in any pharmacy window.

Medical Services: Casa de Socorro, C. Miguel Servet, s/n (tel. 18 42 06). **Ambulatorio San José,** C. Comandante Fontanes, 8 (tel. 22 60 74; urgent care tel. 29 80 18).

Police: Av. Alférez Provisional, s/n (tel. 22 61 00). **Guardia Civil,** C. Lonzas, s/n (tel. 062). **Guardia Municipal,** C. Miguel Servet, s/n (tel. 18 42 25).

ACCOMMODATIONS

The best and most convenient area to look for lodging is one bl. back from **Avenida Marina,** near the tourist office. **Calle Riego de Agua** and the surrounding area (from Pr. María Pita down to Pr. San Agustín) always has available rooms. There are many *pensiones* near the stations—miles away, however, from the *ciudad vieja.*

Marina Española (HI) (tel. 62 01 18), in the town Sada, about 20km east of La Coruña. The Empresa Calpita bus (tel. 23 90 72) runs to Sada (½hr., 220ptas). 3-day max. stay. 685ptas, over 26 900ptas. Meals available. Call first, as students invade in summer.

Albergue Xuvenil "Gandario" (HI) (tel. 79 10 05), in the town Gandario, 19km outside La Coruña. Take the bus to Gandarío (½hr., 200ptas). Marina Española's identical twin.

Hospedaje María Pita, C. Riego de Agua, 38, 3rd fl. (tel. 22 11 87), 1 bl. behind Av. Marina. María Pita held off the attacking British, but the white lace curtains and clean, cheery rooms are anything but unwelcoming. Bathrooms are pristine. Singles (usually full) 1400ptas. Doubles with sink 2500ptas. There are 3 other attractive *hostales* in this building.

Pensión la Alianza, C. Riego de Agua, 8, 1st fl. (tel. 22 81 14). Newly painted white walls contrast with funky brightly-clothed chairs. Spotless gray-tiled bathroom down the hall. Singles 1500-1900ptas. Doubles 2500-3000ptas.

Hospedaje Varela, C. Riego de Agua, 28, 3rd fl. (tel. 22 19 75). Marbleized wallpaper and flamenco-dancer oil painting in the foyer. Flowers everywhere—on papered walls and chintz bedspreads—in the clean, bright rooms. Bathrooms couldn't be cleaner. Doubles 2500ptas. Breakfast available.

Hostal Castelos, C. Real, 14 (tel. 22 29 06), 1 bl. behind Av. Marina. Positively cavernous rooms contain original 1890s mahogany wainscoting. Enter through meticulously hand-carved door frames, and don't forget to check out the little monk on the wall who correctly predicts the weather. Doubles 2500-3500ptas.

FOOD

Sustenance for scrooges comes easy. **Calle Estrella, Calle de la Franja,** and nearby streets lie just behind Av. Marina and are fraught with possibilities. Fresh fruit and vegetables shine in the big **market** in the oval building on Pr. San Agustín, near the old town. (Open Mon.-Sat. 8am-12:30pm.) If you roll out of bed at 12:31pm, buy your groceries in the supermarket downstairs.

Groceries: Supermercados Claudio, C. Menéndez Pelayo, 4-6, off Av. Linares Rivas. Huge. Open Mon.-Fri. 9am-2pm and 5-8pm, Sat. 9am-2pm and 5:30-8:30pm.

Cafetería Pazo, C. Olmos, 26, 2 bl. up from the port, off C. Alta. Sink into their low banquettes for tasty *platos combinados*. Prices start as low as 525ptas for *tortilla*, ham, and croquettes. Open noon-midnight.

Mesón Trotamundos, Pr. España, s/n (tel. 22 16 04). A *ración* of six tasty grilled sardines costs just 400ptas. Sit at the long wooden tables up front and watch them snip the arms off octopi for their *pulpo a la gallega*. *Raciones* 350-800ptas. Open Tues.-Sat. 10am-1am.

Mesón Laporte, C. Franja, 23, on the corner with C. Trompeta. *Tortilla* made with eggs from the owner's nearby farm. *Tapas* galore (80-200ptas), including *pulpo* (octopus, *ración* 710ptas). Open 6am-2am.

Pizzeria Bar Gaby, C. Monteleria, 1, on the corner with C. Estrella. Individual pizzas (600-650ptas) have a larger circumference than the wooden chairs. Wine casks function as tables. *Tapas* begin at the low, low price of 75ptas, and you can wash it all down with dark beer. Open noon-4pm and 7pm-1am. Closed Mon.

Restaurante Varela, C. María Barbeito, 1 (tel. 20 95 39), on a corner of Pr. María Pita. For when you're tired of all those dimly-lit bars and *mesones*. Filling and delicious 4-course *menú* includes chicken noodle soup, *tortilla,* and roast chicken or rabbit (1050ptas). Entrees 800-2500ptas. Open Tues.-Sun. 1-4pm and 8-11:30pm.

Cafetería Piscis, C. Franja, 19-21 (tel. 22 61 07). Not much in the way of atmosphere, but a startling range of *raciones* (350-600ptas). Homemade cod *croquetas* 450ptas. Open 11am-11pm.

SIGHTS AND ENTERTAINMENT

Simple arches and windows surround the cobbled **Praza de María Pita,** named for the heroine who held off the attacking British in 1589. The three red tile domes of the **Pazo Municipal** rise majestically from the north side. Close by, **Prazuela Santa Bárbara** borders a 15th-century convent of the same name. A small Gothic doorway opens to **Igrexa de Santa María del Campo,** with granite columns in the central aisles and a bright rose window. All were built between 1100 and 1500.

The 16th-century **Castelo de San Antón,** now the home of the **Museo Arqueológico** (tel. 20 59 94), juts out into the bay on the southeast side of the peninsula. If the 14th-century stone pig with the large cross on its back isn't enough, the Bronze Age artifacts, bones from the local Roman necropolis, and a reconstruction of a 4th-century wicker and skin boat will make you go hog wild. (Open 10am-2pm and 4-7pm. Admission 200ptas.)

La Coruña's other famous tourist magnet, the **Torre de Hércules,** towers over the western end of the peninsula. Although the original Roman part is visible only from within, this 2nd-century structure is the only Roman lighthouse that still actually shines each night to help guide ships. Legend has it that Hercules himself erected the tower upon the remains of his defeated enemy Gerión. The *Armada Invencible* departed from here in 1588 on its way to Britain, where most of it sank in a storm. (Open Tues.-Sun. 11am-2pm and 4-7pm; Oct.-June Tues.-Sun. 11am-3pm. Free.) The lighthouse is 2km down the Ctra. Torre; walk or take bus #9 or 13 (90ptas).

The **Orzán** and **Riazor** beaches, on the northwest side of the isthmus, pack in tanners, boogie boarders, and surfers. A brand new esplanade connects the two, and has already become a popular stretch for family strolls and teenage groping. An original statue of two surfers hanging ten sits on the north end of the *paseo*.

Back on the other side of the peninsula, the elegant **Jardín Méndez Núñez** interests experts in the fine art of topiary. The verdant park, sandwiched between Av. Marina and the dock, has a clock snipped to botanical perfection, whose arms really work and tell the correct time. Soothing **Jardín de San Carlos,** in the old part of the city, was originally planted in 1843 on the site of old Forte San Carlos. It shelters the tomb of Sir John Moore. Locals say killing this incompetent general cost Napoleon his crown, since Wellington took over Moore's command.

The **Real Academia Gallega** (Royal Galician Academy; tel. 20 73 08) made the family seat of 19th-century novelist **Condesa Emilia Pardo Bazán** its headquarters.

The library contains 25,000 volumes on Galician literature, history, and culture. Next door, at C. Tabernas, 11, the academy devotes part of a museum to Pardo Bazán's work, and part to a rotating exhibition of modern and 19th-century Galician art. (Open Mon.-Fri. 10am-noon. Free.)

Summer nightlife in La Coruña rivals that of Santiago. **Cafe-Bar La Barra,** C. Riego de Agua, 33, offers innocent entertainment all day long. From about 10am on, students and old men gather around its wood tables to play cards, dominoes, and parcheesi. (Open 9am-2am.) The **Teatro Principal** on Av. Marina, next door to the post office, stages local plays and international productions alike. Residents bar hop around **Calle Franja, Calle La Florida,** and surrounding side streets. When bars die at around 2am, discos along the **two beaches** start making a ruckus. Also try the discos and cafés on **Calle Juan Florez** and **Calle Sol. Pirámide,** at Juan Florez, 50 (tel. 27 61 57), plays dance music to rouse the dead. **Picasso** and **Lautrec,** across the street from each other on C. Sol, predictably attract the artistically minded.

Although celebrated in many parts of Europe, **La Noche de San Juan** (June 23) is greeted with particular fervor in La Coruña since it coincides with the opening of sardine season. Locals light the traditional bonfires and spend the night leaping over the flames (contrary to the image that comes to mind, the rite ensures fertility) and gorging on sardine flesh. If you drop an egg white in a glass of water on this night, it will assume the form of your future spouse's occupation; many are led to believe that they'll marry a dairy farmer. The last two weeks of August bring concerts, parades, folk dancing, and a mock naval battle in honor of María Pita.

■ NEAR LA CORUÑA: BETANZOS, MIÑO, AND PONTEDEUME

With several churches and a historic Jewish quarter, **Betanzos** (pop. 12,000) assumes an isolated persona despite its position at a crucial transportation intersection, 23km east of La Coruña and 38km south of El Ferrol. Cafés line the central **Praza García Hermanos,** where a statue of the brothers García, the city's great benefactors, stands. One bl. behind the statue to the left, the **tourist office** in the Ayuntamiento offers a map with a walking tour of the old city, including all the monuments, 14th- and 15th-century churches, and 10th-century nobles' houses. (Open July-Sept. Mon.-Fri. 10am-2pm and 4-7pm, Sat.-Sun. 10am-2pm.) The old Jewish quarter lies across R. Cruz Verde, at the bottom of the hill leading to the old city. Houses here all have two or three stories, since the first floor was always used as a stable. Betanzos's great **festival** involves the launching of the world's largest paper balloon (about 25m high) on the night of San Roque in July.

The **post office** (tel. 77 18 88) is on Pr. Alfonso IX. (Open Mon.-Fri. 8:30am-2:30pm, Sat. 9am-1pm.) For **currency exchange,** try Banco Bilbao Vizcaya. (Open Mon.-Fri. 8:30am-2pm; Oct.-May Mon.-Fri. 8:30am-2pm, Sat. 8:30am-1pm.) For medical assistance, call the **Red Cross** at 77 15 15. **Police** answer at tel. 77 06 02; the **Guardia Civil** at tel. 77 00 53.

Betanzos is a simple ½-day trip from La Coruña. **Buses** run from both La Coruña and El Ferrol (every ½hr., Sun. every hr., 45min., 215ptas). IASA (tel. 23 90 01) also runs to further points along the *rías*. The **train station** sits across the river. About 6 trains per day run between La Coruña and El Ferrol, stopping in Betanzos en route.

Miño, 12km north of Betanzos, is said to have the nicest beach in the Rías Altas. On Saturday afternoons in **Pontedeume,** 22km from Betanzos, workers at the town market cook *pulpo* (octopus) in huge copper urns and mock the citizens of Betanzos for saving that huge balloon. Both towns can be reached on bus lines heading to El Ferrol (every ½hr., 250ptas).

RÍAS ALTAS

Not as isolated as the Costa de la Muerte, these urbane *rías* become increasingly smooth and rolling as they move east. Many of the fishing towns that predominate here have roots deep in the Middle Ages. Old lighthouses, churches, and the remains of a wall or two dot the luscious green countryside. In the misty mountains of Galicia the weather is anything but predictable (even in summer), but views are spectacular year-round. Thanks to a healthy burst of summer tourism from land-locked Spaniards, the Rías Altas have the resources to augment a relatively unspoiled coastline with a transportation system slightly more viable than that of the Dead Coast (for details, see La Coruña Practical Information: Buses).

■■■ RÍAS DE CEDEIRA & VIVERO

On La Coruña's northern coast, where buses and trains seldom tread and hitchhiking is futile, ferny rain forests give way to soft, empty beaches. Thick mists veil and isolate the valleys of the northernmost *rías*. Buses and FEVE train run inland to Vivero from El Ferrol, but the sporadic coastal bus is preferable—you can always hop off if you see a place you like.

VALDOVIÑO

Only 17km northeast from industrial El Ferrol and not on a *ría* at all, Valdoviño is a town of old flagstone farmhouses among eucalyptus trees. The enormous **Praia de Frouxeira** is a hike across the fields from town, but worthwhile for its long, practically deserted stretches of sand. **Hostal A Roda,** on Playa de Meiras (tel. 32 62 61), is the only game in town, and it shows in its prices: 5000ptas for a double with bath. First-class **Camping Valdoñolies** (tel. 48 70 76) is on the highway leading to Cedeira. (Open Semana Santa and June-Sept. 495ptas per person, 525ptas per tent and per car.) Valdoviño is a simple daytrip from either El Ferrol or Cedeira.

CEDEIRA

Legend has it that when cuckolding Lancelot fled England to escape the ire of King Arthur, he landed in Cedeira. There he founded the town and went on to sire many little *del lagos*. Set on its own *ría* 32km northeast of El Ferrol and 84km northeast of La Coruña, this small town of 8000 inhabitants combines pretty beaches and soothing waterside walks with the breathtaking scenery nearby. There's not much to do but watch the tide, but no one seems to mind.

The **Santuario de San Andrés de Teixido** (a steep 12km hike from town) looking out over the sea from 620m in the air, is surrounded by the highest coastline in Europe. Christianity cleverly incorporated animalistic cults, spreading the rumor that if you don't visit this chapel and convert to Christianity during this lifetime, you'll be converted into some lowly animal the next time around.

Closer to town lies the hermitage **San Antonio de Corbeiro,** an easy 2km walk up a gentle slope. From the tourist office, turn left and follow signs to the turnoff (½km farther on the left), then it's up, up, and away. The hermitage is a plain white structure above the *ría*, high enough to send any acrophobe into a cold sweat, and gorgeous enough to impress the most jaded. 6km past the turnoff for San Antonio, and a steep, curving climb, is the lighthouse **Faro de Punta Candieira.**

The **Curro festival** (fourth Sunday in June) entails a round-up of the wild horses that live nearby. Mid-August is devoted to the **Feria de la Virgen del Mar.**

Near the second bus stop, the **tourist office,** C. Ezequiel Lopez, 22 (tel. 48 21 87), hands out snazzy brochures. (Open Semana Santa-Sept. Mon.-Sat. 11am-2pm and 5-8pm, Sun. noon-2pm; July-Aug. afternoons 6-9pm.) **Currency exchange** at Banco Bilbao-Vizcaya, Pr. Galiza, 1. (Open Mon.-Fri. 9am-2pm.) The **post office** is on Av. Zumalacárrequi, 15 (tel. 48 05 52; open Mon.-Fri. 8am-3pm, Sat. 9am-2pm). **Postal code** is 15350. Up the street from the first bus stop is a **telephone** bank, on the Suevos; **telephone code** 981. The **police** can be reached at tel. 48 07 25; the **Red Cross,** C. Muelle, s/n, at tel. 48 26 22; and **taxis** at tel. 48 02 11.

Hostal Chelsea, Pr. Sagrado Corazón, 15 (tel. 48 11 11), hosts guests around the corner from the first bus stop and near the beach. Big, light-filled rooms have TVs and tiled bathrooms. (Singles 1800ptas. Doubles with shower 2800ptas, with bath 3300ptas.) Across the bridge to the right sits **Hostal Brisa,** Arriba da Ponte, 19 (tel. 48 10 54). Rooms here are less modern, but clean and absolutely huge. (Singles 1800-2200ptas, with bath 2200-2800ptas. Doubles with shower 3000ptas, with bath 3300ptas.)

For such a small town, Cedeira serves up a number of local specialties. Open-faced *empanadas* are unique to the town, and locals love to snack on S-shaped sugar cookies called *"eses."* Commendable *bodegas* and *mesones* line both sides of the *ría.* **Taberna da Calexa,** Tras. Elrexa, 7 (tel. 48 20 09), up a tiny staircase off the road leading up to the church, serves Galician wine for 90ptas a glass inside its medieval stone walls, complemented with a wide variety of homemade *raciones,* including rolls of fresh *bonito* (tuna, 400ptas) and mussels in vinaigrette (250ptas).

Bus service is fairly sparse. To get to Vivero or Ortigueira, take an **IASA** bus from C. Ezequiel Lopez, 28, to Campo do Hospital (5 per day, 45min., 110ptas), where you change to another IASA bus, which should arrive soon after. **RIALSA** buses also run from Cedeira to El Ferrol (6 per day, 1hr., 380ptas).

VIVERO (VIVEIRO) AND COVAS

Emblazoned on the tourist office's pamphlet is the bold motto *"No es un sueño. Existe."* ("It's not a dream. It exists.") Sleepy Vivero (pop. 14,000) is not quite dreamy. Still, a respectable share of Spanish tourists come for the nearby beaches.

The nearest beach is in **Covas,** 1km across the river from Vivero. There **Hostal La Terraza,** R. Granxas, 8 (tel. 56 06 06), one bus stop before Vivero, is so close to the beach that the sound of the waves lulls you to sleep. Past the rose gardens, past the TV room, and up the stairs are the capacious, airy rooms. (Singles 2400ptas. Doubles 3500ptas, with bath 5000ptas. Prices lower in winter.) On the same road heading toward Vivero is **Camping Vivero** (tel. 56 00 04). Follow signs to the flagged reception hut. A café and the broad beach are just steps away from this adequate 2nd-class campsite. (Reception open 9am-11pm. 350ptas per person, per tent, and per car. Electricity 400ptas. Open June-Sept.) If you tire of Covas, **Playa de Area** waits 4km from Vivero. **Playa de Sacido** is a bit farther away (6km).

The **tourist office** (tel. 56 04 86) is a snap to find; pass through Puerta de Carlos V (off of Av. Galicia) and it's immediately on the right, up the twisting staircase that leads to a tower. Besides the decent map, they post *pensiones* on their bulletin board. (Open daily 10:30am-1:30pm and 4:30-6:30pm.) This is the only town in the Rías Altas with **motorcycle rentals.** They **rent cars** and **bikes** as well at Viajes Arifran, C. Rosalía de Castro, 54 (tel. 56 04 97 or 56 06 89; open Mon.-Fri. 9:30am-1pm and 4-7:30pm, Sat. 9:30am-1:30pm).

In Vivero proper, **Hospedaje García,** Pr. Maior, 18, 2nd fl. (tel. 56 06 75), offers bare, immaculate rooms, most of which overlook the plaza. (Singles 1700ptas. Doubles 3000ptas. Low-season: 1400ptas; 2500ptas.) **Fonda Bossanova,** Av. Galicia, 11 (tel. 56 01 50), up the street from the bus station, has small, mostly interior rooms and passably clean bathrooms. (Singles 1000ptas. Doubles 2000ptas.) On the first floor, the friendly owner keeps local workers happy with an 800pta *menú,* featuring fish. Budget *mesones* proliferate around Pr. Maior. **Mesón Xoaquín,** up from the square on R. Irmans Vilarponte, 19, serves a 750pta *menú* amid exposed stone walls and classy red tablecloths. (Open daily 1-4pm and 8-11:30pm.) **A Cepa,** R. Fernández Victorio, 7, dishes out incredibly cheap *tapas—chipirones* 175ptas, *patatas bravas* 85ptas, and the mysterious *bikini* 110ptas. (Open noon-3pm and 7:30pm-midnight.)

Bus companies IASA (tel. 56 01 03), at Trav. Marina, and ERSA, Pr. Lugo, 2 (tel. 56 03 90), have recently merged. They serve La Coruña (4 per day, 4hr., 1400ptas); El Ferrol (6 per day, 2hr., 850ptas); Lugo (6 per day, 2½hr., 950-1000ptas); Oviedo (2 per day, 5hr., 1620ptas); and Ribadeo (2 per day except Sun., 1½hr., 450ptas). FEVE **trains** (tel. 55 07 22; down Trav. Marina past Pr. Lugo), chug twice daily to: Oviedo (5hr., 1605ptas); Ribadeo (1hr., 430ptas); then to Ortigueira, Barqueiro, and Vicedo. They also head west to El Ferrol (3 per day, 2hr., 600ptas).

■■■ RÍA DE FOZ

East of Vivero and inland from Ría de Foz, **Mondoñedo** is about 50km from Lugo on the FEVE line. The picturesque town is smack on the river Masma. Stay at **Hostal Padornela,** C. Buenos Aires, 1 (tel. 52 18 92). The 13 rooms have baths. (Singles 2000ptas. Doubles with bath 4000ptas.)

■■■ RÍA DE RIBADEO: RIBADEO

Stunning Galician scenery is the reason to stay in Ribadeo, a town that's inundated with summer residents but still manages to retain a ghostly, deserted feel 25km further east on the *ría* of Río Eo. Choose your mountain-*ría*-Cantabrian Sea view, or enjoy more than one. Pray for a clear day, as the town has little else of interest.

Igrexa de Santa Cruz, 3km from town on a hill overlooking the *ría*. If the climb doesn't take your breath away, the view of the countryside and ocean will.

Praia de Rocas Blancas, 3km in another direction. A *faro* (lighthouse) towers over a small, sweet beach. Both the dock's Paseo Marítimo and the **Praia Os Bloques,** just past the dock, offer super views of the *ría*.

Rua Buenos Aires, off Pr. España in town. More thrilling views for *ría* buffs.

The **tourist office** (tel. 11 06 89), in central Pr. España, distributes a decent map. (Open Mon.-Fri. 9:30am-2pm and 4-7pm, Sat. 9:30am-2pm; Oct.-June Mon.-Fri. 4-7pm.) The **post office** (tel. 11 02 48) is on Av. Asturias, 17. (Open Mon.-Fri. 8am-3pm, Sat. 9am-1pm.) The **postal code** is 27700. For a **taxi,** call 11 01 11. **Rent a car** at Autos Eo, Pasarón Ilasta, s/n (tel. 11 04 89).

Right on Pr. España and across from the church is **Hostal Costa Verde,** 13 (tel. 11 01 13). Ask about vacancies in the bar downstairs; the rooms and bathrooms upstairs are pristine, and some have balconies overlooking the park. (Singles 1500ptas. Doubles 2500-4000ptas, with bath 3500-5000ptas. Owner may lower rates if the place isn't busy.) Down the main street running into town is the grand **Hostal Ribanova,** C. San Roque, 8-10 (tel. 11 06 25), with high ceilings, carpeted stairs, and chenille bedspreads. (Singles 1500-2000ptas. Doubles 3000-3500ptas, with bath 3800-4200ptas.) Westward 14km, **Camping Gaivota** (tel. 12 44 51), in the town of Barreiros, has a ground on Praia de Benquerencia. (375ptas per person, 350ptas per car and per tent. Electricity 300ptas.)

Supermercado El Arbol (tel. 72 58 50) on Av. Galicia is well-stocked. (Open Tues.-Sat. 9:30am-2pm and 5-8pm, Mon. 9:30am-2pm.) A miscellany of low-priced *cafeterías* surround Pr. España. **Restaurante Ros Mary,** C. San Francisco, 3, has *tapas* (300-450ptas), *platos combinados* (675-850ptas), and a *menú* (925ptas). (Open 8am-2am.)

Getting in and out of here isn't all that bad. The FEVE **train station** (tel. 13 01 39) is a 10min. walk from Pr. España along R. Villafranco Bierzo through four name changes. (Information open Mon.-Fri. 8:20am-3:30pm and 4:30-8:15pm, Sat.-Sun. 9am-2:30pm and 4-8:30pm.) Two trains per day crawl eastward on the coastal route from El Ferrol to Ribadeo to Oviedo (Ribadeo to Oviedo 4hr., 1445ptas; to El Ferrol 1010ptas). Trains stop at Ortigueira and Vivero too. IASA **buses** (tel. 22 17 60) run to: Oviedo (6 per day, 4hr., 1335ptas); La Coruña (3 per day, 3hr., 1300ptas); and El Ferrol (1 per day, 1100ptas). The bus stops in Pr. España across from the **travel agency** Viajes Proa (tel. 11 09 10), at Pr. España #9. They give out complete bus and train information. (Open Mon.-Fri. 10am-2:30pm and 4:30-8pm, Sat. 10:30am-1:30pm.)

Asturias & Cantabria

Rugged, rocky, and leafy regions, Asturias and Cantabria are wedged between País Vasco to the east and Galicia to the west. The towering peaks of the Cordillera Cantábrica are ideal for hunting, fishing, and hiking, and are a repository of Europe's best-preserved prehistoric art. Administratively, the coast is divided into two autonomous regions, the Principado de Asturias (the province of Oviedo) and Cantabria (the province of Santander).

Possessing numerous industrial centers and prosperous dairy farms, Cantabria has grown rich as a summer getaway for the Spanish elite. Meanwhile, the decline of the mining, steel, and shipping industries has crippled rainy Asturias, although the traditional Asturian crafts of wood- and iron-working and knife-making are still practiced. Authorities have mobilized to turn the region into a center for scientific research and "green" tourism, promoting an extensive network of country inns in old mansions, *casas de indianos* (rambling Victorian houses built around the turn of the century by Asturians who'd made their fortune in the Americas), and cottages.

After the Moors invaded in 711, Asturias started the Reconquista and became the mountain stronghold of the Christian resistance, chiefly because the Moors ignored these harsh lands. Since the Middle Ages the region has been titular fiefdom of the crown prince, the *Príncipe de Asturias* (Prince of Asturias). As the Christian kingdoms expanded southward, Asturias was gradually absorbed into the kingdoms of León and then Castilla.

Split from the rest of Spain by the Picos de Europa, Asturians maintained their dialect, *bable,* linguistically somewhere between *castellano* and *gallego.* Cantabria is ethnically Castilian, having been Castile's medieval outlet to the sea.

Because of the abrupt terrain, public transport in these regions can be erratic. The roads, however, are striking, winding through deciduous and alpine forests or green valleys now quilted with cornfields and lush pastures. The Atlantic currents might be cool and the weather unpredictable, but Asturias and Cantabria are an idyllic land of flowering valleys, snowy mountains, spectacular seascapes, and pretty wood and tile houses, without the ravages mass tourism inflicts elsewhere.

■■■ OVIEDO

Founded as a monastery on the site of the ancient Roman town of Ovetum, Oviedo was later capital of the kingdom of Asturias for over a century. Unfortunately for the city and its visitors, modernity has taken its toll. Gray, noisy, bustling Oviedo (pop. 200,000) is the mainstay of the Asturian industrial nexus. Located smack in the center of Asturia, the city is a transportation hub for northern Spain, serving Galicia to the west, León to the south, and Cantabria to the east.

ORIENTATION AND PRACTICAL INFORMATION

Two-way **Calle de Uría** bisects the city, running northwest to southeast from its origin at the RENFE train station. On the west side of C. Uría is the leafy, luscious **Campo de San Francisco;** on the east side is the old city, with the **Plaza Mayor** and the tourist office in **Plaza de Alfonso II.**

The first FEVE train station (serving Cantabria and Pais Vasco) is a stone's throw to the left as you leave RENFE, on **Avenida Santander.** To reach the bus stations from here, take **Calle Jerónimo Ibrán,** on which Económicos (EASA) and Turytrans buses make their stops, to **Plaza General Primo de Rivera,** where the bus biggie, ALSA, has its unmarked station underneath the shopping arcade. To reach C. Uría from Pl. General Primo de Rivera, take a right onto C. Fray Ceferino, which ends at C. Uría.

The second FEVE train station (serving the Galicia-Asturias route) is a good deal east of the bus stations on **Calle Victor Chávarri.** To reach C. Uría from here, take

C. Victor Chávarri, which becomes Alcalde García Conde and ends at Pl. Carbayón. On the far side of the plaza, pick up C. Argüelles and you'll hit C. Uría.

Tourist Office: Pl. Alfonso II (tel. 521 33 85). English spoken by helpful, if busy, staff who gives out bus and hostel information plus advice on travel in the Picos de Europa. Their computer next door is open 24hrs. and is an absolute goldmine of information; everything from bus schedules (local, regional, and national) to hotel prices pop up on its multicolored screen. Office open Mon.-Fri. 9:30am-1:30pm and 4:30-6:30pm, Sat. 9am-2pm.

Budget Travel: TIVE, C. Calvo Sotelo, 5 (tel. 523 60 58), past the Campo San Francisco, up from C. Marqués de Santa Cruz. Information on traveling and hiking nearby. They also organize excursions. ISIC 500ptas. HI card 1800ptas. Open Mon.-Fri. 10am-1pm.

Currency Exchange: Barclays Bank, C. Alonso Quintanilla, 35, down the street from the post office. 500ptas charge. Open Mon.-Fri. 8:30am-2:30pm.

American Express: Viajes Cafranga, C. Uría, 26 (tel. 525 56 66). The usual cardholder services, but they don't cash traveler's checks. Open Mon.-Fri. 9am-1:30pm and 4:30-7pm, Sat. 9am-1pm.

Post Office: C. Alonso Quintanilla, 1 (tel. 521 41 86). From C. Uría, turn left onto C. Argüelles and left again. Open for information Mon.-Fri. 9am-2pm; for stamps and Lista de Correos Mon.-Fri. 8am-9pm, Sat. 9am-7pm; for **telegrams** Mon.-Fri 9am-8pm, Sat. 9am-7pm. **Postal Code:** 33080.

Telephones: Telefónica, C. Foncalada, 6. Open summer Mon.-Fri. 9:30am-2pm and 4-10:30pm, Sat. 10am-2pm; rest of the year Mon.-Sat. 10am-2pm and 5-10pm. **Faxes** sent. **Telephone Code:** 98. The telephone company recently added a 5 (as the first digit) to all regional phone numbers. If you see a phone number without a 5 in an old publication, tack one on.

Flights: Aeropuerto de Ranón (Aeropuerto Nacional de Asturias) (tel. 555 18 33). In Avilés, a town northwest of Oviedo. **Aviaco,** C. Uría, 21 (tel. 524 02 50), runs flights to Madrid, Barcelona, Bilbao, and La Coruña. **Prabus,** C. Marqués de Pidal, 20 (tel. 525 47 51), runs frequent buses to the airport.

Trains: RENFE, C. Uría (tel. 524 33 64), at the junction with Av. Santander. Serves points south of León. Pay attention to the kind of train you take: a slow local through the mountains can double your travel time. Information open 7:45am-11:15pm. To: Gijón (every ½hr., last one at 10:15pm, ½hr., 300ptas); León (7 per day, 2½hr., 700-1400ptas); Madrid (3 per day, 6½-8hr., 3300-3900ptas); Barcelona (2 per day, 13hr., 5800-7200ptas). **FEVE,** Av. Santander, s/n (tel. 528 40 96), 2min. from RENFE; turn left as you exit. To: Llanes (3 per day, 3hr., 770ptas); Santander (2 per day, 5hr., 1475ptas); Bilbao (1 per day at 8:15am, 7hr., 2400ptas). Another **FEVE,** C. Victor Chavarri, 19 (tel. 521 90 26), for trains running west as far as Ferrol. To: Ferrol (2 per day, 7½hr., 2150ptas); Viveiro (2 per day, 5¼hr., 1605ptas); Ribadeo (2 per day, 4hr., 1145ptas).

Buses: ALSA, Pl. General Primo de Rivera, 1 (tel. 528 12 00), on the lower level of a shopping arcade, but nothing marks it. To: León (11 per day, 2hr., 935ptas); La Coruña (3 per day, 6hr., 2620ptas); Madrid (13 per day, 6hr., 3420ptas); Vigo (1 per day at 3pm, 9hr., 3870ptas); Santiago (2 per day, 8hr., 3780ptas); Santander (1 per day at 9:15am, 3hr., 1630ptas). **Econòmicos (EASA),** C. Jerónimo Ibrán, 1 (tel. 529 00 39). To: Cangas de Onís (12 per day, 1½hr., 600ptas); Covodonga (5 per day, 1¾hr., 685ptas); Arenas de Cabrales (4 per day, 2¼hr., 850ptas); Llanes (9 per day, 2½hr., 920ptas). Significantly fewer buses on Sundays.

Public Transportation: TVA (tel. 522 24 22) runs **buses** (60ptas). The tourist office has a list of the routes. Buses run about 8am-10pm. #4 goes to bus, FEVE, and RENFE stations; #2 goes to the youth hostel; #2, 3, 5, 7 run from RENFE to near the old part of the city.

Taxis: Radio Taxi (tel. 525 00 00 or 525 25 00).

Car Rental: Avis, C. Ventura Rodríguez, 12 (tel. 524 13 83). Open Mon.-Fri. 9am-1pm and 4-7:30pm, Sat. 9am-1pm. **Europcar,** C. Independencia, 24 (tel. 524 46 16). Open Mon.-Fri. 9am-1:30pm and 4-7:30pm, Sat. 9am-1:30pm. For both, must be at least 21 and have had license 1 year.

Luggage Storage: At the RENFE **train station** (lockers 300ptas). Open 8am-11pm. At the ALSA **bus station** (small locker 200ptas, large locker 300ptas). Open 7am-11pm.

Lost Property: tel. 521 32 05.

English Bookstore: Librería Cervantes, C. Doctor Casal, 3 and 9 (tel. 521 24 55). Penguin Classics at #9; guidebooks at #3. Open Mon.-Fri. 9:30am-1:30pm and 4-7:30pm, Sat. 9:30am-1:30pm.

Youth Center: Dirección Regional de la Juventud, C. Calvo Sotelo, 5 (tel. 523 11 12), in the same building as TIVE (see above). Travel information, including a comprehensive pamphlet on camping, youth hostels, and hiking. Information on cultural activities too. Open summer 7:30am-4pm; winter hours restricted.

Hiking Information: Federación Asturiana de Montaña, Melquíades Alvarez, 16. Good trail maps, mountain guides, and info about weather conditions and the best hiking routes. They also organize excursions. Open Mon.-Fri. 6:30-7:30pm.

Crisis Lines: Alcohólicos Anónimos, tel. 551 16 91, 24hr. **Comité Ciudadano Anti-Sida de Asturias (AIDS Hotline),** tel. 533 88 32.

Red Cross: tel. 521 60 93.

Late-Night Pharmacy: Check listings in *La Voz de Asturias* (local paper, 90ptas).

Hospital: Hospital General de Asturias, C. J. Clavería (tel. 510 61 00). **Emergency Clinic,** C. Tenderina, Baja (tel. 520 19 42). **Ambulance:** tel. 523 50 25.

Emergency: tel. 091 or 006.

Police: Policía Municipal, C. Quintana, s/n (tel. 521 32 05 or 092).

ACCOMMODATIONS AND CAMPING

A superflux of *hostales* crowds the new city near the transport stations, generally much cleaner inside than their discolored facades suggest. Even at the height of summer they rarely fill. Try **Calle Uría** (straight ahead from the RENFE station), **Calle Campoamor** (one bl. to the left, i.e. east), and **Calle Nueve de Mayo** (a continuation of C. Manuel Pedregal, one bl. more to the left, i.e. east).

Residencia Juvenil "Ramón Menéndez Pidal," C. Julián Clavería, 14 (tel. 23 20 54), across from the hospital. Take bus #2 from C. Uría. TV room, library, and dining room. Call first; in summer only 12 beds available. Full *pensión* 1600ptas per person; over 26 2300ptas.

Hospedaje Central, C. Dr. Casal, 8, 2nd fl. (tel. 522 30 55), 2 bl. up on the right coming from the RENFE station along C. Nueve de Mayo. Balconies overlooking a church, and soft beds on hardwood floors. Slightly worn, but cleaner than the stairway suggests. Singles 1000ptas (often full). Doubles 2500-3000ptas.

Pensión Fidalgo, C. Jovellanos, 5, 3rd fl. (tel. 521 32 87), just off Pl. Juan XXIII, 1 bl. northwest of the cathedral. Sunny rooms with frosted glass chandeliers and geraniums on the windowsills. Toilets make scary noises but turquoise bathrooms are clean. Singles 2000-2500ptas. Doubles 3000ptas, with bath 4000ptas.

Pensión Riesgo, C. Nueve de Mayo, 16, 1st fl. (tel. 521 89 45). No risk (*riesgo*) here. Long oriental rug in foyer leads to the smallish but clean rooms with Victorian light fixtures. Singles 1500-1700ptas. Doubles 2700-3200ptas.

Pensión La Armonía, C. Nueve de Mayo, 14, 3rd fl. (tel. 522 03 01), one bl. from the ALSA station, 2 bl. from C. Uría. Light blue spreads on blond wood beds. Pristine bathrooms. Singles 2000ptas. Doubles 3000ptas.

FOOD

Oviedo's proximity to the seashore and the mountains makes for both fresh seafood and hearty country dishes. The specialty is *fabada*, a filling stew of *fabes* (beans) and a tomato base served *a la asturiana* (with chunks of sausage). The *sidra* (hard cider) of Asturias is also celebrated, along with the extensive ritual that accompanies its drinking: keeping the glass at their hips, waiters hold the bottle over their heads and pour an arc of cider—about two fingers worth. The consumer swallows it down in one big gulp and then signals for another go-round. You must order by the bottle, but it shouldn't cost more than 200ptas, and what with all the pouring and chugging and spilling, even featherweights can polish one off. Cheap restaurants line **Calle Fray Cegerino,** which runs between the bus and train stations. The **market** is on C. Fontán, near Pl. Mayor. (Open Mon.-Sat. 7am-3pm.)

Groceries: Supermercado El Arbol, C. Lilalo. Open Mon.-Fri. 9am-9pm, Sat. 9am-3pm.

Mesón de Paco, C. Foncalada, 8 (tel. 522 30 50), up the street from Telefónica. Next door to a snazzier, pricier café; go downstairs. Long benches and tables. Spanish music. Stuffing *menú* (600ptas) changes daily. *Platos combinados* 450-550ptas. Also *bocadillos* and *tapas.* Open Tues.-Sun. 9:30am-midnight.

Mesón-Sidería la Caleya, C. La Lila, 7 (tel. 522 01 15), off C. 9 de Mayo. As the sign says, "Who would believe, in the 20th century, *bonito* with partridge sauce only 400ptas?" Sassy waiters serve innovative *tapas* and 750pta *menú* to go along with the cider. Breakfast with fresh-squeezed OJ (300ptas). Open 9am-1am.

Mesón Luferca, C. Covadonga, 20, around the corner from Telefónica. You may be used to those hanging hams, but nothing, absolutely nothing, can prepare you for the sheer quantity and density of the crazy pig parts in this place. The ceiling positively drips with them. Many meaty *tapas* from 400ptas. Open 10am-1am.

Casa Albino, C. Gascona, 15 (tel. 521 04 45), a right turn from the FEVE-Galicia station. Only a few Real Madrid photos for atmosphere, but the 800pta *menú* extends to *fabada* and braised lamb. 2 dozen shrimp and a *sidra* for the unbelievable price of 475ptas. Open 9:30am-5pm and 7pm-1am.

Restaurante Pinochio, C. Altamirana (tel. 22 35 21), 1 bl. up from the cathedral heading toward Pl. Mayor. A giant Pinocchio (no lie) watches over diners in the airy *comedor.* 1000pta *menú* (only available at lunch) includes steak topped with cheese and a truly delicious nut tart. Filling Italian specialties. Open Tues.-Sun. 1-4pm and 8pm-midnight.

Restaurante Cervantes, C. Jovellanos, 4 (tel. 522 00 11). The dangling hams are interspersed with dried corn husks in a restaurant that serves a huge 1000pta *menú* (4 courses, including roast turkey). Open 11am-midnight.

SIGHTS

In Clarín's 19th-century novel *La Regenta,* Ana Osorio throws herself at the feet of her ecclesiastical lover in Oviedo's **catedral,** Pl. Alfonso II (tel. 522 10 33). Finished for the most part in 1388, the cathedral's 80m **tower** offers great views of the city's rooftops. Lovely **stained glass** windows illuminate the stone interior; the brilliantly blue ceiling above the **altar** was painted with crushed lapis lazuli stone.

In the north transept, the **Capilla del Rey Castro** houses the royal pantheon, designated by Alfonso II as the resting place of Asturian monarchs. The more unusual **Capilla de San Pedro** houses an intense sculpture in metal relief depicting Simon Magnus being dropped from the sky by hideous demons. While the event was instrumental in the conversion of Rome to the Christian faith, records do not indicate whether poor Simon survived his fall. The elaborate masonry of the **Capilla de Santa Eulalia** (the province's *patrona*) is in fine repair.

The curator points out the cathedral's countless peculiar details, dwelling on the Berruguete sculpture of a naked crucified Jesus that had the bishops painting loincloths, and the sexual acrobatics (carvings called *misericordias*) on the old choir stalls. (Cathedral open 10am-1pm and 4-7pm. Free.)

The Cruz de Los Angeles and the Cruz de la Victoria are in a shrine to medieval pilgrims in the **Cámara Santa.** The **Claustro de San Vicente** adjoins the south transept. The **cloister** mourns over a graveyard of pilgrims who never made it to Santiago and back. The **museo** contains pre-Romanesque art. (Open Mon.-Sat. 10am-1pm and 4-7pm. Admission to the Cámara Santa, cloister, museum, and *sala capitular,* 300ptas.)

Nearby in Pl. Alfonso II, **Casa Palacio de la Rúa's** 15th-century facade is the oldest in town; the **Palacio de Campo Sagrado** is now the provincial courthouse. Just up C. Santa Ana from the plaza is the **Museo de Bellas Artes,** at C. Santa Ana, 1 and C. Rúa, 8 (tel. 521 30 61). The two-building, three-story complex displays an ample collection of Asturian art and a small collection of 16th- to 20th-century (mainly Spanish) art, including Murillos and school-of-Rubenses. (Open Tues.-Fri. 11am-1:30pm and 4:30-8pm, Sat. 11am-2pm. Free.) The decent **Archeological Museum,** C. San Vincente, 3 (tel. 521 54 05), in addition to the usual Roman artifacts, also holds exhibits on Asturian anthropology. (Open Tues.-Sat. 10am-1:30pm and 4-6pm, Sun. 11am-1pm.)

Asturian Pre-Romanesque—the first European attempt to blend architecture, sculpture (including representations of humans), and mural painting since the fall of the Roman Empire—was developed under Alfonso II (789-842) and perfected under his son Ramiro I, for whom the style is called *Ramirense.* Two beautiful examples of this style, **Santa María del Naranco** (tel. 529 67 55), and **San Miguel de Lillo** (tel. 529 56 85), tower high above Oviedo on **Monte Naranco.** (Both open Mon.-Sat. 10am-1pm and 3-7pm, Sun. 10am-1pm; Oct.-April Mon.-Sat. 10am-1pm and 3-5pm, Sun. 10am-1pm. Admission 200ptas, Mon. free.) Ask the tourist office for directions to Monte Naranco.

ENTERTAINMENT

The streets around **Plaza del Paraguas** and **Plaza de Fontán,** south of the cathedral, are littered with bars and clubs catering to the young and inebriated. Wine connoisseurs follow **la ruta de los vinos,** from *bodega* to *bodega* along C. Rosal. Tamer entertainment awaits at the **Teatro Filarmónica,** C. Mendizábel, 3 (information tel. 521 27 62), which hosts dramatic productions throughout September, and musical concerts the rest of the year. Oviedo celebrates its patronal fiesta in honor of San Mateo September 13-22. The festival of Ascension in late May brings a livestock market to town. Oviedo also rejoices on the Día de América, usually celebrated around September 19.

■■■ ASTURIAN COAST

Beautiful meadows and hills mark this quaint coastline along the Mar Cantábrico.

LLANES

The most popular **beaches** on the Asturian coast can be found in the secluded coves of Llanes. Small stretches of sand lie nestled within the dramatic remnants of 13th-century walls. Monument fans should peek at the **Iglesia de Santa María del Conceyu's** early 16th-century Plateresque altar and ornately detailed (but badly worn) portal. Violets creep across the walls of the white church in summer. Inside, high stained-glass windows spill colorful light across the pews. (Open for mass Mon.-Fri. 11am and 8pm; Sat. 11am, 8pm, and 9pm; Sun. 9:30am, 11:30am, 1pm, and 7pm.)

Busy **Turismo** (tel. 540 01 64) in the Ayuntamiento office, hands out adorable maps with all the buildings, but without many street names. (Open Mon.-Sat. 9am-2pm and 5-9pm, Sun. 10am-3pm.) The **post office** (tel. 540 01 14) is on C. Pidal. From the tourist office, head left in the direction of the bus station. (Open Mon.-Fri. 8am-3pm, Sat. 9am-1pm.) The **postal code** is 33500. **Telephones** are in Pl. Parres Sobrino. (Open June-Sept. 10am-2pm and 5-11pm.) The **telephone code** is 98. For medical services, call the **Red Cross** (tel. 540 18 57) or **Ambulatorio de la Seguridad Social** (tel. 540 02 20) at C. Nemesio Sobrino, 25 (emergency room of public hospital). For an **ambulance,** call tel. 540 10 60. The **Policía Municipal** (tel. 540 18 87) is on C. Nemesio Sobrino (near the tourist office). For the **Guardia Civil,** C. La Galea, call tel. 540 00 70.

Rooms fill early in the day during the summer. **Casa del Río,** Av. San Pedro, 3 (tel. 540 11 91), in a red house behind light blue iron gates (facing the tourist office, hang a left to the first real street) has wonderful rooms, some with *two* balconies, very close to the beach. (Singles 2200ptas. Doubles 4500ptas. Sept.-June 14: 1700-2000ptas; 3000-3500ptas.) Centrally located **Pensión La Guía,** Pl. Parres Sobrino, 1 (tel. 540 25 77), is beneath the stone archway in the thick of the action. (Singles 1800ptas. Doubles 3000ptas. Triples 3750ptas. Open May-Sept.) Campers may have to eeny-meeny-miny-moe over nearby sites. First-class **Las Barcenas** (tel. 540 15 70), with showers, medical facilities, and currency exchange, sits right past the bus station. (Reception open 8am-11pm. 425ptas per person, 350ptas per car, 325ptas per tent. Open June-Sept.) **El Brao** (tel. 540 00 14), a large site with showers, currency exchange, cafeteria, and supermarket, is a mere 15m outside town. (Reception open 8:30am-midnight. 400ptas per person and per tent, 375ptas per car. Open April-Sept.)

Bar El Muelle, C. Las Barqueras, across the river over the bridge from the old quarter, posts its 900pta *menú* on a tree. Sounds of the terrace café below waft through the windows. Across from El Muelle, charmingly classy restaurants crowd the streets. While entrees are expensive, nearly all the 1000pta *menús* provide the perfect reason to put on your best jeans and enjoy the quiet, relaxing, small-town ambience. Supermarket **Autoservicio Briñasoles** is near Bar El Muelle. (Open Mon.-Sat. 9am-1:30pm and 4-8pm.)

The **bus** and **train stations** are at opposite ends of town. **ALSA-Turytrans** (tel. 540 24 85) runs buses from Santander to Llanes (July-Aug. 6 per day, off-season 4 per day, 2½hr., 760ptas), with stops at San Vicente as well (7 per day, 2hr., 920ptas). From Oviedo, **Económicos (EASA)** will also get you to Llanes (5 per day, 2hr., 820ptas). To reach the center from the bus station exit, take a left and go down C. Cueto Bajo until Correos, then turn left and keep going.

The quirky, capricious **FEVE train station** (tel. 540 01 24) sits at the end of Av. Estación. To find Turismo, exit the station and turn right at the first cross street, C. Egidio Gavito. Trains choo-choo to Santander (2 per day, 2½hr., 705ptas) and Oviedo (3 per day, 2½hr., 770ptas).

PICOS DE EUROPA

As the crow flies it takes only 25km to move from sea level at the Cantabrian coast to heights of over 2600m in the Picos de Europa. While other mountains in Europe may surpass the Picos in altitude, few can match the beauty of the *sierra's* jagged rock profile. The range doesn't enjoy the prestige of the Pyrenees or the Alps—you'll find plenty of peace and quiet here amid untamed nature. The Picos attract many serious mountaineers and hard-core nature enthusiasts, but there are also abundant resources to guide the novice trekker, a number of caves for spelunkers, and plenty of enrapturing views for those who just want to stand around and admire. Organizations devoted to alpine sports flourish in this area. Santander and León have far-reaching buses, but the best place to start is Oviedo, where many *federaciones* are based:

Federación Asturiana de Montaña, Dirección Regional de la Juventud, and **TIVE** travel agency. Referral to mountain guides, organized tour groups, and instructors in anything from paragliding to kayaking and spelunking. See Oviedo: Practical Information for addresses and phone numbers.
ICONA, C. Arquitecto Reguera, 13, 2nd fl. (tel. (98) 524 14 12). Good for general information. They offer free excursions, camping and trail info (including difficulty levels), and a ½hr. video presentation on the flora, fauna, and cheese indigenous to the area. Another office in Cangas de Onís (Av. Covadonga, 35; tel. (98) 584 91 54).
Dirección Regional de Deportes, Pl. España (tel. (98) 527 23 47). Information and referrals for outdoor sports and mountaineering.

A good English **guidebook** to the trails and towns of the area is Robin Walker's *Picos de Europa*. Generally, short (less than half-day) excursions shouldn't cost more than 5000ptas. Some companies (based in various towns throughout the Picos) that offer guided tours are listed below.

Alfredo Fernández, in the town of Arenas de Cabrales (central Picos), Pl. Castañeu (tel. (98) 584 64 45). Organizes a wide variety of excursions—from hard-core mountain climbing to a less strenuous tour (complete with a rest stop at a local *sidrería* and farm, where you can witness the mysteries of the local *queso de cabrales*).

Compañía de Guías de Montaña, in the town of Cangas de Onís (west Picos), C. Emilio Laria, 2, 3rd fl. (tel. (98) 584 89 16).

Spantrek Ltd., in the town of Carreña de Cabrales (central Picos), Casa Corro (tel. (98) 584 55 41). They guide in style, often including a box lunch on a tour led by English-speaking guides. Full-day excursions 3500-5000ptas.

Casa Cipriano, in the town of Sotres, which borders the eastern Picos (tel. (98) 584 55 24). Tours, including one leading to the **teleférico** in Fuente Dé.

Senda, in the town of Llanes (close to the coast), Av. Las Llamas (Ctra Llanes-Cué) (tel. (98) 540 24 30). Bike tours, minivan tours, and plump horse tours.

Often only campers can find beds during the busy months of July and August, and even this can be touch and go—a lot of campgrounds and *refugios* fill up in high season. When in this area, pack warm clothes and rain gear for sudden temperature drops and rainstorms. Contact *hostales* or *pensiones* in June or earlier to make reservations. In a jam, tourist offices can help find a bed in a private residence. Also, if you set off independent of a tour, leave a copy of your planned route so a rescue squad can be alerted if you don't return or call by a certain time.

Getting from various cities to the Picos is relatively easy. The bus company **ALSA,** and its subsidiary **Económicos,** are the best way to get around. For details contact their Oviedo office (see Oviedo: Practical Information).

CANGAS DE ONÍS

Cangas de Onís (pop. 3500) is the gateway to the National Park that spreads across the Western Picos. Founded after the Castilian victory over the Moors at Covadonga in 722, Cangas was the first capital of the Asturian monarchy and a launch-pad for the Reconquista. For the budget traveler, it's a great place to eat and sleep between excursions. The bus from Oviedo passes by Romanesque **Puente Romano,** which arches gracefully over the Río Sella; it's worth backtracking from the bus stop to check it out.

Walking back into Cangas, turn left opposite the park and cross a modern bridge to **Capilla de Santa Cruz.** This reconstruction of a Romanesque chapel was built above the town's oldest monument, a Celtic *dolmen* (monolith). The chapel is almost completely bare, although its exterior is shapely; in a cave underneath, priests hid from invading Moors.

Other sights in the area include **Iglesia de Santa Eulalia** in **Abamia** (11km away), a Romanesque church where King Pelayo and his wife were buried, and the **Cueva del Buxu** (BOO-shoo; 5km away), whose walls bear 15,000-year-old paintings. Only 25 people are admitted to the cave each day; arrive early. (Open Tues.-Sun. 10am-noon. Admission 150ptas, Tues. free.) Both attractions are less than a two-hour walk from Cangas. The **bus** to Covadonga runs near the Cueva del Buxu (ask to be dropped off at the Cruce de Susierra).

The **tourist office** (tel. 584 80 05), in a happening glass kiosk in the small park by the Ayuntamiento (right on Av. Covadonga), has a cute map but little else. (Open 10am-2pm and 5-10pm; Sept.-July 14 10am-2pm and 4-7pm. Closed Sun. and Mon. afternoons.) Hikers and mountaineers generally prefer the **Compañía de Guías de Montaña,** C. Emilio Laria, 2, 3rd fl. (tel. 584 87 16). The staff has a list of mountain refuges and a collection of maps (hrs. variable). Up the street from the tourist office, **Librería Imagen** stocks guides and maps. (Open 8:30am-9pm; Oct.-June Tues.-Sat. 8am-1:30pm and 3:30-7:30pm, Sun. 8am-3pm.) The **post office** (tel. 584 81 96) is down Av. Covadonga; take a right after two bl. onto Av. Constantino González; it's on the left. (Open Mon.-Fri. 8am-3pm, Sat. 9am-1pm.) The **postal code** is 33550. **Telephones** are in a little Telefónica stand behind the tourist office. (Open July-Sept. 10am-2pm and 5-11pm.) The **telephone code** is 98. For police, call the **Guardia**

Civil at tel. 584 80 56 or **municipal police** at tel. 584 80 05. **Taxis** answer at tel. 584 83 68.

A few clean *pensiones* welcome guests on main street Av. Covadonga. **Pensión Audelina,** Av. Covadonga, 6, 4th fl. (tel. 584 83 50), has big sunny rooms with firm beds. (Doubles 3000-4000ptas. Triples 5000-6000ptas.) Down the same street, but with an entrance on Av. Castilla, is **Pensión Carlos Labra,** Av. Castilla, 1, 1st fl. B (tel. 584 90 78). Soft, shiny bedspreads and a new-looking brown tiled bathroom belie the reasonable prices. (Doubles 2500-3000ptas. Less in winter.) **Hostal El Sella** backs into the Puente Romano, Av. Castilla, 2 (tel. 584 80 11). Ask for rooms at the bar downstairs. Rooms as big as the Naranjo de Bulnes is high, some with arch-shaped sliding doors, but slightly dingy bathrooms. (Singles 1800ptas. Doubles 2500-3000ptas.) Campers frequent the second-class **Camping Covadonga** (tel. 594 00 97), on Soto de Cangas about 5km up the road toward Covadonga (5 buses per day). Amenities everywhere: cafeteria, bar, and showers. (475ptas per person, 380ptas per car, 395ptas per tent. Open April 11-16 and June-Sept.) Some people camp illegally in a secluded meadow by the river.

After a rousing hike, few pleasures surpass a substantial meal in the land of *fabes* and *sidra*. Most restaurants, with *menús* slightly over 1000ptas, can be found right on Av. Covadonga. Down the street and on the left side of the park, **Supermercados El Arbol,** El Parque, s/n, sells preparations for a do-it-yourself meal. (Open Tues.-Fri. 9am-2pm and 5-8pm, Sat.-Mon. 9am-2pm.) Hand-painted tiles and dark wood give a comforting feel to **Restaurante El Abuelo,** Av. Covadonga, 31. The 1075pta *menú* includes *fabada* and locally-caught trout. The sauteed wild mushrooms will have you begging for more (*ración* 600ptas).

EASA, Av. Covadonga, s/n (tel. 584 81 33), across from the tourist office, runs frequent **buses** to Oviedo (15 per day, 1½hr., 600ptas). A few others head out to Arenas de Cabrales (4 per day, 1hr., 250ptas). Three per day go to Llanes, and one makes the trip to Madrid.

COVADONGA

"This little mountain you see will be the salvation of Spain," prophesied Don Pelayo in 718 to his Christian army, gesturing to the rocky promontory that was to be the site of the first successful rebellion against the Moors. The Reconquista started in what is now the tiny town of Covadonga. Nationalistic legend claims the Virgin interceded with God on behalf of Don Pelayo's forces.

The **Santa Cueva** (Holy Cave) where Don Pelayo prayed to the Virgin is the most important religious and historical site in Covadonga. The virgin owns a number of lovely cloaks; she changes her outfit every few days in the summer. Pilgrims and tourists crowd the sanctuary at all hours. (Open 8am-10pm. Free.)

The Santuario de Covadonga, a pale pink neo-Gothic **basílica,** towers above the town. (Open 8am-10pm.) The priceless *Corona de la Virgen,* a crown of gold and silver studded with no less than 1109 diamonds and 2046 rubies, is displayed in the **Museo del Tesoro,** directly across the square from the basilica. Underneath is Jesus's crown, also encrusted with sparklers. (Open 11am-2pm and 4-7pm. Admission 50ptas.)

On July 25 the shepherds of Covadonga whoop it up at their annual **festival** with tree-climbing competitions and folksy song and dance.

Mountain climbers in the **information office** (tel. (98) 584 60 35) across from the basilica can inform on local accommodations and sights. But this, like the tourist office at the entrance to Covadonga, is open only July 15-September. Unless you plan to go to the lakes, you won't be able to occupy yourself for more than a half-day in Covadonga. Spending the night in Cangas is cheaper, but if you decide to stay overnight anyway, the light blue shutters of **Hospedería del Peregrino** (on the main highway, tel. (98) 584 60 47) open onto swoon-inducing views of the mountains and basilica. Four bathrooms, each one cleaner than the next, crowd one end of the hallway. (Doubles with 1 bed 2750ptas. Doubles with 2 beds or triples 3000ptas. In Aug.: 4400ptas; 4950ptas.) A few meters down the hill, **Casa Priena** welcomes guests to its sparkling rooms. Upstairs balcony for morning coffee. (Doubles with bath 4000-5000ptas. Breakfast 350ptas.)

For a decidedly more rustic approach, try the nuns' places: **El Mesón** (July-Sept. tel. (98) 584 60 33; Oct.-June tel.(98) 584 60 68; 375ptas per person); **Casa Rosa** (tel. (98) 584 60 68; 375ptas per person); and the **Albergue de Covadonga** (tel. (98) 584 60 68; 200ptas per person). All three are within walking distance of the basilica. The trio offer spartan accommodations (cold water) in ancient buildings with (a few functional) wood-burning stoves; you'll need to bring your own sleeping bag. They often open only for youth groups so call ahead. To find them it's best to ask; all three lie off the main road, down the hill from the basilica.

The only **groceries** in town arrive twice a week (Wed. and Sat.) by truck—you buy them out the back when the driver stops in front of the Hospedería del Peregrino.

EASA buses (tel. (98) 584 81 33) traveling from Oviedo (5 per day, 1¾hr., 689ptas) and Cangas (20 min., 90ptas) grace Covadonga with two stops: one at the Hospedería and one uphill at the basilica.

Near Covadonga: Los Lagos de Enol y Ercina

Two buses per day from Oviedo to Cangas continue 12km higher past Covadonga to **Los Lagos de Enol y Ercina** (the lakes of Enol and Ercina), 1500m above the **Parque Nacional de Covadonga**. They leave from the basilica at Covadonga at 10:40am and noon, and return from Lago Ercina at 1:45pm and 4:45pm (see Covadonga). The ride into the mountains itself is spectacular, if you can stand the hair-raising turns. Encircled by striking rock formations, the lakes are crystal blue and surrounded by mooing cows.

There are three mountain *refugios* on the paths leading from the lakes. In summer, reserve in advance. The **Refugio de Vega de Enol** (tel. 584 82 05 or 584 85 76), close by the lakes, has merely 30 spots, but is open all year and provides meals and guides. To get there, take highway C6312 (Cangas de Onís-Panes, desvío hacia Covadongas y Lagos). Take a right at Lago Enol and keep going until the *refugio* (450ptas per person, *pensión completa* 2500ptas). For solitude, take the two-hour hike to the **Refugio de Villaviciosa-Vega de Ario** (contact the Federación Asturiana de Montañismo in Oviedo for information; tel. 584 41 19 or 584 85 16). Take road A-7 from the Lago Ercina; it's on the left, facing the lake. (Open May 15-Oct. 15. 600ptas.) The **Refugio de Vegarredonda** (contact Refugios de Montaña de Asturias, tel. 584 89 16) is also two hours away and open all year with meals, guides, hot showers, and kitchens (700ptas per night, breakfast 350ptas). To get there from Lago Enol, take highway A-6. Many *refugios* accept reservations only by shortwave radio. Go to the Guardia Civil and ask them to call for you.

ARENAS DE CABRALES

If tourists valued natural beauty as much as famous monuments, Arenas (pop. 800) would be as packed as the Louvre in July. As it is, a fair number of outdoor enthusiasts come to this tiny town between Cangas and Potes in late summer to take advantage of the excellent hiking and climbing. Dwarfed by the rocky green mountains that loom over it, and refreshed by the cold river that cuts through it, Arenas makes an ideal base for exploring the central Picos. It is also *the* place to try *queso de cabrales,* the local, pungent blue cheese, created by mixing goat, cow, and sheep milks, wrapping the resulting mush in leaves, and stewing the whole mess in nearby caves for a few months.

Senda del Cares (Cares Gorge), near the town of **Poncebos,** is a 5km walk from Arenas. Hewn and blasted out of mountain and sheer rock faces, the 12km trail was built by the government to monitor an artificially-made channel of water. At points, the vertical walls of the gorge drop straight down to the Río Cares 500 ft. below. The trail crosses the gorge twice, ending in **Caín,** a town recently hooked to civilization by a paved road. The walk takes about five hours, and the only way back is by foot.

Another shorter and less-traveled path leads south along the Río Tejo to **Bulnes,** a microscopic, roadless village. (Since there aren't any cars in the town, a helicopter must fly in for emergencies.) The blistering hike takes one-and-a-half hours out and one hour back, but is actually more difficult than the Senda del Cares. If Bulnes seduces you, consider tucking in at **Albergue de Bulnes** (tel. 536 69 32). There are 20 beds in three rooms, a bar, a library, games, showers, and guides; meals are served. Reservations are suggested (800ptas per night).

A third path with terrific views leads straight up a cliff from Poncebos to **Cama-rmeña.** For a longer, killer hike (10-12hr.), try the 17km route from Poncebos to **Invernales de Cabao,** then 9km more to the Picos' most famous mountain, **Naranjo de Bulnes.** From here you can see all the major *picos* in the area and the blue waves of the Cantabrian Sea in the distance.

The **tourist office** (tel. 584 52 84) in Arenas is helpful, but small and only open sporadically. Some English spoken. (Open Tues.-Sun. 10am-2pm and 6-9pm.) **Alber-gue de Cabrales,** just off the main road, has hiking information, as do the people at the campground. The rooms with views are gorgeous, but even if you don't stay at **Hotel Torrecerredo,** Los Llambriosos, s/n (tel. 584 66 40), it's well worth check-ing out this one-family outdoors camp: Jim often takes groups off-roading to the best hiking locations, and Pilar and Monchi organize horseback riding excursions of vari-ous lengths, from two hours (3000ptas) to four days. Their parents serve up the most filling meals in town. English spoken (Jim is from the U.K.). Arenas' **post office** is up the street from the bus stop (open Mon.-Fri. 10am-1pm, Sat. 10am-noon). In the other direction from the bus stop are **telephones,** inside the photo shop Foto J. Tomás (open 10am-9:30pm). The **postal code** is 33554; the **telephone code** 98. For **police,** call the **Guardia Civil** in Carreña de Cabrales (tel. 584 50 16).

While many visitors to Arenas choose to camp, the town also has several reason-able *hostales.* **Hostal Naranjo de Bulnes,** Ctra. General, s/n (tel. 584 51 19), has enormous rooms with panoramic views. (Singles 2500ptas, with bath 3000ptas. Doubles with bath 5600ptas.) **Pensión El Castañeu,** Pl. Castañeu (tel. 584 65 73), offers much simpler rooms at modest prices. (Singles 1500ptas. Doubles 3000ptas, with bath 3500ptas.) Both establishments have full restaurants downstairs. One km up the highway heading east toward Panes, the spectacular **Camping Naranjo de Bulnes** (tel. 584 51 78) has a cozy TV room, cafeteria, bar, shower facilities, and reams of info on hiking and assorted mountain sports. A **message board** lists excur-sions and local guides. **Bike rental** also available. (Open March-Oct. 525ptas per per-son, 475ptas per tent and per car.) Numerous **refugios** speckle the Picos; check with Turismo first. **Café La Palma's** owner speaks perfect English and serves *boca-dillos* and *raciones* in a garden courtyard, on the right as you head toward Panes. (Open May-Oct. 3pm-3am.) The setting isn't quite as interesting at **Café Cares,** right across from the bus stop, but the menu is more extensive. (Open 9am-2am.) Both places begin to swing as soon as the sun sets.

Económicos (EASA) buses journey west to Cangas de Onís and Oviedo four times a day. They run twice daily in the other direction to Panes (45min., 210ptas) and Unquera (1¼hr., 220ptas). **Autobuses Palomera** (tel. 88 06 11) leave from the center of Panes to Potes (4 per day, 45min., 210ptas). From Unquera, **Turytrans** travels to Santander (2 per day, 1½hr., 580ptas).

POTES

The most convenient base for exploring the southeastern and central Picos is Potes (pop. 2000), on the Río Deva. Quiet and snow-bound in winter, the town's squares and cafés shimmy in summer with cosmopolitan climbers. Luckily this way-station is also quite beautiful, sheltered by immense white peaks and watered by a burbling stream. The rugged terrain formed the front-line early in the Reconquista. The **Torre del Infantado** stands guard over the main square (open 10am-3pm and 5-7pm); across the river is the **Convento de San Raimundo,** a 17th-century Domini-can monastery.

The **tourist office** on Pl. Jesús de Monasterio (tel. 73 07 87), across the bridge and near the church, has general information about the region, though very little about Potes itself. Ask here about mountain *refugios,* but you'll have to reserve by short-wave radio at the Guardia Civil. (Open Holy Week and June-Sept. Mon.-Fri. 10am-1pm and 4-8pm, Sat. 10am-1pm.) **Actividades Algamientes Inmobilaria,** C. Inde-pendencia, 10 (tel. 73 21 61), next to the *torre,* is a travel agent that also arranges all kinds of excursions, including hiking (3000-4000ptas for daytrip), horseback riding (3500-8000ptas), and paragliding (7000-11,000ptas). They also rent mountain bikes (1500ptas per day). (Open Mon.-Sat. 10am-3pm.) **Bustamente,** C. Dr. Encinas, 10, is a photo shop that sells detailed **maps** and guidebooks to the region, in addition to developing your pictures in 24hrs. The maps published by the *Instituto Geográfico Nacional* and the *Federación Española de Montañismo* are the best, although seri-ous mountaineers may find them a bit vague (500-850ptas). The **post office** is across from Pl. Jesús de Monasterio (open Mon.-Fri. 8am-2:30pm, Sat. 9am-1pm). **Exchange money** at Caja de Madrid, Pl. Jesús de Monasterio. (Open Mon.-Fri. 8:15am-2:30pm.) The **telephone code** is 98.

Several *hostales* and *pensiones* line the road through town; the cheapest rooms fill early in the day—consider reserving in advance by phone. **Hostal Lombraña,** C. el Sol, 2 (tel. 73 05 19), through a passageway off the main road, offers capacious rooms, some overlooking the river. (Singles 2500ptas, with bath 3000ptas. Doubles 3500ptas, with bath 4000ptas.) **Casa Cayo,** C. Cántabra, 6 (tel. 73 01 50), has quaint rooms in its old wing, and bright modern ones in the new part. Look for sign on your right as you walk from second bus stop toward town. (Singles 2500ptas. Dou-bles 4000ptas. Triples 5500ptas.)

There's no official camping in Potes proper. The closest site is 1st-class **Camping La Viorna** (tel. 73 20 21), about 2km up the road to Monasterio Santo Toribio. Besides the restaurant, supermarket, and swimming pool, they also organize hiking, climbing, mountain biking, spelunking, and horseback excursions. (400ptas per person, per tent, and per car. Open April-Oct.) Next closest is **La Isla Picos de Europa** (tel. 73 08 96), 3km down the road to Fuente Dé. (350ptas per person, per tent, and per car. Open April-Oct.) The tourist office has info about other campsites farther out of town. There are also several *casas de labranza* (farm houses available for rent) in the area. **El Barrio** (tel. 73 03 35) in Cabezón de Liébana, 4km southeast of Potes, rents fully furnished apartments with kitchens for six (10,000ptas per day or 56,000ptas per week). **Javier García** offers double rooms with bath overlooking his orchard, 2km from Potes on the road to Fuente Dé (3800ptas per night). Ask at the tourist office for others.

The road through town is packed with cafés and restaurants. Buy you own eats at **Supermercado Autoservicio San Roque,** on C. San Roque (the main street). (Open Mon.-Sat. 9am-3pm and 4-9pm.) **Restaurante El Fogón de Cus** (tel. 73 00 60) hides in a quiet corner below the *pensión. Menú del día* (950ptas) will nourish even the most famished hiker.

Palomera buses (tel. 88 06 11 or 50 30 80) travel from Santander and back three times per day, stopping along the way at San Vincente de Barquera. To Santander (2½hr., 710ptas). Two buses run to and from Fuente Dé, but the timing makes this almost a full-day trip. An **Empresa Fernández** (tel. 21 00 00) bus makes the trip to León in summer. Coming into town, Palomera buses stop twice—once in front of Hotel Rubio and again, further into town, across from Pl. Jesús de Monasterio and the tourist office. They leave, however, only from the plaza near the tourist office.

Excursions

Fuente Dé. A mind-blowing 800m *teleférico* glides up the lunar mountain face to reach a fancy *parador* and spectacular views. There are usually huge lines for the lift in the middle of summer. (Open 9am-8pm; Sept.-June 10am-6pm. Round-trip 1000ptas.) From the top, it's a 4km walk to the **Refugio de Aliva** for a meal or bed—though the rooms in its modern buildings are usually full. Ask about vacan-cies at the lift in Fuente Dé or at the Ayuntamiento in Potes. (500ptas per person.)

So, you're getting away from it all.

Just make sure you can get back.

AT&T Access Numbers
Dial the number of the country you're in to reach AT&T.

*AUSTRIA†††	022-903-011	*GREECE	00-800-1311	NORWAY	800-190-11
*BELGIUM	0-800-100-10	*HUNGARY	00◇-800-01111	POLAND†♦²	0◇010-480-0111
BULGARIA	00-1800-0010	*ICELAND	999-001	PORTUGAL†	05017-1-288
CANADA	1-800-575-2222	IRELAND	1-800-550-000	ROMANIA	01-800-4288
CROATIA†♦	99-38-0011	ISRAEL	177-100-2727	*RUSSIA† (MOSCOW)	155-5042
*CYPRUS	080-90010	*ITALY	172-1011	SLOVAKIA	00-420-00101
CZECH REPUBLIC	00-420-00101	KENYA†	0800-10	S. AFRICA	0-800-99-0123
*DENMARK	8001-0010	*LIECHTENSTEIN	155-00-11	SPAIN •	900-99-00-11
*EGYPT¹ (CAIRO)	510-0200	LITHUANIA♦	8◇196	*SWEDEN	020-795-611
*FINLAND	9800-100-10	LUXEMBOURG	0-800-0111	*SWITZERLAND	155-00-11
FRANCE	19◇-0011	F.Y.R. MACEDONIA	99-800-4288	*TURKEY	00-800-12277
*GAMBIA	00111	*MALTA	0800-890-110	UKRAINE†	8◇100-11
GERMANY	0130-0010	*NETHERLANDS	06-022-9111	UK	0500-89-0011

Countries in bold face permit country-to-country calling in addition to calls to the U.S. **World Connect**℠ prices consist of **USADirect**® rates plus an additional charge based on the country you are calling. Collect calling available to the U.S. only. *Public phones require deposit of coin or phone card. ◇Await second dial tone. †May not be available from every phone. †††Public phones require local coin payment through the call duration. ♦Not available from public phones. • Calling available to most European countries. ¹Dial "02" first, outside Cairo. ²Dial 010-480-0111 from major Warsaw hotels. ©1994 AT&T.

Here's a travel tip that will make it easy to call back to the States. Dial the access number for the country you're visiting and connect right to AT&T. It's the quick way to get English-speaking AT&T operators and can minimize hotel telephone surcharges.

If all the countries you're visiting aren't listed above, call **1 800 241-5555** for a free wallet card with all AT&T access numbers. Easy international calling from AT&T. **TrueWorld Connections.**

AT&T

These people are only a third of the 150 students who bring you the *Let's Go* guides. With pen and notebook in hand, a few changes of underwear stuffed in our backpacks, and a budget as tight as yours, we visited every *penstone*, *palapa*, pizzeria, café, club, campground, or castle we could find to make sure you'll get the most out of *your* trip.

We've put the best of our discoveries into the book you're now holding. A brand-new edition of each guide hits the shelves every year, only months after it is researched, so you know you're getting the most reliable, up-to-date, and comprehensive information available.

But, as any seasoned traveler will tell you, the best discoveries are often those you make yourself. If you find something worth sharing, drop us a line. We're at Let's Go, Inc., 1 Story Street, Cambridge, MA 02138, USA (e-mail: letsgo@delphi.com).

H A P P Y   T R A V E L S !

To return, either retrace your steps to the *teleférico* or walk (3hr.) to **Espinama**. On July 10, a rowdy **festival** brings horse racing and dancing to Aliva. Two **buses** per day drive the 23km route from Potes to Fuente Dé (225ptas).

Monasterio de Santo Toribio de Liébana, 3km west of Potes, claims to hold part of the true (original) cross.

Urdón, 15km north of Potes and on the road to Panes, is the start of a challenging hike to **Treviso.** The trail's steepness and switchbacks are illustrated on posters all over Potes. About 6km; 4 hr.

Peña Sagra is about 13km east and a two-hour walk from the towns of **Luriezo** or **Aniezo;** from the summit you can survey all the Picos and the sea 51km away. On your way down, visit **Iglesia de Nuestra Señora de la Luz,** where the beautifully carved patron saint of the Picos lives 364 days a year. Known affectionately as *Santuca* (tiny saint), the Virgin is honored on May 2.

Panes, on the routes to Santander and Cabrales, is near some spectacular scenery. The Potes-Panes drive through the **Desfiladero de Hermida** (a sharp gorge carved by the Río Deva) is stunning, but the terrifying continuation of that route to Cabrales has been known to induce vomiting.

CANTABRIA

■■■ SANTANDER

In 1941, an enormous fire gutted the entire city of Santander (pop. 200,000). Miraculously, the capital of Cantabria has managed to rebuild itself along modern lines, packing beaches, promenades, a swish casino, and a trendy shopping district into its mini peninsula. A striking combination of natural beauty and modern amenities, Santander is a favorite seaside resort among the Spanish. The presence of the Universidad Internacional Menéndez Pelayo attracts renowned artists and scholars to town.

ORIENTATION AND PRACTICAL INFORMATION

This slender, elongated city sits on the northwestern side of a bay. The small **Plaza Porticada** is its heart. **Avenida Calvo Sotelo** becomes **Paseo de Pereda** to the east, then runs along the waterfront. Buses and trains arrive at **Plaza de Estaciones,** about six blocks west of Pl. Porticada.

Beach activity centers on the neighborhood **El Sardinero,** in the eastern part of town. Municipal buses connect the two parts of the city (frequent service from about 6-8am until midnight, Sept.-June until 10:30pm, 70ptas). The beach is bordered by lengthy **Avenida Reina Victoria** and **Avenida de Castaneda.** Between the two beaches (El Sardinero and Playa de la Magdalena) lies the swanky casino in **Plaza de Italia.**

Tourist Office: Jardines de Pereda (tel. 21 61 20). From the stations, follow C. Calderón de la Barca straight into the park; the office is just off Po. Pereda. Maps and information on Santander and Cantabria. Some English and French spoken. Open Mon.-Fri. 9am-1pm and 4-7pm, Sat. 10am-1pm. Another office in the ferry station has the same hours and services.

Budget Travel: Viajes TIVE, C. Canarias, 2 (tel. 33 22 15), a 20-min. walk northwest from the center. Take bus #5 just off Av. General Camilo Alonso Cela. Travel discounts and flights. English spoken. ISIC 500ptas. HI card 1800ptas. Open Mon.-Fri. 9am-2pm, Sat. 9am-1pm.

Consulate: See Spain Essentials: Embassies and Consulates.

Currency Exchange: When banks close, there's always **Bar Machichaco,** C. Calderón de la Barca, just past C. Isabel II. Open 1pm-midnight.

American Express: Viajes Altair, C. Lealtad, 24 (tel. 31 17 00; fax 22 57 21), at the corner with C. Calderón de la Barca. Cardholder mail held, and the standard services. Open Mon.-Fri. 9:30am-1:30pm and 4:30-8pm, Sat. 10am-1:30pm.

Post Office: Av. Alfonso XIII (tel. 21 26 73; fax 31 02 99), overlooking the Jardines de Pereda on the waterfront. Open for stamps and Lista de Correos Mon.-Fri. 8am-9pm, Sat. 9am-2pm; for **fax** and **telegrams** Mon.-Fri. 8am-9pm, Sat. 9am-7pm. **Postal Code:** 39080.

Telephones: Telefónica, C. Hernán Cortés, 37, up the street from Pl. José Antonio. **Faxes** also sent. Open Mon.-Fri. 9am-3pm and 4-11pm, Sat. 9am-3pm and 4-10pm. Another office is alongside the casino, Pl. Italia. **Telephone Code:** 942.

Flights: Aeropuerto de Santander (tel. 25 10 07 or 25 10 04), 4km away. Daily to Madrid and Barcelona. Accessible only by taxi (1000-1200ptas). **Iberia,** Po. Pereda, 18 (tel. 22 97 00). Open Mon.-Fri. 9am-1:30pm and 4-7pm.

Trains: Pl. Estaciones, on C. Rodríguez. **RENFE station** (tel. 21 02 88). Information open 7:15am-10:30pm. Santander is the northern terminus of one RENFE line, so for service to points north, take FEVE to Bilbao and then pick up RENFE again. To: Madrid (4 per day, 7hr., 3100-5400ptas); Salamanca (5 per day, 7hr., *regional* 2390ptas, *talgo* 4100ptas); Valladolid (7 per day, 5hr., *regional* 1490ptas, *talgo* 3200ptas); Palencia (4 per day, 2¼hr., *regional* 1170ptas, *talgo* 2600ptas). **RENFE ticket office,** Po. Pereda, 25 (tel. 21 23 87). Open Mon.-Fri. 9am-1pm and 4-7pm, Sat. 9am-1pm. **FEVE station** (tel. 21 16 87). Information open 9am-2pm and 4-7pm. To: Bilbao (6 per day, 2½hr., 865ptas); Oviedo (4 per day, 4½hr., 1425ptas).

Buses: Pl. Estaciones (tel. 21 19 95), across C. Rodríguez from the train station. Information open 9am-9pm. To: Santillana del Mar (6 per day, 45min., 250ptas); Potes (3 per day, 2½hr., 750ptas); Bilbao (12 per day, 3hr., 805ptas); Oviedo (2 per day, 4hr., 1440ptas); La Coruña (2 per day, 12hr., 4500ptas); Madrid (6 per day, 6hr., 3200-4000ptas); Llanes (5 per day, 2hr., 705ptas); San Vincente de la Barquera (6 per day, 1½hr., 465ptas); León (1 per day, 3½hr., 1060ptas).

Public Transportation: Buses #4, 5, 6, and 7 run between the city center and El Sardinero (about every 15min., service begins 6am-8am, ends 10pm-midnight, 70ptas).

Ferries: Brittany Ferries, Muelle del Ferrys, near the Jardines de Pereda. All the way to Plymouth, England (2 per week, 14,000-17,000ptas, plus 700-1100ptas for seat reservation). Tickets sold by Modesto Piñeiro, S.A. (tel. 21 45 00), at the ferry station. Information open Mon.-Fri. 7:30am-7pm. In summer reserve 2 weeks in advance, just in case. **Las Reginas** (tel. 21 66 19), from Embarcadero by the Jardines de Pereda. To Pedreña (summer every ½hr., round-trip 250ptas). They also do tours around the bay (summer 2-6 per day, 1½hr., 500ptas).

Taxis: Radio Taxi (tel. 33 33 33, 33 10 37, or 22 20 46).

Car Rental: Avis, C. Nicolás Salmerón, 3 (tel. 22 70 25). Must be at least 23 and have had license 1 yr. Renault 8000ptas per day (includes mileage and insurance). Open Mon.-Fri. 9am-1pm and 4-7:30pm, Sat. 9-11:30am. **Europcar,** C. Rodríguez, 9 (tel. 21 47 06). Must be at least 21 and have had license 1 yr. Ford Fiesta 4800ptas per day, 80ptas per km. Open Mon.-Fri. 9am-1pm and 4-8pm.

Luggage Storage: At the **train station** (lockers 300ptas), by the counter at the ticket window. Open daily 7am-11pm. At the **bus station** (lockers 300ptas). Open 7:30am-10:30pm.

Lost Property: Ayuntamiento building, Pl. Generalísimo Franco (tel. 22 04 64).

English Bookstore: La Estilográfica, C. Hernán Cortés, 1 (tel. 21 19 05). A cramped stationery store with a small but far-flung choice of books in English. Bestselling Book-of-the-Month Club authors. Open Mon.-Fri. 9:45am-3:30pm and 4:30-8pm, Sat. 9:45am-1:30pm.

Women's Center: Instituto de la Mujer, Pasaje de la Puntida, 1 (tel. 31 36 12). Information on gatherings, exhibitions, and talks.

Laundromat: Lavomatique, C. Cuesta de la Atalaya, 18 (tel. 37 41 78), on the corner of San Celedonio. Wash 500ptas per load. Dry 100ptas per 15min. Soap 75ptas. Or let them do it all for you (1000ptas). Open Mon.-Fri. 9am-1:30pm and 4-8pm, Sat. 9am-1:30pm. **El Lavadero,** C. Mies del Valle, 10 (tel. 23 06 07), just off C. Floranes west of the train station. Wash 700ptas per 6kg load. Dry 200ptas per 6kg load. Soap 50ptas. Open Mon.-Fri. 9:30am-2pm, Sat. 10am-1:30pm.

Swimming Pool: Piscinas Municipales, in sports complex Albericias (tel. 33 75 06). Take bus #6 to the end of the line.

Rape Crisis Line: Asociación de Asistencia a Mujeres Violadas, Comisiones Obreras Building, C. Santa Clara, 5, 3rd fl. (tel. 21 95 00). English spoken. Open Mon.-Fri. noon-2pm.

Red Cross: Ambulance, C. Marqués de la Hermida, 23 (tel. 27 30 58).

Medical Emergencies: Clínica Los Escalantes (tel. 21 12 14).

Emergency: tel. 091.

Police: Pl. Verlade, s/n (tel. 22 88 00). **Guardia Civil,** C. Alta, 81 (tel. 22 11 00).

ACCOMMODATIONS AND CAMPING

It's not easy to find affordable rooms in July and August, especially if you arrive late in the day. Highest hotel density is near the market, around **Calle Isabel II,** across from the train station on **Calle Rodríguez,** and along elegant **Avenida de los Castros** in **El Sardinero.** El Sardinero is the modern residential beach neighborhood, a bus ride (see Practical Information: Public Transportation) and worlds away from the hyperactive city center.

Pensión Angelines, C. Rodríguez, 9, 1st fl. (tel. 31 25 84), across the street and to the left as you leave the train station. Comfortable rooms with floral bedspreads. Your choice of shiny bathrooms: blue, pink, tan, or brown. Singles 1200ptas. Doubles 3500ptas. Triples 3600ptas. Sept.-June: Doubles 2500ptas.

Hostal Real, Pl. Esperanza, 1, 3rd fl. (tel. 22 57 87), in peach building at the end of C. Isabel II. Elegant hallway and flowery rooms. Some have balconies, all have hand-carved wood beds. Singles 3000ptas. Doubles 3500ptas, in August 4500ptas.

Hostal Puerto Rico, C. Isabel II, 1, 3rd fl. (tel. 22 57 07). Pretty rooms with subdued white bedspreads, oriental rugs, and teeny-tiny little lamps. Positively swimming in plants. Owner addresses most everyone who comes through her door as *"guapa/guapo"*—pretty/handsome. Singles 3000ptas. Doubles 4400ptas. Prices lower in off-season.

Pensión Fernando, C. Rodríguez, 9, 3rd fl. (tel. 31 36 96), in the same building as Angelines. (Another *pensión* upstairs, as well.) Good size rooms are white-walled and spotless. Must be run by a hunter—boar's head in the foyer and animal skin rugs in some rooms. Singles 2000ptas. Doubles 3000-4000ptas.

Hostal-Residencia Botín, C. Isabel II, 1, 1st fl. (tel. 21 00 94), downstairs from the Puerto Rico. Gigantic rooms with dainty pink bedspreads. Super-clean bathrooms. One single 2000-3000ptas. Doubles 3000-5000ptas.

Fonda Perla de Cuba, C. Hernán Cortés, 8 (tel. 21 00 41), across from the Banesto building past C. Bailén. Decor varies from room to room, but many have balconies. A bit dark, but at these prices, what did you expect? Singles 1000ptas. Doubles 2000ptas. Showers 100ptas. Breakfast 150ptas.

Hostal-Residencia Luisito, Av. Castros, 11 (tel. 27 19 71), 1 bl. from beach. Take bus #4 to Hotel Colón (Pl. Brisas). Beach heaven (but far from downtown). Exceptionally huge rooms, many with huge balconies. Singles 1915ptas. Doubles 3435ptas. Prices don't include IVA. Breakfast 180ptas. Open July-Sept.

Camping: On the scenic bluff called Cabo Mayor, 3km up the coast from Playa de la Magdalena, there are 2 back-to-back sites. Both are *enormes.* Take the "Cueto-Santander" bus from in front of the Jardines de Pereda. **Camping Bellavista** (tel. 27 48 43), a 1st-class site on the beach. 350ptas per person, 325-350ptas per tent. *Parcela* (parking spot) 1500ptas. **Camping Cabo Mayor** (tel. 27 35 66), with pool and tennis courts. 450ptas per person, 350-450ptas per tent. *Parcela* 1400ptas. Open mid-June to Sept.

FOOD

Interesting restaurants crowd the **Puerto Pesquero** (fishing port), serving up the day's catch on a small stretch at the end of **Calle Marqués de la Ensenada.** From the train station, walk eight blocks down C. Castilla and turn left on C. Héroes de la

Armada; cross the tracks and turn right after about 100m (20min.). Don't walk this alone at night; parts are quite deserted. Closer to the city center, reasonable *mesones* and bars line **Calle Daóiz y Velarde** and **Plaza Cañadío.** The **Mercado de Plaza Esperanza,** C. Isabel II, sells produce near Pl. Generalísimo behind the police station. (Open Mon.-Fri. 8am-2pm and 5-7:30pm, Sat. 8am-2pm.)

Groceries: Supermercado BM, C. Calderón de la Barca, 12, 1 bl. up from train and bus stations. Open Mon.-Fri. 9am-1:30pm and 5:15-7:45pm, Sat. 9am-2pm.

Bar Restaurante La Gaviota, C. Marqués de la Ensenada (tel. 22 11 32), at the corner of C. Mocejón in the *barrio pesquero.* Fresh grilled sardines (12 for 900ptas) and *paella de mariscos* (500ptas) are delicious specialties. Watch your 900pta *menú* being prepared in a kitchen, smack in the middle of the cavernous dining room. Open 1-4pm and 7:30pm-midnight.

La Cueva, C. Marqués de la Ensenada (tel. 22 20 87), next door to La Gaviota. Cozier than its neighbors, with more choices on its 900pta *menú. Chipirones encebollados* (baby squid fried in onion, 600ptas). Open noon-4pm and 7:30-11:30pm.

Cervecería Aspy, C. Hernán Cortés, 22 (tel. 31 45 95), just off C. Lope de Vega. Elegant dining room has it all: wine rack, oil paintings, and a signed photo of golf star Seve Ballesteros. Video games up front. *Platos combinados* 500-750ptas. *Menú* 900ptas. Open daily 8am-1am; winter Thurs.-Tues. 8am-1am.

Restaurante-Bar Fradejas, Pl. Cañadío, 1 (tel. 31 48 41). A glorified cafeteria. Exports meals outside. *Bocadillo de tortilla* 200ptas. *Menú* 900ptas, 1000ptas on the *terraza.* Open Tues.-Sun. 9am-2:30am.

Bar-Restaurante Silverio, Pl. Esperanza, 1 (tel. 21 31 25). *Comedor* upstairs is pricey, but *raciones* at the comfortable bar are innovative and reasonable. Stewed quails 350ptas each. Garlic snails 450ptas. Open noon-midnight.

Restaurante Cruz Blanca, C. Hernán Cortés, 16 (tel. 27 30 05), just up from the Aspy. Rice dish *arroz a la cubana* and *pechugas de pollo* (chicken breasts) on their 950pta *menú.* Prussiaphiles dig the Teutonic decor, the German beer, and the bratwurst (375ptas).

Cervecería Santander, C. Lope de Vega, 5, off Po. Pereda near the ferry station. Plaid tablecloths and cloth napkins. Outside tables front the water. Broad 900pta *menú* includes *fabada* (Asturian stew made of pork and beans) and *albóndigas* (meatballs). Open 7:30am-midnight.

SIGHTS

Jutting into the sea between El Sardinero and Playa de la Magdalena, the **Península de la Magdalena** is crowned by an early 20th-century neo-Gothic fantasy **palacio.** Originally Alfonso XIII's summer house, the clifftop palace is a classroom building and dorm for the university. In summer, renowned cultural figures from around the globe arrive for a term of seminars and lectures. There is also a **park** on the peninsula, populated with penguins and sea lions. (Peninsula open 9am-10pm. The *palacio* doesn't have visiting hours. Penguin feeding noon and 6pm. Sea lions 5pm.)

The beaches are truly spectacular. Stretching its powdery sands forever, **El Sardinero,** at the end of town, is the old stand-by. Some fine, less crowded beaches— **Playas Puntal, Somo,** and **Loredo**—fringe the other side of the bay. In summer, Las Reginas **boats** (tel. 21 66 19) run across to Pedreña and sail on 80-minute tours around the bay (see Practical Information: Ferries).

The **Museo Marítimo,** C. San Martín de Bajamar (tel. 27 49 62), stands beyond the *puerto chico* (little port). The traditional fishing boats and salvaged remains on display are dull, but the attached aquarium is pretty nifty. Feeding time is noon. (Open Tues.-Sat. 11am-1pm and 4-7pm, Sun. 11am-2pm; mid-Sept. to mid-June Mon.-Sat. 10am-1pm and 4-6pm, Sun. and holidays 11am-2pm. Free.) Near the Ayuntamiento, the **Museo de Bellas Artes,** C. Rubio, 6 (tel. 23 94 85), exhibits a collection of 16th-through 18th-century paintings. The prize is Goya's portrait of Fernando VII. (Open Mon.-Fri. 10:30am-1:30pm and 5:30-8pm, Sat. 10am-1pm. Free.)

Paleolithic skulls and tools rattle at the **Museo de Prehistoria y Arqueología,** C. Casimiro Sáinz, 4 (tel. 20 71 04). Artifacts from and photographs of the Cuevas de

Altamira (See Cantabrian Coast: Cuevas de Altamira) console the many who won't get to see the real thing. (Open Tues.-Sat. 9am-1pm and 4-7pm, Sun. and holidays 11am-2pm. Free.)

While the 1941 fire scorched the facade of the **catedral** (tel. 22 60 24), the downstairs chapel retains an unusually low Romanesque vaulting. (Open 9:30am-1:30pm and 5:30-8:30pm. Free.)

ENTERTAINMENT

A trendy shopping district centers around Av. Calvo Sotelo. Outdoor cafés overlooking the bay hum on Po. Pereda. A 10-minute walk along the water leads to the **barrio pesquero,** hopping with busy restaurants and their outdoor barbecues. As night falls, Santander starts to drink. Students frequent the area around **Plaza Cañadío, Calle Pedruca,** and **Calle Daóiz y Velarde,** and up the hill from Pl. Cañadío on **Pasadillo de Zorilla.** At **Blues** on C. Gomez Areña in Pl. Cañadío, jazz fans mingle under huge plastic statues of jazz greats.

In the **El Sardinero** district, tourists and students mix all night long. **Plaza Italia** and nearby **Calle Panamá** are the neighborhood hotspots. The **Gran Casino** on Pl. Italia is an imposing white elephant, perfect for an evening of *Belle Epoque* gambling. Passport and proper dress (pants and shoes) required. (Must be 18 to gamble. Open 7pm-4am. Admission 400ptas.) Innumerable students crowd bars **Rebeca** and **Albatros** on C. Panamá. **Amarras,** behind the Casino, is packed with the thirtyish crowd.

The August **Festival Internacional de Santander** brings a myriad of music and dance recitals. The events culminate in the **Concurso Internacional de Piano de Santander.** Daily classical concerts ring through Pl. Porticada; recent festivals have featured the London Symphony Orchestra and the Bolshoi Ballet. Fabulously high-priced tickets are sold in booths on Po. Pereda and Pl. Porticada; a few are under 1500ptas. (Consult the Oficina del Festival, Av. Calvo Sotelo, 15, 6th fl. Tel. 21 05 08 or 21 03 45; fax 31 47 67.) The new **Auditorio,** a grand venue of controversial design for classical music and ballet, opened recently.

■ NEAR SANTANDER

Since only a handful of people each day get into the Cuevas de Altamira, many spelunk in the lesser-known town of **Puente Viesgo,** about 30km south of Santander. The **Cuevas del Castillo** (tel. 59 84 25) display paintings nearly as well-preserved as those in Altamira. (Open Tues.-Sun. 10am-1pm and 3-7pm. Last visits 45min. before closing times. Admission 250ptas.) Continental **buses** stop in Puente Viesgo en route from Santander to Burgos (2 per day, 45min., 440ptas).

■■■ CANTABRIAN COAST

Perfect daytrip material, fishing villages, and beach towns dot the soft and sandy shore of Cantabria. La Cantábrica buses follow the coast and link most of these towns with each other and with Santander.

SANTILLANA DEL MAR

Like Voltaire's Holy Roman Empire, Santillana del Mar is none of the above. Neither *Santa* (holy), *llana* (flat), nor *del mar* (on the sea), the entire town is still a national historical monument, filled with beautifully-preserved stone houses and cobblestone streets. In fact, it is possible to trace the evolution of Spanish architecture from the 15th to the 18th century in the very streets of this village. In the evening, the cows of this town of 1000 (locals, that is) are herded through the streets on their way back from pasture.

Emblazoned above the door of virtually every house is a heraldic shield proclaiming the rank and honor of former noble residents. The shield at **La Casa de los Villa,** near the bus stop, proclaims the glory of honorable death. Many residents have converted their doorways into stands selling the local delectable (if overpriced) sweet milk, *bizcocho* (sponge cake), and ceramics.

The **Colegiata de Santa Juliana,** a 12th-century Romanesque church, occupies one end of C. Santo Domingo. The charming, ivy-covered **claustro** has some fragmented capitals of Jesus and his disciples. The 12th-century reform of the Cistercian Order prohibited the representation of any human form on pillars—hence the vegetable patterns. (Open Thurs.-Tues. 9am-1pm and 4-7:30pm; winter Thurs.-Tues. 10am-1pm and 4-6pm. Admission 100ptas.)

In a town that's a museum itself, the **Museo Diocesano** (tel. 581 80 04) is one of only two official ones. Religious art and artifacts spread throughout the harmonious Romanesque cloister and corridors of the Monasterio Regina Coeli. One display, put together by Benedictine monks from Burgos, explains how polychromed wood sculptures are enameled. Another room is devoted to the process of wood carving. (Museum open 10am-1pm and 4-8pm; winter 10am-1pm and 4-6pm. Admission 100ptas.)

The **Museo Regional,** in the Casa del Aguila y la Parra, across from the *parador,* is Santillana's other indoor exhibition. The eclectic collection contains everything from Roman artifacts to 19th-century tools, with a few stuffed boar's heads thrown in for good measure. (Open Wed.-Sun. 10:30am-1:30pm and 4-7:30pm. Free.)

The **tourist office,** Pl. Ramón Pelayo, is in the same building as the Museo Regional. They offer a map without street names, and can help with lodging and sights. (Open Mon.-Sat. 9:30am-1pm and 4-7pm. Also technically open Sun. 10:30am-1:30pm and 4-7:30pm, but no one is there.) Guided **tours** (tel. 81 82 51) leave from Pl. Ramón Pelayo, in front of the Ayuntamiento. (Summer every ½hr., 10:30am-1:30pm and 4-8pm. In Spanish.) Exiting the tourist office and turning left leads to the **post office** (open Mon.-Fri. 8am-3pm, Sat. 9am-1pm). **Telephones** neighbor the post office, and June-Sept. a phone stand operates down by the municipal parking lot. (Open 11am-10pm.) The **postal code** is 39330; the **telephone code** 942. **Taxis** answer at tel. 88 11 11. For **medical emergencies,** dial 82 06 94.

Santillana's proximity to Santander is especially convenient when rooms fill up in July and August. Don't be lured by the *hostales* on the highway near the bus stop; *casas particulares* right in town are sure to be cheaper. The tourist office can help find one. **Pensión Angélica** (tel. 81 82 38), on C. Hornos off Pl. Ramón Pelayo (look for the *habitaciones* sign), is as beautiful inside as it looks from the outside, with a black iron gate and flowers—it looks sort of like Bob Newhart's inn. (Singles 2500ptas. Doubles 3000ptas.) Nearby **Posada Santa Juliana,** on C. Carrera, 19 (tel. 84 01 06), is equally pleasant. Some rooms have exposed wood beams, and all have TVs, quilts, and downy pillows. (Doubles 4800-6500ptas; Sept.-June 3800ptas.) Less than 1km away on the road to Comillas is **Camping Santillana** (tel. 81 82 50). It'd be easy to mistake this deluxe 1st-class site for a *parador;* not only does it boast a panoramic view of the town, it also has a supermarket, shiny cafeteria, pool, miniature golf, and tennis courts. (Reception open 8:30am-10pm. 495ptas per person, 425-450ptas per tent, 425ptas per car. Golf and tennis 250ptas per person and per hr.)

Just about everyone who comes to **Casa Cossío,** Pl. Abad Francisco Navarro (tel. 81 83 55), across from the church, orders their 950pta *menú* for the ribs. Grilled right in the huge open fire downstairs, they're served with a tasty paprika sauce amid stone walls and wood columns. (Bar open 10:30am-11:30pm. *Comedor* open 1-4pm and 8-11pm.) **Bodega El Porche,** Pl. Juan Infante, has sandwiches (300-500ptas) and *platos combinados* (600-800ptas) which you can eat outside, beneath the stone arches. (Open 11am-4pm and 7-11pm.) The **SPAR** store at Pl. Juan Infante sells groceries amid the souvenirs and film. (Open 9:30am-9pm.)

Santillana is an easy trip from Santander (26km away) by **bus.** La Cantábrica (tel. 72 08 22) sends six buses per day (Sept.-June 4 per day, 45min., 250ptas) from Pl. Estaciones in Santander. When the bus drops you off, walk to Hotel Santillana on the corner, and then head straight uphill. Ask the tourist office for an exact schedule.

CUEVAS DE ALTAMIRA

Bison roam, horses graze, deer prance, and goats butt on the ceilings of the limestone **Cuevas de Altamira** (2km from Santillana del Mar), sometimes called the "Sistine Chapel of Primitive Art." The large-scale polychrome paintings are known for scrupulous attention to naturalist detail (such as genitalia and the texture of hides) and resourceful use of the caves' natural texture. So realistic and carefully wrought are the twenty-five animals, some in inaccessible ceiling areas, that they were originally though to be a hoax, when first discovered at the beginning of the century. To catch a glimpse, you must obtain written permission from the Centro de Investigación de Altamira, Santillana del Mar, Cantabria, Spain 39330 (tel. (942) 81 80 05). Send a photocopy of your passport. **You must write 10 months in advance.** Since the caves have been debased by excess tourism, now only 20 people per day get to make the 15-minute tour. (Tues.-Sun. 9:30am-2:30pm.) When you don't get in, snivel your way through the **museum** of prehistory. (Open Mon.-Sat. 10am-1pm and 4-6pm, Sun. 10am-1pm. Free.)

To walk here, follow the signs from Santillana past the abandoned **Iglesia de San Sebastián,** a hotspot for picnickers. Make a detour through the streets of Herrán, and turn right into the corn field at the wooden barrier on the other side of town.

COMILLAS

Comillas is an understated resort favored by Spain's noble families, who retain their modest palaces along with their anachronistic titles. One of the only places in historically leftist northern Spain where people can refer to themselves as count or duchess with a straight face, the town's conservative nature is diluted only by the thousands of young people tracking sand through the streets each summer.

The broad **Playa Comillas** ends in a small port. The quieter beach of **Oyambre,** 2km away, stretches twice the length and has half the tourists. Many petite palaces and an enormous Jesuit **universidad** rise in Gothic splendor between the sea and Picos de Europa. The neo-Gothic **Palacio de Sobrellano,** on the outskirts of town, dominates a pretty park. Inside, the **Capilla-Pantheon** contains furniture designed by Gaudí. (Open 10am-1pm and 3-8pm. Free.) More Gaudí awaits at multi-colored **El Capricho,** a small stone-and-tile palace that has become a very good, very expensive restaurant. It's one of only three Gaudís outside of Cataluña; the other two are in León and Astorga.

Comillas is an active little town thanks to summer residents and a disproportionate number of clothing stores. It comes to life during the weekend of July 15, when the **fiestas** go up in a blaze of fireworks. Have a go at greased pole-walking, goose-chasing, and dancing in the plaza. Dance the rest of the summer away at **El Bote,** on the sand at the end of the parking lot.

The none-too-helpful **tourist office,** C. Aldea, 2 (tel. 72 07 68), stocks bus and excursion information, as well as a list of *hostales,* but you may have to beg to get them. The only map costs 100ptas and is useless. (Open 10am-1pm and 4-7pm.) The **post office** is on C. Antonio López, 6. (Open Mon.-Fri. 8am-3pm, Sat. 9am-1pm.) **Telephones** ring up the street from the tourist office; take a sharp left up the little hill. (Open 10:30am-2pm and 5-11pm.) The **postal code** is 39520; **telephone code** 942.

Pensión Bolingas, C. El Corro (tel. 72 08 41), off Pl. Ruiz de la Rabia, is a welcome anomaly on the high-priced Comillas accommodations market. Rose-covered archway and bright green trim outside, antiques and the occasional fireplace inside. Excessively clean bathrooms, too. (Doubles 2200ptas.) **Hostal Esmeralda,** C. Antonio López, 7 (tel. 72 00 97), has antique-furnished rooms with windows that stretch from the wood floors to the ceiling moldings. (Singles 4000-5000ptas. Doubles 5000ptas, with bath 6000ptas.) **Camping de Comillas** (tel. 72 00 74) is a first-class site on the water. There's a supermarket, cafeteria, laundromat, and beautiful views. (450ptas per person, 1590ptas per *parcela.* Open June-Sept.) Nearby **Camping El Helguero** (tel. 72 21 24), 3km from Santillana in **Ruiloba,** rivals the Comillas site. In addition to a supermarket, restaurant, café, and laundromat, they've got a swimming pool. **Buses** from Santander's bus station arrive here about five times per day. (350ptas per person and per car, 325-450ptas per tent.)

While upscale restaurants dot the small streets of Comillas, less expensive bars and *cafeterías* fill **Plaza Ruiz de la Rabia,** to the right and up two blocks from the tourist office. **Bodega El Siglo** dishes up a 950pta *menú* and a *ración* of smoky *costillas* (ribs) for 500ptas. *Bocadillos* run 295-450ptas. The supermarket **SPAR** is on the corner of Po. Infantas and C. Solatorre, back from the bus stop. (Open Mon.-Sat. 9am-2pm and 4:30-9pm.)

At 18km from Santillana del Mar and 49km from Santander, Comillas is an easy daytrip from either. La Cantábrica (tel. 72 08 22) **buses** run from Santander (6 per day, Sept.-June 3 per day, 365ptas). Alternatively, the **train** goes as far as **Torrelavega,** where you can catch a bus to Comillas.

SAN VICENTE DE LA BARQUERA

San Vicente (pop. 4750) is a rapidly growing jigsaw puzzle of modern hotels and older houses just west of Comillas. The 12th-century church-fortress **Santa María de los Angeles** has a handsome Romanesque portico and the Renaissance tomb of Antonio Corro, the infamous 16th-century Grand Inquisitor. His effigy lounges jauntily, reading about a nun from Soria whom he ordered burned for heresy. The 8th-century **castillo** lurking above town can be visited from the outside only.

For sandy fun, try beaches **Merón** and **El Rosal.** From the expansive sands of Playa Merón, a 15-minute walk after crossing the 15th-century stone Puente de la Maza, poses fabulous views of the Picos de Europa.

The **tourist office** (tel. 71 07 97), on main street Av. Generalísimo, helps with accommodations. (Open Semana Santa and July-Sept. Mon.-Sat. 9am-9pm.) The **post office** is at C. Miramar, 9 (tel. 71 02 19), on the busy street that runs down the waterfront at right angles to Av. Generalísimo. (Open Mon.-Fri. 8am-3pm, Sat. 9am-1pm.) **Telephones** are in front of the Red Cross stand at the bus stop, by the water. (Open Mon.-Fri. 10am-2pm and 5-11pm, Sat.-Sun. and holidays 10am-2pm.) **Postal code** is 39540; **telephone code** 942. **Taxis** answer at tel. 71 08 80. Tend to hygiene at the **public showers** and **toilets** at the end of Av. Generalísimo, to the right exiting the tourist office (showers 200ptas, toilets 50ptas). The **Red Cross** (tel. 71 09 20) is at the bus stop on Av. Generalísimo. For **medical emergencies,** dial the Centro de Salud at 71 24 56. The **Guardia Civil** (tel. 71 00 07) is at C. Padre Antonio, 8, behind the *murallas*.

Rooms, like everything else in San Vicente, are expensive and often packed during the summer. **Hostal La Paz,** C. Mercado, 2 (tel. 71 01 80), right off the plaza where Av. Generalísimo begins—a yellow sign points the way—is about as cheap as you can get. Big, airy rooms and better than adequate bathrooms. (Singles 1700-2600ptas. Doubles 3900ptas, Oct.-May 3300ptas.) **Pensión Liébana,** C. Ronda (tel. 71 02 11), sits behind La Paz. Popular place, so come early. Deluxe rooms (with TVs) at deluxe prices. (Singles with bath 3500ptas. Doubles with bath 5000ptas.) To find **Camping El Rosal** (tel. 71 01 65), cross the bridge by the bus stop and Red Cross stand and keep going (20min.). An area with stores, like a little town, surrounds the 2nd-class site near the beach: lively *cafetería* and bar, supermarket, laundry, currency exchange, and camping equipment rental. They also provide information on excursions to nearby towns. (Reception open daily 9am-10pm. 400ptas per person and per car, 350ptas per tent. Open Semana Santa-Sept.)

Most restaurants on Av. Generalísimo are generic and overpriced. The **Nameless Bar at #7,** with the tilework out front, however, offers deliciously fresh *raciones* for reasonable prices. Steamed razor clams 500ptas. Fresh grilled anchovies 400ptas.

Six **buses** per day run from Santander to San Vicente in July and August, four the rest of the year (1½hr.). Call **La Cantábrica** (tel. 72 08 22) for schedules. **Turytrans** (tel. 21 56 50) also covers the same dirt. Bus schedules and ticket sales are at **Fotos Noly,** next door to the post office. To Santander (515ptas); Llanes (265ptas).

País Vasco (Euskadi, Euskal Herria)

Cosmopolitan urban centers; colorful fishing villages on the Cantábrico; a rich, living history; natural exuberance, from sylvan mountains to wave-rocked coasts; unique traditions seeped in a deep attachment to the land; and exceptional cuisine rooted in an almost spiritual appreciation of food and drink—the fascinations of the Basque Country are too subtle to count. A green microcosm of vivid detail suspended between France and the Cordillera Cantábrica, the País Vasco is made up of three provinces: Guipúzcoa (Gipuzkoa), whose capital is San Sebastián (Donostia); Vizcaya (Biskaia), centered around Bilbao (Bilbo); and Alava (Araba), whose capital Vitoria-Gasteiz also serves as administrative capital of the whole. Though not officially a part of the País Vasco, sections of Navarra—particularly in the north—consider themselves ethnically Basque. The notoriously rainy coasts of Guipúzcoa and Vizcaya provide respite from the summer sizzle of the central and southern plains.

Basque nationalism was born in the 1890s, although Basque culture and language are much older. (Prior to this time Basques were organized in tribal units and seigneurial domains.) The regional flag is the octogenarian Union Jack-like Ikurriña, created by brothers Sabino and Luís de Arana in 1894. Nationalism grew out of the combination of military defeat (the region had lost three Carlist civil wars in the late 19th century, and in the process, the use of their Medieval *fueros,* or laws) and rapid modernization, which threatened traditional values and forced a search for supposedly pre-modern identities. Outside of País Vasco and northern Navarra, Basques live in sizable concentrations in southwestern France, Idaho, Texas, Nevada, and California.

A minority of Basques seek full independence. Under the Franco regime, Euskadi eta Askatasuna (ETA; Euskadi and Liberty) began an anti-Madrid terrorist movement that has lasted over 30 years. The radical ETA-affiliated party, Herri Batasuna (the United People), draws loud and significant support, though it has declined in recent years; ETA's violent tactics are roundly eschewed. Targets are almost exclusively military, though explosions of car bombs sometimes include civilian areas. Since País Vasco is pushing Madrid for a European-gauge rail link with France, and asking EU countries for aid in adjusting to Maastricht, acts which antagonize foreigners can only be detrimental. With the 100,000 job losses between 1975 and 1982 and the recent recession fresh in mind, the País Vasco government is more concerned with economic acclimation than political independence, and it is trying to foster a "competitive advantage" with value-added steel, machine tools, and food.

Speaking of which, few traditions can match the depth and sophistication of Basque cuisine. Gastronomic clubs (until recently all male) are a tradition in San Sebastián, where members vie with each other in the invention of new dishes. Spaniards throughout the peninsula prize *bacalao a la vizcaina* (salted cod in a tomato sauce), preparations *a la vasca* (in a delicate parsley-steeped white wine sauce), and *chipirones en su tinta* (baby squids in their own ink). *Tapas* in the País Vasco are called *pintxos* (or *pinchos),* and are regional specialties.

As a general rule, choose buses over trains in the region; they are faster and often cheaper. All regional tourist offices stock a guide for Compostelan pilgrims and art lovers called *Los Caminos de Santiago* (The Roads to Saint James), and the comprehensive booklet *Guía de Recursos* (Guide to Tourist Resources) with a wealth of information on museums, festivals, and restaurants. Rural tourism is being heavily promoted by the regional authorities (lodgings in renovated farmhouses and cottages 1250-3500ptas per person), here as elsewhere in Spain; tourist offices in major Basque cities are stocked with brochures on this *agroturismo*.

EUSKERA

Linguists still cannot pinpoint the origin of *euskera*, An agglomerate non-Indoeuropean language with similarities to both Caucasian and African tongues, *euskera's* roots suggest that the prehistoric Basques may have migrated from the Caucasus through Africa. Historically referred to by other Spaniards as *la lengua del diablo* (the devil's tongue)—though supposedly even he could only muster three words—*euskera* has become a symbol of cultural self-determination. It's spoken chiefly in Guipúzcoa, Vizcaya, and northern Navarra by perhaps half a million native speakers, a minority in every region, although it is spreading through *ikastolas* (all-Basque schools), Basque TV, and an increasing number of publications. Because the 1979 autonomy (in which Basques were placed at the helm of all but their foreign affairs) somewhat depoliticized the linguistic question, some of the Basque intelligentsia have begun to question the wisdom of a tongue that cuts them off from the rest of Spanish and Latin American culture.

■■■ BILBAO (BILBO)

Native son and writer Miguel de Unamuno enthused: "the whole world is a great big Bilbao." Indeed, Bilbao (pop. 380,000) is cemented in reality, while conserving an elegance and enthusiasm rare for such a pragmatic city. Few visitors come, but even before the current spree of renovations got underway, those who could see past the smokestacks, abandoned warehouses, and sooty facades delighted in the city's site upon steep hills, its medieval quarter tucked in the crook of a great river estuary, and the grandiose edifices which attest to Bilbao's 19th-century economic and cultural ambitions.

Bilbao is the industrial engine of the entire Basque region. Historically, its ports served as the key shipping link between Castilla and Flanders. In the 16th century, the city was the birthplace of mercantile and commercial law emulated worldwide. As capital of the province of Vizkaya, Bilbao has produced its share of nationalists: Sabino Arana, founder of the Basque nationalist party Herri Batasuna, and José Antonio Aguirre, the first *lehendakari* (president) of the Basque government.

Hard at work as usual, the city forgot to participate in the national primping and preening for the now-legendary 1992. But Bilbao's work will pay off in good time—look out 1996. The Metro (already underway) is scheduled to be ready by then, and plans for a central bus station are also shooting for the millennium. Don't judge the city by the dirt under its nails—with an outstanding art museum, several parks, and orgiastic nightlife, Bilbao rewards the perceptive.

ORIENTATION AND PRACTICAL INFORMATION

Bilbao is divided into two quarters, the modern quarter and the **casco viejo,** across the Ría de Bilbao. In the new quarter, two blocks from the river, the main artery **Gran Vía de Don Diego López de Haro** sprouts from one side of **Plaza de España.** Nearly all important transport terminals, stops, and stations cluster around Pl. España and its offshoots, whereas the city's parks and scenic plazas spread out from the circular **Plaza de Federico Moyúa,** halfway down the Gran Vía.

Puente del Arenal, only two blocks from Pl. España, spans the river to link the new town with the so-called "seven streets" of the *casco viejo.* **Plaza de Arriaga,** at the foot of Puente del Arenal, is the *casco viejo's* main plaza.

From any one of the 16 bus stations, navigate toward the Gran Vía, which leads to Pl. España, Puente del Arenal, and the *casco viejo.*

> **Tourist Office: Oficina de Turismo de Bilbao,** Pl. Arriaga, s/n (tel. 416 00 22; fax 416 81 68), in the enormous Teatro Arriaga. From Pl. España, take C. Navarra to Puente del Arenal. Pl. Arriaga is on the right, just across the river. English-speaking staff gleefully shares truckloads of pamphlets and maps. Their booklet about Bilbao (available in English, 200ptas) practically puts us out of business. Publishes a monthly bulletin on city events. Open Mon.-Fri. 9:30am-1:30pm and 4-8pm, Sat.

9am-2pm, Sun. 10am-2pm. Omnipotent **information service** can be called at tel. (010) 424 17 00 from outside Bilbao.

El Corte Inglés: Gran Vía, 7-9 (tel. 424 22 11), on the east side of Pl. España. They have a **map. Currency exchange:** 1% commission (250pta min. charge). They also offer novels and guidebooks in English, haircutting, supermarket, both cafeteria and restaurant, and **telephones.** Open Mon.-Sat. 10am-9pm.

Budget Student Travel Office: TIVE, Gran Vía, 50 (tel. 441 42 77), 8 bl. east of Pl. España. Open Mon.-Fri. 9am-2pm.

Consulates: See Spain Essentials: Embassies and Consulates.

Currency Exchange: Banks have best rates. Open in the summer Mon.-Fri. 9am-2pm; rest of the year Mon.-Thurs. 9am-5:30pm, Fri.-Sat. 9am-2pm. **Hotel Ercilla,** C. Ercilla, 37 (tel. 410 20 00), from Pl. España down Gran Vía to Pl. Federico Moyúa, then left on C. Ercilla. 1% commission (250ptas min. charge). Open 24hrs. **El Corte Inglés** (see above). Open for exchange Mon.-Sat. 10am-8pm.

American Express: Viaca, Alameda de Recalde, 68 (tel. 444 48 58), off Autonomía. Open Mon.-Fri. 9am-1:30pm and 4:30-7:30pm, Sat. 10am-1pm.

Post Office: Main office, Alameda Urquijo, 19 (tel. 422 05 48; fax 443 00 24). Walk 1 bl. down Gran Vía from Pl. España and turn left after El Corte Inglés; it's on the corner with C. Bertendona. Open for information and Lista de Correos Mon.-Fri. 8am-10pm, Sat. 8am-3pm; for stamps daily 8am-10pm; for **telegrams** and **fax** daily 8am-midnight; 24-hr. telegrams by phone. **Postal Code:** 48071.

Telephones: C. Barroeta Aldamar, 7. From Pl. España walk 2 blocks down C. Buenos Aires, turn left on C. Colón de Larreátegui, then an immediate right. Open Mon.-Fri. 9am-9pm, Sat. 10:30am-1:30pm and 5-9pm. **Telephone Code:** 94.

Flights: (tel. 453 06 40), 9km from Bilbao in Sondica (Sondika). To get there take the Bizkai Bus A-3247 (Transportes Colectivos tel. 475 82 00) from C. Sendeja next to the Ayuntamiento, left after crossing the river into the old town (every 40min. 6am-10:30pm, 40min., 130ptas). Served by all major European airlines. **Iberia office,** C. Ercilla, 20 (tel. 424 43 00; at airport 471 12 10), at the corner of C. Colón de Larreátegui. Open Mon.-Fri. 9am-1:15pm and 3:30-6:45pm.

Trains: Bilbao has 6 train stations, each with at least 2 names; the major ones huddle near Puente del Arenal.

RENFE: Estación de Abando/del Norte, Pl. España, 2 (tel. 423 86 36 or 423 86 23). A monolithic structure. Ticket booth open 7am-11pm. To: Madrid (3 per day, including 1 *talgo* and 2 night, 5¾-8¾hr., 3800-4400ptas); Barcelona (2 per day, including 1 night, 10¾-11½hr., 4500-5000ptas); Sevilla (1 night train per day, 13¾hr., 6100-7500ptas); Salamanca (1 per day, 6¼hr., 2900-3200ptas); La Coruña (3 per day, including 2 night, 12¼-13¾hr., 5000-5800ptas).

FEVE: Estación de FEVE, C. Bailén, 2 (tel. 423 22 66). From Pl. España walk down C. Navarra toward the river and take a right just before the bridge. A huge tiled building on the water. Information open Mon.-Fri. 7am-10pm. To Oviedo (2 per day, 5hr.); change trains in Santander (3 per day, 2½hr., 805ptas).

Ferrocarriles Vascongados (FFVV)/Eusko Trenbideak (ET): Has three train stations. Obscenely slow—take the bus instead. To: Guernica (1hr.); Plentzia beaches; and regional towns. For info, call tel. 433 95 00 or ask at tourist office.

Buses: Bilbao's bus system is even harder to figure out than the trains. The tourist office can help. Of the 20 lines with departure points in the city, 6 stand out.

ANSA (GETSA, VIACAR), C. Autonomía, 17 (tel. 444 31 00). From Pl. España down C. Hurtado de Amézaga to Pl. Zabálburu, bearing right on C. Autonomía for 2 bl.; enter through Bar Ansa. To: Burgos (3-4 per day, 2hr., 1305ptas); Madrid (9 per day, 5hr., 3035ptas); Barcelona (4 per day, 7hr., 4450ptas); León (Mon.-Sat. 1 per day, 7hr., 2655ptas).

Compañía Automóviles Vascongados (CAV), C. Hurtado de Amézaga, Túnel de RENFE (tel. 423 78 06). In Estación de Abando (see Trains above). To Guernica (Mon.-Sat. 5-7 per day, Sun. 2 per day, 270ptas) and Lekeitio (same buses, 1¼hr., 525ptas).

ENATCAR, C. Autonomía, 4 (tel. 444 00 25), off Pl. Zabálburu. Ticket booth open Mon.-Sat. 9am-1pm and 4-8pm, Sun. 9am-noon. Buses depart from adjacent Pl. Zabálburu. To Valladolid (Mon.-Sat. 1 per day, 5hr., 2180ptas) and Badajoz (1 per day, 12hr., 5640ptas).

PESA, C. Hurtado de Amézaga, Edificio RENFE (tel. 424 88 99), in Estación de Abando (see Trains above). To San Sebastián (16-25 per day, 1¼hr., 960ptas).

La Unión, C. Henao, 29 (tel. 424 08 36). From Pl. España walk down Gran Vía 2 bl., turn right onto Alameda Mazarredo, follow for 4 bl., then take the next left on C. Henao. To: Vitoria-Gasteiz (8-10 per day, 1½hr., 595ptas); Logroño (3-4 per day, 1½hr.); Pamplona (3-5 per day, 2hr., 1375ptas); Zaragoza (2 per day, 3½hr., 2400ptas).

ALSA-Intercar, Alameda de Recalde, 68 (tel. 421 03 63), near Pl. Amézola. To: Santander (14 per day, 2¼hr., 845ptas); Irún (6 per day, 2hr., 1065ptas); La Coruña (2 per day, 12hr., 5770ptas); Zaragoza (6 per day, 4hr., 1390ptas).

Public Transportation: Bilbobús (tel. 475 82 00) runs 23 lines across the city (6am-11:30pm, 85ptas, 10-ride coupon 520ptas). The tourist office has a detailed map. **Bizkai Bus** connects Bilbao to suburbs and the airport in Sondica (75-150ptas). (A **subway** running through the center of the new city and the *casco viejo* is scheduled to begin operation by 1996.)

Taxis: Radio Taxi Bizkaia (tel. 416 23 00). **Radio Taxi Bilbao** (tel. 444 88 88). The tourist office map marks taxi queues. To airport 1500ptas.

Car Rental: Avis, Alameda Dr. Areilza, 34 (tel. 427 57 60). From Pl. España walk 9 bl. down Gran Vía (away from the river) and turn left; on the corner of C. Simón Bolívar. Call for reservations. Must be at least 23. Renault Clio *tarifa amiga* (all-inclusive) 7500ptas. Open Mon.-Fri. 8am-1:30pm and 4-7:30pm, Sat. 8am-1pm. **Europcar,** C. Rodríguez Arias, 49 (tel. 442 28 49), 3 bl. past AmEx office at the corner of C. Máximo Aguirre. Must be at least 21. Peugeot 205 4300ptas per day, 43ptas per km. Open Mon.-Fri. 9am-1pm and 4-7:30pm, Sat. 9am-1pm.

Luggage Storage: In **Estación de Abando** (lockers 400ptas). Get tokens at *cercanías* booth. Open 7am-11pm.

Lost Property: tel. 445 03 00.

English Bookstores: Casa del Libro, C. Colón de Larreátegui, 44 (tel. 424 07 04), off Alameda de Recalde. Guidebooks, literature, poetry, trashy novels, and Cliff's Notes. Open Mon.-Sat. 9:30am-1:30pm. **El Corte Inglés** (see above). Always dependable, always convenient.

Gay Information: EHGAM, Escalinatas de Solokoetxe, 4 (tel. 415 07 19). Open Mon.-Fri. 8-10pm, or write them at Apdo. 1667, 48080 Bilbao. Fri.-Sat. it's a gay and lesbian disco. **Gays por la Salud, Asociación T4,** C. Autonomía, 56, 3rd fl. (tel. (908) 67 58 80). Open daily 10am-10pm. Support groups and health info.

Red Cross: C. Ondarrolo (tel. 422 22 22).

Ambulance: tel. 473 16 34.

24-Hour Pharmacy: Check listing on the door of any pharmacy, or call the municipal police.

Medical Services: Hospital Civil de Basurto, Av. Montevideo, 18 (tel. 441 88 00 or 442 40 51). Emergency tel. 442 40 51.

Emergency: dial 088.

Police: Municipal, C. Luis Briñas (tel. 441 10 04, in emergency 092). **National** (tel. 431 00 00, in emergency 091).

ACCOMMODATIONS

Other than during the August festival season (when rates can be higher than those listed below), most areas have never heard the words *temporada alta* (high season). The tourist office has a list of recommended budget *pensiones,* most of which are in the *casco viejo.* Starting points are **Plaza Arriaga,** at the base of the bridge, down the stairs to the right, and **Calle Arenal,** which runs up to the left.

Pensión Ladero, C. Lotería, 1, 4th fl. (tel. 415 09 32). From Pl. Arriaga, take C. Bidebarrieta and turn left on C. Lotería. Each huge room has a chandelier, and most have terraces and oil paintings. Spotless bathrooms. Singles 1500ptas. Doubles 2500ptas.

Pensión Mardones, C. Jardines, 4, 3rd fl. (tel. 415 31 05). From the bridge, take C. Bidebarrieta and turn right. Brand spanking new. Some balconied rooms with geraniums. Singles 1500ptas, with double bed 2000ptas. Doubles 2600ptas, with 2 beds or with bath 3500ptas. Triples 4000ptas.

Pensión Mendez, C. Santa María, 13, 4th fl. (tel. 416 03 64). From the bridge, turn right on C. Ribera; C. Santa María is on the left. Five floors insulate the *pensión* from the raging nightlife below. Glossy bedspreads and firm mattresses. All but 2 rooms have balconies. Singles 1500ptas. Doubles 2500ptas. Triples 3600ptas.

Pensión de la Fuente, C. Sombrería, 2 (tel. 416 99 89). From mid-C. Arenal, turn left on C. Correo, follow 1 bl., then left again. Clean, carpeted halls and large tiled bathrooms. Shoot for the double with couch by the TV room. Singles 1500ptas. Doubles 2500ptas, with bath 3500ptas. Triples 3500ptas.

Hostal Arana, C. Bidebarrieta, 2 (tel. 415 64 11), amid all the trendy shops off Pl. Arriaga. Pink arched halls and nautical style reception area. Mass produced rooms, most with phones. There's even an elevator. Singles 3300ptas, with bath 4500ptas. Doubles 4300ptas, with bath 5500ptas. Breakfast for groups 275ptas. Prices don't include IVA. Closed Dec. 20-Jan. 8.

Hostal-Residencia Jofra, C. Elcano, 34, 1st fl. (tel. 421 29 49), our only listing in the new city. From Pl. España, walk 5 bl. down C. Hurtado de Amézaga past Estación de Abando and turn right. Pleasant rooms off a quiet street. Singles 1600ptas. Doubles 2700ptas. Closed Aug.

FOOD

Restaurants and bars near the sights on the "seven streets" are as cramped as the medieval *casco viejo* itself, but offer hearty local dishes. Dining spots in the modern quarter offer more variety and amenities, but not nearly as much flavor. **Mercado de la Ribera,** on the bank of the river heading left from the tourist office, is the biggest indoor market in Europe. It's worth a trip even if you're not eating. (Open Mon.-Thurs. and Sat. 7:45am-2pm, Fri. 7:45am-2pm and 5-8pm.)

In the Casco Viejo

Charcutería Claudio, C. Esperanza, 18, past the train station. *"La feria del jamón."* Ham, ham, and more heavenly ham. An ominous cane hanging among the hams on the ceiling reads: "If you don't pay, I come down." *Jamón serrano,* cheese, hearty bread, and beverage about 700ptas. Sandwiches 200-400ptas. Open 6-11pm. Their store across the street open 10am-2pm and 5-9pm.

Aitxiar, C. María Muñoz, 8. The best lunch for its price in Bilbao. 3-fork lunch *menú* 900ptas. Open 1:30-3:30pm and 8:30-11pm. Visa, AmEx accepted.

Restaurante Juanak, C. Somera, 10. Hand-painted menu on the wall and blues booming from the speakers. 20-something crowd. 54 *bocadillos* including vegetarian options (325-500ptas), choice array of salads (450-700ptas). Open Sun.-Wed. 1pm-12:30am, Thurs. 1pm-1am, Fri.-Sat. 1pm-3am.

Bar-Restaurante Bizkaia II, C. Jardines, 2. From the river turn left onto C. Santa María, then right on C. Jardines. Sawdust on the floor, kegs and wine cartons all around, and *fútbol*-team photos on the wall. *Bocadillos* 225-400ptas. Lunch *menú* with *paella* 800ptas, Sun. 900ptas. *Platos combinados* 750ptas. Fawning service. Open 1-4pm and 7-11pm. Visa, AmEx accepted.

In the Modern Quarter

Groceries: Eroski, C. Licenciado Poza, between Alameda Dr. Areilza and C. Gregorio Revilla. Open Mon.-Fri. 9am-2pm and 6-8pm, Sat. 9am-2pm. **El Corte Inglés** (5th fl.) is a bit more chic (see Practical Information).

Café La Granja, Pl. España, 3 (tel. 423 08 13), opposite Estación de Abando. Feels like the Orient Express, blood-thirsty Brooks Brothers bankers included. Breakfast of *café* and *tostadas* 200ptas. *Menú* 1100ptas. Open 10am-4pm, *menú* after 1:30pm.

Fük, C. General Concha, 2 (tel. 410 15 64), just off Pl. Pedro Equillor behind Hotel Carlton. The best Fük in town. Spanish fast food with a whisper of German zing. Hamburgers and sandwiches 275-525ptas. Try the *zipi-zape* (meatballs, 350ptas). Breakfast of *café* and a *bocadillo* 310ptas. Open Mon.-Fri. 9am-midnight, Sat. 6pm-2am, Sun. 6-11pm.

SIGHTS

Bilbao's **Museo de Bellas Artes** (tel. 441 95 36), ranked among Europe's best, hordes aesthetic riches behind an unassuming facade. Among its Spanish and Flemish (12th-19th century) holdings are versions of *St. Francis Praying* by El Greco and Zurbarán, Goya's *María Luisa* (wife of Carlos IV) and some of his tragedy engravings, a Gauguin, and numerous canvases by Basque painters. A substantial contemporary abstract art collection and a detail of one of Velázquez's red-nosed Portrait of *Felipe IV* are highlights. The ivy-covered building sits on the edge of **Parque de Doña Casilda de Iturriza,** on the west end of the city. From Pl. Federico Moyúa (with Pl. España behind you), angle right on C. Elcano and follow it to Pl. Museo. (Open Tues.-Sat. 10am-1:30pm and 4-7:30pm, Sun. 10am-2pm. Free.)

The world's 3rd **Guggenheim** museum (after New York and Venice) is currently under construction, and should open by 1997. It will make Bilbao a contemporary art powerhouse.

The **Museo Arqueológico, Etnográfico, e Histórico de Vizcaya,** C. Cruz, 4 (tel. 415 54 23), housed in a beautiful old stone cloister, does Basque culture. The upstairs galleries have displays on hand-weaving, blacksmithing, armaments, and a few rooms devoted to the sea, with a couple of amazingly large well-preserved boats. The museum is in the old city; walk past Pensión de la Fuente away from C. Correo to Pl. Miguel de Unamuno, whence C. Cruz springs. (Open Tues.-Sat. 10am-1:30pm and 4-7pm, Sun. 10:30am-1:30pm. Free.)

Surrounded by a bodyguard of tower blocks, the 16th-century **Basílica de Nuestra Señora de Begoña** sits atop a hill overlooking the old quarter. The *patrona* of the province shines brightly in a long flowing robe over the altar. From Pl. Miguel de Unamuno, a long-distance flight of stairs makes the ascent to heaven, passing by the old cemetery (30min.). Take the first right at the top on C. Virgen de Begoña, which leads to the church. (Open for mass at 7am, 9am, 11am, 6pm, and 8pm.) **Ascensores** (elevators) transport the less athletic (every 10min., 6am-11pm, 20ptas). Go up Plazuela de San Nicolás and turn left on C. Esperanza; the *ascensores* are on the right after the athletic center.

The best view of Bilbao is from the *mirador* on **Monte Archanda,** to the north of the old town. The city's intricate detail spreads out below like the ultimate Lego model. For the *funicular* to the top, turn left from Pl. Arenal with your back to the new town and follow the riverside road past the Ayuntamiento. On Po. Campo de Volantin, turn right on C. Espalza (2nd after the Ayuntamiento) and zig-zag left at its end. (*Funicular* every 15min., 7:15am-10pm, Sun. 7:15am-11pm, one-way 77ptas.)

Beaches are within easy reach by train, north of the city at **Plencia** (Plentzia) or at **Sopelana** along the way. Plencia in particular has cobblestone character. **Getxo** also lies just a little nearer the surf; its illuminated **Puente Colgante** (suspension bridge) fords the river, leading to a spate of all-night bars. The city cashes in on late-night partiers; the bridge carriage costs 25ptas before midnight and 75ptas after. You can also take a **bus** here from Pl. Ensanche in Bilbao (150ptas), near the market. Past midnight, revelers will miss the last train and find themselves obliged to taxi home (2000-2500ptas).

Other sites of interest in Vizcaya include the rock-climbing fishing village of **Elantxobe,** the international surfing capital of **Mundaka,** and the ecological reserve of **Urdaibai.**

ENTERTAINMENT

A city with so many comfortable bars can be expected to have a thriving after-dark scene, especially on weekends. In the **casco viejo** people spill out into the streets to tipple *chiquitos,* small glasses of beer or wine characteristic of the region (the sport is called *chiquiteo).* Youngsters jam C. Licenciado Poza, inflicting teeny-bopperness on everyone in sight. With 200 bars within 200m, **Calle Ledesma** exerts a similar pull. Upscale Bilbao retires to the **Jardines de Albia** to get its *copas.* The coolest, most radical bar in town is **Herriko Taberna** (The People's Tavern), C. Ronda, 20. Unmarked save for an outer wall splattered with militant graffiti, its interior is papered with political posters and photos of Basque detainees. If it's closed, don't despair; they're hanging out six streets over on **Calle Barrencalle.**

For a bit of soccer action, head for "La Catedral," a.k.a. the **Campo de San Mamés,** and watch Athlétic de Bilbao electrify the crowd. The stadium is on C. Felipe Serrate, a 1st right off Av. Sabino Arana at the end of Gran Vía. (Soccer season Sept.-May, games Sat. 8pm and Sun. 5pm, tickets from 1200ptas.) In July, don't miss the bar scene, glued to the tube, with cycling fans watching regional cycling idol and Tour de France champ Miguel Induraín.

The massive blowout *fiesta* in honor of *Nuestra Señora de Begoña* takes place during **Semana Grande,** which starts the weekend after Aug. 15. Music, theater, and bullfights climax in a fireworks display. Documentary filmmakers from the world over gather here in November for the **Festival Internacional de Cine Documental de Bilbao.**

■■■ GUERNICA (GERNIKA)

"If the cities are destroyed by flames, if women and children are victims of asphyxiating gases, if the populations of open cities, situated at long distances from the front, fall victim to the bombs and torpedoes launched by airplanes, then the immediate end to hostilities is possible and a government where nerves resist all tests will not be able to resist such for long."

Such was the philosophy, outlined by M.K.L. Dertzen in 1935, behind the massive aerial bombing that destroyed 70% of Guernica on April 26, 1937. The Nazi "Condor Legion" dumped an estimated 29,000kg of incendiary and shrapnel bombs on market day, killing hundreds of civilians and animals, and demolishing the town. In the course of the three-hour raid, neither the strategic bridge nor arms factory was scratched; mass aerial bombing of undefended civilian populations had made its European debut.

Guernica was etched into world consciousness as the scene of one of the most gratuitously brutal acts of the Civil War. It moved Pablo Picasso to paint his epic *Guernica,* now exhibited in Madrid's Reina Sofía. Fascists pointed to the painting and asked Picasso whether he had done it. "No, you did," he replied. A guidebook to a 1991 Guernica exhibition provides an excellent historical resource (in Spanish, 350ptas). Eduardo Chillida's arresting **La casa de nuestro padre** *(Fure aitareu etxea,* Our Father's House), a monument to peace, plurality, and understanding, was erected on the 50th anniversary of the bombing. From the RENFE station, follow C. Adolfo Urioste as far as it goes. Turn right at the top and cross the little wooden bridge. Farther on is a Henry Moore sculpture called *Great Figure in a Shelter.*

The emotional focus of the town is the **Arbola Zaharra** and its descendants. The remains of this 2000-year-old oak tree stand beneath an 8-pillared dome next to the **Casa de Juntas,** where the Vizkaya General Assembly meets. Medieval Basques gathered to debate community issues under the oak. Later, Guernica became the political center of Vizcaya. When the area passed into Castilian hands, the monarchs were expected to make a ritual voyage to Guernica and its oak and swear to respect the autonomy of the *juntas* (local governments) and local *fueros* (laws). The oak's offspring, an august tree of 300 years, grows next to the building behind the grillwork fence. A grandchild oak was planted in 1979 to celebrate the return of regional autonomy. (Open 10am-2pm and 4-7pm; Oct.-May 10am-2pm and 4-6pm. Free.) Paintings and artifacts on display in the **Museo de Euskal Herria** help with Basque history. (Open Tues.-Sat. 10am-2pm and 4-7pm, Sun. 10am-1:30pm. Free.)

Verdant parks surrounding the Casa de Juntas contrast with the urban sprawl of the rest of town. To get here from the train station, walk 1 bl. up C. Adolfo Urioste and across the tidy flower beds on the hillside to the town's central square, Pl. Pasileskuko. From the top of the stairs, Casa de Juntas is directly ahead; the Museo de Euskal Herria and the monuments are in the park just behind the museum.

To watch the fastest ball sport on earth, a local invention and passion known alternatively, and with slight variations, as Jai-Alai, *Pelota Vasca,* or *Cesta,* head for the

Frontón de Jai-Alai, C. Carlos Gougoti (tel. 625 62 50; Mon. and Fri. nights, 1500ptas).

Practical Information To reach the **tourist office,** C. Artecalle, 8 (tel. 625 58 92), from the train station, walk straight 2 bl. up Adolfo Ucoiste and turn right onto C. Artecalle; the office is on column-lined Andra María Walk, off Artecalle to the right. They've got a list of hotels, *casas particulares,* and restaurants, and a multilingual, indexed map. (Open Mon.-Sat. 10am-2pm and 4-8pm, Sun. 10am-2pm.) The **post office** at Pl. Foruen, s/n (tel. 625 03 87), is across the street from the tourist office. (Open Mon.-Fri. 8am-3pm, Sat. 9am-1pm.) **Public phones** are by the train station. The **postal code** is 48300; the **telephone code** 94. For a **taxi,** call tel. 625 10 02. For a **24-hr. pharmacy,** check listing on the door of the pharmacy at C. Artecalle, 1. **Medical services** are available at the *ambulatorio,* C. San Juan, 1 (tel. 625 42 46). An **ambulance** can be summoned at tel. 088, which is also the general **emergency** number. **Municipal police** are on C. Artecalle, 8 (tel. 625 05 54).

Comprehensive transportation information is available at the tourist office. To get to San Sebastián, it's best to go back to Bilbao and take the bus from there. **Trains** (tel. 625 11 82) journey to Bilbao (every hr., 50min., 250ptas). Compañía de Automóviles Vazcongados (tel. 423 78 06) sends **buses** from a spot 1 bl. left of the train station. To Bilbao (3-17 per day, 45min., 270ptas) and Lekeitio (2-6 per day, 45min., 270ptas).

Accommodations and Food Guernica is best as a daytrip, but if you wish to dally, **Hostal Iratxe,** C. Industria, 4 (tel. 625 64 63), has new, big rooms with TVs. If nobody's home, try Bar Frontón (tel. 625 58 17), down the street; the bartender owns the *hostal.* (Singles 3000ptas. Doubles 4000ptas.) From the train station, go up C. Urioste and turn right on C. Pablo Picasso, which becomes C. Industria.

Market fans go to the huge round building on the pedestrian street next to the tourist office. (Open Mon.-Fri. 9am-1:30pm and 4:30-8:30pm, Sat. 9am-1:30pm.) **Restaurante Julen,** #14 on C. Industria, has unvarnished wood tables and a fine selection of *pinchos. Platos combinados* 550-1800ptas. **Bar-Restaurante Pospolin,** on central C. Artecalle, 4 (underneath the archway on the right), fixes sandwiches (250-400ptas) and multiple *platos combinados* (600-900ptas). (Open 8:30am-1am.)

■ NEAR GUERNICA

Settlement in the area goes back at least 17,000 years, and at the **Cueva de Santimamiñe,** 5km north of Guernica, you can ogle a well-preserved set of prehistoric paintings on cave walls. Some (mainly nationalists) argue that the Basque language originated here when the population abandoned the caves during the Neolithic period, spreading their tongue to the rest of the area. (Admission by free guided tour (in Spanish) only. Mon.-Fri. 10am, 11:15am, 12:30pm, 4:30pm. 15 people max. per tour.) No public transport comes near the cave; the carless must hike or take a cab.

A 3km hike from the caves, the colorful **Bosque Pintado de Oma** has been called a metaphor of Euskal Herria. Completed in 1987, the arboreal artwork is the creation of Basque artist Agustín Ibarrola, who spent years painting the several hundred pine trees. Different groupings of trees make up independent compositions; the intended observation spots are clearly marked. To get to the forest from the caves, follow the well-delineated trail from the parking lot (about 1hr.).

■ ■ ■ SAN SEBASTIÁN (DONOSTIA)

A blue-blood resort town in a come-here-to-die setting, this provincial capital (pop. 207,000) and Franco-Spanish crossing point glitters on the shores off the Mar Cantábrico. Wide boulevards, garden avenues, and stately, ornate buildings give the city a regal air. The mild climate is well-described by Hemingway in *The Sun Also Rises:* "Even on a hot day San Sebastián has a certain early-morning quality. The trees

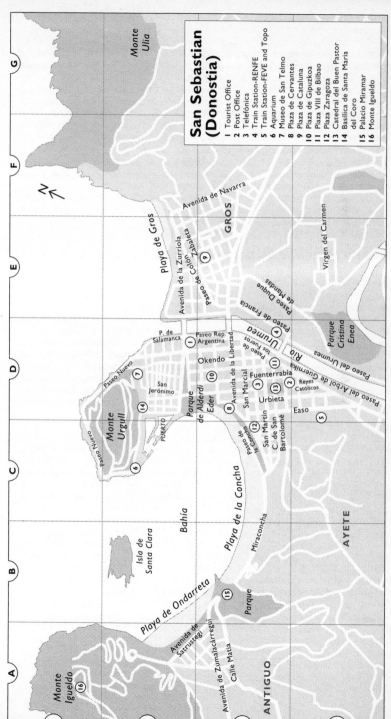

San Sebastian (Donostia)

1 Tourist Office
2 Post Office
3 Telefónica
4 Train Station-RENFE
5 Train Station-FEVE and Topo
6 Aquarium
7 Museo de San Telmo
8 Plaza de Cervantes
9 Plaza de Cataluna
10 Plaza de Gipuzkoa
11 Plaza VIII de Bilbao
12 Plaza Zaragoza
13 Catedral del Buen Pastor
14 Basílica de Santa María del Coro
15 Palacio Miramar
16 Monte Igueldo

seem as though their leaves were never quite dry. The streets feel as though they had just been sprinkled."

By day, crowds flock to La Concha, the crescent-shaped strip of sand that hugs the Mar Cantábrico. On either side of this giant playground, two steep hills elbow their way into the sea. They call San Sebastián "the seashell with the pearl" because La Concha curves like an oyster round an abrupt, wood-capped islet in the bay.

Of course, like any other earthly paradise, San Sebastián has had its troubles. The city has been set ablaze numerous times, and was destroyed in 1813 courtesy of Anglo-Portuguese troops "liberating" it from Napoleon. When the old city was rebuilt, however, it was afforded an internal architectural consistency and a Neo-classical charm. The main square of the *parte vieja* has been a focal point for demonstrations of Basque nationalism. With the granting of regional autonomy for the País Vasco and the dissipation of support for ETA, the tensions that once marred this pleasure-loving city are lessening. Residents and their guests ignore the political graffiti lingering on walls, preferring to enjoy the sun, surf, and sights.

San Sebastián's annual jazz, dance, and film festivals, its tireless nightlife, and its proximity to the French border appeal to visitors of every sort. Enjoy all San Sebastián has to offer, but don't expect to cut corners; over a century and a half of exclusivity is still reflected in the prices.

ORIENTATION AND PRACTICAL INFORMATION

Street and place names on signs are in either *castellano* or *euskera*. The difference can cause slight letter changes (Castilian V becomes B, CH becomes TX). Don't panic: usually both names are present; the street guide on the tourist office map gives both versions in its index.

The Río Urumea splits San Sebastián in two. The city center and most of the monuments are on the west side of the river, in a peninsula that juts into the sea. In the center of the peninsula is the **parte vieja** (old city), where the nightlife rages and budget accommodations and restaurants cluster. To the south, the **Catedral del Buen Pastor** sits on the edge of **Calle de San Martín,** in the heart of the commercial district. Three bridges span the river: **Puente María Cristina** to the south, **Puente Santa Catalina** in the middle, and **Puente Zurriola** to the north. On the west side of the river, **Avenida de la Libertad** runs from Puente Santa Catalina directly to the **Playa de la Concha,** which embraces the large, placid bay. From La Concha, facing the water, the smaller **Playa de Ondarreta** is on the left, **Monte Urgull** on the right.

The east side of the river is home to the **RENFE station** and the **Barrio de Gros.** To get to the *parte vieja* from the station, head straight to Puente María Cristina, cross the bridge, then turn right along the river and walk four blocks north to Av. Libertad. Turn left and follow it to the **puerto** (port); the *parte vieja* fans out to the right, La Concha to the left. To get to the **tourist office** from the station, turn right after crossing Puente María Cristina and continue past Puente Santa Catalina; C. Reina Regente will be on the left.

The **bus station** is in the south of the city in Pl. Pío XII. **Avenida de Sancho el Sabio** runs to the right (north) straight toward the cathedral, the ocean, and the old town. To get to the tourist office, head down Av. Sancho el Sabio for about four blocks; at Pl. Centenario, bear right onto C. Prim, and follow it to Puente María Cristina. From here, follow the directions above.

Tourist Office: Municipal: Centro de Atracción y Turismo, C. Reina Regente, s/n (tel. 48 11 66; fax 48 11 72), in the vast Teatro Victoria Eugenia. Dedicated, English-speaking staff. Gorgeous indexed map. Transit and accommodations info available. Message bulletin board. The *Guía práctica* (500ptas in bookstores) is a gold mine of local information. Open Mon.-Sat. 8am-8pm, Sun. 10am-1pm; Oct.-May Mon.-Fri. 9am-1:30pm and 3:30-6:30pm, Sat. 9am-1pm. **Regional Office:** Po. Fueros, 1 (tel. 42 62 82), at Av. Libertad and Puente Santa Catalina. Info on Gipúzcoa, including *sidrerías* (see Entertainment). Open Mon.-Fri. 9am-2pm and 3-7pm, Sat.-Sun. 10am-7pm.

Budget Travel: TIVE, C. Tomás Gros, 3 (tel. 27 69 34), 1 bl. off Pl. Euskadi down C. Miracruz and then right; below street level. ISIC 500ptas. HI card 1800ptas. They process train, bus, and plane tickets only to international destinations. Message board with some travel info. Open Mon.-Fri. 9am-2pm.

Currency Exchange: Agencia de Cambio, C. San Martín, 35 (tel. 43 03 47), at the corner of C. Easo. Lower rates but no commission. Open daily 9am-9pm.

Banca Besné, C. Fuenterrabía, 4 (tel. 42 04 41), fourth left off Av. Libertad heading away from the river. Open Mon.-Sat. 9am-8pm, Sun. 9:30am-12:30pm; Oct.-June Mon.-Sat. 10am-1pm and 3:30-7pm.

Post Office: C. Urdaneta, s/n (tel. 46 49 14; fax 45 07 94), the street just south of the cathedral. Heading toward the beach on Av. Libertad, take a left on C. Fuenterrabía and walk 5 bl. Open for information and Lista de Correos Mon.-Fri. 8am-9pm, Sat. 9am-2pm; for stamps, **telegrams,** and **fax** Mon.-Fri. 8am-9pm, Sat. 9am-7pm. **Postal Code:** 20007.

Telephones: C. San Marcial, 29, 1 bl. from Av. Libertad, toward the cathedral. Open Mon.-Sat. 9:30am-11pm. Public phones are ubiquitous. **Telephone Code:** 943.

Flights: Airport (tel. 64 22 40). **Aviaco** (tel. 64 12 67). In Fuenterrabía (Hondarribia), 18km east of the city. Interurbanos buses to Fuenterrabía (every 12min., 7:48am-10pm). Information open 8am-1pm and 4-8pm. To Madrid (1-2 per day, 14,050ptas) and Barcelona (1 per day, 14,900ptas).

Trains: RENFE, Estación del Norte, Av. Francia, s/n (tel. 27 92 56), on the east side of Puente María Cristina. Information (tel. 28 35 99) open 7am-11pm. Rates and times vary by train type and date. To: Irún (22-36 per day, 25min., 115ptas); Vitoria-Gasteiz (12-13 per day, 1½-2¼hr., 750-1700ptas); Pamplona (4 per day, 1¾hr., 1200-1700ptas); Burgos (5-8 per day, 3-4hr., 2100-3200ptas); Zaragoza (3-4 per day, 4hr., 2200-2700ptas); Madrid (6 per day, including 1 *talgo* and 2 night, 6-9hr., 4200-5400ptas); Barcelona (1-2 per day, including 1 night, 8-9hr., 4300-4800ptas); Santiago de Compostela (2 per day, including 1 night, 11hr., 5300ptas); Sevilla (via Bilbao or Madrid); Valencia (1 per day, 15hr., 5600-6300ptas); Lisboa (1 per day, 15hr., 7500ptas); Paris (9 per day, including 2 night, 9800ptas; change at Hendaye, France). **RENFE office,** C. Camino, 1, on the corner with C. Oquendo, 1 bl. north of Puente Santa Catalina and one block west of the river. Open Mon.-Fri. 9am-1pm and 4-7pm, Sat. 9am-1pm.

Buses: Several private companies run from different points in the city. Most companies pass through the central station, on Pl. Pío XII, about 13 bl. south of Av. Libertad on Av. Sancho el Sabio. Buy tickets on the bus or at offices along Av. Sancho el Sabio (depending on company). Booklet from the tourist office covers all companies, with phone numbers and routes.

PESA (tel. 29 95 55, ext. 13). To: Bilbao (9-29 per day, 1¼hr., 960ptas); Vitoria-Gasteiz (12 per day, 1¾hr., 935ptas). Tickets next door on Av. Sancho el Sabio

Continental Auto, Av. Sancho el Sabio, 31 (tel. 46 90 74). To: Madrid (6 per day, 6hr., 3360ptas); Burgos (4-6 per day, 3¼hr., 1660ptas); Vitoria-Gasteiz (4-6 per day, 1¾hr., 840ptas).

La Roncalesa (tel. 46 10 64). To Pamplona (5 per day, 1½hr., 685ptas).

Irbarsa, Po. Vizcaya, 16 (tel. 45 75 00). To Barcelona (3 per day, 7hr., 2260ptas).

Turytans (tel. 46 23 60). To Paris (4-7 per week, 10hr., 6800ptas).

Enatcar (tel. 46 80 87). To London (2-4 per week, 22hr., 13,000ptas).

Interurbanos, from Pl. Guipozcoa (tel. 64 13 02). To Fuenterrabía (175ptas) and Irún (160ptas) every 12-15min., 7:45am-10pm, Sun. until 11pm.

Public Transportation: 19 bus routes (85ptas, 10-ride pass available at *tabaco* stores 475ptas). List of routes available at tourist office or call tel. 28 71 00.

Taxis: Radio Taxi Easo (tel. 46 76 66). **A.D.** (tel. 42 66 42).

Car Rental: All agencies are on C. San Martín or its side streets; take Av. Libertad toward the beach, turn left at C. Urbieta, then right after 3 bl. **Avis,** C. Triunfo, 2 (tel. 46 15 27 or 46 15 56), off Pl. Zaragoza. Must be 23 or over. Open Mon.-Fri. 8am-1pm and 4-7pm, Sat. 9am-1pm. **Europcar,** C. San Martín, 60 (tel. 46 17 17; fax 46 09 72). Must be 21 or over. Open Mon.-Fri. 9am-1pm and 4-7:30pm, Sat. 9am-1pm.

Mountain Bike Rental: Comet, Av. Libertad, 6 (tel. 42 66 37 or 42 23 51). ½-day 1500ptas, 1st day 2300ptas, each additional day 1000ptas. Open Mon.-Sat. 10am-9pm, closed Mon. mornings.

Luggage Storage: From RENFE station, cross Puente María Cristina, turn right, walk 1 bl., then take C. San Martín to the left; after 5 bl., left on C. Easo to #22. 175ptas per day. Bikes 350ptas per day. Open June 21-Sept. 21 8:30am-8:30pm.

Bar Self-Service, Po. Duque de Mandas, 49 (tel. 29 14 52), below street level behind RENFE station. 200ptas per day. Open winter Sun.-Fri. 8:30am-10:30pm.

Lost Property: Check with the **municipal police.** At the beach, check the *cabinas* below street level.

English Bookstore: Donosti, Pl. Bilbo, 2 (tel. 42 21 38), 1 bl. west of Puente María Cristina, near the cathedral. *Let's Go,* and mostly modern fiction. Open Mon.-Fri. 9am-1pm and 4:30-8pm, Sat. 9am-1pm. **Azoka,** C. Fuenterrabía, 19 (tel. 42 17 45), off Av. Libertad. Penguin Classics, Agatha Christie, and bestsellers. Open Mon.-Sat. 10am-1:30pm and 4-8pm.

Laundromat: Lavomatique, C. Iñigo, 13, off C. San Juan. Wash 450ptas per 4kg load. Dry 50ptas per 7min. Soap 25ptas. Ironing 50ptas. Open Mon.-Fri. 10am-1pm and 4-8pm, Sat.-Sun. and holidays 10am-1pm.

Public Toilets: Alameda del Boulevard, the pedestrian walk that runs toward the beach from Puente Zurriola. Open 9am-8:30pm. Also near Playa de Oudarreta, in the park at the corner of C. Matia and Av. Zumalacarregui, by the tunnel. Open 10am-2pm and 5-8:30pm. Both 10ptas, urinals free.

Public Showers: Pl. Easo, on C. Easo en route to Estación Amara. Hot showers 60ptas. Soap and towel 75ptas. Open daily 8am-1pm and 3-8pm. Toilets 10ptas.

Hiking Information: Club Vasco de Camping, San Marcial, 19 (tel. 42 84 79), 1 bl. south of Av. Libertad. Below street level. Organizes excursions too. Open Mon.-Fri. 6:30-8:30pm. **Izadi,** Po. Ramón, 20 (tel. 29 35 20). Bookstore of travel guides, hiking guides, and maps; many in English. Organizes tours and rents skis, wetsuits, and hiking equipment. Open Mon.-Sat. 10am-1pm and 4-8pm.

Red Cross: Hospital, C. Matías, 7 (tel. 21 46 00). **Ambulance:** tel. 22 22 22.

24-Hour Pharmacy: Ask the **municipal police** or check page 2 of *Diario Vasco.*

Medical Services: Casa de Socorro, C. Pedro Egaño, 8 (tel. 46 63 19 or 46 41 20).

Emergency: tel. 088.

Police: Municipal, C. Larramendi, 10 (tel. 45 00 00; emergency tel. 092).

ACCOMMODATIONS AND CAMPING

Desperate backpackers are forced to scrounge for rooms in July and August—particularly during *Sanfermines* (July 6-14) and Semana Grande (the week after Aug. 15). If you get away with 2500ptas per night, consider yourself lucky. Budget options congregate both in the **parte vieja** and around the **cathedral;** they're often two or more per stairway, so look for signs on the doors. Many places don't take reservations during the busy summer months. Almost all have winter heating.

The tourist office has lists of budget accommodations, and most *pensión* owners know *casas particulares* that take in guests—so don't be afraid to ask for help. Some people choose to sleep on the beach, but this is illegal and potentially dangerous. The police will kick beach-sleepers out, and the area is reputed to be full of shifty characters. Though it's by no means safe, others try crashing (in groups to discourage thieves) in the park near the RENFE station.

Albergue Juvenil la Sirena (HI), Po. Igueldo, 25 (group reservations tel. 31 02 68, guest phone 31 02 56; fax 21 40 90), near the beach in the far west end of the city. Bus #24 runs from train and bus stations to Av. Zumalacárregui (1st stop after the tunnel). Bus #5 drops you off one street further from hostel on C. Matia. From Zumalácarregui, take the street that angles toward the mountain (Av. Brunei) and turn left at its end. It's the big pink building. Brand-new facilities. Members only (flexible). Arrive early (8-10am). Midnight curfew; mid-June to Sept. 2am curfew. 1500ptas per person; winter 1300ptas. Over 26: 1700ptas; 1300ptas. Breakfast included. Lunch or dinner 650ptas. Sheets 350ptas. Luggage storage and washing machines included. 3-night max. stay in summer.

In the Parte Vieja

A lengthy walk from the stations, the *parte vieja* is brimming with reasonably priced *pensiones*. A prime location because of its proximity to Playa de la Concha and the port, this is where the action is at night; scores of *pensiones* sleep (or try to) above loud *pinchos* bars. The smart money calls ahead. **Alameda del Boulevard,** just west of Puente Zurriola, marks the southern border and is the major artery.

Pensión Amaiur, C. 31 de Agosto, 44, 2nd fl. (tel. 42 96 54). From Alameda del Boulevard, go up C. San Jerónimo to the end and turn left. Gorgeous. Showers last only 5min. Semana Santa and June 22-Sept. 21: Doubles 4500ptas. Triples 6000ptas. After Semana Santa-June 21: 3000ptas; 4200ptas. Sept. 22-before Semana Santa: 2500ptas; 3300ptas. 500pta *Let's Go* discount. Breakfast 200ptas.

Pensión Loinaz, C. San Lorenzo, 17 (tel. 42 67 14). Travelers have been gushing about this *pensión* since it opened in '93. Owners are delightful, the location ideal, the price fair, and the rooms choice. Semana Santa and July-Aug.: Doubles 4000-4500ptas. Triples 6000ptas. After Semana Santa-June: 3000ptas; 4300ptas. Sept. to before Semana Santa: 2500ptas; 3500ptas. 500pta *Let's Go* discount.

Pensión San Lorenzo, C. San Lorenzo, 2 (tel. 42 55 16), a right off C. Narrica from Alameda del Boulevard, on the corner of C. San Juan. Guests can use kitchen and fridge. Doubles 4000ptas. Triples 5000ptas. Sept.-June: 2300ptas; 3000ptas.

Pensión Larrea, Narrica, 21, 1st fl. (tel. 42 26 94). Singles 2500ptas. Doubles 4500ptas. Sept.-June: 2000ptas; 3000ptas.

Pensión Boulevard, Alameda del Boulevard, 24 (tel. 42 94 05). Doubles 5000ptas, with bath 7000ptas. Winter: 3500ptas; 5000ptas.

Pensión Arsuaga, C. Narrica, 3, 3rd fl. (tel. 42 06 81), off the middle of Alameda del Boulevard. Jovial owner runs a cheery *comedor.* Rare singles 2500ptas. Doubles 4000ptas. Sept.-June: 2500ptas; 3500ptas. Breakfast 400ptas. Lunch or dinner 900ptas. Can fill with students Oct.-May.

Pensión Urgull, C. Esterlines, 10, 3rd fl. (tel 43 00 47). From Alameda del Boulevard, right onto C. San Jerónimo, then the 2nd right from there. Singles 2500ptas. Doubles 4500ptas. Triples 5500ptas. Oct.-June except Semana Santa: 2000ptas; 3000ptas; 4000ptas.

Near the Cathedral

These *hostales* are in the heart of the commercial zone. They tend to be quieter, while still fairly close to the port, the buses, the trains, and the beach.

Pensión La Perla, C. Loyola, 10, 2nd fl. (tel. 42 81 23), the street directly ahead of the cathedral. All rooms with balconies and showers. English-speaking owner. Singles 3000ptas. Doubles 4500ptas. Oct.-June: 2500ptas; 3000ptas.

Pensión Urkia, C. Urbieta, 12 (tel. 42 44 36). Urbieta borders the cathedral on the west side; the *pensión* is one bl. north at C. Arrasate. All rooms with showers. Singles 3000ptas. Doubles 4500ptas. Oct.-June: 2500ptas; 3000ptas. Large groups easily accommodated.

Pensión Añorga, C. Easo, 12, 1st fl. (tel. 46 79 45), at C. San Martín. Shares entryway with 2 other *pensiones.* Helpful owner. Singles 2500ptas. Doubles 4000ptas, with bath 5000ptas. Sept.-June: 2000ptas; 3000ptas; 4000ptas.

Hostal Comercio, C. Urdaneta, 24 (tel. 46 44 14), at C. Easo. C. Urdaneta runs behind the church. Three floors and many beds, yet likely to be full by midday in peak season. Singles 3800ptas. Doubles 4500ptas. Oct.-June: 2850ptas; 3375ptas.

Hostal Residencia Easo, C. San Bartolomé, 24 (tel. 46 68 92). From San C. Martín, heading toward the beach, turn left on C. Easo, and left again on C. Triunfo. Doubles 3600ptas, with shower 3800ptas. Nov.-April: Singles 2800ptas. Doubles 3000-3200ptas.

Elsewhere

Pensión La Concha, C. San Martín, 51 (tel. 45 03 89 or 46 13 84), up the street from Pl. Zaragoza, near the beach. All doubles with shower 6000ptas; Oct.-June 4500ptas.

Hostal-Residencia Alameda, Alameda del Boulevard, 23, 2nd fl. (tel. 42 16 87 or 42 41 12). Across a tree-lined walk from the old quarter. Thirty-odd rooms, so there is hope. Singles 3500ptas. Everything else 2500ptas per person, with bath 3500ptas per person. Sept.-June: 2600ptas; 2000ptas; 2600ptas.

Fonda Vicandi, C. Iparraguirre, 3F (tel. 27 07 95), in Barrio de Gros, on the east side of the river. From Puente Santa Catalina, take C. Miracruz and turn right on C. Iparraguirre. Less crowded in summer than elsewhere. Watch TV or the Goya print above it. Doubles 3500ptas. Showers 200ptas.

Hostal Fernando, Pl. Guipúzcoa, 2 (tel. 42 55 75), under the arches, 2 bl. from Alameda del Boulevard. Singles 3500ptas. Doubles 5300ptas. April-June: 3000ptas; 4200ptas. Oct-May: 2700ptas; 3800ptas.

Camping: Camping Igueldo (tel. 21 45 02), 5km west of town. 268 *parcelas* fill in the blink of an eye. Bus #16 "Barrio de Igueldo-Camping" runs between the site and Alameda del Boulevard (roughly every hr., 6:50am-10:30pm, 85ptas). Bear in mind San Sebastián's unpredictable weather; hammer in the rain fly. Bar-restaurant and supermarket. Reception open 8am-midnight. *Parcela* (including tent and up to 2 people) 1378ptas; 395ptas per additional person. Winter: 905ptas; 335ptas. Better rates for longer stays.

FOOD

Pinchos are a religion here. The standard chaser is the strong regional wine *Txacoli*. Bars in the lively old city spread an array of enticing tidbits (called *pintxos* in *euskera*) on toothpicks or bread (8 *pinchos* and a drink, about 1200ptas). Thirty-nine restaurants and bars breathe cheaply on **Calle Fermín Calbetón.** The least expensive hunting ground for a full meal at a *jatetxea* (restaurant in *euskera*) is the **Gros** neighborhood, on the east side of the river. The majority of restaurants offer their best deals on lunchtime *menús del día.*

Many small places in the harbor serve tangy sardines with delicious **sidra,** another regional specialty. A visit to Donostia wouldn't be complete without sampling the strong, slightly bitter *sidra* (see Entertainment). Custom insists on pouring it with arm extended upward, so that the force of the stream hitting the glass will release the *sidra's* bouquet. While not purple-haze-inducing, it'll get you drunk quicker than beer. Vendors also sell small portions of *gambas* (shrimp) in eggcups and *caracolillos* (periwinkles) in paper cones (100-200ptas).

Mercado de la Bretxa inhabits imposing buildings on Alameda del Boulevard at C. San Juan. (Open Mon.-Sat. 8am-2pm and 5-7:30pm.) **Mercado de San Martín** is on C. San Marcial, one block left of Av. Libertad heading to the beach, between C. Loyola and Urbieta. (Open Mon.-Thurs. 7:30am-2pm and 4:30-7:30pm, Fri.-Sat. 6:30am-2pm and 4:30-7:30pm.)

Near the Youth Hostel

Groceries: Todo Todo 3, C. Serrano Anguta, between C. Zumalacárregui and C. Matia. Open Mon.-Fri. 9am-1pm and 4-8pm, Sat. 9am-1pm.

In the Parte Vieja

Groceries: Iñigo Saski, C. Iñigo, 7, in the old city. Open Mon.-Fri. 9am-1:30pm and 4:45-7:15pm, Sat. 9am-1:30pm.

Mariscos el Puerto, C. Pasealekual (tel. 42 71 44), beneath the stone wall past the *marina* in the old quarter. The only affordable seafood in town—cooked and dressed by the kilo (800-3800ptas per kg; min. sale 100 grams). Open Mon.-Sat. 10am-2pm and 5-9pm, Sun. 9:30am-2:30pm and 5-9:30pm.

Bar La Cepa, C. 31 de Agosto, 7-9 (tel. 42 63 94). For history's greatest *pinchos* tour, start here with the to-die-for peppers and a host of other delicacies (*pinchos* 125-250ptas, *bocadillos* 350-700ptas, entrees 900-1250ptas). Then continue across the street at **Gastelv,** C. 31 de Agosto, 22 (tel. 42 14 11), for exquisite seafood confections (*pinchos* 100-200ptas, lunch *menú* 900ptas).

Bar Juantxo, C. Embeltrán, 6, where it meets C. Esterlines in the *parte vieja*. Small and crammed with locals. *The* place for *bocadillos* (235-400ptas)—and they're delivered by a dumbwaiter behind the bar! *Pinchos* 110ptas. Open 9am-11:30pm, later on weekends.

Bar-Restaurante Txalupa, C. Fermín Calbetón, 3, up C. San Jerónimo and the 3rd right. A dazzling selection of *pinchos* (125-150ptas). *Menú* (1450ptas) served in a tranquil room downstairs. Open 1-3:30pm and 8-11:30pm, closed Wed.

Borda Berri, C. Fermín Calbetón, 12, makes the most delectable, unbelievably exquisite *pinchos de foie* in San Sebastián.

Near the Cathedral

La Barranquesa, C. Larramendi, 21 (tel. 45 47 47), 3 bl. behind the cathedral. Soothing pink walls and elegant decor are a break from the madness of the *parte vieja. Menú* with *paella* and chicken 850ptas. Open Mon.-Sat. 1:15-3:30pm and 8:15-11:30pm.

Zakusan (tel. 42 61 46) and **Cachón** (tel. 42 75 07), at #52 and #40 C. San Marcial, are perfect stops on a creative, marine-inspired *pinchos* tour. Yummmm's the word. *Pinchos* and *canapés* 110-175ptas.

Bar Etxadi, C. Reyes Católicos, 9 (tel. 46 07 85), behind the cathedral. Swish as hell. Specialties are *anchoas* or *gambas al ajillo* (anchovies or shrimp with garlic). Tongue-tingling *pinchos* 125-200ptas. *Bocadillos* 350-550ptas. Entrees 500-1200ptas. Open Tues.-Thurs. 11am-11:30pm, Fri.-Sat. 11am-1am. Visa, MC, AmEx accepted.

La Mamma, C. San Bartolomé, 18 (tel. 46 52 93), on the corner of C. Triunfo. Italian, as you inferred. Wine caskets swing from ceiling, checkered tablecloths, etc. Individual pizzas 575-910ptas. Fresh pasta dishes 550-925ptas. *Menú* 1000ptas. Open 1:30-4pm and 8:30pm-12:30am. Visa accepted.

Self-Service la Oka, C. San Martín, 43 (tel. 46 38 84), between C. Triunfo and C. Lezo. Cafeteria-style atmosphere, but the food is good. From basics (*pollo al ajillo,* 475ptas) to the more unusual (*pulpo a la plancha*—grilled octopus—675ptas). Open Sun.-Thurs. 1-3:30pm, Fri.-Sat. 1-3:30pm and 8:30-11pm. Closed for Christmas season and part of June. Visa, MC accepted.

Near the Beach

Café De La Concha, Po. Concha (tel. 47 36 00). Roughly at La Concha's middle. *Très chic,* but affordable for weekday lunches (*menú* 975ptas). Gaze down from the wrought-iron balconies at the proletariat below.

Pizzería La Pasta Gansa, Po. Concha. Fresh pasta (695-755ptas) and wood-oven pizzas (745-775ptas) served in a cool, bright locale right next to La Concha. Open 1:30-3:30pm and 8:30pm-midnight. Closed Tues.

SIGHTS

The most spectacular sight is San Sebastián itself—its green walks and parks, grandiose buildings, and geographical exuberance. The city spreads around a fan-shaped bay. The best view is from the top of **Monte Igueldo** at the far side of the bay. From here you can see the countryside meet the Atlantic in a line of white and azure. The view of the bay—from anywhere—is spectacular after dark, when Isla Santa Clara, lit by floodlights, seems to float on a ring of light, while the mainland's seaside walk acquires an ethereal nimbus. Don't miss native son Chillida's sculpture, *El peine de los vientos* (the winds' comb). The summit of Monte Igueldo vibrates to an **amusement park,** with bumper cars and donkeys for hire. For the **funicular** to the top, take the #16 "Igueldo" bus from Alameda del Boulevard (1 per hr.) or walk along the beach to the end of Ondarreta and turn left just before the tennis courts. (Funicular every 15min.; June 25-Sept. 25 Mon.-Fri. 10am-9pm, Sat.-Sun. 10am-10pm; rest of the year 11am-8pm; 85ptas, round-trip 160ptas.)

At the other end of the bay, gravel paths peppered with monuments, blissful couples, and views galore weave across the shady woods of **Monte Urgull.** The overgrown **Castillo de Santa Cruz de la Mota** crowns the summit with cannons and a chapel, and is itself crowned by the statue of the Sagrado Corazón de Jesús which blesses the city. (Castle open 8am-8pm; winter 8am-6pm.) Other reminders of a tumultuous past litter the mountainside; halfway up, the **Cementerio Británico** faces the sea. The huge monument commemorates British soldiers who died in 1833 defending the Spanish monarchy from the French during the Peninsular War. A more jarring "monument" is the unmarked, white-plaster **smear on a rock** near the *paseo* as it rises above the aquarium. A member of ETA (Basque terrorist organization) accidentally blew himself up here trying to plant a bomb.

Circling the base of Monte Urgull, **Paseo Nuevo** starts at the end of the port and brings you close enough to the waves to feel the spray. At one end, the **Acuario y Museo Naval** (tel. 42 49 77) maintains only a few fish, but has thorough displays on seafaring history. (Open 10am-1:30pm and 3:30-8pm; closed Mon. in winter. Admission 400ptas.)

At the other end of Paseo Nuevo, the **Museo de San Telmo** (tel. 42 49 70) resides in a former Dominican monastery. The serene, overgrown cloister is strewn with Basque funerary monuments. The main museum is beyond the cloister, comprised of a fascinating array of Basque artifacts dating to prehistory, a couple of dinosaur skeletons, some El Grecos, and contemporary art. (Open Tues.-Sat. 9:30am-1:30pm and 4-8pm, Sun. 10am-2pm. Admission 350ptas, students 200ptas.)

Once Isabel II started vacationing here in 1846, the fancy buildings followed. Even the railings on the boardwalk hark back to a time when the city belonged to the languid elite. **El Palacio de Miramar,** built on the land that splits Playa de la Concha and Playa de Ondarreta, passed through the hands of the Spanish court, Napoleon III, and Bismarck. Visitors can stroll through the grounds. (Open 8am-8:30pm; winter 8am-6pm.) A 30-min. walk from the cathedral up Cuesta de Aldapeta (or an 85pta bus ride on #19) heads to another regal love shack, the **Palacio de Ayete.** Again, the residence is closed to the public, but the lush trails aren't.

Near the base of Monte Urgull, at the end of C. Mayor, is the 18th-century **Iglesia de Santa María,** with an intricate concave portal and a statue outside of San Sebastián shot with arrows. The outwardly austere 16th-century Romanesque **Iglesia de San Vicente** is down the street. (Both churches open only for mass.)

Between a lush hill and a dark, gray-green bay, ½hr. from the center, is the onecobbled-street town of **Pasajes de San Juan.** The charming fishing village's woodbalconied houses and small bay crowded with colorful *chalupas* (little boats) make for an enchanting time warp of a visit. To get there, take the Areizaga **bus** (tel. 45 27 06) from C. Regina Regente in front of the tourist office, to **Pasajes de San Pedro** (every 10min., 5:30am-11pm, 85ptas). From here, follow the road toward the sea until you can see Pasajes de San Juan across the bay. Steps lead down to the swift blue boat that will whisk you across (50ptas).

ENTERTAINMENT

San Sebastián's nightlife has suffered somewhat due to the recent recession, though it remains mighty by any standard. Pubs, somewhere between a bar and a disco, are the best bet between midnight and 3am.

Bars

The **parte vieja** pulls out all the stops after dark. **Calle Fermín Calbetón,** 3 bl. in from Alameda del Boulevard, houses oodles of bars.

Bar Uraitz and **Bar Eibartarra,** C. Fermín Calbetón, 26. The two most packed bars on the street; virtually impassable after dark. A human zoo.

Bar Sariketa and **Bar Txalupa,** C. Fermín Calbetón, 23 and 3. Where the music is eardrum-threatening and the climate sweltering.

Bar Colchonería, C. Sant Vicente, 9. More tranquil. Bright modern art and small tables make for intimate conversation.

Akerbeltz, C. Andra Mari, 10, near the port. Shafts of light and a sleek black bar inside a cave-like *bodega* (wine-cellar). Most patrons hang out on the stairs outside the bar.

Taberna Orbela, C. San Jerónimo, 9. Music by erstwhile alternative groups gone blessedly mainstream allows for more relaxed bonding.

The twentysomething crowd packs the streets around the **cathedral.**

Bar Udaberri-Beri, C. Reyes Católicos, 8, and **Splash,** #4, south of the cathedral. "My sister got lucky, she married a yuppy, took him for all he was worth..."
Area, C. Larramendi, 5 and **Txirula Pub,** C. San Martín, 49, are gay bars near the cathedral. **Trigono,** C. General Letxundi, 8, is closer to the beach off San Martín.
Be Bop Bar, Po. Salamanca, 3. Local jazz artists perform once or twice a week.
El Cine, C. San Bartolomé, 21. The place jumps on weekends with spoiled, over-dressed *90210* teenyboppers on their precious motorscooters. Mod music.
Komplot, C. Pedro Egaña, 7, off C. Easo, behind the cathedral. A popular after-hours drinking den. Open until 5am.
El Muro, not near the cathedral. On the east side of the river. Down the *paseo,* past Playa de Gros, the eclectic and hip trudge through a muddy parking lot to listen to the Smiths and the Cure and to sip a large variety of British ales.

Discos

At about 2am, San Sebastián's small but mighty disco scene starts thumping.

Iguana, C. San Jerónimo, in the *parte vieja*. Modern music and dance mixes.
Keops, C. Anoeta, s/n, by the stadium. A beachcomber hangout.
Ku, atop Monte Igueldo. The beach crowd strikes again.

Sidrerías

From the beginning of January until the end of April, the fastidious gourmets of San Sebastián turn their attention to the **sidrerías,** where the slightly bitter *sidra* (see Food) is brewed. The *sidrerías* open to the public, some offering full meals for patrons, others requiring that uncooked food be brought for them to prepare on site, all providing their own delicious *sidra.* Local favorites **Bereziartua** (tel. 55 57 98), **Mendizábal** (tel. 55 57 47), and **Petritegi** (tel. 45 71 88), are all in nearby Asti-garraga. The regional tourist office has transportation info and a list of the 100 or so *sidrerías,* both in and out of the city (some are isolated in the nearby mountains).

Beaches and Sports

Playa de la Concha curves from the port to the **Pico del Loro,** the beak-shaped promontory on which Palacio de Miramar dwells. Unfortunately, the virtually flat beach disappears during high tide; each year the tide comes in a little further. Crowds and parasols jam onto the shorter but steeper **Playa de Ondarreta,** beyond Miramar. Here **Windsurf Donostia** rents windsurfing equipment (800ptas per hr.), surfboards (½-day 800ptas, full-day 1500ptas), and kayaks (800-1100ptas per hr.). (Open mid-June to mid-Sept. 10:30am-8pm.)

Both crowded beaches face **Isla de Santa Clara,** in the center of the bay—an alluring spot for picnics. A **motorboat** leaves from the port (every ½hr., 10am-8pm, round-trip 250ptas, seniors 200ptas, ages 4-8 70ptas). Oarspeople rent **rowboats** (1025ptas for two people and 2hr., 440ptas per additional person and hr.). Both ser-vices operate from the kiosk by the port, the Oficina de Servicios del Puerto (tel. 42 23 36; open June-Sept.).

Information on all summer sports is available in *UDA Verano* brochure, handed out by the tourist office.

Festivals

San Sebastián's five-day **Festival de Jazz** is one of Europe's most ambitious; such giants as Art Blakey, Wynton Marsalis, and Dizzy Gillespie have played here. For information on the 1995 festival, contact the Oficina del Festival de Jazz (tel. 48 11 79) at C. Reina Regente, s/n, 20003 San Sebastián (beneath the tourist office). The tourist office also has the scoop on concerts, schedules, and ticket information. **La Quincena Musical,** in the **Teatro Victoria Eugenia,** C. Reina Regenta, s/n, sponsors more than two weeks of classical music concerts, most of them free.

The tourist office prints a 10-page booklet (in Spanish and *euskera)* with the year's schedule of events: everything from music to regattas to sculpture exhibitions. The city hosts a **marathon** in mid-October; **El Día de San Sebastián** (Jan. 20) with traditional parades; a **carnival** in February; and a **Festival Internacional de Danza** in May (contact Diputación Foral de Guipúzcoa at tel. 42 35 11).

The week of August 15, **Semana Grande** (Big Week) is ablaze with concerts, movies, and an international fireworks festival. Movie stars and directors own the streets in the second fortnight of September during the **Festival Internacional de Cine,** classified among the four most important in the world (along with Venice, Cannes, and Berlin). For information about the film festival, call the Victoria Eugenia Theater (tel. 48 12 12; fax 48 12 18), or write to Apartados de Correos, 397, 20080 San Sebastián, Spain; the office shares the same building as the tourist office.

For more specific information on any of San Sebastián's festivals, call or write to the hyperinformed tourist office, **Centro de Atracción y Turismo,** C. Reina Regente, s/n, 20003 San Sebastián.

■ NEAR SAN SEBASTIÁN

FUENTERRABÍA (HONDARRIBIA)

One hour west of San Sebastián by bus, enchanting Fuenterrabía (pop. 180,000) stretches back along the Franco-Spanish Txingudi Bay from its silky-sanded beach on the Mar Cantábrico.

Fuenterrabía's charm emanates from its brightly painted houses, seaside walks, a gorgeous **casco antiguo** (old quarter), and the old fishermen's town, **La Marina.** The **playa** can become unspeakably crowded with vacationing *Madrileños* during the peak days of summer. The **Parroquia de Nuestra Señora de la Asunción** in the Pl. Armas is the oft-remodeled Gothic church where Louis XIV of France was married by proxy to Spanish Hapsburg Infanta María Teresa. (Open for mass only.) The **museo** on C. Mayor mounts good exhibitions, usually with labels in *castellano* and *euskera,* though sometimes in English and French. (Open Mon.-Sat. 10am-1pm and 5-9pm. Free.)

Fuenterrabía also offers several excursion possibilities. Six km up the avenue of the same name, **Monte Jaizkibel,** the highest mountain on the Costa Cantábrica, guards the **Ermita** and **Fuente de Guadalupe.** The latter is currently closed to visitors, but the environs offer mind-blasting views of the coast. On a clear day you can see as far as Bayonne in France, 45km away. **Boats** shuttle to Hendaye—a French town with a bigger beach—from the pier at the end of C. Domingo Egia, off La Marina (every 15min., 10am-midnight, shorter hrs. in winter, 150ptas).

Bidasoa Turismo is on C. Javier Ugarte, 6 (tel. 64 54 58; fax 64 54 66), off C. Sabina Avana. English-speaking staff has a fair map. (Open Mon.-Fri. 9am-2pm and 3:30-7:30pm, Sat.-Sun. 10am-2pm; winter Mon.-Fri. 9am-1:30pm and 4-6:30pm, Sat. 10am-2pm.) The **post office** is next door on Pl. San Cristóbal (tel. 64 12 04; open Mon.-Fri. 8am-3pm, Sat. 9am-1pm; June-Sept. closed Sat.). The plaza also has **public telephones.** The **postal code** is 20280; the **telephone code** 943. For a **taxi,** call tel. 64 12 56. The **Red Cross** at El Puntal can be reached at tel. 64 40 39. If you need an **ambulance,** call tel. 22 22 22. **Emergency,** tel. 088. The **police** come running when you dial 64 43 00.

The scramble for budget rooms isn't pretty; reservations are vital in the summer. State-of-the-art **Albergue Juan Sebastián Elcano (HI),** Ctra. Faro (tel. 64 15 50; fax 64 00 28), perches on a hillside overlooking the sea. From the town center, head to the beach or take the "Playa" bus. Turn left where the road forks right near the beach entrance (also where the bus swivels) and follow signs to the hostel. 20 beds for travelers; same-day reservations only, so call early. (Members only. 3-day max. stay when full. Flexible curfew 11:30pm. 950ptas per person, over 30 1480ptas. Breakfast included. Sheets 300ptas.) Closer to the center is **Hostal-Residencia Alvarez Quintero,** C. Bernat Etxapare, 2 (tel. 64 22 99), behind a light green garage door on the main intersection. Clean and tasteful. (Singles 3700ptas. Doubles 4900-

6100ptas. Semana Santa-June and Sept. 15-Oct.: 2700ptas; 3900-4900ptas. Closed Nov.-Semana Santa. Breakfast 450ptas.) **Casas particulares** provide alternative accommodations—consult the tourist office. **Camping Jaizkebel** (tel. 64 16 79) spreads 2km from town on the Ctra. Guadelupe towards Monte Jaizkebel. They've got a bar-restaurant, laundry, supermarket, and hot showers. (Reception open 24hrs. 460ptas per person, per tent, and per car.)

There are several **markets** on C. San Pedro in La Marina. An enthusiastic, if somewhat harried staff at **Bar-Restaurante Etxeberría,** C. Mayor, 27 (a.k.a. Kale Nagusia; tel. 64 35 93), serves up Basque entrees (600-1500ptas) and old favorites in epicurean style. (Open 1:15-3:30pm and 8:15-10:30pm, closed Wed.) Beach bums refuel at **Restaurant Gaxen,** C. Mafxin de Arzu, 1, a cute café six bl. from the beach and two from the bay. 39 kinds of sandwiches (300-675ptas). (Open Sun.-Thurs. 9am-11pm, Fri.-Sat. 9am-midnight.)

Interurbanos buses (tel. 64 13 02) run to San Sebastián (every 15min. until 9pm, 1hr., 175ptas). **AUIF** buses (tel. 64 27 91) go to Irún (every 15min. until 10:30pm, 10min., 85ptas).

IRÚN

Irún could be Basque for "I run," which is probably what you'll be doing when you hit this frontier town—most visitors are rushing to their connections to Paris, Madrid, or San Sebastián. Urban sprawl fills the 5km that officially separate Irún (pop. 53,000) from Fuenterrabía. There's an *ermita* on Mt. San Marcial where citizens defeated the entire French army on June 30, 1522.

Irún's **Ayuntamiento** (tel. 62 55 00) at Pl. San Juan Harria dispenses eye-crossing maps. (Open Mon.-Fri. 8:30am-2pm, Sat. 8am-noon.) The **post office** is down the street at Argentinas Errepublika, 6 (open Mon.-Fri. 8am-9pm, Sat. 9am-2pm). For **taxis,** call tel. 61 22 29 or 62 29 71. The **Red Cross** can be reached at tel. 61 12 03, an **ambulance** at tel. 22 22 22. The **police** (tel. 62 03 00; in **emergency** 091) are stationed in Pl. Ensanche, s/n. For other services, call Fuenterrabía (see above).

Several *hostales* near the train station fill quickly in summer. Some people use Irún as a base for visiting San Sebastián, where the *hostal* climate is rougher and pricier. Bear in mind, however, that Irún is not cheap or charming, and public transport back from San Sebastián is scarce after 10pm. Just up the street from RENFE is **Hostal Residencia Lizaso,** C. Aduana, 5 (tel. 61 16 00), with a TV room and clean, unremarkable rooms. (Singles 1975ptas, with shower 3400ptas. Doubles 3325ptas, with bath 4975ptas.) **Restaurant Itxaso** next door serves a decent 900pta *menú*. *Platos combinados* 550-850ptas. (Open Sat.-Thurs. 9:30am-10:30pm.) The **mercado** is up C. República de Argentina, 12. (Open 8:30am-1:30pm.)

RENFE trains (tel. 61 22 36) flounce out to all of Spain; connections to San Sebastián are frequent (25min., 115ptas). Information (tel. 61 67 08) open 7am-11pm. The station has **currency exchange,** a **post office,** and some stores.

■ ■ ■ VITORIA-GASTEIZ

Though Vitoria-Gasteiz has been the capital of País Vasco for well over a decade, the city still feels like a well-kept secret. With more than 15 square meters of *zona verde* per person, slow-paced Vitoria-Gasteiz (pop. 210,000) is perhaps the greenest city in Europe. Not just for tree huggers and squirrels, the city is replete with airy shopping plazas, tree-canopied avenues, magnificent churches, and world-class museums. Indeed, Vitoria-Gasteiz has the charm of an old city packaged in a sleek cosmopolis.

In 1181, the Navarrese king Sancho el Sabio (the Wise) changed the town's original name from Gasteiz to Villa de Nueva Vitoria, promoting it to the status of a city in a single stroke. Because of its strategic location on the plain between the Kingdoms of Navarra and Castille, Vitoria found itself caught in a tug-of-war between the two jealous crowns in the 12th and 13th centuries. The critical Battle of Vitoria was fought in 1813 by the Duke of Wellington and the Spanish General Alava, who drove out Bonaparte's troops from their positions just north of the town and secured the Basque provinces.

As Castilla's commercial routes took on increasing importance, *castellano* came to displace *euskera* in everyday discourse; to this day, the province of Alava ("Araba" in *euskera*) speaks almost exclusively Castilian. On recovering administrative autonomy in 1979, the Basques made this city (now officially called Vitoria-Gasteiz to incorporate the original name) the seat of their government.

ORIENTATION AND PRACTICAL INFORMATION

Vitoria-Gasteiz is sensibly laid-out and user-friendly: signs to all major sights are clear and accurate, and street names are actually posted on clearly visible signs.

The medieval **casco viejo** (old city) is the egg-shaped epicenter of the city. **Plaza de la Virgen Blanca,** at the base of the old city, marks the center of town. Around the old city lies an expansive quarter built according to the Enlightenment urban planning recipe, with wide tree-lined pedestrian streets. From the train station, follow **Calle Eduardo Dato** to its end, turn left, and head straight to the plaza.

Pending the renovation of the old bus station on C. Francia (1-2 yrs.), buses now head for the frustratingly symmetrical concrete and glass contraption on a traffic island in **Calle de los Herrán,** between **Calle Prudencio María Verastegui** and **Calle de Arana.** All directions will be given assuming you exit on its west side, in which case you should be facing stores across the street (there are none on the east side), and C. Verastegui should be on your left. To get to Pl. Virgen Blanca, follow C. Verastegui, turn left when it ends on C. Francia, follow for 4 bl. through its rebaptism as C. Paz, and turn right on C. Postas, which leads straight to the plaza.

Tourist Office: Parque de la Florida, s/n (tel. 13 13 21). From train station, take 2nd left on C. Florida and follow it to the edge of the *parque*. From bus station, head toward Pl. Virgen Blanca, but follow C. Francia/Paz 2 bl. past C. Postas to C. Ortiz de Zárate on the right, which leads to C. Florida and to the park. In the park, follow the tree-lined perimetral path to the left; the tourist office is in a squat, gray stone house. Request *"paseo por el casco viejo"* map. Open Mon.-Fri. 8am-7:30pm, Sat. 10am-2pm and 5-7pm, Sun. 10am-2pm; Oct.-May Mon.-Fri. 9am-1:30pm and 3-6pm. When closed, use polyglot audiovisual information server. A smaller, less informative **municipal tourist office** is in Edificio Europa, Av. Gasteiz, s/n (tel. 16 15 98). From Parque de la Florida, take C. Luis Heinz to C. Sancho el Sabio and bear right on Av. Gasteiz. Open Mon.-Sat. 10am-7pm, Sun. 11am-2pm.

Budget Travel: TIVE, C. General Alava, 19 (tel. 14 22 20). Sell ISIC (500ptas). Open Mon.-Fri. 9am-2pm.

Post Office: C. Postas, 9 (tel. 23 05 75; fax 23 37 80), on pedestrian street that leads to Pl. Virgen Blanca from the east. Open for info Mon.-Fri. 8am-9pm, Sat. 9am-2pm; for stamps, **telegrams,** and **fax** Mon.-Fri. 8am-9pm, Sat. 9am-7pm. For Lista de Correos, walk around corner to C. Nuestra Señora del Cabello side of the building to unmarked door (open Mon.-Fri. 8am-9pm, Sat. 9am-2pm). **Postal Code:** 01080.

Telephones: Telefónica, Av. Gasteiz, 69. From the tourist office bear right on C. Luis Heinz, walk through Pl. Lovaina and onto C. Sancho el Sabio until Av. Gasteiz; it's on the corner of C. Beato Tomás de Zumárraga. **Fax-sending service.** Open Mon.-Sat. 9am-2pm and 4-9pm. **Telephone Code:** 945.

Flights: Aeropuerto Vitoria-Foronda (tel. 16 35 00), 9km away from town. Accessible only by car or taxi (1500ptas). **Iberia** (tel. 16 36 14), information open 6am-11pm. To: Madrid (Mon.-Sat. 1 per day, 50min., 12,500ptas); Palma de Mallorca (Tues. 1 per day, 1hr., 18,650ptas); Tenerife (Tues., Thurs. 1 per day, 3½hr.). Check p. 2 of *El Correo Español* (local paper) for current flights. Charter flights to international destinations.

Trains: RENFE, Pl. Estación (tel. 23 02 02), at the end of C. Eduardo Dato, south of the old city. Information open 8am-10pm. To: Pamplona (4-5 per day, 1-1½hr., 400-1100ptas); San Sebastián (12-14 per day, 1½-2½hr., 765-1600ptas); Burgos (12-15 per day, 1½-2hr., 715-1400ptas); Zaragoza (2-3 per day, 3hr., 1770-

2000ptas); Madrid (6 per day, including 1 *talgo* and 3 night, 4½-7¾hr., 3500-4500ptas); La Coruña (2 per day, 11hr., 5300ptas); Lisboa (1 per day, 13hr., 6630ptas); Paris (2 per day via Hendaye, France, 11,000ptas).

Buses: C. Herrán, on a traffic island east of the old city. Tons of companies. **La Burundesa** (tel. 25 55 09). To: San Sebastián (4-6 per day, 1½hr., 835ptas); Barcelona (3 per day, 6hr., 3020ptas); Pamplona (9-11 per day, 1½hr., 790ptas); Zaragoza (5 per day, 3hr., 1150ptas). **La Unión** (tel. 26 46 26). To Bilbao (7-13 per day, 1hr., 595ptas). **Compañía Automóviles Alava** (tel. 25 84 07). To Logroño (4 per day, 2hr., 885ptas). **Turytrans** (tel. 28 32 74). To Santander (3 per day, 3hr., 1320ptas). **Viajes Bascotour** (tel. 25 02 49). To Málaga (1 per day, 13hr., 5600ptas); Valencia (1 per day, 10hr., 5600ptas including meal). **Continental Auto** (tel. 28 64 66). To: Burgos (5-8 per day, 1½hr., 850ptas); San Sebastián (3-6 per day, 1½hr., 840ptas); Madrid (6-7 per day, 4½-5hr., 2545ptas).

Public Transportation: Buses cover the entire metropolitan area, including suburbs (75ptas). Tourist office has a pamphlet with routes.

Taxis: Radio-Taxis (tel. 27 35 00 or 25 30 33).

Car Rental: Avis, Av. Gasteiz, 53 (tel. 24 46 12), just past C. Adriano VI. Opel Corsa Swing 7000ptas (all-inclusive). Must be at least 23 and have had driver's license 1 yr. Open Mon.-Fri. 9am-1:30pm and 4-7pm, Sat. 9am-1pm. **Hertz,** C. Nicaragua, 10 (tel. 24 77 83), off the right side of Pl. Constitución coming from Av. Gasteiz. Ford Fiesta 7647ptas (all-inclusive). Must be at least 25. Open Mon.-Fri. 9am-1pm and 4-8pm, Sat. 9am-1pm.

English Bookstore: Linacero, C. Fueros, 17-19 (tel. 25 06 88), left off C. Postas heading toward Pl. Virgen Blanca. Classics, travel guides, and some juicy stuff. **Study,** across the street, has an impressive collection of Penguin classics. Both open Mon.-Fri. 9:45am-1:30pm and 4:30-8pm, Sat. 9:45am-1:30pm; Sept.-May also Sat. 5-8pm.

Youth Center: Instituto Foral de la Juventud, Pl. Provincia, 18 (tel. 26 69 86). From Pl. Virgen Blanca, turn left onto C. Diputación, which ends at Pl. Provincia. Information on trips, camping, travel. Open July-Aug. Mon.-Fri. 11am-2pm; Sept.-June Mon.-Fri. 11am-2pm and 5-7pm.

Laundromat: Lavomatique, C. Torno, 2 (tel. 27 65 30). From the bus station turn left on C. Francia, then right on C. Abrevadero, then right again. Wash and dry 1200ptas per load. Open Mon.-Fri. 9am-7pm.

Swimming Pool: Complejo Polideportivo Mendizorroza, Pl. Amadeo García Salazar, s/n (tel. 16 10 68), off Portal de LaSarte behind the train station. "Circunvalación" bus runs here (75ptas). Admission to the sports complex 600ptas.

Red Cross: Portal de Castilla (tel. 13 26 30), **emergency** (tel. 22 22 22).

24-Hour Pharmacy: tel. 23 07 21. Check pharmacy doors (there's one at C. Eduardo Dato, 24) or p. 2 of *El Correo Español* for listing.

Medical Services: Hospital General de Santiago, C. Olaguíbel (tel. 25 36 00). With your back to the bus station, take a left one block after C. Francia becomes C. Paz. **Ambulance** (tel. 16 11 11 or 27 98 97).

Emergency: Medical or otherwise (tel. 088).

Police: Municipal (tel. 16 11 11 or 092). **National** (tel. 091).

ACCOMMODATIONS AND CAMPING

As Vitoria-Gasteiz is not a common stop on the budget traveler's path, finding an affordable place to crash can be difficult—particularly for solo travelers who are sometimes forced to take double rooms at 80% of the regular double rate. The tourist office keeps an up-to-date list of the scarce budget *pensiones* and *casas de huéspedes*. Most are clustered near the bus and train stations. If you plan to come during the *fiestas* in early August, make reservations at least a month ahead.

Hostal-Residencia Nuvilla, C. Fueros, 29, 4th fl. (tel. 25 91 51). From the bus station, follow directions to Pl. Virgen Blanca but take the first left off C. Postas. Relaxing, well-kept rooms. Fills up quickly in summer, so call ahead. Very rare singles 1850ptas. Doubles 3400ptas. Showers 150ptas.

Pensión Araba (2), C. Florida, 25 (tel. 23 25 88). On the road to the tourist office from the bus station; a right turn on C. Florida from the train station. Persian-style rugs, wood floors and furniture, and beautiful tile bathrooms. TV in every room. Doubles 3500ptas, with bath 4500ptas. Triples 4725ptas, with bath 6075ptas.

Hostal Savoy, C. Prudencio María de Verástegui, 4 (tel. 25 00 56). Turn left from the bus station then an immediate right. Large, modern rooms with phones in a new building. Singles with bath 3500ptas. Doubles with bath 5200ptas. Triples with bath 7000ptas. *Menú* 1000ptas, breakfast 350ptas. Rooms in **Pensión Fuentes,** on the 4th fl., lack these amenities, but they are comfortable and far cheaper. Singles 1900ptas. Doubles 3200ptas. Triples 4300ptas.

Pensión Zurine, C. Florida, 24 (tel. 14 22 40). Across the street from Pensión Araba. Low, firm beds, new furniture, and ice-blue bathrooms. Winter heating. Singles 2300ptas. Doubles 3700ptas.

Pensión Florida, C. Florida, 46, 4th fl. (tel. 23 38 87), on the way to the tourist office from train or bus station. Clean and affordable. Call ahead, as permanent residents can fill it in the summer. Singles 2240ptas. Doubles 2800ptas.

Hotel Amarica, C. Florida, 11 (tel. 13 05 06), on the other side of C. Eduardo Dato from Pensión Araba. Poised between the shopping zone and Parque de la Florida, this Amarica the beautiful has carpeted halls and large, impeccable rooms. Singles with shower 4000ptas. Doubles with bath 6000ptas, with double bed 5500ptas.

Camping Ibaya (tel. 13 04 94), 5km from town toward Madrid. Follow Portal de Castilla out west from the tourist office intersection. Supermarket, café-restaurant, hot showers. Reception open 8am-2pm and 4-10pm. 400ptas per person, per tent, and per car. Open June-Sept.

FOOD

Plunge into the **casco viejo** for the most interesting options. **Calle Cuchillería** is lined with budget bar-restaurants—and you'll find a young SoHo-esque crowd. From the train station, take C. Eduardo Dato, turn right on C. Postas, and then left past the post office and uphill, where C. Cuchillería and other old-town streets radiate from C. San Francisco. Fresh produce and food are traded at the 2-level market, **Mercado de Abastos,** on Pl. Santa Bárbara. From the bus station, take C. Francia to C. Paz and turn left on C. Postas. (Open Mon.-Thurs. 9am-2pm and 5-8pm, Fri. 9am-2pm and 5-8:30pm, Sat. 8am-1pm.)

In the casco viejo

Restaurante Casa Paco, C. Mateo Moraza, 17, under the arches near C. San Francisco. Elegant arches, lace curtains, and wall-bound woodcuts mark this epicurean *comedor. Merluza a la vasca* is a specialty. Entrees 800-1500ptas. Lunch *menú* 800ptas. Open 1:30-3:30pm and 9-11pm. Closed Tues. and early Aug.

Amairu, C. Cuchillería, 11. Ideal for those mid-bacchanal munchies. Busloads of *ambiente.* Burger with the works, cone of fries, and cup of wine 550ptas. Open Thurs. 6:30-11:30pm, Fri.-Sun. 6:30pm-1 or 2am.

Bar Trafalgar, C. Herrería, 11, off the far end of Pl. Virgen Blanca from the post office. A clean, well-lit place with outside seating. *Pinchos* 110-150ptas, beer 135ptas.

Restaurant Hirurak, C. Cuchillería, 26, off C. San Francisco on the right. Old stone walls bedecked with modern art. Hip, young clientele bops to reggae and blues. Staff have their hands full. Lunch *menú* 900ptas. Entrees 950-1400ptas. Open Tues.-Fri. 1-3:30pm and 9-11pm, Sat.-Sun. 2-3:30pm and 9-11:30pm.

Amboto Oleagarena, C. Cuchillería, 29. Small dining room in a stone tavern with benches that come out of the wall. Modern music and traditional food. 850pta lunch *menú* (1100ptas on Sat.). Entrees 650-1800ptas. Open Tues.-Sun. 1:30-3:30pm, Fri.-Sat. also 9:30-11:30pm.

Elsewhere

Groceries: Simago, C. General Alava, 10, between C. Eduardo Dato and C. San Antonio. Open Mon.-Sat. 9am-8pm. **Eroski,** C. Florida, 56, a right off C. Eduardo Dato. Open Mon.-Fri. 9am-1:30pm and 5-8pm, Sat. 9am-2pm.

Museo del Organo, C. Manuel Iradier, 80. Take C. Florida east from the park to the Pl. Toros, then turn right. Veggie food, classic rock, and thirtysomething crowd in a plant-filled haven. Savory *tarta de cebolla* (onion pie) and do-it-yourself salad in a 4-course *menú* (900ptas). Open for lunch only Mon.-Sat. 1-4pm.

Bar La Bodega, C. Florida, 36. From the park, walk past Pensión Araba (see Accommodations). Traditional-looking enough to be cliche if it weren't the real thing. *Bacalao a la vizcáina* (cod, 550-650ptas) is a specialty. A good place for *tapas* (125-150ptas). Open Tues.-Sun. 9am-11pm (later Fri.-Sat.).

Dolomiti, C. Ramón y Cajal, 1 (tel. 23 34 26), left off C. Florida as it hits the park. Fresher ingredients and you would be eating garden dirt. Wood-oven pizzas (750-1100ptas), rich pastas (800-1000ptas), and other Italian specialties. *Menú* 1200ptas. Open Tues.-Sat. 1:15-3:30pm and 8:30-11:30pm, Sun. 1:15-3:30pm.

SIGHTS AND ENTERTAINMENT

Vitoria-Gasteiz is a city to be taken in slowly, on a walk, stopping every so often for a few *copas*. Vast and airy **Plaza de la Virgen Blanca** is the focal point of the *casco viejo* and site of Vitoria-Gasteiz's *fiestas*. At its side sits broad, arcaded **Plaza de España,** which divides the old town of concentric streets and balconied seigneurial houses on the hill from the new town's broad avenues (beginning with C. Eduardo Dato) and grid streets.

When Gasteiz became Vitoria, it was necessary to join the hill to the rest of the town below; architects Sefurola and Olaguíbel pulled this off with **Los Arquillos,** above C. Mateo de Moraza, a set of arches that merge old and new Vitoria-Gasteiz through stairs and streets arrayed like terraces. The *casco viejo* begins uphill through the arches. Down C. Cuchillería, the 15th-century **Casa del Cordón,** so-called because of the stone *cordón* (rope) that embellishes its central arch, now houses a museum. Skirting the left side of the old Catedral de Santa María and downhill is the **Museo Provincial de Arqueología,** with artifacts from the Paleolithic Era. A loop-de-loop left through the plaza next to the archeology museum onto C. Siervas de Jesús deposits the looper at the **Museo de Ciencias Naturales,** with its geological, botanical, and zoological exhibits.

The **Museo Provincial de Armería,** on Po. Fray Francisco de Vitoria, has a weapons collection featuring battle plans and uniforms from the Battle of Vitoria. To get there, take Po. Senda from Parque de la Florida (on the right when facing C. Florida), and make successive right and left turns at its end. Opposite the museum, the gorgeous, stained-glass Casa de Araba houses the **Museo de Bellas Artes,** with sculptures in the garden, and a collection of Romanesque and polychrome works by Ribera, Miró, and Picasso. A collection of playing cards dates back six centuries. (Museums open Tues.-Fri. 11am-2pm and 4-6:30pm, Sat.-Sun. 11am-2pm. Free.)

Any evening of the year sees all of Vitoria-Gasteiz head, lemming-like, to the watering holes of the *casco viejo*. On weekdays the action settles down by midnight, but the thrashing weekend scene lasts till dawn. Early in the evening, the bar scene centers on **Calle Cuchillería.** For more space but no less attitude, head for **Calle Herrería,** where many bars have courtyard seating. Then it's on to **Calle Zapatería,** also in the *casco viejo,* and **Calle San Antonio,** where *marcha* like there's no tomorrow continues until the morrow.

The monthly *Guía del Ocio* (125ptas) is an excellent guide to bars, entertainment, and special events in the city. World-class jazz comes to Vitoria-Gasteiz in mid-July for the week-long **Festival de Jazz de Vitoria-Gasteiz.** 1994 performers included B.B. King and Natalie Cole. (Tickets 500-2000ptas; for information call tel. 14 19 19 or write to C. San Antonio, 16, 01005 Vitoria-Gasteiz. Box office open 8:30am-2pm prior to and during the festival. English spoken.) The **Fiesta de la Virgen Blanca** (Aug. 4-9) includes dancing and *a capella* singing. Revelry is launched in Pl. Virgen Blanca with a rocket.

Other sites of interest in Alava include the **Natural Parks** of **Urquiote, Urbea,** and **Valdrejo,** and the town of **La Guardia** which, though in Alava, produces Rioja wine with *denominación de origen.*

La Rioja and Navarra

Navarra sits between Euskadi and Aragón, beneath the lush Pyrenean valleys which reach toward France. After demolishing Charlemagne's rear guard at Roncesvalles in revenge for their tearing down a segment of Pamplona's walls, Navarra came into its own as a kingdom in the 9th century. In the early 11th century, under King Sancho the Great (1000-1035), it was the most powerful kingdom in Iberia, reuniting all of the Christian states except Galicia and Cataluña. Fernando el Católico annexed Navarra to a recently unified Spain in 1512, but he allowed it to maintain its traditional privileges embodied in the *fueros* (medieval laws)—including exemption from military service. Ironically, Navarra's active role in the Peninsular War, in which Spain expelled Napoleon, ushered in a period of centralism and a political climate hostile to special regimes such as Navarra's. Navarra added insult to injury by persistently supporting the losing conservative cause in the 19th-century Carlist wars, and siding with Franco in the Civil War. In 1982, Navarra regained status as an autonomous region; strong regionalist sentiment is limited to a small group of Basque towns in the north.

The Navarrese have a strong epicurean reputation and love to cite a medieval code which mandates treatment of prisoners condemned to death: they should be served "good food, game, mutton, fish, jams, and chocolate" as well as wine between meals until final hour. Popular stews include bull stew and *calderete* (potato stew). *Ajoarriero* (salted cod fried with tomato, peppers, and garlic) and fresh trout are common fish dishes.

An extensive network of *casas rurales* (individual houses, subsidized by the regional government, and made available for travelers) renders visits to small towns easy and flavorful—among other reasons, because home-cooked meals are often part of the deal. The *Guía de alojamientos de turismo rural* is available at any tourist office.

Tucked under Navarra, La Rioja is synonymous with great wine, produced here since the 12th century. The western section of the region benefits from its proximity to the rainy hills of País Vasco, and irrigation ensures that even the acrid plains near Navarra produce bumper crops. The name "La Rioja" derives from the Ebro tributary Río Oja, whose muddy waters trickle through the vineyards.

Logroño, capital of La Rioja, lies in the center of the region. Haro, in the western Rioja Alta, offers most of the best *bodegas* (wine cellars). Trying to find a picturesque town with a *bodega* here is like trying to find a tipsy tourist in Pamplona during *Sanfermines*. The Camino de Santiago—which commences in Navarra—traverses this region; all tourist offices stock the pamphlet *El Camino de Santiago por La Rioja* (The Way of St. James through La Rioja), available in many languages. The mountainous Sierra region, with tranquil fields at the feet of lunar-like peaks, stretches along La Rioja's southern border. Ask at any tourist office about the *zonas de acampada*, three scenic zones in which the government has provided basic camping facilities on the unspoiled land. For the sweet tooth, local fruits *al vino* (marinated in wine) make a delectable dessert.

■■■ LOGROÑO

Logroño (pop. 110,000), the pleasant capital of La Rioja and wine country, is fighting its over-industrialized image. While some areas of the city have become derelict, gentrification and government intervention have restored much of the *casco antiguo* (old quarter) and many of the 17th- and 18th-century homes which line the river. Residents emphasize Logroño's history as a stopover for Compostela-bound pilgrims, and the outlying area's *bodega* tradition. There is little in the city itself to warrant a journey, but Logroño's rail and bus connections make it the best entry point to the small wine and monastery towns of La Rioja.

ORIENTATION AND PRACTICAL INFORMATION

The town, both old and new, radiates out from the **Parque del Espolón**, a tree-lined set of gravel paths with a large fountain at its center. The **casco antiguo** spreads between the park and the **Río Ebro**, on the far north side of the city from the bus and train terminals. Just about everything of interest to budget travelers sleeps in or around the old quarter.

To reach the park from the train station, cross the major traffic artery of **Avenida de Lobete** and angle left on **Avenida de España**. The bus station is on the right at the next major intersection; its doors face toward **Calle del General Vara del Rey**, which runs north-south. A right turn on C. General Vara leads north to the park. To reach the river from the park, turn left from C. General Vara at the north end of the park and follow the arcaded store fronts to **Calle de Sagasta** on the park's west end. Turn right and follow this street as it slopes downhill to the river.

Tourist Office: C. San Miguel Villanueva, 10 (tel. 26 06 65; fax 25 60 45), left off C. General Vara on the street that borders the near (south) end of Parque Espolón. Out-of-their-league staff speaks English but has only basic information on the wine and monastery routes and a decent map of Logroño. Open Mon.-Sat. 10am-2pm and 4:30-7:30pm, Sun. 10am-2pm; Nov.-May Mon.-Fri. 9am-2pm.

Budget Travel: Dirreción General de Juventud, C. Portales, 1 (tel. 29 11 00). Info about youth discounts and special city events. Open Mon.-Fri. 9am-2pm.

Currency Exchange: Many banks crowd around C. San Miguel Villanueva. Open Mon.-Fri. 9am-2pm.

Post Office: Pl. San Agustín (tel. 22 00 66 or 20 50 88), next to the *museo*. Open for stamps, **telegrams,** and Lista de Correos Mon.-Fri. 8am-9pm, Sat. 9am-2pm, telegrams Sat. until 7pm. **Postal Code:** 26070.

Telephones: C. Portales, 75, just past the post office. Open Mon.-Sat. 9am-1pm and 5-9pm. **Telephone Code:** 941.

Trains: RENFE, Pl. Europa (tel. 24 02 02), off Av. España on south side of town. Information open 7am-11pm. To: Haro (4-5 per day, 40min., 315ptas); Tudela (7-9 per day, 1½hr., 595ptas); Burgos (1-2 per day, 2¼hr., 1000ptas); Zaragoza (7-9 per day, 2-2½hr., 1000ptas); Bilbao (2-3 per day, 3hr., 1500-1700ptas); León (1-2 per day, 5hr., 2000-3500ptas); Madrid (1 per day, 5½hr., 3100ptas); Barcelona (3 per day, 6-8hr., 3600-4400ptas); Valencia (daily late June-late Sept., Fri. and Sun. rest of the year, 9½hr., 5700ptas); La Coruña (1 per day, 11¼hr., 5500-6600ptas).

Buses: Av. España (tel. 23 59 83), on the corner of C. General Vara and Av. Pío XII. Several companies; check information board for the appropriate counter. Information open 6:30am-10:30pm. To: Haro (5 per day, 45min., 320ptas); Santo Domingo de la Calzada (9 per day, 1hr., 325ptas); San Millán de la Cogolla (2 per day, 1hr., 280ptas); Vitoria-Gasteiz (4-6 per day, 1-2hr., 885ptas); Soria (4-5 per day, 2hr., 770ptas); Pamplona (3-5 per day, 2hr., 815ptas); Zaragoza (6 per day, 2hr., 1145ptas); Bilbao (4 per day, 2¼hr., 1300ptas); Burgos (7 per day, 3-5hr., 875ptas); Santander (3 per day, 4-5hr., 2000ptas); Madrid (4-5 per day, 4¾hr., 2335ptas); Barcelona (2-4 per day, 6hr., 3635ptas); Estella (4 per day, 1hr., 445ptas). Most leave 7:30am-7pm.

Public Transportation: City buses (55ptas) are generally unnecessary for tourists.

Car Rental: Avis, Gran Vía del Rey Don Juan Carlos I, 67 (tel. 20 23 54), left from C. General Vara. Open Mon.-Fri. 9am-1pm and 4pm-6pm, Sat. 10am-1pm. **Hertz,** C. General Vara, 67 (tel. 25 80 26), left from Av. España with the stations behind you. Open Mon.-Fri. 9am-2pm and 4pm-6pm, Sat. 9am-1pm.

Luggage Storage: Consignas, at **bus station** (200ptas; open 6am-11pm; 15-day max) and **train station** (400ptas; open 24hrs.; token at ticket booth 7am-11pm).

English Bookstore: Librería Gumersindo Cerezo, C. Portales, 23 (tel. 25 17 62). Small selection of novels. Open Mon.-Fri. 10am-2pm and 4-8pm, Sat. 10am-1pm.

Public Toilets: In Parque del Espolón. Open 9am-8pm.

Red Cross: C. Beneficiencia (tel. 22 22 22; information tel. 22 52 12).
Medical Services: Hospital de la Rioja, Av. Viana, 1 (tel. 29 11 94), on the edge of town in the direction of Pamplona.
Police: tel. 091. Call them or the Red Cross in an **emergency. Municipal police** (tel. 092). **Guardia Civil** (tel. 062 or 22 11 00).

ACCOMMODATIONS AND CAMPING

The *casco antiguo* brims with budget *pensiones* and *hostales*. Try **Calle San Juan,** the second left past Parque de Espolón from the stations, and **Calles San Agustín** and **Laurel,** a little deeper into the old quarter past the far corner of the Parque. Although some lodgings look a bit shabby from the street, most are family-run and very clean. Reservations are crucial for the *fiesta* weeks of June 11 and Sept. 21.

Fonda Bilbaína, C. Capitán Eduardo Gallarza, 10 (tel. 25 42 26). The facade is the only part that hasn't been renovated. Brilliantly white stucco walls, flowered bed-spreads, and high ceilings. Some rooms have glassed-in balconies. Singles 1500ptas. Doubles 2500ptas, with shower 3000ptas.
Pensión Blanca, C. Laurel, 24 (tel. 22 41 48). Homey, immaculate rooms. Rare singles 2000ptas. Doubles 3000ptas. Oct.-June: 1600ptas; 2500ptas.
Hostal Sebastián, C. San Juan, 21 (tel. 24 28 00). Large doubles with paper-thin walls, sinks, and industrial strength beds. Winter heating. Sparkling bathrooms. Front rooms have balconies. Singles 2000ptas. Doubles 3200ptas.
Camping La Playa, Av. Playa, s/n (tel. 25 22 53), off the main highway across the river from the *casco antiguo*. A riverbank site with a sandy beach. Municipal swimming pools next door are free. 500ptas per person, per tent, and per car. Open June-Sept.

FOOD

Scads of bars happily uncork a bottle of the region's wine (1991 and 1987 vintages are very good, 1982 excellent). Restaurants in the *casco antiguo* stock La Rioja's veggie-heavy gastronomical delights, including *patatas en salsa picante* (potatoes with melted cheese in a slightly spicy sauce) and *pimientos a la Riojana* (sweet peppers with minced meat). **Calles Laurel** and **San Juan** brim with bars and cafés. The local **market** is in the large concrete building on C. Capitán Eduardo Gallarza, left off C. Sagasta en route to the river. (Open Mon.-Sat. 9am-2pm and 5-8pm; winter Mon.-Sat. 9am-2pm.)

Supermarket: Simago, Av. La Rioja, a left off C. Miguel Villanueva past the tourist office. A megamarket that eats up half the block. Open Mon.-Sat. 9am-8pm.
Restaurante La Cueva, C. San Juan, 13 (tel. 24 27 48). Imitation stalactites dripping from the low, stucco ceiling make this small restaurant feel like the Bat Cave. Entrees 550-1200ptas. Open Fri.-Tues. 1:30-3pm and 9-11pm.
El Arca de Noé, C. Oviedo, 6 (tel. 25 60 40), off Av. España, 1 bl. from the bus station. A vegetarian paradise. *Menú* 900ptas. Open Mon.-Sat. 1:30-3:45pm, Thurs.-Sat. also 9:30-11:45pm.
Bar Soriano, Trav. Laurel, 2 (tel. 22 88 07), a right at the end of C. Laurel in the *casco antiguo*. Specialty *pincho, champiñones con gambas* (sauteed mushrooms and shrimp on bread, 80ptas), borders on the transcendental. Bartenders shovel shrimp and 'shrooms out the window to eager crowds in the street. Open all day.

SIGHTS AND ENTERTAINMENT

Catedral de Santa María de la Redonda, on Pl. Mercado, wears a nondescript 18th-century facade and an engraved tribute to Franco's so-called "crusade against communism." From C. General Vara turn left on C. Portales; the cathedral is two blocks away on the right. (Open 8am-1pm and 6-8:30pm. Free.)

Another three blocks along C. Portales is the **Museo de La Rioja,** Pl. Agustín, 23 (tel. 22 27 35), which owes its existence to the rifling of the area's monasteries and convents under the Disentailment Law of 1835. (Open Tues.-Sat. 10am-2pm and 4-9pm, Sun. 11:30am-2pm. Admission 200ptas, EU citizens under 21 free.) The grassy lawns along the **Río Ebro** provide good strolling; two bridges, the **Puente de Hierro** and the **Puente de Piedra,** and a pedestrian path allow access to the other side.

Those in search of a great *bodega,* dwelling of Dionysus, need look no further than the outskirts of Logroño. **Bodegas Marqués de Murrieta, S.A.,** Ctra. Zaragoza (tel. 25 81 00), founded in 1872, is the most appealing. To arrange a visit, you must call at least 1-2 days beforehand; greater flexibility will improve your chances of getting a tour in English. They want wine aficionados only, but the requirements aren't too stringent. The more you know, however, the better you will fare. (Open 9am-2pm and 4-7pm.)

At night the partying begins in the *casco antiguo,* moving later to C. Argentina (across Gran Vía del Rey Don Juan Carlos I). Thank the Pez brotherhood for the one fish and piece of bread donated to the **Ferias de San Bernabé** the week of June 11. The **Ferias de la Vendimia,** complete with bull-running, are held in mid-September.

■ NEAR LOGROÑO

SANTO DOMINGO DE LA CALZADA

When Santo Domingo retired to the woods southwest of Logroño in the 11th century, he certainly didn't renounce his entrepreneurial spirit. Seeing first-hand from his hermitage the trials and travails of the pilgrims crossing the river, he built a bridge for them, drove a road (the *calzada,* or causeway) through the woods, and converted his hermitage into a hospice. Soon business was booming in the town of Santo Domingo de la Calzada (pop. 6000). The town honors its founder the first 12 days of May in a series of rituals that symbolically reenact episodes from his life.

King Alfonso VI noticed the work of this monastic reject and donated resources for the construction of the grand **Catedral de Santo Domingo,** on the site of the original temple. The king lay the first stone himself in 1098. With some Romanesque features, the current form dates from the 12th and 13th centuries. The *retablo mayor* is now being renovated and can be seen, in pieces, in the museum's *claustro* (open 10am-6:30pm, 250ptas). Romanesque engraved pillars have been discovered behind where the *retablo* stood. The hen and rooster display alludes to the miracle of Santo Domingo, known as "the cock that crows after it has been roasted."

As the legend goes, an innkeeper's daughter fell madly in (unrequited) love with a pilgrim named Hugonell. The heartbroken girl slipped a silver cup into Hugonell's bag and reported the "robbery" to the mayor. Hugonell was hanged. When his distraught parents visited the gallows, they heard their son's voice insisting that he was alive, and that Santo Domingo had saved him. They rushed to the mayor's house and related the bizarre series of events. The skeptical mayor scoffed that Hugo was as dead as the roasted chicken on his plate. The mayor ate his words when the cooked cock suddenly sprouted feathers and crowed Hugo's innocence.

From the bus stop at Pl. Beato Hermosilla, cross Av. Rey Don Juan Carlos I and follow C. Alcalde Rodolfo Varona. Take the next left—unmarked C. Pinar—for one block, then turn right on C. Hilario Pérez, which ends at the cathedral square. Entrance to the cathedral is from C. Cristo, the second door from the left corner of the west facade. (Can be visited during mass or *claustro* hours—see above.)

Practical Information The **tourist office** sits in Casa de Trastámara, C. Mayor, 70 (tel. 34 33 34), under the long stone arch ½ bl. from the cathedral square. Lame maps, but a detailed brochure in English with info about the city's monuments. (Open June-Oct. Mon.-Sat. 10am-2pm and 4:30-7:30pm, Sun. 10am-2pm.) The **Casa del Santo,** C. Mayor, 42 (tel. 34 33 90), off the cathedral square, has information for pilgrims and an *hospedería,* where 70 beds, potatoes, cooking oil, and kitchen-use are free for the journeying. (Casa open 9am-11pm, though schedule varies widely.) The **post office** is on Av. Calahorra (tel. 34 14 93; open Mon.-Fri. 9am-2pm, Sat. 9am-1pm). The **postal code** is 26250; the **telephone code** 941. The **Red Cross** answers at tel. 34 02 61; the **Centro de Salud** at tel. 34 21 73. In an **emergency,** call the local **police** at 34 00 05. The **Guardia Civil** are at tel. 34 03 91.

Buses run to and from Logroño (Mon.-Sat. 9 per day, Sun. 2 per day, 1hr., 325ptas). The bus stop is in Pl. Beato Hermosilla.

Accommodations and Food   Unless you're hoping to withdraw in contemplation, Santo Domingo is best as a daytrip. If you do hang around, **Hostal Río,** C. Alberto Etchegoyen, 2 (tel. 34 00 85), features spotless, barren rooms. Turn right off Av. Juan Carlos I, and walk 1 bl. (Singles 1800ptas. Doubles 3000ptas.) More worldly pilgrims can afford **Hospedería Santa Teresita,** C. Pinar, 2 (tel. 34 07 00), staffed by solicitous nuns. It lies at the end of C. Pinar, a right turn from C. Alcalde Rodolfo Varona. (Singles 1775ptas, with bath 2435ptas. Doubles 3330ptas, with bath 4530ptas.) The nearest camping is 5km away toward Logroño at **Camping Bañares** (tel. 34 28 04; 550ptas per person, per tent, and per car).

Numerous restaurants hover near the cathedral, luring hungry pilgrims with generous, low-priced *menús.* From the cathedral walk toward the bus stop and take a right on C. Pinar, then a left onto C. Navarra; the town **market** is held near Pl. Beato Hermosilla. The owners of Hostal Río serve up a storm (*paella,* ½-roast chicken, bread, wine, and dessert) for a hospitable 900ptas. (Sat. 9am-2pm.)

SAN MILLÁN DE LA COGOLLA

The enshrined remains of another hermit, the shepherd *de la cogolla* (of the hood), Millán, became the seed of San Millán (pop. 200). Two nationally registered monasteries now grace the town. **Monasterio de Suso** is a Mozarabic structure dating from the 10th century. The library contains a Codex with 12 lines scrawled in the lower right hand margin—today known to be one of the first ever Castilian texts. (Open Tues.-Sun. 10am-2pm and 4-7pm. Free.) Erected in the 16th and 18th centuries, **Monasterio de Yuso,** also known as **El Escorial de La Rioja** (after Felipe II's severe palace), features several Romanesque and Byzantine ivory plaques of San Millán and San Felices. (Open Tues.-Sun. 10:30am-1:15pm and 4-6:15pm. Guided tours in Spanish 300ptas.) While there is no tourist office, you can call the Monasterio de Yuso for information (tel. 37 30 49). The **telephone code** is 941. **Buses** (tel. 22 42 78) shuttle to and from Logroño (2 per day, Sat.-Sun. 1 per day, 1hr., 280ptas).

■■■ HARO

Ninety-six wine-makers overwhelm Haro (pop. 10,000), drawing international merchants and acclaim. At least half a dozen of these **bodegas** offer tours of their facilities, in large warehouses grouped around the RENFE station (across the river from the town center). Tours are generally held between 9am and 2pm. Calling 1-2 days in advance is a good idea; the tourist office can also help in this endeavor. Bodegas Encùna and Muga are among the few with English-speaking guides.

Between 7 and 10pm, while the rest of Spain goes on the evening *paseo,* Haro's citizenry opts for the sedentary custom of *chiquiteo*—drinking wine in the **bars** on the streets between Pl. Paz and Pl. Iglesia. The tourist office distributes an official classification of vintages (the *Vinícola Riojana Comercial* booklet). June 24-29 the wine flows continually in honor of patron saint San Felices, and it cascades during the **Fiesta Mayor** (Sept. 7-11), which honors the Virgen de la Vega.

Haro is so thoroughly steeped in the tradition of wine-making that some streets actually bear a winey bouquet. Still, it's possible to amuse yourself without so much as sniffing a cork. A beautiful stained-glass window radiates through the *retablo* of the **Basílica de Nuestra Señora de La Vega.** The church gardens command a view of the surrounding valley and wine-covered hills. To get to the church from the tourist office, turn left and follow C. Vega for about three blocks. (Church open for services only.) An appealing Plateresque exterior is the outside of the **Iglesia Parroquial de Santo Tomás,** on Pl. Iglesia, a left from Pl. Paz as you face the non-winey Ayuntamiento. Behind the Basilica, in the Estación Enológica, is the **Museo del Vino.** (Guess what it's about? Open daily 10am-1pm, Sat. also 5-7pm. 300ptas, Wed. free.)

Practical Information The **Centro de Iniciativas Turísticas,** Pl. Monseñor Florentino Rodríguez, s/n (tel. 31 27 26), dispenses info on La Rioja and a useless map of Haro. With your back to the Ayuntamiento, take C. Vega from the far left corner of Pl. Paz. The office is in the plaza to the left after you round the bend. (Open June-Sept. Mon.-Sat. 10am-2pm and 4:30-7:30pm, Sun. 10am-2pm. If closed, get a map and brochures from the Ayuntamiento.) The **post office** (tel. 31 18 69) is at the corner of Av. Rioja and C. Alemania, a left from C. Ventilla. (Open for stamps and Lista de Correos Mon.-Fri. 9am-2pm, Sat. 9am-1pm.) The **postal code** is 26200 and the **telephone code** is 941. **Luggage storage** is at the train station. **Public toilets** squat beneath the gazebo in Pl. Paz. The **Red Cross** is at C. Siervas de Jesús, 2 (tel. 31 18 38); the **Centro de Salud** on C. Manuel Bartolomé Cossío (tel. 31 14 77, **emergency** tel. 31 05 39). The **municipal police** are at C. Sánchez del Río, 11 (tel. 31 01 25).

RENFE **trains** (information tel. 31 15 97) run to: Logroño (4-5 per day, 1hr., 370ptas); Bilbao (2-3 per day, 2¼hr., 1200-1500ptas); Zaragoza (4-5 per day, 3½hr., 1200ptas); Tudela (4-5 per day, 2-2½hr., 800ptas). To reach Pl. Paz from the train station, take the road downhill, turn right and then left across the river, and let C. Navarra lead you uphill to the plaza. The **buses** all stop at the circle at the end of C. Ventilla. The last bus to Logroño leaves Haro around 8pm (5-6 per day, ¾-1hr., 320ptas). To get to Pl. Paz from the bus stop, follow the signs to *centro ciudad* along C. Ventilla and bear left from Pl. Cruz.

Accommodations and Food Accommodations are limited in Haro; you might be better off daytripping from Logroño (43km away). **Hostal Aragón,** C. Vega, 9 (tel. 31 00 04), a right from tourist office, has spacious old rooms with high ceilings, creaky wood floors, princess-and-the-pea-style beds, and winter heating. (Singles 1500ptas. Doubles 2700ptas. IVA not included. Showers 200ptas, up a spiral staircase. Breakfast 300ptas.) **Camping de Haro,** Av. Miranda, s/n (tel. 31 27 37), is on the same riverbank as the train station, to the left from the bridge coming from town. (410ptas per person, per tent, and per car; Sept.-June 300ptas.)

Restaurants in the side streets off **Plaza Paz** offer satisfying meals at good prices and, in a surprise turn, great wine. Bars in the **Herradura** quarter around the Iglesia Parroquial de Santo Tomás serve more modest meals and excellent *tapas.* Also on C. Santo Tomás, many **wine shops** sell the region's fruit of the vine; the best vintages list for around 6500ptas per bottle, but others cost as little as 200-500ptas.

■■■ PAMPLONA

Long, long ago, Pamplona's *fiestas* in honor of its patron saint San Fermín were just another Spanish religious holiday. Known to locals as *los Sanfermines* and misnamed by most English speakers, "The Running of the Bulls," the week of July 6-14 is now as undiluted and gripping an expression of lunacy and joy as ever careened down a city's streets. Ever since Ernest Hemingway brought the festival to international attention in *The Sun Also Rises,* clouds of visitors from around the world have come to witness and experience the legendary *encierro* (running of the bulls). At the city's bullring, a huggable statue of the Nobel-prize-winning author welcomes *aficionados* to Europe's biggest and most primal party: eight days of dancing, drinking, dashing, and satiating the wild beast within.

During non-*Sanfermines* time (the other 51 weeks of the year), a different but no less enchanting side of Pamplona emerges. The city is all elegance, with its broad, airy Enlightenment streets and the historic alleyways of the old Jewish quarter. Watered on two sides by the Río Arga and flanked and livened by verdant parks, Pamplona (pop. 183,000) is known to Spaniards for its high-powered university, one of the premier medical institutions in Europe. The best base for exploring Navarra, it is also one of the greenest and (excepting that fateful week) cleanest cities in the region.

PAMPLONA

Pamplona was founded by sons of Pompey (hence its name) and was brought into the Christian fold by a priest named Honesto, who converted senator Firmo and his son Fermín. Fermín became a bishop at an early age and evangelized Gaul until he was decapitated and immortalized in Amiens. Pamplona's strong religious tradition continued through San Ignacio de Loyola, who conceived the idea of the Jesuit order here, and through the conservative order Opus Dei, who have made the city its home.

ORIENTATION AND PRACTICAL INFORMATION

Everything liable to interest visitors is concentrated in the narrow, meandering streets of the **casco antiguo**, the northeastern quarter of this provincial capital. **Plaza del Castillo**, marked by a bandstand, lies in this neighborhood's center. To get there from the bus station, turn left onto Av. Conde Oliveto. At the traffic island on Pl. Príncipe de Viana, take the second left onto Av. San Ignacio, follow it four bl. past a statue on the left, which marks the end of pedestrian thoroughfare **Paseo Sarasate**, and bear right. To reach Pl. Castillo from the train station, take bus #9 from the station (75ptas); disembark at the last stop, traverse Po. Sarasate, then walk diagonally left of the statue to Pl. Castillo. To the north of Pl. Castillo, the Baroque red and gold **Casa Consistorial** (a.k.a. Ayuntamiento) makes a handsome marker amid the swirl of medieval streets in the old quarter. From Pl. Castillo walk downhill on C. Chapitela and turn left on the second street, C. Mercaderes. Incidentally, the *encierro* route begins north of Pl. Consistorial and passes near Pl. Castillo as it roars down **Calle Estafeta**, one street over, and winds up in the Pl. Toros.

A right onto Av. Conde Oliveto from the bus station leads to the **Ciudadela**, a sprawling fort in park grounds (home to a couple of Chillida sculptures) that guards the southeastern border of the *casco antiguo*.

Although Pamplona is usually a very safe city, crime skyrockets during *Sanfermines*, when even assaults and muggings are not unheard of. Never be alone at night, and take extreme care in the parks and streets shadowed by the city's old walls in the *casco antiguo*. Enthused revellers who pass out can say good-bye to wallet, money belt, and, thanks to thieves who know the system, the luggage they left in the *consignas*. Many stores close during *Sanfermines*, and many restaurants and bars close after the *fiestas* for a well-deserved rest.

Tourist Office: C. Duque de Ahumada, 3 (tel. 22 07 41; fax 21 27 49). From Pl. Castillo, take Av. Carlos III 1 bl., turn left on C. Duque de Ahumada, and cross C. Espoz y Mina. Functional but unimpressive map, and minute by minute guides to the festivities. During *Sanfermines* the line forms by 9am. English spoken. Currency exchange, public baths, and buses to campsite are posted on a bulletin board outside. Open Mon.-Sat. 9:30am-2:30pm and 3:30-7:30pm, Sun. 9:30am-2:30pm; Oct.-June Mon.-Fri. 10am-2pm and 4-7pm, Sat. 10am-2pm. **City Information Office,** in the rear of the Ayuntamiento (tel. 10 01 50), off the plaza by the market, offers a map and basic city information. Open Mon.-Fri. 8am-3pm.

Budget Travel: TIVE, C. Paulino Caballero, 4, 5th fl. right (tel. 21 21 97). In the direction of Pl. Castillo, take Av. San Ignacio, turn right on C. Roncesvalles and follow for 2 bl., then turn right on C. Paulino Caballero. Discount travel tickets, ISIC cards (500ptas), and HI cards (1800ptas). Open Mon.-Fri. 9am-1:30pm.

Currency Exchange: Reception desk at **Hotel Tres Reyes,** Jardines de la Taconera, s/n (tel. 22 66 00) changes money 24hrs. 10% discounts from the market rate. From the bus station turn right, then right again on Av. Taconera 5 bl., and bend left; hotel to the left where the road forks. Better rates during *Sanfermines* at **Caja de Ahorros de Navarra** central branch, with special extended weekday hours. July 8-12 open Mon.-Fri. 9:30am-12:30pm and 4-6pm; otherwise Mon.-Fri. 9:30am-1pm. From Pl. Castillo take Av. Carlos III; the bank is at C. Roncesvalles on the right. During *Sanfermines* other banks open Mon.-Fri. 9:30am-1pm.

Post Office: Central office at Po. Sarasate, 9 (tel. 22 12 63, after hours (944) 24 20 00), at corner of C. Vínculo. Open for stamps and **telegrams** Mon.-Fri. 8am-9pm, Sat. 9am-7pm; *Sanfermines* Mon.-Sat. 8am-2pm. Lista de Correos around the corner in the branch office, C. Estella, 10, next to the RENFE office. Same hours. **Postal Code:** 31001.

Telephones: Po. Hemingway, next to the Pl. Toros. From the tourist office, turn left, then bear left at Pl. Toros. Open *Sanfermines* daily 8am-10pm; July-Sept. daily 9am-3pm and 4-10pm; Oct.-June Mon.-Fri. 9am-1pm and 5-9pm, Sat. 9am-1pm. **Telephone Code:** 948.

Flights: Aeropuerto de Noaín (tel. 31 71 82), 6km away and accessible only by taxi. To Madrid (1-2 per day) and Barcelona (Mon.-Fri. 1 per day, 30min., 12,000-13,000ptas).

Trains: Estación RENFE, off Av. San Jorge, 20min. from the *casco antiguo* by bus (#9 from Po. Sarasate, 75ptas). Information (tel. 13 02 02) open Mon.-Fri. 8:30am-1:30pm and 4-7pm. Another ticket/information office (tel. 22 72 82) behind the bus station. Exit the bus station and go around the left corner; office is across C. García Ximinez to the left. Open Mon.-Fri. 9am-1:30pm and 4-7pm, Sat. 9am-1pm. Pamplona is miserably connected by rail. No *talgo* service; reservations are often mandatory on longer trains during *Sanfermines*. (It's much faster and easier to take the bus.) To: Olite (2-3 per day, ¾hr., 400ptas); Tudela (6-8 per day, 2hr., 630-1200ptas); Vitoria-Gasteiz (4-5 per day, 1¼hr., 400-1100ptas); Zaragoza (4-7 per day, 2-3hr., 1100-2000ptas); San Sebastián (3 per day, 1¾hr., 1200-1700ptas); Madrid (3 per day, 5-6hr., 3400-5100ptas); Barcelona (2-3 per day, 7-9hr., 3600-4000ptas). For Logroño you must go first to Castejón de Ebro (6-8 per day, 1hr., 630-1200ptas) or Tudela.

Buses: Estación de Autobuses, C. Conde Oliveto at the corner with C. Yanguas y Miranda. Nearly 20 companies. Tourist office has an excellent if not quite complete guide, or consult the bulletin board's alphabetized list of destinations for the appropriate ticket window. Ticket booths for less frequent buses usually open only ½hr. before departure. To: Sangüesa (1-3 per day, 45min., 380ptas); Javier (Mon.-Sat. 1 per day, 1hr., 405ptas); Yesa (Mon.-Sat. 1 per day, 1hr., 405ptas); Estella (5-12 per day, 1hr., 380-440ptas); Tudela (6-9 per day, 1½hr., 750ptas); Roncal (Mon.-Sat. 1 per day, 2hr., 805ptas); Isaba (Mon.-Sat. 1 per day, 2¼hr., 860ptas); Vitoria-Gasteiz (7-11 per day, 1½hr., 720-795ptas); Burguete (Fri.-Sat. 1 per day, 1¼hr., 480ptas); Orbaiceta in Aezcoa Valley (Mon.-Sat. 1 per day, 1¾hr., 510ptas); Ochagavía (Mon.-Sat. 1 per day, 2½hr., 695ptas); Logroño (4-5 per day, 2hr., 815ptas); San Sebastián (7 per day, 1½hr., 635ptas); Zaragoza (7-9 per day, 3½hr., 1330-1465ptas); Bilbao (2-6 per day, 2¼hr., 1300ptas); Madrid, through Soria (5 per day, 5½hr., 2905ptas); Barcelona (3-6 per day, 5½hr., 3480ptas).

Public Transportation: 14 inter-city bus lines dodge between the *casco antiguo* and all corners of the city. Excellent, foreign-user-friendly route guide available at tourist office. #9 from Po. Sarasate to train station (every 10-15min., 6:30am-10:30pm, 20min., 75ptas). During *Sanfermines,* some routes run extra night shifts. (Night fare 100ptas. Inquire at tourist office.)

Taxis: Radio-dispatched at tel. 23 21 00 or 23 23 00.

Car Rental: Europcar, Hotel Blanca Navarra, Av. Pío XII, 43 (tel. 17 60 02). Bus lines #1, 2, and 4 go here; get off after the traffic circle on the way out of town. Must be 21. Seat Ibiza 7000ptas per day. **Hertz** is in Hotel Tres Reyes (tel. 22 35 69). Must be at least 25. **Avis** (tel. 17 00 68) rents from the airport. Ask for promotional rates.

Hitchhiking: Tourist office claims that hitching to Logroño and France is more feasible here than elsewhere. *Let's Go* does not recommend hitchhiking.

Luggage Storage: July 4-15 there's 24-hr. luggage storage at the **bus station** (tel. 22 88 47). 200ptas for each time luggage is fetched; allow ½-1hr. Huge, but can fill up. Also during *Sanfermines,* **RENFE** (tel. 13 13 04) stores bags for 300ptas per day. Open 5:30am-1:30am. The rest of the year, in the bus station (115ptas per bag per day, large packs 170ptas). Open 6:15am-9:30pm, Sun. 7am-9:30pm.

Lost Property: Check with the Municipal Police.

English Bookstore: Librería Gómez, Pl. Castillo, 28 (tel. 22 67 02). Small selection of novels, magazines, and newspapers. Open Mon.-Sat. 9am-1:30pm and 4:30-8pm; closed during *Sanfermines*.

Gay and Lesbian Organization: EGHAM, Apdo. 1667, Pamplona 31080.

Laundromat: Lavomatique, C. Descalzos, 28 (tel. 22 19 22). From Pl. San Francisco follow C. Hilarión Eslava to the end, then turn right. Harried staff during *Sanfermines* can even get the bull blood out: wash, dry, and soap for 800ptas; open Mon.-Sat. 11am-4:30am, closed the 7th. At other times: wash 400ptas, dry 50ptas per 5min., soap 50ptas; open Mon.-Fri. 10am-2pm and 4-8pm.

Public Toilets and Baths: Ubiquitous sets of squat-variety **toilets booths.** Use them! (25,000pta fine for using the street as a urinal.) **Casa de Baño,** C. Hilarión Eslava, 2, at the corner with Jarauta; up from Pl. San Francisco, on the left past C. Mayor. 100ptas, with towel and soap 200ptas. Open daily 8am-9pm.

Swimming Pool: Piscinas de Aranzadi, 15min. from Pl. Castillo on Vuelta de Aranzadi (tel. 22 30 02). From the tourist office walk round the left corner, take C. Estafeta to Pl. Mercaderes, turn right, then turn left on C. Carmen, following it out of the city. Open 10:30am-9pm. Admission 450ptas, under 14 150ptas. During *Sanfermines:* 700ptas; 225ptas.

Hotlines (all Spanish unless otherwise noted): **Andrea, Centro de Atención a la Mujer** (tel. 22 77 14); **Comisión Anti-SIDA** (tel. 21 22 57); **S.O.S. Racismo** (tel. 21 15 21, some English and French spoken).

Red Cross: C. Yanguas y Miranda, 3 (tel. 22 64 04 or 22 92 91). Also sets up stands at the bus station and the *corrida* during *Sanfermines.*

24-hr. Pharmacy: Check for *Diario de Navarra* listings or call Municipal Police.

Medical Services/Emergency: In any emergency call tel. 088 or 092. Call these also for 24-hr. pharmacy and **ambulance. Hospital de Navarra,** C. Irunlarrea, s/n (tel. 10 21 00).

Police: National Police, C. General Chinchilla (tel. 092), to the right on Av. Taconera with your back to the statue on Po. Sarasate. **Municipal Police,** C. Monasterio de Irache, 2 (tel. 25 51 50). Some English spoken.

ACCOMMODATIONS AND CAMPING

If you have Jedi powers of mind control, the sort of luck that wins Ed McMahon sweepstakes, truckloads of cash, or a large gun, you *may* be able to find a room during the first few days of *Sanfermines.* For solo travelers, even these will probably not be enough. Diehard *sanferministas* book their rooms for next year before going home. In most cases, you must reserve about two months ahead and pay rates (up front) two to three times higher than those listed below. Arriving several days before the *fiestas* start can help too. Check newspapers *(Diario de Navarra)* for **casas particulares.** Hordes of people with dollar signs for eyes accost visitors at the train and bus stations, offering couches and floor space; use extreme caution with this course of action—accommodations and prices vary tremendously, and you might find yourself blowing your food money for a blink of sleep on a dirty floor in a bad part of town. Because of past scams, the tourist office will neither recommend nor aid in this effort. Many who can't find rooms sleep outside on the lawns of the Ciudadela and the Pl. Fueros traffic circle (from the bus station turn left, then left again at the traffic circle). Park-sleepers recommend extreme caution: if you can't leave your belongings at the *Consigna* in the bus station (it fills fast), they urge you to sleep on top of them. Always sleep in groups. It can be safer to nap during the day—when it is warmer and brighter—and stay up through the night.

When the bulls stop running, finding a room is no problem. Rooms line **Calle San Gregorio** and its continuation, **Calle San Nicolás,** off Pl. Castillo.

Hostal Bearán, C. San Nicolás, 25 (tel. 22 34 28). Comfortable, clean white rooms with pink trim, all with phone, TV, and safe box. Action *encierro* photos on the walls. Singles with bath 4500ptas. Doubles with bath 5000ptas. Friendly proprietor rents rooms without baths across the street at **Fonda La Aragonesa;** the narrow, decrepit entrance belies new, large, Quaker-like rooms inside. Singles 3000ptas. Doubles 3500ptas. Oct.-May: 2500ptas; 3000ptas.

Hostal Otano, C. San Nicolás, 5 (tel. 22 50 95). This former prison has reformed—it's a really nice place now, with gorgeous rooms, tasteful furniture, and oil paintings. Restaurant downstairs. Singles 2000ptas, with bath 2700ptas. Doubles 3500ptas, with bath 5000ptas. Visa, MC, AmEx accepted.

Casa Santa Cecilia, C. Navarrería, 17 (tel. 22 22 30), follow C. Estafeta to its end in Mercaderes, turn right, then left at a 30° angle. Don't judge by its entryway. Bright, spartan rooms in a clean wood-floor apartment. At the heart of the English-speaking action during *Sanfermines.* Single 2000ptas. Doubles 3000ptas.

Fonda La Union, C. San Nicolás, 13 (tel. 22 13 19). Unmarked entrance next to Restaurante San Nicolás. Look for banana-yellow paint job. Smart, tidy rooms, many with iron balconies, preside over the bustling crush below. 1500-2000ptas per person.

Fonda La Montañesa, C. San Gregorio, 2 (tel. 22 43 80). Spotless, frill-less quarters vary in size, from claustrophobic cubicles to spacious, balconied rooms. There may be hope for early-birds without reservations. 1500ptas per person.

Camping: Camping Ezcaba (tel. 33 03 15), in Eusa, 7km outside Pamplona on the road to Irún. From Pl. Toros, La Montañesa bus runs to Eusa (4 per day, get off at the gasoline station, the last stop). Capacity for 714. Fills as fast as other accommodations during you know what. 425ptas per person, per tent, and per car. Open June-Oct. No reservations accepted.

FOOD

While Pamplona shares the rest of Navarra's epicurean reputation, *Sanfermines* means unremarkable food at inflated prices. Try side streets in the neighborhood of Casa de Huéspedes Santa Cecilia, the cathedral area above Pl. San Francisco, and off Po. Sarasate opposite the post office. **Calle Navarrería,** near the cathedral, overflows with small bars and restaurants. More restaurants crank away on **Calles Estafeta, Mayor,** and **San Nicolás;** the last is longer on crowds and alcohol than solid food. Navarrería, San Lorenzo, and Po. Sarasate house *bocadillo* bars. During *fiestas,* cheap drinks and cheaper ideology can be found at *barracas políticas* (bars organized by political interest groups) set up next to the amusement park on the west end of the *cuidadela.* A fine Navarrese finish is the dessert liqueur *Patxaran* (*Pacharán*). More popular with the natives is *Calimocho,* a mix of wine to keep you happy and Coca-Cola to keep you up, allowing you to drink yourself to oblivion without fear of sleep getting you there first. Many cafés and restaurants close for one to two weeks after *Sanfermines.*

The **market** on C. Mercado is to the right of Casa Consistorial's facade and down the stairs. (Open Mon.-Thurs. and Sat. 8am-2:30pm, Fri. 8am-2:30pm and 4-7:30pm.)

Supermarket: Autoservicio Montserrat, at the corner of C. Hilarión Eslava and C. Mayor. Open Mon.-Fri. 9am-2pm and 5-7:30pm, Sat. 9am-2pm; during S.F. Mon.-Sat. 9am-2pm. Visa, MC accepted.

Restaurante Sarasate, C. San Nicolás, 19-21 (tel. 22 57 27), above the seafood store. Indian tapestries and Dylan tunes for vegetarian beatniks. Boho crowd settles in early. Nutritious *menú* 1175ptas. Open Mon.-Thurs. 1:15-4pm, Fri.-Sat. 1:15-4pm and 9-11pm.

Bar-Restaurante Lanzale, C. San Lorenzo, 31 (tel. 22 10 71), between C. Mayor and C. Jarauta, above Pl. San Francisco. Good-natured service, better-than-average food. Entrees from 850ptas. Open Mon.-Sat. 1:30-3:30pm and 9-11pm.

Bar-Restaurante Casa Paco, Rincón de San Nicolás, s/n (tel. 22 51 05). Small but over-achieving restaurant behind C. San Nicolás (facing Pl. Castillo, go right). No stools at the bar, but if there were, Norm would be sitting on one. Lunch and dinner *menú* 1200ptas. *Bocadillos* (night only) 350-450ptas.

Self-Service Estafeta, C. Estafeta, 57 (tel. 22 16 05). Service so quick you can stop, get some chow, and the bull *still* won't catch you. *Pimientos rellenos* (stuffed peppers, 700ptas), roasted ½-chicken (500ptas). Open Mon.-Tues. and Thurs.-Sat. 1-4pm and 8:30-11pm, Wed. & Sun. 1-4pm. Visa, MC, AmEx accepted.

BLOOD, SIGHTS, AND TEARS

¡Uno de enero, dos de febrero, tres de marzo, cuatro de abril,
Cinco de mayo, seis de junio, siete de julio es San Fermín!
¡A Pamplona hemos de ir! Con una bota, con una bota,
¡A Pamplona hemos de ir! Con una bota y un calcetín.

There's ample reason to visit Pamplona even outside of that mythical week. The clatter of cranky bovines tends to obscure Pamplona's rich and diverse architectural legacy. In the late 14th century, Carlos III el Noble endowed the city with a proper Gothic **catedral;** he and Queen Leonor remain dead within the ornately sculpted mausoleum. The cathedral is at the end of C. Navarrería. Neighboring streets are dense with palaces, Baroque mansions, and artisan houses from different periods. Aside from the cathedral, there are the fortified Gothic 13th-century **Iglesias de San Cernín** and **San Nicolás,** and the 16th-century **Iglesia Santo Domingo,** with its sumptuous *retablo* and brick cloister.

Near this basilica is the site where Ignacio de Loyola fell wounded in a war, a brush with mortality that radically changed Church history. Expansion in the 17th century deposited the Baroque **Palacio Arzobispal** and **Casa Consistorial,** and the Neoclassical **Palacio de la Diputación** at the east end of Pl. Castillo. Navarra's ancient laws—along with other manuscripts and artifacts related to the kingdom's history—are exhibited in the Diputación's annex, the **Archivo de Navarra.**

The **Museo de Navarra** (tel. 22 78 31), up C. Santo Domingo from Casa Consistorial, shelters Roman funerary steles and mosaics, architectural fragments from the cathedral, mural paintings from all over the region, and a collection of 14th- to 18th-century paintings, including Goya's portrait of the Marqués de San Adrián. (Open Tues.-Sat. 10am-2pm and 4-7pm, Sun. 11am-2pm. Shorter hours during *Sanfermines.* Admission 200ptas, students free.)

The pentagonal **Ciudadela,** built by Felipe II and sprawled next to botanical highlight **Jardines de la Taconera,** hosts free exhibits and concerts in the summer. The most scenic route to the Ciudadela from the old quarter, known as the *Vuelta del castillo,* follows the city's third set of **walls,** built between the 16th and 18th centuries. When Charlemagne dismantled the walls in the 9th century, the Navarrese and Basques joined at the pass of Roncesvalles to massacre his rear guard (and his nephew Roland). This violence was the basis of the French medieval epic *La chanson de Roland* (The Song of Roland). At the far end of the cathedral plaza, pick up C. Redín, which runs to the walls. A left turn follows the picturesque walls, past the gardens of Parque de la Taconera on the right, until they meet the Ciudadela, where there's an open *pelota* pitch, a pond for ducks, some sitting deer, and gravel paths for strollers. (Open 6:30am-9:30pm. Closed during *Sanfermines.* Free.)

For another view of the fortress, exit the old city by one of two gateways, **Portal de Francia** or **Portal de Guipúzcoa,** and stroll along the **Río Arga,** following the curve of the walls. These awesome structures scared off Napoleon himself, who refused to attack frontally and staged a trick snowball fight instead. When Spanish sentries came to join them, the French entered the city through the gates.

Throughout the year, **Plaza Castillo** is the city's social heart, with people of all ages congregating in and around its bars and cafés (**Iruña** is the critic's pick). **Café Roch,** on Comedias, 6, off Pl. Castillo, makes the most scrumptious *pimentos rellenos* (stuffed peppers) in Navarra—this is not light praise. Youth activity concentrates on bars in the *casco antiguo.* **Calle Jarauta** is a nighttime favorite. **Herriko Taberna,** C. Carmen, 34 (tel. 22 28 28), mixes hard-core music with posters demanding amnesty for ETA prisoners. Claustrophobes escape the cramped streets of San Gregorio and San Nicolás to bars in **Barrio San Juan,** beyond Hotel Tres Reyes on Av. Bayona. If you want to take the wine with you, check out wineskin store **Botas las Tres ZZZ,** C. Comedias 7, right off Pl. Castillo.

The tourist office has ample information on the concerts, theater, dance, Festivales de Navarra, and organized excursions into rural Navarra. Ask about **El Topillo,** a new government-sponsored bus program which prepares beautiful excursions into difficult to reach places in the Pyrenees, at extraordinarily reasonable prices (300-600ptas).

Los Sanfermines (July 6-14)

Visitors from the world over crowd Pamplona for the **Fiestas de San Fermín**—known to locals as **Los Sanfermines** and to many visitors as the Running of the

Bulls—in search of Europe's greatest party. Pamplona orgiastically delivers, with an eight-day frenzy of parades, wine, bullfights, wine, parties, wine, fireworks, wine, rock concerts, and wine to topple even the most Dionysian ne'er-do-wells. As a popular song illustrates: *"¡En Pamplona por San Fermín!/Riau, Riau, Riau que trabaje la Guardia Civil!"* ("In Pamplona for *San Fermín,* Let the Guardia Civil work.") The Pamplonese, uniformly clad in blinding white garb with red sashes and bandanas, throw themselves into the merry-making with inspired abandon, displaying unheard of levels of physical stamina and alcohol tolerance. Keep up with them at your own risk.

The mayor kicks off the festivities at noon on July 6, firing the first rocket, the *chupinazo,* from the Ayuntamiento's balcony. A barbaric howl explodes from the rolling sea of expectant *Sanferministas* in the plaza below, and within minutes the streets of the *casco antiguo* are flooded with improvised singing and dancing troupes. The *peñas,* taurine societies more concerned with Bacchus than bullfighting, lead the brouhaha. At 4pm on the 6th, and at 9:30am every other day, they are joined by the *Comparsa de Gigantes y Cabezudos,* a troupe of *gigantes* (giant wooden monarchs), *kilikis* (swollen-headed buffoons), and *zaldikos* (courtiers on "horseback"), many armed with play clubs. These harlequinesque misfits, together with church and Ayuntamiento officials, escort San Fermín on his triumphant *procesión* through the streets of the *casco antiguo.* The saint's 15th-century statue is brought forth from the Iglesia de San Lorenzo at 10am on the 7th, the actual day of San Fermín.

The Running of the Bulls

The actual running of the bulls, called the **encierro,** has become the symbolic core of *Sanfermines.* The first *encierro* takes place at 8am on the 7th, and is repeated at that time each day of the festival. Hundreds of bleary-eyed, hung-over, hyper-adrenalized runners flee from very large bulls, as bystanders cheer, provoke, and make mischief from barricades, windows, balconies, and doorways.

Rockets mark the bulls' progress on their 825m dash down Cuesta de Santo Domingo, through Pl. Consistorial, C. Mercaderes, and C. Estafeta to Pl. Toros. Barricades go up along Calles Santo Domingo, Mercaderes, and Estafeta. The entire *encierro* lasts only about as long as the 1990 Tyson-Spinks fight (3min. from the first release rocket to the final *encierro* rocket). Six steers accompany the six bulls—and they have horns, too. Both the bulls and the mob are dangerous. Terrified runners, each convinced that a bull is breathing on their tush, flee for dear life—with no concern for their peers who might get trampled in the process, or for what was once considered an athletic art form performed only by Pamplona's youth.

If you decide to run (you must be at the course no later than 7:45am), give up on getting near the bulls and concentrate on getting to the bullring in one piece. Try not to cower in a doorway; people have been trapped and killed by bulls this way. Be particularly wary of isolated bulls, since they run into crowds looking for company. Many people are injured at the end of the course, where the river of adrenaline cascades through a terribly narrow opening. Avoid running in the dangerous weekend traffic jams at all costs. Touching the animals is considered a major offense—you're likely to get the bejeezus kicked out of you by the locals.

Hemingway had the right idea: don't run, watch the *encierro* from the bullring (be there by 7am). To live a day like the Nobel Prize-winning tough guy, give up on sleep and any inkling of a budget. Hemingway rose early to get good bullring seats for the *encierro;* breakfasted on ham and peppers; roamed through town; settled down for serious talk and drink in one of the outdoor cafés on Pl. Castillo (of those he frequented, **Txoko** and **Iruña** are still there); returned after lunch to the bullring for the afternoon fight (tickets today *start* at 1500ptas and are difficult to come by); and dined and bar-hopped until the wee hours of the morning.

Day and Nightlife

After the taurine track-meet, the insanity spills into the streets, gathering steam until it explodes at nightfall, with singing in the bars, dancing in the alleyways, spontaneous parades, and a no-holds-barred party in Pl. Castillo, southern Europe's biggest open-air dance floor. Most English-speakers congregate in front of **La Mejillonera** (a.k.a. The Mussel Bar) at the corner of C. Navarrería and C. Carmen, in front of Casa Santa Cecilia (see Accommodations above). A word to the wise: beware of fountain-jumping (you'll know it when you see it). Several people have died after being on the giving or receiving end of this idiotic stunt.

The truly inspired carousing takes place the first few days of *Sanfermines*. After that, the crowds begin to thin and Pamplona assumes the air of the inside of your head after your 21st birthday bash. The end of the festivities is marked on midnight of the 14th by the singing of the *Pobre de mí* ("Poor Me"): *Pobre de mí, pobre de mí, que se han "acabau" las Fiestas de San Fermín.*

Nearby towns sponsor *encierros* as well. Tudela holds its festival during the last week of July, Estella for a week from the first Sunday in August, Tafalla during the week of August 15, and Sangüesa for a week beginning September 12. Many Pamplonese opt for these instead, preferring to watch their own *"en la televisión."*

■ NEAR PAMPLONA

ZUGARRAMURDI

According to Navarrese lore, in the majestic caves of Zugarramundi *brujos* and *brujas* (evil sorcerors) convened and brooded, presided over by a diabolical he-goat. The *akelarres* (meetings) in these impressive caves were so feared that in 1610 the Inquisition brought to trial and burned 12 *brujos*—of both genders. The caves are about 80km from Pamplona, on highway N-121 to France, through Dancharinea. The sign to Zugarramundi is on the left just before the international bridge at the border. Also accessible from San Sebastián.

OLITE

Enchanting Olite (pop. 3000) is absurdly close to what you'd expect a little Spanish town to be like before knowing any better. The Río Cidacos trickles by the slender walls of the **Palacio Real,** which rises proudly out of the flatlands 42km south of Pamplona, in the very center of **Plaza Carlos III el Noble.** Intrigue and sabotage have lurked about the palace of the kings of Navarra for centuries. In the early 15th century, King Carlos III made this sumptuous palace of pointed turrets, arched windows, soaring stone walls, and flowery courtyards the focus of Navarrese courtly life. Ramparts, spiral staircases, guard towers, lookout perches, moats, alligators, distressed damsels, dragons, armored attackers, poison-dipped arrows, and court jesters—this is the medieval palace of your dreams. Burned during the Napoleonic wars, the palace has been restored and was made a national monument in 1925. (Palace open Mon.-Sat. 10am-2pm and 5-7pm, Sun. 10am-2pm; Oct.-March Mon.-Sat. 10am-2pm and 4-5pm, Sun. 10am-2pm. Free.)

The palace chapel, **Iglesia de Santa María,** is noted for its 14th-century Gothic facade and its belfry. **Iglesia de San Pedro** is fitted with an octagonal tower; for San Pedro turn right on R. Villavieja and follow it to its end. (Both open only during mass, 10am and 8pm.)

Practical Information The bus unloads on Ctra. Zaragoza, which runs through Olite. From there, turn left (if coming from Pamplona) to reach Pl. Carlos III. The metal staircase in the middle of the plaza leads to the helpful **tourist office** (tel. 71 24 34; open April-Sept. Mon.-Sat. 10am-2pm and 4:30-7:30pm). A series of *galerías,* old escape tunnels, now house art exhibitions (same hours as tourist office). The **post office** is on the left side of the plaza, as you face the palace (tel. 74 05 82; open Mon.-Sat. 9-11:30am). The **postal code** is 31390. **Telephone booths** are in Pl. Teobaldos; the **telephone code** is 948. **Taxis Villar** can be reached at tel. 74 01 43. **Public bathrooms** are next to the post office. For medical attention, call the **pharmacy** in the plaza at tel. 74 00 36; it will open after hours if you call. The **Centro de Salud** (medical center; tel. 71 23 64) is on the outskirts of the old city on Ctra. Zaragoza. **Emergencies** in all of Navarra are directed to tel. 061. The three **municipal police** have no permanent office, so call the **Guardia Civil** at tel. 74 00 07.

Trains run to Pamplona (2-3 per day, 35min., 400ptas), Tudela, and other points on the Vitoria-Gasteiz-Zaragoza line. To get from the RENFE station to Pl. Carlos III, take C. Estación and turn left, following the sign to Zaragoza. The next left is C. El Portillo, which leads to the plaza. Conda (tel. 82 03 42) and La Tafallesa (tel. 70 09 79) run **buses** to Pamplona (6-12 per day, 45min., 380ptas) and Tudela (4-5 per day, 45min., 390ptas). Note that the return buses stop a little farther down the road.

Accommodations and Food The luxurious and rarefied air of the court lingers in many of Olite's restaurants and accommodations. An exception is the budget-minded **Fonda Gambarte**, R. Seco, 13, 2nd fl. (tel. 74 01 39), off Pl. Carlos III. (Doubles 3000ptas.) The second option is **Pensión Cesareo Vidaurre**, Pl. Carlos III, 22, 1st fl. (tel. 74 05 97), to the right of the tourist office staircase with your back to the battlements. The nondescript entrance and teeny *"camas"* sign belie bright rooms upstairs. (Doubles 3000ptas, lower in off-season and for longer stays.) Both are small and can fill up, especially during *Sanfermines*, so call ahead. **Camping Ciudade Olite** (tel. 71 24 43), 8km northwest from Olite, has a restaurant, swimming pool, and other modern conveniences. Follow the signs from the Pamplona-Zaragoza highway. (400ptas per person, per tent, and per car.)

There are several **supermarkets** on C. Mayor, off Pl. Carlos III. Downstairs from the *fonda*, **Restaurante Gambarte** serves a royal 3-course *menú* for 1000ptas. (Open 1-3:30pm and 8-11pm.)

Near Olite

Ujué crowns a hill 20km from Olite. Perched at the top, and with splendid views, is **Iglesia Fortaleza de Santa María de Ujué,** an 11th-century Romanesque fortress-basilica. The church guards Carlos II's heart. (Call the *parroquia* at tel. 73 81 28 (Spanish only) for information on visits.) At the close of April, a solemn procession of the faithful, shoeless and dressed in tunics, some bearing crosses, climbs silently to the top to worship the **Imágen Románica de la Virgen** (Romanesque Image of the Virgin) inside. Tafallesa **buses** from Pamplona to Olite (see Olite for details) pause in Tafalla, where a bus connects to Ujué (Mon., Wed., Fri. 7pm, 150ptas; return to Tafalla Mon., Wed., Fri. 8:45am).

The hard-luck **Monasterio de la Oliva,** 28km from Olite, has survived numerous sackings and years of wear-and-tear since it was built in 1164. The result is an architectural palimpsest of Romanesque, Gothic, and Baroque. Despite the centuries of turbulence, monks continue to monk along here. Tafallesa buses (tel. 70 09 79) run from Pamplona to Olite and continue on to **Carcastillo,** a town 2km from the monastery (2-3 per day, 1½hr., 565ptas).

TUDELA

Tudela exemplifies Navarra's distinction as a crossroads of cultures. Coming into its own in the 9th century, Tudela was a major Muslim center until 1119, when Christian forces under King Sancho the Strong regained control of the land. Both Muslim and Jewish populations remained strong throughout the Middle Ages. The town's *morería* and *judería* were the most important in Navarra, and furnished such figures as poet and philosopher Jehuda Haleví, scholar Abraham ben Ezra, and celebrated globe-trotter and son of a rabbi, Benjamín de Tudela, who in the 12th century traveled as far as the western frontier of China before Marco Polo. Today Navarra's second largest city, Tudela (pop. 30,000) welcomes with airy plazas, pedestrian-friendly streets, and a myriad of comfortable cafés. If urban roaming is your thing, but park sleeping and mobs of drunken revelers are not, Tudela is an ideal alternative to Pamplona during *Sanfermines* (July 6-14).

Old town and new meet in **Plaza de los Fueros,** erstwhile sight of the town's bullfights. The **Casa del Reloj,** with its distinctive clock (hence the name), presides on the western end. North of the plaza is the *cazco antiguo,* overlooked by the **Castillo de Sancho el Fuerte** and the **Monumento al Corazón de Jesús,** which crown a hill at the edge of town. To the south stretches the modern town, capped by the **Atalaya** (literally lookout), also known as the Torre de Monreal, built under Muslim rule in the 9th century and reformed in the 19th and 20th centuries. These two highpoints face off over the plaza and provide panoramas of Tudela and its surroundings.

In the heart of the *casco antiguo,* site of the old *morería* and *judería,* rises the airy Gothic **catedral,** built over the town's old mosque. An amalgam of building periods, the cathedral features a Romanesque cloister, several 15th-century Gothic *retablos,* and two ornate, cupola-crowned *capillas.* The more elaborate of these is the multi-colored *capilla de Santa Ana,* built in the 18th century. The cathedral is on Pl. Vieja. To get there from Pl. Fueros, go north on C. Concarera to Pl. San Jaime, then turn right. (Open Tues.-Sat. 9am-1pm and 4-7pm, Sun. 9am-1pm.)

Winding through the *cazco antiguo,* the monumental tour of Tudela is rounded out by the 12th-century **Iglesia de la Magdalena** on its northeast edge; the 16th-century **Palacio del Marqués de San Adrián,** which today houses the *Universidad a distancia;* the 18th-century **Palacio del Marqués de Huarte,** home to the town's library and archives and a Rococo carriage that once belonged to the Marqués de San Andrián; and the **Iglesia de San Nicolás,** whose Romanesque portico alone is worth a side trip.

Tudela's **nightlife** is lively and nomadic. Early in the evening, friends gather in bars and cafés between Pl. Fueros and the cathedral to chat over a *caña* or a glass of wine. Then it's on to **Calle San Marcial,** east of the plaza, and **Calle Aranaz y Vides,** stretching north from the bus station (toward the old town), where pits of perdition function until the wee hours. For intense relaxation, check out the cafés on **Calle Herrerías,** off Pl. Fueros at the end of C. Yanguas y Miranda.

Practical Information The **tourist office** (tel. 82 15 39) on C. Muro, about 1 bl. east of Pl. Fueros, has a great indexed map and information on budget accommodations. (Open Mon.-Sat. 10am-3pm.) The **post office** is on C. Juan Antonio Fernández, 4 (tel. 41 05 95), a right at the end of C. Eza D. Miguel, off Pl. Fueros. The **postal code** is 31500. There are **public phones** in Pl. Fueros; the **telephone code** is 948. The **Red Cross** is on Po. Pamplona (tel. 82 74 11). **Hospital Comarcal Reina Sofía** (tel. 82 75 00) provides health care outside of town on the road to Tarazona. More accessible is the **Ambulatorio Santana,** C. Juan Antonio Fernández, 11 (tel. 82 06 93), near the post office. In an **emergency,** dial 092. The **Guardia Civil** are at C. Aranaz y Vides, 8 (tel. 82 00 73); the **municipal police** on C. San Marcial (tel. 82 04 93); and the **national police** on Pl. Padre Lasa (tel. 82 09 85).

With solid transportation connections, Tudela makes a good base for exploring southern Navarra and its surroundings, especially Olite and Tarazona in Aragón. Two RENFE **train** lines run through Tudela: one connects La Rioja to Zaragoza, via Castejón de Ebro; the other connects Zaragoza to Vitoria-Gasteiz, via Pamplona. **RENFE information** (tel. 82 06 46). To Pamplona (4-7 per day, 1¼hr., 630-1200ptas). To get to Pl. Fueros from the train station, cross the plaza past the statue, make a second right on Av. Zaragoza, follow the *avenida* for 5 bl., then turn left near its end on C. Gatzambide-Carrera, which leads west to the plaza.

Conda **buses** (tel. 22 10 26) run to: Pamplona (6-9 per day, 1½hr., 720-795ptas); Olite (4-5 per day, 45min., 390ptas); and Tarazona (Mon.-Sat. 5 per day, 45min., 190ptas). Also to Madrid, Soria, Zaragoza, and San Sebastián. To get to Pl. Fueros from the bus station (which is on the street that leads to its railway sister), turn left on Cuesta de la Estación, then make an immediate right on Av. Zaragoza and follow instructions from the train station (above).

Accommodations and Food The tourist office has comprehensive information on accommodations; ask them to recommend budget options. **Hostal Remigio,** C. Gaztambide, 4 (tel. 82 08 50), off Pl. Fueros on the way to the train and bus stations, has modern rooms with phones and pristine bathrooms. Restaurant downstairs serves a 1150pta 4-course *menú.* (Singles 1750ptas, with bath 2550ptas. Doubles 3400ptas, with bath 4500ptas. AmEx accepted.) Restaurants offering affordable *menús* abound on and around Av. Zaragoza and in the winding alleys of the *cazco antiguo.* Every picnicker's dream, the **Mercado de Abastos,** off Pl. San Jaime near the cathedral, sells everything from hams to cheeses to fruits to cow brains to breads. (Open Mon.-Fri. 8am-1:30pm and 5-8pm, Sat. 8am-2pm.)

Near Tudela: The Bardenas Reales

The awesome desert of the Bardenas Reales, with titanically textured hills and cliffs wrought by erosion, stretches for over 400 sq. km off the beginning of the road connecting Tudela to Pamplona. The area vistas are best contemplated from a mountain bike or car. To rent one of the former, take the bus from Tudela to Pamplona and ask to be let off in the unremarkable, sun-blasted town of **Arguedas** (15min., 110ptas). There, **Ciclos Marton,** C. San Ignacio, 2 (tel. 83 15 77 or 83 00 85) has mountain bikes for full-day rental (2000ptas for first day, 1000ptas per additional day). Don't forget the Bardenas are a desert; call ahead about weather conditions, as the heat, especially in summer, can be prohibitive. The tourist office in Tudela can provide tips and directions.

ESTELLA

Suspended between the robust cities of Logroño and Pamplona, intimate Estella (pop. 13,000) is working overtime to earn respect on the Camino block. What it lacks in size and glamour, this quiet town more than makes up for in cheerful hospitality toward pilgrims of all types. Just remember that this is the place where, in the 17th century, the Ayuntamiento properly attired every citizen for a visit by Felipe III (and went broke in the process.) A number of monuments to Estella's medieval dynamism remind visitors that it was once the second largest market town in Europe (c. 13th century). The town still bears traces of its heyday as a multi-ethnic metropolis, with Jewish, Frankish, and Navarrese quarters.

In the "modern" quarter, the 12th century **Iglesia de San Miguel,** whose five-arch doorway dons capitals of the baby Jesus, commands a view of the town from the hilltop Pl. San Miguel. Up the stairs opposite the tourist office, the **Iglesia de San Pedro de la Rúa** towers above **Calle de la Rúa,** the main street of the original mercantile center. This elderly Gothic church flaunts a Romanesque baptismal font. Behind the building, a 100-ft. cliff rises above the Romanesque cloister. Left from the tourist office at the end of C. Rúa lurks the street's crowning glory, the restoration-hungry **Iglesia del Santo Sepulcro,** whose 14th-century facade features a monstrous Satan swallowing the damned by the mouthful. Outside of mass hours, the first two churches can only be visited through tours in Spanish organized by the tourist office (½-hr. tour of San Pedro, 125ptas; 1½-hr. tour of San Pedro, San Miguel, and the outside of Santo Sepulcro, 250ptas). Several tours per day; ask at the tourist office for information (see below).

Across from San Pedro, next to the tourist office, the oldest stone Roland in the world jousts with Farragut the Moor on the capitals of the 12th-century **Palacio de los Reyes de Navarra.** (Tel. 54 60 37; open Tues.-Sat. 11am-1pm and 5-7pm, Sun. 11am-1pm. Free.) Several **craft artists** on C. Rúa recreate medieval Navarrese carved-wood furniture and knick-knacks, including *templetas* (wooden knockers used to clack the hours of mass during Lent) and *argisaiolas* (human-shaped sculptures used by Navarrese witches and the Catholic clergy). Towering above, **Monte Amaya** provides a spectacular panorama of the valley.

The week-long **Fiestas de la Virgen del Puy y San Andrés** kick off the Friday before the first Sunday in August. Estella has its own *encierro* with heifers, smaller and less ferocious than Pamplona's *toros*. Kiddie entertainment, a fair, and Navarrese *gaitas* (bagpipes without the bags) in the streets round out the *fiestas*.

Practical Information Estella snuggles into a bend in the Río Ega. Two perpendicular axes define the town. **Calle San Andrés/Calle Baja Navarra** runs SW-NE from the bus station on Pl. Coronación to **Plaza de los Fueros,** the *Autobahn* of the evening *paseo*. **Paseo de la Inmaculada Concepción** runs NW-SE from C. Dr. Huarte to the **Puente del Azucarero** (right if coming from the bus station), which spans the river to the old town, most sights, and the tourist office.

The **tourist office** is on C. Rúa, 3 (tel. 55 40 11), straight from the bridge through Pl. San Martín, and around the corner to the right. Indexed map and good information on the Camino and surrounding areas. (Open Mon.-Sat. 10am-2pm and 4-7pm, Sun. 10am-2pm.) The **post office** is on Po. Inmaculada, 5 (tel. 55 17 92; open for stamps, Lista de Correos, and **telegrams** Mon.-Fri. 8am-3pm, Sat. 9am-1pm). The **postal code** is 31200. **Phone booths** line Po. Inmaculada; the **telephone code** is 948. The **Centro de Salud** heals at Po. Inmaculada, 39 (tel. 55 07 37). For **ambulances,** call tel. 55 04 68; for the **Red Cross,** tel. 55 10 11. The **police** are in the Ayuntamiento, Po. Inmaculada, 1, and can be reached at tel. 55 08 13 or 092. The **emergency** phone number for all of Navarra is 061.

Most of the **buses** running from the former RENFE station on Pl. Coronación belong to La Estellesa (tel. 55 01 27). To: Pamplona (5-11 per day, 1hr., 380ptas); Logroño (5-7 per day, 1hr., 445ptas); San Sebastián (3-4 per day, 2¼hr., 450-1060ptas); Zaragoza (Mon.-Sat. 1 per day, 3hr., 1460ptas). Autobuses Pinedo goes to Vitoria-Gasteiz (3-4 per day, 1½hr., 540ptas).

Accommodations and Food Close to Pamplona, Estella can be a good place to catch some shut-eye during *Sanfermines*. Reservations are advisable during the town's August *fiesta*. **Pensión San Andrés,** Pl. Santiago, 50 (tel. 55 04 48 or 55 41 58), has an elevator and happy little rooms, some with TVs. A first left off C. Baja Navarra after crossing Po. Inmaculada takes you down C. Mayor to Pl. Santiago. (Singles 1600ptas. Doubles 3180ptas, with bath 5000ptas. Triples with bath 6000ptas.) **Fonde Izarra,** C. Calderería, 20 (tel. 55 06 78), off Pl. Fueros, offers simple, clean rooms. Its restaurant has a 1000pta *menú*. (Rare singles 1500ptas. Doubles 2800ptas. Visa accepted.) For the wild at heart, there's **Camping Lizarra** (tel. 55 17 33), on C. Ordoiz, left from the tourist office and 1km down river. Supermarket, pool, and mountain bike rentals. (390ptas per person, 1200ptas per *parcela,* which includes tent, car, and electricity.)

Estella is known throughout the region for its *gorrín asado* (roast piglet, also called *gorrín de Estella)*. If the thought of chowing on Winnie the Pooh's best buddy makes you uncomfortable, go for one of their vegetarian classics: *menestra de verduras* (mixed, cooked vegetables) or *alubias blancas* (white beans). Picnickers can stock up at **Autoservicio Moreno,** C. Zapatería, at the corner with C. Navarrería. To get there, take a first right off C. Baja Navarra and cross Po. Inmaculado, then straight 3-4 bl. (Open Mon.-Fri. 8am-1:30pm and 4-7:30pm, Sat. 8am-2pm.) **Restaurante Casanova,** C. Fray Wenceslao de Oñate, 7 (tel. 55 28 09), a left as you enter Pl. Fueros, has overwhelming portions that are sure to slow down any pilgrim's progress. Lunch and dinner *menú* 1000ptas. Entrees 400-1700ptas. (Open Mon.-Fri. 1-3:30pm and 9-11pm, Sat. 9am-2am.)

NAVARRESE PYRENEES

Navarra has the most topographically diverse range of the Pyrenees. While truly forbidding peaks reach as far as Valle de Roncal, the mountain slopes to the west lose their ferocity and height, allowing easier access to the streams, waterfalls, and verdant meadows which dot the area. Navarrese slopes are lusher and greener than their Aragonese and Catalan counterparts. The valleys fill with mist and fog even on summer mornings, obscuring visibility; you should bring your raincoat and sweater if you plan to get up before noon. Navarrese villages remain largely isolated; their main industries are cattle and logging.

Tourism is also a booming business. **El Camino de Santiago** (El Camino, or St. James Way) is the celebrated cross-kingdom supertrek of intrepid pilgrims who clambered over these peaks from France (see Santiago de Compostela: El Camino de Santiago). The most popular pilgrimage route crosses the French border at Ronces-valles, and continues to Santiago de Compostela in Galicia. Many free or cheap *refugios* cater to weary, modern-day pilgrims along the way. To follow the route, get the best available guide (in Spanish), the *Guía práctica del peregrino,* published by Edi-ciones Everest (2500ptas). For information on the extensive and well-managed net-work of Navarrese *casas rurales,* refurbished farmhouses that lodge travelers, ask for the free *Guía de alojamientos de turismo rural* in any of Navarra's tourist offices. For reservations, call the central office at (948) 22 93 28.

From Pamplona, you can head east toward Valle de Roncal (via Sangüesa), or north toward Roncesvalles. Buses are one-a-day affairs (if at all) through most of the area; Pamplona is the only sensible base. New government-sponsored **El Topillo** buses, which organize excursions throughout the Pyrenees, are an alternative option (for info, ask at a tourist office).

SANGÜESA

Set in the arid foothills 44km east of Pamplona, Sangüesa attracts vacationing Span-iards and hikers en route to either the Pyrenees or the spectacular Lumbier and Arbayún gorges, which have made Navarra's monumental landscape famous. Although the city's economy is traditionally agricultural, on bad days it reeks of its industrial side, the paper factory.

The legacy of the Camino de Santiago appears first and foremost in the main entrance to the **Iglesia de Santa María,** a veritable triumph of Romanesque sculp-ture. The central relief depicts the Day of Judgment, with fanged devils casting the damned into the cavernous mouth of Lucifer. The woman nursing a toad on one breast and a snake on the other is a conventional iconographic rendering of Lust. Inside is a hairy Baroque Madonna whose human locks are changed every 10 to 15 years. Beware the sound of scissors. To get to the church from the bus stop, go left on C. Mayor off C. Alfonso El Batallador and continue to the river.

On the way you'll pass the Gothic stone St. James, straddling a large conch before the **Iglesia de Santiago.** Behind him, two giggling cloaked pilgrims hold staffs and cockleshells in homage to him. St. Francis himself is supposed to have sojourned in Sangüesa during his pilgrimage to Compostela, home of the first Franciscan hermit-age outside of Italy.

The town's **Fiesta Mayor** falls September 11-17 and includes a communal dance to the C. Mayor every night at midnight and 1:30am.

The **tourist office,** C. Alfonso el Batallador, 20 (tel. 87 03 29), is on the right as you enter the Palacio de Vallesantoro. The staff is fluent in English. (Open Oct.-June Mon.-Sat. 10am-2pm and 4-7pm, Sun. 10am-2pm.) The **post office** is at Fermín de Lubián, 17, pass the tourist office on Pl. Fueros. The **postal code** is 31400. The **tele-phone code** is 948. The **Red Cross** (tel. 87 05 27) is on C. Mercado, s/n, past the tourist office. For **medical services** there's a Centro de Salud (tel. 87 03 38) on the road to Cantolagua. The **municipal police** can be called at tel. 87 03 10; the **Guardia Civil** (tel. 87 00 55) is posted at Benabé Armendaríz, 17. In **emergencies** of any kind, dial 061 in all of Navarra.

Considering Sangüesa's proximity to popular tourist sites, the paucity of afford-able lodging is surprising—and potentially frustrating. One option is **Pensión Las Navas,** C. Alfonso el Batallador, 7 (tel. 87 00 77). Flamboyant pink curtains and bed-spreads simper in the clean and comfortable rooms (1750ptas per person, with bath 2000ptas). Ask at the tourist office for a guide to *casas particulares*; some visitors have luck with the houses on C. Mayor. For campers, the only game in town is

Camping Cantolagua (tel. 43 03 52), located near the Ciudad Deportivo outside of town. (400ptas per person, 350ptas per car, 375ptas per tent. Open all year.) **Restaurant Acuario,** C. Santiago, 9, off C. Mayor, serves a simple but satisfying *menú* (1000ptas) amid the dulcet strains of Spanish muzak. The town's **market** is held on Pl. Toros (Fri. 9am-2pm), at the end of C. Alfonso el Ballatador away from C. Mayor.

Veloz Sangüesina **buses** (tel. 87 02 09) go to and from Pamplona (3 per day, Sun. 1 per day, 45min., 380ptas) and deposit passengers on C. Alfonso el Batallador near the corner with C. Gil de Jaz.

Near Sangüesa

Two fantastic gorges lie within 12km of Sangüesa. The **Foz de Lumbier** (Lumbier Gorge) is 2km outside of the little town of **Liédena,** on the bus route from Sangüesa to Pamplona. Hundred-and-fifty-foot walls, home to a large flock of griffin vultures, surround one side of this yawning gorge on the Río Irati. About 2km from the opposite edge of the gorge sits the town of **Lumbier.** A 12km ride from here brings you to **Iso** and to the mouth of an even more impressive gorge, the **Foz de Arbayún** (Arbayún Gorge). If the Río Salazar is low enough in the late summer, you can swim, or even hike your way through this 4km chasm; at other times of year, the petrifying cold water forces hikers to raft or canoe it. There is no pre-blazed trail here, so watch your step. Ask locals in Iso about conditions before setting up the TNT, sharpening the machete, or attempting any kind of expedition. The tourist office in Sangüesa provides more detailed information on how to reach these gorges. If you have a car, look for the signs off N-240 in the direction of Pamplona.

Castillo de Javier

Near the small village of **Yesa,** 8km from Sangüesa by the even smaller village of **Javier,** is the restored **Castillo de Javier.** Poised on the border between Navarra and Aragón, the castle has changed hands numerous times over the last millennium. Today it belongs to the Jesuit order, which has made it a monument to St. Francis Xavier, the missionary who was born here in 1506. Priests and apprentices conduct tours of the Disney-esque castle in Spanish only. The Tower of the Holy Christ houses a 14th-century effigy which allegedly has spontaneous blood-sweating fits. The castle also provides the very best in moat-crossing and boiling-oil-pouring prac-tice. (Open Mon.-Sat. 9am-1pm and 4-7pm, Sun. 10-11:15am, 1:15-2:30pm, and 4-7:30pm. Tours every ½hr. Free.)

La Tafallesa (tel. 22 28 86) runs a **bus** to Javier from Pamplona (Mon.-Fri. at 5pm, Sat. at 1pm, 1hr., 465ptas) continuing to nearby Yesa and on to Roncal and Isaba (see below).

MONASTERIO DE LEYRE

Windswept and austere, miles from any other settlement, the Monasterio de Leyre silently surveys the foothills of the Pyrenees and the fabricated Lago de Yesa. Hang-gliders launch themselves off the very same hills where great wealth and power once presided. Several centuries back, medieval Navarrese kings took up residence in the **monasterio medieval.** Because monks still live at Leyre, you cannot enter this part of the complex, nor the 20th-century **monasterio nuevo.** However, the rather dank, subterranean **cripta** eagerly welcomes the public (open daily 10:30am-1:30pm and 4-6:30pm, admission 100ptas). The architectural highlight of the monastic complex is the ghoulish **Portal de la Iglesia.** Outside the monastery, there is a path to the **Fuente de San Virila.** The fountain occupies the site where, according to legend, the abbot of San Virila, attempting to determine the nature of heaven, swung into a 300-year trance induced by the singing of a little bird (call the monk voice lackey tel. 88 40 11 for more information).

Outside the monastery, the **Hospedería de Leyre** (tel. 88 41 00) offers vast, gleaming rooms that make the nearby monks' cells look like, well, monks' cells. (Singles 3600ptas. Doubles 6400ptas. July-Aug. and Semana Santa: 3900ptas; 7800ptas.) **Bar Restaurant Yamaguchy 2,** at the intersection of the roads to Pamplona and Sangüesa, has a 1200pta *menú* and al fresco dining. The **Red Cross** (tel. 88 41 52) is back a bit towards Huesca. The **telephone code** is 948.

The monastery lies about one hour away from Pamplona, off the highway to Huesca. To get to it, take the La Tafallesa **bus** (tel. 22 28 86) from Pamplona to Yesa (1 hr., 465ptas). From Yesa, follow the road back to Pamplona for about 1km and turn right at the clearly marked sign. From there, it's about 4km uphill—not too strenuous in fine weather, but a real grind in one of the frequent gales that wrack the region.

RONCESVALLES

The somber, mist-enshrouded monastery of Roncesvalles rests amid miles of thickly wooded mountains in imperturbable magnificence. Welcome to Avalon. The Valley of the Thorns is 48km from Pamplona, 20km the French border, and eons from reality. Its cold stone walls are a monument to the continuing primacy of myth over history. For more than 1000 years, pilgrims, poets, and romantics have been drawn by the legend and spiritual shrine planted in the rugged slopes of **Puerto Ibañeta** (1057m), about 1½km up the main road from the monastery.

The mythical site of Roland's last hours, Roncesvalles is filled with remembrances of the legendary warrior. According to legend, the stone split in two on the road in Ibañeta was cut by Roland himself, as he tried in vain to destroy his beloved sword Durandal to keep it from falling into the hands of the enemy upon his death. A different popular source—his song—claims that the Moor Marsillo killed Roland, embracing his sword. Charlemagne's nephew actually fell in 778 at the hands of the Navarrese, who were perturbed that the Emperor had razed the walls of Pamplona, but no one seems to care that the battle didn't take place here. The heavily restored **Capilla de Sancti Spiritus** stands over the remains of a bone-heap (courtesy of dead soldiers and pilgrims), marking the spot of Roland's unanswered plea for help. The gates are always closed, as is the entrance to the tiny 12th-century **Capilla de Santiago** next door to the left. The light switch will illuminate a statue silhouetted against an alabaster window.

Inside the **Colegiata** (tel. 76 00 00), just up the driveway from the *capilla,* tombs of King Sancho El Fuerte (the Strong) and his bride rest in solitary splendor, lit by huge stained-glass windows. Sancho was so tall (over 7 ft.) and strong, that legend has it with his own hands he broke the chains which protected the tent of the Arab leader in the decisive battle of the Navas de Tolosa. The heavy iron chains, which hang from the walls of the chamber, are represented in Navarra's flag. The monastery's Gothic church, endowed by the dead king and consecrated in 1219, is its main attraction; the elegant vaulting and comic-book vivid stained-glass battle scenes were ahead of their time. Beneath a soaring canopy weeps the golden and silvery **Virgen de las Lágrimas** (Virgin of Tears). (Church and cloister open daily 8am-8pm.) To the right under the first arch on the monastery, a small **museo** houses religious artifacts. (Open Tues.-Sun. 11am-1:30pm and 4-6pm; Oct.-June Sat.-Sun. 11am-1:30pm and 4-6pm. Admission 200ptas.)

A shiny, well-stocked **tourist office** (tel. 76 01 93), in the tin-roofed mill behind Casa Sabina Hostería, has excellent maps and guides to the Camino de Santiago. (Open 10am-2pm and 3-6pm; Oct.-May 10am-3pm.) The **telephone code** is 948.

Those undertaking the Camino de Santiago love to start from Roncesvalles. The **monastery** has free lodging for Camino followers—enter the door to the right as you face the monastery. Youth groups and hikers crowd **Albergue Juvenil Roncesvalles (HI)** (tel. 76 00 15; guests' public phone 79 04 03), at the back of the monastery and to the right. (Members only. 800ptas. *Pensión completa* 2000ptas. Over 26: 1000ptas; 2500ptas. Breakfast 300ptas. Visa, MC accepted.) **Casa Sabina Hostería** (tel. 76 00 12 or 79 04 38), uphill from the monastery on the main road, offers doubles with bath (4500ptas) and a 1500pta *menú.* It's small, so call ahead.

Near Roncesvalles: Burguete

It's a pleasant 2½km walk to Burguete (pop. 300), the nearest town braved by public transportation. Accommodations in Burguete are generally easy to find. Hemingway's rest stop on his way back from *Sanfermines*, **Hostal Burguete**, C. Unica, 51
(tel. 76 00 05), has rooms with high, plump beds off hallways large enough to host
pelota vasca games. (Doubles 3400ptas, with bath 4200ptas. Breakfast 400ptas.)
Further downhill on C. Unica, **Hostal Juandeaburre** (tel. 76 00 78) is similarly
quaint. (Singles 1450ptas. Doubles 3350ptas.) **Camping Urrobi** (tel. 76 02 00),
2½km downhill from Burguete in Espinal, has tennis courts and a small grocery
store. (Open April-Oct. 375ptas per person, per tent, and per car.) La Montañesa
buses (tel. 22 15 84) run from Pamplona to Burguete Friday at 6pm and Saturday at
4pm, continuing to Roncesvalles if asked (1¼hr., 480ptas). The return bus leaves
Burguete Saturday and Monday at 7:15am. Burguete's **Guardia Civil** (tel. 76 00 06)
serves the valley and its environs. Call them in an **emergency,** or dial 061.

VALLE DE AÉZCOA

An 8km crow flight east of Roncesvalles, the Valle de Aézcoa welcomes hikers and
nature lovers with mist topped forests, wandering brooks, and whispering bird
songs that mingle with the remains of spoken Basque. By car, the coffee table book
town of **Arive,** a small collection of white houses with steep red roofs 25km from
Burguete, is the point of entry into the valley. From there, a narrow road winds
north through the woods, following the course of the Río Irati, past the equally picturesque villages of **Orbara** and **Orbaiceta** to the hamlet of **Barrio Larraún,** whose
refugio makes a good base for hikers in the area. 9½km from Arive, **Refugio Mendi-
tatz** offers winter heating, hot showers, and *literas* (800ptas per person). The restaurant downstairs has a 1000pta *menú* and 200pta breakfast. The staff is an
excellent source for hiking advice. **Camping de Orbaiceta,** at the entrance to Orbaiceta 3km south, should be open by 1995. *Casas rurales* provide alternative accommodations (ask at a nearby tourist office). Because of its relative proximity and the
trails connecting it to Aézcoa, **Roncesvalles** can make a good base as well.

The area is characterized by its rivers, thick, humid woods, and ecological wealth.
Deer sightings are not uncommon, and ancient ruins dot the mountains. The essential *Editorial Alpina* map is available at the *refugio* (500-600ptas). The area's most
traditional hike connects Barrio Larraún to Roncesvalles, passing through the beautiful forest and prairies (5-6hr. each way). An easier and more well-defined trail (also
great on **mountain bike)** leads east from Barrio Larraún to the artificial but striking
Embalse de Irabia (dam of Irabia), and from there to the **Ermita de Nuestra Señora
de las Nieves** following the Río Irati (8hr. round-trip from the *refugio).* A more
strenuous hike begins on the same trail that leads to Roncesvalles, but continues
straight north to **Monte Urkulu** (1423m). Right on the French border and crowned
by a mysterious round tower, it provides glorious panoramas on both sides of the
frontier (6hr. round-trip from the *refugio).* Shorter but scenic excursions can be
done by car. Ask at the *refugio* about road conditions.

The closest **tourist office** is in **Garralda,** about 4km from Arive on the road to Burguete. (Open July-Sept.) There's a **pharmacy** in Arive across from the exit to Orbaiceta. (Open Mon.-Fri. 9am-2:30pm and 5-9pm; Sat. 9am-2:30pm.) In an **emergency,**
call the **Guardia Civil** in Burguete (tel. 76 00 06) or dial 061.

OCHAGAVÍA

Set on the banks of the Río Andena, Ochagavía (pop. 622) is 40km (but a draining
90km bus ride) from Pamplona. The biggest town in the **Valle de Salazar,** Ochagavía's charm stems from cobblestoned streets and bleached stone buildings with
ochre roofs. The restored 16th-century **Hermita de Musquilda** is a 30-min. hike.

The **tourist office** (tel. 89 00 04) on the main road opens during Holy Week and
July-Sept. 20 (Tues.-Sat. 10am-2pm and 4-7pm, Sun. 10am-3pm). The **post office** is
open Mon.-Fri. 10am-2pm; Sat. 11-noon for urgent **telegrams** only. The **postal code**

is 31680. There are public **phones** across the main road from the tourist office. The **telephone code** is 948. In **emergencies** call 061.

Across the river from the main road is **Hostal Laspalas,** C. Urrutia, s/n (tel. 89 00 15). Some rooms have views of the river, others have bathrooms like soccer fields. (Singles 1650ptas, with bath 3000ptas. Doubles 3000ptas, with bath 4000ptas.) Over the river and through the woods, the **Pensión Auñamendi** (tel. 89 01 89) is on the left some distance after the bridge. Geraniums in balconies outside; pleasant, simple decor inside. (Doubles 3700ptas, with bath 4200ptas. Triples 4700ptas, with bath 5200ptas.) **Camping Osate** (tel. 89 01 84), at the entrance to town, provides a modern campsite on the river (400ptas per person, per tent, and per car). They also rent **mountain bikes** (500ptas per hr., 1500ptas per ½-day, 2500ptas per full day).

Río Irati (tel. 22 17 40) runs **buses** to and from Pamplona (from Ochagavía Mon.-Sat. 1 per day at 7am; from Pamplona Mon.-Fri. 1 per day at 6pm, Sat. 2 per day at noon and 6pm; 640ptas).

RONCAL AND ISABA

If you don't know who Julián Gayarre is, maybe you should skip ahead to Isaba. Tiny **Roncal** (pop. 200), at the heart of Navarra's easternmost valley, is famous for two products: *Queso Roncal* and the world-renowned tenor Julián Gayarre. Every grocery store in the valley sells the former, a sharp cheese made from sheep's milk. Numerous sculptures and monuments scattered about town commemorate the latter. Gayarre's tomb, an ornate flourish of dolorous cherubs and muses, blooms in the town cemetery, 800m along C. Castillo, which runs behind the *pelota* court from Pl. Julián Gayarre. Roncal won out over Queen María Cristina, who would have just died to have the fab mausoleum in front of the Teatro Real in Madrid. Hardcore Gayarre-heads thrill at the **Casa Museo Julián Gayarre,** a small museum in the house where the singer was born. Signs lead from the main (only) street. (Open Tues.-Sun. 11:30am-1:30pm and 5-7pm.) Along the way to the cemetery, you'll pass the **Casa de Junta de Valle,** which displays the town's traditional festival clothing. If its wrought-iron door won't open, schlep to the Casa Consistorial on the main road and ask for a key.

The **tourist office** (tel. 89 32 34) in the Ayuntamiento building on Pl. Julián Gayarre, is open July-Sept. and weekends year round. (Open 10am-2pm and 4:30-7:30pm, Sun. 10am-2pm.) Ask them about nearby hiking trails. The **post office** is uphill from Pl. Julián Gayarre near the smaller bridge across the river. (Open Mon.-Sat. 10am-2pm.) The **postal code** is 31415. Public **phones** are in front of the Ayuntamiento. The **telephone code** is 948. **Banco Central,** on the left on the main road on the way to Isaba, doles out *pesetas*. (Open June-Sept. Mon.-Fri. 8:30am-2:30pm.) There's a **pharmacy** diagonal from the bank. The **Guardia Civil** is at (tel. 47 50 05).

Across the river from the *pelota* court is **Hostal Zaltúa,** C. Castillo, 23 (tel. 47 50 08), with wood floors and full-size shower stalls. (Doubles 3200ptas, with bath 4600ptas.) You can also stay in a family's house by requesting the *casa particular* brochure at the tourist office. Free **camping** is permitted in the valley, but permission must first be received from the Ayuntamiento (tel. 47 50 49).

The more populous (pop. 300) village of **Isaba** straddles the highway 7km north of Roncal. Isaba's history consists of border disputes (fueled by wandering French livestock) that gripped the valley from 125 BC through the Middle Ages. These ancient squabbles are commemorated once a year with the **Tributo de las Tres Vacas (Tribute of the Three Cows).** Nearly every year since 1375, the French have donated three cows to the town on July 13. French and Spanish officials, dressed in traditional costume, join hands and solemnly pray for peace as the bovine harbingers of harmony switch nationalities. On any other boring cowless day, Isaba's main attraction is the large, 16th-century **Iglesia de Santa Engracia,** with a grandiose, 18th-century organ.

The **post office** is uphill from Albergue Oxanea (zig-zag left; open Mon.-Sat. 9-11am). The **postal code** is 31417. Public **phones** are in the small park with red benches at the entrance to town. The **telephone code** is 948. In an **emergency,** call the **Guardia Civil** (tel. 89 30 06) or dial 061.

Albergue Oxanea, C. Bormapea, 47 (tel. 89 31 53), left up the stone staircase uphill past the Centro de Salud, across from the red benches, is run by a group of young, friendly locals. Neat wooden *literas* (bunks) fit 8 and 14 to a room, and there's a VCR in the TV room. (800ptas per night with your own locker, 700ptas if you bring your own sleeping bag. Hot showers and sheets included.) For a bit more luxury, **Hostal Lola** (tel. 89 30 12) has sizable, tastefully decorated rooms with baths. (Singles 3000ptas. Doubles 5000ptas.) **Camping Asolaze** (tel. 89 30 34), 6km toward the French border, houses a restaurant and a store. (Open June-Sept. 425ptas per person, per tent, and per car.) Eight km north of Isaba, the earth opens up into the **Valle de Belagua.** A refuge/shelter operates near the valley. (Open June-Sept.) Check also in the guide to *Casas Rurales,* at any Navarrese tourist office, for local houses offering lodging.

La Tafallesa **buses** from Pamplona and Javier continue to Roncal (2hr., 800ptas from Pamplona) and on to Isaba (2¼hr., 810ptas).

■ Aragón

Comprising the provinces of Huesca, Zaragoza, and Teruel, this former kingdom embraces the towering central Pyrenees, the deeply ravined terraces of the Ebro basin, and the tawny, windswept plateaus of the south. Sheltered in green valleys amid the snow-capped peaks, 12th-century Romanesque churches and monasteries mark the pilgrims' progress toward Santiago de Compostela. In the flatlands below, hydroelectric and irrigation schemes harness the mountain streams and the Río Ebro, transforming large areas of the reddish desert into a vast green *huerta* (orchard). Both the names of towns and regional artwork reflect the Muslim influence here; from the fusion of Christian and Muslim cultures in this region, the intricate Mudejar architectural style developed.

The harsh terrain and climate couple with the region's strategic location to engender a martial culture, known among Spaniards for its obstinacy. (Did you hear the one about the *Aragonés* on the train tracks?) Established as a kingdom in 1035 and united with the commercially enterprising Catalans in 1137, Aragón forged a far-flung Mediterranean empire that brought Roussillon, Valencia, Murcia, the Baleares, Naples, Sicily, and even the Duchy of Athens under its sway. Aragonese kings were held in check by the nobility, *cortes* (parliaments), and cities with restrictive *fueros* (laws). From the 12th century on, an elected *Justicia* (magistrate) defended commoners' rights against overbearing royal or seignorial fiat. Aragón retained these privileges, even after union with Castile in 1492, until Felipe II marched into Zaragoza in 1591 and seized the Justicia Juan de Lanuza for giving sanctuary to his fallen minister Antonio Pérez. Economic decline followed the political humiliation; as all eyes and hands turned to the New World in the 16th century, people and capital fled from Aragón to the Atlantic coast.

Regional specialties take advantage of the abundant fresh-water fish from northern rivers and produce from the Ebro basin's orchards. *Ternasco* (roast lamb) and preparations with *chilindrón* (pepper and tomato) sauce are especially good here. Possibly the most famous local products are the strong, full-bodied red and white wines from the Cariñena-Daroca vineyards. *Frutas de Aragón* are dried fruits dipped in semi-sweet chocolate.

The omniscient *Guía de servicios turísticos de Aragón,* available at any tourist office in the kingdom, makes roaming easy, with comprehensive information on accommodations (including *casas rurales, refugios,* and campgrounds), tourist offices, and some emergency numbers.

■■■ ZARAGOZA

Zaragoza (pop. 620,000) is Spain's forgotten urban center. Augustus founded the city in 19 BC—naming it Cesaraugustus after himself—as a retirement colony for veterans, but Zaragoza rejected the slow-pulsed life, opting instead for expansion and industry. Zaragoza became, along with Mérida and Valencia, the base of Roman efforts to make Spain Rome's greenery. In Moorish times, Zaragoza was a *taifa* (tributary state) which developed into a full-fledged emirate, and was also the only part of Al-Andalus which refused to be incorporated into the Almoravid empire. The Almoravids were evangelical Muslims whose religious zeal doubtless made Zaragoza, more into profits than prophets, nervous. More recently, General Motors got serious industrial vibes from the city and set up its Spanish base here, cementing an already strong manufacturing sector.

Zaragoza's heritage, cultural wealth, and large university have not given it airs: it remains above all a genuine, pragmatic Iberian city. By the same token, Zaragoza's open spirit makes it the ideal place to experience urban Spain without the price tag and cosmopolitan hassle of metropoli like Madrid and Barcelona.

Z A R A G O Z A

ORIENTATION AND PRACTICAL INFORMATION

Zaragoza is laid out like a bicycle wheel. Five spokes radiate from the hub at **Plaza Basilio Paraíso.** Facing the center of the plaza with the IberCaja bank building at your back, the spokes going clockwise are: **Paseo de Sagasta; Gran Vía,** which turns into Po. Fernando el Católico; **Paseo de Pamplona,** which leads to Po. Marí Agustín and the train station; **Paseo de Independencia,** which ends at **Plaza de España** (the entrance to the *casco antiguo*); and **Paseo de la Constitución.**

The *casco antiguo,* or the old quarter, lies to the north of Pl. Paraíso at the end of Po. Independencia, stretching between Pl. España and Pl. Nuestra Señora del Pilar (commonly known as **Plaza del Pilar).** Several key museums and sights frame this plaza's borders, the most central and important being the grandiose **Basílica de Nuestra Señora del Pilar,** whose blue-and-yellow tiled domes are a good landmark.

To reach Pl. Pilar from Pl. Paraíso, walk down Po. Independencia to Pl. España, and take C. Don Jaime I (a bit to the right), which runs to the plaza. The user-friendly public bus system, plus city map blow-ups at major intersections, make touring easy.

Take care at night around the red-light and drug-dealing districts of C. Ramón Pignatelli and C. Agustina de Aragón, 4-5 bl. to the left of Pl. España facing the old quarter. Women travelers, especially solo, should be wary.

Tourist Office: City: Pl. Pilar (tel. 20 12 00; fax 20 06 35), in the black glass cube in front of the basilica. Request the *plano callejero* (indexed street map), as well as the tourist map. English speaking staff offers several useful guides to the city. The *Sitios de Zaragoza* booklet set (200ptas), available in English, has comprehensive info on restaurants, sights, and nightlife. Open Mon.-Sat. 9:30am-1:30pm and 4:30-7:30pm, Sun. 10am-1:30pm. **Regional: Torreón de la Zuda,** Glorieta de Pío XII (tel. 39 35 37), imprisoned in the squat tower to your far right as you face the basilica. Covers all of Aragón. Open Mon.-Fri. 8:15am-2:45pm and 4:30-8pm, Sat. 10am-2pm and 5-8pm, Sun. 10am-2pm; Oct.-June Mon.-Fri. 8:15am-2:45pm and 4-7:30pm, Sat. 9am-1:30pm, Sun. 9am-2pm.

El Corte Inglés: Po. Sagasta, 3 (tel. 22 93 01), near Pl. Paraíso. They have a **map. Currency exchange:** No commission, but lower raters. They also offer novels and guidebooks in English, haircutting, both cafeteria and restaurant, **supermarket,** and **telephones.** Open Mon.-Sat. 10am-9pm.

Budget Travel: TIVE, Residencial Paraíso, building 4, local 40 (tel. 21 83 15 or 22 98 46). From behind El Corte Inglés (see above), through the courtyard, up the stairs, and left; office on left. ISIC 500ptas. HI card 1800ptas. Usually deals only with foreign travel destinations, along with the Baleares. Open Mon.-Fri. 9am-1:30pm; Oct.-May Mon.-Fri. 9am-2pm.

Currency Exchange: Banks open 9am-2pm; some open afternoons in winter. Some luxury hotels will change currency in emergencies.

American Express: Viajes Turopa, Po. Sagasta, 47 (tel. 38 39 11; fax 25 42 44), 6 bl. from Pl. Paraíso; entrance around the corner on Camino de las Torres. Bus #33 from Pl. España stops nearby. Full services. Cardholder mail held. Slightly better exchange rates than banks, but service depends on cash availability. Open Mon.-Fri. 9am-1:30pm and 4-7:30pm, Sat. 9am-1pm.

Post Office: Po. Independencia, 33 (tel. 22 26 50), 1 bl. from Pl. Aragón on the right. Information booth open Mon.-Fri. 8:30am-3pm. Open for stamps, **fax,** and **telegrams** Mon.-Fri. 8am-9pm, Sat. 9am-7pm, Sun. 9am-2pm. For Lista de Correos (downstairs at window 4) Mon.-Fri. 8am-9pm, Sat. 9am-2pm. **Postal Code:** 50001.

Telephones: Public phones in Pl. España. **Telephone Code:** 976.

Flights: tel. 34 90 50. The Ebrobus (tel. 32 40 09) shuttles between the airport and its terminal on Pl. Aragón, 10, off Pl. Paraíso at the beginning of Po. Independencia (3-7 per day, 6:45am-9:30pm, 75ptas). A taxi (see Taxis below) to the airport costs about 1000ptas. Flights to: Barcelona (1 per day, except Sat.); Madrid (2 per day, Sat.-Sun. 1 per day); Jerez (1 per day, except Sat.); Paris (1-2 per day); London (3 per week). Check p. 2 of local paper *El Heraldo de Aragón* for current flight schedules. **Iberia,** C. Canfranc, 22-24 (tel. 21 82 59; domestic reservations tel.

(901) 33 31 11, international tel. (901) 33 32 22). From Pl. Paraíso, 3 bl. down Po. Pamplona on the right near Puerta del Carmen arch. Open Mon.-Fri. 9:30am-2pm and 4-7pm, Sat. 9:30am-1:30pm.

Trains: Estación Portillo, Av. Anselmo Clavé (information tel. 28 02 02). To find Pl. Paraíso from here, start upstairs, bear right down the ramp and walk across Av. Anselmo Clavé. Head 1 bl. down C. General Mayandía and turn right on Po. María Agustín; continue 7 bl. as the street becomes Po. Pamplona ending at Pl. Paraíso. (Bus #21 from Po. María Agustín.) Information booth open 6am-10pm. **RENFE** information and ticket office also at C. San Clemente, 13 (tel. 23 38 02). From the post office, turn right and follow Po. Independencia 2 bl., then turn right again. Open Mon.-Fri. 9am-2pm and 5-7pm, Sat. 9am-2pm. To: Tudela (14-18 per day, 45min., 400-460ptas); Huesca (3 per day, 1¼hr., 410-570ptas); Jaca (3 per day, 3½hr., 1065-1600ptas); Logroño (7-9 per day, 1½-2½hr., 955-1100ptas); Pamplona (6-8 per day, 2½hr., 955-1700ptas); Teruel (2-3 per day, 2½hr., 1065-1220ptas); Madrid (12 per day, 3-4hr., 2400-3500ptas); Vitoria (2-3 per day, 3hr., 1770-2000ptas); Barcelona (10-13 per day, 4½hr., 2400-7500ptas); Lérida (5-6 per day, 1¾-2¼hr., 1600-2200ptas); San Sebastián (1-2 per day, 4hr., 2200-2500ptas); Valencia (2 per day, 5-6hr., 2000-4100ptas); Bilbao (3 per day, 5hr., 2500-2700ptas); La Coruña (1 per day, 13hr., 6400ptas).

Buses: Various bus companies each have their own terminals. The tourist offices stock schedules for all companies. The most important lines are accessible by city bus from Pl. Paraíso.

Agreda Automóvil, Po. María Agustín, 7 (tel. 22 93 43). (Bus #21 stops directly in front, across the street if coming from Pl. Pilar.) To: Madrid (15 per day, 3hr., 1115ptas); Barcelona (9 per day, 3½hr., 1980ptas); Bilbao (5 per day, 4hr., 1450ptas); Vitoria (5 per day, 3hr., 1200ptas). From **second terminal** at Av. Valencia, 20 (tel. 55 45 88) to: Muel (2 per day, ½hr., 240ptas); Cariñena (Mon.-Sat. 1 per day, 1hr., 275ptas); Daroca (2-3 per day, 2hr., 665ptas); Lérida (4 per day, 2½hr., 1100ptas).

Arión Express, C. Asalto, 53 (tel. 39 70 82). From Pl. Paraíso down Po. Constitución 6-7 bl., then left on Po. Mina, which becomes C. Asalto. To: Valencia (6 per day, 5hr., 1435ptas); Alicante (6 per day, 8hr., 2240ptas).

CONDA, Av. Navarra, 81 (tel. 33 33 72). From Pl. Paraíso follow Po. Pamplona to Po. María Agustín; turn left at 2nd major intersection onto Av. Madrid. Cross the highway and railbed on the blue pedestrian bridge; hang a right on Av. Navarra, then left after a long stretch. (Bus #25 from Po. Pamplona; watch for the station on the left.) To: Tudela (5-6 per day, 1hr., 625ptas); Pamplona (7-8 per day, 2½hr., 1465ptas); San Sebastián (5 per day, 4hr., 2145ptas).

La Oscense, Po. María Agustín, 7 (tel. 22 93 43). Shares a terminal with Agreda Automóvil. To: Huesca (9-10 per day, 1hr., 625ptas); Jaca (2-3 per day, 2½hr., 1305ptas).

Samar Buil, C. Borao, 13 (tel. 27 61 79). From Pl. Paraíso down Po. Pamplona, the 1st left after 1st major traffic intersection. (Bus #21 from Pl. Pilar and Po. Pamplona to the stop in front of the Jefatura Superior building, then walk.) Office is mid-block on the left. Ticket booth opens ½hr. before departure. To Fuendetodos (1-2 per day, 1hr., 340ptas).

Therpasa, C. General Sueiro, 22 (tel. 34 31 58). From Pl. Paraíso ½ bl. down Po. Constitución, then right for 2 bl. Open Mon.-Fri. 9am-1pm and 4:15-7:30pm, Sat. 9am-1pm. To: Empalme de Vera (see Near Tarazona) (5 per day, 1¼hr., 530ptas); Vera de Moncayo (Mon.-Fri. 1 per day, 1½hr., 565ptas); Tarazona (5-6 per day, 1½hr., 595ptas); Soria (4-7 per day, 2½hr., 1000ptas).

Zuriaga, C. San Juan Pablo Bonet, 13 (tel. 27 61 79). From Pl. Paraíso 7 bl. down Po. Sagasta, then right. (Bus #33 from Pl. España; seek out road sign for C. San Juan Pablo Bonet after 2 stops on Po. Sagasta.) To: Logroño (2-6 per day, 1¾hr., 1260ptas); Teruel (5 per day, 2¾hr., 1180ptas); Burgos (2-4 per day, 4-5½hr., 1845-2015ptas); Santander (1-2 per day, none Sat., 6hr., 3195ptas).

Public Transportation: Red **TUZSA** buses (tel. 22 64 71) cover the city (75ptas, 10-ride ticket 470ptas from booth in Pl. España). Route information in *Guía Tuz* at tourist offices. Bus #21 is particularly useful, running from near the train station to Po. Pamplona, Pl. Paraíso, Pl. Aragón, Pl. España, Pl. Pilar, then back up C. San

Vicente de Paúl. #33 more central, going through Po. Sagasta, Pl Paraíso, Po. Independencia and Pl. España.

Taxis: Near the train station. **Radio-Taxi Aragón** (tel. 38 38 38). **Radio-Taxi Zaragoza** (tel. 42 42 42). **Radio-Taxi Cooperativa** (tel. 37 37 37).

Car Rental: Hertz, at train station and C. Luis del Valle, 26 (tel. 35 34 62). From Pl. Paraíso take Gran Vía, follow Po. Fernando El Católico 2 bl., turn right on Corona de Aragón, then take 3rd right. **Avis,** Po. Fernando El Católico, 9 (tel. 55 50 94). From Pl. Paraíso take Gran Vía, which becomes Po. Fernando El Católico. Ford Fiestas 4995ptas per day plus 39ptas per km. MIn. age 23. **Atesa,** Av. Valencia, 3 (tel. 35 28 05). Take Gran Vía to Av. Goya, turn right, then left.

Luggage Storage: At the **train station.** *Equipaje* office sells locker tokens (400ptas). Open 24hrs. At **Agreda Automóvil** bus station, 100ptas per piece (open 8am-8pm). At **Therpasa** bus station, 125ptas per piece (open Mon.-Fri. 9am-1pm and 4:15-7:30pm, Sat. 9am-1pm).

English Bookstore: Librería General, Po. Independencia, 22 (tel. 22 44 83). Surprisingly large selection downstairs. Open Mon.-Fri. 9:30am-1:30pm and 4:45-8:30pm, Sat. 10am-2pm. **El Corte Inglés** (see above).

Women's Services: Casa de la Mujer, Don Jaime de Aragón, 2 (tel. 39 11 16). Offers judicial assistance and general information. Open Mon.-Fri. 9am-2:30pm; Sept.-June Mon.-Fri. 9am-9:30pm.

Gay and Lesbian Services: LYGA (Lesbianas y Gays de Aragón), C. San Vicente de Paúl, 26 (tel. 39 55 77). Office hours Wed. 7-10pm.

Youth Organization: CIPAJ (Centro de Información y Promoción de Actividades Juveniles), C. Bilbao, 1 (tel. 21 39 60). From Po. Independencia turn left on C. Casa Jiménez 2 bl. past Pl. Aragón, then left. Clearinghouse for sundry youth information. Great monthly bulletin of city happenings (available at tourist office). Some English spoken. Open Mon.-Fri. 11am-2pm.

Laundromat: Lavandería Rossell, C. San Vicente de Paul, 27 (tel. 29 90 34). A right on C. Coso, 4 bl., then left 4½ bl. Wash and dry 950-1700ptas per load, depending on size. Open Mon.-Fri. 9am-1pm and 4-8pm, Sat. 9am-1pm.

Swimming Pool: 16 of them. *Centros deportivos,* available at tourist offices, features a comprehensive guide to the city's pools. A cool pool in an even cooler park is **C.D.M. Salduba,** Parque Primo de Rivera, s/n (tel. 55 36 36), at the very end of Po. Fernando El Católico. (Buses #29, 30, 35, 40, 42, and 45.) Open May-Sept. 15 11am-9pm. Admission 250ptas, over 65 100ptas, ages 6-17 150ptas.

Late-Night Pharmacy: Check listings in *El Heraldo de Aragón* (local paper), or posted notices on pharmacy doors.

Medical Services: Hospital Miguel Servet, Po. Isabel La Católica, 1 (tel. 35 57 00). In **emergencies,** turn to Ambulatorio Ramón y Cajal, Po. María Agustín, 12 (tel. 43 41 11). **Casa de Socorro,** Po. de la Mina, 9 (tel. 23 02 91). **Ambulance** (tel. 35 85 00).

Emergency: dial 006.

Police: Jefatura Superior, Po. Rosales, 24 (tel. 59 30 88). **Municipal Police,** C. Domingo Miral, s/n (tel. 092). **National Police,** Po. María Agustín, 36 (tel. 091).

ACCOMMODATIONS AND CAMPING

Hostales and *pensiones* cram the narrow streets of the *casco antiguo,* especially within the rectangle bound by **Calle Alfonso I, Calle Don Jaime I, Plaza España,** and **Plaza del Pilar.** Hunting can be frustrating, as many *pensiones* prefer long-term residents. *Casas particulares,* too, are scarce. It pays to travel in company. Fortunately, help is on the way. After interminable renovations, **Residencia Juvenil Baltázar Gracián (HI)** is expected to re-open by 1995 (knock on wood). Call tel. 55 15 04 to check on progress or ask at the tourist office.

Be wary the week of October 12, when Zaragoza celebrates the *Fiesta de la Virgen del Pilar;* make reservations as early as possible. Also know that *ferias* (trade shows) go in February through April. The biggest is the agricultural machinery show FIMA, usually in late March or early April, during which the tourist office has to scour everything within a 100km radius to find rooms.

Casa de Huéspedes Elena, C. San Vicente de Paúl, 30 (tel. 39 65 80), across the street from Lavandería Rossell. Capacious, modern rooms and a superior hall bathroom. An unmatched deal on doubles. Singles 1800ptas. Doubles 2000ptas.

Hostal Ambos Mundos, Pl. Pilar, 16 (tel. 29 97 04; fax 29 97 02), at the corner with C. Don Jaime I. Perfect location. Plain but clean and comfortable rooms. Some doubles have balconies on the plaza. Elevator. Singles 1900ptas, with shower 2100ptas. Doubles with shower 3500ptas. Breakfast (9-11am) 250ptas.

Hostal Plaza, Pl. Pilar, 14 (tel. 29 48 30). Could be next door neighbor Ambos Mundos's older brother. Clean and well-maintained. Some doubles face the plaza. Singles 2014ptas, with shower 2120ptas. Doubles with shower 3180ptas. Breakfast 300ptas.

Hostal Venecia, C. Estebanes, 7 (tel. 39 36 61), the first left off C. Don Jaime I heading toward Pl. Pilar. Nice rooms with tile floors and "woody" furniture in the heart of the *Tubo* (see Food below). 1500ptas per person.

Pensión Rex, C. Méndez Núñez, 31 (tel. 39 26 33), on the corner of C. Don Jaime I. Roomy rooms, many with balconies, in the heart of the *casco antiguo*. Easy access to nightlife. Singles 1800ptas, with shower 2400ptas. Doubles 3200ptas, with shower 4000ptas. Showers 350ptas.

Camping: Casablanca, Barrio Valdefierro (tel. 33 03 22), down Ctra. Nacional 2. (Bus #36 from Pl. Pilar or Pl. España to the suburb of Valdefierro.) Ask the driver to let you know when you've arrived, as it's notoriously difficult to find. By car, take the road to Madrid, then the Valdefierro exit, and from there follow the signs. Good facilities, including pool. June-Sept. 5 525ptas per person, per tent, and per car; otherwise 475ptas. Open April.-Oct.

FOOD

Tapas bars, inexpensive restaurants, and *bocadillo* factories crowd the area known as **El Tubo** (Calles Mártires, Cinegio, 4 de Agosto, and Estebanes), off Pl. España. Several *marisquerías* serve seafood *raciones* at good prices on C. Don Jaime I, near Pl. Pilar. Many of Zaragoza's most enticing restaurants lie at rather remote points off the beaten track. For the scoop on restaurants, lay your hands on the *Places to Eat* brochure, part of the *Sitios de Zaragoza* collection. The **market** thrives in the long green building on Av. César Augusto off Pl. Pilar. Fresh fruit and veggies, cow's tongue, and live squid exchange hands. (Open Mon.-Sat. 9am-2pm and 5-8pm.)

Supermarket: Galerías Primero, C. San Jorge, the 2nd left off C. Don Jaime I. Open Mon.-Sat. 9am-1:30pm and 5-8:30pm. The mega-market in **El Corte Inglés'** basement is well stocked but pricey.

Restaurante Alcarabea, C. Zumalacárregui, 33 (tel. 22 47 76). From Pl. Paraíso take Po. Sagasta 3 bl. and turn right. How a veggie restaurant got to this out-of-the-way location is beyond us. Revel in heaping, delicious, colon-cleansing portions. Veggie-only *paella* is heavenly. Substantial 700pta *menú*, 500ptas for students. *Platos combinados* 550ptas. Lunch only. Open daily 1-4pm; Aug. closed Sat.-Sun.

Restaurante Savoy, Coso, 42 (tel. 22 49 16), left off Pl. España facing the old quarter. We don't normally list restaurants where a full meal comes to 2000ptas, and we probably wouldn't but for those magical words: "all you can eat." Chicken, peppers, fish, pork, veggies, beef, shrimp, ham, mussels, fruit, desserts... it's all here and it's all exquisite. Buffet 1690ptas. Open daily 1-4pm and 8:45-11:30pm. AmEx, Visa, MC accepted.

La Zanahoria, C. Tarragona, 4 (tel. 35 87 94). From Pl. Paraíso take Gran Vía, turn right on Av. Goya, then the 1st left after crossing Av. Teruel/Valencia. Yuppie vegetarians. Excellent salads and quiches. Lunch *menú* 900ptas. *Platos combinados* 850ptas. Two-course dinner with beverage about 1500ptas. Open 1:30-4pm and 9-11:30pm. For dinner, arrive before 10pm or call for reservations.

Restaurante Triana, C. Estebanes, 5, across the street from Hostal España. Good, honest Aragonese food. *Menú* 900ptas. Entrees 500-1200ptas. Open Mon.-Sat. 1-4pm and 8:30-11pm, Sun. lunch only.

SIGHTS

The monumental spread of **Plaza del Pilar** lies in sun-bathed opulence. The massive 17th-century Baroque **Basílica del Pilar** defines the skyline with towers and brightly colored tile domes decorated with frescoes by Goya, González Velázquez (a contemporary of Goya's), and Bayeu. A pillar inside the central chapel was a gift from the Virgen Mary to St. James in 40 AD. Its legend gives birth to the most popular of Spanish composite names: María del Pilar. Where it isn't covered, the pillar has been eroded by pilgrims' kisses in homage to the Virgin's continued protection of the city. Two bombs hang down the hall from the right entryway, part of a trio dropped on the basilica on August 3, 1936— none of which exploded—in tangible evidence of this protection. The **Museo del Pilar** (in the basilica) displays the glittering *joyero de la Virgen* (Virgin's jewels) and a collection of original sketches of the ceiling frescoes. (Museum open 9am-2pm and 4-6pm. Admission 150ptas. Basilica open 6am-8:30pm.) An elevator to the top allows a giraffe's-eye view of the city and surrounding plains. (Open Aug.-July 14 9:30am-2pm and 4-7pm. Closed Fri. Admission 150ptas.)

Sadly, the **Catedral de la Seo** has been tinkered with a few times since it was erected as a mosque. The first changes brought the Gothic style, with important Mudejar elements such as the brick wall and *azulejo* tiles. Later alterations introduced the Plateresque, Renaissance (interior), and Baroque (facade, belfry). Under restoration, the building, which sits across C. Don Jaime I from the basilica, is closed to the public, but the tower and Mudejar north (left) face are worth the side trip.

Between the cathedral and the Ayuntamiento, Zaragoza's 16th-century Gothic and Plateresque **Lonja** (stock exchange) is distinguished by star vaulting and a forest of soaring Ionic columns that rise to a ceiling of gilt crests. It now houses occasional art exhibits. (Open Mon.-Sat. 10am-2pm and 5-9pm, Sun. 10am-2pm.) Mudejar art shows in the **torres** of the Iglesias de San Pablo, San Gil, San Miguel, and la Magdalena. Numerous seignorial mansions, the medieval baths, and several old university buildings embellish **Calle del Coso,** the southern boundary of the old city.

In addition to an extensive collection of medieval Aragonese paintings, the **Museo Provincial de Bellas Artes** (tel. 22 21 81) hangs works by Ribera, Lucas van Leyden, and Claudio Coello, along with a Goya self-portrait and likeness of Carlos IV and María Luisa. From the post office, turn right and walk around the corner; the museum is five blocks away to the left in Pl. Sitios. (Open Tues.-Sat. 9am-2pm, Sun. 10am-2pm, archaeology section Sun. 10am-noon. Admission 200ptas.)

The **Museo Pablo Gargallo,** dedicated to one of the most innovative sculptors of the 1920s, houses a small but marvelous collection of his works in the graceful Palacio de Arguillo. From C. Don Jaime I in the direction of Pl. Pilar, take the 2nd left on C. Casto Méndez Núñez; the museum is on Pl. San Felipe, which is on the left five bl. down. (Open Tues.-Sat. 10am-1pm and 5-9pm, Sun. 11am-2pm. Free.) The **Fundación Pablo Serrano,** Po. María Agustín, 26, honors a second native sculptor with sexy abstract works and reinterpretations of works by Picasso, Velázquez, and Goya. (Museum open Mon. and Wed.-Sat. 10am-2pm and 5-8pm, Sun. 10am-2pm. Free. Guided tours in Spanish.)

Following the Muslim conquest of the Iberian Peninsula in the 8th century, a crisis over succession smashed the kingdom into petty tributary states called *taifas.* The **Palacio de la Aljafería,** on C. Castillo, remains the principal relic of Aragón's *taifa.* Previous alterations and renovations have encumbered the building's original grace, but its awesome stone walls and serene interior are still worth a visit. The ground floor has a distinctly Moorish flavor in contrast with the Gothic second floor. The fortified tower imprisoned *El Trovador* in García Gutierrez's drama, source of Verdi's opera. Buses #21 and 33 both stop here, or head left on Coso through its incarnation as C. Conde de Aranda to the pedestrian street that leads to the castle. (Open Tues.-Sat. 10am-2pm and 4-8pm, Sun. 10am-2pm; Oct.-May Tues.-Sat. 10am-2pm and 4:30-6:30pm, Sun. 10am-2pm. Free.)

Those hungering for green should head for the shaded walks and fountains of the **Parque Primo de Rivera,** on the end opposite the old quarter from Pl Paraíso. At night the park is transformed as its fountains are lit up.

ENTERTAINMENT

Young Zaragozans brag that their city has *mucha marcha* (lots of action). *Night Spots* (part of *Sitios de Zaragoza)* is a slick brochure that covers the gay and straight scene. Herds of *casco antiguo* goers begin around **Coso** and **Calle San Miguel,** and get it goin' on (around midnight) in the market area, on **Calles Predicadores, El Olmo, El Temple, Contamina,** and **Manifestación.** Teeny-boppers and *militares* favor **Calle Dr. Cerrada,** off Po. Pamplona, while the more affluent and mature patronize **Residencial Paraíso** and Calles Doctor Casas, Bolonia, and La Paz. University students storm **Paseo Sagasta** and its offshoot, C. Zumalacárregui. Gulping beer from *litros* (literally liters—about 350ptas a pop) is the primary sport around **El Rollo,** the zone bounded by C. Moncasi, C. Bonet, and C. Maestro Marquina at the southern end of Po. Sagasta. The bars rule supreme in Zaragoza, but a small disco scene draws late-night (early morning) partiers. **Torreluna,** C. Miguel Servet, 193, is the only disco that has dancing *al aire libre* all night long. **Pachá,** C. Sevilla, 6, is a popular indoor version. Gay bars and discos lie around the west side of the *casco antiguo.*

The city erupts for a week of unbridled hoopla around October 12 in honor of *La Virgen.* City patrons San Valero (Jan. 29) and San Jorge (April 23) are also feted. In May, Zaragoza hosts an international festival of dance, music, and theater. The city tourist office distributes information on the *fiestas.*

■ EXCURSIONS FROM ZARAGOZA

Tourist offices have information on excursions through Aragón, such as the *Ruta del Vino* (route of the wine) and the *Ruta de Goya.* Teruel and Tarazona (see below) are good daytrips from Zaragoza. Fans of the Romanesque should inquire about visits to the **Cinco Villas,** particularly **Sos del Rey Católico** and **Uncastillo.**

MONASTERIO DE PIEDRA

An oasis of waterfalls and trees springs out of the dry Aragón plain in Nuévalos around the **Monasterio de Piedra** (tel. 84 90 11), about 110km southwest of Zaragoza. The monastery itself was founded in 1195 by an order of Cistercian monks from Tarragona. Abandoned under government orders in 1835, a hotel now occupies what is left of the monastery. The 12th-century **Torre del Homenaje,** the only part of the existing building that hasn't been restored, still stands strong overlooking the valley.

The main attraction is the surrounding **park.** The **Río Piedra** plunges down a valley, creating numerous waterfalls and lakes. A path leads through, under, and over segments of this watery paradise. Starting out early is essential if you wish to enjoy the path. No fishing is allowed. (Park open daily 9am-nightfall. Admission 900ptas.)

Nuévalos, 2km from the park, is a tiny town with just one paved street and a few services. **Automóviles Zaragoza buses,** C. Almagro, 18 (tel. 21 93 20), leave from Zaragoza at 9am and pass by on their way to the Monasterio de Piedra.

FUENDETODOS

The Goya route begins at the painter's birthplace, Fuendetodos, 50km south of Zaragoza. Close to his birthplace, **La Casa de Goya** recreates Goya's life and times by dressing itself up with period furnishings and curiosities. (Open Tues.-Sun. 11am-2pm and 4-7pm; Nov.-March Tues.-Sun. 11am-2pm and 3-6pm. Admission 300ptas, under 16 free.) The village itself (pop. 183), is authentic and unremarkable. Samar Buil **buses** make the run (see Zaragoza: Practical Information).

NUÉVALOS

CARTUJA DE AULA DEI

Woefully, only men are allowed to enter the Cartuja de Aula Dei, a 16th-century Carthusian monastery 12km from Zaragoza. Here the young Goya completed one of his first major works, a series of 11 tableaux depicting the life of Mary. The monastery is undergoing renovations, but should be open by 1995—call ahead if you have that pesky Y chromosome (tel. 15 42 11) or check with a tourist office. Take **bus** #28 (every ½hr., 20min., 75ptas) from the stop alongside the Roman walls (near Zaragoza's regional tourist office) to the leafy entrance of *la cartuja*. Look for the large complex in the open on the left after passing the Universidad de la Cartuja de Aula Dei sign. (Cartuja open Wed., Sat. 10am-noon and 2-4pm.)

TARAZONA

Owing to its ubiquitous Arabic-influenced architecture, Tarazona (pop. 11,000) has earned the name "La Ciudad Mudéjar" (The Mudejar City). Buildings everywhere display the intricate Arabic brickwork of the 16th century. A great daytrip from Zaragoza, Tudela, or Soria, Tarazona is best visited mid-July to mid-August, when monuments open their doors to host **Tarazona Foto** (yup, photographic exhibitions, free).

Like so many monuments here, the splendid Gothic 13th- to 15th-century **cathedral** is being painstakingly restored (most of it is closed, even during the exhibitions). The glorious towers, belfry, lantern, and plasterwork tracery in the inner cloister are particularly fine examples of Mudejar work. From the bus station, turn right onto Av. Navarra and follow to Pl. San Francisco, then head right (following signs to Soria and Zaragoza); the first left leads up a flight of stairs to the cathedral. Skirt the right side of the cathedral and follow C. San Antón for half a block or so. The 18th-century **Plaza de Toros Vieja,** now multi-colored private residences, has a balconied and arcaded upper tier. From the cathedral, take a left at the sign for Soria, then turn right and pursue for a block.

Tarazona was a seasonal residence of medieval Aragonese kings until the 15th century; their Alcázar has since served as the **Palacio Episcopal.** The bishop's home lies across the bridge nearest the Pl. Toros, left 1 bl., and then up the twisting stairs of the Recodos and the Rúa Baja. The former dungeons of the palace, known as the **Bajos del Palacio,** lie downhill on R. Alta de Bécquer; they've since been gentrified by the **Centro de Estudios Turiasonenses** (Center for Tarazona Studies) and its temporary exhibitions. (Open Mon.-Sat. 11am-2pm and 5-9pm, Sun. 11am-2pm. Free.) The Renaissance facade of the **Ayuntamiento** on Pl. España is worth a side trip from the Mudejar tour. From Bajos del Palacio, continue down R. Alta de Bécquer and, at its end, zig-zag left.

Opposite the Palacio Episcopal in the heart of the medieval quarter, "El Cinto," rises **Iglesia de la Magdalena,** with a Romanesque east end and a Mudejar tower that dominates the old town. The entrance is a left up Cuesta de Palacio and another left (open only for mass). **Murallas** (walls) surround the quarter's heart; push up the hill from La Magdalena past the remarkable Renaissance facade of **Iglesia San Atilano** until you hit Pl. Puerto, where you should exit left. Your reward for the effort is the panoramic vista of the broad Valle del Moncayo, which on a clear day even takes in the distant Aragonese Pyrenees.

During Tarazona's **fiestas** (Aug. 27-Sept. 1), crowds congregate in Pl. España to pelt each other and a polychromatic costumed character (the *cipotegato)* with tomatoes.

The **tourist office** has cornered the left side of the cathedral at C. Iglesias, 5 (tel. 64 00 74). From the bus station, turn right on Av. Navarra; at circular Pl. San Francisco follow the Soria/Zaragoza signs; at the tree-shaded Pl. Seo turn left and go up the steps. Ask for the indexed map in the *Tarazona* booklet. (Open Tues.-Fri. 9am-1:30pm and 4-7pm, Sat. 9am-1:30pm, Sun. 11am-1pm.) The **post office** is at Av. Navarra, 19 (tel. 64 13 17; open Mon.-Fri. 9am-2pm, Sat. 9am-1pm). The **postal code** is 50500. **Public phones** are in Pl. San Francisco; the **telephone code** is 976. The **Red Cross** is outside town on Ctra. Zaragoza (tel. 64 09 26). In **medical emergen-**

cies also turn to **Ambulatorio San Atilano,** Av. Paz, 29 (tel. 64 12 85). The **municipal police** are next to the library on Pl. San Francisco (tel. 64 16 91, **emergency** tel. 092). They provide maps when the tourist office is dead.

The decidedly un-touristy Tarazona has a grand total of three hotels. **Hostal Residencia María Cristina,** Carrera de Castilla, 3 (tel. 64 00 84), is on the highway to Soria from Pl. San Francisco. Hardly sumptuous, but it's quiet and affordable. (Curfew 11:30pm. Doubles 2400ptas; March-May 2200ptas; Oct.-Feb. 2100ptas. Solo travelers pay more than half the double rate.)

Grocery store **Tutienda,** C. Laureles, 2, is about ½ bl. left of the cathedral following the Soria/Zaragoza signs. (Open Mon.-Fri. 9:30am-1:30pm and 5:30-8:30pm, Sat. 9:30am-2pm; winter afternoon hours are 5-8pm.) **Bar Avenida,** on Av. Navarra, just down the street from the bus depot toward Pl. San Francisco, serves zesty *tapas* (100ptas) and *bocadillos* (300-375ptas).

Therpasa **buses** (tel. 64 11 00) operate from the station on Av. Navarra. To Soria (4-6 per day, 1hr., 470ptas) and Zaragoza (4-7 per day, 1hr., 595ptas). The 7am bus to Zaragoza stops in Vera de Moncayo (15min., 110ptas; see below). Other buses to Zaragoza pause at Empalme de Vera (10min., 65ptas), 4km from Vera de Moncayo. **Conda** buses go to Tudela from outside the Therpasa bus station (Mon.-Sat. 5-6 per day, Sun. 1 per day, 30min., 190ptas). If you ask nicely, you'll probably be allowed to leave your **luggage** for a few hours at the ticket window in the bus station, although it's not an official storage area.

Near Tarazona: Monasterio de Veruela

The romantic walled monastery of Veruela slumbers in the Sierra de Moncayo, 15km south of Tarazona. Its golden stone walls guard a Romanesque-Gothic church and an almost transcendentally peaceful cloister. Nineteenth-century poet Gustavo Adolfo Bécquer sought the mountain air here and penned his *Cartas desde mi celda* (Letters from my Cell) within these walls. The Cistercian monastery participates in the Tarazona Foto exhibitions. (Grounds open Tues.-Sun. 10am-2pm and 4-7pm. Admission 200ptas.) Catch the bus to Zaragoza that stops 2km from the monastery at **Vera de Moncayo** (see Tarazona bus info). Otherwise, ask to be dropped off near Vera at the *empalme* (junction, 6km from the monastery).

■■■ LA RUTA DEL VINO: MUEL, CARIÑENA, DAROCA

The ideal grape-growing climate about 100km south of Zaragoza has wine for water. Cool nights and scorching days keep the vines happy. A booklet from the regional tourist office in Zaragoza answers commonly asked questions: What is the history of winemaking in this region? What are the best vintages? Why is this night different from all other nights?

Agreda Automóvil **buses** cover all three towns from Zaragoza; Zuriaga's bus service to Teruel from Zaragoza is faster, but doesn't always include all three towns (see Zaragoza: Practical Information).

Besides its Dionysian charm, **Muel** is noteworthy as home to a world-renowned school of ceramics, and to the **Ermita de Nuestra Señora de la Fuente,** which features frescoes painted by Goya. **Cariñena's** church is a fragment of a fortress built by the Orden de los Caballeros de San Juan (Order of the Knights of St. John); its Capilla de Santiago did duty as a mosque.

Last stop on the line, **Daroca** (pop. 2600) is a coffee-table-book-cute town founded by Muslims and surrounded by ruins of a 4km wall punctuated by 114 towers. The two main gates in the wall, **Puerta Alta** and **Puerta Baja,** still provide the only access to the main part of town; the glazed red-tile towers of the latter have been declared a national monument. Footpaths shadow the wall, so hikers can get a sentry's-eye view of the town and the whole valley from the towers. C. Arrabal is one approach to the wall; exit the Puerta Baja and turn right. Go up, then right, then up (and up and up).

Religious art fills the museum of the **Colegiata de Santa María,** a 16th-century Renaissance church. (Church and museum open 11am-1pm and 7-8pm. The tourist office arranges guided tours; call ahead for more info.) To reach the church, take either of the two Calles Juan de la Huerta from C. Mayor.

The town transubstantiates most feverishly on the **Fiesta de Corpus Christi,** held every year in late May or early June. Daroca also hosts the annual **Curso Internacional de Música Antigua** the first two weeks of August, when musicians from the world over gather in Daroca to teach, learn, and give free ancient music concerts (if you thought harpsichords were exotic...).

The **tourist office** is at Pl. España, 7 (tel. 80 01 29), opposite Colegiata Santa María. To get here from Puerta Alta, pursue C. Mayor for 4-5 bl., and hang a right on C. San Juan de la Huerta. The map (100ptas) is superfluous. (Open Tues.-Sat. 11am-2pm; during the *Curso de Música* 9am-2pm and 7-8pm.) The **post office,** C. Mayor, 157 (tel. 80 02 15), is near Puerta Baja. (Open Mon.-Fri. 9am-2pm, Sat. 9am-1pm.) The **postal code** is 50360. **Telephone booths** are located at various points along C. Mayor and near Hostal Legido on Av. Escuelas Pías. The **telephone code** is 976. The **Red Cross** (tel. 80 03 36) is outside Puerta Alta and across the highway. The **Guardia Civil** (tel. 80 11 86) has headquarters on the highway next to the swimming pool.

To bed down, try **Pensión El Ruejo,** C. Mayor, 88 (tel. 80 11 90), complete with a disco and intimate courtyard restaurant. (Lone single 1500ptas. Doubles 3000ptas, with bath 4000ptas.) The *roca* of the **Restaurante La Roca,** C. Mayor, 107 (tel. 80 04 09), juts defiantly into the dining room. The 800pta *menú* presents a scrumptious *trucha con champiñones* (trout with mushroom sauce). (Open 1-4pm and 9-11pm.) The town **market** vends in Pl. Santiago, off C. Mayor (Thurs. 9am-2pm).

Buses back to Zaragoza or on to Teruel depart from in front of Mesón Felix, C. Mayor near Puerta Baja. Buses arriving in Daroca stop at Puerta Baja, or occasionally on the highway by Hostal Legido. To reach C. Mayor from the highway stop, walk past the *hostal* to Av. Escuelas Pías, turn left, and continue downhill. Bear right at the traffic circle on Av. Libertad to pass through Puerta Alta and onto C. Mayor.

■■■ TERUEL

A sun-baked town poking out of the plains of southern Aragón, Teruel (pop. 28,000) is famous for its magnificent examples of Mudejar architecture. When Aragonese King Fernando II el Sabio conquered Teruel in 1171, it was still royal policy for Christian kings to respect Muslim religious customs. Teruel's last mosque did not close until 1502 (the Jewish community remained until 1486). Mudejar architecture, the fruit of co-mingling of Hispano-Muslim and Christian aesthetic traditions, is like a Greatest Hits of Spanish Form album: bricks, ornate tiles, and geometric patterns from the Moors, and Romanesque and Gothic grandeur from their successors.

Muslim artisans built the brick-and-glazed-tile **Torres Mudéjares** (Mudejar Towers) between the 12th and 15th centuries. The Christian churches adapted the structure of the Almohad minarets to their own purposes. The two more intricately designed of the three towers are the richly tiled 14th-century **Torre de San Martín,** in Pl. Pérez Prado near the post office; and the **Torre de San Salvador,** on C. El Salvador, built around 1277. In the latter, 123 skinny steps climb through several chambers to the panoramic *campanario* up top. (Open 11am-2pm and 5-7pm; winter Sat.-Sun. only. Admission 250ptas, includes optional guided tour.)

The tombs of Diego de Marcilla and Isabel de Segura in the **Mausoleo de los Amantes,** next to Torre San Pedro, explain why Teruel is known as the *ciudad de los amantes* (City of Lovers). To prove his worth to Isabel's wealthy family, Diego set out to win fame and fortune, only to return five years later just in time to watch Isabel marry his rival. Diego's request for one last kiss was refused, and he promptly died. At the funeral, Isabel kissed the corpse, and, overcome with grief, also died.

Life-size alabaster statues of the lovers reach out over their tombs to touch hands, but, in Grecian urn fashion, never do. From Pl. Castell/Torico, take the alleyway to the left of the purple *Modernista* house. Stairs from there lead directly to the *mausoleo*. (Open Tues.-Sat. 10am-2pm and 5-7:30pm, Sun. 10:30am-2pm. Admission 50ptas.)

The summa of Teruel's Mudejar is the 13th-century **Catedral de Santa María de Mediavilla,** in Pl. Catedral. The *capilla mayor* is octagonal, its ambulatory rectangular. The magnificently decorated square brick tower is a mere preface to the wonderment of the 14th-century stylized *artesonado mudéjar* (Mudejar coffered ceiling) roofing the central of three naves. All roads left of Pl. Castell/Torico lead one block away to Pl. Catedral. (Cathedral open 11:30am-2pm and 5:30-9pm. Free.)

The **Museo Provincial,** Pl. Fray Anselmo Polanco (tel. 60 11 04), is housed in the 16th-century porticoed **Casa de la Comunidad.** From Pl. Castell/Torico walk up C. Joaquín Costa/del Tozal and turn left on C. Rubio. Several floors of exhibition space are given over to the history and folklore of the area. The rooftop view is unparalleled. (Museum open Tues.-Fri. 10am-2pm and 4-7pm, Sat.-Sun. 10am-2pm.)

The **Palacio Episcopal,** Pl. Cristo Rey/Monjas, 1 bl. in the direction of Pl. Castell/Torico from Pl. Pérez Prado, has a Renaissance entrance and patio. The soaring **viaducto** joining old town and new is worth a visit.

The yearly **Fiestas del Angel** explode the week following the first Monday in July, and feature a 500kg bull-on-a-rope in Pl. Torico (Papa Hemingway would be proud). The **Feria del Jamón** in September is also festive, drawing motorcycled people from all over Spain.

Orientation and Practical Information Isolated atop a hill 926m above sea-level, Teruel is still very accessible, linked by train and bus to Valencia (163km southwest) and Zaragoza (184km north). Teruel's nonsensical layout can confound even the most finely tuned sense of direction. The tourist office's pitiful map covers only the historic center of town. Street signs, where they exist at all, are in semi-legible script. Worse yet, several major streets and plazas go by two names. Look for street maps posted at the train station and on major streets in the old quarter.

The **casco histórico** perches on a hilltop, linked to modern Teruel by bridges. The center of the *casco* is **Plaza de Carlos Castell,** affectionately known as **Plaza del Torico** for the fountain crowned by a tiny iron bull. Teruel is renovating its bus station, which should be ready by 1995 (and if you believe this...). Currently, the RENFE station remains the more convenient access to the *casco antiguo*. To reach Pl. Castell/Torico from the **train station,** take the *Modernista* flight of stairs leading out of the park, cross Po. Ovalo, and follow signs to the *centro histórico* through C. Nueva. If the new **bus station** is done, arrivals will be on Ronda de Ambeles, at the edge of town. To get to Pl. Castell/Torico, head straight up C. Abadía through the parking lot, and follow the road to the steps that lead to the plaza. Until the new station is finished, arrivals are in the modern quarter. For Pl. Castell/Torico, go left from the station, take the first right and follow the curve to its end, then turn right and go straight to the pedestrian *viaducto* (5-10min.). Cross the bridge and head uphill on C. General Pizarro, walk across Pl. San Juan past the pyramid bearing left, and follow C. Ramón y Cajal/San Juan to the plaza.

The **tourist office** (tel. 60 22 79) is at C. Tomás Nogues, 1, at the corner with C. Comandante Fortea/del Pozo. From Pl. Castell/Torico, follow C. Ramón y Cajal/San Juan and take the first left; the office is 1 bl. away on your right. English spoken. (Open Mon. 9am-2pm, Tues.-Sun. 9am-2pm and 5-9pm; Sept. 16-July 14 Mon-Sat. 8am-2:30pm and 5-7:30pm.) The **post office** (tel 60 11 92) is at C. Yagüe de Salas, 17, in the Seminario Conciliar building. Open for stamps, **telegrams,** and **fax** Mon.-Fri. 8am-9pm (fax starts 9am), Sat 9am-7pm; for Lista de Correos Mon.-Fri. 8am-9pm, Sat. 9am-2pm. The **postal code** is 44001. The **telephone office** rings at C. San Andrés, 13, two consecutive rights from the tourist office; the **telephone code** is 974. **Luggage storage** at the train station (lockers 400ptas) and the bus station (125ptas per piece, 2 or more 100ptas each; open Mon.-Sat. 9am-3pm and 4:30-

7pm). For a **24-hr. pharmacy,** consult p. 2 of *El Heraldo de Aragón* or call the municipal police. **Red Cross** are at C. San Miguel, 3 (tel. 60 26 09; emergency tel. 60 22 22); **Hospital Provincial** at tel. 60 53 17 or 60 53 68; and **Casa de Socorro** at tel. 60 53 68. **Municipal police** answer at tel. 60 21 78 (emergency tel. 092). **Guardia Civil** guard at C. San Francisco, 1 (tel. 062). In an **emergency,** call the **national police** (tel. 091).

The **train station** (info tel. 61 02 02) is at Camino de la Estación, 1, down the stairs from Po. Ovalo. To: Zaragoza (2-3 per day, 3hr., 1065ptas); Valencia (2-3 per day, 2¾hr., 955ptas). Several **bus** companies work out of whichever station is open (see Orientation above). Dial tel. 60 10 14 for general information. Round-trip tickets are generally less than twice the one-way fare. **La Rápida** (tel. 60 20 04). To: Barcelona (2 per day, Sun. 1 per day, winter Mon.-Sat. 1 per day, 5½-6½hr., 2875ptas). **Samar** (tel. 60 34 50). To: Valencia (2-4 per day, 2-3hr., 1105ptas); Madrid (2-3 per day, 5hr., 2115ptas). **Zuriaga** (tel. 60 28 28). To: Zaragoza (3-4 per day, 2¾hr., 1180ptas). **Autotransportes Teruel** (tel. 60 15 90). To: Albarracín (Mon.-Sat. 1 per day, ¾hr., 265ptas). **Furio** (tel. (964) 60 01 00). To: Mora de Rubielos (1hr., 214ptas); Rubielos de Mora (Mon.-Fri. 1 per day, 1½hr., 285ptas).

Accommodations and Food Lodging is scarce only during Semana Santa and the *fiestas* in early July. **Hostal Aragón,** C. Santa María, 4 (tel. 60 13 87), has attractive rooms and ultra-firm beds. (Singles 1600ptas. Doubles 2750ptas, with bath 4450ptas. Oct.-June singles 1500ptas.) Head in the direction the Torico is facing, but take the first left as you leave the plaza. The nearest **campgrounds** are in Albarracín, 37km away, and in Mora de Rubielos, 42km away (see Near Teruel below). If you clear it first with the Ayuntamiento (next to the cathedral in Pl. Catedral), and with the Guardia Civil, you may be allowed to pitch a tent for free at Parque de la Fuente Cenada, about 3km down the road to the coast. (Unfortunately, this is even harder than it sounds.)

Restaurant standards and prices are high; the *casco viejo* is the place to look. *Tapas* bars on Pl. Castell/Torico are satisfying and cheap. Teruel is famous for its salty, flavorful cured ham, *jamón de Teruel.* A **market** is on Pl. Domingo Gascón. From Pl. Castell/Torico take C. Joaquín Costa/del Tozal. (Open Mon.-Sat. 8am-1:30pm.) **Supermercado Muñoz** at Pl. Castell/Torico, 23, is open Mon.-Fri. 9:30am-2pm and 5-7:30pm, Sat. 9:30-2pm. **Restaurante La Parrilla,** C. Esteban, 2 (tel. 60 52 63) is the best restaurant in town. Walk right and uphill 2 bl. from the tourist office.

■ NEAR TERUEL

Protected by ancient walls, medieval townships are suspended in Teruel's countryside amid acres of feral land. Getting to these mystical hamlets is an ordeal. Only one bus per day ventures to them from Teruel and returns the next morning (see Teruel: Bus and Train above). Unless you have a car, you'll have to spend the night. The almighty *Guía de servicios turísticos,* available at any Aragonese tourist office, has information on accommodations throughout the area. Some hitch, though *Let's Go* does not recommend it. Amid the reddish desert hills, traffic is heaviest between Teruel and Albarracín; hitchers have posted themselves with placards at the end of Camino de la Estación, the beginning of the road for Zaragoza. For Mora de Rubielos and Rubielos de Mora, hitchers favor the end of the aqueduct bridge on the road to Valencia. The telephone code for the whole province of Teruel is 978.

ALBARRACÍN

35km west of Teruel, castellized Albarracín was once a powerful Islamic city; it now lives mainly on fading grandeur amid its stone houses, small churches, and dispersed towers. The **tourist office** is at Pl. Mayor, 1 (tel. 71 02 51). Ask about tours to the *pinturas rupestres,* post-paleolithic shelter paintings dating from 5000 BC. (Open July-Sept. Mon.-Sat. 10am-2pm and 5-7:30pm, Sun. 10am-2pm. In the summer, free guided tours at 2:30 and 5:30pm.) In the off-season, consult the Ayuntamiento (tel. 70 04 00; open Mon.-Fri. 9am-3pm). The **post office,** on C. Catedral, 3, can be reached at tel. 71 07 77. The **Red Cross** is at Ctra. Teruel, s/n (tel. 71 00 02). The **Guardia Civil** is stationed on C. San Juan, s/n (tel. 71 00 03). **Camping Ciudad de Albarracín** stakes out here (tel. 71 01 97; 350ptas per person, per tent, and per car).

MORA DE RUBIELOS

Mora de Rubielos, 42km on the other side of Teruel, has the largest and best-preserved 15th-century castle in the neighborhood. During the summer, a **tourist office** sets up on C. Diputación (tel. 80 00 00). The **post office** is at C. Las Parras, 20 (tel. 80 01 71). There's **camping** at **El Morrón-Barrachinas** (tel. 80 03 62; 200ptas per person and per car, 500ptas per tent; open June 15-Sept. 15).

RUBIELOS DE MORA

Local connoisseurs insist the most *precioso* of the medieval towns around Teruel is **Rubielos de Mora,** 15km east of Mora de Rubielos. All of its 600 souls live in an unrestored and unscathed architectural setpiece from medieval days, complete with two city gates and a handsome 16th-century town hall (courtyard, dungeon, and all).

The **tourist office** is in the Ayuntamiento building, Pl. Hispano América, 1 (tel. 80 40 96; open 10am-2pm and 5-7pm; Sept.-June Mon.-Fri. 10am-2pm). The **Guardia Civil** is at Av. Mártires, s/n (tel. 80 40 02).

HUESCA

A convenient pit stop en route to the Pyrenees, the hastily overdeveloped Huesca is about as spectacular as watching *Star Wars* on a Sony Watchman. Suspended between Jaca to the north and Zaragoza to the south, Huesca (pop. 47,000) does not pretend to be a powerful tourist magnet, but there's enough to keep visitors satisfied while waiting for connections to more scenic elsewheres.

The massive Gothic **cathedral,** with its striking portal, and neighboring **Museo Diocesno** display a few Gothic *retablos* and other churchly artifacts. (Cathedral open 9am-1pm and 4-6pm. Museum open Mon.-Sat. 10am-1pm. Free.) Travelers may choose to use Huesca as a springboard to **Castillo de Loarre** (see Near Jaca) or the nearby ruins of **Castillo de Montearagón.** The ruins are 3km east of town down Ctra. 245. (Always open and free.)

The **Coso Alto** and **Coso Bajo** bound the *casco antiguo* on the east, south, and west, and are the main commercial arteries. The train station is a 10-min. walk down C. Zaragoza (Porch Galicia on the map) from the center (go left from the station); the bus station is roughly at the midway point, set back to the left across Pl. Navarra. At the top of C. Zaragoza, Coso Alto diddles off to the left, and Coso Bajo to the right. Most of the shops, cafés, and budget accommodations cluster around this boundary between the old city and the new.

On the Coso Alto, at #23, the English-speaking staff atthe **tourist office** (tel. 22 57 78) supplies pamphlets on the mountains and a pitiful map of Huesca. (Open Mon.-Fri. 9am-2:30pm and 5-8pm, Sat. 9am-2pm and 5-8pm, Sun. 9am-2pm.) The **post office** (tel. 22 59 87) is at Coso Alto, 14-16, at the corner of C. Moya. (Open Mon.-Fri. 9am-9pm, Sat. 9am-6pm; for Lista de Correos Mon.-Fri. 9am-2pm.) The **postal code** is 22002. There's a **telephone** *locutorio* at C. Caspe, 3, off Pl. Navarra. (Open Mon.-Sat. 9am-1pm and 5-10pm.) The **telephone code** 974. There are **lockers** at the RENFE station (open 7am-9pm, 400ptas). For the **municipal police** dial tel. 22 30 00. The **Red Cross** is at tel. 22 11 86, or in an **emergency,** tel. 22 22 22.

Many *hostales* and *casas particulares* live off Pl. Lizana, 3 bl. down Coso Alto on the right, and on the bar- and disco-filled streets several blocks to the right of C. Zaragoza (facing the Coso). Finding accommodations is only difficult during the *Fiestas de San Lorenzo* (Aug. 9-15)—call ahead during this week. The recently renovated **Hostal El Centro,** C. Sancho Ramírez, 3 (tel. 22 68 23), a right from Coso Bajo, has tasteful rooms in an area with enthusiastic (and loud) nightlife. (Singles 2200ptas, with bath 3000ptas. Doubles with bath 4200ptas. Sept. 16-June: 2000ptas;

2800ptas; 4000ptas.) **Camping San Jorge** (tel. 22 74 16) is in a bushy grove in the outskirts of town, to the left of the road to Jaca, by the **municipal pool.** (400ptas per person, per tent, and per car. Open mid-April to mid-Oct.)

For **groceries** hit **Aldi,** on C. Zaragoza, 11, a couple blocks from the train station toward the Coso. (Open 9am-1:30pm and 5-8pm, Sat. 9am-1:30pm.) Several restaurants off Pl. Lizane serve Aragonese *menús* hearty enough to put hair on one's chest. Star-children smooth out their auras at the veggie-food-and-new-age-muzak **Restaurante Ceres,** C. Padre Huesca, 37 (tel. 24 26 21). Feast your karma on tasty specialties like *canelones rellenos de verdura* (stuffed vegetable cannelloni, 715ptas). Entrees 600-985ptas. (Open Mon.-Sat. 1-4pm and 8:45-11pm.)

RENFE trains (tel. 24 21 59) run to: Jaca (3 per day, 2¼hr., 600-1300ptas); Sabiñánigo (3 per day, 1¾hr., 545-1200ptas; catch the early train to connect with the 10:50am mail bus to Torla, the closest point to the Ordesa Park); Zaragoza (3 per day, 1¼hr., 490-1100ptas); Valencia (1 per day, 7hr., 2335ptas); and Madrid (1 per day, 5hr., 2800ptas). **La Oscense** (tel. 21 07 00) runs **buses** to: Jaca (3-4 per day, 1¼hr., 680ptas); Lérida, the western entry to the Catalan Pyrenees (4 per day, 2½hr., 1025ptas); Pamplona (Mon.-Sat. 2 per day, 3hr., 1025ptas); and Zaragoza (6-10 per day, 1hr., 625ptas). **La Alta Aragonesa** (tel. 21 07 00) runs to and from Benasque (1-2 per day, 3½hr., 1180ptas).

ARAGONESE PYRENEES

Fans of political geography look at the Pyrenees, consider the infrequency of Northern invasion into Spain, and say it all makes sense. Most everyone else looks at the Pyrenees and is rendered speechless. With jagged cliff faces, grand canyons, icy snow-melt rivers, and serpentine ravines, the Aragonese Pyrenees stupefy with their majestic exuberance and variety. Despite the scanty train and bus transportation, the area draws both mountaineering aficionados and daystrollers to its famous peaks. While the Aragonese Pyrenees are more popular with tourists than their cousins in Cataluña and Navarra, they abound with isolated stretches. Jaca is attractive; but to truly enjoy the area, explore the cobbled streets and meandering trails of the outlying villages and their valleys. The region's spectacular features build to a crescendo at the magical Ordesa, the grand old national park.

Hikers should beg, borrow, or steal an *Editorial Alpina* map. Tourist offices in Huesca and Jaca also hoard information on local mountain-climbing clubs. Skiers have five major resorts at their poletips: Astún, Cerler, Panticosa, Candanchú, and Formigal. The pamphlets *Ski Aragón* and *El Turismo de Nieve en España,* free at tourist offices, give the low-down on all of these. Huesca and Jaca provide very limited, infrequent access through the area by bus. The most efficient and enjoyable way to explore the valleys is, of course, by car, and Jaca is one of the few places where those under 21 can rent one. Even if you lack access to a car, Ordesa is worth the sluggishly slow connection by mail bus.

■■■ JACA

Pilgrims to Santiago once recuperated from the trek through the Pyrenees at this first major stop on their route, the ancient capital of the Kingdom of Aragón. Today the pilgrimage goes both ways, as travelers on the Camino de Santiago continue to rest in Jaca (pop. 15,000), while most people now head through Jaca *toward* the Pyrenees for spectacular hiking and skiing. The valleys of Hecho and Ansó make wonderful excursions from Jaca. The "Pearl of the Pyrenees" is now primping itself in hopes of hosting the 2002 Winter Olympics. As practice, it will hold the 1995 Winter University Games during the fourth week of February.

ORIENTATION AND PRACTICAL INFORMATION

If you arrive by bus, you'll be dropped conveniently at the edge of the city's center on **Avenida de la Jacetania,** which loops around downhill to become **Avenida de Oroel.** When Av. Oroel reaches the bottom of the hill it connects with **Avenida Regimiento de Galicia,** which becomes **Avenida Primer Viernes de Mayo,** a broad street that completes the circle by running back uphill to Av. Jacetania. Within this circle, the central artery for shops and restaurants is **Calle Mayor.** The shuttle bus from the train station will either drop you off at the Ayuntamiento, in the middle of C. Mayor, or at the intersection of C. Mayor and Av. Regimiento de Galicia.

Tourist Office: Av. Regimiento Galicia, 2, local 1 (tel. 36 00 98), left off C. Mayor. English-speaking staff. Useful map, lots of hiking info. Open Mon.-Fri. 9am-2pm and 4:30-8pm, Sat. 9am-1:30pm and 5-8pm, Sun. 10am-1:30pm; mid-Sept.-June Mon.-Fri. 9am-1pm and 4:30-7pm, Sat. 10am-1pm and 5-7pm. The **Ayuntamiento** at C. Mayor, 24, proffers a city plan when the tourist office is closed.

Travel Agent: Viajes Abad, Av. Regimiento Galicia, 19 (tel. 36 10 81). **Viajes Arán,** C. Mayor, 46 (tel. 35 54 80 or 35 55 10). Both schedule bus tours to San Juan de la Peña (July-Aug. only; around 1000ptas).

Currency Exchange: Banks cluster on Av. Jacetania. Afternoons and summer weekends try **Fincas Rapitan,** Av. Primer Viernes de Mayo, 14 (tel. 36 20 59). Open 10am-1:30pm and 5:30-9pm.

Post Office: C. Correos, 13 (tel. 36 00 85), Av. Regimiento Galicia heading down-hill from C. Mayor. Open Mon.-Fri. 9am-2pm, Sat. 9am-1pm. Lista de Correos in same building, open Mon.-Fri. 8am-3pm. **Postal Code:** 22700.

Telephones: Ask the tourist office for the location of the summer phone center. Phone booths by bus station and in front of tourist office. **Telephone Code:** 974.

Trains: Shuttle buses run from downtown to the train station roughly ½hr. before each train leaves. They stop at the Ayuntamiento on C. Mayor or (if closed) at the taxi stop, and at the bus station. If you're walking, take Av. Juan XXIII from the station past 3 ornate traffic islands before joining Av. Primo de Rivera at the fork (just past Restaurante La Abuela 2); stay right until the Ciudadela comes into view, then take the left fork (Av. Primo de Rivera), which eventually crosses C. Mayor. **RENFE** (tel. 36 13 32) is at northeast end of Av. Juan XXIII. Ticket booth open 10am-noon and 5-7pm. To: Ayerbe to connect to Loarre (3 per day, 1½hr., 400ptas; Inter-City 1000ptas); Huesca (3 per day, 2hr., 600ptas; I.C. 1200ptas); Zaragoza (3 per day, 3hr., 1065ptas; I.C. 1600ptas); Madrid (1 per day, 6½hr., 3200ptas).

Buses: La Oscense (tel. 35 50 60). To: Sabiñánigo, where mail buses connect to Torla, near Ordesa and Aínsa (2-5 per day, 15min., 150ptas); Huesca (2-3 per day, 1hr., 630ptas); Zaragoza (2-3 per day, 2½hr., 1210ptas). **Josefa Escartín** (tel. 36 05 08). Mon.-Sat. 1 per day to: Hecho (1½hr., 275ptas); Siresa (1¾hr., 340ptas); and Augó (2hr., 375ptas). Also to Puente La Reina (125ptas), where there is ser-vice to Pamplona (1-3 per day, 2hr., 640ptas).

Taxis: Taxis line up at the intersection of C. Mayor, Av. Regimiento Galicia, and Av. Primo de Rivera (tel. 36 28 48).

Car Rental: Aldecar, Av. Jacetania, 60 (tel. 36 07 81), left from the bus station and downhill. Seat, Ford, or VW 3500ptas per day, 25ptas per km. Semi-mandatory insurance 600ptas per day, 15% tax. Valid international license required. **Viajes Abad** (see travel agents). 6325ptas per day includes 100km, insurance, and sales tax. 25ptas per additional km. Neither place has a minimum rental age, and both require that you return the car to Jaca.

Bike Rental: Lokoski, Av. Francia, 55B (tel. 35 59 20) rents mountain bikes and skis.

Laundromat: Lavomatique, Av. Escuela Militar de Montaña, 1 (tel. 36 01 12), part of Bar Santi to the left of the bus station. Wash and dry 650-700ptas. Open Mon.-Sat. 10am-10pm.

Hiking Club: Transpirineos, Av. Regimiento Galicia, 2 (tel. 36 49 98; fax: 36 48 26). Organizes biking, rafting, and mountaineering excursions throughout the Pyrenees.

Sports Center: Polideportivo, Av. Perimetral (tel. 35 53 06). Pool, skating rink, and just about everything else.

Ski Conditions: Teléfono blanco (tel. (976) 20 11 12).

24-Hour Pharmacy: Check listings in local paper, *Pirineo Aragonés*. Otherwise, take your medical prescription to the local police in the Ayuntamiento on C. Mayor (tel. 092); they will escort you to one.

Medical Services: Centro de Salud, Po. Constitución, 6 (tel. 36 07 95).

Red Cross: (tel. 36 11 01), outside town on Llano de la Victoria.

Emergency: tel. 092.

Police: Policía Local, C. Mayor, 24 (tel. 092), in the Ayuntamiento. **Policía Nacional,** tel. 091. **Guardia Civil** (tel. 36 13 50), on the highway to France, following Av. Primer Viernes de Mayo from town toward the train station.

ACCOMMODATIONS AND CAMPING

Jaca's *hostales* and *pensiones* are mainly grouped around C. Mayor and the cathedral. It pays to travel with company, as doubles and triples offer the best deals. Lodgings are scarce mainly during the town's *fiesta* June 24-29 and the bi-annual Festival Folklórico in late July and early August. Book rooms weeks ahead.

Albergue Juvenil de Vacaciones (HI), Av. Perimetral, 6 (tel. 36 05 36). Follow Av. Jacetania-Oroel to the left (facing town) halfway around the town's perimeter, and go down the broad stone steps capped by the modern metal sculpture. The hostel is then across the street and to the right. Swarming with youth groups, these barracks just scream "summer camp," and are a ways from the train station and everything else. Winter heating. 950ptas per person, over 26 1100ptas. *Media pensión:* 1800ptas; 2000ptas. Non-members pay 100ptas more. Sheets 250ptas. Reception open 8am-4pm and 7pm-midnight.

Albergue Villanúa (HI) (tel. 37 80 16), on Camino de la Selva in Villanúa, about 15km north of Jaca. Buses and trains to Canfranc stop here. Open Christmas-Aug. Call ahead, as it fills with groups July-Aug. 3-day max. stay. 950ptas per person, over 25 1400ptas.

Hostal Sompart, C. Echegarery, 11 (tel. 36 34 10). Several centuries worth of cleanliness and comfort, and only 100-200ptas more than surrounding *pensiones*. TV in every room. Restaurant downstairs serves a 900pta *menú*. Doubles 4000ptas, with bath 4500ptas. Triples 6000ptas. Low-season: 3600ptas; 4000ptas; 5500ptas. Visa, MC, AmEx accepted.

Habitaciones Martínez, C. Mayor, 53 (tel. 36 33 74). Feisty, gregarious management gushes over *Let's Go* travelers. Bright new rooms with happy floral bedspreads in annex down the street. 1800ptas per person. Avoid smaller, unappealing—albeit cheaper—rooms above the bar (1500ptas per person).

Hostal Residencia El Abeto, C. Bellido, 15 (tel. 36 16 42), 1 bl. toward Av. Jacetania from C. Mayor. Nice rooms, nice beds, nice scarlet blankets, 'nuff said. Singles 2400ptas. Doubles 3700ptas, with bath 4700ptas.

Camping: Peña Oroel (tel. 36 02 15), 3½km down the road to Sabiñánigo. Wooded grounds. 1st-rate facilities. 490ptas per person, per tent, and per car. Open Holy Week and mid-June to mid-Sept. **Camping Victoria** (tel. 36 03 23), 1km from Jaca on Highway C-134 (direction of Pamplona). Groovy view of the foothills. 400ptas per person, per car, and per tent. Open year-round.

FOOD

Most of Jaca's restaurants radiate from **Calle Mayor,** with a few along Av. Primer Viernes de Mayo and Av. Juan XXIII. Regional specialties include *costillas de cordero* (lamb chops) and *longanizas* (short spicy sausages). There is a produce **market** on C. Fernando el Católico, Fri. 9am-2pm. From C. Mayor head down Av. Primer Viernes de Mayo and turn right.

Supermarket: ALDI, C. Correos, 9, next to the post office. Open Mon.-Sat. 9:30am-1:30pm and 5-8pm.

Crepería El Bretón, C. Ramiro I, 10. The French owner makes authentic dinner crepes *(galettes,* 350-800ptas) and dessert crepes (275-600ptas). Salads 650ptas. Open Tues.-Sat. 6pm-1am.

Croissanterie Cafetería Demi-Lune, Av. Regimiento Galicia (tel. 36 36 19), in same clump of shops as the tourist office. Name suggests proper order of consumption: dessert, then dinner, then moonlight. Popular with locals. Substantial croissant sandwiches 200-300ptas, sweet dessert ones 50-200ptas. Warning: croissant *vegetal* comes with ham. Open 7:45am-2pm and 3:30-11:30pm.

Bar Restaurant La Campanilla, C. Mayor, 43 (tel. 36 14 48), in a small hive of shops and restaurants set off the street. Proves the adage: *"Patata y caña, lo mejor de España." Patatas asadas* (broiled potatoes) and *caña* (draft beer) each 110ptas.

SIGHTS AND ENTERTAINMENT

The pentagonal fortress referred to as **La Ciudadela** or Castillo de San Pedro puts Jaca on the tourist map. Built by King Felipe II in 1590 and sheltered in a grassy knoll, the citadel originally served to protect Jaca from French Huguenot attacks. It overlooks the battlefield known as *Las Tiendas* (The Tents), where Moors were repelled around 760. The victory is celebrated every first Friday in May with a reenactment that highlights the heroic role of the city's women in its defense. (Open 11am-1:30pm and 5-6:30pm; Sept.-June 11am-noon and 4-5pm. Tours in Spanish available.)

The Romanesque **catedral** is modest but noteworthy. Begun in 1063, it influenced most designs for churches built along the Jacobean route. The Baroque period brought a new altarpiece and the clashing ribbed vaulting. Four masses are held roughly every hour each morning, an evening mass at 7pm. In the sealed cloister, the **Museo Diocesano** has intricate 13th-century ironwork and Romanesque wall paintings. (Open Tues.-Sun. 11am-1:30pm and 4-6:30pm. Admission 200ptas.)

The **Fiestas Patronales de Santa Orosia** (June 24-29) draw dozens of youth groups, bands, and costumed street performers to the city. Every odd-numbered year at the end of July and beginning of August, people from all over the world come with bells on their toes for the **Festival Folklórico de los Pirineos.**

■ NEAR JACA

MONASTERIO DE SAN JUAN DE LA PEÑA

The Monasterio de San Juan de la Peña is difficult to reach, but suck it up and find a way. About 22km from Jaca, the monastery has been wedged into its mountainside for nearly 1000 years. Inside is the end of the line for all of Aragón's kings. Be careful not to confuse the *monasterio viejo* with the new *monasterio* 1km uphill. Check at the tourist office for information about travel agencies that organize excursions in July and August. During the same months, you can get partway there by taking the Jaca-Fuenterrabía bus as far as Desvío de Santa Cruz, which leaves 11km to cover. (Monastery open 10am-1:30pm and 4-8pm; Oct.-March Wed.-Sun. 11am-2:30pm; April-May Tues.-Sun. 10am-1:30pm and 4-7pm. Free.)

EL CASTILLO DE LOARRE

In the 11th century, King Sancho Ramírez built a castle to protect himself from Moorish attacks. El Castillo de Loarre (5km from the town of Loarre), perched atop a solid rock mount, is made nearly impenetrable by sharp cliffs at its rear and 400m of thick walls to the east. The building's outer walls follow the turns and angles of the rock so closely that at night an attacker might have only seen the silhouette of an awesome stone monolith.

A crypt opens to the right of the steep entrance staircase. The remains of Demetrius were stashed here after the French saint died in Loarre. A narrow staircase leads from the crypt into the magnificent **capilla.** A strip of checkered masonry curves directly above the several dozen capitals that line the apse, and a maze of passages and chambers honeycomb the rest of the castle. You can climb up to the battlements of both towers; the only access designed for the larger of the two is a narrow, arched footbridge from the smaller tower. Be careful when climbing the wobbly steel rungs to the roof. Use equal caution descending into the dark and doorless **sótano** (dungeon), probably used to hoard supplies. (Same hours as San Juan de la Peña (see above), closed Mon. year-round. Free.)

Reaching **Loarre** isn't easy. By **train,** the closest town is **Ayerbe,** 7km away. Trains run from Jaca (see Jaca: Trains) and Huesca. From Ayerbe, you can trek all the way to Loarre (about 2hr.) or walk to Bar Pirineos on the main plaza and ask for a taxi. A **bus** from Huesca to Ayerbe passes through Loarre. You can **camp** near the castle in the lovely pine forests. The castle is 5km from the town by a very circuitous road; the more direct walk from Loarre takes 45 minutes.

■■■ VALLE DE HECHO

This unspoiled, craggy valley cuts the Aragonese Pyrenees with the **Río Aragón Subordán** roughly 20km west of Jaca, the closest hiking area to the city. From early July to early August, villages in the valley host the **Simposio de Escultura y Pintura Moderna.** Artists come from far and wide to work here, turning the surrounding hills into a huge open-air museum. Villagers come to Hecho to feast on roast lamb and fried bread at the enormous festival kick-off party. By the end of August, the symposium splatters nearly all of the valley's towns with modern painting and sculpture. The rest of the year, the fruits of this labor lie scattered about the village, particularly next to the brightly painted studio on the *carretera.*

A **bus** leaves Jaca (see Jaca: Buses) Mon.-Sat. at 4:45pm, stopping at Hecho (6:15pm) and Siresa (6:30pm), before continuing on to Ansó. Mon.-Sat. morning the bus returns from Ansó through Siresa (7am) and Hecho (7:15am), on its way to Jaca.

HECHO

The town of **Hecho,** the valley's geographical and administrative center, cultivates its rustic charm. Although diehard service-oriented restaurants translate their menus for foreign guests, the majority of residents *(chesos)* brush tourists off like flies. The bus drops off in Pl. Fuente. Up the hill from the plaza on C. Aire, and light years from the tourist caravan, is the **Museo Etnológico,** which displays old photographs of valley residents and the meanest-looking collection of farming implements you'll ever see. (Open 11am-2pm. Admission 100ptas.)

The valley's lone **public phones** are in Hecho's main plaza, to the left of Pl. de la Fuente facing Casa Blasquicio. The **phone code** for the valley is 974.

While Hecho's rural environs aren't wholly welcoming to wanderlust travelers, the town does harbor numerous small *hostales,* such as **Casa Blasquicio,** Pl. Fuente/Pl. Palacio, 1 (tel. 37 50 07), an unmarked white house with balconies like Babylon in front of the bus stop. Follow your nose—the proprietor's cooking skills are formidable, as is her command of English and French. The six rooms are frequently full, so call ahead. (Singles 2000ptas. Doubles 3500ptas. IVA not included.) **Camping Valle de Hecho** (tel. 37 53 61), at the entrance to Hecho, has new facilities in a convenient location (450ptas per person, per car, and per tent).

SIRESA

Only 2km up the road from Hecho is tranquil **Siresa,** where octogenarians chatter in every precious spot of shade. Townspeople (not the current ones) built **Iglesia de San Pedro de Siresa** way back in Charlemagne's day. The church's caretaker lives in the white house around the corner and holds the key. The **Hostal Pirineo** (tel. 31 51 13), above the bar of the same name, right up the cobbled street at the very entrance to town, offers large rooms for up to four people for 3000ptas. Inquire for rooms at the restaurant past the bar, which has a 900pta *menú.*

HAPPY TRAILS

Between Hecho and Siresa, carved wood signs mark the beginning of trails to Picoya, La Reclusa, Lenito, Fuente de la Cruz, and Ansó. Although not particularly difficult, these are overgrown with brambles, eroded in places, covered with rocks, infested by flies, and scorched by the sun.

From Siresa, the road weaves up the valley, passing through a number of tunnels and the river-rock formation known as **La Boca del Infierno** (The Mouth of Hell), in which the river slips into a profound gorge. After about 9km, you'll reach **Valle de Oza,** a crescent of meadows with the grounds of **Camping Selva de Oza** (tel. 37 51 68; open June to mid-Sept. Mid-July to mid-Aug. 500ptas per person and per tent, 565ptas per car. Otherwise: 465ptas; 530ptas. Reception open 9am-2pm and 4-10pm.) The site has hot showers, a store, and even a restaurant. Fishing allowed in the river nearby.

Trails into the mountain leave from near the campground; go prepared with the red *Guía Cartográfica de los Valles de Ansó y Hecho,* published by *Editorial Alpina.* Nearly every bookstore, grocery store, and general store carries it (400-500ptas). The campsite arranges excursions, but you'll have more fun on your own. North of the site, you can hike along the peaks of the French border, from **Pic Rouge** (2177m) to **Pic Lariste** (2168m) to **Pic Laraille** (2147m), which has a stupe-fying view of the **Ibón de Acherito,** a glimmering lake framed by alpine brush. If you follow the guidebook and take a car part of the way, the actual hiking time for these should be around three hours to the summit. To climb **Castillo de Acher** (2390m), a square-topped mountain that resembles a waitress in the sky, follow the forest road toward the **Torrente de Espata,** amble along the path by this stream, cut up the mountainside on the zig-zag path to the ridge, follow the ridge past the **Refugio Forestal,** and go left at the fork. Several steep, narrow paths ascend to the summit (3½-4hr. to the top). For a real romp, consider scaling **Bisaurin,** the highest peak in the neighborhood. From the rocky, snow-capped peak you can practice casting parental looks over Old Aragón, the sumptuous Peña Forca (2391m), the iso-lated Pico Orhy (2015m), and the cosmic Castillo de Acher (2390m).

■■■ VALLE DE ANSÓ

ANSÓ

The absurdly adorable town of **Ansó,** a collection of tidy stone and white plaster houses with wrought-iron balconies and colorful garden boxes, presides over its very own valley 12km east of Hecho. Finally elected into the Kingdom of Aragón at the end of the 10th century, this placid town has never seen many visitors. Until recently, residents wore traditional costumes and spoke their own dialect. In 1900, the town boomed with 1700 residents; it's now down to around 300 (but who's counting?). Sheep-herding dogs are let lie on most street corners, ocular proof of the village's rural economy.

At Ansó's **Museo de Etnología,** inside the town church, mannequins model tradi-tional garb next to candlesticks, spinning wheels, weaving looms, costume jewelry, wood carvings, and religious books. The multi-layer bridal dress on display weighs over 30kg. (Open daily Mon.-Fri. 10:30am-1:30pm and 3:30-8pm; mid-Sept.-June talk to the priest *(mosen)* in the stone house in front of the church with the papal coat of arms relief. Admission 200ptas.)

The **bus** making the rounds of these valleys from Jaca drops off at C. Mayor (6:50pm), and leaves for Jaca at 6:30am (375ptas). For info on the town, call the **Ayuntamiento** at tel. 37 00 03. The **post office** is next door on Pl. Mayor (open Mon.-Fri. 9am-1pm, Sat. 10am-1pm). **Phones** are in the same plaza. The **telephone code** is 974. In an emergency, call the **Guardia Civil** (at the edge of town) at tel. 37 00 04.

Although few travelers decide to spend the night here, Ansó still maintains won-derful *hostales.* The **Posada Magoría,** C. Chapitel, 8 (tel. 37 00 49), is a clean and cozy old stone house. Owner Enrique Ipas is fluent in English and French and, as vice-president of the Pyrenean Conservation Society, will regale you with extensive stories of local flora and fauna. (2000ptas per person. Breakfast 500ptas.) Around the corner of the cobbled street (look for the wooden sign), is the comfortable, family-run **Posada Veral,** C. Cocorro, 6 (tel. 37 01 19). (Singles 1800ptas. Doubles 3200-3600ptas, with bath 4500ptas. Rates lower off-season. Breakfast 375ptas.)

ZURIZA

Fifteen km north of Ansó, **Camping Zuriza** (tel. 37 01 96 or 37 00 77) rubs elbows with a mountain stream 2km away from the Río Veral, a broad river suitable for fishing and rafting or kayaking. The site also provides a supermarket and *hostal.* (The campsite costs 425ptas per person, per tent, and per car. In the *hostal:* double 4000ptas; bunk in *literas* 800ptas. Visa, MC accepted.) From the campground, it's a dayhike to the **Mesa de los Tres Reyes,** a series of peaks close to the borders of France, Navarra, and Aragón (hence the three kings). From Zuriza, the Fountain of Linza lies north, and east of the Collado de Linza, a break between two smaller peaks. Hereabouts the terrain alternates between the shallow **Agujero de Solana** (Hole of Solana), the steep summit of **Escoueste,** and other quirky peaks. From Zuriza, you can also make the arduous trek to **Sima de San Martín** on the French border. To enjoy the area without a strenuous hike, walk 2km south of Ansó to the fork in the road. Just above the tunnel toward Hecho, you can see the striking, weather-sculpted rock formation called **El Monje y la Monja** (The Monk and the Nun). Sweep all lurid thoughts from your mind.

■■■ PARQUE NACIONAL DE ORDESA Y MONTE PERDIDO

Getting to Ordesa can mean riding along with the mail for an hour, and then hiking 9km. We would gladly crawl twice that distance to experience the park's primeval majesty, with cascades, rivers, and miles of trails crossing sheer, poplar-covered mountain faces. Located just south of the French border, roughly midway between Jaca and Aínsa, Ordesa cuts deeply into the highest mountains of the Pyrenees, rising from a valley etched by the Río Arazus toward some of the most magnificent peaks in the country. The park is a perfect base for hikers of all levels. Hiking boots are a must for even the most well-trodden trails. Arrive early (7-8am) to avoid the crowds on the principal paths.

Buses go only as far as **Torla,** a small stone village 9km short of the park; a mail-delivery bus leaves Sabiñánigo Mon.-Sat. at 10am, stopping in Torla at 11:55am before continuing to Aínsa. The bus passes through Torla again at 3:30pm on its way back to Sabiñánigo (arrives 4:30pm). Sabiñánigo connects easily by bus or train to Jaca and Huesca (2-5 buses per day from Jaca, 15 min., 150ptas; all trains on the Zaragoza-Huesca-Jaca line stop in Sabiñánigo). From Torla, the park is accessible only on foot or by car (hitchhiking is common, though not recommended). July and August, drivers should arrive at the park by 9am or earlier, as parking space is limited. For hikers, the lovely riverside path is accessible by crossing the main bridge in Torla itself, at the bottom of a very rocky path leading down past the Hostal Bella Vista. Once you've crossed the bridge, follow the track off to the left for about 1km: the tracks turn into the steep path, which later becomes gentler and shadier.

The Instituto Nacional para la Conservación de la Naturaleza **(ICONA)** is the control center for the park. They have an office in Torla during the summer on Ctra. Ordesa, just beyond C. Francia (tel. 48 63 48; open 9am-2pm and 4-8pm). The **information booth** at the park entrance is also open in summer. Both sell a trail map (300ptas). The indispensable *Editorial Alpina* guide is on sale at the souvenir shop by the parking lot for a hefty 650ptas. Ask the tourist office for their collection of pamphlets on local fauna *Animales del Parque Nacional de Ordesa y Monte Perdido* (free). You could come across wild boar, vipers, griffins, eagles, and vultures.

The **post office** is on C. Francia at Pl. Ayuntamiento (open Mon.-Fri. 10am-1pm). The **postal code** is 22376. Public **phones** are in Pl. Ayuntamiento and Pl. Nueva, also on C. Francia. The **telephone code** is 974. A **supermarket** sits on C. Francia, just past L'Atalaya (open 9am-2pm and 4-9pm, though actual hrs. vary). Jorge Soler (tel. 48 62 43) rents **mountain bikes** (2hr. 1000ptas, half-day 1400ptas, full-day 2300ptas). He can be found at the disco on C. Fatas, on the left as you enter town from the non-park side. In an **emergency,** call the **Guardia Civil** (tel. 48 61 60), at edge of town just before the ICONA office, who also offer park info when ICONA is closed.

In the park, one can only **camp** for the night and only at heights over 2200m, above the Soaso Steps. Many **refugios** (mountain huts, usually without facilities) facilitate overnight stays. The 120-bed **Refugio Góriz,** about 4hr. from the parking lot, has winter heating and meager hot showers. (950ptas per person.)

Torla's range of accommodations is greater. Cobblestoned C. Francia is the only road in Torla off the highway to the park—go left up it at the second entrance to town; on your right after 1 bl., under some wooden beams, lies the **Refugio L'Atalaya,** C. Francia, 45 (tel. 48 60 22). The *refugio* name and feel while still in town; 21 beds are clumped together in several large wooden bunks. (900ptas per person. Hot showers included.) Owners also serve a good *menú* (1300ptas) and breakfast (400ptas). If you fancy a room of your own, consider **Fonda Ballarín,** C. Capuvita, 11 (tel. 48 61 55), with comfortable beds, thick wool blankets, clean, checkered wooden floors, and an English-speaking owner. (Singles 1500ptas. Doubles 2700ptas. Mid-Sept.-June: 1400ptas; 2500ptas. Breakfast 370ptas.) To get there continue up past Refugio L'Atalaya to the small plaza and go up the hill to the left of the building with the stone arches—you'll see the bright flowers and sign. Two **campgrounds** lie just outside of "town." There's angling in the river at **Camping Río Ara** (tel. 48 62 48), about 1km down the paved path from its sign off Ctra. Ordesa, right before the bridge. (Open March-Nov. 380ptas per person, per tent, and per car.) Stay on the paved road. More upscale with a hotel, pool, and tennis courts is **Camping Ordesa** (tel. 48 61 46), 750m farther along Ctra. Ordesa. (Open April-Oct. 450ptas per person, per tent, and per car; children 300ptas; tax not included; 30% off in low-season.)

CIRCO DE SOASO AND OTHER HIKES

If you only have a day to spend in Ordesa, the **Soaso Circle** is the most practical hike, especially for virgin mountaineers. Frequent signposts along the wide trail clearly mark the six-hour journey. The trail slips through more topographical zones than Biosphere II: forests, waterfalls, cliffs, and plateaus. Although delightfully simple and satisfying in sunny weather, the trail becomes slippery and rather dangerous after rainfall. Check weather forecasts before starting out, and remember that in the winter, heavy snow can make the trail impassable. Less intrepid types who want to cut the hike by two-thirds (to about 2hr.) may return to the parking lot instead of continuing on. Whichever route you choose, try to arrive at the park early, since the entire Soaso Circle resembles Picadilly Circus by noon.

If you prefer a private mountain hike to a communal, multilingual parade, try the **Circo Cotatuero** or the **Circo Carriata**—both two-hour hikes which can also be done as a single five-hour hike. More experienced hikers might attempt the **Torla-Gavarnie** trail, a six-hour haul (one-way) all the way to Gavarnie, France. The **Ordesa-Gavarnie** trail is longer; plan to spend at least 10 hours. An even more rugged climb begins at the Refugio Góriz and climbs Monte Perdido (3355m; mountaineering equipment recommended). Count on eight hours there and back from the *refugio* (for details call tel. 48 63 79 or 48 63 75). For any of these hikes, the *Editorial Alpina* topographical map is an absolute must. Those who would rather enjoy the mountain splendor without strenuous involvement can hitch a **mule ride** around Ordesa Valley during July and August; inquire at the information office.

■ NEAR PARQUE NACIONAL DE ORDESA

AÍNSA

The same mail-delivery bus that stops off at Torla later continues, rain or snow or wind or shine, to the delightful village of Aínsa. It's difficult to imagine that Aínsa was once a major city; but a thousand years ago it was the undeniable capital of the Kingdom of Sobrarbe (incorporated into Aragón in the 11th century). The subtly restored **casco antiguo**, or old city, sits high above the Río Ava on a dry plateau.

The city's strategic strength is evident in the ruins of the 11th-century **castillo.** A little mountaineering allows for a sensational view from the top of its ancient walls at the far end of the *casco antiguo* across the **Plaza Mayor** (whip and fedora optional). The main plaza used to be the center of town, until houses between it and the castle were destroyed in the 1860s. Today a grassy park separates the plaza, while the rest of the *casco antiguo* stretches back on the opposite side.

In 1811, priests consecrated **Iglesia de Santa María,** just across the Pl. Mayor from the castle. Its expansion in the 16th century pilfered the masonry of nearby Iglesia de San Salvador. Several column bases transformed into capitals for the new church portal; the inscriptions consequently read upside-down. Inside you'll find the crypt's six original 16th-century capitals. Only short non-claustrophobes should brave the **torre.**

Every odd-numbered year the town holds a *fiesta* celebrating the victory against the Moors in 724. The **Morisma** takes place September 14-16, and includes theatrical representations of the battle, in which outnumbered townspeople vanquish the occupying Moorish forces with the help of a miraculously burning cross.

Practical Information The mail-delivery bus from Sabiñánigo stops at the crossroads of the highways that run through Aínsa: **Carretera a Ordesa** to the west, **a Campo-Graus** to the east, **a Francia** to the north, and **a Barbastro** to the south. Follow signs from there for the *casco antiguo* and Pl. Mayor to get to the old section of town. The stairs right next to the post office go up the hill; when you pass under an archway, C. Mayor is the left-hand fork, and it curves around uphill to Pl. Mayor. The **tourist office,** Av. Pirenáica, 1 (tel. 50 07 67), is at the highway crossroads. Helpful staff advises on transportation and excursions. Large supply of regional brochures. (Open Tues.-Sat. 10am-1:30pm and 4:30-8pm, Sun. 10am-1:30pm, Mon. 4:30-8pm. Closed Nov.-Easter; irregular hrs. except July-Aug.) The **post office,** Av. Ordesa (tel. 50 00 71), is opposite the bus stop on the way to the old town. (Open Mon.-Fri. 9am-2pm, Sat. 9am-1pm.) The **postal code** is 22330. A **telephone center** is on Av. Central before the bridge, past Hostal Dos Ríos. The **telephone code** is 974. The **Red Cross** (tel. 50 00 26) is located on Av. Ordesa on the outskirts of town. The **Guardia Civil** is posted in Barrio Banasto (tel. 50 00 55 or 50 01 74).

The **mail bus** from Sabiñánigo arrives at 1pm; it leaves at 7am for Barbastro and points south (with connections to Benasque), and at 2:30pm for Torla and Sabiñánigo (with train connections to Jaca and Huesca). The tourist office has up to date information on bus schedules.

Accommodations and Food Hostal Residencia Ordesa, Av. Ordesa, 22 (tel. 50 00 09), past the post office, has gleaming rooms with terraces, A/C, big hallway bathtubs, and a 1000pta *menú.* (1500ptas per person. Doubles with bath 3500ptas. Oct.-June: 1350ptas; 3200ptas. Breakfast 400ptas.) At the crossroads is **Hostal Dos Ríos,** Av. Central, 2 (tel. 50 00 43), with compact, well-kept modern rooms painted bright white. (Singles 20000ptas, with bath 3300ptas. Doubles 3500ptas, with bath 4300ptas. Oct.-May: 1900ptas; 2950ptas; 3300ptas; 3800ptas.) **Camping Aínsa,** Ctra. Aínsa-Campo km 1.8 (tel. 50 02 60) has a store, pool, and hot showers in a shady site. Take a left 300m after the bridge as you leave town toward the east, and then follow the unpaved road. (450ptas per person, per tent, and per car.)

Restaurant Bar Alaska is on Av. Ordesa right across from Hostal Ordesa. Not exactly Northern Exposure, but the air-conditioning works. Serves *bocadillos* (350-500ptas) beneath the glow of an immense TV.

■■■ VALLE DE BENASQUE

The Valle de Benasque is a hiker's dream come true. Countless trails of all levels wind through the surrounding mountains, and the area teems with *refugios*, allowing for longer expeditions. Soft-core strollers are often scared away by the valley's serious mountaineering reputation, but the Río Esera gorge and the astounding variety of mountain landscapes universally titillate. Snow-covered peaks 2km high tiptoe down the edges of the valley; cascades shoot over the sides of pine-covered hills. As always, be sure to get *Editorial Alpina*'s excellent topographical map of the valley (400-500ptas) in any of Benasque's stores before starting your hike.

BENASQUE

The village of Benasque rests lazily in the valley's abrupt soaring cradle. At the valley's center, it makes a practical base: most trailheads originate from the paved roads between Benasque and **Cerler,** a ski resort 8km north. If you start early from Benasque, you can hike just over 8km down the valley road, cross the river on the camping area bridge, and climb up, up, and away following the falls of the Río Cregueña. Four sweaty hours later you will reach **Lago de Cregueña** (2657m), the largest and, you'll be convinced, highest lake in the Maladeta massif.

The pilgrimage to **Mount Aneto** (3404m), the highest peak in the Pyrenees, begins each morning at about 5am, when the experts set out from the **Refugio de la Renclusa** to conquer the mountain. To reach the *refugio,* take the main road north, take the 4th exit to the right, and follow the paved road for 8km. From where it ends, it's a 30-min. trek. If lugging heavy supplies and equipment up a mountain face isn't your idea of fun, head downhill to the road and follow signs to **Forau de Aigualluts.** This tranquil pond, 50 minutes from the *refugio* trailhead at the end of a tumbling waterfall, stoically withstands the onslaught of hundreds of gallons per minute. Two gaping black holes (*foraus* in Aragonese) keep the pond calm by pulling the water underground and releasing it in Val d'Arán. Another strenuous hike from the *refugio* leads to the peak of **Sacroux** (2675m). Even if snow prevents you from reaching the top and peering into France, the rush of the **Torrents de Gorgutes** and the sight of Lago Gorgutes make the four-hour climb worthwhile. (*Refugio* open June 22-Sept. 24. 950ptas per person, discount for club members. Breakfast 450ptas. No showers, but a nice hose.) Call tel. 55 12 15 for information about any of the valley's *refugios.*

Practical Information To get to the **tourist office,** and volumes of info on local hiking, face the Galerías Barrabés mountain supply store at the main highway intersection and go past it down the alley on the right for 1 bl. (Tel. 55 12 89; open Mon.-Fri. 10am-2pm and 5-8:30pm; daily July-Aug.) There's a mapboard of the town near the fountains by the bus stop if the office is closed. The **post office** (tel. 55 12 37) is in the Ayuntamiento building (open Mon.-Fri. 10am-1pm, Sat. 11am-noon for urgent **telegrams** only). The **postal code** is 22440. A **telephone center** is on C. Mayor near the bus stop (open July-Sept. 10am-1:30pm and 5-9pm). The **telephone code** is 974. **Vit's,** Pl. Major, s/n (tel. 55 02 88) rents **mountain bikes** (500ptas per hr., half-day 1200ptas, full-day 2000ptas; open 10am-2pm and 4-9pm, July-Aug. 9:30am-9pm). The **Red Cross** is at tel. 55 12 85, the **ambulance** at tel. 55 10 01. Signs point to the **Guardia Civil** (tel. 55 10 08) from the main highway intersection.

La Alta Aragonesa (tel. 21 07 00) runs **buses** to and from Huesca (1-2 per day, 3hr., 1120ptas).

Accommodations and Food Inexpensive lodgings are available in the town proper. At the literal rock bottom are the cement floors of the *literas*. In **Fonda Bar-**

rabés, C. Mayor, 5 (tel. 55 16 54), off Pl. Mayor, left from the bus stop and straight 200m, 700ptas gets you a spot in one of their *literas,* a well-used mattress, a blanket, possibly three bedfellows on the same wooden bunk, a sink with water melted from the surrounding peaks, and access to a hot shower. For just a little more than twice the price, you can get a real room, floor, and winter heating. (Singles 1500ptas. Doubles 2950ptas.) English spoken. Restaurant downstairs serves *bocadillos* (300-400ptas) and *platos combinados* (650-950ptas). **Camping Aneto** (tel. 55 11 41), 3km out of town up the hill past the Cerler turnoff, has facilities for both summer and winter camping. (370ptas per person, per tent, and per car.) **Camping Ixeia** is a little farther past Aneto. (Open June-Sept. 400ptas per person, per tent, and per car. Call tel. (96) 154 68 09 in Valencia for info during off-season.) Both have stores and hot water. You can also pitch your tent in the wide open spaces, but only for a night and never in Plan del Hospital/Plan d'Estany.

Supermarket Super Spar is on C. Horno, off Pl. Iglesia, a 2-min. walk to the left from Pl. Mayor facing the main road. (Open daily 9am-2pm and 4:30-9:30pm; Sept.-June closed Sun.)

Andorra

Perched high in the Pyrenees, the tiny principality of Andorra (pop. 62,000, area 462 sq. km) remains one of Europe's most intriguing geographical and political anomalies. While Andorra has soaring peaks and near-pristine wilderness, it is not the grandeur of its sights but the humility of its sales taxes that draws most visitors. A string of duty-free shops soaked with the light of neon signs has transformed this diminutive nation into Europe's largest department store. To best appreciate Andorra, keep your money in your wallet, break away from the capital, and visit the picturesque Lilliputian villages cradled within a Brobdignagian mountain range.

Sandwiched between France and Spain, Andorra depends on its two larger neighbors for the tourism and trade that feed its economy—it accepts both *pesetas* and francs, and has no native currency. Still, Andorra clings fiercely to its individuality. The country has its own distinct culture and language (Catalan).

According to legend, Charlemagne founded Andorra in 784, in gratitude to the area's inhabitants for helping his army against the Arabs. In 839, Charles II, Charlemagne's grandson, transferred sovereignty to the Spanish Counts of Urgell, who gradually ceded their power over the region to the Church of Urgell. The church has retained its hold for more than seven centuries. On the secular side, a series of complex marriages delivered some power to the King of France, who ultimately lost it (and his head) to the French president. Thus it is that today French President François Mitterrand and Bishop of Urgell Dr. Joan Martí Alanis share the title "Co-Princes" of Andorra, with Andorrans still paying their "guardians" a tribute tax called the *Questia.* A popularly elected "General Council of the Valleys," which consists of 28 members and a Cap de Govern (Prime Minister) elected by the council, conduct the legislative and executive functions of government.

Politically, Andorra is far less progressive than other industrialized western European nations. Through 1970, only third-generation Andorran men older than 25 could legally vote. Only in the last twenty years has suffrage been extended to women, younger voters, and recent immigrants. Not until 1990 did Andorra create a comission to draft a constitution, adopted on March, 14, 1993, that liberalized the political system and created political parties. Also in 1990, the General Council voted to give Spain responsibility for representing Andorra in international organizations.

Andorran cuisine closely resembles that of Spanish Cataluña. A pork-lover's paradise, Andorra produces piggy wonders like *butifarra* (sausage), *bringuera,* and *llonganiça*. These, along with *paella* (rice flavored with saffron and mixed with seafood, sausage, and chicken) comprise the staples of the local diet. *Trinxat*, a mashed potato and green cabbage concoction, is a local specialty more subtly flavored than its ingredients would suggest. Trout is the backbone of Andorra's fishing industry; when grilled it provides respite from the pungent spices which usually spike local dishes. With festivals come a great variety of *coques* (cakes), all endowed with mysterious names.

Andorra's unabated attachment to its traditional Catalan culture manifests itself every summer when each of the seven parishes holds its own festival, a three-day jubilee. These spectacles start the third weekend of July and continue until mid-September. (Contact a tourist office for more info.) The national *festa* is on Sept. 8, in honor of patron *Nostra Señora de Meritxell* (Our Lady of Meritxell).

Most Andorran towns are scattered along the principality's three branches of "highways." Additionally, an extensive network of hiking trails and cabins make the country's beauty accessible to those on foot. Several Gallo-Roman churches, often topped by cylindrical bell-towers, huddle near the Spanish border. North of the capital, clear lakes and icy mountain peaks shelter tiny villages. Many Andorran towns, notably Canillo and La Massana, provide a base for skiing from December to April on a wide range of downhill and cross-country terrain. As major towns are separated by mere kilometers, most of the country can be accessed on local buses.

GETTING THERE

French and Spanish border police require presentation of a valid passport or an EU identity card to enter the country. No train tracks run through Andorra, and no planes brave its peaks. Instead, two highways—one from Spain and one from France—provide access to the principality. All traffic from France must enter Andorra at the town **Pas de la Casa;** the gateway town on the Spanish side is **Sant Julià de Lòria**.

La Hispano-Andorra (tel. 213 72) run between Spanish town La Seu d'Urgell to Andorra la Vella (6-7 per day, ½hr., 270ptas). **Alsina Graells** buses (tel. (973) 35 00 20 in La Seu, tel. (3) 265 68 66 in Barcelona, and tel. 273 79 in Andorra) connect La Seu to the rest of Spain via Catalan towns Puigcerdà and Lérida. To: Puigcerdà (3 per day, 1hr., 505ptas, Sat.-Sun. 575ptas); Lérida (2 per day, 2½hr. 1400ptas, Sat.-Sun. 1585ptas). Also direct buses between Andorra la Vella and Barcelona (3-4 per day, 3¾-4½ptas, 2245-2555ptas). **Andor-Inter/Samar** buses (tel. (91) 230 31 31 in Madrid, tel. 615 814 53 in Toulouse, tel. 262 89 in Andorra) make the Madrid-Andorra la Vella run (3 per week, 9hr., 4300ptas) via Zaragoza (6hr., 2100ptas). Most buses leave from the **bus station** at Pl. Guillemó (known to locals as Pl. Arcades) off Av. Princep Benlloch, at the end of C. Doctor Negüi. Buses from La Seu drop passengers off at the bus stop on Av. Princep Benlloch, 6, off Pl. Princep Benlloch. The Barcelona and Madrid buses leave from another bus station on C. Bonaventura Riberaygua. To get to the station from Pl. Princep Benlloch, follow Av. Meritxell to the other side of the river. Make an immediate right after crossing, an immediate left, then a fourth right and go straight 4-5 bl. (20min.).

GETTING AROUND

An efficient system of **inter-city buses** connects villages lying along the three major highways that meet in Andorra la Vella; the entire country is navigable in an hour or two via public transportation. The main bus stop is on Av. Princep Benlloch, 6, off Pl. Benlloch. It's a 10-min. ride from Andorra la Vella to **La Massana, Encamp, Ordino,** or **Sant Julià de Lòria** (roughly every ½hr.). Those who wish to reach more distant points within Andorra will have a more difficult time, simply because bus service is less frequent. Buses run one to three times per day to **Pas de la Casa, Arinsal,** and **El Serrat** from Andorra la Vella. Buses cost 75-525ptas, though most are around 100ptas. Bus lines are not indicated by number or color; pay careful attention to the direction signs posted in the front window. For more information, contact **Cooperative Interurbana Andorrana,** Av. Princep Benlloch, 15 (tel. 204 12). The tourist office's pamphlet, though in Catalan, is easy to decipher.

ONCE THERE

Within Andorra, an extensive and superb network of tourist offices (indicated by *Informació* signs) provides information on lodgings, excursions, and skiing facilities. In the capital, the office provides an adequate, indexed *plànol* (street plan) of Andorra la Vella with a list of emergency telephone numbers and services. Ask for the brochure published by the Andorran Ministry of Tourism and Sports, containing what must be the world's second most detailed map of Andorra (the first being the *Editorial Alpina*, which all hikers should procure). The staffs in these offices generally speak fluent Spanish, decent French, and passable English.

All establishments are legally bound to accept French and Spanish currencies in every transaction. In practice, however, dominant trading ties with Spain have resulted in a conspicuous preference for *pesetas,* so it pays off to change *francs* into *pesetas.* All prices (except on a few touristy menus) appear in *pesetas.*

Dual French and Spanish administration of the postal system has resulted in separate **post offices,** overseen by France and Spain, within a few blocks of one another. Correspondence forwarded to the **Poste Restante** in Andorra la Vella will arrive at the French post office; **Lista de Correos** at the Spanish office. The tourist office recommends the French service (except for Spain-bound mail).

Phone communications in Andorra are handled exclusively by the **STA** network. You must purchase an STA *teletarjeta* (telecard) for a minimum of 500ptas, which provides 50 units of calling time. The cards are available in any post office or kiosk. Spanish Telefónica phone cards do not work in Andorran payphones, and those which accept *pesetas* are being phased out. Collect calls are not available, and AT&T does not maintain an access network with Andorra (despite what the Access Number Guide may say). For **directory assistance** within Andorra, dial 111. From Spain, Andorra is dialed as if it were a regular province, with **telephone code** 9738.

Accommodations in Andorra take after their Spanish counterparts in just about every respect. While there are no HI youth hostels, affordable *pensiónes* abound, there is an *albergue* in La Massana, and 20 *refugios* dot mountain trails. Campgrounds are also plentiful, but tend to fill quickly in summer months with French and Spanish vacationers. The helpful tourist office guide *Hotels i Restaurants* lists prices and facilities of all accommodations in Andorra.

■■■ ANDORRA LA VELLA

Avinguda Meritxell, Andorra la Vella's main thoroughfare and the Hong Kong of the Pyrenees, manages to disguise the fact that the city is the permanent home of only 15,000 residents. What Andorrans refer to as a "city" is little more than a narrow stretch of perfumeries, electronics shops, clothing stores, and a host of other boutiques which sprout along this short boulevard overlooking the placid Gran Valira River. Marvel at Europe's largest shopping mall and move on. Climb the roads leading away from the city, where residents in the tiny mountain villages still practice sheep-husbandry and cultivate tobacco.

ORIENTATION AND PRACTICAL INFORMATION

The city's main thoroughfare, **Avinguda Meritxell,** rushes through the city on a riverbed of neon lights, flashing from Pl. Princep Benlloch in the heart of the tiny **barri antic** (old quarter). To the left (west) of the *plaça* facing the Eglésia (Church) of Sant'Esteve, Av. Meritxell becomes Av. Princep Benlloch. C. Dr. Negüi, the first right (a sharp turn) off Av. Princep Benlloch from the *plaça,* leads to Pl. Guillemó. To get to the tourist office from the bus stop on Av. Princep Benlloch, continue east (away from Spain) just past the *plaça* on your left, then take C. Dr. Villanova, which curves down to the right.

Tourist Office: Av. Doctor Villanova, 22 (tel. 202 14; fax 258 23). Excellent guides to hiking, mountain biking, and horseback riding available in English. Open Mon.-Sat. 9am-1pm and 3-7pm; Oct.-June Mon.-Sat. 10am-1pm and 3-7pm, Sun. 10am-1pm. There is an **information booth** at Av. Meritxell, 33 (tel. 271 17); open Mon.-Sat. 9am-1pm and 4-8pm, Sun. 9am-1pm and 4-7pm.

Currency Exchange: Banc Internacional, Av. Meritxell, 32 (tel. 206 07). No commission. Open Mon.-Fri. 9am-1pm and 3-5pm, Sat. 9am-noon.

American Express: Viatges Relax, Carrer Roc dels Escolls, 12 (tel. 220 44), a third right off Av. Meritxell from Pl. Princep Benlloch. Open Mon.-Fri. 9am-1pm and 3:30-7pm, Sat. 9:30am-1pm.

Post Offices: French Post Office, Carrer Pere d'Urg, 1 (tel. 204 08). Poste Restante. Open Mon.-Fri. 9am-5:30pm, Sat. 9am-noon; June-Sept. Mon.-Fri. 8am-2pm, Sat. 9am-noon. **Spanish Post Office,** Carrer Joan Maragall, 10, a few blocks away. Lista de Correos. (Open Mon.-Fri. 9am-1pm and 4-5pm, Sat. 9am-1pm.) Both at the eastern end of town, on the other side of the river from Pl. Princep Benlloch.

Taxis: Stations at Pl. Guillemó and at Pl. Rebés (tel. 269 00 for pick-up).

Late-Night Pharmacy: Each pharmacy has the "duty roster" posted on its door, listing which is open on a given night. Or, call the police.

Hospital: Clínica Verge de Meritxell, Av. Fiter I Rossell (tel. 680 00). **Ambulance,** tel. 118.

Police: C. Prat de la Creu, 16 (tel. 212 22). **Emergency,** tel. 110.

ACCOMMODATIONS, CAMPING, AND FOOD

Since most people zoom in and out of Andorra, finding a room is no problem. If your stomach starts to growl, your best bet is the **mega-market,** on the 2nd floor of Grans Magatzems Pyrénées, Av. Meritxell, 10, the country's biggest department store. (Open Mon.-Fri. 9:30am-8pm, Sat. 9:30am-9pm, Sun. 9am-7pm.) Mediocre *menús* are the rule in Andorra la Vella, though at least they're cheap. Hunt for restaurants along the busy **Avinguda Meritxell** and in the quieter streets around **Plaça Princep Benlloch.** Most restaurants have supplementary charges on certain items in their *menús*.

Residència Benazet, C. Llacuna, 21 (tel. 206 98), a left and immediate right off Pl. Guillemó, facing the Banc d'Andorra. Large, no frills rooms. Cold showers. 1300ptas per person. In quads 1000ptas.

Pensió La Rosa, Antic Carrer Major, 18 (tel. 218 10), just south of Av. Princep Benlloch. Provides immaculate, fresh rooms, all with cheery wallpaper. Exceptional hallway bathroom. Singles 1700ptas. Doubles 3000ptas. Breakfast 350ptas.

Camping: Camping Valira (tel. 223 84), located behind the **Estadi Comunal d'Andorra la Vella,** offers shade, video games, hot showers, and an indoor pool. 450ptas per person, per tent, and per car. Reception open 8am-1pm and 3-9pm. Call ahead—it gets full. 2½km down the road, **Camping Santa Colomba** (tel. 288 99)has about the same prices but no video games and pool.

Restaurant Navarra, Cap del Carrer, 1 (tel. 212 01), on the alley off Pl. Princep Benlloch, has authentic Catalan fare. *Menú* 975ptas.

Restaurant Marti, Av. Meritxel, 44, sells good cheap food.

SIGHTS AND ENTERTAINMENT

Although *vendo ergo sum* appears to be Andorra la Vella's motto, a token 20 minutes can be spent outside of the shopping vortex. **Casa de la Vall** (House of the Valleys), the tiniest little parliament this side of Hobbiton, is at the end of the stone alley that goes west from Pl. Princep Benlloch past the church. This 16th-century building, a private home until it was sold to Andorra's General Council in 1702, still contains many of the original fixtures. The Hall of the Council, where the Consell meets twice a month, contains the chapel of Sant Ermengol and the "seven-keyed" cupboard. Each of Andorra's seven parishes holds a key to the cupboard, which contains documents of the General Council. (Obligatory guided tour every hour Mon.-Fri. 10am-1pm and 3-6pm, Sat. 10am-1pm. Free.) The tourist office sells tickets for Andorra la Vella's annual **Festival Internacional de Música i Dansa,** highlighting an international array of ballet, jazz, and classical concerts. For information contact the **Collectiu d'Activitats Culturals,** Av. Princep Benlloch, 30 (tel. 202 02). The annual festival colors the capital on the first Saturday, Sunday, and Monday in August.

■ NEAR ANDORRA LA VELLA

LA MASSANA

The *parròquia* of La Massana (pop. 5000) provides an excellent base for exploring Andorra's spectacular mountains. Though a good 1252m above sea level, it is easily accessible by bus from Andorra la Vella (every ½hr. until 8:30pm, 10min., 95ptas).

La Massana is home to Andorra's tallest peak, **Pic Alt de la Coma Pedrosa** (2946m). The *Grande-Randonnée* 11 goes through **Arinsal,** northwest of the town on the way to Spain; a multitude of trails criss-cross the area. From the tiny **Cortals de Sispony,** 3km west of Sispony, the climb to **Cap del Cubil** (2364m), on the Spanish border, takes 1½hr. (Consult the tourist office for details on hikes.) Or, perambulate leisurely through the countryside, visiting the old town of La Massana and its **Església Parroquial de Sant Iscle i Santa Victoria,** a reconstructed Romanesque church with an impressive Baroque altar.

The ski resort **Pal** (tel. 362 36), 10km from La Massana, **rents mountain bikes** (700ptas per hr., 1850ptas per ½-day, 2600 per day). A bus runs to Pal from La Massana at 10am; the return bus leaves Pal at 5pm (250ptas each way).

The trans-Pyreneic **Alta Ruta dels Pirineus** (occupying 53km of trails in Andorra) passes through La Massana and is complemented by a number of shorter mountain bike trails. **Club Hipic L'Aldosa** (tel. 373 29), on the road to Andorra la Vella from La Massana, and **Estació d'Esqui de Pal** rent horses and organize **horseback riding** expeditions (call ahead). All tourist offices stock information in English on trekking, biking, and horseback riding around La Massana.

The **tourist office** in La Massana (tel. 356 93) is in a steep-roofed cabin by the bridge, just ahead of the bus stop (open Mon.-Sat. 9am-1pm and 3-7pm, Sun. 9am-1pm and 3-6pm). For emergency and health services, call Andorra la Vella.

La Massana is a 20- to 30-min. climb from the **Alberg Borda Jovell,** Av. Jovell, s/n (tel. 365 20; fax 357 76) in **Sispony,** a mountain-clinging hamlet of gray stone houses. To get there from La Massana's bus stop, go back towards Andorra la Vella 75m and turn right at the main intersection. Follow the signs south for 1.3km until the *alberg,* a 700-year-old stone house, appears on the left. The renovated all-wood interior has large bunk-bed filled rooms and immaculate bathrooms with stand-up toilets(!). The friendly owner holds court in the restaurant downstairs and is a good source of information on the area. (1050ptas per person. Sheets 550ptas. Visa, MC, AmEx accepted. Curfew midnight.) **Camping STA Catarina** is on the uphill outskirts of La Massana; contact the tourist office for info. **Establiments Mohis,** on the road to Andorra la Vella across from the exit to Sispony, can furnish your grocery needs (open Mon.-Sat. 8:45am-2pm and 4:30-8pm, Sun. 9am-1pm).

■■■ ELSEWHERE IN ANDORRA

Sadly, too few of the sale-zealots shift their eyes from the boutique windows toward the rocky, forested mountains, and realize what they are missing. Andorra is dotted with hamlets, mountain lakes, and some of the best ski slopes in Europe (see Getting Around for transportation info, and La Massana for bike rentals).

Santa Coloma, five minutes from Andorra la Vella by bus, features a solitary 12th-century church notable for its unique cylindrical Romanesque bell tower. The curious stone bridge of the Margineda arches gracefully over the diminutive **Gran Valira River** in **Sant Julià de Lorià,** just north of the Spanish border. **Ordino** rests comfortably past La Massana in a valley in the shadow of the imposing Pic de Casamanya. The least populated of Andorra's seven parishes, Ordino is distinguished by its status as former home to the principality's **seignorial mansions** *(pairals).* The town's nobles built a small fortune in the regional iron industry; the home of Don Guillem, a prominent Andorran iron magnate, stands near the church. The colossal **Palau de Gel D'Andorra** (Andorran ice palace; tel. 515 15), an eclectic recreational facility, dominates the tiny town of **Canillo.** The facilities of the "palace," including an overflowing swimming pool, ice-skating rink, squash courts, and cinema, are accessible by individual admission tickets. (Palace open Mon.-Fri. 8:30am-midnight, Sat.-Sun. 11am-midnight. Each facility has independent hours. 400ptas for pool, 800-850ptas for skating, 950ptas per ½hr. squash plus 250ptas for racket rental. Schedule and prices subject to change; call before you go.)

During the winter, Andorra is transformed from a giant Rolex into a giant ski-slope, harboring five outstanding ski resorts within its boundaries (all rent equipment). On the French border, **Pas de la Casa** boasts 530 hectares of skiable land, with 42 different trails for all levels of ability. The resort (tel. 203 99) provides 27 mechanical lifts, downhill instruction, two medical centers, and night skiing. Health-minded cross-country aficionados flock to the slopes of **Soldeu-El Tarter** (tel. 211 97). 15km from the French border, between Andorra la Vella and Pas de la Casa, the resort packs a 840m vertical punch and includes 12km of cross-country trails. Other, smaller resorts are **Arinsal** (tel. 358 22) and **Ordino-Arcalis** (tel. 363 20). Andorra's tourist office publishes the rather lyrical *Mountains of Snow,* a guide to all its ski resorts. **SKI Andorra** (tel. 643 89) can answer miscellaneous questions. During the winter, there are **white phones** in Spanish (tel. 488 52) and French (tel 488 53), as well as Catalan.

When most of the snow has melted away, a wealth of **hiking** opportunities spring to life all over Andorra. The *Grandes-Randonnées* trails 7 and 11 traverse nearly all of the country. The G-R 7 stretches from Portella Blanca on the French border to Suberri on the Spanish border, hitting an altitude of 2411m at Els Estangs about one-third of the way through. The kinder, gentler G-R 11 moves alongside the river Valira from Port de Sigeur in the northwest corner of Andorra to the Col d'Ordino in Andorra's (tiny) heartland. Cabins and mountain refuges dot each trail, providing shelter for the weary hiker. The booklet *Andorra: The Pyrenean Country,* supplied by Andorra's tourist office, provides a complete list of cabin and refuge locations within the principality.

Cataluña (Catalunya)

Confined by the Pyrenees to the north and the Rio Ebro delta to the south, Cataluña is a privileged land. This prosperous region has always proudly held itself apart from the remainder of the country, retaining its own culture and tongue.

Colonized by Greeks and Carthaginians, Cataluña was one of Rome's favored provinces. Only briefly subdued by the Moors, Cataluña's counts achieved independence in 874 and were recognized as sovereign princes in 987. Having nabbed the throne of Aragón in 1137, Cataluña was thenceforth linked to the rest of Spain; yet Catalan *usages* or *fueros* (legal codes) remained in effect. It took a Bourbon, Felipe V, to suppress Cataluña's privileges as punishment for siding against him in the War of the Spanish Succession (1700-1713).

A revival of fortunes accompanied the opening of the American empire for trade with all Spanish cities (late 18th century), when Cataluña rapidly developed into one of Europe's premier textile manufacturing centers. Industrial expansion through the 19th century underpinned a flowering of the arts and sciences that came be to regarded as a Catalan *Renaixença* (Renaissance).

Having fought on the losing side in the Civil War, Cataluña lost its autonomy in 1939; Catalan instruction was widely suppressed (except in universities) and publication in the language was limited to specialized areas. Since autonomy was recovered in 1977, media and arts in Catalan have flourished. The language is once again official in Spain and currently some are pushing for the right to speak Catalan in the Madrid Senate, though the region itself is almost entirely bilingual.

Some worry that the use of Catalan in institutions such as universities will discourage talented Spaniards elsewhere from teaching, studying, or doing research there, effectively sealing off the principality from the wider world. Others, however, clamor for more autonomy for the region, arguing that the tenor of Catalan regionalism has consistently been progressive and that Spain should emulate rather than stifle its regional practices. For example, Cataluña's successful attraction of foreign investment—it already receives 40% of the foreign industrial investment in Spain—and its recent nine-fold increase in trade promotion offices abroad are touted as instances of the region's adroit handling of diplomatic and contemporary economic issues. The most visible display of Catalan spirit was the 1992 Olympics: Catalan president Jordi Pujol took out full-page ads in newspapers around the world that referred to the "country" of Cataluña, and "Freedom for Cataluña" banners were not an uncommon sight.

Lovers exchange books and roses to honor the region's patron, St. George, on the Fiesta de Sant Jordi (April 23). On September 11, Catalans really whoop it up for Diada, La Festa Nacional de Catalunya, set aside to affirm the region's political autonomy.

Whether by air, rail, bus, ferry or road, transportation in Cataluña is superb; only in the Pyrenees and on the Costa Brava do you need a car.

■■■ BARCELONA

Grand, sprawling, and self-confident, Barcelona consolidates Cataluña's artistic genius and commercial resourcefulness. By reputation and tradition, it is the nation's most cosmopolitan, sophisticated, and progressive city.

Barcelona (pop. 1,700,000) was a Carthaginian enclave until the Romans elbowed in sometime during the 4th century BC. By the Middle Ages the city was the capital of a fat commercial empire. But with the discovery of the Americas, Barcelona found itself poorly located to partake of the New World feeding frenzy. Not until the 19th century did Cataluña's Industrial Revolution textile mills restore Barcelona's glory, feeding a budding bourgeoisie and a pioneering generation of architects, artists, and musicians.

The city tore down its medieval walls in 1859. While authoritarian planner Ildefons Cerdà laid out a stiff grid of streets, the architects of *Modernismo,* led by native son Antoni Gaudí, filled them with exuberant, fantastical creations. The 20th century brought political unrest and the rise of anarchism: during the Spanish Civil War, the anti-Fascist coalition operated out of Barcelona. Still politically charged in the latter part of the 20th century, Barcelona is an activist center for Catalan nationalists, feminists, gays, and many others.

Barcelona took advantage of the 1992 Olympics to redesign itself as a European capital. Substandard hotels fell to the wrecking ball, new parks and sculpture gardens were planted, pedestrian zones expanded, and over 50 monuments restored. The city accused of 'turning its back' to the Mediterranean transformed its gritty, concrete, rust-and-smog coastline into a seaside promenade with parks, palms, benches, beaches, and cafés. Catalan and foreign architects continue to transform the city into a showcase of contemporary urban design and aesthetic coherence. Much as Paris has been described as the capital of the 19th century, self-possessed Barcelona may be remembered as the capital of the 1990s.

ORIENTATION

The hub of the city, **Plaça de Catalunya,** is easily accessible from either of Barcelona's two train stations. Most trains come into **Estació Sants.** Sants is handily on the green L3 Metro line, which whisks travelers to Pl. Catalunya (Direction: Montbau. For Metro times, see Getting Around: Metro and Bus.) For late arrivals, the N2 bus of the Nitbus service shuttles to Pl. Catalunya as well (every ½ hr. 11:30pm-4:30am,

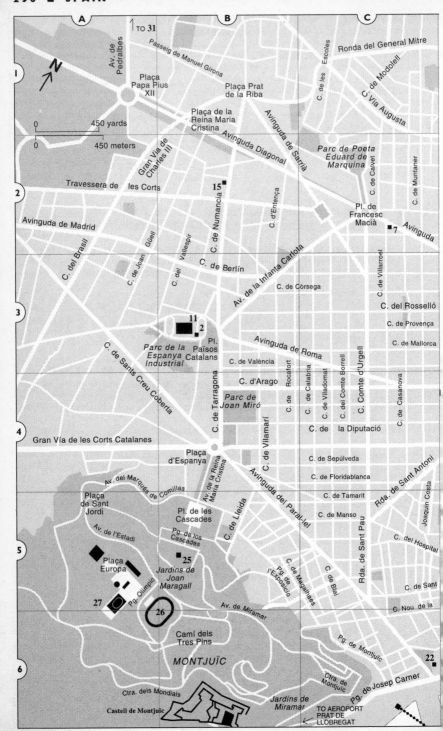

Barcelona

1 Regional Tourist Office
2 City Tourist Office
3 City Tourist Office
4 Budget Travel: TIVE
5 American Consulate
6 Canadian Consulate
7 U. K. Consulate
8 American Express Office
9 Main Post Office
10 Estació de França
11 Estació de Sants
12 Estació de la
   Plaça de Catalunya
13 Estació del Passeig de Gràcia
14 Police Station
15 Youth Hostel
16 La Seu
17 Palau de la Generalitat

18 Ajuntament
19 Santa María del Mar
20 Museu Picasso
21 Gran Teatre del Liceu
22 Museu Marítim
23 Temple Expiatori de la
   Sagrada Familia
24 Palau de la Música Catalana
25 Palau Nacional
26 Estadi Olímpic
27 Palau Sant Jordi
28 Vila Olímpica
29 Auditori Municipal
30 Teatre Nacional de Catalunya
31 Museu-Monestir de Pedralbes
32 Museu d''Art Modern
33 Museu d'Art Contemporani
34 Hospital de Sant Pau

120ptas). To get to the N2, exit Sants to Plaça Joan Peiró, then walk down Carrer de Sant Antoni to Plaça de Sants. Cross Carrer de Sants (which cuts through the plaza) to catch the bus.

Other trains arrive at **Estació de França.** The quickest route to Pl. Catalunya is the Metro from Barceloneta (turn left as you exit the station and take the third left) on the yellow line (L4). Take L4 in the Roquetes direction and switch to the red line (L1) at Urquinaona in the Feixa Llarga direction; Pl. Catalunya is the next stop.

Flying travelers arrive at **Aeroport El Prat de Llobregat,** 12km southwest of Barcelona and well connected to the city by train, bus, and taxi. (See Getting There: By Plane.)

Accommodations are most easily reached on foot from Estació de França. The narrow and winding streets of **Barri Gòtic** (Gothic Quarter) are a 10- to 15-minute walk away, while the more centrally located *hostales* of **Las Ramblas** are 15 minutes away. From the exit of França, both neighborhoods lie to the left down Av. Marquès de l'Argentera, which becomes Passeig d'Isabel II. At Plaça d'Antoni López (marked by the enormous central post office labeled *Correos*), the wide street to the right, Via Laietana, runs along the edge of Barri Gòtic. (Barri Gòtic is on the left as you head up Via Laietana away from Pl. Antoni López.) To reach Las Ramblas from Pl. Antoni López, continue down the palm-tree-lined Passeig de Colom toward the Monument a Colom (Columbus: the guy in the raincoat standing on top of a tall pole pointing south over the water). Las Ramblas, a wide, tourist-shop and tree-lined boulevard, lies on the right. (Barri Gòtic is on the right as you head up Las Ramblas from Sr. Columbus toward Pl. Catalunya.)

Barcelona's layout is quite simple and is best described by imagining yourself perched atop Columbus's head, viewing the city with the Mediterranean at your back. The city slopes gently upward from the harbor to the mountains; on most *avingudas* (avenues) keeping this in mind should help you get your bearings. From the harbor, **Las Ramblas** proceed directly to Pl. Catalunya in five indistinguishable yet differently-named segments: Santa Monica, Caputxins, Sant Josep, Estudis, and Canaletas. To the right of Las Ramblas lies Barri Gòtic—bordered on the other side by Via Laietana. Beyond Via Laietana lies the labyrinthine neighborhood **Ribera,** which touches Parc de la Ciutadella and Estació de França. Past Parc de la Ciutadella is the **Vila Olímpica,** with its two new towers (the tallest buildings in Barcelona), and a shiny assortment of malls and hotels.

On the left side of Las Ramblas is **Barri Xinès** (officially, El Raval), the city's red-light district. Beyond rises **Montjuïc,** a picturesque hill crammed with gardens, museums, stadiums, castles, and other tourist traps.

From Pl. Catalunya, fanning up toward the mountains away from Las Ramblas, the **Eixample** is bordered along its lower edge by the Gran Via de les Corts Catalanes and bisected by Passeig de Gràcia, with its numerous shops and cafés. Avinguda Diagonal marks the upper limit of the grid-planned neighborhoods, separating the Eixample from **Gràcia,** an older neighborhood in the foothills of the mountains that encircle Barcelona. In this mountain range, the peak of **Tibidabo,** the highest point in Barcelona, provides the most privileged aerie from which to view the city.

Barcelona is relatively safe; safety concerns should not prevent you from enjoying the city at all hours. The city has largely succeeded in its vigorous efforts to rid itself of petty thieves, but pickpocketing—mainly around Las Ramblas and in the train stations—is still the most common crime. Distraction is the pickpocket's primary tool. Standard ploys include dropping coins on the ground, smearing mustard on a victim's shirt and offering to clean it off, borrowing money without returning it, grabbing at men's crotches, and, in a kinder and gentler vein, giving women flowers. Keep valuables in your lap while sitting in an outdoor café and firmly in hand while watching the street shows on Las Ramblas. Barri Xinès is not safe for lone walkers at night, but most areas with lively night life (see Entertainment) are well patrolled, well lit, and safe.

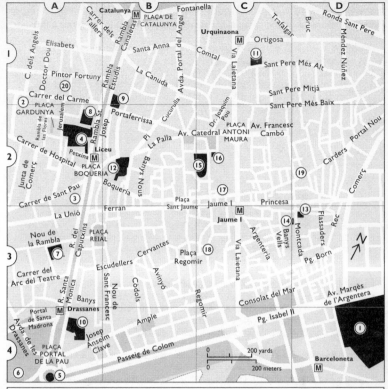

Las Ramblas

1 Estació de Francia
2 Santa Creu
3 Gran Teatre del Liceu
4 Mercat de Sant Josep o de la Boquería
5 Monument a Colom
6 Museu Marítim

7 Palau Güell
8 Palau de la Virreina
9 Palau Moja
10 Palau March
11 Palau de la Música
12 Santa María del Pí
13 Museu Picasso

14 Museu Textil i d'Indumentària
15 Catedral
16 Museu Frederic Mares
17 Museu Historia de la Ciutat
18 Barri Gòtic
19 La Ribera
20 El Raval

GETTING THERE

By Plane

All domestic and international flights land at **El Prat de Llobregat** (tel. 478 50 00), 12km southwest of Barcelona. The quickest and easiest way to the center of town (Pl. Catalunya) or Estació-Sants is by **Aerobus** (every 15min., 425ptas). Benches sit right outside the customs door, next to the cabs. From the airport, the bus runs 6am-11pm, Sat.-Sun. 6:30am-10:50pm. From Pl. Catalunya to the airport, the bus runs 5:30am-10pm, Sat.-Sun. 6am-10:20pm.

RENFE trains provide slightly cheaper transportation to and from the airport (every ½hr., 20min., 260ptas). The first train to Barcelona leaves at 6:13am and the last one at 10:43pm, with stops at **Estació Central-Sants** (Metro: L1, L5; on the southwestern edge of the city), then **Plaça de Catalunya** (Metro: L1, L3; smack in the middle of Barcelona). The red **automatic purchase machines,** which have instructions only in Catalan or Castilian and take only ptas, are otherwise the most convenient way to buy tickets. The elevated, enclosed walkway to the trains is accessible from inside the national terminal, less than 100m to the right of the new international terminal entrance.

Trains to the airport from Pl. Catalunya run between 6:37am and 10:07pm. Those from Sants run between 5:43am and 10:13pm. Buy tickets to the airport at the "Aeroport" window in Sants (5am-11pm); otherwise wait at the Recorridos Cercanías window or purchase a ticket from one of the automatic ticket machines.

The **bus** is the only inexpensive late night service available besides a taxi. From the airport to Plaça de Espanya (Metro: L1, L3), take bus EN between 9pm and 2:40am, or from Pl. Espanya to the airport from 9:40pm to 3:15am. The stop at Pl. Espanya is on the corner between Gran Via de les Corts Catalanes and Av. Reina María Cristina. A taxi ride between Barcelona and the airport costs 2000-3500ptas. (See Taxis below.)

Iberia, Pg. Gràcia, 30 (tel. 412 56 67; national reservations 412 70 20). Metro: Pg. Gràcia (L3, L4), at the intersection of Pg. Gràcia and Pg. Diputació. To: Madrid (frequently, 15,200ptas); Valencia (3 per day, 17,850ptas); Sevilla (4 per day, 31,200ptas); Lisboa (1 per day, 40,535ptas); New York (1 per day, 96,500ptas); London (3 per day, 38,000ptas); Paris (3 per day, 40,000ptas); Rome (2 per day, 41,000ptas); Geneva (1 per day, 38,000ptas). Open Mon.-Fri. 9am-6pm. Prices quoted here for round-trip international flights are student rates (under 25).

By Train

Call RENFE for general train information (tel. 490 02 02; open 7:30am-10:30pm). Tickets can be purchased at either of Barcelona's two stations. For travelers under 26 to: Madrid (60 per day, 3900ptas); Sevilla (8 per day, 12-14hr., 6900ptas); Valencia (14 per day, 4½hr., 3000ptas); Milan (1 per day, 18hr., 8825ptas); Zürich (1 per day, 13½hr., 12,700ptas); Paris (5 per day, 9650ptas); Geneva (1 per day, 7575ptas).

Estació Sants, Metro: Sants-Estació (L3, L4), is the main terminal for domestic and international traffic. Open 6am-11pm.

Estació França, Av. Marqués de L'Argentera, s/n. Metro: Barceloneta (L3). All domestic trains leaving França pass through Sants. França has international services to Milan, Zurich, and France. Open 6am-11pm.

Ferrocarrils de la Generalitat de Catalunya (FFCC) (tel. 205 15 15), or Catalan State Railways, are commuter trains with main stations at Pl. Catalunya and Pl. Espanya. Indispensable to get to Montserrat, Sant Cugat, or Tarrassa. Connections with the Metro are marked by a double-arrow symbol. The commuter line until Tibidabo charges the same as the Metro (10-ride Metro pass valid); beyond here fares go up.

By Bus

Most buses arrive at the brand new **Estació del Nord,** (C. Ali-bei, 80; Metro: Arc de Triomf (L1); tel 265 65 08; open 6am-1am), but some companies still refuse to make the move. For those without Eurorail passes, buses offer a cheaper and sometimes more direct mode of travel than trains.

Enatcar, Estació del Nord (tel. 245 25 28). Open daily 6am-1am. To: Madrid (5 per day, 8hr., 2600ptas); Valencia (9 per day, 4hr., 2650ptas).

Linebús, Estació del Nord (tel. 265 07 00). Open Mon.-Sat. 8:30am-2pm and 3-8pm. To: London (3 per week, 25hr., 13,450ptas); Paris (6 per week, 14hr., 10,250ptas).

Julià Via, C. Viriato (tel. 490 40 00), to the right of Estació-Sants. Metro: Estació-Sants (L3, L5). Open daily 9am-8pm. To: Paris (6 per week, 15hr., 9225ptas); Frankfurt (3 per week, 19hr., 11,160ptas).

Sarfa, Estació del Nord (tel. 265 11 58). Open daily 8am-8pm. Services many beach towns along the Costa Brava.

By Ferry

Transmediterránea, Av. Drassanes, 6 (tel. 317 42 62). Metro: Drassanes (L3). Open Mon.-Fri. 9am-1pm and 4-6pm, Sat. 9am-noon. From the Metro, Columbus points the way from his perch to Estació Marítima, behind the *Aduana* building on the wharf. During the summer, voyages most days between Barcelona and Mallorca (8hr.), Menorca (9hr.), and Eivissa (9½hr.). A *butaca* seat, about the size of an airline seat, is the cheapest at 6100ptas, but cabins are reasonably priced as well. Boats fill up quickly in the summer.

By Rideshare and Thumb

Barnastop, C. Sant Ramon, 29 (tel. 443 06 32), on the corner of Non de Rambla. Metro: Liceu (L3). Matches drivers with riders and can hook you up with other *Mitzfahrzentrales* (ride-share associations). 3ptas per km to driver in Spain, 4ptas per km outside Spain. 1-2pta per km commission to Barnastop (min. 200ptas, max. 2000ptas). To: Paris (6200ptas); Amsterdam (8200ptas); Rome (7700ptas); Berlin (9400ptas). Open Mon.-Fri. 11am-2pm and 5-8pm, Sat. 5-8pm, or call and leave a message on the machine.

Let's Go does not recommend hitchhiking as a safe mode of travel. Those who hitch to France can take the Metro to Fabra i Puig, then Av. Meridiana to reach A-7. Those en route to Tarragona and Valencia take bus #7 from Rambla Catalunya at Gran Via. *Autopista* access lies near here. With the proper sign, this process also puts hitchers on the A-2 to Zaragoza. Hitchhiking on *autopistas* (toll roads, marked by the letter A) is illegal. Hitchhiking is permitted, however, on national (N) highways.

GETTING AROUND

Maps

Everything geographic you need to know about Barcelona is on one of the free *Ajuntament de Barcelona* (city government) maps, available in Catalan, Castilian, English, French, German, and Italian at all tourist offices.

Metro and Bus

Barcelona's extensive public transport system (tel. 412 00 00) will get you within walking distance of any point in the city quickly and cheaply. *Guía del Transport Públic,* available free at tourist offices and at the transport information booth in Pl. Catalunya, maps out all four of the city's Metro lines and bus routes (both day and night). Metro and bus rides cost 120ptas. A 10-ride Metro pass is 600ptas; a 10-ride T1 pass, valid for bus and Metro, is 625ptas. Automatic vending machines and ticket windows sell Metro passes; T1s are available at ticket windows and *estancos* (tobacco stores). Make sure to hold on to your ticket or pass until you leave the Metro—riding without a receipt carries a fat 5000pta fine. Metro open Mon.-Thurs. 5am-11pm, Fri.-Sat. and holidays 5am-1am, Sun. 6am-midnight. Day buses usually run 5am-10pm and night buses 11pm-4am, but individual bus routes vary.

Taxis

Taxis are everywhere and have a *Libre* sign in the windshield or a lit green light on the roof if they're not occupied. The yellow and black taxis can also be summoned by phone (tel. 358 11 11, 330 08 04, 357 77 55, or 300 38 11). The first six minutes or 1.9km cost 250ptas; then it's 88 or 102ptas per km, depending on when you ride.

Car Rental

Docar, C. Montnegre, 18 (tel. 322 90 08, 24-hr. reservations). Free delivery and pickup. 2300ptas per day, 23ptas each additional km. Mon.-Fri. 9am-2pm and 4-8pm, Sat. 9am-2pm.

Tot Car, C. Josep Terradellas, 93 (tel. 405 34 33). Free delivery and pickup. 2100ptas per day, 21ptas each additional km. Insurance 1100ptas per day. Mon.-Sat. 9am-2pm and 4-8pm.

Bicycle and Moped

Bike Rental: Biciclot, Sant Joan de Malta, 1 (tel. 307 74 75). Metro: Clot (L1). Bikes 350ptas per hr., 1400ptas per day. Mountain bikes too. Open Mon.-Fri. 9am-2pm and 5-8pm, Sat. 10am-2pm.

Moped Rental: RR Serveis, C. Camprodon, 24 (tel. 207 33 48), off C. Girona. Metro: Verdaguer (L5). Mopeds 2900ptas per day, weekend special (Fri.-Mon.) 5500ptas. Includes helmet and insurance. Open Mon.-Fri. 10am-1pm and 4:30-8pm., Sat. 10am-noon.

PRACTICAL INFORMATION

Tourist Information

For general city information dial 010. For general destination information dial 412 00 00. For general tourist information dial 412 20 01. Information on **cultural events** is dispensed at Palau de la Virreina, Las Ramblas, 99. (Metro: Liceu (L3), between La Boquería and C. Carme. Tel. 301 77 75. Open Mon.-Sat. 10am-2pm and 4-8pm.) Year-round tourist offices are:

Estació Central de Barcelona-Sants, Pl. Països Catalans, s/n (tel. 491 44 31). Metro: Sants-Estació (L1, L5). Run by the Ajuntament de Barcelona with information only on Barcelona. Open Mon.-Fri. 8am-8pm, Sat.-Sun. 8am-2pm.

Aeroport El Prat de Llobregat, International Terminal (tel. 478 47 04), 25m to the left of the customs exit. Run by the Generalitat de Catalunya with information about Barcelona, Cataluña, and the rest of Spain. Open Mon.-Sat. 9:30am-8pm, Sun. 9:30am-3pm.

La Gran Via de les Corts Catalanes, 658 (tel. 301 74 43). Metro: Urquinaona (L1, L4) or Pl. Catalunya (L1, L3, L5). Two blocks from the intersection with Pg. Gràcia, in the Eixample. Also run by the Generalitat office. Open Mon.-Fri. 9am-7pm, Sat. 9am-2pm.

A tour bus is an alternate way to obtain city information.

Tourist Bus: Marked *Bus Turístic,* four air-conditioned buses (bus #100) have 15 stops at points of interest. The whole circuit (28km) takes two hours, with buses passing each stop every 20 minutes. The easiest place to get on the bus is at Pl. Catalunya in front of El Corte Inglés department store. Tickets can be purchased on the bus. In service mid-June through Sept. 9am-8:40pm (last bus leaves Pl. Catalunya at 6:30pm). Full day 1000ptas.

Budget Travel Offices

TUJUCA (TIVE), C. Calàbria, 147 (tel. 483 83 78). Metro: Rocafort (L1), 2 bl. from the Metro. Come early and come fast: in summer there's often a wait. Eurotrain tickets, cheap buses, flights, and ISICs. Open 9am-1pm and 4-5:30pm.

Centre d'Informació: Assesorament per a Joves, C. Ferran, 32 (tel. 402 78 03). More of a local student assistance office than a travel agency. No tickets for sale, but plenty of free advice and a bulletin board with events for youths. Excellent library of travel guides, including *Let's Go.* Open Mon.-Fri. 10am-2pm and 4-8pm.

Consulates

See Spain Essentials: Embassies and Consulates.

Money

American Express: Pg. Gràcia, 101 (tel. 217 00 70; fax 415 37 00). Metro: Diagonal (L3, L5). The entrance is on C. Rosselló, around the corner from this address. Mail held 1 month free of charge for card and check holders. Multilingual ATM machine outside for 24-hr. service. Open Mon.-Fri. 9:30am-6pm, Sat. 10am-noon.

Currency Exchange: The best rates can be obtained at the **banks** in the Eixample; they work off 1% commission on greenbacks (min. 300ptas). General banking hours are Mon.-Fri. 8:30am-2pm. **American Express** office also charges 1% commission on bills (no commission to change traveler's checks). **El Corte Inglés** in Pl. Catalunya changes traveler's checks with zero commission and no minimum. Open Mon.-Sat. 9am-9pm. On Sun. you can change money at **Estació de Sants** (tel. 490 77 70) for a 1% commission on checks and bills (500pta min.). Open daily 8am-10pm, except Dec. 25, 26, and Jan. 1, 6. The currency exchanges on Las Ramblas may be temptingly convenient on Sun., but they normally charge a scary 9.8% commission.

Communications

Post Office: Pl. Antoni López (tel. 318 38 31), at the end of Via Laietana near the port. Metro: Jaume I or Barceloneta (L4). Open for stamps Mon.-Fri. 8am-10pm, Sat. 8am-2pm; for Lista de Correos (general delivery) Mon.-Fri. 8am-9pm, Sat. 9am-2pm; for **telegrams** Mon.-Sat. 8am-8pm. **Emergency telegrams** (dial 322 20 00) open 24hrs. Most neighborhoods also have post offices; a useful one near the city center is at Pl. Urquinaona, 6. Metro: Urquinaona (L1, L4). Open Mon.-Fri. 8am-3pm, Sat. 9am-1pm. **Postal Code:** 08002.

Telephones: Central Telephone Exchange, C. Fontanella, 2, just off Pl. Catalunya. Metro: Catalunya (L1, L3). Open Mon.-Sat. 8:30am-9pm. Another telephone service is at Estació Sants (tel. 490 76 50). Metro: Sants-Estació (L3, L5). Also, **faxes** received for 150ptas and sent (490 82 73). Open 7:45am-11pm. **Telephone Code:** 93.

Emergency, Health, and Help

Police: New police station at Las Ramblas, 43 (tel. 301 90 60), right across from the entrance to Pl. Real and next to C. Nou de la Rambla. Metro: Liceu (L3). Installed to deal with tourist concerns (English, French, German, and Italian spoken) and clean up the port end of Las Ramblas. **Municipal Police:** tel. 092. **National Police:** tel. 091.

Fire: tel. 080.

Ambulance: tel. 061.

Hospitals: Hospital Clínic, Villarroel, 170 (tel. 323 14 14). Metro: Hospital Clínic (L5). Main entrance at intersection of C. Roselló and Casanova. **Hospital de la Santa Creu i Sant Pau,** at intersection of C. Cartagena and C. Sant Antoni Moria Claret (tel. 347 31 33). Metro: Hospital de Sant Pau (L5). **Médicos de Urgencia,** C. Pelai, 40 (tel. 412 12 12). Metro: Catalunya (L1, L3), close to the end of the street that meets Las Ramblas and Pl. Catalunya. Hospitals also useful as an emergency drug store.

Late-Night Pharmacy: Pharmacies stay open late on a rotating basis. Check signs in pharmacy windows for current listings.

Crisis Services: Oficina Permanente de Atención Social, (tel. (900) 30 90 30). Open 24hrs.

STD treatment, Av Drassanes, 17-21 (hotline tel. 441 29 97).

Gay and Lesbian Association: Grup de Lesbianes Feministes de Barcelona, Gran Via de les Corts Catalanes, 549, 4th fl. (tel. 323 33 07). Metro: Catalunya (L1, L3). Less than 1 bl. from Pg. Gràcia heading away from Pl. Catalunya.

Other

El Corte Inglés: Pl. Catalunya (tel. 302 12 12). Full-fledged department store. They have a good **map. Currency exchange:** 250pta min. charge. Also offer novels and guidebooks in English, haircutting, rooftop cafeteria, grocery store, and **telephones.** Open daily 9am-9pm.

Luggage Storage: At Estació Sants (Metro: Sants-Estació (L1, L3)); small lockers 400ptas, large lockers 600ptas. At Estació França (Metro: Barceloneta (L1)), small lockers 300ptas, large 500ptas. Open 6:30am-11pm. At Estació del Nord (Metro: Arc de Triomf (L1)), lockers 300ptas. Open Mon.-Fri. 7:30am-7pm, Sat. 8am-noon. Many hostels hold bags for about 150ptas per bag per day.

Lost Property: Objets Perduts (tel. 301 39 23), on the ground floor of the Ajuntament, Pl. Sant Jaume. Metro: Jaume I (L4). Open Mon.-Fri. 9:30am-1:30pm.

English Bookstore: Librería Francesa, Pg. Gràcia, 91 (tel. 215 14 17). Metro: Diagonal (L3, L5). Between C. Provença and C. Roselló. Good selection, including

Let's Go. Open Mon.-Fri. 9:30am-2:30pm and 4-8:30pm, Sat. 9:30am-2pm. **LAIE,** Av. Pau Claris, 85 (tel. 318 17 39), 1 bl. from the Gran Via. Metro: Urquinaona (L1, L4) or Pl. Catalunya (L1, L3, L5). Collection more extensive, but also more expensive. Open Mon.-Sat. 10am-9pm. **LAIE Rooftop Cafe** provides aromatic teas (275ptas) and a pleasant setting for the erudite to read and brood over Dalí's infamous autobiography. Open Mon.-Wed. 9am-1am, Thurs.-Sat. 9am-2am.

Library: Institut d'Estudis Norteamericans, Via Augusta, 123 (tel. 200 75 51). Take the FFCC commuter train to Pl. Molina. Lots of **American newspapers** and periodicals, as well as a strong reference section. Open Sept.-July Mon.-Fri. 11am-2pm and 4-9pm. **Biblioteca Central,** C. Hospital, 57 (tel. 317 07 78), next to Hospital de Santa Creu off Las Ramblas. Open Mon.-Fri. 9am-8pm, Sat. 9am-2pm.

Foreign Periodicals: Try the newsstands along Las Ramblas and Pg. Gràcia.

Women's Services: Ca La Dona Women's Center, Gran Via de les Corts Catalanes, 549, 4th fl. (tel. 323 33 07). **Librería de Dones Prolèg,** C. Dagueria, 13. Metro: Jaume I. Open Mon.-Fri. 10am-8pm, Sat. 10am-2pm. Women's bookstore stocks a large feminist collection. Current and second-hand books. Works in English, French, and German. Workshops, seminars, and notice board. **Informatia Dona,** C. València, 302 (tel. 487 80 92). Metro: Passeig de Gràcia (L3, L4). Information and advice on women's issues. Mon.-Fri. noon-2pm.

Religious Services: Catholic Mass in English, C. Anglí, 15 (tel. 204 49 62). **Anglican Mass** in English, St. George's English-Speaking Church, C. Horacio, 38 (tel. 417 88 67), off C. Sant Joan de la Salle. Sun. 11am. **Jewish services,** Sinagoga de la Comunidad Judía, C. Avenir, 24 (tel. 200 61 48). **Muslim services,** Comunidad Musulmana, Mezquita Toarek Ben Ziad, C. Hospital, 91 (tel. 441 91 49).

Laundromat: Lava Super, C. Carme, 63, off Las Ramblas by the Palau Virreina. Wash and dry 1000ptas per 5kg. Open Mon.-Fri. 8am-8pm, Sat. 8am-2pm. **Lavandería Ramblas,** Ramelleres, 15 (tel. 318 83 31). Wash, dry, and fold 1100ptas per 6kg. Open Sun.-Fri. 9am-2pm and 5-8pm.

Showers: Public showers are nonexistent, but municipal swimming pools have shower facilities. (See Entertainment: Recreational Sports.)

ACCOMMODATIONS AND CAMPING

Hostal and *pensión* signs hit wandering travelers in the face every three doors. Quality varies tremendously, but the benefits of the 1992 Olympic frenzy—newly-painted walls, upgraded bathrooms, and new beds—are still evident. Rooms are scarce during the peak season (July-Aug.).

Hostels

Barcelona's hostel scene offers a surprisingly wide range of living environments. All, however, offer the cheapest beds in town and the best way to get acquainted with the personal habits of complete strangers.

Albergue de Juventud Kabul, Pl. Reial, 17 (tel. 318 51 90). Metro: Liceu (L3). Head toward the port from the Metro; turn left after C. Ferran to enter Pl. Reial. Upon entering the plaza, turn right and walk to the end. Though Pl. Reial used to be quite dangerous at night, constant vigilance by the mobile-home police station adjacent to the hostel door has reduced the area to a tolerable level of creepiness. Inside, Kabul offers, in the words of their own brochure, "a great party atmosphere," complete with pool table, foozball, chess boards, beer and cigarette vending machines, music, satellite TV, and a happy cast of regulars. Showers and freshly painted rooms. 1000ptas per person. Sheets 200ptas. 5kg laundry 500ptas. Baggage storage 100ptas per day. 5-night max. stay. Open 24hrs.

Albergue Juvenil Palau (HI), C. Palau, 6 (tel. 412 50 80). Metro: Jaume I (L4). 1 bl. from Pl. Sant Jaume: take C. Ciutat to C. Templaris, then take the 2nd left. Friendly, small hostel in the heart of the Barri Gòtic. Offers a full kitchen and a spacious dining salon where you can meet fellow backpackers or catch some TV. Kitchen open 7-10pm. 2-8 people per room. 1100ptas per bed, breakfast included. Sheets 150ptas. 6-night max. stay. Reservations with one night's deposit. Hostel open 7am-midnight and 3-3:15am.

Albergue Mare de Déu de Montserrat (HI), Pg. Mare de Déu del Coll, 41-51 (tel. 210 51 51), beyond Park Güell. Bus #28 from Pl. Catalunya stops across the street from the hostel. Otherwise take the Metro to Vallcarca (L3), walk up Av. República Argentina and across C. Viaducte de Vallcarca; from there, signs point the way up the hill. This renovated villa comes complete with its own private woods and a hilltop view of Barcelona. A gorgeous neo-Moorish entrance and detailed Baroque salons contrast with institutional sleeping areas. Reception open 7:30-9:30am, 5-7:30pm, and 8:30-10pm. Bedrooms closed 10am-1:30pm for cleaning. Move in at 5pm. Midnight curfew, but doors open at 1 and 2am sharp for the late-night crowd. No showering 11pm-7am. No eating, drinking, or smoking in bedrooms. 1300ptas per person, over 25 1925ptas, and 500pta deposit for ID card. HI members only. Breakfast (8-9am) included. Sheets 350ptas. 5-night max. stay. No reservations.

Albergue Internacional Pensión Colón-3, C. Colón, 3 (tel. 318 06 31). Metro: Liceu (L3). Just off Las Ramblas at Pl. Reial. Metal bunk beds cramp small rooms with balconies. 24-hr. reception. 1000ptas per person. Sheets 200ptas. Laundry 500ptas. Must be under 30. Credit cards accepted.

Barri Gòtic and the Ramblas

Barcelona's *ciutat vella* (old quarter) has a wealth of accommodations for the impoverished traveler.

Casa de Huéspedes Mari-Luz, C. Palau, 4 (tel. 317 34 63). Metro: Jaume I (L4) or Liceu (L3). 1 block from Pl. Sant Jaume. Take C. Ciutat to C. Templaris, then take the 2nd left. After dark it is safer not to approach from Escudellers. Amicable Mari-Luz and Fernando offer basic rooms, sparkling new showers, use of their refrigerator, keys for 24-hr. entry, and a li'l extra TLC. 1200ptas per person (less in winter). Reservations accepted from repeat visitors only.

Hostal Levante, Baixada de San Miguel, 2 (tel. 317 95 65). Metro: Liceu (L3). Walk down C. Ferran and turn right on C. Avinyó; Bda. San Miguel is the first left. New sparkly tiled floors and bathrooms. Handsome wood interior and large windows. Singles 2000ptas. Doubles 3200ptas, with shower 4000ptas. Reservations and credit cards accepted.

Pensión Bienestar, C. Quintana, 3 (tel. 318 72 83). Metro: Liceu (L3). 2 blocks from Las Ramblas, off C. Ferran. This quiet *pensión* offers 27 rooms with high ceilings and freshly painted walls. Bathrooms large enough to sleep in. Singles 1500ptas. Doubles 2400ptas. Triples 3600ptas.

Hostal Residencia Marmo, C. Gignás, 25 (tel. 315 42 08). Metro: Jaume I (L4). From Via Laietana, C. Angel Baixeras narrows into C. Gignás. Spacious rooms with oversized, polished furniture and vaulted ceilings possess an antique charm. Keys for 24-hr. entry. Singles 1500ptas. Doubles 3000ptas.

Hostal Marítima, Las Ramblas, 4 (tel. 302 31 52). Metro: Drassanes (L3). At port end of Las Ramblas; follow the signs to *Museo de Cera* next door. Prime location on the main drag has noisy drawbacks. Bathrooms leave a bit to be desired. Singles 1500ptas. Doubles 2600ptas, with shower 3500ptas. Laundry 800ptas.

Pensión Fernando, C. Volta de Remei, 4 (tel. 301 79 93). Metro: Liceu (L3). Fourth left off C. Ferran walking from Las Ramblas. Also run by Mari-Luz and Fernando, this *pensión* offers small, affordable rooms stuffed with furniture. Those in for longer hauls get use of kitchen and other amenities. Keys for 24-hr. entry. 1300ptas per person. Reservations accepted.

Hostal Residencia Romay, C. Avinyó, 58 (tel. 317 94 14). Metro: Drassanes (L3). Toward the end of Las Ramblas, turn left onto C. Josep Clavé; C. Avinyó lies on the left after the church. Directly above Pensión Albi. Marble reception, starch white halls, a large comfy chair, some beds. Keys for 24-hr. entry. Singles 1500ptas. Doubles 2000ptas, with bath 2500ptas.

Hostal Layetana, Pl. Ramón Berenguer el Gran, 2 (tel. 319 20 12). Metro: Jaume I (L4). Less than 1 bl. from the Metro, on the far side of the *plaça*. Balconies open to a view of ancient Roman walls, which never imagined they would be so close to immaculate bathrooms with individually wrapped bars of soap. Singles

2000ptas. Doubles 3500ptas, with bath 4800ptas. Shower 200ptas. Reservations recommended July-Aug.

Hostal Residencia Segura, Junta de Comerç, 11 (tel. 302 51 74), off C. Hospital. Metro: Liceu (L3). You can be *segura* that beds are firm and bathrooms clean. Ask for a room with a sink. Singles 1500ptas, with shower 2000ptas. Doubles 2500ptas, with shower 3000ptas. Triples 3500ptas, with shower 4000ptas.

Pensión Aviñó 42, C. Avinyó, 42 (tel. 318 79 45), next door to Hostal Residencia Romay. Metro: Drassanes (L3). Faux stained-glass windows brought down a peg (and up a few centuries) by pink bathrooms. Singles 1500ptas. Doubles 2000ptas, with shower 3000ptas. Prices vary according to length of stay and time of year.

Hostal Retorno Medinaceli, Pl. Duque de Medinaceli (tel. 317 10 66). Metro: Drassanes (L3). Off the port end of Las Ramblas on C. Josep Anselm Clavé. Average establishment saved by two rooms with port views and ocean breezes. Singles 1500ptas. Doubles 3000ptas.

Hostal Rey Don Jaime I, C. Jaume I, 11 (tel. 315 41 61). Metro: Jaume I (L4). Every room has a bathroom. Every bed has a double mattress. Every luxury has a price. Singles 3800ptas. Doubles 5500ptas. Triples 6500ptas. Prices do not include IVA.

Hostal Nogaró, C. Cervantes, 2 (tel. 318 81 48). Metro: Liceu (L3). Take C. Ferran to C. Avinyó, then the second left. Small, one-man operation in the thick of the Gothic Quarter. Dark, languid hallways lead to 27 big rooms. Keys for 24-hr. entry. Singles 1300ptas. Doubles 2500ptas.

Pensión Albi, C. Avinyó, 58 (tel. 302 50 03). Metro: Drassanes (L3). Directly below Hostal Residencia Romay. 10 simple, clean rooms a little closer to the ground. Keys for 24-hr. entry. Singles 1500ptas. Doubles 2500ptas, with bath 3000ptas.

Hotel Joventut, Junta de Comerç, 12 (tel. 301 84 99; fax 412 08 19), across the street from Hostal Residencia Segura. Ideal for large groups. Big lounge. Telephone and new shower in every room. Singles 2500ptas, eight days 16,000ptas. Doubles 4000ptas. Triples 7000ptas. Quads 8500ptas. Quints 9000ptas. Sexts 10,000ptas. Breakfast 300ptas. Wheelchair accessible. Credit cards accepted. Reservations 8 days in advance recommended July-Aug.

Near Plaça de Catalunya

A bit pricier than in the Barri Gòtic, accommodations here are safer and more modern, while still close to the action (and rumble) of Las Ramblas. Ideal for groups of two or more. The Metro stop is Pl. Catalunya (L1, L3) unless otherwise specified.

Hotel Toledano/Hostal Residencia Capitol, La Rambla, 138 (tel. 301 08 72; fax 412 31 42). Facing Las Ramblas from Pl. Catalunya, it's 50m away on the left. This family owned, split-level hotel-*hostal* has been making tourists happy for 76 years. Rooms with cable TV, private phone, and balcony. Reception has leather couches and English-speaking owner. Keys for 24-hr. entry. Singles 2500ptas. Doubles 3800ptas, with shower 4300ptas. Quads 5600ptas, with shower 6300ptas. Prices are for *hostal* only and don't include IVA. Reservations and credit cards accepted.

Pensión Noya, La Rambla, 133 (tel. 301 48 31). Above noisy restaurant Nuria, so you can nibble to induce sleepiness. This 10-room retreat welcomes backpackers with open arms. Singles 1600ptas. Doubles 2600ptas. Reservations accepted.

Residencia Australia, Ronda Universitat, 11 (tel. 317 41 77). A gregarious English-speaking owner shows that she cares with embroidered sheets and curtains, a spotless bathroom, ceiling fans in rooms, and winter heating. Singles 2350ptas. Doubles 3450ptas, with bath 4200ptas. Prices don't include IVA.

Pensión L'Isard, C. Tallers, 82 (tel. 302 51 83), directly opposite the University. Metro: Universitat (L1). Quiet, relaxing rooms with new mattresses, tiling, sinks, and balcony. Keys for 24-hr. entry. Singles 1800ptas. Doubles 3500ptas, with bath 4500ptas. Triples 4500ptas. Reservations with deposit.

Hostal Residencia Lausanne, Av. Portal de L'Angel, 24 (tel. 302 11 39). Amid the shopping promenade, a quiet back terrace provides Swiss-like sanctuary from Barcelona's evening intensity. Couches and chairs in many rooms, and new wallpaper. Singles 2000ptas. Doubles 3000ptas, with shower 3990ptas. Triples with shower 4500ptas.

Pensión Nevada, Av. Portal de L'Angel, 16 (tel. 302 31 01), just past Hostal Lausanne. Your cozy bedroom away from home on the range, complete with matching throw pillows, firm beds, comfortable chairs, flowers on the balcony... and the list goes on. Try to get the room with the Dungeons & Dragons figure. Keys for 24-hr. entry. Singles 2000ptas. Doubles 4400ptas.

Residencia Victoria, C. Comtal, 9 (tel. 317 45 97). Walking from Pl. Catalunya, take the first left on Av. Portal de L'Angel. Popular with foreign students. Full kitchen, TV, washer/dryer, and open-air dining room. Singles 2000ptas, one month 48,000ptas. Doubles 3000ptas. Five-day minimum stay. Reservations required at least 15 days in advance.

Pensión Santa Ana, C. Santa Ana, 23 (tel. 301 22 46). What this place lacks in size and ambience, it makes up with clean bathrooms and firm beds. Singles 2000ptas. Doubles 3000ptas. Triples 3500ptas.

Pensión Aris, C. Fontanella, 14 (tel. 318 10 17), 2 bl. past the Telefónica on the right. Memories of the Olympics hang on white-washed walls with light blue trim. Huge rooms with little more than beds. 21st-century windows shut out all sound. Singles 2000ptas. Doubles 3500ptas, with bath 4500ptas. Triple 4500ptas.

Hostal Fontanella, Via Laietana, 71 (tel./fax 317 59 43). Go 3 bl. past El Corte Inglés and hang a right. *Hostal* (except the bed covers) weathered renovations well. Bathrooms up to surgical hygiene standards. Singles 2385ptas, with bath 2800ptas. Doubles 3600ptas, with bath 5200ptas. Credit cards accepted.

Pensión Comtal-7, C. Comtal, 7 (tel. 302 42 44). Metro: Catalunya (L1, L3) or Uriquanaona (L1, L4). Next to Residencia Victoria. TV room with the latest Spanish magazines and a fantasy-inducing view of beach paradises. Winter heating, fans in summer. Studied cleanliness in bathroom. Keys for 24-hr. entry. Singles 2000ptas. Doubles 3500ptas, with shower 4000ptas.

Hostal Sena, Ronda Universitat, 29 (tel. 412 38 91), on the corner of C. Balmes. Metro: Universitat (L1). Large beds and clean bathrooms ease the pain in your wallet. Singles 2500ptas. Doubles 4000ptas, with bath 4500ptas.

Hostal Plaza, C. Fontanella, 18 (tel. 301 01 39), down the street from Pensión Aris. Adopted by eager-to-please Americans just starting in the Spanish *pensión* business. 18 rooms with American art and 3-speed fans. Public phone, fax, vending machine, and TV room with music and A/C. Discounts with local restaurants and discos. Singles 2500ptas. Doubles 3500ptas, with bath 4000ptas. Triples 6000ptas. Prices may vary. 5kg laundry 1000ptas. Credit cards accepted.

Pensión Estal, C. Santa Anna, 27 (tel. 302 26 18). Rooms offer views of Iglesia Santa Anna. French-speaking owner. Singles 1500ptas, with view 2000ptas. Doubles 3000ptas, with bath 4000ptas.

The Eixample

The most beautiful *hostales* are found here along wide, safe *avingudas*. Most have huge entryways with colorful tiles and steel and wood *Modernista* elevators.

Hostal Residencia Oliva, Pg. Gràcia, 32, 4th fl. (tel. 488 01 62), on the intersection with C. Disputació. Metro: Pg. Gràcia (L4, L3). Sedate lounge with a long, polished wooden table encourages guests to write the great 20th-century novel. New bathrooms and frilly curtains and bedspreads. Some doubles are cramped. Singles 2650ptas. Doubles 4770ptas, with bath 5830ptas.

Hostal Residencia Palacios, Gran Via de les Corts Catalanes, 629bis (tel. 301 37 92), across from the main tourist office. Metro: Catalunya (L1, L3) or Urquinaona (L1, L4). Rooms are well-furnished, if a little dark. Singles 2300ptas, with shower 3300ptas, with bath 3750ptas. Doubles 3500ptas, with shower 4000ptas, with bath 4500ptas. Breakfast 300ptas. Prices do not include IVA. Reservations and credit cards accepted.

Hostal Residencia Windsor, Rambla Catalunya, 84 (tel. 215 11 98), above the Hostal Líder. Metro: Pg. Gràcia (L4, L3). Aristocratic *hostal* lives up to its name with crimson carpets and palatial quarters. Each room decorated differently— cheers for Anglo-Saxon individualism. Singles 2900ptas, with bath 3700ptas. Doubles 4900ptas, with bath 6000ptas.

Hostal Residencia Montserrat, Pg. Gràcia, 114 (tel. 217 27 00). Metro: Diagonal (L3, L5, FFCC). Hidden on the right side of Diagonal as you face Tibidabo. Small lounge in the reception area with bloated leather couches. Private phone line. Singles 3000ptas. Doubles 4715ptas. Breakfast 400ptas. Reservations held 24hrs.

Gràcia

In Gràcia, an area five to 10 minutes on foot from Diagonal, families and travelers mingle in a calm, neighborhood setting. The accommodations listed here are small and elegant. Neighborhood bars and *pastelerías* remain "undiscovered."

Pensión San Medín, C. Gran de Gràcia, 125 (tel. 217 30 68). Metro: Fontana (L3). Hallways are lined with faux-corkboard wallpaper and long Persian rugs. Each room has new furniture and a phone. Singles 2500ptas, with bath 3500ptas. Double 4300ptas, with bath 5300ptas. Showers 200ptas.

Hostal Bonavista, C. Bonavista, 21 (tel. 237 37 57). Metro: Diagonal (L3, L5). In a lush neighborhood off the northern end of Pg. Gràcia. Well-kept rooms dotted with pictures of horses and their successors (old-fashioned cars). Keys for 24-hr. entry. Singles 1887ptas. Doubles 2642ptas, with bath 3680ptas. Showers 300ptas.

Pensión Norma, C. Gran de Gràcia, 87 (tel. 237 44 78). Metro: Fontana (L3). Rooms with life-size dressers and tables, but your own house could never be this clean. So newly-renovated as to be austere. Singles 1500ptas. Doubles 3000ptas, with bath 4000ptas.

Camping

While there is no camping in Barcelona, inter-city buses (150ptas) run to all the following locations in 20 to 45 minutes. Campsites are classified according to size and the number of services offered.

El Toro Bravo (tel. 637 34 62), just south of El Prat in Vildecans, accessible by bus L93 from Pl. Universitat or L90 from Pl. Goya. 550ptas per person, 400ptas per child, 600ptas per tent. Reception open 8:30am-1:30pm and 4-8pm. 1st-class site. Camping year-round. **Filipinas** (tel. 658 28 95) at 550ptas per person, 400ptas per child, 600ptas per tent (reception open 9am-10pm; camping year-round) and **La Ballena Alegre** (tel. 658 05 04) at 500ptas per person, 250ptas per child, 1100ptas per tent (reception open 9am-6pm; camping April-Aug.) are also excellent another km down the road.

Gavá, south of Barcelona, has several campgrounds, all 1st-class sites and accessible by bus L90 from Pl. Universitat. **Albatros** (tel. 662 20 31) costs 520ptas per person, 380ptas per child, 795ptas per tent. Reception open 8am-midnight. Camping May-Sept. **Tortuga Ligera** (tel. 662 12 29) is 525ptas per person, 420ptas per child, 630ptas per tent. Reception open 9am-10pm. Camping year-round. Both sites are near the "Tortuga Ligera" bus stop. **Tres Estrellas** (tel. 662 11 16) is 2km closer to town, 1 stop past "Ballena Alegre." 540ptas per person, 430ptas per child, 690ptas per tent. Reception open 24hr. Camping year-round.

Camping Don Quixote (tel. 389 10 16), north of Barcelona. Take a RENFE train from the Cercanías station. Get off at Monsolis, one stop past Mongat, 15min. from the city. A 3rd-class site. 450ptas per person, 315ptas per child, 450ptas per tent. Reception open 9am-2pm and 4-9pm. Camping June 15-Sept. 15.

FOOD

Barcelona is teeming with restaurants; almost every block has four or five places to eat. In the Eixample, *patisseries* and cafés offer luscious (but expensive) treats under shady trees. Closer to the port, bars and cafés are more crowded and harried. The Barri Gòtic is plastered with 850-950pta *menús*. **Bakeries** are a cheap alternative to sit-down dining, and often sell cold *bocadillos* (sandwiches). Catalan specialities include *mariluz a la romana* (white fish in tomato sauce), *butifarra con judías blancas* (sausage with white beans), and *crema catalana* (Catalan pudding).

Consult the weekly *Guía del Ocio* (available at most newsstands, 95ptas) for dining options beyond those listed here. This guide provides mini-reviews and listings by specialty for hundreds of restaurants, including sections on *servicio a domicilio* (delivery), *para llevar* (take-out), *abiertos en domingo* (restaurants open on Sun.), and *cenar de madrugada* (late-night dining).

Groceries: La Boquería, officially **Mercat de Sant Josep,** off Rambla Sant Josep, 89, is Barcelona's best market, with fresh fish and produce in an all-steel *Modernista* structure. Packed food stalls sell everything from dried fruit to pigs' feet. (Open Mon.-Sat. 7am-8pm.) **Simago,** Rambla des Estudis, 113. Open Mon.-Fri. 9:30am-8:30pm, Sat. 9:30am-9pm.

Be aware that food options shrink drastically in August, when restauranteurs and bar owners—a la Freud—close up shop and take their vacations.

Barri Gòtic

You'll find oodles of *menús* for around 850ptas in the narrow and dark streets between the cathedral and the port. Carrer de Avinyó runs through the middle of the *barri,* between C. Ample and C. Ferran. Metro: Liceu (L3) or Jaume I (L4).

Restaurante Bidasoa, C. Serra, 21. (tel. 318 10 63). Metro: Drassanes (L3). Take 3rd left off C. Josep Anselm Clavé heading from Las Ramblas. This well-managed family place will stir up whatever your heart desires if you're not satisfied by their 43 permutations of eggs, salad, and fish. A full meal for under 1000ptas. Open Sept.-July Tues.-Sun. 1:30-4pm and 8-11pm.

Can Conesa, C. Llibreteria, 1 (tel. 315 33 09), on the corner of Pl. Sant Jaume. This little nook distinguishes itself from myriad other sandwich shops with ultra-low prices and trademark crispy grilled *bocadillos* and *sobrasada* (ground sausage). Cheap pizza (245-325ptas) too. Open Mon.-Sat. 8am-9pm. Closed first half of Aug.

El Gallo Kirko, C. Avinyó, 19 (tel. 412 48 38). Metro: Liceu (L3). Walk down C. Ferran, and it's the 4th right. Built around part of a Roman stone wall erected around Barcelona in the 4th century, EGK specializes in *couscous* (with vegetables, 450ptas) and curry (with beef and rice, 450ptas). Mango fruit shakes 350ptas. Open daily noon-midnight. Credit cards accepted.

Els Quatre Gats, C. Montsió, 3bis (tel. 302 41 40). Metro: Catalunya (L1, L3). Walk down Av. Portal de L'Angel and take the 2nd left. This frequently touristed spot was once the hangout of Picasso and other Lost Generation-ers. Their works adorn the walls. Live music 9pm-1am. *Menú* 1500ptas served Mon.-Fri. 1-4pm. Open Mon.-Sat. 8am-2am, Sun. 5pm-2am. Credit cards accepted.

Restaurante Self-Naturista, C. Santa Anna, 11-15 (tel. 318 23 88). Metro: Catalunya (L1, L3). Self-service vegetarian cafeteria with a jazz background. A wide selection of desserts and salads spills over the counter. Variety of bread, mushroom, and artichoke dishes, most under 400ptas. Open Mon.-Sat.11:30am-10pm; count on a line during siesta.

Restaurante El Cid, C. Princesa, 11 (tel. 319 28 25). Metro: Jaume I (L4). C. Jaume I becomes C. Princesa at the intersection with Via Laietana. Dimly lit tables, mirrored walls, and a polished wooden bar make for a relaxing dinner. *Paella con espárragos* with appetizer 1100ptas. *Menú* 825ptas. Open Mon.-Sat. 8am-10pm.

Bar Restaurante Cervantes, C. Cervantes, 7 (tel. 317 33 84), 2 bl. down C. Avinyó off C. Ferran. Metro: Jaume I (L4). Rub elbows with those quixotic government officials from the buildings next door. Scrumptious chicken croquettes or a gigantic plate of macaroons 275ptas. Open Mon.-Fri. 1-4pm and 6-8pm.

Restaurante Cafeteria Nervión, C. Princesa, 2 (tel. 315 21 03), near the corner of C. Princesa and Via Laietana. Metro: Jaume I (L4). Neighborhood "diner" has the big rule of life printed on the menu: "eat well, live well." *Menú* 800ptas, cheap *platos combinados* (375-625ptas), and breakfast. Open Sept.-July Mon.-Fri. 6-10am and 11am-10pm, Sat. 6-10am and 11am-3pm. Credit cards accepted.

Restaurant Pitarra, C. Avinyó, 56 (tel. 301 16 47). Metro: Drassanes (L3). Turn left down C. Clavé at the end of Las Ramblas, and take 3rd left after a church. In the former home of great Catalan poet-dramatist Pitarra, art lives on in epic dishes concocted by Queen Sofía's former chef Señor Marc. The *escalopines ternera* (veal) is the most delicious 975ptas you can spend in Spain. *Paella* 1300ptas.

Vino de la casa 750ptas. Open Sept.-July Mon.-Sat. 1-4pm and 8:30-11pm. Credit cards accepted.

La Fonda, C. Escudellers, 10 (tel. 301 75 15). Metro: Drassanes (L3) or Liceu (L3). C. Escudellers enters Barri Gòtic halfway between Liceu and Drassanes. Waiting in line outside is painful enough without the large windows through which patrons may be seen ordering classic Catalan cuisine prepared and served by professionals for less than the price of a compact disc. Try to snag a *silla* (seat) on the balcony. Lunch *menú* 875ptas. Dinner 1500-2000ptas. Open Sept.-July Tues.-Sun. 1-3:30pm and 8:30-11:30pm. Credit cards accepted.

Restaurante Porto Mar, C. Josep Anselm Clavé, 19 (tel. 301 82 27), ½bl. from the port end of Las Ramblas. Metro: Drassanes (L3). Decorated with boats, but not strictly seafood. Chicken, fish, and pizza tolerated on board. 2-course *menú* with bread, wine, and dessert 900ptas. Open Mon.-Wed. 1-4pm and 8-11pm, Thurs.-Sat. 1-4pm and 8pm-1am.

Between Las Ramblas and Ronda de Sant Antoni

Students and workers cluster here at lunch. The area around Calles Tallers and Sitges, just one block off Rambla de les Canaletes, overflows with inexpensive places to eat; some advertise specials on chalkboards outside. Good Galician food is served off C. Luna and C. Joaquín Costa. Barri Xinès, the red-light district, begins roughly below C. Hospital.

Restaurante Riera, C. Joaquín Costa, 30 (tel. 442 50 58). Metro: Liceu (L3) or Universitat (L1). Off C. Carme coming from Liceu, or off Rda. de Sant Antoni coming from Universitat. The Riera family supplies a feast fit for a hungry, poor king. Flocks of gregarious regulars. Meals change daily, but a heaping plate of *paella* is always available. 3-course gorge-fest with dessert 600ptas. Open Sept.-July Sun.-Thurs. 1-4pm and 8:30-11pm, Fri 1-4pm.

Bar Restaurante Los Toreros, C. Xuclá, 3-5 (tel. 318 23 25), on a narrow alley between C. Fortuny and C. Carme, both off Las Ramblas. Metro: Catalunya (L1, L3). The floors, faded from red to brown, would no longer anger the bull. And who could be angry when *platos combinados* start at 500ptas? Open Mon.-Fri. 8am-1am, Sun. 8am-5pm.

Pizzeria Restaurante Ideal, C. Unió, 4 (tel. 302 30 31), right off Las Ramblas, past the Teatre del Liceu. Metro: Liceu (L3). Founded in 1840; the restaurant's history is pictured on the wall. Serves up a romantic combination of Italian, French, and Spanish food. Pizzas around 775ptas. *Menú* 850ptas.

Restaurante Biocenter, C. Pintor Fortuny, 24 (tel. 302 35 67). Metro: Catalunya (L1, L3). Across the street from the store of the same name, off Las Ramblas. This alter-ego to Los Toreros sounds threateningly futuristic; it's actually a small and friendly vegetarian restaurant. *Menú* with trip to the salad bar, a bowl of soup, a vegetarian dish, and dessert 975ptas. Open Mon.-Sat. 1-5pm and 8:30-11pm.

Raim D'or Can Maxim, C. Bonsuccés, 8 (tel. 302 02 34), off the right-hand side of Las Ramblas when facing the port. Metro: Catalunya (L1, L3). Smoked hams hang in hoof-ed glory over the bar. Fresh fish from 475ptas, meat dishes 500-700ptas, and crowd-pleasing pizzas 575-800ptas. Open Oct.-Aug. Mon.-Sat. 9am-5pm and 8pm-midnight. Credit cards accepted.

Restaurante Nuria, Las Ramblas, 133 (tel. 302 38 47), 2 doors down from Burger King at the upper end of Las Ramblas. Metro: Catalunya (L1, L3). This big operation doubles as an expensive grocery store. Sandwiches downstairs and meals upstairs. Menu includes 8 meat and 8 fish dishes (most under 1000ptas) and 19 desserts (including orange juice, 300ptas). Open 8am-1am.

Restaurante la Garduña, C. Morera, 17-19 (tel. 202 43 23). Inside the meat and produce market, this restaurant is a sight in itself—and acquires the freshest and best-priced daily offerings. Though crowded and confusing on the ground floor, the restaurant is simple and relaxing. Typical Catalan food in both *menú* (975ptas) and special of the day (1375ptas).

Restaurante Pollo Rico, C. Sant Pau, 31 (tel. 441 31 84), several blocks off Pl. Boquería on Las Ramblas. Metro: Liceu (L3). For the price of an asparagus tip with mayonnaise at some other restaurants, take home your very own chicken

(800ptas). Half-chicken, fries, and bread 550ptas. Take out available and advised. Open Thurs.-Tues. 1pm-midnight.

Can Segarra, Ronda Sant Antoni, 102 (tel. 302 44 22). Metro: Universitat (L1). *Menú del día* (800ptas) served in the refreshingly air-conditioned 2nd-floor dining room. Open Mon.-Sat. 8am-1am.

The Eixample

The chi-chi aura is ever so soothing, although restaurants tend to be pricier than those in the old quarter. Metro: Pg. Gràcia (L3, L4) or Diagonal (L3, L5).

Restaurant Les Corts Catalanes, Gran Via de les Corts Catalanes, 603 (tel. 301 03 76), just off Rambla Catalunya. Metro: Catalunya (L1, L3). Groceries in front, food and drink in back. Earthy-crunchy vegetarian staples include *tarta de espinacas con guarnición* (savory spinach cake) and *zumo de zanahorias* (carrot juice). Salads 700-1000ptas. Most pastas around 1000ptas. Desserts such as sweet spinach cake around 425ptas. Restaurant open 1-4pm and 8-11pm. Bar and store open 9am-midnight. Credit cards accepted.

Restaurante Comedia Club, Gran Via de les Corts Catalanes, 609 (tel. 301 33 99), between Rambla Catalunya and Pg. Gràcia. Metro: Catalunya (L1, L3). All-you-can-eat buffet for more-than-you-can-afford (1800ptas, Sat.-Sun. 2000ptas). Open Mon.-Thurs. 1-3:30pm, Fri.-Sun. 1-3:30pm and 9-11:30pm.

Pizzeria Argentina El Ceibo, C. Mallorca, 279, 1 bl. from Pg. Gràcia. Metro: Diagonal (L3, L5) or Pg. Gràcia (L3, L4). Outdoor tables in summer. South American specialties such as *empanadas* (meat turnovers). Assorted pizzas 700ptas. *Menú* 820ptas. Open Sept.-July Mon.-Sat. 1-4pm and 8-11pm.

Charcutería L. Simó, Pg. Gràcia, 46 (tel. 216 03 39). Metro: Pg. Gràcia (L3, L4). On the right as you walk up the street from the Metro. Gourmet eatery with A/C. Culinary options displayed in the window. Meat dishes 700ptas. Salads and casseroles 400ptas per *ración* (portion). Open Mon.-Sat. 8am-8pm.

Gràcia and Nearby Neighborhoods

You know you're in Gràcia when you hear fellow diners speaking Catalan, instead of Spanish, English, French, or German. The food is likewise authentic.

Can Suñé, C. Mozart, 20 (tel. 218 54 86). Metro: Diagonal (L3, L5). Take C. Goya off C. Gran de Gràcia, and then take the 2nd right. A petite, family-run restaurant with marble tables and ceiling fans. Neighbors gather to spin yarns and eat a different meal each day (including wine and dessert, 875ptas). Fried *calamares* (squid, 350ptas). Open Sun.-Thurs. 7am-5pm, Fri-Sat. 7am-5pm and 9-11pm.

Taverna El Glop, C. Sant Lluís, 24 (tel. 213 70 58). Near the Joanic Metro stop (L4) off C. Escorial. This 2-story rustic tavern has become *muy* popular with the local bourgeoisie for its *chorizo* (a Spanish sausage) cooked over an open flame. Carbo-load on gigantic *torradas* (slices of toasted catalan bread with tomato and cheese or sausage, 295-945ptas). If there's a long line (as there often is after 10pm), let the staff direct you to **Taverna El Nou Glop,** for an equally gloppy experience. Open Sept.-July Tues.-Sun. 1-4pm and 8pm-1am.

La Ceba/La Perla, C. La Perla, 10 (tel. 217 06 01). Metro: Fontana (L3). Down the street from El Glop (C. La Perla becomes C. Sant Lluís as you head toward Joanic), in the direction of Fontana. An elegant little restaurant which specializes in *truiterias* (Catalan for tortillas, most around 575ptas)—36 kinds at last count—and ice cream desserts. Open Mon.-Sat. 1-4pm and 8:30pm-midnight.

Restaurante Crêperie, C. Bonavista, 2, off C. Gran de Gràcia. Metro: Diagonal (L3, L5). Crepes. Sketchings on the wall provide a whirlwind tour of Barcelona. Open 8am-1am.

SIGHTS

During the summer (June 13-Sept. 27), the easiest way to take in the major sights of Barcelona is to hop on the **Bus Turístic,** sponsored by the city's Patronat de Turisme. (For fare and schedule information see Tourist Information: Tourist Bus. Ajuntament tourist offices have a free pamphlet that maps out the bus route.) The tourist offices have a wealth of information and pamphlets. *Barcelona: One and Only* is a *barri*-by-*barri* description of the city; *El Barcelonés* is a quick-and-dirty glance. For a thematic look, peruse *Discovering Romanesque Art in Catalonia, Routes of Gothic Art in Catalonia,* or *Discovering Modernist Art in Catalonia. Barcelona: Urban Spaces* is downright strategic in its layout of various walking itineraries. And don't leave the office without the Ajuntament's large map of the city, which lists all the museums and Gaudís in Barcelona.

Las Ramblas

Dubbed "the most beautiful street in the world" by W. Somerset Maugham, this tree-lined boulevard runs from Pl. Catalunya to the Monument a Colom at the port. Originally composed of five distinct segments (Santa Monica, Caputxins, Sant Josep, Estudis, and Canaletas), its broad pedestrian lane is a veritable urban carnival: street performers dance flamenco, fortune-tellers survey palms, beggars hold out their hands, merchants hawk their wares, and tourists fiddle with their packs. The superstitious make wishes at **Font de Canaletes** at the top of Las Ramblas near Pl. Catalunya.

About halfway down Las Ramblas toward the port, the **Gran Teatre del Liceu,** Las Ramblas, 61 (tel. 318 91 22), stands on the right. On opening night here in 1892, an anarchist launched two bombs from the upper balcony into the crowd of aristocrats, killing 22 and wounding many more. After executing five others for the crime, authorities finally found the real culprit, who cried "*Viva la anarquía*" before being hanged. The *teatre* was once one of Europe's leading stages, having nurtured the likes of José Carreras. Ravaged by a fire on January 31, 1994, the *teatre* is not expected to reopen until 2001.

At the far end of C. Sant Pau stands Barcelona's oldest Romanesque church, the 10th-century **Església de Sant Pau,** once attached to a Benedictine monastery. The church is noted for the capitals of the entrance, the carved tympanum, and particularly the ornate **cloister** with lobed arches, dating from the 11th and 12th centuries. (No regular hours. Try calling 441 00 01 to make reservations, or inquire next door at C. Sant Pau, 101, Mon.-Fri. 6-8pm.)

Designed by Gaudí, the **Palau Güell,** Carrer Nou de la Rambla, 3-5 (off of Rbla. Caputxins) houses the **Museu de les Arts de l'Espectacle,** with exhibits relating to the world of performing arts. **Plaça Reial,** to the left off Rbla. Caputxins (facing the port) was once crawling with pickpockets during the day and worse at night. Now with a police station, two youth hostels, two discos, and a handful of bars and restaurants, those seeking the thrill of that wrong-side-of-the-tracks experience will find more success elsewhere. The area to the right of Rambla Santa Mónica and Rambla de Caputxins (facing the port), officially El Raval, is known as the **Barri Xinès,** or Barrio Chino, Barcelona's red-light district.

At the port end of Las Ramblas the **Monument a Colom,** erected in 1888, towers over the city. Spotlights turn the statue into a firebrand at night. (Elevator to the top open 9am-9pm; Oct.-Mar. Tues.-Sat. 10am-2pm and 3:30-7pm, Sun. 10am-7pm; April-May Tues.-Sat. 10am-2pm and 3:30-8pm, Sun. 10am-8pm. Admission 225ptas, children 125ptas. Ticket office open until ½hr. before closing.) The **Museu Marítim** is nearby on Pl. Porta de la Pau, 1 (see Museums).

Barcelona's drive to recover and refurbish its seafront has not only resulted in Vila Olímpica, but also in **Moll de la Fusta,** which lies between Pg. Colom and the water. Shoving the coastal road underground, the city opened a wide pedestrian zone that leads down to the docks past new, scenic, and pricey restaurant-cafés. The cobblestone docks are ideal for a slow evening *passeig.*

The small ferry **Las Golondrinas** (tel. 412 59 14) leaves Barcelona's busy harbor, to flaunt Montjuïc and the isolated peninsula at the breakwater. (Every ½hr. Daily 11am-8:30pm; Nov.-Mar. Sat.-Sun. 11am-6pm; Apr. and Oct. daily 11am-6pm; June daily 11am-7pm. Round-trip 355ptas.)

Barri Gòtic

Strictly speaking, the **Barri Gòtic** (Gothic Quarter) is the area surrounding the cathedral, the Ajuntament, and the Generalitat, but the name also extends to the area between Las Ramblas and Via Laietana. While streets such as **Carrer de la Pietat** and **Carrer del Paradis** have managed to preserve their medieval charm, cheap *pensiones,* souvenir stands, and bars swamp much of the area. The intrusion of the tourist economy, however, gives the area a liveliness—and a livelihood—it would otherwise lack.

The handsome **Plaça de Sant Jaume**—Barcelona's main square since Roman times—took its present form in 1823. The *plaça* is dominated by two of Cataluña's most important buildings: the **Palau de la Generalitat** (seat of Cataluña's autonomous government) and the **Ajuntament** (city hall; tourist information and lost and found also here).

Jagged spires fly high over the old city, supported by the Gothic **Església Catedral de la Santa Creu,** on C. Bisbe between the Generalitat and smallish **Plaça de la Seu.** Charles Galtés designed its facade in the 15th century, almost 200 years after the first stone was set; Josep Mestres didn't finish the *església* until 400 years later. The coats of arms painted on Pere Ca Anglada's elegant upper pews mark the gathering of the Knights of the Golden Fleece in 1519 at the summons of Carlos I, who that year became the most powerful ruler in the world. The marble choir screen in the chancel illustrates the death of Barcelona's patron saint and martyr, St. Eulàlia. The cathedral's **claustre** has magnolias growing in the middle and geese waddling around the periphery. The petite **museu** (tel. 315 35 55) off the cloister houses religious treasures and 15th-century *La Pietat,* painted by Bartolomé Bermejo. (Cathedral open 8am-1:30pm and 4-7:30pm. Cloister open 8:45am-1:15pm and 4-6:45pm. Museum open 11am-1pm. Admission 50ptas. Ask a guard to let you see the *coro* (choral chamber) for 25ptas.)

On the opposite side of the Església Catedral, on C. Comtes, is the **Palau Reial** (Royal Palace), which belonged first to the counts of Barcelona, then to the kings of Aragón. Inside, the **Museu Frederic Marès** and **Museu d'Historia de la Ciutat** (see Museums) hold court. (Chambers of the royal palace can be visited with admission to history museum.)

Also on C. Comtes, the distinguished late-Gothic **Palau del Lloctinent** (Lieutenant's Palace) has a Renaissance-influenced courtyard and fountain. The **Arxiu de la Corona d'Aragó** (Archives of the Kingdom of Aragón), one of the world's major repositories of medieval documents, molders inside the palace. Behind looms an imposing ensemble of buildings that form **Plaça del Rei.** The Renaissance tower, wherein a rebellious peasant tried to assassinate King Fernando el Católico, is the square's landmark.

Barri de la Ribera

Turn-of-the-century urban planners separated this vivacious part of the old city from the Barri Gòtic proper when they built the Via Laietana in 1907. The area grew with Barcelona's development as a major sea power during the Middle Ages. With its horizontal lines, octagonal towers, and large, unadorned surfaces, the **Església Santa María del Mar** on Pl. Santa María is perhaps the zenith of 14th-century Catalan Gothic design. Entrance around back on Pg. Born, 1. (Tel. 310 23 90; open Mon.-Sat. 8:45am-12:30pm and 4:30-8:15pm.)

The monumental palaces on **Carrer de Montcada,** which begins around the back of the *església,* exemplify Barcelona's secular architecture. Especially interesting is **Palau Berenguer d'Agüilar** at #15. This same palace also houses the **Museu Picasso** (see Museums), one of Barcelona's greatest tourist attractions. The **Museu Tèxtil i d'Indumentària** is across the street (see Museums).

Nearby soars the **Palau de la Música Catalana,** Sant Francesc de Paula, 2, just off of the intersection of Via Laietana and C. Jonqueres. The palace was designed by *Modernista* architect Lluís Domènech i Montaner, and completed in 1908. The music hall is festooned with stained-glass cupolas, flowing marble reliefs, intricate woodwork, and dazzlingly colorful ceramic mosaics on the ceilings, walls, and floors. (Tel. 268 10 00; open to the public Sept.-July Tues. and Thurs. 3pm, Sat. 10 and 11am. By appointment only; call ahead. 200ptas. English spoken.)

Parc de la Ciutadella and Vila Olímpica

Fierce fighting and damage to the city convinced Felipe V to construct a large citadel in 1716 on what is now Pg. Picasso. Citizens left homeless by the fires that ravaged Barcelona relocated here, and the fortress later became a symbol of the Bourbon king's strict treatment of Catalan insurgents. The fortress was razed in 1868, and replaced by the peaceful promenades of **Parc de la Ciutadella.** Host of the 1888 Universal Exposition, the park now harbors several museums, well-labeled horticulture, the fabulous **Cascada** fountains, a pond (rowboat rental 10am-8pm, 225ptas per person per ½hr.), and a zoo. EXPO '88 also bore the triumphantly small **Arc de Triomf,** just across Pg. Pujades from the park. Today the nearby tree-lined plaza is frequented by elderly locals who sip *café* and play yahtzee. Little Snowflake (*Copito de Nieve*), the world's only albino gorilla behind bars, is the main attraction at the **Parc Zoològic** (tel. 221 56 06), south of the Plaça Armes. Dolphin and whale shows too. (Open 9:30am-7:30pm; winter 10am-5pm. Admission 900ptas.) On Pl. Armes is Barcelona's **Museu d'Art Modern** (see Museums).

Beyond the east side of the zoo is the site of the **Vila Olímpica,** which housed 15,000 athletes for the 25th edition of the Summer Games in 1992, and is now a rising yuppie village known as **La Nova Icària,** with several public parks, a shopping center, offices, strategically placed monumental buildings, in-line skate rental (Marina, 22; tel. 221 16 66; 750ptas per hr.), and a ring road connecting the East and West ends of the city. The new dock has opened the city to 5km of the seafront (once covered by railroad tracks and warehouses), attempting to correct Barcelona's inclination to ignore the sea.

The Eixample

The 1859 demolition of Barcelona's medieval walls symbolically ushered in the *Renaixença* (renaissance) of Catalan culture. The design of Catalan architect Ildefons Cerdà's for a new Barcelona, *Pla de Reforma i Eixample* (plan for renovation and broadening), is revealed in an aerial view of the Eixample area: a regular grid of squares, softened by the cropped corners of streets, forming octagonal intersections. Meanwhile, the flourishing bourgeoisie commissioned a new wave of architects to build their houses, reshaping the face of the Eixample with *Modernismo* architecture. The best way to approach this macro-museum of Catalan architecture is with two handy-dandy pamphlet guides available free at the tourist office: *Discovering Modernist Art in Catalonia* and *Gaudí.*

Antoni Gaudí (1852-1926) led the Modernists with his curving, organic surfaces and with his blurring of the roles of artist and artisan. His nature-inspired designs and outlandish yet structurally sound building contours were made possible only by the invention of new building materials—sheet iron and concrete. Surpassing the role of architect, Gaudí designed every last detail of his works, including the furniture, light fixtures, decorative mosaics, and iron grill work. His methods were unconventional. The vault of the Colònia Güell was created using a method only an engineer would understand: sand bags were hung from a wire model of the ceiling, the inversion of which was perfectly balanced against structural stress. One of his most controversial works, *Casa de Cartas,* was never completed due to recurring winds. Fellow Modernista luminaries include **Luis Domènech i Montaner,** noted for his profusely decorated surfaces, and **José Puig y Cadafalch,** who developed an antiquarian style mingling local and foreign traditions.

Many modernist buffs argue that the **Casa Milà** apartment building (popularly known as **La Pedrera**—Stone Quarry), Pg. Gràcia, 92 (tel. 487 36 13), is Gaudí's masterpiece. The entrance to this buckling mass of rock is around the corner on C. Provença. Note the intricate ironwork around the balconies and the diversity of the front gate's egg-shaped window panes. The roof sprouts chimneys that resemble odd geological formations. Rooftop tours provide a closer look at the *cascs prusians* (Prussian helmets), spiral chimneys inspired by the helmets worn in Wagner's operas. (Rooftop tours Tues.-Sat. 10am-1pm on the hour. Same day reservations accepted in the early morning. Free.)

Gaudí's most famous work is unequivocally the **Temple Expiatori de la Sagrada Familia,** on C. Marina between C. Mallorca and C. Provença (Metro: Sagrada Familia, L5). Gaudí seized another architect's neo-Gothic plans for the church and made it look like no other building on the face of the earth. For 43 years Gaudí obsessed over the Sagrada Familia, living in a small room there for his last 11 (he was killed by a trolley in a possible suicide in 1926). The church's three proposed facades symbolize Jesus's nativity, passion, and glory; only the first is finished. Gaudí estimated that the project would take at least 200 years to complete—but he wasn't counting on the confusion which followed his death. Since 1926 construction has progressed erratically, and with tremendous controversy. A furor has arisen over recent additions, such as the streamlined pyramid arch on C. Sardenya, that some say don't flow with the rest of the structure. Elevators and a maze of symmetrical staircases lead to the towers, bridges, and crannies of the nativity facade. In the **museum** is a model of the completed structure and various artifacts relating to its construction. (Open June-Aug. 9am-9pm; May and Sept. 9am-8pm; March-April and Oct. 9am-7pm; Nov.-Feb. 9am-6pm. Admission to church, museum included, 700ptas.)

The odd-numbered side of Pg. Gràcia (called *la manzana de la discordia*—the apple of discord, a mythological reference to the judgement of Paris), between C. Aragò and Consell de Cent, offers an overview of the peak of the *Modernista* movement. The bottom two floors of the facade of **Casa Lleó i Morera,** by Domènech i Montaner, were destroyed to house a store, but the upper floors sprout flowers and winged monsters which snarl on the balconies. Puig i Cadafalch opted for a cubical pattern on the facade of **Casa Amatller** at #41. Gaudí's balconies undulate and the tiles sparkle on #43, **Casa Batlló.** A letter of permission from Cátedra Gaudí, Av. Pedralbes, 7 (tel. 204 52 50; open Mon.-Fri. 8am-2pm), allows access to the *casa principal* (main apartment), where bent and swollen wood doors and the mushroom-shaped arch in front of the main fireplace make you think you're in a German Expressionist film. **Fundació Antoni Tàpies** is just around the corner from *la manzana de la discordia,* and the **Museu de la Música** is nearby on Av. Diagonal, 373 (see Museums).

Montjuïc

Throughout Barcelona's history, whoever controlled this strategically located mountain ("hill of the Jews") ruled the city. Over the centuries, dozens of despotic rulers have modified the **fortress** built atop the ancient Jewish cemetery at Montjuïc. Felipe IV's troops overcame rebelling citizens here in the 1640s, Felipe V snatched it away from the Catalans in 1714, and in the 20th century Franco made it one of his local interrogation headquarters. Somewhere deep in the recesses of the structure, his *beneméritos* ("honorable ones," a.k.a. the Guardia Civil) shot Cataluña's former president, Lluís Companys, in 1941. Only in 1960 did Franco return the fortress to the city for recreational purposes. This act was commemorated with a huge stone monument expressing Barcelona's thanks; the reminder of forced gratitude is visible from the castle battlements. To get to Parc de Montjuïc, take bus #61 from Pl. Espanya (Metro: L1, L3). The bus runs about every 10min. to Montjuïc and back, with stops at various points on the mountain. The bus stop at Montjuïc is on Av. Reina María Cristina (flanked by large brick towers).

The **Fonts Luminoses** (Illuminated Fountains), dominated by the huge central **Font Mágica** (magic fountain), are visible from Pl. Espanya up Av. Reina María Cristina. (Temporarily closed for repairs.) The **Museu d'Art de Catalunya,** housed in the stately **Palau Nacional** (see Museums), is also partially closed for renovations.

Up Av. Marquès de Comillas from the base of the fountains, is the **Pavelló Mies van der Rohe,** designed by the German architect for his country's 1929 EXPO pavilion. Its simple lines and building materials (marble, onyx, chrome, glass, and water) were the talk of the show (open 9am-8pm). Just across the hillside is **Poble Espanyol** (tel. 325 78 66), a "town" which features replicas of famous buildings and sites from every Spanish region: a Plaza Mayor (with a self-service cafeteria), a Calle de la Conquista, a Plazuela de la Iglesia, and so on. Prices here are high, but this is the only chance in Barcelona to see glassblowers and potters plying their trades. Bars and clubs here are a favorite nighttime spot on the weekend. (Open Sun.-Mon. 9am-8pm, Tues.-Thurs. 9am-3am, Fri.-Sat. 9am-4am. Craft shops open daily 10am-8pm. Admission 650ptas.)

In 1929 Barcelona inaugurated the **Estadi Olímpic de Montjuïc** in its bid for the 1932 Olympic games. Over 50 years later, Catalan architects Federic Correa and Alfons Milá—who were also responsible for the overall design of the **Anella Olímpica** (Olympic Ring) esplanade—and Italian Vittorio Gregotti renovated the shell (open 10am-6pm). Designed by Japanese architect Arata Isozaki, the **Palau d'Esports Sant Jordi** is the most technologically sophisticated of the Olympic structures. About 100m down the road from the Olympic stadium is the **Fundació Miró** (see Museums).

Parc del Migdia, on the opposite side of the Olympic Ring from the Palau Nacional, is remote and peaceful, with a long view of the sea nibbling at the plains south of Barcelona. A team of architects, landscape architects, botanists, and horticulturists were hired in 1989 to design a new **Jardí Botánic** (currently closed for renovations) respectful of the mountain's topography on the southern slopes of Montjuïc. The **Museu Arqueològic** is on the far side of the mountain (see Museums).

Farther along Pg. Miramar, where the park comes nearest to getting wet, is the popular **Parc d'Atraccions.** From the Fundació Miró, walk down Av. Miramar and take the *teleferic* (cable car) halfway up. (11:30am-9:30pm; off-season Sat.-Sun. 11:30am-2:45pm and 4-7:30pm. Fare 325ptas, round-trip 525ptas.) From Barcelona, take the funicular (tel. 412 00 00; fare 165ptas, round-trip 275ptas) from Pl. Raquel Meller (Metro: Paral-lel (L3)) to Av. Miramar, where you can hop on the *teleferic.* The amusement park (tel. 241 70 24), C. Montjuïc at the cable car's mid-station, amuses with every sort of ride, including bumper cars, a roller coaster, a ferris wheel, and a turkish bath. (Open Mon.-Thurs. 6pm-midnight, Fri.-Sat. 6pm-2am, Sun. noon-midnight; Sept. 15-March Sat.-Sun. noon-8pm; April-June 20 Sat.-Sun. noon-10pm.) Uphill, at the highest *teleferic* stop, the historically rich **castell** guards the **Museu Militar** (see Museums).

Gràcia

Located just beyond the Eixample, Gràcia charms—even as it confuses—with narrow alleys and numerous plazas. The **Torre del Reloj** (Clocktower) on popular **Plaça Rius i Taulet** is a symbol of the Revolution of 1868. **Plaça del Diamant,** on nearby C. Astúries, is a poetic landmark made famous by Mercè Rodoreda's eponymous novel. At night local youths swarm to **Plaça del Sol** and the cafés and bars that skirt its edge.

Modernismo brushed across Gràcia, as you'll see at #13 and #15 Carrer Astúries. One of Gaudí's youthful experiments, **Casa Vicens,** stands at C. Carolines, 24-26. The house incorporates audacious variations on Islamic motifs. To get to Gràcia, take the Metro to Fontana (L3).

Parc Güell

This park, conceived as a garden city for 60 houses with a splendid view of Barcelona and the sea, was designed entirely by Gaudí (including the promenades, walls, and service buildings), and—in typical Gaudí fashion—not completed until after his death. Inside, an elegant white staircase, lined with patterned tiles and a joyous *(trippi* in Catalan), multicolored salamander, leads to a pavilion supported by 88 pillars—apparently unrelated to Gaudí's love for the piano. In the back of the park, sweeping elevated paths, supported by columns shaped like palm trees, swerve through large hedges and prehistoric plants. The **Casa-Museu Gaudí** is here (see Museums). The easiest way to reach the park is bus #24 from Pg. Gràcia to the upper park entrance. The other way is to take the Metro to Lesseps (L3), walk down Travessera de Dalt for about ½km, and turn left up C. Larrad. The entrance is on C. d'Olot. (Like all city parks, open May-Aug.10am-9pm; April and Sept. 10am-8pm; March and Oct. 10am-7pm; Nov.-Feb. 10am-6pm. Free.)

Sarrià

Sarrià is the home of Barcelona's old money; well-to-do residents still talk about "going down to Barcelona." Sarrià was the last *barri* to lose its independence and merge into Barcelona in 1921. A walk through the shady, peaceful streets reveals elegant mansions with manicured gardens, and a host of exclusive Modernist *colegios* (private schools). Gaudí designed one of these, the **Colegio-Convento de Santa Teresa,** C. Ganduxer, 85, in the 1880s. The brick facade is composed of high windows elongated by rows of distinctive parabolic arches. Inside, arched corridors flank the courtyard.

The villa of **Bellesguard,** at C. Bellesguard, 46, is a good example of Gaudí's creative interpretation of Gothic Revival. The walls surrounding the villa used to belong to the royal summer residence of Margarita de Prades, wife of Martín I, King of Aragón. The **Finca Güell,** on Av. Pedralbes, 7, near Pg. Tilos and Pg. Manuel Girona, has an iron gate encrusted with a Gaudí dragon.

Off Pg. Bonanova, the **Planetarium Barcelona,** C. Escoles Pies, 103, reaches for the stars. (Currently closed for renovations.) To reach the building, take bus #22 from Pg. Gràcia or bus #64 from C. Aribau near the university.

The **Monestir de Pedralbes,** Baixada del Monestir, 1 (tel. 204 25 45), at the end of Pg. Reina Elisenda, has a Catalan Gothic single-aisle church and 14th-century three-story cloister. The artistic highwater is in the Capella Sant Miquel, where murals by Ferrer Bassa depict Mary's seven joys as well as some of her low moments. The monastery recently received a part of the Thyssen-Bornemisza collection, purchased by Spain in 1993. (Open Tues.-Fri., Sun. 10am-2pm, Sat. 10am-5pm. 500ptas, collection only 300ptas.)

Tibidabo

The odd name could only come from the devil. *"Haec omnia tibi dabo,"* he promises to Jesus, referring to the smashing view the area commands over Cataluña, *"si cadens adoraberis me."* ("All this I will give to you if you fall down and worship me.") Tibidabo's huge **Temple del Sagrat Cor** has received little artistic attention. The souvenir shop and telescopes tucked away in the building's spires make its religious function an afterthought. The view of Montserrat and the Pyrenees from the bust of Jesus is an eyebrow raiser (round-trip elevator ride 75ptas). 500ptas purchases a view of the **Torre de Collserola,** 560m above sea level, a communications tower built in 1992 by British architect Norman Foster. The **Parc d'Atraccions** (tel. 211 79 42) here doesn't compare to Montjuïc's. (Consult newspaper or call for times. Admission with unlimited use of 12 selected rides 950ptas, unlimited use of any ride except the Passage of Terror 1950ptas.)

Designed to appeal to all ages and interests, the **Museu de Ciéncia** rests on its laurels in Tibidabo (see Museums). An FFCC train or buses #17, 22, and 58 from Pl. Catalunya run to Av. Tibidabo. To reach the mountain top, either wait 15 minutes for the **Tramvia Blau** (blue streetcar) or walk up Av. Tibidabo in almost the same time. (Tramvia Blau runs June-Sept. 9:05am-9:35pm, Oct.-May Sat.-Sun. 9:05am-9:35pm. Mon.-Fri. 120ptas or use a T-1 pass, Sat.-Sun. 165ptas, round-trip 275ptas.) At the top of the street, you have to take a funicular. (Operates 7:15am until 30min. after the amusement park closes. Round-trip 400ptas.)

MUSEUMS

Municipal museum admission is 300ptas, Wed. 150ptas, students under 25, pensioners, and the unemployed 150ptas, children under 16 free, 1st Sun. of the month free. Many privately owned museums offer similar discounts.

Casa-Museu Gaudí, Park Güell, C. Olot (tel. 284 64 46). Metro: Pg. Gràcia (L3, L4), then bus #24 (see Sights: Park Güell). Designed by Gaudí's associate Francesc Berenguer, the house where he lived from 1900-26 has an eclectic *Modernista* collection of designs, sensual furniture, and portraits. Open 10am-2pm and 4-7pm; Nov.-March 10am-2pm and 4-6pm. Admission 200ptas.

Fundació Joan Miró, Parc de Montjuïc, Pl. Neptú on Av. Miramar, s/n (tel. 329 19 08). Metro: Espanya (L3), then bus #61 from Pl. Espanya (see Sights: Montjuïc). Designed by renowned Catalan Josep Luís Sert and winner of an international competition, the unobtrusive white concrete building commands a panoptic view of Barcelona. Permanent collection covers all periods of Miró's career. Two new wings display his sculptures. The library and well-stocked art bookstore attract young artist-types and intellectuals. Open Tues.-Sat. 11am-7pm, Thurs. 11am-9:30pm, Sun. 10:30am-2:30pm. Admission 500ptas, students 250ptas.

Fundació Tàpies, C. Aragó, 255 (tel. 487 03 15). Metro: Pg. Gràcia (L3, L4), between Pg. Gràcia and Rambla de Catalunya (see Sights: Eixample). Well-marked with an enormous array of tangled wire hanging over the entrance. Features prestigious exhibitions of Tàpies and other 20th-century artists. Open Tues.-Sun. 11am-8pm. Admission 400ptas, students 200ptas.

Museu Arqueològic, Parc de Montjuïc, Pg. Santa Madruna, s/n (tel. 423 21 49). Metro: Espanya (L1, L3), then bus #61. East of the Palau Nacional (see Sights: Montjuïc). A fine collection of Carthaginian art from Ibiza. Several rooms dedicated to relics found in the excavation of the Greco-Roman city of Empúries (near Girona). Open Tues.-Sat. 9:30am-1:30pm and 3:30-7pm, Sun. 10am-2pm. Admission 200ptas, Sun. free.

Museu d'Art de Catalunya, Palau Nacional, Parc de Montjuïc (tel. 423 71 99). Metro: Espanya (L1, L3), then bus #61 (see Sights: Montjuïc). The world's finest Romanesque art collection. Also Gothic altarpieces and paintings of Cataluña's medieval churches scavenged from the world's museums. The museum is partially closed for renovations. Consult the tourist office for details.

Museu d'Art Modern, Plaça d'Armes in the Parc de la Ciutadella (tel. 319 57 28). Metro: Ciutadella (L4) (see Sights: Parc de la Ciutadella). A potpourri of paintings and sculptures, most by recent Catalan artists. Noteworthy works include *Plein Air* by Casas, *Els Primers Freds* by Blay Fabregas, Josep Llimona's *Desconsol,* and Isidre Nonell's paintings of Gypsy women. Open Wed.-Mon. 10am-9pm.

Museu de Cera de Barcelona, Rambla 4-6 (tel. 317 26 49). Where Cleopatra mingles with C3P0. Open daily 10am-8pm; off-season Mon.-Fri. 10am-1:30pm and 4-7:30pm, Sat.-Sun. 10am-1:30pm and 4:30-8pm. Admission 750ptas.

Museu de Ciéncia, C. Teodor Roviralta, 55, Tibidabo (tel. 212 60 50). FFCC train or buses #17, 22, and 58 from Pl. Catalunya to Av. Tibidabo, walk 2 bl. and turn left onto C. Teodor Roviralta, then continue to the end of the street and up the stairs (see Sights: Tibidabo). Knob twisting, button pushing, and rod pulling open the mysterious world of science. If you can't understand the Catalan and Castilian instructions, stand back and let the first-graders show you the ropes. Open Tues.-Sun. 10am-8pm. Admission 500ptas, students 350ptas. Admission to ½hr. planetarium show 250ptas extra.

Museu de Geologia, near the corner of Pg. Picasso and Pg. Pujades in the Parc de la Ciutadella (tel. 319 68 95). Metro: Ciutadella (L4). The rock displays are geared toward jocks who already know their rocks. Open Tues.-Sun. 10am-2pm.

Museu de la Música, Casa Vidal-Quadras, Av. Diagonal, 373, in the Eixample (tel. 416 11 57). Metro: Diagonal (L3, L5). The building by Puig i Cadafalch conceals a collection of odd antique instruments. Open Tues., Thurs.-Sun. 10am-2pm, Wed. 5-8pm.

Museu de les Arts de l'Espectacle, C. Nou de la Rambla, 3-5 (tel. 317 39 74). Metro: Liceu or Drassanes (L3). (See Sights: Las Ramblas.) The Palau Güell, bought by the city to house this museum of 19th- and 20th-century theater memorabilia, is one of the few Gaudí buildings you can actually enter. Open Mon.-Sat. 10am-2pm and 4-8pm. Admission 200ptas.

Museu de Zoologia (tel. 319 69 12), at the corner of Pg. Picasso and Pg. Pujades in the Parc de la Ciutadella. Metro: Ciutadella (L4). An amusing reminder of the antiquated stuff-and-tag approach to museum displays. Open Tues.-Sun. 10am-2pm.

Museu d'Historia de la Ciutat, entrance at C. Verguer (tel. 315 11 11). Metro: Jaume I (L4), next to Pl. Rei (see Sights: Barri Gòtic). 6th-century Visigoths buried the Roman ruins to make room for their cemetery; their buildings, in turn, became the foundations for medieval structures. Ruins of the Roman colony are in the basement; some well-preserved floor mosaics and villa walls with interesting inscriptions are all that remain. On the upper floors of the museum is the **Capella de Santa Agueda,** built to store the king's holy relics. Open July-Sept. Tues.-Sat. 10am-8pm, Sun. 10am-2pm; Oct.-June Tues.-Sat. 10am-2pm and 4-8pm, Sun. 10am-2pm.

Museu Etnològic, Parc de Montjuïc, Pg. Santa Madruna, s/n (tel. 424 64 02). Metro: Espanya (L1, L3), then bus #61. Temporary exhibitions on Asian and Latino cultures. Open Tues. and Thurs. 10am-7pm, Wed. and Fri.-Sun. 10am-2pm.

Museu Frederic Marès, entrance at Pl. Sant Iu, 5-6 (tel. 310 58 00). Metro: Jaume I (L4). Housed in the Palau Reial, on the opposite side of the cathedral (see Sights: Barri Gòtic). An idiosyncratic personal collection of the sculptor Marès. The crypt has an Old Testament air, with a series of reliefs illustrating Adam and Eve. The 2nd and 3rd floors contain exhibits about daily life from the 15th to the 20th centuries. Open Tues.-Sat. 10am-5pm, Sun. 10am-2am.

Museu Marítim, Av. Drassanes, 1 (tel. 318 32 45), at the port end of Las Ramblas. Metro: Drassanes (L3) (see Sights: Las Ramblas). Recounts Barcelona's maritime history. The museum fills the old *drassanes,* the only extant example of a medieval shipyard in Europe. Open Tues. and Sat. 9:30am-1pm and 4-7pm, Wed.-Fri. 9:30am-2pm and 4-8pm, Sun. 10am-2pm.

Museu Militar, Castell de Montjuïc (tel. 329 86 13). Metro: Parallel (L3), then funicular from Pl. Raquel Meller to Av. Miramar, then cable car all the way up to the *castell* (see Sights: Montjuïc). Antique and modern Spanish army weapons, models of castles, and lead soldiers. Open Tues.-Sun. 9:30am-1:30pm and 3:30-7:30pm. Admission 150ptas.

Museu Picasso, in Palau Berenguer d'Agüilar, C. Montcada, 15-19 (tel. 315 47 61). Metro: Jaume I (L4) (see Sights: Barri de la Ribera). Paintings and drawings fill 30 rooms. Masterpieces include the *Maids of Honor* series and Picasso's reinterpretation of Velázquez's *Las Meninas.* Lithographs and early works (especially Blue Period, which he initiated while living in Barcelona) make up a large part of the collection. Not a comprehensive museum, but gives insight into the artist's beginnings. Some little-known ceramic work. Open Tues.-Sat. 10am-8pm, Sun. 10am-3pm. Admission 500ptas.

Museu Tèxtil i d'Indumentària, C. Montcada, 12-14 (tel. 310 45 16), almost across the street from the Museu Picasso (see Sights: Barri de la Ribera). Metro: Jaume I (L4). A rich assemblage of 16th-century Spanish attire in a 14th-century palace. Open Tues.-Sat. 10am-5pm, Sun. 10am-2pm.

Palau de la Virreina, Las Ramblas, 99 (tel. 301 77 75), on the corner of Carrer del Carme. Metro: Liceu (L3). This 18th-century palace, once a Peruvian viceroy's residence, displays the excellent Colecció Cambó with works by Raphael, Tintoretto, Titian, Van Dyck, Goya, and Zurbarán on the 2nd floor. Changing exhibitions (often photographic) as well. Open Tues.-Sat. 11am-9pm, Sun. 11am-3pm. Admission 500ptas, students 250ptas.

ENTERTAINMENT

Every evening around 5pm, a man sets up a box in the middle of C. Porta de l'Angel before the Galerías Preciados and, as a crowd gathers, intersperses opera with voluble commentary. Nightlife in Barcelona starts then and there, and winds down about 14 hours later.

The best source of information on movies, concerts, cultural events, and bars is the weekly *Guía del Ocio* (95ptas, available at all newsstands). Although in Spanish, the listings are comprehensible even if you don't speak the language. The *Cine* section designates subtitled films with *V.O. subtitulada;* other foreign films are dubbed. The *Arte* section lists the whens and wheres of current exhibitions. The *Tarde/Noche* section has bars and discos galore. Listings include the name, location, phone, and hours, but do not provide reviews.

Discos and Bars

The *passeig* (n. walk, stroll; drive) is divided into two shifts: post-siesta (around 5-7pm) and then a second wave (around 9-11pm). The later *passeig* is fueled by alcohol. After the bars wind down around 2am, the crowds flood the discos for another four- or five-hour stint. The more swish bars and discos tend to discriminate on the basis of hair and dress styles. Bouncers may invent a cover charge for men to prevent their numbers from overwhelming those of the women. Don't make the mistake of calling a *disco* a *club*—the latter refers to a brothel.

Where to take your *passeig* is an issue of overwhelming importance. Outdoor cafés and bars on Las Ramblas or Plaça Pi in *Barri Gòtic* provide front row seats for some of the best entertainment. Other options include a more serene setting on Montjuïc or the trendy Rambla Catalunya and the Gran Via de les Corts Catalanes.

The most fashionable and safe discos are located in the **Eixample.** Fish out your hippest garb and head out along **Carrer de Balmes, Avinguda Diagonal,** or any of their cross streets. (Metro: Diagonal, L3, L5.)

Bars

La Fira, C. Provença, 171 (tel. 323 72 71). Metro: Diagonal (L3, L5). On the block between C. Aribau and C. Muntaner. Stationary bumper cars, swings, ferris wheel benches, and fun house mirrors salvaged from amusement parks. No carnival dress: avoid shorts or sandals. Open Mon.-Thurs. 7pm-3am, Fri.-Sat. 7pm-4am, Sun. 6pm-midnight.

La Línea 6,25, C. Enric Granados, 52 (tel. 323 75 58). Metro: Diagonal (L3, L5). One bl. past C. Balmes near the corner of C. Provença. Sports theme with basketball hoops, lighted trails on the floor, and that most aerobic of exercises—dance. Beer 450ptas. 2-for-1 drinks daily 11pm-midnight. Open Sun.-Thurs. 7pm-2:30am.

L'Ovella Negra, Sitges, 5 (tel. 317 10 87). Metro: Catalunya (L1, L3). From Pl. Catalunya, down Las Ramblas and the first right at C. Tallers; Sitges is the first left. Rustic tavern where the locals and travelers mix freely over pool and foozball. Beer 250ptas. Open Mon.-Thurs. 9pm-2am, Fri.-Sat. 9pm-3am, Sun. 5pm-3am.

Nick Havana, C. Rosselló, 208 (tel. 215 65 91). Metro: Diagonal (L3, L5). On the block between C. Balmes and Rambla Catalunya. The latest in audio-technical devices, the dance floor gyrates with blaring video screens and flashing lights. Mixed drinks 900ptas. Cover (starts at midnight) 900ptas. Open Mon.-Thurs. 8pm-4am, Fri.-Sat. 8pm-5am, Sun. 7pm-3am.

Mirablau, Pl. Funicular, Av. Tibidabo, s/n (tel. 418 58 79). Take the FFCC to Av. Tibidabo and then hop on the Tramvia Blau, or just hail a taxi from Pl. Catalunya (1200ptas). Amazing view of Barcelona in a covered but open-air bar. Open midnight-5am.

Miramelindo, Pg. Born, 15 (tel. 319 53 70), right behind Església Santa María del Mar. Metro: Jaume I (L4). 2-floor Spanish colonial-style tavern with soothing jazz in the background. Open 8pm-3am.

Discos

Otto Zutz, C. Lincoln, 15 (tel. 238 07 22). Metro: FFCC Muntaner. Uptown near Pl. Molina where C. Balmes intersects Via Augusta. Large and flashy. Cover 2000ptas. Drink included. Open until 4:30am.

Fibra Optica, C. Beethoven, 9 (tel. 209 52 81). Metro: Hospital Clinic (L5). From Metro walk up C. Comte Urgell, turn left at Diagonal; it's in Pl. Wagner, 1 bl. up on the right. A twenty-something crowd. Cover 1700ptas. Drink included. Open Fri.-Sun. 6pm-9:30am and Mon.-Sun. midnight-5am.

Zeleste, C. Almogàvers, 122 (tel. 309 12 04), a 15-min. walk from Pg. Lluís Companys, or take the NL bus (11pm-4:30am). Metro: Llancuna (L4). Located in an old warehouse, this dance club has rooftop terraces and live performances (separate charge) on occasion. Cover 1000ptas. The shindig takes off at 2:30am.

KGB, C. Alegre de Dalt, 55 (tel. 210 59 04). Metro: Joanic (L4). C. Alegre de Dalt is the first left off C. Pi i Margall from the Metro. Caters to those who like their rock and roll loud and hard. Open Fri.-Sun. 10pm-4:30am.

La Paloma, C. Tigre, 27 (tel. 301 68 97). Metro: Universitat (L1). Friendly people *bailan* to Spanish and Latin music. Open Thurs.-Sun. 6-9:30pm and 11:30pm-4am. Cover for late session 700ptas.

La Boîte Mas i Mas, Av. Diagonal, 477 (tel. 419 59 50). Metro: Hospital Clinic (L5). More emphasis on the dance than the flash. Live music Tues., Thurs., and Fri. Big names sometimes come to perform in the relatively intimate disco setting. Open 10pm-5am.

Jamboree, Pl. Reial, 17 (tel. 301 75 64). Metro: Liceu (L3) or Drassanes (L3). Pl. Reial lies just off Las Ramblas, via C. Colom. Turn right upon entering, it's toward the end on the right. The Mas i Mas musical entertainment empire offers 2 concerts nightly at 9pm (500ptas) and midnight (1000ptas). Drink included. Jazz, blues, be-bop, reggae, pop-funk, and jazz-funk. Call or visit for a schedule, or call the Mas i Mas main office (tel. 318 59 66). Dancing after the 2nd concert.

Xampanyeríes

Often translated "champagne bars," they're upscale bars that serve *cava* (champagne).

Xampú Xampany, Gran Via de les Corts Catalanes, 702 (tel. 265 04 83). Metro: Pg. Gràcia (L3). The upwardly mobile of Barcelona swing to 40s tunes in an urbane atmosphere. *Cava brut nature* 500ptas per glass. Open 6pm-3am.

Xampanyet, C. Montcado, 15, off Pg. Borne behind La Església Santa María del Mar. Cozy, ceramic-tiled place with a few always occupied tables. Bubbly proprietor could teach a mini-course on *cavas*. Open Tues.-Sun. 7pm-1am.

Music, Theater, and Film

The **Gran Teatre del Liceu,** Rambla de Caputxins, 61 (tel. 318 92 77), founded in 1847, was, until recently, one of the world's leading opera stages: its interior was destroyed in a fire in 1994, and the theater is not expected to reopen until the 21st century. Many performances that would have occurred here have been moved to the **Palau Sant Jordi** (tel. 426 20 89; see Sights: Montjuïc). Classical music is performed at the **Palau de la Música Catalana,** an extraordinary brick *Modernista* building, tucked away on C. Francesc de Paula, 2 (tel. 268 10 00), off Via Laietana near Pl. Urquinaona. Concerts include all varieties of symphonic and choral music. Tickets run 800-1500ptas. Ask about free Tuesday night winter concerts and about the October music festival. (Box office open Mon.-Fri. 5-8pm.; Sept.-May Mon.-Fri. 11am-1pm and 5-8pm.) The **Conservatorio,** C. Bruc, 112, in the Eixample, is the only indoor classical music venue that operates during the summer.

Theatrical offerings in Barcelona are no less satisfying, if you understand Catalan. The **Teatre Lliure,** C. Montseny, 47 (tel. 218 92 51), in Gràcia, claims notoriety and respect with years of innovative productions. (Metro: Fontana L3.) Tickets range from 600-1100ptas, depending on the day. The season runs from Oct. to June. The **Teatre Poliorama,** or Teatre Català de la Comèda, offers lighter fare. Look for it at Rambla Estudis, 115 (tel. 317 75 99).

A new domed **Auditori** (concert hall) is going up on Plaça de les Glòries. Next door on Plaça dels Arts will be Ricard Bofill's **Teatre Nacional de Catalunya,** a cyclopean, glass-enclosed Classical temple. It's estimated to be at least a year before the two are functional.

Barcelona doesn't close its stage doors when summer arrives, the theater simply moves outdoors. The **Teatre Grec,** on Montjuïc, the **Mercat de les Flors,** and the **Velòdrom d'Horta** (for the fabulous *Grec* season) are the three biggies. **Grec,** the summer festival of classical Greek theater, produces tragedies, comedies, music, dance, folklore, and a special program for young adults (*Grec Jove*). Performances are in many languages. For times and prices, consult local papers or the Palau de la Virreina (see Practical Information: Tourist Information). For **rock concerts** held in the main soccer stadium or the sports palace, tickets are available in the booth on Gran Via at C. Aribau, next to the university (open 10:30am-1:30pm and 4-7:30pm).

Films are popular in Barcelona. Besides Spanish and Catalan features, the newest American flicks are everywhere. Also check the schedule of the **Filmoteca,** Av. Sarrià, 33 (tel. 430 50 07), run by the Generalitat, which screens classic, cult, exotic, and otherwise exceptional films. (Always subtitled if not a Castilian- or Catalan-language film. Metro: Hospital Clínic, L5. Admission 300ptas.) Movie theaters which tend to screen American films include: **Alexis,** Rambla Catalunya, 90 (tel. 405 22 22; 600ptas, weekends 650ptas, Mon. 400ptas); **Casablanca,** Pg. Gràcia, 115 (tel. 218 43 45; 625ptas, weekends 650ptas, Mon. 375ptas); **Maldà,** Pi, 5 (tel. 317 85 29; 525ptas, Mon. 350ptas); and **Verdi,** Verdi, 32 (tel. 237 05 16; Tue.-Thurs. 600ptas, Sat.-Sun. 650ptas, Mon. 400ptas).

Recreational Sports

Guía de l'esport, available free at the tourist offices, lists (in Catalan) information about swimming, cycling, tennis, squash, sailing, hiking, scuba diving, white-water rafting, and kayaking. Information is also available over the phone (tel. 237 34 01, Catalan or Castilian).

Swimming Pools: Piscina Municipal Marítim, Pg. Marítim, 35 (tel. 221 00 10), next to the hospital across the street from the beach. Metro: Ciutadella (L4). Covered; swimming cap required. Open Mon.-Fri. 7am-9pm. Admission 350ptas. **Piscina Bernat Picornell,** Av. Estadi, s/n. Metro: Espanya (L1, L3), and then bus #61 up Montjuïc. Olympic pool. Admission 700ptas. Open Mon.-Fri. 7am-11:30pm, Sat. 7am-8:30pm, Sun. 7am-2:15pm.

Beaches: Several between Vila Olímpica and the sea, all accessible from the Ciutadella Metro stop. The closest and most populated is **Platja Barceloneta,** off Pg. Marítim. Metro: Ciutadella (L4). The basics: water and sand.

Shopping

There's a lot of style walking around in Barcelona—none of it accessible to the average *Let's Go* reader. Barcelona's reputation as a fashion capital second to Paris and Milan has led to outlandish prices in the elegant shops along **Passeig Gràcia** and the **Rambla de Catalunya.** Things you can probably afford but may not want jam the tacky tourist traps along Las Ramblas.

Markets: An **antique market** is held Thurs. 9am-8pm in Pl. Nova. The famous **Els Encants** flea market bites Mon., Wed., Fri.-Sat. 8am-8pm on C. Consell de Cent at C. Dos de Maig, near Pl. Glòries. Metro: Glòries (L1). A **stamp and coin market** is held Sun. 9am-2:30pm in Pl. Reial. A **coin and book market** is held at the same time in the Mercat de Sant Antoni, Comte d'Urgell, 1.

Carrer Banys Nous, in the Barri Gòtic. Prices and quality vary widely on this street of tiny antique shops. Painters gather in Pl. Pi to sell their masterpieces Sat. 11am-8pm, Sun. 11am-2pm.

El Corte Inglés, Pl. Catalunya (tel. 302 12 12). The top department store in Barcelona. Huge, crowded, well-stocked, and staffed by multilingual salespeople. Rooftop cafeteria has heavenly views and celestial prices. Open Mon.-Sat. 10am-9pm.

Galerías Preciados, C. Portal de l'Angel. Inglés' department store rival. The bird-ridden pet shop wins points, but the rooftop cafeteria (serving a good buffet lunch) is a Corte Inglés wannabe. Open Mon.-Sat. 10am-9pm.

VIPS, Rambla Catalunya, above Pl. Catalunya. Only a fraction of the size of the department stores, but this late-night locale is crammed with books, records, food store, and café. Open Sun.-Thurs. 8am-1:30am, Fri.-Sat. 8am-3am.

English Bookstores: see Practical Information.

La Lidia, Sardanas, and Fiestas

Although the best matadors rarely venture out of Madrid, Sevilla, and Málaga, and few Catalans are true fans, Barcelona does maintain **Plaça de Toros Monumental,** a *Modernista* bullring on Gran Via at Pg. Carles I. Buy tickets at local travel agencies, or at the box office before the start of the *corrida.* (Tel. 453 38 21; open 10:30am-1:30pm and 4-8pm. Tickets 1600-9000ptas. Metro: Marina (L1).) Don't waste money

LET'S GO TRAVEL

CATALOG

1995

WE GIVE YOU THE WORLD... AT A DISCOUNT

Discounted Flights, Eurail Passes,
Travel Gear, Let's Go™ Series Guides,
Hostel Memberships... and more

Let's Go Travel

a division of

Harvard Student
Agencies, Inc.

Bargains
to every
corner of
the world!

Travel Gear

A
Let's Go T-Shirt..........$10
100% combed cotton. Let's Go logo on front left chest. Four color printing on back. L and XL. Way cool.

B
Let's Go Supreme..........$175
Innovative hideaway suspension with parallel stay internal frame turns backpack into carry-on suitcase. Includes lumbar support pad, torso, and waist adjustment, leather trim, and detachable daypack. Waterproof Cordura nylon, lifetime gurantee, 4400 cu. in. Navy, Green, or Black.

C
Let's Go Backpack/Suitcase..........$130
Hideaway suspension turns backpack into carry-on suitcase. Internal frame. Detachable daypack makes 3 bags in 1. Waterproof Cordura nylon, lifetime guarantee, 3750 cu. in. Navy, Green, or Black.

D
Let's Go Backcountry I..$210
Full size, slim profile expedition pack designed for the serious trekker. New Airflex suspension. X-frame pack with advanced composite tube suspension. Velcro height adjustment, side compression straps. Detachable hood converts into a fanny pack. Waterproof Cordura nylon, lifetime guarantee, main compartment 3375 cu. in., extends to 4875 cu. in.

E
Let's Go Backcountry II..........$240
Backcountry I's Big Brother. Magnum Helix Airflex Suspension. Deluxe bi-lam contoured shoulder harness. Adjustable sterm strap. Adjustable bi-lam Cordura waist belt. 5350 cubic inches. 7130 cubic inches extended. Not pictured.

800-5-LETSGO

Discounted Flights

Call Let's Go now for inexpensive airfare to points across the country and around the world.

EUROPE • SOUTH AMERICA • ASIA • THE CARRIBEAN • AUSTRALIA •
AFRICA

Eurail Passes

Eurailpass (First Class)

15 days	$498
1 month (30 days)	$798
2 months (60 days)	$1098

*Unlimited rail travel anywhere
on Europe's 100,000 mile rail network.
Accepted in 17 countries.*

Eurail Flexipass (First Class)

*A number of individual travel days
to be used at your convenience
within a two-month period.*

Any 5 days in 2 months	$348
Any 10 days in 2 months	$560
Any 15 days in 2 months	$740

Eurail Youthpass (Second Class)

15 days	$398
1 month (30 days)	$578
2 months (60 days)	$768

*All the benefits of the Eurail Pass
at a lower price. For those passengers
under 26 on their first day of travel.*

Eurail Youth Flexipass (Second Class)

*Eurail Flexipass at a reduced rate
for passengers under 26
on their first day of travel.*

Any 5 days in 2 months	$255
Any 10 days in 2 months	$398
Any 15 days in 2 months	$540

Europass (First & Second Class)

First Class starting at	$280
Second Class starting at	$198
For more details	CALL

*Discounted fares for those passengers
travelling in France, Germany, Italy,
Spain and Switzerland.*

Hostelling Essentials

F Undercover Neckpouch............$9.95
Ripstop nylon with soft Cambrelle back. Three
pockets. 6 x 7". Lifetime guarantee. Black or Tan.

G Undercover Waistpouch.........$9.95
Ripstop nylon with soft Cambrelle back. Two
pockets. 5 x 12" with adjustable waistband.
Lifetime guarantee. Black or Tan.

H Sleepsack.................................$13.95
Required at all hostels. 18" pillow pocket.
Washable poly/cotton. Durable. Compact.

I Hostelling International Card
Required by most international hostels. For U.S.
residents only. Adults, $25. Under 18, $10.

J Int'l Youth Hostel Guide.......$10.95
Indispensable guide to prices, locations, and
reservations for over 4000 hostels in Europe
and the Mediterranean.

K ISIC, ITIC, IYTC..........$16,$16,$17
ID cards for students, teachers and those people
under 26. Each offers many travel discounts.

800-5-LETSGO

Order Form

Please print or type — Incomplete applications will not be processed

Last Name	First Name	Date of Birth

Street	*(We cannot ship to P.O. boxes)*

City	State	Zip

Country	Citizenship	Date of Travel

( ) -

Phone	School (if applicable)

Item Code	Description, Size & Color	Quantity	Unit Price	Total Price
			SUBTOTAL:	

Domestic Shipping & Handling

Order Total:	Add:
Up to $30.00	$4.00
$30.01 to $100.00	$6.00
Over $100.00	$7.00

Call for int'l or off-shore delivery

Shipping and Handling (see box at left):	
Add $10 for RUSH, $20 for overnite:	
MA Residents add 5% tax on books and gear:	
GRAND TOTAL:	

MasterCard / VISA Order

CARDHOLDER NAME _____

CARD NUMBER _____

EXPIRATION DATE _____

Enclose check or money order payable to:
Harvard Student Agencies, Inc.
53A Church Street
Cambridge, MA 02138

Allow 2-3 weeks for delivery. Rush orders guaranteed within
one week of our receipt. Overnight orders sent via FedEx the same afternoon.

Missing a Let's Go Book from your collection?
Add one to any $50 order at 50% off the cover price!

Let's Go Travel
1-800-5-LETSGO

(617) 495-9649   Fax: (617) 496-8015
53A Church Street
Cambridge MA 02138

on expensive seats: the ring is small enough so that everyone can see. Bullfights normally take place on Sunday at 6:30pm; the season runs June to October. There's also a **museu** of bullfighting history here (open 10am-1pm and 3:30-6pm).

The **sardana,** Cataluña's regional dance, is one of Barcelona's most popular sights. Teenagers and grandparents join hands to dance in a circle in celebration of Catalan unity in front of the cathedral, Pl. Sagrada Familia, or at Parc de la Ciutadella near the fountains Sun. at noon. Dances are also held in Pl. Sant Jaume Sun. at 6:30pm, at Parc de l'Espanya Industrial Fri. at 8pm, in Pl. Catedral Sat. at noon and 6:30pm, and in other locations throughout the city on Tues., Thurs., and Fri. Consult papers for current info.

Fiestas are abundant in Barcelona. Before Christmas, **Feria de Santa Lucía** fills Pl. Catedral and the area around the Sagrada Familia with stalls and booths. **Carnaval** is celebrated wildly from February 7th to the 13th, but many head to the even more raucous celebrations in Sitges and Vilanova i la Geltrú. Soon thereafter comes the **Festa de Sant Jordi** (Saint George) on April 23, the feast of Cataluña's patron saint and Barcelona's St. Valentine's Day. Men give women roses, and women reciprocate with a book. On May 11 is the **Festa de Saint Ponç,** when a traditional market of aromatic and medicinal herbs and honey is set up in C. Hospital, close to Las Ramblas. In the summer, Barcelona erupts on June 23, the night before **Día de Sant Joan.** Bonfires roar throughout the city, unsupervised children play with *petardos* (fireworks), and the fountains of Pl. Espanya and Palau Reial light up in various colors in anticipation of fireworks on Montjuïc. Next, city folk kick up their heels at Gràcia's **Festa Major** (Aug. 15-21). Lights blaze in the plazas and streets, while rock bands play all night.

In September, the **Feria de Cuina i Vins de Catalunya** brings wine and *butifarra* (sausage) producers to the Rambla Catalunya. For one week you can sample fine food and drink for a pittance. On the **Festa de la Verge de la Mercè,** celebrated Sept. 24, fireworks again light up the city while the traditional *correfocs,* manic parades of people dressed as devils, whirl pitchfork-shaped sparklers. Buckets of water are hurled at the demons from balconies overlooking the fiery streets. In November, a **festival de jazz** swings the city's streets and clubs.

■ NEAR BARCELONA

MONTSERRAT

An hour northwest of Barcelona, the unmistakable profile of the Montserrat mountain range—legendary site of the Holy Grail and inspiration of Wagner's *Parsifal*—juts out from the flat Riu Llobregat valley. In the 10th century, a wandering mountaineer had a blinding vision of the Virgin Mary here. The story immediately attracted pilgrims, and in 1025 the bishop-abbot Oliba founded a local **monastery** to worship the blessed Virgin, the spiritual patroness of Cataluña. The present buildings date from the 19th century, although two wings of the old Gothic cloister survive. Today some 80 Benedictine monks tend the shrine, work in ceramics and goldsmith workshops, and distill the herbal liqueur *Aromes de Montserrat.*

The most important buildings stand one level above Plaça Creu in **Plaça Santa María.** The **basilica's** spacious courtyard contrasts with the dark, cavernous interior, reverently aglow with dozens of suspended votive lamps (each one a gift from a city or institution). To the right of the main chapel glimmers the sacred 12th-century polychrome figure of Mary and child, *La Moreneta.* Legend has it that an image of Mary carved by St. Luke was hidden in the caves of Montserrat by St. Peter. (Basilica open 7am-8:30pm. Free.) Twice a day, members of the *Escalonia* (a boy's choir) brighten the basilica with song as only little boys can (Aug.-June at 1 and 6:45pm).

Plaça Santa María also boasts the **Museu de Montserrat,** which exhibits an eclectic range of art—from Mesopotamian artifacts to paintings by El Greco, Caravaggio, and Picasso. Various artifacts from biblical lands are also on display, including a mummified crocodile more than 2000 years old. (Antiquities section open 10:30am-

2pm. Modern section open 3-6pm. Ticket valid for both museums 300ptas, students 150ptas, children 50ptas.)

Some of the most beautiful areas of the mountain are accessible only on foot. A lookout over Barcelona sits 20 min. down the path between the Pl. Creu and Sant Joan funicular stations; another 40 minutes on the same bucolic path leads to the latter station (otherwise take the funicular to Sant Joan, every 20min., 730ptas). From here, a network of overgrown paths extends over the mountain. The dilapidated **Sant Joan monastery** and **shrine** are only a 20-min. tromp away. But the real prize is **Sant Jerónim** (the area's highest peak at 1235m), with its mystical views of Montserrat's celebrated rock formations—enormous domes and serrated outcroppings resembling human forms, including "The Bewitched Friars" and "The Mummy." The hike is a hot two hours, but on a clear day the spectacular view of the Baleares and the eastern Pyrenees will have you singing hosannas all the way.

The other funicular from Plaça Creu descends to **Santa Cova,** or "Holy Grotto" (every 20min., 295ptas), where the mountaineer allegedly discovered the image of the Madonna. The path to the shrine, **Via Crucis,** is lined with religious works by Catalan artists (e.g. Gaudí) which illustrate the stations of the cross. (Chapel open 9am-6:30pm.) The path from the cable car station doubles as a cheap way to Santa Cova.

Practical Information For more details on navigating your way through the mountains, go to the **information booth** in Pl. Creu (tel. 835 02 51, ext. 586), a providential and multilingual source of advice and the *Official Guide to Montserrat* (360ptas). (Open 10am-2pm and 3-6pm.) Other conveniences include a **post office** (open Mon.-Fri. 9am-1pm and 3-6pm, Sat. 9am-1pm) and a place to **change money** ("La Caixa" automatic exchange machine accepts Visa, AmEx, MC, and Eurocard). For an **ambulance** or mountain rescue team call 835 02 51 (ext. 562). The **Guardia Civil** is headquartered in the main square (tel. 835 01 60).

Trains to Montserrat leave from Barcelona's Pl. Espanya (L1, L3) stop (every 2hr., 9:10am-5:10pm, 1485ptas, children 890ptas; with funicular to Sant Joan 2010ptas, children 1390ptas). These FFCC trains are on the Manresa line; be sure to get off at the Aeri de Montserrat stop, *not* the Olesa de Montserrat stop just before it. The trains stop at the base of the mountain, where a funicular ascends on a lengthy wire up the slope. Upon exiting the upper funicular station, turn left and walk about 100m to reach **Plaça Creu,** Montserrat's tourist-oriented commercial area.

Accommodations and Food If you choose to spend the night, stop at the building marked **Despatx de Celiles,** on the walk from Pl. Santa María down to Pl. Creu (tel. 835 02 51, ext. 230; open 9am-1pm and 3-6pm). More a series of apartments than an *hostal;* up to 10 people (8950ptas with bath) may room together for extended periods of time. The rooms are ascetic, the view stupefying. (Singles 1250ptas. Doubles 2950ptas. Reservations recommended for Aug.) An adequate **campground** (tel. 835 02 51, ext. 582) lies five minutes up the hill beyond the Sant Joan funicular. Showers. Closed in winter. (350ptas per person and per tent.)

The fresh fruit and baked goods at the **market** next to the Despatx de Celiles may look like food—but they're actually souvenirs, and priced accordingly. Instead try the **Bar de la Plaça** behind the market (sandwiches 300-450ptas; open Mon.-Fri. 10am-5:30pm, Sat.-Sun. 9:30am-6:45pm, closed 2-3:30pm except in July) or the **pastisseria** and **autoservei** for baked goods and groceries (on the left when walking from the market to Pl. Creu; open 9am-1:45pm and 3-5:45pm).

SANT CUGAT DEL VALLÈS

Devotees of Romanesque art and architecture can happily worship the church at **Sant Cugat del Vallès,** just over the Serra de Collserola on Barcelona's coattails. This church boasts one of the largest Romanesque cloisters in Cataluña, with a double-decker forest of 13th-century columns supporting the breathtaking upper gallery, which wasn't completed until the 16th century. The most striking feature of the church is also its oldest: the soaring 11th-century Lombard bell tower, visible from any corner of the town. Visigothic, Biblical, and mythological motifs mingle in its intricate carvings, while the rose window breathes life into its facade. Arnau Gatell sculpted all the figures in the cloister. (Cloister open Tues.-Sat. 9:30am-1:30pm and 3:30-5:30pm, Sun. 9:30am-1:30pm. Admission 100ptas.) FFCC trains depart Barcelona's Pl. Catalunya (Metro: L1, L3) for Sant Cugat (every 15min., 5am-midnight, Sat.-Sun. every 20min.).

■■■ GIRONA

A world-class city waiting patiently for the world to notice, Girona rules without vainglorious ceremony over the 235-municipality province of Girona from the banks of the Riu Onyar. The wonderfully schizophrenic Girona is really two cities in one: a hushed Medieval masterpiece of stone alleyways on one river bank and a thriving, modern city on the other. Girona was named for the Roman city Gerunda, but owes as many connotations to the renowned *cabalistas de Girona,* who for centuries spread the teachings of Kabbalah (mystical Judaism) in the West. Still a center of culture and home to a large university, it is a magnet for artists, intellectuals, and activists. Girona lures visitors to wander its alleyways and discover cached treasures.

ORIENTATION AND PRACTICAL INFORMATION

The coffee-colored **Riu Onyar** divides the new city from the old. The **Pont de Pedra** connects the two banks and leads directly into the old quarter by way of C. Ciutadans, C. Carreras Peralta, and C. Força, off of which the **cathedral** and the historic Jewish neighborhood known as **El Call** are located.

Girona is the transportation hub of the Costa Brava: all trains on the Barcelona-Portbou-Cerbère line stop here; seven different lines send scores of buses daily to the Costa Brava and nearby cities; and the major national and international car companies have offices here. Girona is the ideal jumping-off place for the Catalan Pyrenees. RENFE and bus terminals are situated off **Carrer de Barcelona** on the modern side of town. To get from there to the old city, pass through the commercial district by heading straight out of the station through the parking lot, turning left on C. Bailen, and left again on C. Barcelona. Follow C. Barcelona for two blocks until it forks at the traffic island. The right fork runs via C. de Santa Eugenia to the **Gran Via de Jaume I.** Cross this at the Banco Central Hispano to get on **Carrer Nou,** which runs directly to the bridge Pont de Pedra.

Tourist Office: Rambla de la Llibertat, 1 (tel. 22 65 75; fax 22 66 12), directly on the left as you cross Pont de Pedra from the new town. Vies for best in Cataluña; the staff has made Girona tourism its guiding passion. Transit schedules, restaurant and accommodations listings with locations marked on maps, and piles of brochures. English and all major European languages spoken. Open Mon.-Fri. 8am-8pm, Sat. 8am-2pm and 4-8pm, Sun. 9am-2pm. **Train station branch:** tel. 21 62 96. Downstairs, on the left as you face away from the RENFE ticket counter. Nifty electronic information server with zoom-able information maps opposite it. Open July-Aug. Mon.-Fri. 9am-2pm. When closed, the office posts indexed street map with directions to main office.

Budget Travel: Direcciò General de Juventut, C. Juli Garreta, 14 (tel. 20 15 54), 1 bl. from the train station, off C. Bisbe Tomás de Lorenzana. In an unmarked building, 1 flight up on the *entresol* (mezzanine). Railpasses, buses to Europe, HI cards (1800ptas), ISICs (500ptas), *Guide to Budget Accommodations* (500ptas). These portfolio experts also run Girona's youth hostel. Open mid-June to mid-Sept. Mon.-Fri. 9am-2pm; low-season 9am-1:30pm and 3:30-5:30pm.

Currency Exchange: Throw a peseta in the new city and you'll probably hit a major bank. Remember that they close at 2pm.

Post Office: Av. Ramón Folch, 2 (tel. 22 21 11), at the beginning of Gran Via de Jaume I. Turn right on the Gran Via if coming from the old city. Open Mon.-Fri.

8am-9pm, Sat. 9am-2pm for stamps and Lista de Correos—letters and packages must be picked up at the **second office** on Ronda Ferran Puig, 17 (tel. 21 07 71). **Telegrams** upstairs in main office Mon.-Fri. 8am-9pm, Sat. 8am-7pm. **Postal Code:** 17070.

Telephones: Currently, no Telefónica office. Ubiquitous phone booths (some to the right of Port de Pedra as you enter the old town). **Telephone Code:** 972.

Airport: (tel. 47 43 43), 13km out of Girona. Charter flights only.

Trains: RENFE, Pl. Espanya (tel. 20 70 93). Frequent trains to: Figueras (26-52min., 260ptas); Portbou (50-70min., 400ptas); Barcelona (including 2 *talgos,* 1-2hr., 600ptas, *talgo* 1660ptas). Also to: Zaragoza (9 per day, 3-4hr., night train 6½hr., 2400-3500ptas); Valencia (1 per day at 7:45am, 8hr., 3500ptas); Madrid (2 per day including 1 *talgo,* 12hr., *talgo* 9-10hr., 5100ptas, *talgo* 6500ptas). To Jaca or Huesca: change in Zaragoza.

Buses: (tel. 21 23 19), around the corner from the train station (to the left). **Sarfa** (tel. 20 17 96) has services to: Tossa de Mar (July-Aug. 3 per day, regularly 2 per week, 480ptas, Sat.-Sun. 505ptas); and Palafrugell (13 per day, mid-Sept. to June 8 per day, 1hr., 425ptas, Sat.-Sun. 480ptas). From Palafrugell, you can make connections to Begur, Llafranc, Calella, and Tamariu. **Fills de Rafael Mas** (tel. 21 32 27) runs to: Lloret (3-5 per day, 55min., 415ptas, Sat.-Sun. 475ptas). **Teisa** (tel. 20 02 75) to: Olot (6-8 per day, 1¼hr., 525ptas, Sat.-Sun. 600ptas); Ripoll (4-5 per day, 2¾hr., 855ptas, Sat.-Sun. 975ptas); St. Feliu (15 per day, 355ptas, Sat.-Sun. 405ptas). **Barcelona Bus** (tel. 20 24 32). Express service to: Barcelona and Figueras (4-9 per day).

Car Rental: Most companies cluster around C. Barcelona near the train station. Must be over 21 (some companies 24) and have had a license for at least 1-2 years. **Hertz** (tel. 21 01 08), at the train station next to the branch tourist office. Rents Ford Fiestas and Peugots. **Avis,** C. Barcelona, 35 (tel. 20 69 33). Rents Renaults and Opels. **Melció,** Sant Joan Bta. La Salle, 33-38 (tel. 20 04 43). Rents Marbellas. Fancy models available. Rates improve the longer car is kept. All agencies charge approx. 1000-1500ptas per day for mandatory insurance. Credit cards generally required.

Automobile Club: Reial Automòbil Club de Catalunya, C. Barcelona, 22 (tel. 22 36 62), left from the train station. Travel agent will help you rent a car. Open Mon.-Fri. 9am-1:30pm and 4-7:30pm.

Luggage Storage: Lockers in train station (600ptas). Station open 6am-11pm.

English Bookstore: Girona Books, C. Carme, 63. Rambla Llibertat runs into C. Carme as you walk with the Riu Onyar on your right. Small but tasteful selection of new and used paperbacks. Open Mon.-Fri. 9am-1pm and 4-6:30pm.

Mountain Bike/Moped Rentals: Lluis Casademont S.A., C. Figuerola, 34 (tel. 20 53 15). Mountain bikes 1500ptas per half-day, 2400ptas per day, 3500ptas per weekend. Scooters 3500ptas per day if less than 3 days, 2500ptas if more.

Gay Services: F.A.G.C. (Front d'Alliberament Gai de Catalunya): Aportat Correus, 681 (tel. 22 38 16).

Red Cross: Bonastruc de Porto, 11 (tel. 22 22 22).

Medical Services: Hospital Municipal de Santa Caterina, Pl. Hospital, 5 (tel. 20 14 50), across from library. **Hospital Doctor Josep Trueta** (tel. 20 27 00), on the highway to France. Interpreter in summer.

Police: Policía Municipal, C. Bacià, 4 (tel. 092). From Banco Central turn right on the Gran Via, then right on Bacià.

ACCOMMODATIONS

Rooms are hardest to find in June and August. The majority of the budget accommodations are sprinkled in and around the old quarter.

Alberg-Residència Cerverí de Girona (HI), C. Ciutadans, 9 (tel. 21 80 03). In the heart of the old quarter, on the street which runs left after Pont de Pedra. A college dorm most of the year (shhhh! they're studying), this 5-yr.-old is ultramodern inside, repainted stucco outside. High-caliber staff, high-fashion sheets. No lights-out in VCR/TV room downstairs. 11pm curfew, but door opens every ½hr. until 1am, and the guard may be convinced to let you in even later. 1200ptas, July-Aug.

1300ptas. Over 25: 1625ptas; 1925ptas. (Real) breakfast included. Get lunch or dinner (all-too-familiar dining hall fare) for a measly 300-450ptas, over 25 460-675ptas. Laundry (wash and dry) 500ptas; detergent sold at reception. Reservations should be made at the Barcelona office (tel. (93) 483 84 11) June- Aug.

Pensió Viladomat, C. Ciutadans, 5 (tel. 20 31 76). Blindingly white and sparklingly clean rooms and bathrooms. Primarily a student residence until late June. Dining area with TV. *Menú* 950ptas. Breakfast 400ptas. Singles 1800ptas. Doubles 3500ptas. Triples 4000ptas.

Pensió Residencia Reyma, Pujada Rei Marti, 15 (tel. 20 02 28), 2 bl. from the cathedral on the corner of C. Ballaire. Bland but immaculate rooms on a soporific alley. Singles 1500ptas. Doubles 3000ptas, with bath 4500ptas.

Pensió Coll, C. Hortes, 24 (tel. 20 30 86). Turn left on C. Santa Clara just before Pont de Pedra; C. Hortes is 2 bl. farther on the left. In the modern sector—more nightlife but less character. Institutionally clean rooms. Winter heating in halls. Avoid the annex down the street, where rooms are small, and off a dark hallway. Singles 1800ptas. Doubles 2200ptas, with bath 3200ptas. IVA tax not included.

Pensió Residencia Bellmirall, C. Bellmirall, 3 (tel. 20 40 09), go straight from the door on the right side of the cathedral (angle left) until the blue sign appears. The delightful and creative project of two Gironese artists bound in matrimony, these stone rooms are a florid mix of the husband's oil paintings and the wife's colorful needlework. Juice, croissants, and coffee served in intimate breakfast room. Singles 3674ptas, with bath 3891ptas. Doubles 5813ptas, with bath 6308ptas.

FOOD

Partly because of Girona's blessed obscurity, the city's restaurants serve authentic, inexpensive Spanish cuisine. Some of the best restaurants huddle about the cathedral, especially along **Calle Força.** Others—including several al fresco—are found on **Plaça Independència,** at the end of C. Santa Clara in the modern section of the city. A score of cafés lie along **Rambla de la Llibertat.** Many restaurants offer deliciously priced lunch *menús* that disappear by nightfall. Several cafés and bars in the old quarter cater to university students.

Supermarket: Valvi, C. Sequia, 10. Off the Gran Via, one street north of C. Nou. Open Mon.-Sat. 9am-1:15pm and 5-8:30pm.

Café la Torrada, C. Ciutadans, 18 (tel. 21 71 04), 1 bl. from the youth hostel. Local student crowd. Catalan menu features mostly *torradas,* those delectable toasts with toppings. Entrees 450-1250ptas. Open Mon.-Fri. 9am-4pm and 7pm-1am, Sat.-Sun. 7pm-midnight.

L'Anfora, C. Forçà, 15 (tel. 20 50 10). Upstairs dining hall with wicker chairs and exposed stone walls was once the secret site of Jewish religious ceremonies. Downstairs (irony of ironies), large hunks of decidedly un-kosher ham hang over the bar. Lunch *menú* 800ptas. Entrees 500-1650ptas. Open 12:30-4pm and 7-11pm. Visa, MC accepted.

L'Arcada, Rambla de la Llibertat, 38 (tel. 20 10 15). Tables right on the Rambla. In true Spanish style, linger over your meal as you watch amorous couples flaunting their bliss. Try their crispy, tangy variation on the pizza theme (650-900ptas).

El Racò, C. Santa Clara, 47 (tel. 22 16 89). Take C. Santa Clara left just before Pont de Pedra into the old town and continue 4 bl. Don't be deterred by the fast-foody exterior. Pasta (490-750ptas), pizza (500-725ptas), salads (560-630ptas), and dessert crepes (340-515ptas) prepared at counters while you watch. Open 1-4pm and 8pm-midnight. Visa, MC accepted.

SIGHTS

Most of Girona's sights lie in the old city, across the Riu Onyar from the train station. To take an historical tour, begin at the Pont de Pedra and turn left at the tourist office down tree-lined **Rambla de la Llibertat.** At the end of the Rambla, turn right on C. Argenteria, cross C. Cort-Reial, and continue on C. Bonaventura Carreras i Peralta. Up a flight of stairs, C. Força begins on the left.

El Call

El Call, a Catalan word meaning "passage," is the Jewish Medieval neighborhood. It begins at C. Sant Llorenç, a right turn off C. Forçà onto a narrow alleyway before the cathedral. The entrance to the **Centre Bonastruc Ça Porta,** also known as the **Casa de Isaac el Cec** (the Blind), is off C. Sant Llorenç about halfway up the hill. Probable site of the last synagogue in Girona, it now serves as a museum linking the baths, butcher shop, and synagogue, all of which surround a serene central patio. (Tel. 21 67 61; open 10am-6pm; Nov.-May Tues.-Sun. 10am-2pm. Free.)

Girona's Jewish community became a leading center for the practice of Kabbalah. Its most influential teacher was Moses Ben Nahman, or Nahmanides, born in Girona in 1194. Kabbalah is a mystical reading of the Scriptures in which number values are assigned to each Hebrew letter, and numerical sums are interpreted to reveal spiritual meaning. Interestingly, Kabbalah flourished in the 13th century, and was thus contemporaneous with the development of Bhakti (a form of Hindu mysticism) and the proliferation of Sufism (Islamic mysticism). The Jewish community grew during the Middle Ages despite increasing conflict with the city's Christian sector. In 1391, during an economic crisis when Jews were accused of deliberately spreading the plague and sapping the community's wealth, a mob of Girona's Christians killed 40 residents of the Jewish quarter. By the 16th century, the 1492 expulsion by Isabel and Fernando, mass emigration, conversion, and the Inquisition's *autos-de-fé* had virtually wiped out the once thriving Jewish community. The city blocked off the streets of the *aljama,* or neighborhood, and converted the buildings for its own use. The process of reopening the streets and alleys that were once El Call started after Franco's death in 1975. The area off C. Forçà is the best place to see what little is left of Jewish Girona's architecture.

Cathedral Complex

Further uphill on C. Forçà and around the corner to the right, Girona's imposing Gothic **catedral** rises up a record-breaking 90 steps (the largest Rococo stairway in Europe) from its *plaça.* The northern **Torre de Charlemany,** best viewed from the *claustro,* is the only structure which remains from the 11th century; the leftover was designed in the 15th century. The cavernous interior has but one rather than the customary three naves, making it the world's widest Gothic vault at 22m.

A door on the left leads to the trapezoidal cloister and the **Museu del Claustre,** which hoards some of Girona's most precious possessions: seven 15th-century sculptures by Mercadante de Bretaña, and Beato de Liébana's 10th-century *Libre de l'Apocalipsis,* an illuminated commentary on the end of the world. The museum's (and possibly Girona's) most famous piece is the intricate and animated **Tapis de la Creació,** which takes up the entire wall of Room IV. Woven in the 11th or 12th century, its illustrations depict biblical scenes and the creation cycle. (Tel. 21 44 26; cathedral and museum open May-Oct. 15 10am-2pm and 4-7pm; Oct.16-Jan. 7 and Feb.-April Tues.-Sun. 10am-2pm and 4-5pm. Admission to museum 300ptas, students 200ptas.)

Elsewhere

From Pl. Catedral, head out through the Roman arch on the left and take a right to the Romanesque **Banys Arabs** (Arab Baths) on C. Ferran el Catòlic. Dating from the 13th century, each of the four rooms was kept at a different temperature for truly salubrious bathing. (Open Tues.-Sat. 10am-7pm, Sun. 10am-2pm; Oct.-May Tues.-Sun. 10am-2pm. Admission 100ptas.)

To reach the **Museu Arqueològic,** turn left from the Banys Arabs and climb down the stairs. From the foot of the stairs walk through the gates of the Pl. Jurats and over the bridge. The museum is the final resting place for the medieval tombstones that once marked nearby Jewish burial sites. A small section is dedicated to artifacts from Empúries. (Tel. 20 26 32; open Tues.-Sat. 10am-1pm and 4:30-7pm, Sun. 10am-1pm. Admission 100ptas.)

Near the University of Girona is the beginning of the **Passeig de la Muralla.** Railed steps lead up onto the walls of the city, from which you can get a sea gull's perspective of old Girona's ochre tapestry. The walk ends 2 bl. to the left of the Pont de Pedra. The trees and meadows of the **Val de Sant Daniel** stretch north along the banks of the Galligant. Partly stepped and lined with cypresses, pines, and flower beds, the **Passeig Arqueològic** (archeological promenade) skirts the medieval wall on the eastern side of the river and overlooks the city. To reach the promenade, exit the Banys Arabs and take the stairs to the base of the turret.

On the way back to the cathedral, turning right, the view of the river valley from the Portal de Sant Cristòfol is sure to slow your pace. On its eastern side, the **Museu d'Art** houses a large collection of 12th-century Romanesque wood sculpture and the *teballa de vitraller* (14th-century workbench to make stained-glass), the only known vestige of the laborious medieval stained-glass making process. Each page of the 15th-century book *Martirologi* is adorned with five delightfully humane paintings of abused martyrs. On the fourth floor, moody 19th-century landscapes and portraits of farmers hang side by side with contemporary Catalan works. (Tel. 20 38 34; open Tues.-Sat. 10am-7pm, Sun. 10am-2pm; Oct.-Feb. Tues.-Sat. 10am-6pm, Sun. 10am-2pm. Admission 100ptas, 1st and 3rd Sun. of the month and students free.)

For other buildings of interest, including contemporary works, ask at the tourist office.

ENTERTAINMENT

Girona takes its evening *passeig* seriously. The Rambla is the place to see and be seen, to chat amicably, to gossip, to politic, to flirt, and to dance: there's a live band here every Wednesday in July at 10pm, and *sardanas* most Fridays all summer long.

After the *passeig* there's dinner, and after dinner there's bar-hopping, when the throngs move to the newer part of the city. Bars near Pl. Ferran el Catòlic draw big crowds, but during the summer, **Parc de la Devesa,** across the river from the old town and several blocks to the left, has all the *ambiente.* Against a backdrop of towering 140-year-old trees and broad paths, local bars stand in all their splendor. Of Girona's four discotheques, the mightiest is **La Sala de Cel,** C. Pedret, 118 (tel. 21 26 64), off Pl. Sant Pere in the northern quarter of the city. It's in a building with a small pool and garden. (Open Sept.-July Thurs.-Sun. nights. Cover 2000ptas, includes 2 drinks.) Artsy folk mill around bars and cafés in the old quarter.

For nine days in May, flower exhibitions are held in the city, local monuments are bathed with flora, and the courtyards of Girona's fine old buildings open to the public. (Contact tourist office for this year's dates.) In July, the city hosts the **Curs Internacional de Música,** a series of six concerts in La Mercè. The concert hall is at Pujada de la Mercé, 12 (tel. 22 33 05). In June and July, **concerts** take place in front of the cathedral, in the Jardins de la Devesa, and various other points in the city. Check with the tourist office for a schedule of events. (Admission 0-1500ptas. For information, call 41 94 10.) The **Parc de la Devesa,** on the western side of the river, is the largest urban park in Cataluña. It also houses the **municipal swimming pools.** (Open Mon.-Fri. 10am-8pm, Sat. 10am-7pm. Admission 600ptas.)

On Rambla Llibertat near the tourist office peddlers sell jewelry and flowers on Saturday mornings. The complete *sardana* guide, the *Guia d'Aplecs Sardanistes de les Comarques Gironines,* can be found at the tourist office, along with a complete listing of observed holidays and festivals. Girona's two local holidays are July 25 for Sant Jaume, and Oct. 29 for the Festa Major. On June 23, Girona and all of Cataluña light up for the Focs de Sant Joan, a pan-Catalan party featuring fireworks, campfires, and oodles of tradition.

Frequent and quick RENFE service makes the **Teatre-Museu Dalí** in Figueras a good daytrip, and provides easy access to the **beaches** around Portbou and Llansá.

COSTA BRAVA

The jagged cliffs of the Costa Brava cut into the Mediterranean Sea from Barcelona north to the French border. Coined by Catalan poet Ferran Agulló, the name for this "savage coast" rings of danger and natural isolation. Craggy precipices and hairpin turns render parts of the coast unnavigable even for the most modern land transportation; many buses zigzag between the coastal towns and safer inland routes. In winter the *tramontana,* a bitterly cold wind from the Pyrenees, can screech at 45 mph for days. In July and August, the coast turns its other cheek to attract vacationing Europeans with warm sun, cool breezes, and idyllic seaside vistas. The juxtaposition of mountains and sea, trees and rocks, make it the paradise of the perambulatory naturalist. The rocky shores traditionally also entrance artists; Chagall set up his canvas here, and Surrealist icon Salvador Dalí was a native of the region. Dalí's house in Cadaqués and a museum in Figueras house the largest collections of his work in Europe. Early June and late September are the perfect times to visit the area: the water is still warm, but the beds—without many tourists to fill them—are cool.

Schedules here are fickle. Services are most regular during July and August, somewhat less so the rest of the tourist season (May-Oct.), and drop to bare subsistence levels during winter. Prices, especially for lodging, also tend to vary along this timeline. Call ahead for precise information on accommodations and transportation.

RENFE trains stop at the southern tip of the coast at Blanes, at Figueras, and again at Llansá and Portbou (up near the French border). Bus is the preferred mode of transportation here, especially through Sarfa (beautiful buses, beautiful rides). Some of the more tortuous rides might warrant medication for those vulnerable to car sickness. Tossa de Mar is the crown of southern Costa Brava and makes a good exploration base for the area. For the northern swath, Figueras is linked with Cadaqués by bus and Portbou by rail. Palafrugell is an inland connection to central Costa Brava. Local tourist offices distribute maps of off-road sights, camping areas, and trails along the coast

■■■ TOSSA DE MAR

In 1951, during the filming of "The Flying Dutchman" in Tossa de Mar, Ava Gardner fell in love with Mario Cabrera, a Spanish bullfighter turned actor. Falling in love in, and with, Tossa is easy. Appropriately called the "flower of the sea," Tossa boasts unspoiled beaches and a lively, labyrinthine old quarter, which culminates in the Vila Vella (Old Town), a walled, sun-baked cluster of 12th- to 14th-century buildings nestled in a rocky peninsula and overlooking the sea. The town lives seasonally, with many pensiones, restaurants, and bars open only from May to October, when Spanish and Western European visitors invade. As for Ava, her hubby at the time (code name "Old Blue Eyes") found out about Tossa's spell and flew in with a group of toughies to chaperone what remained of the film's shooting.

ORIENTATION AND PRACTICAL INFORMATION

Tossa is near the southern corner of the Costa Brava, about 40km north of Barcelona (90km of winding roads). **Sarfa's** bus service is relatively frequent from Barcelona in the summer (6-8 per day), but is so limited from Girona during low- and mid-season that many travelers head for Lloret de Mar (10km south) first, and then catch the bus (15min.) from there to Tossa.

Buses arrive at **Plaça de les Nacions Sense Estat,** at the corner of **Avinguda Pelegrí** and **Avinguda Ferran Agulló;** the town slopes gently down from there to the waterfront (10-min. walk). Two routes from the terminal lead to the beach. Av. Pelegrí winds its way gradually through the **old quarter,** and through several name changes. For a more direct route, walk away from the station on Av. Ferran Agulló, turn right on **Avinguda Costa Brava,** and continue until your feet get wet. **Passeig

del Mar, at the end of Av. Costa Brava, curves along the **Plátja Gran** (Tossa's main beach) to the foot of the old quarter.

Tourist Office: Av. Pelegrí, 25 (tel. 34 01 08; fax 34 07 12), in bus terminal building at the corner of Av. Ferran Agulló and Av. Pelegrí. Handy town map with indexed streets, accommodations, campsites, and services. English spoken. Open Mon.-Sat. 9am-9pm, Sun. 10am-1pm; Nov.-May Mon.-Fri. 10am-1pm and 4-7pm, Sat. 10am-1pm.

Currency Exchange: Ubiquitous. Try **Caixa de Girona,** Av. Costa Brava, 19 (tel. 34 01 71).

Post Office: C. Bernats at corner with C. María Auxiliadora off Av. Pelegrí (tel. 34 04 57). Open Mon.-Fri. 8am-3pm, **telegrams** Mon.-Fri. 8am-2pm, Sat. 9am-1pm. **Postal Code:** 17320.

Telephones: Av. Costa Brava, 2, to the left just before the statue of Neptune. Open 10am-1pm and 3-8pm. **Telephone Code:** 972.

Buses: Av. Pelegrí at Pl. Nacions Sense Estat. **Pujol i Pujol** (tel. 36 42 36) to: Lloret del Mar (every ½hr., 15min., 130ptas, Sat.-Sun. 145ptas). **Sarfa** (tel. 34 09 03) to: Girona (2 per week or 3 per day depending on season, 1hr., 515ptas, Sat.-Sun. 585ptas); and Barcelona (every 2hr. 7:40am-7:10pm, 1½hr., 830ptas, Sat.-Sun. 945ptas).

Ferries: The only direct means to St. Feliu and other northern points, as buses first travel inland by way of Girona. **Cruceros** (tel. 34 03 19) has its booth on the main beach. To: St. Feliu (5 per day, 45min., 950ptas round-trip). Costa Brava schedules vary frequently due to the cliffs. Sun. service is sporadic. Poor weather may cancel all service. Check with the ticket booth near the Vila Vella end of the Platja Gran.

Mountain Bike and Moped Rentals: Road Runner, Av. de la Palma, 7 (tel. 34 05 03). April-Oct. Mon.-Sat. 9am-9pm. Bring passport and license (for moped). 2-hr. mountain bike rental 1000ptas. 2-hr. moped rental 1500ptas.

Laundromat: Lavandería Valentí, Av. Catalunya, 25 (tel. 34 13 60), off Av. Ferran Agulló at Av. Costa Brava. Open 10am-noon and 4-8:30pm.

Medical Services: Casa del Mar, C. Catalunya (tel. 34 18 28). Primary health services and immediate attention. Nearest hospital is in Blanes.

Emergency/Police: In an emergency, medical or otherwise, call the **municipal police,** C. Església, 4 (tel. 34 01 35), in the Ajuntament building, 1st fl. to the rear. English spoken. They will escort you to the **24-hr. pharmacy.** The rules say you must have a doctor's prescription or they cannot help you get medicine. **Guardia Civil,** Ctra. Sant Feliu (tel. 34 03 29).

ACCOMMODATIONS AND CAMPING

Tossa fills as quickly as the best of the big-time resorts in the summer. Reservations by phone, letter, or through the multitude of travel agencies are advisable, as some establishments are booked solid from July-Aug. The tourist office provides a list of travel agencies and helps find rooms during this period. Few rooms have winter heating. The alleys and cobblestone streets of the **old quarter** are the only areas worth contemplating for lodging.

Fonda Lluna, C. Roqueta, 20 (tel. 34 03 65). Turn right off Pg. del Mar onto Peixeteras, through C. Estalt until it ends, then left and straight until you're there and hugging "mama." Charming grandparent-like management has kept some guests coming for almost three decades. Pristine rooms; beds, and bathrooms. Heart-stopping rooftop view of the Vila Vella and the sea. 1500ptas per person with full bath and breakfast. Lunch and dinner available. Open March-Oct.

Pensión Moré, C. Sant Telmo, 9 (tel. 34 09 39). Downstairs, a dim and cozy sitting room. Upstairs, large rooms with wash basins and views of the old quarter below. 1200ptas per person; Sept.-June 1000ptas per person.

Camping: Tends to be pricey; often costs as much as or more than *pensiones* for those not traveling in large groups. The tourist office has listings of nearby campgrounds. The closest is **Cau Martí** (tel. 34 08 51; fax 34 07 12), at the end of Av.

Pau Casals, off Av. Ferran Agulló (10 to 15-min. walk from the bus station). June 20-Aug. 650ptas per person and per tent, otherwise 500ptas.

FOOD

Restaurants on Av. Ferran Agulló and other main drags prove the Chevy Chase theorem that tackiness breeds tourists and tourists breed tackiness. The best cuisine and ambience rest in the alleys of the old quarter. Most places specialize in local seafood, but other fare is also available. For a special treat, try the traditional *crema catalana*, something like the ultimate roasted marshmallow, only better.

> **Supermarket: Supermarkets Valvi,** C. Enric Granados, 4. Follow beachside road to Av. Ramón Penyafort and take second left. Open Mon.-Sat. 9am-9pm, Sun. 9am-1pm. **Centi,** Av. Ferran Agulló in front of C. Enric Granados. Good selection, same hours, and competitive prices. Both accept MC, Visa
>
> **Restaurant La Salsa,** Pg. Sa Sassola, s/n (tel. 34 08 85). Turn right off Pg. del Mar onto Peixeteres, to C. Estalt and the first right. Seafood Poseidon would covet and a plethora of other options. Owner Giorgio is multi-lingual, friendly, and full of lore. Vegetarian rice 700ptas, *paella* 950ptas (2 person minimum).
>
> **Restaurant Marina,** C. Tarull, 6 (tel. 34 07 57). Faces the new Església de Sant Vicenç—look for the striped awning and tables out front. Family from Fonda Lluna cooks up a *paella* as good as you can get anywhere. *Menú* 875ptas, *paella menú* a steal at 1000ptas. Both include 2 courses, bread, and a ½ bottle of wine.
>
> **Dino's Restaurant and Cova,** C. Sant Telm where it meets C. Rosa, 2 bl. from the new church. Walk around inside to inspect the walls Dino fashioned himself—but save your pesetas for the downstairs Dante-esque bar, a fantastic grotto of hand-shaped plaster. Beer 150ptas. Open 8pm-3am or later.

SIGHTS AND ENTERTAINMENT

The **Vila Vella** is a *Monumento Artístico-Histórico Nacional* dating from the 12th to 14th centuries. Inside its golden stone walls, a spiral of medieval alleys leads to the remains of a Gothic church poised atop the cliff, the old **Església de Sant Vincenç.** Also in the Vila Vella, on tiny Plaça Pintor J. Roig y Soler, the **Museu Municipal** (tel. 34 07 09) has a nifty collection of 20s and 30s art, including the only Chagall painting currently in Spain and works by Olga Sakharov, Georges Kars, Togores, and Solá. Tossa's 4th- to 1st-century BC Roman mosaics and other artifacts from the nearby **Vila Romana** keep cool in the museum basement. The excavation site off Av. Pelegrí displays the buildings' foundations and more mosaics. (Museum open Tues.-Sun. 10am-1pm and 4-7pm, shorter hours Oct.-May. Admission 200ptas.)

In Tossa, the placid Mediterranean lazily laps onto four resplendently clean **beaches** and seven nearby **calas** (small bays) accessible by foot. The tourist office supplies maps of nearby hiking paths, which double as challenging mountain bike trails. They are easy to follow (though not always to find) and side-trips can lead to ruins and staggering views of cliffs and sea. The tourist office also provides information on scuba diving and mountain bike expeditions. Several companies offer **glass-bottom boat** outings to nearby beaches and caves (7-8 per day, 1hr., 800ptas). Tickets are available at booths on the Platja Gran.

Fashionable discos in town are **Ely,** C. Bernats, 2 and Av. Costa Brava, 5 (tel. 34 00 09), and **Paradis,** C. Pou de la Vila, 12-14 (tel. 34 07 55), at the end of Pg. del Mar in Hotel Rovira. For information about outdoor concerts and cultural festivals, contact the **Casa de Cultura,** Av. Pelegrí, 8 (tel. 34 09 05), in an historic red-tile roof building (open 4-6pm). Local festivals take place on Jan. 20 and 21, when the townsfolk make a 42km pilgrimage from Tossa to Santa Coloma in honor of St. Sebastian. Jan. 22 then brings the **Festa del Hivern** (Winter Fair) celebrating the feast day of St. Vincent, Tossa's patron saint. The **Festa del Estiu** (Summer Fair) is held June 29 to July 2 in honor of St. Peter. Tossa's residents make for the hills on Oct. 13 for a traditional picnic on **Aplec Sant Grau.** Make reservations for accommodations if you plan to come on these dates.

■ NEAR TOSSA

LLORET DE MAR

If Hemingway had first entered Spain through modern-day Lloret, *The Sun Also Rises* would be a very short book, and *For Whom the Bell Tolls* would never have been written. 12km south of Tossa, Lloret is sloppier, more crowded, and less chic than its neighbor. This high-rise-intensive beach town of 17,000 bloats to 210,000 during July and August. By day, tourists cram into winding back streets to buy everything from sunblock to three-foot sombreros. By night, Lloret hooks 'em up with 23 discos, 21 dance clubs, and six gay bars. To wind down, take the winding path up the rocks on the right side of **Platja de Lloret** (the main beach).

Orientation and Practical Information Buses arrive at the intersection of **Carrer de Blanes** and **Avinguda Just Marlés.** The latter is a neon-lit string of clubs and hotels leading to the waterfront (turn left off C. de Blanes, about a 5-min. walk). The main beach, **Platja de Lloret,** is surprisingly pristine for such a promiscuous town, but in July and August the sand disappears under all the oiled hides. Platja de Lloret runs the length of the shopping district, whose center is **Plaça de L'Església,** right behind the tourist office. The **main tourist office,** Pl. Vila, 1 (tel. 36 47 72), is housed in *Casa de la Vila,* a yellow stucco building midway down the beach. (Open June-Sept. Mon.-Fri. 9am-9pm, Sun. 9am-2pm; low-season Mon.-Sat. 9:30am-1pm and 4-7pm.) The **terminal branch** (tel. 36 57 88) is to the right as you exit the bus station. (Open Mon.-Sat. 9:30am-1pm and 4-8pm.) English spoken in both offices. **Post office** is at Vincens Bou, 10. (Tel. 36 46 78; open Mon.-Fri. 8:30am-2pm, Sat. 8:30am-1pm; June-Sept. closed on Sat.) **Postal code** is 17310. **Telephones** are in the bus terminal. (Open Mon.-Fri. 9:30am-1pm and 4:30-9:30pm, Sat.-Sun. 10am-1pm and 5-8:30pm.) **Telephone code:** 972. The **Red Cross** is on C. Blanes (tel. 33 03 36). Primary health care is available at the **C.A.P. (Centro de Atención Primaria),** C. Gerona, 8-10 (tel. 37 29 09). In an emergency, call the **municipal police** at (tel. 092), or drop in at C. Verge de Loreto, 3 (tel. 37 91 00). English-speaking personnel accompany you to the emergency room or the **24-hr. pharmacy.**

There are plenty of ways to get out of Lloret, most of them from the **bus station** on C. de Blanes (tel. 36 44 76). **Rafael Mas** (tel. 36 41 42) runs to Girona (3-5 per day, 50min., 415ptas, Sat.-Sun. 475ptas). Tickets on sale 15min. before departure. **Sarfa** (tel. 36 42 95) goes to Barcelona (6-10 per day, 70min., 720ptas, Sat.-Sun. 820ptas). **Pujol i Pujol** (tel. 36 44 76) makes the frequent jaunt to Tossa (every ½hr. 8:15am-8:15pm, 15min., 130ptas, Sat.-Sun. 145ptas). For travel by water, **Cruceros** (tel. 36 44 99) has stands on the beach in front of the tourist office. Ferries to: Tossa (7-9 per day, 45min., 850ptas round-trip); St. Feliu (1-5 per day, 1½hr., 1150ptas round-trip); and a host of other towns between Calella to the south and Palamós to the north.

Accommodations and Food Those determined, or forced, to stay in Lloret should be warned that lodgings are neither cheap nor easy to find. Summer travelers make reservations one to two months in advance; compulsive types reserve as early as March. Most of the cheaper hotels and *pensiones* are stacked atop one another behind and to the right (with your back to the sea) of the church. Ask at the tourist office for a complete list (on the backside of their map) and call ahead. **Hostal La Rosa** is on C. de la Fábrica, 41 (tel. 36 44 92), a right turn on C. Conilli Salsa off C. de la Vila. Pink building with restaurant downstairs. (Breakfast 350ptas. Lunch and dinner *menús* 850ptas. Singles 1600ptas. Doubles 3000ptas. Sept.-June: 1100ptas; 1900ptas.) The waterfront area is a Babel of restaurants and fast food joints. For a break from glossy, illustrated menus, try **Raimon's II,** Ctra. Tossa, 5, three bl. from the bus station. Offers simple, generous servings of traditional Catalan poultry and fish dishes. Two-course *menús* with salad, dessert, and drink 850-1350ptas, more on Sun.

SANT FELIU DE GUÍXOLS

A perilous but panoramic road twists 23km north between golden cliffs and frothy blue sea from Tossa to Sant Feliu (pop. over 17,000). While its smaller neighbors have become dependent on tourism, Sant Feliu still relies heavily on its cork and boat-building industries.

Traces of Sant Feliu's 1000-year history have been slowly obliterated by successive invaders. The **Monestir** church and monastery at Pl. Monestir (take Av. de Juli Garreta from the beach) is an architectural potpourri patched together from the remains of various buildings, including the **Torre de Fum,** which stands over Visigothic and Roman walls. The **Museu d'Història** stands to the right of the monastery walls. (Open Mon.-Sat. 11am-2pm and 6-9pm; Oct.-May Sat. 11am-2pm and 5-8pm, Sun. 11am-2pm. Admission 100ptas, students and retirees free.)

If you've come for Sant Feliu's three beaches, stake out your grain of sand by 11am. It's a 20-min. walk to the **Platja de Sant Pol.** Green **Viñolas** shuttle beachgoers from P. Marítim (every ½hr., 80ptas). Without any commercial docking, the cove has unmediated access to the sea. Next to Sant Pol, a 2km path scampers across the rocky hills, past picturesque coves and lagoons to **La Conca,** another popular beach.

In summer, Sant Feliuians dance *sardanas,* the Catalan folk dance, one bl. from the beach in Pl. Espanya (July-Sept. Fri. 10:30pm). Throughout July and August, classical music fills Sant Feliu's municipal theater in Pl. Monestir for the **Festival Internacional de Música de la Porta Ferrada,** the oldest in Cataluña.

Orientation and Practical Information Buses arrive at the Sarfa **bus station** on Ctra. Girona. If entering Feliu by sea, you'll disembark mid-beach in front of **Passeig del Mar,** a tree-lined waterfront promenade and pedestrian path. **Rambla D'Antoni Vidal,** between the two arrival points, connects the pedestrian street to **Placeta de Sant Joan.** From the beach, take a left onto Pg. del Mar, then a right onto Rambla D'Antoni Vidal, following it to the semicircular *placeta.* A right again at the sign for Girona leads to Ctra. Girona and the bus station (3 bl.).

The **tourist office** (English spoken) is on Pl. Monestir, 54 (tel. 82 00 51). From the beach, take a left on Pg. del Mar and a right on Av. Juli Garreta to the *plaça.* (Open Mon.-Fri. 8am-2pm and 4-8pm, Sat. 9am-1pm and 4-8pm; July-Sept. also Sun. 9am-1pm; Oct.-May Mon.-Sat. 9am-3pm.) The **post office** is on Ctra. Girona, 15 (tel. 32 11 60; open Mon.-Fri. 8am-3pm, Sat. 9am-1pm). **Telegrams** may be sent from the post office during the same hours (tel. 32 06 78). **Telephones** are located at Rambla Antoni Vidal, 44. (Open Mon.-Sat. 10am-1pm and 5-8:30pm; July-Aug. also Sun. 10am-1pm and 6-8pm.) The **telephone code** is 972. The **municipal police,** C. Callao, s/n (tel. 32 42 11), are on the outskirts of town; from Pl. Monestir head past the theater and across the parking lot on Ronda Martirs.

Sarfa, Ctra. Girona, 35 (tel. 32 11 87), runs **buses** to: Girona (9-10 per day, 1½hr., 640ptas, Sat.-Sun. 735ptas); Palafrugell, on Girona line (9-10 per day, 45min., 215ptas, Sat.-Sun. 245ptas); and Barcelona (6-9 per day, 2hr., 1075ptas, Sat.-Sun. 1220ptas). **Teisa,** Pl. Monestir, has no office, so buy your tickets on the bus. To see a schedule, take two rights out of the tourist office and look through the grate on the left (or call Girona's office at tel. 20 02 75). Teisa runs buses to: Girona (13 per day, 45min., 355ptas, Sat.-Sun. 8 per day, 405ptas; Sept.-June Mon.-Fri. 10 per day). **Cruceros ferries** (tel. 32 00 26) have a stand on the beach and sail south to: Tossa (4 per day, 45min., round-trip 950ptas); Lloret (1¼hr., round-trip 1150ptas); and Blanes (1¾hr., round-trip 1300ptas). One-way fares are substantially more than half the round-trip price.

Accommodations and Food Many hotel owners discount prices for stays of five days or more. Reservations are suggested for July and August. Two bl. from the beach and three from the Ramblas is **Pensión Geis,** C. Especieros, 27 (tel. 32 06 79). Spotless rooms have full baths. Restaurant downstairs. (1700ptas per person. Sept.-June 1400ptas.) **Habitaciones El Gas Vell** is on C. Sta. Magdalena, 29 (tel. 32

10 24); ring doorbell before Coca-Cola sign. Spartan rooms off spacious hallways in a working-class neighborhood 15min. from the beach. (1300ptas per person.) For more chic and less economical accommodations, try **Hostal Zürich,** Av. Juli Garreta, 43-45 (tel. 32 10 54). English spoken. (Singles 2500ptas. Doubles 4400ptas, with bath 5800ptas. Breakfast included.) The **market** is in Pl. Mercat, the town's main square (Mon.-Sat. 8am-2pm). Many restaurants near the beach serve *bocadillos* at middling to outlandish prices. **Nou Casino La Costancia,** Rambla Portalet, 2 (tel. 32 10 92), is a striking neo-Mudejar café-bar and casino, replete with spires and balconies. Beers start at 125ptas, coffee 80ptas. (Open 8am-1am; Oct.-May 9am-midnight. Closed one month in winter.)

■■■ PALAFRUGELL

The town of Palafrugell (pop. 17,000) nestles in a fertile valley between the Gavorres Range and the Coastal Begur Massif, 40km east of Girona. Around it stretch fields of golden wheat dotted with hamlets—but beach towns **Calella de Palafrugell, Llafranc,** and **Tamariu,** 3km away, monopolize all attention in this area. With sparkling sands and rocky outcroppings, they attract thousands of affluent European tourists every summer. To vacation like the European aristocracy without the expense, stay in Palafrugell and sojourn regularly to the coast. Inexpensive accommodations, a friendly atmosphere, and beautiful streets and plazas make it an ideal base for forays into the area. Minuscule Tamariu is isolated from the other two beach towns, and is thus likely to be less crowded. Calella is the largest and liveliest of the three, and is connected to Llafranc by one of several **Caminos de Ronda,** a series of small stone footpaths that allow one to explore the coast and can lead to gorgeous sights.

ORIENTATION AND PRACTICAL INFORMATION

Most visitors arrive at Palafrugell by bus from Girona, Sant Feliu, Barcelona, and Figueras (via L'Escala). **Carrer Torres i Jonama** runs past the Sarfa **bus station,** from whose doors you should turn right and walk until you reach **Carrer de Pi i Margall.** Turn right and walk past the **Guardia Civil** and the **market** until you hit **Plaça Nova,** the hangout of the town's pensioners and pigeons.

From the Palafrugell Sarfa station, buses frequently (4-23 per day) dash the paltry 3km to Llafranc and Calella. They leapfrog Llafranc to stop in Calella first, turning around to catch Llafranc on the way back to Palafrugell. There are multiple stops in Calella—watch for the inflatable beach balls to know when to get off. Bus service to Tamariu, also with Sarfa, is far less frequent (3-4 per day). Other options are mopeds and mountain bikes, or a pleasant, if time-consuming, walk through the countryside (45min.-1hr. to each of the coastal towns).

Tourist Office: C. Carrilet, 2 (tel. 30 02 28). From the bus station take a left on C. Torres i Jonama, left again at the traffic circle, and walk about 200 yards. English-speaking staff inundates weary, bewildered travelers with fantastic maps and brochures, including the indispensable *Guía Municipal* and an enlightening Catalan dictionary. (Open Mon.-Sat. 10am-1pm and 5-8pm, Sun. 10am-1pm; Oct.-May Mon.-Sat. 10am-1pm and 5-7pm.) Branches with the same summer hours are located in **Llafranc,** C. Roger de Llúria (tel. 30 50 08); **Calella,** Les Voltes, 4 (tel. 61 44 75); and **Tamariu,** C. Riera (tel. 30 50 07).

Post Office: C. Torres i Jonama, 16 (tel. 30 06 07). Open for stamps, **telegrams,** and Lista de Correos Mon.-Fri. 8am-3pm. **Postal Code:** 17200.

Telephones: Pl. Camp. d'en Prats, at the end of C. Sant Sebastià, next to the bar in the middle of the *plaça.* Open daily 9am-10pm, Sept.-June 10am-1pm and 5-9pm. **Telefono Fax,** Pi i Margall 29 (tel./fax 61 19 08). **Telephone Code:** 972.

Buses: Sarfa, C. Torres i Jonama, 67-79 (tel. 30 06 23). To: Calella and Llafranc (4-23 per day, 90ptas); Tamariu (3-4 per day, 90ptas); Girona (10-16 per day, 1hr., 425ptas, Sat.-Sun. 480ptas); Sant Feliu (7-14 per day, 45min., 215ptas, Sat.-Sun. 245ptas); Barcelona (4-9 per day, 2hr., 1265ptas, Sat.-Sun 1440ptas); Figueras (2-4 per day, 1½hr., 635ptas, Sat.-Sun. 725ptas); and L'Escola (take the Figueras bus, 45min., 350ptas, Sat.-Sun. 400ptas).

Taxis: Ràdio Taxi, 24-hr. service (tel. 61 00 00) throughout the area.

Mountain Bike and Moped Rental: El Pedal, C. Tarrús, Galerías Pirroig #4, in Calella. Mountain bikes 700ptas for 2hr., 100ptas each additional hr. Scooters 3000ptas for 2hr., 500ptas each additional hr.

English Bookstore: None really, but check **Llibreria Mediterrànea,** Tarongeta, 24 (tel. 30 04 78), off Pi i Margall.

Laundromat: C. Constancia, 16 (tel. 30 28 63), off C. La Caritat. 6½kilos 1425ptas, 10kilos 1825ptas. Open Mon.-Fri. 9am-1pm and 4-8:30pm, Sat. 9am-1pm.

Medical services: Red Cross, C. Ample, 1. Call 30 19 09 for **ambulance.** The **ambulatorio,** Av. Josep Pla (tel. 30 48 16), provides more general medical care.

Municipal police: Av. Josep Pla and C. Cervantes (tel. 61 31 01). Call them for **24-hr. pharmacy.** One of two places on the Costa Brava with an *oficina de atención extranjera* (office for assistance to foreigners), the answer to the penniless, documentless, or clueless tourist's prayers. In an **emergency** dial 092.

ACCOMMODATIONS AND CAMPING

While even one-star Costa Brava *hostales* cheerfully relieve visitors of 5000-6000ptas for a high-season double, Palafrugell's clean, caring, and largely family-run operations are more reasonable, as are some of the nearby campsites.

Fonda L'Estrella, C. Quatres Cases, 13-17 (tel. 30 00 05), under the pink sign at the corner of C. La Caritat, off C. Torres Jonama. Exterior rooms have rounded ceilings over wood-framed beds, and the brighter interior rooms border a courtyard of Moorish arches. May-Sept. 1500ptas per person. Lower winter rates. Breakfast 425ptas. Parking 200ptas.

Pensió Familiar Ramirez, C. Sant Sebastià, 29 (tel. 30 00 43), 2 bl. from and within earshot of Pl. Nova. Halls are papered in blue with printed white "paint spatters." Sparkling tiled bathrooms. 1600ptas per person. Sept.-June 1400ptas. Reservations recommended in summer.

Hostal Plaja, C. Sant Sebastià, 34 (tel. 30 05 26). Ornate arched entryway and quiet rooms. Terraces overlook a vast courtyard filled with lush, vibrant flowers. Common lounge with TV. Singles with bath 2200ptas. Doubles with bath 4200ptas. Sept.-June: 2000ptas; 3800ptas. Breakfast 450ptas. (6% tax not included.)

Camping: Camping Moby Dick, C. Costa Verde, 16 (tel. 61 43 07), on bus route off Av. Costa del Sol in Calella. Cheaper than surrounding grounds, it's a tree-filled park 5min. from the beach. Good showers. 470ptas per person and per car. Small tent 365ptas, large 480ptas. Cheaper in low season. Open April-Sept.

FOOD

Restaurants near the beach are predictably expensive—bringing your own lunch is generally a good idea. You might want to treat yourself to some local specialties, however. Palafrugell has a gastronomical penchant for unusually seasoned and textured seafood, such as delicacies octopus in onion sauce and *garoines* (sea urchin). The town **market** is held on C. Pi i Margall, off Pl. Nova (Tues.-Sun. 7am-1pm).

Supermarket: Super Stop, Torre i Jonama, 33, is a basic well-stocked supermarket. Open Mon.-Sat. 8:30am-1:30pm and 4:30-8:30pm, Sun. 8:30am-1:30pm

Restaurant Bar L'Espasa, on the beautiful seaside walk connecting Calella and Llafranc. The food quality equals the views. Seafood specialties. *Menú* 1100ptas.

Restaurant La Clau, C. Pi i Margall, 31, 2 bl. toward C. Torres i Jonama, close to Pl. Nova. A wood and stucco eatery. Watch a televised bullfight as you tear through a savory steak (675ptas). ¡Viva la bloodlust! *Bocadillos* in the 200-400pta range. Entrees 545-1450ptas. Open Tues.-Sun. 1-4pm and 8-11pm.

The Penguins, Pl. Nova, 12 (tel. 61 16 93), directly off the Pl. Nova. Outside tables are perfect for surveying the activity on Pl. Nova. Serves hot and cold *bocadillos* (250-350ptas) and, for the homesick, hamburgers with the works (375ptas). Beer 145ptas. Open Sun.-Thurs. 8am-midnight, Fri.-Sat. 8am-1am.

Forn de Pa, Torres i Jonama, 27, 30m down from Super Stop. Oven-fresh bread from 35ptas. Open Tues.-Sat. 7:30am-1pm and 5-8:30pm, Sun. 7:30am-1pm, July-Aug. open Mon. 7:30am-1pm.

SIGHTS AND ENTERTAINMENT

The tourist office provides maps of the paths and trails that criss-cross the area and join the coastal towns, including the **Rondas** (incredible climbs near the coast), as well as info on nearby scuba diving sites. From the bus stop in front of Calella's Hotel Garbí, the botanical gardens at **Castell i Jardins de Cap Roig** are a 45-min. walk. Russian Colonel Nicolas Voevodsky, after fleeing his homeland during the revolution, came to Spain and built this castle on the sea. He and his wife planted and pruned a splendid maze of paths and flower beds with their own hands. (Open dawn to dusk all year. Admission 200ptas.) The first sign for the castle points to the right at the fork of Av. Costa Daurada and C. Consolat del Mar. The castle also hosts the **Festival de Jazz de la Costa Brava** every July (ask the tourist office for detail).

On Calella's waterfront, anglers spend the first Sat. in July crooning the old sea chanties of the **Cantada d'Habaneras,** effectively scaring away most of the fish.

A 40-min. walk up the road from Llafranc, the **Iglesia-Hostería de San Sebastià** crowns the mountain of the same name (about 50m from the lighthouse) and provides views of the entire Palafrugell valley, beaches, and sea.

And what Costa Brava town would be complete without an homage to that most versatile of vegetable products, cork. Palafrugell outshines all competitors with its **Museu del Suro,** C. Tarongeta, 31, an institution devoted to the continuing study of the industrial, ecological, and cultural aspects of cork. (Tel. 30 39 98; open Tues.-Sat. 5-9pm, Sun. 10:30am-1:30pm; Sept.-June Tues.-Sat. 5-8pm, Sun. 10:30am-1:30pm. Admission 200ptas, students and retirees 100ptas.)

Palafrugell's Friday evening *passeig* ends up at the *plaça,* where young and old do the *sardana* at 10pm. Don't be afraid to join, all it takes is a little coordination and a truckload of gumption. For dancing of the more familiar sort, check out **Discoteca X qué** (pronounced *por qué*), 1km down the old road to Calella. The town's biggest party takes place July 20-22, when the dance-intensive **Festa Major** bursts into the streets. Calella's festivities take place on June 29 in honor of Sant Pere, Tamariu's on August 15, and Llafranc's on August 27-30 in honor of Santa Rosa.

■ NEAR PALAFRUGELL

EMPÚRIES

In the 7th century BC, Greek traders landed on a small island on the northeast Iberian coast. As the settlement grew it moved to the mainland and became the prosperous colony of Emporion ("marketplace"), falling into Roman hands four centuries later when Scipio moved in to try to divert Hannibal's march away from Rome. Remnants of both Greek and Roman cities, as well as a Visigothic early Christian basilica, today form the ruins of **Empúries,** a 40-hectare site. Excavation of the ruins continues, recently fueled by the 1992 Olympic Games whose torch formally entered Spain through the ancient Greek port. Small but rich **Museu Monogràfic d'Empúries** (tel. 77 02 08) showcases a large collection of ceramics, artifacts, and weirdly complex doorlocks. Plaques throughout the ruins indicate the ancient urban plan without marring the overall effect of fountains, mosaics, and columns set against a backdrop of cypress trees and the Mediterranean Sea. (Grounds and museum open Mon.-Sun. 10am-7pm; Oct.-May Tues.-Sun. 10am-5pm. Admission 400ptas, students free.)

Only half a km to the north of the ruins starts the 47 sq. km **Parc Natural dels Aiguarnolls de l'Empordà,** a protected habitat with miles of marshland, lakes, and animal and plant species found only in this area (the unhappily named *fartet* fish, for example). Bird-watchers should gaze upwards mornings and early evenings from March to May and August to October. For more information, contact **El Cortalet information center** (tel. 25 42 22; fax 45 44 74).

Orientation and Practical Information Most travelers arriving in Empúries from Palafrugell, Figueras, Girona, and Barcelona, disembark at the **Sarfa bus stop** on **Avinguda Ave María**. The **tourist office,** about 150m up the road at **Plaça les Escoles,** 1 (tel. 77 06 03; fax 10 33 85), provides a decent map, information on tourist sites, an accommodations list, and even a fax service. (Open Mon.-Sat. 8:30am-8:30pm, Sun. 9:30am-1:30pm; Oct.-June Mon.-Wed. and Fri.-Sat. 10am-1pm and 4-7pm, Thurs. 10am-1pm.) The **post office** is on Pl. Rei Marti, s/n (tel. 77 16 51; open Mon.-Fri. 8am-1pm, Sat. 9am-1pm). The **postal code** is 17130. Near the waterfront on Av. Ave María is a **Telefónica.** (Open Mon.-Sat. 10am-1pm and 5-9pm, Sun. 10am-2pm and 6-9pm.) The **telephone code** is 972. For an **ambulance,** call 10 81 00. The **municipal police,** C. Pintor Joan Massanet, 24, take calls at 10 81 00. The HI Hostel rents **mountain bikes** (400ptas per hr., 1200ptas per half-day, 1700ptas per day; groups greater than nine 700ptas per half-day, 1400ptas per day).

Sarfa buses (tel. 77 01 29) depart from Av. Ave María, s/n, near the tourist office to: Figueras (3-4 per day, 45min., 350ptas, Sat.-Sun. 400ptas); Palafrugell (3-5 per day, 45min., 290ptas, Sat.-Sun. 330ptas); Girona (2 per workday, 1½hr., 445ptas, Sat.-Sun. 505ptas).

Accommodations and Food Finding a room in L'Escala is taxing; many *pensiones* require that their summer guests pay full board. The **HI youth hostel,** Les Coves, 41 (tel. 77 12 00), is set 100m from the ruins in a grove of trees. Facing the tourist office, follow the road on the right toward the coast and the Olympic monument; from there follow signs to **Alberg De Juventut.** Lunch and dinner offered. Often filled with groups mid-June to Aug. (Members only. Rates vary by season and age. High season: under 25 1300ptas per person including breakfast. Call Barcelona youth office (tel. 83 83 83) for reservations one month in advance.) **Hostal Poch,** C. Gràcia, 10 (tel. 77 00 92), is indeed posh, with antique furniture styles and ceramic tiles. (Doubles 3700ptas; low-season 3500ptas. Visa, MC accepted.) **Hostal Mediterrá,** C. Riera, 24 (tel. 77 00 28), is one of those barren but clean slumberamas with baths in many rooms and a dining area downstairs. (Singles 1625ptas, with bath 2025ptas. Doubles 3200ptas, with bath 4000ptas. Sept.-June: 1250ptas; 1625ptas; 2500ptas; 3075ptas.) **Town market** is held daily from 7:30am-1:30pm in **Plaça Victor Català,** or fill your basket at supermarket **Maxor,** Pl. Les Escoles. (Mon.-Fri. 8:30am-1pm and 5-8:15pm, Sat. 9am-1:15pm and 5-8:30pm, Sun 9am-1:15pm. MC, Visa accepted.) Nostalgic **Restaurant El Gavìa,** C. Enric Serra, 16 (tel. 77 03 55), 2 bl. up from the *platja,* combines historical pictures on the wall of L'Escala and tuneful 40s Spanish swing (seafood specialties, *paella* 850ptas, *menú* 950ptas).

L'ESCALA

Thanks to archeological sites and extensive beaches, which are rare in Costa Brava, the former fishing village of **L'Escala** has boomed into a fairly commercialized, if not overly tacky tourist town. Large groups of students join Spanish and other European families, usually staying for at least a night to enjoy the rocks and sand. Daytrips (especially from Figueras and Palafrugell) can be a good option.

■■■ FIGUERAS(FIGUERES)

Tourists once ignored the rather unwelcoming, beachless sprawl of Figueras, 36km north of Girona. But since the egomaniacal Salvador Dalí built a museum for his works here in 1974, art buffs swarm to see the largest single collection of Spain's loudest Surrealist. Figueras seems ambivalent toward its newfound guests; while the city is long on museums, it is short on the enthusiastic hospitality characteristic of the Costa Brava.

ORIENTATION AND PRACTICAL INFORMATION

Roughly 20km inland from the coast, Figueras marks the center of the Costa Brava's breadbasket; just follow your nose to the earthy fragrance that envelops you as you approach the town. Otherwise, follow the RENFE or bus schedule. Either way you'll arrive at **Plaça Estacio** on the edge of town. Take a left on **Carrer Sant Llàtzer.** Walk seven bl., to **Carrer Nou,** and take a right. C. Nou leads directly to Figueras's arboreal **Rambla.** To reach the **tourist office,** walk up the Rambla and continue on **Carrer Lasauca.** Across the rather treacherous intersection with **Ronda Frial** emerges the all-important big blue "i".

Tourist Office: Pl. del Sol (tel. 50 31 55). Offers a good city map, list of accommodations, and ranking of restaurants. Open Mon.-Sat. 8:30am-8pm; Oct.-June 20 Mon.-Fri. 8:30am-3pm; from Easter on also Mon.-Fri. 4:30-8pm, Sat. 9am-1pm. During the summer use the **branch office,** in the bus station across the park from the train station. Open Mon.-Sat. 9:30am-1pm and 4:15-7pm.

Post Office: Pl. del Sol (tel. 50 54 31). Open Mon.-Sat. 8am-2pm. **Postal Code:** 17600.

Telephones: Pl. del Sol, open Mon.-Sat. 9am-1:30pm and 4:30-9pm. **Telephone Code:** 972.

RENFE trains (tel. 20 70 93) make for: Girona (24 per day including 2 *talgos,* 25min.-1hr., 260ptas); Portbou (19 per day including 2 *talgos,* ½hr., 185ptas); and Barcelona (24 per day, 1½-2hr., 850ptas; less Sat.-Sun. and low-season).

Buses: All lines leave from the Estació Autobuses at Pl. Estació. **Sarfa** (tel. 67 42 98) to: Cadaqués (4 per day, Sept.-June 2-3 per day, 1¼hr., 390ptas, Sat.-Sun. 440ptas); and Llansá (2-3 per day, 240ptas, Sat.-Sun. 270ptas). **Barcelona Bus** (tel. 50 50 29) to: Girona (325ptas one-way, 525ptas round-trip); and Barcelona (6 per day, Sat.-Sun. 4 per day, 1¼hr., 1200ptas one-way, 1450ptas round-trip). **Teisa** buses connect with Olot (2-3 per day, 1hr., 400ptas, Sat.-Sun. 510ptas), where there's service to Ripoll, an entrance to the Catalan Pyrenees.

Luggage Storage: at train station, large lockers 600ptas. Open 6am-10pm. Also at bus station.

Laundromat: check HI Youth Hostel.

Bike Rentals: HI Youth Hostel (400ptas per hr., 1200ptas per half-day, 1700ptas per day).

Emergencies: Red Cross, Albeut Cotó, 1 (tel. 50 17 99 or 50 56 01). The **local police** (tel. 51 01 11) are at Ronda Final, 4, 100m from the tourist office; the **emergency** number for the **municipal police** is 092.

ACCOMMODATIONS AND FOOD

Finding a place to sleep can be a surreal experience. Though the town is reorganizing to accommodate the influx of tourists, Figueras is still surprisingly lacking in affordable hotels and *pensiones*. Aside from the ones listed, some lie on **Carrer del Rec Arnau,** though they involve some trekking. Don't stay at the notoriously unsafe Municipal Park, however; *Let's Go* has been made aware of assaults there. Tourist-oriented restaurants near **Plaçà del Sol** serve expensive yet bland meals. Better ones reside a few minutes away in the streets surrounding the Rambla. The **mercado** opens Tues., Thurs., and Sat. 7am-1pm at Pl. de la Palmera and nearby Pl. del Grano.

HI Youth Hostel, C. Anicet de Pagés, 2 (tel. 50 12 13; public phone 50 41 01; fax 67 38 08), a bit of a hike from the train and bus stations. Follow C. Sant Llàtzer past the park on the left, turn right on Ronda de Barcelona, turn left into the tourist office parking lot, and finally take a left on C. Poeta Marquinà. Kitchen facilities and friendly hosts. Hot showers and French TV. Lock-in midnight (opens for 10min. at 1, 2, 3, and 4am). Lockout—and they mean it—10am-4pm, Sat.-Sun. 10am-5pm. Members only. Rates vary by age and season. Under 25 1300ptas. Sheets 350ptas. Breakfast included. Reserve 1 month in advance in July and Aug. through the Barcelona office at (93) 402 11 66 or call the hostel 2-3 days prior to arrival.

Pensión Mallol, C. Pep Ventura, 9 (tel. 50 22 83). Follow the Rambla toward the tourist office, leave it to the right on Castell, and take the second left. Despite the unfortunate sickly green motif, this *pensión* offers spacious rooms with sinks, four bl. from the Dalí Museum on the way to the tourist office. Single 1700ptas. Doubles 2950. Low-season rates lower.

Supermarket: MAXOR, Pl. del Sol 6. Open Mon.-Sat. 9am-1pm and 4-8pm. Visa, MC accepted.

Restaurante La Torrada, La Rosa, 6 (tel. 50 95 66). Left off the Rambla on C. Vilatant; then take second right. A meat lover's haven in the Costa Brava. Steak and fries 500ptas. Great *torradas* (toasted bread with toppings). A number of vegetarian options on the appetizer list. Open 9am-11pm.

La Barretina, Lasauca, 13 (tel. 67 34 25). Right off the Rambla, this restaurant is named after the traditional Catalan cap. Serves *bocadillos* of various sizes (150-600ptas) and a variety of meat, chicken, and fish entrees (350-1250ptas).

SIGHTS AND ENTERTAINMENT

Surrealist scandal-monger Salvador Dalí was inspired by dreams and the new theories of Sigmund Freud—or so he claimed. Though perpetually challenged by members of the surrealist movement, he remains its most popular exponent, and the cult of his personality is eternalized here. Transformed from old municipal theater into Surrealist funhouse, the **Teatre-Museu Dalí** (tel. 51 17 96; fax 50 16 66) in Pl. Gala i S. Dalí, parades the artist's capricious projects: erotically nightmarish drawings, extra-terrestrial landscapes, and even a personal rock collection. Probably nowhere else in the conscious world can you walk up a set of stairs to stand underneath a camel, look through a peephole, and see a room with a giant nose on the floor. And Dalí is not the only featured act—**Evarist Vallés's** thing for nails really digs. Follow C. Sant Llàtzer (to the train station) for six bl., turn right on C. Nou and follow it to its end at the Rambla. Go diagonally to the right and take C. Girona, which goes past Pl. Ajuntament and becomes C. Jonquera. A flight of steps by a Dalí statue on the left leads to the museum. (Open 9am-7:15pm; Oct.-June 10:30am-5:15pm. Admission 900ptas, students and seniors 700ptas; Oct.-June 700ptas, 500ptas. Closed Mon.) From mid-July to mid-September, avoid the crowds (5000 visitors a day) and get a few extra spooky peeks during night hours (10pm-12:30am, 1200ptas, 500 person maximum).

Museu de l'Empordà, Rambla, 1 (tel. 50 28 00), explores local history with an impressive collection of amphoras, urns, and a pack rat-like assortment of archeological finds and other whatzits, including paintings from the 19th-century Catalan *Renaixença.* (Open Tues.-Sun. 11:30am-1:30pm and 3-7pm; Oct.-June Tues. 11am-1pm and 3:30-7pm., Sat. 11am-3pm and 4:30-8pm. Free.)

If Dalí's playfulness doesn't sate you (or suit you), you can reclaim your childhood at the **Museu de Joguetes,** Rambla, 10 (tel. 50 45 85), an historical toy collection. (Open Mon.-Sat. 10am-12:30pm and 4-5:30pm, Sun. 11am-1:30pm and 5-7:30pm. Oct.-June. closed Tues. Admission 350ptas, students and groups 250ptas, children under 12 150ptas.)

The nearest body of water is one of the municipal **swimming pools,** C. Cusi i Fortunet (tel. 50 90 01 or 50 93 39), just behind the city park in the northeastern quarter of Figueras, across town from the train and bus station. (Outdoor Olympic-sized pool open June 20-Sept. 20 Mon.-Sat. 10am-8pm. Admission 350ptas, under 14 250ptas. Indoor pool one bl. away open year-round Mon.-Fri. 7am-11pm, Sun. 9am-2pm. Admission 300ptas. Special deals for hostelites.)

In September, Figueras hosts classical and jazz music at the **Festival Internacional de Música de l'Empordà.** (Call Joventuts Musicals at 50 01 17 for info and tickets or ask for brochure at the tourist office.) In the first week of May, the **Fires i Festes de la Santa Creu** offers cultural events and art and technology exhibitions. Merrymaking at the **Festa de Sant Pere,** held June 28-29, honors the town's patron saint.

■ NEAR FIGUERAS

CADAQUÉS

This strikingly beautiful array of whitewashed houses around a small bay has attracted artists, writers, and musicians since Dalí built his summer house here in the 1930s. To preserve its aesthetic, Cadaqués has just said no to condos, huge hotels, and trains. A largely affluent, pseudo-bohemian crowd of property owners and renters shares the pebbly beaches with day-trippers from all walks of life.

The **Museu Municipal d'Art** on C. Monturiol, currently closed for repairs, is due to re-open by 1995. Ask for information at the tourist office about this collection of local and Dalí-esque art. The **Museu Perrot-Moore,** C. Vigilant, 1 (tel. 25 82 31), near the center of town, hoards a load of odd Dalí memorabilia, as well as some of Pablo Picasso's ephemera, including part of his sketchbook for the monumental *Guernica.* (Open April-Oct. Mon.-Sat. 10:30am-1:30pm and 4-8pm, Sun. 11am-2pm.) For either museum follow the signs from the mapboard on Pl. Frederic Rahola; otherwise, head toward the bay, hang a right on the waterfront road and another on C. Vigilant. For Dalí's house, stay on the waterfront road past the bars and restaurants until C. Miranda appears on the left. Follow this road out of town and take a right onto Av. Salvador Dalí. The house is being renovated to open as a museum in the summer of 1995.

The **Festival Internacional de Música** sponsors 10 concerts in late July and early August, two given by students. (Tel. 25 83 15. Tickets around 1000ptas.) Throughout the summer, locals dance *sardanas* outdoors (Sun. 4pm) and occasionally hip-hop to live rock. Those determined to catch some rays can try the **Platja Gran,** near the town center, or, even better, **Sa Concha,** a 5-min. walk to the south of town.

Practical Information The bus to Cadaqués halts at a shack outside of town, where an excellent guidebook with detailed maps and a wealth of information (including a Catalan glossary) sells for 300ptas. From the bus station, walk downhill toward the left along Av. Caritat Serinyana until the waterfront **Plaça Frederic Rahola.** There, a signboard map with indexed services and accommodations will orient you. The **tourist office,** C. Cotxe, 2 (tel. 25 83 15), off Pl. Frederic Rahola opposite the *passeig,* informs on local events and hands out a less than ideal map. (Open Mon.-Sat. 10am-1pm and 4-9pm, Sun. 10am-1pm; winter Mon.-Sat. 10am-1pm and 4-8pm, Sun. 10:30am-12:30pm.) The **post office** is on Av. Rievasa, in front of Disco Paradis; it has no phone. (Open Mon.-Sat. 9am-1pm.) The town's **postal code** is 17488. **Telephone** cabins are on the beachwalk in Pl. Frederic Rahola; the **telephone code** is 972. **Bikes and in-line skates** can be rented at **Espacro** at C. Fort Vellay, 2 (tel. 25 90 52), off Av. Caritat. (Open daily 9am-9pm. Mountain bikes 500ptas per hr., 2500ptas per day, 8500ptas per week. In-line skates 400ptas per hr., 2000ptas per day.) The **laundromat** tel. is 25 84 89. In an **emergency,** contact the **local police** (tel. 25 81 94) on Pl. Frederic Rahola beside the promenade. For **medical assistance,** call 25 80 07.

Sarfa buses (tel. 25 87 13) run to: Figueras (2-5 per day, 1¼hr., 390ptas, Sat.-Sun. 440ptas); and Barcelona (2-4 per day, 1705ptas, Sat.-Sun. 1940ptas). Buses drop passengers at the junction of Ctra. Port Lligat and Pg. Caritat Serinyana; the latter leads to the town center.

Accommodations and Food Sleep is dear in Cadaqués because of the dearth of budget accommodations. Cadaqués is a comfortable daytrip from Figueras, and due to frequent RENFE service between Figueras and Girona, a possible excursion from there as well. Rooms are nearly always available except on major Catalan weekend holidays. **Hotel Ubaldo,** C. Unió, 13 (tel. 25 83 24), has brightly decorated doubles (4800ptas, 5500ptas with bath; Sept.-June rates lower; breakfast 450ptas). Near the water is **Hostal Marina,** C. Riera de Sant Vicenç, 3 (tel. 25 81 99), directly ahead as you face the mapboard on Pl. Frederic Rohola. Its rooms are clean, some even balconied. (Singles 2200ptas, with bath 3100ptas. Doubles 3800ptas, with bath 5800ptas; low-season lower rates. Breakfast 450ptas.) **Camping Cadaqués,** Ctra. Portlligat, 17 (tel. 25 81 26), is on the left on the way to Dalí's house from town; or ask the bus driver to let you off near it before you arrive in town. The grounds, only ½km from the beach, have a supermarket, pool (July-Aug.), and warm showers (100ptas). (Open March 15-Sept. 30 450ptas per person, 700-1800ptas per tent.) Their "no frills" bungalows offer budget beds for the tent-deprived. (Doubles 2300ptas. Triples 3000ptas. Quads 3500ptas. Two-day minimum.) **Bar La Cala,** partly downhill on C. Caritat Serinyana, serves behemoth *bocadillos* of all types (200-450ptas), as well as salads and seafood dishes.

LLANSÁ

9km south of the French border, **Llansá** (pop. 3700) is the northernmost resort of magnitude on the Costa Brava, with many beaches and coves and a smattering of minor historical sights. The main beach, **Platja del Port,** opens onto a protected harbor. The town center lies in the opposite direction; look for the **església** and the 14th-century **Torre de Llansá** to find the central **plaça.** The town's annual festival takes place on the outskirts, in the chapel of the 11th-century Romanesque hermitage **Sant Silvestre de Valleta i del Terrer.** To get there from town, take a right from the train station onto Ctra. Bisbal, cross the river on a bridge opposite the soccer field, and continue on the path up the hill. Near the top take the left fork for the hermitage (1hr.).

From the bus and train stations, cross the highway and bridge and continue on Av. Europa until it forks: right leads into town, left to the port. For the harbor and beaches, follow the curve to the left and walk about 1km, watching for signs for the port. The first street you'll encounter in the town center is C. Rafael Estela. Follow it to the **telephones** (open 9:30am-1:30pm and 4:30-9:30pm) and to **Plaça Major.** A second phone office with similar hours is at the port parking lot to the right of the beach.

The English-speaking staff in the **tourist office,** Av. Europa, 37 (tel. 38 08 55; fax 38 12 58), on the road to the port, distributes a detailed but largely superfluous map; you don't need to be Lewis and Clark to get your bearings in this little hamlet. (Open daily 9:30am-9:30pm; June and Sept. 10am-1pm and 4:30-7:30pm; Oct.-May Mon., Wed., Fri. 10am-1pm and 5-7pm. Closed Sun. Sept.-June.) The **post office** is in the municipal building on C. la Selva, 17. (Tel. 38 12 68; open Mon.-Fri. 8am-3pm, Sat. 8am-2pm.) The town's **postal code** is 17490. The **Red Cross** is at Platja Crifeu, s/n (tel. 38 08 31). The **local police** take calls at 38 13 13. The **Guardia Civil** is installed at Pl. Major (tel. 38 01 22).

Habitaciones Can Pau, C. Puig d'Esquer, 4 (tel. 38 02 70), was built laboriously on weekends by the owner and his son for 10 years; comfortable and clean, it's got a rooftop view. To get there take the second left as you enter town, C. Cabrafiqa, for three bl., then turn left on C. Deciana; almost immediately, turn right on C. Puig d'Esquer. (1300ptas per person in groups of two or more. Singles 1700ptas. IVA not included.) **Hostal Beri,** C. Creu, s/n (tel. 38 01 98), has magnificent, clean rooms, winter heating, and bathrooms to get lost in. You can practice sweeping entrances on the wide tile staircase. From Pl. Major, bear right and follow C. Nicolás Salmerón to the edge of town. At the crossroads take a sharp left till the sign comes into view. (Singles with bath 2000-2500ptas. Doubles with bath 4000-4600ptas. Prices vary by season. Breakfast 500ptas.)

Llansá's waterfront eateries are generally overpriced, although *bocadillos* and reasonably priced *menús* can be found, both there and in town. Stock up your picnic basket at **Valvi Supermercats,** a large supermarket on Av. Europa, on the right as you head toward the beach. (Open 9am-1:30pm and 4:30-8:30pm, Sun. 9am-1:30pm.) **Pizzeria Le Provençal,** Paseo Marítimo, 1 (tel. 38 06 40), at the corner of C. Castellar, has creatively seafood-laden pizzas (650-850ptas).

RENFE trains (tel. 38 02 55) run to and from: Portbou (16 per day, 15min., 115ptas); Figueras (18 per day, 20-30min., 125ptas); Girona (18 per day, 1hr.,

315ptas); and Barcelona (18 per day, 1½hr., 955ptas). **Sarfa** (tel. 12 06 76) run 2-6 **buses** per day to Port de la Selva (20min., 140ptas, Sat.-Sun. 175ptas).

SANT PERE DE RODA

The glorious ruins of the monastery **Sant Pere de Roda** are 9km south of Llansá on the coast. On a clear day you can easily see Portbou to the north and Cadaqués to the south from the Benedictine monastery, built in the 10th and 11th centuries. Getting there can be something less than half the fun. The tourist office at Llansá organizes excursions every Tuesday during July and August (750ptas)—anybody who finds this schedule inconvenient and lacks a car should be prepared for some serious climbing. Committed hikers can consider trekking from Llansá (a strenuous 3-hr. hike with splendid vistas along the way). For the rest, take the Sarfa bus from Llansá to Port de la Selva and ask to be dropped off on the road to the monastery. From there, make the far less arduous 1½-hr. climb. (Monastery open Tues.-Sun. 10am-7pm; Oct.-May 10am-1:30pm and 3-5:30pm. Admission 200ptas.)

PORTBOU

Fifteen km north of Llansá, **Portbou** (pop. 1800) suffered a sea-change about a hundred years ago when the Barcelona-Cerbère railroad opened. The tentacles of the sprawling train station all but choked the life and character out of Portbou. The recent arrival of European economic unity has induced the latest identity crisis, rendering customs jobs obsolete. Now this confused pitstop for fly-by-day tourists on their way somewhere else is trying to sell itself as a beach resort town. To its credit, Portbou has managed to preserve its pleasant, rock-framed small **beach.** To get to the water, head out the lower level of the train station down tree-lined C. Mercat and take the first left past the post office. **Plaça Lluis Companys** is near the water.

The **tourist office** on the water is well-stocked. (Open Mon.-Sat. 10am-1pm and 5-8pm.) The **post office** is at Pg. Enric Granades, 10 (tel. 39 01 75). The **postal code** is 17497. The **police** (tel. 39 02 84) and the **health center** are housed in the **Ayuntamiento** at the end of Pg. Sardanes, on the end of the beach.

Hostal Juventus, Av. Barcelona, 3 (tel. 39 02 41), stands near the waves two bl. from the train station and left on Av. Barcelona. The outer rooms just manage views of the nearby bay and bluffs. The same owners run a *croissanterie* downstairs with a panoply of baked goods in the morning. (Singles 1500ptas. Doubles 2800ptas. Triples 3600ptas. Low-season rates less.) **Hostal Plaza,** C. Mercat, 15 (tel. 39 00 24), is on the left, half a block from the train station. The rooms and facilities are clean. (Doubles 2650ptas, with shower 3340ptas. Open April-Sept. Call to reserve July-Aug.) For a restorative drink, try one of many **cafés** lining Pg. Marítim—ask for directions at the tourist office or just turn to the right.

RENFE trains go to Barcelona via every town with a train station in Western Cataluña, including Figueras (19 per day, ½hr., 185ptas). At the two stops prior to Portbou are better beaches, if fewer trains, than in town.

CATALAN PYRENEES

Around the turn of the last millennium, a number of virtually independent counts ruled the mountains of upland Cataluña. By and large, the old counties of Pallars, Urgell, and Cerdanya remain in idyllic isolation. Sheep and cows outnumber people here, wandering unattended through the rocky outcrops and snow-covered crags that cut through the steep green slopes. Limited bus service and circuitous roads prevent easy access to this section of the Pyrenees (230km long), but the splendor of Parc d'Aigüestortes, filled with clear glacial lakes and waterfalls, renders even the most arduous journey worthwhile.

Besides Catalan and Spanish, inhabitants of the ancient Catalan villages often speak French, while people in the Val d'Aran (the westernmost area of the Catalan

Pyrenees) speak Aranese, a variant of the Gascon spoken in the Comminge region of France. French influence permeates the food as well; the pâtés, civets, and crepes (*Zut alors!*) give way to local hearty dishes such as *trinxat amb rosa* (creamed spinach and salt pork) in areas farther from the French border.

Romanesque castles, churches, and monasteries fill the old medieval counties. This style emerged after the breakup of the Carolingian Empire in the latter part of the 10th century and dominated Europe until the end of the 13th century. Romanesque architecture mixed Roman building traditions (such as the vaulted roofs) with newer techniques (such as massive masonry to uphold the barrel vault) necessary for edifices suitable for an expanding society. The buildings are famous for the arched doors and windows, and are characterized by modest (as compared to Gothic) heights. Benedictine monks and the Knights Templar hired builders to spread Romanesque influence far and wide; it is the first truly pan-European architectural style.

For each Catalan *comarca,* the Department of Commerce and Tourism distributes pamphlets with information on local winter sports or areas of scenic grandeur. Skiers will find the English-language guide *Snow in Catalonia* (free at tourist offices) especially useful. Cyclists should ask for *Valles Superiores del Segre/Ariège,* which covers the Alt Urgell, Cerdanya, and the Val de Ribas. Editorial Alpina publishes a series of indispensable topographical maps bound in red booklets.

For those coming from the east, Ripoll is the point of entry to the area, while those coming from the west and south enter through Lérida (Lleida). From Girona or the Costa Brava you can connect to Ripoll by bus; RENFE runs from Barcelona through Ripoll and ski resort Núria to Puigcerdà, where buses continue to La Seu d'Urgell. Lérida, too, is connected by bus to La Seu d'Urgell and by train to Barcelona, and provides the only public transportation (bus) to the lakes and trails of the Parc Nacional d'Aigüestortes i Estany de Sant Maurici.

■■■ RIPOLL

The ear-popping road up to Ripoll passes by sleepy hamlets and pastoral villages and over mountain streams running undisturbed through the valleys. It is surprising, then, when around the bend emerges the relative sprawl of Ripoll with its multistory buildings. Both trains and buses stop smack dab on the border between modern Ripoll and its rustic tubers.

Almost everyone comes to Ripoll to see the 11th-century portal of the **Monestir de Santa Maria.** This archway depicts monstrous gargoyles and local animals in a 12-month calendar. These days you may need to squint and exercise some imagination; time has taken its toll on the stone. The figures of Christ and the apostles shepherding away are still decipherable. The 12th-century **claustre** inside is surprisingly well-preserved. (Church open daily 9am-1pm and 3-9pm. Free. Cloister open Tues.-Sun. 9am-1pm and 3-7pm. 50ptas.)

In the building to the left of the church, stands a second wonder atop a long spiral staircase, the **Museu-Arxiu Folklòric.** Your mere ambulatory presence sets off working scale models of old Ripollese mills, and encourages sing-alongs with a monastic choir as you read from a 16th-century songbook honoring the town's patron saint, Sant Eubaldo. Birds' eggs, toy soldiers, human bones, funny hats—it's all here. (Open Tues.-Sun. 9:30am-1:30pm and 3:30-7:30pm; winter 9:30am-1:30pm and 3:30-6:30pm. Admission 200ptas.) The monastery and museum are both in Pl. Abat Oliba, the center of town. From the train or bus station, turn left on C. Progrés and follow the road through several incarnations until it ends at the monastery.

Hobbits and fans of Antonio Gaudí enjoy the tiny **Capilla de Sant Miquel de la Roqueta,** built by the architect's disciple, Joan Rubió. The chapel is usually closed, but to inspect the outside, walk left down C. Progrés from the train station, turn right on C. d'Olot, the first light after the train station, and left on C. Industria. It's on the right.

Ripoll's **Festa Major** falls on May 11; the following Sunday, the **Festa de la Llana** (Festival of Wool) amuses the town with shearing of indignant sheep in Pl. Ajuntament. On July weekends, the **Festival de Música** brings six evenings of classical music to the cloisters. For more information, call the tourist office.

Practical Information The well-stocked **tourist office** (tel. 70 23 51) is next to the monastery on Pl. Abat Oliva. Don't bury any treasures using their map. (Open Mon.-Fri. 10am-1pm and 5-7pm, Sat. 10am-1pm; Oct.-June Mon.-Fri. 11am-1pm and 4-6pm, Sat. 11am-1pm.) The **post office** (tel. 70 07 60) is at C. Sant Bartolomeu, 6, at the corner with C. Progrés. (Open Mon.-Fri. 8am-3pm, Sat. 9am-1pm; June-Sept. closed Sat.) The **postal code** is 17500. The **telephone code** is 972. **Medical services** are administered at the Ambulatori de la Seguretat Social, C. Macià Bonaplata (tel. 70 01 59). An **ambulance** can be summoned at the **Red Cross** (tel. 70 04 71). The **municipal police** are at Pl. Ajuntament, 3 (tel. 71 44 14).

RENFE trains, Pl. Nova, 1 (tel. 70 06 44), serve Puigcerdà (6 per day, 1½hr., 290ptas) and Barcelona (11-12 per day, 2hr., 600ptas). To reach Ribas de Freser and the Cremallera to Núria, take the Puigcerdà train (125ptas). **Teisa** (tel. 20 02 75), one bl. down from RENFE, runs **buses** to Girona via Olot (6-8 per day, 2¾hr., 855ptas, Sat.-Sun. 975ptas). Buses also travel to Sant Joan de les Abadesses (7-9 per day, 20min., 115ptas, Sat.-Sun. 130ptas).

Accommodations and Food If gaping at the church portal took longer than you planned, try winter-heated **Hostal Habitacions Paula,** C. Pirineus, 6 (tel. 70 00 11), Pirineus runs off Pl. Abat Oliba; *hostal* at the corner of C. Berenguer. Some of the big rooms face the monastery, but the interior singles are more like closets than cloisters. (1300ptas per person plus tax. Visa, MC accepted.) There is camping 2km south of town at **Solana de Ter,** Ctra. Barcelona (tel. 70 10 62), in Colònia Santa Maria; follow the road from Pl. Gran, since there is no bus. (Open Dec.-Oct. 530ptas per person and per tent. 1000ptas for both tent and car.) Many eateries around the monastery's *plaça* serve scrumptious *bocadillos* and *tapas*. Try **Bar Stop** on Pl. Tomàs Raquer, 15 (tel. 70 21 16), down C. Raquer Font for *platos combinados* (650-700ptas) and a snappy art deco interior done all in primaries. Ripoll's food and clothing **market** sets up all over town Sat. 9am-1pm. Supermarket **Valvi** is on C. Mossèn Cinto Verdaguer, next to Pont D'Olot at the end of C. Bisbe Morgader. (Open Mon.-Sat. 9am-1:30pm and 5-8:30pm.)

■ NEAR RIPOLL

SANT JOAN DE LES ABADESSES

In the 9th century Comte Guifré el Pelós ("the Hairy"), an equal-opportunity patron, endowed a convent 10km away to complement Ripoll's first monastery. His daughter Emma became the first abbess for Benedictine nuns. In the 12th century the Augustinians set up here, expanding and rebuilding most of the pre-existing structures. A labyrinthine and thoroughly charming town gradually developed around it. The **Santíssim Misteri,** a seven-piece polychromatic modern sculpture, is kept in the monastery's Romanesque church. Admission to the church and cloister (200ptas) allows a visit to the **museu** (tel. 72 00 13), a showcase for richly embroidered cassocks, a gigantic mortuary cloth crafted for a bishop, and humorous 16th-century choir stall carvings. (Open daily 10am-2pm and 4-7pm; mid-March to mid-June and mid-Sept. to Oct. daily 11am-2pm and 4-6pm; Nov. to mid-March Mon.-Fri. 11am-2:30pm, Sat. and holidays 11am-2pm and 4-6pm.) The monastery may be reached by following the *rambla* to the circle at the end. At the other end of the *rambla,* and a right on the highway out of town, the untended ruins of *Sant Pol* are an unofficial picnic ground. The miniscule **tourist office,** at Rambla Comte Guifré, 5 (tel. 72 00 92), offers a guide and a map, although you really won't need either. (Open 11am-1pm and 5-7pm.) Buses connect Sant Joan de les Abadesses to Ripoll (see above).

NÚRIA

Heidi could have been set in Núria. Near the French border and some 35km north of Ripoll, these sky-scraping hills used to attract only the religious hard-core, on foot or horseback during the summer, to the **Santuario** of the Virgen Maria. Yet the installation in 1931 of a second-hand funicular, the **Cremallera** ("the zipper"), left over from the 1929 World's Fair in Barcelona, brought major changes. By 1934, a luxurious lodge had been erected at the top of the new cable ride. After the Civil War, Núria enjoyed about 20 years of fame for its international ski competitions, but because of the popularity of bigger mountains and longer slopes, the town temporarily declined. Núria has carved a new market niche for itself as a resort area with year-round, right-at-your-doorstep hiking and skiing. The Cremallera zips from the Ribas de Freser stop on the Ripoll-Puigcerdà line; the 45-min. ride scales 800m through virgin mountain faces to which stubborn sheep, goats, and pine trees cling (6-11 per day depending on season 7:20am-9:30pm, 1750ptas round-trip). If the Cremallera ride whetted your ocular appetite, relive it at your own pace by following the stone path (1½-2-hr.) to Quebradillas.

The lake near the shrine greets picnickers. Climbers prefer the 4-hr. hike to **Puigmal** (2913m). In 1988, 11 ambitious mountaineers climbed the peak on 6-ft. stilts, setting a new world record. **Pic d'Eina** is a shorter but equally strenuous hike through a stone gorge littered with yellow wildflowers.

Ten ski trails offer slopes ranging from *molt facil* (very easy) to *molt difficil* (very difficult or expert) at **Estació de la Vall de Núria.** The "white phone" for ski conditions is in Barcelona at tel. (93) 301 97 77. (Weekend lift tickets 1500ptas, weekdays 1200ptas.)

Information for the whole valley is available at tel. (972) 72 70 31. Núria is equipped with full 24-hr. medical services, including a first aid dispensary, a pharmacy and a rescue group. The **Guardia Civil** in Ribas de Freser is posted at C. Eres, 2 (tel. (972) 72 70 38).

From Núria, a modern cable line (670ptas) whisks straight to **Alberg de Joventut Pic de l'Aliga** (tel. (972) 73 00 48), the alternative being an arduous 20-min. climb (10-min. down). The modern three-story youth hostel loyally maintains Núria's training-camp atmosphere with ping-pong, volleyball, and basketball. (1300ptas per person, over 25 1925ptas. Hot showers. Breakfast included. Closed Nov.) For reservations, especially July-Aug. and (if there's snow) Jan.-March, call Barcelona office at (93) 483 83 63. **Hotel Vall de Núria** (tel. (972) 73 03 26) is the only other real building in the valley. (Singles from 3500ptas in winter and 7500ptas in summer. Doubles from 5000ptas in winter to 9500ptas in summer.) Free **camping,** with hot showers and toilets, is permitted near the hotel. Bring up a well-stocked picnic basket, as there are no markets in the valley and only a handful of eateries.

■■■ PUIGCERDÀ

There are few towns in Catalunya whose names are more difficult to pronounce and whose RENFE stations are more inconveniently placed. One and a half hours northwest of Ripoll by train, on the French border, Puigcerdà (something like Pooh-chair-DAH) commands the best vantage point from which to explore the teeny *comarca* of Cerdanya. With hiking, fishing, hunting, kayaking, and other such Conradian challenges, this is the sort of town that will help you conquer the fire in your belly. Puigcerdà sated its own thirst for glory in 1993 by entering the Guinness Book of Records with the world's longest *butifarra* (sausage), a Freudian nightmare measuring 5200 meters. Non-culinary and non-outdoor types can happily gape at the delicious view of the valley, within a stone's throw of half a dozen bars.

ORIENTATION AND PRACTICAL INFORMATION

Puigcerdà's center squats squarely on top of a hill. It is roughly boxed in by C. Alfons I to the south, the **Passeig 10 d'Abril** to the east, three *plaças* (Santa María, dels

Herois, and de Barcelona) to the north, and the **Plaça Ajuntament** to the west. This *plaça* is nicknamed *el balcón* (balcony) *de Cerdanya;* its commanding view of the valley makes it a wickedly lovely place to watch bedraggled newcomers struggle up the hill from the RENFE station at the foot of the west slope. Most buses also drop off at the bottom of the hill (if you're lucky, they might continue to the top).

To reach Pl. Ajuntament from the train station, walk past the stairs in the station's *plaça* to the first flight of *real* stairs (between two buildings). Turn right at the top of these, and then look for the next set on your left, just before a sign for C. Hostal del Sol. Climb these to the top and turn left on C. Rabadans, where the final set of stairs winds up to the right.

With your back to the wall, **Carrer Alfons I** runs straight out of the left-hand corner of the *plaça.* It will lead you after one block to **Carrer Major,** the principal commercial street. Left on C. Major will convey you to **Plaça Santa Maria,** where road signs for Barcelona point to Pl. Herois, then Pl. Barcelona. Continuing straight across C. Major on C. Alfons I leads you to Pg. 10 d'Abril, the other main square in town.

Tourist Office: C. Querol, 1 (tel. 88 05 42), a right turn off Pl. Ajuntament with your back to the view. Good map packed with accommodations, entertainment, and daytrip listings. English spoken. Open Mon.-Sat. 10am-8pm, Sun. 10am-2pm; Oct.-June Tues.-Fri. 10am-1pm and 4-7pm, Sat. 10am-1:30pm and 4-8pm.

Post Office: Av. Coronel Molera, 11 (tel. 88 08 14), off of Pl. Barcelona on your left after 1½ bl. Open Mon.-Fri. 9am-2pm, Sat. 9am-1pm for **telegrams** only. **Postal Code:** 15720.

Telephones: C. D'Espanya, 41, directly off Pl. Herois. Open 9am-1:30pm and 4-9pm. **Telephone Code:** 972.

Trains: RENFE (tel. 88 01 65) runs to: Ribas de Freser to connect to Núria (7 per day, 50min., 250ptas, 2-way train and Cremallera package 2245ptas); Ripoll (7 per day, 1¼hr., 315ptas); Barcelona (7 per day, 3½hr., 850ptas). To get to Jaca or Huesca you must first go to Zaragoza from Barcelona, a good full day of travel.

Buses: Alsina Graells (tel. (973) 35 00 20) runs 3 buses per day to La Seu d'Urgell, where there is passage to Andorra and, through Lérida, to Aragón (1hr., 505ptas, Sat.-Sun. 575ptas). First bus departs Puigcerdà at 7:30am; last returns from La Seu at 7pm. **Cerdanya** (tel. 302 65 45 or 302 40 86) runs to Llivia (2 per day). Buses depart from in front of the train station; tickets are purchased on board. See schedule on the side of cigarette machine in Bar Estació, left of the train station.

Car Rental: Suzuki off-road vehicle from **Turning Cerdanya,** C. Escoles Pies, 19 (tel. 88 06 02), off Pl. Cabrinetty. 12,000ptas per day, 50ptas per km. Must be returned to Puigcerdà. Must be at least 25 and have had license 2 yrs. Open Mon.-Sat. 9am-1pm and 3:30-8pm.

Bike Rental: Import-Bikes, Ponsi Gausch (tel. 14 00 30), off Pl. Barcelona. 500ptas per hour, 1500ptas per half-day, 2500ptas per day. Visa, MC accepted.

24-hr. Pharmacy: A pharmacy is located on C. Alfons I, 16 (tel. 88 01 60). Pharmacy doors, local paper *Reclam,* and police all list current 24-hr. pharmacy.

Medical Services: Centre Hospitalari, on Pl. Santa Maria (tel. 88 01 50 or 88 01 54). English spoken. **Red Cross,** Av. Segre, 8 (tel. 88 05 47 or 89 41 53), on the outskirts of town to the right of Pl. Ajuntament with your back to the view.

Ambulance: Pl. Indus. la Closa (tel. 88 21 35).

Municipal Police: Pl. Ajuntament, 1 (tel. 88 19 72).

ACCOMMODATIONS

Since many visitors daytrip to Puigcerdà, you should be able to find a room easily if not cheaply; call for reservations in August. Most cheaper *pensiones* await in the old town, off Pl. Santa María; most rates lower in off-season. The closest **HI youth hostel** is the Mare de Déu de les Neus in La Molina-Alp on Ctra. Font Canaleta (tel. 89 20 12), 500m from the RENFE station (go left) at La Molina, 20 minutes by train or car from Puigcerdà. (112 beds. Members only. 1300ptas, over 25 1925ptas. Breakfast included. Slopes only 4km away; take Alsa bus every ½hr.)

Hostal Residencia Alfonso, C. D'Espanya, 5 (tel. 99 02 46). Large, carpeted rooms with bathrooms, full-length mirrors, and ridiculously comfortable beds. Winter heating. 2500ptas per person; Sept.-June 2000ptas.

Hostal Residencia La Muntanya, C. Coronel Molera, 1 (tel. 88 02 02), off Pl. Barcelona. Paintings of pearly-teared waifs weep at your bedside, which explains why the rooms feel so freshly cleaned. 3500ptas per person, including breakfast and dinner. Off-season rates negotiable.

Hostal Residencia Estació (tel. 88 03 50), to the left of the train station. Location ideal if passing through; otherwise it's a strenuous hike along a rollercoaster road to town and back. 1991 renovations left attractive rooms with wood floors and tasteful decor. Singles 2500ptas. Doubles 4000ptas, with bath 5000ptas.

Camping: Camping Stel (tel/fax 88 23 61). Full-service camping about 1km from Puigcerdà on the road to Llivia. Supermarket and pool. 525ptas per person, 600ptas per tent (space fills up early). Open June 17-Sept. 26.

FOOD

The neighborhood of C. Alfons I is a picnicker's paradise of bakeries, markets, and butcher shops—in addition to inexpensive restaurants. The **market** is at Pg. 10 d'Abril, Sun. 9am-2pm.

Supermarket: Bon Preu, diagonally across from the post office on Av. Colonel Molera, 12. Open Tues.-Sat. 9am-1pm and 4-8pm, Sun. 10am-2pm.

Gourmet Cerdà, C. Alfons I, 9 (tel. 88 14 85). A well-stocked deli. Fresh bread next door at the bakery **Palau** to make a giant, self-empowered *bocadillo*. Both open Tues.-Sat. 9am-1:30pm and 4-8pm, Sun. 9am-2pm.

Bar-Restaurant Sant Remo, C. Ramón Cosp, 9 (tel. 88 00 05). Serves a wide variety of *tapas* and *bocadillos*. Bluntly named but generous *menú turístico* 900ptas.

SIGHTS AND ENTERTAINMENT

Puigcerdà calls itself the capital of snow—you can indeed ski in your country of choice (Spain, France, or Andorra) at one of 19 ski areas within a 50km radius. The closest one on the Spanish side is at La Molina.

Between runs, dash over to the **campanario,** the octagonal bell tower in Pl. Santa Maria. This 42m-high 12th-century tower is all that remains of the Església de Santa Maria, destroyed in the 1936 Civil War. Now open to the public, it offers an unmatchable view of all Cerdanya. (Open July-Sept. 10am-2pm and 4-8pm. Free.) Along Pg. 10 d'Abril, off Pl. Heroes, is the 13th-century **Convent de Sant Domènec,** whose large-scale renovation brought a regional museum, library, and archives to the town. **Església de Sant Domènec,** the largest church in Cerdanya, hulks next door. Its most interesting holdings are several Gothic paintings, probably by Guillem Manresa, and considered to be some of the best of their genre. On the outskirts of town, spanning the Riu Querol, is the **Pont de Sant Martí d'Aravó,** with a Romanesque base and a Gothic superstructure.

Even travelers with a 4 x 4 may want to park it and go for pony or paddle boat-rides around the **Estany** (a.k.a. Lake Brilliant) up Av. Pons i Guasch from Pl. Barcelona. The **Festa de l'Estany** is usually held the next to last Sun. of August. On September 8, the town goes *sardanas* at the **Festivitat de la Verge de la Sagristia.** In July and August, devotees gather for said dance every Wed. at 10pm. More concentrated dancing takes place during the **Festa Major** in the first weekend of July.

■ NEAR PUIGCERDÀ

PARC NACIONAL D'AIGÜESTORTES

Ice-cold mountain lakes, gushing waterfalls, and stream-crossed trails make up the splendor of Parc Nacional Aigüestortes. 100km east of Ordesa and adjacent to the French border, the park is punctuated with some challenging peaks, but most hikes are easy enough for everyone to enjoy. A 2500m range divides the park in half. Informally, the eastern half is considered the Estany de Sant Maurici (the central lake), and the western half the Aigüestortes. Don't rely on the streamlined freebie maps from the information offices; the red *Editorial Alpina* guides, one each for Montardo and Vall de Boí and Sant Maurici, are essential for trails and *refugios* (400-500ptas at any bookstore in the Pyrenees). *Refugios,* government-maintained dormitories (900-950ptas), and *Casas de Pagés,* like farm houses, are good accommodations options. The park brochure published by the Generalitat de Catalunya, available at tourist offices throughout Cataluña, is useful. For information on the park, contact the park tourist offices (tel. (973) 62 40 36 in Espot and (973) 69 61 89 in Vall de Boí, or (973) 69 60 00 for general information).

The park deserves at least two days, and if you rely on public transport, it's hard to see much in fewer than three. Drivers must rise early, as there is no access to the park after 10am or after the 175-car parking lot fills (whichever is first). The mountains are deceptive from afar, particularly in spring and fall. A couple hikers die each year when they lose the trail in a freak spring blizzard. Listen to local advice: bring warm clothing even for July and August and check with the Espot or Boi park office before heading out.

ESPOT AND ESTANY DE SANT MAURICI

Surrounded by buffeted terraces, the official gateway to the eastern half of the park is the little town of **Espot.** Espot is actually a good 8km from the entrance proper, an arrangement that respects the tranquility of the park but disturbs the tranquility of the traveler. Unfortunately, the Alsina Graells **bus** (tel. (973) 26 85 00 or (933) 02 65 45) from Lérida—the only public transport to the area—does not come any nearer than 7km from the *other* side of Espot, on Highway C-147. Buses leave Lérida's bus station Mon.-Sat. at 4:30pm (3hr., 1570ptas). A **jeep service** (tel. (973) 62 41 05) taxis into the park from Espot, and will even collect you from the bus stop if you call ahead (1500ptas to Espot per 7-8 person jeep). From Espot, jeeps run to Estany Sant Maurici (5000ptas) and to Amitges, another lake in the north that houses the park's best and biggest *refugio* (12,000ptas). Estany Sant Maurici is the launch pad for most hikes; the 2hr. hike from there to Amitges is one of the park's best. The **park information office** (tel. (973) 62 40 36), on the main road on the right as you enter town, provides good brochures and advice on the park. (Open 9am-1pm and 3:30-7pm.)

A night's rest in Espot allows hikers an early start on the park trails; several small **supermarkets** supply picnic materials. Many residences in the area take in travelers; contact the tourist office for information or ask at the *Casas de Pagés.* **Residència Felip** (tel. (973) 62 40 93), a *Casa de Pagés,* packages rooms with breakfast. (1900ptas per person, with bath 2400ptas. Oct.-June rates negotiable.) Cross the main Espot bridge, follow the road 2 bl., then turn left. **Càmping la Mola** (tel. (973) 62 40 01), lies about 2km from Espot. **Càmping Sol i Neu** (tel. (973) 62 40 24), is about 1km from La Mola en route to the village. (Both open July-Sept. 425ptas per person, per tent, and per car. Good facilities. La Mola has a pool.)

AIGÜESTORTES AND VALL DE BOÍ

Gentle inclines in the western half of the park attract more cows and casual strollers than the Sant Maurici side. To compare the two halves of the park, take the main trail along the Riu de Sant Nicolau from Aigüestortes to the **Portarró de Espot,** the 2400m gateway between the two sides. The descent to Estany de Sant Maurici is steep and covered in patches of snow at the higher altitudes. This 6- to 8-hour hike crosses the whole park, passing the **Estany Llong,** a llong llake indeed. Near its western tip is the park's first *refugio,* also called **Estany Llong.** (Open mid-June to Oct. 10.) Near the end of the paved road at the entrance of Aigüestortes are pine groves circled by winding streams, a tranquil sanctuary of twisted waters which is the park's namesake.

Entering the park from its western side isn't much easier than the eastern approach. When it's running (July-Sept.), the bus from Lérida drops off in **Boí,** a community of 150 people, 7km from the park's entrance. **Taxis** (tel. (973) 69 60

36) go from the town's main *plaça* to the park (500ptas per person). The **park information office** is near the bus stop in the town *plaça* (tel. (973) 69 61 89).

An inordinate number of Romanesque churches dot the valley. **Sant Climent of Taüll,** uphill from Boí, is the most noted. Boí maintains its pastoral feel, despite the nearby ski resort in Taüll. Amid low arches and cobblestoned streets stand accommodations run by local families. Recommended is **Casa Guasch** (tel. (973) 69 60 42), whose proprietor lets you use her kitchen if the house isn't too full. Leave the plaza through the stone arch, turn right through the next arch, then bear left and turn left again where street ends. Follow the street looking for the multicolored entryway on the left. The family knows the mountains well and can give you pointers in Spanish or Catalan (1500ptas per person, 1300ptas if you don't use the kitchen).

Pont de Suert, 17km south of Boí, offers most emergency services. The **Red Cross** can be reached at (973) 69 02 85; **Guardia Civil** at (974) 69 00 06.

COSTA DORADA (COSTA DAURADA)

SITGES

Forty km south of Barcelona, and light years away on the activity meter, resort town Sitges has become famous for its long oceanside walks, cobbled streets, whitewashed houses, fertile tanning ground, numerous cultural festivals, and international gay community.

Water is pervasive under Sitges's sun; the beach is a direct 10-min. walk from the train station via any street. In summer, the main **beaches** get crowded, but you can walk to less busy areas on your right as you face the water (west). Walk along the shore to the Solarium Club on your right, then over the hill or through the train tunnel and left. The beach is mixed stone and sand with some surf. The gay beach is over the next hill.

Complementing the salty *agua,* the several museums are remnants of the village's avatar as an artists' colony. Behind Església del Evangelista, which hangs on the water's edge, the **Museu Cau Ferrat** (tel. 894 03 64) lounges on C. Fonollar. This former house of Catalan *Modernista* Santiago Russinyol contains numerous paintings by him and his cronies Picasso and Casas. Next door, the **Museu Maricel del Mar** (tel. 894 03 64) has a fine collection of medieval paintings and sculpture. The **Museu Romàntic** (Can Llopis), C. Sant Gaudenci, 1 (tel. 894 29 69), a bourgeois 19th-century house filled with period pieces, displays music boxes and 17th- to 19th-century dolls. Take C. Bonaire from the waterfront. (All 3 open Tues.-Sat. 9:30am-1pm and 4-6pm, Sun. 9:30am-2pm. Admission to each 200ptas. Students free; Sun. free.)

Sitges celebrates holidays with all-out style. During the **Festa de Corpus Christi,** neighbors join together for one day to create intricate carpets of hundreds of thousands of flowers in the streets. For raucous fun (papier-mâché dragons, devils, and giants dancing in the streets), visit during the **Festa Major,** held each year August 23-27 in honor of the town's patron saint Bartolomé. Yet nothing compares to the wonderful **Carnaval** during the first week of Lent, when Spaniards of every ilk and province crash the town for a frenzy of dancing, outrageous costumes, vats of alcohol, and an antique car race from Barcelona to Sitges.

The modern **tourist office** at Bus Terminal "Oasis" waits behind the Oasis shopping mall, Pg. Vilafranca (tel. 894 12 30). It has a "super" map of the town with extraordinary information on services. From the train station, turn right and go downhill until Oasis signs appear on the right. (Open Mon.-Sun. 9am-9pm; Sept. 16-June Mon.-Fri. 9:30am-2pm and 4-6:30pm, Sat. 10am-1pm.) The **post office** (tel. 894 12 47) headquarters on Pl. Espanya. (Open Mon.-Fri. 9am-2pm.) The **postal code** is 08870. There are **telephones** for international and domestic calls at C. Jesus, 10 (open 10am-10pm). The **telephone code** is 93. The **hospital** is on C. Hospital (tel.

894 00 03). The **municipal police,** on Pl. Ajuntament, answer at tel. 811 76 25. **Trains** link Sitges to Barcelona (2 per hr., 50min., round-trip 550ptas).

Due to Sitges's popularity, accommodation prices are so steep they warrant a day trip from Barcelona. **Hostal Parelladas,** C. Parelladas, 11 (tel. 894 08 01), one bl. from the beach, is as cheap as they come here. Standard rooms with no surprises. (Singles 2100ptas. Doubles with bath 4500ptas.) **Hostal Mariangel,** C. Parelladas, 78 (tel. 894 13 57), just down the street, has 18 rooms of varying description. A small lounge with wicker furniture sits by the sea breeze. (Singles 2000ptas, with bath 2500ptas. Doubles 3750ptas, with bath 4600ptas. Prices lower in off-season.)

CASTELLDEFELS

On the same train line as Sitges, **Castelldefels** has more grit and less glitter. The enormous beach, only 20 minutes from Barcelona, is perfect for young children and hydrophobes—the water takes its time to get deep.

Beware of afternoon rush hours—train cars are often packed. The L93 **bus** leaves Barcelona's Pl. Espanya for Castelldefels (one-way 180ptas).

VILANOVA I LA GELTRÙ

Cataluña's most important port after Barcelona and Tarragona, **Vilanova i la Geltrù** (90km southwest of Barcelona) is actually two cities blended into one. La Geltrù, dating back to 1070, is the elder, while large and bustling Vilanova was born in 1274. The industrial side of the city cooperates graciously with its well-groomed **beaches** (10-min. walk from train station) and vibrant cultural life. The **Passeig Marítim** is the nightly setting for leisurely seaside promenades.

In the **Museu Balaguer,** Av. Victor Balaguer, s/n (tel. 815 42 02), opposite the train station, an Egyptian mummy sidles up to paintings from the 17th century to the present, including El Greco's *Anunciación.* (Open Mon.-Sat. 10am-2pm and 4-7pm. Free.) Deep in the old city, the 13th-century **Castell de la Geltrù,** C. Torre, s/n (tel. 893 00 13), now safeguards a bronze mortar that maybe, just maybe, was used by 12th-century alchemists to grind drugs. Also some 20th-century paintings. (Open same hrs. as Museu Balaguer. Free.) **Casa Papiol,** C. Major, 32 (tel. 893 03 82), is a 19th-century house that takes you down memory lane to the tastes of turn-of-the-century bourgeoisie. (Open Tues.-Sat. 10am-1pm and 4-6pm, Sun. 10am-2pm. Admission 200ptas.)

The **tourist office** (tel. 815 45 17), right on the beach, can help find lodgings. (Open Mon.-Sat. 9:30am-1:30pm and 4:30-8:30pm, Sun. 10am-1pm.) **Taxis** can be summoned by phone (tel. 893 32 41). **Ambulances** (tel. 893 12 16) provide medical assistance. The **municipal police** can be reached at tel. 893 00 00.

■■■ TARRAGONA

A plentitude of pitchers, pillars, and pendants from the praetorian past provide this prehistoric port's primary pull. The Romans anointed Tarragona a provincial capital; this rocky mountain on the sea was strategic for trade and invulnerable in war. One of the empire's finest cities, Tarragona provided respite for Augustus and Hadrian. Several hundred years later, the city remains a pivotal point of maritime activity and a popular tourist center for Roman ruins aficionados.

ORIENTATION AND PRACTICAL INFORMATION

The older part of the city sits on a hill surrounding the cathedral in view of the sea. The main thoroughfares, **Ramblas Nova** and **Vella,** run parallel to each other and perpendicular to the shore. Most of the city's sights are north of Rambla Vella (on the other side of Rambla Nova). Rambla Nova runs from the edge of the city to **Plaça Imperial Tarraco** (home of the bus station).

To reach the center of the old quarter from the train station, take a right and walk 200m to the vertiginous (killer) stairs parallel to the shore. At the top of the stairs, walk past Rambla Nova, one block down Pg. Palmeres to Rambla Vella. Turn left on Rambla Vella. The third right ends at **Plaça de la Font,** a center of activity. Alternatively, take the bus to Via de l'Imperi Romà and take a left onto Rambla Vella. The second left off Rambla Vella leads to Pl. Font.

Tourist Office: Rambla Nova, 46 (tel. 23 21 43). Maps, brochures in English on every aspect of the city. Open Mon.-Sat. 9:30am-8:30pm; Oct.-June Mon.-Fri. 9am-2pm and 4-7pm, Sat. 10am-2pm. Another **branch** at C. Major, 39 (tel. 24 19 53), below the cathedral steps. Open Mon.-Sat. 10am-2pm and 4-8pm, Sun. 11am-2pm. **Generalitat,** C. Fortuny, 4 (tel. 23 34 15), off Rambla Nova, 5 bl. from the sea end. Best for regional info. Open Mon.-Fri. 8am-2:30pm and 4-7pm, Sat. 9am-2pm.

Consulates: See Spain Essentials: Embassies and Consulates.

Post Office: Pl. Corsini (tel. 21 01 49), 1 bl. below Rambla Nova off C. Canyelles. Stamps sold Mon.-Fri. 8am-9pm, Sat. 9am-2pm. Lista de Correos and **telegrams** open Mon.-Fri. 8am-9pm, Sat. 9am-7pm. **Postal Code:** 43070.

Telephones: C. Fortuny, 1, marked by a street sign on Rambla Nova, 74. Open Mon.-Fri. 10am-10pm, Sat. 11am-8pm. **Telephone Code:** 977.

Trains: Pl. de la Pedrera (tel. 24 02 02), on the waterfront at the base of the hill. Information office open 6am-10pm. To: Sitges (14 per day, 1hr., 315ptas); Barcelona (28 per day, 1½hr., 490ptas); Lérida (7 per day, 2hr., 490ptas); Zaragoza (4 per day, 3½hr., 1490ptas); Valencia (13 per day, 4hr., 1595ptas); Madrid (2 per day, 8hr., 3600ptas); Córdoba-Sevilla (2 per day, 6500ptas to Sevilla). **RENFE office,** Rambla Nova, 40 (tel. 23 25 34). Tickets and inquiries. Open Mon.-Fri. 9am-1pm and 4-7pm.

Buses: Pl. Imperial Tarraco (tel. 22 91 26). **Transportes Bacoma** (tel. 22 20 72) serves most of these destinations. To: Barcelona (8 per day, 1½hr., 780ptas); Lérida (4 per day, 2½hr., 970ptas); Valencia (7 per day, 3½hr., 2055ptas); Alicante (7 per day, 6½hr., 3465ptas); Málaga (3 per day, 14hr., 7515ptas).

Public Transportation: EMT Buses (tel. 54 94 80) runs 8 lines all over Tarragona. The tourist offices have a map with the routes. Runs 7am-10pm, until 11pm on some routes. One ride 80ptas, 10-ride "bono" ticket 525ptas at tobacco shops.

Car Rental: Gaui, C. Ramón y Cajal, 61 (tel. 21 42 97), off Rambla Nova. Seat Marbella 2300ptas per day, plus 14ptas per km. Weekend special (Fri.-Mon.) 6180ptas with 250km free mileage. Open Mon.-Fri. 8am-1pm and 4-7:30pm, Sat. 9am-noon.

Luggage Storage: At the train station, 200ptas per bag. Open whenever the station is (24hrs. in summer, variable otherwise).

Taxi: Radio Taxi, tel. 22 14 14 or 23 60 64.

Medical Assistance: Hospital de Sant Pau i Santa Tecla, Rambla Vella, 14 (tel. 23 50 12). **Protecció Civil,** Pl. Imperial Tarraco (tel. 006), for any emergency.

Emergency: tel. 091 or 092.

Police: Comisaría de Policía, Pl. Orleans (tel. 23 33 11 or 091). From Pl. Imperial Tarraco on the non-sea end of Rambla Nova, walk down Av. Pres. Lluis Companys, which runs between the bus station and the Govern Civil building. Take the 3rd left to the station.

ACCOMMODATIONS AND CAMPING

Tarragona is not famous for its cheap beds. Some budget accommodations do rest in the area behind **Plaça de la Pedrera,** outside the train station. Also investigate the tourist office's updated list of accommodations.

Residencia Juvenil Sant Jordi (HI), Av. Pres. Lluis Companys, 5 (tel. 24 01 95). At the end of Rambla Nova, past Pl. Imperial Tarraco, Rambla Nova changes into Av. Pres. Lluis Companys. The entrance is on Marqués de Guad-el-Jelú, the 2nd right after the traffic circle. A youth recreation complex on the outskirts of Tarragona houses boisterous local college students. Institutional dormitory rooms come with desks and large closets. Other facilities include outdoor pool (225ptas), tennis courts, lounge with pool table, and washing machine. Reception open 7am-11pm. Doors close at midnight, but arrangement can be made for later entrances given a sufficiently worthy cause. 1200ptas per person, breakfast included. 26 and over 1675ptas. Sheets 350ptas. Make reservations for July-Aug.

Pensión Marsal, Pl. Font, 26 (tel. 22 40 69), in the heart of the historic town. Tough beds with floral printed sheets. Sparkling communal bathrooms. Singles 1500ptas. Doubles 3000ptas. 5th-floor rooms are cheaper. Breakfast 230ptas.

La Pilarica, C. Smith, 20 (tel. 24 09 60). From the train station, turn left and cross Pl. Pedrera to C. Barcelona, which becomes C. Sant Miguel. Turn left on C. Misericòrdia, and then take the third right. Talkative owner offers big rooms and family atmosphere in a somewhat dingy building. Singles 1500ptas. Doubles 3000ptas.

Pensión Mariflor, C. General Contreras, 29 (tel. 23 82 31). From the train station, turn left down Pl. Pedrera, right onto C. Barcelona, then a sharp right onto C. Contreras. Dim rooms. Singles 1400ptas. Doubles 2700ptas. Hot showers 100ptas, cold ones free.

Camping: Several sites line the road toward Barcelona (Via Augusta or CN-340) along the beaches north of town. To reach any of them, take bus #1 or 9 from Pl. Corsini, opposite the market (every 20min., 80ptas). The closest is **Tarraco** (tel. 23 99 89), at Platja Rabassada. Facilities are well-maintained, and the beach is out the tent door. 465ptas per person, per tent, and per car. Open April-Sept.

FOOD

The tourist office has a list of restaurants with prices. **Ramblas Nova** and **Vella** are the most promising streets, but true seafood freaks with fishy priorities take bus #1 from Rambla Nova to **El Serrallo** (see Sights for walking directions), where the fresh daily catch is served up in the pricier restaurants of this fishers' neighborhood. Tarragona's **indoor market,** next to Pl. Corsini by the post office, moves food and many other wares: plants, goldfish, baby ducks, candy, spiders. (Open Mon.-Thurs. 8am-2pm, Fri. 8am-2pm and 5-8pm.)

Groceries: Simago, C. Augusta at Comte de Rius (tel. 23 88 06), parallel to and running between Ramblas Nova and Vella. Open Mon.-Sat. 9:30am-8:30pm.

Bar Turia, Pl. Font, 26 (tel. 22 40 69), under Pensión Marsal. Crowded local hangout with color TV and outdoor seating on the *plaça*. 3-course *menú*, always with a fish or meat option, 650ptas. *Bocadillos* 250-325ptas. Open 1-4pm and 8:30-11pm.

Mesón El Caserón, Trinquet Nou, 4 (tel. 23 93 28), parallel to Rambla Vella (off Pl. Font). Decorous ceiling fans cool plain, stomach-stuffing, family-style eats. Steak platter 825ptas. Appealing seafood *paella* 950ptas. *Menú* 950ptas. Open Mon.-Sat. 1-3:30pm and 8:30-10:30pm; July-Sept. also open Sun. nights.

C'an Peret, Pl. Font, 6 (tel. 23 76 25). Not unlike a baseball park: small sandwiches (150ptas), junk food, and desserts—and people at first base in the back. Open Mon.-Sat. 9am-3pm and 6pm-midnight, Sun. 9am-3pm.

Cap i Cua, C. Colom, 17 (tel. 24 00 39). C. Colom intersects Rambla Nova at Font del Centenari, 7 bl. from the water, and also borders the indoor market on the opposite side from Pl. Corsini. This fabulously ordinary bar offers a 2-course *menú* with bread, drink, and dessert Mon.-Sat. 1-3:30pm (750ptas). *Platos combinados* 250-575ptas. Open Mon.-Fri. 6:30am-9:30pm, Sat. 6:30am-5pm.

SIGHTS

Countless Roman and medieval remains lie on the city's Mediterranean edge. **Balcó del Mediterràni,** fringing Rambla Nova, commands a view of the lazy sea. From here as you face the water, the **Amfiteatre Romà** (Roman amphitheater) and the **Circ Romà** (Roman circus where chariots raced) are off to the left down Pg. Palmeres. In the 12th century, in disdain for the excess that the amphitheater represented, Christians built the **Church of Santa María** right over it. (Open Tues.-Sat. 10am-8pm, Sun. 10am-3pm; Oct.-March Tues.-Sat. 10am-5:30pm, Sun. 10am-3pm. Admission 400ptas, students free.)

Continuing past the ruins, Pg. Sant Antoni winds its way up into the medieval quarter of the city. The first stop is the **Museu Arqueològic,** Pl. Rei (tel. 23 62 09), with a collection of ancient utensils, statues, friezes, and mosaics, including a ravishing *Cap de Medusa* (Head of Medusa). (Open Tues.-Sat. 10am-1pm and 4:30-8pm, Sun. 10am-2pm; Oct. 16-June 15 Tues.-Sat. 10am-1:30pm and 4-7pm, Sun. 10am-

2pm. Admission 100ptas, Tues. free.) The museum adjoins the **Pretori Romà** (tel. 24 19 52), the governor's palace in the 1st century BC. Rumor has it that Pontius Pilate was born here. Tunnels link the palace with the Roman circus. The vaults were used as dungeons, both by the Romans and centuries later by Franco's Fascists. (Open Tues.-Sat. 10am-8pm, Sun. 10am-2pm; Oct.-June Tues.-Fri. 10am-6:30pm, Sun. 10am-2pm. Admission 400ptas, students free.)

Nearby, cornered by narrow streets and lit by a huge rose window, is yet another Romanesque-Gothic **catedral,** down C. Major at Pl. Seu. Dominating the ornate apse is the extravagantly detailed altarpiece, carved around 1430. The 19 chapels have representatives from a number of centuries. The **Museu Diocesà** (tel. 23 86 85), in the east gallery, contains Roman and Iberian pottery, medieval and Renaissance religious icons, and medieval tapestries. (Cathedral and museum open Mon.-Sat. 10am-7pm; Nov. 16-March 15 Mon.-Sat. 10am-2pm; March 16-June and Oct. 16-Nov. 15 10am-12:30pm and 4-6pm. Admission 300ptas, students 75ptas.)

Following the walls that encircle the old city, the **Passeig Arqueològic** winds through Tarragona's history. The ruins of the Roman city walls date from the 3rd century. Moorish and Christian towers guard the ancient gates. Entrance at the top of Via de l'Imperi Romà. (Open Tues.-Sat. 10am-midnight, Sun. 10am-3pm; Oct.-March Tues.-Sat. 10am-5:30pm, Sun. 10am-3pm; April-June Tues.-Sat. 10am-8pm, Sun. 10am-3pm. Admission 400ptas, students free.)

For more ontological visitors, on Pg. Independència on the edge of town are the **Necròpolis** and **Museu Paleocristià** (tel. 21 11 75). The enormous early Christian burial site has yielded a rich variety of urns, tombs, and sarcophagi, the best of which go to the museum in its center. (Both open Tues.-Sat. 10am-1pm and 4:30-8pm, Sun. 10am-2pm; Sept. 16-June 15 Tues.-Sat. 10am-1:30pm and 4-7pm, Sun. 10am-2pm. Admission 100ptas, Tues. free.) The **Pont del Diable** (Devil's Bridge) is a perfectly preserved Roman aqueduct. Take municipal bus #5 from the corner of C. Christòfor Colom and Av. Prat de la Riba (every 20min., 80ptas); it will drop you off right at the aqueduct.

El Serrallo, Tarragona's fishing district, fans out next to the port. Fishers return in the late afternoon to auction off the daily catch. Take bus #1 (Naútico) or walk (from the train station, take C. Comerç and turn a long right on C. Reial—which starts as C. A. Clavé—until it hits C. Pere Martell; turn left, go one block, then duck under the bridge).

The rather hidden access to **Platja del Miracle,** directly below town, is along Baixada del Miracle, starting off Pl. Arce Ochotorena, beyond the Roman theater. **Platjas Rabassada,** with dirt-like sand; **Sabinosa,** full of families; and **Llarga,** with its strong winds, are larger beaches. To reach them, take bus #1 or 9 from Pl. Corsini.

ENTERTAINMENT

The town is dead by midnight, though cafés along Rambla Nova entertain until the wee hours.

Moto Club Tarragona, Rambla Nova, 53 (tel. 23 22 30), near C. Comte de Rius, is a popular sidewalk café. (Open 7am-midnight.) Tarragona's hippest disco is **La Canela,** in a warehouse on C. Sant Magí, 6 (tel. 21 76 00), off C. La Unió. (Open 7pm-2:30am.) Serious dance clubs are in **Salou** and **Torredembara,** two beach towns 10km south and north of Tarragona, respectively (easily reached by Plana bus from the main bus station, though the last bus returns at 10pm).

July and August usher in **Festivales de Tarragona**—rock, jazz, dance, theater, and film—at the Auditori Camp de Mart near the cathedral. A booth on Rambla Nova sells tickets for the 10:30pm performances (700-1500ptas). Try the location itself one hour before the performance (contact the municipal tourist office for details).

On even-numbered years, the first Sunday in October brings the **Concurs de Castells,** in which groups of acrobats build human towers. They appear amidst dragons, beasts, and fireworks during the annual **Festa de Sant Tecla** on September 23.

■ NEAR TARRAGONA

MONESTIR POBLET

Monestir Poblet (tel. (977) 87 00 89), one of the largest Cistercian abbeys in Europe and a celebrated monastic complex, is famed for its magnificent architecture. Ramón Berenguer IV founded the monastery in 1151, and the community grew rapidly. A favorite stopover between Zaragoza and Barcelona for the kings of Aragón, it was eventually selected as the royal burial place.

Guided **tours** showcase the 12th-century kitchens and refectory, the cloister, the chapter house, the 13th-century library, and the royal tomb. The church's severe grandeur complements its most remarkable ornaments, a 16th-century carved alabaster altarpiece and the immense low arches in the cross vault. The four-tiered *retablo* was painstakingly created in 1527; the adjacent cloisters swathed in lovely scrollwork complete the serenity. (Open 10am-12:30pm and 3-6pm. Admission 250ptas, students 100ptas. Closed Christmas Day.)

The town, 48km from Tarragona, is a stop on the Autocares Parellada, S.A. **bus** route from Tarragona to Lérida (3 per day, 1hr.).

MONESTIR SANTES CREUX

Monestir Santes Creux (tel. (977) 63 83 29) was founded under the reign of Alfonso II, thanks to the generosity of Catalan nobles who donated the land. The Cistercian monastery survived invasions from Felipe and Napoleon, but when abandoned by the monks in 1835, the buildings were sacked. A 20th-century restoration has preserved this architectural treasure that spans from Romanesque to Gothic. (Open 10am-noon and 3:30-6pm.) To get here, catch a **bus** (tel. 22 20 72) from Tarragona to Valls, and switch there for Santes Creux (about 40km from Tarragona).

Islas Baleares

Dreaming, perhaps, of the vast fortunes to be made in the 20th-century tourist industry, nearly every culture with boats and burly men to spare has tried to conquer the Baleares. Imperialist efforts of England and Germany notwithstanding, the islands have been essentially Spanish since the thirteenth century. Discos, ancient history, and beaches—especially the beaches—draw 1.7 million almost exclusively European tourists to the islands each year.

Mallorca is home to the province's capital, Palma, and absorbs the bulk of invaders. Jagged Sierra de Tramontana's limestone cliffs line the north coast, while lazy bays scoop into the rest of the coastline. Condominiums on the coast obscure beaches with clear turquoise water, while orchard upon orchard spring from fertile soil inland. Ibiza, once a haven of the counter-culture, successfully plays the entertainment capital of the islands and has an active gay community. Its smaller neighbor Formentera is more peaceful and unspoilt. Wrapped in green fields and stone walls, Menorca leads a private life with empty white beaches, hidden coves, and mysterious Bronze Age megaliths.

Language and folklore distinguish these islands from the rest of Spain. The regional dialect spoken on all the Islas Baleares, *mallorquín,* is similar to *catalán.* Island cuisine is relatively simple, but mayonnaise, a Menorcan innovation, puts the Baleares in the culinary hall of fame. *Pa-amb-oli* (bread with oil, plus ham, tomato, or egg) makes a filling snack (it's what Michael Douglas misses most when away from his home in Mallorca). More substantial foods include *sopes mallorquines,* a stocky vegetable soup ladled over thinly sliced brown bread, and *escaldums,* an appetizing chicken dish. Soft, spicy sausages, such as *camaiot, sobrasada* (*chorizo* spread), and *botifarrons* are picnickable. Sweet tooths die for *ensaimadas,* doughy, candied pastries smothered in powdered sugar, and liquor lovers are crazy about Menorca's gin and sweet liqueur.

Summers tend to be hot, dry, and crowded—spring and autumn are gorgeous, and the easiest times to find budget accommodations.

GETTING THERE

By Plane

Charters are the cheapest and quickest means of round-trip travel. Most deals entail a week's stay in a hotel, but some charter companies (called *mayoristas*) sell fares for unoccupied seats on flights booked primarily with full-package (meaning airfare and hotel) passengers. The leftover spots, called "seat only" deals, can be found in newspaper ads or by asking at various travel agencies (check TIVE and other budget travel havens) in any Spanish city. Summer and Semana Santa prices are more than double standard off-season (Oct.-May) fares. The 1993 *Liberalización del Transporte* Act may mean the relaxation of stringent you-pay, you-stay policies if new companies get involved in the charter business.

Scheduled flights are far easier to book. Frequent departures cruise from Barcelona, Madrid, and Valencia, as well as Düsseldorf, London, Frankfurt, Hamburg, and Paris. **Iberia** and **Aviaco** handle all flights from Spain to the isles. From Barcelona, a one-way ticket to Palma costs 8950ptas, to Menorca 9250ptas, and to Ibiza 10,200ptas. From Valencia, a one-way ticket to Ibiza runs 8450ptas, to Palma 10,500ptas, and to Menorca 12,400ptas. From Madrid the one-way fares are a bit steeper: to Ibiza 14,400ptas, to Palma 15,900ptas, and to Menorca 18,600ptas.

Another option, the *tarifa-mini* fare, discounts round-trip tickets by 40%. The catch is that only five or six seats open up per flight, and they often sell out almost six months beforehand. If you manage to swing one of these tickets, you are usually required to stay on the island at least one weekend (no changes allowed).

MALLORCA

By Boat

Boat fares are comparable price-wise to charter flights—although naturally, longer time-wise; fun in a disco and small swimming pool help while away the longer passage. **Transmediterránea** monopolizes water transportation between the mainland and all the islands except Ibiza and Formentera. Ships depart from Barcelona (office at Estació Marítima, tel. (93) 443 25 32) and Valencia (office at Av. Manuel Soto Ingeniero, 15, tel. (96) 367 65 12); any travel agent in Spain can book a seat. Ships sail from both ports to Palma, Mahón, and the city Ibiza. All connections are direct except Valencia-Mahón, a painful 18-hour trip via Palma. Ships follow this schedule: Barcelona-Palma 7-10 per week; Barcelona-Ibiza 4-5 per week; Barcelona-Mahón 2-6 per week; Valencia-Palma 6-7 per week; Valencia-Ibiza 1-6 per week. The journey to the islands takes about 8-9 hours. The one-way fare for a *butaca* (airplane-style seat) is 6100ptas. Reservations made a few days in advance help, although seats are often available until an hour before departure.

Flebasa in the city of Denia, conveniently located for rail, bus, and boat transportation between Valencia and Alicante, challenges Transmediterránea's corporate colossus. The trip from Denia to Ibiza (3hr.) is the shortest, and boats dock in Puerto de San Antonio rather than Ibiza City. Denia lies on the FEVE rail line between Valencia and Alicante. The high-speed ferry ticket comes with a bus connection from either of those cities or from Madrid, Albacete, or Benidorm (in summer). A one-way ticket from Madrid costs 7610ptas, from Alicante or Valencia 5570ptas. Offices are at the ports of Denia (tel. (96) 578 40 11 or 78 42 00), Alicante (tel. (965) 22 21 88), and San Antonio (tel. (971) 34 28 71). Travel agents also book for Flebasa.

GETTING AROUND

Flying is the best way to island-hop. **Iberia** flies from Palma to Ibiza (3-4 per day, 20min., 4800ptas) and Mahón (2-3 per day, 20min., 4850ptas), and from Menorca to Ibiza, but be aware that the stop-over in Palma can last up to four hours (2-3 per day, 10,650ptas). Planes fill a couple of days in advance in summer, so make reservations. If flying round-trip, ask if the *tarifa-mini* fare is applicable.

Seafarers sail **Transmediterránea,** whose ships connect Palma with Ibiza (1-2 per week, 4½hr., 4509ptas) and Mahón (1 per week, 6½hr., 4509ptas). **Flebasa** ferries connect Palma to Puerto San Antonio in Ibiza (7-14 per week, 2-4½hr., 2950ptas), and Alcudia in Mallorca to Ciudadela in Menorca (14-42 per week, 1-3½hr., 2950ptas). All the islands operate extensive intra-island bus systems. Mallorca also has two narrow-gauge train systems that don't accept Eurailpasses.

Travel costs on Mallorca, Menorca, and Ibiza add up, as bus fares between cities range from 100ptas to 700ptas each way. You might want to try self-operated transport for greater mobility and access to islands' remote beaches. For groups, car rental may be the cheapest travel option. A day's **car rental** of a SEAT Panda should cost around 5000ptas, including insurance; Vespa or **moped rental,** 2200ptas; and **bicycle rental,** about 800ptas.

MALLORCA

Of all possible resorts fit for a king, Spanish monarch Juan Carlos chooses Menorca as his holiday spot. The island is filled with wealth, royalty, and romance. British author Robert Graves wrote eery stories about the superstitious and wonderful Mallorcan towns. Polish pianist Frédèric Chopin and French novelist George Sand spent months of their steamy love affair in the island's smaller towns. Royalty and artists, however, are hard to pick out among the package-tour European vacationers who stuff the 500km coastline, particularly in July and August.

The jagged edge of Sierra de Tramontana stretches along the island's northwestern coast, hiding its white sand beaches and frothy water. Lemon groves and ancient olive trees cling to the hillsides in terraced plots. To the east, expansive beaches, some as long as 6km, open onto smooth bays, while the southeastern coast hides its beauty underground in giant caves. The calmer inland plains, dotted with windmills drawing up water for the almond and fig trees, form the agricultural heartland of a thriving economy. Mallorca's natural beauty—both inland and along the shore—draws the highest percentage of the islands' visitors, many of whom use the less appealing capital city as a base from which to explore. For more specific bus information, see Palma Orientation and Practical Information: Buses.

■■■ PALMA

Mallorca's capital (pop. 303,485) is the showy Balearic upstart, a city that delights in quashing every image of serene island living ever to grace a travel agency's wall. Palma is a concrete jungle. Its streets hustle with shoppers consuming conspicuously. Shops hawk leather coats and bags, designer clothes, jewelry, silverware, and car stereos. Even the city's namesake palm trees have gone commercial, picked up their plastic roots, and moved to cheap hotel lobbies. Palma remains one of Spain's wealthiest cities, a true metropolis with a large year-round population, a well-preserved old quarter, fancy restaurants, and a swinging nightlife.

ORIENTATION AND PRACTICAL INFORMATION

To get to the town center from the airport, take bus #17 to **Plaça d'Espanya** (every ½hr., 6:10am-1:15am, 15min., 210ptas, after 9pm and Sun. 250ptas). From the dock, walk outside the parking lot and turn right on Pg. Marítim, then left onto Av. Antoni Maura, which leads to **Plaça de la Reina** and **Passeig des Born.** Pg. Born leads away from the sea to **Plaça del Rei Joan Carles I. Avinguda Rei Jaume III,** the business artery, runs to the left. To the right, **Carrer de la Unió** leads after some stairs to the **Plaça Major,** the center of the pedestrian shopping district. C. Sant Miquel connects Pl. Major to Pl. Espanya, where you can catch a bus.

Tourist Office: Govern Balear, Av. Rei Jaume III, 10 (tel. 71 22 16), off Pl. Rei Joan Carles I. Superb information about all the islands. Map, readable bus and train schedules, a multilingual list of all sporting and cultural events on the island, and a pamphlet with 20 hiking excursions. English spoken. Open Mon.-Fri. 9am-2:30pm and 3-8pm, Sat. 10am-1:30pm. Branch office at the **airport** (tel. 26 08 03) with similar information. Open Mon.-Sat. 9am-2pm and 3-8pm, Sun. 9am-2pm. English-speaking staff at **municipal branch,** C. Sant Dominic, 11 (tel. 72 40 90), is likewise helpful. *A Palma,* their monthly cultural calendar, is brimful with facts. Open Mon.-Fri. 9am-8pm, Sat. 9am-1:30pm. The **information booth** (tel. 71 15 27) in Pl. Espanya is a branch of this operation. Open Mon.-Fri. 9am-8pm, Sat. 9am-1pm.

Budget Travel: TIVE, C. Jerónim Antich, 5 (tel. 71 17 85), near Pl. Bisbe Berenguer de Palou toward Pl. Espanya. ISIC (1500ptas), HI cards (1800ptas), and mainland flights. Go elsewhere for inter-island travel and charters. Open Mon.-Fri. 9:30am-1:30pm.

Consulate: See Spain Essentials: Embassies and Consulates.

American Express: Viajes Iberia, Pg. Born, 14 (tel. 72 67 43). Can't accept wired money. Holds mail for 1 year. Cashes all traveler's checks with 2% commission. Open Mon.-Fri. 9am-1:30pm and 4-7pm, Sat. 9:30am-1pm.

Post Office: C. Constitució, 6 (tel. 72 10 95). Parcels upstairs. Lista de Correos downstairs at window #3. Open Mon.-Fri. 9am-9pm, Sat. 9am-2pm. **Postal Code:** 07001.

Telephones: C. dels Paraires, right off Pl. Reina. Credit cards accepted. Open Mon.-Fri. 9am-8pm, Sat. 9am-2pm. **Telephone Code:** 971 for all the Baleares.

Flights: Aeroport Son San Juan (tel. 26 41 62), 8km away from downtown Palma. Bus #17 goes to Pl. Espanya. **Iberia,** Pg. Born, 10 (tel. 72 61 24). Open Mon.-Fri. 9am-3:15pm and 4-7:15pm, Sat. 9am-12:45pm. **Aviaco** (tel. 26 02 73). Open Mon.-Fri. 9:30am-3pm and 4-5pm, Sat. 7am-3pm, Sun. 7am-3pm.

Trains: Ferrocarril de Sóller, C. Eusebio Estada, 1/6 (tel. 75 20 28), off Pl. Espanya. To Sóller (5 per day, 360ptas). Avoid the 10:40am "tourist train"—prices inflate to 690ptas for the privilege of a 10-min. stop in Mirador del Pujol d'en Banya. **Servicios Ferroviarios de Mallorca (SFM)** (tel. 75 22 45), on Pl. Espanya, goes inland to Inca (Mon.-Fri. almost every 40min., Sat.-Sun. every hr., 215ptas).

Buses: A lot of companies; the tourist office distributes a complete inter-city bus schedule that orders the confusion. **Transportes de Palma** (tel. 29 57 00) runs municipal buses with the main terminal at Pl. Espanya. Standard city fare 130ptas, 10 tickets 590ptas. Prices to outlying areas are slightly higher. Buy tickets aboard or in Pl. Espanya kiosks. Service 6am-10pm. **Inter-city buses** are an individual and autonomous nightmare. **Autocares Llompart,** C. Arxiduc Lluís Salvador, 1 (tel. 27 69 06), near Pl. Espanya, links Valldemosa, Puerto de Sóller, and Deyá. **Autocares Grimalt,** Av. Alejandro Rosselló, 32 (tel. 58 11 35), off Pl. Progrés, serves towns in southeastern Mallorca. **Autocares Carbonell,** C. Arxiduc Lluís Salvador, 24 (tel. 28 54 04), covers southwestern Mallorca, including Banyalbufar. **Autocares Armenteras,** Pl. Espanya (tel. 54 56 96), serves Alcudia and other ports in northern Mallorca. **Autocares Aumasa,** Pl. Espanya (tel. 55 07 30), provides solid links to the eastern seaboard, including Porto Cristo.

Ferries: Transmediterránea, Estación Marítim, 2 (tel. 40 50 14). Bus #1 runs along Pg. Marítim to the Moll Pelaires. Tickets sold Mon.-Fri. 9am-1pm and 5-7pm, Sat. 9am-noon. Ferries dock at Moll Pelaires (part-way around the bay south of the city), where you can buy tickets until shortly before departure. To: Ibiza (Thurs., 4½hr., 4590ptas); Mahón (Sun., 6½hr., 4590ptas); Barcelona (10 per week, 8hr., 6099ptas); Valencia (6 per week, 8½hr., 6099ptas).

Taxis: tel. 75 54 40 or 40 14 14. Airport fare is about 2000ptas.

Car Rental: Mascaro Crespi, Av. Joan Miró, 9 (tel. 73 61 03).

Moped Rental: RTR Bike Rental, Av. Joan Miró, 338 (tel. 40 25 85). From Pl. Espanya, take bus #3 to Pl. Gomila. Mopeds 2300ptas per day, 3900ptas for 3 days. Open Mon.-Sat. 9am-9pm.

Luggage Storage: SFM office, Pl. Espanya. Small locker 200ptas, big locker 300ptas. 24-hr. automatic system.

English Bookstore: Book Inn, C. Horts, 20 (tel. 71 38 98), right off La Rambla. An impressive selection of literature. Children's books too. Open Mon.-Fri. 10am-1:30pm and 5-8pm; Oct.-May Mon.-Fri. 10am-1:30pm and 5-8pm, Sat. 10am-1pm.

Laundromat: Fast Laundry, Av. Joan Miró, 5 (tel. 45 46 14). 5kg wash, dry, and fold 1300ptas. Open Mon.-Fri. 8am-8:30pm, Sat. 8am-2pm.

Women's Center: Central Informació Drets de la Dona, C. Portella, 11, 2nd fl. (tel. 72 25 51), near Parc de la Mar. At the end of Av. Antoni Maura by the waterfront, turn left up the stairs to D'alt Murada and take the 2nd left; 3 doors down from the Museu de Mallorca. Rape crisis assistance available. Open Mon.-Fri. 9am-2pm. **24-hr. hotline,** tel. (900) 19 10 10.

Medical Assistance: Hospital Provincial Sa Misericordia, Pl. Hospital, s/n (tel. 17 35 01). From Pl. Espanya walk to C. Olmos (OMS on most maps), turn right on Pg. Rambla, left on C. Bisbe Campins, and another left onto C. Misericordia.

24-hr. Pharmacy: See listings in local paper, *Diario de Mallorca* (100ptas).

Emergency: tel. 091 or 092.

Police: Municipal, on Av. Sant Ferran, s/n (tel. 28 16 00).

ACCOMMODATIONS

For cheap rooms, check out the back streets of the **Barri Gòtic.** For 500-600ptas more and a bus commute (#3 from Pl. Espanya, every 10min.) from the center of town, some *hostales* by **Parc Gomila** on Av. Joan Miró offer fairly luxurious lodging five minutes from the city's nightlife. Make reservations for late July and August.

Alberg Juvenil Platja de Palma (HI), C. Costa Brava, 13 (tel. 26 08 92), in the beach town El Arenal. Take bus #15 from Pl. Espanya (130ptas) and ask the driver to let you off at Hotel Acapulco. Poorly-lit. Showers only a water conservationist could love. Dunk at the beach instead (2 bl. away). 1000ptas per person. Members only. Breakfast 200ptas. Curfew midnight, weekends 3am. Open Jan.-Nov.

Hostal Bonany, C. Almirante Cervera, 5 (tel. 73 79 24), in El Terreno, 3km from the center of town and 5min. from the nightlife. Take bus #3, 20, 21, or 22 from Pl. Espanya to the beginning of Av. Joan Miró, walk up C. Camilo José Cela, take the first right, then the first left. Rooms resemble those in the island brochure—spacious, with full bath and a balcony overlooking the private pool and patio. Singles 2200ptas. Doubles 3850ptas. Hearty breakfast (bread, coffee, eggs, cheese, and juice) 400ptas. Open Feb.-Nov. Credit cards accepted.

Hostal Ritzi, C. Apuntadores, 6 (tel. 71 46 10), off Pl. Reina. Meticulous British owner keeps a classy *hostal* with ritzy throw pillows and wall-to-wall carpeting. Parlor jammed with knick-knacks and English books. Well-heated in winter. Singles 1700ptas. Doubles 2800ptas, with shower 3200ptas, with bath 3500ptas. Keys for 24-hr. entry. Call 2 weeks ahead to ensure a reservation.

Hostal Residencia Pons, C. Vi, 8 (tel. 72 26 58), at the end of C. Apuntadores, which starts at Pl. Reina. This quiet retreat looks like a Victorian museum, with room after room of luxurious antique furniture and collectibles. Beware of morning rush-hour traffic as 21 rooms share a single bath. 1400ptas per person. Showers 250ptas.

Hostal Goya, C. Estanc, 7 (tel. 72 69 86), off Pg. Born. Cheapest thing you'll find with Goya's name on it. Bare-walled, aging *hostal*. Singles 900ptas.

Hostal Brondo, C. Brondo, 1 (tel. 71 90 43), just off Pl. Rei Joan Carles I in the center of the old city. Singles 2000ptas, with bath 3000ptas. Doubles 3500ptas, with bath 5000ptas. Triples 7000ptas. Keys for 24-hr. entry. Credit cards accepted.

Camping: Platja Blava (tel. 53 78 63) is located at km 8 of the highway between Alcudia and C'an Picafort. 550ptas per person and 600ptas for a 3-by-6 meter plot. Ten buses leave daily for C'an Picafort from Palma (600ptas). **Club San Pedro** (tel. 58 90 23) is a 3rd-class site 2km outside of Colònia de Sant Pere. 450ptas per person and 975ptas per tent. Open April-Oct. To get here from Palma, hop on a C'an Picafort bus and take a connecting bus to Colònia de Sant Pere.

FOOD

Menus come in German, French, Hittite, and English, as well as *mallorquín* and Spanish, but the food is rarely as international. Mom-and-Pop operations serve tourists and locals alike along side streets, especially around **Passeig Born.** Two **markets** vie for customers, one in Pl. Olivar, off C. Padre Atanasio near Pl. Espanya; the other across town by Pl. Navegació in Es Jonquet. (Both open Mon.-Sat. 7am-2pm.)

Groceries: Servicio y Precios (SYP), C. Felip Bauzà (tel. 72 78 11). Just a little larger than the corner store at home. Open Mon.-Fri. 9am-2pm and 5:15-8:30pm, Sun. 9am-2pm.

Celler Pagès, C. Felip Bauzà, 2 (tel. 72 60 36), at the end of C. Pintor Guillem Mesquida off Pl. Reina. A Mallorcan bourgeois midday crowd. Bowl of spiced olives with every 900pta *menú*. Open Mon.-Fri. 1-4pm and 8:30-11pm, Sat. 1-4pm.

Bodega Casa Payesa, C. Moliners, 3, in an alleyway off C. Sant Miguel, 4 streets from Pl. Major. An informal verbal *menú* allows the owner to whip up most anything your heart desires (limited to food). *Menú* 600ptas or *paella* with bread, drink, and dessert 460ptas. Open Mon.-Fri. 8am-8:30pm, Sat. 8am-3:30pm.

Celler Sa Premsa, Pl. Bisbe Berenguer de Palou, 8 (tel. 72 35 29), between Via Roma and Pl. Espanya off Carrer OMS. Traditional *mallorquín* food served by superhumanly efficient waiters on platters with vegetables. Veal steak 695ptas. Famous *sopas mallorquinas* (hearty vegetable soup, 460ptas). Open Mon.-Fri. noon-4pm and 7pm-midnight.

Bon Lloc, C. Sant Feliu, 7 (tel. 71 86 17), off Pg. Born. Excellent vegetarian restaurant serves up *nouveau riche* morsels of proteins and vitamins. Midday 4-plate *menú* 1075ptas. No smoking. Open Tues.-Sat. 1-4pm and Fri. (*a la carte*) 9-11pm.

Merendero Minyones, C. Minyones, 4. An infinitesimal booth on a small street 1 bl. from and parallel to C. Constitució. *Pa-amb-oli i tomate* (tomato and olive oil on bread, 95ptas). *Sobrasada* (soft Mallorcan *chorizo* spread, 130ptas). They'll wrap up large selection of sandwiches (130-195ptas). Open Mon.-Fri. 7:30am-8:30pm, Sat. 8am-2pm.

C'an Joan de S'aigo, C. Sanç, 10 (tel. 71 07 59), near Pl. Coll. Children from 7 to 107 enjoy this old-fashioned ice cream parlor, housed in the city's oldest building. Mallorca's specialty is *gelado de almendra* (almond ice cream, 170ptas). Open Tues.-Sun. 8am-9pm.

Yate Rizz, Pg. Born, 2 (tel. 72 62 46). Perhaps it was for this establishment's oft-greasy food that the term "greasy spoon" was coined. Serious 2-course *menú* with bread, wine, and dessert (600ptas). Open Mon.-Sat. 12:30-3:30pm.

SIGHTS

Inaugurated in Dec. 1992, **Fundació Joan i Pilar Miró,** C. Saridakis, 29 (tel. 70 14 20), is essentially a collection of the works found in the Catalán artist's Palma studio (open to the public) at the time of his death. (Open Tues.-Sat. 10am-7pm, Sun. 11am-2pm; Sept.-Apr. Tues.-Sat. 11am-6pm, Sun. 11am-2pm. Admission 400ptas.) **Col·leccio March, Art Espanyol Contemporani,** C. Sant Miquel, 11 (tel. 71 26 01), has a collection of 36 works, each by a different 20th-century Spanish artist, including Picasso, Dalí, Miró, Juan Gris, and Antoni Tàpies. The curator kindly and patiently answers the befuddled questions of those who thought art ended with Monet. (Open Mon.-Fri. 10am-1:30pm and 4:30-7:30pm, Sat. 10am-1:30pm. Admission 300ptas.) The **Palau Sollerich,** C. Sant Gaietà, 10 (tel. 77 20 92), frequently opens to the public with contemporary art exhibits. (Free.)

The **Barri Gòtic** (medieval quarter) around the cathedral and Palau Almudaina is a tangle of tight streets, half-covered by the overhanging carved wooden eaves of elegant townhouses still occupied by aristocracy. At the top of the hill at C. Palau Reial, the **catedral** (tel. 72 31 30)—one of the largest Gothic cathedrals in the world—dramatically overlooks Palma and its bay. Begun in 1230, the cathedral wasn't finished until 1601. Gaudí then modified the interior and the ceiling ornamentation in *Modernista* fashion so it would blend smoothly with the stately exterior. (Cathedral and **tresor** of Palma's patron saint San Sebastián open Mon.-Fri. 10am-6pm, Sat. 10am-2:30pm; Nov.-Mar. Mon.-Fri. 10am-3pm, Sat. 10am-2pm. Admission for both 300ptas.)

The **Museu Diocesà** (tel. 71 40 63), behind the cathedral on C. Palau, is pure eclecticism. Highlights of the collection include 15th-century statues and tableaux; an alligator killed and stuffed in 1776; the autographs of Napoleon Bonaparte, Emperor Maximilian of Mexico, Queen Victoria, and Louis Philippe D'Orléans; and, perhaps for connoisseurs of 18th-century ale, a collection of American quarters. (Open Mon.-Fri. 10am-1:30pm and 3-8pm, Sat.-Sun. 10am-1pm; Nov.-Mar. Mon.-Fri. 10am-1pm and 3-6pm, Sat.-Sun. 10am-1pm. Admission 300ptas.)

Mallorca's only well-preserved Moorish legacy are the un-thrilling **Banys Arabs** (Arab sauna baths), located in the same area on C. Serra. (Tel. 72 15 49; open 9:30am-8pm. Admission 100ptas.) On the opposite side of Av. D'Antoni Maura is the graceful **Llotja** (tel. 71 17 05), on Pg. Sagrera near the waterfront, a 15th-century merchants' association. Currently, exhibitions flow through the preserved building regularly. (Open Tue.-Sat. 11am-2pm and 5-9pm, Sun. 11am-2pm. Free.) **Basilica de Sant Francesc,** in the *plaça* of the same name, is a cavernous 13th-century Gothic structure altered in the 16th and 17th centuries with the incorporation of a Plateresque and Baroque facade. (Open Mon.-Sat. 9:30am-noon and 3:30-6:45pm, Sun. 9:30am-noon.) Right next to the *catedral,* **Palau Reial Almudaina** (tel. 72 71 45) was constructed by the Moors, and later adopted by the Christian kings. Guided tours, which include the museum, are given in numerous languages, except when King Juan Carlos is tromping about the halls on business. (Open Mon.-Fri. 10am-7pm, Sat.-Sun. 10:30am-2pm; Oct.-Mar. Mon.-Fri. 10am-2pm and 4-6pm, Sat.-Sun. 10:30am-2pm. Admission 400ptas, students 275ptas.)

Overlooking the city and bay and set in a park, **Castell de Bellver** (tel. 73 06 57) served as summer residence for the 12th-century royalty; for centuries thereafter it housed distinguished but unwilling guests. The castle contains a **Museu Municipal** of archaeological displays. Buses (#3, 21, 22, or 23) leave from C. Joan Miró. (Castle, grounds, and museum open 8am-8pm; Oct.-Mar. 8am-6pm. Admission 150ptas.) A little way outside of town is Palma's **Poble Espanyol,** C. Poble Espanyol, 39 (tel. 73 70 75), a smaller reproduction of its parent in Barcelona, with scaled-down samples of Spanish architecture. Buses #4 and 5 pass nearby along C. Andrea Doria. (Open Mon.-Sat. 9am-8pm; Arts & Crafts Mon.-Sat. 10am-6pm. Admission 350ptas, under 12 250ptas.)

ENTERTAINMENT

The municipal tourist office dutifully keeps a comprehensive list of sporting activities, concerts, and exhibits. Every Friday, *El Día de Mundo* newspaper (100ptas) publishes an entertainment supplement with numerous listings of bars and discos all over Mallorca. The **Centre de Cultura "Sa Nostra,"** C. Concepció, 12 (tel. 72 51 10), sponsors daily and free cultural events such as lectures, concerts, and movies, and displays a hall of temporary art exhibits. (Center open Mon.-Fri. 10:30am-9pm, Sat. 10:30am-1:30pm. Exhibition hall open Mon.-Fri. 10:30am-1:30pm and 5-9pm, Sat. 10:30am-1:30pm. Admission free.)

Enact your fantasies of the aristocratic life in the *casa antigua*-turned-bar **ABACO,** C. Sant Joan, 1 (tel. 71 59 11), in the Barri Gòtic near the waterfront. Drinks appear amid elegant furniture, cooing doves and ducks, piles of fresh fruit and flowers, and hundreds of dripping candles, all to the accompaniment of Handel, Bach, et al. Fruit nectars cost 750ptas, cocktails 1300-1400ptas; but wandering the chambers is fun and free.

Salsa is chic in Palma, and those who have the gusto and hips head to **El Rincón Latino** (tel. 45 59 92) on C. Industria near Pg. Mallorca and C. Argentina. *Caipirinha,* a zingy Brazilian lemon cocktail (700ptas), oils the hips until the 6am coda (Wed.-Sat. 11pm-4am, no cover). The rest of Palma nightlife is in the **El Terreno** area, with a motherlode of nightclubs centered on Pl. Gomilia and along C. Joan Miró. **Minim's,** Pl. Gomilia, 3A (tel. 73 16 97), is a magnet for the rich and extravagant, a favorite watering hole of King Carlos's children. **Plato,** across the street at Pl. Gomilia, 2, keeps a lower, more local profile. At Pl. Gomilia, 1, **Tito's Palace** (tel. 73 76 42) is an indoor coliseum of mirrors and lights with windows overlooking the water (open 11am-6am, cover 1500ptas). Hats off to the gay bar **Sombrero,** at C. Joan Miró, 26. (Tel. 73 16 00; open 9pm-3am. No cover.) The divine **Baccus** (tel. 45 77 89), around the corner on C. Lluis Fábregas, 2, attracts lively lesbian and gay hedonists (open until 3am). Finally, the thirtysomething crowd heads to the waterfront for **Victoria Boite,** Pg. Marítim (tel. 45 12 13), directly below Tito's. Fluorescent blue lights and 70s tunes are staying alive in this couch-filled pad (cover 1500ptas).

Though better **beaches** spread throughout the expanse of the island, decent ones are a mere bus ride from Palma. The beach at **El Arenal** (Platja de Palma, bus #15), 11km to the southeast, is popular—a little over-touristed perhaps. The clear-watered **Palma Nova** and **Illetes** beaches (buses #21 and 3 respectively) are 15 and 9km southwest.

Residents use any and every occasion, even a national holiday, as an excuse to party. One of the more colorful bashes, **Día de Sant Joan** (June 24), involves a no-expense-spared fireworks display the night before, followed by singing, dancing, and drinking in Parc del Mar below the cathedral.

■■■ WESTERN COAST

The westernmost end of Mallorca, punctuated by the small Isla Dragonera (Dragon Island), plunges abruptly into the water from the Sierra de Tramontana. Stone walls stitched across the slopes support terraced olive groves, and villages (in spite of encroaching development) crouch in protected pouches on the hillside.

The best way to explore the region is to choose a destination along the gorgeous coast, and then meander on foot. The Playa-Sol company (tel. 29 64 17) runs buses from stops around Pl. Espanya in Palma to as far south as Magaluf, about 8km from the end of Cabo de Cala Figuera, and to the handy transport base Andraitx, 30km from Palma. Nord Balear buses depart from C. Arxiduc Lluis Salvador, 24 (tel. 20 21 25), also near Pl. Espanya, for Banyalbufar's beaches and quiet hills.

A Rambler's Paradise, available at the tourist office (tel. 13 91 09; open Mon.-Fri. 9am-2pm) in Calvia, a city southwest of Palma, has helpful suggestions.

VALLDEMOSA

Valldemosa's weathered houses huddle in the harsh yet beauteous Sierra de Tramontana. Little in this ancient village hints at the passion that shocked the townsfolk in the winter of 1838-39, when tubercular Frédèric Chopin and his lover George Sand (with her two children in tow) stayed in the **Cartoixa Reial** (tel. 61 21 06), loudly flouting the monastic tradition of celibacy. The monastery's museum assembles innumerable Chopin memorabilia, including a picture of the famous hands and the piano upon which they played. There are short piano recitals here in the summer (8 per day, one by a famous pianist the last Sunday in July; Mallorcan dance on Mon. and Thurs. mornings).

The **Museu Municipal** inside the monastery collects dust and documents on the royalty that once lived in town. Next door is **Palau del Rei Sancho,** a Moorish residence converted into a palace by Mallorcan kings. (Cartoixa Reial open Mon.-Fri. 9:30am-1pm and 3-6:30pm; Nov.-Feb 9:30am-1pm and 3-5:30pm; Oct. and March 9:30am-1pm and 3-6pm. Admission to everything 900ptas.)

Valldemosa lacks many basic services (no tourist office), but the **post office** is at Pl. Ruben Carío, 21, down the street from the museum. (Open Mon.-Fri. 8:30am-11:30pm.) Bus Nord Balear **buses** (tel. 20 21 25) to Valldemosa leave from Palma at the bar at C. Arxiduc Salvador, 1 (5 per day, 175ptas).

Near Valldemosa, 10km north on the bus route to Sóller, vogues the artists' hangout, **Deyá** (5 buses per day, 95ptas). Tourists frequent its overpriced restaurants, all on the main road, for lunch. Walks through this unspoiled town and surrounding area afford a sensational view of miles and miles of twisted olive trees. Cryptic Mallorcan folklore holds that only the thousand-year-old trees have witnessed the true history of the island. Said trees, however, were unavailable for comment.

SÓLLER AND PUERTO DE SÓLLER

Another 30km up the coast, **Sóller** basks in a mountain valley that opens 3km to its golden port and the aqua Mediterranean Sea. The endpoint of a train ride through the pine covered "alps" of Mallorca, the town hums with tourists all day long. Every available plot of land is lined with citrus groves. Tall glasses of freshly squeezed OJ are a local specialty and ritual. The tangy nectars and shady *plaças* make Sóller a refreshing escape from the concrete and heat of Palma.

There's not much to see but a sand castle-like **catedral** in Pl. Constitució. (Open Mon.-Fri. 10am-12:30pm and 2:30-5pm, Sat. 10am-12:30pm.) In August, the Ajuntament hosts an international **Festival de Dança Folclorica** with dancers from all of Europe, and Asia (1995 festival dates to be determined).

The **tourist office** in the town hall on Pl. Constitució, 1 (tel. 63 02 00; open Mon.-Sat. 9:30am-1:30pm), supplies a map and keeps a list of the few **accommodations** in Sóller. They can suggest scenic hikes through the valley's handsome citrus and olive orchards; one manageable route steps to **Fornalutx,** about an hour up the valley. The **post office** is on C. Cristobal Piza at C. Rectoria, about two bl. from Pl. Constitució. (Open Mon.-Fri. 9am-2pm, Sat. 9am-1pm.) The **police** (Guardia Civil) can be reached at tel. 63 02 03, the **Red Cross** at tel. 63 30 11. Five **trains** per day bound to Sóller from Palma (360ptas; tel. 75 20 28 for information).

The half-hour walk to **Puerto de Sóller** from the beach is free exercise, but many people prefer to rumble along on the **trolley** (110ptas). The port, at the bottom of the valley, absorbs most of the tourists. A white-sand beach lines the small, semicircular bay, where windsurfers zip back and forth. Numerous hotels hang at the base of the mountains, floored by foreign package-tourists. **Hotel Miramar,** C. Marina, 12-14 (tel. 63 13 50), provides modern comforts, including full bath and bright, orange beds in every room. Patio restaurant in front. (Singles 2090ptas. Doubles

3275ptas. Triples 3800ptas.) Restaurants of all sorts and sizes file along the beach. **Restaurante Bar La Pirata,** C. Santa Catalina, 8 (tel. 63 14 97), near the next trolley stop, stands out for its 800pta *menú* and the numerous spoils of a pirate ship spilled on the walls. (Open Jan.-Oct. Fri.-Wed. 11am-4pm and 7pm-midnight.)

Exploring the rest of the coves on the coast is easiest by **boat. Tramontana** and **Barcos Azules** on the port near the last trolley stop (tel. 63 20 61) sail four times daily to Sa Calobra (May-Oct.15, round-trip 1600ptas) and Cala Deyá (June-Oct. 15, round-trip 1100ptas). Nord Balear **buses** link Puerto de Sóller to Palma via Vall-demosa (5 per day, 415ptas).

SA CALOBRA

If your parents saw the road to **Sa Calobra,** they'd reach for the Valium. This asphalt serpent drops 1000m to the sea over ten hairpin km, writhing back underneath itself in the process. The **boat** from Puerto de Sóller is easier on the nerves (see above). If you don't suffer from vertigo or claustrophobia, try Sa Calobra: a 5-minute hike through tunnels cut in cliffs leads to the **Torrent de Pareis,** a pebble-strewn canyon which ends in a bit of coast. In winter it becomes a river, but in summer it is a super beach with water so clear you can see the shadows of boats on the bottom.

LLUC

The **Monestir de Lluc** (tel. 51 70 25), 20km inland in Escorca, tucks into the moun-tains, remote from the frenetic coastal bustle. Lluc is Mallorca's Montserrat, home of the 700-year-old image of *La Verge de Lluc,* whose carved wood has turned a dark brown over the years (hence its nickname, *La Moreneta,* The Dark Lady). She dark-ens in a room behind the main altar in the basilica. The in-house **museu** aggregates somewhat interesting prehistoric remains, 15th-century ceramics, and 14th-century religious treasures. (Open 10am-5:30pm. Admission 250ptas.) Behind the monas-tery, **Via Crucis** winds around a hill with a view of the valley's olive trees and jin-gling goats. Gaudí designed the path's stations of the cross.

Monks, pilgrims, and a few privileged guests stay overnight at Lluc's **monastery** (tel. 51 70 25). (True pilgrims stay for a donation. Everybody else: doubles with bath 2350ptas. Quads 2450ptas, with bath 3000ptas.) The monks can also point you to **campgrounds** nearby. The monastery's small food store sells **groceries,** and its res-**taurant,** pricey food. To get to the monastery from Palma, take the 10am or 4pm **train** to Inca, which arrives in time for the two daily connecting **buses** to Lluc.

■■■ NORTHERN GULFS

Two peninsulas of land point rudely at Menorca, forming large, beautiful bays on Mallorca's northern edge. The package tours and condo developments that overrun these beaches have missed a secluded cove or two in their haste. Many towns are well connected to and easiest to reach through Inca.

POLLENÇA

Puerto de Pollença's long beaches and short strip of residential development make for a relatively uncrowded beach of fine white sand and rambunctious surf. The area hosts a **festival de música** from July to September. A complete schedule of events and list of ticket vendors is available at the tourist office (tickets 2000-3000ptas, stu-dent discount of 25% available with *Carnet Joven*).

Hostal Corro, C. Joan XXIII, 68 (tel. 86 50 05), has expansive rooms with sinks. (Singles 1500ptas. Doubles 2500ptas. Triples 3500ptas.) Closer to the beaches, **Hos-tal Residencia Bauza,** C. Juan de la Cosa, 32 (tel. 86 54 74), pleases with firm beds and a balcony view of the bay from the third-floor rooms. (Doubles 2200ptas; July-Aug. 2400ptas.)

The **tourist office,** at Pl. Miquel Capllonch, 2 (tel. 53 46 66), off C. Atilio Bover from the waterfront, weeds through bus schedules and plans excursions in a single bound. (Open May-Oct. Mon.-Fri. 9am-1pm and 4-7pm, Sat. 9am-1pm.) The **post office** is on C. Llevant, 15. (Open for stamps Mon.-Fri. 9am-9pm, Sat. 9am-2pm; for **telegrams** Mon.-Fri. 8am-9pm, Sat. 9am-2pm.) Maria's, C. Joan XXIII, 52 (tel. 53 24 68), near Hostal Corro, rents two-wheelers. (**Bikes** 600ptas per day, 2200ptas per week. **Mopeds** 2000ptas per day, 10,500ptas per week. Open March-Oct. Mon.-Sat. 9am-1pm and 3-7:30pm, Sun. 9am-1pm and 6-7:30pm.) Right on the beach, a summertime **telephone kiosk** handles international calls (open April-Oct. 9:30am-10pm). **Laundry service** available at Launderette Poles, C. Verge del Carme, 19, for 900ptas complete (open daily 9am-9pm).

At the end of **Cabo Formentor,** 15km northeast of Puerto de Pollença, *miradores* (lookouts) overlook spectacular fjords. Before the final twisting km, the road drops down to **Platja Formentor,** where a canopy of evergreens runs nearly to the edge of the water. Here the sand is softer, the water calmer, and the crowds smaller than at Puerto de Pollença. Armenteras **buses** (tel. 54 56 96) connect Palma to Alcudia, which in turn connects to many neighboring cities, including Puerto de Pollença (every 15min. 8:30am-8pm, 110ptas). Hydrophiles can also take the boat to Formentor from Puerto de Pollença (tel. 86 40 14; 5 per day, 650ptas).

ALCUDIA

14th-century ramparts encircle one side of **Alcudia,** and dazzling isolated coves and beaches string their way around the other. The spiritual center of the town, **Ermita de la Victoria,** is tucked away in a pine grove near the notable **Museu Arqueológic,** C. de Sant Jaume, 30 (tel. 54 63 13), next to the church. (Open Tues.-Sat. 10am-1:30pm and 5-7pm, Sun. 10am-1:30pm. Admission 200ptas.)

The **tourist office** (tel. 89 26 15) is near the waterfront at Av. Pere Mas Reus, on the corner with Ctra. Arta, at the 3rd stop on the bus after the tourist port. English spoken. (Open April-Sept. Mon.-Sat. 9am-7pm.) An equally helpful and much more mobile **tourist van** parks outside the tourist port. (Open Tues.-Sun. 10am-1pm and 5-8pm. Parks at the town market on Tues. and Sun. mornings.) The summertime **telephone kiosk** tinkles at the tourist port (open 9am-1pm and 4-10pm). Rent bikes at 600ptas per day from **Reina Bike Rental,** C. Teodoro Canet, 27 (tel. 54 55 72; open in summer 9am-1pm and 5-8pm). **Medical attention** in Puerto de Alcudia can be had at **Casa del Mar,** C. Ciudadela (tel. 54 59 68) or **Ambulatorio** (tel. 54 63 71). Municipal **police** can be reached at tel. 54 51 49.

The only HI youth hostel outside of Palma resides in Alcudia. Signs to the **Alberg Victoria,** Ctra. Cap Pinar, 4 (tel. 54 53 95), lead east from the town center, up a hillside road, 4km from Alcudia (1-hr. walk or 800pta taxi ride). The hostel lolls only 100m from an empty beach on the Bahía de Pollença. Reserve at least six months in advance to get a bed in July or August. (Members only 1900ptas. Breakfast included. Open mid-June-Sept.) **Puerto de Alcudia,** the beach and boating area 1km south, has less crowded and only slightly more expensive accommodations; the trusty tourist office has the master list. At C. Teodoro Canet, 29, on the road that leads up to Alcudia, **Hostal Puerto** (tel. 54 54 47) offers multi-star hotel-quality rooms with private baths and cable TV in the downstairs lounge. (Open May-Oct. Singles 1500ptas. Doubles 2600ptas.)

Armenteras **buses** (tel. 54 56 96) for Alcudia (485ptas) and Puerto de Alcudia (505ptas) leave Pl. Espanya in Palma (Mon.-Sat. 10 per day, Sun. 5 per day). The bus between Alcudia and Puerto de Pollença runs reliably, and some buses continue on to Cabo Formentor. Bus service to the south goes only as far as C'an Picafort.

■■■ EASTERN COAST

As the tourist swarm sweeps east, it swallows dozens of small coastal towns in its path, then seeps underground to the eerie Plutonian landscapes of the region's many caves. Buses connect most of the major towns and beaches.

ARTÁ

Mallorca's best caves, the **Covas de Artá** (tel. 56 32 93), burrow 10km away from Artá itself. The labyrinth of vaulted chambers with imposing stalactites and stalagmites (mites go up, tites go down) draws far fewer explorers than the Covas del Drach and exudes a macabre and mysterious beauty (tours daily, every ½hr. 10am-7pm; winter daily 10am-5pm; 750ptas). Aumasa **buses** (tel. 55 07 30) leave Pl. Espanya in Palma for Artá (Mon.-Sat. 4 per day, Sun. 2 per day, 685ptas) and continue to Cala Ratjada (120ptas more).

PORTO CRISTO

Porto Cristo itself has nothing but excursion buses and annoyed tourists. 25km to the south, however, are the famous **Covas del Drach.** These Caves of the Dragon (tel. 82 07 53) are enormous, spectacular, and fantasy-inducing—a good thing, too, since in real life you'll be marching through the caverns in lockstep with thousands of package tourists. One-hour tours include a break at the edge of a big lake, where cunningly lit boats float back and forth carrying musicians who play classical music. (Tours daily on the hr. 10am-5pm. Admission 800ptas.)

Porto Cristo's **aquari** (tel. 82 09 71) is just off the road to the caves (1km outside town). Its dinginess and general failure to inform or entertain are excused by virtue of its being one of the largest marine life collections in Europe, including a very big turtle. (Open 10am-7pm; off-season 11am-3pm. Admission 500ptas.) For your own human marine pleasure, hop on a boat to Cala Romántica (3 per day, round-trip 800ptas) or Cala Millor (midday, 1200ptas).

The **tourist office,** C. d'En Gual, 31-A (tel. 82 09 31), behind the town church, has a map as well as a list of superb restaurants and accommodations. (Open summer Mon.-Fri. 8:30am-3pm.) The **post office** is at C. Zanglada, 10 (tel. 82 16 07), off C. Navegantes. (Open Mon.-Fri. 9am-2pm, Sat. 9am-1pm.) For **medical attention,** call the **Red Cross** at 82 07 84.

Aumasa **buses** (tel. 55 07 30) connect Porto Cristo with Ca'n Picafort (3 per day, 565ptas); Palma, via Manacor (Mon.-Sat. 7 per day, Sun. 2 per day, 1hr., 675ptas); and various **beaches** nearby, including **Cala Ratjada** (Mon.-Sat. 8 per day, 450ptas).

■■■ SOUTHEAST

The eastern coast of Mallorca's southeastern peninsula is a scalloped fringe of bays and caves. Many harbor the island's most recent resort developments, where new hotel towns aspire to some architectural integrity. A walk of 1-2km, however, puts plenty of sand between you and the thickest crowds.

Rounding **Cap de Salinas,** Mallorca's southernmost point, the long leg of coastline back to Palma begins. Miles of inaccessible and isolated sand lie between here and **Cap Blanc,** beyond which ill-humored, rocky cliffs fend off Palma's southern suburbs. The grandsons of Joan March, an infamous Spanish banker, own most of the southeastern interior.

Autocares Grimalt buses leave Cafetería Alcalá, Av. Alejandro Rosselló, 32 (tel. 46 35 27), in Palma, for a number of recommendable destinations in the southeast: **Santanyí,** an inland town whose Porta Murada (defensive wall) testifies to the piracy that once plagued the region; **Cala d'Or,** an inlet of pinewoods and massive boulders; **Porto Petro,** on the beach; and **Colonia Sant Jordi.**

From Colonia Sant Jordi, a boat ventures to **Cabrera,** the largest island (30 sq. km) in a small archipelago of 17. (Grimalt buses do not arrive early enough to catch the boat. For boat info, call Excursiones a Cabrera; tel. 64 90 34.) Uninhabited except for a small military installation, it has a gruesome history. Besides the many shipwrecks that poke up from the ocean floor, 8000 French prisoners of war died here during the Peninsular War in 1809; the Spanish abandoned them on the island with no food. A monument to the dead stands by the port. Nearby looms a 14th-century fortress used as a pirates' den.

■■■ INLAND

Orchards, vineyards, and wheat fields make up Mallorca's heartland. Ancient stone walls, crumbling and rudimentary, divide inland valleys into individual farms, where windmills and haystacks dot hillside fig, olive, and almond groves. Pastel almond blossoms flourish in February, their petals covering the island like fragrant confetti.

INCA

Inca lies just south of the Sierra de Tramontana, panting for the moisture barred by the mountains. Halfway between Palma and Alcudia and at the end of a railway, it attracts visitors with inexpensive leather goods and a busy Thursday morning market. Snack-food connoisseurs flock to Inca for authentic *galletes d'oli,* locally produced cookies that resemble overfed American goldfish crackers. The main streets parallel to the railroad tracks—**Carrer de Colom** and **Carrer de Vicent Ensenyat**—are lined with factory-outlet leather shops, which sell everything from books and combs to whips and chains.

Inca lies 35 minutes by **train** (tel. 50 00 59) from Palma (Mon.-Sat. 20 per day, Sun. 16 per day, 215ptas). Five **buses** per day make the trek from Inca to Alcudia.

MANACOR

As part of its grand scheme to lure the masses away from the beaches, Manacor has developed a booming faux-pearl industry. Factories open for visits and purchases. The largest one, **Perlas Majorca,** Via Roma, 48 (tel. 55 02 00), is on the road to Palma on the edge of town. (Open Mon.-Fri. 9am-1pm and 3-7pm, Sat.-Sun. 10am-1pm. Free.) **Perlas Orquídea,** on Pl. Ramón Llull, 15 (tel. 55 04 00) is a bit closer to town. (Open Mon.-Fri. 9am-7pm, Sat. 9am-1pm, Sun. 9:30am-1pm. Free.) There's not much else to see except for a turreted Gothic **catedral** and adjoining **Museu Arqueológic** (tel. 84 30 65; open Tues.-Thurs. 9am-1pm).

Aumasa **buses** depart from Pl. Cos, 4 (tel. 55 07 30) for: Palma (7 per day, Sun. 2 per day, 495ptas) and Porto Cristo (8 per day, Sun. 3 per day, 140ptas).

PETRA

Rocking nearby is **Petra,** the hometown of Fray Junípero Serra, the man responsible for the Spanish presence in California. The house of this ecclesiastical Johnny Appleseed, who founded a chain of West Coast Franciscan missions—the seedlings of San Francisco and San Diego, among others—is now a museum. The unadorned **Ermita de Bonany,** or "cathedral of the mountains," is a 1-hr walk into the gorgeous hills.

Aumasa **buses** leave Pl. Espanya in Palma for Petra (3/day, Sun. 2 /day, 490ptas).

FELANITX

About 15km south of Manacor, on route C714, lies **Felanitx** and its 16th-century convent of San Antonio. The town lounges at the foot of Puig de San Salvador, capped by the **Santuari de Nostra Senyora de San Salvador** (tel. 58 06 56) and the **Castell de Santuari,** which overlook the island Cabrera and the Bahía de Alcudia. Some accommodations are available.

Should you take a liking to the sequestered life, another monastery, the **Santuari de Nostra Señora de Cura** (tel. 66 09 94), goes about its humble routine 30km east of Palma. The sanctuary is open most daylight hours; if it's closed (usually around lunchtime), ask to be let in at the convent. If you don't have a car or motorbike, you'll have to take a **bus** to Lluchmajor and then hike or take a taxi.

MENORCA

This northernmost and easternmost of the Baleares has been part of the Catalan world since 1287, when Alfonso the Liberal, King of Cataluña and Aragón, liberally conquered its people. In the ensuing years, the island has seen pirates, Turkish, French, Spanish, and British visitors of varying degrees of friendliness. Nowadays Menorca's premier industry is that tricky business of convincing people to come and then convincing them to leave—tourism.

Aside from the tremendous suction power generated by the condominiums, apartment complexes, and luxury hotels which blanket the southern shore, Menorca's ability to attract tourists lies in its 700 square km of UNESCO-protected (Menorca was declared a Biosphere Reserve by UNESCO in 1983), Bronze Age monument-festooned, stone-walled, gently sloping... parking lots. No, pastures. Beautiful beaches, pristine natural harbors, and provincial fishing villages in the north don't hurt matters either. Menorca is greener and rainier than the other Baleares. Many hillsides, crossed with old stone walls and splotched by whitewashed houses, remain unpopulated and ideal for hiking.

Menorca's two main cities, Mahón in the east and Ciudadela in the west, serve as gateways to the island's natural and archeological wonders. A small chapel dedicated to Menorca's saint caps Mont Toro, the island's highest peak. At the foot of the road leading to the shrine is Mercadal, a brilliantly white town and departure point for the road to Fornells. Excellent topographical maps (250ptas per quadrant) are sold at Cós 4, Cós de Gràcia, 4 (tel. 36 66 69), in Mahón. (Open Mon.-Fri. 10am-1pm and 6-8pm, Sat. 10am-1pm.) The maps mark island houses as well as archeological sites.

■■■ MAHÓN (MAÒ)

Perched atop a steep bluff, Mahón (pop. 22,150) overlooks a deep, well-trafficked harbor. The white-splashed houses and mellow inhabitants of Menorca's capital evince a gentility long forsaken by most tourist-plagued cities. The British occupied Mahón for almost a century in the 1700s and left Georgian doors, brass knockers, and wooden shutters in their wake. Gin distilleries, British-style pubs, and the city's early bedtime testify to a continuing influence.

Mahón is the place to eat, drink, sleep, shop, rent a moped, or take a bus to the beach (no beaches are within easy walking distance). The city's fascinating history and culture are evident during the major festivals (see Sights and Entertainment).

ORIENTATION AND PRACTICAL INFORMATION

If you arrive in Mahón by air, you have only the choice of which taxi to take into town (7km, 850ptas); there is no other pubic transportation to or from the airport. If you arrive by sea at the **ferry station,** walk to the left about 150 yards, then turn right at the steps which cut through the twisty **Costa de ses Voltes.** The steps top off between Pl. Conquesta and Pl. Espanya.

Plaça de S'Esplanada is the transportation center for taxis, buses, and kids. Mahón is a maze of twisty, identical streets. Luckily for new arrivals, just about every plaza in the city sports a map kiosk. The tourist office gives away maps for free.

Tourist Office: Pl. S'Esplanada, 40 (tel. 36 37 90), across the plaza from the taxi stand. Marked only by a small government shield. Maps, bus schedules, church schedules, lists of restaurants and hotels, car rental services, and pamphlets on archeological sites. Some English spoken. Open Mon.-Fri. 8am-3pm and 5-7pm, Sat. 9:30am-1pm. Summer office at the **airport** (tel. 36 01 50) purveys similar materials. Open May-Oct. 8am-11pm. **Municipal information:** (tel. 36 90 99). English operator available upon request.

American Express: Viajes Iberia, C. Nou, 35 (tel. 36 28 48), 2 doors from Pl. Reial. No commission on traveler's checks. Cardholder mail held for 2 months. Open Mon.-Fri. 9am-1:30pm and 4:30-7:30pm, Sat. 9:30am-1pm.

Post Office: C. Bonaire, 11-13 (tel. 36 38 92), on the corner with C. Esglésias. From Pl. S'Esplanada, take C. Moreres (C. Dr. Orfila) until it becomes C. Hannover, then take the 1st left. Open for stamps (1st fl.) Mon.-Fri. 9am-9pm, Sat. 9am-1pm; for Lista de Correos (2nd fl.) Mon.-Sat. 9am-2pm. **Postal Code:** 07700.

Telephones: A **telefónica service** behind the playground in Pl. S'Esplanada. Open Mon.-Sat. 10am-1pm and 5-9:30pm, Sun. 6-10pm. **Telephone Code:** 971.

Airport: 7km out of town (tel. 36 01 50). Main office open 7:15am-9:30pm. Aviaco or Iberia to Palma (5 per day, 20min., 5050ptas, round-trip 9200ptas) and in summer, Barcelona and Madrid. Any travel agent issues tickets. In summer advance booking is essential. Call Aviaco at the airport (reservations tel. 36 56 73, info tel. 36 90 15). Many travel agencies offer charter flights.

Buses: Transportes Menorca (TMSA), C. Josep M. Quadrado, 7 (tel. 36 03 61), off Pl. S'Esplanada. To: Alayor (5 per day, 130ptas); Son Bou (5 per day, 215ptas); Mercadal (6 per day, 205ptas); Ferrerias (6 per day, 265ptas); Ciudadela (6 per day, 415ptas); Platja Punta Prima (9 per day, 170ptas); and Castell (every ½hr., 85ptas). Some depart from Pl. S'Esplanada, some from C. Quadrado; check signs posted at the bus stop. **Autocares Fornells** (tel. 37 66 21) are blue buses that depart from C. Vassallo, kitty-corner from Pl. S'Esplanada. To: Fornells (3 per day, 205ptas); Platja Es Grau (3 per day, Sun. 6 per day, 100ptas). The tourist office and the local paper *Menorca Diario Insular* (100ptas) have complete bus schedules with exact times. Buy all tickets aboard the buses.

Ferries: Transmediterránea (tel. 36 29 50), at Estació Marítima along Moll (Andén) de Ponent. To: Barcelona (6 per week, Oct.-May 2 per week, 9hr., *butaca* 6100ptas) and Palma (1 per week, 6½hr., 4750ptas), continuing to Valencia (9 more hr.). Open Mon.-Fri. 8:30am-noon and 5-7pm, Sat. 8:30am-noon, Sun. 1 hr. before departure to Palma.

Taxis: Taxi stand (tel. 36 12 83 or 36 28 91), or radio taxi from anywhere on the island (tel. 36 71 11). Flat rates for any given route. Taxi stop at Pl. S'Esplanada.

Car Rental: English-speaking car rental at **British Car-Hire,** Pl. S'Esplanada (tel. 36 24 32), with 24-hr. help service. Tourist office has list of all vehicle rental places and 9 gas stations on Menorca. Gas stations open 6am-10pm; Oct.-May 7am-9pm. Rotating 24-hr. service (one of them is always in Mahón) is listed in *Menorca Diario Insular*.

Bike and Moped Rental: Scores of places in town, all with similar prices. For a bike try **Just Bicicletas,** C. B., C. Infanta, 19 (tel. 36 47 51). 1 day 950ptas, 3 days 2500ptas. For mopeds, **Autos y Motos Valls,** Pl. Reial, 4 (tel. 36 28 39). 2-Person Suzuki 2800ptas per day, 6600ptas for 3 days. Open 9am-1:30pm and 5-8pm.

English Bookstore: English-Language Library, C. Vasallo, 48 (tel. 36 27 01), a few bl. off Pl. S'Esplanada. Sells and lends a good selection of books. Open Mon., Wed., Fri. 9am-1pm and 5-7pm; Tues., Thurs., Sat. 9am-1pm.

Laundromat: 215, Antic Estació Marítima, at the port in a large yellow building behind the food market of the same name. 7kg wash and dry 1700ptas. Open 9am-1pm and 6-9pm.

Red Cross: tel. 36 11 80.

24-hr. Pharmacy: See listings in *Menorca Diario Insular* (local paper, 100ptas at newsstands in Pl. S'Esplanada).

Medical Assistance: Residencia Sanitaria, C. Barcelona, s/n (tel. 15 77 00). Near the waterfront, 1 bl. in from Pg. Marítim. English spoken.

Emergency: tel. 091 or 092. **Fire:** tel. 36 39 61.

Police: Municipal (tel. 092), Pl. Constitució. **Guardia Civil** (tel. 062), Ctra. Sant Lluís.

ACCOMMODATIONS

Space is a problem only in August. Call a few days in advance. The tourist office keeps a list of accommodations. Prices below are for high season only, unless otherwise specified.

Hostal Orsi, C. Infanta, 19 (tel. 36 47 51). From Pl. S'Esplanada, take C. Moreres straight as it becomes C. Hannover. Turn right at Pl. Constitució, and follow C. Nou through Pl. Reial. Hard-working English couple offers invaluable gems about the island's hidden treasures. Recently renovated rooms are clean and inviting.

Rooftop patio with view. Laundry service. Keys for 24-hr. entry. Singles 1950ptas. Doubles 3100ptas, with shower 3600ptas. Breakfast 350ptas.

Hotel la Isla, C. Santa Catalina, 4 (tel. 36 64 92). Take C. Concepció from Pl. Miranda. Family-run bar-restaurant-hotel with a marginally successful "hour of disco." Clean bathrooms with powerful running water. Singles 1650ptas, with bath 1800ptas. Doubles 3000ptas, with bath 3600ptas. Breakfast 250ptas.

Hostal-Residencia Jume, C. Concepció, 6 (tel. 36 32 66; fax 36 48 78), near Pl. Miranda. TV room, lounges on each floor, ice-cream freezer, bar, and pool table. Newish rooms all have full baths. Toiletries on sale at reception. Singles 1800ptas. Doubles 3500ptas.

Hostal Sheila, C. Santa Cecilia, 41 (tel. 36 48 55), off C. Concepció at C. Sant Nicolau. This family-run operation shines all around from the skylight in the hallway to the clay-tiled breakfast terrace. During July and August, full *pensión* (breakfast and dinner) required, 3500ptas per person; Sept.-June 1500ptas per person.

FOOD

Bars around **Plaças de la Constitució** and **S'Esplanada** serve filling *platos combinados* (400-650ptas). Mahón-*esa* was invented in Mahón, and mayonnaise lends its subtle overtones to a wide variety of edibles in this city. A polite, yet firm, *"sin mahonesa, por favor,"* is the mantra of the gastronomically timid. Local favorites (not all with the blessed white spread) are *formatge maonès* (a local cheese), *sobrasada* (soft *chorizo* spread), *caldereta de langosta* (lobster stew), *crespells* (biscuits), and *rubiols* (pastry turnovers filled with fish or vegetables). The **market** off Pl. Carme hawks fruits, vegetables, and sandwich meats.

Restaurante La Huerta, C. Rovellada de Baix, 64 (tel. 36 28 85). Take C. Rovellada de Dalt off Pl. Esplanada and make a sharp right at the 1st intersection. Toothsome dining on fresh fish and salads in front of a wide-screen TV. Enticing 2-course meal with salad, bread, wine, and dessert 825ptas, 975ptas on Sun. Open Mon.-Fri. 1-3:30pm and 8:30pm-12:30am, Sat.-Sun. 1-3:30pm.

Pizzería La Dolce Vita, C. Sant Roc, 25 (tel. 36 48 24), off Pl. Bastió. Inviting and casual, less pretentious than the film. Large plate of pasta 475-725ptas. Pizza 475-1100ptas. Take-out available. Open 1-4pm and 8pm-midnight.

Il Porto Grill, Anden de Levante, 225 (tel. 35 44 26), on the water. Classy and mellow, with a gurgling fountain, background music, and a canopied patio. Specializes in roasted meats (700-2900ptas). Open 12:30pm-12:30am.

El Turronero, C. Nou, 22-26 (tel. 36 28 98), off Pl. Reial. "Do not say that you know the island and its delights unless you have tried our ice creams and the famous lemon-ice drink." El Turronero's been churning out *turrón* (nougat) candy and ice cream since 1894. Double scoop of *turrón*-flavored ice cream 175ptas. Also *sangría* (245ptas per liter). Open Mon.-Fri. 9am-2pm and 4-9:30pm, Sat. 9am-2pm and 7-9:30pm, Sun. 10am-2pm and 7-9:30pm.

Tea Cosy, Es Cos de Gràcia, 1st right off C. Moreres from Pl. Esplanada. A charming attempt at the British thing: breakfast with egg, sausage, bacon, tomato, beans, and more (600ptas). Hamburgers (225ptas). Open Mon.-Fri. 8:30am-2pm and 5:30-10pm, Sat. 7:30-10pm.

SIGHTS AND ENTERTAINMENT

The **Museu Arqueològic Provincial de Belles Artes,** in the cloister of Església de Sant Francesc, displays chiefly Spanish ceramics from Alcora and Talavera, plus Aztec, Mayan, and Roman artifacts. (Currently closed for repairs.)

Església de Santa María la Major in Pl. Constitución, founded in 1287 and rebuilt in 1772, trembles to the 51 stops and 3006 pipes of its disproportionately large **organ,** built by Maese Juan Kilburz in 1810. A **festival de música** in July and August showcases this immense instrument. Festival concerts are given Fridays at 10pm; seat prices are minimal, and the sound carries into the surrounding streets.

Up C. Sant Roc, **Arc de Sant Roc** straddles the streets, reminding those who pass under it of the fortifications necessary to defend the city from marauding Catalan pirates. Closer to Pl. S'Esplanada, the private cultural society **Ateneu Científic, Lit-**

erari y Artístic, C. Comte de Cifuentes, 25 (tel. 36 05 53), has a collection of books, ancient Menorcan newspapers, pirate maps, stuffed birds, and preserved fish. (Open Mon.-Sat. 10am-2pm and 3-10pm. Free.) For the live version (fish, that is), head down to the **aquarium** at the port, Moll de Ponent, 73. (Tel. 35 05 37; open 10am-7pm. Admission 225ptas.) The aquarium is lined with small tables because every evening at 9pm it spins around three times, runs into a telephone booth, clicks its heels together, and slides down a metal pole, becoming the **aquarium bar,** where you can tipple under the stare of unblinking fish (open nightly 9pm-3am).

For those with different taste in water recreation, Mahón provides an hour-long **boat tour** of the harbor. (Mon.-Sat. 7 tours per day, 800ptas, under 12 400ptas.) Buy tickets at the Xoriguer Gin Distillery, Moll de Ponent, 93 (tel. 36 21 97; see hrs. below), or the Mad Hatter Bar, Moll de Ponent, 62 (tel. 36 58 65; open Mon.-Sat. 9am-7pm, Sun. 9am-3pm). A more satisfying trip leaves from the harbor to the island beach **Illa d'en Colom.** The steep price (2500ptas, under 12 1250ptas) covers lunch on the boat with wine and a splash of Menorcan gin. Ships leave at 10am and return by 5pm. Buy tickets at the aquarium.

The **Xoriguer distillery** brews its celebrated Menorcan gin on the waterfront at Moll de Ponent, 93 (tel. 36 21 97), in huge copper vats bubbling over wood fires. There are 15 subtly different local brews (free samples). (Distillery and store open Mon.-Fri. 8am-7pm, Sat. 8am-1pm.)

From May to September, artisans display their work alongside neon T-shirts in **mercadillos** held every day in the main square of at least one locale on the island. (Mahón Tues. and Sat.; Ciudadela Fri. and Sat.; Alayor Thurs.; Mercadal Sun.; Ferrerias Tues. and Fri.; Castell Mon. and Wed.; and Migjorn Wed.) The art is cheaper than the T-shirts.

Mahón is not famed for its nightlife, though a number of bars cluster along the port across from the ferry. One favorite is **Baixamar,** Moll de Ponent, 17 (tel. 36 58 96; open 7am-3am; Oct.-May 10am-1am). The disco **Si,** C. Virgen de Gracia, 16 (tel. 36 13 62), just off C. Infanta, has low vaulted ceilings, a small dance floor, and strange, undulating benches along the sides. People squeeze (really squeeze) in only on Saturdays after 2am. (Open midnight-5am; cover with drink 1000ptas.) For a livelier scene, try neighboring Castell (formerly Villacarlos).

Mahón's **Verge del Carme** celebration, July 16, floats a colorful armada of trimmed boats into the harbor. The **Festa de Nostra Senyora de Gràcia** swings out September 7-9.

Prehistoric settlements stand like monumental rock gardens on the island's grassy slopes. Visit near dusk when these cities are eeriest. Particularly creepy is the **Torre d'en Gaumes,** 14km from Mahón off the route to Son Bou. To get there, hike or take the Son Bou bus. Walk 20 min. from Mahón's town center to **Trepuco,** the most accessible site off the road to Castell. The tourist office provides a brochure in English describing the major monuments on the island and how to locate them.

■■■ CIUDADELA (CIUTADELLA)

Ciudadela, 45km west of Mahón, is Menorca's erstwhile capital. 20,785 people in one place may seem like urban chaos by this island's standards, but the port, arcaded streets, stately residences, and 14th-century Gothic cathedral make Ciudadela a pleasing base for excursions to nearby sights and fantastic beaches.

ORIENTATION AND PRACTICAL INFORMATION

The 1-hr. bus ride from Mahón drops visitors off at C. Barcelona. To reach **Plaça des Born,** which connects directly with **Plaça de S'Esplanada/Plaça deis Pins,** turn left off C. Barcelona onto C. Maò and walk straight until you hit Pl. Born.

Tourist Office: In a mobile home between Pl. S'Esplanada and Pl. Born (tel. 38 10 50). Open Mon.-Fri. 9am-1pm. Same truck at **Castell de Sant Nicolau,** at the end of Camí de Sant Nicolau. Open Mon.-Fri. 7:30-9:30pm.

Post Office: Pl. Born (tel. 38 00 81). Open Mon.-Fri. 9am-2pm, Sat. 9am-1pm.
Postal Code: 07760.

Telephones: Plexiglass telephone office in Pl. Pins. Open June-Oct. 15 Mon.-Sat. 10am-1pm and 5:30-10pm, Sun. 6-10pm. **Telephone Code:** 971.

Buses: Transportes Menorca, C. Barcelona, 7 (tel. 38 03 03). To Mahón (6 per day, 415ptas). **Torres,** C. Barcelona, 1-3 (tel. 38 47 20), offers daily service to surrounding beaches. To: Cala Blanca (9 per day, 105ptas); Sa Caleta Santandria (9 per day, 100ptas); Cala Blanes (12 per day, 105ptas); Cala Bosch and Son Xoriguer (12 per day, 130ptas). Torres ticket booth and bus departure point located at Pl. Pins.

Taxis: tel. 36 71 11. Try Pl. S'Esplanada/Pins.

Bike/Moped Rental: Bicicletas Tolo, C. Sant Isidor de ses Cadufes, 28-34 (tel. 38 15 76). Bike 500ptas per day, 2900ptas per week. Moped 3400ptas for 2 days, 10,600ptas per week. Open Mon.-Fri. 8am-1pm and 3:30-8pm, Sat. 6-7pm, Sun. 10-11am.

Red Cross: tel. 38 19 93.

24-Hour Pharmacy: Farmàcia Martí, Pl. Pins, 20 (tel. 38 03 94), posts a list of night pharmacies in the window.

Medical Assistance: Ambulance (tel. 38 19 93).

Police: Pl. Born, Ajuntament building (tel. 38 07 87).

Guardia Civil: tel. 36 58 88.

ACCOMMODATIONS AND FOOD

Pensiones are packed only during peak season (July-Sept.). Choice eateries spread their umbrellas and chairs along **Carrer Marina,** on the town's narrow harbor. Nondescript sandwich bars enclose **Plaça des Born** and its meaty environs. Prices below are for peak season only.

Hostal Residencia Oasis, C. Sant Isidore, 33 (tel. 38 21 97). Off Av. Jaume I El Conqueridor. And *what* an oasis it is. Walk through the figurative desert of aimless travel up the driveway to a floral masterpiece. Clean, breezy rooms with large wooden windows. Doubles with bath 2700ptas.

Hotel Geminis, C. Josepa Rossinyol, 4 (tel. 38 58 96). Take C. Sud off Av. Capital Negrete, then a quick left onto C. Rossinyol. Matching bedcovers and curtains. Phone and full shiny bathroom in each room. Singles 3000ptas. Doubles 5600ptas. Breakfast 275ptas.

Pensió Bar Ses Persianes, Pl. Antrux, 2 (tel. 38 14 45), off Av. Jaume I El Conqueridor. Bright white walls in smallish scrubbed rooms. Below bar with A/C serves breakfast. Doubles 3500ptas.

Bar La Guitarra, C. Dolores, 1 (tel. 38 13 55). Golden oldies like rabbit in onion sauce and ox tongue with peas, in a restaurant that challenges patrons to "try our meals the way *we* do them." Rustic wood and stone bar. 2-person *paella* 1300ptas. Open summer daily 11:30am-3:30pm and 7-11:30pm; winter Tues.-Sun. same hours. Credit cards accepted.

Restaurante El Horno, C. Forn, 12 (tel. 38 07 67), off C. Mirador. On the site of the city's first bakery. Low, arched ceilings and cloth tablecovers provide the setting for an intimate, relaxing dinner. A variety of French and Spanish dishes. Mouthwatering Sole Colbert 1550ptas, juicy Chicken Kiev 1100ptas, grilled trout 900ptas. Lunch *menú* 1000ptas. Open Nov.-Sept. Mon.-Sat. 7am-11pm. Credit cards accepted.

Café Balear, C. Marina (tel. 38 00 05), on the harbor's mouth. The only place to satisfy that craving for beer—ask for a *caña.* Open 6am-3am.

SIGHTS AND ENTERTAINMENT

The archeological sites of **Torre Trencada** and **Torre Llafuda** preserve Bronze Age remnants just 6km inland from Ciudadela. Formerly *talayot* (rounded towers for overlooking the countryside) settlements, both protect Stonehenge-ish **taulas.** (The *taulas* are two enormous rectangles of rock, carefully balanced on each other—for 3000 years—in the shape of the letter "T.") The **Naveta dels Tudons,** the most important prehistoric site on Menorca and the oldest building in Europe (despite some cosmetic restoration), crumbles 4km from the city. These community-tomb ruins are today the most complete of the ruins on the island. Buses don't come near these sights; consider hiking (about 5km) along tranquil C. Cami Vell de Maò.

Ciudadela's 16th-century law requiring all citizens to be asleep by midnight (still officially in the books, by the way) has generated a community of early-to-bedders. Don't come here for nightlife.

From the first week in July to the first week in September, Ciudadela hosts the **Festival de Música d'Estiu,** featuring some of the world's top classical musicians and ensembles, in the Claustre del Seminari. Tickets (900-1500ptas) are sold at Foto Born, C. Bisbe Vila, 14 (tel. 38 17 54). Every June, the **Festival of Sant Joan** fills a weekend with festivities, as the citizens of Ciudadela flood the streets to see the horse riders do their tricks.

■■■ NORTHERN COAST

FORNELLS

A small fishing village, famous for its lobster farms, Fornells is starting to attract foreigners, providing a calm base from which to explore this area of sandy white coves and jagged cliffs by car or bike (buses only run to Mahón). The beaches of **Cala Tirant** and **Binimella** are a few km to the west, and there are countless private coves to discover.

Fornells itself is alluring for its water sports rather than its beaches. Helpful municipal **maps** are posted in key spots around town. **Currency exchange** is possible only at Sa Nostra, C. Gabriel Gelabert, 4, near the *plaça.* (Open June-Sept. Mon.-Fri. 8:15am-1:30pm.) **Police** can be reached at tel. 37 55 76 and **Red Cross** at tel. 37 53 00. For other services go to Mercadal, 8km away. Most of the limited accommodations here are pricey, but **Casa de Thespedes La Palma,** Pl. S'Algaret (tel. 37 51 34), provides tidy, inexpensive rooms with terraces. (Singles 1200ptas. Doubles with bath 4500ptas. Triples with bath 6000ptas. Closed Oct.-March.) Lobster restaurants in town are prohibitively expensive. *Bocadillos* are an option at *bares* on **Plaça S'Algaret,** or deal your own meal with **groceries** from **Supermercado Ca'n Digas,** C. Major, 24. (Open Mon.-Sat. 8am-1:30pm and 4-8pm, Sun. 8am-noon.)

Autocares Fornells runs **buses** to Mahón (2 per day, 205ptas) from Pl Algaret.

■■■ BEACHES

Some of the more popular Menorcan beaches are accessible by bus from Mahón and Ciudadela. (For more information, see Practical Information: Buses under both cities.) Many of the best, however, require a vehicle and sometimes even legwork. Don't take the easy way out—they are worth the extra hassle.

Es Grau is a small bay about 8km north of Mahón, with unexciting brown sand. Popular with native Menorcans. Autocares Fornells buses leave from C. Vasallo (3 per day, 100ptas). Once there, catch a boat out to the **Illa d'en Colom,** a tiny island with more beaches. (Tickets on sale at Bar C'an Bernat at the beach.)

Punta Prima, to the south, is a wide, often crowded beach served by Transportes Menorca buses (6 per day, 170ptas).

Platges de Son Bou is a gorgeous string of beaches with crystal waters on the southern shore. There is a 5th-century Christian **basílica** in the nearby settlement of Son Bou. Transportes Menorca buses (5 per day, 215ptas).

Cala Santa Galdana is the narrow beach 9km south of Ferrerias, from which you can walk to the untouched **Cala Macarella,** about ½hr. west. Galdana is accessible by public transportation from Ferrerias.

Cala'en Porter's huge bluffs are closer to Mahón and connected by bus. Open beaches curve underneath. Here the **Covas d'en Xoroi,** a Swiss cheese of spooky prehistoric dwellings, gaze down on the sea.

Cales Cores is a ½-hr. walk to the east (left facing the sea) from Porter's, with the best sand to tan ratio on the shore.

Cala Bosc's jagged cliffs plummet into the clear pale-blue water, a perfect backdrop for a refreshing Mediterranean swimming hole.

Arenal d'en Castell, a sandy ring around calm water perfect for unofficial camping (although near hotels), sits on Menorca's northern shore behind a thin barrier of pine trees. Coastal ravines and cliffs are honeycombed with caves where prehistoric Menorcans lived. Autocares Fornells buses to Castell leave from C. Vasallo.

Cala Tirant is a wide strip of beach nudged between two cliffs. Popular with the Brits, it's only accessible by vehicle or bike.

IBIZA (EIVISSA)

"Dress the way you want to but with good taste." This statement, offered by a tourist pamphlet as an example of the "total freedom" of Ibiza, symbolizes the island. Once a hippie enclave, Ibiza is now a summer camp for disco maniacs and tourists with bohemian pretensions. Although the existence of a thriving gay community lends credence to Ibiza's self-image as a "tolerant" center, the island's high cost-of-touring precludes a true human diversity. The Carthaginians founded the dry, smoldering island in 654 BC after being kicked out of Phoenicia. From then on, the list of conquerors reads like a "Who's Who of Ancient Western Civilization," each one leaving a mark on the island's character. The 1235 invasion by the Catalans, who constructed the massive Renaissance walls that still fortify the capital city Ibiza today, and incorporated Christianity into the island, was the last until the hippie influx of the '60s.

Small, pine-covered peaks provide the island with a bit of greenery. The little water that flows tastes like the surrounding sea. Beaches placate the heat with a warm blue surf, and are reached in minutes by bus. Formentera, a tiny, sparsely populated island annex of Ibiza, is a convenient day trip by ferry.

■■■ IBIZA

Nobody in their right mind hangs out in this bare city during the day when there are so many beaches about. When the sun sets, however, Ibiza turns into the SoHo of the Mediterranean. Tourists and locals alike jam the outdoor cafés and boutiques clad in outrageously scanty attire: hip-huggers, bangles, and nipple rings.

ORIENTATION AND PRACTICAL INFORMATION

Three sections comprise Ibiza City. **Sa Penya** is directly ahead when you are standing on the Transmediterránea dock at Estació Marítima with your back to the port. This former fishing village (stretching from Estació Marítima along the waterfront to the old walls) is now the soul of the old city and the center of most nighttime activity. **La Marina,** the commercial district, is down Pg. Marina to the right toward the center of town. Pg. Vara de Rei and Av. Espanya are the main promenades. The ancient **Dalt Vila** (high city) climbs up and behind the old walls.

Buses to the **airport** (7km south of the city) run from Av. Isidor Macabich, 20 (every hr., 7am-10pm). Buses run to town (every hr. on the ½hr., 7:30am-10:30pm, ½hr., 85ptas). To get to the waterfront, walk down Av. Isidor Macabich, which becomes Av. Bartolomé Roselló and runs straight down to La Marina.

The local paper *Diario de Ibiza* (100ptas) has an *Agenda* page that lists: the bus schedule for the whole island; the complete ferry schedule; the schedule of all domestic flights to and from Ibiza for the day; water and weather forecasts; 24-hr. pharmacies in the imortant cities; 24-hr. gas stations on the island; and phone numbers for the police, Red Cross, ferry companies, and taxis.

Tourist Office: Pg. Vara de Rei, 13 (tel. 30 19 00), on the long promenade that runs southeast from the harbor. Good maps and advice. Open Mon.-Fri. 9:30am-1:30pm and 5-7pm, Sat. 10:30am-12:30pm. Also a small booth at the **airport** (tel. 30 22 00), across from international arrivals. Open May-Oct. 8am-midnight.

Consulate: See Spain Essentials: Embassies and Consulates.

Post Office: C. Madrid, 23 (tel. 31 13 80), off Av. Isidor Macabich. Open for stamps and Lista de Correos Mon.-Fri. 9am-9pm, Sat. 9am-1pm. Open for **telegrams** (tel. 72 20 00) Mon.-Fri. 9am-9pm, Sat. 9am-7pm. **Postal Code:** 07800.

Telephones: Telefónica, Av. Sta. Eulalia, 17, on the corner with C. D.J. Ribas, opposite the Formentera ferries. For international and domestic calls. Open April-Oct. 10am-1pm and 5-10pm. Another telephone service at **Extra,** Av. Sta. Eulalia, 27 (tel. 19 17 17). Receive calls at tel. 19 04 08; **fax** 19 01 60. Open July-Aug. daily 8am-10pm; Sept.-June daily 8am-9pm. **Telephone Code:** 971.

Flights: tel. 30 22 00. **Iberia,** Av. España, 34 (tel. 31 13 54) has flights to Palma, Barclona, Valencia, Madrid, and Alicante. Open for tickets and reservations Mon.-Fri. 9:30am-1:15pm and 4:30-7:45pm, Sat. 8am-1pm. Airport booth open 7am-10pm.

Buses: The 2 main bus stops are on Av. Isidor Macabich, one at #42, the other in front of #20. For an exact schedule consult the tourist office or *El Diario Agenda* page. Intercity buses run from #42 (tel. 31 20 75) to: San Antonio (Mon.-Sat. every 15min., Sun. every ½hr., 150ptas); Santa Eulalia (Mon.-Sat. 9 per day, Sun. 4 per day, 150ptas). Buses to nearby beaches (85-95ptas) leave from #20 (tel. 34 03 82) to: Salinas (every hr.); Platja d'en Bossa (every ½hr.); Cap Martinet (Mon.-Sat. 10 per day, Sun. 8 per day); Can Misses (Mon.-Sat. 7 per day, Sun. 2 per day).

Ferries: Estació Marítima, at the end of Av. Bartolomé Roselló (tel. 31 16 50). All boats except Flebasa's leave from here. **Transmediterránea,** Av. B. V. Ramón, s/n (tel. 31 41 73), at C. Ramón y Cajal. In summer to: Barcelona (5 per week, 6100ptas); Valencia (6 per week, 5100ptas); Palma (2 per week, 4500ptas). **Pitra** (tel. 34 50 68) connects San Antonio to Formentera and Denia (11 per week, 5220ptas). Private boats leave for San Antonio, Santa Eulalia, and some east coast beaches, but their schedules are erratic—bus is quicker and cheaper. To get to **Flebasa** (tel. 34 28 71), take the bus from Ibiza to San Antonio. The office is at the docks in Edificio Faro I. Open 9am-1:30pm and 4:30-8pm. June-Sept. 15 to: Denia (5 per day, 3hr., 5220ptas), with bus connections to Valencia (350ptas), Alicante (350ptas), and Benidorm (250ptas). April-Sept to: Formentera (10 per day, 20min.-1hr., 850-1600ptas).

Taxis: tel. 30 70 00 or 30 66 02.

Car and Motorbike Rental: Most places in town have similar prices. **Casa Valentín,** Av. B.V. Ramón (tel. 31 08 22), the street parallel to and 1 bl. off Pg. Vara de Rei. Mopeds 2500ptas per day, 2200ptas per day for more than 6 days. Panda or Marbella car 5500ptas per day. Open Mon.-Fri. 8:30am-1pm and 3:30-8pm, Sat.-Sun. 9am-noon and 5:30-8pm.

Luggage Storage: Extra, Av. Sta. Eulalia, 27 (tel. 19 17 17). 300ptas per 24hr. Open July-Aug. daily 8am-10pm; Sept.-June daily 8am-9pm.

Laundromat: Master Clean Lavandería, C. Felipe II, 12. Wash and dry 1000ptas per 5kg. Open Mon.-Fri. 9am-1:30pm and 4-9pm, Sat. 9am-2pm.

Red Cross: tel. 30 12 14

Hospital: Hospital Can Misses, Av. Espanya, 49 (tel. 39 70 00). Heading out of town on Av. Espanya, the hospital is on the left at the corner with C. Extremadura. **Emergency Medical Clinic,** Pg. Vara de Rei, 18 (tel. 30 31 31).

Police: In emergency tel. 091. **Policía Municipal,** C. Madrid (tel. 092), by the Post Office. **Guardia Civil,** C. Aeropuerto (tel. 30 11 00).

ACCOMMODATIONS

Decent, cheap accommodations in town are rare, especially in the summer when gobs of Britons et al. vie for the few that do exist. "CH," which stands for *casa de huespedes,* marks many doorways, but often the owner must be reached through the phone number tacked on the door. Ibiza's relative safety and up-all-night mentality ensure that owners offer keys for 24-hr. entry.

Hostal La Marina, C. Andenes del Puerto, 4 (tel. 31 01 72), across from Estació Marítima. Convenient location. Salty air floats through the window. Brown, dim rooms keep the temperature down. Reception area is a seafood restaurant. The unlucky are exiled to annex housing near the bus station (but nothing else). Singles 1500ptas. Doubles 3000ptas, with bath 4500ptas. Credit cards accepted.

Hostal Residencia Sol y Brisa, Av. Bartomeu v. Ramón, 15 (tel. 31 08 18), parallel to Pg. Vara de Rey, off Av. Ignasi Wallis. The sun and breeze have done wonders for this place's health: the wood-panelled entrance, bedrooms, and bathrooms are recently brushed up. Singles 1800ptas. Doubles 3400ptas. Off-season: 1400ptas; 2600ptas. Hot showers 200ptas.

Hostal Residencia Ripoll, C. Vicente Cuervo, 14 (tel. 31 42 75), right off Av. Bartomeu de Roselló. Rooms less homey than at Sol y Brisa. Singles 2100ptas. Doubles 3300ptas. Off-season: 1900ptas; 3000ptas.

Camping: Camping is popular in Ibiza, a leftover from the hippie '60s. **Es Cana** (tel. 33 21 17) and **Cala Nova** (tel. 33 17 74) are close to Santa Eulalia (see Santa Eulalia). **Cala Bassa** (tel. 34 45 99) is 6km west of San Antonio on the bay.

FOOD

There is little supply of or demand for cheap eats. Full meals rarely cost less than 1200ptas in the port and downtown areas; **Sa Penya** and **Dalt Vila** proffer exquisite fare in elegant settings for no less than 1500ptas per person. A **fruit and vegetable market** usurps Pl. Constitució, near the old gate to the Dalt Vila in Sa Penya. (Open April-Sept. Mon.-Sat. 9am-2pm; some stands stay open until 8pm.)

Some Ibizan dishes worth hunting down are *sofrit pagès,* a deep-fried lamb and chicken dish; *flao,* a lush lemon- and mint-tinged cheesecake; and *graxonera,* the celebrated cinnamon-dusted pudding made from eggs and bits of *ensaimada* (candied bread). Vegetarians soak up *sopas mallorquines,* an almost waterless vegetable "soup" ladled over thin slices of brown bread.

Comida Bar San Juan, C. Montgrí, 8 (tel. 31 07 66). The 2nd right on the Puerto Moll walking from Pg. Vara de Rey. Minuscule, family-run restaurant. Surprisingly cheap selection of foods. *Paella* 325ptas, *gambas a la plancha* 650ptas. Open Mon.-Sat. 1-3:15pm and 8-10:15pm.

Restaurante Ca'n Costa, C. Cruz, 19 (tel. 31 08 65), down the street from Victoria. Rows of tables tucked away in a basement eatery. Meats 450-800ptas, fishies 600-1400ptas, lunchtime *paella* 450ptas—all cooked in a cozy wood-burning stove. Open Feb.-Dec. Mon.-Sat. noon-3pm and 8pm-midnight.

Restaurante Rocky's, C. Virgen, 6 (tel. 31 01 07), off the port in Sa Penya. An elegant establishment specializing in *paella* (6 kinds, 1250-1500ptas). Friendly English-speaking owner, and lots of info on area gay restaurants, bars, and discos. Open daily 7pm-1am.

Restaurante Cock's, C. Vicente Soler, 5 (tel. 31 01 73), off the port. An up-and-coming restaurant—*Let's Go*-friendly management promises a surprise for book users. The outdoor café offers a front-row view of the harbor and an ample *menú.* Pizza, too. Open Mon.-Sat. noon-4pm and 7pm-midnight, Sun. 7pm-midnight.

Restaurante Victoria, C. Riambau, 1 (tel. 31 06 22), at the end of Pg. Vara de Rey as it turns into La Marina. *Sopa mallorquín* 375ptas. *Graxonera* 325ptas. *Platos* hover around 500ptas. Open Mon.-Sat. 1-4pm and 8:30pm-midnight.

SIGHTS AND ENTERTAINMENT

The original city of Ibiza, **Dalt Vila** ("High Town"), presides over 20th-century urban bustle wrapped inside 16th-century walls. Its twisty, sloped streets lead up to the 14th-century **cathedral,** which offers super views of the city and beyond. (Open Mon.-Sat. 10am-1:30pm.) Right in the middle of the antique action sits the **Museu D'Art Contemporani D'Eivissa,** C. Sa Carrosa, with a wide range of current art exhibitions. (Open Mon.-Fri. 10am-1:30pm and 5-8pm, Sat. 10am-1:30pm. Admission 200ptas, students free.)

The archeological museum, **Puig des Molins,** is in the western part of the city on Via Romana, which runs off the Portal Nou at the foot of the Dalt Vila. The museum displays Punic, Roman, and Iberian art, pottery, and metals from the island, and sells replicas. Tours every 45min. to the 4th-century BC Punic-Roman **necropolis** behind the building. (Both open Mon.-Sat. 10am-1pm and 5-8pm; Oct.-May Mon.-Sat. 10am-1pm and 4-7pm. Admission to both 200ptas.)

The crowds return to Ibiza City by nightfall, when even the clothing stores feel like clubs, with throbbing music and headache-inducing lights. The elbows push into most **bars** along C. Major and the next street parallel, C. de la Verge. Live jazz wails through the smoky air of **La Cantina** under Teatro Pereyra on C. Comte Roselló every night after 10pm. Gay nightlife hovers around Sa Penya; the bars **Exis** and **Gallery** are especially throbbing.

Ibiza's **disco** scene is world-famous and ever-changing. The best information sources are regulars; the second, posters and the *Diario de Ibiza* newspaper (100ptas). Elusive and invaluable is the schedule for the **Discobus,** which runs to and from all the major hotspots (midnight-5am, 200-300ptas). Cover ascends to 3500ptas for the unlucky at megaplexes like **KU,** just outside town on the road to San Antonio, and **Pacha,** on the other side of the port on Pg. Perimetral (tel. 31 36 12). More economical and less mainstream goings-on may be found with a little asking around.

The power of the rising sun draws thousands of solar zombies to the nearby tanning grounds. No beach is within quick walking distance, but **Platja de Talamanca, Platja des Duros,** and **Platja de Figueretes** are close enough to be on the larger city maps. Many more good beaches are accessible by bus (see Buses), including clean **Salinas,** former hippie hangout **Cala Llonga,** and **Cala Olivera.**

■■■ SAN ANTONIO ABAD (SANT ANTONI DE PORTEMANY)

British package tourists storm San Antonio's huge crescent beach, busy harbor, and stirring night scene. During the day it's too hot to be anywhere but the beach. Since sand space dwindles exponentially towards noon, many people relocate to beaches further out. All buses and boats leave San Antonio from the central part of the waterfront, **Passeig de la Mar.** They go to **Cala Bassa,** a sandy beach on a thin strip, and **Cala Conta,** a slightly rocky beach. Boats sail for Portinatx and Formentera. Buses serve **Cala Tarida,** a protected inlet at the base of forested hills, as well as Cala Gració, Port des Turrent, and Santa Eulalia.

A national monument on the outskirts of town north of the waterfront, the underground **Capella de Santa Inés** haunts visitors with eerie devotion (ask about tours at the tourist office). If you have your own wheels, explore **Cueva de Ses Fontanelles,** just north of Platja Cala Salada, where faintly colored prehistoric paintings cover the walls (free).

San Antonio's rollicking nightlife is a welcome alternative to hellishly sunny days. **Cafés** line C. Balanzat, one street in from the waterfront. The **bar** scene prevails on C. Vara de Rey and Pg. Mar. Those in the know head to **Es Paradis** (tel. 34 28 93), off Av. Dr. Fleming, a large semi-enclosed garden of bushy plants and white pillars where exhausted patrons crash on the pillows around the dance floor. (Open June-Sept. 11:30pm-6am. Cover with drink 1500ptas, Aug. 2000ptas.)

The well-equipped, multilingual **tourist office** (tel. 34 33 63), on the waterfront, at the beginning of Pg. Fonts, can help with local transport. (Open Mon.-Fri. 10am-8:30pm, Sat.-Sun. 9:30am-1pm; Nov.-Apr. Mon.-Sat. 9:30am-1pm.) The **post office** (tel. 34 02 86) is on C. Mar at C. Sant Rafael (open Mon.-Fri. 8am-2pm).

Rooms in San Antonio are better values than those in the capital. High-quality **Hostal Nicolao** is on C. Valencia, 9 (tel. 34 08 45), numerous blocks inland from the port, parallel to C. Progrés. Large, modern rooms have comfortable beds, terrace, and full bath (1500ptas per person; low-season 1250ptas per person). Closer to the waterfront, simpler but cheaper accommodations await at **Casa de Huespedes**

Serra, C. Roselló, 13 (tel. 34 13 26), directly off C. Progrés. Elevated beds and cool floor tiles add to the ancient charm. (Singles 1200ptas. Doubles 2000ptas.)

Pizzerias and hamburger stands line the shore and work their way inland. The indoor **Mercat des Clot Mares** stalls at the corner of C. Progrés and C. Santa Rosalia. (Open Mon.-Fri. 8am-2pm and 6-9pm, Sat. 8am-2pm; Sept.-May Mon.-Thurs. 8am-2pm, Fri. 8am-2pm and 6-8pm, Sat. 8am-2pm.)

■■■ SANTA EULALIA DEL RÍO

Small, easily navigable, and lined with palm trees, Santa Eulalia provides respite from the more hard-core tourist haunts on the southern and western coasts. Though generally less exploited, northeastern Ibiza contains some of the island's most popular beaches. The island's only river evaporates into the sea south of the town.

Boats and buses connect Santa Eulalia to the northern beaches. Buses leave from Av. Dr. Ricardo Gotarrendona, up C. Mariano Riquer Wallis from the beach; boats leave from the waterfront near the edge of the boat basin. **Cala Llonga,** a long sandy cove, lies 5km south (10 buses per day, 85ptas; 9 boats per day, 20min., 250ptas). Five km north of town, the overpopulated **Es Cana** sucks in backpackers and families alike with white sand and an overpriced Wednesday craft market (buses every ½hr., 85ptas; boats every hr., 250ptas). **Cala Nova** is a 10-minute walk from Es Cana. Four buses per day serve **Cala Llenya** (170ptas). Most awestruck visitors to **Aigües Blanques** are moved to strip by its beauty. To get here, ask to be let off nearby on the bus route to Figueretas (Mon.-Fri. 6 buses per day, 170ptas).

The award-winning **tourist office** is just down from the bus stop, C. Mariano Riquer Wallis, 4 (tel. 33 07 28). (Open Mon.-Fri. 9:30am-1:30pm and 5-8pm, Sat. 9:30am-1:30pm.) The **post office** is at Av. Generalísimo, 1 (tel. 33 00 95; open Mon.-Fri. 9am-2pm, Sat. 9am-1pm). The international and domestic **telephone kiosk** rings at the end of Av. Dr. Ricardo Gotarredona at C. Juan Tur. (Open April-Oct. 10am-2pm and 4-10pm.) The **medical emergency** center neighbors the tourist office at C. Mariano Riquer Wallis, 6 (tel. 33 24 53). The **municipal police** protect and serve at C. Sant Jaume, 72 (tel. 33 08 41).

The town's two-star **Hostal Rey,** C. Sant Josep, 17 (tel. 33 02 10), is fit for a queen. Spacious rooms with modern bathrooms. (Singles 2200ptas. Doubles 4200ptas. Low-season: 1600ptas; 3200ptas. Breakfast 400ptas.) **Hostal Central,** C. Sant Vincent, 24 (tel. 33 00 43), serves breakfast with eggs, bread with three marmalades, salami, and pots of coffee (300ptas). The flower-tiled bathroom in each room glimmers. (Singles 1500ptas. Doubles 3000ptas. Low-season: 1000ptas; 2500ptas.) Cala Nova's **campsite** (tel. 33 17 74) is just 50m from the beach, and 1km from a large hippie-market. (439ptas per person, 425ptas per tent.) Or try **Es Cana** (tel. 33 98 72), on the bus route to Es Cana. (480ptas per person, 650ptas per tent. Open May-Oct.) Local sources say there's only one place to eat—**Restaurante Ca'n Miquel,** C. Sant Vincent, 49 (tel. 33 03 29), off Pl. Espanya. The 800pta *menú* includes two juicy courses, bread, wine, and dessert. (Open noon-4pm and 6pm-midnight.)

Boats and **buses** dash between Santa Eulalia and Ibiza City. The bus stops on C. Mariano Riquer Wallis. (Buses every ½hr., 145ptas; boats 14 per day, every ½hr., 45min., one-way 450ptas.) Boats drift from Santa Eulalia to Formentera (3 per day, round-trip 1900ptas).

Valencia

Take any train around Valencia and you'll see why it's known as the *huerta* (orchard) of Spain. Miles of geometrically-laid fruit trees suggest an Eden that has gone through the copier machine. Water is important for the people of this eastern (Levant) region, and they have made an aesthetic of their necessity. Lovely fountains and pools grace carefully landscaped public gardens in many cities. Spring and autumn river floods bring soil down the alluvial plain. Since Roman times, irrigation canals have formed a broad network for water distribution. Dunes, sand bars, rock promontories, and lagoons (including the celebrated rice-growing Albufeira) mark Valencia's great bay. The traditional *Tribunal de les Aigües* governs water distribution, using an intricate set of rules to decide each grove's allotment. Each Thursday at noon, the *Tribunal* congregates in the capital by the Apostle's Door of the cathedral in Plaça de la Mare de Deu.

An unusual melange of Phoenicians, Carthaginians, Romans, Visigoths, and Moors all had relations with Valencia. Even El Cid made it over here to rule for five years (and marry off his daughters) in the 11th century. Although conquered by Aragón in the 13th century, the region retained a large, *morisco* population. Valencia suffered for joining the losing sides in both the War of the Spanish Succession and the Civil War, not recovering its autonomy until 1977. Regional pride has subsequently caused an increasing usage of *valenciá*, a regional language similar to Catalan. The language is spoken more in the north than the south, more inland than on the coast.

Valencia is the birthplace of the most celebrated of Spanish dishes, *paella* (saffron rice with meat or fish). Alicante's varied nougat *turrones* are the traditional Christmas candy throughout Spain.

■■■ VALENCIA

As if to provide the sharpest possible contrast between itself and the lazy orchards surrounding it, Valencia, Spain's third-largest city, bustles with activity and commercialism. Somewhat non-descript in appearance, the city is not Spain's most beautiful—but it is post-industrial rather than grimy; marked by snazzy buildings and dress-for-success people, rather than pollution or anomie. In Valencia, ancient and modern are intertwined with great determination, if not any particular skill—noisy traffic courses through the city's mostly one-way streets at all hours. Pockets of lushness mitigate Valencia's business-like "normalcy." Parks, gardens, and orange trees dot the city.

Founded by the Greeks, Valencia has been conquered by Carthaginians, Romans, Visigoths, and Moors at one time or another. El Cid took the city in 1094, but lost it eight years later. Jaume I of Aragón eventually seized it back from the Moors in 1253 and remains a local hero. In the Middle Ages, the silk industry flooded the city with stupendous wealth, transforming Valencia into an agricultural and industrial capital.

ORIENTATION AND PRACTICAL INFORMATION

Those with foresight arrive in Valencia by train, since Estació del Nord is close to the town's center. **Avinguda M. de Sotelo** runs from the train station to **Plaça del Ajuntament,** where the city tourist office is located. The avenue then splits into **Avinguda Maria Cristina,** which leads to the Central Market, and **Carrer de Sant Vicent,** which leads to **Plaça de la Reina** and the cathedral.

The ancient quarter of the city, which is still the town's center, is nestled into a bend in the Río Turia. Before it was diverted, the river wound its way down to the coast from the edge of the old city. Now the enormous length of dry riverbed is slowly being converted into the largest urban park in the world.

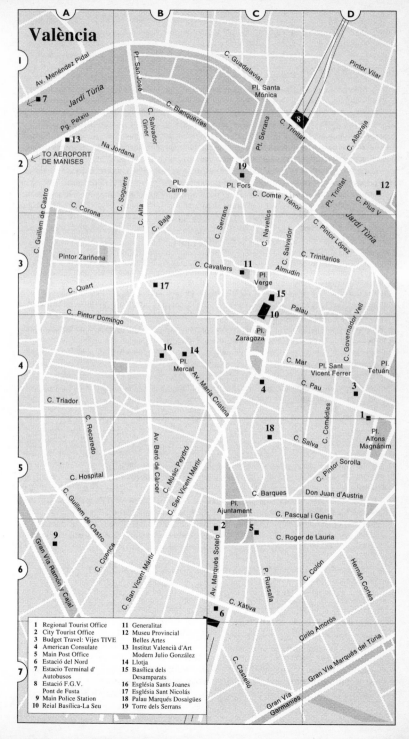

València

A Av. Menéndez Pidal
Jardí Túria
■ 7
Pg. Petxu
■ 13
TO AEROPORT DE MANISES
C. Guillem de Castro
C. Corona
Pintor Zariñena
C. Quart
C. Pintor Domingo
C. Triador
C. Recaredo
C. Hospital
C. Guillem de Castro
9 ■
Gran Via Ramón y Cajal

B Pl. San José
C. Blanqueries
C. Salvador Giner
Na Jordana
C. Soguers
C. Alta
C. Baja
Pl. Carme
C. Serrans
C. Cavallers
17 ■
16 ■ 14 ■
Pl. Mercat
Av. Maria Cristina
Av. Baró de Càrcer
C. Músic Peydró
C. San Vicent Màrtir
C. Cuenca
C. San Vicent Màrtir

C C. Guadalaviar
Pl. Santa Mònica
Pt. Serrans
19 ■
Pl. Fors
C. Comte Trénor
C. Navellos
C. Salvador
11 ■ Almudín
Pl. Verge
15 ■
10 ■
Palau
Pl. Zaragoza
4 ■
Pl. Sant Vicent Ferrer
C. Mar
C. Pau
18 ■
C. Salvà
C. Barques
Pl. Ajuntament
2 ■ 5 ■
Av. Marqués Sotelo
6 ■
C. Xàtiva
C. Castelló
C. Comèdies
Gran Via Germanies

D Pintor Vilar
8 ■
C. Alboraia
C. Trinitat
Pt. Trinitat
C. Plus V.
12 ■
Jardí Túria
C. Pintor López
C. Trinitarios
C. Governador Vell
Pl. Tetuàn
3 ■
1 ■
Pl. Alfons Magnànim
C. Pintor Sorolla
Don Juan d'Austria
C. Roger de Lauria
P. Russafa
C. Colón
Hernàn Cortés
C. Pascual i Genís
Cirilo Amorós
Gran Via Marqués del Túria
Gran Via Germanies
C. Guillem de Castro

1 Regional Tourist Office
2 City Tourist Office
3 Budget Travel: Vijes TIVE
4 American Consulate
5 Main Post Office
6 Estació del Nord
7 Estació Terminal d' Autobusos
8 Estació F.G.V. Pont de Fusta
9 Main Police Station
10 Reial Basílica-La Seu

11 Generalitat
12 Museu Provincial Belles Artes
13 Institut Valencià d'Art Modern Julio González
14 Llotja
15 Basílica dels Desamparats
16 Església Sants Joanes
17 Església Sant Nicolás
18 Palau Marqués Dosaigües
19 Torre dels Serrans

Valencia's scale, sprawl, tangle, and public maplessness make an unaided geographical assault worse than futile. El Corte Inglés' map wins the annual *Let's Go* Cartographical Excellence In the Face of Bitter Adversity award, and is free. The tourist office's map (unwieldy and unhelpful) and the indexed Bayarri map sold at newsstands (unwieldy and 450ptas) lose out.

Regional Tourist Office: Estació del Nord, C. Xàtiva, 24 (tel. 352 85 73), on the right as you walk off the train. Plenty of pamphlets and maps on any little town in the Comunidad de Valencia. English spoken. Open Mon.-Fri. 10am-6pm. **City Tourist Office:** Pl. Ajuntament, 1 (tel. 351 04 17). Dedicated crew. Open Mon.-Fri. 8:30am-2:15pm and 4:15-6:15pm, Sat. 9am-12:45pm.

El Corte Inglés: C. Pintor Sorolla, 26 (tel. 351 24 44). From Pl. Ajuntament, walk down C. Bareas as it turns into a pedestrian walk; El Corte Inglés sits on the left. **Currency exchange,** novels and guidebooks in English, haircutting, cafeteria, restaurant, **telephones,** and **grocery store.** Open Mon.-Sat. 10am-9pm.

Budget Travel: IVAJ, C. Hospital, 11 (tel. 386 97 00). From the train station, head left on C. Xàtiva, which becomes C. Guillem de Castro, and turn right on C. Hospital. The last word on student travel discounts. Several travel handbooks in English. ISIC 500ptas. HI card 1800ptas. Open Mon.-Fri. 9am-1:30pm; Sept.-June Mon.-Fri. 9am-1:30pm and 4:30-6:30pm.

American Express: Duna Viajes, C. Cirilo Amorós, 88 (tel. 374 15 62; fax 334 57 00). Next to Pl. América on the edge of Río Turia. No commission on AmEx traveler's checks. Accepts wired money. Mail held (1 yr.) and **fax** service for cardholders. Open Mon.-Fri. 9:30am-2pm and 5-8pm, Sat. 10am-2pm.

Post Office: Pl. Ajuntament, 24 (tel. 351 67 50). Open for stamps and Lista de Correos Mon.-Fri. 8am-9pm, Sat. 9am-2pm; for **telegrams** during off-hrs. (tel. 352 20 00). **Postal Code:** 46080.

Telephones: Estació del Nord, C. Xàtiva, 24. Open daily 8am-10pm. **Faxes** (fax 394 27 44) sent and received. **Telephone Code:** 96.

Flights: The airport is 15km southwest of the city (tel. 350 95 00). CVT buses (tel. 340 47 15) link the airport with the bus station in Valencia (almost every hr., 6am-8:20pm from airport, 200ptas). **Iberia,** C. Pau (Paz), 14 (tel. 352 05 00). Open Mon.-Fri. 9am-2pm and 4-7pm, Sat. 9am-1:30pm. To: Palma de Mallorca (3 per day, 10,500ptas); Barcelona (3 per day, 11,900ptas); Madrid (7 per day, 12,250ptas); Sevilla (3 per day, 16,050ptas).

Trains: Estació del Nord, C. Xàtiva, 24 (tel. 351 36 12). Information open 7am-10:30pm (24hrs. by phone). To: Barcelona (15 per day, 4-6hr., 2020-3700ptas); Madrid (11 per day, 5-7½hr., 3000-4500ptas); Sevilla (3 per day, 8½-9½hr., 4900-6000ptas).

Buses: Estació Terminal d'Autobuses, Av. Menéndez Pidal, 13 (tel. 349 72 22), across the river, a 25-min. walk northwest of the town center. From town center, get on municipal bus #8 (80ptas) at Pl. Ajuntament, 22. **Autores** (tel. 349 22 30) sends 15 buses per day to Madrid (5hr., 2645ptas). **Bacoma** (tel. 347 96 08) runs buses to Málaga (3 per day, 11hr., 5550ptas) and Sevilla (2 per day, 12hr., 5625ptas). **Enatcar** (tel. 340 08 55) offers 10 trips daily to Barcelona (4½hr., 2650ptas). **Ubesa** (tel. 340 08 55) makes several stops along the Costa Blanca on its way to Alicante (6 per day, 2¼-3hr., 1760ptas). International service with **Julia Tours** (tel. 351 33 36) to: Paris (1 per day, 14,200ptas); Rome (2 per week, 17,000ptas); Geneva (3 per week, 11,000ptas); and London (3 per week, 17,000ptas).

Ferries: Transmediterránea, Av. Manuel Soto Ingeniero, 15 (tel. 367 07 04). To Palma (Mon.-Sat., 9hr., 6099ptas). Advance ticket sales open Mon.-Fri. 9:30am-2pm and 5-7pm, Sat. 9:30am-2pm; or buy tickets on day of departure at the port office, Estació Marítima (tel. 367 39 72). Take bus #4 from Pl. Ajuntament. Ask travel agent for **Flebasa** (Denia office tel. 578 42 00) ferry schedule to Ibiza, leaving from Denia (5220ptas, includes 3-hr. bus ride to Denia port).

Taxis: tel. 370 33 33 or 357 13 13.

Public Transportation: EMT Buses (tel. 352 83 99). Most leave from Pl. Ajuntament, 22. Bus #8 runs to the bus station at Av. Menéndez Pidal. Bus #19 runs to Las Arenas and Malvarosa. Buy tickets aboard or at any newsstand (80ptas, 10-ride ticket 550ptas). Regular service stops around 10:30pm. Late-night buses run (every 40min., 7 per night, 10:30pm-1:40am). Bus **map** available at EMT office, C. En Sanz, 4 (open Mon.-Fri. 8am-3:30pm).

Car Rental: Furgo Car, C. Linares, 15 (tel. 385 15 38), on bus #70 route from Pl. Ajuntament. Fiesta 2200ptas per day plus 22ptas per km. Open Mon.-Fri. 8am-1:30pm and 4-7:30pm, Sat. 8am-1:30pm.

Luggage Storage: At the **bus station,** lockers 200ptas and 400ptas. Or at the **train station,** lockers 300ptas and 600ptas. Both open 24hrs.

English Bookstore: The English Book Centre, C. Pascual y Genis, 16 (tel. 351 92 88), off C. Barcas. Open Mon.-Fri. 10am-1:30pm and 4:30-8pm, Sat. 10am-1:30pm.

Laundromat: Lavanderia El Mercat, Pl. Mercat, 12 (tel. 391 20 10), on the left past the market. Self-service wash or dry 425ptas. Open Mon.-Sat. 10am-8pm.

Women's Center: Instituto València de la Dona, C. Naquera, 9 (tel. 391 48 87). Open Mon.-Fri. 8am-3pm; Sept.-June Mon.-Fri. 8am-8pm.

Rape Crisis Hotline: tel. (900) 58 08 88 for hotline and free legal counsel.

24-hr. Pharmacy: Check listing in the local paper *Levante* (100ptas) or the *farmacias de guardia* schedule posted outside any pharmacy.

Hospital: Hospital Clínico Universitario, Av. Blasco Ibañez, 17 (tel. 386 26 00), at the corner of C. Dr. Ferrer. Take bus #30 or 40 from Av. M. de Sotelo in front of the train station. English-speaking doctor is often on duty.

Emergency: tel. 091. **Ambulance** (tel. 352 67 50). **First Aid,** Pl. América, 6 (tel. 322 22 39).

Police: Jefatura Superior, Gran Via de Ramón y Cajal, 40 (tel. 091).

ACCOMMODATIONS

The business of Valencia is business, not tourism, so rooms are not hard to find during the summer. If coming in March for the papier-mâché orgy, Las Fallas, reserve well in advance. Avoid the areas by the *barrio chino* (red-light district) around Pl. Pilar. The best options cluster around **Plaça Ajuntament** and **Plaça Mercat.**

Alberg Colegio "La Paz" (HI), Av. Port, 69 (tel. 369 01 52), nearly halfway between town and the port. Take bus #19 from Pl. Ajuntament and ask the driver to signal the stop. Forbidding fortress safeguards the peaceful ambience inside. 2-4 people and a bathroom in every room. HI membership required. 950ptas per person, over 26 1300ptas. Breakfast included. Sheets 300ptas. Lockout 10am-5pm; lock-in before 8am. Reception open 9am-1pm and 5-8pm. Curfew midnight. Open July-Sept. 15.

Near Plaça del Mercat

Hostal del Rincón, C. Carda, 11 (tel. 391 60 83). Walking from Pl. Ajuntament, Pl. Mercat extends to the right of the market fortress; its continuation is C. Carda. Ample *hostal* with starched white bed sheets and clean bathrooms. Rooms cleaned daily. Singles 1000ptas. Doubles 1800ptas.

Hostal-Residencia El Cid, C. Cerrajeros, 13 (tel. 392 23 23), second left off C. Vicente Mártir between Pl. Ajuntament and Pl. Reina. *Faux* wooden floors and little dog Snoopy create a homey feel. Some English with special effects spoken. Singles 1200ptas. Doubles 2500ptas, with shower 2800ptas, with bath 3500ptas.

Hospedería del Pilar, Pl. Mercat, 19 (tel. 331 66 00). Past the market and Llonja, on the far right-hand side. Founded in 1886, sagging beds don't look as if they could support healthy 20th-century bods. Sinks antiquated too. Singles 1000ptas, with shower 1600ptas. Doubles 1800ptas, with shower 2900ptas.

Near Plaça del Ajuntament

Hostal Moratin, C. Moratin, 15 (tel. 352 12 20), first street on the left off C. Barcas coming from Pl. Ajuntament. Brilliantly white rooms with petunias on the windows. Owner serves up great *paella* in blue-tabled dining room. Singles 1850ptas. Doubles 3000ptas. Triples 4500ptas. Breakfast 250ptas. Dinner 900ptas.

Hostal-Residencia Universal, C. Barcas, 5 (tel. 351 53 84), conveniently off the plaza. Three floors of spacious rooms featuring balconies, ornate ceilings, and

VALENCIA

new sinks. Family-run. One free shower per day. Singles 1800ptas. Doubles 2800ptas, with shower 3400ptas. Triples 3900ptas.

Pensión Paris, C. Salvá, 12 (tel. 352 67 66), off C. Poeta Querol, which crosses C. Barcas. 13 bedrooms with light wooden furniture. Clean, clean, clean. Singles 1800ptas. Doubles 2800ptas, with shower 3400ptas, with bath 3800ptas. Triples 3900ptas.

Hostal España, C. Embajador Vich, 5 (tel. 352 93 42). Take C. Barcelonina off Pl. Ajuntament and go left when it ends. Rooms are an endearing mix of textured wallpaper, plaid blankets, shiny new mirrors, and antique desks. Only 7 rooms. Keys for 24-hr. entry. Singles 1500ptas. Doubles with shower 2500ptas. Prices include IVA.

FOOD

The taste (meat-shellfish-lemon-saffron-rice-chicken). The connotations (unadulterated Spain). The birthplace (Valencia). The word (*paella*). The experience.

Unbeknownst to most tourists, *paella* is just one of 200 Valencian rice specialties. Other local specialties include *arroz a banda* (a rice and fish dish with garlic, onion, tomatoes, and saffron) and *all i pebre* (eels fried in an oil, paprika, and garlic sauce).

Another regional favorite is *horchata,* a sweet, milky-white drink pressed from locally grown *chufas* (earth almonds). **Alboraya,** a neighborhood 4km from the city center, pushes *horchata* like Michigan sells ale (with a vengeance). Pick up a cartoon history of the brew while developing an addiction at **Horchata Daniel,** C. La Horchata, 41 (tel. 185 88 66; bus #70 from Pl. Ajuntament stops right in front). *Horchata* 175ptas. (Open March-Nov. 10am-2:30am; Dec. and Feb. Sat.-Sun. 4pm-1am.)

Buckets of fresh fish, meat, and fruit sell at the **Mercat Central** on Pl. Mercat. (Open Mon.-Thurs. 7am-2pm, Fri. 7am-2pm and 5-8:30pm, Sat. 7am-3pm.)

Groceries: El Corte Inglés, C. Pintor Sorolla, 26 (tel. 351 24 44), on the fifth floor. Open Mon.-Sat. 10am-9pm.

Restaurante La Utielana, Pl. Picadero Dos Aguas, 3 (tel. 352 94 14). Take C. Barcelonina off Pl. Ajuntament, turn left at its end, then a sharp right onto C. Procida. Devilish to find, but worth it. Ideal service, SoHo ambience, and not a plate on the menu over 650ptas. Choose from a super scoop of scrumptious seafood *paella* (a shocking 325ptas) or *gambas a la plancha* (425ptas). A meal you won't forget. A/C. Open Sept.-July Mon.-Fri. 1:15-4pm and 9-11pm, Sat. 1:15-4pm.

Comidas Eliseo, C. Conde de Montornes, 9 (tel. 392 33 58), off Pl. Ferrer, at the end of C. Mar from Pl. Reina. Narrow, white-tiled hall accommodates an onslaught of locals at midday. Two-plate *menú* for the price of a sandwich and *agua* elsewhere (575ptas). Open Mon.-Sat. 1-4pm and 8-11pm.

La Lluna, C. Sant Ramón (tel. 392 21 46), in El Carme district near IVAM. Behind the hanging-bead curtain is a veggie restaurant to moon over. A 4-course *menú* and whole-grain bread served only weekday afternoons (750ptas). Natural juices 175ptas. Open Mon.-Sat. 1:30-4:30pm and 8pm-midnight.

Cafés Valiente, C. Xàtiva, 8 (tel. 351 21 17). From the train station, 2 bl. to the left. Stainless steel bar winds around the *restaurante,* accommodating patrons with one ambition—a large helping of *paella* scooped fresh from giant round pans (with chicken 490ptas, with seafood 560ptas). Expect a good 10-15-min. wait. *Paella* served religiously 1-4pm. Open Mon.-Sat. 1-4pm and 7-10pm, Sun. 1-5pm.

Cafeteria Játiva, C. Xàtiva, 14 (tel. 394 19 64), 1 bl. from train station. Bingo parlor turned restaurant bulges with rowdy customers. A slew of *platos combinados* (625-800ptas) tacked to the walls. Delicious desserts. Open 9am-11pm.

Comidas Esma, C. Zurradore, 5 (tel. 391 63 52), off C. Correjería, which runs in front of the *catedral.* Full meal with hefty bowls of homemade soup and freshly grilled *emperador* (swordfish) 650ptas. A la carte dishes at rock-bottom prices. Open mid-Sept. to mid-Aug. Mon.-Fri. 1-3:30pm and 8:30-11:30pm, Sat. 1-3:30pm.

Centro Aragonés, C. Don Joan d'Austria, 18 (tel. 351 35 50), off C. Barcas. A one-room clubhouse 2 fl. up. Join other folks at the wide communal table. High-quality *menú* (including—surprise!—*paella*) 800ptas. Open Mon.-Sat. 1:30-4pm.

SIGHTS

Touring Valencia on foot is complicated; maps are essential. Most of the sights line the Río Turia or cluster near Plaça de la Reina.

Valencia's parks are impressive. Taxonomists marvel at the **Jardí Botànic,** C. Beato Gaspar Bono (tel. 391 16 57), on the western end of Río Turia. This university-maintained open-air botanical garden cultivates 43,000 plants (300 precisely labeled species) from around the world. (Open 10am-9pm; Oct.-May 10am-6pm. Admission 50ptas, students free.) Off C. Monforte over the Pont del Real bridge, the neoclassical **Jardí Monteforte** (tel. 360 48 33) offers the bliss of (relative) seclusion among its sculpted bonsai-laden paths. (Open Mon.-Fri. 10:30am-6pm, Sat.-Sun. 10:30am-2:30pm and 4:30-6pm. Free.) One block farther, Valencia shows the world what should be done with dry riverbeds. A series of pillared public recreation areas mark the banks of the now diverted **Río Turia,** terminating with hundreds of children climbing up and sliding down a gigantic reification of Jonathan Swift's "Gulliver." (Gulliver open Tue.-Sun. 10am-2pm and 5-9pm; Sept.-June 10am-dusk.)

At the **Jardins del Real** (tel. 362 35 12), off C. Sant Pius V on the north bank, yaks, emus, baboons, swans, and flamingos go about their bodily functions in a small zoo. (Open 10am-7pm. Admission 330ptas.) Next to the park, on C. Sant Pius V, the compelling **Museu Provincial de Belles Artes** (tel. 360 57 93) displays superb 14th- to 16th-century Valencian primitives (influenced by Flemish painters' marked attention to clothing) and works by later Spanish and foreign masters—a Hieronymous Bosch triptych, El Greco's *San Juan Bautista,* Velázquez's self-portrait, Ribera's *Santa Teresa,* and a slew of Goyas. (Open Oct.-July Tues.-Sat. 10am-2pm and 4-6pm, Sun. 10am-2pm; Aug. Tues.-Sun. 10am-2pm. Free.)

Across the old river and west, the **Institut València d'Art Modern Julio González (IVAM),** C. Guillem de Castro, 118 (tel. 386 30 00), has a permanent collection of works by 20th-century sculptor Julio González and frequent temporary exhibits of cutting-edge art and photography. (Open Tues.-Sun. 11am-8pm. Admission 250ptas, students 150ptas. Sun. free.) The institute also administers another small modern art museum in a rehabilitated convent, the **Centre del Carme,** C. Museo, 2, to the east off Pl. del Carmen. (Open Tues.-Sun. noon-3:30pm and 4:30-8pm. Free.)

On the edge of the former Río Turia at Pl. Serrans, the **Torre dels Serrans** (Watchman's Tower) stands watch, a 16th-century fortified entrance to the city. The Aragonese began the **seu** (cathedral) in Pl. Zaragoza shortly after the *Reconquista.* The three different entrances represent centuries of architectural styles, including Gothic, Baroque, and Romanesque. Seized by a fit of Romantic hyperbole (or perhaps "new math"), French novelist Victor Hugo counted 300 bell towers in the city from the **Micalet** (the cathedral tower) in Pl. Reina—actually, there are only about 100. (Tower open Mon.-Fri. 10am-1pm and 4:30-8pm, Sat.-Sun. 10am-2pm and 5-8pm. Admission 100ptas.) The **Museu de la Seu** (Cathedral Museum, tel. 391 81 27) squeezes a great many treasures into very little space. Check out the overwrought tabernacle made from 1200kg of gold, silver, platinum, emeralds, and sapphires; the Holy Grail; two Goyas; and the withered left arm of San Vicente, who was martyred in 304 AD. (Open Mon.-Sat. 10am-1pm and 4:30-6pm; Dec.-Feb. 10am-1pm. Admission 100ptas.)

Behind the cathedral on Pl. Mare de Deu, elliptical **Basílica de la Mare de Deú dels Desamparats** (Basilica of Our Lady of the Forsaken) houses a shining golden altar. Immediately on the right, the **Palau de la Generalitat** (Provincial Palace) at C. Cavallers, 2, boasts ceilings of a gilded, Asian-Renaissance blend. (Courtyard open Mon.-Fri. 9am-8pm. Views of the ceiling possible for groups only, by appointment Mon.-Fri. 9am-2pm; call 386 34 61.)

Next to the train station and linked to the bullring is the original **Museu Taurino** (Bullfighting Museum), at C. Dr. Serra, 16. Among displays of bulls' heads and matador equipment hang several gory photos of the death of Manuel Granero, last of the great Valencian bullfighters, killed in 1922. (Open Mon.-Fri. 10:30am-1:30pm. Free.)

In Plaça del Mercat, the old **Llotja de la Seda** (Silk Exchange, tel. 391 36 08) in one of the foremost examples of Valencian Gothic architecture, testifies to Valencia's medieval prominence in the silk trade. (Open Tues.-Sat. 10am-1:30pm and 5-9pm, Sun. 10am-2pm. Free.)

A few blocks east stands the old **Universitat.** Valencia recently inaugurated the **Palau de la Mùsica** (concert hall), a dead ringer for England's Crystal Palace, in the middle of the Jardi del Turia.

ENTERTAINMENT

In the area around the **Plaza de los Fueros** (at the foot of the Puente de Serrano) clusters of bars, with their tables spilling into the narrow streets, look like fireflies on a summer's night. The bars and cafés of **Carrer Roteros** buzz the loudest. It's wiser to tackle the labyrinth of the old city in groups; the dark areas in between the clusters can be dangerous. For information on activities in the city, consult the *Qué y Dónde* weekly magazine, available at newsstands (125ptas), or *La Cartelera,* a weekly entertainment supplement to the daily paper *Levante* (125ptas for both).

The newer sections of the city around Pl. Cánovas del Castillo and over the Turia near the university on Av. Blasco Ibañez are fertile ground for discos. One favorite is **Woody,** C. Menéndez y Pelayo, 137 (tel. 361 85 51), with a blinking 70s-type dance floor. (Open Fri.-Sat. 11:30pm-7am. Cover 1000ptas.) **Distrito 10,** C. General Elío, 10 (tel. 369 48 62), is another hotspot, with mirrors, three floors of balconies, and a gigantic video screen. (Open Sept.-July Thurs.-Sat. 6-9:30pm and midnight-7am, Sun. 6-9:30pm. Early session 400ptas, late session 1500ptas.) Meanwhile, **Club Perdido,** C. Sueca, 17, past the train station, jazzes it up. Lesbians favor **Carnaby Club,** Poeta Liern, 17. Gay men congregate at **Balkiss,** C. Dr. Monserrat, 23 (tel. 391 70 80).

Movies are popular: ask at the tourist office for information on the Mostra de València de Cine Mediterrani and the Independent Film Festival.

During **Semana Santa** (Holy Week), the streets are clogged by lavishly attired monks riding platforms enacting Biblical scenes, and children performing the miracle plays of St. Vincent Ferrer. The festival of **Corpus Christi** features *Rocas,* intricate coaches that double as stages for religious plays. The **Fira de Juliol** (July Fair) brings fireworks, cultural events, bullfights, and a **batalla de flors,** a violent skirmish in which girls on passing floats throw flowers at the crowd, which in turn flings them back.

LAS FALLAS

If you can choose any time of the year to come to Valencia, make it March 12-19. Valencia's most illustrious traditional event is undoubtedly **Las Fallas.** The city's neighborhoods compete to build the most elaborate and satirical papier-mâché effigy; over 300 such *ninots* spring up in the streets. Parades, bullfights, fireworks, and street dancing enliven the annual excess. On the final day—*la nit del foc* (fire night)—all the *ninots* simultaneously burn in one last, clamorous release. The inferno exorcises social ills and brings luck for the agricultural season. Accommodations are packed in March.

■ NEAR VALENCIA

SAGUNTO

Sagunto (25km north of Valencia) provoked the Second Punic War. Spaniards still puff with pride over the courage of the city's inhabitants. In the third century BC, residents of Sagunto held out for months on end against Hannibal's besieging Carthaginians. There are conflicting opinions about the outcome of this violent story of local pride and valor. Some sources say that on the brink of total destruction, Sagunto's women, children, and elderly threw themselves into a burning furnace; others insist that the residents chose starvation over defeat. Roman ruins still mark the hill just above town.

To get to the center of town from the train station, turn right at the exit. Then turn left at the traffic lights onto the diagonal street (C. Vicent Fontelles), heading the wrong way down a one-way street to La Glorieta next to the **Ajuntament.** On the opposite side of the Ajuntament from La Glorieta, the town slopes upward to the old town and peaks at the refurbished medieval **castell.** (Open Tues.-Sat. 10am-8pm, Sun. 10am-2pm; Oct.-May Tues.-Sat. 10am-2pm and 4-6pm, Sun. 10am-2pm.) Along the way, the once-crumbling **Teatre Roman** has survived a fiercely contested restoration to become an impressive modern performance stage, built entirely on the still-visible skeleton of the Roman structure. The **Museu Arquelògic,** a national monument, boasts a collection of epigraphs; the Roman, Iberian, and Hebrew inscriptions go back to the Bronze Age. (Currently closed for restorations.)

   Beaches, including the Puerto de Sagunto (which won an EU beach award) and Almarda, beckon by the port (4km away). Buses leave from outside the Ajuntament (every ½hr., 80ptas). In summer, a number of nameless restaurants set up shop on the beach along Av. Mediterrani and Pg. Marítim.

   The **tourist office** (tel. 266 22 13), Pl. Cronista Chabret, proudly answers questions. (Open Mon.-Sat. 9:30am-2pm and 4-8pm, Sun. 10:30am-1pm.) Frequent RENFE **trains** from Valencia (headed for Castellón and Barcelona) stop in Sagunto (tel. 266 07 28; ½hr., 300ptas), as do Vallduxense **buses** (tel. 349 37 38; ½hr., 250ptas).

MANISES

The province of Valencia is famous for its colorful, hand-decorated ceramics, thanks largely to the small town of **Manises,** which fairly bursts with family-owned ceramics ateliers and stores. The town's main square is a sop to those who detest souvenir hunting. CVT **buses** (tel. 340 47 15) leave from Valencia (almost every hr., ½hr., 150ptas), but **trains** from Valencia along the line to Riba-Roja de Turia (20min., 145ptas) are more frequent and arrive at Manises's decorative ceramic-filled train station. You can also find fine ceramics closer to Valencia at the famous **Fábrica Lladró** workshop in Tavernes Blanques (take bus #16 from Pl. Ajuntament in Valencia).

ALBUFEIRA

The **Albufeira,** Spain's largest lagoon, is 13km south of Valencia. Rice fields rim the edges, fish and wild fowl populate the waters, and the scenery is splendid. Mediterráneo Urbano **buses** (tel. 349 72 22) from C. Alicante, on the right side of the Valencia train station, stop here on the way to El Perello (every ½hr., 40min., 150ptas). *All i pebre* (garlic eels fried in pepper sauce) are particularly delectable in the nearby village of **El Palmar,** another stop on the bus route from Valencia (50min., 150ptas).

CULLERA

The rapidly growing town of **Cullera,** south of Valencia, glories under the protective glare of its 13th-century **castell.** Those who survive the 15-min. zig-zag hike are rewarded with a 360-degree postcard view, which takes in the mountains, sea, river, and city. Attached to the castle is the 19th-century **Santuari de la Verge,** displaying sundry religious treasures "collected" by the castle's residents over the years. (Open 9am-9pm; off-season 8am-6pm. Free.) Cullera lies on the Cercanías **train** line between Valencia and Gandía (every hr., 35min., one-way 300ptas). From the train station, take the bus into the city and pester the driver for the correct stop.

MORELLA

Amid miles of rolling green hills, a lone massive rock holds court, with an ancient village sprinkled about its outcroppings. On the peak, cliffs mingle with grand stone walls in a truly superlative Spanish castle. The **Castell de Morella** is unlike any other in the world; the sight of it dazzles even the most jaded castlemasters. This stunning natural fortress has attracted settlers from Celts to Romans to Moors. El Cid stormed it in 1084, and Don Blasco de Alagón took the town in the name of Jaume I in 1232. Weather-worn walls twirl in an almost vertical spiral to the pinnacle. The walk is rigorous, but the view of the surrounding countryside, including the ancient Roman aqueducts behind the mountain, is priceless. (Entrance is on C. Hospital, uphill from

JÁTIVA

the basilica with two Gothic portals. Open Mon.-Fri. 10:30am-2pm and 3:30-6:30pm, Sat.-Sun. 10:30am-6:30pm. Admission 200ptas.) The **Torres de San Miguel** allow entrance through the surrounding walls. (Open Sat.-Sun. 11am-2pm and 4-7pm. Admission 200ptas.)

Oldest among the town's noteworthy remains are the Paleolithic **pinturas rupestres** (cave paintings) in Morella la Vella (4km away). Halfway there, leftovers of the 13th-century Gothic **acueducto,** with 16 towers and six gates, arch above the road. The best time to visit is during **Sexeni,** Morella's most famous *fiesta,* celebrated every six years in honor of the Virgen de Vallivana.

The **tourist office** (tel. 17 30 32) is at Puerta de San Miguel (climb along the wall uphill from the bus stop). (Open Mon.-Sat. 10am-2pm and 4-7pm, Sun. 10am-2pm.) The **telephone code** is 964. The **post office,** C. San Nicolás, 13 (tel. 16 03 13), off C. San Juan, offers basic services Mon.-Sat. 9am-2pm. The **postal code** is 12300. C. Blasco Alagón has the town's only **pharmacy** (tel. 16 00 04) and a couple of banks for **currency exchange** (generally open Mon.-Fri. 9am-2pm). For all emergencies call the **Guardia Civil** (tel. 16 00 11) or the **Red Cross** (tel. 16 03 08).

If you're staying overnight, **Fonda Moreno,** C. San Nicolás, 12 (tel. 16 01 05) has ancient rooms, polished, uneven floors, and wooden ceilings. (Doubles with 3 meals 2500ptas.) Also inexpensive is **Hostal El Cid,** Puerta San Mateo, 3 (tel. 16 00 08), directly down from the bus stop. Offers guests flower-clad bedspreads and a balcony view of the hilly frontier. (Singles 1100ptas. Doubles 1900ptas, with shower 2800ptas, with bath 3200ptas. Breakfast 250ptas.)

Bus services operate between Castellón—two RENFE stops away from Valencia on the Barcelona-Cádiz line—and Morella. The bus stop in Castellón lies on the other side of the park, outside the train station. If going by **car,** highway N-232 links Morella to the coastal routes and Valencia.

BEACHES

The polluted, overcrowded **platjas** close to Valencia lie along the coastal strip known as the **Levant.** Most popular are **Les Arenes** and **Malvarosa,** both on the bus #19 route from Pl. Ajuntament. Equally crowded, but more attractive, is **Salér,** a long, pine-bordered strand 14km from the city center. Cafeterias and snack bars line the shore, with shower and bathroom facilities nearby. Mediterráneo Urbano **buses** (tel. 349 72 22) make for Salér (on the way to El Perello) from Valencia's C. Alicante, on the right side of the train station (every ½hr., 25min., 150ptas).

■■■ JÁTIVA (XÀTIVA)

The last foreigner of note to come through Játiva was Felipe V, who burned it to the ground. With an imposing mountainous backdrop and land that lends itself equally to *huertas* (orchards) and to vineyards, it's no wonder that Felipe was just one in a long line of conquerors. Although it's quite accessible as a daytrip from Valencia, few tourists visit the city, and its quiet charm remains intact.

Once the second-most populous city in Valencia, this city of palaces and churches sits amidst verdant hills. Játiva's varied distinctions include being the birthplace of European paper production, Baroque painter José Ribera, and the Borja Popes Calixtus III and Alexander VI.

ORIENTATION AND PRACTICAL INFORMATION

Játiva is an inland town 64km south of Valencia and 102km north of Alicante, easily accessed by rail. **Avinguda de Jaume I** divides the town into two parts: the old village, at the foot of the hill with the castles and ancient walls, and the modern village. To reach the old section from the train station in the modern section, go straight up Baixada de L'Estació and turn left at its end.

Tourist Office: C. Noguera, 10 (tel. 227 33 46). From Av. Jaume I, take Portal de Lleó and continue straight up the hill as it becomes C. Peris. Open Tues.-Sun.

9am-2:30pm; Sept. 16-June 14 Tues.-Fri. 9am-2pm and 4-6pm, Sat.-Sun. 10am-2pm. City maps also available any time of day at the **Policía Nacional.**

Post Office: Av. Jaume I, 33 (tel. 227 51 68). Open for stamps and Lista de Correos Mon.-Fri. 9am-2pm; for **telegrams** Mon.-Fri. 8am-3pm, Sat. 9am-1pm. **Postal Code:** 46800.

Telephone Code: 96.

Trains: RENFE, Av. Cavaller Ximén de Tovia (tel. 227 33 33). To Valencia (35 per day, 1hr., 365ptas, round-trip 730ptas) and Madrid.

Buses: At corner of Av. Cavaller Ximén de Tovia and C. Don Carles Santhou; down the street to the left of the train station. Many companies serve the small nearby towns. **Iberbus** (tel. 287 41 10) goes direct to Gandía (2 per day, 1¼hr., about 325ptas). Call the bus station in Valencia (tel. 349 72 22) for a schedule from there to Játiva.

Red Cross: tel. 227 02 39.

Hospital: Lluis Alcanyis, Ctra. Alzira (tel. 228 91 00), about 2km from the town center.

Medical Assistance: Ambulance (tel. 227 10 95).

Police: Baixada del Carme behind the Ajuntament at Av. Jaume I, 33 (tel. 092).

ACCOMMODATIONS AND FOOD

Call before coming if you plan to stay the night. Játiva's traditional desserts are unmistakably Arabic in origin. *Harnadi* is a pudding of squash, sweet potato, nuts, and raisins. *Al Monchamena* tastes like a sweetened omelette. The city's version of *paella* is *arroz al horno,* baked, slightly drier, and loaded with chick peas. Tuesdays and Fridays are **market** days on Pl. Mercat. (Open 8am-1pm.)

Margallonero, Pl. Mercat, 42 (tel. 227 66 77), which looks out on the city's active market plaza, offers large, well-furnished, utterly flowery rooms at reasonable prices. (1400ptas per person.) The **restaurant** below is one of the most economical in town (full meal 1000ptas).

Casa Floro, Pl. Mercat, 46 (tel. 227 30 20), next door to the Margallonero. Their *menú* is 1000ptas. (Open Mon.-Sat. 1-4pm.)

SIGHTS AND ENTERTAINMENT

The 18th-century mansions of **Carrer Moncada,** one block in and parallel with Av. Jaume I, reflect Játiva's formerly-capital glory. At the end of the street, where C. Moncada meets Pl. Trinitat, the small 15th-century **Font Gòtica** dribbles out water, looking more like an upside-down ice cream cone than the city's sole medieval remnant. Behind it, the 18th-century Baroque **Palau d'Alarcó,** with its angled courtyard, once housed the city's richest family.

A walk up C. Sanchis is the **Colegiata de Santa María,** a giant church known in town as *La Seu.* In front, the city's two popes scheme in bronze. Constructed from 1596 to 1920, the ornate *colegiata* is more a religious museum—paintings and figurines lurk in numerous nooks and crannies, as well as on the ceiling. (Open 7:30-10:45am and 7-9pm.)

The **Museu Municipal l'Almodí,** in a 16th-century palace on C. Corretgeria, 46 (tel. 227 65 97), off Pl. Calixto III, holds four floors of Spanish paintings, including three Riberas. Here the townspeople avenged Felipe V's 1707 destruction of the town by hanging his portrait upside down. (Open Tues.-Sun. 9am-2:30pm; Oct.-May Tues.-Fri. 11am-2pm and 4-6pm, Sat.-Sun. 11am-2pm. Free.)

The striking ramparts atop the hill in back of town lead to the city's awe-inspiring **castell** (2km). The castle is made up of two sections: the **castell machor** (larger), on the right as you come in, and the pre-Roman **castell chicotet** (smaller). The former, used from the 13th through 16th centuries, bears the scars of many a siege and earthquake. Its arched stone **prison** has held some famous wrongdoers, including King Fernando el Católico and the Comte d'Urgell, would-be usurper of the Aragonese throne. Referred to in Verdi's *Il Trovatore,* the Comte spent his final decades here before being buried in the castle's chapel. (Open Tues.-Sun. 10:30am-2pm and 4:30-7pm; off-season Tues.-Sun. 10:30am-2pm and 3:30-6pm. Free.)

Although Játiva is a small town, partying people refuse to be tied down. **El Verde Limón,** Pl. Cayetano, a tavern inside an ancient house, blends a mean *agua de Valencia* (O.J., champagne, gin, and whatever else the owner feels like splashing in; open 7:30pm-2:30am, Fri.-Sat. 7:30pm-4am.) Walking distance from the town center on Ctra. Xàtiva Novetlé, **Almassera** is a huge ex-factory and the first choice of Generation X-ers. (Opens at 1am. Cover 300ptas.) Spanish music bursts from **Elite** (cover 300ptas).

■■■ GANDÍA

Gandía (pop. 53,000) is the capital of La Sofor, a verdant region of Valencia. Winter hardly exists here; the only white covering the ground are the long stretches of absolutely white beaches. Before everyone became so fascinated by beaches, Gandía was best known as the hangout of the Borjas, who settled here in the 15th century. The fourth Borjan Duke Francisco became a Jesuit and took vows of poverty and celibacy—as Gandía and the other Borjas took vows of jeopardy, and monopoly. Francisco died a saint, the others grew rich. Five centuries later, as an agri-business and mercanto exchange nexus, Gandía still yields cash crops galore: sugar cane, oranges, silk, burlap, beach condos, daffodils, and mulberries.

ORIENTATION AND PRACTICAL INFORMATION

Everything you need is a stone's throw from the train station on **Marqués de Campo.** Everything you want is at the **beach,** 4km away.

Tourist Office: Marqués de Campo (tel. 287 77 88), across from the train station. Detailed map. Open Mon.-Fri. 10am-2pm and 4:30-8pm, Sat. 10am-2pm. A beach **branch** (tel. 284 24 07) at Pg. Marítim, on the water. Open March 15-Oct. 15 Mon.-Fri. 10am-2pm and 4-8pm, Sat.-Sun. 10am-2pm.

Post Office: Pl. Jaume I, 7 (tel. 287 10 91), a few bl. behind the Ajuntament. Open for stamps and Lista de Correos Mon.-Fri. 9am-2pm; for **telegrams** 8:30am-8:30pm. **Postal Code:** 46700.

Telephone Code: 96

Trains: the **RENFE** variety (tel. 286 54 71) depart from Marqués de Campo to Valencia (31 per day, every ½hr., 1hr., 460ptas, round-trip 920ptas).

Buses: UBESA (tel. 287 16 54) leaves from Marqués de Campo, just down the street from the train station, to: Valencia (14 per day, 1¼hr., 625ptas); Alicante (5 per day, 3hr., 1050ptas); Barcelona (1 per day, 7-8hr., 3455ptas); Costa Brava towns (several per day). **Auto Res,** Marqués de Campo, 12 (tel. 287 10 64). Buses stop at the beach at Pg. Marítim en route to Madrid (6 per day, 6hr., 2955ptas, round-trip 5335ptas).

Ferries: Pitra, Port de Gandía (tel. 284 45 00). Chugs to San Antonio on Ibiza Mon.-Fri. and Sun. 11pm (5220ptas).

Bike/Windsurfer Rental: At the HI hostel in Platja de Piles (see Accommodations). Bike 500ptas per day. Windsurfer 600ptas per hr.

Emergency: tel. 091.

Hospital: C. Sant Pere and Pg. Germanies (tel. 295 92 00).

Police: tel. 287 88 00.

ACCOMMODATIONS AND FOOD

HI cardholders rejoice at Gandía's hostel, especially with the number of expensive *hostales* about. Make reservations in the summer, especially in August, or go bedless. Gandía offers a seafood speciality called *fidueà,* a shellfish and pasta dish covered with hot broth, and the invariably expensive but tempting *zarzuela,* a platter of assorted shellfish and squid in broth.

Alberg Mar i Vent (HI), C. Doctor Fleming, s/n (tel. 289 37 48), in Platja de Piles, a town 10km south of Gandía. Take the La Amistad bus (tel. 287 44 10), which departs from the right of the train station (for exact times check with the tourist office, 85ptas). From Sept.-June, the bus only runs to the town of Piles, 3km short of the beach. Simple flattery does not do justice to this hostel/beachfront resort. Water laps at the door, there's an outdoor patio and basketball court, and they rent bikes and windsurfers (see Practical Information). Alcohol is strictly prohibited. No smoking indoors (except for one lecture hall). 3-day max. stay. Curfew midnight. 770ptas per person, with 3 meals 1700ptas. Over 26: 915ptas; 2225ptas. Sheets 170ptas. Open Feb.-Nov.

Hotel Europa, C. Levante, 12-14 (tel. 284 07 50). From the tourist office, hop on the La Marina bus and ask the driver to let you off at the C. Levante stop (100ptas). A regal hotel with elevator, solarium, and many newly designed rooms. Doubles with shower 3000ptas, with bath 5000ptas. Breakfast 300ptas.

Camping: The tourist office has directions to and details about the 3 campsites near the beach. The cheapest is **L'Alqueria** (tel. 284 04 70), on the La Marina bus route between Gandía and the beach. 420ptas per person and 460ptas per tent. Open April-Sept.

Asador Josman, C. Ermita, 16 (tel. 284 05 30). From the tourist office, take the La Marina bus and ask for the C. Levante stop; Levante becomes C. Ermita as it nears the highway. On weekends this *pollería* (chicken store) is an unbelievable deal. Whole chickens 700ptas; Sat.-Sun. whole chickens with french fries for 4 people 900ptas. Open Mon.-Sat. 9:30am-2:30pm and 6:30-9:30pm, Sun. 9:30am-2:30pm.

Bar-Restaurante Nati, C. del Mar, 25 (tel. 289 34 09), in Platja de Piles near the HI hostel; right at the bus stop. *Paella* 650ptas. *Bocadillos* 200-350ptas. Open noon-3:30pm and 9:30-11:30pm.

SIGHTS AND ENTERTAINMENT

Not much aside from the **beach,** but who cares? Wedged between blue sea and tiled Pg. Marítim, fine sands stretch for several km from the port to the condos. La Marina buses (tel. 287 18 06) leave from Marqués de Campo, 14, next to the tourist office, and make various stops along Pg. Marítim, which runs the length of the beach (every ½hr., 105ptas).

For a taste of Gandía's former glory, visit the **Palau de Sant Duc** (tel. 287 12 03), on C. Sant Duc in town (5min. from the train station; head south on C. Magistrat). Its mix of Gothic, Renaissance, and Baroque styles reflects renovations from the 14th to the 17th centuries. Now a Jesuit college, the palace was once inhabited by the Borja family, as well as Doña Constanza, the ne'er-do-well old aunt of King Jaume II. (Guided visits Mon.-Sat. 11am, noon, 6pm, and 7pm; Oct.-June 11am, noon, 5pm, and 6pm. Admission 200ptas. Groups call ahead for reservations.) A **Museu Arquelògic** should open by 1995. Check with the tourist office.

No discos strobe in Gandía proper, although numerous **bars** line C. Gutiérrez Más. (Follow Marqués de Campo to the end, turn right onto C. Magistrat Catala, and take the fifth right onto C. Gutiérrez Más.)

Gandía has been honoring its patron saint (San Francisco) every September since 1310. The town also revs up for its version of **Las Fallas** on March 19.

■■■ ALICANTE (ALACANT)

Lanky palm trees and shady cafés line Alicante's glossy avenues, and white sand beaches bask in the balmy sea breezes. It's hard to imagine today that Alicante (pop. 250,000) once had to earn its "city" status. Fernando finally relented when *alicanti-nos* helped reconquer the last Muslim outpost in Granada. Alicante is now confident enough in its urbanity to emphasize its relaxing provincial aspects—particularly the waterfront. Beneath the famous *castillo,* this city offers a trail of history in the snarl of lively, antiquated streets. Lodgings are plentiful and cheap here, and the nightlife moves at a good clip.

A
L
I
C
A
N
T
E

ORIENTATION AND PRACTICAL INFORMATION

Avenida la Estación (site of the train station) runs straight out from the train station and becomes **Avenida Alfonso X el Sabio** after passing through **Plaza de los Luceros**. **Esplanada d'Espanya** stretches along the waterfront between **Rambla Méndez Núñez** and **Avenida Federico Soto,** which reach back up to Av. Alfonso X el Sabio, forming a box of streets where nearly all services cluster.

Tourist Office: Regional Tourist Office, Esplanada d'Espanya, 2 (tel. 520 00 00). Information about the entire coast and the city. The friendly staff will bend over backwards to help the weary traveler get a bed or bite. Open Mon.-Sat. 10am-8pm; Sept. 16-June 14 Mon.-Sat. 10am-7pm. **Municipal Tourist Office,** C. Portugal, 17 (tel. 514 92 95), next to the bus station. Ask for *Alicante at your Fingertips,* a helpful guide to local services. Open Mon.-Fri. 9am-2pm. Also an **airport branch** (tel. 528 50 11, ext. 367).

El Corte Inglés: Maisonnave, 53 (tel. 511 30 01). Their usual wonderful **map. Currency exchange:** zero commission. Novels and guidebooks in English, hair-cutting, cafeteria and restaurant, and **telephones.** Open Mon.-Sat. 10am-9pm.

Budget Travel: TIVE, Av. Aguilera, 1 (tel. 513 11 58), near the train station off Av. Oscar Esplá. ISIC 500ptas. HI card 1800ptas. Open Mon.-Fri. 9am-1:30pm.

Consulate: See Spain Essentials: Embassies and Consulates.

Post Office: Pl. Gabriel Miró (tel. 521 99 84), off C. Sant Ferran. Open Mon.-Fri. 8am-9pm, Sat. 9am-2pm. For **telegrams** (tel. 514 20 01), open Mon.-Fri. 8am-9pm, Sat. 9am-7pm, Sun. 9am-2pm. **Postal Code:** 03000.

Telephones: Av. Constitució, 10. Open 9am-10pm. Another office at the **bus station.** Open Mon.-Fri. 9:30am-2pm and 5-9:30pm, Sat.-Sun. 10am-2pm and 5-9pm. **Telephone Code:** 96.

Flights: Aeroport Internacional El Altet (tel. 528 50 11), 10km from town. **Alcoyana** (tel. 513 01 04) sends 13 buses per day between the airport and Av. Constitució (from town 7am-10pm, from airport 6:30am-9:20pm, 150ptas). **Iberia,** C. F. Soto, 9 (tel. 521 44 14). To: Palma (4 per day, 11,700ptas); Barcelona (3 per day, 13,650ptas); Madrid (4 per day, 12,600ptas); Sevilla (2 per day, 15,400ptas).

Trains: RENFE, Estació Término, Av. Salamanca (tel. 592 02 02), west of the city center. Information open 7am-10pm. Most destinations require a transfer. Direct to: Murcia (1½hr., 420ptas); Valencia (2hr., 1500-2000ptas); Madrid (4hr., 3400-4400ptas); Barcelona (6hr., 4000ptas). **Ferrocarrils de la Generalitat Valenciana, Estació de la Marina,** Av. Villajoyosa, 2 (tel. 526 27 31), a 15-min. walk down Esplanada d'Espanya, away from Rambla Méndez Núñez; it's on Po. Marítimo. (Bus C-1 from Pl. Espanya.) Local service along the Costa Blanca to: San Juan (90ptas), Villajoyosa (285ptas), Benidorm (370ptas), Calpe (565ptas), and Denia (820ptas). Railpasses not accepted. Departures every hr., 6:15am-8:15pm; only 7 as far as Calpe and Denia. Round-trip tickets discounted 15%. Also **night trains** to discos on the beaches near Alicante.

Buses: C. Portugal, 17 (tel. 513 07 00). To reach Esplanada d'Espanya, turn left onto Carrer d'Italia and right on Av. Dr. Gadea; follow Dr. Gadea until the park, then left on the waterfront. Each company serves different destinations, including international ones. For the Costa Blanca, **UBESA** (tel. 513 01 43) sends 22 buses per day to Villajoyosa (300ptas) and Benidorm (390ptas). Also to: Calpe (565ptas); Denia (910ptas); Valencia (1770ptas). **Molla** (tel. 513 08 51) to: Elche (every ½hr., 185ptas). **Enatcar** (tel. 512 56 22 or 592 95 10) to: Madrid (5½hr., 2895ptas); Granada (6hr., 3090ptas); Málaga (8hr., 4180ptas); Sevilla (10hr., 5130ptas); Barcelona (8hr., 4290ptas).

Ferries: Flebasa, Estació Marítima, Puerto de Denia (tel. 578 42 00). Service from Denia (includes bus from Alicante) to Ibiza (3 per day, 3½hr., 5220ptas). Open Mon.-Fri. 9am-1pm and 4:30-8pm, Sat. 9am-noon.

Taxis: tel. 525 78 37. 900-1000ptas to Platja Sant Joan.

Luggage Storage: At the **bus station** (200ptas per bag). Open 6:45am-9pm.

Medical Services: Hospital Clínico, Maestro Alonzo, 109 (tel. 590 83 00). **Ambulance** (tel. 511 46 76).

Emergency: tel. 091.

Police: Comisaría, C. Médico Pascual Pérez, 27 (tel. 514 22 22). **Office for Tourist Assistance,** C. Sant Ferran, 18. Open Mon.-Fri. 9am-2pm.

ACCOMMODATIONS AND CAMPING

Although there seem to be *pensiones* and *casas de huéspedes* on every corner in town, the number of clean rooms is considerably smaller. The tourist office keeps accommodations listings. Stay away from most places along C. Sant Ferran (where theft and prostitution are common) and around the Església de Santa María; opt instead for the newer section of town. Arrive early for a good room.

Residencia Juvenil (HI), Av. Orihuela, 97. Take bus G (85ptas, make sure you go in the right direction) and get off at the last stop, directly behind the large *residencia*. Really a college dormitory, it offers all the conveniences of a 1-star hotel—individual rooms, private bath, A/C. Cheap snack bar inside (wine 50ptas). HI card required. 3-day max. stay. 770ptas per person, with breakfast 850ptas, with three meals 1700ptas. Over 25: 910ptas; 1240ptas; 2225ptas.

Pensión Las Monjas, C. Monjas, 2 (tel. 521 50 46). Follow C. San Isidro off Rambla Méndez Núñez until it turns into C. Monjas. In the center of the historic district and only a few bl. from the beach. Each lovely room is individually decorated in the owner Pedro's taste. Singles 1500ptas, with sink 1700ptas, with shower 2000ptas, with bath 2500ptas. Doubles 3000ptas, with sink 3200ptas, with shower 3500ptas, with bath 4000ptas.

Habitaciones México, C. General Primo de Rivera, 10 (tel. 520 93 07), off the end of Av. Alfonso X El Sabio. Pristine rooms. Friendly owners organize a book swap, and allow use of kitchen. Laundry service (600ptas per load). Singles 1450ptas. Doubles 2800ptas, with bath 3400ptas. Triples 3600ptas, with bath 4000ptas.

Hostal-Residencia Portugal, C. Portugal, 26, (tel. 592 92 44), across from the bus station. Angular rooms with cushy beds and cool sheets. Dining room/lounge has picnic-style red and white checked tablecloths, and color TV. Singles 2000ptas. Doubles 3400ptas, with bath 3800ptas. Hearty breakfast 250ptas.

Hostal Ventura, C. Sant Ferran, 10 (tel. 520 83 37), off the end of the Rambla near the water. Singles 1800ptas. Doubles with bath 3200ptas. Triples with bath 4800ptas.

Camping: Camping Bahía, Playa Albafereta (tel. 526 23 32), 4km away on the road to Valencia. Take bus C-1. 450ptas per person and 500ptas per tent. Open March 15-Oct. 15.

FOOD

Most tourists eat on the main pedestrian thoroughfare. Less traveled are the smaller family-run establishments in the **old city** (between the cathedral and the steps to the castle). Locals devour *tapas* in the **Calle Mayor.**

The **market** near Av. Alfonso X El Sabio sells fresh fish, meats, and produce, plus sandwich meats and bread.

Groceries: Supermarket Maercadona, C. Alvarez Sereix, 5 (tel. 521 58 94), off Av. Federico Soto. Open Mon.-Thurs. and Sat. 9am-8pm, Fri. 9am-8:30pm.

Mesón de Castilla, C. Sant Nicolau, 12 (tel. 520 06 84). The owner juggles 10 plates through the dining room to accommodate the regulars. *Menú especial*—3 courses, fruit, bread, and drink—800ptas. *Paella* option Thurs. and Sun. Open Mon.-Fri. 1-4pm and 7-10pm, Sat.-Sun. 1-4pm.

Restaurante Mixto Vegetariano, Pl. Santa María, 2. Creative vegetarian fare; some meat plates as well. Salad bar and only whole-wheat pizza crust in Spain. *Menú* 975ptas. Open Tues.-Sun. 1-4:30pm and 8pm-midnight; fewer hours in off-season.

La Venta del Lobo, C. Sant Ferran, 48 (tel. 514 09 85). A 2-room neighborhood grill ambitious enough to prepare specialties from all over Spain. Try *gazpacho andaluz* for a taste of the south (370ptas) or Valencian *paella. Menú* 900ptas. Multilingual menu. Open Tues.-Sat. 1-5pm and 8:30pm-12:30am, Sun. 1-5pm.

La Pavilla de Cordero, C. San Francesc, 12 (tel. 521 19 59). One of 6 adjacent outdoor eateries. Romantic evening dining or mid-day *menú* (3 plates and dessert, 950ptas). Open daily 1-4pm and 8pm-midnight; Sept.-June closed on Wed.

SIGHTS

Complete with drawbridges, clandestine tunnels, passageways, and dungeons, the **Castell de Santa Bárbara** isn't just another castle. Built by the Carthaginians and recently reconstructed, the 200m-high fortress has a dry moat, a dungeon, a spooky ammunition storeroom, and an amazing view of Alicante. Inside the castle, the minuscule, dull **Museu de les Fogueres de Sant Joan** (St. John) displays statuettes of the famed martyr. A paved road from the old section of Alicante leads to the top; most people take the elevator (200ptas) by the beachfront. (Castle and museum open 10am-8pm; Oct.-Mar. 9am-7pm. Free.)

The **Concatedral de San Nicolás de Bari,** one block north of Méndez Núñez on C. San Isidro, reflects the sober Renaissance style of Agustín Bernadino, while the Baroque communion chapel lavishly compensates. (Open Mon.-Sat. 8am-2:30pm and 6-8:30pm, Sun. 9am-1:45pm.) For keen contrast, visit the **Església de Santa María,** built on the ruins of an Arab mosque, harmonizing a Gothic nave, a Baroque facade, and a Renaissance marble baptismal font. (Closed for restoration.)

Inside the Neoclassical **Diputación Provincial,** a **Museu Arqueològic** (tel. 512 13 00) houses artifacts that include Bronze Age dowries and Roman Statues from excavations throughout the province. (Open Mon.-Fri. 9am-1:30pm. Free.) In direct temporal contrast, a crowd of Valencian modernist art pieces, along with a few Mirós, Picassos, Kandinskys, and Calders fraternize in the **Museu de Arte Sigo XX "La Asegurada"** (tel. 521 45 78), at the east end of C. Mayor. The original collection was donated to the city by Valencian artist Eusebio Sempre. (Open Oct.-Apr. Tues.-Sun. 10am-1pm, 5-8pm; May.-Sept. Tues.-Sun. 10:30am-1:30pm, 6-9pm. Closed Sun. pm. Free.)

If Alicante's own beach doesn't suit you, hop on bus C-1 in Pl. Espanya (75ptas) or board the Alicante-Denia train (85ptas) for 6km-long **Platja de Sant Joan.** If crowds have soiled every square inch, try the **Platja del Saladar** in Urbanova. Buses from the Alicante bus station make the trip to Urbanova (3 per day, 35min., 100ptas).

ENTERTAINMENT

In summer, nightlife centers on the **Playa de San Juan. Ferrocarriles de la Generalitat Valenciana** runs special **Trensnochador** night trains from Estació de la Marina to several points along the beach (every hr., 11pm-7am, 85-280ptas). A taxi from Alicante (900-1000ptas) to Playa de San Juan and can be shared by up to four people. **Voy Voy** on Av. Niza at the "Discoteca" stop on the night train, swings with outdoor bars, decibels of music, and dancing. (Open until 6am. Beer 350ptas.) **Copity** and **Va Bene** are other discos, both along Av. Condomina, a long walk or short taxi ride away from the "Condomina" stop on the night train.

In Alicante itself, discos charge 1000pta cover on weekends, but disco employees sometimes hand out free passes in Pl. Esplanada. The hottest one is **Buggatti,** C. Sant Ferran, 27 (tel. 521 06 46), featuring neon-lined bars and candle-lit tables. (Cover including 1 drink 1000ptas. Open nightly until 5:30am.) Gay men convene at **Jardineto** on C. Baron de Finestrat; for dancing, try **Rosé,** on C. Sant Joan Bosco.

From June 21 to 29, the town bursts with bacchanalian celebration for the **Festival de Sant Joan,** comprised of romping *fogueres* (symbolic or satiric effigies). The figures burn in a *cremá* on the 24th; but the charivari continues with breathtaking and hazardous nightly fireworks, and lights and decorations that festoon the streets. On the last day, a marching band and parade of candy hurlers whet people's appetites for next year's festival. The **Verge del Remei** takes place one week after Semana Santa; pilgrims trek to the monastery of Santa Faz the following Thursday.

■ NEAR ALICANTE

Monestir de Santa Faz (tel. 526 49 12), 5km from Alicante, has a shred of the controversial handkerchief of Sta. Verónica, which preserves an imprint of the face of Jesus. Pick up the **bus** for "Muchamiel" at the beginning of the beach. Open 10am-1pm and 4-8pm. Call ahead.

Tabarca, an island 11 miles south, makes a fine beachy daytrip. Crucero Kon-Tiki boats (tel. 521 63 96) leave from in front of the Esplanada d'Espanya (6 per day, winter 1 per day, round-trip 1150ptas).

Jijona, 37km away from Alicante, is the home of the wondrous **Turrones El Lobo** (tel. 561 02 25), a nougat factory. Drool over free samples of the traditional Spanish Christmas candy *turrón,* that has turned Jijona into a household word. Guided tour every ½hr. Open 9:30am-1pm and 4-8pm.

Agost, 15km northwest of Alicante, has a **pottery museum** (tel. 569 11 99) and a **bojitos** (white clay jars) **factory.** Factory open Tues.-Sun. 11am-2pm and 5-8pm; off-season Tues.-Sat. noon-2pm.

Covas de Canalobre (tel. 569 92 50) are spectacular stalagmited caves 24km north of Alicante. The caves lie 700m above the tiny village of **Busot,** hanging over the splendid coastline. Open 10:30am-8:30pm; Oct.-March 11am-6:30pm. Admission 425ptas.

Villajoyosa, a happy and unspoiled town, sits north of Alicante, on the route to Calpe. Nationally famous for its chocolate factories, it's the ideal spot for *churros y chocolate* in the mid-evening. Ferrocarrils de la Generalitat Valenciana **trains** (every hr., 270ptas) and OBESA **buses** (22 per day, 285ptas) run from Alicante.

COSTA BLANCA

The "white coast," which extends from Denia through Calpe, Alicante, and Elche down to Torrevieja, derives its name from the fine, clear granules that cover the shores, although it could also refer to the complexions of its summer visitors (mainly Northern Europeans). Areas of great natural beauty, including the alternating lush and dry mountain range, border the tourist spots. Those with a car are truly set; but not to worry—the extensive rail line out of Alicante (not RENFE) connects most towns and snakes through the mountains, hugging the picturesque coast. UBESA bus line offers quicker service with less show.

CALPE (CALP)

Stepping into Calpe is like stepping into a Dalí landscape. Ten km south of Moraira and 62km northeast of Alicante, the town cowers beneath the **Peñó d'Ifach** (327m), a gargantuan flat-topped protrusion of rock whose sheer faces drop straight to the sea. The throngs that stampede neighboring resorts mercifully spare Calpe. Sparkling **Platja Levant** has plenty of room and is ripe for windsurfing.

If you decide to climb the big rock (2hr.), wear sneakers and bring water (don't bring excess baggage). Hike during the day, since ghosts in goats' clothing haunt the rock and butt unwary travelers over the cliff at full moon. Farther north hang the hard rock and caves of the easterly **Cabo de la Nao,** from which you can see Ibiza. Around the bend from the *cabo,* a castle and watchtower have protected the old fishing village of **Moraira** from freeloading pirates for centuries (several buses from Calpe per day). The fortress village of **Guadalest,** 25km inland from Calpe, towers above the surrounding countryside and a clear blue lake that fills an entire valley.

The **tourist office** on Av. Ejércitos Españoles, 62 (tel. 583 12 50), between the old town and the beach, though far away, has all the info you need on Costa Blanca beaches. (Open Mon.-Sat. 9am-9pm; off-season hours vary.) A second **branch** at C. José Antonio, 36 (tel. 583 67 12), offers a map. (Open 10am-1:30pm and 6-9pm.) The **post office** lies in the old town on C. 18 de Julio (tel. 583 08 84; open Mon.-Sat. 9am-1:30pm). The **American Express,** at **Viajes Gandía,** Av. Gabriel Miró, 25 (tel.

583 04 12; fax 583 51 51), holds mail for six months and cashes AmEx checks for a 2% fee. (Open Mon.-Fri. 9:30am-1:30pm and 5-9pm, Sat. 9:30am-1:30pm; winter Mon.-Fri. 9:30am-1:30pm and 4-7pm, Sat. 9:30am-1:30pm.)

The most reasonable inns and restaurants march up the steep incline toward the older *pueblo*. Beware of bland food and high prices by the seaside. Hang your hat at the bright and comfortable, English-run **Pensión Céntrica,** Pl. Ifach (tel. 583 55 28), at the top of Av. Gabriel Miró. TV lounge and carpeted floors are a refreshing welcome after a day in the sun (1500ptas per person). Tent-toters can try **Camping La Merced** (tel. 583 00 97), a 2nd-class site 400m from the beach (440ptas per person).

Bar El Toro Blanco, on a small side street off C. Mar (tel. 583 14 20), offers a 4-course *menú* for 750ptas and a famous Scottish vegetable soup (285ptas). (Open 11am-3pm and 7:30pm-very late.)

Fourteen UBESA **buses** per day zip from Alicante to Calpe (545ptas), stopping 2km from the beach at C. Capitán Pérez Jorda. **Trains** also connect the two cities (1¾hr., 535ptas). From the train station, take a municipal bus downhill through old Calpe past the bus station and to the beach (1 per hr., 85ptas)—it's an arduous walk.

DENIA

Halfway between Valencia and Alicante on the promontory that forms the Golfo de Valencia, Denia is primarily a family resort where only bright rowboats interrupt the sweep of *platja*. Named by the Greeks for Diana (goddess of the hunt, the moon, and purity), Denia's sheer and sandy coves swarm with fish.

If you tire of the beach, a **museo arqueológico** resides within the dungeon of the 18th-century **castell.** Enter off C. Sant Francesc. (Castle open 10am-1:30pm and 5-8:30pm; Oct.-May 10am-1pm and 3-6pm. Admission 100ptas, Thurs. free. Museum open Fri.-Wed. 10:30am-1pm and 4-7pm; Oct.-May Fri.-Wed. 10:30am-12:30pm and 3-5:30pm. Admission 200ptas.) One bus per day travels 9km down the coast to the hidden cove of **Jávea** (Xàbia). To return, take the bus from Játiva to Gata and the train from Gata to Denia. Denia holds a mini **Fallas** festival March 12-19, burning effigies at midnight on the final day. During the second week of July, the **Fiestas de la Santísima Sangre** (Holy Blood) include street dances, concerts, mock battles, and wild fireworks over the harbor. From August 14-16 are the colorful parades and religious plays of the **Fiestas de Sant Roque.**

The **tourist office,** on. C. Glorieta Oculista Baigues, 9 (tel. 578 07 24), near the train station, directs the weary toward beach and bed. (Open Mon.-Fri. 9:30am-1:30pm and 4:30-7:30pm, Sun. 10am-1pm; Oct.-June Mon.-Fri. 9:30am-1:30pm and 4:30-7:30pm, Sat. 10am-1pm.) The **post office** also does **telegrams** at C. Patricio Ferrándiz, 59, west of the tourist office. (Open Mon.-Sat. 10am-2pm.) A **telephone** service operates next to the train station in summer. (Open 9am-2pm and 5-10pm.)

Denia is no haven for the budget traveler. The tourist office has a list of accommodations; otherwise try **Pensión el Comercio,** C. La Vía, 43 (tel. 578 00 71), about halfway between the tourist office and bus station. Roomy rooms have baths tiled in a brilliant shade of blue. (Singles 2100ptas. Doubles 4200ptas.) Several campgrounds have sprouted in the area. **Camping Las Marinas** (tel. 578 14 46) is the closest to town, a 3km bus ride (75ptas) from **Platja Jorge Joan.** (440ptas per person and per tent, inclusive price 1300ptas; low-season prices vary, closed in Oct.) **Calle Marqués de Campo** cooks inexpensive fare. The morning **market** operates on C. Magallanes, one block north of C. Marqués de Campo.

The **train station** (tel. 578 04 45), down the road at C. Calderón, has service to Alicante (7 per day, 780ptas). The UBESA **bus station** at Pl. Arxiduc Carles serves Valencia (5 per day, 1760ptas) and Alicante (4 per day, 830ptas). Denia is the embarkation point for Flebasa **ferries** (tel. 578 40 11) to Ibiza (4 per day, off-season schedule varies, 3hr., 5220ptas).

ELCHE (ELX)

Although most residents spend their days making shoes, Elche is best known for its 500,000 palm trees. The male palms produce enough fronds to supply the entire country on Palm Sunday, and the females bear enough dates to fill gift boxes around the world. The *Dama de Elche,* Spain's finest example of pre-Roman sculpture, hails from this town (23km from Alicante) although it rests at the Museo Arqueológico in Madrid (see Madrid Entertainment: Museums).

If possible, come to Elche Aug. 11-15, and witness the **Misteri de Elx,** a medieval mystery play performed in **Basilica de Santa María.** (The *fiesta* **Nit de l'Alba** falls on August 13.) During even-numbered years, repeat performances occur Oct. 31 and Nov. 1. Of the parks and public gardens that fill odd corners of the city, the most beautiful is the **Hort del Cura** (Orchard of the Priest), where magnificent trees shade colorful flower beds.

The municipal **tourist office** (tel. 545 38 31) helps at Pg. Estació, Parque Municipal (open Mon.-Fri. 9am-2pm and 5-8pm, Sat. 9am-1:30pm; winter Mon.-Sat. 9am-2:30pm). The **post office** (tel. 544 25 02) is in Parque Project, near the Pont de Canalejas. **First aid** can be obtained from the **Red Cross** (tel. 545 90 90). The **police station** (tel. 545 13 53) is in Parque Project (tel. 545 13 53). The central **train station, Estació Parque,** is at Pl. Alfons XII, but there's also the **Estació Carrus** on Av. Llibertat. The **bus station** on Av. Llibertat serves Alicante (every hr., 180ptas).

Murcia

Murcia has had its share of outrageous fortune. Four centuries ago, mysterious forces unleashed a bizarre wave of plagues, floods, and earthquakes. The earthquakes uncovered a rich supply of minerals and natural springs, which have been converted into a system of irrigation canals that water every acre from the capital city to the wine towns of Yecla and Jumilla. Thermal spas, paprika mills, and pottery factories pepper the lively coastal towns and orange- and apricot-filled countryside. Suddenly Murcia's nickname is "La Huerta de Europa" (Europe's Orchard).

You'd think the epithet would make neighboring Valencia nervous, but apparently not. Murcia is an autonomous province simply because no one else wanted it, not even in the post-Franco zeal of regional strengthening. Indeed, in spite of being flanked by the Mediterranean and the Mar Menor, much of Murcia still suffers from dryness. Further isolating factors include its poverty and its persistent use of *murciano,* a dialect akin to *andaluz.*

■■■ MURCIA

Amid a carpet of citrus orchards, the town of Murcia roasts in the summer. Unnoticed until the 13th century, when the Moors and then the Christians spontaneously declared it the region's capital, today's Murcia is an uninspiring city. Tourist officials are currently targeting it, promoting the city's unspoiled Costa Cálida (hot coast)—which some Murcian apologists maintain refers to the water.

ORIENTATION AND PRACTICAL INFORMATION

To the dismay of weary travelers, most places of interest scatter around the town's periphery. The Río Segura cuts the town into north and south halves, with most sights and services in the northern half. **Gran Vía de Alfonso X El Sabio** is a broad avenue running from Pl. S. Domingo north to the giant Pl. Circular. The cathedral is in **Plaza Cardenal Belluga.**

The **train station,** across the river at the southern edge of the city, and the **bus station,** at the western edge, are both 15min. from the center.

Tourist Office: C. Alejandro Séiquer, 4 (tel. 21 37 16; fax 21 01 53), off Pl. Cetina. Enthusiastic and not yet bored by foreigners. Truck loads of slick pamphlets on the city and province. Open Mon.-Fri. 10am-1pm and 5-8pm, Sat. 10am-1pm.

El Corte Inglés: Av. Libertad, s/n (tel. 29 80 50). The old standby gives away **maps. Currency exchange:** commission rates similar to banks. Also offers novels and guidebooks in English, haircutting, both cafeteria and restaurant, and **telephones.** Open Mon.-Sat. 10am-9pm.

Budget Travel: TIVE, C. Conde Roche, 5 (tel. 21 32 61). Open Mon.-Fri. 9am-2pm.

Post Office: Pl. Circular, 8a (tel. 24 12 43), at the end of Gran Vía Alfonso X El Sabio, in a modern building on the far left side of the giant traffic plaza. Open for stamps Mon.-Fri. 9am-2pm and 5-8pm, Sat. 9am-2pm; for Lista de Correos (in back) Mon.-Fri. 10am-2pm, Sat. 10am-1pm; for **telegrams** Mon.-Fri. 8am-9pm, Sat. 9am-7pm. **Postal Code:** 30001.

Telephones: C. San Lorenzo, 16, 1 bl. up C. Alejandro Séiquer and right from Turismo. Open Mon.-Fri. 10am-2pm and 6-9pm. **Telephone Code:** 968.

Flights: Airport in San Javier, 40km southeast of Murcia on the Mar Menor (tel. 57 05 05). Buses from Murcia's bus station (21 per day, 305ptas) only go to San Javier, 2km short of the airport. Taxi it from there. **Iberia,** Av. Libertad, next to El Corte Inglés (24-hr. reservations: national tel. (901) 33 31 11; international tel. (901) 33 32 22). Open Mon.-Fri. 9:30am-2pm and 4-7:30pm, Sat. 9:30am-1:30pm.

Trains: Estació del Carmen, C. Industria (tel. 25 21 54). For the tourist office, take bus #9 or 11 to the town center; or walk straight on C. Diego Hernández, right on C. Floridablanca, left on Alameda de Colón, and cross the Puente Viejo (15min.). To: Lorca (1hr.); Alicante (1½hr.); Valencia (*talgo* 3hr., express 4½hr.). **RENFE office,** C. Barrio Nuevo, 6 (tel. 21 28 42). Open Mon.-Fri. 9am-1pm and 4:30-7:30pm.

Buses: Sierra de la Pila (tel. 29 22 11), behind the Museo Salzillo. For the tourist office, take bus #3 from the station to the center (10min.). Ask the information window which sells tickets to your destination. (Open 8am-10pm.) To: Elche (50min.); Granada (4-5hr.); Sevilla (9¾hr.); Cádiz (12¼hr.); Córdoba (9hr.); San Javier (1¼hr.); Lorca (1½hr.); Valencia (3¾hr.).

Public Transportation: Municipal bus system has 33 routes to get folks anywhere, including the outskirts (within 15km). Fare 85ptas.

Taxis: tel. 29 77 00.

Luggage Storage: At the **bus station** (300ptas per bag). Open Mon.-Sat. 8am-10pm.

Late-Night Pharmacy: Check listings in *La Opinión de Murcia* (local paper, 85ptas).

Hospital: Hospital General Universitario, Av. Intendente, Jorge Palacios, 1 (tel. 25 69 00).

Emergency: tel. 23 75 50.

Police: Municipal, C. Isaac Albéniz, 10 (tel. 092). **Nacional** (tel. 091).

ACCOMMODATIONS AND FOOD

As Murcia steams up and empties out in summer, finding a room is a breeze. When winter blows in, competition is a bit stiffer. The prices are high year-round. **Plaza San Juan** is nothing but restaurants. Most Murcians don't have potassium, iron, or vitamin deficiencies because they load up on veggies produced in the surrounding countryside. *Paella murciana* means vegetarian *paella*. Along with the greenery, locals nibble on *hueva de mujo* (millet roe), a local delicacy. Sample the harvest at the **market,** on C. Verónicas near the river. (Open Mon.-Sat. 9am-1pm.)

Hostal Legazpi, Av. Miguel de Cervantes, 8 (tel. 29 30 81). Take #3 bus to Ronda Norte, get off at Renault dealership, and follow Ronda Norte around the corner to the left; look for the *hostal's* eyesore sign. Cheapest reputable lodgings you're likely to find. Rooms have TVs and large beds. Singles 1600ptas, with bath 2400ptas. Doubles 3200ptas, with bath 3600ptas. Triples with bath 5100ptas. Garage 500ptas per day.

Hostal-Residencia Murcia, C. Vinadel, 6 (tel. 21 99 63), off Pl. Santa Isabel. Rooms with TVs and phones, but a bit rundown with '70s decor. Prices tend to be negotiable. Singles 2500ptas, with shower 3500ptas. Doubles 4500ptas, with shower 5500ptas, with bath 8000ptas.

Señorio de Jomelsu, C. Isidoro de la Cierva, 3 (tel. 21 21 33), the continuation of C. Alejandro Séiquer. Looks more like a cellar than a bar. Try finding the bartender behind rows of dangling meat and cheese products. *Menú* 995ptas. The best brunch/lunch deal in town: 9am-noon, *bocadillo* and beer, wine, or mineral water (225ptas). Open 9am-3pm and 8pm-midnight.

Casino de Murcia, in the casino at C. Trapería, 22 (tel. 21 22 55). Dine among opulence and splendor and feel like a member of an exclusive Victorian wine-tasting or hunting club. *Menú* for casino members 700ptas, non-members (hint: that's you) 1000ptas. Open daily 1:30-4pm; July-Aug. closed Sat.

Mesón el Corral de José Luís, Pl. Santo Domingo, 23-24 (tel. 21 45 97). Chefs in the open kitchen toss together Murcian cuisine. Local handicrafts complement the regional specialties. *Tapas* 150-450ptas. Daily *menú* 1000ptas at bar, 1150ptas at table. Open 11am-4pm and 8pm-midnight.

El Tío Sentao, C. La Manga, 12 (tel. 29 10 13), near the bus station, hidden on a teensy street off Pl. San Agustín. After 80 years of services, this warm, family restaurant still cooks up authentic Murcian fare at reasonable prices. Beware of the powerful chaser of local *vino de jumilla*. Open daily 1-4pm and 7pm-midnight.

SIGHTS AND ENTERTAINMENT

Museo Salzillo, Pl. San Agustín, 1 (tel. 29 18 93), on bus route #3 and 8, is devoted to the 18th-century polychrome wood sculptures by Murcian Francisco Salzillo. (Open Mon. 9:30am-1pm, Tues.-Sat. 9:30am-1pm and 4-7pm, Sun. and holidays 11am-1pm; off-season Mon. 9:30am-1pm, Tues.-Sat. 9:30am-1pm and 3-6pm, Sun. and holidays 11am-1pm. Admission 200ptas, free on Sun.) The **Museo de Arqueología de Murcia,** Gran Vía Alfonso X El Sabio, 5, one of the finest in Spain, chronicles the province from prehistoric times. (Open Mon.-Fri. 10am-2pm; Sept.-June Mon.-Fri. 9am-2pm and 5-8pm, Sat. 11am-2pm. Admission 75ptas.) The **Museo de Bellas Artes,** C. Obispo Frutos, 8 (tel. 23 93 46), leaps to Spanish art of the 19th and 20th centuries. (Open Mon.-Fri. 9am-2pm and 5-7pm, Sat. 10am-2pm.)

The palatial **Casino de Murcia,** C. Traperiá, 18 (tel. 21 22 55), began life as a social club for the town's 19th- and 20th-century bourgeoisie. Rooms inside were each designed according to a particular theme. Mammoth, impossibly ornate chandeliers fill the Versailles ballroom. A handsome English billiard room offers a whiff of Pall Mall, while the Arabic patio and its multicolored glass doors simulate the Alhambra. Look for the Oxfordian library with plush leather chairs and a luxurious gilt powder room. (Free.)

Next door to the casino, 400 years of procrastination made Murcia's **catedral** in Pl. Cruz, 2 (tel. 21 63 44; buses #2 and 3) an odd confusion of architectural styles: an oft-photographed Baroque facade, a Gothic entrance, and Renaissance tower. (Cathedral open 7am-1pm and 5-8pm; tower open 10am-1pm.)

Beaches on the Costa Cálida are a snap to reach. **La Manga** (the sleeve) is the beach-peninsula 40km long and only 500m wide that closes off the shallow Mar Menor. Another large and popular beach is **Puerto de Mazarrón,** farther south. Buses for both beaches leave from the bus station in Murcia. Just outside of Murcia, the Río España courses through rocky mountains dotted with the pines and sagebrush of the Parque Natural Sierra España (highest elevation 1585m). The flowers explode into dazzling color in springtime, the best season to visit the park. Accommodations range from camping and a hostel to mountainside refuges. Ask about **camping** at the tourist office. From Murcia's bus station you can travel as far as Alhama or Totana.

On Wednesday and Saturday nights students from the local university blow off work, starting at the bars near **Calle Saavedra Fajardo,** then moving on to discos on **Gran Vía Alfonso X el Sabio.** On the day before Easter starts the **Exaltación Huertana,** a week-long harvest celebration that brings jazz and theater to the already crowded streets.

■■■ LORCA

Lorca compensates a bit for Murcia's lack of historic monuments, though many are unfortunately deteriorating into the dry landscape. Battles between Romans and Visigoths, and Christians and Muslims, left Lorca without an orange grove, much less a full-fledged *huerta* (orchard), to its name. Yet each conquering force left its own peculiar imprint on the large, piecemeal **castillo** on Lorca's central hill. The Moors built the **Torre Espolón** shortly before the city fell to Alfonso el Sabio of Castilla, who in self-adulation ordered the counstruction of the **Torre Alfonsín.** The ruins of Lorca's first church, the **Ermita de San Clemente,** deteriorate at the castle's eastern edge. (Open daily 9am-sunset. Free.)

Once Granada fell in 1492, inhabitants left the fortresses and moved to the bottom of the slope, leaving in their wake three idyllic churches, **Santa María, San Juan,** and **San Pedro.** Starting anew, Lorcans erected six monasteries and the **Colegiata de San Patricio.** Of the many well-preserved private residences, **Casa de Guevarra's** curving pillars and intricate carvings have a special flair. (Closed for renovations. Ask at tourist office.)

The **tourist office,** in Casa de Guevarra on C. Lópes Gisbert (tel. 46 61 57), gives out a detailed **map.** (Open Mon.-Fri. 10am-2pm and 5-8pm.) The **post office** is across the street on C. Musso Valiente. (Open Mon.-Sat. 9am-2pm.) **First aid** pampers the wounded at C. Abad Los Arcos (tel. 46 60 79). In **emergency,** call 091. The **police** come running from C. Villascusa, s/n (tel. 092).

Accommodations are cheap in this arid area. Shining ceramic tiles and rooms with new wicker furniture are the siren calls of **Hostal del Carmen,** C. Rincón de los Valientes, 3 (tel. 46 64 59), off C. Nogalte (1300ptas per person). **Hostal Felix,** Av. Fuerzas Armadas, 146 (tel. 46 76 50), on the far side of the river, has air-conditioned halls, winter heating, phones, desks, and tightly made beds. (Singles 1100ptas, with bath 1950ptas. Doubles with bath 3500ptas, with A/C 4000ptas.)

Andalucía

Between the jagged Sierra Morena and the deep blue sea, Andalucía is an intoxicating amalgamation of cultures and physiques. The ancient lost kingdom of Tartessos—the Tarshish mentioned in the Bible for its fabulous troves of silver—grew wealthy on the Sierra Nevada's rich ore deposits. Greeks and Phoenicians colonized and traded up and down the coast, and Romans later cultivated wheat, olive oil, and wine on the fertile soil watered by the Guadalquivir (Betis to the Romans). Andalucía owes its name and not much more to the Vandals, who flitted through on their way to North Africa, where they were promptly exterminated. The Arabs, by contrast, arrived in 711 and stayed for almost eight centuries, establishing a yet unbroken link with Africa and the Muslim world, and generating the Moorish Spain of *cante jondo*, flamenco dance and gypsy ballads. Under their reign, which lasted until 1492, the cities of Andalucía flourished: Córdoba became the most culturally influential center of its time, and Sevilla and Granada the pinnacle of Islamic artistry.

The Moors maintained Roman techniques in irrigation and architecture, perfecting them to create what became characteristically Andalusian—the cool patios and the alternation of red brick and white stone (as in the Córdoba Mosque)—and assimilated the wisdom and science of Classical Greece and the East, which made the European Renaissance possible. The architectural and artistic style which arose was called *Arte Mudéjar*, an art by Christians modelled in Arab style. *Arte Mudéjar* is essentially an art of mixture, with Romanesque and later Gothic influences added to the typical Arab designs and materials. Decorations on stone, brick, wood and plaster are often extremely complex and intricate.

However rich in history and art, Andalucía has been one of the poorest regions of Spain. The practice of holding land in large tracts—started in Roman times, continued by the Church, and sanctioned by 19th-century law—created an elite (often absentee) group of landowners who employed laborers on semi-feudal and economically inefficient terms. Many chose to migrate rather than face a future of indigence, and even today mobility is one effect of Andalucía's endemic poverty. In the 1960s, Andalucía lost 14% of its population to emigration, arguably the largest European peacetime migration in the 20th century.

Owing to the long summers, regional cooking is light, depending on such delicacies as *pescaíto frito* (lightly fried fish) and cold soups such as *gazpacho* served *con guarnición* (with garnish), often spooned by the waiter at your table. There are many varieties besides the tomato-based one, but perhaps the most sublime is attributed to Málaga. Called *ajo blanco* (white garlic), it is a bread and garlic soup lent a creamy white color by puréed blanched almonds and garnished with peeled grapes.

■■■ SEVILLA

Site of a small Roman acropolis founded by Julius Caesar, thriving seat of Moorish culture, focal point of the Spanish Renaissance, and guardian angel of traditional Andalusian culture, Sevilla has never failed to spark the imagination. Jean Cocteau included it with Venice and Peking in his trio of magical cities. St. Teresa denounced it as the work of the devil. Moorish historian al-Saqundi proclaimed that even the milk of birds could be found here. *Carmen, Don Giovanni, The Barber of Seville,* and Zorilla's tragically racy play *Don Juan Tenorio* are only a few of the artistic works inspired by the metropolis. The 16th-century maxim *"Qui non ha visto Sevilla non ha visto maravilla"*—who has not seen Sevilla has not seen a marvel— remains true five centuries later. The charm of this city is infectious.

ORIENTATION

Although Sevilla has almost a million inhabitants, it retains a peaceful and intimate feeling. Among orange trees and date palms, this sunny and affable city goes to sleep every summer afternoon for a few hours. Only the people are warmer than the weather. In the past few centuries the city has expanded to incorporate a number of neighboring villages. But these communities, now *barrios* of the city, have not lost their distinctive character. **Río Guadalquivir** flows roughly north-south through Sevilla. Most of the city, including the alleyways of the old **Barrio de Santa Cruz,** are on the east bank; some of the most active nightlife and least expensive food are on the west bank in **Barrio de Triana** and **Barrio de los Remedios.** The **catedral,** next to Barrio de Santa Cruz, marks Sevilla's center. If ever disoriented, look for the cathedral's conspicuous *giralda* (the minaret turned bell tower). **Avenida de la Constitución** skitters alongside the cathedral. The main tourist office, post office, banks, and travel agencies line it. Sevilla's **shopping district** lies north of the cathedral where Constitución fades into **Plaza Nueva,** bordered by a busy pedestrian zone; **Calle Sierpes** cuts through the district. The neighborhoods surrounding Plaza Nueva, as well as those northeast of the Barrio de Santa Cruz **(Barrio de la Puerta del Carne** and **Barrio de la Puerta de Carmona)** are hunting grounds for *pensión* and restaurant seekers.

To reach the center from Estación Santa Justa (a 40min. walk), catch bus #70 or C2, to the left as you enter the station. Both proceed to the main bus station at Prado de San Sebastián. The city bus network is extensive, and Sevilla is large enough to justify mastering it.

To walk to the cathedral from the bus station at Prado de San Sebastián (15 min.), exit the station and walk straight ahead one block to C. Menéndez Pelayo. Take a left here, an immediate right on C. San Fernando, then a right at the Puerta de Jerez on Av. Constitución.

Alternatively,walking from Estación Santa Justa (40 min.), exit through the main, parabolic front door and take the right on Calle José Laguillo past the apartment buildings. When this road ends, turn left on C. María Auxiliadora. Continue straight ahead on this road for 25-30 minutes as it turns into C. Recaredo and C. Menéndez Pelayo, bordered on the right by Jardines de Murillo. When the park ends at C. San Fernando, turn right. At the end of this long block, take a soft right at the Puerta de Jerez onto Av. Constitución. The regional tourist office is ahead on the right; the cathedral looms about two blocks farther.

Unfortunately, Sevilla lives up to its reputation as the Spanish capital of pickpockets and car thieves. Don't leave valuables unattended.

The Centro, Triana, and Los Remedios are often crowded and safe by night. Don't spend much time on your own in the windy and dark alleys of Santa Cruz or the vicinities of Jardines de Murillo after dark; and never ever set foot in the poverty and crime stricken Barrio de las Tres Mil Viviendas at night.

GETTING THERE

By Plane

All flights land at **Aeropuerto San Pablo** (tel. 451 61 11, ext. 1240), 12km out of town on Ctra. Madrid. A taxi to the airport from the center of town costs about 1800ptas.

Iberia, C. Almirante Lobo, 2 (tel. 422 89 01; reservations: national 901 333 111, international 901 333 222), in front of Torre de Oro. To: Madrid (7 per day, 13,100ptas); Barcelona (4 per day, 20,600ptas).

By Train

All train service is now centralized in modern **Estación Santa Justa,** Av. Kansas City, s/n (information tel. 454 02 02, reservations tel. 454 03 03). Services: Information booth, luggage storage, telephone office, cafeteria, ATM for Visa, Mastercard, AmEx

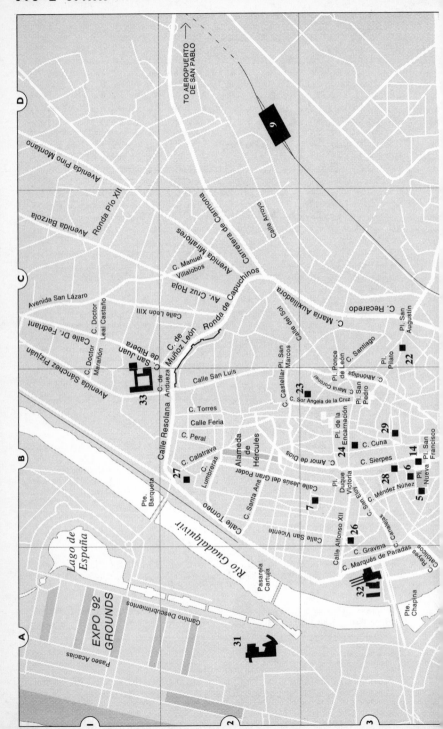

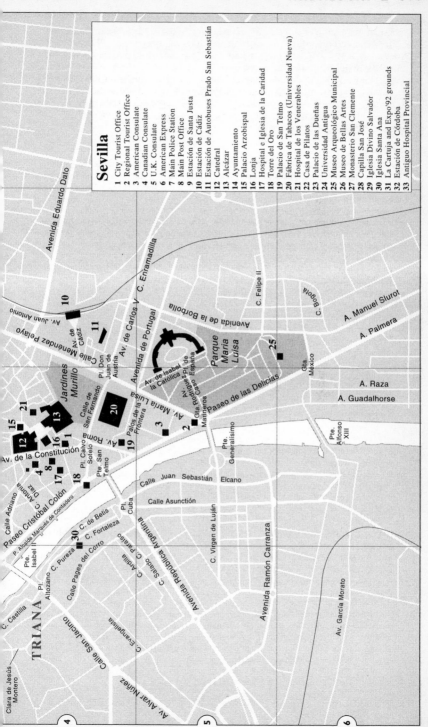

Sevilla

1 City Tourist Office
2 Regional Tourist Office
3 American Consulate
4 Canadian Consulate
5 U.K. Consulate
6 American Express
7 Main Police Station
8 Main Post Office
9 Estación de Santa Justa
10 Estación de Cádiz
11 Estación de Autobuses Prado San Sebastián
12 Catedral
13 Alcázar
14 Ayuntamiento
15 Palacio Arzobispal
16 Lonja
17 Hospital e Iglesia de la Caridad
18 Torre del Oro
19 Palacio de San Telmo
20 Fábrica de Tabacos (Universidad Nueva)
21 Hospital de los Venerables
22 Casa de Pilatos
23 Palacio de las Dueñas
24 Universidad Antigua
25 Museo Arqueológico Municipal
26 Museo de Bellas Artes
27 Monasterio San Clemente
28 Capilla San José
29 Iglesia Divino Salvador
30 Iglesia Santa Ana
31 La Cartuja and Expo'92 grounds
32 Estación de Córdoba
33 Antiguo Hospital Provincial

cash card, and others. Bus #70 links Estación Santa Justa and the Prado de San Sebastián bus station. It stops on Av. Kansas City, to the left as you exit the station.

The main **RENFE office** is located at C. Zaragoza, 29 (tel. 421 79 98), near Pl. Nueva. Open Mon.-Fri. 9am-1:15pm and 4pm-7pm, Sat. 9am-1pm. Strikes may alter current schedules and prices. To: Madrid (14 per day; *AVE* 2¾hr., 6800-9100ptas; *talgo* 3½hr., 4600-5200ptas); Cádiz (12 per day; *talgo* 1½hr., 1500-1700ptas; *Andalucía Exprés* 2hr., 1000ptas; *regional* 2hr., 880ptas); Córdoba (6 per day; *Andalucía Exprés* 1¾hr., 980ptas; *regional* 2½hr., 880ptas); Málaga (4 per day; *regional* 4hr., 1600ptas); Granada (3 per day; *regional* 4hr., 1580ptas); Huelva (3 per day; *regional* 1¾hr., 790ptas).

By Bus

The older bus station at **Plaza de San Sebastián,** C. José María Osborne, 11 (tel. 441 71 11), serves mainly Andalucía. Bus #70, C1 and C2 link Estación Santa Justa and Plaza de San Sebastián. Information service, luggage service (*consigna*). Open 6:30am-10pm, 90-180ptas

Transportes Alsina Graells, (tel. 441 88 11). To: Córdoba (Mon.-Fri. 13-15 per day, Sat. 9 per day, Sun. 12 per day, 2hr., 1100ptas); Granada (8 per day, 3½-4½hr., 2505ptas); Málaga (10-12 per day, 4hr., 2065ptas); Murcia (3 per day, 7¼-9½hr., 4730ptas).

Prado de San Sebastián, C. José María Osborne, 11 (tel. 441 71 11). Bus #70 and C2 link Estación Santa Justa and Prado de San Sebastián. Has helpful information service. Luggage service too (160ptas).

Transportes Comes, (tel. 441 68 58). Tickets sold Mon.-Sat. 6:30am-10:30pm, Sun. 6:30-10:45pm). To: Cádiz (10 per day, 1¾hr., 1200ptas); Algericas (5 per day, 3½hr., 2000ptas); Jerez de la Frontera (2-9 per day, 1¾hr., 825ptas); Rota (2 per day, none on weekends, 2hr., 1160ptas); Puerta de Santa María (2-7 per day, 2hr., 950ptas).

Bacoma Enactar, (tel. 441 46 60). To: Valencia (2 per day, 12hr., 5675ptas); Barcelona (1 per day, 17hr., 8500ptas); Alicante (1 per day, 22hr., 5360ptas); Benidorm (1 per day, 23hr., 5635ptas).

Los Amarillos, (tel. 441 52 01 and 441 56 11). To: Arcos de la Frontera (1-2 per day, 2hr., 840ptas); Ronda (3 per day, 2½hr., 1145ptas); Fuengirola (2 per day, 1910ptas); Marbella (2 per day, 1555ptas).

The newer bus station is at **Plaza de Armas,** Puente Cristo de la Expiración corner with C. Arjona (tel. 490 80 40), on the river bank, facing the ghost-town remnant of Expo92. New and modern, it covers buses leaving Andalucía and Spain. Services: ATM, cafeteria, photocopies, drugstore, luggage service (open Mon.-Fri. 8am-10pm, Sat. 8am-2pm; 25ptas first day, 75ptas per day after that), and lockers (300ptas).

Sevibus, (tel. 490 11 60; fax 490 16 92). To: Madrid (13 per day, 6hrs. non-stop, 2305ptas).

Damas, (tel. 490 80 40 and 490 77 37). To: Huelva (11-14 per day, 1¼hr., 810ptas); Málaga (1 per day, 3hr., 2800ptas); Badajoz (4 per day, 4hr, 1500ptas).

Alsa Internacional, (tel. 490 78 00). Thurs. and Sat. year round, 1 each per day to: Toulouse (21hr., 10,900ptas); Nîmes (23½hr., 13,600ptas); Lyon (28½hr., 15,500ptas); Geneva (30½hr., 16,800ptas); Zurich (32½hr., 19,100ptas).

By Thumb

Hitchhiking: Not recommended. Those who choose to hitch toward Madrid and Córdoba take bus #70 out of Av. Kansas City by the train station. This road becomes the highway. Those heading to Granada and Málaga take bus #23 to Parque Amate and walk away from the park to the highway (about 20min.). Those hitching to Cádiz take bus #34 to Heliopolis and walk west to the bridge. Those heading for Huelva take bus C1 to Pachina; they cross the bridge and walk straight ahead until they reach the highway.

GETTING AROUND

City Buses: Extensive network. Most lines converge on Pl. Nueva, Pl. de la Encarnación, or in front of the cathedral on Av. Constitución. Most buses run every 10min., 6am-11:15pm. Limited night service departs from Pl. Nueva every hr. midnight-3am. City bus guides stocked at the regional tourist office, city tourist office, the information booth at Estación Santa Justa, and at most tobacco shops and kiosks. Fare 110ptas, 10-trip *bonobús* 500ptas. Three day pass 750ptas, 7 day pass 1250ptas. Specially useful are C1 and C2 (*circulares interiores,* which circle through the Centro).

Taxis: Tele Taxi (tel. 462 22 22). **Radio Taxi** (tel. 458 00 00). All Sevillian cabs are metered. Starting fare 250ptas, service 10pm-6am and on Sun. 25% surcharge.

Car Rentals: Avis, Av. Constitución, 15B (tel. 421 65 49), next to the regional tourist office or at Santa Justa train station. Both open Mon.-Fri. 9am-1pm and 4-7pm, Sat. 9am-1pm. **Ital,** Av. República Argentina, 9 (tel. 427 75 51). Open Mon.-Fri. 9am-1pm and **Hertz,** Av. República Argentina, 3 (tel. 427 88 87), and at the airport (tel. 451 47 20). Open Mon.-Fri. 9am-1:30pm and 4pm-7pm, Sat. 9am-1pm. Most companies require a credit card, a minimum age of 23 yrs., and 1 yr. of driving experience.

Bike Rental: El Ciclismo, Paseo Catalina de Ribera, 2 (tel. 441 19 59), in Puerta de la Carne, at north end of Jardines de Murillo. Also sells and repairs bikes. 1500ptas per day (some mountain bikes available). Open Mon.-Fri. 10am-2pm and 5-8pm, Sat. 10am-2pm.

PRACTICAL INFORMATION

Tourist Information

Tourist Offices: Regional, Av. Constitución, 21B (tel. 422 14 04; fax 422 97 53), 1 block south of the cathedral. Make this your first stop in Sevilla—an absolute must. Gushing staff with excellent regional and city information. Stocks separate maps for Sevilla and Barrio de Santa Cruz. English spoken. Most crowded at opening and in afternoon. Open Mon.-Fri. 9am-2pm, Sat. 10am-2pm. **City,** Po. Delicias, 9 (tel. 423 44 65), across from Parque de María Luisa by Puente del Generalísimo. Open Mon.-Fri. 9am-1:15pm and 4:30-6:45pm. The **information booth** in Estación Santa Justa stocks city maps and bus guides.

Budget Travel: Viajes TIVE, C. Jesús de Veracruz, 27 (tel. 490 60 22). Downtown near El Corte Inglés. Also offers language courses and organized excursions. Open Mon.-Fri. 9am-2pm. Another near Reina Mercedes.

Interjoven, Adriano, 23 (tel. 456 37 92). Behind the Plaza de la Maestranza. HI card, youth and student fares

Consulates

See: Spain Essentials: Embassies and Consulates.

Money

American Express: Viajes Alhambra, Teniente Coronel Seguí, 6 (tel. 421 29 23), north of Pl. Nueva. Two counters of efficient, English-speaking service. Holds mail (postal code: 41001). Emergency check-cashing for cardholders and 24-hr. outside cash machine. Open Mon.-Fri. 9:30am-1:30pm and 4:30-8pm. Sat. 9:30am-1pm.

Currency Exchange: El Corte Inglés (see below) is the only place that doesn't charge a commission, but it adjusts the rates to compensate. **Banks** offer the best rates, charging 1% commission or 500ptas, whichever is greater. Most open Mon.-Fri. 8:30am-2pm year-round, during the winter additionally Sat. 8:30am-1pm. Oficina de Cambio Banesto, Av. Constitución, 30 (tel. 422 26 23), across from the cathedral. Open Tues.-Sun. 9:30am-7pm.

Communications

Post Office: Av. Constitución, 32 (tel. 421 95 85), across from the cathedral. Open for stamps and most mail services Mon.-Fri. 8am-9pm, Sat. 9am-7pm. Open for Lista de Correos Mon.-Fri. 8am-9pm, Sat. 8am-2pm. Open for **telegrams** (national

tel. 422 00 00, international tel. 422 68 60) Mon.-Fri. 8am-9pm, Sat. 9am-8pm. Open to send **faxes** Mon.-Fri. 8am-midnight, Sat. 9am-8pm. **Postal Code:** 41070.
Telephones: Pl. Gavidia, 7, near Pl. Concordia. Open Mon.-Fri. 10am-2pm and 5:30-10pm, Sat. 10am-2pm. **Telephone Code:** 95.

Emergency, Health, and Help

Police: (tel. 461 67 76), Av. Paseo de las Delicias. English theoretically spoken.
24-Hour Pharmacy: 5-6 pharmacies are open each night, all night, on a rotating basis. Check list posted at any pharmacy in the city.
Hospital: Hospital Universitario Virgen Macareno, Av. Dr. Fedriani, s/n (tel. 437 84 00). English spoken.
Medical Assistance: Casa de Socorro, C. Menéndez Pelayo, facing the Jardines de Murillo (tel. 441 17 12).
Emergency: tel. 091.

Other

El Corte Inglés: one at Pl. Duque de la Victoria, 10, near C. Alfonso XII; another at C. Luis de Morales, 122, near the football stadium. Offer excellent **map** of Sevilla.
Currency exchange: (See above.) They also offer novels and guidebooks in English; haircutting; both cafeteria and restaurant; and **telephones.** Open Mon.-Sat. 10am-9pm.
VIPS, C. República Argentina, 25, three blocks from Pl. Cuba. A modern convenience store where you can read a non-Spanish newspaper, use a clean restroom, buy a cassette tape, or purchase non-perishable groceries. Good sales on art books and best-sellers in Spanish. Adjoining café serves expensive hamburgers (650-695ptas) and *platos combinados* (875-1195ptas). Open 9am-3am. Open Sun.-Thurs. 8am-2am, Fri. 8am-3am, Sat. 9am-3am.
Luggage Storage: At Plaza de San Sebastián bus station, Plaza de Armas bus station, and Santa Justa train station (see Getting There).
Lost Property: C. Almansa, 21 (tel. 421 15 64). Or contact municipal police (tel. 461 54 50).
English Bookstore: Decent selection of novels and Penguin Classics at any **Librería Beta.** Two centrally located ones are at Av. Constitución, 27 (tel. 456 07 03), and at Av. República Argentina, 15 (tel. 427 59 24). Open summer Mon.-Fri. 10am-2pm and 5pm-8:30pm, Sat. 10am-2pm; winter Mon.-Fri. 10am-2pm and 5-8pm, Sat. 10am-2pm and 5-8:30pm. **Librería Vértice,** C. Mateos Gago, 24A, behind the cathedral. Choice literature and Penguin Classics. Open Sept.-June Mon.-Fri. 10am-1pm and 5:30-8pm, Sat. 11am-2pm; July Mon.-Fri. 10am-1:30pm and 6-9pm, Sat. 11am-2pm; Aug. Mon.-Fri. 10am-1pm, Sat. 11am-2pm.
Women's Center: C. Alfonso XII, 52 (tel. 490 47 76 and 490 61 12; fax 490 83 93). Information on feminist and on gay and lesbian organizations, as well as legal and psychological services for rape victims. Also employment listings for women.
Religious Center: Iglesia del Señor San José, C. San José, 17 (tel. 422 03 19). Catholic mass in English Sat.-Sun. 7pm; confession in English daily.
Laundromat: Lavandería Robledo, C. F. Sánchez Bedoya, 18 (tel. 421 81 32), 1 block west of the cathedral, across Av. Constitución. Wash and dry 5kg, 950ptas. Open Mon.-Fri. 10am-2pm and 5-8pm, Sat. 10am-2pm. **Lavandería Sevilla,** C. Castelar, 2 (tel. 421 05 35), 2 blocks off Av. Constitución. Self-service and full service same price: 5-6 kg, 1000ptas. Open Mon.-Fri. 9:30am-1:30pm and 4:30-8:15pm, Sat. 10am-1pm.
Public Toilets: Off Av. Constitución, underground, between the cathedral and the Palacio de la Lonja. Semi-clean and completely free.
Swimming Pool: Piscina Municipal "Sevilla," Av. Ciudad Jardín, 81 (tel. 463 58 92), near the Gran Plaza (bus #232 or 25). Admission 450ptas, children under 10 325ptas. Open June-Sept. 11am-7pm.

ACCOMMODATIONS AND CAMPING

During *Semana Santa* and the *Feria de Abril,* rooms vanish and prices soar. Make reservations if you value your footleather. Usually, a call a day or two ahead suffices, but for *Semana Santa* and the *Feria de Abril,* call several months before. Tourist officials have lists of *casas particulares* which open on special occasions. Be sure to ask about prices in all accommodations; they may be negotiable.

Sevilla Youth Hostel (HI), C. Isaac Peral, 2 (tel. 461 31 54), a few km out of town. The #34 bus stops around the block. You can get on at Plaza Nueva or in front of the tourist office; disembark at the first stop after the bus leaves the large avenue and takes a right onto narrower streets. After midnight, take the bus labeled "Helio-polis" from Pl. Nueva. Although there is a 3 day max. stay, there is no curfew or lockout. English spoken. No camping, but the facilities include refreshing balconies and banana palms in the yard. All rooms are triples. Members 1007ptas, over 26 1484ptas; non-members 1484ptas, over 26 2650ptas; breakfast 160ptas.

Barrio de Santa Cruz

Hostales cluster along C. Mateos Gago and C. Archeros. Charming and conveniently located, these ordinarily quiet streets turn into a madhouse during the April *Feria*.

Huéspedes Buen Dormir, C. Farnesio, 8 (tel. 421 74 92). From the cathedral follow C. Mateos Gago, bearing left on the main thoroughfare, then turn right on Fabiola; look for the alley opposite #10. Room size varies radically. Tropical birds chirp in the lobby. English spoken. Singles 1500ptas (cheaper and hotter in upstairs terrace). Doubles 2500-3000ptas, with spotless bath 3500ptas. Triples with bath 4500ptas.

Hostal-Residencia Córdoba, C. Farnesio, 12 (tel. 422 74 98). Family-run with spacious rooms, wood doors, and modern, clean bathrooms. A bit posher than the average Eurail joint—hotel comfort at an affordable price. Singles 2500ptas. Doubles 3500-4500ptas. Triples 4800ptas, or request extra beds.

Hostal Toledo, C. Santa Teresa, 15 (tel. 421 53 35), off Pl. Santa Cruz, just west of the Jardines de Murillo. Located on a quiet street, this recently renovated *hostal* has a private bath in each room. Singles 2650-3180ptas, depending on bath size. Doubles 5300ptas.

Hostal-Residencia Monreal, C. Rodrigo Caro, 8 (tel. 421 41 66). From the cathedral, walk northeast on C. Mateos Gago to the 1st block on your right. A large, hotel-style place with dark but clean rooms—most with A/C. Perpetually open bar and restaurant. Singles 2500ptas. Doubles 3500-4800ptas, with shower 5000-6000ptas. Triples 6500-7800ptas.

Hostal Bienvenido, C. Archeros, 14 (tel. 441 36 55), near Pl. Curtidores, just off C. Menéndez Pelayo. Welcoming, English-speaking managers are willing to negotiate prices. Rather small, dark rooms offset by a beautiful view from upstairs terrace. Singles 1500ptas. Doubles 3000ptas.

Pensión Archero, C. Archeros, 23 (tel. 441 84 65). Spacious rooms face an open, fern-laden patio. Singles 2000ptas. Doubles 3000ptas, with shower 3500ptas.

Hostal Javier, C. Archeros, 16 (tel. 441 23 25). Decorated with oil-paintings and prints. Rooms are well-furnished and comfortable, with fans. Singles 1500ptas. Doubles 3000ptas, with bath 4000ptas. Triples with bath 4500ptas.

Hostal Goya, C. Mateos Gago, 31 (tel. 421 11 70). Kitschy lobby, with shiny brown leather furniture beneath a glass ceiling. Ample rooms with fans. Doubles with shower 5035ptas, with bath 5620ptas. Triples with shower 7050ptas, with bath 7865ptas.

Pensión Fabiola, C. Fabiola, 16 (tel. 421 83 46). Basic, clean rooms—many recently refurbished. All have fans, much needed in some particularly hot interior rooms. Huge rooms on top floor can accomodate entire groups of backpackers. Singles 2000ptas. Doubles 3000ptas. Triples 4500ptas. One shower per day included in room price; subsequent showers are 200ptas each.

El Centro

The *casco viejo* of El Centro is comprised of narrow, winding streets radiating from the Plaza de la Encarnación. A pretty, albeit disorienting neighborhood.

Hostal Galatea, C. San Juan de la Palma, 4 (tel. 456 35 64; fax 456 35 17). From the west end of Pl. Encarnación, take C. Regina; make a right on C. San Juan de la

SEVILLA

Palma. Young polylingual managers captivate patrons with their warmth and their clean, new *hostal* with patio, TV room, and peaceful *terraza*. Laundry services negotiable. All rooms with fan. Summer rates: Singles 2900ptas. Doubles 4700ptas, with shower 5800ptas. Triples 6100ptas.

Hostal Lis, C. Escarpín, 10 (tel. 421 30 88). Brightly tiled eye-bugging entry and patio—Sevillian tiles on acid. Small *hostal* with large rooms, all with shower. Singles 2000ptas. Doubles 4000ptas. Triples 5600ptas.

Hostal La Gloria, C. San Eloy, 58 (tel. 422 26 73). Striking exterior with ornate wood trim in brick orange. Flawlessly tiled floors and firm beds. Hot showers. A/C upstairs where it's most needed. Singles 2500ptas, with bath 3000ptas. Doubles 3500ptas.

Hostal Bonanza, C. Sales y Ferre, 12 (tel. 422 86 14), in the depth of a maze—from Pl. Pilatos, head down C. Caballerizas and through Pl. San Ildefonso, where the street becomes C. Descalzos. From Pl. Cristo de Burgos, Sales y Ferre is on the left. In a dark apartment building, but all the rooms have showers and A/C. Singles 1500ptas. Doubles 3000ptas. Triples 4000ptas.

Near Plaza de Armas

The backstreets around the erstwhile Estación de Córdoba, now the Pl. de Armas bus station, still have a track of rooms. Most are on C. Gravina, parallel to C. Marqués de las Paradas, and one block farther from the old station.

Hostal Romero, C. Gravina, 21 (tel. 421 13 53). Potted plants, antique furniture, and hanging brass pots embellish the typically Sevillian inner courtyard. Rooms are basic. Singles 2500ptas. Doubles 4500ptas. Triples 5200ptas.

Hostal Residencia Gala, C. Gravina, 52 (tel. 421 45 03). Shiny wood front door. Clean bathrooms. Some rooms lack windows, but the place manages to stay cool. Singles 2500ptas, with bath 3600ptas. Doubles 3600ptas, with bath 5200ptas.

Elsewhere

Pensión Hostal Nevada, C. Gamazo, 28 (tel. 422 53 40). From Pl. Nueva, take C. Barcelona, and turn right on C. Gamazo. Located near several *bodegas* and *tabernas*. Naturally cool courtyard with leather sofas and large fan collection. Dark, tapestry-laden rooms. Singles 2500-3000ptas. Doubles 4500ptas, with shower 5000ptas, with bath 6000ptas. Triples with shower 7000ptas, with bath 8000ptas.

Camping Sevilla, Ctra. Madrid-Cádiz, km 534 (tel. 451 43 79), 12km out of town near the airport. From Estación Prado de San Sebastián, take the Empresa Casal bus toward Carmona (approximately every hr. 7am-9:30pm, 225ptas) or bus #70, which stops 800m away at Parque Alcosa. A happy medium between metropolis and outback. Grassy sites, hot showers, supermarket and swimming pool. 525ptas per person, 500ptas per car and per tent. Children 425ptas.

Club de Campo, Av. Libertad, 13, Ctra. Sevilla-Dos Hermanas (tel. 472 02 50), 12km out of town. From C. Infante Carlos de Borbón, at the back of the Auditorium in the Prado de San Sebastián, take the Los Amarillos bus (the direct one) to Dos Hermanas (about every 45min., 6:30am-midnight, 130ptas). Grassy site, swimming pool. 400ptas per person, per car, and per tent. Children 300ptas.

Camping Villson, Ctra. La Marisma (better known as Ctra. Sevilla-Cádiz), km 554 (tel. 472 08 28), closer to Itálica than to Sevilla, about 14km out of the city. Take the Los Amarillos bus which goes to Dos Hermanas via Barriada (every 20-25min. 6:30am-midnight, 130ptas). Adults 400ptas. 425ptas per car and per tent. Children 350ptas. Hot showers included. Free pool.

FOOD

Sevilla features the best of Andalusian cuisine. This city is particularly renowned for its jams, pastries, and candy, sold fresh from convent kitchens at several stores in **Plaza del Cabildo. Calle Arjona** and **Avenida Marqués de Paradas** (near Pl. de Armas bus station), the entire **Barrio Santa Cruz,** and many streets in **El Arenal** (between the Real Maestranza bullring and Pl. Nueva) are all saturated with good *bar-restaurantes.* After hours the **Centro**, particularly the area around **C. Sierpes** and the **Barrio Triana** have the most to offer.

Barrio Triana is Sevilla's favored venue for the *tapeo* (*tapas*-bar hopping), a gloriously active alternative to sit-down dining. Places overlooking the river on C. Betis are popular and expensive; cheaper alternatives can be found by exploring deeper into the neighborhood.

Sangría in Sevilla is especially delicious (thirst is the best garnish). During the summer heavenly *tinto de verano,* a cold blend of red wine and Casera (sweetened, citrus-flavored tonic water) is consumed at all hours in gargantuan volumes. A couple of glasses a day are essential for those tough *siesta* hours.

A number of inexpensive, student-oriented restaurants and bars operate during the school year (Sept.-June) on **Av. Reina Mercedes,** near the technical university and the Sevilla Youth Hostel. No gourmet experience here, but the bars and food joints become quite lively late at night on the weekends.

Mercado del Arenal is near the bullring on C. Pastor y Leandro, between C. Almansa and C. Arenal. Look there for fresh produce, *toro de lidia* (fresh bull meat from next door) and screaming vendors. Merchants also hawk excellent fresh produce, fish, meat, and baked goods at **Mercadillo de la Encarnación.** (Both open Mon.-Sat. 9am-2pm.)

> **Groceries: El Corte Inglés** (see Practical Information: Other). Huge supermarket in the basement. Open Mon.-Sat. 10am-9pm. **% Día,** C. San Juan de Avila, on the Pl. de la Gravídia, across the street from Telefónica. Discount supermarket. Open Mon.-Thurs. 9:30am-2pm and 6-9pm, Fri.-Sat. 9am-2:30pm and 5:30-9pm.

Near the Cathedral

Restaurants next to the cathedral cater exclusively to tourists. Food and prices improve in the back street establishments between the cathedral and the river, and in those a few blocks north of the cathedral.

> **Bodega Santa Cruz,** C. Rodrigo Caro, 1 (tel. 421 32 46). Take C. Mateos Gago, on the north end of the cathedral; the Bodega is on the first corner on your right. Casual and crowded—locals come at all hours to sample the varied and tasty *tapas* (150ptas), washing them down with beer (110ptas). Particularly busy on weekend nights. Open 8am-midnight.

> **Restaurante-Bar El Baratillo/Casa Chari,** C. Pavia, 12 (tel. 422 96 51), on a tiny street off C. Dos de Mayo. Don't miss this tiny restaurant. Friendly owner circulates among the customers, talking faster than the AVE and proudly offering tasty samples of her cooking in a room covered by early-eighties posters. An experience as well as a meal. Huge *menú,* including wine or beer 500ptas. Excellent *platos combinados* 450-750ptas. Meals served Mon.-Fri. 8-10pm, Sat. noon-5pm.

> **Mesón Serranito,** C. Antonia Díaz, 11 (tel. 421 12 43), beside the bullring. Take C. García Vinuesa across from the cathedral and turn left on C. Antonia Díaz. Stuffed bull heads from the nearby Maestranza bullring line the walls; behind the bar, the Virgin Mary sits with hanging hams and other bullfighting paraphernalia. Prices 20% higher at tables than at the bar. If the fresh fish dishes, such as the *pez espada a la plancha* (grilled swordfish, 900ptas) seem too pricey, opt for the yummy *serranito* (a pork, prosciutto, and green pepper sub, topped by a mountain of french fries, 375ptas). *Platos combinados* 750-800ptas. Open Mon.-Sat. noon-4:30pm and 8pm-midnight. Also at C. Alfonso XII, 7, near the Corte Inglés at Plaza del Duque de la Victoria (same prices and hours).

> **Pizzería Renato,** C. Pavia, 17 (tel. 421 00 77), on the corner of C. Dos de Mayo. Facing the post office, take the first right and continue straight through the golden archway onto C. Dos de Mayo, or follow your nose. *Lasagna al borno* (750ptas) comes sizzling straight out of the oven, smothered with superb cheese sauce. Several-topping pizzas will stuff (480-725ptas). Pasta 500-775ptas. Open Sun.-Tues., Thurs. and Fri. 1:15-3:45pm and 8:30-11:45pm, Sat. 8:45pm-midnight.

> **Mesón La Barca,** C. Santander, 6, off Paseo de Cristobal Colón, up from Torre del Oro. Small restaurant, ample portions. Bambi gone classy: *estofado de venado*

(venison, red wine, garlic, and vegetable stew) 800ptas. *Platos combinados* from 650ptas. Open Sun.-Fri. 11am-midnight.

Cafetería Postal, C. Almirantazgo, 10 (tel. 422 03 92), across Av. Constitución from the cathedral. Don't leave Sevilla without trying this café. For the perfect breakfast, post with dispatch here to get thick, rich *chocolate* and crispy, grease-less *churros. Churros* with *chocolate* or *café* 250ptas per *ración.* Open 8am-1pm.

El 3 de Oro, C. Santa María la Blanca, 34 (tel. 442 68 20), down from C. Menéndez Pelayo. Loud self-service cafeteria with ceramic art. Superb and abundant *paella* 550ptas, huge *raciones* 550-900ptas, *menú* 1200ptas. Open 8am-1am.

Casa Diego, Pl. Curtidores, 7 (tel. 441 58 83). Casa Diego's renowned *brochetas de pescado y carne* (fish and beef skewers, 800ptas) have attracted tourists and locals alike for the last thirty years. Open April-Oct. Mon.-Fri. 1-4pm and 8:30-11:30pm, Sat. 1-4pm; Nov.-March Mon.-Fri. 1-4pm and 8-11pm, Sat. 1-4pm.

El Centro

Just beyond the usual tourist coops, this area belongs to business people and shoppers by day and young people on their *paseo* by night.

Jalea Real, Sor Angela de la Cruz, 37 (tel. 421 61 03), near Pl. Encarnación. From Pl. Encarnación, head 150m east on C. Laraña, and turn left immediately before Iglesia de San Pedro. Hard to find, but definitely worth the effort. Young, hip management caters to young, hip clientele in this casual vegetarian place. Huge selection of interesting salads and homemade desserts. Excellent, 2-course lunch *menú* with whole-wheat bread, wine, and dessert 1200ptas. Monumental *platos combinados* 700ptas. Open Oct.-May Tues.-Sat. 1:30-5pm and 8:30-11:30pm, Sun. 1:30-4:30pm; June-Sept. Mon.-Fri. 1:30-5pm and 8:30-11:30pm, Sat. 1:30-5pm.

La Bodeguita de Pollos, C. Azofaifo, 9 (tel. 421 30 44), off C. Sierpes in a quiet alley. Tame but TVed atmosphere. Cramped unless you have drumsticks for legs. Zesty food. *Gazpacho* in a glass 180ptas. Half-chicken, bread, salad, and beverage 700ptas. Meals served 1-4:30pm and 7-11pm.

Rincón San Eloy, San Eloy, 24 (tel. 421 80 79). Waiters can barely be heard above the din of the crowds. Airy courtyard, old wine barrels, massive beer taps, and bullfight posters. *Tapas* 175ptas. *Raciones* 900ptas. Pork chop and fries 400ptas. *Menú* with wine or beer 800ptas. *Sangría de la casa:* 1½liters 900ptas, stein 175ptas. Open Mon.-Sat. noon-4:30pm and 7pm-midnight.

Bar El Camborio, C. Baños, 3 (tel. 421 75 34), directly off Pl. Gavidia. Standard Sevillian decorative triumvirate: the bullfighting wall, the flamenco wall, and the religious imagery wall. Lunch *menú* 650ptas, supper *menú* 750ptas. *Platos combinados* from 400ptas. A/C. Open Mon.-Sat. 1-4pm and 7:30-11pm.

Bodegón Alfonso XII, C. Alfonso XII, 33, near the Museo de Bellas Artes. Dark-stone walls with columns and arches. Fleet waiters sprint the dizzying circuit from kitchen to counter to you. Breakfast with ham and eggs about 350ptas. *Serranito* 300ptas. Ponderous *tortilla de patatas* (egg and potato omelette) with bread and tomato 350ptas. *Menú* 625ptas. Meals served Mon.-Sat. 8am-noon, 1-4pm, and 8-10pm.

Barrio de Triana

This charming old *barrio,* on the far side of the Río Guadalquivir, was once a separate village. Avoid overpriced C. Betis and the main avenues; plunge instead into smaller side streets to find *freidurías* (fried-fish vendors) and *bar-restaurantes* by day, *tapas* bars by night.

Freiduría Santana, C. Pureza, 61 (tel. 433 20 40), parallel to C. Betis, 1 block away from the river. 11 kinds of fried fish, all fresh and delicious. Free-samples ease the wait in line. *Pescado* (local fish) 1000ptas/kg. *Calamares* (squid) and *gambas* (shrimp) 1600ptas/kg. Open Sept.-July Tues.-Sun. 7pm-midnight.

Casa Manolo, C. San Jorge, 16 (tel. 433 47 92), north of Puente Isabel II. This local favorite is wild and crazy during *fiestas.* A meat locker displays the merchandise for inspection. *Pescado frito* (fried fish) 850ptas; *menú de la casa* 1600ptas. Meals served Tues.-Sun. 9am-midnight.

Café-Bar Jerusalem, C. Salado, 6, at Virgen de las Huertas. Kick-back bar with an international crowd and inventive *tapas. Shoarmas,* a.k.a. *"el bocadillo hebreo"* (the Hebrew sandwich) 300-525ptas. A savory change from standard Sevillian fare, though hardly kosher. Open Wed.-Mon. 8pm-3am.

Barrio Los Remedios

This neighborhood and shopping district, across the river from the center and south of Barrio Triana (Av. República Argentina is the divide), is lively, modern, and middle-class. Particularly animated on weekend nights, when Sevillian youth crowd its bars, and during the *Feria,* held at the east end of the *barrio.*

Sloppy Joe's Snack Bar, C. Asunción, 62 (tel. 427 77 28 or 428 36 48), six blocks from Pl. de Cuba, between C. Virgen de Luján and C. de Fernando IV. A favorite of students. Large portions, small prices, late hours. Take-out or sit-down service. Thin-crusted pizzas with mile-high toppings serve four (or three starving Let's Goers) 700-975ptas. Burgers 300-600ptas. Open Sun.-Thurs. 8am-2am, Fri. and Sat. 8am-3am. Also at C. Periodista Ramón Resa, 2 (tel. 423 66 78 or 423 65 60), near the Sevilla Youth Hostel (same food, crowd, prices, and hours).

La Tasca de Panchito, C. J. Sebastián Elcano, 10 (tel. 428 10 09), on a small commercial alley between C. J.S. Elcano and C. Monte Carmelo, about 2 blocks east of Pl. de Cuba. Casual and fun. Aztec-design tapestries within. Outdoor tables on large plaza. *Tacos* 225-350ptas. Mexican *platos* 325-550ptas. Open Sun.-Thurs. 12:30pm-2am, Fri.-Sat. 12:30pm-4am. Three other locations: C. Padre Tarín, 6 (tel. 490 79 53), near Pl. de la Gavidia (same hours); Av. Reina Mercedes, 5 (tel. 462 29 82), near the Youth Hostel (same hours); and C. Fernando IV, 38, in Barrio de los Remedios (open Sun.-Thurs. 7pm-2am, Fri.-Sat. 7pm-4am).

El Amanecer, C. Asunción, 76 (tel. 445 93 79). Cross Puente de San Telmo, head left down C. Asunción 9-10 blocks. Tourists dissolve in the local clientele like salt in water. Outdoor dining also available. Enchiladas 400-495ptas, large selection of hamburgers 275-600ptas, *platos combinados* 250-400ptas. Open Sun.-Thurs. 1pm-2am, Fri. and Sat. 1pm-4am.

SIGHTS

The Cathedral and Surroundings

Renaissance-era and later urban planning is manifest in the broad avenues and wide open squares of Menéndez Pelayo, Constitución, Alfonso XII, and Reyes Católicos. Traditional Spanish and Arab architectures are also integrated here to create a Mudejar urban landscape which is characteristically Andalusian.

Christians razed an Almohad mosque to clear space for Salvias **cathedral** in 1401, although the famed minaret known as **La Giralda** survived. The tower and its twins in Marrakech and Rabat are the oldest and largest surviving Almohad minarets (the lower walls are 2.5m thick). In 1565, it was crowned by a Renaissance belfry with Classical arches and a bronze orchestra of 25 bells. A well-preserved stone ramp— built to permit ascent on horseback—leads to the tower and belfry. (Entrance to the left after entering the cathedral's main door.) The conquerors demonstrated their religious fervor by constructing a church so great that, in their own words, "those who come after us will take us for madmen." It took more than a century to build this fourth-largest cathedral (after St. Peter's in Rome, St. Paul's in London, and the pastiche of St. Peter's in the Ivory Coast) and largest Gothic edifice ever built. Black and gold coffin-bearers block the entrance, guarding one of Sevilla's most cherished possessions, the **Tumba de Cristóbal Colón** (Columbus's Tomb).

Green and gold floor tiles lay geometrically across the gilt oval chamber of the **cabildo** (chapter house) to the east, a magnificent Renaissance space. Paintings by Murillo and Ribera cover the walls of the **Sacristía Mayor.** Behind the wooden partitions on either side, a disembodied head of John the Baptist watches visitors enter the **tesoro** and guards two keys that Jewish leaders presented to the city of Sevilla after King Fernando III ousted the Muslims in 1248. The neighboring **Sacristía de**

los Pintores maintains a collection of minor canvases by old masters, including Zurbarán and Goya. The Baroque organ in the center of the cathedral is a colossal piece of hand-me-down mahogany left over from a 19th-century Austrian railway.

The barred **Portal Principal** at the back of the cathedral faces Av. Constitución. North of the portal, the **Capilla de San Antonio de Padua** celebrates the Portuguese-born saint notorious for demonstrating his exuberance by preaching to fish. Just before the exit is the **Capilla Real** (Royal Chapel). (Tel. 456 33 21; cathedral complex and Giralda open Mon.-Sat. 11am-5pm, Sun. 2-5pm; Giralda also open Sun. 10am-2pm. Tickets sold until one hour before closing time. Joint admission 550ptas, students 200ptas, senior citizens free.)

Outside of the cathedral, on its northeast end, the **Patio de los Naranjos** (orange trees) evokes the bygone days of the Arab caliphate. The tortuous alleys of the **Judería** (old Jewish quarter) run from the Patio de los Naranjos to the Jardines de Murillo, along the walls of the Alcázar.

The 9th-century walls of the **Alcázar**—the oldest palace still used by European royalty—face the south side of the cathedral. The walls and several interior spaces, including the exquisitely-carved **Patio de las Muñecas** (Courtyard of the Dolls, whose rooms display handfans and a bed purportedly slept in by Queen Isabel) and the **Patio del Yeso** (Courtyard of Plaster), remain from the Moorish fortress. Of later Christian additions, one of the most exceptional is the **Patio de las Doncellas** (Maids' Court). Court life in the Alcázar traditionally revolved around this spacious, colonnaded quadrangle ringed by foliated archways, adorned with glistening tilework, roofed with coffered ceilings, and soothed by a central fountain. Still more impressive is the golden-domed **Salón de los Embajadores** where Fernando and Isabel welcomed Columbus upon his return from America. Labyrinthine **jardines** stretch away from the residential quarters in all directions. (Tel. 422 71 63; open Tues.-Sat. 10:30am-5pm, Sun. 10am-1pm. Admission 600ptas, students free.)

Between the cathedral and the Alcázar, the 16th-century **Lonja** was built by Felipe II as a *Casa de Contratación* (commercial exchange) for the American trade. In 1784 it was turned into the *Archivo General de Indias* (Archive of the Indies), a collection of over 30,000 documents relating to the discovery and conquest of the "New World." Highlights include letters from Columbus to Fernando and Isabel. Today, the **Archivo** is both a museum and a center for historical research. (Tel. 421 12 34; exhibits open Mon.-Fri. 10am-1pm. Free. Researcher institute open Mon.-Fri. 8am-3pm.) The **Museo de Arte Contemporáneo** next door (C. Santo Tomaso, 5) has some celebrated Mirós on the top floor. (Tel. 421 58 30; open July-Sept. Tues.-Fri. 10am-2pm; Oct.-June Tues.-Fri. 10am-7pm, Sat.-Sun. 10am-2pm. Free.)

On the northwest end of the cathedral and facing the Pl. Virgen de los Reyes, the **Palacio Arzobispal** was built in the 16th century; the sumptuous Baroque staircase and facade were added a century later. Opposite the palace and screened by orange trees is the **Convento de la Encarnación,** whose 14th-century church integrates the lobed windows of a mosque, visible from outside.

On C. Temprado, off C. Santander, two blocks west of the Lonja, is the **Hospital de la Caridad,** a compact 17th-century complex of arcaded courtyards. Its founder, Don Miguel de Marañe, is popularly believed to be the model for legendary Sevillian Don Juan. He was allegedly converted to a life of piety and charity after stumbling out of an orgy into a funeral cortège that he was told was his own. Inside the **Iglesia de San Jorge** hang paintings and frescoes by Valdés Leal and Murillo, including Leal's *Finis Gloria Mundi* which depicts corpses of a peasant, a bishop, and a king putrefying beneath a stylized depiction of Justice and the Seven Deadly Sins. The ornate **altar mayor** (main altar) includes a grisly sculpture of Jesus. Don Miguel is buried in the crypt. (Tel. 422 32 32; open Mon.-Sat. 10am-1pm and 3:30-6pm. Admission to church 200ptas.)

Barrio de Santa Cruz

The tourist office has a special map for this neighborhood of winding alleys, flower pots, wrought-iron *cancelas* (gates), befountained courtyards, and excellent art galleries. King Fernando III forced Jews fleeing Toledo to live in this ghetto. Haloed with geraniums, jasmine, and ivy, every street corner in the *barrio* bears a reminder of history and legend. On **Calle Susona,** a glazed skull above a door recalls the beautiful Jewess Susona who fell in love with a Christian knight. Susona warned her lover when she learned her father and friends planned to kill several inquisitors, including her knight. When bloody reprisal was unleashed on the ghetto, Susona's whole family was slaughtered. The distraught woman requested her skull be placed above her doorway in atonement for her betrayal. According to legend, the actual skull remained there until the 18th century. This street leads to **Plaza Doña Elvira,** site of a theater where Sevillian Lope de Rueda's works, precursors of Spain's Golden Age drama, were staged. A turn down C. Gloria leads to Pl. Venerables, location of the 17th-century **Hospital de los Venerables,** a hospital-church adorned with a choice ensemble of Sevilla School art including Leal and Montañés. (Tel. 456 26 96; open July-Sept. Tues.-Sun. 10am-2pm and 5-9pm; Oct.-June Mon.-Sun. 10am-2pm and 4-8pm. Admission 500ptas.)

Calle Lope de Rueda is graced with two noble mansions, beyond which lies **Plaza de Santa Cruz. Convento de San José** on C. Santa Teresa (off Pl. Santa Cruz) religiously cherishes a cloak of Santa Teresa of Avila, along with a portrait of the saint by Father Miseria. The Pl. Santa Cruz church houses the grave of artist Murillo, who died in what is now known as the **Casa Murillo,** after falling from a scaffold while painting ceiling frescoes in Cádiz's Iglesia de los Capuchinos. (Open Tues.-Sat. 10am-2pm and 6-8pm.) **Iglesia de Santa María la Blanca** in the nearby square was built in 1391 on the foundations of a synagogue. It features red marble columns, Baroque plasterwork by Pedro and Miguel Broja, and a Murillo *Last Supper*.

Sierpes and the Aristocratic Quarter

The **Ayuntamiento** on Pl. San Francisco has 16th-century Gothic and Renaissance interior halls, a richly decorated domed ceiling in the chapter room, and a Plat'-esque facade. Off Pl. San Francisco, pedestrian **Calle Sierpes** is shoppers' turf. At the beginning of the street, a plaque marks the spot where the royal prison was once located; some scholars believe Cervantes began *Don Quijote* there.

Fronted by a Montañés sculpture, **Iglesia de El Salvador** stands on the square of the same name one block east of Sierpes. The 17th-century church was built on the foundations of the city's main mosque, of which the courtyard and the belfry's base remain. As grandiose as a cathedral, it's adorned by outstanding Baroque retables, sculpture, and painting, including Montañés's *Jesús de la Pasión.* (Open Mon.-Sat. 6:30-9:30pm-Sun. 10am-1pm and 6:30-9:30pm.)

The brick **Iglesia de la Anunciación,** on the somewhat degraded Pl. Encarnación, served for two centuries as church of the adjacent **Antigua Universidad.** A pantheon here honors illustrious Sevillians, including poet Gustavo Adolfo Bécquer.

North of Barrio Santa Cruz off Pl. Pilatos, the **Casa de Pilatos** is a palace with a considerable collection of Roman antiquities, Renaissance and Baroque paintings, period furniture, several courtyards, and a pond. (Tel. 422 52 98; open 9am-7pm. Admission 1000ptas.) Use the metal bell pull if the gate is closed during visiting hours. Sundry palaces at #2 and #5 on C. Esteban lead to **Iglesia de San Esteban.** The lobed arches and 16th-century Mudejar altar tiles make it one of Sevilla's finest Gothic Mudejar churches.

La Macarena

This neighborhood, named for the Román Macarios who owned an estate here, is a richly endowed quarter often overlooked by tourists. *Macarena* is at once the name of a Sevillian virgin and of a popular rumba which advises women to give their bodies *"alegría y cosas buenas"* (happiness and good things). C. María Coronel leads to **Convento de Santa Inés,** whose courtyard boasts the revolving window from which cloistered nuns sell patented puff pastry and coffee cakes. Legend has it the founder was pursued so insistently by King Pedro el Cruel, she poured boiling oil on her face to disfigure it.

The *ruta de los conventos* (route of the convents) traverses this quarter. **Convento de Santa Paula** includes a church with Gothic, Mudejar, and Renaissance elements, a magnificent coffered ceiling, and sculptures by Montañés. The **museo** has a *St. Jerome* by Ribera. Nuns here push scrumptious homemade marmalades and angel hair pastry. (Tel. 442 13 07; open Tues.-Sun. 9:30am-1pm and 4:30-6:30pm.) Opposite the belfry of the Iglesia de San Marcos rises **Convento de Santa Isabel.** The Baroque church has a retable done by Montañés. Nearby on C. San Luís stands the exuberantly Baroque **Iglesia de San Luis** with octagonal glazed-tile domes.

Nearby C. Dueñas leads to yet another great Sevillian mansion, **Palacio de las Dueñas,** birthplace of 20th-century poet Antonio Machado. He likened the passage through life to the impact of footsteps on water; luckily his erstwhile home has endured more successfully.

Between the Puertas de Macarena and Córdoba on the Ronda de Capuchinos ring road is a stretch of restored **murallas,** built by the Almohads in the 12th century and successively enlarged by the Almoravids and the Christians. A large garden beyond the walls leads to the **Hospital de las Cinco Llagas,** a spectacular Renaissance building, primped to house the Andalusian parliament.

Back within the walls toward the river is **Alameda de Hércules,** in a quarter punctuated by many Mudejar churches and adjacent to the city's red-light district.

El Arenal, San Lorenzo, and Triana

The **Torre del Oro** (Gold Tower), on P. Cristóbal Colón, beside the river, is a 12-sided crennelated tower built by the Almohads in 1220 to reinforce a wall leading from the Alcázar. A glaze of golden tile once sheathed its squat frame; today a tiny yellow dome is the only reminder of its original splendor. For an attack of acrophobia, climb to the top and visit the **Museo Náutico,** with engravings and drawings of Sevilla's port in its heyday. (Tel. 422 24 19; tower and museum open Tues.-Fri. 10am-2pm, Sat. and Sun. 11am-2pm. Admission 100ptas.)

The inviting riverside esplanade **Marqués de Contadero** stretches along the banks of the Guadalquivir from the base of the tower. Bridge-heavy one-hour boat tours of Sevilla leave from here (700ptas). Immortalized by Golden Age writers Lope de Vega, Quevedo, and Cervantes, **Arenal** and (across the river) **Triana** were Sevilla's bustling and chaotic seafaring quarters in the 17th century. The tiled boardwalk leads to **Plaza de Toros de la Real Maestranza,** a veritable temple of bullfighting. Home to one of the two great schools of *tauromaquia* (the other is in Ronda), the plaza fills to capacity for the 13 *corridas* of the *Feria de Abril* and for weekly fights in the summer (on Thurs. and Sun.). (Tel. 422 45 77; open to visitors April 24-Oct. 12 Mon.-Sat. on non-bullfight days from 10am-1:30pm. Tours every ½hr. Admission 250ptas.)

The **Museo Provincial de Bellas Artes,** Pl. Museo, 9, contains Spain's finest collection of works by Sevilla School painters, notably Murillo, Leal, and Zurbarán, and aliens, El Greco and Dutch master Jan Breughel. To reach the museum, walk toward the river along C. Alfonso XII which is lined with a number of palaces. (Tel. 422 07 90; open Tues.-Sun. 9am-3pm. Admission 250ptas. EU citizens under 21 free.) The Museo de Bellas Artes has been undergoing major renovations for the last few years.

Several blocks away in Pl. San Lorenzo is the **Iglesia del Gran Poder de San Lorenzo,** remarkable for Montañés's lifelike sculpture *El Cristo del Gran Poder.* Worshipers kiss Jesus' ankle through an opening in the bulletproof glass. Semana Santa culminates in a procession bearing this statue. (Tel. 438 54 54; open 8am-1:30pm and 6-9pm. Free.)

Across the river is the former potters', tilemakers' and gypsy quarter called **Triana,** now much gentrified. The riverside promenade **Calle Betis** with its many outdoor terraces is an ideal spot from which to view Sevilla's monumental profile. Originally commissioned by King Alfonso X el Sabio (the Wise or the Learned), the **Iglesia de Santa Ana** (two blocks from the river) was renovated three times between the 13th and 16th centuries.

Elsewhere

In 1929, Sevilla made elaborate plans for an Iberian-American world fair. When Wall Street crashed, so did the fair, but the event left the city the lovely landscapes of the **Parque de María Luisa.** Innumerable courtyards, turquoise-tiled benches, and tailored tropical gardens fill this expanse of manicured greenery, ideal for picnics or early afternoon *siestas.*

On the park's northeastern edge, the twin spires of **Plaza de España** poke above the Sevillian skyline. The plaza's colonnade, checkered with terracotta tiles, curves toward the neighboring park; a narrow moat, spanned by four bridges, encircles the pavilion. The enclosed area is overlaid with brickwork and punctuated in the center by a large fountain. Boaters putt around the miniature canal (300ptas per hr.). By night the *Plaza* is spectacularly lit against the background of the 18th-century **Antigua Fábrica de Tabacos** (Old Tobacco Factory, now part of the University of Sevilla), location of Bizet's *Carmen*.

Sevilla's **Museo Arqueológico,** inside the park at Pl. de América, shows off a small collection of pre-Roman and Roman artifacts excavated in the surrounding provinces. (Tel. 423 24 01; open Tues.-Sun. 10am-2pm. Admission 250ptas. EU members under 21 free.) A block or so toward the river down Palos de la Frontera is the 17th-century **Palacio de San Telmo,** built as a training school for sailors. St. Telmo, patron saint of sailors, hovers over the door amid a maelstrom of marine monsters and allegorical figures. The courtyard within encloses a pillared hall and chapel with a large Zurbarán.

Although it is soon due to become a science and technology park as well as a cultural area for theater and concerts, the EXPO is now only a ghost town, lit up at night, an architectural hangover from the '92 party.

ENTERTAINMENT

The tourist office distributes *El Giraldillo,* a free monthly magazine on entertainment in Sevilla with complete listings on music, art exhibits, theater, dance, fairs, and film.

Movies, Theater, and Music

Avenida 5 Cines, C. Marqués de las Paradas, 15 (tel. 422 15 48), and **Cine Cristina,** C. Almirante Lobo, 1 (tel. 422 66 80), both show predominantly foreign (i.e. American) films dubbed into Spanish. **Cine Corona,** in the mall between C. Salado and C. Paraiso in Barrio de Triana, screens subtitled films, often in English. Shows at most theaters run from early afternoon to late at night and cost around 600ptas, Wed. half price, Thurs. two for one. For information on all three cinemas, call 427 80 64.

For theater, the venerable **Teatro Lope de Vega,** near Parque María Luisa, has long been the city's leading stage. (Ask about scheduled events at the tourist office or check the bulletin board in the university lobby on C. San Fernando.) The grand new **Teatro de la Maestranza,** on the river next door to the Plaza de Toros, is a splendid concert hall designed to accommodate both orchestral performances and full-fledged opera. Tickets can be purchased from 11am-2pm and 5-8pm at the box office in front of the theater. On spring and summer evenings, neighborhood fairs are often accompanied by free **open-air concerts** in Barrios de Santa Cruz and Triana.

Nightlife

Nightlife is active all year in Sevilla, reaching its apotheosis during summer weekends. On warm nights after sundown, Sevillians gather in *bars, terrazas,* and *chiringuitos.* The latter, outdoor bars that pulsate to *bacalao* (techno-dance music), cluster on the riverside, along Paseo de Cristóbal Colón, between Puente del Generalísimo and Puente de Isabel II. **Bar Capote,** next to Puente de Isabel II, is always worth a visit—so packed it overflows into nearby streets and parking lots. (Beer 125-200ptas. Open Mon.-Thurs. until about 5am, Fri.-Sat. until about 6:30am.) **Plaza del Salvador,** C. Alvarez Quintero, three blocks north of the cathedral, fills with revelers toting drinks from the two tiny bars on the plaza. Others flock a few blocks to the east on C. Alcaicería to **Plaza Alfalfa,** a district brimming with *tapas* bars and cafés. The locales on and around **Calle Mateos Gago** and **Calle Argote de Molina** of Barrio Santa Cruz are always worth a late-night visit, as is the smaller area across from the tourist office. A bevy of *terrazas* take over Barrio de Triana near Puente Isabel II and line **Calle Reina Mercedes** and the **Jardines de las Delicias,** both down Po. Delicias away from the cathedral. On Po. Delicias, **Alfonso XII, Líbano,** and **Chile** are the bars of choice for ending an evening of bar-hopping. Some quieter, more traditional bars include:

La Carbonería, C. Levies, 18, a few blocks west of C. Menéndez y Pelayo, off C. Santa María la Blanca. Established 30 years ago to encourage artists and musicians censored during Franco's dictatorship, the locale now functions as a popular nightspot, with jazz, folk, and other shows nightly (flamenco Sun.-Tues.). On hot nights the large garden courtyard is packed with a crowd of mixed ages.

Antigüedades, C. Argote de Molina, just north of the cathedral. A new decorative theme every other week (such as hanging bones and flying golden trumpets) and modern-art oddities displayed through upstairs balconies. Beer 150ptas, mixed drinks 400ptas. Open weeknights until 3am, Fri.-Sat. until about 4am.

Las Columnas, corner of C. Mateos Gago and C. Rodrigo Caro. Hordes of people block access inside most nights; try joining the overflow outside.

Abades, C. Abades, 15 (tel. 421 50 96). Not just another bar in Barrio de Santa Cruz; it's your excuse to visit an 18th-century mansion. For background music you can choose between the fountain in the elegant courtyard or the strains of classical music in one of the comfortable dens. Pretty pricey.

Casa Morales, C. García de Vinuesa, 11, one block from the cathedral. Small tables dwarfed by 5m-high barrels form the setting for regional wine sampling (100-130ptas per glass).

A typical Sevillian sampling of *marcha* (the term for the endless revelry) begins with visits to several bars, followed by nightclubs for dancing, and culminating in an early-morning breakfast of *churros* and *chocolate*. Most clubs, catering to the post-bar throngs, don't expect business until well after midnight; the real fun often starts after 3am. Women and foreigners, especially Americans, are frequently admitted to discotheques without paying the cover charge. Ask bartenders or patrons at Alfonso XII, Capote, Líbano, or Chile to recommend hot spots.

The gay scene is coming out strong in Sevilla; several gay and lesbian bars have opened in the last couple of years. Most can give you information on the others, and some carry a local guide to gay life in Sevilla. Rumor has it that **Itaca,** C. Amor de Dios, near C. Lope de la Vega in el Centro, is the best gay disco in town (show Wed. at 1am). **Conos,** C. Santa Ana, in el Centro, is a disco bar with a video room. Popular disco-bars with a mostly international clientele include **Lamentable** and **Cátera,** on Pl. Alfalfa; **Poseidón,** on C. Marqués de las Paradas; and **Califas,** on C. Menéndez Pelayo (by C. Santa María la Blanca).

Flamenco

Lightning-fast footwork of Sevilla's flamenco *bailaores* dazzles the eye while rhythmic guitar, pulsating handclaps, and wailing *cantaores* overwhelm the ear. Unfortunately for the budget traveler, good flamenco doesn't come cheap (unless you catch the *Feria de Abril,* when dancers take over the city). Show times change every few weeks; call ahead for listings. The best show in town, and the only one with professional dancers, is on the western edge of Barrio Santa Cruz at **Los Gallos,** Pl. Santa Cruz, 11 (tel. 421 69 81). Cover starts at 3000ptas and includes one drink. Arrive early to get a good seat. You'll find similar prices at **El Arenal,** C. Rodó, 7 (tel. 421 64 92), and **Patio Sevillano,** P. Cristóbal Colón, 11 (tel. 421 41 20). Some folk music and flamenco is performed at **La Gitanilla,** C. Ximénez de Encisco, 11, in Barrio de los Remedios, across the river; take bus #42 from Pl. Encarnación, Pl. Nueva, or Av. Constitución.

La Lidia (bullfighting) and Festivals

To avoid the scalper's 20% markup, buy bullfight tickets at the ring. For a good *cartel* (line-up), however, one of the booths on C. Sierpes, C. Velázquez, or Pl. Toros might be the only source of advance tickets. Ticket prices, depending on the coolness of both your seat and the matador, can run from 1600ptas for a *grada de sol* (nosebleed seat in the sun) to 10,000ptas for a *barrera de sombra* (front row seat in the shade). *Corridas de toros* (bullfights) or *novilladas* (cut-rate fights with young bulls and novice bullfighters) are held on the 13 days around the *Feria de Abril* and into May, often during Corpus Christi in June, nearly every Sunday in June, and again during the Feria de San Miguel near the end of September. For information on dates and prices, go to **Plaza de la Real Maestranza,** commonly known as **Plaza de Toros,** or call 422 31 52.

Sevilla swells with tourists during the *fiestas*. The world-famous **Semana Santa** (Holy Week) lasts from Palm Sunday to Good Friday. Penitents in hooded cassocks guide bejeweled floats, lit by hundred of candles, through the streets. Book your room well in advance of the festivities, and expect to pay at least triple the ordinary price. Two or three weeks after Semana Santa, the city rewards itself for its Lenten piety with the six-day carnivalesque **Feria de Abril** (April Fair). Circuses, bullfights, and flamenco shows roar into the night in a showcase of local customs that began in the 19th century as part of a popular revolt against foreign influence. The fairgrounds are on the southern side of Barrio Los Remedios, near the river. A spectacular array of flowers and lanterns festoons over 1000 kiosks, tents, and pavilions. Don't even dream of getting any sleep during this week.

The **Romería del Rocío** takes place 50 days after Easter on Pentecost and involves the veneration of the *Blanca Paloma* (white dove) through candle-light parades and traditional dance. The festival culminates with a peregrination from Sevilla to the nearby village of Rocío, a mere 80km away. Hundreds of Sevillians participate in the two-day trek, accepting food from strangers and camping by the road at night. In the best Spanish fashion, the *Romería* is half religious penitence, half party: singing and dancing break out around campfires after a long day of walking, and *sevillanas* (flamenco songs) are played until sunrise.

■ NEAR SEVILLA

ITÁLICA

The village of **Santiponce** (pop. 6200), a mere 9km northwest of Sevilla, holds the ruins of the first important Roman settlement in Iberia, Itálica. Founded in 206BC, this city was the birthplace of emperors Trajan and Hadrian. The Romans promptly became the town's aristocracy, the Iberians its underclass. The city walls, Nova Urbs, and other edifices were constructed between 300 and 400AD, otherwise known as the *apogeo* (apogee). In the centuries that followed, Itálica's power declined, and by the 5th century Sevilla had become the region's seat of power.

Archeological excavations begun in the 18th century continue today. The well-preserved **anfiteatro,** one of Spain's largest, seats 25,000. Classical theater is still performed here; check Sevilla's *El Giraldillo* for schedules. A handful of colorful **suelos de mosaicos** (mosaic floors) remain in some buildings. (Tel. 599 73 76; open April-Sept. Tues.-Sat. 9am-6:30pm, Sun. 9am-3pm; Oct.-March Tues.-Sat. 9am-5:30pm, Sun. 10am-4pm. Admission 250ptas. Students under 21 free.)

Take Empresa Casal's bus toward Santiponce, and tell the driver you want to go to Itálica. Catch the bus in front of #33 C. Marqués de las Paradas, near 'Sevilla's old Plaza de Armas or Córdoba train station. (Buses run every ½hr. Mon.-Fri. 6am-11pm, every hr. Sat.-Sun. 7:30am-midnight, 30min., 120ptas.)

CARMONA

Just east of Sevilla, the ancient city of Carmona (pop. 24,000) presides over a tall hill above the gold and green countryside. Once a thriving Arab stronghold, it was later the favorite 14th-century retreat of Pedro el Cruel. Moorish Mudejar palaces mingle with Christian Renaissance mansions amidst a skein of streets still partially enclosed by fortified walls. **Puerta de Sevilla,** a horseshoe-shaped passageway, burrows through the ramparts, to the right and up C. San Pedro from the bus stop. The adjoining **Alcázar de la Puerta de Sevilla** dates back to the reign of Augustus in the first century BC. (Open Fri.-Sat. 11am-1pm, Sun. 11am-2pm. Admission 165ptas.) Opulent Baroque mansions lie farther uphill past the Alcázar, while the **Alcázar del Rey Don Pedro,** a fortress of Almohad origin, is at the eastern edge of town. Just west of the town limits, by the ruins of the most important **Necrópolis Romana,** is the **Museo Arqueológico.** The museum contains urns and such from over a thousand tombs (including some pre-Roman burial mounds) unearthed at the necropolis. (Tel. 414 08 11. Roman necropolis and museum open Tues.-Fri. 10am-2pm and 4-6pm, Sat.-Sun. 10am-2pm. Free.)

Tourist information is available from the **Casa de la Cultura,** Pl. Descalzas, s/n (tel. 414 22 00). From the bus stop, head right down C. San Pedro, pass through the Puerta de Sevilla, and take C. Prim to the left. Keep going until Pl. San Fernando, then take C. Martil L. (on the far size of the plaza) down to Pl. Descalzas. (Open Mon.-Fri. 8am-2pm, Sat. 9am-1:30pm.) The **post office** is at C. Prim, 29 (tel. 414 10 24; open for stamps, Lista de Correos, and **telegrams** Mon.-Fri. 8am-3pm, Sat. 9am-2pm). **Postal code** is 41410; **telephone code** 95. For **medical assistance,** at C. Paseo de La Feria, s/n, call 414 09 97. The **police,** Pl. San Fernando, s/n, take calls at 414 00 08.

Accommodations are generally cheaper and easier to find than in Sevilla. Overlooking the Alcázar, **Pensión Comercio,** C. Torre del Oro, 56 (tel. 414 00 18), favors guests with spic, span, and spacious rooms. Breakfast in restaurant 350ptas, *platos* 500-700ptas, *menú* 1100ptas. (Singles 1500ptas, with bath 2000ptas. Doubles 3000ptas, with bath 4000ptas.) **Pensión Casa Carmelo,** C. San Pedro, 15 (tel. 414 05 72), to the right of the bus stop, houses several rooms in a vintage 19th-century casino. (Singles 1200-1600ptas. Doubles 2700-3700ptas, with bath 4000-6000ptas.)

Carmona is a convenient, one-hour **bus** ride from Sevilla. (Mon.-Fri. 21 per day, Sat. 10 per day, Sun. 7 per day, 250ptas.) In Sevilla, buses leave across the street from the south side of the Prado de San Sebastián, in front of the Plaza de España. In Carmona, buses leave from in front of Bar La Parada at C. San Pedro, 31. For information call Empresa Casal at 441 06 58.

OSUNA

Julius Caesar founded the town Osuna (pop. 17,000), naming it after the *osos* (bears) that once lumbered about the land. Today only the remaining stone mansions reveal the former status of this peaceful little town as a cushy ducal seat.

Protectors of a number of artists, the Dukes of Osuna brought important works to their town, including the four Riberas which hang in the **Iglesia Catedral,** atop the high hill. Goya's portrait of the family—his most assiduous private patrons—now hangs in the Prado. The dukes had their very own private chapel built beneath the main one, complete with pulpit and choir. The neighboring 16th-century mausoleum guards the treasures of this family. **Panteón Ducal,** a morbid sepulchre with low ceilings, is the most intriguing of the chambers. Only three empty spaces await the remaining nobility. The sole duke not buried here lies in a marble sarcophagus upstairs because his coffin couldn't fit through the sepulchre's entrance. (Open Oct.-May Tues.-Sun. 10am-1:30pm and 3:30-6:30pm; June-Sept. Tues.-Sun. 10am-1:30pm and 4-7pm. Admission 200ptas. It's much easier for large groups to gain entrance; you'll need to be friendly and very persuasive to gain access to the church on your own.)

Facing the church's entrance is the **Monasterio de la Encarnación.** A resident nun will show you room upon room of polychromed wooden sculptures and silver crucifixes, but the must-sees are the 18th-century statue of *Cristo de la Misericordia* in the adjoining Baroque church and the Sevillian *azulejo* tiles in the shadow of the sun-filled patio. (Open same hours as church. Admission 150ptas. Divine sweets made by monks 300-400ptas.)

The **Museo Arqueológico,** on the road to the hilltop from Plaza Mayor, houses a collection of Roman artifacts found in the vicinity and replicas of pieces sent on to Madrid and Paris. (Same hours as the church and monastery. Admission 150ptas.)

To reach the **tourist office** make a right on Avda. de la Constitución as you exit the bus station and walk for five minutes. (Open Tues.-Sun. 11am-2pm.) Maps and schedules available upon request. Mail away at the **post office,** C. San Agustín, 4 (tel. 481 09 61), between Pl. Santa Rita and Pl. Mayor (open Mon.-Sat. 9am-2pm). The **postal code** is 41640; the **telephone code** 95. For **medical assistance,** call Hospital Ntra. Sra. de la Merced, C. Carrera, 84 (tel. 481 09 00). In an **emergency** dial 091. The **municipal police** are at 481 00 50, on Pl. Mayor.

Best suited to daytrippers, Osuna has few beds. **Hostal Cinco Puertas,** C. Carrera, 79 (tel. 481 12 43), is comfortable but noisy. (Singles 1300ptas. Doubles 2700ptas, with shower 3000ptas.) The convenient restaurant charges faintly stiff prices. **Restaurante Mesón del Duque,** Pl. Duquesa, 2 (tel. 481 13 01), on the road to the Museo Arqueológico and Iglesia Colegial, supplies a *menú* (1000ptas), several fish dishes (600-700ptas), and a panoply of *tortillas* (500-600ptas). View of sun-flower and olive tree fields from an outdoor terrace. (Open Tues.-Sun. 1-4:30pm and 9-11:30pm.) The **market** adjoins Plaza Mayor (open Mon.-Sat. 8am-2pm).

Osuna is an easy daytrip from either Sevilla or Antequera. **Trains** stop at the small, desolate station on Av. Estación (tel. 481 03 08), a 15-minute walk from the center. To reach Pl. Mayor from the train station, walk up Av. Estación, which curves right onto C. Mancilla. After a small plaza with Hostal Granadino, turn left onto C. Carmen and then right onto C. Sevilla. Trains run to Sevilla (4 per day, 1¼hr., 600ptas); Málaga (2 per day, 1¾hr., 725ptas); Granada (2 per day, 3¼hr., 1100ptas). The **bus station** is at Av. de la Constitución, s/n (tel. 481 01 46), a 10-minute walk from the center. To reach Pl. Mayor, make a right upon exiting the bus station and walk downhill, following signs pointing toward *Centro Urbano*. Pass little Pl. Santa Rita, staying on C. Carrera Caballos all the way to Pl. Mayor. **Empresa Dipasa** and **Linesur** (tel. 481 01 64) run buses to Sevilla (12 per day, Sat. 8 per day, Sun. 6 per day, 1½hr., 750ptas one way, 1000ptas round trip). **Alsina Graells** stops here for connections to Málaga (2 per day, 2½hr., 1200ptas); Granada (3 per day, 3½hr., 1500ptas), and Antequera (5 per day, 1hr., 675ptas).

■■■ CÓRDOBA

The legend of graceful Córdoba, *"lejana y sola"* (lone and distant) as Frederico García Lorca immortalized the city in his renowned poem, has enticed many into an intriguing labyrinth of history and streets. One of the oldest cities on the Iberian Peninsula, Córdoba (pop. 330,000) has seen Christianity, Islam, and Judaism meet variously in harmony and strife for centuries. The city's first inhabitants lived in the caves of the nearby Sierra Morena. In 152 BC Roman Praetor Claudius Marcellus, considered by many the founder of Córdoba, proclaimed the city capital of Roman Ulterior Spain. With Romanization, Córdoba became a major cultural center, producing such luminaries as the playwright Seneca. It was under the Muslims (711-1263) that Córdoba once again emerged as a seat of intellectual and political power, capital of the western Caliphate (929-1031) when the Ummayads broke with Baghdad. During and following its medieval "Golden Age," Córdoba was birthplace of many of Spain's most illustrious figures, including Jewish philosopher and theologian Maimonides, poet Luís de Góngora, and painter Bartolomé Bermejo. Although the Christians reconquered Córdoba in the 13th century, vestiges of *convivencia* (coexistence) remain. On the anniversary of the Mezquita's (mosque's) construction, Muslims and Catholics still gather for joint services.

ORIENTATION AND PRACTICAL INFORMATION

Córdoba diverges into two geographic parts: a modern and commercial northern half, extending from the train station on **Avenida de América** down to **Plaza de las Tendillas** in the center of the city; and an older and touristy maze in the southern half called the **Judería** (old Jewish quarter). This tangle of beautiful and disorienting narrow streets extends from Pl. Tendillas down to the banks of the Guadalquivir, winding past the Mezquita and Alcázar.

Tourist Offices: Oficina de Turismo de la Juventud, C. Torrijos, 10 (tel. 47 12 35; fax 49 17 78), on the western side of the Mezquita. From the train station, take bus #12 (bus stop is on Av. de América, 500m to the left of the station) along the river and until Puerta del Puente, the large stone portal to your right. Office is one block up C. Torrijos. Abundant information on Córdoba and all of Andalucía. English spoken. Open April-Sept. Mon.-Fri. 9:30am-2pm and 5pm-7pm, Sat. 10am-1pm; Oct.-March Mon.-Fri. 9:30am-2pm and 3:30pm-5:30pm, Sat. 10am-1pm. Less crowded, the newly renovated **Oficina Municipal de Turismo y Congresos,** Pl. Judas Levi (tel./fax 20 05 22), next to the youth hostel, provides free maps, schedules, and cultural info. English spoken. Open June-Oct. Mon.-Sat. 9am-2pm and 5:30pm-7:30pm, Sun. 9am-2pm; Nov.-May Mon.-Sat. 9am-2pm and 4:30-6:30pm.

Currency Exchange: Cajasur, corner of C. Medina y Corella and C. Torrijos, near the tourist office. 1% or 500ptas commission, whichever is greater. Open 8:30am-2:30pm. Dozens of banks along Av. del Gran Capitán, Ronda de los Tejares, and near Pl. Tendillas also change money. Open Mon.-Wed. and Fri. 8:30am-2:30pm, Thurs. 8:30am-2:15pm and 4:30-7:30pm.

Post Office: C. Cruz Conde, 15 (tel. 47 82 67), just north of Pl. Tendillas. Open for stamps and Lista de Correos Mon.-Fri. 8am-9pm, Sat. 9am-7pm. **Telegrams:** tel. 47 03 45. Open Mon.-Fri. 8am-9pm, Sat. 9am-7pm. **Postal Code:** 14070.

Telephones: Pl. Tendillas, 7. Open Mon.-Fri. 9:30am-1:55pm and 5-10:55pm, Sat. 9:30am-1:55pm. **Telephone Code:** 957. **Information:** 003.

Trains: Av. América, 130 (**Information:** tel. 49 02 02). To: Sevilla (16 per day, *AVE* 45min., 1800-2500ptas; *talgo* 1hr., 1700-2000ptas; *regional* 2½hr., 710ptas); Málaga (8 per day, *talgo* 2½hr., 1800-2100ptas; *regional* 3hr., 1800ptas); Madrid (24 per day, *AVE* 1¾hr., 5000-6600ptas; *talgo* 2¼hr., 4600-5200ptas; *expreso* 6¾hr., 3200ptas); Cádiz (10 per day, *talgo* 3hr., 3200-3700ptas; *expreso* 5 hr., 2000ptas.). For international tickets, visit or call the main **RENFE**, Ronda de los Tejares, 10 (tel. 47 58 84).

Buses: Transportes Ureña and **Empresa Bacoma,** Av. Cervantes, 22 (tel. 47 23 52), travels east to Cataluña. To: Valencia (3 per day, 4500ptas); Barcelona (1 per day, 7500ptas). **Alsina-Graells Sur,** Av. Medina Azaliara, 29 (tel. 23 64 76), covers southern Andalucía. To: Sevilla (15 per day, 2hr., 1605ptas); Málaga (4 per day, 3-3½hr. 1395ptas). **Autocares Priego** (tel. 29 01 58 and 29 07 69) runs anywhere on the Sierra Cordobesa; **Empresa Carrera** (tel. 23 14 01) functions in the Campiña Cordobesa; and **Empresa Ramírez** (tel. 41 01 00) runs buses to nearby towns and camping sites.

Taxis: Tendillas (tel. 47 02 91) or **Gran Capitán** (tel. 47 51 53).

Car Rental: Hertz, Av. América, s/n (tel. 47 72 43), next to the train station. Open Mon.-Fri. 8:30am-1pm and 5-8pm, Sat. 9:30am-noon. Reservation center in Madrid (tel. 900 100 111). Must be 25 or older to rent.

Luggage Storage: Paquete-Exprés, next to the train station, 300ptas per locker.

English Bookstore: Windsor, C. Santa Victoria, 4 (tel. 48 53 11).

Late-Night Pharmacy: On a rotating basis. Refer to list posted outside every pharmacy or to local newspaper.

Medical Assistance: Urgencias Avenida de América, Av. América, s/n (tel. 47 23 82), ½km east of the train station. **Urgencias Santa Victoria,** C. Jerez, s/n (tel. 20 38 05), in *sector sur* on the other bank of the Guadalquivir. **Ambulance:** tel. 29 55 70. **Red Cross Hospital** (tel. 29 34 11). English spoken. **Emergency Medical Team** (tel. 27 22 80). English spoken. **Los Angeles de la Noche** (tel. 25 24 50). English spoken.

Fire: tel. 080.

Emergency: National Police, tel. 091. **Municipal Police,** tel. 092.

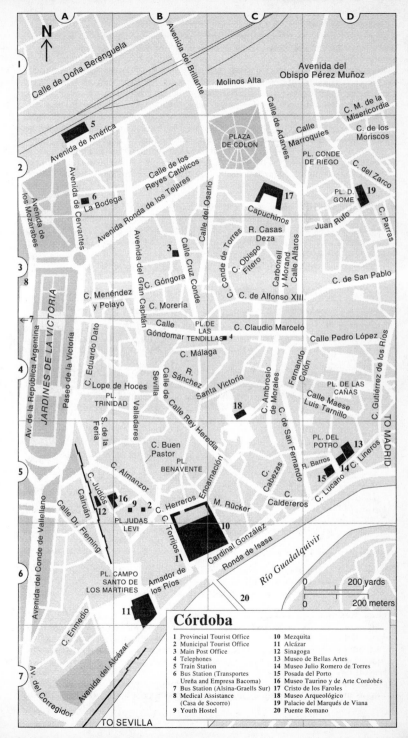

Córdoba

1 Provincial Tourist Office
2 Municipal Tourist Office
3 Main Post Office
4 Telephones
5 Train Station
6 Bus Station (Transportes Ureña and Empresa Bacoma)
7 Bus Station (Alsina-Graells Sur)
8 Medical Assistance (Casa de Socorro)
9 Youth Hostel
10 Mezquita
11 Alcázar
12 Sinagoga
13 Museo de Bellas Artes
14 Museo Julio Romero de Torres
15 Posada del Porto
16 Museo Taurino y de Arte Cordobés
17 Cristo de los Faroles
18 Museo Arqueológico
19 Palacio del Marqués de Viana
20 Puente Romano

TO SEVILLA

ACCOMMODATIONS AND CAMPING

Córdoba is especially crowded during *Semana Santa*, and May through September, so call ahead for reservations. The following prices include hot showers.

Residencia Juvenil Córdoba (HI), Pl. Judas Levi (tel. 29 01 66; fax 29 05 00). Go up C. Torrijos, on the west side of the Mezquita, and turn left on C. Medina y Corella. Take the first left onto C. Manríquez. The hostel is one block down on the right. Hostel heaven: impeccably clean, brand-new, no curfew, English spoken. Hostel hell: thick plastic divisions instead of walls. Bring earplugs or listen to the person six rooms down snore. All rooms are doubles, but some (two single beds, new mattresses, sink) are nicer than others (bunk beds, foam and springs). Be sure to request newer rooms. Call ahead in the summer, and confirm a day before arriving. 1007ptas per person, over 26 1484ptas. With breakfast 1166ptas, over 26 1643ptas. *Media Pensión* 1908ptas, over 25 2385ptas. *Pensión Completa* 2650ptas, over 25 3127ptas. Non-members pay more.

In the Judería

The Judería's white-washed walls, narrow twisting streets, and proximity to the major sights make it the most pleasing and convenient area to stay in Córdoba. For those without Ariadne's thread, another approach to labyrinths might be useful: never lift your left hand from the walls and if worst comes to worst, you'll resurface where you began. Remember here that no price is ever final. Most places lower rates for those staying a couple of nights or if business is slow. Though a bit more expensive, many *hostales* also line C. de San Fernando, 5 min. from the Judería.

Hostal-Residencia Séneca, C. Conde y Luque, 7 (tel. 47 32 34), 2 bl. north of the Mezquita. Impeccably maintained by a vivacious English- and French-speaking owner with an endless list of interesting places to visit. Breakfast in the beautiful patio 250ptas. Only single is 1800ptas. Doubles 3350ptas, with bath 4350ptas. Triples 4800ptas, with bath 6250ptas. Lower rates in winter.

Huéspedes Martínez Rücker, Martínez Rücker, 14 (tel. 47 25 62), just east of the Mezquita. Airy, arboreal courtyard. Charming rooms and owners. Singles 1500ptas. Doubles 3000ptas (one even has a balcony with flowers).

Hostal Mari 2, C. Horno de Porra, 6 (tel. 48 61 85 or 48 60 04), between C. Cardenal González and C. Calderos. As cheap as it gets. Simple, clean rooms. No check in 2-4pm. English spoken. Some parking. Washing machine available (about 400ptas per load). Singles start at 1000ptas. Doubles 2000ptas. Triples 3000ptas.

Fonda Rey Heredía, C. Rey Heredía, 26 (tel. 47 41 82), on a narrow street parallel to the northeastern corner of the Mezquita. Clean, modern bathrooms. Some windowless rooms get a bit stuffy in the summer, but most have fans. Singles 1500ptas. Doubles 3000ptas. Triples 4000ptas. Quads 5000ptas. All prices negotiable. Usually closed Nov.-Feb., but call to check.

Hostal El Portillo, C. Cabezas, 2 (tel. 47 20 91), off C. Caldereros, the continuation of C. Rey Heredía near the river. As everywhere in Córdoba, lush patio. Lone, small single 1200ptas. Doubles 2600ptas. Triples 3900ptas.

Off Plaza de las Tendillas

Rooms in this busy plaza are imbued with the atmosphere of modern Córdoba although they are only five minutes north of the Judería. In the afternoons, locals gather in the *terrazas* bordering the plaza for conversation and over-priced drinks.

Hotel Residencia Boston, C. Málaga, 2 (tel. 47 41 76; fax 47 85 23), on Pl. Tendillas. This 2-star hotel's prices are more suited for a *hostal*. Amenities to please Boston Brahmins: A/C, winter heating, TV, telephones and baths in modern rooms. Laundry service available, but outrageously expensive. Full-time concierge. Singles with small bath and TV, 2600ptas. Doubles with bath 4300ptas.

Hostal Residencia La Paz, C. Morería, 7 (tel. 47 61 79), off the plaza on a pedestrian side street beside C. Cruz Conde. Old paintings, antique lamps, and the religious memorabilia from *pueblos* around Córdoba create an eerie atmosphere.

Large tapestry-laden rooms with winter heating, away from the noisy street. Doubles 2650ptas, with shower 3180ptas, with bath 3445ptas. Triples with shower 4770ptas, with bath 5167ptas.

Hostal Las Tendillas, C. Jesús y María, 1 (tel. 47 30 29), on Pl. Tendillas. Not distinctive, but rooms and bathrooms are respectable. Deafening plaza revelry below. Refrigerator in hall; overnight laundry service. Singles 1600ptas. Doubles 2800ptas. Triples 3600ptas.

Near the Train Station

Most places are cheap and feel safe, but bring the earplugs.

Casa de Huéspedes Córdoba, Av. Cervantes, 22 (tel. 47 72 04), diagonally across from the train station. Trapezoidal rooms on perhaps the noisiest street in existence. Singles 1200ptas. Doubles 1700ptas. Triples 2500ptas.

Hostal Perales, Av. Mozárabes, 15 (tel. 23 03 25). Turn right down Av. América as you exit the train station, and go past the park until you reach Av. Mozárabes and the big yellow sign on the left. Clean, verging on institutional. Singles 1300ptas. Doubles 2400ptas.

Elsewhere in Córdoba

Hostal Maestre, C. Romero Barros, 16 (reservations: 47 24 10; tel./fax 47 53 95), five-minute walk from the Judería. Recently renovated. Maintains intimate hostal feeling though the rooms belong in a hotel: new beds, full bathrooms, some with A/C. Parking. Singles 2000ptas. Doubles 3500-4000ptas. Triples 4000-500ptas.

Camping: Camping Municipal, Av. Brillante (tel. 47 20 00; ask for *Camping Municipal*). From the train station: turn left on Av. América, left again at Av. Brillante, then walk about 2km uphill. Or take bus #10 or #11, both of which leave from Av. Cervantes near the station and run to the campsite. Public pool is indefinitely closed for restorations. 519ptas per person, per tent and per car. Under 10 375ptas.

Camping Los Villares, Carretera Vecinal Córdoba-Obejo (commonly known as Carretera de Los Villares) (tel. 26 14 08 or 25 70 32). Inaccessible by public transportation, yet the best camping option if the Municipal is full. Drive past Camping Municipal and follow signs for 8km. 300ptas per car, 350-500ptas per tent, 350ptas per person, under ten 250ptas.

FOOD

Calle Doctor Fleming, demarcating the west side of the Judería, is sprinkled with little *mesones* where *menús* cost about 600ptas. Students and student-priced eateries abound in **Barrio Cruz Conde,** around Av. de Menéndez Pidal and the area approaching the Hospital General. The famous Mezquita attracts more high-priced eateries than Muhammed did followers, but a five-minute walk away from it—in any direction except south where you'll taste de Guadalquivir—yields local specialties at reasonable prices and copious *platos combinados.* For an afternoon beer, try one of the numerous *Sociedad de Plateros* or any **café** to the northwest of the Judería.

The regional specialties include *gazpacho, salmorejo* (a *gazpacho*-like cream topped with hard-boiled eggs and pieces of ham), and *rabo de toro* (bull's tail simmered in tomato sauce). The nearby towns of Montilla and Moriles produce superb sherries (about 150ptas per glass): a light, dry *fino;* a darker *amontillado;* a sweet *oloroso;* and a creamy *Pedro Ximénez.* For non-alcoholic drinks, locals favor the delicious and refreshing *horchata de chufa,* so sweet that it is the closest one could get to drinking *turrón.* Other favorites are *horchata de almendra* (a bitter almond drink), and *granizados* (slushies in every flavor). For about 175ptas, you can indulge your sweet tooth in a light *pastel cordobés* (Cordoban pie).

Groceries: Small *tendejones* can be found every five blocks; just ask for the nearest one to stock up on bottled water, fruit, and groceries. Or go to **Supermercado Simago,** C. Jesús María s/n, ½ block south of Plaza Tendillas. Attention: groceries are downstairs. Open Mon.-Sat. 9am-2pm and 5-9pm. **Supermercado Gama,** is on C. Medina Azahara, 3 (tel. 23 36 36). Open Mon.-Fri. 9am-1:30pm and 5:30-8:30pm, Sat. 8am-2pm.

Sociedad de Plateros, C. San Francisco, 6 (tel. 47 00 42), between C. San Francisco and the top end of Pl. Potro. Big and bustling. Casual atmosphere, good food and drink have attracted visitors since 1872. Wide selection of *tapas* 150-200ptas. *Raciones* 300-600ptas, with fresh fish every day. Half-glass of wine 70ptas, beer 115ptas. Bar open 8am-4pm and 7pm-1am; meals served 1-4pm and 8pm-midnight. Others scattered throughout Córdoba, a few in the Judería.

Taberna Salinas, C. Tundidores, 3 (tel. 48 01 35), just south of the Ayuntamiento. A shining example of traditional Cordoban cooking: extraordinary *salmorejo,* fish, and an eye-popping spinach and garbanzo mash. Service a bit rushed, but the indoor patio setting and the fountain secure tranquility. Delectable *raciones* 600-700ptas. Desserts, such as the *natilla de la casa,* 250ptas. Half glass of wine 60ptas. Beer 100ptas. Open Mon.-Sat. 12:30-4:30pm and 8:30pm-midnight; during the winter Mon.-Sat. 12:30-4:30pm and 8pm-midnight.

Mesón de las Cabezas, C. Cabezas, 17 (tel. 47 83 56). Dark, musty, weird and wonderful. Great place to drink wine—not much else is served. Cheerful host, quiet patio fountain, and a surreal collection of decorations: bullfight posters, nude calendars, old metal signs, a stuffed owl and a boar's head. A nearby rooster crows all day long. Half-glass of wine 50ptas. Open Tues.-Sun. 11am-3pm and 7-11pm, but hours are as unpredictable as the tastes of the owner and patrons.

Mesón-Restaurante El Tablón, C. González, 75 (tel. 47 60 61). On the southern corner of the Mezquita. Slowish service and touristy atmosphere, but A/C makes the wait enjoyable. *Platos combinados* (750ptas) are big enough to fill a budgeting (or burgeoning) belly. Open noon-4pm and 7-11pm.

El Pincantón, C.F. Ruano, 19. Just a block east of the top of C. Judíos, the *menú* in this little room includes nothing above 225ptas. Specializing in *salsas picantes.* Huge *bocadillos* start at 110ptas. Beer 100ptas. Open Fri.-Wed. 10am-1:30pm and 6pm-midnight.

La Hostería de Laurel, C. Sevilla, 2 (tel. 47 30 40), 1 block west of Pl. Tendillas. Large, friendly bar with *tapas* (175-225ptas). Wine from local grapes and wall decorations from local deer. Room with pool table frequented some weeknights by English and Irish locals. Half-glass of wine 85ptas, liter 600ptas. Open Mon.-Sat. 8am-4pm and 8pm-midnight.

Bodega Guzmán, C. Judíos, 7, ½ block north of the Sinagogue (tel. 29 60 09). A wine cellar decorated with barrels, bullfight posters, and mosaics. Frequented by retired men who sit for hours, talking and drinking house wines. Hard-core *andaluz.* Beer 100-120ptas, half-glass of wine 80-120ptas. Reasonably priced *tapas* and *raciones.* Open Fri.-Wed. 11am-3pm and 8-11:30pm.

Bodega Taberna Rafaé, Deanes s/n, corner with C. Buen Pastor, two blocks north of the Mezquita. Abundant *raciones* (300-500ptas) and no-nonsense personnel make this an appealing place for a meal while visiting the Judería. A cheap option for afternoon wine: ½-glass is 75ptas, and prices decrease as volumes increase. Open Wed.-Sun. 10am-8pm.

SIGHTS

Begun in 784 under the reign of Abderramán on the site of a Visigothic basilica, the **Mezquita** was intended to surpass all other mosques in grandeur. Over the next two centuries the spectacular golden-brown building was gradually enlarged to cover an area equivalent to several city blocks—the largest mosque in the Islamic world of that time. The airy space is enclosed by a massive wall reinforced with thick, square towers. The 14th-century Mudejar door, **La Puerta del Perdón,** opens to the north. A high crenellated wall on the north side of the Mezquita encloses the fabulous **Patio de los Naranjos** (oranges), which is open to the public all day. Arcaded on three sides, the courtyard features carefully spaced orange trees, palm trees, and fountains. Inside, 850 pink and blue marble, alabaster, and stone columns—no two the same height—support hundreds of red-and-white-striped two-tiered arches. Caliphal vaulting, greatly influential in later Spanish architecture, appears for the first time in the **Capilla Villaviciosa,** in the center of which is the **Mihrab** (lighted central dome where the Koran was guarded), whose prayer arch faces Mecca. The intricate gold, pink, and blue marble Byzantine mosaics shimmering across its arches were given by the Emperor Constantine VII to the Córdoba caliphs.

When Córdoba was conquered by the Christians in 1236, the Mezquita was converted into a church. The **Capilla Mayor** (High Chapel) was enlarged in 1384 with the substitution of ogival elements for arches and columns. In 1523 more drastic alterations placed a full-blown Renaissance cathedral in the middle of the mosque. The odd hybrid disappointed even Carlos V, who had originally authorized it. "You have destroyed something unique to create something commonplace," he reportedly griped. You can survey the whole cathedral/mosque melange (along with the city's white houses and Indian-corn colored roofs) from the **torre,** which should be fully renovated and open to visitors by 1995. (Tel. 47 05 12; open April-Sept. 10am-7pm; Oct.-March 10am-1:30pm and 3:30-5:30pm. Admission 700ptas, ages 8-11 350ptas. Free during masses: weekdays 8:30-10am and Sun. 9:30am-1pm. Admittance and ticket sales stop twenty minutes before closing.)

Just west of the Mezquita and closer to the river lies the **Alcázar.** This palace for Catholic monarchs was constructed in 1328 during the campaign for the conquest of Granada; between 1490 and 1821 it served as headquarters for the Inquisition. Its walls surround a manicured hedge garden with flower beds, terraced goldfish ponds, multiple fountains, and palm trees. Inside, the museum displays 1st-century Roman mosaics and a 3rd-century Roman marble sarcophagus. (Tel. 42 01 51; open May-Sept. Tues.-Sat. 9:30am-1:30pm and 5-8pm, Sun. 9:30am-1pm; Oct.-April 9:30am-1:30pm and 4-7pm. Gardens illuminated May-Sept. 10pm-1am. Admission 300ptas, or 450ptas combined ticket to the Alcázar and the Museo Taurino. Admittance stops half an hour before closing time. Free Tues.) Although the building will be undergoing renovations until 1996, exhibitions are open to the public.

The **Museo Taurino y de Arte Cordobés,** at Pl. Maimonides, is dedicated to *la lidia*, with galleries full of the heads of bulls who killed matadors and other unfortunates. Some rooms are devoted to legendary Cordoban matadors, including Manolete. (Tel. 20 10 56; same hours and prices as the Alcázar.)

The **Torre de la Calahorra,** south of the Alcázar and down the Puente Romano across the river, is a museum offering a kitschy multi-media review of Córdoba's history. One room houses a large-scale, detailed model of the Mezquita in its pre-cathedral heyday. Headphones are available in four languages. (Tel. 29 39 29; open May-Sept. 10am-2pm and 5:30-8:30pm; Oct.-April 10am-6pm. Tower tour 350ptas; with multivision film, 500ptas.)

Tucked away on C. Judíos, 20, in one of the most beautiful areas of the Judería, the **Sinagoga** is a solemn reminder of the expulsion of Spanish Jewry in 1492. The temple is decorated with Mozarabic patterns and Hebrew inscriptions from the psalms. The statue of Maimonides on nearby C. Doctor Fleming, was used as the model for the New Israeli Shekel. (Tel. 20 29 28; open Tues.-Sat. 10am-2pm and 3:30-5:30pm, Sun. 10am-1:30pm. Admission 50ptas.) Half a block down C. Judíos and to the left sits **El Zoco,** a series of leather, ceramics, and silversmithing workshops within a beautiful courtyard. (Open Mon.-Fri. 10am-2:30pm and 4:30-8pm, Sat.-Sun. 10am-2pm.)

The **Museo Arqueológico** is on Pl. Paz, several blocks northeast of the Mezquita. Housed in a Renaissance mansion, the museum contains a chronological exhibit of tools, ceramics, statues, coins, jewelry, and sarcophagi, including intriguing stone carvings of lions that date from 500 BC. (Tel. 47 10 76; open mid June-mid Sept. Tues.-Sat. 10am-2pm and 6-8pm, Sun. 10am-1pm; mid Sept.-mid June Tues.-Sat. 10am-2pm and 5-7pm, Sun. 10am-1pm. Admission 250ptas. EU citizens free. Admittance stops 20 min. before closing time.)

The **Museo de Bellas Artes** in Pl. Potro now occupies the building that was King Fernando and Queen Isabel's Charity Hospital. Its small collection displays a couple of original Goya prints, an early 17th-century sculpture of a christ-child by Juan de Mesa y Velasco, and canvasses by Cordoban "primitives." (Tel. 47 33 45; open mid June-mid Sept. Tues.-Sat. 10am-2pm and 6-8pm, Sun. 10am-1pm; mid Sept.-mid June

Tues.-Sat. 10am-2pm and 5-7pm, Sun. 10am-1pm. Admission 250ptas.) Housed in the same building, the **Museo Julio Romero de Torres** exhibits the major works (all portraits of Cordoban women) of this native artist. (Tel. 49 19 09; open May-Sept., Tues.-Sat. 9:30am-1:30pm and 5-8pm, Sun. 9:30am-1:30pm; Oct.-April Tues.-Sat. 9:30am-1:30pm and 4-7pm, Sun. 9:30am-1:30pm. Free; admittance stops ½-hr. before closing time.) Facing the museums and also in the plaza is the **Posada del Potro,** a 14th-century inn mentioned in *Don Quixote*. It now contains the excellent collection of *guadameciles* formerly in the Museo Taurino. North of the Palacio del Marqués de Viana, in Pl. Capuchinos, is the **Cristo de los Faroles.** The plaza, one of the most famous religious shrines in Spain, is frequently the site of all-night vigils.

Townspeople take great pride in their traditional *patios,* many dating from Roman times. These open-air courtyards offer tranquil pockets of orange and lemon trees, flowers, and fountains in the old quarter of the city. **Calleja del Indiano,** off C. Fernández Ruano at Plaza Angel Torres, is distinguished for its beauty. The **Palacio del Marqués de Viana** on Pl. de Don Gome, 2, displays the quintessence of Cordoban courtyards with fourteen elegant structures. (Tel. 48 22 75; open June-Sept. daily 10am-2pm; Oct.-May Mon.-Sat. 10am-1pm and 4-6pm, Sun. 10am-2pm. Admission 200ptas, children 100ptas.)

ENTERTAINMENT

For some of the best **flamenco** in Spain, join the masses of tourists at the **Tablao Cardenal,** Cardenal Herrero, 14 (tel. 48 03 46), facing the Mezquita. Professionals dance passionately in an intense and intimate room. (Shows Tues.-Sat. at 10:30pm. 2500ptas, including one drink.) The tourist office keeps a schedule of **bullfights** at Los Califas bullring. (Prices range from 800 to 12,000ptas.)

For classical or traditional music, Córdoba's Municipal Orchestra gives Sunday morning **concerts** in the Alcázar. In the summer, the **Palacio de Viana** has frequent, free chamber music concerts on Fridays at 8:30pm. The city's open-air theater hosts concerts and festivals, including the irregularly scheduled **Festival Internacional de Guitarra** in June or July. For information and tickets stop by the F.P.M. Gran Teatro, Av. Gran Capitán, 3. (Tel. 48 02 37 or 48 06 44. Admission 400-1200ptas).

The **Filmoteca,** on C. Medina y Corella, 5, just west of the Mezquita, screens movies in their original language, with subtitles in Spanish. A beautiful old palace houses the Filmoteca, a *phoneteca* and a film library. (Tel. 48 18 35. Admission 150ptas, 10-show pass 1000ptas.)

During most of the year, Córdoba's youth frequent the pubs and clubs around the **Pl. Tendillas** at night. From the first weekend of June until the heat subsides, the **Brillante** area (uphill from and north of Av. América, or a 500-900pta cab ride) is the place to be: the Sierra is cool, the beer cold, and the prices not too high. The most recent additions to Córdoba's nightlife are the bars and *terrazas* in the new **Recinto Ferial,** along the riverside.

Of Córdoba's festivals, **Semana Santa,** with its floats and parades, is the biggest. But **May** is a never-ending party. During the **Festival de los Patios,** in the first two weeks of that month, the city erupts with classical music concerts, flamenco dances, and a city-wide decorated-*patio* contest (don't forget to ask the owners of your hostel how theirs ranked this year). Late May brings the week-long **Feria de Nuestra Señora de la Salud** (Fair of Our Lady of Good Health, commonly known as the *Feria*), for which thousands of Cordoban women don colorful, traditional apparel. A carnival, dozens of stands, dancing and drinking animate the crowds the whole week. In early September, Córdoba celebrates its patroness with the **Feria de Nuestra Señora de la Fuensanta.** The **Concurso Nacional de Arte Flamenco** (National Flamenco Contest) is held every third year during May.

■ NEAR CÓRDOBA

MEDINA AZAHARA

Built into the Sierra Morena by Abderramán III for his favorite wife, Azahara, this 10th-century *medina* was considered one of the greatest palaces of its time. The *medina* was divided into three terraces—for the palace, servants' living quarters, and an enclosed garden replete with almond groves, intended for the enjoyment of the prefered wife. Azahara had been born in Granada and missed the snow in the Sierra Nevada; when spring came, the almond groves turned white, reminding beloved Azahara of her beloved snow. The site, whose existence had been mere rumor until its discovery, was excavated in 1944. The **Salón de Abd al-Rahman III,** the grand hall on the lower terraces, is almost completely reconstructed to its original intricate and geometrical beauty. (Tel. 23 40 25; open May-Sept. Tues.-Sat. 10am-2pm and 6-8:30pm, Sun. 10am-2pm; Oct.-April Tues.-Sat. 10am-2pm and 4-6:30pm, Sun. 10am-2pm. Admission 250ptas, EU citizens free.)

Reaching Medina Azahara takes some effort; call ahead to make sure it's open. The O-1 bus (schedule information tel. 25 57 00, or see list in the tourist office) leaves from Av. Cervantes for Cruce Medina Azahara, stopping 3km from the site itself (about every hr. 6:30am-10:30pm, 90ptas). The walk from the bus is mostly uphill. A taxi costs about 600ptas one-way.

ALMODÓVAR DEL RÍO

Thirteen km from Córdoba on the rail line to Sevilla, the impenetrable **castillo** at Almodóvar del Río crowns a solitary, rocky mount, commanding views of the countryside and the whitewashed houses of the village spiral below. The castle is a remarkably well-preserved example of Mudejar architecture. On the second Sunday in May, the town celebrates the **Romería de la Virgen de Fátima** with a parade from Cuatro Caminos to Fuen Real Bajo roads. Frequent trains run to Almodóvar del Río from Córdoba (5 per day, last train back at around 11pm, 20min., 180ptas).

■■■ JAÉN

The hills near Spain's olive capital Jaén are covered by a checkerboard of olive trees, interspersed with barley hops and wheat fields. Surrounded by the Sierra Morena and Valdepeñas to the north, Sierras Segura and Zazorla to the east, and Sierras de Huelma and Noalejo to the south, this town named *Geen* (caravan route) by the Moors, became known as the "gateway to Andalucía." Today, Jaén (pop. 100,000) boasts an Universidad de Granada campus. Famous for its *chorizo* and *jamón,* Jaén produces *El Alcázar* beer, and continues to profit wildly from the olive oil business.

ORIENTATION AND PRACTICAL INFORMATION

Jaén lies a solitary 105km north of Granada and 57km southwest of Ubeda. The town center revolves around **Plaza de la Constitución. Calle Bernabé Soriano** leads uphill from the plaza to the cathedral and old town. **Paseo de la Estación** and **Avenida de Madrid,** the two main arteries which dominate the new quarter, wag downhill. From the bus station, turn right (uphill) on Av. Madrid, directly to Pl. Constitución. The Castillo de Santa Catalina presides over the town (3km vertical climb). From the cathedral, take **Maestra Madre,** then **Aldana,** then **San Lorenzo;** take a left when you reach the **Carretera de Circumvalación,** for it eventually turns into **Carretera al Castillo y Neveral** which leads to the castle.

Tourist Office: C. Arquitecto Berges, 1, after Pl. Batallas but before Pl. Constitución. From train station, walk uphill on Po. Estación and turn right on C. Arquitecto Berges. From the bus station, walk uphill and take the first right on C. Pio XII, which 2 bl. later becomes C. Arquitecto Berges. Staff is fluent in French and English, has boundless info, free maps, and brochures. Open Mon.-Fri. 8:15am-2:15pm; winter Mon.-Sat. 8:15am-2:45pm. After Sept. 1994, open more hrs.

Post Office: Pl. Jardinillos, s/n (tel. 22 01 12), west of Pl. Constitución. Open Mon.-Sat. 9am-2pm. **Postal Code:** 23071.

Telephone Code: 953.

Trains: Po. Estación, s/n, at the bottom of the slope. **RENFE** (tel. 27 02 02) has cut most southbound trains. To Madrid (2 per day, 4-5hr., 2160ptas) and Sevilla (1 per day, 1830ptas). For other points outside Andalucía, take Madrid-Sevilla line through Esperluy (3 per day, ½hr.). For other points in Andalucía, go via Estación Linares-Baeza, north and east of Jaén.

Buses: Pl. Coca de la Piñera (tel. 25 01 06). From Pl. Constitución go down Av. Madrid and take the third left; it's just off Pío XII. To: Ubeda (9 per day, 1½hr., 560ptas); Baeza (9 per day, 1hr., 450ptas); Granada (13 per day, 2hr., 925ptas); Málaga (4 per day, 4hr., 1800ptas).

Public Transportation: Although almost everything is within walking distance, a private company called **Urbanos** runs a local bus service from stops such as Pl. Batallas and Pl. Constitución (7am-11pm).

Taxis: Taxis gather at Pl. Coca de Piñera (tel. 25 10 26) in front of the bus station. A ride to the *castillo* is about 700ptas.

Pharmacy: ½ block downhill from Pl. Constitución on Po. Estación. Open 9:30am-2pm and 4:30-8pm.

Emergency: tel. 091.

Red Cross: C. Carmelo Torres, 1 (tel. 25 15 40).

Hospital: Hospital del S.A.S., Av. Ejército Español (tel. 22 24 08).

Police: tel. 26 18 50.

ACCOMMODATIONS AND FOOD

Budget accommodations in Jaén are few and far between (a couple cluster around Pl. Constitución), since there isn't usually a very high demand for rooms. Vegetarians have to make do with local olives and specialties like *ensalada de pimientos* (roasted sweet pepper salad). Try **Calle Nueva,** a pedestrian side street a half-block downhill from Pl. Constitución, for good food.

Hostal Carlos V, Av. Madrid, 4 (tel. 22 20 91), 2 doors down from a record store. Big, clean rooms with embroidered bedspreads. Baths in hall. Singles 2000ptas. Doubles 3000ptas.

Hostal Martín, C. Cuatro Torres, 5 (tel. 22 06 33), off Pl. Constitución. Big beds in slightly dark rooms. Blaring TV. Singles 2000ptas. Doubles 3000ptas.

Supermarket: Simago, C. San Clemente, 7-9 (tel. 26 31 02), on the 2nd floor of the department store on a street off of Pl. Constitución.

Café-Bar Ideal II, C. Arquitecto Berges, 8. Wood-paneling makes the place look darker than it actually is. Not the cheapest watering hole in town (mixed drinks 450ptas), but reasonable rotating *menú* (800ptas).

Freiduría Pitufos, C. Nueva, 2. Portions do not reflect the name *pitufo* (dwarf). Pictures of smurfs on the wall. *Platos combinados* of meat and fish (600-900ptas). *Churros* to turn Hefty's muscles to lard. *Caña* (dwarfish beer) 100ptas. Open 7am-midnight.

La Gamba del Oro, C. Nueva, 3 (tel. 26 16 13). Great bar and fresh seafood market. Savor a cold beer and ¼kg *calamares* for 500ptas. Open noon-4pm and 8:30pm-midnight.

SIGHTS

The **Museo Provincial** on Po. Estación, 29, north of Pl. Batallas, although hardly provincial, is certainly eclectic. Works range from prehistoric artifacts to expressionist paintings. The loot from a Tartessian necropolis includes the morbid *Sarcófago Paleocristiano de Martos*. (Open Tues.-Fri. 10am-2pm and 4-7pm, Sat.-Sun. 10am-2pm. Admission 100ptas or free with EU passport or student ID.)

   Palacio de Villadompardo, in Pl. Luisa Marillac, is a Renaissance edifice which houses the **arab baths** and a museum. The recently-restored 11th-century **hamman** (baths) are Spain's largest, though not as elaborate as the baths of Granada or Córdoba. The **Museo de Artes y Costumbres Populares** displays a multicultural bonanza of costumes from the world over. (Open Tues.-Fri. 10am-2pm and 4-7pm, Sat.-Sun. 10am-2pm. Admission 100ptas or free with EU passport or student ID.)

Catedral de Santa María, a few blocks southwest of Pl. Constitución, was built between 1492-1802. The spell-binding beauty of the *Imagen de Nuestro Padre Jesús* behind the altar is reputed to have saved it from destruction during the mass burning of churches at the beginning of this century. The **Museo de la Catedral** displays sculptures by Martínez Montañés and canvases by Alonso Cano. (Cathedral open 8:30am-1pm and 4:30-7pm. Museum open Sat.-Sun. 11am-1pm. Both free.)

Iglesia de la Magdalena and **Iglesia de San Juan** were both built on the foundations of mosques. They are in the northwest of the city, just east of the Ctra. Circunvalación. The *Cristo del bambú* of the **Monasterio de Santa Clara,** just west of the tourist office, near the Pl. Jardinillos, has been attributed to the School of Quito. (Ring the convent bell and a concierge will open the monastery.)

Jaén's most imposing and least accessible sight is the **Castillo de Santa Catalina,** a 3km climb from the center of town (for directions see Orientation). The former Arab fortress was recently restored and now houses a four-star *parador* (10,400ptas a night). (Open to the public Sun. 10am-2pm. Free.)

■ NEAR JAÉN

The idyllic towns of northern Andalucía are beautiful and relatively tourist-free. Numerous whitewashed villages and ruins dot the mountainous countryside to the east and south, outside *Let's Go's* turf. Quesada, 15km south of Cazorla, is a balm to the urbanite seeking blissful oblivion among Roman, Islamic, and Christian ruins. Orcera, less than 100km east of Ubeda, is a traditional highland village devoted to the wood trade. These scraps of Eden lie amid the national parks in the Sierras de Cazorla y Segura. A roving, albeit infrequent bus service makes these jaunts into day trips from Jaén, or even Granada and Córdoba.

UBEDA

On a ridge above the olivey Guadalquivir valley, Ubeda encloses narrow cobbled streets, ivied remnants of medieval walls, and a passel of old palaces and churches. A stop on the crucial trade route linking Castilla to Andalucía in the 16th century, the town fattened on the American gold shipped up from Sevilla. The resulting showpiece is one of the best preseved gems of the Spanish Renaissance, and one of the best preserved secrets in Spain.

Sights clutter around the **Plaza del Ayuntamiento** and the neighboring **Plaza Vázquez de Molina.** At the epicenter of historic Ubeda is the **Palacio de las Cadenas,** which now houses the Ayuntamiento, police, the **Museo Alfarería de Ubeda,** and a new pottery museum. (Open 8:30am-2:30pm. Museum open Tues.-Sat. 10:30am-2pm and 4:30-7pm, Sun. 10:30am-2pm. Admission 200ptas. Ubeda residents and groups of 15 or more 100ptas each. Students 25ptas.)

To the south of the Palacio de las Cadenas, at the wide end of Pl. Vázquez de Molina, is the Gothic **Iglesia de Santa María de los Reales Alcázares,** with chapels enclosed by grilles wrought by maestro Bartolomé. (Currently being restored.) Just as impressive is the contemporaneous **Iglesia de San Pablo,** on Pl. 1 de Mayo, with its Plateresque, concave southern portal. The magnificent chapels within are embellished with intricate wrought-iron grilles. (Open 9am-1pm and 7-9pm. Free.)

Carlos V commissioned an enormous palace here, but when the architect died (shortly after finishing the plans) construction fell to his lackey, Vandelvira, a developer of the Spanish Renaissance style. The result is a characteristically severe, monumental profile. Only the **Sacra Capilla del Salvador,** at the narrow end of the square, and the main facade remain. (Chapel open 5-7pm. If the front door is closed, go around the side and ring the sacristy bell.)

The town is centered around **Plaza de Andalucía;** the old town and the Pl. Ayuntamiento lie to the east; the newer section, including the bus station, lies to the west. To reach Pl. Andalucía from the bus station, walk a block right (downhill).

Take a left on **Avenida Cristo Rey,** which turns into **Calle Obispo Cobos** and **Calle Mesones** and heads right into Pl. Andalucía. To reach C. Ramón y Cajal, walk two bl. left (uphill) to **Avenida Ciudad de Linares,** then two blocks right to a treacherous six-way intersection. C. Ramón y Cajal is the second road on the left.

Practical Information The **tourist office** in Pl. Ayuntamiento, next to the police, is a jackpot—oodles of multilingual maps and brochures. (Open Mon.-Fri. 8:15am-2:15pm). The **post office,** on C. Trinidad, 4 (tel. 75 00 31), opens for mail and **telegrams** Mon.-Fri. 8:30am-2:30pm, Sat. 9am-1:30pm. The **postal code** is 23400. **Telephones** are on C. San José, across from the bus station. (Open 10am-2pm and 4-7pm.) The **telephone code** is 953. **Luggage storage:** 300ptas per day in the bus station lockers. The **pharmacy,** Isabel Liñán de la Hoz, C. Ramón y Cajal, 16 (tel. 75 06 72), opens Mon.-Fri. 9am-2pm, Sat. 10:30am-1pm. The **Hospital San Juan de la Cruz** has emergency medical services across the street from pharmacy; hospital itself is on Carretera Linares (tel. 79 71 00). **Red Cross** answers tel. 75 56 40. **Police** can be reached at tel. 75 00 23. **Emergency,** tel. 091.

There's no **train** service to Ubeda; the nearest station is **Estación Linares-Baeza** (tel. 65 02 02), 40min. northwest by bus. **Buses,** C. San José, s/n (tel. 75 21 57) travel to: Baeza (6 per day, 15min., 100ptas); Linares station (6 per day, 40min., 180ptas); Jaén (8 per day, 1½hr., 485ptas); Córdoba (3 per day, 2½hr., 1160ptas); Sevilla (3 per day, 5hr., 2275ptas).

Accommodations and Food Budget accommodations and food can be found along **Calle Ramón y Cajal.** Lodgings are often out of the way. The roster of regional specialties include *andrajos* (a soup made with ground chickpeas) and *pipirrana* (a sauté of tomato, green pepper, onion, egg, and tuna salad). The **market** is down C. San Fernando from Pl. Andalucía. (Open Mon.-Sat. 8am-2:30pm.) **Hostal Victoria,** C. Alaminos, 5, 2nd fl. (tel. 75 29 52), is the best deal in town. Rooms are new, have TVs, A/C (500ptas extra), and private baths. (Singles 1900ptas. Doubles 3000ptas. Visa, MC accepted.) **Hostal Sevilla,** C. Ramón y Cajal, 9 (tel. 75 06 12), has decent-sized rooms, and a large TV lounge set up theatre-style. (Singles 1800ptas. Doubles with bath 3400ptas.) A reasonably priced *cafetería* is just next door.

BAEZA

Called Biatia by Romans and Bayyasa by Arabs, this town reached its highest splendor as Baeza, during the Spanish Renaissance (16th and 17th centuries). Modern-day Baeza has a noteworthy monument on practically every street corner. Backpackers are rare and services accessible and affordable.

Most sights lie on the hill northeast of **Plaza del Pópulo.** If a monument is closed, ask in the tourist office and the Ayuntamiento may open it. To find monuments, and to stumble upon death-defying views, just wander around. In the heart of the city, north of Pl. Constitución, is the **Palacio de Jabalquinto,** now the Seminario. Somewhere on the ornate Plateresque facade and sober patio are written the names of its graduates, along with a caricature of an unpopular professor, in bull's blood. Across from the Palacio, poet Antonio Machado taught French at the **Universidad** (founded in 1595 and disbanded in the 19th century). The amphitheater bears a fine Mudejar ceiling. (Open 9am-2pm.)

The **Ayuntamiento,** formerly the town jail and court, is pierced with magnificent Plateresque windows. Other Renaissance structures line the Cuesta de San Felipe on its way to the soaring, brightly-colored **catedral,** whose interior was remodelled by Vandelvira. The **Iglesia de San Andrés,** faced with a Plateresque portal, houses Gothic paintings in its **sacristía.** The glint of gold in the cathedral's *retablo* is blinding from the **Plaza de la Fuente de Santa María**— named for its 16th-century fountain. (Church open 10am-2pm and 5-7pm. Free, but 100ptas donation requested.)

The **tourist office,** Pl. Pópulo, s/n (tel. 74 04 44), hands out free maps and brochures. English is spoken. (Open Mon.-Fri. 9am-2:30pm. More hrs. after Oct. 1994.)

The **post office** is on C. Julio Burell, 19 (tel. 74 08 39). The **postal code** is 23440. The **telephone code** is 953. A **pharmacy** is on C. Julio Burell, 41 (tel. 74 03 93; open 9:30am-1:30pm and 5-8pm). The **hospital,** Centro de Salud Comarcal is on Av. Alcalde Puche Pardo, s/n (tel. 74 09 17). **Police,** on C. Cardenal Benavides, 7, answer tel. 74 06 59.

Accommodations and restaurants are scarce—but then, so are tourists. All of Baeza congregates on **Paseo de la Constitución** in the evenings to take refreshment. **Hostal Residencia Comercio,** C. San Pablo, 21 (tel. 74 01 00), furnishes large, attractive rooms with fin-de-siècle antiques. Poet Antonio Machado snored here in 1912—and it looks as if it hasn't been painted since. (Singles with shower 1300ptas, with bath 1500ptas. Doubles with bath 3000ptas.) The patio of **Pensión el Patio,** C. Romanones, 13 (tel. 74 02 00), serves as a comfortable lounge for guests with over-stuffed chairs and sofas. (Singles with shower 1500ptas. Doubles 2500ptas, with shower 3000ptas, with bath 3500ptas.) **Las Vegas Bar,** C. Portales Tunidores, 1 (tel. 74 00 87), deals big sanwiches (225-275ptas) and *caña y caracoles* (beer and snails, 125ptas). (Open 8:15am-1am.)

Trains leave **Estación Linares-Baeza** (tel. 65 02 02), 8km from town on the road to Madrid. **Buses** run from Av. Alcalde Puche Pardo, 1 (tel. 74 04 68), at the uphill end of C. San Pablo, in the north of the city. To get to the station, walk north on Po. Constitución to Pl. España. C. San Pablo leads north out of the plaza. To: Ubeda (6 per day, 15min., 100ptas); Jaén (9 per day, 1hr., 450ptas). To reach most other major cities, switch in either Jaén or Ubeda.

CAZORLA

Cazorla is a typical, lovely *pueblecito blanco* (very small whitewashed town), with three main squares all within shouting distance of each other. It's too small even for sights, although two ancient castles stand like forlorn sentinels within hiking distance of town.

Why, you ask, is Cazorla in this book?

The **Parque Natural de las Sierras de Segura y Cazorla,** which covers 214,000 hectares of protected mountains and waterways and, almost like Scarborough Fair, is scented with Mediterranean flora—lavender, rosemary, and thyme. The mighty Río Guadalquivir—Andalucía's lifeline—wells up here. Hunting, fishing, and camping are permitted in designated areas, and hiking along marked paths. An impressive variety of animal species makes for an interesting ecosystem. For more info on the park, storm its office at **Oficina del Parque Natural,** C. Martínez Falero, 11 (tel. 72 01 25), the white building with green trim a few blocks uphill from Pl. Constitución. (Open daily 11am-2pm and 5-7pm.) **Buses** run to Cotorios **camping,** in the middle of the park. (Mon.-Sat. 2 per day, 7:30am and 2:30pm, 1½hr., 225ptas.)

The town of Cazorla is small and manageable. Buses arrive at the main square, **Plaza de la Constitución,** from which **Plaza de Corredera** lies (if you face the peaks) to the right, and **Plaza del Mercado** behind and downhill. Although Cazorla has no tourist office, a private tour guide company named **Quercus,** C. Juan Domingo, 2 (tel. 72 01 15), associated with the Forestry Department, provides tourist information free from its second-floor office in Pl. Constitución. (Open 10am-2pm and 5-8pm.) They also sell detailed maps of Cazorla and the Parque Natural (400ptas) and topographic maps (1200ptas). The **post office** is at C. Mariano Extremera, 2 (tel. 72 02 61), behind the Ayuntamiento in Pl. Corredera. The **postal code** is 23470; the **telephone code** 953. There's a **pharmacy** at Pl. Corredera, 17 (tel. 72 00 09), to the right after entering the square. (Open 9am-2pm and 5-8pm.) The nearest **hospital** is Centro de Salud, Av. Ximenez de Rada, 1 (tel. 72 10 61), a few km away. The **police** are in Pl. Corredera (tel. 72 01 81).

Hostal Betis, Pl. Corredera, s/n (tel. 72 05 40), has vast rooms with good views of the mountains. (Single 1200ptas. Doubles range from 2000-2200ptas.) The owner also runs a *comedor* for guests (*menú* 750-900ptas). **La Estrella,** Tercia, 8 (tel. 72 02 08), offers comfortable rooms at a reasonable price. (Doubles 2300ptas.) *Tapas* bars and cafeterias rule on Pl. Corredera and Pl. Constitución. A fresh fruit and veggie **market** resides in Pl. Mercado. (Open Mon.-Sat. 8am-2pm.) Sorry, no cheap restaurants in town.

The easiest way to Cazorla is by **bus** from Ubeda (3 per day, 1¼hr., 710ptas); Jaén (3 per day, 2¼hr.); or Granada (2 per day, 4hr.).

■■■ GRANADA

When ruler Boabdil was fleeing beautiful Granada, the last Muslim stronghold in Spain, he cast a longing look back, for which he was reproached by his mother: "Weep like a woman for what you could not defend like a man." Though he lost Granada, Granada never lost Boabdil. The last hill he passed through is still called the Cuesta de Lágrimas (hill of tears), a rock on which he reclined the Suspiro del Moro (the sigh of the Moor), and the gate he locked remains closed to this day. Granada, *"ay, mi Granada,"* as poet Lorca repeated, casts a spell on all who pass through. Placido Domingo's rendition of Enrique de Lara's "Granada" evokes the essense of that Arab past. Even throughout all of Spain, where remnants of Mudejar architecture are ubiquitous, where an Arab influence is arresting, Granada and its glorious Alhambra stand out.

After it was conquered by the Moors in 711, the town blossomed into one of Europe's wealthiest and most refined cities. Granada's rulers took increasing precautions as the Christians fought back, adding layer upon layer of fortifications. In the 15th century, however, Granada was surrounded and besieged by Fernado and Isabel's troops, at a time when the ruling Sultan Moulay Abdul Hassan was experiencing troubles of his own. He was so in love with a concubine named Zoraya that he ignored civic duty and began publicly repudiating his wife. When Aïcha (the queen) caught on, she drummed up local support, had him deposed, and thrust her young son Boabdil on the throne. Fernando and Isabel took advantage of the disarray and defeated Boabdil, winning the city.

Though Christians burned mosques and most of the lower city, covering and converting others to Christian churches, the Arab quality was impossible to eliminate entirely. Spain's most famous attraction, the spectacular palatial fortress known as the Alhambra, built by the Moors at the brilliant pinnacle of their culture and civilization, was abandoned for hundreds of years until its rediscovery in the 19th century. The Albaycín, a maze of Moorish houses and twisting alleys, is Spain's best-preserved Arab settlement and the only part of the Muslim city that survived the Reconquista intact. More recently it was the center of Granada's Republican resistance during the Civil War. Nearby, footpaths in the Gypsy Quarter wind up to cactus-dotted caves atop the hill of Sacromonte. The top of the hill has scattered ruins of the Muslim city walls.

ORIENTATION AND PRACTICAL INFORMATION

The center of Granada is **Plaza Nueva,** framed by handsome Renaissance buildings and outfitted with a wide variety of hotels and restaurants. Pl. Nueva sits just north of **Plaza de Isabel la Católica,** which is at the intersection of the two main arteries, **Calle Reyes Católicos** and **Gran Vía de Colón.** A few blocks south of that, **Puerta Real** is the five-way intersection of C. Reyes Católicos, C. Recogidas, C. Mesones, C. Acera de Darro, and C. Angel Ganivet.

The Alhambra is on a steep hill north of the city. To get there, take C. Cuesta de Gomérez, a side street off Pl. Nueva, up-up-up hill. Or take bus #2 from Pl. Isabel Católica. The Alhambra is on your left.

From RENFE and all bus stations except Alsina Graells, follow Av. Constitución to Gran Vía de Colón, turn right and walk the 15-20 minutes into town. From the Alsina Graells bus station, turn right on Camino de Ronda and left three full blocks later at the gas station onto C. Recogidas, which becomes C. Reyes Católicos at Puerta Real. It's a schlep.

Municipal **buses** (see Public Transportation) cover nearly all areas of town. Bus #11 connects a number of major streets, including Carretera de Madrid, the train

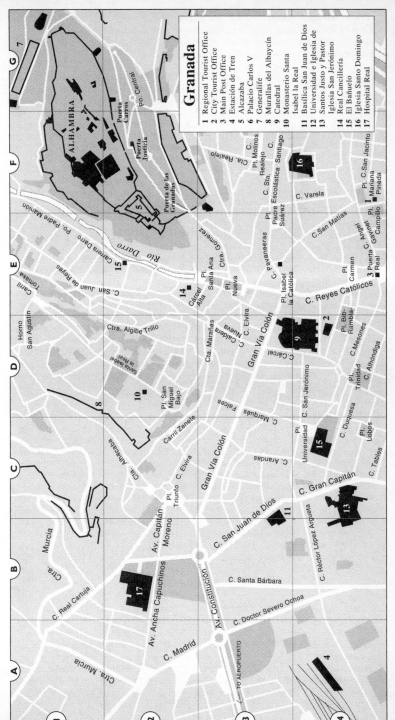

Granada

1 Regional Tourist Office
2 City Tourist Office
3 Main Post Office
4 Estación de Tren
5 Alcazaba
6 Palacio Carlos V
7 Generalife
8 Murallas del Albaycín
9 Catedral
10 Monasterio Santa
   Isabel la Real
11 Basílica San Juan de Dios
12 Universidad e Iglesia de
   Santos Justo y Pastor
13 Iglesia San Jerónimo
14 Real Cancillería
15 El Bañuelo
16 Iglesia Santo Domingo
17 Hospital Real

and bus stations, and the town center. Since the Alhambra, Albaycín, and Sacromonte hills are all near each other and the town center, the best way to explore is on foot. If solo, avoid the small streets at the foot of the Albaycín northeast of Pl. Nueva after dark.

Tourist Office: Pl. Mariana Pineda, 10 (tel. 22 66 88). From Puerta Real turn right onto Angel-Gavinet, and then the 3rd right again. The office is in the Patronato bulding. Helpful staff speaks English, French, and German, and has tons of brochures and photocopies on Granada, city and province (free posters are yours for the taking). Ask for a map of the Alhambra and the Albaycín since the palace complex itself does not provide one. Open Mon.-Fri. 9am-2pm and 4:30-7pm, Sat. 10am-1pm. **Branch Office:** C. Mariana Pineda, s/n (tel. 22 59 90). From Puerta Real, take C. Reyes Católicos to Pl. Carmen. C. Mariana Pineda is the 1st street on the left. Inside the plaza, in the Coral del Carbon building. Maps and list of accommodations readily available. Open Mon.-Fri. 10am-8pm, Sat. 10am-2pm.

Budget Travel: Viajes TIVE, C. Martínez Campo, 21 (tel. 25 02 11), off C. Recogidos. BIJ tickets and assorted information. Open Mon.-Fri. 9am-1pm (they are open 1-2pm for information, but not sales).

Currency Exchange: Look for the **banks** all along Gran Vía, and compare rates. **Hipercor supermarket,** C. Arabial, has poor rates but long hours. Open Mon.-Sat. 9am-9:30pm.

American Express: Viajes Bonal, Av. Constitución, 19 (tel. 27 63 12), at the north end of Gran Vía de Colón. Entrance on side street, C. María Luisa de Dios. If you're a cardholder, you can buy traveler's checks with personal checks. 1% commission on changing AmEx traveler's checks; worse rates than many banks. Cardholder mail held for 3-6 months. Open Mon.-Fri. 9:30am-1:30pm and 5-8pm, Sat. 10am-1pm.

Post Office: Puerta Real, s/n (tel. 22 48 35; fax (58) 22 36 41), on the corner between Acera de Darro and C. Recogidos. Open for stamps and Lista de Correos Mon.-Fri. 8am-9pm, Sat. 9am-2pm; for **telegrams** Mon.-Fri. 8am-9pm, Sat. 9am-6pm. **Faxes** also sent and received. **Postal Code:** 18080.

Telephones: C. Reyes Católicos, 55, 1 bl. towards Pl. Nueva from Pl. Isabel la Católica, on corner of C. Abenhamar. Open Mon.-Sat. 9am-2pm and 5-10pm. **Telephone Code:** 958.

Flights: (tel. 44 70 81), 17km west of the city. Salidas bus (tel. 13 13 09) shuttles there from Pl. Isabel la Católica (2 per day, Sun. 1 per day, 300ptas). Call them or ask tourist office for departure times. Taxi to the airport about 1800ptas. **Iberia,** Pl. Isabel la Católica, 2 (tel. 22 75 92). Open Mon.-Fri. 9am-1:45pm and 4-7pm. To Madrid (2 per day, 45min., 12,650ptas) and Barcelona (2 per day, Sun. 1 per day, 1¼hr., 18,050ptas).

Trains: RENFE Station, Av. Andaluces, s/n (tel. 27 12 72). From Pl. Isabel la Católica, follow Gran Vía de Colón to the end, then bear left on Av. Constitución. Turn left on Av. Andaluces. RENFE is at the end of the street. To Madrid (2 per day, 6-8hr., 3400-5200ptas); Barcelona (2 per day, 14hr., 6500ptas); Algeciras (3 per day, 5hr., 1595ptas); Almería (3 per day, 3hr., 1065ptas.); Cádiz (3 per day, 6hr., 2100ptas); Ronda (3 per day, 3¼hr., 1065ptas). The **RENFE office** for information and ticket sales is on C. Reyes Católicos, 63 (tel. 22 71 70).

Buses: For the time being, the various companies are scattered throughout the southwestern quarter of the city. However, the rumor around town is that the Ayuntamiento is building an all-encompassing mother-bus station.

Alsina Graells, Camino de Ronda, 97 (tel. 25 13 58). From Puerto Real, walk all the way down to C. Recogidas (prepare to huff and puff); turn right on Camino de Ronda Or take #11 bus from the cathedral and save yourself the lung-ache. To: Algeciras (2 per day, 5hr., 2235ptas); Antequera (4 per day, 2hr., 805ptas); Cádiz (2 per day, 6½hr., 3310ptas); Córdoba (7 per day, 3hr., 1475-1605ptas); Jaén (12 per day, 1¾hr., 800ptas); La Linea (2 per day, 5hr., 2180ptas); Málaga (14 per day, 2hr., 1045ptas); Sevilla (8 per day, 4½hr., 2110-2505ptas).

Bacoma, Av. Andaluces, 12 (tel. 28 42 51), off Av. Constitución. To: Alicante (5 per day, 7hr., 3090ptas); Valencia (5 per day, 9hr., 4500ptas); Barcelona (4 per day, 14hr., 7290ptas).

Autedía, C. Rector Martín Ocete, 10 (tel. 28 05 92). To: Almería (2 per day, 3½hr., 1000ptas); Baeza (9 per day, 2¼hr., 875ptas).

Autocares Bonal, Av. Constitución, 34 (tel. 27 31 00). Tickets sold only between 8:30-9am at Ventarillo Bar. To: Veleta in the Sierra Nevada (round-trip departs at 9am, returns at 5pm, 1hr., 610ptas). Departs from Palacio de Congresos on Po. Violón.

Enatcar: Av. Andaluces, 12 (tel. 28 42 51). To Madrid (4 per day, 5½hr., 2550-3750ptas).

Public Transportation: Municipal buses (85ptas, book of 10 tickets 550ptas). The buses you will grow to love are: #2 (8am-10pm, every 20min.) from Acero Darro to Pl. Isabel La Católica to La Alhambra; #4 (7:15am-11pm, every 20min.) from Camino de Ronda to C. Recogidas, C. Reyes Católicos, and Gran Vía de Colón; #11 (7:25am-10:50pm, every 10min.) from Fuente de las Batallas to Camino de Ronda, Gran Vía de Colón, and Pl. Isabel La Católica. Stops are practically on every other block and can't be missed.

Ridesharing: Mitzfahrzentrale, C. Elvira, 85 (tel. 29 29 20), off Pl. Nueva. An unofficial agency that helps arrange rides. Give them at least 2 days' notice. Open Mon.-Fri. 11am-1pm and 5-7pm.

Hitchhiking: The tourist office has information on buses to places where some people sometimes supposedly allegedly conceivably maybe possibly hitch. *Let's Go* does not recommend hitchhiking as a safe means of travel.

Taxis: tel. 28 06 54, 15 14 61, or 20 14 61.

Car Rental: Atesa, Pl. Cuchilleros, 1 (tel. 22 40 04). Cheapest car 2950ptas per day, plus 25ptas per km and 970ptas for insurance. Must be at least 21.

Luggage Storage: At the **train station** (200ptas). At the Alsina Graells **bus station** (300ptas).

English Bookstore: Librería Urbano, C. Tablas, 6 (tel. 25 29 09), off Pl. Trinidad. Decent selection of literature and fiction, plus some guidebooks. Open Mon.-Fri. 9:30am-2:30pm and 4:30-9:30pm, Sat. 9:30am-2:30pm.

Laundromat: Lavandería Autoservicio Emperatriz Eugenia, C. Emperatriz Eugenia, 26 (tel. 27 88 20). Exit Alsina Graells bus station to the left and turn at the first right. Wash 300ptas and dry 200ptas per load. Open Mon.-Sat. 9am-2pm and 4-8pm, Sat. 9am-2pm.

Women's Services: Servicio Sociales, C. Lepanto (tel. 24 81 65), in the Ayuntamiento off Pl. Carmen. Open Mon.-Fri. 8am-2pm.

Swimming Pool: Piscina Neptuno (tel. 25 10 67), next to flamenco club Jardines Neptuno, near the intersection of C. Recogidas and Camino de Ronda. Adults 600ptas, children 300ptas. Open June-Sept. 11am-7:30pm.

Red Cross: C. Escorianza, 8 (tel. 22 22 22, 22 20 24, or 22 21 66).

Pharmacy: Farmacia Nuña González, Camino de Ronda, 83 (tel. 25 48 43), down 1 full bl. from Alsina Graells bus station. Exit bus station to the right. Open 9:30am-12:30pm and 5-8pm. For late-night pharmacies, check listings in any local paper or on signs posted in pharmacies.

Medical Services: Clínica de San Cecilio, C. Doctor Oloriz, 16 (tel. 28 02 00), on the road to Jaén.

Police: Municipal, C. Duquesa, 21 (tel. 092). **Guardia Civil,** Av. Puliana Pol. Almanjayar, s/n (tel. 25 11 00). **Policía Nacional,** Pl. Campos (tel. 091). English and French theoretically spoken.

ACCOMMODATIONS AND CAMPING

Granada has more cheap accommodations than shoe stores. Lodgings pose a problem only during Semana Santa. During this week, definitely call ahead.

Albergue Juvenil Granada (HI), Ramón y Cajal, 2 (27 26 38; fax 28 52 85). From Alsina Graells station, walk down Camino de Ronda for about 15min., take the right fork to the end, then turn down a gravel road and walk through the tall peach and gray gate. Or take the #11 bus from the center. The hostel is the new peach building across the field on the left. Freshly renovated in 1994. Rooms are all doubles with baths (with heat lamps), except six singles with handicapped access. Tiny windows and winter heating. No curfew. 1007ptas per person; over 26 1488ptas. Non-members: 1488ptas; 2500ptas.

In the Alhambra

Pensión Doña Lupe, Av. Generalife, s/n (tel. 22 14 73). From Pl. Nueva, turn right onto Cuesta de Gomérez and walk up and up. Keep walking up (or take the #2 bus from Pl. Nueva, Pl. Isabel la Católica, or Puerta Real). Very close to the Alhambra, but far from everything else. English spoken. It's not fancy, but it's cheap and they'll always find a spot for you—even if its in a room with 6 other people. Rooms all have baths, a few have TVs. Not new or sparkling clean, but there *is* a pool on the roof. Calling ahead would be wise. 900ptas per person in shared room. Singles 1000ptas. Doubles 1950ptas. Includes free continental breakfast. Brand new **annex,** on Cuesta de Escoriaza, is more central, and should have its own pool by 1995. Make all reservations and arrangements through Doña Lupe, and bring your own sheets and sleeping bag for firm, new bunkbeds. Doubles 1400ptas. Shower included.

Along Cuesta de Gomérez

Hostales blanket **Cuesta de Gomérez,** the street that leads uphill to the Alhambra, near Pl. Nueva. Crashing in this area is especially wise for those who plan to spend time at the Alhambra Complex. To reach Cuesta de Gomérez from Pl. Isabel Católicos, pass Telefónica and the RENFE office on the left, and look for Hostal Residencia Britz's huge vertical sign on the right.

Hostal Navarro-Ramos, Cuesta de Gomérez, 21 (tel. 25 05 55). Ring the buzzer to be let in by a rope/pulley home invention. Quarters are comfortable and cool in the evening. Terraces are a great place to eat pastries and spy on the Alhambra-bound passers-by below. Singles 1200ptas. Doubles 1900ptas, with bath 2900ptas. Triples with bath 3900ptas.

Hostal Austria, Cuesta de Gomérez, 4 (tel. 22 70 75). Wow. Remodeled last year. If there had been dust, it wouldn't have had time to settle. Funky tiles and glass everywhere. All rooms have baths and 8-ft windows. The place sparkles. Singles 1500-2000ptas. Doubles 2500-3000ptas.

Hostal Residencia Britz, Cuesta de Gomérez, 1 (tel. 22 36 52). On the corner of Pl. Nueva. Sister *hostal* to Lisboa in Pl. Carmen—you've seen one, you've seen them both, which is by no means a bad thing. Large rooms, sturdy wooden furniture. Friendly management. Rad soft-drink machine in the lobby says *"Gracias."* Singles 2120ptas. Doubles 3286ptas, with bath 4505ptas. 6% discount for *Let's Go* readers, but you've got to show them the book or no deal. Visa, MC accepted.

Huéspedes Gomérez, Cuesta de Gomérez, 2 (tel. 22 63 98). Spacious rooms with balconies have seen better days. Singles 1300ptas. Doubles 2200ptas. Triples 3300ptas.

Near the Cathedral/Near University

Scoring a room in this quadrant of Granada won't put you any closer to train or bus stations, but if you're looking to park it near the cathedral or Puerta Real, these places are your ticket. The *hostales* concentrated around C. Mesones are usually inhabited during the school year, but free up during the summer.

Hostal Mesones, C. Mesones, 44 (tel. 26 32 44). Flowery curtains and bedspreads, perfumey smell, and flora in the stairwell. Rooms all have winter heating, hot water, and balconies. Singles 1500ptas. Doubles 2500ptas.

Huéspedes Romero, C. Sillería de Mesona, 1 (tel. 26 60 79). From Puerta Real, follow C. Mesones into Pl. Trinidad. C. Sillería is on the right. Each room is unique. Large double beds and tiled floors. Quiet with lots of light. Singles 1300ptas. Doubles 2500ptas.

Hostal-Residencia Lisboa, Pl. Carmen, 29 (tel. 22 14 13). Take C. Reyes Católicos from Pl. Isabel Católica; Pl. Carmen is on the left. Luxurious forest-green tiled baths. Rooms well-furnished and stocked with phones and fans. Prices for *Let's*

Go users: Singles 2120ptas, with bath 3286ptas. Doubles 3233ptas, with bath 4346ptas. Reduced rates only if you flash the book.

Hostal Residencia Zacatín, C. Ermita, 11 (tel. 22 11 55). Not new, but rooms are good-sized and baths immense. Singles 1300ptas, with bath 2100ptas. Doubles 2500ptas, with shower 3000ptas, with bath 3600ptas.

Hostal Plaza Isabel, C. Colcha, 13 (tel. 22 30 22). Above Bar La Viña. From Pl. Isabel la Católica, C. Colcha is first side street on the right. It's got the basics. Clean and pretty cheap. Singles 1500ptas. Doubles 2300ptas.

Off Calle San Juan de Dios

This area is the closest to the train station. From the station, head straight along Av. Andaluces, turn right onto Av. Constitución, then right onto C. San Juan de Dios (10min.). Although the neighborhood is generally safe, this is the seediest area that we list.

Hostal Residencia San Joaquín, C. Mano de Hierro, 14 (tel. 28 28 79), 5th street on the left off C. San Juan de Dios. Paths to rooms are labyrinths of tiles, mosaics, and steps. The beautiful rooms have double beds, baths, and TVs. Three patios covered with flowers. 1700ptas per person. Lunch or dinner with a tub of wine 800ptas.

Hostal las Cumbres, C. Cardenal Mendoza, 4 (tel. 29 12 22), the 3rd left off C. San Juan de Dios. A bit expensive, but pretty and clean. Squeaky clean bathroom. Winter heating. Singles 2000ptas. Doubles 3000ptas.

Along Gran Vía de Colón

The Gran Vía de Colón is the main throughfare that links Pl. Isabel la Católica with Av. Constitución. Building facades are lost behind colorful plastic signs. Many of these *hostales* house students during the school year and are open for visitors July-September.

Hostal los Montes, C. Arteaga, 3 (tel. 27 79 30). Going down Gran Vía de Colón from Pl. Isabel la Católica, it's on the 8th street on your right. Very, very quiet. High cathedral ceilings. TV room. Singles 1300ptas. Doubles 2300ptas. Bath down the hall.

Hostal Gran Vía, Gran Vía de Colón, 17 (tel. 27 92 12), about 4 bl. from Pl. Isabel la Católica. Siamese cats standing guard and apparently hold the entire place to feline standards of cleanliness. Rooms looking onto Gran Vía are more noisy than those in the back. The usual TV room. Singles 1500ptas, with shower 1800ptas. Doubles 2500ptas, with shower 2800ptas, with bath 3500ptas.

Hostal-Residencia Londres, Gran Vía de Colón, 29 (tel. 27 80 34). Further down on the same side of the street as Hostal Gran Vía. Big terrace with views of the Albaycín and the Alhambra. London was never this exciting. Many students live here during the school year. Singles 1500ptas. Doubles 2500ptas.

Camping

Buses serve four campgrounds within 5km of Granada; check the departure schedules at the tourist office. Ask bus drivers to alert you to approaching stops.

Sierra Nevada, Av. Madrid, 107 (tel. 15 09 54). Take #3 or 5 bus. Lots of shady trees, modern facilities, and free hot showers. If the town fair is here stay elsewhere, or forget about REM sleep. 460ptas per person, per tent and per car. Youngsters 360ptas. Also a hotel (doubles with bath 5300ptas).

María Eugenia, Ctra. Nacional, 342 (tel. 20 06 06), at km 292, on the road to Málaga. Take Santa Fé or Chachina bus from the train station. 385ptas per person, per tent, and per car. Kiddies 275ptas.

Los Alamos (tel. 20 84 79), next door to María Eugenia at km 290. Same buses. 350ptas per person, per tent, and per car. Offspring 300ptas. Open April-Oct.

G
R
A
N
A
D
A

Reina Isabel, Ctra. Granada at km 4 (tel. 59 00 41). 400ptas per person, per tent, and per car. Kids 300ptas. Open March-Oct. Shuttle bus running between Granada and La Zubia leaves from Pasillo del Salón (75ptas).

FOOD

Seafood, seafood, sea-feud! As in the rest of Andalucía, the accent is on fresh (usually fried) fish. *Tapas* rule. Most of Granada hits the bars on **Campo del Príncipe** (several blocks south of Pl. Nueva) late in the evening. Ice cream fans head to popular **La Veneciana** (commonly called "Los Italianos"), Gran Vía, 4 (150-450ptas). The **market** overflows from Pl. Romanilla beside the cathedral, until the architectural dig at the usual spot on C. San Augustín is done. (Open Mon.-Sat. 8am-3pm.)

Tortilla Sacromonte is an omelette composed of calf brains, ham, shrimp, and numerous green vegetables. Other *platos típicos* include *sesos a la romana* (batter-fried calves' brains) and *rabo de toro* (bulls' tail).

Groceries: C. Ribera del Genil, s/n, next to Galerías Preciados. Open Mon.-Sat. 9:30am-1:30pm and 5-8:30pm.

Near Plaza Nueva

Central, but no bargain bin of restaurants. Casual family-type joints offer a good selection of bars and *comedores* (dining areas). Explore the little alleys around the plaza and check out the bars **Makeba** and **La Taberna del Irlandés** near Placeta de San Gil.

Restaurante Alcaicería, C. Oficios, 6 (tel. 22 43 41). One of the most highly regarded eateries in town, spills into the little side street. Enter through the vine-covered archway and follow the sounds of the guitar. *Menú* 1450ptas. Roast or grilled chicken 850ptas. Open 1-4pm and 8-11:30pm.

Rincón de Pepe, Escudo de Carmen, 17 (tel. 22 07 63), off Pl. Carmen. Unassuming facade hides good food and better prices. *Menú* 525-975ptas. Savory *pollo ajillo* (chicken in garlic sauce) 475ptas. Open noon-4pm and 7:30-11pm.

La Nueva Bodega, C. Cetti-Meriem, 3 (tel. 22 59 34), on a small side street parallel to C. Reyes Católicos and 1 bl. toward town from Pl. Nueva. Dining room and bar, separated by wrought-iron partition. Charming local flavor. *Caña* (small beer) 125ptas. Tangy *menús* 725-1000ptas. Eminently munchable *bocadillos* around 350ptas. Prices much lower at the bar. Open noon-midnight.

Restaurante León, C. Pan, 3 (tel. 22 51 43), on a small side street parallel to C. Reyes Católicos and 1 bl. toward town from Pl. Nueva. The kind of place where you want to settle in for a while. Meals start at 750ptas, sky's the limit. *Chuleta de cerdo* (pork chop) 675ptas. Open late-July to mid-June Thurs.-Tues. 1-4pm and 7:30-11pm. *Tapas* at bar Thurs.-Tues. 12:30-4pm and 7-11pm.

Cafetería Lisboa, C. Reyes Católicos, near Pl. Nueva. Enter on an empty stomach and you'll never want to leave. Delicious pastries (200ptas) and coffee.

Elsewhere

El Ladrillo, Placeta de Fátima (tel. 29 15 65) off C. Pagés in the Albaycín. Follow the main street from the foot of the Albaycín to the top of the hill (15min.). Thunderous evening hangout. Whopping rations of delicious fresh seafood. Mountainous *barco* (a platter of diverse fried fish for 2) 1200ptas. Open 1-4pm and 8pm-midnight.

Restaurante Pizzería Lago di Como, Campo de Principe, 8 (tel. 22 61 54). Upstairs, downstairs, and a terrace. Pizzas and pasta start at 500ptas. Bottle of *vino de la casa* (house wine) a bargain at 550ptas. Home delivery. Open 1-3pm and 9pm-midnight.

Pulcinella Trattoria, Dr. Martín Lagos, 3 (tel. 25 52 60), at the corner of C. Frailes, off C. Recogidas. Blaring classical music and dapper waiters. Copious Italian menu and food *para llevar* (to go). Open 1:30-4pm and 8pm-midnight.

Las Girasoles, C. San Juan de Dios, 24 (tel. 29 34 10), on the corner with Cardenal Mandoza. Dull interior, unbeatable prices and hours. Wall of mirrors gives the illusion of a large dull interior. *Menú* 600ptas. Lasagna 700ptas. Open 7am-midnight.

SIGHTS

The Alhambra Complex

The **Alhambra** (tel. 22 75 27) is both the name for the hill that dominates Granada and the sprawling palace-fortress atop it. From the Arabic for "red," it refers to the clay extracted from the hill used for building. Enter the Alhambra through Puerta de Granada, off Cuesta de Gomérez, and climb to the well-marked main entrance. Some monuments are closed to the public and viewing time is limited. Ask for a map at the tourist office before coming. (Alhambra open Mon.-Sat. 9am-7:45pm, Sun. 9am-5:45pm; Oct.-May daily 9am-5:45pm. Admission 600ptas, Sun. after 3pm free. Separate 650pta ticket required for illuminated nighttime admission: Tues., Thurs., and Sat. 10pm-midnight; winter Sat. 8-10pm. Daytime admission to Generalife only, 150ptas. Box office shuts down about 45min. before closing time.)

The Alcazaba

Against the silvery backdrop of the Sierra Nevada, the Christians drove the first Nazarite King Alhamar from the Albaycín to this more strategic hill. Here he built a fortress called the Alcazaba, the oldest section of today's Alhambra.

In the Alcazaba, the **Torre de la Vela** (watchtower) has the finest view of Granada and the Sierra Nevada. The bells of the tower were rung to warn of impending danger and to control irrigation phases. The Alcazaba was once a separate palace with its own entrance; its massive battlements were later transformed into a guard house and palace garrison. Napoleon stationed his troops here, but before leaving he blew up enough of the place to ensure the end of the palace's reign as an effective military outpost. Exit through the **Puerta del Vino** (wine gate), where inhabitants of the Alhambra once bought tax-free wine.

The Alcázar

The next addition to the Alhambra, the Alcázar (Royal Palace), was built for the great Moorish rulers Yusuf I (1333-1354) and Mohammed V (1354-1391). Legend has it that an unexplained force murdered Yusuf I in an isolated basement chamber of the Alcázar, so his son Mohammed V was left to complete the palace.

The entrance is east of the Patio de Machuca, leading into the **Mexuar,** a great pillared council chamber. This area was demolished after an explosion in a nearby gunpowder mill. The Mexuar opens onto the Patio del Cuarto Dorado (Patio of the Gilded Hall). Off the north side of the patio, foliated horseshoe archways of successively diminishing width open onto the **Cuarto Dorado** (Gilded Hall) itself, decorated by Carlos V in Mudejar style. Its opulent starry wooden ceiling is inlaid with ivory and mother-of-pearl.

To the east lies the **Patio de los Arrayanes** (Courtyard of Myrtles), a wide open space with a bubbling fountain at either end. Also at either end, the palace shows an elaborately carved wood facade, the 14th-century **Fachada de Serallo.** The long and slender **Sala de la Barca** (Boat Gallery), with a boat-hull ceiling, flanks the north side of the courtyard.

Adjoining the Sala de la Barca to the north, the **Sala de los Embajadores** (Hall of Ambassadors) is where King Fernando and Christopher Columbus discussed the route to India. This perfectly square hall is one of the most magnificent rooms in the palace, every surface intricately wrought with inscriptions and ornamental patterns and topped by an incredible carved wooden dome. On the ground floor of the **Torre de Comares,** it's interrupted by enormous, rounded windows that offer views in all directions.

East of the Patio de los Arrayanes, the Galería de los Mozardos leads to the **Patio de los Leones** (Courtyard of the Lions), the most photographed swatch of the palace and once the center of the sultan's domestic life. The grandeur continues: a symmetrical arcade of horseshoe arches and white marble columns borders this courtyard, while a fountain supported by 12 marble lions tinkles in the middle.

At the far end of the courtyard, the **Sala de los Reyes** (Hall of the Kings) shelters the sultan's bed. South of the courtyard, in the **Galería de Abencerrajes,** Sultan Moulay Abdul Hassan piled the heads of the sons of his first wife (16 of them) so that Boabdil, son of his second, could inherit the throne. The (metaphorically) blood-stained room has another doozy of a ceiling. On the north side of the courtyard, the resplendent **Sala de las Dos Hermanas** was named for twin marble slabs embedded in its floor. It also has a staggering honeycomb dome made of thousands of tiny cells. From here a secluded portico overlooks the Jardines de Daraxa.

Passing the room where Washington Irving resided, a balustraded courtyard leads to the 14th-century **Baños Reales** (Royal Baths), the center of court social life. Light shining through star-shaped holes in the ceiling once refracted through steam to create indoor rainbows.

Torres and Gardens

Just outside the east wall of the Alcázar, in the **Jardines del Partal,** lily-studded pools drip beside terraces of roses shadowed by the soaring **Torre de las Damas** (Ladies' Tower). And this is just the beginning: the area between the Alcazaba and El Generalife is one garden and tower after another. They had towers for everything and everyone: *Infantas* (crown pricesses), *Cautivas* (captives), etc. The gardens are floral masterpeices and would merit a visit even if possibly the most magnificent sight in Spain was not on the premises.

The Palacio de Carlos V

After the Christian Reconquista drove the Moors from Spain, Fernando and Isabel respectfully restored the Alcázar. Little did they know, two generations later omnipotent Emperor Carlos V would demolish part of it to make way for his Palacio de Carlos V, a Renaissance masterpiece by Pedro Machuca (a disciple of Michelangelo).

Although glaringly incongruous amidst all the Moorish splendor, experts seem to agree that the Palacio is one of the most beautiful Renaissance buildings in Spain. Ringed with two stories of Doric colonnades, it's Machuca's only surviving effort. Inside, a **museum** of Hispano-Arabic art contains the only original furnishing from the Alhambra, a spectacular vase.

Upstairs there is the **Museo de Bellas Artes,** which contains some religious sculpture and paintings from the 16th to the 18th century. (Both open Mon.-Sat. 10am-2pm. Admission 250ptas.)

El Generalife

Up the hill past the Alhambra's main entrance and through **Callejón de los Cipreses** and the shady **Callejón de las Adelfas** is the lush palace greenery of the Generalife, the spacious summer retreat of the Sultans that crowns the Alhambra's twin hill, *el cerro del sol* (the sun hill). Aben Walid Ismail designed El Generalife in 1318. The two buildings converse across the **Patio de la Acequia** (Courtyard of the Irrigation Channel), embellished with a narrow pool fed by fountains forming an aqueous archway. Canals, fountains, and water jets criss-cross the lovely gardens.

The Cathedral Quarter

Back down from heaven, in the town proper, is the **Capilla Real** (Royal Chapel), Fernando and Isabel's private chapel. During their prosperous reign, they funneled almost one-quarter of the royal income to the chapel's construction. The rich Gothic carvings and gilded floral ornaments attest that they weren't ripped off.

Inside, the cool gray marble figures of the 16th-century **royal mausoleums** repose behind an elaborate screen. The figures of Fernando and Isabel recline to the right; beside them sleep their daughter Juana la Loca (the Mad) and her husband Felipe el Hermoso (the Fair). The tombs lie in the crypt directly below, accessible by a small stairway on either side. To the horror of the rest of the royal family, Juana insisted on keeping the body of her husband with her for an unpleasantly long time after he died. Friends had a hard time convincing the insanely jealous wife that Felipe was actually dead. After they pried him from her arms, the remains of his body were laid to rest here. This ghoulish story possibly inspired Faulkner's story "A Rose for Emily."

The highlight of the chapel, Queen Isabel's private **colección de arte,** is exhibited next door in the sacristy. The collection favors Flemish and German masterpieces of the 15th century, especially the exquisite Memling, Bouts, and Roger van der Weyden. The glittering **alhajas reales** (royal jewels) shine in the middle of the sacristy: the queen's golden crown, scepter, and jewelry box, and the king's sword. (Open 10:30am-1pm and 4-7pm; Oct.-Feb. 10:30am-1pm and 3:30-6pm. Admission 200ptas, Sun. morning free.)

The adjacent **catedral** dwarfs the Capilla Real. The first purely Renaissance cathedral in Spain boasts massive Corinthian pillars supporting an astonishingly high vaulted nave. Its frosty whiteness gives it the look of an overexposed snapshot. You can adjust the lighting with coin-operated electric switches beside each chapel. Admission also good for the cathedral's **tesoro** and **museo.** (Open 10:30am-1pm and 4-7pm; Oct.-Feb. 10:30am-1pm and 3:30-6pm. Admission 200ptas.)

The 16th-century **Hospital Real** is divided into four tiled courtyards. Above the landing of the main staircase, the Mudejar coffered ceiling echoes those of the Alhambra. Nearby rise the twin spires of **Basílica de San Juan de Dios,** a very Baroque temple. The 14th-century **Monasterio de San Jerónimo** is just around the corner; badly damaged by Napoleon's troops, it has recovered admirably. (All three are at the end of C. San Juan de Dios. *Monasterio* open 10:30am-1pm and 4-7pm; Oct.-Feb. 10:30am-1pm and 3:30-6pm. *Basílica* open 8:30-10am and 6:30-8:30pm. Hospital open Mon.-Fri. 8am-3pm. Free.)

The Albaycín

Don't miss the Albaycín, the old Arab quarter, where the Moors built their first fortress. After the Reconquista, a small Moorish population clung to the neighborhood on this hill until their expulsion in the 17th century. Ask for the tourist office map before you come. Be cautious here at night.

The best way to explore the maze is to proceed along C. Darro off Pl. Nueva, climb up Cuesta del Chapiz on the left, then wander aimlessly through Muslim ramparts, cisterns, and gates. On Pl. Nueva, the 16th-century **Real Cancillería** (or Audiencia) was the Christians' Ayuntamiento. The arcaded patio and stalactite ceiling are notable. Behind the Plateresque facade of Casa Castril is the **Museo Arqueológico,** C. Darro, 41, with funerary urns, coins, Classical sculpture, Carthaginian alabaster vases, Muslim lamps, and ceramics. (Open 10am-2pm.)

Cármenes—traditional whitewashed Arab villas with luxurious walled gardens— characterize the neighborhood. Bus #12 travels from beside the cathedral to C. Pagés, at the top of the Albaycín. From here, walk down C. Agua through the **Puerta Arabe,** an old gate to the city at Pl. Larga. The terrace adjacent to **Iglesia de San Nicolás** affords the city's best view of the Alhambra, especially in winter when glistening snow covers the Sierra Nevada. To the west of San Nicolás, **Monasterio de Santa Isabel la Real,** founded by Queen Isabel in 1501, is a domed church with an exceptional coffered ceiling and Plateresque Gothic facade.

ENTERTAINMENT

Entertainment listings are near the back of the daily paper, the *Ideal* (90ptas), under the heading *Cine y Espectáculos.* The Friday supplement lists even more bars, concerts, and special events. The tourist office distributes a monthly culture guide. Discos tend to be overpriced and unpopular.

Avoid the **Cuevas Gitanas de Sacromonte** (gypsy caves). Once home to a thriving Gypsy community, the hill is now just a snare for gullible tourists.

The Albaycín is a great place to start. Exclusive **Casa de Yanguas,** on C. San Buenaventura off Cuesta del Chapiz, with terraces, balconies, and even a rotating art exhibit surrounding its 15th-century Moorish patio, competes with **Carmen de**

Aben Humeya, off Pl. San Nicolás, for the title of Most Romantic Bar in Spain. (Drinks at both start at 600ptas.) **Casa Arabe,** also in the Albaycín off C. Pages, is nothing to sneeze at. If you want to discuss China's economic future, try **Restaurante-Bar Poetas Andaluces II,** C. Pedro A. Alarcán, 43 (tel. 26 30 50).

Granada's **Corpus Christi** celebrations, processions, and bullfights are well-known. The **Internacional Festival de Música y Danza** (mid-June to early July) sponsors open-air performances of classical music and ballet amid towering shrubbery in the gardens of the Alhambra's Generalife. Prices for seats run 2000-7500ptas. Some performances are free, however. This refined culture bit has also taken over the new **Auditorio Manuel de Falla** (tel. 22 00 22), one of Spain's premier concert halls. Cheaper seats for most performances are available from Edificio Hermanitas de los Pobres, Gran Capitán, 24, Granada 18002 (tel. 20 68 47). Their office is at C. Gracia, 21 (tel. 26 74 42). Travel agencies can also hook you up for a small fee.

■ NEAR GRANADA: LA CARTUJA AND FUENTEVAQUEROS

On the outskirts of Granada stands **La Cartuja,** a 16th-century Gothic Carthusian monastery. A marble with rich brown tones and swirling forms (a stone unique to nearby Lanjarón) marks the sacristy of Saint Bruno. To reach the monastery, take **bus** #8 (85ptas) from in front of the cathedral. (Open 10:30am-1pm and 4-7pm; Oct.-Feb. 10:30am-1pm and 3:30-6pm.)

Author of *Bodas de sangre* (Blood Weddings) and *Romancero Gitano* (Gypsy Ballads), poet and playwright Federico García Lorca was born outside of town in tiny **Fuentevaqueros,** near the airport. The ancestral house-*cum*-**museo** has photographs, manuscripts, and even some sketches by the great poet-and dramatist, who was shot by right-wing forces near Granada at the outbreak of the Civil War. The museum is a psychoanalyst's dream—García Lorca spent his formative years there—but few others can get that excited about a place where he lived only nine years. (Open to 15 people; every ½hr. Tues.-Sun. 10am-1pm and 6-8pm; Oct.-March Tues.-Sun. 10am-1pm and 4-6pm; April-June Tues.-Sat. 10am-1pm and 5-7pm. Admission 100ptas.) **Buses** (150ptas) run to the house from the train station almost every hour.

■■■ SIERRA NEVADA

The peaks of Mulhacén (3481m) and Veleta (3470m), the highest mountains of the Sierra Nevada (Snowy Range) and of all Spain, sparkle with snow and groan with tourists most of the year. The most popular approach to the Sierra Nevada is the highway from Granada to Veleta. The alternative is the southern approach through the Alpujarras. The first option is quick and easy; the second time-consuming and circuitous, but more rewarding. Sierra Nevada is currently expanding its ski facilities to accommodate the 1995 Alpine Ski Championships.

Librería Estudios, C. Mesones, 53 (tel. 26 74 08), in Granada, sells a detailed but pricey 4-part map of the Sierra Nevada printed by the Dirección General del Instituto Geográfico Nacional (1400ptas). (Open Mon.-Fri. 10am-1:30pm and 5-8:30pm.)

Before you go, call to check on **road and snow conditions** (tel. 48 01 53 in Spanish and English) as well as hotel vacancies. Bring warm clothes.

VELETA

Near the foot of Granada's Alhambra, the highest road in Europe begins its ascent to one of the highest peaks. The road starts as a normal everyday *camino* through the arid countryside, then climbs the face of the Sierra wall. Due to snow, the very top of Veleta is driveable only in August and September.

The **Autocares Bonal Bus** (tel. 27 31 00) from Granada to the top of Veleta is a fantastic bargain (9am, round-trip 590ptas). Buy tickets in the bar El Ventorrillo, next to Palacio de Congresos. (See Granada: Practical Information: Buses for details.) The bus runs only up to the resort community of **Prado Llano** (19km from the peak), stopping at a **cabina-restaurante.** From mid-June on, the road is clear up to an altitude of at least 2700m, leaving a snowy, treacherous, three-hour hike to the top. The bus driver sometimes will drive to the top if a few people request it (extra 200ptas charge). The bus stops for four hours before the return (at 5pm, 1hr.). Those bored by hiking after the first five minutes shouldn't attempt this excursion, as there's no escape other than the return bus.

During ski season (Nov. to mid-May), a network of **ski lifts** operates from the cabin-restaurant to the peak of Veleta and several intermediate points (all-day lift ticket 3000-6000ptas). **Ski rentals** are in the Gondola Building and in Pl. Prado Llano. This is the brightest and southernmost ski resort in Europe—wear sunscreen or suffer DNA mutations. The entire resort of Prado Llano closes in summer. Check **weather conditions** through Federación Andaluza de Esquí, Po. Ronda, 78 (tel. 25 07 06) or through the station on the mountain (tel. 44 91 00). The cheapest of the area's accommodations is the lodge **Albergue Universitario,** Peñones de San Francisco (tel. 48 01 22; mandatory *pensión completa* 3500ptas; reserve early in winter).

When the snow has melted, peak-shaded **Capileira** in the southern valley of the Alpujarras is hikeable. The walk is a good 25km among rock-strewn meadows with wild goats and birds behind every boulder. Even in summer, the wind is severe and temperatures drop considerably at night.

LAS ALPUJARRAS

The small white houses of the poor, secluded Alpujarra villages huddle together on the southern slopes of the Sierra Nevada. Settled by mountain Berbers in the Middle Ages, they are of an architectural style found only here and in the Algerian and Moroccan Atlas. The beauty of these settlements is due to their isolation; until the '50s, travel there was possible only by foot or mule. Even industry was aesthetic— silkworms love the climate of the Alpujarra, and villagers used to spin the silk in-house. Now, they send cocoons directly to Almería and Granada. Local gastronomic specialties include *sopa alpujarreña* (broth with eggs, croutons, and ham) and *plato alpujarreño* (ham, fries, eggs, sausages, and salad).

Even by **bus** you should plan on at least a two-day trip. The Estación Alsina Graells in Granada, Av. Constitución, 19, runs buses to all the major villages; to reach the most elevated—such as Pampaneira, Bubión, Capileira, Portugos, and Trevélez— take the Murtas bus (2 per day, noon and 5pm). Plan for a night in the mountains; the single return bus to Granada leaves early the next morning. From July to September, **Viajes Ecomar** (tel. 22 30 91) organizes a Sunday excursion from 9am to 8pm (3500ptas, midday meal included). Reservations are required. Unfortunately, this is the only form of public transportation between the villages. The locals, aware of the transportation problem, often sympathize with hitchers. *Let's Go* does not recommend hitchhiking as a safe means of travel.

Lanjarón

Lanjarón is famed throughout Spain for its mineral water, gulped by the gallon throughout Andalucía. Spaniards used to flock to the village to cure themselves of kidney ailments and rheumatism. A town of 4200 people and 23 hotels, not-so-secluded Lanjarón is close to the highway connecting Granada to the coast. If you're stuck here overnight, try **Hotel El Sol,** Av. Generalísimo, 32 (tel. 77 01 30), which has firm beds, marble floors, winter heating, and phones in all rooms. (Singles with bath 3700ptas. Doubles with bath 7400ptas.) If driving, take the left-hand turn just before Orjiva. If taking the **bus** to Ugijar via the main highway, you'll have to disembark here to take advantage of the tourist route.

Pampaneira

As the road winds in serpentine curves up to Pampaneira, the lowest of the Alpujarras villages (1059m), the scenery suddenly becomes dramatic. **Casa Alfonso,** José

Antonio, 1 (tel. 76 30 02), is the best place to stay. The large, clean rooms—all doubles, 3300ptas—are kept warm in winter by knit quilts and central heating.

Capileira

Three km up the road lies the wonderful village of Capileira, a good base for exploring the region and the closest thing to a tourist center in the Alpujarras. Jagged, cobbled alleys wind up the slope amid ivy and chirping birds; on either side, the peaks loom above while the valley plummets below. You can enjoy the latter vista from your bedroom window at **Mesón-Hostal Poqueira,** C. Dr. Castillo, 6 (tel. 76 30 48), with fresh, wainscoted rooms, all with bath and winter heating. (Doubles 3500ptas. Breakfast included.)

The road through Capileira continues up the mountainside. By June, the road may be clear enough to make the two-hour climb to **Mulhacén,** Spain's highest peak. Proceed with extreme caution when approaching the summit; the wind is gusty, the snow slippery, and the drop to the other side unpleasantly murderous. To reach the trail, follow the signs marked "Sierra Nevada"; the well-marked fork for the road to Mulhacén branches to the right after 20km. The hike from Capileira down to the **gorge** is also scary. There's no clearly marked trail and at times the going is rough. For the most comfortable (and indirect) route, take the road to Bubión and the path from there to Pampaneira (3 times faster than the road).

Trevélez

The highway stops at the township of Trevélez (1476m), continental Spain's highest community, renowned for its cured ham. Covens of witches used to cast spells in this village; supposedly there is a direct correlation between the number of witches in an Alpujarran village and its altitude above sea level. For a wonderful view of the village, cross the stone bridge over the Río Chico de Trevélez and continue along the opposite side of the gorge. On the road into town, clean and modern **Hostal Mulhacén,** Ctra. Ugijar, s/n (tel. 85 85 87). Spacious rooms and terrace with a view of the valley. (Doubles 5000ptas. Good meals reasonably priced.) **Camping Trevélez** (tel. 76 50 75), Ctra. Trevélez-Orgiva, km 1, is open year-round with a bar, restaurant, and lots of shade. (Adults 400ptas, children 300ptas.)

On June 13, Trevélez celebrates the **Fiesta de San António** with a costumed dramatization of the Moorish-Christian conflict. Skilled actors on horseback make their horses rear up and neigh.

Yegen, Laroles, and Ugijar

On a mountaintop outside Berchules, **Yegen** is the world's most scenic playground, and offers a nameless cheap *pensión.* Thereafter, the road forks to the larger agricultural villages of **Laroles** to the north and **Ugijar** to the south. In Ugijar on the road to Almería rests **Pensión Vidaña,** Ctra. Almería, s/n (tel. 76 70 10). (Doubles 2800ptas.) Odysseus supposedly stopped in Ugijar one day to patch up his ships. Although it's far from the sea, he picked this village becauseof the river bed's reputed gold content. If you're driving, this eastern portion of the Alpujarras is most directly accessible via the somewhat dilapidated highway originating in the village of Lacalahorra.

■■■ MÁLAGA

Hanging from the mountains and pierced by the river Guadalmedina, Málaga's Mediterranean lustre has caused many a local and visitor to wax poetic. Yet this second largest city in Andalucía (pop. 50,000), celebrated by Hans Christian Andersen, Rubén Darío, and native poet Vicente Aleixandre, has recently lost some of its gleam. The temptation to bypass the aluminum cans, dirtiness, and auspicious shop signs reading *'se alquila'* (for rent), shines bright when the Costa del Sol is just around the corner. Málaga is the transportation hub of Andalucía, and its residents some of the most lively, genial people you are likely to meet.

Industrial Málaga divides the Costa del Sol in two. To the northeast, the hills dip straight into the ocean. Here the scenery is less spoiled, but beaches are usually rocky. To the southeast, the coast is more built up and water washes almost entirely against concrete. However, even industrialization and urbanization cannot take away the coast's major attraction: abundant sun that makes for eight months of spring and four of summer per year.

ORIENTATION AND PRACTICAL INFORMATION

To see the city at its best, stroll the length of the palmy **Paseo del Parque;** it'll take you below the **Alcazaba,** the local Moorish palace. Po. Parque turns into **Alameda Principal** just east of the **Plaza de la Marina.** The city center, containing most sights and the cathedral, is north of Alameda Principal. The Río Guadalmedina flows north-south through the town.

Tourist Office: Pasaje de Chinitas, 4 (tel. 221 34 45), off Pl. Constitución. Enter through Pasaje Chinitas (under Hotel Residencia Chinita's big yellow sign) and take the 1st right; at the corner with C. Nicasio Calle. Curiously supplies more information on other parts of Spain than on Málaga. English spoken. Open Mon.-Fri. 9am-2pm, Sat. 9am-1pm.

El Corte Inglés: Av. Andalucía, 4-6, (tel. 230 00 00), across from the post office and next to Barclay's Bank. **Map,** map, map. **Currency exchange:** No charge. Free. *Gratis.* They abolished their commission policy last year. **Supermarket.** *The* place for compact discs, health and beauty aids, English language books, tobacco, telephones, clothes—you name it. Watch for big sales. **Telephones** every 50 ft. all over town, and here, too. Open Mon.-Sat. 10am-9pm (9:30pm during summer months).

Budget Travel: Viajes TIVE, C. Huéscar, 2 (tel. 227 84 13), next to El Corte Inglés. Books, international plane, train, and bus tickets. ISIC 500ptas. HI card 1800ptas. Open Mon.-Fri. 9am-1pm. Reservations only from 1-2pm.

Consulates: See Spain Essentials: Embassies and Consulates.

Currency Exchange: 24-hr. ATM machine: Banco Zaragozano, Pl. Marina, 3 (tel. 222 79 06), on the corner of Pl. Marina and C. Molina Lario. If you've got a Cirrus, Plus, Visa, MC (or any number of cards indigenous to Europe), you're in business.

American Express: Viajes Alhambra, C. Especerias, 10 (tel. 222 22 99; fax 221 46 36), near C. Nueva. 2% commission on cash. Mail held 1 yr. for card holders. Accepts wired money. Open Mon.-Fri. 9am-1:30pm and 5-8pm, Sat. 9am-2pm.

Post Office: Av. Andalucía, 1 (tel. 235 90 08), a tall building just over the bridge (Puente Tetuán), running over a dry river, from the city center. Open for stamps and Lista de Correos Mon.-Fri. 8am-9pm, Sat. 9am-7pm. For **telegrams** Mon.-Fri. 9am-9pm, Sat. 9am-3pm. **Postal Code:** 29070.

Telephones: Telefónica, C. Molina Lario, 11, next to the cathedral. Open Mon.-Sat. 9am-9pm, Sun. (and holidays) 10am-2pm. **Telephone Code:** 95, recently changed from 952.

Airport: (tel. 224 00 00). From the airport, wait for bus #19 (at the "City Bus" sign). The bus leaves the airport every ½hr. on the hr. (6:50am-midnight, 115ptas) and stops at the bus station and the corner of C. Molina Lario and Postizo Abades. The RENFE train is cheaper (100ptas) and quicker (12min. to get to Málaga; 7:15am-11:45pm). **Iberia,** C. Molina Larios, 13 (tel. 221 82 04; national reservations (901) 33 31 11, international reservations (901) 33 32 22). Open Mon.-Fri. 9am-1:15pm and 4:30-7:15pm.

Trains: Estación de Málaga (tel. 231 25 00). To get to the station, hop on bus #3 at Po. Parque or bus #4 at Pl. Marina. **RENFE** (office for reservations and information), C. Strachan, 4 (tel. 260 23 66 or 236 02 02), is less crowded, and more convenient for getting tickets and information. Open Mon.-Fri. 9am-1:30pm and 4:30-7:30pm. To: Fuengirola (30 per day, ¾hr., 260ptas); Torremolinos (30 per day, ½hr., 125ptas); Córdoba (3 per day, 3hr., 1700ptas); Valencia (3 per day, 8hr., 5100ptas); Barcelona (3 per day, 14hr., 6400ptas); Valladolid (2 per day; 9hr., 5300ptas); Bilbao (2 per day, 13hr., 6300ptas); Madrid (2 per day, 7-10hr.,

MÁLAGA

4200ptas); Baeza (2 per day, 4½hr., 2500ptas). Prices and hours are for RENFE's slower and cheaper trains.

Buses: Po. Tilos, s/n, (tel. 235 00 61), one block north of RENFE station. To: Fuengirola (10 per day, ½hr., 270ptas); Algeciras (4 per day, 1¾hr., 1190ptas); Marbella (8 per day, 1hr., 505ptas); Madrid (4 per day, 7hr., 2680ptas); Barcelona (4 per day, 16hr., 8340ptas); Valencia (5 per day, 11hr., 5500ptas); Murcia (5 per day, 2hr., 3555ptas); Alicante (5 per day, 8hr., 4140ptas); Granada (12 per day, 2hr., 1100ptas); Córdoba (4 per day, 3½hr., 1350ptas); Sevilla (6 per day, 3hr., 2100ptas).

Horse-and-Buggy: On the corner of C. Molina Larios and the Alameda Principal. Don't bother. You'll be scammed—a 4000-5000pta ride.

Taxis: Tele-Taxi (tel. 233 64 00). From Pedregalejos to town center 400-700ptas. From town center to airport 1100ptas.

Luggage Storage: Lockers at the **train station,** 300ptas per day. Open 7am-10:45pm. At the **bus station,** 300ptas per day. Open 6:30am-11pm.

Outdoor/Camping Equipment: Colonel Tapioca Viajes y Aventuras, C. Antonio Baena Gomez, 6 (tel. 221 32 13). Everything the forgetful (or adventurous) traveler needs, including "emergency food pills." Open Mon.-Fri. 10am-1:30pm and 5-8:30pm, Sat. 10:45am-1:45pm. Visa, MC, Eurocard accepted.

Women's Services: Centro Asesor de la Mujer, C. Carretería, s/n (tel. 221 93 39), the street off Po. Sta. Isabel near the bridge. Open Mon.-Fri. 9am-2pm.

Crisis Lines: Fundación de Ayuda Contra la Drogadicción (tel. (900) 16 15 15).

Red Cross: tel. 225 04 50.

Pharmacy: Farmacia y Laboratorio Laza, C. Molina Lario, 2 (tel. 222 75 97), close to the cathedral. Clinics capable of blood, water, hormonal, immunological, and biochemical analyses. Open Mon.-Fri. 9:30am-1:30pm and 5-8:30pm, Sat. 10:30am-1:30pm. Analyses clinics open Mon.-Fri. 9-11am.

Medical Assistance: tel. 222 44 00. **First Aid:** tel. 229 03 40 or 222 64 98.

Emergency: tel. 091, 092, or 062.

Police: tel. 231 71 00.

ACCOMMODATIONS AND CAMPING

Málaga's affordable rooms tend to look somewhat run-down. *Pensión* owners often frequent the train station in hopes of enticing travelers to rent. If the price seems high (over 1600ptas for a single), straighten your spine and bargain like crazy. When asked about room prices, hostel *dueños* in Málaga rarely—if ever—give a direct answer. Lodging rates are approved by the city *ayuntamientos,* so while many hostels are willing to let their rooms for fewer *pesetas,* they are not permitted to post discounts. Finally, when approaching reception desks, scrub up. Some *pensión* owners will turn away shady-looking potential guests. With this in mind, head toward **Avenida de las Américas, Plaza de la Constitución,** or **Calle Córdoba** for a good night's rest. Many budget establishments cluster north of **Paseo del Parque** and **Alameda Principal.** Be particularly wary of the following neighborhoods after dark: **Alameda de Colón, El Perchel** (streets NW of C. Cuarteles), **Cruz de Molnillo,** streets around **market,** and **La Esperanza/Santo Domingo** (north of El Corte Inglés).

Hostal La Palma, C. Martínez, 7 (tel. 222 67 72), off C. Marqués de Larios. 30-sec. walk from McDonald's. Owned by a mother and her two daughters. Big bathroom. Ceiling fans. Singles 1500-1800ptas. Doubles 2500-2800ptas. Triples 3300-3600ptas. Quads 4400-4800ptas.

Hostal Residencia Larios, C. Marqués de Larios, 9, 3rd fl. (tel. 222 54 90). Near Pl. Marina and C. Molina Lario. Spacious rooms, many with 8-ft. windows. Peachy-pink paint thankfully restricted to hallways. Singles 1500-2000ptas, with bath 2100-2600ptas. Doubles 3400ptas. Use of half bathroom 350ptas.

Hotel Carlos V, C. Cister, 10 (tel. 221 51 20/27/28; fax 221 51 29). A 30-sec. walk southeast of the cathedral. A bit swanky for budget travelers. 24-hr. reception. Telephones and heaters in all rooms. TVs in about half. Soft beds. Fax service (225ptas for 1st page). Garage (1095ptas per day). Singles 2682-2926ptas. Dou-

bles 5300-6070ptas. 250ptas extra per day during Semana Santa. Reservations recommended. Visa, MC, AmEx, Diner's Club accepted.
Hostal Residencia Chinitas, Pasaje Chinitas, 2, 2nd fl. (tel. 221 46 83), on an alley
off Pl. Constitución. Look for the big yellow sign. Centrally located. Amiable
owner. A little dreary but clean. Singles 1600ptas. Doubles 3400ptas.
Hostal Residencia Lампérez, C. Santa María, 6 (tel. 221 94 84), off Pl. Constitución, on a small alley beside Pasaje Chinitas. Dilapidated entrance and stairwell,
guarded by Chihuahua Rocky. *Hostal* doesn't get much better. Singles 1500ptas.
Doubles 2400ptas. Triples 3300ptas.

FOOD

Twenty feet from the sands of **Playa de las Acacias** in **Pedregaleje** cluster restaurants specializing in—what else?—seafood. Eateries around the perimeter of the
cathedral, and off **Calle Granada,** boast more diverse menus. Quench your thirst
and engage in more serious people-watching at one of the multitude of bars and
cafés on **Paseo Marítimo.** For the truly homesick, a McDonalds awaits in Pl. Marina.
  Most restaurants take their daily menus straight out of the Mediterranean. *Espetos
de sardina* (sardines) are roasted over an open flame (usually in old rowboats) right
on the beach. *Calamares fritos* (fried squid) are house specialties throughout the
city. Wash your *cena* down with either *malagueño* or *moscatel,* Málaga's sweet
wines.

Groceries: El Corte Inglés, Av. Andalucía, 4-6. Open Mon.-Sat. 10am-9pm
(9:30pm during the summer).
Restaurante La Paloma, Po. Marítimo, El Pedregal, 20, (tel. 229 79 94). Take bus
#11. Wow. *So* good. Blue and white nautical decor, indoor/outdoor seating. Some
of their best dishes include *boquerones fritos* (fried anchovies) and *calamaritos
a la plancha* (grilled baby squids in garlic sauce). Open noon-4:30pm and 8pm-
12:30am.
Cafetería El Jardín, C. Cañón, 1 (tel. 22 04 19). On the corner of C. Cañón and C.
Cister, next to cathedral gardens. Laura Ashleyesque emporium decor, complete
with ceiling fans and piano. *Platos combinados* 600-850ptas. *Menú* 900ptas.
Don't leave without trying the *granizado de limón* (lemon slushy). Open 8am-
midnight. AmEx, Visa, MC accepted.
La Cancela, C. Denis Belgrano, 3 (tel. 221 01 50), off C. Granada. Their 4-page, sin-
gle-spaced, 2-column menu satisfies any conceivable gastronomical craving—a
haven for vegetarians. Dine inside the *salón* or out on the *terraza,* but take heed:
the *terraza* costs an average of 100ptas more. *Menú* 925ptas (*terraza* 1075ptas).
Open 12:30-5pm, and 8pm-midnight. Visa, MC, AmEx accepted.
Bar Malacca, Po. Marítimo, 9 (tel. 222 80 43). Hip, urban bar with cityscape
murals and loud dance music (even during the day). Clientele ranges from teens
to mid-40s. Celestial dessert menu (300-400ptas). Open 9am-5:30am during summer and on winter weekends;winter weekends closes a few hours earlier.
Restaurante El Tintero II, Playa del Dedo. *Dim Sum,* Málaga style. Patrons order
a variety of seafood platters and eat family-style. Loud. 500ptas per plate. Open
11am-5pm and 7:30pm-1am.

SIGHTS AND ENTERTAINMENT

Filled with labyrinthical concentric walls, the **Alcazaba** was constructed in the 11th
century as a fortified palace for Moorish kings. Along the eastern end of Po. Parque,
this building is Málaga's highlight. The attached **Museo Arqueológico** contains a
good collection of neolithic pottery. (Open Mon.-Fri. 9:30am-1:30pm and 4-7pm,
Sat. 10am-1pm, Sun. 10am-2pm. Closed Monday afternoons in summer, and all day
Monday in winter.) Thieves and other shifty types prowl the castle walls at night;
think twice about strolling here come evening.
  For a breathtaking view of Málaga and the Mediterranean, climb up to the **Castillo
Gibralfaro,** originally constructed by the Phoenicians and later rebuilt by the Arabs.
To get there, take bus #35 from the Po. Parque (10 per day, 11am-7:05pm, 100ptas).
On Pl. Obispo, 6, the **catedral** (tel. 221 59 17), a pastiche of Gothic, Renaissance,

and Baroque styles, houses organs built by Julián de la Orden in 1781. Constructed between the 1st half of the 16th-century and the last half of the 18th, the cathedral's second tower remains unfinished even today because architect Pedro de Mena died before its completion. The cathedral also contains the **Virgen de los Reyes,** an anonymous 16th-century work of the first patron saint of Málaga. (Open Mon.-Fri. 10am-12:45pm and 4-5:30pm. Museum is currently closed for restoration.)

The **Museo de Bellas Artes,** C. San Agustín, 8 (tel. 221 83 82), in the old palace of the Counts of Buenavista, hoards a wealth of mosaics, sculptures, and paintings, including works by Murillo, Ribera, and native son Picasso (born in Pl. Merced). (Open Tues.-Fri. 10am-1:30pm and 5-8pm, Sat.-Sun. 10am-1:30pm. Admission 250ptas, EU students under 21 free.) According to the tourist officials, even though Picasso beat it out of Málaga when he was quite young, he always "felt himself to be a true *malagueño.*" Diehard fans can visit **Picasso's birthplace,** soon to be converted into a museum. (Tel. 228 39 00; open 11am-2pm and 5-8pm.) East of the Po. del Parque is the **Plaza de Toros de Málaga,** Po. Reding, s/n. Tickets for bullfights range from 1000-11,000ptas. Young *malagueños* have two destinations after the sun goes down: either the beaches and nightclubs at **Pedregalejos** (take bus #11), or the bars and discos *"del centro"*—particularly around **Calle Comedia.** The *Guía de Ocio* (160ptas), sold at newsstands, lists the week's events around town.

■ NEAR MÁLAGA

GARGANTA DEL CHORRO

In the hierarchy of remarkable geological formations, the **Garganta del Chorro** (a.k.a. El Chorro, 70km northwest of Málaga) stands high. One of Spain's premier natural wonders, the gorge is overwhelming and the walk exhilarating; best of all, virtually no tourists spoil the experience. The gorge is remote, the entrance to the walkway hard to find, and the route dangerous. Those susceptible to vertigo or afraid to stroll through functioning train tunnels are guaranteed to be scared stiff. If none of this dampens your appetite for adventure, bring some rope, update your will, and talk to the bartender at El Chorro's train station for directions.

TORREMOLINOS

Something about Torremolinos (pop. 30,000) just screams *Love Boat:* hordes of shoppers peering into Duty-Free stickered windows, and tourists downing drinks at kiosk bars, tapping their feet to the likes of Gloria Estefan. Travelers and residents of Málaga intermingle and collectively exude an "I'm-on-vacation" attitude, which evolves from a daytime, beachside lassitude into nocturnal energy. An old fishing village now entirely consumed by tourists, Torremolinos is all laughter, loud upbeat music, drinking, and people milling about.

Formerly known for its **Torre de los Molinos** (Tower of the Windmills, still standing at the end of C. San Miguel), this village became a district of the city of Málaga (12km away) in 1924. By 1988, it had become its own township. **Calle San Miguel**—from the RENFE **train station,** walk down C. Antonio Girón, turn right onto Av. Palma de Mallorca, and then another right onto C. San Miguel—is a shopper's heaven, if you're in the market for Lladró figurines, Mallorca pearls, or gold jewelry. In the opposite direction on C. Palma de Mallorca (turn left rather than right), turn down **Calle Guetaria** and point your nose in the direction of the best bird's-eye view of **Bajondillo** beach. This street leads to C. Santos Arcángeles, where an archway marks the entrance to **Camino de La Playa,** a brick-and-tile paved walkway and observation deck that ends on Po. Marítimo in Bayondillo. The spot is romantic, but if you don't have someone to hold your hand after dark, you may run across a few undesirable characters.

The **tourist office** is at C. Guetaría, s/n (tel. 238 15 78). Stick outgoing letters into the lions' heads at the **post office,** Plaza de Mallorca, s/n (tel. 238 45 18), across from the pink Palladium Discoteca. (Open Mon.-Sat. 8am-3pm; **telegram** service available 9am-9pm.) The **postal code** is 29602. The **ATM machine** at **Banco Sabadell,** on the corner of Av. Plaza de Mallorca and C. Guetaría, services Visa, AmEx, MC, PLUS, and Cirrus users, and has instructions in English. The **pharmacy** is located at Pl. Mallorca, 39. (Open Mon.-Fri. 9:30am-1:30pm and 5-8:30pm, Sat. 10am-1:30pm.) Look for 24-hr. *farmacia de guardia* listings on the window. For a **taxi,** dial 238 10 30 or 238 31 52. **Police** answer at tel. 238 99 99 or 238 14 22. In an **emergency,** call 061.

If you're not renting an apartment or condominium for the summer, **Hostal La Palmera,** Av. Palma de Mallorca, 37 (tel. 237 65 09), makes a fine home away from home. Located above La Caixa Savings Bank (entrance is around the corner next to the pharmacy). Pleasant smelling quarters are 5min. from the beach. Rooms have windows and big closets; showers have hot water. TV and bar in reception room. English spoken. (Singles 2000-3000ptas. Doubles 3000-4000ptas. Triples 4000-5000ptas. Cots 600ptas. Breakfast 350ptas.) **Hostal Pizarro,** Pasaje Pizarro (tel. 238 71 67 238 71 85), is only a block or two past C. San Miguel, off Pl. Costa del Sol. Looks like a real hotel lobby, with schmaltzy gold-brown linoleum walls. All rooms have full bathrooms (with bathtubs!), but furniture is small and shaky-looking. (Singles 2500ptas. Doubles 3500ptas. Triples 5000ptas. Quads 6000ptas. Prices may be 400-600ptas more per person during Christmas, Semana Santa, and July-Aug.) Check out the restaurants that dot **Avenida Palma de Mallorca. La Carihuela** is *the* place to be when the sun goes down by virtue of its diverse selection of dishes and see-and-be-seen ambience.

Buses and **trains** run frequently to and from Málaga. Portillo Bus Co. can be reached at tel. 238 09 65.

ALMUÑÉCAR

A steadily growing town with character, Almuñécar is a rarity on the Costa Tropical, an extension of the Costa del Sol. Brightly colored boats moor alongside the beach and the well-preserved old quarter makes up for the high-rises in the background.

Still in use, the 1900-year-old 8km-long **acueducto** (1km to the west off the highway, a 20min. walk) watered the ancient Roman town and its salt-manufacturing industry. More than 400 varieties of plants imported from Cuba and Brazil grow in **Parque El Majuelo,** and lots of folks enjoy the wooden benches shaded by palm trees.

Almuñécar is justly proud of its **Parque Ornitológico: Loro Sexi,** below El Castillo de San Miguel (100m from the beach), where nearly 100 species of birds perch. (Open daily 11am-2pm and 4-8pm. Admission 300ptas, children 150ptas.)

The extensive **beaches** blend fine gray sand and fist-sized stones, but at least they're not glitzy. The two main ones are **Puerta del Mar,** on the east side of the **Peñón del Santo,** and **San Cristóbal,** on the west. Most streets from the bus station eventually lead toward the beach; the easiest way to get there is via Av. Europa, straight from the bus station (signs points to "Playa San Cristóbal").

For more beach, walk down Po. Puerta del Mar to the east, to **Playa de Velilla,** with its beautiful landscape. Eight buses per day go through **La Herradura,** on the way to Málaga. The largest official **nude beaches** on the Costa Tropical are **Playa Cantarrijan** and **Playa Almuñécar Trópico de España.** If you get off at La Herradura, it gets you 3-4km closer, but there is no direct transportation. If you're into that kind of thing, telephone the Asociación Naturista de Andalucía at (951) 25 08 05, or write to Apdo. 301, Almería, 04070.

The **tourist office** (tel. 63 11 25) is stuck in a hideous mauve mansion called La Najanra, on Av. Europa, s/n, off Av. Costa del Sol. (Open Mon.-Fri. 10am-2pm and 4-9:30pm.) The **post office** (tel. 63 04 59) is on Pl. Livry Gargan, 2. (Open Mon.-Fri. 9am-2pm, Sat. 9am-noon.) The **postal code** is 18690; the **telephone code** is 58. In a medical emergency, rush to the **Centro de Salud,** Ctra. Málaga (tel. 63 20 63). The **police** can be reached at tel. 63 06 49.

The cheapest accommodations cluster around Av. Europa. **Hotel Residencia Goya** (tel. 63 05 50; fax 63 11 92), Av. Europa, s/n, across the street from the tourist office, has spacious rooms and well-lit halls. 2 blocks from the beach. (Singles 1700ptas, with bath 2800ptas. Doubles 3000-5500ptas. Visa, MC, Eurocard accepted.) Further up the road from the tourist office is **Hotel R. Carmen,** Av. Europa, 19 (tel. 63 14 13 or 63 25 11), on the left side of the street if you're walking toward the beach (before you reach the tourist office). Faux marble tiles lead from a plant-filled entryway through a homey TV room. All rooms have gigantic baths tiled in soothing blue floral prints. (Singles 1700-3000ptas. Doubles 2830-4717ptas. Visa, MC, AmEx accepted. Breakfast 283ptas.) **Residencia Tropical,** Av. Europa, s/n (tel. 63 34 58), ½ bl. from the beach. Bar in reception area. Well-furnished rooms have bathrooms. (Singles 2000-2800ptas. Doubles 3000-4500ptas. Visa, MC, Eurocard accepted.)

Plenty of restaurants stud Po. Puerta del Mar (a.k.a. Po. Altillo), where you can enjoy the day's catch from a terrace peering over the coast. Try **Bar Avenida Lute y Jesús,** Av. Europa, 24 (tel. 63 42 76), almost across from Hotel Carmen. Specializes in *fritura de pescado* (fried fish, 600ptas). *Menú* with soup, main course, drink, bread, and dessert is only 800ptas.

Buses run to: Málaga (9 per day, 1¼hr., 685ptas); Granada (7 per day, 1¼hr., 700ptas); Madrid (2 per day, 8hr., 2500ptas); and Nerja (10 per day, 45min., 265ptas). The station (tel. 63 01 40) is at the corner of Av. Costa del Sol and Av. Europa.

NERJA

Though renowned in Spain for its beaches and caves, peaceful Nerja has managed to resist total commercialization. Strangely, you'll hear more English than Spanish in this town (52km east of Málaga). Home to some of the most breathtaking panoramas on the Costa del Sol, Nerja may be just your cup of tea if a fantastic beach is all you require for the perfect holiday.

The most hyped (overrated?) attraction in town is the **Balcón de Europa,** a wide-open brick patio that looks out over the Playa de la Caletilla. Follow signs from the street across from the bus station. Below the cliff is a really remarkable series of small caves, best explored from the marvelous promenade **Paseo de los Carabineros** (off the stairs right of the tourist office).

Long **beaches,** mostly of gravel, coarse sand, and pebbles, have clear, brilliant turquoise water. To reach them from the Balcón, cut through town westward to the Playa Torrecilla apartments; from there follow the shoreline for 15 minutes. Much closer but even more packed is **Playa del Salón,** through an alley off the Balcón to the right of Restaurante Marisal. **Playa Burriana** is a large, pebbly beach a sweaty 15-min. hike to the east. From the tourist office, follow C. Hernando de Corabeo to a dirt road behind a few newly constructed apartments.

Practical Information The **tourist office** (tel. 252 15 31) is at Puerta del Mar, 2, beside the Balcón de Europa. English, French, and German spoken fluently. (Open Mon.-Sat. 10am-2pm and 6-9pm.) The **post office** (tel. 252 17 49) is at C. Almirante Fernández, 6. (Open Mon.-Fri. 9am-2pm, Sat. 9am-1pm.) The **postal code** is 29780. The **telephone kiosk** is next to the Ayuntamiento by the Balcón de Europa. (Open summer 10am-2pm and 5:30-10pm; winter 11am-2pm and 5:30-9pm.) The **telephone code** is 95. An **ambulance** can be reached at C. Carlos Millión, 1 (tel. 252 09 35). **Police** headquarters are on C. Pescia (tel. 252 15 45).

The small bus station is at C. San Miguel, 3 (bus schedules posted in the window). Inquiries should be directed to the Nerja bus ticket window, on Av. de Pescia (tel. 252 15 04). **Buses** travel from here to: Málaga (12 per day, 1½hr., 400ptas); Almuñécar (7 per day, 45min., 275ptas); Almería (4 per day, 3hr., 1310ptas); Granada (3 per day, 2hr., 850ptas); Sevilla (2 per day, 4hr., 2140ptas); Cádiz (1 per day, 13hr., 2880ptas).

Accommodations and Food For those not willing to sacrifice the amenities of the U.K. when on holiday, **The Fountainebleau,** C. Alejandro Bueno (fax 252 14 75), is the place to find a room. Clientele almost exclusively the 40+ British set, and owners are themselves British. Rooms have telephones, coffee makers, complimentary wine, and—what do you know?—British room service, along with English A/C. Unfortunately the decor is drabby and the WCs Barbie-sized. (Double-occupancy rooms 1925-2695ptas per night. 1100pta per night surcharge for a single-occupancy room.) If that isn't your kind of crumpet, check out **Hostal Azahara,** Av. Pescia, 1 (tel. 252 04 26). Look for the green awning directly across the street from the bus stop. Marbly bathrooms and a terrace may be worth the distance to the beach. (Singles with bath 2500-4000ptas. Doubles with bath 3000-5000ptas.) A number of other hostels are on **Calle Pintada,** though the appeal of these establishments seems inversely proportional to their proximity to the surf and sand.

Overpriced restaurants along the Balcón de Europa tempt passers-by with terraces and views. If raw vegetables or do-it-yourself cooking appeal, pick up lunch every Tues. at the **market,** 2 bl. up C. San Miguel from the bus stop. **Restaurante Montemar,** on Playa de Burriana, with the least touristy clientele of the beachside restaurants, prepares delicious *paella* (700ptas), fish, and beef. Keep your eyes peeled for the blue-and-white street awning. *Espeto de sardina* is a specialty (500ptas). English breakfast (350ptas).

Near Nerja

Just 5km east of Nerja poses the tremendous **Cueva de Nerja.** The cave is a huckster's paradise, with piped-in music and photographers snapping and selling your picture in cave-shaped frames. The caverns consist of large chambers winding around a huge column of limestone. Filled with weird rock formations created over millions of years by deposit and erosion, one reputedly has the world's largest stalactite (65m). (It's technically the widest column, a merged stalagmite and stalactite. Refer to the 1989 edition of the *Guinness Book of World Records* for more details.) One cave is used as an amphitheater for music and ballet performances in July and August. Intrepid explorers have just discovered a new section of caves, reportedly four times as large as the already known one. Look for the archeological exhibit of primitive art and tools in the cave. (Open daily 10:30am-2pm and 3:30pm-6pm. Admission 600ptas, ages 6-12 300ptas.)

Buses run to and from Nerja (8:15am-8:10pm, every 50min.-1hr., 80ptas).

Maro is an unspoiled speck of a village near the cave with paths that lead to nearly empty rocky beaches and coves. North of Nerja, the tiny village of **Frigiliana** crowns a hill 5km away. Only two small gift shops have put down tourist-hungry roots among the glistening white buildings and patterned, cobblestoned streets.

FUENGIROLA

Beauty parlor. Health food store. Pet store. Beauty parlor. Beauty parlor. Shoe store. Boutique. The 50th ice cream kiosk you've seen in as many minutes. Pet beauty parlor. A neon, lemon-lime colored bus whizzes by—all this against a backdrop of picture-perfect chalk-hued resort *villas.* No, you're not dreaming. You're in Fuengirola, 29km southwest of Málaga, and you're probably sweating like crazy.

Although suffocated by merchants who encourage vanity, the citizens of Fuengirola dress casually and frequent the beach behind the **Plaza de Castilla** and bars on the **Paseo Marítimo.** Residents and tourists alike flock the beachside with good reason: temperatures on the coast can be as much as 15°F cooler than they are a mere three blocks inland. Yay Mediterranean!

The air-conditioned **tourist office** (tel. 246 74 57) is on Av. Jesús Santo Reino. (Open Mon.-Fri. 9:30am-1:30pm and 4-8pm.) A **24-hr. ATM machine** can be found at Caja de Madrid on Av. Jesús Santo Reino, right outside RENFE station. (Visa, MC, Eurocard, PLUS—but no Cirrus—accepted). The **post office** is on Pl. Chinorros, s/n (tel. 247 43 83; open Mon.-Fri. 8am-3pm, Sat. 9am-1pm). The **postal code** is 29640; the **telephone code** 95. The 24-hr. **medical clinic,** C. Alfonso XIII, 41a, can be reached at tel. 258 30 00. A 24-hr. **emergency service** can be reached at the corner of Av. de Mijas and Av. Jesús Santos Rein (tel. 831 60 60). The number for the **local police** is 247 31 57. They can be reached at C. Alfonso XII, 1, a 7-min. walk from RENFE. (Walk down Av. Jesús Santos Rein; street is on the left.)

Fuengirola's reputation as a tourist trap for jet-setters is largely exaggerated. Although it's true that some *villas* can cost as much per night as an airline ticket from the U.S. to Spain, reasonable *pensiones* and *hostales* abound in **Los Boliches,** and in the streets surrounding **Plaza de la Constitución. Hostal Costabella,** Av. Boliches, 98 (tel. 247 46 31) is only one bl. north of the beach, and one bl. south of the Los Boliches stop on RENFE. Owners are doting grandfatherly-types. Hall bathrooms. Some rooms have beach views. (Singles 1200-2000ptas. Doubles 2200-3000ptas.) Non-beach aquamaniacs should head to the 13-room **Hostal Pensión Jomarijo,** Dionisia Redondo, 5-6 (tel. 246 44 21), off Av. Ramón y Cajal. Guests permitted to use swimming pools of Residencia Las Camelias next door. Rooms with bathrooms have bathtubs. (Singles 3100ptas. Doubles 2200-4200ptas. Triples 3200-4900ptas. Rooms with bathrooms 300ptas extra.) Eateries are easy to come by on the **Calles de Hambre**—you'll run into them south of Pl. Constitución. Folks at the tourist office talk up the local **market,** reportedly the greatest thing since *churros con chocolate.* (Tues. 9:30am-2pm at the **fairground** north of Av. Jesús Santo Reino.) Supermarket **Cayetano Supermercado,** on Av. Ramón y Cajal, 43 opens Mon.-Fri. 9am-2:30pm and 4:30-9pm, Sat. 9am-9pm, Sun. 10am-2pm. Visa, MC accepted. For nightlife, hit the bars on Po. Marítimo and the area around **Calle Miguel de Cervantes** and **Calle Oviedo.** The **Bowling Palmeras** strikes on Av. Martínez Catena, s/n, with a sauna, jacuzzi, gym, roller skating, bowling alley, and much more. (Tel. 246 06 41; behind Hotel Las Palmeras).

About 24 **buses** run to and from Málaga each day (every 45min., 270ptas); the Málaga-Fuengirola route on **RENFE** costs 260ptas and takes only 40min.

■■■ MARBELLA

Glamorous Marbella, popularly considered the jewel of the Costa del Sol, is all tourist attraction, resort, and spectacle. The flashy rich and famous descend upon this city, at a price: Marbella extorts *pesetas* quickly, efficiently, painlessly, and in many different languages, though it's also possible to steal away from Marbella with a budgety good time. Once encircled with towers and battlements, Marbella's walls frame an attractive and well-preserved old city. Of late, its controversial mayor has "cleaned up" the "marginal" elements (drug dealers, prostitutes, fellow politicians, etc.). Marbella is now reputed to have the lowest crime rate in all of Europe for cities of pop. 100,000 or more.

ORIENTATION AND PRACTICAL INFORMATION

Marbella glitzes 56km south of Málaga. To get to the town center from the bus station, take a left on Av. Ricardo Soriano until it becomes **Avenida Ramón y Cajal.** The old town is on the left; the waves crash to the right.

Tourist Office: C. Glorieta de la Fontanilla, s/n (tel. 277 14 42). Open Mon.-Fri. 9:30am-9pm, Sat. 10am-2pm; winter Mon.-Fri. 9:30am-8pm, Sat. 10am-2pm. Another tourist office in Pl. Naranjos (tel. 282 35 50). Open same hours. New **branches** have opened at the arches at entrance of city. Open 10am-2am. Av. Miguel Cano, 1 (tel. 277 14 42), behind the Alameda Park.

American Express: Av. Arias Maldonado, 2 (tel. 282 14 94 or 282 28 20), off Av. Ricardo Soriano. Holds mail for cardholders and changes money. Open Mon.-Fri. 9:30am-1:30pm and 4:30-7:30pm, Sat. 10am-1pm.

Post Office: C. Alonso de Bazán, 1 (tel. 277 28 98). Open Mon.-Fri. 9am-2pm, Sat. 9am-1pm; for **telegrams** Mon.-Fri. 8:30am-8:30pm, Sat. 9am-1pm. **Postal Code:** 29600.

Telephones: Kiosks every couple of blocks along the beach. Open June-Sept. 10am-2pm and 5-10pm. **Telephone Code:** 95.

Buses: Av. Ricardo Soriano, 21 (tel. 277 21 92). To: Málaga (30 per day, 1½hr., 505ptas); Fuengirola (41 per day, ½hr., 250ptas); San Pedro de Alcántara (33 per day, 15-20min., 85ptas); Estepona (38 per day, 1hr., 225ptas); Granada (4 per day, 2½hr., 1550ptas); Ronda (4 per day, 1½hr., 520ptas); Sevilla (2 per day, 2½hr.,

1555ptas); Cádiz (3 per day, 3hr., 1710ptas); Madrid (4 per day, 8-11hr., 2965-4845ptas); Barcelona (3 per day, 20hr., 8435ptas).
Taxis: Cánovas del Castillo, s/n (tel. 277 44 88).
Red Cross: tel. 277 45 34.
Hospital: Hospital Europa, Av. Severo Ochoa, 22 (tel. 277 42 00).
Emergency: tel. 092 (municipal police).
Police: Pl. Los Naranjos, 1 (tel. 282 24 94).

ACCOMMODATIONS AND CAMPING

If you don't have reservations, especially from mid-July through August, arrive early and pray. The area in the old part of town, behind Av. Ramón y Cajal, is loaded with little *hostales* and *fondas,* all of which fill up quickly. Several cheap guest houses line **Calles Ancha, San Francisco, Aduar,** and **de los Caballeros,** all of which are uphill off C. Huerta Chica, across C. Ramón y Cajal from the tourist office road. People at bars often know of *casas particulares:* the lively **English Pub** and **The Tavern,** face to face on C. Peral, can offer advice in English.

Hostal del Pilar, C. Mesoncillo, 4 (tel. 282 99 36), in an alley behind the English Pub. C. Mesoncillo is the 2nd left off C. Huerta Chica. Friendly English management and a relaxing bar/lounge make for a sociable scene. Mattresses on the roof (in warm months) from 800ptas per person. Singles 1500-2300ptas. Doubles 2500-4000ptas. Triples about 3500-5000ptas. English breakfasts (served until 4pm) 500ptas. Bar serves food until midnight. "Hot meal of the day" 500ptas.
Casa-Huéspedes Aduar, C. Aduar, 7 (tel. 277 35 78). The verdant courtyard overflowing with roses puts a positive tint on the unexceptional rooms. Balconied rooms upstairs. Singles 2000ptas. Doubles 2000-2900ptas.
El Castillo, a couple bl. uphill from the Aduar. Same owners. The windowless rooms get a little stuffy in summer, but the others are fine. All have stupendous bathrooms inside. Singles 1000-2000ptas. Doubles 2000-4000ptas.
Camping Marbella (tel. 283 39 98), 2km east on N-340. Coming by bus from the Fuengirola direction, it's on the left just before Mirabella; push the button to signal the driver to stop. A 2nd-class site. 455ptas per person, 805ptas per tent. Open all year.

FOOD

The municipal **market** is off C. Huerta Chica.

Restaurante Sol y Sombra, C. Tetuán, 7 (tel. 277 00 50). Good fresh fish dishes (650-1200ptas) and a 1000pta *menú.* Open 1-4pm and 8-11:30pm.
Bar Taurino, C. Leganitos, 1, toward the top of C. Aduar. Boisterous local crowd inspired by bullfighting posters. Mountain of *paella* 450ptas. Tasty *tapas.* Open Wed.-Mon. 9am-11pm.
Bar El Gallo, C. Lobatas, 46 (tel. 282 79 98). Loud TV and louder locals, but lip-smacking good food. *Ensalada mixta* 300ptas. *San Jacobo* (pork stuffed with ham and swiss) and fries 400ptas. Open 9am-midnight.

SIGHTS AND ENTERTAINMENT

Marbella caters to fat-walleted sun-worshipping tourists. Aside from some 3rd-century **baños** at the western city limits, don't look for much in the way of historical titillation. The eastern section of the old town, just up from the church, is worth exploring. A massive Arab wall once protected the town, and numerous houses with beautiful courtyards huddle against its crumbling remains.

The chic promenade over the beach leave's Marbella most sizzling asset starved for space. If the press of flesh stifles, hop on the Fuengirola bus, stop at **Playa de las Chapas,** 10km east, and walk in either direction to find an open stretch. Even here, the sand is rough and the beaches are rocky. If you choose to stay in Marbella for the evening, visit **Old Vic,** Av. Ansol, 2, a Spanish neon disco. The **Feria y Fiesta de San Bernabé** (mid-June) is the big event of the year, with fireworks and concerts.

■■■ ANTEQUERA

The whitewashed houses and occasional church towers of Antequera broil in a valley below a Moorish fortress. Although Romans named the city, civilization here began much earlier—*dólmenes* (funerary chambers built from rock slabs; the oldest of their kind in Europe) constructed 5000 years ago stud the outskirts of town. Few sunsets more beautiful than those captured through the hills from the top of the Moorish fort. Antequera makes a fine bivouac for forays into the surrounding mountains.

ORIENTATION AND PRACTICAL INFORMATION

Antequera straddles the crossroads of Córdoba, Granada, Ronda, and Málaga (rail travelers, however, will notice that RENFE has made Bobadilla the major switching point). It's a 10-minute hike up a shadeless hill (Av. Estación, which becomes a different street at practically every block) from the station to town. At the top, forge dead ahead to Pl. Descalzas, just east of the Museo Municipal. Turn right at C. Encarnación to reach **Plaza San Sebastián,** the town center.

The **bus station** sits atop a neighboring hill. To reach Pl. San Sebastián from the bus station, walk down the hill (to the right as you exit) to the bullring, then turn left onto **Alameda de Andalucía.** At the fork, follow **Calle Infante Don Fernando** (the right branch) until it runs into the plaza. If you dislike climbing with luggage in the heat, arrive by bus and leave by train—or take a cab (about 350ptas).

Tourist Office: C. Infante Don Fernando, s/n, Edificio San Luis (tel. 270 04 05). From the bullring, go down Av. Andalucía and bear right when the road forks. Unbelievably helpful staff has maps, transportation schedules, information on Antequera and a few nearby cities as well. Open summer 10am-2pm and 5-8pm; and winter 9:30am-1:30pm and 4-7pm. **Branch** office is located on Pl. Coso Viejo, s/n (tel. 284 21 80), just inside the Museo Municipal, off C. Nájera near Pl. Descalzas. They distribute maps and information about the countryside, and house a **museum** (see Sights). Open Tues.-Fri. 10am-1:30pm, Sat. 10am-1pm, Sun. 11am-1pm.

Post Office: C. Nájera (tel. 284 20 83), down the street from the Museo Municipal. Open for stamps, *certificados,* Lista de Correos, and **telegrams** Mon.-Fri. 8am-3pm, Sat. 9am-1pm. **Postal Code:** 29200.

Trains: Av. Estación (tel. 284 32 26), in the north of the city. To: Granada (3 per day, 1½-2hr.); Málaga (3 per day, 1hr.); Sevilla (3 per day, 2½hr.); Algeciras (2 per day, 4hr.); Bobadilla (3 per day, 115ptas). A number of other connections from Bobadilla. Call the nearby Bobadilla station (tel. 272 00 22) for info.

Buses: Po. García del Olmo (tel. 284 31 82), near the Parador Nacional. To: Málaga (Mon.-Fri. 14 per day, Sat. 10 per day, Sun. 9 per day, 1hr.); Almería (2 per day, 4½hr.); Cádiz (1 per day); Córdoba (3 per day); Granada (4 per day); Jaén (1 per day); Ubeda (1 per day); Murcia (2 per day); Sevilla (5 per day).

Taxis: tel. 284 10 76 or 284 10 08.

Hospital: Hospital Municipal San Juan de Dios, C. Infante Don Fernando, 135 (tel. 284 44 11).

Emergency: tel. 091.

Police: Municipal (tel. 284 11 91 or 284 12 89). **Civil,** C. Infante Don Fernando, 140 (tel. 284 50 90).

ACCOMMODATIONS AND FOOD

Most establishments lie between the Museo Municipal and the **market,** on Pl. Abastos. Also snoop around on the side streets off **Calle Infante Don Fernando.** Most places to eat are economical. Stop by the market (open 8am-2pm) for a savory nibble of *queso de cabra* (goat cheese). Also try *porra,* the local, thicker version of *gazpacho.*

Residencia Colón, C. Infante Don Fernando, 29 (tel. 284 45 16). So nice that there's no reason to stay anywhere else. Combination of antiquated rooms in the old quarters, and new quarters with A/C. Rooms and bathrooms could each contain their own dance floors. Singles 1000-2000ptas, with bath 2000-3000ptas. Doubles 2900-3200ptas, with bath 4000-5000ptas. Visa, MC, AmEx accepted. Wheelchair accessible.

Pensión Madrona, C. Calzada, 25 (tel. 284 00 14). Walk through Bar Madrona to *pensión's* kitchy hallway. A/C and central heating in every room. Singles cramped; doubles roomy. Singles 1400ptas, with bath 2500ptas. Doubles with bath 3350ptas.

Pensión Toril, C. Toril, 5 (tel. 284 31 84), off Pl. Abastos. Clean, bright rooms and free parking in garage. Singles 1200ptas. Doubles 2200ptas. While you're here enjoy the well-prepared and inexpensive fare. Larger-than-life *menú* (700ptas), whopping *platos combinados* (500ptas), and generous drinks (75ptas). Open 1-4pm and 7:30-9:30pm.

Mesón-Restaurante Amigos de Chaplín, C. San Agustín, 8 (tel. 270 39 59). On the right side of a narrow brick street off C. Infante Don Fernando. Bar downstairs, restaurant upstairs. Guess whose likeness adorns the entrance? *Menú* 1000ptas. Bar open from 11am. Restaurant open 1-5pm and 7:30-11:30pm.

Bar Madrona, C. Calzada, 25 (tel. 284 00 14). Chrome bar. Seriously. Beverages slightly more expensive than usual (150ptas for a Coke), but *menú* (800ptas) is pretty reasonable.

Bar Vidal, C. Infante Don Fernando, 80-84 (tel. 284 30 90). An Antequera sports bar. Big screen TV mounted on wall. Bar and table seating. Open Mon.-Sat. 7pm-midnight.

La Espuela, Ctra. Córdoba, s/n, Pl. Toros (tel. 270 26 76 or 270 26 33). Outdoor seating fenced by white lamp posts. Quite pricey. Specialty is *rabo de toro* (bull's tail). *Menú* 1200ptas. Open noon-4pm and 9pm-midnight.

SIGHTS

Antequera's three ancient **cuevas de dólmenes** dodder along as the oldest and best-preserved tombs in Europe. Crudely cut rock slabs form both the antechamber (the storeroom for the dead's possessions) and the burial chamber. **Cueva de Menga** dates from 2500 BC. Pious and muscular ancients lugged the mammoth 200-ton roof over five miles to the burial site. The four figures engraved on the chamber walls typify Mediterranean Stone Age art. The elongated **Cueva de Viera,** discovered in 1905, bears equally monstrous proportions. Bring a flashlight to explore the dark recesses. Small, flat stones cement the circular interior walls and domed ceiling of **Cueva de Romeral,** which dates from 1800 BC.

To reach the Cuevas de Menga and Viera, follow the signs toward Granada to the edge of town (a 10-min. walk from the market), or catch the bus for Barrio de los Dólmenes (50ptas) and watch for a small sign on C. Granada next to the gas station. To reach Cueva de Romeral from the other *cuevas,* continue on the *carretera* to Granada for another 2km or so. Just past Almacenes Gómez, one of the last warehouses after the flowered intersection, a gravel road cuts left and bumps into a narrow path bordered by 50-ft. fir trees. Take this path across the train tracks to reach the cave. (All caves open Tues.-Fri. 10am-2pm and 3-5:30pm, Sat.-Sun. 10am-2pm.)

Back in town, all that remains of the **castillo** are two towers and the wall between them. At the top of the wall you can feast your eyes on the beautiful view of farmland capped by a neighboring mountain peak. Along a shady, cypress-lined stairway downhill looms the Renaissance **Colegiata de Santa María.** (Open Tues.-Sat. 10am-2pm and 4-6pm, Sun. 10am-2:30pm.)

Down the street from Pl. San Sebastián in Pl. Coso Viejo, the deserted **Museo Municipal** is home to one of the tourist offices. The building still houses some local pieces, such as the *Efebo de Antequera,* a 1st-century Roman bronze figure, and native artist Cristóbal Toral's *El paquete.* (Open Tues.-Fri. 10am-1:30pm, Sat. 10am-1pm, Sun. 11am-1pm. Admission 100ptas.)

■NEAR ANTEQUERA: SIERRA DE TORCAL

A gargantuan garden of wind-sculpted boulders, the misty Sierra de Torcal glows like the surface of a barren and distant planet. The central peak of **El Torcal** (1369m) hogs most of the horizon, but the smaller clumps of rounded rocks are even more spectacularly unusual. Don't wear sandals on these hot but rocky trails in summer, and bundle your feet up well in winter.

Close to the summit, two circular trails await wisely-shod feet. The path marked with yellow arrows takes about an hour and is 2½km long; the path marked with red arrows takes over two hours and is 4½km long. Both paths begin and end 13km from Antequera at the *refugio* at the base of the mountain. Two-thirds of the 13km can be covered by **bus;** take the bus (from Antequera) for Villanueva de la Concepción, and ask the driver to let you off at the turnoff for El Torcal. Buses leave Antequera (Mon.-Sat. 1 per day, 1830ptas); the return bus leaves Villanueva de la Concepción (Mon.-Fri. 3 per day, Sat. 1 per day). Call Empresa for details (tel. 233 92 47).

There are no towns or turnoffs before Antequera, so anyone heading east on the road is going all the way. Taxi to the *refugio*—with time to watch the sun set— costs about 1800ptas.

■■■ RONDA

Ronda (pop. 45,000) tops a rocky massif split by a spectacular 100m gorge, while far below the Río Guadalevín shimmers. An earthquake split the rock and made the city a natural fortress and a national monument. Ronda's *casco antiguo* is one of Spain's loveliest.

Ronda's history runs as deep as the gorge. Called Arunda (surrounded by mountains) by Pliny and Ptolemy, the city was a pivotal commercial center under the Romans. During the Muslim occupation, the Machiavellian Al Mutadid ibn Abbad annexed the city for Sevilla by asphyxiating the previous lord in his bath. Modern bullfighting (on foot rather than horseback) was started here by Pedro Romero. German poet Rainer Maria Rilke wrote his *Spanish Elegies* here, and Orson Welles had his ashes buried on a bull farm outside of town.

Only an hour from the resorts of the Costa del Sol, Ronda, with its bountiful monuments, is both a welcome diversion from crowded beaches and a good base for exploring some of the *pueblos blancos* to the south.

ORIENTATION AND PRACTICAL INFORMATION

Ronda sits 125km southeast of Sevilla, 60km northwest of Marbella, 75km west of Antequera, and 98km north of Algeciras. The old and new parts of the city connect by three bridges: one Roman, one Moorish, and one modern (the **Puente Nuevo**— 1735, rebuilt in 1793). On the new side of the city, Carrera Espinel (the main east-west drag) runs perpendicular to **Calle Virgen de la Paz.** Carrera Espinel is more commonly known as **Calle la Bola,** so named 50 or 60 years ago when a snowstorm formed a huge snowball that blocked the street and caused several deaths.

Both the **train** and **bus stations** rumble on the western side of the new city. To reach the tourist office and the center of town from the train station, turn right on Av. Andalucía and follow it past the bus station (where the name changes to C. San José) until the street ends. Here, take a left on C. Jerez, follow it past the Alameda del Tajo (city park) and Pl. Toros (C. Jerez changes to C. Virgen de la Paz at the **Plaza de la Merced)** until it hits **Plaza de España.** Carrera Espinel intersects C. Virgen de la Paz between the *corrida de toros* and Pl. España.

Tourist Office: Pl. España, 1 (tel. 287 12 72). English- and French-speaking staff has information on Ronda and surrounding towns. Pamphlets in English, German, French, and, of course, Spanish. Open Mon.-Fri. 9am-2pm.

Post Office: C. Virgen de la Paz, 20 (tel. 287 25 57), across from Pl. Toros. Open for stamps, Lista de Correos, and **telegrams** Mon.-Fri. 8:30am-2:30pm, Sat. 9:30am-1pm. **Postal Code:** 29400.

Telephones: Orbase, S.L., C. Mariano Soubirón, 5 (tel. 287 46 70), off C. Virgen de la Paz. A few booths in a tobacco shop. Expensive, but they accept plastic. Open 9am-2:30pm and 5-9:30pm. **Telephone Code:** 952.

Trains: Station, Av. Andalucía (tel. 287 16 73). **Ticket office,** C. Infantes, 20 (tel. 287 16 62). Open Mon.-Fri. 10am-2pm and 5-7pm, Sat. 10am-1:30pm. To: Málaga (3 per day, 2hr., 765ptas); Algeciras (4 per day, 2hr., 700ptas); Granada (4 per day, 3hr., 1075ptas); Sevilla (3 per day, 3hr., 1273ptas). Change at Bobadilla for destinations other than Algeciras.

Buses: Pl. Concepción García Redondo, 2 (tel. 287 26 57). To: Málaga (4 per day, 2½hr., 975ptas); Cádiz (3 per day, 9hr., 1475ptas); Marbella (1 per day, 1½hr., 520ptas); Fuengirola (2 per day, 2hr., 755ptas); Torremolinos (2 per day, 1½hr., 895ptas).

Taxis: tel. 287 23 16. Train station to center of town about 300ptas.

Car Rental: Velasco, C. Lorenzo Borrego, 11 (tel. 287 27 82).

Hitchhiking: *Let's Go* does not recommend hitchhiking as a safe means of travel. Those heading to Sevilla, Jerez, and Cádiz follow C. Sevilla out of the Mercadillo. Those aiming for Granada walk up Carrera Espinel and take the third right after the tree-lined Av. Martínez Stein. Those destined for Málaga and the Costa del Sol zip across the highway leading downhill from Barrio de San Francisco.

Luggage Storage: At the **bus station** (100-150ptas). Open 8am-7:45pm.

Laundromat: Lavandería Andaluza, C. Almendra, 23, 1 bl. past Hostal Ronda Sol on the same street. Dry clean only. About 200ptas per item. Open Mon.-Fri. 9:30am-2pm and 5-8:30pm, Sat. 9:30-2pm.

Swimming Pool: Piscina Municipal, on Av. Málaga (the continuation of Carrera Espinel). On the left as you enter the city from Málaga or Marbella. Admission 225ptas, children 175ptas. Open June 5-Sept. 5 10am-8pm.

Medical Services: Hospital General Básico de la Serranía, Ctra. El Burgo, 1 (tel. 287 15 40). **Emergencies: Notfall,** C. Espinillo, s/n (tel. 287 58 52), or simply dial 091.

Police: Pl. Duquesa de Parcent, s/n (tel. 287 32 40 or 287 32 42).

ACCOMMODATIONS

Almost all accommodations are bunched in the new city near the train station, along the streets perpendicular to **Carrera Espinel,** like **Calle Sevilla** and **Calle Molino.** Expect room shortages only during the Feria de Ronda in September.

Pensión La Purísima, C. Sevilla, 10 (tel. 287 10 50), a block or two from C. Bola. Run by two attentive women. Walls covered with pictures of saints and grandchildren. Hallways resemble the Garden of Eden. Singles 1500ptas. Doubles 3000ptas. Triples 4500ptas.

Hostal Morales, C. Sevilla, 51 (tel. 287 15 38), near the corner with C. Lauria. Friendly management. Modern bathrooms (but cold showers), a tiled courtyard, and spotless rooms—some with balconies. Singles 1200ptas. Doubles 2400ptas.

Huéspedes La Española, C. José Aparicio, 3 (tel. 287 10 52), on a side street around the corner from tourist office. What a deal! Rooms are tidy, if cramped. Curfew 1am. 1200ptas per person. Shower included.

Virgen de los Reyes, C. Lorenzo Borrego, 13 (tel. 287 11 40). One block from C. Bola. Great setup: A/C, elevator, huge closets, and bathtubs. Rooms have TVs, radios, and phones (or some combination of the above). Rooms get nicer in proportion to the number of people they accommodate. Singles 2500ptas. Doubles 4500. Triples 6000.

Pensión Virgen del Rocio, C. Nueva, 18 (tel. 287 74 25), off Pl. España. Newly remodeled family-owned *pensión*. Singles 1300-1500ptas. Doubles 2500-3000ptas. Breakfast 200ptas; lunch or dinner 600ptas.

FOOD

Affordable eateries may at first seem few and far between, but you're probably just looking in the wrong places. Best bargains are found on alleys behind the tourist office on **Plaza de España**. Snack bars and bakeries line **Carrera Espinel**. **Gestoría Harillo,** #36, serves pastry to flaky perfection. The ice cream at **Heladería La Ibense,** next door, is creamy and delicious. **Café Alba** at #44 serves very tall *churros* in the morning.

Restaurante El Alhambra, C. Pedro Romero, 9 (tel. 287 69 34), off Virgen de la Paz. Not the Alhambra, but you're treated like royalty nonetheless. Filling *menú* 775ptas. Ask for owner José Luis' unnamed specialty drink (available only to *Let's Go* readers): cream, Tía María, and Málaga sweet wine. Heaven. Open summer 11am-4:30pm and 7:30-11pm or midnight. In winter, they close either Mon. or Tues. Visa, MC, Eurocard, Diners Club accepted.

Restaurante Flores, C. Virgen de la Paz, 9 (tel. 287 10 40), behind tourist office. Tent-covered outdoor tables allow a super view of tourists on their way to the Pl. Toros. *Menú* 700ptas. MC, Eurocard accepted. Open 1-4pm and 8-11:30pm.

Restaurante Mediterraneo, C. Virgen de La Paz, 7 (tel. 287 10 58), off Pl. España, next to Restaurante Flores. Quiet, tastefully decorated. Indoor/outdoor tables. *Menú* 750ptas.

La Ibense, C. Bola, 42. Look for the glittery disco sign. Ice cream parlor/café decked in black and white. Patronized by both young people and families. The *granizado de café* (coffee slushy, 150ptas) will do you right. Open 8am-3pm.

SIGHTS

Ronda's most dramatic sight, the precipitous gorge carved out by the Río Guadalevín, dips under three stone bridges. The most impressive of these, the 18th-century **Puente Nuevo,** hangs nearly 100m high and binds the city's old and new quarters. During the Civil War, prisoners were sometimes thrown into the gorge when jails became overcrowded.

In the old city (to the left across the bridge), a colonnaded walkway leads to the **Casa del Rey Moro** (House of the Moorish King), which, notwithstanding its name and Moorish facade, dates from the 18th century. From the gardens in back, 365 zigzag steps descend to *la mina* (the mine), a spring that once served as the town's water supply. Four hundred Christian prisoners were employed at one time to perform the arduous task of drawing water. "In Ronda," it was said fearfully across the countryside, "they die carrying stacks of water." Across the street, behind a forged iron balcony and a stone facade portraying four Peruvian Incas, stands the 18th-century **Palacio del Marqués de Salvatierra.** The palace floor sparkles with ceramic tiles. (Open Mon.-Wed. and Fri.-Sat. 11am-2pm and 4-6:30pm, Sun. 11am-1pm. Tour every ½hr., 6 people min. Admission 200ptas. Closed, but may reopen in 1995.)

Cobbled steps descend from the Puente San Miguel turnoff to Ronda's sci-fi **baños árabes.** The roofs are punctured with star-shaped holes and capped with skylights. The 14th-century saunas still function, but are currently undergoing restoration (may reopen in late 1994). Enter through the unmarked brown door under the dilapidated plaster wall at the bottom of the street; a yellow sign reads "Ministerio de Cultura Monumento en Restauración." (Open Tues.-Sun. 10am-2pm. Free.)

On the way back up the cobbled steps, Ronda's second and third bridges appear on the right: the architecturally innovative **Puente Viejo** (rebuilt in 1616 over an earlier Arab bridge) and the Roman **Puente San Miguel.**

C. Marqués de Salvatierra leads to the **Iglesia de Santa María la Mayor,** a large 16th-century hall-church crowned by a Renaissance belfry, in the heart of Ronda's old city. The small arch just inside the entrance and the Koranic verses behind the Sacristy are the only vestiges of the mosque once on the site. The even fainter sign announcing *"Julius Divo, Municipe"* reveals this historical site's original incarnation as a church consecrated for Caesar. Inside the cathedral is *Virgen de los Dolores* by Martínez Montañés. (Open 9am-6pm. Knock for the caretaker, who'll admit you for

100ptas.) The balcony on the tower side of the church overlooks Pl. Cuidad, former parade grounds of the castle.

Back toward the new city, **Giralda de San Sebastián** pokes out as part of a former mosque converted into a church after 1485, when Ronda was captured by the Christians. Nearby, toward the Puente Nuevo, is **Palacio Mondragón,** once owned by Don Fernando Valenzuela (one of Carlos III's ministers), and the resting spot of Queen Isabel on her visit to Ronda to stifle a Moorish rebellion. The Baroque facade, bracketed by two Mudejar towers, hides 15th-century Arab mosaics. (Open 8am-2pm; off-season 8am-3pm.)

Ronda's beautiful **Plaza de Toros,** the oldest in Spain, is the site where local hero Pedro Romero invented modern bullfighting *a pie* (on foot) and used the *muleta* (red cape) for the first time. Inside the 1784 structure, the **Museo Taurino** tells his glorious story and that of Cayetano Ordónez, apotheosized by Hemingway's Romero in *The Sun Also Rises.* (Open 10am-7pm; Oct.-May 10am-2pm. Admission 200ptas; children and seniors free Fri. after 3pm.)

Perhaps the calmest, and certainly the coolest, spot in town is the shady green **Alameda del Tajo** on C. Virgen de la Paz. Complete with drinking fountains, flower gardens, subtropical plants, and a view of the gorge, the park is overrun by ducks, swans, canaries, doves, roosters, pheasants, and the occasional vulture. **Paseo de Blas Infante,** at the bottom of Carrera Espinel by the bull-ring, has the better view.

ENTERTAINMENT

It's pretty quiet at night. Excitement lurks in the discos and pubs near Pl. España. **Café Tenorio,** C. Tenorio, 1, to the right of the bridge in the old quarter, blasts rock music in a rustic bar with a pool table. In early September crowds flock to the **Plaza de Toros,** where *corridas goyescas* (bullfights in traditional costumes) and flamenco contests explode as part of the **Feria de Ronda** celebrations. The **Corpus Christi** festivities revolve around Alameda del Tajo and C. Virgen de la Paz.

■ NEAR RONDA

CUEVAS DE LA PILETA

A subterranean prehistoric museum of bones, stalactites, stalagmites, and paleolithic paintings, the Cuevas de la Pileta hollow out 22km west of Ronda along the road to Ubrique. The caves were populated by the late Ronda-ites 25,000 years ago. The highlight of the expedition is surely the "Cámara del Pez" (Chamber of the Fish), named for its enormous prehistoric painting. Bring a flashlight or torch, bundle up, and don't wear sandals, high heels, or ill-fitting footwear. Upon arrival at the caves, climb to the mouth to see if the guide is inside. If no one is about, walk to the farm below and rouse the owner, who'll make appropriate arrangements. (Open 9am-1pm and 4-7pm; winter 10am-2pm and 4-6pm. Admission and 1hr. tour for individuals 600ptas, group rate 500ptas per person, school groups 300ptas per person.)

To reach the caves from Ronda, take the **train** to **Benaoján** (4 per day—the 7am will spare you the midday heat on the hike, 340ptas) and steel yourself for the grueling 7km uphill climb to the cave entrance. From the station, take the wide dirt road leading uphill and bear right at the rotary in the middle of town. The 2-3km uphill road to the cave is just outside of town. You'll have to ask directions in town. By **car,** take highway C-339 north (Ctra. Sevilla heading out of the new city). About 13km out of town is the turnoff to Benaoján and the caves, in front of an abandoned bar-restaurant. Don't leave valuables in your car during the tour.

You can also take the Amarillo **bus** to Benaoján (4 per day, 22min., 200ptas). The last two are useless unless you want to spend the night in Benojoán and tour the next morning, since they run after the caves have closed. The approach through the barren stone massifs of the Serranía de Ronda is stupendous. The road winds through the town of Montajaque; the turnoff to the caves is just outside of town.

SERRANÍA DE RONDA

South of Ronda, the rocky Serranía de Ronda extends east to west. With the exception of the area between Ronda and Ubrique, where wind and rain have created a polymorphic landscape, the terrain is composed of mountainous brown rock and sparse vegetation. Only at the heights do the *pinsapos*, famous native pines, spruce up the mountains with greenery.

The southern stretch from Ronda south to San Pedro de Alcántara climbs up along a fantastic coast overlooking the valley of the Guadalmedina. Explore other routes as well:

Highway toward Málaga: The **Mirador de Guardia Forestal** lookout point is spectacular.

Road to Jerez and Sevilla: Winding among the Serranía foothills, the road passes through the village of **Zahara de la Sierra,** dominated by the lovely **Iglesia de Santa María de la Mesa.** Legend has it that women who wish to bear the child of the man with whom they have just been, come here to pray.

Highway C-341: Dazzling local scenery and three choice *pueblos blancos* (Knights Templar country) to boot. **Benadolid** has a handsome, cliffside Moorish castle to its credit; **Algatocín** chimes with a 18th-century stone bell tower; and **Gaucín** wraps around a humongous rock scattered with Moorish ruins.

OLVERA

Olvera's wave of white houses washes up a hill and breaks over the green and gold of surrounding farmlands, in bright contrast to the rows of orange houses lining the hillside. Procure the key to the **Castillo Arabe** from the town hall. The top of the castle has a fabulous view of the town set against acres of olive groves.

The best place to stay is **Pensión Maqueda,** C. Calvario, 35 (tel. (956) 13 07 33; 1000ptas per person). **Pensión Olid,** Llana, 13 (tel. (956) 13 01 02), proffers immaculate rooms and friendly management. (Singles 1000ptas. Doubles 2000ptas. Showers 150ptas.) **Bar-Restaurante Manolo,** in Pl. Andalucía, 2, between the hotels and the castle, stirs up a *menú* (650ptas) and entrees (500-700ptas). Other good, and affordable, restaurants can be found on **Avenida Julian Besteiro.** Los Amarillos **buses** take on Olvera from Ronda (1 per day, 1:15pm, 385ptas).

SETENIL DE LAS BODEGAS

Nearby, the village of **Setenil de las Bodegas** perches on a mountain encrusted with caves. Troglodytes first inhabited Setenil's caves. Facades and then free-standing houses branched off the grottoes. There are still long rows of chalk-white houses built into the hillsides. The village stretches along a dramatic gorge cut by the waters of the sparkling Río Guadalporcún. The riverside streets or *cuevas* burrow under the gorge's cliff walls, creating long, covered passageways: **Cuevas Sombra, Cuevas del Sol,** and **Cuevas de Cabrerizos.** The 15th-century **Iglesia de la Encarnación,** atop the biggest rock, has darling views of the village below.

From Ronda, Ferron-Coin **buses** serve Setenil (Mon.-Fri. at 8:45am and 9:30am). By **car,** take Ronda's C. Sevilla to C-339 North. For Olvera and Setenil, take either the turn for El Gastor or the longer route by the dramatic outcropping of the village of Zahara.

■■■ ALGECIRAS

Most people come to Algeciras, a sordid, polluted port town, to leave. Scores of Moroccan migrant laborers pass through Algeciras on their way to and from Europe. If Morocco is next on your agenda as well, consider spending your last Spanish evening in windsurfing haven Tarifa or in beautiful Vejer de la Frontera. Algeciras does make a sensible jumping-off point for exploring Gibraltar, however. Buses run between the two every half-hour, and the city appears not quite so uninhabitable when the alternative is spending your last *pesetas* in overpriced Gibraltar accommodations. If you do stay, venture into the city, where health and company improve exponentially as you move away from the dope fiends at the port.

ORIENTATION AND PRACTICAL INFORMATION

Avenida Virgen del Carmen, street of the banks, hotels, and restaurants, stretches all along the coast. The train tracks (now a parking lot) and **Calle Juan de la Cierva** run perpendicular to the coast and to Av. Virgen del Carmen—whose name changes to **Avenida La Marina** near the port. The **train station** and **Comes bus station** are located on its extension. To reach the **tourist office** on C. Juan de la Cierva from either one, follow the tracks toward the **port** for a few hundred meters. From the port itself, cross the tracks as you exit and the tourist office is just up on the right.

All services necessary for transit to Morocco are clustered around the port, accessible by a single driveway. No advance purchase necessary. Be wary of imposters who peddle ferry tickets. You'll need about a half-hour to clear customs and board, an hour and a half if you have a car.

Tourist Office: C. Juan de la Cierva (tel. 57 26 36), the gigantic, tube-shaped, pink-and-red building. French and English spoken. Big map with all essentials clearly marked. Lots of Andalucía brochures. Message board to contact your ever–mobile friends. Open Mon.-Fri. 9am-2pm, Sat. 10am-1pm.

Budget Travel: No office, but many of the travel agencies sell BIJ tickets. Try **Tourafrica,** Av. Marina, 8 (tel. 65 22 00). Open Mon.-Sat. 7am-9pm, Sun. 9am-1pm and 4-8pm.

Currency Exchange: For *pesetas* or *dirhams,* go to a bank along Av. Virgen del Carmen around the market or Pl. Alta. Travel agencies get away with atrocious exchange rates.

Post Office: C. Ruiz Zorilla, s/n (tel. 66 31 76). From the train station, hang a left on the street leading to Málaga. It becomes C. Ruiz Zorilla. Open for Lista de Correos and **telegrams** Mon.-Fri. 9am-8pm, Sat. 9am-6pm. Another, smaller post office on C. José Antonio Primo de Rivera, 4, has the same services and hours. **Postal Code:** 11080.

Telephones: On C. Pescadería and Av. Virgen del Carmen. Open Mon.-Sat. 10am-2pm and 6-10pm, Sun. 11am-2pm and 6-10pm. **Telephone Code:** 956.

Trains: RENFE (tel. 63 02 02 or 63 20 45), all the way down C. Juan de la Cierva and its connecting street. To: Granada (3 per day, 5½hr.,1600ptas). With connections in Bobadilla to: Málaga (3 per day, 5½hr., 1380ptas); Sevilla (3 per day, 6hr., 1805ptas); Madrid (3 per day, 7-9hr., 7300-7700ptas; night train 12 hr., 4900ptas).

Buses: Empresa Portillo, Av. Virgen del Carmen, 15 (tel. 65 10 55), 1½ bl. to the right as you leave the port complex. To: Marbella (11 per day, Sun. 1 per day, 1½hr., 680ptas); Granada (2 per day, 5hr., 2235ptas); Málaga (11 per day, Sun. 1 per day, 3hr., 1190ptas); Almería (1 per day, 6hr., 2955ptas). **Empresa La Valenciana,** Viajes Koudubia, C. Juan de la Cierva, 5 (tel. 60 11 89). To: Jerez de la Frontera (6 per day, 2hr., 975ptas); Sevilla (6 per day, 3½hr., 1795ptas); Madrid (2 per day, 10hr., 3385ptas). **Empresa Comes** (tel. 65 34 56), under Hotel Octavio on C. San Bernardo, the continuation of C. Juan de la Cierva. To: Tarifa (Mon.-Fri. 10 per day, Sat. 9 per day, Sun. 4 per day, ¾hr., 200ptas); La Linea (every ½hr 7am-9:30pm, ¾hr., 200ptas); Cádiz (Mon.-Sat. 9 per day, Sun. 8 per day, 2½hr., 1135ptas); Sevilla (4 per day, 3½hr., 2000ptas). **Empresa Bacoma,** at the Tourafrica office on the port, Av. Marina, 8 (tel. 65 22 00). To Barcelona (4 per day, 19½hr., 9500ptas). Shortened schedule weekends and holidays.

Ferries: To: Ceuta *(buque ferry* daily, every hr. on the hr. 7am-10pm, 1½hr., 1834ptas per person, children 917ptas, 8442-14583ptas per car, 1814-2940ptas per motorcycle; *embarcaciones rápidas* Mon.-Sat. 8 per day, Sun. 4 per day, ½hr., 2914ptas per person, children 1457ptas, 8442-14,583ptas per car, 1814-2940ptas per motorcycle) and Tangier (every hr. on the hr., 8am-10pm, 2½hr.; Class A 3440ptas per person, 1720ptas per child; Class B 2700ptas per person, 1350ptas per child; 8500ptas per car, 2400ptas per motorcycle). 20% discount with Eurail pass. No cars on board in stormy weather. Limited service in winter.

Luggage Storage: At **Empresa Portillo** bus terminal. Large lockers, 300ptas per day. Open 7:30am-10pm.

English-Language Periodicals: Kiosk on C. Juan de la Cierva across from the tourist office, next door to the Casa Alfonso Restaurant. Limited selection.

Pharmacy: C. Cayetano del Toro at C. Tarifa. Open Mon.-Fri. 9am-1:30pm and 5-8:30pm. *Farmacias de guardia* listed on windowpane.

Hospital: Residencia Sanitaria (tel. 60 57 22).

Emergency: tel. 091.

Police: Municipal, C. Ruiz Zorilla (tel. 66 01 55), next to Pl. Andalucía.

ACCOMMODATIONS AND FOOD

Lots of convenient *casas de huéspedes* and *hostales* bunch around **Calle José Santacana,** parallel to Av. Marina and one block inland, and **Calle Duque de Almodóvar,** two blocks farther from the water. Consider asking for a back room, as would-be mods cruise the narrow streets on Vespas at ungodly hours. The beach in Algeciras isn't the best place to camp. Police patrol the waterfront and when they don't, unsavories do. Relish your final taste of *paella,* or welcome yourself back from Morocco with a *medio pollo asado* (baked ½-chicken) sold in many places along Av. Virgen del Carmen, near the port, and C. Juan de la Cierva.

Hostal Vizcaino, C. José Santacana, 9 (tel. 65 57 56). From the port, follow the train tracks and take the 2nd street to the right. Attractive foyer and front TV room. Rooms on top floor glow with outside light, but the lower rooms are rather gloomy. Owners may allow you to store your things for a few weeks if you're coming back to town. Singles with bath 1200ptas. Doubles with bath 2400ptas.

Hostal Residencia González, C. José Santacana, 7 (tel. 65 28 43). Another decent bargain close to the port. Roomy, tasteful quarters and new wood furnishings. Singles 1500ptas, with bath 2000ptas. Doubles 3000ptas, with bath 4000ptas.

Hostal Levante, C. Duque de Almodóvar, 21 (tel. 65 15 05), 2 streets inland from C. Jose Santacana. Modern, multi-fauceted bathrooms, with demonic miniature soaps. Brightly lit rooms. Enormous color TV gets all 6 Spanish channels. Beds sag a tad. Singles 1500ptas, with bath 2000ptas. Doubles 2500ptas, with bath 3500ptas. Showers free.

Casa Alfonso, C. Juan de la Cierva (tel. 60 31 21), the big green building near the tourist office. For no-nonsense eating with the people who run the port. *Tortillas* (350-500ptas) make a substantial meal. You can assemble a personalized *menú* (900ptas). Open Sun.-Fri. noon-11pm; winter Sun.-Fri. noon-11pm.

Restaurante Casa Sanchez, Av. Segismundo Moret, 6 (tel. 65 69 57), on the corner of C. Río, 1 bl. inland from C. José Santancana. Lively local joint with low-key service. *Menú* with salad, 2 courses, fruit, bread, and wine 800ptas. *Gazpacho andaluz* 275ptas. Open Fri.-Wed. noon-11:30pm.

SIGHTS

Some of the Spaniards forced to leave Gibraltar in 1704 (over trouble with the British) settled in Algeciras around the beautiful **Plaza Alta,** crowned in the middle by a handsome blue- and gold-tiled fountain. Many outdoor cafés and *heladerías* line nearby **Calle Regino Martinez,** the main *paseo.*

Accessible only by car, the nicest beach around borders the tiny village of **Getares,** 5km south of Algeciras off the main road. The mile-long sand strip is relatively uncrowded. A city bus (tel. 66 22 57) swings out that way in summer.

■ NEAR ALGECIRAS

TARIFA

The southernmost city in continental Europe ranks with the streets of downtown Chicago and the moors of England as one of the world's great windsurfing centers—many windsurfers, in fact, prefer Tarifa since it has a beach. Only a 45-minute bus ride west of Algeciras, Tarifa is a clone of a California surf town. T-shirts announce that Tarifa has "365 windy days a year." But the same winds that thrill surfers taunt those who would otherwise overrun the uncongested beaches.

To reach **Plaza de Mateo,** the main square, exit to the right of the bus station and take a right on Av. Andalucía, before the stone arch that is the main gateway to the Moorish old town. The stone pile to the left is the **castillo** of Guzmán el Bueno. In the 13th century, the Moors kidnapped Guzmán's son and threatened to kill him if Guzmán didn't relinquish the castle. Guzmán, like Abraham, didn't surrender his "principles." The castle is not open to visitors, but you can look out from its ramparts to Morocco (entrance July- Aug. Mon.-Fri. noon and 2pm). To get here, follow the street on your left from the castle's main gate and climb the stairs through the gardens of **Plaza de Santa María.** The wetter action treks 200m north at **Playa Lances,** 5km of cool orange sand and turquoise water. Beware of high winds and the undertow.

The small **information kiosk** near the intersection of Batalla del Salado and Av. Andalucía (by the arch) is reached through the **Ayuntamiento** (tel. 68 41 86, ext. 51). It functions as the **tourist office,** and is usually open Mon.-Fri. 11am-1pm and 6-8pm; if closed, head to the Ayuntamiento for a map and advice. The **post office,** C. Colonel Moscardó, 9 (tel. 68 42 37), is near the town center. (Open Mon.-Fri. 8am-3pm, Sat. 9am-2pm.) The **postal code** is 11380. **Telephones, fax,** and international press can be found at the kiosk at C. Batalla del Salado, 8 (open 10:30am-2pm and 5-9pm), or in virtually every exchange bureau on that street. In case of **medical emergency,** dial **Casa del Mar** at tel. 64 37 79. The **police** uphold law and order from the Ayuntamiento building (tel. 68 41 86).

Affordable rooms line the main strip, **Batalla del Salado.** If you visit in August, call ahead or arrive early. **La Casa Concha,** C. San Rosendo, 4 (tel. 68 49 31), one block off Pl. El Bravo, offers inexpensive lodging. From the bus station, take an immediate left onto C. Silos after the aforementioned arch, and take the first right. (Singles 1500ptas. Doubles with bath 4000ptas.) A number of official **campgrounds** lurk a few km to the north on the beach (400-450ptas per person). The police seem remarkably tolerant of unofficial camping.

For simple yet sating victuals, head to **Méson el Carnicero,** Av. Edificio 3, for the filling 700pta *menú.* Exit the bus station to the left and take the 6th right off Batalla del Salado. *Tubo de cerveza* 100ptas, with *tapa* 150ptas. (Open 8pm-midnight.)

Transportes Generales Comes buses make for Algeciras (10 per day, Sat. 9 per day, Sun. 4 per day, ½hr., 200ptas) and Cádiz (8 per day, Sat.-Sun. 5 per day, 2hr., 930ptas) from the **bus station** at Batalla del Salado, 19 (tel. 68 40 38).

VEJER DE LA FRONTERA

Vejer de la Frontera is the *pueblo blanco* of your dreams, charming and (almost) tourist-free. Whitewashed houses scatter at the base of a handsome Moorish castle, and an elegant church pokes above an imposing rock spike. The view from the outskirts of town is smashing. (Perhaps the best countryside vista is along the Corredera near the bus stop.) Favorite evening pastimes in Vejer include gaping at the colorful sunset from the esplanade and gulping at the colorful bars around **Plaza de España,** the **Mercado de Abastos,** and especially the **Plazuela** just uphill from the bus stop.

The **Castillo Moro** offers the usual assortment of battlements and crenellated walls, along with a blinding view of the town's glowing white houses. (Open July-Aug. 10am-2pm and 4-9pm, rest of the year 10am-2pm.) **Iglesia del Divino Salvador** is a stand-out mix of Romanesque, Mudejar, and Gothic styles. The castle and the church are brilliantly illuminated at night. (Open Mon.-Fri. 11am-1pm and 7-9pm, or for mass Mon.-Fri. 8:30pm, Sat. 9pm, Sun. 11am.)

The village throws brilliant *fiestas.* As soon as the **Corpus Christi** revelry ends in June, Vejer shoots off the **Candelas de San Juan,** in which a firecracker-filled mannequin (prepared by village children in a fierce competition) is burnt over a huge bonfire. A marching band escorts the inanimate winner through the village before its demise. In spring come the delirious **Semana Santa** and **Feria de Abril** celebrations, with dancing in the streets and the running of a bull *(toro embolado)*.

Pay a visit to the **tourist office** on C. Juan Relinque (tel. 44 73 85 or 44 72 24), off the *plazuela*, to receive maps, information, and free and delicious cookie samples *(tortas vejeriegas)*. (Open Mon.-Fri. 10am-2pm and 6-9pm. In summer, also open Sat. 11am-1pm.) The **post office** (tel. 45 02 38) is located at C. Juan Bueno, 22 (open for **telegrams** and Lista de Correos Mon.-Fri. 8am-3pm, Sat. 9am-2pm). The **postal code** is 11150. Call home from the **telephones** at Plazuela, 2B (open Mon.-Fri. 10am-2:30pm and 6-11pm, Sat.-Sun. 10am-2:30pm and 7-11pm). In case of **medical emergency,** call the **Centro de Salud** at tel. 45 01 07; or visit them at Av. Andalucía, 8. **Police** are at tel. 45 04 00.

The best accommodations in Vejer are in **casas particulares.** Sra. Luisa Doncel keeps clean and pretty rooms, with almost-private bath and a sitting room with color TV, on C. San Filmo, 12 (tel. 45 02 46). C. San Filmo begins at the stone stairs to the right of the Autoservicio, across form the bus stop; walk two blocks uphill. If Doña Luisa is not at #12, look in #16. (Singles 1250ptas. Doubles 2500-3000ptas.) Sra. Isabel López offers similar **lodgings** on C. Amaro, 8 (tel. 44 71 09). Uphill the bus stop to the Plazuela, then one block up C. Teniente Castejóu. Make a right on C. Altozano, then a left on C. Sagasta, off of which veers tiny C. Amaro.

The cheapest way to eat is to have *tapas* or *raciones* at one of the bars around the Plazuela, such as **Bar Julián,** C. Juan Relinque, half a block from the tourist office (open 6pm-1am). If you're in the mood for a sit-down meal, go to **La Posada** (tel. 45 01 11), on the Corredera a few buildings downhill of the Plazuela and the bus stop. Bar and ornate dining room, with 900pta *menú*, 700pta *huevos a la flamenca* (eggs cooked in tomato sauce and topped with asparagus and prosciutto), and a 350pta monster tuna-topped *ensalada mixta*. (Open 1:30-4pm and 8-11pm.)

By night the old quarter houses some lively bars **(El Joplin** and **La Bodeguito** on C. Marqués de Tamarón, **El Callejón** on C. Arco de las Monjas, **El Patio** on C. Sagasta, and **El Altillo** on C. Altozano), as well as a discotheque **(La Cilla,** on C. Sagasta).

Bus info at the Comes office on Plazuela, a tiny window with green ironwork (tel. 45 00 30). To: Cádiz (7 per day, Sat.-Sun. 3 per day, 1¼hr., 500ptas); Sevilla (2 per day, Sat.-Sun. 1 per day, 3hr., 1600ptas); Algeciras (1¼hr., 610ptas). Sadly, some buses let you out by the highway at **La Barca de Vejer.** Taxis charge 500ptas to take you up the hill, a fee that can be split among several passengers. It's money well spent, as the walk up can be torturous with a backpack. If you do decide to make the 30-minute trek, climb up the stone steps to the left of the restaurant. Leaving Vejer, you won't have to walk downhill, since all buses come to a stop on the **Corredera,** the main road running on and along the mountain.

■■■ GIBRALTAR

Anglophiles and homesick Brits get jolly well excited at Gibraltar's amenities, its fish'n'chips, changing of the guard, and Marks and Spencer. The gateway to the Atlantic commands a breathtaking view of the Straits of Gibraltar all the way to the Moroccan coast. Nicknamed "Gib" by the locals, this British colony (pop. 36,000) takes its Britishness very seriously; citizens switch in and out of the Queen's English and Andalusian Spanish. The history of the Rock leaves tension unresolved today: residents look up to Britain and down on the mainland Spanish; there's a massive British military presence; and Moroccans work in horrific conditions at sweatshop wages.

The ancients considered the Rock of Gibraltar one of the Pillars of Hercules, marking the very end of the world. The Moors fortified Gibraltar into an important strategic base following the 711 invasion. After they recaptured the Rock from the Moors in 1462, the Spanish Christians pocked the peninsula with military wares to ward off Barbary pirates and Moorish retaliation. English troops stormed Gibraltar's shores during the War of the Spanish Sucession, and the Treaty of Utrecht (1713) solidified Britain's hold on the enclave. When control of Hong Kong passes to China in 1997, Gibraltar will become the last outpost of Britain's empire.

A 1967 vote showed that the populace overwhemingly favored its British ties over becoming part of Spain (12,138 to 44). In 1969, General Franco sealed off the border and forbade any contact between Spain and Gibraltar. After a decade of negotiations and 16 years of isolation, however, the border reopened at midnight on February 4, 1985. Tourists and residents now cross *la línea* freely. Spanish government, however, seems far from relinquishing its claim to *El Peñón* (rock).

ORIENTATION AND PRACTICAL INFORMATION

From the bus stop on the Spanish side, walk directly toward "the Rock;" the border is 10 minutes away. After passing through Spanish customs and Gibraltar's passport control, walk across the airport tarmac and cross the overhead pedestrian bridge.

To get downtown, continue along Ave. Winston Churchill until the road forks to Corral Lane. Follow Ave. Winston Churchill (bear left) and go through **Landport Tunnel.** Gibraltar's **Main Street,** a commercial strip containing most services and hotels, begins at the far end of the large parking lot past the shops on the left.

Although *pesetas* are accepted everywhere (except in pay phones), the pound sterling is clearly the preferred method of payment. Merchants sometimes charge a higher price in *pesetas* than is the pound's exchange equivalent; more often than not, change will be given in English currency rather than Spanish.

Tourist Office: 18-20 Bomb House Lane (tel. 748 05), in the Gibraltar Museum. Bomb House Lane is across the street from Marks and Spencer on Main Street. Open Mon.-Fri. 10am-6pm, Sat. 10am-2pm. This office is a bit better equipped than the information office, though maps (£1.50) leave a bit to be desired. **Information Center,** Main St., The Piazza. Open Mon.-Fri. 9am-6pm, Sat. 10am-2pm.

Currency Exchange: (see Orientation, last paragraph). Banks on Main St. Most close at 3:30pm, reopening Fri. only 4:30-6pm. **Gib Exchange Ctr., Ltd.,** John Mackintosh Sq., 6A (tel. 735 17), has comparable rates. Open Mon.-Fri. 9am-1pm and 3-7pm, Sat. 9am-6pm.

American Express: Bland Travel, Irish Town (tel. 726 17; after-hours emergency calls are forwarded to England if necessary). Holds mail and sells traveler's checks, but doesn't cash them. Open Mon.-Fri. 9am-6pm.

Post Office: 104 Main St. Sells Gibraltar stamps in sets for collectors. Possibly the easiest Poste Restante address on earth (not one number): Name, Poste Restante, Gibraltar (Main Post Office). Open for most services Mon.-Fri. 8:45am-2:15pm, Sat. 10am-1pm; winter Mon.-Fri. 9am-5pm, Sat. 10am-1pm.

Telephones: Conspicuous red booths on many corners and pay phones in most pubs—none accept *pesetas*. More expensive but without the hassle of coins is **Gibraltar Telecommunications International Ltd.,** 60 Main St. (tel. 756 87). **Faxes** also sent. To US: £3.50 for the first page, £2.50 for each additional page. Open Mon.-Fri. 9am-5pm. **Telephone Code:** From Britain (010) 350. From Spain first dial 07 (or from Algeciras *only* 7), as the Rock is considered a foreign destination. The USA Direct code is 88 00.

Buses: Buses run to **La Línea,** the nearest Spanish town on the border, from the **Empresa Comes** station in Algeciras behind Hotel Octavio (every ½hr., 40min., 195ptas). Buses also run from Málaga to La Línea (5 per day, 2½hr., 1135ptas).

English-Language Bookstore: The Gibraltar Bookshop, 300 Main St. (tel. 718 94). Superior choice of classics such as *Let's Go* (£13.95). Open Mon.-Fri. 9:30am-7pm, Sat. 11am-4pm. **The Book Centre,** 219 Main St. (tel. 756 49). Books (*Let's Go* is only £13.50 here) as well as stationery and greeting cards. Open Mon.-Fri. 9:30am-7pm, Sat. 9:30am-1pm.

English-Language Periodicals: Sacarelo News Agency, 96 Main St. (tel. 787 23). The most globe-trotting selection of papers and magazines in town. Open Mon.-Fri. 9am-7pm, Sat. 9am-2:30pm, Sun. 1:30-5pm.

Hospital: St. Bernard's Hospital (tel. 797 00), on Hospital Hill.

Police: 120 Irish Town St. (tel. 725 00 or 199), behind MacKintosh Sq.

Emergency: tel. 112.

ACCOMMODATIONS

Camping is illegal, and the two affordable places in the area are often full, especially between July and September. If worse comes to worst, crash at one of the *hostales* in La Línea, a 20-minute trudge over the border.

Toc H Hostel, Line Wall Rd. (tel. 734 31). Toward the Rock on Main St., right just before the arch at Southport Gate, then left in front of the Hambros Bank. Everyone in Gibraltar knows of Toc H, a whitewashed maze of plants, cats, and young people—confusion worth overlooking for such a bargain. Make friends with the hospitable proprietors; they tell great stories. Check-out at noon. Cold showers only. £3 per person. £15 per week.

Miss Serruya Guest House, 92/1a Irish Town (tel. 732 20). From Main Bank St., turn right onto Tuckey's Lane, then left before the stairs. Small, makeshift rooms do for a cheap night's sleep. Ruckus from neighboring pubs breezes in. Shower of extremities: freezing or scalding. £8 per person; you may have to share a room. £16 single. Reservations held only with deposit.

Queen's Hotel, 1 Boyd St. (tel. 740 00; fax (350) 400 30), through Southport Gate. Bear right. Only slightly preferable to living under the Rock, but there are phones in each room, and some have TVs. Special rates for *Let's Go* readers (ask for them) are more than 50% less than their regular rates. Twin bedded room £12, with bath £14. Single £16, with bath £18. Free parking. Common bathrooms aren't quite as nice. Breakfast £3-4.

Continental Hotel, 1 Engineer Lane (tel. 769 00; fax 417 02). Off Main St., turn left at the Corner House Cafe. Closets are bigger than bathrooms. Comfortable, carpeted rooms with color TVs, phones, and A/C. Elevator. Single £42. Double £55. Triple £70. Quad £85. Continental breakfast included. 5% discount for cash.

White's Hotel, Govenor's Parade (tel. 705 00; fax 702 43). Fancy. There's a sauna, pool, and gym on the 8th floor. Rooms all have double or king-sized beds, as well as TV, phone, and A/C. Expensive, but they are almost always running specials that knock prices down somewhere in the £49-60 range. Singles £95. Doubles £99. Extra person £10. Senior citizen rates available.

FOOD

Visitors can scarf Chinese, English, French, Indian, Spanish, and Italian cuisine—all for a considerable price. Even fast food is expensive. For the cheapest eats, check out the small restaurants and pubs in the alleys of **Main Street.** A bit of advice to Gibraltar's weekend visitors: eat early, as almost all restaurants are closed by 4pm.

Smith's Fish and Chips, 295 Main St. (tel. 742 54). Run by a cheerful lad who dishes out rotund servings of chicken and fish. Fish and chips (£2.95) plus some vegetarian dishes. Open Mon.-Fri. 11am-9:30pm, Sat. noon-3pm.

Uptown Chicago, 10 Cannon Lane (tel. 789 51), off Main St. Decorated with model cars and pictures of the Windy City. Fine English grub and fab service. American burger with fries and salad £2.50. English breakfast £2.95. Take-away cheaper. Open Mon.-Fri. 9am-10pm, Sat. 9am-5pm. Closes a bit earlier in the winter.

The Cannon, 27 Cannon Lane (tel. 772 88). Off Main St.; turn left at Marks and Spencer. Menu of the day £4.75 (includes salad, entree, ice cream or coffee, and a glass of wine). Sunday lunches £5. English, Spanish, French, and German spoken. Open 9am-midnight, weekends 9am-1am. Food not served at all hours.

Ye Olde Rock, Mackintosh Sq. (tel. 718 04), off Main St. Pub with beer mugs hanging from the rafters. Burger with chips and salad £2. Sandwiches a mere £1.25-1.50. Open Mon.-Thurs. 10am-1am, Fri.-Sat. 10am-2am. Meals served all day.

Maharala, 5 Tuckey's Lane (tel. 752 33), off Main St., turn right at Barday's Bank onto Tuckey's Lane; it's on your left. Pink and white "Indian" decor. Relatively cheap, but "extras" such as rice and bread jack up the price. Entrees £3.80-6. Open late on Sunday nights. Take-away available. Open noon 12-3pm and 7-11:15pm.

The Leanse Kosher Restaurant, 7 Bomb House Lane (tel. 417 51; fax 403 04), in the gray building adjacent to the Gibraltar Museum. Surely the only Glatt Kosher *tapas* (£70) in the entire Iberian peninsula. Appetizers £0.80-4. Entrees £6-10.50. Under the supervision of the Rabbi of the Jewish Community of Gibraltar. A/C. Open Sun.-Thurs. 11am-3:30pm and 7:30pm-midnight, Fri. 11am-3:30pm.

SIGHTS

From the northern tip of the massif known as **Top of the Rock,** there's a truly remarkable view of Iberia and the Straits of Gibraltar. **Cable cars** carry visitors from the southern end of Main St. to the Top of the Rock, making a stop at Apes' Den (every 10min., Mon.-Sat. 9:30am-6pm). You can't buy tickets after 5:15pm. (Round-trip £4.65 per person, children £2.30; one-way £3.45 per person, children £1.70). Get the one-way ticket and walk down. The price of the cable car includes admission to St. Michael's Cave and the Apes' Den. Newly-installed toll booths charge £3 per car and £3 per walker. Tickets for the Nature Reserve on the Upper Rock are £5 for adults and £2.50 for children; £1.50 if you drive in your own car. This ticket includes admission to St. Michael's Cave, the Apes' Den, the Great Siege Tunnels, the Arts & Crafts Centre, the Miltary & Heritage Centre, the "Gilbraltar: A City Under Siege" exhibit, and the Moorish Castle. (Open 9:30am-7pm. Last entries at 5:30pm. Cars allowed in only after 2:30pm.)

The ruins of a Moorish wall crumble down the road from the cable car station to the south, where the spooky chambers of **St. Michael's Cave** cut into the rock. The deep cave metamorphosed into a hospital during the 1942 bombardments; now it's an auditorium with the requisite colored lights and corny music. If lucky, you'll hear a flute arrangement of Hall and Oates' "Maneater." The first Neanderthal skull was unearthed here. To reach St. Michael's from the Top of the Rock, take gravelly St. Michael's Road and stick to the right. (Open 9:30am-8pm; off-season 9:30am-7pm. No entrance 15min. before closing. Admission £1.50.)

Take a U-turn down Queen's Rd. to the **Apes' Den,** where a colony of monkeys clamber lithely about the sides of rocks, the tops of taxis, and tourists' heads. The tail-less Barbary apes have inhabited Gibraltar since before the invasion of the Moors. The British believe they'll control the peninsula only as long as these animals survive. When the ape population came dangerously close to extinction in 1944, Churchill put Yalta aside and ordered reinforcements from North Africa.

Farther north on Queen's Road, the **Moorish Castle,** built in 1160, has flown the British flag since 1704. (Closed to the public.) A labyrinth of steep stone alleyways through Gibraltar's **old town** leads back to the commercial rush on the north end of Main St.

The **Gibraltar Museum** at the tourist office on Bomb House Lane has hedonistic 14th-century **Moorish baths** and other items of interest about Gib's history. (Open Mon.-Fri. 10am-6pm, Sat. 10am-2pm. Admission adults £2, children £1; includes a 15-min. film on Gibraltar.)

At the southern tip of Gibraltar, **Europa Point** commands a seemingly endless view of the straits, guarded by three machine guns and a lighthouse. On a clear day you can see Africa. Take buses #3 or 1B from Line Wall Rd., just off Main St., all the way to the end (every 15min., £35).

Tucked at the foot of the great white cliff on the northern end of the peninsula, **Catalan Bay** is a beach swarming with British tourists. Several seaside cafés and grocery stores sell snacks and beverages. Smaller but slightly less crowded, **Sandy Bay Beach** is just a short hike up the road. You can get to the most spacious crescent of sand, **Eastern Beach,** by foot from Catalan Bay. The Eastern Beach bus is £35. To reach the beach, take buses #1B, 4A, or 4B from Line Wall Rd. toward Catalan Bay (every 15min., 8:45am-8:45pm, £30).

ENTERTAINMENT

Pubs linger along Main St. The early evening crowd people-watches from **Angry Friar,** 287 Main St. (across from the Governor's Residence), also known as **The**

Convent (tel. 715 70), which occasionally has live music, and a jazz band most summer Sunday nights. The name alone warrants patronage by ecclesiastophiles. Don't miss having your photograph taken with the picture of the fist-shaking monk. (Open 10am-midnight, food served 10am-3pm.) As evening wears into night, pubhoppers slide on down to the **Horseshoe Bar** with its video jukebox at 193 Main St. (tel. 774 44; open Sun.-Thurs. 9:30am-midnight, Fri.-Sat. 9:30am-1am).

Films screen at the **Queen's Cinema,** Boyd St. (tel. 737 61), near the Queen's Hotel down the street from the cable car station. (Wed.-Fri. at 10pm. £3 stalls, £4 dress circle). The **Casino** (tel. 766 66; fax 424 74) lies up the hill from the cinema at 7 Europa Road. Entrance is free; no membership or passport required. Dress is "Smart Casual." Bingo Sessions nightly at 9:30pm. (Open: Cocktail Bar 7:30pm-3:30am; Terrace Restaurant 8pm-1am; Casino Gaming Rooms 9pm-4am; Gaming Machines Parlour 10am-2am.)

■■■ CÁDIZ

The fortunes of Cádiz have always been linked to the Spanish sea trade. After the Phoenicians landed here in 1100 BC, founding what is thought to be the oldest city in Western Europe, Cádiz thrived as the gate to the West Coast of Africa and was eventually frequented by the ubiquitous Hannibal. When Rome fell, however, so did this port city. Cádiz plummeted until the 16th century, when trade with the Americas provided the impetus for its economic revival. The departure point, this "City of Explorers" became the wealthiest port in Europe; the flower-filled alleys of the *casco viejo* (old town) date from this period. Unfortunately for Cádiz, it was targeted by England in its struggle against Spain. Sir Francis Drake came here in 1587 to "singe the King of Spain's beard," and the port was then repeatedly invaded by the British Navy during the 17th century. When Napoleon occupied Spain, Cádiz resisted (as did other regions) by proclaiming a provisional *junta* to rule the country. All of the *juntas* met here in 1810, and the radical *Constitución de 1812* (providing universal suffrage even in the colonies) was drawn up in Cádiz while French cannons bombarded the peninsula. Here irony once again played the muse of history: the very colonies which had suffered under Spanish exploitation were inspired by the Cádiz document to take action. The era of Latin American Nationalism began, as the New World colonies resisted Napoleon and Fernando VII in rapid succession. By the 1820s, most Latin American countries were independent.

During the 1930s, Cádiz's inhabitants fought fiercely against the Fascists in the Civil War. Today they consistently vote for leftist parties. Socially, the city has a reputation for a vibrant nightlife, a large gay scene, and the most extravagant carnival in all of Spain—reputedly the only one Franco could not suppress. The primacy of the sea has remained, and many of the current population of 154,500 are merchants.

Cádiz makes an excellent base from which to explore the Costa de la Luz—the coast that curves around Spain's southwestern edge to Portugal. Although light can't compete with sun for warm waters, the Costa de la Luz's long, sandy beaches are relatively tourist-free compared to the ever-popular Costa del Sol.

ORIENTATION AND PRACTICAL INFORMATION

Cádiz is accessible by bus and train from Sevilla and nearby towns. To reach **Plaza San Juan de Dios** (the center of town) from the bus station, head to the left along Av. Puerto past a park (Po. Canalejas), and then walk almost two blocks. From the train station, walk about four blocks to the right, keeping the port on your right side. Pl. San Juan de Dios is the first plaza on the left. The tangled streets of Cádiz's *casco viejo* are disorienting—tourists and locals alike stop and ask for directions.

Tourist Office: Municipal, Pl. San Juan de Dios, Pozos de Miranda building (tel. 24 10 01). Bright yellow "i" marks the spot. Provides only available, and utterly essential (though sometimes incomplete) map of the *casco viejo,* as well as listings of cultural events. English spoken. Open Mon.-Fri. 9am-2pm and 5-8pm, Sat.

10am-2pm. **Regional,** C. Calderón de la Barca, 1 (tel. 21 13 13). From the bus station, cross over to Pl. España and walk uphill on C. Antonio López. The office is across Pl. Mina, on the corner of C. Calderón de la Barca. From the train station, follow Av. Puerto north toward the town center all the way to Pl. España, then follow directions given above. Some English spoken. Same hours as Municipal.

Currency Exchange: Banks on Pl. San Juan de Dios and Av. Ramón de Carranza (next to the *plaza* and facing the port) exchange for the usual 1% or 500pta commission. Most open Mon.-Fri. 8:30am-2pm.

Post Office: Pl. Flores, next to market (tel. 22 94 32). Open for Lista de Correos Mon.-Fri. 9am-3pm, Sat. 9am-2pm; for stamps Mon.-Fri. 9am-9pm, Sat. 9am-2pm; for **telegrams** Mon.-Fri. 9am-9pm, Sat. 9am-7pm. **Postal Code:** 11080.

Telephones: C. Sacramento, 41, near the post office. Open Mon.-Fri. 10am-2pm and 6-10pm, Sat. 10am-2pm. **Telephone Code:** 956.

Trains: Pl. Sevilla, s/n, off Av. Puerto. **RENFE** (tel. 25 43 01). To: Jerez de la Frontera (16 per day, 45min., 350ptas); Sevilla (cheapest is *regional*, 8 per day, 2hr., 850ptas); Málaga (3 per day, 5hr., 1700ptas); Granada (3 per day, 6hr., 2020ptas); Córdoba (3 per day, 4½hr., 1830ptas); Valencia (2 per day, 6000-6900ptas); Madrid (nightly *expreso* 10hr., 4800ptas; *talgo* 8hr., 7700-8800ptas; AVE 6hr., 8500-9700ptas); Barcelona (nightly *expreso* 18hr., 6700-8200ptas; *rápido* 15hr., 7500ptas; *talgo* 10hr., 9000ptas).

Buses: Transportes Generales Comes, Pl. Hispanidad, 1 (tel. 22 42 71). To: Puerto de Santa María (Mon.-Fri. 18 per day, Sat.-Sun. 11 per day, 30min., 175ptas); Rota (Mon.-Fri. 8 per day, Sat.-Sun. 5 per day, 1¼hr., 415ptas); Arcos de la Frontera (Mon.-Fri. 7 per day, Sat.-Sun. 3 per day, 1½hr., 615ptas); Jerez de la Frontera (Mon.-Fri. 15 per day, Sat.-Sun. 11 per day, 1hr., 325ptas); Algeciras (8 per day, 2½hr., 1135ptas); Sevilla (11 per day, 1¾hr., 1200ptas); Córdoba (daily at 4:30pm, 5hr., 2020ptas); Granada (2 per day at 1:30pm and 9pm, 7hr., 3705ptas). **Transportes Los Amarillos,** leave from ticket office (open Mon.-Fri. 10:30am-1:30pm) on Av. Ramón de Carranza, 31 (tel. 28 58 52), across from Jardines de Canalejas, facing the port. Tickets can also be purchased on board. To: Sanlúcar de Barrameda (Mon.-Fri. 9 per day, Sat.-Sun. 5 per day, 1¼hr., 350ptas); Chipiona (4 per day, 1½hr., 430ptas); Puerto de Santa María (Mon.-Fri. 8 per day, Sat.-Sun. 5 per day, 30min., 160ptas); Arcos de la Frontera (2 per day, 2hr., 710ptas).

Taxis: tel. 21 21 21, 26 26 26, or 22 10 06.

Luggage Storage: Lockers at train station, 300ptas. Open 8am-10pm.

Bookstore: Librería Manuel de Falla, Pl. Miras, 2. Has 3½ shelves of Penguin books. Photocopies. Open Mon.-Fri. 10am-2pm and 5-9pm, Sat. 10am-2pm.

Laundromat: Lavandería Industrial, C. Santo Domingo, 17 (tel. 25 73 98). No self-service. Charges per item. Open Mon.-Fri. 9am-1pm and 3-8pm, Sat. 9am-2pm.

Pharmacy: Farmacia S. Matute, Pl. San Juan de Dios, 2. Open Apr.-Sept. Mon.-Fri. 9am-1pm and 5-8:30pm; Oct.-March Mon.-Fri. 9:30am-1:15pm and 4:30-8pm, Sat. 10am-1pm. *Farmacia de guardia* (night pharmacy) rotates; look for list posted outside pharmacies.

Medical Assistance: Hospital Puertal del Mar, Av. Ana de Viya, 21 (tel. 24 21 00; emergencies 25 90 11). **Red Cross,** C. Sta. María Soledad, 10 (tel. 25 42 70).

Emergency: tel. 091 or 092.

Police: National, Av. Andalucía, 28 (tel. 28 61 11). **Municipal,** Campo del Sur (tel. 22 81 06). Both are in new city.

ACCOMMODATIONS

Hostales huddle around the harbor and **Plaza San Juan de Dios,** as well as on **Calle Marqués de Cádiz** and **Calle Flamenco.** Singles and triples are scarce, although more negotiable in the off-season. Call months in advance for February's carnival.

Hostal Colón, C. Marqués de Cádiz, 6 (tel. 28 53 51), off Pl. San Juan de Dios. Recently renovated. Spotless rooms with shiny floors, sinks, and colorful tiles. Doubles 2800-3200ptas. One triple 3300ptas. In off-season solo travelers may be able to get a room with a double bed for 1500ptas.

CÁDIZ

Hostal Cádiz, C. Feduchy, 20 (tel. 28 58 01), near Pl. Candelaria. Comfortable and friendly. Ask knowledgeable and amicable owner for tips on cheap eateries and hip nightlife. Everything labeled in three languages. Doubles 2500-3000ptas. Triples 3600-4500ptas.

Camas Cuatro Naciones, C. Plocia, 3 (tel. 25 55 39), in a corner of Pl. San Juan de Dios. Same 2-tone decor as the cathedral, in deeper shades of pale. Rooms facing the street get a lot of light. This place is somehow still afloat, though prices are rock-bottom. Singles 1200ptas. Doubles 2500ptas.

Pensión Matilde, C. Sagasta, 18 (tel. 22 14 48), near the telephone office, in the middle of the maze. Ample, clean rooms. Lobby decorated with illustrations of boats and amphibians. Doubles 2000ptas. Triples 3000ptas.

Camas Marqués, C. Marqués de Cádiz, 1 (tel. 28 58 54), off Pl. San Juan de Dios. Glaring green and white interior. Three identical floors of identical rooms. Plants on the balconies. One single 1500ptas. Doubles 2500ptas.

FOOD

The area around **Plaza San Juan de Dios** is fertile foraging territory. Dozens of stands and bars (called *peñas*) near **Playa de la Caleta,** in Barrio de la Viña to the southwest, and on **Calle La Palma,** sell the city's notorious *pescado frito* (fried fish).

Supermarket: Supermercado Cádiz, corner of C. Sacramento and C. Sagasta, near the telephone office. Open Mon.-Fri. 9am-2pm and 6-9:30pm, Sat. 9am-2pm; winter Mon.-Fri. 9am-2pm and 5-9pm, Sat. 9am-2pm.

Bar-Restaurante Pasaje Andaluz, Pl. San Juan de Dios, 9 (tel. 28 52 54). Our favorite on the plaza. The bare decor, metal tables on the plaza, and white tiled walls disguise one of Cádiz's best restaurants as a shower stall. *Menú* with lots of *paella,* veal chop, fries, bread, wine, and dessert (725-900ptas). Fish and seafood dishes 350-900ptas. Open Sat.-Thurs. 1-4:30pm and 8-11:30pm.

Freiduría Sopranis, C. Sopranis, 2 (tel. 25 64 31), off Pl. San Juan de Dios. Every imaginable type of fried fish and seafood goes for 1200-2000ptas/kg (half of that will stuff two). Fresh from the port, try *chocos, acedías, pijotas,* or *puntillitas* for the best of Andalusian fast food. Open 11am-4:30pm and 7-11pm.

Restaurante Fanny, C. Barrocal, 2, near Pl. Candelaria. The first corner on the left off C. Obispo Urquinaona. Flashy white tablecloths, paneling, and friendly service. *Paella* or fried fish, a veal chop, fries, bread, and dessert (800ptas). Open Mon.-Sat. 1-4pm and 8:30-10pm.

SIGHTS AND ENTERTAINMENT

The winding, cobbled streets of the **ciudad vieja** form a labyrinth of seaside dives and tiny shops. In Pl. Mina, the **Museo de Cádiz** displays works by Murillo, Rubens, and Zurbarán. (Tel. 21 22 81; open Tues.-Sun. 9:30am-2pm. Admission 250ptas; EU citizens free.) To the south on C. Santa Inés, 9, the **Museo Histórico Municipal** flaunts an enormous, painstakingly-wrought 18th-century ivory-and-mahogany model of the city. (Tel. 22 17 88; open Tues.-Fri. 9am-1pm and 5-8pm, Sat.-Sun. 9am-1pm; winter Tues.-Fri. 9am-1pm and 4-7pm, Sat.-Sun. 9am-1pm. Free.) Around the corner and two blocks downhill on C. Rosario, the art of Goya, Cavallini, and Camarone hangs at **El Oratorio de Santa Cueva.** (Tel. 21 36 09; open Mon.-Fri. 10am-1pm. Admission 50ptas.)

Continue down C. Rosario and turn right on C. Padre Elejarde to reach the 18th-century **catedral,** with an imperious gold dome and Baroque facade. The treasury bulges with stupefying valuables. One piece, the *Custodia del Millón,* is said to be set with a million precious stones. Composer Manuel de Falla is buried in the crypt. (Tel. 28 61 54; museum open Mon.-Sat. 10am-1pm; guided tours every ½hr. Cathedral mass Mon.-Sat. 6:30pm, Sun. noon and 6:30pm. Admission 250ptas, children 125ptas. No shorts or bare shoulders allowed during mass.)

Cádiz's balustraded **seaside paseo** runs along the north and east sides of the city, fronting the panoramic Atlantic and the far shore of the bay of Puerto de Santa María. Exotic trees, fancifully sculpted hedges, and even a couple of chattering monkeys fill the neighboring **jardines públicos.** To reach the finest part of the beach, catch local bus #1 (toward Cartadura) at Pl. España, get off at "Balneario," and turn right on C. Glorieta Ingeniero La Cierra. On foot (about ½hr. from Pl. España), walk east to Pl. Constitución and continue along Av. Cayetano del Toro. Sprawling **Paseo Marítimo,** along the beach east of Pl. Constitución, has some of the city's best bars, discos, cafés, and *terrazas.* **Punta San Felipe,** reached by walking north along the sea from Pl. España, is a new favorite area. The hip bars that cluster on **Calle Manuel Rances,** between Pl. Mina and Pl. España, including **Mikro** (#19) and **No!** (#9), make room for funky tunes.

If you can pick any one time to come to Cádiz, make it during **Carnaval.** The gray of winter gives way to dazzling color in February when Cádiz hosts one of the most Rabelaisian *carnavales* in the world. Costumed dancers, singers, residents, and folks from all over take to the streets in a week-long frenzy of festivity that makes New Orleans's Mardi Gras look like Thursday night bingo.

■■■ EL PUERTO DE SANTA MARÍA

Protected from winds and the city bustle in the Bahía de Cádiz, El Puerto de Santa María boasts the only functioning casino on the Costa de la Luz. Columbus's second voyage to the New World commenced here because one of his pilots essentially owned much of the area. As trade with the New World developed, El Puerto became Spain's largest mercantile center.

Traders and prominent families used the riches to build palaces and monuments still open to the public. **Iglesia Mayor Principal** has a Baroque front topped with a one-armed nude and two sidekicks. (Open 9am-noon and 7-9pm. Free.) Alfonso X El Sabio (The Wise) constructed the **Castillo de San Marcos** in the 13th century. Visitors can survey the city from the castle's tower. (Open Tues., Thurs., and Sat. 11am-1pm; Oct.-June Sat. 11am-1pm. Free.) The **Museo Municipal Arqueológico** displays local artifacts and paintings. (Tel. 54 27 75; open Mon.-Sat. 10am-2pm. Free.) **Casa Museo de Rafael Alberti,** C. Santo Domingo, 25 (tel. 85 07 11; free) displays the poet's books, correspondance, and personal belongings. Two of El Puerto's *bodegas* offer tours (Mon.-Fri. 10am-1pm); to visit, make a reservation with **Bodega Terry** (tel. 48 30 00) or **Bodega Osborne** (tel. 85 52 11).

Practical Information El Puerto's **tourist office** is at C. Guadalete, 1 (tel. 54 24 13 or 54 24 75), off Av. Bajamar near the port. From the train station, take a left on Ctra. Madrid and then right onto C. Pozas Dulces. Follow the water for about five to 10 minutes; the tourist office is on the right. From the bus stop in front of Pl. Toros, bear right on C. Muros, turn left on C. Pagador, follow it until you reach Pl. España, and turn right on C. Palacios toward the port. The tourist office is on the right after you cross C. Aramburu de Mora. (Open 10am-2pm and 6-8pm; winter 10am-2pm and 5:30-7:30pm. Guided city tours in Spanish depart Sat. 11am.) The **post office** (tel. 85 53 22) is at Pl. Polvorista, 7. (Open Mon.-Fri. 8am-9pm, Sat. 9am-2pm). The **telephone kiosk** (tel. 54 26 02) is in the middle of the palm-lined *paseo del parque* between train station and tourist office. (Open 10am-3pm and 6pm-midnight; off-season 10am-2pm and 6-10pm.) The **telephone code** is 956. **Taxis** can be summoned at tel. 87 25 55. The **pharmacy,** on the corner of C. Palacias and C. Micaela Aramburu (open 9:30am-1:30pm and 5-9pm), hangs lists of the city's 24-hr. pharmacies. In case of a medical emergency, rush to the **Clínica Santa María del Puerto,** C. Valdés, s/n (tel. 54 00 11). The **Red Cross** is on C. Micaela Aramburu, a block from the tourist office. The **national police** are on Av. Constitución (tel. 091), while the **municipal police** can be alerted at C. Manuel Alvarez, 58 (tel. 092).

El Puerto's bus station is more of a **bus stop,** in front of Pl. Toros. Try to get off closer to the port for greater proximity to the tourist office and the *centro.* The bar on the corner lists current bus schedules. Buses connect El Puerto to: Cádiz (every ½hr., 8am-9:30pm, 40min., 185ptas); Jerez de la Frontera (10 per day); Rota (8 per day, 250ptas); Sanlúcar (7 per day, 35min.); and Chipiona (7 per day, 50min.). If arriving by bus from Jerez or from Cádiz, you may be dropped off in front of El

Puerto's **train station** on Pl. Estación, at the intersection of Av. Estación and Ctra. Madrid. Trains depart for: Jerez (23 per day, 11min., 130ptas); Cádiz (19 per day, ½hr., 255ptas); Sevilla (12 per day, 1½hr., 600-1060ptas); Madrid (1 *expreso* per day 9½hr., 5200ptas; 1 *talgo* per day, 7½hr., 7180ptas); and Barcelona (1 *rápido* per day, 14hr., 9500ptas; 1 *expreso* per day, 17½hr., 6600ptas). A ferry ("El Vapor") links El Puerto with Cádiz, departing near the bus stop and tourist office. (4 per day, Sun. 5 per day, 45min., 180ptas. Departures from Cádiz 4 per day, Sun. 5 per day.)

Accommodations and Food Several *hostales* lie off C. Virgen Milagros and C. Palacios in the town center. To get to the town center from the train station (about 10min.), follow the signs straight ahead and then go left on C. Virgen de los Milagros. From the bus stop, simply walk away from the water. The tourist office keeps up-to-date listings of available accommodations. Family-run **Pensión Santamaría,** C. Nevería, 8 (tel. 85 36 31) is clean, cool, and comfy, but only has two singles. (Singles 1500ptas. Doubles 3000ptas, with bath 3500ptas. Triples with bath 4500ptas.) **Camping Las Dunas** is on Po. Marítimo de la Puntilla, in a beautiful, beach-front pine forest. Cafeteria, supermarket, clean showers. (490ptas per adult and per tent, 425ptas per child, 420ptas per car.)

Avoid the numerous overpriced restaurants near the water. **Casa Adriano,** C. Pozas Dulces, 20 (tel. 54 34 17), is on the way from the train station to the tourist office. Rabbit's 1001st enemy because it sells hare meat so cheap (600ptas). Its fish also gets rave reviews from locals. *Menú* 800ptas. (Open Tues.-Sun. 1-4:30pm and 8pm-midnight.) **La Tortillería,** C. Palacios, 4, famous for its outstanding *tortilla* sandwiches (125-200ptas), is a must. (Open Mon.-Sat. 6am-3pm and 8:30pm-closing, Sun. 8pm-closing.) Baked whole chickens are sold from the stand at C. Ganado, 29 (575-600ptas; irregular hours, but generally open 7-10pm, sometimes early afternoon). El Puerto's nightlife explodes during the summer, particularly on weekends, when locals and tourists gather in the **bars** on Pl. Herrería, C. Jesús de los Milagros, and C. Micaela de Aramburu.

■■■ JEREZ DE LA FRONTERA

A curious and captivating town in southeastern Andalucía, Jerez is the fusion of two obsessions, wine and horses; the composite of two cultures, Spanish and British. Since the English discovered Jerez during the reign of Henry VII, mangling the name to "sherry," British families have elbowed in on the production of the local wine. You can still visit the *bodegas* (wine cellars) throughout Jerez (their names might be British, but the fermenting sherry is certanly Andalusian). One of Andalucía's most commercial cities, Jerez (pop. 180,000) is also handy for exploring four popular tourist circuits: the *ruta de los pueblos blancos* (route of the white villages); *ruta del toro* (route of the bulls); *ruta de la Sierra* (route of the Sierra); and, of course, *ruta del vino* (wine route).

ORIENTATION AND PRACTICAL INFORMATION

From the bus station, exit left onto C. Cartuja. C. Cartuja becomes C. Medina, which beelines for **Plaza Romero Martínez** (the city's commercial center). **Plaza del Arenal** is two blocks left on C. Lencería. Exit from the train station and take the first right on C. Herrera; the bus station is one block up (follow the directions above).

Tourist Office: C. Alameda Cristina, 7 (tel. 33 11 50 or 33 11 62), on a palm-lined *paseo*. From Pl. Romero Martínez take C. Honda to the right and continue as it swerves to the right. Friendly and well-staffed, with highly technical data on brandy and sherry production, *bodegas* tour info, brochures on *bodegas,* the royal equestrian school, etc. English spoken. Open Mon.-Fri. 8am-3pm and 5:30-8pm, Sat. 10am-1:30pm; winter Mon.-Fri. 8am-3pm and 5-7pm, Sat. 10am-2pm.

Post Office: Main Office is on C. Cerón, 2 (tel. 34 22 95; fax 32 14 10), off Pl. Romero Martínez. Open for stamps and Lista de Correos Mon.-Fri. 8am-9pm, Sat.

9am-2pm. Open for **telegrams** Mon.-Fri. 8am-9pm, Sat. 9am-7pm (tel. 34 16 92). Another office beside the train station sells stamps and accepts packages. **Postal Code:** 11480.

Flights: Ctra. Jerez-Sevilla (tel. 15 00 00 or 15 00 83). Airport is 7km from town. Connections to Madrid, Valencia, Tenerife, Palma, Zaragoza, and Barcelona. **Iberia,** Av. Albaro Domecq, s/n (tel. 18 43 94). For tickets, go to any travel agency. **Aviaco** (tel. 15 00 10) has flights to London (the "sherry express") every Mon., Wed., and Fri.

Trains: Pl. Estación (tel. 34 23 19), at the eastern end of C. Medina after its name changes to C. Cartuja. **RENFE,** C. Tornería, 4 (tel. 33 48 13). To: Cádiz (11 *regionales* per day, 1½hr., 215ptas; 1 *talgo* per day, ¾hr., 1300-1500ptas); Sevilla (11 *regionales* per day, 1½hr., 400ptas; 1 *talgo* per day, 1hr., 1300-1500ptas); Madrid (1 *estrella* per day, 10hr., 4400ptas; 2 *talgos* per day, 4½hr., 7200-8100ptas); Barcelona *(2 diurnos* per day, 13½-14½hr., 8000-10,000ptas; 1 *talgo* per day, 10hr., 12,000ptas; 1 *estrella* per day, 15hr., 7200ptas).

Buses: C. Cartuja, the continuation of C. Medina, at the corner of C. Madre de Dios (two blocks from train station). **T.G. Gomes** (tel. 34 21 74). To: Arcos de la Frontera (6 per day, Sat.-Sun. 4 per day, ½hr., 250ptas); Cádiz (18 per day, Sat.-Sun. 9 per day, 1hr., 325ptas); Sevilla (9 per day, Sat.-Sun. 4 per day, 1½hr., 825ptas); Ronda (3 per day, 2½hr., 1160ptas); Puerto de Santa María (6 per day, Sat.-Sun. 4 per day, ½hr., 140-165ptas); Vejer de la Frontera (1 per day, 1½hr., 730ptas). **Amarillos** (tel. 34 78 44). To: Córdoba (1 per day, 4hr., 1715ptas); Arcos de la Frontera (16 per day, Sat.-Sun. 11 per day, ½hr., 255ptas). **Linesur** (tel. 34 10 63). To: Sevilla (6 per day, 1½hr., 800ptas); Algeciras (6 per day, 2hr., 975ptas); Sanlúcar de Barrameda (hourly 7am-10pm, ½hr., 195ptas). **Sevibus** (tel. 30 50 05). To: Madrid (6 per day, 7hr., 2605ptas).

Urban buses: In a coquettish shade of mauve, the 12 lines run every ¼hr. (80ptas). Bonobus, good for 10 rides, sold at tobacco stores (500ptas). Information office located in Pl. Arenal.

Taxis: tel. 34 48 60.

Car Rental: Hertz, at the airport (tel. 15 00 38). Open Mon.-Fri. 7:30am-8:30pm. **Avis,** C. Sevilla, 25 (tel. 34 43 11). Must be at least 21.

Bookstore: La Luna Nueva, C. Caballeros, 36 (tel. 33 17 79). Two shelves of books in English. Open Mon.-Fri. 9:30am-1:30pm and 5-8:30pm, Sat. 9:30am-1:30pm.

Red Cross: Av. Cruz Roja (tel. 30 74 54).

Medical Assistance: Ambulatorio de la Seguridad Social, C. José Luis Díez (tel. 34 84 68).

Fire: tel. 085 or 33 66 00.

Police: National Police (tel. 091), **Municipal Police** (tel. 092).

ACCOMMODATIONS AND FOOD

Finding a bed in Jerez is as easy as finding wine. Look along **Calle Medina,** near the bus station, and **Calle Arcos,** which intersects C. Medina at Pl. Romero Martínez. *Tapas*-hoppers bounce in, out, and all around **Plaza del Arenal,** or northeast on Av. Alcalde Alvaro Domeqo around **Plaza del Caballo.** *Jerez,* the local wine of which natives are justifiably proud, is ubiquitous and inexpensive.

Albergue Juvenil (HI), Av. Carrero Blanco, 30 (tel. 34 28 90). In an ugly urbanization, a 25-min. walk from downtown, or 10-min. bus ride (bus L-8 leaves near the bus station, every 15min., 80ptas; or bus L-1 from Pl. Arenal). Definitely worth the ride. Clean and modern, with spacious doubles (in low-season you might have the room to yourself), pool, tennis and basketball courts, mini-soccer field, library, TV and video room, and a rooftop terrace. Doubles as a university dorm. 1007ptas per person, 1166 with breakfast, *pensión completa* 2650ptas. Over 26: 1484ptas; 1643ptas; 3127ptas. Nonmembers: 2650ptas; 2809ptas; 4293ptas. Only Spanish citizens can buy HI here.

Hostal San Andres, C. Morenos, 12 (tel. 34 09 83). Take C. Fontana (off C. Medina) for 1 bl., and turn left; C. Morenos is the first right. Two beautiful patios, one with stained glass and palm trees, the other with hanging grapes and an array

JEREZ DE LA FRONTERA

of baby cacti. Possibly the most beautiful *hostal* in town, tended by an amiable couple. Singles 1500ptas. Doubles 2500ptas. Triples can be arranged.

Pensión Los Amarillos, C. Medina, 39 (tel. 34 22 96), two streets down from the bus station. At 60, the oldest *penisón* in Jerez. Furniture and baths are only a couple of years old, though. Clean, convenient, simple. Singles 1200ptas. Doubles 2200ptas. Triples 3000ptas. Prices negotiable for longer stays.

Casa Pepa, (tel. 32 49 06) on a nameless little street off C. Madre de Dios, 1 bl. from the bus and train stations. A meeting place and a landmark. There's an unofficial move to name the street after the owner, who serves scrumptious *menús* (625ptas), *platos combinados* (250-275ptas), and *tapas* (150-175ptas). Open, and serving meals, 9:30am-midnight.

Mesón Alcazaba, C. Medina, 19 (tel. 32 34 76). Looks a bit posh, with its antique armor and low leather-and-velvet couches, but is affordable. *Menú* 800ptas, fish plates start at 600ptas. Open 11am-midnight.

SIGHTS AND ENTERTAINMENT

Like Napa Valley, California, the main tourist attractions here are the *bodegas.* Multilingual tour guides distill the complete sherry-making process, and you tipple free sherry. The best time to visit is early September, during the harvest; avoid August when many *bodegas* close down for the annual hangover. Maps showing *bodega* locations are available in many of the town's travel agencies. Group reservations for the hour-long tours must be made at least one week in advance; reservations for individual visitors are recommended, if not required. All wine cellars are open to the public Monday through Friday during certain hours only. All conduct tours in English, but exact times vary. Call ahead.

Harveys of Bristol: C. Arcos, 53 (tel. 15 10 30). Particularly charming tour guides. Admission 200ptas. Closed the first 3 weeks of Aug.

González Byass: Manuel María González (tel. 34 00 00). Admission 300ptas.

B. Domecq: San Idelfonso, 3 (tel. 33 18 00). Gratis!

Williams and Humbert, Ltd.: Nuño de Cañas, 1 (tel. 34 65 39). Admission 300ptas.

Wisdom and Warter, Ltd.: C. Pizarro, 7 (tel. 18 43 06; fax 18 11 79). Guided tours in English and French. Admission 250ptas.

Jerez's love for wine is closely followed by its passion for horses. During the last week of April or the first week of May, the **Real Escuela Andaluza de Arte Equestre** (Royal Andalusian School of Equestrian Art), located at Av. Duque de Abrantes (tel. 31 11 11), sponsors a **Feria del Caballo** (Horse Fair) with shows, carriage competitions, and races of Jerez-bred Carthusian horses. During the rest of the year, shows every Thurs. at noon. (Admission 1425-1750ptas.) Dress rehearsals are almost as impressive (Mon.-Wed. and Fri. at 11am and 1pm; admission 425ptas). The **Centro Andaluz de Flamenco,** Palacio Pemartín in Pl. San Juan (tel. 34 92 65), has audio-visuals and displays showcasing Andalusian flamenco. (Open Mon.-Fri. 10am-2pm, Tues. also 5-7pm. Audiovisuals on the hour. Free.)

Also worth a visit is the 16th-century **Iglesia de Santo Domingo** on C. Marqués de Casa Arizón, near the tourist office. (Open Mon.-Fri. 10am-1:30pm and 4:30-8:30pm. Free.) To the south, 1 bl. past Pl. Arenal, lies the 11th-century **Mosque,** the Moorish **Torre Octagonal** (Octagonal Tower), and the Almohad **baños árabes** (Arabic baths). (Complex open Mon.-Fri. 10:30am-2pm and 4:30-7pm, Sat. 10am-1:30pm. Free.) Near the elaborate Arabic complex is the imposing Baroque **catedral,** built on the site of a major Arab mosque with a Mudejar belfry. (Open Mon.-Fri. 6am-8pm, Sat. 11am-2pm and 6-8pm, Sun. 11am-2pm and 7-8:30pm. Free.) **The Museo de Relojes,** which exhibits functioning old clocks, ticks away at C. Cervantes, 3. (Tel. 18 21 00; open Mon.-Sat. 10am-1:30pm. Admisssion 300ptas.) The **Zoológico Alberto Durán,** C. Taxdirt, s/n (tel. 18 23 97), is both a huge park with botanical gardens and the King of Andalucía's zoos. (Open Tues.-Sun. 10:30am-6pm; Sept.-

May Tues.-Sun. 10:30am-5pm. Admission 500ptas, children 300ptas, seniors 200ptas. Group rates are avaliable for 100-200ptas cheaper.)

At night, a series of student **bars** shapes up the scene at the triangle formed by C. Santo Domingo, C. Salvatierra, and Av. de Méjilo.

As for festivals, the **Festival de Teatro, Música, y Baile** in September celebrates flamenco dancing, which supposedly originated in Jerez. During the second week in September, the town toasts the pagan roots of religious celebration with the **Fiestas de la Vendimia,** a celebration of the season's harvest.

■ NEAR JEREZ DE LA FRONTERA: SANLÚCAR DE BARRAMEDA

The best way to approach Sanlúcar de Barrameda is by sea. Unfortunately, you'll be approaching from the opposite direction, so be prepared for a disappointment. Rugged small-town charm *is* tucked behind those industrial outskirts. The city is celebrated primarily for its huge *langostinos* (king prawns) and *manzanilla*—a savory sherry, served at any *bodega* (wine cellar) in the old city, with a unique tangy aftertaste ascribed to the sea salt in the soil. Sanlúcar bops with people sitting at terraces and outdoor bars until after midnight. Numerous festivals testify to the residents' fondness for merrymaking. The **Feria de la Manzanilla** in May liberates the most alcohol, but **Corpus Christi,** in June, explodes with the biggest fanfare. In August, horseracing thunders along the beach, and the **Festival de la Exaltación del Río Guadalquivir** enlivens the streets with poetry readings, a flamenco competition, popular dances, and bullfights in tribute to Andalucía's great river.

Two impressive palaces grudge-match with the enormous 14th-century **Iglesia de Nuestra Señora de la O** for the attention of sun-struck tourists. The **Palacio Medina Sidonia** was inhabited until recently (tel. 36 01 61; open for visits Wed. 10am-1pm). The 19th-century **Palacio Infantes de Orleans** now houses the Ayuntamiento (open for visits Mon.-Fri. 10am-2pm).

Parque Nacional de Doñana, one of the largest and most important natural reserves in Europe, extends north of Sanlúcar and requires an expensive but worthwhile tour (4hr., 3300ptas). Contact **Tourafrica,** C. San Juan, 8 (tel. 36 25 40) or **Agencia de Viajes Ocio y Vacaciones,** Calzada del Ejército, s/n (tel. 36 02 25). The office of Parque Doñana in El Acebuche (tel. (959) 43 04 32) offers significantly cheaper tours (2400ptas). Call ahead for reservations. To reach Doñana, take a boat from the Sanlúcar beach (200ptas) or a bus from Sevilla. (Park closed during the week-long festival of the Romería del Rocío in May.)

Practical Information The **tourist office,** Calzada del Ejército, s/n (tel. 36 61 10) provides information on the city and Parque Nacional de Doñana. (Open Mon.-Fri. 10am-2pm and 6-8pm, Sat. 10am-1pm. Closed weekends in winter.) The **post office** is on Av. Cerro Falón, 61 (tel. 36 09 37), 3 bl. east of the tourist office. (Open for Lista de Correos, stamps, **telegrams,** and packages Mon.-Fri. 8am-3pm, Sat. 9am-2pm.) **Telephones** are on C. Bolsa, off Pl. Cabildo (open Mon.-Fri. 9:30am-1:30pm and 6-10pm, Sat. 9:30am-1:30pm). **Telephone code** is 956. The **pharmacy** is on C. San Juan, 26 (tel. 36 04 25; open Mon.-Fri. 9am-1:30pm and 5:30-9pm; winter 9:30am-1:15pm and 5-8pm). **Hospital de San Diego** is at Centro de Salud (tel. 36 74 88). **National police** are at Juan de Argüeso, 11 (tel. 36 40 43); **municipal** at Av. Constitución (tel. 36 01 02).

Buses leave from **Los Amarillos,** Pl. Salle (tel. 36 04 66), at the end of C. San Juan. To: Chipiona (7 per day, Sat.-Sun. 4 per day, 30min., 80ptas); Cádiz (8 per day, Sat.-Sun. 4 per day, 1¼hr., 350ptas); Sevilla (9 per day, Sat.-Sun 5 per day, 2hr., 825ptas). **La Valenciana** (tel. 36 01 96) has buses operating from Calzada del Ejército, by the tourist office. To: Chipiona (17 per day, Sun. 12 per day, 25min., 85ptas); Jerez de la Frontera (17 per day, Sun. 11 per day, 40min., 190ptas); Sevilla (3 per day, 870ptas). Buy tickets on the bus. For **taxis** call tel. 36 11 02 or 36 00 44.

Accommodations and Food No true budget accommodations exist, and most places try to extort double room fees from lonesome travelers if only double rooms remain. Try **Hostal La Blanca Paloma** at Pl. San Roque, 15 (tel. 36 36 44). Spacious, clean rooms have white marbley floors, some with jumbo balconies. (Singles 2000-2500ptas. Doubles 3500-4000ptas.) Another option is **Pensión La Bohemia** at C. Don Claudia, 1 (tel. 36 95 99), just off C. Santo Domingo, whose beige carpet and bedspreads tame all bohemian urges. (No singles. Doubles 3300-3700ptas, with bath 4300-5000ptas.) Bar-restaurants and *tascas* serving *tapas* and *raciones* fill **El Barrio,** the area uphill and away from the river, circumscribed by Calles San Nicolás, Bolsa, Rubiños, Barrameda, and San Antonio Pirrado. For a sit-down meal, head for the side streets off **Calle San Juan. Bar-Restaurante El Cura,** C. Amargura, 2 (tel. 36 29 94), between Pl. San Roque and Pl. Cabildo, serves up divinely-ordained *paella* (450ptas) in a family atmosphere. (Open 7am-1am.) **Bar-Restaurante La Parada,** Pl. Paz, 4-5 (tel. 36 11 60) is always crowded with locals. Tremendously big *raciones* (400-900ptas). (Open Oct.-Aug. Tues.-Sun. noon-5pm and 8pm-12:30am.)

Near Sanlúcar de Barrameda: Chipiona

A quiet seaside village for nine months of the year, Chipiona transforms into a crowded tourist trap during the summer, when thousands of visitors—mostly German and British—creep across the beaches and invade the *pensiones*. This trend began in the 19th century, when Chipiona's extremely salty sea (you can smell it all over) was reputed to have curative powers. **Iglesia de Nuestra Señora de la O,** constructed in 1640, stands in gorgeous Pl. Juan Carlos I, Chipiona's shadiest, most fragrant, and colorful spot. Gothic architecture buffs may prefer the **Santuario de Nuestra Señora de Regla.** (Irregular hours; knock loudly and ask for admission.)

Chipiona's **Casa de Cultura** (tel. 37 08 80) is a de facto **tourist office.** It's in the municipal library at Pl. Pío XII, on pedestrian shopping street C. Isaac Peral. (Open Mon.-Fri. 10am-1pm and 6-9pm, Sat. 10am-1pm; winter 10am-1pm and 5-8pm, Sat. 10am-1pm.) Meanwhile, the **Ayuntamiento,** Pl. Juan Carlos I (tel. 38 01 00), near C. Isaac Peral, two blocks from the beach, gives away maps. **Currency exchange** at any of the numerous banks on C. Victor Pradera and C. Isaac Peral. The **post office** is on C. Padre Lerchundi, 15A (tel. 37 14 19), near Pl. Pío XII (open Mon.-Fri. 8am-2pm, Sat. 9am-1pm). The **postal code** is 11550. **Telephone** service at Librería Benítez, on C. Victor Pradera, 6, facing Los Amarillos bus station (open 9am-2pm and 6-10pm; off-season closed Sat. afternoons and all day Sun.). **Taxis** are summoned at tel. 37 00 18 or 37 11 20. In a **medical emergency,** call an **ambulance** at tel. 37 17 04, or find the **Red Cross** at Av. Cruz Roja, 35 (tel. 37 04 81), one block inland from Pl. Regla. For **local police** (tel. 37 10 88), go to C. Virgen de Consolación.

A municipal **campground,** on Ctra. Rota at 3km (tel. 37 23 21), 800m from the beach, is the only affordable place to sleep. It has a pool and supermarket. (480ptas per person and per tent, children under 11 415ptas, electricity 400ptas, car 425ptas.) The **mercado,** C. Victor Pradera, to your left as you exit Los Amarillos bus station, is teeming with fresh produce and small eateries. (Open 8am-2pm.) Restaurants line Po. Cruz del Mar (at the end of C. Isaac Peral) and the area around Pl. Palomas and Pl. Pío XII. **Restaurante El Gato,** C. Pez Espada, 11 (tel. 37 07 87) may be Chipiona's best. Lap up its specialties, local seafood, and *bellota* ham (from acorn-fed piggies). Most dishes cost 700-900ptas. (Open 1-5pm and 8pm-midnight.)

Los Amarillos buses (tel. 37 02 92) operate from Av. Regla to: Sanlúcar (8-14 per day, 30min., 80ptas); Sevilla (5-9 per day, 2½hr., 900ptas); Cádiz (9 per day, 1½hr., 430ptas). **La Valenciana** buses (tel. 37 12 83) depart from Pl. San Sebastián.

■■■ ARCOS DE LA FRONTERA

The road to Arcos snakes through fields of sunflowers and sherry-grape vines. The town appears abruptly on a giant spike, undercut on three sides by the Río Guadalete. The premier *pueblo blanco* on the *ruta de los pueblos blancos* (route of the white villages), Arcos de la Frontera (pop. 25,000) is a historic monument—a maze of alleyways, medieval ruins, and stone arches.

ORIENTATION AND PRACTICAL INFORMATION

Arcos twiddles its thumbs on the highway between Jerez (30km away) and Antequera, accessible by bus from both cities and from Cádiz. To reach the center of town from the bus station, walk uphill 20min., exit to the left, make the first left, then turn right on the second street, C. Munoz Vásquez. Keep walking uphill as this street turns into C. Debajo del Corral, which later turns into **Calle Corredera** and leads into the old quarter. The tourist office is even higher uphill, as C. Corredera turns into C. Cuesta de Belén at the beginning of the old quarter. Most of the town's restaurants and hotels are on (or off) C. Corredera, halfway to the old quarter. Walk on the shady side of the street, or wait at the bus station for one of the urban buses (more or less every ½hr., 55ptas); those labeled **La Paz** stop 10min. from the tourist office.

Tourist Office: C. Cuesta de Belén (tel. 70 22 64), on the continuation of C. Corredera. As you exit the bus station, turn left, left again at the end of the street, and walk uphill 15-20min. Or take the urban bus (La Paz). Incredible detailed map of the old city and all essential information on food and lodgings. Some English spoken. Open Mon.-Fri. 9am-2pm and 5-7pm, Sat. 10am-2pm; winter Mon.-Fri. 9am-3pm and 5-7pm, Sat. 10am-2pm.

Post Office: C. Boliches, s/n (tel. 70 15 60), parallel to the Corredera, near the tourist office. Open Mon.-Fri. 9am-2pm, Sat. 9am-1pm. Open for **telegrams** Mon.-Fri. 9am-3pm, Sat. 9am-2pm. **Postal Code:** 11630.

Telephones: Bazar-Casa Ceuta, C. Debajo del Corral, next to the taxi stop, facing the little park—half-way up, known to everyone by name. Open Mon.-Fri. 10am-2pm and 6-9:30pm, Sat. 10am-2pm. **Telephone Code:** 956.

Buses: On C. Corregidores. **T.G. Comes** (tel. 70 20 15) to: Cádiz (7 per day, Sat.-Sun. 3 per day, 1½hr., 615ptas); Jerez (7 per day, Sat.-Sun. 4 per day, ½hr., 255ptas); Ronda (4 per day, 2hr., 875ptas); Costa del Sol (1 per day, 1310-1900ptas depending on destination). **Los Amarillos** (tel. 70 02 57) to: Sevilla (2 per day, 2½hr., 840ptas); Cádiz (2 per day, 1hr., 710ptas); Jerez (19 per day, Sat. 9 per day, Sun. 6 per day, ½hr., 255ptas).

Taxis: tel. 70 13 55 or 70 00 66.

Medical Assistance: Red Cross, Av. Cruz Roja (tel. 70 03 55). **Casa de Socorro,** C. Calvario (tel. 70 05 55). **Emergencies: Polimédica** (tel. 70 04 98).

Police: C. Nueva, s/n (tel. 70 16 52), **Guardia Civil** (tel. 70 00 52).

ACCOMMODATIONS AND FOOD

Arcos has surprisingly few budget beds for a city that thrives on tourism. Call ahead at the height of summer. Restaurants huddle at the bottom end of the Corredera by the rotunda, while *tapas* heaven is uphill in the old quarter.

Fonda del Comercio, C. Debajo del Corral, 15 (tel. 70 00 57). Sign outside massive wooden door reads "Fonda." Old building with thick white–washed walls, incredibly high ceilings with wooden beams, and rather new furniture. Simple and adequate. Singles 1500ptas. Doubles 2600ptas. Call ahead or arrive early.

Hostal Callejón de las Monjas, C. Dean Espinoza, 4—known by everyone as Callejón de las Monjas (tel. 70 23 02). In the old quarter, 1 bl. from tourist office and behind the Iglesia de Santa María. Cutesy rooms with new beds and baths. Owner's barber shop downstairs. Singles 2000ptas. Doubles 3000-3500ptas, with bath 4500ptas.

Hostal Voy-Voy, Av. Ponce de León, 9 (tel. 70 14 12 or 70 13 20). A 20-min. walk from bus station. Exit to the right, take an immediate right uphill, then a left uphill onto Av. Manuel Mancheño. At the intersection, take a sharp right onto the highway, which becomes Av. Ponce de León. Or take urban bus "La Paz" from the bus station, and tell the driver *"Voy al Voy-Voy."* Obviously, management is sick of "I go" jokes. (Tell us about it.) Recently renovated rooms strut their stuff with A/C,

TV, phone, and sharp bathrooms. Singles 2000-3000ptas. Doubles 4000-6000ptas. Good restaurant below has a huge menu from 700ptas and a TV with a sports channel in English. Open Fri.-Wed. 1:30-4:30pm and 8:30-11:30pm.

Los Faraones, C. Debajo del Corral, 8 (tel. 70 19 16). An Egyptian-Spanish couple serve Egyptian and Spanish dishes amid Middle Eastern decor. *Menú del día* 1250ptas. Felafel and lamb shish-kebab 725ptas. A/C. Open 11:30am-5pm and 8pm-12:30am.

Café-Bar El Faro, C. Debajo del Corral, 14 (tel. 70 00 14). Filling meals in this hermitage with A/C and color TV, loved by locals. *Platos combinados* 400-600ptas. Gigantic *menú*, with *gazpacho, pollo en salsa* (chicken in sauce), *pescado frito* (fried fish), a drink, and bread (900ptas). Open for meals Wed.-Mon. 1-5pm and 8-11pm.

Bar Típico Alcaraván, C. Nueva, 1 (tel. 70 33 97). Take C. Nueva down from Pl. Cabildo. In a cave carved into the side of the mountain. Solid rock ceiling and walls. *Tapas* 200ptas. Open Tues.-Sun. 11am-3pm and 8pm-1am.

SIGHTS

The most beautiful sight might be the old quarter itself, with winding white alleys and hanging flower pots. The monuments begin, and abruptly end, at **Plaza del Cabildo,** a rectangular esplanade hanging over a cliff. **Iglesia de Santa María** and a privately owned **Castillo Ducal** face the dandy view of olive groves and low hills. Built in 1553, the church's unique interior melange of Gothic, Renaissance, and Baroque styles is sheathed by a late-Gothic facade. Christians built the late-Gothic **Iglesia de San Pedro,** on the site of an old Arab fortress on the northern edge of the old quarter. Murillos, Zurbaráns, Riberas, and Pachecos decorate the interior. (Both churches open 10am-1pm and 4-7pm. Admission 150ptas. Or go during mass: summer Mon.-Sat. 8pm, Sun. 11am and 8pm; winter Mon.-Sat. 7:30pm, Sun. noon and 7:30pm.) In the attached **tower,** the town bell-ringer might, if you are persistent and convincing, let you climb the tight spiral staircase that leads to the belfry. Even the spindly-legged find the view worth the effort. (Open 9am-3pm and 4:30-9pm.) In the twisting alleys of the old quarter, heraldic emblems mark medieval *palacios* or nobles' dwellings. Also, the tourist office can make arrangements for tours of 16th- and 17th-century **convents.**

Arcos has an inordinate number of artisans and workshops, which can be visited. **Jali,** C. Maldonado, 7 (tel. 70 02 64) weaves and sells rugs and tapestries. (Open Mon.-Fri. 9:30am-1:30pm, Sat. 11am-1:30pm.) **Galería de Arte,** C. Marqués de Torresoto, 11 (tel. 70 12 98) exhibits and sells work from local artists and artisans. (Open 10am-2pm and 6-10pm.) **Alfarería Ramón Carrillo,** C. Boticas, 11 (tel. 70 25 68) sells its very own hand-painted ceramics, including beautiful vases and replicas of medieval tiles. Ask to see the studio with its furnace, aberrations (messed up pieces), and tons of clay. (Open 10am-2pm and 3-9pm.)

Bornos, a hillside hamlet 11km to the northeast, is the next town along the *ruta de los pueblos blancos.* To dip in its freshwater lake, climb down the hill and turn left on the dirt road. A bar at the end of the road is cleverly disguised as a straw hut. Swim only in the area directly in front of the bar; dangerous whirlpools swirl other parts of the lake. **Buses** for Bornos are run by both Comes and Los Amarillos from the bus station (12 per day, Sun. 5 per day, 20min., 125ptas).

Extremadura

The poorest region in Spain derives its name from its position on the "far end" of the Río Duero, which flows from Western Spain into Portugal. The river's qualities are those that define the region: it is harsh; it is extreme (temperatures above 100°F in this region are common in summer); it is huge. The value of naming the region after a body of water is more than symbolic. Extremadura's life blood is its large number of reservoirs (this dry-plained region is ironically one of the wettest spots in Western Europe). For his controversial 1932 film *Tierra sin pan (las Hurdes)*, intended to depict the poverty of rural Spain, Spanish filmmaker Luis Buñuel chose a village in Extremadura; he made a film so sordid and harsh that it was banned by the Republican government.

A strategic frontier zone for centuries, Extremadura fell to Tartessians, Celts, Romans, Muslims, and Christians, all of whom left behind monuments, bridges, and castles. From Extremadura came most of the *conquistadores* who forged into the New World, such as Hernán Cortés and Francisco Pizarro (exploiters of Mexico and Peru). Also from Extremadura, María Escobar was the first person to plant wheat in Peru, and Inés de Suárez helped capture Santiago del Nuevo Extremo (today Santiago de Chile) by beheading imprisoned Araucanians as a threat to other defending indigenous tribes. Yet just as Extremadura prospered during the Age of Empire, its fortunes sagged with Spain's decline.

Extremadura is administratively and culturally divided into the provinces of Cáceres (also known as Alta Extremadura) and Badajoz (Baja Extremadura). During the Spanish Civil War, Cáceres fell with virtually no fighting while the province of Badajoz fiercely resisted Franco, provoking one of the more horrifying massacres perpetrated by the Nationalist troops.

Towns are few and far between. As the tourist infrastructure improves each year—brochures and street maps for all the region's towns are available at any town's tourist office—more and more visitors have discovered Extremadura's wide brown landscape and vast skies. Prices remain low by Spanish standards.

The most traditional dishes of Extremaduran cuisine come from the wild: rabbit, partridge, lizard with green sauce, wild pigeon with herbs, and *faisán a la Alcántara* (pheasant with a truffle and port wine sauce). *Extremeño* soups are scrumptious: *cocido* (chickpea stew) warms in winter, while the many varieties of *gazpacho* (including an unusual white one) cool in summer. Consomés and tomato-fig soup are enjoyed year-round. Cáceres favors a *migas* (spicy bread) and *chorizo* (spicy sausage) concoction. Montánchez sausages are renowned in Spain—hence the nickname for an Extremaduran: *choricero* (sausage-maker). Fruit, especially melon, is remarkable throughout the region.

■■■ CÁCERES

Founded by the Romans in 34 BC, the thriving provincial capital and university town of Cáceres (pop. 80,000) is the closest thing to a big city in the wilds of Extremadura. The walls of the medieval old city enclose a wonderfully preserved complex of churches, palaces, and museums. Down below, the rapidly expanding and industrializing new city boasts attractive parks and plazas, plus a healthy dose of nightlife.

Cáceres's central location makes a good base for exploring the rest of Extremadura. From here you can enter Portugal via Badajoz, with several daily bus and rail connections to Elvas, or by train via Valencia de Alcántara, due west of here. Valencia de Alcántara's station is the last Spanish stop on the Madrid-Lisboa line.

ORIENTATION AND PRACTICAL INFORMATION

The **ciudad monumental** (old city) lies east of **Plaza Mayor** (Pl. General Mola on old maps). The plaza is 3km north of the bus and train stations, which face each other across the intersection of Av. Hispanidad and Av. Alemania, in the south of the city. Bus #1, from the stop to the right as you emerge from the bus station, runs to a small plaza just up stone steps from Pl. Mayor (every 15min., 75ptas). Alternatively, a shuttle bus from the bus station runs to **Plaza de América** (south and west of Pl. Mayor), hub of the new downtown area.

Walkers face an ugly and noisy 10- to 15-min. walk to Pl. América; from the train station turn left, from the bus station right (that is, north from either station) along Av. Alemania until you reach Pl. América, from which it's a further 10-15 minutes, albeit more pleasant ones, to Pl. Mayor. From Pl. América, purple *Ciudad Monumental* signs point north up the grassy and tree-lined Av. España toward Pl. Mayor. When the avenue ends, bear right on C. San Antón, then right again on C. San Pedro.

Tourist Office: Pl. Mayor, 33 (tel. 24 63 47), east side of the plaza, to the right of steps up to the old city gate. Ask for the big fold-out *ayuntamiento* map instead of the tourist map. Open Mon.-Fri. 9am-2pm and 5-7pm, Sat.-Sun. 9am-2pm.

Post Office: C. Miguel Primo Rivera, 2 (tel. 22 50 71), just off Av. España on the left as you walk from Pl. América (in building with the Caja Postal Argentaria sign). Open for stamps Mon.-Fri. 8am-4pm, Sat. 9am-2pm; for Lista de Correos and **telegrams** Mon.-Fri. 9am-9pm, Sat. 9am-2pm. For telegrams by phone call 22 20 00. In the same building, the Caja Postal handles **currency exchange** for a 100pta commission. Open Mon.-Fri. 8am-2pm. **Postal Code:** 10004.

Telephone Code: 927.

Trains: Av. Alemania (tel. 22 50 61), across the highway from the bus station, 3km south of the old city. Madrid-Badajoz *regionales* to: Mérida (3 per day, 1hr., 415ptas); Badajoz (4 per day, 2hr., 850ptas); Madrid (1 per day, 4½hr., 1900ptas). 2nd-class *talgos* and *estrellas* (seats, not sleepers) run to: Lisboa (1 *talgo* per day, 4½hr., 3000ptas; 1 *estrella* per day, 4½hr., 2530ptas); Sevilla (1 *talgo* per day, 4hr., 1810ptas); Madrid (4 *talgos* per day, 3 *estrellas* per night, 4-5hr., 2675-3600ptas).

Buses: Ctra. Sevilla (tel. 24 59 54 or 24 49 50), across the highway from the train station, 3km south of the old city. Information window open 7am-midnight. To: Madrid (8-12 per day, 4-5hr., 2230ptas); Sevilla (5-7 per day, 4½hr., 2030ptas); Salamanca (3-6 per day, 4hr., 1630-1810ptas); Badajoz (3 per day, 2hr., 815ptas); Mérida (2-3 per day, 1hr., 730ptas); Trujillo (6-10 per day, 45min., 370ptas); Valencia de Alcántara (2 per day, 2½hr., 795ptas); Valladolid (4-6 per day, 5½hr., 2415ptas).

Public Transportation: Autobuses Urbanos de Cáceres (75ptas). #1 runs from a stop just to the right as you exit the bus station access road onto Ctra. Sevilla to the plaza just above Pl. Mayor (every 15min.).

Taxis: Pl. Mayor (tel. 24 84 44); Pl. San Juan, in the old city (tel. 24 90 37); Av. España (tel. 22 19 73); bus station (tel. 24 49 50); train station (tel. 22 50 61); radio taxi (tel. 24 30 63).

Car Rental: Avis, in train station. Open Mon.-Fri. 9am-2pm and 5-7pm, Sat. 9am-2pm. **Hertz,** Agencia de Viajes Marsans, Av. Virgen de Guadalupe, 3 (tel. 22 43 45).

Luggage Storage: At the **train station** (500ptas per day). At the **bus station** (50ptas per item per day).

Pharmacy: Four in Pl. Mayor: Pl. Mayor, 36 (tel. 24 52 82); Pl. Mayor, 4 (tel. 24 59 24); Pl. Mayor, 17 (tel. 24 50 97); Pl. Mayor, 18 (tel. 24 52 36). All have *farmacia de guardia* list posted in window.

Medical Services: Red Cross (tel. 24 78 58); **Residencia Sanitaria** (tel. 25 62 00); **Hospital Provincial** (tel. 24 01 51 or 24 23 00).

Emergency: tel. 091 or 092.

Police: Municipal, C. General Margallo (tel. 24 84 24). **Nacional,** Av. Virgen de la Montaña, 3 (tel. 22 60 00).

ACCOMMODATIONS

Hostales, hotels, and *pensiones* line Pl. Mayor, and more are scattered throughout the new city. Call ahead for stays on summer weekends.

Hostal Residencia Almonte, C. Gil Cordero, 6 (tel. 24 09 25 or 24 09 26), 15min. south of Pl. Mayor, off Pl. América. A gigantic, hotel-like, 90-room monster with unrestrained luxuries in every room: full bath or shower, phone, fluffy towel, firm bed. Garage. Hell, the fan even oscillates. Singles with bath or shower 2500ptas. Doubles with bath or shower 4000ptas. Jan. until (not including) Semana Santa: 2500ptas; 3700ptas. Breakfast 300ptas. Visa, MC, AmEx accepted.

Pensión Márquez, Gabriel y Galán, 2 (tel. 24 49 60), sign visible at low end of Pl. Mayor. All 9 rooms with balconies. Faded floor tiles, candle holders, and miniatures clutter the walls. Bathrooms not much larger than the wall decorations. Singles 1250ptas. Doubles 2500ptas. Showers (hot water) 250ptas.

Fonda Soraya, Pl. Mayor, 25 (no phone). Huge rooms with balconies and big windows in a ramshackle old building. Friendly management. 1300ptas per person for doubles, triples, and quads (no singles). However, depending on how things look when you show up, they just may let you hog a double for 1300ptas.

Hostal Residencia La Princesa, C. Camino Llano, 32 (tel. 22 70 00). From Pl. América, head down Rda. Carmen to Pl. Conquistadores, bear left on C. Colón, and turn left on the last unmarked street. From Pl. Mayor, take C. Pintores past Iglesia de San Juan, follow the left-hand branch down onto C. Camino Llano. Hallways are long and dark. Antiseptic-smelling rooms, some with phones. Garage. Singles 1800ptas, with bath 2010ptas. Doubles with bath 3000-3200ptas. Triples with bath 4500ptas. Breakfast 200ptas. Prices do not include IVA.

FOOD

Like any Plaza Mayor worth its salt, Cáceres' is full of restaurants and cafés with *terrazas* ready to wine and dine the populace—for a price, of course. In this case, the price isn't too hefty since the eateries in Pl. Mayor are by and large unpretentious establishments with cheap *bocadillos* and *raciones* (300-600ptas) and *menús* (800-1100ptas). Within the old city walls there's only a pair of expensive restaurants and a couple of taverns, catering largely to the *parador* clientele (see the notable exception below). On Wednesdays the weekly **market** lets loose on Pl. Marrón, two and a half blocks north of Pl. Mayor. The permanent local market, **Mercado de Abastos,** is on C. San José at C. Piedad. (Open Mon.-Sat. 8am-2pm and 4-7pm.)

Groceries: Mostazo, several locations. Most central at Pl. Duque, just behind the low end of Pl. Mayor. Open Mon.-Sat. 9am-2pm and 5:30-8:30pm, Sun 10am-2pm. **Super Spar,** C. Parras, 4, at junction of C. San Antón and C. San Pedro. Larger and much less expensive, but farther from Pl. Mayor. Open Mon.-Fri. 9:25am-2pm and 5:30-8pm, Sat.-Sun. 9:25am-2pm.

La Callejina del Beso Extremeño, C. Ancha, in the *ciudad monumental,* up the street from the *parador.* Shares an entrance with the Restaurante Palacio del Vino. Music and decently-priced *raciones* like *champiñones al ajillo* (375ptas). The iron cages lining the wall are hopefully nothing worse than the remnants of a 16th-century pet store. Open noon-1am.

El Gran Mesón Restaurante, C. General Ezponda, 7 (tel. 24 77 26), just off Pl. Mayor. A dilemma of a *menú* choice (900 or 1200ptas) in a "typical" *mesón* with swinging hammocks and the requisite wooden tables and bar. Bar open noon-midnight. Meals served 1:30-4pm and 9-11pm. Visa, MC, AmEx accepted.

Mesón del Jamón, Av. Virgen de Guadalupe, 5 (tel. 22 10 17), first street parallel to Av. España (to your right as you face Pl. América). Extr-ham-aganza! A stylish *tapas* bar and restaurant with a great selection of *tapas* (250-600ptas), *bocadillos* (300-400ptas), and *raciones* (400-700ptas), plus heftier fare. Open 1:30-4pm and 8pm-midnight. Visa, MC, AmEx accepted.

SIGHTS

The stork-filled, golden **barrio antiguo** (a.k.a. *ciudad monumental* or old city) is one of the most heterogeneous architectural ensembles in Europe. Surrounded by Almohad walls built on Roman foundations, the *barrio* is Arabic in its narrow, winding streets opening onto small squares, and feudal in the churches, towers, ancestral mansions, and fortified palaces introduced by rival clans. Roman, Arabic, Gothic, Renaissance, and even Native American influences have left their stamps.

Churches and Cathedrals

In front of Arco de la Estrella, **Plaza de Santa María** suns itself between stone buildings. A statue of San Pedro de Alcántara, one of Extremadura's two saints, eyes the plaza from an outside corner pedestal of **Catedral de Santa María.** His big toes are shiny because locals have rubbed or kissed off all the dirt, bird turd, and oxidation—touching them is said to bring good luck. The cathedral itself, built between 1229 and 1547, has Romanesque and Gothic architecture, with a Renaissance ceiling. The *retablo mayor* is an amazing example of Plateresque style, executed in pine and cedarwood. Cáceres' nobility are buried beneath the cathedral floor. In the cathedral's small **museum,** various items of religious significance are displayed. (Cathedral open daily 10am-2pm and 4-8pm. Free. Museum open Mon.-Thurs., Sat. 10am-2pm and 4-6:15pm, Fri. 10am-2pm, 4-6:15pm, and 7-8pm, Sun. 10:45-11:45am and 5-6:15pm. Admission 100ptas.)

Legend has it that the Orden de Santiago—first known as Los Frailes de Cáceres (The Friars of Cáceres)—was established in the **Iglesia de Santiago Matamoros,** outside the city walls on Pl. Santiago. A Gothic retable by Berruguete can be viewed during services only.

Towers and Palaces

The Almohad **Torre del Horno** and **Torre de Bujaco** are two of five rectangular towers preserved in the western wall. The star-shaped lantern near the entrance marks the spot where Queen Isabel la Católica swore she would respect the *fueros* (city charters) in exchange for recognition of her sovereignty.

Between the 14th and 16th centuries, Cáceres was flooded with *hidalgos* (nobles) who built dozens of fortified palaces and towers, including Palacio de la Generala, Casa de los Ovando-Perero, Casa Espadero-Pizarro, and Casa del Mono. The aristocracy resolved their disputes more often than not through violence, prompting the monarchs to remove all battlements and spires from local lords' houses as punishment. Due to Don Golfín's loyalty to Isabel, his **Casa y Torre de las Cigueñas** (the House and Tower of Storks) was the only one allowed to keep its battlements. Storks build impressive nests on its spires every spring. The Golfín clan's showy **Palacio de los Golfines de Abajo** gratefully bears the coat of arms of Isabel and Fernando. The **Palacio de los Golfines de Arriba,** another Golfín-owned palace farther uphill, is near C. Olmos and C. Adarros de Santa Ana. Here, on October 26, 1936, Francisco Franco was proclaimed head of the Spanish state and Generalísimo of its armies.

Other

In the 15th and 16th centuries, the taste for fortified palaces gradually yielded to one for smaller, comfier mansions. Examples include Casa de Aldana, Casa del Sol, Casa de Ulloa, and Casa de Carvajal. The **Casa de los Toledo-Moctezuma** is outside the old town through Arco de la Estrella, down the street to the right. Inside the **Casa de las Veletas** (House of Weathervanes), the absorbing **Museo de Cáceres** (a.k.a. Museo Arqueológico Provincial; tel. 24 72 34) exhibits fascinating memorial stones *(estelas),* a few Celtiberian stone animals (relatives of the bull in Salamanca), Roman and Visigothic tombstones, one El Greco, and a variety of randomish crafts. The museum's *pièce de résistance* is the 11th-century Arab *aljibe* (cistern) downstairs, which supplied Cáceres with water until 1935. (Open Tues.-Sat. 9:30am-2:30pm, Sun. 10:15am-2:30pm. Admission 200ptas.)

Uphill is **Plaza de San Jorge,** named for the dragonslayer and patron saint of the city whose likeness is bolted to its niche, lest it be pinched by rival Plasencians eager to rob the city of its saint's protection. Near the plaza, on the Cuesta de Marqués, is the **Casa y Colección Yusuf Al Borch,** a charming little place decorated with period pieces to look like an 11th-century Arab residence, complete with steam baths, wine cellar, verdant courtyard, and a miniature version of the Koran, which you can read with a magnifying glass. (Open Tues.-Sun. 10am-2pm and 4-8pm. Suggested donation 100ptas.)

ENTERTAINMENT

On warm evenings residents and tourists stroll along **Avenida de España,** and pack *terrazas* at **Parque de C. Sotelo** (the end of Av. España closest to Pl. Mayor) and the fringes of **Plaza Mayor,** especially those at the lower end (such as **Mesón Los Portales, Mesón Los Arcos,** and **Berlin**). As the night heats up and temperatures drop, sometimes even below 40°F, the town drifts toward the discos along **Calle General Ezponda** and the crowded pubs that line the two tiny alleys connecting Pl. Mayor with Pl. Duque. (Try the raucous **El Que Faltaba,** C. Gabriel y Galan, 10.)

El Corral de las Cigüenas, Cuesta de Aldana, 6 (tel. 21 58 36) is one of the few places for drinks and socializing after dark in the *ciudad monumental. Melrose Place* types frequent its sizable *terraza,* surrounded by high ivied walls. Dining here is expensive, but drinks are average (beers 400ptas, mixed drinks 500ptas and up). (Open from 8:30pm.) The nearby **Bar La Machacona "Café Latino,"** C. Andrada, 8 (tel. 21 67 52) is a touch cheaper and less self-consciously classy. (Open 1pm-1am.)

The 1st Sunday in May, Cáceres celebrates the day of **Nuestra Señora de la Montaña,** and during the final week of May, the city explodes in a general chaos of fairs, **festivales,** and partying in the streets.

■ NEAR CÁCERES

TRUJILLO

Rising high on a granite hill, Trujillo (pop. 10,000) looks the part of the "Cradle of Conquistadors." Over 600 plunderers of the New World, including Francisco Pizarro, the Conquistador of Peru, hailed from here. Established by the Romans and dominated later by the Arabs, Trujillo was reconquered in 1232 by the forces of Fernando III. In 1430, Juan II honored Trujillo with the title, *"Muy noble y muy leal ciudad"* (very noble and very loyal city). An important seat of Judaism, Trujillo was home to a school of Talmudic studies (which no longer exists), and base of operations for Samuel Ha-Levi, Pedro I's treasurer. Despite the town's rich history, the majority of the monuments and edifices within the medieval walls date from the 15th and 16th centuries, when wealthy soldiers and their descendants constructed sumptuous residences here.

Trujillo's **Plaza Mayor** inspired the one built in Cuzco, Perú, after Francisco Pizarro defeated the Incas: palaces, arched passageways, and one wide flight of steps surround an ample, stone-paved space and center fountain. The **Estatua de Pizarro,** the gift of an American couple, was erected in 1927 to honor the town's most famous native son. At night the eerie church clock tower keeps vigil over the lit fountain and statue.

Festooned with storks' nests, **Iglesia de San Martín** dominates the northeastern corner of the plaza. The church contains several historic tombs, but not—contrary to the dearly held Extremaduran belief—the tomb of Francisco de Orellana, the first European to explore the Amazon. Conquistador graves in Spain are few; Orellana, like most of his fellow explorers, died abroad. (Open 9am-1pm and 5-8pm.)

Across the street, the **Palacio de los Duques de San Carlos** was given by its owners to the few remaining Hieronymite cloistered nuns, who became homeless when their convent rotted. Ring the bell hard to be shown around the patio (whose 18th-century stonework includes a couple of Visigothic chunks) and up a winding staircase. One ancestor of the Duke is said to have climbed it on horseback. Emperor

Carlos V stayed here a couple of times and had his coat of arms painted on the ceiling. The seven smokestacks atop the house signify the different religions defeated by conquering Spaniards in the New World. (Open 9am-1pm and 4-6pm. Donation of at least 100ptas requested.)

Up the hill from the Iglesia de San Martín stands the **Casa-Museo de Pizarro.** The bottom floor reproduces the living quarters of a 15th-century *hidalgo;* the top floor houses a display illustrating the life and times of Francisco Pizarro. (Open Tues.-Sun. 11am-2pm and 5-8pm. Admission 250ptas.) A short trudge away are the spectacular ruins of a 10th-century Arab **castillo.** Here on the summit of Trujillo's 517m granite hill, the air is thick with swallows, storks, and buzzards. Some of the castle walls are extremely well-restored. The battlements and ramparts offer a view of the unspoiled landscape that overwhelms even the most jaded of travelers. Inside the walls lie remnants of the castle's *aljibe* (cistern) and the entrance to the lower-level dungeons. In 1232, the Virgin Mary infused Fernando III's troops with the strength to drive the Moors from the city; in return, the town erected a shrine to her inside one of the castle turrets. The **Madonna** twirls round (for 50ptas). (Castle open dawn to dusk.)

West on C. Ballesteros is Gothic **Iglesia de Santa María.** The caretaker points out the places assigned to Fernando and Isabel for mass during their brief residence in the city. Pizarro is said to have been christened on a stone font here. Legend has it that the giant-soldier Diego de Paredes picked up the fountain and carried it to his mother at age 11; the giant was buried here after he twisted his ankle and fell to his death. The church's 27-panel Gothic retable at the high altar was painted by master Fernando Gallego. (Open Mon.-Sat. 9am-2pm and 5-8pm, Sun. mass at 11am. Admission 100ptas. If the church is closed, inquire at the house directly to the right of the church steps.)

The fascinating and free **Museo de la Coria** (with your back to Santa María's facade, walk two blocks up and turn right) explores the historical relationship between Extremadura and Latin America. (Open Sat.-Sun. 10:30am-2pm.)

Orientation and Practical Information Trujillo is 45min. east of Cáceres by bus (there's no train station). To get to the **Plaza Mayor,** turn left up C. Marqués de Albayda as you exit the station and go uphill on C. Pardos, past the Iglesia y Convento de la Encarnación and the small Pl. Aragón, onto C. Romanos. Turn right at the end of C. Romanos onto C. Parra, then left on C. Carnicería (15min.). Across the plaza and directly in front of you is the **tourist office** (tel. 32 26 77; open Mon.-Fri. 9am-2pm and 5-7pm, Sat.-Sun. 9:15am-2pm and 5-7pm). The **post office** (tel. 32 05 33) is on Po. Ruiz de Mendoza—you'll see it as you walk from the station to Pl. Mayor. (Open Mon.-Fri. 9am-3pm, Sat. 9am-1pm.) For **telegrams** by phone dial 22 20 00. **Postal code** is 10200. The **telephone code** is 927. The **Red Cross** is at tel. 32 11 77. The municipal **police** (tel. 32 01 08) are in Pl. Mayor (in an **emergency,** dial 091). For an **ambulance,** call 32 00 89.

The bus station is on the road to Badajoz at the foot of the hill. Six to ten buses per day make the trip there and back (370ptas).

Accommodations and Food If you want to extend your stay, you'll find spacious, spic-and-span rooms at **Pensión Boni,** C. Domingo de Ramos, 7 (tel. 32 16 04), off the right-hand corner of Pl. Mayor. (Single 1500ptas. Doubles 2500ptas, luxury double with full bath and A/C 4000ptas.) Otherwise, try the less centrally located **Hostal Trujillo,** C. Francisco Pizarro, 4 (tel. 32 22 74 or 32 26 61), off C. Encarnación near the bus station. Nice rooms, all with fans. (Singles 2000ptas, with bath 2500ptas. Doubles 3000ptas, with bath 3500ptas.) Pl. Mayor has many restaurants and cafés. For a delicious and luxurious repast, check out **Mesón-Restaurante La Troya,** Pl. Mayor, 10 (tel. 32 14 65), decorated to look like a typical Spanish house. Three-course *menú* 1800ptas, a la carte entrees 1400-2000ptas. (Open 1-4:30pm and 9-11:30pm.)

Near Trujillo: Guadalupe

One fine day in 1300, as cowherd Gil Cordero was about to skin his just-found cow on the banks of the Río Guadalupe, the Virgin Mary appeared and told him to find the local priests, for in the ground under the cow's body lay an image of the Holy Mother. This image had, according to the story, been a gift of Pope Gregory the Great to St. Isidore of Sevilla, and had been buried before the Islamic conquest. The cow revived, the cowherd fled, the image was found, and the pilgrims haven't stopped coming.

In 1340 at the Battle of Salado, Alfonso XI invoked the Virgin's aid and defeated a superior Muslim army. In gratitude he commissioned the sumptuous **Real Monasterio de Santa María de Guadalupe,** a fortress to house the shrine on the site. The monastery and town came to unite all of *hispanidad* in the 15th century; it became customary to grant all licenses for foreign expeditions here, including the prototypical contract between Fernando and Isabel and Christopher Columbus. Columbus named the island of Turugueira "Guadalupe" in 1493 and also brought the first Native American converts to be baptized here in 1496. The rest of the *Conquistadores* took with them the Virgin's new nickname, Guadalupe. In 1836, the monastery was temporarily dissolved, and part of the complex was used for stables. The Franciscans moved into the lavish monastery early in this century.

Construction began in the 14th century, but haphazard renovations and additions continued through the 18th. The **basílica** of the monastery hulks over Pl. Mayor, connected by a wide set of stairs. Inside is a severe, 18th-century retable, designed by El Greco's son. You'll see the *coro* (choral area) on the official tour, wherein lie ornate Churrigueresque wood chairs and the magnificent ceiling painting of Juan de Flandes. (Basílica open 8:30am-8:30pm; Oct.-May 9am-6pm. Four masses per day. Free.)

Plaza Mayor is the place to be. Finding a room is difficult only during Semana Santa. **Mesón Típico Isabel,** Pl. Mayor, 18 (tel. (927) 36 71 26), offers modern rooms, all with newly renovated private baths. (Singles 2000ptas. Doubles 3000ptas. Breakfast 150ptas. Lunch 900ptas. Dinner 800ptas). The bar serves huge *raciones* (400ptas) and toothsome *caldereta* (350ptas). (Open 8am-1am). Dreamy **Hostal Cerezo,** Gregorio López, 12 (tel. (927) 36 73 79), is between the Ayuntamiento and the plaza. An immaculate collection of rooms, all with baths and many with views. Bare it all for the strong, hot showers. (Singles 2200-2500ptas. Doubles 3250-3800ptas. Prices do not include 6% IVA. Visa accepted. Restaurant-bar *menú* 750ptas.)

Two hours east of Trujillo and a three-hour bus ride southwest of Madrid, Guadalupe rests on a mountainside in the Sierra de Guadalupe. From Madrid, most travelers rush through the monastery as a daytrip, although the transportation can be tricky. Others go with organized bus tours or simply drive. From Trujillo, bus schedules force an overnight stay.

■■■ BADAJOZ

Big, bad Badajoz (pop. 120,000) is somewhat of an industrial wasteland, and the most populous city in Extremadura. This border town had its 15 minutes when an 11th-century poet with a bizarre sense of analogy sung its praises: "the valley of your delightful river opens out like a split in an embroidered tunic." That was a long time ago. Although the town deserves merit for bravely resisting Franco in one of the bloodiest battles of the Civil War (many citizens were brutally executed in the old bullring), it hasn't coped gracefully with urbanization, modernization, and emigration. An urban planner's nightmare come true, the city is an unsightly sprawl of industry and commerce, with only a few pleasant parks, plazas, and museums to balance. However, the nightlife is the region's best, and Badajoz is often a necessary stopover en route to or from Portugal—the border is only 6km to the west, and the town of Elvas, Portugal, only 11km beyond.

ORIENTATION AND PRACTICAL INFORMATION

The monumentally unaesthetic **Plaza España** is the heart of the old town, across the Guadiana River (read: festering swampland) from the train station. From Pl. España, C. Juan de Rivera leads to **Plaza Libertad** (5min.), home of the tourist office. Between Pl. España and Pl. Libertad lies **Plaza San Francisco,** with the post office, a big supermarket, and the restaurants and *terrazas* which Pl. España lacks. To get from the train station to the center of town, follow Av. Carolina Coronado straight to the Puente de Palmas, cross the bridge, and continue straight along C. Prim and its continuation. Turn left on C. Juan de Rivera for Pl. España, right for Pl. Libertad (35min.). To Pl. España from the bus station, turn left out of the station, take a quick right, and then left on the main C. Damión Tellez Lafuente. It becomes C. Fernando Cazadilla, passes through Pl. Constitución, becomes Av. Europa, and then C. Pedro de Valdivia, which runs uphill to the plaza (20min.).

Tourist Office: Pl. Libertad, 3 (tel. 22 27 63). City maps and mountains of glossy brochures. Staff helps with lodgings. English and French sometimes spoken. Open Mon.-Fri. 9am-2pm and 5-7pm, Sat.-Sun. 9:15am-2pm; winter Mon.-Fri. 9am-2pm and 4-6pm, Sat.-Sun. 9:15am-2pm. **Municipal Tourist Office,** Pasaje de San Juan, s/n (tel. 22 49 81), just off the top end of Pl. España. Open Mon.-Fri. 8am-3pm, Sat. 10am-1pm.

Post Office: Po. San Francisco, s/n (tel. 22 02 04). Main entrance on Pl. San Francisco. Open for stamps, Lista de Correos, and **telegrams** Mon.-Fri. 8am-9pm, Sat. 9am-2pm. For telegrams by phone call 22 31 57; 9pm-8am call (955) 22 20 00. **Postal Code:** 0605.

Telephones: No Telefónica, just lots of little booths and a few shops. One on Pl. Constitución in the "Hoy" Kiosk. Open 8am-3:30pm and 7-11:30pm. From the tourist office, walk right on Av. Ramón y Cajal, then right on Av. Europa. Shops in the bus station and Pl. España also have phone services. **Telephone Code:** 924.

Flights: Aeropuerto de Badajoz, Carretera Madrid-Lisboa, km 19 (tel. 44 00 16). Buses leave hourly from bus station to the airport (20min., 300ptas). A small, national airport with flights daily to Madrid, twice-weekly (Tues. and Thurs.) to Barcelona, and to the Islas Canarias in July-Aug.

Trains: Av. Carolina Coronado, s/n (tel. 23 71 70). To: Madrid (2 *regionales* per day, 8hr., 2500ptas; 2 *talgos* per day, 5hr., 3400ptas); Barcelona (3 per day); Mérida (8 per day, 1½hr., 360ptas); Cáceres (3 per day, 2½hr., 830ptas); Lisboa (3 per day, 5½hr., 1835ptas); Zafra (2 per day via Mérida, 700ptas).

Buses: Ctra. Valverde, s/n (tel. 25 86 61). Information open 7:45am-9pm. To: Zafra (7 per day, 1hr., 685ptas); Mérida (8 per day, 1½hr., 685ptas); Cáceres (3 per day, 1¾hr., 825ptas); Madrid (10 per day, 4hr., 2860-3440ptas); Sevilla (5 per day, 4½hr., 1610ptas).

Public Transportation: Buses (60ptas). Bus #1 (every ½hr.) runs from train station to Pl. Libertad; buses 6a and 6b run between bus station and Pl. Libertad.

Taxis: Cluster in Pl. España, the bus station, and the train station when arrivals are expected. **Radio-Taxi,** tel. 24 31 01 (open 24hrs.).

Luggage Storage: In the **bus station** (50ptas per item). In the **train station** (lockers 300ptas).

Red Cross: Av. Pardalevas, 2 (tel. 23 50 00 or 23 33 91).

Hospital: Pl. Minayo, 2 (tel. 22 47 43), between Pl. Libertad and Pl. España.

Emergency: tel. 091 or 092.

Police: Av. Ramón y Cajal, s/n (tel. 23 02 53), the street that runs in front of the tourist office. **Frontier Guards:** Caya (tel. 27 12 53).

ACCOMMODATIONS

Most *hostales* lie near **Plaza España.** Three acceptable *pensiones* (some with curfew) and a lone *hostal* huddle on **Calle Arco Agüeros,** in the heart of the open-air party (described in Sights and Entertainment below). You won't sleep here until 3, 4, or 5am unless you get an interior room and put your pillow over your head. For slightly more upscale accommodations, check out **Plaza Cervantes.** Except for Pensión Orrego, prices do not include IVA.

Hostal Victoria, C. Luis de Camoes, 3 (tel. 27 16 62), a 2-min. walk from the train station just down the boulevard, on a quiet side street to your left. Modern rooms with powerful A/C (when arbitrary powers turn it on) and phones. Lounge has TVs and so do doubles. Singles 1600ptas, with shower 2000ptas. Doubles with bath 3500ptas. Breakfast 200ptas. Lunch or dinner 900ptas.

Pensión Orrego, C. Arco Agüeros, 41 (tel. 22 08 32). Follow directions for Hostal Niza below. Pleasant rooms improved by faded photographs on the wall. Singles 1100ptas. Doubles 2000ptas.

Hostal Niza, C. Arco Agüeros, 34 (tel. 22 38 81), the street off C. San Blas to the right, coming from Pl. España. Solid beds, large rooms, and lofty ceilings. Singles 1250ptas. Doubles 2200ptas.

FOOD

Mediocre cafés and restaurants adorn the city. Check around **Plazas España, Libertad,** and **San Francisco,** especially the latter.

Groceries: Simago, Pl. San Francisco, next to the post office. Open Mon.-Sat. 9am-8pm. Visa accepted. **Maxcoop,** C. Ramón y Cajal, 6b, diagonally across from the Puerta de Palmas. Open Mon.-Fri. 9am-2pm and 5-8pm, Sat. 10am-2pm and 6-9pm.

La Bellota de Oro, C. Zurbarán, 5 (tel. 22 10 25). A lively, smoky atmosphere. Named after a golden acorn, but the only acorn-sized items are the yummy *tapas.* Open 1-4pm and 8pm-midnight.

Café Bar La Ría, Pl. España, 7 (tel. 22 20 05). Another popular hangout, with large picture-coded *platos combinados* (775-1200ptas). Intimate *comedor.* A/C. Open 8am-1am.

SIGHTS AND ENTERTAINMENT

Badajoz complies perfunctorily with the requisite cathedral/castle/museum points of interest. In one of Spain's least attractive Plazas de España, the bleak 13th-century **catedral** looms. Each of the 85 chairs is carved to represent a saint. There are also some hand-carved wooden choir stalls and an impressive pipe organ. (Open 8am-1pm, with two masses per day.) The **museo catedralico** houses a small collection of paintings, including some by Morales. (Open irregularly; sometimes someone will be lurking around the cathedral to let you in.) The **Puerta de Palmas** and **Puente de Palmas** (both 16th-century) confront you as you cross the Guadiana coming from the RENFE station. The attractive **Parque de la Legión** contains some of the original city walls.

To the west of Pl. España on C. Meléndez Valdés is the **Museo de Bellas Artes** (tel. 21 24 69), ashamed at the silly copies of Zurbarán and Caravaggio that fill its ground floor. Works by local 19th-century artists hang above. (Open Mon.-Fri. 7am-2:30pm, Sat. 9am-1pm. Free.)

The ruins of the **Alcazaba** now house the newly reopened **Museo Arqueológico,** which displays fragments of Roman and Visigothic architecture from local digs. (Open Tues.-Sun. 10am-3pm. Admission 200ptas; EU citizens with ID, students with ID, and all under 21 free.) Nearby hovers the **Torre del Apéndiz,** nicknamed **Torre de Espantaperros** ("to shoo away Christian dogs"), which served as the Alcazaba's watchtower. Its octagonal shape is similar to the Torre de Oro in Sevilla. Heading uphill from the center of town, the neighborhood becomes increasingly poor and deserted. **Plazas Alta** and **San José,** just outside the castle walls, are particularly ruinous, and the walls of the Alcazaba aren't in great shape. Avoid the area after dark. To get to the Alcazaba, follow the road leading uphill (parallel to the highway) from the Puerta de Palma. The road eventually runs into C. San Antón, which leads up to the right past the walls to the main entrance.

Nightlife spills out from the bars and literally fills the streets of the *centro* for several blocks; the fun-loving come from kilometers around, even Portugal, to partake in this bar and club scene—a sad comment on Extremadura for Spanish standards. **Calle San Blas,** off Pl. Mayor, is stuffed with teens passing around *minis* of *cerveza* or *sidra* (300ptas). **Calle Zurbarán,** off Pl. Mayor and perpendicular to C. San Blas, is wall-to-wall with twenty-somethings milling about. Barhoppers also clog the zone between these two streets, especially along **Calle Martín Cansado.**

For a more sedate afternoon drink or ice cream, head for shaded **Plaza San Francisco** (there's a Baskin Robbins!), lined with restaurants and shops.

■■■ MÉRIDA

If you liked *Spartacus,* you'll love Mérida (pop. 25,000), the town with the most Roman ruins in all of Spain. As a reward for services rendered, Caesar Augustus granted a group of veteran legionnaires the privilege of founding a city in Lusitania, comprised of Portugal and part of Spain. They chose a lovely little place surrounded by several hills on the banks of the Río Guadiana and called their new home "Augusta Emerita." However, they weren't content to rest on their laurels. Itching to gossip with fellow Patricians in Sevilla and Salamanca, the soldiers built what was then the largest bridge in Spain. The nostalgic crew also adorned their "little Rome" with baths, aqueducts, temples, a hippodrome, an arena, and the famous amphitheater where plays are still performed.

Mérida's ruins and world-class *Museo Romano* both merit at least a day. In July and August, the *Festival de Teatro Clásico* attracts some of Europe's finest classical and modern troupes, which perform tragedies by the flawless three: Aeschylus, Euripides, and Sophocles.

ORIENTATION AND PRACTICAL INFORMATION

Deep in the heart of Extremadura, Mérida is 73km south of Cáceres and 59km east of Badajoz. **Plaza de España,** the town center, is near the Río Guadiana, two bl. up from the **Puente Romano.** To get to the plaza from the bus station, cross the suspension bridge directly in front of the station and turn right on Av. Guadiana. Walk along the river until you reach the Puente Romano, then take a left on C. Puente, which leads straight into Pl. España (20min.). From the train station, walk down C. Cardero, which leads out of the station, and continue as it becomes C. J. Cela and C. Camilo. Angle right onto C. Felix Valverde Lillo, and follow it to Pl. España. From Pl. España to the tourist office, head up C. Santa Eulalia, which becomes a pedestrian shopping street, and bear right at the little circle onto C. J. Ramon Melida. The tourist office is on the right, across the street from the Museo Romano next to the Teatro Romano entrance.

Tourist Office: C. P.M. Plano, s/n (tel. 31 53 53). Friendly, multilingual staff in air-conditioned office. Small maps and theater schedules (but no tickets). Lists of accommodations. Open Mon.-Fri. 9am-2pm and 5-7pm, Sat.-Sun. 9:15am-1:45pm; winter Mon.-Fri. 9am-2pm and 4-6pm, Sat.-Sun. 9:15am-1:45pm.

Post Office: Pl. Constitución, s/n (tel. 31 24 58). Follow signs to the *parador;* the office is directly opposite. Open for **telegrams** and Lista de Correos Mon-Sat 8am-8pm; for stamps Mon-Sat 8am-2pm. **Postal Code:** 06800.

Telephones: Telefónica has some weird porta-phones down the street from the theater. Unattended, but at least you can sit down. **Telephone Code:** 924

Trains: C. Cardero (tel. 31 63 23). Information booth open 7am-midnight. To: Madrid (1 *regional* per day, 6hr., 2230ptas; 2 *talgos* per day, 6hr., 2100ptas); Barcelona (3 per day, 12hr., 6500ptas); Cáceres (1 *regional* per day, 1hr., 335ptas; 1 *talgo* per day, 1hr., 835ptas); Badajoz (6-10 per day, 1hr., 335-950ptas); Sevilla (1 per day, 4hr., 1350ptas). For trains to Lisboa, transfer in Cáceres or Badajoz.

Buses: Av. Libertad, s/n (tel. 37 14 04), in the so-called Polígono Nueva Ciudad. To: Cáceres (2 per day, 1hr., 630ptas); Badajoz (5-10 per day, 1½hr., 685ptas); Sevilla (6-9 per day, 3hr., 1850ptas); Madrid (7-9 per day, 5½hr., 2510ptas); Salamanca (8-10 per day, 3hr., 1775ptas); Valladolid (8-10 per day, 8hr., 5210ptas); Barcelona (1 per day, 12hr., 6720ptas).

Taxis: tel. 37 11 11 or 31 89 58. 24-hr. service.

Car Rental: Avis, in the Hotel Trip Medea (tel. 37 33 11).

Luggage Storage: In the **bus station** (300ptas per day) or the **train station** (lockers 500ptas per day).
Medical Services: Residencia Sanitaria de la Seguridad Social Centralita (tel. 38 10 00). **Ambulance,** El Madrileño (tel. 31 57 58 or 31 11 08).
Emergency: tel. 092 or 091.
Police: Ayuntamiento, Pl. España, 1 (tel. 38 01 00) or at the **Comisaría,** C. Almendialejo, 48 (tel. 091).

ACCOMMODATIONS

Plenty of rooms for all.

Pensión El Arco, C. Santa Beatriz de Silva, 4 (tel. 31 01 07). Follow signs to the *parador;* just before passing under the arch, look right. Wacky Mérida-Baroque decor. Rooms are small, simple, neat, painfully decorated, and the least expensive in town. Electric fans, too. During July, call ahead to make sure owners haven't closed down for vacation. Singles 1600ptas. Doubles 2900ptas. Showers 125ptas.
Hostal Nueva España, Av. Extremadura, 6 (tel. 31 33 56 or 31 32 11), 1 bl. from the train station, at the end of C. Cardero. Spacious, tidy rooms with bath, phone, and enough closet space for an army. Singles 2500ptas. Doubles 4500ptas. Off-season: 2200ptas; 3800ptas. For triples, negotiate the price of an extra bed.
Hostal-Residencia Senero, C. Holguín, 12 (tel. 31 72 07), take street to left of Hotel Emperatriz (on Pl. España) through its twists to C. Holguín. Spanish tile interior. Clean and comfortable. Plain rooms, all with space-saving baths. Rooms overlooking the patio can get a bit hot and stuffy. Singles 2500ptas. Doubles 4000ptas. Off-season: 2200ptas; 3500ptas.
Hostal Bueno, C. Calvario, 9 (tel. 31 10 13), on a quiet street, a bit out of the way. From Pl. España, pass under the arch and continue past the *parador* and around the corner of the post office to C. Almendralejo. Turn left, then a quick right on C. Calvario. A modest establishment which knows better than to call itself *Hostal Excelente:* rooms are a bit dim and cramped, but are clean and have baths. Singles 2500ptas. Doubles 4000ptas. Off-season: 2200ptas; 3500ptas.

FOOD

Restaurant options are plentiful—for those not on a budget. Sleuth out meals and pop *tapas* around **Plaza de España** and **Calle Juan Ramón Melida.** The **market** is on C. San Francisco, off C. Lillo (open 8am-2pm and 4-7pm).

Groceries: No centrally located supermarket—you'll have to settle for one of many little stores selling everything from hunks of ham to water guns. Across from the Museo Romano, a rather expensive shop (without a name) sells meat, cheeses, and wine. Open Mon.-Fri. 10am-2pm.
Casa Benito, C. San Francisco next to the market. Gawk at the photos, prints, and posters of all things taurine covering every inch of wall space—some images date back to the beginning of the century—while sipping *caña* (yeast water, 80ptas) and munching a spicy *pincho* (200ptas). Ivy-shaded terrace. Open for eating 1-4pm and 9-11pm. Bar open all day and into the night.
Bar Restaurante Briz, C. Félix Valverde Lillo, 5 (tel. 31 93 07). Typical Extremaduran fare. Hefty *menú* (800ptas) specializing in *callos* (tripe). Frogs 1000ptas. Open Mon.-Sat. 1-5:30pm and 9:15pm-midnight.
Cafeteria Lusi, on a little plaza just behind Pl. España on the Hotel Emperatriz side. The *menú* (900ptas) is uninspired, but it's a popular spot in the evening to see people and consume *tapas* (175-200ptas) and cool drinks *(caña,* 100ptas). Also does well in the breakfast department: *café con leche* or *chocolate* with *churros* (225ptas).

SIGHTS

Put on your swankiest toga. The Romans have come and you'll *amo, amas, amat* what they left behind. The best view of the **Acueducto de los Milagros** is from the road from Cáceres. Farther up the river are the three remaining pillars of the **Acue-**

ducto de San Lázaro. Over the wide, shallow Río Guadiana, the **Puente Romano,** one of the Romans' largest bridges, is still the main access to town from the south.

Mérida's acclaimed **Museo Nacional de Arte Romano,** designed by Rafael Moneo, is a well laid-out museum with all the Romemorabilia you could ask for: statues, dioramas, household utensils, remains of wall paintings, learned disquisitions on the nature of the city-state, and more. Tombstone remains and tool fragments might bore those without an overriding interest in all things Roman. A Roman road passes under and through the museum. To get here, follow C. Santa Eulalia from Pl. España and bear right up C. Juan Ramón Melida. (Open Tues.-Sat. 10am-2pm and 5-7pm, Sun. and holidays 10am-2pm; Oct.-May Tues.-Sat. 10am-2pm and 4-6pm, Sun. 10am-2pm. Admission 200ptas, EU citizens and students with ID free.)

The **Teatro Romano** lies across the street, a gift from Agrippa to the city. The semicircle of tiers (seating for 6000) faces a *scaenaefrons,* an impressive marble colonnade built backstage. The notion that conquered Greece took captive her own fierce conqueror (Rome) is never more apparent than in theater; the building could easily be *griego* and not *romano.* Seats are divided into three sections, originally used to separate social classes. The **Teatro Clásico** performances take place here June-Aug. at 11pm. (Tickets 800-2000ptas. Box office tel. 31 25 30; open 10am-1pm and 6-11pm.) Next to the theater and in worse shape is the 14,000-seat **Anfiteatro Romano.** Inaugurated in 8 BC, the amphitheater was used for man-to-man gladiator combat and contests between men and wild animals. Corridors at both ends of the ellipse hold gloomy pre-combat waiting rooms. (Both open same hrs. as the museum. Admission 800ptas, EU citizens and students with ID 100ptas. Hold onto your ticket, as it will get you into the Alcazaba and the Basílica de Sta. Eulalia—see below.)

Northeast of the theater complex is the **Circo Romano** or hippodrome. Once filled with 30,000 crazed spectators cheering their favorite charioteers, the arena now resembles a large parking lot. Diocles, the all-time best Lusitanian racer, got his start here and wound up in Rome with 1462 victories. (Free.)

Down the banks of the Guadiana, near the elegant *terrazas* of Pl. España, is the **Alcazaba,** a Moorish fortress built to guard the Roman bridge. The Moors showed their usual canny good sense by using building materials left behind by the Romans and Visigoths. The *aljibe* (cistern) held water filtered from the river. (Open Mon.-Sat. 9am-2pm and 5-7pm, Sun. 9am-2pm; Oct.-March Mon. 9am-1pm, Tues.-Sat. 9am-1pm and 3pm-6pm. Admission (with same ticket for *teatro* and *anfiteatro)* 300ptas, EU citizens and students with ID 100ptas.)

At the end of C. Rambla Martir Sta. Eulalia (from Pl. España, take C. Sta. Eulalia and angle left onto the *rambla),* stand the **museo, basílica,** and **iglesia** of the martyr Santa Eulalia. In 1990, in the course of repairs to the church of Sta. Eulalia (which was originally constructed in the 6th century, abandoned in 875 AD to the Arabs, and rebuilt in 1230 during the Reconquista), a hodge-podge of ruins and remains built willy-nilly atop one another were discovered: Roman houses dating from the 3rd to 1st centuries BC; a 4th-century necropolis; and a basilica dedicated to Sta. Eulalia. You can visit this fascinating mix of left-overs from centuries past, plus a nice little museum which explains their provenance. (Open 10am-2pm and 4-6pm. Admission with same ticket for *teatro, anfiteatro,* and Alcazaba. Church open only during services, daily at 8:30am and 8pm. Free.)

■■■ LOS PUEBLOS BLANCOS

So named for their blindingly whitewashed walls, the *pueblos blancos* are a series of small, tranquil towns in southern Extremadura, any of which makes a good daytrip from Mérida or Badajoz.

Zafra: Zafra has been a major market town since the Middle Ages. It's **Plaza Grande** has some austere stone 17th- and 18th-century mansions, while its verdant **Plaza España** houses a Renaissance **Alcázar.** 5 buses per day (1hr., 630ptas) from Mérida and 8 per day (1hr., 620ptas) from Badajoz voyage here.

Llerena: Once the center of the military Orden de Santiago, Llerena had 14th-century importance as a frontier town. Its **Plaza Mayor** is a textbook of Mudejar architecture. From Zafra, buses run here (4 per day, 1¼hr., 480ptas).

Jerez de los Caballeros: This areas is considered to be some kind of mysterious prehistoric settlement. Numerous inscriptions, funerary steles, and mosaics remain from the Romans. Check out the Templar-built 13th-century **Castillo Fortaleza,** with its decorated brick and painted stucco. The Knights were later put to death in their very own church towers. Open mid-morning-8pm. 4 buses per day go to and from Zafra and 1 per day to and from Mérida.

Olivenza: Founded by the strong, brave Portuguese Knights Templar, this town is still rich in the Portuguese Manueline style (see Portugal Essentials: Art and Architecture). Call the tourist office (tel. (924) 49 01 25) for transportation details.

PORTUGAL

US $1 = 158.23 escudos ($)	**100$ = US $0.63**
CDN $1 = 115.70$	**100$ = CDN $0.86**
UK £1 = 244.38$	**100$ = UK £0.41**
AUS $1 = 117.26$	**100$ = AUS $0.85**
NZ $1 = 95.93$	**100$ = NZ $1.04**
SA R1 = 44.38$	**100$ = SA R2.25**

 Essentials

■■■ TOURIST OFFICES

The national tourist board is the **Direcção Geral do Turismo (DGT).** Their offices are in virtually every city; look for the **"Turismo"** sign. They'll give you free maps that usually include brief descriptions of sights and useful phone numbers. Many Turismos keep lists of approved accommodations and can point you to a *quarto*. They may stock maps and brochures for the whole area, even for the whole country. Finding an English speaker at these offices should be no problem.

The principal student travel agency is **TAGUS Juvenil** (for addresses, see Planning Your Trip: Useful Addresses: Travel Services). English is spoken at these offices.

■■■ EMBASSIES AND CONSULATES

If you're seriously ill or in trouble, contact your consulate, not your embassy (whose function is solely diplomatic). They can provide legal advice and medical referrals and can contact relatives. In extreme cases, they may offer emergency financial assistance. Embassies are in Lisboa; consulates are in other major cities. Both are usually open Monday through Friday; call for specific business hours.

U.S. Embassy: Av. das Forças Armadas, 1600 Lisboa (tel. (1) 726 66 00).
Canadian Embassy: Av. Liberdade, 144/56, #4, 1200 Lisboa (tel. (1) 347 48 92).
British Embassy: R. São Domingos à Lapa, 37, 1296 Lisboa CODEX (tel. (1) 396 11 91; fax (1) 397 07 69). **Consulates,** Av. Zarco, 2, CP 417, 9000 Funchal, Madeira (tel. (91) 22 12 21; fax (91) 22 98 03). Av. da Boavista, 3072, 4100 Porto (tel. (2) 618 47 89; fax (2) 610 04 38).
Irish Embassy: Rua da Imprensa, à Estrela, 1-4., 1200 Lisboa (tel. (1) 60 45 19).
Australian Embassy: The Australian Embassy in Lisboa has been closed; refer to the Australian Embassy in Paris.
New Zealand Embassy: Refer to the British Embassy in Lisboa or the New Zealand Embassy in Rome.
South African Embassy: Av. Luís Bivar, 10, 1097 Lisboa CODEX (tel. (1) 353 50 41; fax (1) 353 57 13). **Consulate,** R. Julío Dinis, 772, 1st fl., 4000 Porto (tel. (2) 69 89 68).

■■■ GETTING AROUND

TRAIN

Caminhos de Ferro Portugueses, Portugal's national railway, operates throughout the country, but aside from the Braga-Porto-Coimbra-Lisboa line, it's wisest to take

the bus. Trains are less comfortable, less frequent, often slower, and reach fewer destinations than buses.

Unless you own a Eurailpass, the return on round-trip tickets must be used before 3am the following day. The fine for riding without a ticket is at least 3500$. Tykes under 4 travel free; ages 4-11 pay half price for their own seat. **Youth discounts** are only available to Portuguese citizens; this stipulation is strictly enforced.

BUS

Buses are often the way to go. They run frequently and are super cheap. **Rodoviária,** the national bus company, has recently been privatized and broken up by region. (Names now usually correspond to the region, such as Rodoviária Alentejo, Rodoviária Minho e Douro, with notable exceptions such as EVA in the Algarve.) In most places Rodoviária is still known by its old name, and links just about every town. A superflux of private regional companies—**Cabanelas, AVIC,** and **Mafrense,** among them—cover the more obscure routes. Express coach service *(expressos)* between major cities is especially good. City buses are really inexpensive and may run to small nearby villages. Rodoviária's headquarters in Lisboa are at Av. Casal Ribeiro, 18-B (tel. (1) 54 58 63).

CAR

Portugal has the highest accident rate per capita in Western Europe. Off the main arteries, the narrow, twisting roads may prove difficult to negotiate. Moreover, parking space in cities is nonexistent, and drivers fulfill their reputation for rash and risky maneuvers. The Portuguese AAA is called the **Automóvil Clube de Portugal.**

Gas comes in super (97 octane), normal (92 octane), and unleaded. Prices are high by North American standards (about 160$ per liter). Officially you need an **international driver's license** to drive in Portugal (see Planning Your Trip: Documents and Formalities).

Renting a car involves the extra costs of insurance and tax. A major rental company in Portugal and Europe is **Europcar,** whose U.S. affiliate is National Car Rental. **Avis, Hertz,** and other major companies are in the larger cities and in airports. Rates vary, depending on whether insurance, tax, and a per km charge are included. Shop around; local companies may be less expensive. It costs less (for some reason) to reserve your rental in the U.S. before coming to Portugal. The driving age is 18, but you must be 21 to rent a car and have had a driver's license for at least one year. The following companies offer information on reservations.

Auto-Europe, P.O. Box 1097, Camden, ME 04843 (tel. (800) 223-5555; fax (800) 235-6321).

Avis (tel. (800) 331-1084). You must reserve while still in the U.S.

Europe By Car, Rockefeller Plaza, New York, NY 10021 (tel. (800) 223-1516 or (212) 581-3040). Student and faculty discounts.

Hertz Rent-A-Car (tel. (800) 654-3001).

Kemwel Group (tel. (800) 678-0678).

National Car Rental (tel. (800) 227-7368).

MOPED AND BICYCLE

Touring by **moped** is less popular here than in the rest of Europe, so don't expect to find rentals easily.

Although in coastal areas and on the flatlands **bicycles** are an obvious choice, roads are often in deplorable condition; often only a mountain bike will do. Also, watch out for motorists who aren't used to driving alongside cyclists. Even experienced pedal-pushers should beware of the hot Mediterranean climate of southern Portugal. There are few bike stores outside of Portugal's major cities. You'd best be packing a suitable bike helmet and a tough bike lock (the best are made by Kryptonite, US$35-US$50), a strong pump, and various spare parts and tools. Wise cyclists bring along a basic bike repair book and the relevant gadgetry. Bike Nashbar, 4112

Simon Rd., Youngstown, OH 44512 (tel. (800) 627-4227) offers excellent prices on equipment—generally the best deal around.

Airlines count a bicycle as your second free piece of checked luggage. As a third piece, it'll cost US$85 each way. The bike can't weigh over 70 lbs. and must be boxed (normally boxes are available at the airport). Policies vary, so call individual airlines.

A number of books about bicycle travel in Europe recommend scenic and cyclable roads. *Europe by Bike,* by Karen and Terry Whitehill (The Mountaineers Books, Seattle, WA (tel. (800) 553-4453); US$14.95), with detailed info on biking in 11 countries, is a fantastic reference for planning your trip and outfitting your bike.

HITCHHIKING

Let's Go does not recommend hitching as a means of travel. The information presented below and throughout the book is not intended to do so.

Opportunities to hitch are few and far between. Although some tourists try to hitchhike, most locals stick to buses, which are already inexpensive. Rides are reportedly easiest to come by between smaller towns. Thumbers often get results by approaching people for rides at gas stations near highways and rest stops.

The dangers of hitchhiking should not be underestimated. Drivers have raped, sexually assaulted, and killed passengers. If you choose to solicit a ride, avoid doing it alone. Experienced hitchers sit in the front, and never get in the back seat of a two-door car. If the driver begins to harass them, they ask firmly to be let out. They report that, in an emergency, opening the door on the road may surprise a driver enough to slow down. Pretending you're about to vomit may also help, they say.

■■■ ACCOMMODATIONS

Tourist offices keep lists of all recognized youth hostels, hotels, *pensões, pousadas,* and campgrounds. Sometimes they can inform on *quartos* (rooms in private homes).

YOUTH HOSTELS

The **Associação Portuguesa de Pousadas de Juventude (APPJ),** the Portuguese Hostelling International affiliate, runs the country's HI hostels. A bargain bed in a *pousada de juventude* costs 1300-2000$ per night; 1100-1750$ in off-season. (Breakfast included.) Lunch or dinner cost 750$. Rates are slightly higher for guests 26 or older. Hostels are often some distance away from the town center. Check-in hours are 9am-12:30pm and 6-9pm. Most hostels enforce a lockout 10:30am to 6pm, and early curfews (11pm or midnight) may cramp your style if you club-hop. Don't expect much privacy.

To reserve beds in high season (July and August), obtain an **International Booking Voucher** from APPJ (or your home country's HI affiliate) and send it to the desired hostel four to eight weeks in advance of your stay. If traveling between October 1 and April 30, make sure the hostel's open. Groups should contact APPJ's national reservation service (address below) at least 30 days in advance, giving the exact number of males and females in the group and the dates desired.

To stay in a hostel, an **HI card** (3000$) is mandatory. In Portugal they're sold only by APPJ's Lisboa office (see address below), so you may want to get one before leaving home (see Planning Your Trip: Documents: HI Membership). Also required is a **sleepsack,** so either bring your own or rent one from the hostel—in listings we'll write "Sheets 200$." (To make a cheap sleepsack, see Planning Your Trip: Packing.) Don't confuse *pousadas de juventude* with their sneakily-named opposites, *pousadas* (the Portuguese equivalent of the Spanish *parador,* historic buildings that were converted into pricey hotels).

For **information** such as hostel addresses, contact **APPJ,** Av. Duque D'Avila, 137, 1000 Lisboa (tel. (1) 355 90 81; fax (1) 352 86 21). (See also Planning Your Trip: Documents and Formalities: Hostelling Organizations.)

PENSÕES AND RESIDENCIAS

Pensões, also called *residencias,* will likely be your mainstay. They're far cheaper and offer fewer amenities than hotels and are only slightly more expensive than crowded youth hostels. All are rated on a three-star scale and required to prominently post their category and legal price limits. During high season, many *pensão* owners won't reserve rooms by phone. Travelers with foresight book at least one month in advance and get written confirmation.

HOTELS

Hotels in Portugal are expensive. A quality establishment typically includes showers and breakfast in the price. Most rooms without bath or shower have a sink. Generally you must vacate your room by noon. When business is slack, try bargaining down in advance; the "official price" is merely the maximum allowed.

CAMPING

The Portuguese see camping as a social activity rather than a solitary survival exercise, and their 168 official campgrounds *(parques de campismo)* come brimful with amenities and comforts. Virtually all have a supermarket and café and most enjoy access to a beach. Many inland sites possess river bathing or pools. With such facilities, it's wise to arrive early; urban and coastal parks may require reservations. Recently police have been cracking down on illegal camping, so don't try it near one of the official campgrounds. Larger Turismo branches stock the **Roteiro Campista** (550$), an indispensable multilingual guide to all official campgrounds; or write to the Federação Portuguesa de Campismo, Av. 5 Outubro, 15-3, Lisboa CODEX (tel. (1) 315 27 15; fax (1) 54 93 72).

Orbitur-Intercâmbio de Turismo, S.A., a private company, administers 18 of Portugal's poshest, best-run, and most expensive campgrounds (may have bungalows, pool, restaurant, and supermarket). For reservations write to Orbitur at R. Diogo Couto, 1-8, 1100 Lisboa (tel. (1) 815 48 71 or (1) 815 49 51; fax (1) 814 80 45).

ALTERNATIVE ACCOMMODATIONS

Quartos: Rooms in private residences, just like *casas particulares* in Spain. Sometimes the only choice in small or less touristed towns, particularly in southern Portugal. Turismo can usually help find them, although at times officials prefer to direct tourists to hotels. Restaurant proprietors and bartenders often supply names and directions.

Pousada (literally, resting place): A castle, palace, or monastery converted into a luxurious government-run hotel. Portugal's version of the Spanish *parador nacional.* Pricey "historical" *pousadas* play up local craft, custom, and cuisine. You pay for the exceptional surroundings: they generally cost as much as the most expensive hotels. Most require reservations. Priced more cheaply are *regional pousadas,* which are situated in national parks and reserves. For information contact ENATUR, Av. Santa Joana Princesa, 10-A, 1700 Lisboa (tel. (1) 848 90 78).

Turismo de Habitação Regional helps tourists find rooms, apartments, or entire houses, many of them mansions. This practice is most common in the Algarve and the provinces north of the Ribatejo.

■■■ FOOD AND DRINK

Olive oil, garlic, herbs, and sea salt routinely season local specialties. As a whole, the aromatic Portuguese cuisine is heavy on herbs and light on spices.

TYPICAL FARE

Sopas (soups) are hearty and filling. Thick *caldo verde,* a potato and kale mixture with a slice of sausage and olive oil, is a northern specialty. **Sandes** or **sandwiches** (sandwiches) here are smaller than their Spanish counterparts, but a *bifana* or *prego no pão* (a meat sandwich) is a *festa* on a roll. Seafood lovers get their fix from grilled *peixe espada* (swordfish), *lagosta suada* (steamed lobster), *pescada frita* (fried fish, usually hake, a particularly delicious Atlantic fish), *linguado grelhado* (grilled sole), *polvo* (boiled or grilled octopus), and *mexilhões* (mussels). Cod lovers snarf *bacalhau* (roasted, boiled, or fried cod served with potatoes). Bold gourmands shouldn't miss *chocos grelhadas* (grilled cuttlefish) or *lulas grelhadas* (grilled squid), a Portuguese specialty.

Pork fiends indulge in *bife de porco à alentejana,* made with beef, clams, and potatoes in a coriander sauce. Those who prefer chicken fork into *frango assado* (roasted on a spit) and *frango no churrasco* (on the grill). The entire country feeds on *cozida à portuguesa* (boiled beef, pork, sausage, and vegetables) in winter. Ballsy connoisseurs plop a dollop of *piri-piri* (mega-hot) sauce on the side. In the country, an expensive delicacy is freshly roasted *cabrito* (baby goat). There are scores of variations on *feijoada,* bean stew with pork and sausage. No matter what you order, *batatas* (potatoes), prepared in a billion different ways, will accompany it.

Queijos (cheeses) are fresh and delectable. The soft, chewy *serra* comes from ewe's milk and costs many a ducat, while tangy *cabreiro* takes its name from goat's milk. *Alvorca* is a blanket term for hard cheeses made from cow, goat, or ewe's milk. The only cheese reminiscent of cheddar is *queijo São Jorge* from the Açores.

Portugal's favorite **dessert** is *pudim,* a rich caramel custard. The Costa Verde's own *toucinho de céu* (bacon of heaven) combines egg, almond, and sugar in a prodigiously sweet tart. The almond groves of the Algarve produce their own version of marzipan. For something different, try *peras* (pears) bathed in sweet Port wine and served with a sprinkling of raisins and filberts on top. Countless varieties of ice cream also feed the Portuguese sweet tooth—vendors post the colorful, ubiquitous "Olá" sign. *Pastelarías* (bakeries) are the social centers of most towns, and display a tantalizing array of deliciously cheap (70-150$) pastries in their windows.

DINING HOURS AND RESTAURANTS

The Portuguese eat the midday meal (dinner, "lunch" to Americans) between noon and 2pm, supper between 7:30 and 10pm.

A good meal costs 1000-2000$ just about anywhere. Oddly, prices don't vary much between ritzy and economy restaurants in Portugal. Half portions **(meia dose)** cost more than half-price but are often more than adequate—a full dose is often enough for two. Other cheapo options? The ubiquitous **prato do dia** (special of the day) and **menú** (appetizer, bread, entree, and dessert) satisfy hungry people. The **ementa turística** (tourist *menú*) is usually a way to rip off foreigners, and inevitably the most expensive option, although it's a lot of food. The standard pre-meal bread, butter, cheese, and pâté usually served at restaurants will up your bill.

Concocting a meal from the outdoor food stalls is the most inexpensive option. Attention vegetarians: every town you visit is likely to have a **mercado municipal** (open-air market); get there before noon for the choicest produce. For groceries, shop at the **supermercado** (supermarket).

DRINKS

Portuguese **vinho** (wine) costs a pittance by North American standards. Sparkling *vinho verde* (literally "green wine"—the name refers to its youth, not its color) comes in red and white versions; the red may be obnoxious to the unaccustomed palate but the white is brash and delicious by anybody's standards. The Adega Cooperatives of Ponte de Lima, Monção, and Amarante make the best. Excellent local table wines are Colares, Dão, Borba, Bairrada, Bucelas, and Periquita. Ordering the overpriced Mateus Rosé marks you instantly as an ignorant foreigner. If you can't decide, experiment with the **vinho de casa** (house wine); either the *tinto* (red) or the *branco* (white) is a reliable standby.

Vinho do Porto (port), pressed (by feet) from the red grapes of the Douro Valley and fermented with a touch of brandy, is a dessert in itself. Chilled white port makes a snappy aperitif, while the ruby or tawny port makes a typical digestif. A unique heating process gives **Madeira** wines their odd "cooked" flavor. Try the dry Sercial and Verdelho as aperitifs, and the sweeter Bual and Malmsey as dessert wines.

Bar lingo is rather specialized. If it's beer you want, order bottled Sagres or Super Bock. Ask for it **fresco** (cool), or it may come *natural* (room temperature). A tall, slim glass of draft beer is a **fino** or an *imperial,* while a larger stein is a **caneca.** When it's time to sober up, order a **bica** (cup of black espresso), a **galão** (coffee with milk, served in a glass), or a **cafe com leite** (coffee with milk, served in a cup).

■■■ COMMUNICATIONS

MAIL, TELEGRAPH, AND FAX

The most reliable way to send a message is actually via telegram (see below); the least is by surface mail, which may take over two months. Mail sent from small towns takes longer than from major cities such as Lisboa; overall, mail service tends to be faster than Spain's. Stamps are sold only at post offices *(correios)*. A "CTT" sign at the post office indicates that it does **telegrams** and has telephones—nearly all do. A telegram costs about the same as a three-minute international call: a message of 10-15 words costs a flat fee of about 1614$ plus a 84$ per word charge. **Fax** is becoming more common in Portuguese business establishments, and is frequently used by hotels and other accommodations. However, to *send* a fax is difficult as only large city post offices have machines for public use.

Air mail: *Via aerea.* Takes 6-8 business days to reach the U.S. or Canada. Postage 130$.
Surface mail: *Superficie.* Takes up to 2 months.
Postcards: *Cartão postal.* Takes a bit longer than a letter. Postage 130$.
Registered mail: *Registrado* or *certificado.* The most reliable way to send a letter or parcel home. Takes about 5 business days.
Overnight mail: Also called "EMS" or "Express Mail." Only available in large cities. Takes approximately 2 days to reach the U.S. and costs a fortune. Is it really that urgent?
General Delivery mail: *Posta Restante.* Letters or packages held for pick-up at the post office that handles general delivery for a town. Letters should be addressed as follows: LAST NAME, First Name; Posta Restante; City Name; Postal Code; COUNTRY; AIR MAIL. When you pick it up, always ask for mail under both your first and last names to make sure it hasn't been misfiled. You can have mail forwarded to another Posta Restante address if you must leave town while expecting mail. Takes 2 wks. Charge of 55$ per piece picked up.
American Express: Mail (no packages) for cardholders may be sent to some AmEx offices, where it will be held. This service may be less reliable than Posta Restante. A directory of which offices hold mail can be had from any AmEx office, or contact their main office at American Express Tower C, Royal Financial Center, 200 Vesey St., New York, NY 10285 (tel. (800) 528-4800). They'll keep mail for 1-3 months after receipt.

TELEPHONE

Country Code: 351.
Directory Assistance: 118.
Local Operator: 142.
International Operator: 099 for inside Europe; 098 for elsewhere.
Emergency (Police, Fire, Medical): 115.

Phone booths are located at phone offices, on the street, and in some post offices, marked by signs saying "Credifone." The **Credifone** system uses magnetic cards rather than coins (few pay phones accept coins any more) that are sold at locations posted on the phone booth. Local calls cost 17.5$ by Credifone, or 20$ by coin. Phone calls from bars and cafés cost whatever the proprietor decides to charge, typically 30-40$; there's usually a posted sign that indicates the rates.

Direct-dialing from a phone booth is the least expensive way to make an international call. You may have difficulty reaching the U.S. from anywhere other than Lisboa. Call the operator beforehand to get an idea of how much your call will cost. Then dial 098 for Europe, 097 for everywhere else; + country code + city code + phone number. Handy calling cards let you make calls even when you don't have a pocket full of coins, but their rates are higher.

> **AT&T calling card:** Two services offered: USADirect for calling from overseas to the U.S. and AT&T World Connect for calling between two countries other than the U.S. Callers must have an AT&T card. To call the U.S., dial toll-free 05 017 1288; then give the operator the number you want to reach and your calling card number.
>
> **MCI calling card:** WorldPhone allows callers to access MCI service and bill calls to their calling cards. To call the U.S., dial toll-free 05 017 1234; then give the operator the number you want to reach and your calling card number.

Collect calls *(pago no destino)* are charged according to person-to-person *(chamada pessoa à pessoa)* rates but are still cheaper than calls from hotels.

Telecom Portugal is an overpriced telephone office, similar to *Telefónica* in Spain.

Overseas Access is a telephone service offered by EurAide, P.O. Box 2375, Naperville, IL 60567 (tel. (708) 420-2343). Between May 2 and Octoberfest, European travelers can have phone messages collected for them at a "home base" in Munich. They can then call and retrieve their messages at any time. Particularly useful for travelers without a set itinerary. The cost is US$15 per week or US$40 per month, plus US$15 registration fee.

■■■ MORE MONEY

Bills come in denominations of 500, 1000, 2000, 5000, and 10,000$. Coins come in 1, 2½, 5, 10, 20, 50, 100, and 200$.

Banking hours are officially Monday through Friday 8:30am-3pm, but play it safe and visit between 8:30-11:45am and 1-2:45pm. All banks are closed on Saturdays.

VALUE-ADDED TAX (VAT)

The Value-Added Tax (VAT) is a sales tax levied on goods and services in the EU, at a rate that depends on the item. Stores, restaurants, and lodgings include VAT in posted prices, unless otherwise noted. In Portugal the rate is 2-16%. The *factura* is an official bill which lists the price of your purchase separately from the amount of VAT. Ask at stores and tourist offices about VAT refunds—a rare possibility with many restrictions (e.g., hefty minimum amount spent). Prices quoted in *Let's Go* include VAT except where noted.

TIPPING

Most restaurants add 10% to your bill. It's customary to round off the sum to the next highest unit of currency and leave the change as a tip. Everyone else deserves a tip as well: train or airport porters 100-150$ per bag, taxi drivers 15% of the meter fare, and hotel chambermaids 200$ per day (optional).

■■■ LIFE AND TIMES

HISTORY AND POLITICS

Portugal was colonized by a succession of civilizations—Phoenicians, Celts, Greeks, and Carthaginians—long before the **Romans** won the peninsula in the Second Punic War (218-202 BC). The Romans brought the Latin language to the land they called "Lusitania."

The Moors and the Reconquista

When the Roman Empire crumbled in the early 5th century, Visigoth invaders assumed a shaky dominance, then fell to the Moors in 711 AD. Four centuries of Moorish rule left heavy stone castles throughout the country and hundreds of Arabic words in the Portuguese language. With the help of the Crusaders, **Dom Afonso Henriques** eventually overpowered the Moors and declared himself ruler of the Kingdom of Portugal at Guimarães, site of the first Christian victory (1143). The speedy Christian **Reconquista** ("reconquering") united Portugal by the 13th century, as **Dom Dinis** (1279-1325) ensured the unity of the nation, established a university, and exterminated those powerful, mysterious **Knights Templar.**

The Age of Discovery

In 1415, Portuguese forces captured the North African city of Ceuta. Ambitious Prince Henry, his imagination fired by this new conquest, launched a famous school of navigation and exploration at Sagres, earning himself the nickname **Henry the Navigator** and inaugurating the Age of Discovery.

Portuguese adventurers drove into Africa in search of wealth, glory, and a mysterious messianic figure named Prester John, the mythical ruler of a Christian paradise thought to be hidden in the African interior. Portugal established colonies in Madeira, the Açores, and Guinea-Bissau before Bartolomeu Dias found an ocean route around Africa's Cape of Good Hope in 1487. **Vasco da Gama** led the first European naval expedition to India in 1498, and Portugal beefed up its empire with numerous colonies along the East African and Indian coasts. Two years later **Pedro Alvares Cabral** stumbled into Brazil; next Portugal became the first European nation to establish trading contacts with Japan. With riches pouring in from far and near, Lisboa blossomed into one of Europe's most ornate cities. King Manuel the Fortunate commissioned buildings and monuments, artists slapped on symbols of maritime conquest, and *voilà*, Portugal had perfected its **Manueline** style.

The House of Bragança

Meanwhile, Spanish, English, and Dutch merchant fleets competed ferociously with Portugal for control of the **spice** trade. By the late 16th century, the debt-ridden country had lost it and the Golden Age of Portugal went out with a whimper. In 1580, paper-pushing Hapsburg Felipe II inherited the Portuguese crown, uniting the entire Iberian peninsula under Spanish rule. For 60 years the Hapsburgs dragged Portugal into their ill-fated wars; when the dust cleared, Portugal had lost a good part of its empire.

In 1640 the **House of Bragança** engineered a nationalist rebellion, assumed the throne, and erected a pole topped by a stone pig in their hometown (see Trás-Os-Montes: Bragança). The clever dynasty handed over Tangier and Bombay to the English, sealing an alliance with Spain's worst enemy. In the next two decades the nation gave up Ceylon and Malabar to the Dutch. Still, Portugal's empire was not entirely defunct. Brazil's gold, not to mention the booming slave trade (the first slave market was in Lagos), financed the "enlightened" despotism of **João V** (1706-1750), who lavished the dough on massive, flamboyant architectural projects.

The great **Earthquake of 1755** devastated Lisboa and killed as many as 50,000. The catastrophe, unparalleled in Portuguese history, shook European faith in both God and humanity; some even suggest that it brought an end to the more naively cheery aspects of Enlightenment thought. Dictatorial minister **Marquês de Pombal** led Lisboa's reconstruction, rebuilding the capital (or at least the Baixa district) in typically griddy Neoclassical style.

Napoleon, Then More Trouble

When Napoleon's army invaded in 1807, the Portuguese royal family fled to Brazil, where they remained until the French were driven out. The timid monarchs returned to Lisboa in 1821, only to face even more problems. One year later, in the New World's only bloodless revolution, Brazil declared its independence.

As the empire disintegrated, behind-the-scenes machinations at court left Portugal itself in disarray. When Prince Pedro flubbed the marriage arrangement between his seven-year-old daughter Maria da Gloria and his brother Miguel, a squabble over succession to the crown mushroomed into the **War of the Two Brothers** (1826-1834). Eight gory years later, with Pedro pushing up the daisies and Miguel in exile, Maria ascended to the throne at the age of 15. But even **Queen Maria's** staunch opposition could not stop the formation of a shaky party government.

Recent History

The monarchy wasn't ended, nor the **First Republic** established, until 1910. The new government granted universal male suffrage and managed to wrangle some power from the Catholic Church. The world disapproved when the Republic booted out the Jesuits and other religious orders, while governmental conflicts with workers' movements heightened tensions at home. The Republic wobbled along until it was overthrown in a 1926 military coup led by Antonio Carmona.

When Carmona died in 1951, conservative economist and star University of Coimbra student **António Salazar** succeeded to the dictator's chair. His *Estado Novo* (New State) gave women the vote for the first time, but did little else to end the country's authoritarian tradition (his secret police, the PIDE, had a ball). Although Salazar balanced the budget at first, he refused to take economic measures that would help the country grow. The regime improved life for the wealthy while the working class, peasantry, and colonized peoples of Africa suffered. Salazar spent money on costly wars that quelled colonial rebellions.

A slightly more liberal **Marcelo Caetano** continued the increasingly unpopular African wars after Salazar's death in 1970. On April 25, 1974, a left-wing military coalition overthrew Caetano in a quick coup. The insurgents waited for a radio station to play the popular song "Grandola Vila Morena" and attacked in sync. The **Captain's Revolution** sent Portuguese splashing euphoric graffiti on government buildings; today, every town in Portugal has its own Rua 25 de Abril. The Marxist-socialist armed forces established a variety of civil and political liberties and withdrew from Africa by 1975. But civil wars in Angola and Mozambique continued, and hundreds of thousands of *crioulos* (overseas Portuguese) and African refugees streamed into the country. This flow into Portugal is atypical; the trend over the past thirty years has been for emigration out of Portugal as people searched for better jobs. Some estimates hold that close to two fifths of the resident domestic population went to live and work abroad; many are now returning.

Portugal's first elections (1978) plopped the more conservative Social Democrats into power under charismatic **Mario Soares.** Foreign debt, inflation, and unemployment skyrocketed. Soares instituted "100 measures in 100 days" to resuscitate the country by stimulating industrial growth. The year 1986 brought Portugal into the European Union, ending its long isolation from more affluent Northern Europe. Soares won Presidential elections in 1986 and 1991.

ART

The Age of Discovery (15th-16th centuries) promoted cultural exchange with the rest of Renaissance Europe. Flemish masters such as **Jan van Eyck** brought their talent to and left their influence in Portugal, and Portuguese artists polished their skills over in Antwerp. King Manuel's favorite, **Jorge Afonso,** the most famous High Renaissance artist, whipped up typically ordered, realistic portrayals of human anatomy. Afonso's best work hangs at the Convento de Cristo in Tomar and the Convento da Madre de Deus in Lisboa. In the late 15th century, **Nuno Gonçalves** revived a primitivist school that went against the humanist grain of the Renaissance.

The Baroque era spawned intricate woodwork. Many a tree died for **Joachim Machado's** elaborately carved creches in the early 1700s. On canvas, the portrait flourished. The very busy nineteenth-century artist **Domingos António de Sequeira** painted historical, religious, and allegorical subjects too; his technique would later inspire French Impressionists. Porto's **António Soares dos Reis** brought Romantic sensibility to sculpture in the 1800s.

Cubism, Expressionism, and Futurism trickled into Portugal despite vicious censorship by Salazar's henchmen. In recent years, **Maria Helena Vieira da Silva** has won international recognition for her abstract paintings; **Carlos Botelho** is well-known for his street scenes of Lisboa.

ARCHITECTURE

Few Moorish structures survived the Christian Reconquista, but Moorish elements survive in the tilework, church ceilings, and castle windows of later periods. Colorful **azulejos** grace many walls, ceilings, and thresholds. Carved in fabulous relief by the pre-Reconquista Moors, these ornate tiles later took on flat, glazed Italian and Northern European design.

Portugal's "national style," the **Manueline,** celebrates the exploration and imperial expansion that took place under King Manuel the Fortunate. This hybrid style frappes an Islamic and Gothic heritage with the influences of Italy, Flanders, and the Spanish Plateresque—and a sprinkle of marine motifs (anchors, knotted ropes, seaweed). The amalgamation found its most elaborate expression in the church and tower at **Belém,** built to honor Vasco da Gama. Close seconds are the **Mosteiro dos Jerónimos** in Lisboa and the **Abadia de Santa Maria de Vitória** in Batalha. Groups of architects collaborated to design these, among them **Diego Boytac, João de Castilho,** and the brothers **Diego** and **Francisco Arruda.**

Today Portuguese architect **Alvaro Siza** blends diverse Portuguese traditions, relying heavily on Modernism's functionality. His adorned houses line the streets of Porto and the Malagueira District in Evora.

LITERATURE

Poetry holds a proud place in Portugal's literary tradition. Bards and balladeers entertained royalty with troubadour art for centuries and it was the poet-king **Dinis I** who made Portuguese the region's official language in the 12th century. Portuguese poetry bloomed with the Age of Discovery, most notably in the verse letters of **Francisco de Sá de Miranda** (1481-1558) and the musical lyrics of **Antonio Ferreira** (1528-1569). **Luís de Camões** celebrated the Indian voyages of Vasco da Gama in the greatest epic poem of Portuguese literature, *Os Lusíadas* (The Lusiads, 1572).

Prose historians used great flourish and varying degrees of accuracy to chronicle the exploits of the Portuguese discoverers. An explorer himself, **João de Barros** detailed his wild adventures in *Asia.* **Gil Vicente,** the country's first known playwright, wrote light if idealized dramas about peasants, the pastoral life, and nature. The witty realism of Vicente's *Barcas* trilogy (1617-1619) influenced his contemporaries Shakespeare and Cervantes, and his works in Castilian earned him a distinguished place in the Spanish literary pantheon.

Spanish hegemony, intermittent warfare, and imperial decline conspired to make the literature of the 17th and 18th centuries somewhat less triumphant in tone. But **Almeida Garrett,** the dandy leader of the Romantic school, breathed life into patriotic literature with his accounts of Portuguese heroism. A lyric poet, dramatist, politician, revolutionary, frequent exile, and legendary lover, Garrett is credited with reviving drama in Portugal; his most famous play is *Frei Luís de Sousa* (Brother Luís de Sousa, 1843).

Political thinkers dominated the rise of the literary **Generation of 1870.** The Generation's most prominent novelist, **José Maria Eça de Queiroz,** inaugurated Portuguese social realism in works such as *O Primo Basilio* (Cousin Basilio, 1878) and *A Cidade e as Serras* (The City and the Mountains, 1901).

Portuguese modernism has not forsaken the tradition of lyric poetry. **Fernando Pessoa** wrote in English as well as Portuguese and developed four distinct styles under four different pseudonyms: Pessoa, Alberto Caeiro, Ricardo Reis, and Alvaro de Campos. This multiple personality of the literary world introduced free verse to Portuguese poetry and lent a distinctly anti-bourgeois tone to the vanguard. **José Regio** waxed messianic in the collection *Poemas de Deus e do Diabo* (Poems of God and the Devil), in which poets are frequently compared to Jesus. Contemporary writers **Aquilino Ribeiro** and **Miguel Torga** have risen to international fame with their wonderfully satirical novels.

MUSIC

The best known expression of Portuguese music is **fado,** solo ballads accompanied by acoustic guitar. Symbolically named for fate, *fado* is identified with the Portuguese emotion *saudade* (yearning or longing), and is characterized by tragic, romantic lyrics and mournful melodies. (See Entertainment: Lisboa and Coimbra.)

Apart from its folk tradition, the music of Portugal never been famous internationally. Opera, under the sponsorship of the Jesuits, soon assumed its position as the most popular and sophisticated Portuguese musical form. **António José da Silva,** who eventually fell victim to the Inquisition in 1739, was one of the most celebrated operatic composers. Music for keyboard instruments flourished as well, thanks in large part to the influence of Italian composer **Domenico Scarlatti,** who was brought to Lisboa by King João V. Scarlatti's preeminent Portuguese contemporary, Coimbra's **Carlos Seixas,** thrilled 18th-century Lisboa with his talent and contributed to the development of the sonata form. Sousa Carvalho's student **Domingo Bontempo** introduced new symphonic innovation from abroad and helped establish the first Sociedade Filarmónica, modeled after the London Philharmonic, in Lisboa in 1822.

The French invasion and civil war in the 19th century meant bankruptcy for the Church and the court, the two main sources of patronage. Since then, musical activity has been limited to local and popular spheres. New composers such as **Luís de Freitas Branco,** leader of the Neoclassical movement, have helped revitalize the Portuguese music scene.

FINAL NOTE

Note: *Let's Go* provides a glossary in the back of the book for all terms used recurrently in the text.

Lisboa (Lisbon)

Although modern problems assail Lisboa—traffic, smog, and urban decay noticeable to most visitors—the city retains a certain imperial grandeur. Its appeal stems from a combination of relaxed urbanity and the care with which Lisboans have retained many of their traditions. The city constantly renovates its beautiful and historic monuments, and meticulously maintains the black and white mosaic sidewalks, pastel building facades, and cobbled medieval alleys (some barely an arm's length wide). Streetcars weave between buses, motorcycles, cars, and pedestrians down broad avenues and narrow lanes.

While legend claims that Odysseus founded the city, historians and archeologists assert that the Phoenicians were the first to stick their flag in Lisboa's soil, sometime in the 12th century BC. Successively conquered by Greeks, Carthaginians, Romans, and Arabs, Lisboa later flourished as a trade center during 300 years of Moorish rule. By 1255, however, Dom Afonso III had completed the Moorish expulsion in the Algarve and made Lisboa the capital of the Kingdom of Portugal.

The city's golden age began toward the end of the 15th century, when Portuguese navigators pioneered explorations of Asia and the New World. Then, on November 1, 1755, a huge earthquake struck. Hundreds of citizens at Mass perished immediately as churches collapsed on their congregations. A tidal wave gulped the lower part of the city and drowned those who fled to the Tejo. Close to 50,000 ultimately died in the catastrophe, and Lisboa was reduced to a pile of smoldering rubble. Under the authoritarian leadership of the Prime Minister, the Marquês de Pombal, the city quickly recovered, and magnificent new squares, palaces, and churches were speedily rebuilt.

When Mozambique and Angola won their independence in 1974, hundreds of thousands of refugees converged upon the Portuguese capital. This immigration, combined with the openness resulting from the demise of the long-standing dictatorship in 1974, lends Lisboa a cosmopolitan air.

■■■ ORIENTATION

Getting around Lisboa's seven hills requires patience and stairmaster training. The **Baixa** (Lower Town) is Lisboa's downtown and the old business district. Its grid of small streets begins at the **Rossio** (the main square, comprised of the connecting **Praça Dom Pedro IV** and **Praça da Figueira)** and ends at **Praça do Comércio,** near the Rio Tejo (Tagus River). **Praça dos Restauradores,** a bustling square, is just north of the Rossio. Elegant Art Nouveau buildings color the newer business district, which centers on the broad avenues radiating from the northern **Praça Marquês de Pombal.** The old and new business districts are connected by **Avenida da Liberdade,** a tree-lined boulevard which begins its uphill climb at Pr. Restauradores.

Lisboa's upscale shopping district, the **Chiado,** lies to the west of the Baixa and is linked by the Ascensor de Santa Justa, an elegant, historic elevator. Rua do Carmo and Rua Garrett are the two most famous streets in this area.

West of Rua da Misericórdia is the **Bairro Alto** (Upper District), a populous, working-class area of narrow streets, tropical parks, and Baroque churches. To the east of the Baixa, the **Alfama,** Lisboa's famous medieval moorish quarter, stacks tiny whitewashed houses along a labyrinth of narrow alleys and stairways beneath the Castelo de São Jorge. **Belém** (Bethlehem), formerly an autonomous town (about 6km west of Praça do Comércio), is home to the Mosteiro dos Jerónimos, as well as several museums and palaces.

A detailed map is an absolute necessity in this town. The twisting streets change names about every three steps. The tourist office's map is fairly detailed, but the street-indexed **Falk city map** (sold in Estação Rossio and numerous magazine stands, 950$) is the best guide to Lisboa's geography. If you plan to stay for any length of time, consider investing in a *bilhete de assinatura turístico* (tourist pass), good for unlimited travel on CARRIS buses, trolleys, funiculars, and the subway (7 days 2030$, 4 days 1440$, 3 days 850$, 1 day 400$). Passes are sold in CARRIS booths (open 8am-8pm), located in most network train stations and the busier metro stations (e.g. Restauradores).

■■■ GETTING THERE

BY PLANE

All flights land at **Aeroporto de Lisboa** (tel. 80 20 60), on the northern outskirts of the city. Local buses #44 or 45 stop to the right and then upstairs as you exit the airport (20min. to downtown). The express bus (Aero-bus or line 91) is expensive at 400$ but faster; it stops directly in front of the exit. All 3 lines head for the Baixa. The final Aero-bus stop at Pr. Restauradores is directly in front of the tourist office. Taxis are cheaper for more than 2 people (about 800$ to the Baixa). Major airlines have offices at Pr. Marquês de Pombal and along Av. Liberdade.

TAP Air Portugal (airport tel. 848 91 81; information 848 91 82). To: Faro (24,000$); Funchal (31,200$); Porto (25,800$); London (43,200$); New York (93,500$); Madrid (32,400$); Barcelona (42,000$).
Iberia (tel. 358 20 16; reservations 847 50 34).

BY TRAIN

Train service in Lisboa is confusing because there are a bunch of stations. For info call (tel. 888 40 25).

Santa Apolónia (on banks of the Tejo near Alfama) for international, northern, and eastern lines.
Cais do Sodré for Estoril and Cascais (every 15min., 40min., 155$).
Barreiro for the Algarve and southern lines. To reach Barreiro, take a ferry across the Tejo (110$, free if coming into Lisboa from the south); ferries leave from Pr. Comércio every 5-10min.
Rossio (between Pr. Restauradores and Pr. Dom Pedro IV) to Sintra and on western lines. Schedules and assistance available. English spoken. (Open 8am-11pm.) To: Sintra (every 10min., 45min., 165$); Evora (4 per day, 3hr., 820$); Portalegre (4 per day, 4hr., 1200$); Porto (4 per day, 5hr., 1690$); Lagos (5 per day, 6½hr., 1540$); Faro (6 per day, 7hr., 1540$); Badajoz, Spain (4 per day, 5hr., 2850$); Paris (1 per day, 27hr., 21,135$).

BY BUS

Rodoviária, Av. Casal Ribeiro, 18 (tel. 54 58 63), is a private company. Metro: Picoas. From Pr. Marquês de Pombal, take Av. Fontes Pereira de Melo to Pr. Duque de Saldanha and bear right at a roundabout. A ½-hr. walk from Pr. Restauradores. To: Evora (7 per day, 2½hr., 1100$); Coimbra (8 per day, 3hr., 1200$); Portalegre (3 per day, 4hr., 1250$); Lagos (5 per day, 5hr., 1900$); Porto (5 per day, 5hr., 1600$); Faro (5 per day, 5½hr., 1800$); Braga (2 per day, 6hr., 1800$).
Caima, R. Bacalhoeiros, 16 (tel. 87 50 61), runs express buses to the Algarve and Porto (with movies). Fastest way to the Algarve from Lisboa. To: Porto (6 per day, 1700$); Lagos (6 per day, 2100$).

■■■ GETTING AROUND

City Buses: CARRIS (tel 36 32 02). 140$ within the city. From Estação Santa Apolónia, take #9, 39, or 46 to Pr. Restauradores and to Estação Rossio. From Estação Cais do Sodré, take #1, 44, or 45 to Pr. Restauradores, #28 to Estação

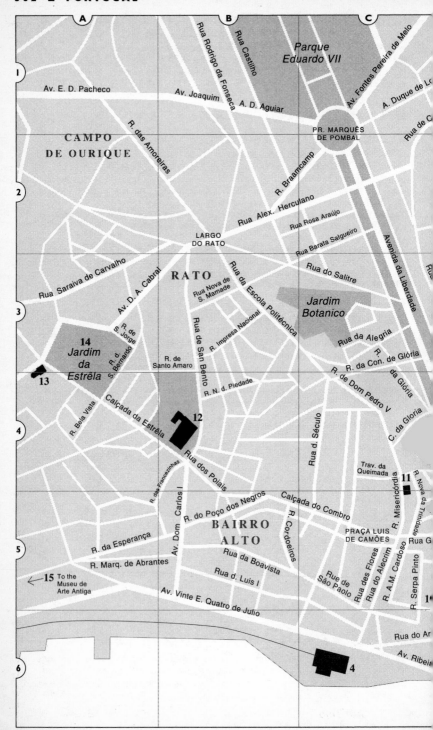

A
B
C

1

Rua Rodrigo da Fonseca

Rua Castilho

Av. Fontes Pereira de Melo

Parque Eduardo VII

A. Duque de Lo

Av. E. D. Pacheco

Av. Joaquim A. D. Aguiar

PR. MARQUÊS DE POMBAL

Rua de C

R. das Amoreiras

CAMPO DE OURIQUE

R. Braamcamp

2

Rua Alex. Herculano

Rua Rosa Araújo

Avenida da Liberdade

Rua Saraiva de Carvalho

LARGO DO RATO

Rua Barata Salgueiro

Rua do Salitre

Rua

Av. D. A. Cabral

RATO

Rua Nova de S. Mamede

Rua da Escola Politécnica

Jardim Botanico

3

R. de S.ª Jorge

R. Impresa Nacional

Rua da Alegria

R. da Con. de Glória

R. d. S. Bernardo

R. de Santo Amaro

Rua de San Bento

R. de Dom Pedro V

da Glória

14 *Jardim da Estrêla*

R.N. d. Piedade

C. da Gloria

13

R. Bela Vista

Calçada da Estrêla

12

Rua d. Século

4

Rua dos Poiais

Trav. da Queimada

R. Misericórdia

11

R. Nova da Trindade

R. das Francezinhas

R. do Poço dos Negros

Calçada do Combro

R. Dom Carlos I

BAIRRO ALTO

R. Cordoeiros

PRAÇA LUIS DE CAMÕES

Rua G

5

R. da Esperança

Rua da Boavista

Rue de São Paolo

Rua das Flores

Rua do Alecrim

R.A.M. Cardoso

R. Serpa Pinto

R. Marq. de Abrantes

Rua d. Luis I

15 To the Museu de Arte Antiga

Av. Vinte E. Quatro de Julio

Rua do Ar

6

Rua do Ar

Av. Ribei

4

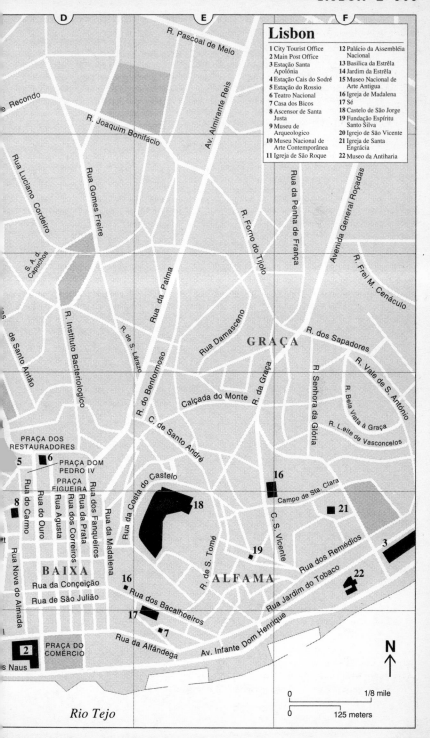

D **E** **F**

R. Pascoal de Melo

e Recondo

R. Joaquim Bonifácio

Av. Almirante Reis

Lisbon

1	City Tourist Office	**12**	Palácio da Assembléia Nacional
2	Main Post Office	**13**	Basilica da Estrêla
3	Estação Santa Apolónia	**14**	Jardim da Estrêla
4	Estação Cais do Sodré	**15**	Museo Nacional de Arte Antigua
5	Estação do Rossio	**16**	Igreja de Madalena
6	Teatro Nacional	**17**	Sé
7	Casa dos Bicos	**18**	Castelo de São Jorge
8	Ascensor de Santa Justa	**19**	Fundação Espíritu Santo Silva
9	Museu de Arqueologico	**20**	Igrejo de São Vicente
10	Museu Nacional de Arte Contemporânea	**21**	Igreja de Santa Engrácia
11	Igreja de São Roque	**22**	Museo da Antiharia

Rua Luciano Cordeiro

Rua Gomes Freire

Rua da Penha de França

Avenida General Roçadas

R. Frei M. Cenáculo

S. A. d. Capuchos

R. Instituto Bacteriologico

R. de S. Lázaro

Rua da Palma

R. Forno do Tijolo

Rua Damasceno

GRAÇA

R. dos Sapadores

R. Vale de S. António

de Santo Antão

R. do Bentormoso

Calçada do Monte

R. da Graça

R. Senhora da Glória

R. Bela Vista à Graça

R. Leite de Vasconcelos

C. de Santo André

PRAÇA DOS RESTAURADORES

5 ■ **6**

PRAÇA DOM PEDRO IV

PRAÇA FIGUEIRA

8 ■

Rua do Carmo

Rua do Ouro

Rua da Prata

Rua Augusta

Rua dos Correiros

Rua dos Fanqueiros

Rua da Madalena

Rua da Costa do Castelo

18

16 ■

Campo de Sta. Clara

21 ■

C. S. Vicente

3

R. de S. Tomé

19 ■

ALFAMA

Rua dos Remédios

22

Rua Nova do Almada

BAIXA

Rua da Conçeição

Rua de São Julião

16 ■

Rua dos Bacalhoeiros

17 ■

Rua Jardim do Tobaco

2

PRAÇA DO COMÉRCIO

7 ■

Rua da Alfândega

Av. Infante Dom Henrique

s Naus

N
↑

Rio Tejo

0 _____ 1/8 mile

0 _____ 125 meters

Santa Apolónia. From the airport, take #44, 45, 83, 90 or express bus (Aero-bus or line 91, 400$) to the town center.

Subway: 65$ at window, 60$ from vending machines. Book of 10 tickets 500$ at window, 475$ from machines. "M" marks Metro stop. The Metro follows Av. Liberdade, then branches into lines covering the modern business district. Pickpocket galore—watch out.

Trolleys (eléctricos): Everywhere. Offer beautiful views of the harbor and older neighborhoods. Many cars appear to be of pre-World War I vintage. Line #28 is good for sight-seeing (stops in Pr. Comércio, 140$).

Funiculars (elevadores): Link the lower city with the hilly residential area (50-150$).

Taxis: Rádio Táxis de Lisboa (tel. 815 50 61), **Autocoope** (tel. 793 27 56), and **Teletáxi** (tel. 815 20 16). 24-hr. service. Taxis swarm like pigeons along Av. Liberdade and throughout the Baixa, but are scarce elsewhere. Fare 600$ from Rossio to central bus station. Be careful—taxi drivers may attempt to overcharge.

Car Rental: AABA, R. Padre António Vieira, 44 (tel. 65 38 40). 2900$ per day, 29$ per km, 1300$ insurance per day, plus 17% tax. Must be 23 and have had license 1 yr. Hair-raising traffic in the city (it's dangerous enough just being a pedestrian).

■■■ PRACTICAL INFORMATION

TOURIST INFORMATION

Tourist Office: Palácio da Foz, Pr. Restauradores (tel. 346 33 14 or 342 52 31). Metro: Restauradores. English spoken. Bus schedules and *pensão* listings. Open Mon.-Fri. 9am-8pm, Sat.-Sun. 10am-7pm. Branch office at the airport (open 24hr.).

Budget Travel: Tagus (Youth Branch), Pr. Londres, 9B (tel. 848 53 63). Metro: Alameda. From metro, walk up Av. Guer. Junquiero. Books flights on TAP and British Airways. English spoken. **Tagus (Main Office),** R. Camilo Castelo Branco, 20 (tel. 352 55 09). Both offices open Mon.-Fri. 9am-1pm and 2:30-5:30pm.

EMBASSIES

See Portugal Essentials: Embassies and Consulates.

MONEY

Currency Exchange: Estação Santa Apolónia, on the platform. Enormous lines often form here and at the airport branch. Both open 24hr. The main post office, most banks, and travel agencies also change money (often for a 1000$ fee and 152$ tax). Banks open Mon.-Fri. 8:30-11:45am and 1-2:45pm.

American Express: Top Tours, Av. Duque de Loulé, 108 (tel. 315 58 85). Metro: Rotunda. Exit toward R. Rod. Sampa and walk up Av. da Liberdade toward the Marquês de Pombal Statue, then hang a right. This sole Top Tours office handles all AMEX services. Traveler's checks sold and cashed. Mail held. English spoken. Long line. Open Mon.-Fri. 9am-1pm and 2:30-6:30pm.

COMMUNICATIONS

Post Office: Correio, Pr. Comércio (tel. 346 32 31). Open for Posta Restante Mon.-Fri. 9am-7pm. Branch office at Pr. Restauradores open for **telegrams,** international express service, stamps, and telephones 8am-10pm. **Postal Code:** 1100 for central Lisboa.

EMERGENCIES, HEALTH, AND HELP

Police: R. Capelo, 3 (tel. 346 61 41). English spoken.

Late-Night Pharmacy: Throughout the city. Emergency service only. Police will direct you to the nearest one.

Medical Services: British Hospital, R. Saraiva de Carvalho, 49 (tel. 60 20 20; at night 60 37 85).

Crisis Lines: Poison (tel. 795 01 43). **Drug Abuse** (tel. 726 77 66).

Emergency: call 115 from anywhere in Portugal.

OTHER

Telephones: Central exchange at Pr. Dom Pedro IV, 68. Metro: Rossio. On the corner to the right of the National Theater as you face away from the theater. Staff explains the arcane telephone system in Portuguese only. **Credifone cards** come in 50 units (750$) or 120 units (1725$) and can be purchased here and at neighborhood book stores and stationers. Local calls consume at least 1 unit. Do not confuse this card with the TLP card, which is valid in Lisboa and Porto only. Note that the central exchange is mainly a TLP office. Make sure to request a credifone or they will automatically issue a more limited TLP card. One phone (marked with stickers) also accepts MC, Visa, and Eurocard. Open 8am-11pm. For **telegrams,** dial 183. **Telephone Code:** 01.

Luggage Storage: At **Estação Rossio** and **Estação Santa Apolónia.** Lockers 350$, 450$, and 750$ for up to 48hr. At the **bus station,** 130$ per bag per day.

Shopping Center: Amoreiras Shopping Center de Lisboa, Av. Duarte Pacheco. 330 shops including a humongous Pão de Açucar supermarket, a couple of English bookstores, and a 10-screen cinema.

English Bookstore: Livraria Clássica Editora, Pr. Restauradores, 17. Metro: Restauradores. Wide selection of paperback classics, best-sellers, and travel books. Mostly Portuguese with some French and English titles. **Livraria Británica,** R. São Marçal, 83 (tel. 32 84 72), across from the British Institute in the Bairro Alto. A good collection of classics and popular novels. Open June-Aug. Mon.-Fri. 9:30am-7pm. **Livraria Bertrand,** R. Garrett, 75 (tel. 346 86 46). Good collection of best-sellers and (mostly fashion) magazines. International maps and travel guides (including *Let's Go*). Open Mon.-Fri. 9am-7pm, Sat. 9am-1pm.

Library: Av. Duque Loulé, 22-B (tel. 57 01 02). English-language books. Open Aug.-June Mon. 2-8pm, Tues.-Fri. 12:30-6pm.

Laundromat: R. Augusto Rosa, 11. Wash 550$ per 5kg load. Large dryers 350$ per load. **Lavatax,** R. Francisco Sanches, 65A (tel. 82 33 92). Metro: Arroios. Wash, dry, and fold 800$ per 5kg load. Open 9am-1pm and 3-7pm, Sat. 9am-noon.

Public Toilets: In the Rossio and other major squares. Some subway stations.

Weather and Sea Conditions: tel. 150.

■■■ ACCOMMODATIONS AND CAMPING

A price ceiling supposedly restricts how much hotel owners can charge for particular types of rooms, so if you think you're being overcharged, ask to see the printed price list. During low- or mid-season, you might be charged quite a bit less than the official minimum depending on room availability and the whim of the *pensão* owner—try coughing up a little Portuguese. Establishments are also required to post their rating according to a four-star system. Most places have rooms only with double beds and charge per person for the same room. Expect to pay about 2500$ for a single and 4000$ for a double depending on features and the area.

The vast majority of hotels are in the center of town on **Avenida Liberdade** and adjacent side streets. Lodgings near the Castelo de São Jorge or in the Bairro Alto are quieter and nearer to the sights, hence more expensive. Be especially cautious in the Bairro Alto, the Alfama, and the Baixa after dark. Many streets are isolated and most are poorly lit. If the central accommodations are full, head east to the *pensões* along **Avenida Almirante Reis.**

Beach aficionados with lots of cash may want to use **Estoril** or **Cascais** as a base. These affluent suburbs are about 20km away from Lisboa and mercifully free of the capital's noise and smog. Food and lodging prices are up to 50% higher than those in the city.

Pousada da Juventude de Lisboa (HI), R. Andrade Corvo, 46 (tel. 353 26 96; fax 352 86 21). Metro: Picoas. Take a left out of the station and then make 2 successive right turns. Newly renovated and reopened in 1993, this ultra-hip and ultra-clean youth haven has abandoned some of the typical HI restrictions (there is no curfew or lockout) so you can revel at all hours with impunity. Six floors accessible by elevator. Meeting room, TV room, and dining room. Handicapped access. Noticeable noise from the busy street. English spoken. Check out by noon. Lockers 350$. Multiples 2000$ per person. Doubles with bath 5000$. Winter: 1750$; 4500$. Breakfast included. Lunch and dinner each 800$. Reservations (by letter or fax only) highly recommended. IYHF card required.

Pousada da Juventude de Catalazete (HI), Estrada Marginal (tel. 443 06 38), in the coastal town of **Oeiras**. Take a train from Estação Cais do Sodré to Oeiras (20min., 95$). Exit through the train station underpass from the side of the train coming *from* Lisboa. Cross the street and follow signs to Lisboa and Cascais. The street curves through a residential district. At the intersection across from a bus stop (no street signs), make a left and go downhill. At the underpass, go straight and follow HI signs to the INATEL complex. Enter the complex and walk to the end of the path; the hostel is to the left beyond the fence. Beautiful ocean views from the patio and more quiet than the city. Guard all belongings. Reception open 9:30-10:30am and 6-11pm. Curfew midnight. June-Sept. multiples 1600$. Doubles 3600$, with bath 4000$. Low-season: 1300$; 3000$; 3500$. Breakfast included. Lunch and dinner each 750$. Reservations recommended and can be made through Lisboa's HI office, R. Andrade Corvo, 46 (tel. 353 26 96).

BAIXA

Dozens of *pensões* surround the three connected *praças*—**Praça Restauradores, Praça Dom Pedro IV,** and **Praça Figueira**—that form the nexus of Lisboa's downtown. Many pre-war buildings with decrepit exteriors have been renovated within. Most have fewer than 20 rooms. For a good night's sleep, bring soundproofing.

Pensão Prata, R. Prata, 71, 3rd fl. (tel. 346 89 08), 2 bl. from Pr. Comércio. A yellow awning hides the sign. Eleven sun-kissed rooms in a peaceful apartment setting. Centrally located and clean. English spoken. All rooms with double bed 3800$, with shower 4300$, with bath 5000$.

Residencial Florescente, R. Portas de Santo Antão, 99 (tel. 342 66 09), 1 bl. from Pr. Restauradores. Across from a disco and next to an arcade. 120 rooms. Rooms with windows are cleaner and better furnished. Waterfall with fish pond in the lobby. Singles and doubles 5000$, with shower 6000$, with bath, TV, and phone 7500$. Large room with full bath and A/C 8500$.

Residencia do Sul, Pr. Dom Pedro IV, 59 (tel. 342 25 11). Through the shops, up two flights of stairs. Renovated inside. Clean, tasteful rooms overlooking the square. Singles 3500$. Doubles 4500$.

Pensão Arco Bandeira, R. Arco Bandeira, 226, 4th fl. (tel. 342 34 78), south of Pr. Dom Pedro IV, under the Arco Bandeira on the left, four flights up. Very quiet for the central location with views of the *praça*. Singles 3500$. Doubles 4500$.

Pensão Campos, R. Jardim do Regedor, 24, 3rd fl. (tel. 346 28 64), on busy pedestrian street between Pr. Restauradores and R. Portas de Santa Antão. Cozy rooms and clean baths. Singles 3000$. Doubles 3500$, with bath 4500$.

Pensão Iberica, Pr. Figueira, 11, 2nd fl. (tel 886 70 26 or 886 74 12), on the farthest side from the Rossio. Basic rooms with wood floors. Toiletries sold at the reception desk. Doubles 2800$, with window 3200$, with shower 5000$. Triples 3900$, with window 5100$, with shower 6000$. Prices variable. Breakfast included.

Pensão Beira Minho, Pr. Figueira, 6, 2nd fl. (tel. 346 90 29), beside the Rossio at the northern end of the *praça* through a flower shop. Decently renovated rooms with telephones. Singles well-lit to make up for being windowless. Singles 2500$, with bath 4000$. Doubles 4000$, with bath 5000$. Breakfast included.

IN AND AROUND THE BAIRRO ALTO

The Bairro Alto is quieter than the Baixa and has a sense of community which the town center lacks; but the uphill hike is inconvenient and daunting to luggage-holders. Don't wander off alone here at night—this area has a reputation for muggings.

Pensão Globo, R. Teixeira, 37 (tel. 346 22 79), on a small street parallel to R. S.P. Alcántara at the top of the funicular. From the entrance to the park, cross the street to Tr. da Cara and make a right onto R. Teixeira. Spacious, well-furnished, homey rooms 2500-4500$.

Pensão Estrela de Chiado, R. Garrett, 29, 4th fl. (tel. 342 61 10). The climb up the 95 stairs would tire even Sisyphus, but the rooms are clean, the water hot, and the singles large. Rooms with veranda have views of the castle. If possible, opt for rooms with bath; the common shower is not so appealing. Singles 2000$. Doubles 3500$, with bath 4000$.

Pensão Londres, R. Dom Pedro V, 53 (tel. 346 55 23; fax 346 56 82). Take the funicular by Palácio da Foz in Pr. Restauradores. Facing away from the funicular, walk across to R. Dom Pedro V. Travel lightly or drive. Near parks and good inexpensive restaurants. Rooms of varying sizes. Colorful tile bathrooms. Singles 3000$, with bath 4000$. Doubles 5000$, with bath 7000$. Breakfast included.

NEAR THE CASTELO (MOURARIA)

Narrow thoroughfares, flowered balconies, and amazing views abound in this neighborhood. Steep streets torture those who don't travel lightly. Grimy facades misrepresent *pensões* with pleasant interiors. Tourists traveling to and from the *castelo* keep the area relatively crowded and safe in the daytime, but beware here at night.

Pensão Beira-Mar, Largo Terreiro do Trigo, 16 (tel. 87 15 28). One of the best values in Lisboa. Clean spacious rooms, some with ocean view. Friendly owner speaks English and picks guests up from the train station. Laundry facilities available. Singles 1500$. Doubles 3000$.

Pensão Ninho das Aguias, R. Costa do Castelo, 74 (tel. 886 70 00), near Escada do Marquês da Ponte de Lima. This *pensão's* spectacular views of Lisboa are worth the long hike and additional staircase. Splendid outdoor terrace with small garden and bird cages. Cheerful rooms are in high demand—make reservations weeks in advance. Phones in rooms. Singles 4500$, with shower 5000$. Doubles 5500$, with shower 6500$. Triples 6500$, with shower 7000$.

Pensão Residencial Brasil Africano, Tr. Pedras Negras, 8, 2nd fl. (tel. 886 92 66), off R. Madalena. Close to the cathedral and the Baixa. Don't judge this *pensão* by its cover; it's been renovated. Spacious, comfy rooms with balconies. Singles 2000$. Doubles 3000$, with shower 4500$. Discounts for multiple-night stays.

CAMPING

Although camping is a "social activity" in Portugal, campers are considered prime targets for thieves. Guard all valuables carefully.

Parque da Câmara Municipal de Lisboa-Monsanto (tel. 70 20 61; fax 70 74 74), on the road to Benfica. Take bus #43 from the Rossio to the Parque Florestal Monsanto. Lisboa's municipal campground has a swimming pool and a reasonably priced supermarket. 350$ per person, 300$ or more per tent (depending on size), 230$ per car.

Clube de Campismo de Lisboa Costa da Caparica (tel. 290 01 00), 5km out of Lisboa (take the bus from Pr. Espanha; Metro: Palhavã). Beaches. Shade. Pool. Fun. 700$ per person, per tent, and per car.

■■■ FOOD

Lisboa has some of the least expensive restaurants and best wine of any European capital. A full dinner costs about 1500$ per person. The *prato do dia* (special of the day) is often reasonably priced. Finish off your meal with a tempting Portuguese pastry—they're sinfully cheap.

Restaurants in the **Baixa,** catering largely to tourists, are more elegant and more expensive than those in other districts. The **Bairro Alto** feeds many locals. Restaurants there, as in the **Alfama,** are correspondingly small, dark, and (relatively) cheap. Dine on seafood specialties such as *bacalhau cozido com grão* (cod with chick-peas and boiled potatoes), a local classic. Other culinary delights include *amêijoas à bulhão pato* (a steamed clam dish), and *creme de mariscos* (seafood chowder with tomatoes).

Mercado Ribeira, a market complex on Av. 24 de Julho outside the Cais do Sodré (bus #40), is open Mon.-Sat. until 2pm. There's a larger market in Cascais on Wednesday morning (5min. from the train station, follow the signs for "mercado"). Go early for the freshest selection. For groceries, try the jumbo **Supermarket Pão de Açucar,** in Amoreiras Shopping Center de Lisboa, Av. Duarte Pacheco.

BAIXA

The nearer the water, the cheaper the restaurants. The southern end of town near the port and the area bordering the Alfama is particularly inexpensive. Some bargain eateries line **Rua dos Correiros,** parallel to R. Prata, and neighboring streets. One block from Pr. Restauradores, on **Rua das Portas de Santo Antão,** several superb seafood restaurants stack the day's catch in their windows. Many of the Baixa's restaurants are not open on Sunday and close around 9 or 10pm on weekdays.

Groceries: Supermercado Expresso, R. Jardim do Regidor, 34-36 (tel. 346 73 70), a bl. around the corner from R. das Portas de Santo Antão. Conveniently located, medium-sized market. Stocks some imported foods (perfect for the homesick). Open Mon.-Fri. 9am-10pm, Sat. 9am-9pm, Sun. 10am-9pm. **Self-Service Market,** Pr. Dezembro, 65 (tel. 342 24 63), off C. do Carmo. Upstairs from the health food restaurant Celeiro. Market stocks "macrobiotic foods," granola, and other healthy staples. Also organic toiletries. Open Mon.-Fri. 8:30am-8pm, Sat. 8:30am-7pm.

Restaurante Bonjardim, Trav. de Santo Antão, 12 (tel. 342 74 24), on a side street off Pr. Restauradores. Outrageously delicious roast chickens (995$) and *chouriço asado na brasa* (roast sausage, 290$). Entrees 800-1600$. Open noon-3pm and 6:30-10:30pm.

Porto de Abrigo, R. Remolares, 16-18 (tel. 346 08 73), near Estação Cais do Sodré. One of the most popular riverside eateries. *Pato com arroz* (duck with rice and olives, 1190$). Entrees 950-1480$. Open Mon.-Sat. noon-3pm and 7-10pm.

Lua de Mel, R. Prata, 242-248 (tel. 87 91 51), corner with R. Santa Justa. Perhaps the most delicious pastries in Lisboa. Ogle the beautiful cakes in the window, and make a bee-line for the fresh, honey-laden pastries (85$). Sandwiches 200-400$. Fruit salads and ice cream sundaes 450$. A/C. Open Tues.-Sat. 7am-midnight.

Celeiro, Rua 1 de Dezembro, 65, right off the Rossio. This "macrobiotic" restaurant located beneath a health food supermarket will satisfy the strictest herbivore. Cafeteria-style. Salads, soufflés, and sandwiches all self-serve. Entrees 100-570$. Open Mon.-Fri. 9am-7pm.

Adega Popular 33, R. Conceiçao, 33 (tel. 84 94 72), 2 bl. from Pr. Comércio. Popular because it's a bargain. Simple interior, simply great food. *Lulas grelhadas* (grilled squid, 720$). Entrees 500-850$. ½-portions available. Open Mon.-Fri. 8am-9:30pm.

Adega do Atum, R. Bacalhoeiros, 8D (tel. 87 03 19), off R. Madalena, 1 bl. north and parallel with R. Alfandega. A local hangout in a sun-splashed square not far from the port. Very, very fresh fish. Try their *chocos assados com tinta* (roast squid in their own ink, 650$). Entrees 500-850$. Open Mon.-Sat. 7am-midnight.

Cervejaria Baleal, R. Madalena, 277 (tel. 87 21 87), 1 bl. toward the Mouraria from Pr. Figueira. Enter through a passage flanked with tanks of lobsters. Exceptionally clean, bright, and cheery. Fresh fish entrees 800-1800$. Open Mon.-Sat. 8am-midnight.

BAIRRO ALTO

Although the Bairro has its share of glamourous restaurants, it also has far more small and medium-sized eateries than the Baixa. The district's hilly, narrow streets are quieter and less congested. Many inexpensive local haunts line **Calçada do Combro,** the neighborhood's main westward artery. Climb **Rua Misericórdia** to the adjacent side streets for mustier, cheaper restaurants and quieter, dimmer dinners.

Cervejaria da Trindade, R. Nova Trindade, 20c-d (tel. 32 35 06), make a left coming off R. Misericórdia. Regal imagery on shiny *azulejos* in an elegant but noisy atmosphere. The *espetada de tambroil con gambas* (fish and prawn kebab, 1300$) is particularly yummy. Grilled specialties and fish entrees 950-1600$. Open Mon.-Sat. 9am-11:30pm.

Bota Alta, Trav. Queimada, 37 (tel. 342 79 59), on the far side of R. Misericórdia. Suck it up as you walk by the wafting aromas of rivals. Worthwhile if expensive. *Sopa Alentejana* (garlic soup, 300$). Wide range of fish dishes. Entrees 1000-2200$. Open Mon.-Fri. noon-2:30pm and 7pm-midnight. Reservations accepted.

A Pérola do Bonjardim, R. Cruz dos Poiais, 95A (tel. 60 84 80), off R. Poiais, a continuation of Calçada do Combro. Stucco-and-tile family restaurant in a neighborhood of pastel colored high-rises. *Pratos do dia* (700-1200$) and delectable entrees (500-1500$). Open Mon.-Sat. 7am-midnight.

Lua Nova, Trav. Queimada, 4 (tel. 346 57 92), off R. Misericórdia, a couple bl. down from Calçada da Gloria. Bring a flashlight so you can read the menu. Great for a cheap dinner before hitting the nearby *fado* houses (see Entertainment). Entrees 800-1000$. Open July 16-June 30 Mon.-Sat. 10am-10pm.

Xêlê Bananas, Pr. Flores, 29. Walk down R. S. Marçal from R. Escola Politécnica. Right on Pr. Flores, facing a small park. Flowered terraces look out onto the picturesque square. Pricey entrees 1600-3100$. Open Mon.-Fri. 12:30-3:30pm and 7:30-11:30pm, Sat. 7:30-11pm.

Casa de Pasto de Francisco Cardoso, R. Século, 244 (tel. 342 75 78), off R. Dom Pedro V. Small restaurant with hearty food. Genuine neighborhood hangout. Walls inscribed with food-for-thought proverbs such as "He who talks much says little." Omelettes 700$. Mouth-watering pastries 150-300$. Entrees mostly 700-950$. Sangria 600$. Open 8am-midnight.

ALFAMA

The winding streets of the Alfama conceal a number of extremely small, unpretentious restaurants. Lively discussions and chatter echo through the damp, narrow alleys. Theft plagues the Alfama, so come here by day and without handbags, cameras, or snatchable diamond earrings.

Malmequer Bemmequer, R. de São Miguel, 23-25 (tel. 87 65 35). The name means "He loves me, loves me not." Friendly owner trained on cruise ships serves delicious, reasonably priced seafood dishes. Entrees 800-1300$. Open noon-3:30pm and 7-11pm.

Dragão da Alfama, R. Guilherme Braga, 8 (tel. 86 77 37), near Igreja São Estevão. Around 10pm a woman with a woolly-mammoth voice belts out tear-welling *fado. Peixe espada grelhada* (grilled swordfish, 950$). Huge fish entrees (700-1400$). Open Mon.-Fri. noon-4pm and 7pm-midnight, Sat. noon-4pm.

Mestre André, Calçadinha de Sto. Estevão, 6 (tel. 87 14 87), off R. Remédios. Eclectic adornment of old movie posters and stills. Brazilian background music. Outdoor seating. Their *murcela frita,* an ugly, but savory little blood sausage (400$), and *truta grelhada* (grilled trout, 800$) are favorites among regulars. Entrees 700-1200$. Open Mon.-Sat. noon-3pm and 7-10:30pm.

Os Minhotos, R. Remédios, 31 (tel. 87 55 80), next to Mestre André. Less chi-chi than its neighbor, with food cooked on an outdoor grill. Fresh *lulas* (squid) or *bacalhau cozido* (boiled cod, 700$). Entrees (600-900$) are a steal. Open Mon.-Sat. 11am-4pm and 7pm-midnight.

■■■ SIGHTS

OLD CENTER

Today Lisboa's modern and sophisticated side is evident in the 18th-century heart of the city. The center of bustle is the **Rossio,** or **Praça Dom Pedro IV,** the city's main square. Once a cattle market with a public execution stage, bullfight arena, and carnival ground, the *praça* is now the domain of drink-sipping tourists. Limestone and tile buildings, built under the Marquês de Pombal's edict after the 1755 earthquake, line three sides. On the fourth, the **Teatro Nacional** marks the former site of the Palace of the Inquisition. A statue of Gil Vicente, Portugal's first dramatist, straddles the building. Dom Pedro IV's statue maintains a remarkably stoic countenance, considering his position perched atop a tall Corinthian column in the square's center.

After the earthquake, Marquês do Pombal created the **Baixa,** the grid of streets south of the Rossio, to facilitate communication between the town center and the river. At the very height of Enlightenment urban design, each street was designated for a specific trade. Two centuries later, the Baixa is one of the most crowded, touristy areas of town. Pedestrians toss litter on the wide mosaic sidewalks, cars drag race down the Marquês' stately avenues, and visitors swarm upscale shops along pedestrian sidestreets. A bustling center of activity, the neighborhood caters to ice cream eaters (countless vendors line the streets in the summer) and window shoppers. **Rua Augusta,** now restricted to pedestrians, is lined with shops selling furs, shoes, and perfume, and leads past a triumphal arch to **Praça do Comércio.** According to a Lisboa saying, "God gave the Portuguese the Tagus, and in gratitude they made the Terreiro do Paço." Known by its popular name, Pr. Comércio lies before the towering statue of Dom José I, cast from 9400 pounds of bronze in 1755. The *praça's* center has since been converted to a sports pavilion.

From the northwest corner of Pr. Comércio, R. Alfândega leads to the late Gothic **Igreja da Conceição Velha.** Its effusively Manueline portal represents Mary protecting miscellaneous clerics and royals with her mantle. The church's interior has a handsome vaulted chancel and a statue (in the second chapel on the right) of Nossa Senhora de Rastelo. The figure came from a small church in Belém, where the great Portuguese navigators spent their last terrified night in prayer before embarking.

North of the Rossio, **Praça dos Restauradores** commemorates the 1640 "restoration" of Portugal's independence from Spain with an obelisk and a bronze sculpture of the Spirit of Independence. Here begins **Avenida da Liberdade,** Lisboa's most imposing boulevard. Its malls of flowering shrubs, palm trees, swan ponds, and fountains were at one time the city's favorite promenade. Although this mile-long avenue has seen better days, it's still shady and peaceful. The avenue ends at **Praça do Marquês do Pombal** in the center of a bustling commercial district.

CHIADO AND BAIRRO ALTO

Boxed in a fanciful Gothic tower, the beloved **Ascensor de Santa Justa** connects the Baixa to the Chiado. The elevator ride costs 140$ each way: tourists ride only to admire the view from the upper levels, while for many locals the elevator is a means of transportation into the hilly Bairro Alto. From the upper terrace, a narrow walkway leads under a huge flying buttress to the 14th-century **Igreja do Carmo.** Although the 1755 earthquake left the church roofless, it retains its dramatic Gothic arches. The ramshackle **Museu Arqueológico** here includes Dom Fernando I's tomb, black from a treatment inflicted for photographic purposes. (Open Mon.-Sun. 10am-6pm. Admission 300$.)

One block south, posh **Rua Garrett** abounds with nouveau coffee houses and bakeries. Portuguese writer Eça de Queiroz used to caffeinate at **A Brasileira** at #120-122, perhaps the most famous of the city's 19th-century coffee houses. Two blocks south (left) on R. Serpa Pinto, the **Museu Nacional de Arte Contemporânea** (under renovation) displays Portuguese paintings and sculpture from 1850-1950, as well as temporary exhibits of photography and drawings. (Open Tues.-Fri. 10am-12:30pm and 2-5pm. Admission 300$, students free.)

Back to R. Garrett, past a square (Pr. Camões) guarded by two churches, and right on R. da Misericórdia is **Igreja de São Roque,** dedicated to the saint who is believed to have saved the Bairro Alto from the devastation of the great quake. The notorious **Capela de São João Baptista** (fourth from the left), ablaze with precious gems and metals, caused a stir upon its installation in 1747. It took three different ships to deliver the chapel to Lisboa after it was built in Rome from agate, lapis lazuli, alabaster, verde antica, and mosaics. Adjoining the church, the small **Museu de São**

Roque, with its own share of gold and silver, features European religious art from the 16th to 18th centuries. (Open Tues.-Sun. 10am-5pm. Admission 150$, students and seniors free, Sun. free.)

At the end of the Travessa do Convento de Jesus (off Calçada do Combro), flowered balconies and hanging laundry frame **Igreja das Mercês,** a handsome 18th-century travertine building. Its small *praça* overlooks the neoclassical **Palácio da Assembléia Nacional** (House of Parliament).

Past the Parliament on Calçada da Estrela, the ornate **Basilica da Estrela** (1796) steals the sky with an exquisitely shaped dome poised behind a pair of tall belfries. Half-mad Maria I, desiring a male heir, made fervent religious vows promising God anything and everything if she were granted a son. When a baby boy was finally born, she built this church. Ask the sacristan to show you the gigantic 10th-century *presépio* (manger scene). (Open 8am-1pm and 3-8pm. Free.)

Across from the church, **Jardim da Estrêla's** wide asphalt paths wind through lush flora and flocks of pigeons. Park walkways are popular for Sunday strolls, and the benches for lascivious smooching. Behind the park, tropical plants, cypress trees, and odd gravestones mark the **Cemitério dos Ingleses** (English Cemetery; ring bell for entry). Its musty Victorian chapel dates from 1885. The cemetery's most famous grave belongs to novelist Henry Fielding (of *Tom Jones* fame), who came to Lisboa in 1714 on a rather unsuccessful convalescence trip.

It's a half-hour walk down Av. Infante Santo and a 10-minute jaunt to the left of Calçada da Pampulha to find Portugal's national museum, the **Museu Nacional de Arte Antiga,** on R. Janelas Verdes. A representative collection of European paintings ranges from Gothic primitives to 18th-century French masterpieces. The most prized possession is the six-panel *Adoration of St. Vincent* by Nuno Gonçalves, one of Portugal's greatest painters. Other notable works are ghoulish 16th-century *O Inferno* and a few choice Breughels. (Open Tues.-Sat. 10am-1pm and 2-5pm. Admission 250$, students free.) Buses #40 and 60 stop to the right of the museum exit and head back to the Baixa.

ALFAMA AND MOURARIA

The **Alfama,** Lisboa's medieval quarter, covers the hill in tiers beneath Castelo de São Jorge on the southern slope facing the Rio Tejo. Between the Alfama and the Baixa is the quarter known as the **Mouraria** (Moorish quarter), established after Dom Afonso Henriques and the Crusaders expelled the Moors in 1147. A few words of advice: don't even think about walking through the Alfama without getting lost; wandering aimlessly among the winding medieval streets is a delightful way to spend the rest of your life (though at night watch out for muggers).

The best way to enter this part of the city is from R. da Madalena alongside the 16th-century **Igreja de Madalena** at the eastern end of the Baixa's R. Conceição. Uphill from the Madalena rises the delicately proportioned **Igreja de Santo António da Sé** (1812), built over the saint's alleged birthplace. The construction was funded with money collected by the city's children, who fashioned miniature altars bearing images of the saint to place on their doorsteps—a custom still re-enacted annually on festive June 13, the saint's feast day. Near the entrance is a small **museum** featuring religious artwork devoted to the saint's life and miracles. (Tel. 86 04 47; open Tues.-Sun. 10am-1pm and 2-6pm. Free.) Beyond the church is the huge 12th-century **sé** (cathedral) with its beautiful garden.

From the church, follow the signs for a winding uphill walk to the restored **Castelo de São Jorge,** which offers spectacular views of Lisboa and the ocean. Built in the 5th century by the Visigoths and enlarged by the 9th-century Moors, this castle was the principal lap of luxury for the royal family from the 14th to the 16th centuries. The castle gardens, with an assortment of birds, a small swan pond, and enticing nooks in which to sit, relax, and enjoy the view, are a wonderful place to explore—and to exploit, as numerous vendors have discovered. (Open April-Sept. 9am-9pm; Oct.-March 9am-7pm. Free.)

From the castle, walk down the hill and turn left onto Largo de São Vicente to reach the **Fundação Espírito Santo Silva (Museo de Artes Decorativas Portuguesas),** a decorative arts museum which seeks to recreate its former days as a palace. Rooms filled with impressive furnishings and decorations represent 18th-century palatial luxury. Museum also features a tea room and bookstore with Portuguese art books in English. (Tel. 886 21 83; open Wed., Fri.-Sun. 10am-5pm, Tues. and Thurs. 10am-8pm. Admission 500$, 50% discount for those under 12 or over 65.)

Exiting the museum, make a left onto Tr. de São Tomé and follow the trolley tracks (even as the street changes names and winds uphill and leftward) to the **Igreja de São Vicente de Fora** (1582-1627), dedicated to Lisboa's patron saint. Ask to see the deathly still *sacristia,* with fabulous 18th-century walls inlaid with Sintra marble—perhaps the only part of the complex worth the admission. (Open 9am-1pm and 3-7pm. Admission 200$.) **Igreja de Santa Engrácia** is further down toward the coast from São Vicente. Walk along the same street, and consistently stay on the right as the road branches. This church took so long to build (1682-1966) that it gave rise to the famous expression, "endless like the building of Santa Engrácia." Impressive Portuguese Baroque domes elegantly commemorate the country's heroes, including Henry the Navigator and Vasco da Gama. The church has been designated the Portuguese National Pantheon. (Open Tues.-Sun. 10am-5pm. Admission 150$.)

Take a #13 bus from Estação Santa Apolónia for the 10-minute ride to **Convento da Madre de Deus.** The 16th-century convent complex houses an excellent tile museum, the **Museu Nacional do Azulejo.** The Baroque interior of the church, reached through a fine Manueline doorway, is a riot of oil paintings, *azulejos,* and gilded wood. The rapturous excess continues in the *coro alto* (chapter house) and the **Capela de Santo António,** where bright *azulejos* and paintings make the place eye-buggingly busy. (Complex open 10am-5pm, Sun. 10am-2pm. Admission 200$, students 80$.)

From the Castelo de São Jorge, a walking tour without monuments and museums leads through the neighborhood of the **Alfama,** former home to the Moorish aristocracy. The outline of the pre-urban planning tangle is visible in the labyrinth of balconies, archways, terraces, and courtyards. The neighborhood became the noisy residence of fishers and sailors after the *Reconquista,* yet the fervent voice of the *fado* recalls this district's past.

To walk through the Alfama, make a left from the *castelo,* leading to Largo das Portas do Sol (beyond the museum). Take a ramp or stairway down to Beco de Santa Helena and turn left on R. Castelo Picão to reach Largo do Salvador. From here, R. Regueira descends to a small *praça.* The square adjoins the narrow **Beco do Carneiro** and **Beco do Mexias,** where a doorway leads to a fountain in which the local women do their washing. R. Regueira ends at R. Remédios. Turn right past an open square to **Rua de São Pedro,** the Alfama's main fish market street. A small opening (to the right, midway down the street) leads to **Igreja de São Miguel,** with a Rococo gilt altar screen and a ceiling crafted of Brazilian jacaranda wood. (Ask the sacristan to turn on the lights.) R. de São Pedro ends at Largo de São Rafael, enclosed on one side by the remains of an old Moorish tower. To return to Largo das Portas do Sol, climb R. da Adiça.

BELÉM

Belém (Bethlehem) is about 6km west of Praça do Comércio. Take tram #15 or 17 from Praça do Comércio (20min., 140$) or the train from Estação Cais do Sodré (every 15min., 10min., 100$). From the train station, cross the street to go into town and make a left. The **Mosteiro dos Jerónimos** (5-min. walk) rises from the banks of the Tejo behind a sculpted garden worthy of a king. Initially cultivated by Manuel I in 1502 to give thanks for the success of Vasco da Gama's voyage to India, the monastery stands as Portugal's most refined celebration of the Age of Discovery—a monument to the exuberant age when Portuguese navigators mapped the world. The monastery showcases Portugal's own Manueline style, combining Gothic forms with early Renaissance details. Sailor symbolism—including ropes, anchors, coral, and algae—is everywhere.

The south door of the church is a sculptured anachronism—Henry the Navigator mingles with the Twelve Apostles under carved canopies on both sides of the central column. In the vast interior, six octagonal columns spring open like palm trees to support an elaborately creased roof 25m above. The pagoda-style tombs in the chancel and transepts, as well as the various fruit and vegetable encrustations throughout the church, typify Manueline exoticism.

The symbolic tombs of Luís de Camões and navigator Vasco da Gama lie in two opposing transepts. Camões, who chronicled his nation's discoveries in lyric verse, is considered the Portuguese Shakespeare. The studly poet had so many affairs with ladies of the court that he was forced to flee to North Africa to escape their vengeful husbands. He died a pauper somewhere in Asia, and to Portugal's chagrin his body was never recovered.

Even flashier than the church's interior are the octagonal cloisters, some of the most overdone in Europe. Two stories are lavishly decorated with fantastic sculpture. (Open Tues.-Sun. 10am-5pm; Oct.-May 10am-1pm and 2:30-5pm. Admission 400$, Oct.-May 250$; students free.)

The monastery building also houses the **Museu Nacional de Arqueología,** which features a small, unremarkable collection of pottery, jewelry, and other archeological tidbits. (Open Tues.-Sun. 10am-5pm. Admission 500$, under age 25 250$.)

Next door to the monastery complex are the petite **Museu da Marinha** and the **Planetário C. Gulbenkian.** The museum exhibits a slightly unusual collection of nautical maps and replicas. (Open Tues.-Sun. 10am-6pm. Admission 250$, students 150$, seniors free.) The planetarium has show in English and French Sat. and Mon; Wed. at 11am, 3pm, and 4:15pm in Portuguese. (Admission 300$, age 10-18 200$, seniors free.)

Across the street from the museums on the coast stands the sword-shaped **Monumento dos Descobrimentos.** Built in 1960 to honor Prince Henry the Navigator, the monument features an elevator which transports visitors 70m up to a small terrace with views of Lisboa and the sea. Also temporary exhibits and films. (Tel. 301 62 28; open Tues.-Sun. 9:30am-6:45pm.)

The **Torre de Belém,** built to protect the seaward entrance of the Portuguese capital, rises from the Tejo's north bank. It's a 20-min. walk (heading away from Lisboa) along the railroad tracks from the monastery. The six-cornered turrets, copied from originals in India, and the Venetian balconies and windows typify the crafty eclecticism of Manueline architects. Climb the narrow, winding steps to the top of the tower, surrounded by the ocean on three sides, for a magnificent panoramic view. (Open Tues.-Sun. 10am-1pm and 2:30-5pm. Admission 400$, Oct.-May 250$; students and seniors free.)

Before leaving Belém, consider visiting the **Museu Nacional dos Coches,** across from the train station, 1 bl. into town. The museum is the retirement home of 54 carriages, ranging from the gilded Baroque coach that bore the Portuguese ambassador from Rome in 1716 to the simpler carriages of the late 18th century. (Open Tues.-Sun. 10am-6pm; Oct.-May Tues.-Sun. 10am-1pm and 2:30-5:30pm. Admission 400$, students 14-25, teachers, and seniors free.) The **Palácio Nacional da Ajuda,** a royal palace constructed in 1802, is a short bus ride away in the hills overlooking Belém. The 54 rooms make a rather telling display of decadence. (Open Tues., Thurs.-Sun. 10am-5pm. Admission 250$, Sun. morning free, students free.) Take bus #14 from in front of the Museu Nacional dos Coches. Alternatively, trolley #18 ("Ajuda") stops behind the palace and returns to town.

■■■ ENTERTAINMENT

The weekly paper **Sete,** available from kiosks in the Rossio (215$), publishes listings of concerts, movies, plays, exhibits, and bullfights. More comprehensive, though less hip, the **Cultura Agenda** is available free from kiosks in the Rossio and at the tourist office. It contains similar information, along with lists of museums, gardens, and libraries.

The **Teatro Nacional de Dona Maria II** (tel. 32 37 46) at Pr. Dom Pedro IV stages performances of classical Portuguese and foreign plays (tickets 700-2000$, 50% student discount). **Folk concerts** and **dance performances** move and shake the Palácio de Congressos de Estoril most nights in June and less frequently during the rest of the summer. The Fundação Gulbenkian also sponsors classical and jazz concerts year-round. Opera reigns at Lisboa's largest theater, the **Teatro São Carlos,** R. Serpa Pinto (tel. 346 59 14; open 1-7pm) from late September through mid-June.

NIGHTLIFE

While most nightlife revolves around the bars and *fado* joints in Lisboa, those seeking more active revelry won't be disappointed. June is the month of *feiras populares,* outdoor night fairs with plenty of eating, drinking, and dancing to live music. There's a lively one called "Oreal" at **Campo das Cebolas,** near the waterfront in the Alfama. (Open June Mon.-Fri. 10pm-1am, Sat.-Sun. 10pm-3am.) The Elevador da Glória stops at a *feira* in the **Bairro Alto** with a view of the illuminated Av. Liberdade. This one goes until 3am every night in June, except on June 13 (the **Festa de Santo António),** when it continues all night.

Fado

Lisboa's trademark, *fado* is an expressive art which combines elements of singing and narrative poetry. *Fadistas* perform sensational tales of lost loves and faded glory; their melancholy wailing is expressive of *saudade,* an emotion of nostalgia and yearning. Indeed, listeners are supposed to feel the "knife turning in their hearts." On weekends, book in advance by calling the venues or the municipal tourist offices. The Bairro Alto, with many *fado* joints off **R. Misericordia,** particularly on side streets radiating from the Museu de São Roque, is the best region in the city for quality *fado.*

Arcadas do Faia, R. Baroca, 56 (tel. 312 19 23). Cover charge 2500$. Open Mon.-Sat. 8pm-2am.

Sr. Vinho, R. Meio a Lapa, 18 (tel. 347 26 81), in nearby Madregoa. Minimum food and drink charge 2500$—with appetizers at 1200-2800$, it's not hard to reach. Open 8:30pm-2am.

Cafés

Most cafés close before your grandparents go to bed. Dawdlers linger at the **Pastelaria Suiça,** on the eastern side of Pr. Dom Pedro IV (the Rossio), a boisterous gathering place mobbed until midnight. Bring your well-thumbed Camões volumes across the square to **Café Nicola,** once a famous meeting spot for 19th-century Portuguese writers. **A Brasileira,** on R. Garrett in the Bairro Alto, attracts a more bohemian crowd. On weekends a roving guitar player serenades late-night coffee drinkers.

Bars

Those in search of rowdier nightlife shouldn't be deceived by the after-dinner lull. Nothing really starts up until after midnight—primarily on weekends, of course. Nightspots cluster around **Rua Diario das Notícias** in the Bairro Alto, where revelers wander the streets from club to club until morning.

Boris, Travessa Agua da Flor, 20. A small but trendy place where the drunken singing carries into the street. Open 9pm-2am.

Cena de Copos, R. da Barroca, 105. Postmodern decor, technopop music, and the requisite smoky air. Enigmatic cubist painting on the wall makes more sense as the night progresses. Jammed after midnight. A "tourist menu" (750$) is good for 3 drinks. Open 10pm-2am.

Mascote do Bairro, R. Diario das Noticias, 136. Diagonally across the street from Boris—calmer, roomier, and more down-to-earth.

Artis, R. do Diario das Noticias, 95 (tel. 342 47 95). Sip beer with a cosmopolitan crowd under the sultry red lights. Eclectic mix of posters and musical instruments adorn the walls. Open 8:30pm-2:30am.

Keops, R. da Rosa, at the intersection of Tr. dos Inglesinhos. Small and hip, with Egyptian decor and a miniature dance floor. Open 10pm-2am.

Discos

La Folie Discoteca, R. Diario Noticias, 122-4. Crazy fun with a bar, A/C, and the latest international music. 900$ cover charge includes two beers or one mixed drink. Open Tues.-Sun. 10pm-4am.

Do Outro Lado, R. Barroca, 129B. Easy-going atmosphere with the latest dance music. A young, trendy crowd. Expensive bar but no cover charge. Ring the bell. Open 10pm-3am.

Loucuras, Av. Alvares Cabral, 35 (tel. 68 11 17), southwest of Largo do Rato. A multi-room mirrored extravaganza decorated entirely in black. Cover 650$ for pub, 1000$ for disco. Open Fri.-Sat. 11pm-4am as a disco, plus Sat.-Sun. 4-8pm as a pub.

Memorial, R. Gustavo de Matos Sequeira, 42A (tel. 396 88 91), 1 bl. south of R. Escola Politécnica in the Bairro Alto. A hip gay and lesbian disco-bar. The lights and Europop blast from 10pm, but the fun starts after midnight. The 1000$ cover charge includes two beers or one mixed drink. Open 10:30pm-4am.

■■■ SHOPPING

Feiras are *the* way to combine shopping and cultural involvement. The open-air markets come in many kinds, and bargaining is the name of the game. Bookworms burrow for three glorious weeks in the **Feira do Livro** (Parque Eduardo VII, late May-early June). In June the Alcântara holds the **Feira Internacional de Lisboa,** while in July and August the **Feira de Mar de Cascais** and the **Feira de Artesania de Estoril** take place near the casino. *Fritadas* (Portuguese doughnuts) and freshly baked bread are served. Prowlers, and packrats should catch the **Feira da Ladra** (flea market), held at Campo de Santa Clara (Tues. and Sat. 7am-3pm; take bus #12 or trolley #28).

Mercado Ribeira, an open-air market just outside Estação Cais do Sodré, is festive with fresh fruit and abundant food. (Open Mon.-Sat. until 2pm. Freshest pickings in the morning.) The **Amoreiras Shopping Center de Lisboa,** at Av. Duarte Pacheco, boasts 330 shops (see Practical Information). To reach the shopping center, take bus #33 from Pr. Comércio or M. Rotunda and catch bus #11, 23, 48, or 53 for a short ride to the modern beige complex (you can't miss it).

Estremadura

An angry Atlantic foams below the sharp cliffs and whitewashed fishing villages along the Costa de Prata (Silver Coast) of Estremadura. Mornings are misty and grey, but the gloominess dissipates by midday. The people of Costa de Prata cling tightly to their traditions, despite or perhaps because of the tourists. Along the coast this culture thrives in such towns as Nazaré and Peniche. Inland, medieval strongholds and monumental monasteries remain at Obidos and Alcobaça.

The eclectic Costa de Lisboa has a variety of charms and styles. Wealthy beach towns of Estoril and Cascais are part suburb and part resort. These, along with the castles of Queluz, Mafra, and Sintra, make pleasant day trips from Lisboa. Below the Tejo and south of Lisboa lies the Setúbal Peninsula, an industrial and fishing center often bypassed by tourists. Setúbal itself is the best base for daytrips to the picturesque fishing village of Sesimbra; the Serra da Arrábida, a mountainous area with sparkling beaches; and the beaches of Tróia. Accommodations are quite expensive in these smaller towns.

■■■ SINTRA

Sintra (pop. 200,000) is as old as Portugal itself. Dom Afonso Henriques, the first king of Portugal, conquered the city from the Moors in 1147. After Lord Byron sang its praises in the epic poem *Childe Harold,* dubbing it "glorious Eden," Sintra became a must for 19th-century English aristocrats on the Grand Tour. Set in the midst of the hills, Sintra's beautiful views and fascinating palaces and museums continue to attract visitors.

ORIENTATION AND PRACTICAL INFORMATION

Sintra (30km northwest of Lisboa and 15km north of Estoril) is connected by train to Lisboa's Estação Rossio (every 8min., 45min., 165$). From the train station take a left and follow signs down a winding road to the town center (15min.). Be aware that theft is common in this heavily traveled area; many backpackers stow their gear in the tourist office for safety during the day.

Tourist Office: Pr. República (tel. 923 11 57; fax 923 51 76). A long winding walk, so try to travel lightly. From the town center, follow signs toward the Palácio Nationale; the tourist office is beyond the palace. English-speaking staff provides a map and lists of accommodations. They can also help you find a room in a private home. Housed in the same building as the **regional museum,** so check out exhibits while waiting. Open 9am-8pm; Oct.-May 9am-7pm.

Currency Exchange: Banco Totta e Açores, R. Padarias, 4 (tel. 924 19 19), on a side street off the main *praça.* Open Mon.-Fri. 8:45-11:45am and 1-2:45pm.

Post Office: Pr. República (tel. (01) 923 52 52), across from the tourist office. Small office with local **telephones.** Open Mon.-Fri. 9am-12:30pm and 2:30-6pm. **Postal Code:** 2710.

Trains: Estação de Caminhos de Ferro, Av. Dr. Miguel Bombarda (tel. 923 26 05), at the northern end of the city. To: Lisboa (every 16min., 45min., 165$); Obidos; Figueira da Foz (8 per day); and the northern beaches (change at Cacém). No direct service to Estoril or Cascais (see Buses).

Buses: Rodoviária, Av. Dr. Miguel Bombarda (tel. 921 03 81), across the street from the train station. Open 7am-8pm. To: Cascais (10 per day, 1hr., 500$) and Estoril (13 per day, 40min., 300$). Green-and-white **Mafrense** buses depart from stops to the right of the train station as you exit. To: Mafra (11 per day, 45min., 340$), with connections to points north.

Hospital: Largo Dr. Gregório de Almeida (tel. 923 34 00).

SINTRA

Emergency: tel. 115.
Police: Largo Dr. Virgilio Horta on corner of R. Costa (tel. 923 07 61).

ACCOMMODATIONS AND CAMPING

The youth hostel is inexpensive but far away from the city center. *Pensões* are pricier here than almost anywhere else in the country. Tourist office has a list of *quartos* (rooms in private homes; singles 3000$, doubles 3500$).

Pousada da Juventude de Sintra (HI), Sta. Eufémia (tel. 924 12 10), an uphill walk (2km) out of town beyond São Pedro. Streets are winding and difficult to navigate; have the tourist office show you the route on a map. Be wary of cab drivers who may over-charge. Meals served. TV lounge. Reception open 9am-noon and 6pm-midnight. Lockout at midnight. Multiples 1300$ per person. Doubles 3000$. Winter: 1100$; 2500$.

Casa de Hóspedes Adelaide, R. Guilherme Gomes Fernandes, 11 (tel. 923 08 73). From the train station, turn left and walk to the yellow *câmara;* the *pensão* is around the corner to the left opposite the police station. Central location. Clean rooms with A/C. Common bathrooms. Singles 2500$. Doubles 3000$.

Piela's, R. João de Deus, 70-72 (tel. 924 16 91). Make a left out of the train station and another left onto the uphill street behind the station. Piela's five rooms are spacious and well-furnished. Friendly, English-speaking owner. Café downstairs. Single 3500$. Doubles 5000$. Winter: 2500$; 4000$.

Pensão Nova Sintra, Largo Afonso d'Albuquerque, 25 (tel. 923 02 20), facing the square east of the train station. Charming terrace, tidy rooms—some with stupendous views of the *castelo.* Common bathrooms. Singles 3000$. Doubles 5000$. Breakfast included.

Camping: Camping Capuchos (tel. 86 23 50), near Convento da Capuchos, 9km from Sintra. Nestled in the mountains quite a ways from town, has a beautiful landscape, but very few of the usual amenities. 330$ per person.

FOOD

Cheap places fill the street behind the train station on the other side of the tracks. In the town center, narrow side streets such as **Rua Padárias** offer a wider range of eateries. There's a daily **Mercado Municipal** (8am-1pm) in the small square behind the buildings facing the Paço Real.

Casa da Avó, R. Monserrate, 44 (tel. 923 12 80). From the main *praça* down the hill from the tourist office, turn right on R. Monserrate; past a dilapidated fire station on the right. Fewer tourists than most local restaurants, thus all the more *frango assado* (roast chicken, 800$) to yourself. *Pratos do dia* up to 1200$. Open Fri.-Wed. 8am-10pm.

Casa da Piriquita, R. Padarias, 5 (tel. 923 06 26), up small side street off the Praça República. Delicious bakery, snack bar, and candy counter, flanked by a marble-floored coffee and tea room. Sintra's traditional tiny pastries with cheese and cinnamon or egg filling 100-200$. Open Thurs.-Tues. 9am-10:30pm.

Restaurante Alcobaça, R. Padarias, 9 (tel. 923 16 51). Specializes in fresh fish dishes, but *Ensopada de borrego* (lamb stew, 1200$) recommended too. Entrees 850-1800$. Open Thurs.-Tues. noon-4pm and 7pm-midnight.

SIGHTS

Between the train station and the town center stands a storybook village hall; the conical chimneys of the **Paço Real (Palácio Nacional)** loom behind. Once the summer residence of Moorish sultans and harems, the palace and its complex gardens were torn down during the Reconquista and replaced with a vaguely Moorish, mostly Gothic and Manueline building. Not much to look at on the outside (the chimneys look like giant bullhorns), the palace's interior is pure architectural whimsy.

According to legend, the impressive **Sala das Pêgas (Hall of Magpies)** came to be when Dom João I's wife caught him kissing one of the ladies of the court. Although he claimed that it was merely a gesture of friendship, the court ladies made it a subject of scandalous gossip. To spite them, the king caricatured them as magpies. A more serene bird motif is echoed in the **Sala dos Cisnes (Hall of Swans),** a banquet hall where 27 swans in different positions decorate the ceiling. The patio is a work of Moorish genius. (Open Thurs.-Tues. 10am-12:30pm and 2-4:30pm. Tickets sold 10am-4:30pm. Admission 400$, Oct.-May 200$, Sun. free.)

For more recent art, the **Anjos Teixeira Museum-House** (tel. 923 61 23), in the forested area below the Paço Real, displays 20th-century sculptures by two of Portugal's most revered artists: Master Anjos Teixeira and his son, Pedros Anjos Teixeira. Exquisite sculptures are often models for commissioned monuments showcased throughout Portugal. Pedros Anjos Teixeira greets visitors himself. Open Tues.-Sun. 9am-noon and 2-6pm.

From the Paço Real, the 3km ascent to the **Castelo dos Mouros** and the **Palácio da Pena** (crowning one of the highest peaks in the Sintra range) begins. Taxis swarm outside the Paço Real (fares vary), but the lush flora is best seen on foot. Word on the street is that hitchhiking to and from these attractions is possible, but *Let's Go* does not recommend it.

To reach the Castelo dos Mouros, walk up R. Monserrate and take the first right (signs point to Monserrate and Seteais); hang a left shortly thereafter on Calçada dos Clérigos. Continue climbing a short distance past the small 12th-century Igreja de Santa Maria until the sign for the *castelo.* From here, follow the trail through the dense forest. The 7th- to 8th-century castle of the Moors commands a glorious view of the countryside. Returning to the fork in the forest path, take a right turn and walk (20min.) until the path exits onto a road where you can either continue the climb to the Palácio da Pena (30min.) or make a slight detour to a small park. Take care: this path, though scenic, is steep and strenuous. It shouldn't be attempted if you're tired, a heavy smoker, lazy, very pregnant, or in poor health. Also avoid taking this route after dusk, when a tortuous maze of paths becomes a tortuous maze of invisible paths.

The Palácio da Pena was built in the 1840s by Prince Ferdinand, the queen's German consort, on the site of a 17th-century convent. Nostalgic for his country, the prince commissioned an obscure German architect to design this folly, which combines the aesthetic heritages of both Germany and Portugal. The utterly fantastic result would do loony King Ludwig proud: a Bavarian castle embellished with Arab minarets, Gothic turrets, Manueline windows, and a Renaissance dome. The meticulously restored rooms inside contain an awe-inspiring assortment of royal Portuguese, Indo-Portuguese, and Sino-Portuguese furnishings, plus overstuffed Victorian junk. Definitely worth a visit, if only for the cloister and chapel, which remain from the original convent. (Open Tues.-Sun. 10am-5pm, none admitted after 4:30pm. Admission 400$, Oct.-May 200$; students and seniors free.)

To get back to town take the narrow road straight down. A 15-minute detour up a trail to the right along this road (look for the "Sta. Eufémia" sign) leads past a ruined convent to a **capela,** built on a ridge to mark the miraculous appearance of Santa Eufémia in the 18th century. The view from here is incredible—Lisboa, the Rio Tejo, Cascais, and the coastline—but an even more impressive scene can be spied along the path to the **Cruz Alta** (a stone cross built on a rocky peak 520m above sea level). The trail down passes the **Igreja de São Pedro,** which preserves 17th-century *azulejos* of Bible scenes. From there, R. Trindade leads past a small convent and then rejoins the road that you came up on.

A less arduous way to experience Sintra and the surrounding area, including Cabo de Roca (see below), is to embark on the half-day **bus tour** which departs from the Paço Real. (Tues.-Sat. 2-6pm. 4500$, students 2225$.)

The **Feira do São Pedro** takes place on the 2nd and 4th Sundays of each month in the Village of São Pedro, 1.5km from Sintra (8am-8pm).

■ NEAR SINTRA

MAFRA

The quiet, unremarkable town of Mafra houses one of Portugal's most impressive sites: a huge **complex**, like Spain's El Escorial, including a palace, royal library, marvelous cathedral-sized church, and hospital. With 2000 rooms, the monstrous building took 50,000 workers 13 years (1713-1726) to complete under the whip of architect Johann Friedrich Ludwig. This Herculean task gave rise to a school of sculpture known as the Mafra School.

The exterior of the magnificent Baroque **igreja** has fallen into grime-covered disrepair, but the belfries remain eloquent. Two of the finest bell complexes in Europe are here. Legend has it that Emperor D. João V, upon hearing the astronomical price of one bell tower, replied "I didn't expect it to be that cheap. I'll have two." Although he may have meant to be sarcastic, the result was 217 tons of bronze bells—a highlight of the complex. The design for the church's extravagant dome was actually snagged from Bernini's unexecuted plan for St. Peter's in Rome. The richly decorated interior—with bas-reliefs and statues of Carrara marble—is one of Portugal's finest. (Open Wed.-Mon. 10am-1pm and 2-5pm, closed on national holidays. Admission June-Sept. 400$, Oct.-May 200$; students free. Mandatory tour in Portuguese.)

Access to the building's interminable corridors and extravagant living quarters is through a door to the right near the church exit. The **hospital's** beds are arranged like side-chapels, for patients to hear mass. The **sala dos troféus,** furnished with stag antlers and skins from chandeliers to chairs, is a must-see. The **biblioteca** (library) also headlines with 38,000 volumes printed in the 16th, 17th, and 18th centuries, displayed on 290 feet of Rococo shelves.

To reach the ultramodern **turismo** (tel. (061) 81 20 23) in the Auditório Municipal Beatriz Costa building on Av. 25 de Abril, walk right after exiting the museum and take the first left. Staff distributes brochures and info on accommodations in surrounding areas (Mafra has only one hotel) such as the popular coastal town of **Ericeira.** (Open daily 9:30am-7:30pm; Oct.-May 9:30am-6pm.) For **police,** call 067 520 69.

Green and white Mafrense **buses** stop in front of the church. They serve Lisboa's Largo Martim Moniz (1 per hr., 1½hr., 500$) and Sintra (1 per hr., 1 hr., 340$).

QUELUZ

Tourists come to **Queluz**, 14km west of Lisboa, to see the **Palácio Nacional de Queluz,** built on the orders of D. Pedro III in the late 18th century. Portuguese architect Mateus Vicente de Oliveira and French sculptor João Baptista Robillan collaborated to build this pink-and-white Rococo wedding cake of a palace. The building and furnishings are clearly French in inspiration; the well-ordered garden, Classical. Highlights are the garden's marble pond and the ornate throne room. Of historical interest is the room where Pedro I, first emperor of Brazil, was born and died. Each room includes a printed description in English. The **tourist office** (tel. 436 34 15) is also in the Palácio. (Both open Wed.-Mon. 10am-1pm. Admission 400$, Oct.-May 200$. Garden admission 50$. Students free.) To **train** here from Lisboa, take the Sintra line from Estação Rossio (every 15min., ½hr., 145$) or the same line from Sintra (every 15min., ½hr., 135$). Turn left from the station and follow the signs to the palace, a 10 to 15-min. walk.

CABO DA ROCA

Cabo da Roca, 18km from Sintra, is the western-most point on the European continent. The cape offers spectacular views of the ocean hurling itself against the cliffs. Authentic (expensive!) certificates from the tourist office will officially certify your presence on this westerly point. Mobbed on Sunday. Accessible by bus from Sintra (10 per day, 1hr., 300$). Alternatively, a 3km hike or bus ride from Cascais (see Estoril and Cascais).

■■■ COSTA DE LISBOA

Just half an hour west of Lisboa, the beach resorts of Estoril and Cascais offer less crowded, more upscale alternatives to staying in the capital city. Although the area's reputation as a playground for the rich and famous raises prices and draws tourists, both towns retain a certain charm, beauty, and playfulness, and are worth a visit.

ESTORIL

With an internationally renowned casino, flashy shows, and a beautiful beach, Estoril is reputed to be Portugal's "most famous tourist resort." High-priced restaurants and hotels, well-known golf courses, and a nearby Formula 1 track, the Autodromo, round out the town's luxury image.

The glass and marble **casino** tempts from just above the park. Reportedly the largest and most luxurious in Europe, this grandiose gaming-palace contains a restaurant, bars, a cinema, and a room of slots. Foreigners must cough up a passport; all must be 18 years old for the slots and 21 for the game room. (Entrance fees: bingo room 20$, game room 500$, slot machine room 180$. Open 3pm-3am.) The flowery paths of **Parque do Estoril,** in front of the casino, offer less material pleasure.

The **tourist office,** Arcadas do Parque (tel. 468 01 13), across from the train station and to the left, offers detailed maps and schedules of events in the area. English spoken. (Open Mon.-Sat. 9am-8pm, Sun. 10am-6pm; Oct. 15-June 16 Mon.-Sat. 9am-7pm, Sun. 10am-6pm.) **Police** are on Av. Biarritz (tel. 468 13 96). **Emergency:** tel. 115. **Radio Taxi:** tel. 468 70 95.

For lodging, try **Pensão Marylus,** R. Maestro Lacerda, 13 (tel. 468 27 40). From the train station, walk uphill on Av. Marginal. At the intersection, make a left onto Av. Bombeiros Voluntários and walk 3 bl. until R. Maestro Lacerda; the seven-room *pensão* is on the right. Rooms with sinks and toilets. (Singles 2500$. Doubles 6000$. Oct.-May: 2000$; 4000$. Breakfast in pleasant dining room included.) **Pensão Costa,** R. Olivença, 2 (tel. 468 16 99), on the corner of Estrada Marginal uphill from the train station, has airy, simply furnished, reasonably priced rooms. Some overlook the crashing Atlantic. (Singles and doubles 4500$, with shower 6000$.) If the casinos are kind, the **Estalagem Belvedere Guest House,** R. Dr. António Martins, 8 (tel. 406 02 08; fax 467 14 33), is a step up from the *pensões*. Features a small pool, modest fitness room, full bar and restaurant, and well-furnished, airy rooms with views. English spoken. Reservations recommended. (Singles with shower 7500$. Doubles with shower 8800$, with balcony 11,250$. Reduced rates Oct.-June.)

The **Yate Restaurant and Bar** (tel. 468 26 61) borders the park and provides simple meat dishes, sandwiches, and pastries in a relaxed outdoor atmosphere. Menus in English. (Entrees 600-1200$. Open 8am-2am.) **Restaurante Esplanada** (tel. 468 18 54) is up Estrada Marginal from the station, east of the park on the corner of Av. Bombeiros Voluntários. Here you can gobble a hefty dinner of baked fish or barbecued meat. (Menu 1400$, entrees 100-900$. Open noon-2pm and 7-9pm.)

Trains to Estoril leave from Lisboa's Estação Caís do Sodré (every 15min., ½hr., 165$). **Buses** to Sintra depart from in front of Estoril's train station (every hr., 40min., 300$).

CASCAIS

Cascais is a 15-minute walk from Estoril along a beautiful coastline promenade, or two train stops away on the same line originating in Lisboa's Caís do Sodré. Home to a fishing port and aristocratic residences, Cascais also has several historic sites and gardens. The lush municipal garden is a wonderful place to walk and picnic. Nestled within is the **Museo do Palácio de Castro Guimarães,** Av. Rei Humberto II De Itália Estrada da Boca do Inferno (tel. 438 08 56). Formerly the turn-of-the-century home of a Portuguese Count, the palace was converted into a museum in 1931, and contains an excellent collection of 17th-century Portuguese and Indo-Portuguese silver and furniture, as well as paintings and archeological findings. (Open Tues.-Sun. 10am-5pm. Admission 160$.)

About 1km west of town (a 20-min. walk along the coast) lies the **Boca do Inferno** (Mouth of Hell), a huge mouth carved in the rock by the incessant Atlantic surf. Sadly, the ominous sight is swamped with tourists. Less crowded is **Praia do Guincho,** an immense stretch of sandy beach 8km to the west. Its dangerous undertow and cold water may give swimmers pause, but it's perfect for windsurfing and offers a good view of **Cabo da Roca** (see Near Sintra). Here the Serra de Sintra ends abruptly in a sheer cliff 150m above the sea. 2km farther from Praia do Guincho, at a bend in the way flanked by small restaurants, a road leads to another beach, **Praia do Abano. Buses** to Praia do Guincho leave from the train station in Cascais (every hr. beginning at 7:35am, 20min., 150$, book of 5 tickets 1440$, book of 10 tickets 2880$). Tickets may be purchased in a booth attached to the outside of the station.

The pastel yellow **tourist office** is on R. Visconde Da Luz (tel. 486 82 04), at Av. Combatentes da Grande Guerra (Av. Valbom begins just outside the train station and leads to the office). The English-speaking staff operates on the site of an archeological dig in Paços do Concelho, and will supply detailed maps and a list of hotel rates. (Open Mon.-Sat. 9am-8pm, Sun. 10am-6pm; Oct.15-June 16 Mon.-Sat. 9am-7pm, Sun. 10am-6pm.) Rodoviária **buses** run from Sintra to Cascais. Buses leave from Av. Dr. Miguel Bombarda, across the street from the train station in Sintra (10 per day, 1hr., 300$).

Residencial Palma, Av. Valbam, 15 (tel. 483 77 97; fax 483 79 22), is quaint and centrally located. Well-appointed rooms, all with surprisingly large bathrooms. A cozy sitting room, and small yard with tables and a pond in front. (Singles and doubles 8000$. Breakfast included.) **Restaurante Pereira,** R. Bela Vista, 30 (tel. 483 12 15) serves plain but hearty Portuguese fare in a bright, informal atmosphere. Walk uphill on Visconde da Luz, turn right on R. C. Ribeiro, and immediately left on R. Bela Vista. A new menu daily (entrees 700-1500$). (Open Fri.-Wed. noon-4pm and 7pm-midnight.) For a taste of the Middle East, dine at **Joshua's Shoarma Grill,** R. Visconde da Luz, 19 (tel. 484 30 64); left on R. Viscondeda Luz, ½ bl. uphill from the tourist office. A full Middle Eastern menu including falafel (395$) served in an upbeat atmosphere. (Open Mon.-Fri. noon-4pm and 6pm-2am, Sat.-Sun. 1pm-2am.)

■■■ SETÚBAL

Setúbal is the home of spanking new Ford and Renault factories, but wait—don't turn the page yet. Thanks to these factories, exhaust-sputtering salt and cement plants, and a port, the city has become a key commercial center, and the government's favorite example of how foreign industry can address Portugal's chronic unemployment problem (it had reached 30% here). Industry doesn't net tourists, most of whom head straight for the Algarve, but the city's proximity to the mountainous Serra da Arrábida and the beaches of Tróia render it a perfect base for daytrips.

From the first to the fourth centuries AD, Setúbal was a Roman port connecting the iron mines of the Alentejo and the merchant ships of the Mediterranean. Abandoned and then occupied by the Moors in later centuries, the town became part of the Portuguese kingdom in the 13th century.

ORIENTATION AND PRACTICAL INFORMATION

Avenida Luísa Todi, a broad boulevard with a strip of park and cafés down its middle, runs parallel with the Rio Sado through the city. **Praça do Quebedo** (home to the train station and tourist office) and the bus station are both on **Avenida 5 de Outubro,** which runs north of Av. Todi. Between Av. Todi and Av. 5 de Outubro sits the **Praça de Bocage,** in the heart of the city. Av. Todi, Av. 5 de Outubro, Pr. Quebedo, and Pr. Bocage bound the **old city.** This neighborhood of narrow streets, cafés, bars, and upscale shops is a favorite place for an evening stroll.

Tourist Office: There are two. The **city government office** is on Largo do Corpo Santo (tel. 53 42 22), off Pr. Quebedo and across from the train station. Open

Mon.-Sat. 9am-12:30pm and 2-6pm. The **regional office,** run by Costa Azul, is on Tr. Frei Gaspar, 10 (tel. 52 42 84), off Av. Todi. Open Mon.-Sat. 9am-7pm, Sun. 9am-12:30pm. English spoken at both offices. Pamphlets and maps of Setúbal and the Costa Azul.

Currency Exchange: Numerous banks along Av. Todi advertise exchange rates in their windows. **Banco Borges e Irmão,** Av. Todi, 290. Coming from Pr. Bocage onto Av. Todi, it's on the left. Open Mon.-Fri. 8:30am-3:30pm.

Post Office: Av. Mariano de Carvalho (tel. 52 27 78), on the corner with Av. 22 de Dezembro. Open for Posta Restante and telephones Mon.-Fri. 8:30am-6:30pm, Sat. 9am-12:30pm. New **branch office** in Pl. Bocage (tel. 25 55 55). Open for similar services (no Posta Restante) Mon.-Fri. 9am-noon and 2-8pm. **Postal Code:** 2900.

Telephones: In the post office, or along Av. Todi. **Telephone Code:** 065.

Trains: Pr. Quebedo, across from the city tourist office, for local trains. **Estação de Setúbal,** Pr. Brasil (tel. 52 68 45). To: Lisboa (31 per day, 1½hr., 250$); Faro (4 per day, 4hr., 1240$); Evora (13 per day, 2hr., 735$).

Buses: Rodoviária Subalentejo, Av. 5 de Outubro, 44 (tel. 52 50 51). From the city tourist office, walk up the street toward traffic and turn left. To: Lisboa (every ½hr., 1hr., 500$); Evora (5 per day, 2½hr., 770$); Faro (7 *expressos* per day, 4hr., 1600$); Porto (6 *expressos* per day, 6hr., 1800$); Vila Nova de Milfontes (6 per day, 3hr., 1150$).

Ferries: Transsado, Doca do Comércio (tel. 52 33 84), off Av. Todi at the east end of the waterfront. 36 trips back and forth between Setúbal and Tróia per day (15min., 100$ per person, 50$ per child, 450$ per car).

Taxis: tel. 333 34, 314 13, or 523 55.

Luggage Storage: At the **bus station,** 90$ per bag per day.

English Bookstore: Livraria Telis, R. Serpa Pinto, 8 (tel. 52 85 55), on a street off Pr. Bocage to the east. Petite stock of maps and paperbacks in English. Open Mon.-Fri. 9am-7pm, Sat. 9am-1pm.

Laundromat: Tinturária Domini, R. Tenente Valadni, 9 (tel. 52 42 77), off Pr. Bocage to the north. Dry cleaning only. 500$ per shirt, 600$ per pants. Open Mon.-Fri. 9am-1pm and 3-7pm, Sat. 9am-1pm.

Hospital: R. Camilo Branco (tel. 52 21 33).

Emergency: tel. 115.

Police: Av. Todi (tel. 52 20 22), at the corner with Av. 22 de Dezembro, on the roundabout across the street from the Mercado Municipal.

ACCOMMODATIONS AND CAMPING

Summer prices are higher, but space is no problem. Several *pensões* in town almost always have vacancies.

Residencial Alentejana, Av. Luísa Todi, 124 (tel. 21 398). Homey, well-furnished rooms. Clean common bathrooms with plenty of hot water—no need to pay extra for a room with basic shower. Doubles 2400$, with shower 3000$.

Residencial Bocage, R. São Cristão, 14 (tel. 52 15 98; fax 52 18 09). Good-sized, tidy rooms overlooking a quiet square 1 bl. north of Av. Todi and 1 bl. east of Pr. Bocage. Central location. All rooms with bath and telephone. Singles 3900$. Doubles 5200$. Oct.-June: 3600$; 4800$. Breakfast included.

Residencial Todi, Av. Todi, 244 (tel. 52 05 92). Clean rooms and central location. The noisy ones overlook the street. Doubles 3500$, with bath 4500$. Triples 5000-6000$, or about 1000$ per person over the price for doubles. Prices drop about 1000$ in winter.

Pensão Residencial Avenida, Av. Todi, 87 (tel. 52 25 40). Wood floors, high ceilings, and huge windows (if you're lucky). Distinctly spartan with a common bathroom—it's all clean and there are gallons of hot water. Some rooms with shower. Singles 2400$. Doubles one bed 3700$, two beds 4200$. Triples 6500$.

Camping: Toca do Pai Lopes, R. Praia da Saúde (tel. 52 24 75), run by the Câmara Municipal de Setúbal. At the western end of Av. Todi on the road to Outão. Right on the beach. Standard amenities and crowds. Reception open 8am-10pm; Sept.-

May 9am-9pm. 200$ per person, 160$ per tent, 200$ per car. Sept.-May: 150$; 110$; 150$. Free hot showers.

FOOD

Cheap meals lurk in the narrow streets of the old town, especially off **Rua A. Castelões** (off Pr. Bocage). Fresh grilled seafood costs more on Av. Todi. The **mercado municipal** vends fresh produce at open stands on the corner of R. Ocidental do Mercado and Av. Todi, next door to Pingo Doce supermarket.

Groceries: Pingo Doce, Av. Todi, 149 (tel. 52 61 05). Large market with its own bakery. Open daily 8am-9pm. Late-night groceries at **Loja Extra 22,** Av. Todi, 89 (tel. 52 30 19). Open daily 7am-3am.

Jardim de Inverno, R. Alvaro Luz, 48-50 (tel. 393 73), off R. A. Castelões. Green garden, walls, and lights—a go signal to this bustling and reasonably priced *cafetaria-restaurante-bar. Menu* 700$. Entrees 700-1100$. Open 8am-11:30pm.

Laçarote, R. Alvaro Luz, 34 (tel. 380 84), down the street from Jardim de Inverno. Vast miscellany of foods colors up the jaundiced decor. Pizza from 370$. Crepes from 200$. *Pratos do dia* 720$. Open 8:30am-7pm.

A Torre, Av. Todi, 275 (tel. 308 01). The left half, called **Brazuca,** is fancier and more pricey, yet shares a common kitchen with A Torre, an unremarkable *cafetaria* and *cervejaria.* At Brazuca, entrees 800-7500$. At A Torre, mediocre budget meals 490-570$. Open 8am-midnight.

SIGHTS AND ENTERTAINMENT

The most impressive sight in town is the **Castelo de São Filipe.** Take Av. Todi to its western end, turn right, and continue to the crossroads. Then take R. Estrada do Castelo uphill about 600m (30min.). Built by Spanish King Felipe II in 1590, this national monument is a luxury *pousada.* The views from the walls of Setúbal, the Tróia across the river, and the Serra da Arrábida mountains are worth the climb. (Always open. Always free.)

The **Igreja de Jesús,** at Praça Miguel Bombarda at the western end of Av. 5 de Outubro, was begun in the 15th century as part of a larger monastic complex. Maritime-motif decorations and faux-rope pillars and vaulting mark the beginnings of the Manueline style.

Next door, the **Museu de Setúbal** (a.k.a. Convento de Jesús) houses a noteworthy collection of 15th to 18th-century *azulejos.* (Closed for renovations.) The age-flaunting **library** boasts 12,000 volumes of valuable first editions, municipal archives as far back as the 14th century, and a celebrated collection of autographs. (Open Tues.-Sun. 9am-noon and 2-5pm. Free.)

Setúbal is known for fast cars, not the fast lane. Take in a flick at **Cinema Charlot,** R. Dr. António Gamito, 9-11 (tel. 367 59; 350$). **Copus** and **Pierrot** are among the popular bars along Av. Luísa Todi. The **Feira de Santiago** in the last week of July and first week of August is an industrial and agricultural party. More entertaining are the amusement park, bullfighting, and folk dancing that accompany it.

■ NEAR SETÚBAL

SERRA DA ARRÁBIDA

Convento da Arrábida nestles in the nearby mountain range. Founded in 1542 by Franciscans, the convent offers a striking panoramic view of the cliffs and sea. For beachgoers, the **Portinha da Arrábida,** between the top of Serra da Arrábida and the sea, features a beautiful, less-touristed stretch of white sand, breathtaking views, windsurfing, sailing, and submarine hunting. Between the Portinha and Setúbal is another popular beach, **Praia de Figuerinha,** with windsurfing, sailing, and sport fishing.

SESIMBRA

Tucked between the mountains, Sesimbra retains a tranquil and refreshingly quaint atmosphere despite its recent, extensive development. The tourist industry has grown rapidly, but Sesimbra has held onto its roots as a fishing center; you'll be hard pressed to find fresher seafood. Those prepared for a steep half-hour hike above town to the **Moorish Castle** will be rewarded with an incredible panoramic view of the ocean and surrounding mountains. The castle houses various museums, as well as the **Santa Maria do Castelo Church.** On Av. Liberdade, the **Municipal Museum** contains archeological and ethnographic finds of the region. (Open 10am-6pm. Free.) Sesimbra's popular **beach** is a main attraction.

Maps, regional information, and lists of accommodations are available at the **tourist office,** Av. Naufragos, 27 (tel. 223 57 43), along the waterfront. English spoken. (Open 9am-8pm; Oct.-April 9am-12:30pm and 2-5:30pm.) The **telephone code** is 01. The **hospital** is on Largo 5 de Outubro (tel. 223 36 92). In an **emergency,** dial 115. The **police** are on Largo Gago Coutinino (tel. 223 02 69).

Inexpensive accommodations can be difficult to find, particularly in summer. The best option is to check for private rooms with the tourist office. Otherwise, **Residencial Chic,** Trav. Xavier da Silva, 2-6 (tel. 223 33 10), offers simple, breezy rooms. One of the better deals in town. (Doubles 5000-9000$, depending on demand. Winter 3500$. Breakfast included.) **Pensão Espadarte,** Av. 25 de Abril, 11 (tel. 223 31 89), has spartan rooms with gorgeous ocean views. All rooms with bath. (Singles 7500$. Doubles 9600$. Winter: 4000$; 5700$.) For excellent seafood, follow the local fishermen to **Restaurante Sesimbrese,** R. Jorge Nunes, 19 (tel. 223 01 48). People drive from kilometers around for their exquisite fisherman's stew (1200$). (Entrees 800-1500$. Open Wed.-Mon. 9am-10pm.)

Regular **buses** leave for Sesimbra from Lisboa's Praça de Espanha (505$), but due to heavy traffic in the summer, you should probably take a ferry from Lisboa across to Cacilhas (90$) and then catch a bus to Sesimbra (415$). Regular buses also leave from Setúbal. For more information, call the bus companies in Sesimbra: **Carasefilhos** (tel. 22 30 72) or **Rodoviária Nacional** (tel. 223 30 71).

■■■ PENICHE

Portugal's second-largest fishing fleet is based in Peniche, a seaport 24km west of Obidos. The town crests (and is named for) a high and rugged peninsula. Wide beaches skirt the cliffs. Many travelers overlook Peniche as they hurry through to the Ilhas Berlengas, but the town's monuments and beaches have recently been attracting tourists in greater numbers. The local museum's coverage of Portugal's Fascist and anti-Fascist history has been sparking historical interest, and the bounteous supply of domestic electronics stores comes as a relief after all the natural marvels to the south.

ORIENTATION AND PRACTICAL INFORMATION

Peniche's town center, enclosed on one side by **Largo Bispo Mariana** and on the other by **Rua de San Marcos,** radiates in a tidy grid-like fashion from the bustling seaside **Avenida Do Mar.** The new **bus station** is on an isthmus outside the town walls. To reach the tourist office, make a right exiting the station and cross the small river (on Ponte Velha) to enter town. Make a left onto R. Alexandre Herculano and walk for a couple blocks alongside the public garden, following signs to the office.

Tourist Office: R. Alexandre Herculano (tel. 78 95 71), hidden in a garden behind the gas pumps. Chock full of brochures and photos of the region. Helpful English-speaking staff. Open 9am-8pm; winter 9am-noon and 2-7pm.

Currency Exchange: Banco Nacional Ultramarino (tel. 78 96 03), just off Pr. Jacob Rodrigues Pereira. 1000$ commission on cash exchange; 2180$ for traveler's checks.

Post Office: R. Arquitecto Paulino Montez (tel. 78 70 11). Exiting Turismo, make a right on R. Herculano, then a left onto R. Arquitecto Montez. Posta Restante and **telephones** lie within. Open 9am-6pm. **Postal Code:** 2520. **Telephone Code:** 062.

Buses: R. Estado Portugues da India. Express and regular service to: Lisboa (14 per day, 2½hr., 820$); Caldas (10 per day, 1hr., 370$); and Santarém (2 per day, 1½hr., 740$).

Taxis: tel. 78 44 24. They cluster around Pr. Jacob Rodrigues Pereira.

Luggage Storage: in the **bus station,** 90$ per day.

Laundromat: Lavandaria "a primeira," R. Arquitecto Paulino Montez, 17, down the street from the post office. Dry cleaning only. Shirts 150$. Pants 650$.

Hospital: tel. 78 17 00 or 78 17 08. On R. Gen. Humberto Delgado, off R. Arquitecto Paulino Montez.

Emergency: tel. 115.

Police: tel. 78 95 55. On R. Marquês de Pombal, off Pr. Jacob Rodrigues Pereira.

ACCOMMODATIONS AND CAMPING

Pensões fill up quickly in July and August; try to arrive early in the day. Extremely aggressive women and children roam the streets offering beds in their homes, but enough prime-location, budget *pensões* have popped up to make private houses a last resort. Before accepting a room in a private home insist on seeing the place and inquire about hot water and other amenities. Many rooms thankfully cluster near the tourist office, but also look for signs on Av. Mar.

HI Youth Hostel, Praia da Areia Branca, 13km south (tel. 42 21 27). The hostel is accessible by the local bus to Lisboa (9 per day, ½hr., 275-450$). Multiples 1300$. Doubles 3000$. Oct.-May: 1100$; 2500$.

Residencia Mira Mar, Av. do Mar (tel. 78 16 66), above a yummy restaurant of the same name. Tells you to look at the sea but it has nothing to hide: cheerful rooms, oak furniture, clean bath, and a prime location near the beaches. Singles 2000$, with bath 2500$. Doubles with bath 4000$. Triples 5000$. Winter discount.

Pensão Felita, Largo Professor Francisco Freire, 12 (tel. 78 21 90). From the tourist office, walk past Pr. Jacob Pereira several blocks; Felita is across from the school. Multi-room doubles with small covered balcony. Clean, comfortable bedrooms. Doubles 2500$, with bath 3500$, with sitting room and bath 4000$. Winter discount.

Residencial Cristal, R. Gomes Freitas de Andrade, 14-16 (tel. 78 27 24), 3 bl. inland from Pr. Jacob Pereira. Simple, clean rooms. Private baths are considerably more appealing than the common ones. Singles 3000$. Doubles with bath 4000$. Triples 6000$.

Camping: Municipal campground (tel. 78 95 29), 1½km outside of town, fronts a beach and has a small market. Eight buses per day speed to the campground from a stop 1 bl. to the right of the tourist office. (Ask tourist office for times or check at the bus station.) Otherwise it's a 40-min. walk through the *jardim público* and across the Ponte Velha; once across turn right, then left at the T in the road. Go straight ahead a long, long time until the Mobil station, behind which you can collapse in the comfort of the *campismo*. **Camping Peniche Praia,** Estrada Marginal Norte (tel. 78 34 60). Closer to the town and beach with bungalows, snack bar, and showers.

FOOD

Portions of immense proportions sizzle on outdoor grills all along **Avenida do Mar.** The outdoor cafés on **Praça Jacob Rodrigues Pereira** are lively hangout spots, particularly on Sundays, when the rest of the town is virtually comatose. The animated **market** has fresh produce; from the tourist office walk up R. Paulino Montez, then turn right on R. António da Conceição Bento. (Open Tues.-Sun. 7am-1:30pm.)

Casa Canhoto, R. 13 de Infantaria, serves savory treats from an outdoor grill. The *espetadas de lulas grelhadas* (squid kebab, 800$) and the *sopa de peixe* (fish soup, 120$) are especially good. Entrees 750-1400$.

Restaurante Beiramar, Av. Mar, 106-108 (tel. 78 24 79). Delectable grilled fare served on wood tables in the midst of stone walls. The 2nd floor has some cheery balcony tables. *Espetada de Carne* (meat kebab, 800$). Open 10am-11pm.

SIGHTS AND ENTERTAINMENT

Salazar, Portugal's longtime Fascist dictator, chose Peniche's formidable 16th-century **Fortaleza** as the site for one of his four high-security political prisons. Its high walls and bastions later became a camp for Angolan refugees and now house the **Museo de Peniche.** The highlight of the museum is undoubtedly the fascinating anti-Fascist Resistance exhibition. A series of photo panels, accompanied by Portuguese text, trace the dictatorship and underground resistance movements from the seizure of power in 1926 to the coup that toppled the regime on April 25, 1974.

The round lookout tower perched above the ocean contains the notorious **Segredo de Peniche** (Secret of Peniche) punishment cell, the scene of a more dramatic liberation story. In 1954 Communist political prisoner Dias Lourenço made a breakout from the isolation cell, plunged into the icy waves below, and waded through a sewage tunnel to the town. He was eventually recaptured. An international campaign for his release drew attention to the tribulations of the Portuguese. The fortress is at the far end of R. José Estevão, near the dock where boats leave for the Berlengas. (Tel. 78 18 48; museum open Tues.-Sun. 10am-noon and 2-5pm. Admission 100$, under 15 free.)

The largest church in town is **Igreja de São Pedro** (2 bl. from the docks where R. Marquês de Pombal hits R. Nossa Senhora de Conceição), a 16th-century Manueline building with paintings of the life of St. Peter. The **Parque do Murraçal** winds over to the Baroque **Igreja de Ajuda,** gilded with *azulejos* depicting Classical as well as biblical and medieval scenes.

For sun and surf, head to any of the town's three beaches. **Praia de Peniche de Cima,** along the northern crescent, is beautiful and has warmer water, but tends to get windy. The beach merges with another at **Baleal,** a small fishing village popular with tourists. The southern **Praia do Molho Leste** is colder but slightly safer, and a good escape from the wind. Beyond it is the crowded **Praia da Consulação.** The strange humidity at this beach is supposed to cure all sorts of bone diseases. In the past decade an improved economy has revived the art of tatting hand-made lace, once an important craft. The **Festa de Nossa Senhora da Boa Viagem,** held Saturday through Tuesday on the first weekend in August, brings arts and crafts, *fado,* fireworks, and a temporary amusement park.

■ NEAR PENICHE

THE PENINSULA

The best way to savor the rough ocean air is to walk all the way around the peninsula (8km). Start hiking at **Papôa,** a small, rocky peninsula that juts out to the north of Peniche. Stroll out to the tip, where orange cliffs protrude from a swirling blue sea. Nearby lie the ruins of an old fortress, **Forte da Luz.**

The 12-pewed **Santuário de Nossa Senhora dos Remédios** stands at the edge of a Portuguese ghost town. Signs invite pilgrims to seek reconciliation with God and to be quiet.

Cabo Carvoeiro, the most popular and dramatic of Peniche's natural sights, and its **farol** (lighthouse), punctuate the extreme western end of the peninsula. Next door is a conveniently situated snack bar where you can watch the waves crash on the rocks below as you relish *ginja* (the syrupy cherry liquor of Obidos). The **Nau dos Corvos** (Crow's Ship), an odd rock formation and a popular bird roost, also provides stunning views.

ILHAS BERLENGAS

Out of the Atlantic Ocean, 12km northwest of Peniche rises the rugged, terrifying beauty of the Ilhas Berlengas (Berlenga Islands). One minuscule main island, numerous reefs, and isolated rocks form an archipelagic home for thousands of screeching seagulls, wild black rabbits, and a small fishing community.

The main island, encircled by sparkling surf, is traced with deep gorges, natural tunnels, and rocky caves. For 3000$, a **motorboat** chugs from the castle pier and explores the island's scenic wonders (for info, call tel. 78 99 60). The island is fringed with several protected beaches, but the only one accessible by foot lies in a small cove by the landing dock. The water in the cove is calm and clear; for beachgoers willing to brave the cold, quick dips and dives offer respite from the heat. For hikers, the tiring trek to the top of the island yields a gorgeous view of the 17th-century **Fortaleza de São João Batista,** now a hostel on an islet.

The community-run **hostel** in the old fortress is a spectacular place to sleep. The government tried running it as a luxury *pousada,* but the effort failed due to the utter lack of facilities and the strenuous 20-min. hike from the ferry landing. Bring a sleeping bag. The hostel has a kitchen, but no cooking utensils; the small canteen and snack bar stock basic food. Spartan doubles 1000$ per person. Open June-Sept. 21. Advance reservations must be made through Club Naval (tel. 78 25 68).

The island has a small, barren **campground** on a series of rocky terraces above the ferry landing and beach. If you stay here, be prepared to be shat upon by scores of seagulls. (The seven-year's good luck is not worth this unpleasant experience miles away from your own tub.) Always look mean and carry a stick to ward them off. Inquire and make reservations in-person at the tourist office in Peniche. (Open June-Sept. 20. 2-person tent 800$ per night, 3-person tent 1500$, 4-person tent 1600$. Seven-day max. stay.) **Pavilhão Mar e Sol** (tel. 75 03 31), the main restaurant on the island, also rents rooms. (Doubles 10,000-12,000$. Breakfast included.)

Near the boat landing there are **public bathroom** facilities. From Peniche's public dock, the Berlenga **ferry** makes three trips per day to the island in July and August (9am, 11am, and 5pm, returning 10am, 4pm, and 6pm), and one per day in June and September 1-20 (10am, returning 6pm). In late-July and August, the ferry gets so crowded that you may have to queue up at 7am; at other times 1 hr. in advance should be sufficient. A same-day round-trip ticket (2000$) for the 9am ferry means you'll return on the 4pm ferry; if you go at 11am, you return at 6pm unless there is space on the other boat. To stay overnight, buy a 1200$ one-way ticket for the 5pm boat and pay your return fare on board a 10am return boat. The crossing can be rough—sickness bags handed out to all passengers at the beginning of the trip are frequently appreciated. If you intend to stay the night, bring a flashlight. The half-hour walk from the bar near the boat landing to the hostel is lit only by periodic flashes from the lighthouse.

■■■ INLAND

OBIDOS

In 1282, Queen Isabel so admired Obidos' beauty that her husband, King Dinis, gave it to her, beginning a tradition (lasting until 1834) in which Obidos was part of the queen's dowry. Long a favorite retreat of royal couples, Obidos died and rose again as a luxury resort turned national monument. No tourist pamphlet can honestly claim that this town of fantastically clean streets, expensive restaurants, multilingual inhabitants, and vendors of *Beverly Hills, 90210* lollipops is "typically Portuguese." Obidos is an exhibition piece: mosey around the walls, appreciate its beauty, snap some pictures and, after a few hours, leave. You'll eat and sleep more cheaply in nearby towns such as Caldas da Rainha (6km), and have more fun at the beaches around Peniche (20km).

When you see the formidable **walls,** you'll understand why Portugal's first king was humbled in several attempts to capture the town from the Moors. He only succeeded when forces at the main gate diverted the guards' attention, while others, disguised as cherry trees, tiptoed up to the castle. Taking notice of the advancing trees, an astute Moorish princess asked her father if trees walked. The distracted king just didn't listen. By the time he realized what was happening, Afonso's men had broken through the castle door. You can walk around the entire town on the walls. Arboreal attire is, of course, optional.

The main entrance to the town has always been **Porta Da Vila.** R. Direita, the main street, runs from here through the entire walled town to the Sant'Iago Igreja and the inner fortress. The 17th-century *azulejo* bonanza **Igreja de Santa Maria** in the central *praça* was built on the foundations of a Visigothic temple and later used as a mosque. Nun Josefa de Obidos' graceful, vividly colored canvases fill the retable to the right of the main altar. The church was the site of the 1444 wedding of 10-year-old King Afonso V to his 8-year-old cousin, Isabel. (Open 9:30am-12:30pm and 2:30-7pm; Oct.-May 9:30am-12:30pm and 2:30-5:30pm. Free.) The nearby pillory bears the arms of Queen Leonor. Slightly below and to the right of the church, the **Museu Municipal** houses Portuguese paintings and Gothic religious sculptures from the 16th to 18th centuries. (Open 10am-12:30pm and 2-6pm. Admission 100$; students, seniors, under 12, and Wed. free.)

Igreja de São Pedro was built on the site of a Gothic temple that toppled in the earthquake of 1755. Nearby are the remains of the **castelo,** built in the 12th century as a fortress on the Atlantic coast. The stronghold gradually lost its strategic importance as the ocean receded 7km through silting, but has all but made up for that in soft power as a luxury **pousada.**

Obidos hosts an annual **festival of ancient music** in the first two weeks of October, and a **festival of modern art** every other year (Sept.-Nov.). The **market** sets up every Sat. morning outside the main town gate, Porta de Vila.

Practical Information   The **tourist office** (tel. 95 92 31) is in an adobe house on R. Direita, right before Pr. Santa Maria. The helpful staff speaks English. (Open 9:30am-1pm and 2-6pm.) The **post office** (tel. 95 91 99), nearby in Pr. Santa Maria, is open for **telegrams** and telephones as well as basic services. (Open Mon.-Fri. 9am-12:30pm and 2:30-6pm.) The **postal code** is 2510 and the **telephone code** 062. The nearest **hospital** is in Caldas da Rainha (tel. 83 21 33), 6km away. In an **emergency,** call tel. 115. For **police,** dial tel. 95 91 49.

Frequent **buses** connect Obidos to Peniche (8 per day, 5 on Sun., 40min., 330$). Also, via Caldas da Rainha (6 per day, 20min., 130$) to Lisboa, Santarém, and Nazaré. The bus stops down some stairs from the main gate. Wait across from the shelter to catch the bus for Peniche, under the shelter for Caldas de Rainha. Obidos is an easy **train** ride from Lisboa's Estação Rossio (2hr.). Take a commuter train to Torres Vedras, then change trains for Obidos (8 per day, 2¾hr., 590$). The train station is 10 minutes outside town to the north. To get there from the town center, at the far end of R. Direita from the Porta da Vila, walk out the gap in the walls. Turn right, then left, then walk down a steep flight of stairs on the hillside. When walking from the station to town, be sure to climb the stairs across from the station rather than walking along the length of the town wall. The station is unattended; buy tickets aboard the train.

Accommodations and Food   Places to stay are few and dear. Private rooms are the best option; look for advertisements along R. Direita. **Agostino Pereira,** R. Direita, 40 (tel. 95 91 88), rents four cozy, wood-floor rooms; some have window seats to enjoy the view of the nearby *igreja.* Pleasant lounge with TV and small bar, washing machine, and kitchen for guest use. Winter heating. (Singles 3000$. Doubles 4000-4500$. Triples 5000$. Reserve at least 3 days in advance.) Outside the walls about 500m from town, **Residencial Martim de Freitus,** Estrada Nacional, 8 (tel. 95 91 85) offers relatively affordable rooms. (Doubles 5000$, with bath 7000-8000$.)

The fact that the tourist office staff (and other locals) bring lunch to work should tell you something about the price of restaurants. There's a tiny **mini-market** near the town's main gate and two larger ones wedged between handicraft shops on R. Direita. Otherwise, **Café Restaurante I de Dezembro,** Largo São Pedro (tel. 95 92 98), serves food simply and well in its snack-bar and *restaurante.* Various *pratos do dia* around 990-1330$ (½-portion 600$). (Open Fri.-Wed. 8am-10pm.) Obidos patents a wild cherry liqueur called *ginja,* even sweeter and more syrupy than the national norm. It may make you thirstier than you already are. Turismo sells gulp-sized bottles for 150$.

CALDAS DA RAINHA

Most famous for its sulfur springs, the town takes its name, "Baths of the Queen," from Queen Leonor, who luxuriated in the thermal springs here in 1484. The first lady then sold her jewels to finance the construction of the world's first **thermal hospital,** where victims of rheumatism, respiratory ailments, and skin afflictions came to be cured. Though the site is still primarily intended for those who suffer from arthritis, you can still sample the treatments at the Hospital Thermal Rainha Dona Leonor. (Simple bath 370$; pay at the cashier upstairs.) Downstairs, in a small private room, you can languish in a marble tub and soak up the steaming, sulfurous (ergo smelly) water. All tubs are equipped with an optional water massage. An hour-glass marks time in 20-minute segments, but you can stay as long as you like, provided there's no wait. After your bath, the attendant makes sure you lie down in a reclining chair and drink liquids—all to regain your body's precarious equilibrium. To reach the hospital, walk downhill on R. Liberdade from Pr. República, the town's main square. The hospital is at the bottom of the ramp on the left. (Tel. 83 21 33 or 83 21 44; open for baths Mon.-Fri. 8am-6pm, Sat. 8am-noon. Try between 3pm and 4pm.)

Through the tunnel on the left side of the hospital facade is its old chapel, **Igreja de Nossa Senhora do Pópulo**—another Leonor commission, perhaps the spiritual counterpart to the baths' physical therapy. Arabic tiles and arches shine out from the early Manueline design. (Inquire at the hospital for permission to visit; usually open only for mass, 11am-12:30pm. Free.)

Caldas is best known for its traditional ceramics. The town's prestige in ceramics has long been unrivaled, and most art museums throughout the country house at least a few characteristic pieces from Caldas; its kilns produce for handicraft shops nationwide. You can shop here for high quality pieces at low, low prices, or view the finished products at the **Casa da Cultura** on Largo Rainha Dona Leonor, across from the hospital. (Under construction in 1994. Free.) More pieces are displayed at the **Associação de Artesãos das Caldas da Rainha** gallery in the building just inside the park gate from the Casa da Cultura. A leaflet here lists the local artists and their *ateliers.* (Open June-Sept. 10:30am-1pm and 3:30-8pm.) Caldas hosts the **Feira Nacional de Cerâmica** for four days in the middle of July.

Believe it or not, well-rounded Caldas is also a center of modern sculpture. The work of native son António Duarte occupies the beautiful, modern, and undiscovered **Atelier-Museu Municipal António Duarte.** Most of Duarte's sculpture explores the range of facial and anatomical expression. (The museum has no fixed hours. Ring the doorbell at any reasonable hour; you'll probably have the whole place to yourself. Free.) The **Museu de Cerâmica** across the street traces the history and manufacturing process of Caldas clay. Yawn. (Open Tues.-Sun. 10am-noon and 2-5pm. Free.) A park separates the two museums from the town center. From R. Camões or Largo Rainha Dona Leonor, walk clockwise around its periphery.

The **Museu de José Malhôa** houses a collection of modern Portuguese paintings, sculpture, and ceramics. (Open Tues.-Sun. 10am-12:30pm and 2-5pm. Admission 200$; students with ID, seniors, and Sun. morning free.)

Practical Information The **tourist office** (tel. 83 10 03) is at Pr. 25 de Abril, 1 bl. from the bus station walking along R. Eng. Duarte Pacheco. (Open Mon.-Fri. 9am-

7pm, Sat.-Sun. 9am-12:30pm and 2-7pm; winter 9:30am-12:30pm and 2-7pm.) There is also a **summer tourist office** (tel. 345 11) on Pr. República (look for Turismo sign; open Mon.-Fri. 9am-7pm, Sat.-Sun. 10am-1pm and 3-7pm). The **post office,** R. Heróis da Grande Guerra (tel. 246 81-C.T.T.), is across the street from the bus station. (Open Mon.-Fri. 8:30am-6:30pm.) The **postal code** is 2500 and the **telephone code** 062. **Taxis** (tel. 83 24 55) run 24hrs. You may want one from the train station to the campground (250$). Dirty laundry is deloused at **Lavandería Press,** R.Capitão Filipe de Sousa, 50 (tel. 338 88). Dry cleaning only (shirts 400$, pants 530$). The **hospital** (tel. 83 21 33) is on the first street to the right after the police station. In an **emergency,** call tel. 115. The **police** (tel. 83 20 22) are headquartered at Frei de São Paulo, just off Pr. República.

The **bus station** (tel. 83 10 67) is on R. Heróis da Grande Guerra. For the tourist office, turn left as you exit the station and left again two bl. later onto R. Almirante Cândido dos Reis. Frequent bus service to Obidos (14 per day, 20min., 125$) and Lisboa (8 per day, 1½hr., 850$). The **train station** (tel. 236 93) is on the northwestern edge of town on Largo de Estaçao. From Av. 25 de Abril, take Av. 1 de Maio. Eight trains per day connect Caldas to Lisboa (2¼hr., 690$). The train station has **luggage storage** facilities (200$ per 4hr., 1000$ per day).

Accommodations and Food Pensão Residencial Estremadura, Largo Dr. José Barbosa, 23 (tel. 83 23 13; fax 336 76), off Pr. República. From the bus station, turn left on R. Heróis da Grande Guerra and then left onto Almirante Cândido. Slightly worn but comfortable rooms. (Singles and doubles 4000$, with bath 5000$; prices vary according to demand.) **Pensão Residential Central,** Largo Dr. José Barbosa, 22 (tel. 83 19 14; fax 84 32 82) has the same owner as Estremadura, but more upscale rooms with TVs and telephones. A good deal for those looking for a bit of the red carpet treatment. (Singles and doubles with showers 5000$, with bath 6000-7000$. Off-season discount. Breakfast included.) **Orbitur** (tel. 223 67) runs a **campground** in Parque Dom Carlos I. From the Hospital Thermal, continue on R. Camões and turn left on Av. Visconde de Sacavem, walk past the tennis courts and *voilà.* (Reception open 8am-11pm. 250$ per person, 200-400$ per tent, and 200$ per car. Hot showers free. Open Jan. 16-Nov.)

Caldas is the fruit capital of Portugal. Even if you don't want to buy any produce, visit the large and colorful **Mercado da Fruta,** where frenzied local vendors and shoppers haggle each morning in Pr. República. No-frills meals are wolfed at **Churrasqueira Zé do Barrete,** Trav. Cova da Onça, 16 (tel. 83 27 87), off the busy pedestrian shopping thoroughfare R. Almirante Cândido dos Reis. *Frango no churrasco* (barbecued chicken) is just 880$, 580$ for a ½-dose. (Open Mon.-Sat. 9am-10:30pm.) The town's sweets (*cavacas,* like Burgos' sugared egg yolks) are famed and loathed throughout the country.

■■■ NAZARÉ

Nazaré has always lived for the sea; now it fishes for tourists. In the height of summer the beach quarter explodes with foreigners, trinket vendors and overpriced restaurants line the streets, and bathers jostle each other for a tiny spot on the sand. In the meantime, the *Nazarenses* attempt to uphold their traditions: ,they still paint their long, narrow wooden boats in bright colors and preserve their unique form of dress. The male fisher, barefoot and clad in plaid pants rolled up to the knees, wears a black stocking cap chock full of tobacco, matches, hook, line, and money; women typically don seven petticoats, a thick shawl, and large gold earrings. The boats have now moved to a new harbor ten minutes from the town, however, and are pulled ashore by modern machinery rather than oxen. Visitors seeking a quaint fishing town will be sorely disappointed. Come to share the beach with the masses, and be prepared to open your wallet.

ORIENTATION AND PRACTICAL INFORMATION

Nazaré is situated on a long, populated, and windy beach. On a cliff north of town lies the **Sítio,** the old town, which preserves a sense of calm and tradition less prevalent in the crowded resort further south. To get from the bus station to the tourist office, walk toward the beach and make a right onto **Avenida República.** The office is a 10-min. walk along the beach, between the two major *praças.* The nearest **train station** (Valado), 5km away on the Lisboa-Figueira da Foz line, serves both Nazaré and Alcobaça. Regular buses shuttle between the three points (125$).

Tourist Office: Av. República (tel. 56 11 94). English-speaking staff provides maps and little else. Open 10am-10pm; Sept.-June 9:30am-12:30pm and 2-6pm.

Currency Exchange: Maré Agencia de Viagens e Turismo, LDA, Centro Comercial Maré, Store #10 (tel. 56 19 28), next to Hotel Maré on R. Mouzinho de Albuquerque, off Pr. Souza Oliveira (the next square after Pr. Arriaga from the bus station). Commission: cash 700$, traveler's checks 1350$. Open Mon.-Fri. 9am-7pm.

Post Office: Av. Independência Nacional (tel. 56 16 34). From Pr. Souza Oliveira walk up R. Mouzinho de Albuquerque, which veers to the right. The post office is 1 bl. past Pensão Central. Open for Posta Restante and **telephones** Mon.-Fri. 9am-12:30pm and 2:30-6pm. **Postal Code:** 2450. **Telephone Code:** 062.

Trains: tel. 57 73 31, in the town of Valado dos Frades on the Nazaré-Alcobaça bus line. To Lisboa (9 per day, 3hr., 820$) and Figueira da Foz (8 per day, 2hr., 550$). Change in Figueira da Foz for other destinations.

Buses: Av. Vieira Guimarães (tel. 511 72), perpendicular to Av. República. Express service to: Lisboa (8 per day, 2hr., 1050$); Coimbra (6 per day, 2hr., 1000$); Porto (7 per day, 3½hr., 1300$). Regular service to: Valdos dos Frades (11 per day, 125$); Alcobaça (15 per day, ½hr., 180$); Caldas da Rainha (9 per day, 1¼hr., 400$); Tomar (3 per day, 1½hr., 720$); Leiria (13 per day, 1¼hr., 650$) with connections to Obidos and Peniche.

Car Rental: Avis, Centro Comercial Maré, Store #10 (tel. 56 19 28), next to Hotel Maré on R. Mouzinho de Albuquerque, in Maré Agencia de Viagens. The easiest way to take in Alcobaça, Fátima, and Batalha without pitching a tent in the bus station. Summer minimum 9339$ per day, winter minimum about 5600$ per day; rates decrease the longer you rent. 7500$ deposit. Must be at least 21. Reserve at least a day in advance. Open Mon.-Fri. 9am-7pm.

Luggage Storage: In the **bus station,** 100$ per bag per day.

Laundromat: Lavanderia Nazaré, R. Branco Martins (tel. 55 27 61), off R. Trineiras, which is in turn off Av. República. Wash and dry 1200$ per 3kg load. Dry clean: shirt 500$, pants 650$. Open Mon.-Sat. 9am-7pm.

Hospital: In the Sítio district on the cliffs above the town center (tel. 56 11 40).

Emergency: tel. 115.

Police: One bl. from the bus station at corner of Av. Vieira Guimarães and R. Sub-Vila (tel. 55 12 68).

ACCOMMODATIONS AND CAMPING

By stepping off the bus, you unwittingly signal a phalanx of room-renters to stampede. Although prices (singles 2500$, doubles 4000$) are lower than at *pensões,* a "room" may be anything from a comfortable bedroom with bathroom and shared kitchen to a prison-like cell. Insist on seeing your quarters before settling the deal. Once the owners take you home, though, they consider the deal a *fait accompli.* As always, bargain, and never pay more than the lowest prices for a room in a *pensão.*

Residencial Marina, R. Mouzinho de Albuquerque, 6A (tel. 55 15 41). Modern, carpeted rooms with tidy baths. English spoken. Doubles 3500-5000$, with bath 4000-6000$. Open May-Oct.

Pensão Leonardo, Pr. Dr. Manuel de Arriaga, 25-28 (tel. 55 12 59), above Restaurante Mar Alto, on a main square parallel to beach. Cramped rooms with pale pink walls and wood furniture. Singles 3000$. Doubles 3500$, with bath 5000$.

NAZARÉ

Pensão Central, R. Mouzinho de Albuquerque, 85 (tel. 55 15 10). Adequately furnished, comfortable rooms, all with TVs. Singles with bath 5000$. Doubles 5000$, with bath 8500$. Winter discount.

Camping: Orbitur's Valado site (tel. 56 11 11), a 2km uphill climb from town. 480$ per person, 400$ per tent, 410$ per car. Hot showers 50$ in July only. Pines shade the bungalows. Bus service is sketchy, so take a taxi at night (400$). A newer and closer site, **Vale Paraíso,** Estrada Nacional, 242 (tel. 56 15 46), has swimming pools, a restaurant-bar, and a supermarket. 520$ per person, 530$ per tent, 430$ per car. 20-40% off-season discount. Open year-round.

FOOD

As long as you stick to fresh fish, you'll eat well anywhere. Pardon the platitude—the tourist restaurants along the beach are more expensive than the small places along side streets. For fresh fruit and vegetables, shop at the large **market** across from the bus station. (Open 8am-1pm; winter Tues.-Sun. 8am-1pm.) Small supermarkets line R. Sub-Vila, which is parallel to Av. República. Some are open 24hrs.

A Casinha da Graça, Av. Vieira Guimarães, 30L (tel. 55 22 11), across the street from the bus station. Fresh flowers atop every checkerboard picnic table. Delicious *caldeirada* (fish stew, 900$). Entrees 700-1200$. Open 11am-11pm.

Forno d'Orca, Largo Caldeiras, 11 (tel. 55 18 14). From Pr. Souza Oliveira, follow Trav. Elevador toward the funicular. The outdoor patio is in the small square immediately on your right. A good beach-quarter restaurant. A whale of a helping of *lulas à Sevilhana* (squid) 750$, or *ameijos ao natural* (clams) 750-1300$. About 1000-1500$ per person for a full meal. Open 11am-2am.

Meu Jardin, R. Gil Vicente, 67B (tel. 56 17 84), a street perpendicular to Av. República. Placid peach walls adorned with hanging plants and slick art. Typical meat and fresh fish dishes, but also a wide variety of filling thin-crust pizzas (650-950$) and salads. Entrees 850-1150$. English spoken. Open March-Oct. noon-3:30pm and 6:30-11pm.

Casa Santos, R. Occidental, 19A, a narrow street perpendicular to Av. Vieira Guimarães, 1 bl. toward the water from the bus station. Sardines and salad (550$) served in a small, narrow, family-run restaurant. *Sopa de peixe* (fish soup, 135$). Open noon-midnight.

O Frango Assado (a.k.a Casa dos Frangos), Pr. Dr. Manuel de Arriaga, 20 (tel. 55 18 42). A small food bar mainly for take-out. Heavenly barbecued chicken *piri-piri* (1100$ per kg—to go only). Even though they cut the chicken, you'll still have to rip, peel, and gnaw like a beast. Open 9am-1pm and 3-8pm.

SIGHTS AND ENTERTAINMENT

The demented, stairway-shaped funicular (every 15min. until 1am, 60$) climbs from R. Elevador off Av. República to the less refined quarter of the **Sítio,** whose uneven cobbled streets and weathered buildings were all there was of Nazaré before the tourists arrived. The striking facade of **Igreja de Nossa Senhora da Nazaré** fronts a large square, site of the annual festival dedicated to Nazaré's patron saint (second week in Sept.). An elegant coffered dome shelters the interior, which is carved with grapevines. The motif is repeated on the twisted columns of the high altar.

On a side street leading off the *praça* to your right facing the church, the mini **Museu Etnografico e Arqueológico do Dr. Joaquim Manso** displays miniature fishing boats, massive nets, and other fishing paraphernalia. (Tel. 56 12 46; open 10am-12:30pm and 2-5pm; Oct.-May Tues.-Sun. 9:30am-12:30pm and 2-5pm. Admission 150$; students, seniors, and Sun. free.)

The tiny, whitewashed **Ermida da Memória** stands in a corner of the square diagonally across from the church. Dom Fuas Roupinho built the chapel out of gratitude to Our Lady of Nazaré, who chanced upon him as he was falling off a cliff while hunting a deer—and saved him. 120 meters above the sea is a breathtaking aerie from which to view the lower town's orange-tiled roofs, the town profile, and the coastline.

ALCOBAÇA

Around 7:30pm, fishing boats return to the **port** at the southern end of the Praica quarter; head over to the shore front market and witness the local restaurateurs' spirited bidding for the tastiest catches of the day.

Back in the tourist quarter, Av. República, the cluttered **beach-side promenade,** fills with cars, tour buses, local vendors, and those elbowing their way to the beach. Stay in the populated area if you're swimming, as sewage collects on the water surface elsewhere. **Cafés** in Pr. Souza Oliveira bustle with *bica*-sippers until 1am. You might want to graduate to **Discoteca Jeans Rouge** (Sat. only, opens at 11:30pm), up the street from the *praça,* and dance away the early morning. For lively Brazilian and Portuguese tunes, imbibe with the locals at **Bar "a Ilha,"** on R. Mouzinho Albuquerque. (Open 7pm-about 3am.) Every Thursday and Friday in July at 10pm, a local group performs **traditional dances** called *viras* at the Casino, a festival hall, on R. Rui Rosa. (Admission 500$.) Every Friday night, **Hotel Maré** (tel. 56 12 26), 2 bl. up Pr. Souza Oliveira where R. Mouzinho de Albuquerque begins, hosts a Portuguese folklore jam session including dinner, music, and *viras* (8:30pm, 2500$). Bulls fight at the **Praça de Touros** (bullring) in the Sítio every other Saturday or Sunday in early summer and every Saturday from mid-July to mid-September. Tickets (from 1300$) go on sale at the kiosk in Pr. Souza Oliveira.

■■■ ALCOBAÇA

Unlike Nazaré, Alcobaça is a peaceful little town built on rolling hills away from the sea and its devotees. Dom Afonso Henriques donated the land in 1178 for the great limestone Cistercian Mosteiro de Santa Maria, one of the finest sights in Portugal, as an offering of thanks for the recapture of Santarém from the Moors.

ORIENTATION AND PRACTICAL INFORMATION

To reach the tourist office from the **bus station,** turn left from the station exit, walk down the slope, then turn left again. Follow R. Dr. Brilhante across the bridge to Pr. República. Through the portal, the sight of the monastery towers will guide you to **Praça 25 Abril,** the square in front of the monastery.

Tourist Office: Pr. 25 Abril (tel. 423 77), opposite the monastery steps. Helpful, multilingual staff distributes maps and keeps a list of accommodations. Open 9am-7pm; Oct.-May 10am-1pm and 3-6pm.

Post Office: Pr. 25 Abril (tel. 59 74 35), on an adjacent corner. Posta Restante and **telephones.** Open Mon.-Fri. 8:30am-6pm. **Postal Code:** 2460.

Telephone Code: 062.

Trains: 5km north in Valado dos Frades, halfway between Nazaré and Alcobaça (tel. 57 73 31). Frequent buses make the jaunt (14 per day, 125$).

Buses: Av. Manuel da Silva Carolino (tel. 422 21) a 5-min. walk from the center of the old town. Buses to: Nazaré (14 per day, ½hr., 180$); Batalha (6 per day, ¾hr., 330$); Leiria (5 per day, 1hr., 450$); Lisboa (3 *expressos* per day, 2½hr., 950$).

Luggage Storage: at the **bus station** (100$ per bag per day).

Hospital: R. Afonso de Albuquerque (tel. 59 74 16).

Emergency: tel. 115.

Police: R. Olivença (tel. 433 88).

ACCOMMODATIONS AND FOOD

Consult the tourist office for budget accommodations. For inexpensive dining, try the hearty, self-serve restaurants across from the bus station. The **market,** just across the small park north of the bus station, reputedly sells the freshest fruit in Portugal (measured in time from tree to market). (Open Tues.-Fri. 9am-1pm.) Monday and Saturday are the town's big market days (8am-4pm).

Pensão Mosteiro, Av. João de Deus, 1 (tel. 421 83), just up from the tourist office, has bright, simple rooms. Upstairs from two restaurants. Singles 3000$, with bath 5000$. Doubles 5000$. Breakfast included.

Pensão Alcoa, R. Araújo Guimarães, 3 (tel. 427 27), by Pr. República. Modest accommodations between dark wood floors and ceilings. The murmuring Rio Alcoa behind the building lulls guests to sleep. Singles 700$. Doubles 1400$.

Camping: A **municipal campground** (tel. 422 65) spreads near a stand of trees behind the market, about 15-min. walk from bus station. The site is woefully sandy and barren. 230$ per person, 750$ per tent, 220$ per car. Showers 60$.

Celerios dos Frades, Arco de Cister, 2 (tel. 422 81), under an arch in Pr. Don Afonso Henriques. Stylish restaurant and a cool *cervejaria-café* all in one. Stone vaulted ceilings and columns are much like the neighboring monastery. Regional chicken dish, *frango no púcara,* is the house specialty. Entrees 800-1200$. Open Fri.-Wed. 10am-2am.

SIGHTS

Behind the **Mosteiro de Santa Maria's** handsome Baroque facade, only the main doorway and rose window remain from the original Gothic structure. Inside, the 350-ft. long and 70-ft. high nave—the largest in Portugal—dozes in elegantly diffuse light. In the transept are the two jewels of the church: the 14th-century **sarcophagi** of Inês de Castro and Dom Pedro I. While Pedro was prince, he fell in love with Inês, the daughter of a Spanish nobleman. Pedro's father, Afonso IV, forbade their marriage to keep Spanish influence away from the Portuguese throne. Nonetheless, Pedro and Inês were secretly wed in Bragança. To stifle the politically dangerous romance, Afonso IV had Inês put to death. Upon attaining the crown, Pedro personally ripped out the hearts of those who had slit Inês' throat and ate them (hence his nickname, "the Cruel"). Then, in a ghoulish ceremony, he had her body exhumed, meticulously dressed in royal robes, and brought to court, where he plopped her on a throne and made her his queen. She was reinterred in an exquisitely carved tomb in the king's favorite monastery. The king had his own tomb placed opposite hers so that they could reunite face to face at the moment of resurrection. Their tombs are inscribed with *"Até ao Fim do Mundo"* (Until the End of the World). How romantic.

A doorway on the north side of the church leads to the **claustro.** The central courtyard is the *claustro do silêncio,* where monks ate in silence. A six-ton marble table hulks at the center of the room; at its feet flows a branch of the Rio Alcoa, amazingly routed into the kitchen floor.

Enormous terra-cotta statues painted by monks in the 17th and 18th centuries fill the **sala do capítulo** (Room of the Chapter) next door. The last of the chambers is the **sala dos reis** (Room of the Kings), whose 17th-century *azulejos* depict the founding of the convent. Larger than life statues of the kings of Portugal, sculpted by more of these artistic monks, look down from an upper ledge. To get to the monastery from the bus station turn right, then right again, cross the river and pass through tree-lined streets with many restaurants. (Monastery open 9am-7pm. Admission 400$; Oct.-March 200$. Students, teachers, and seniors free.)

The **Museu Nacional do Vinho** (tel. 422 22), Portugal's only museum devoted to the history and production of wine, lies about 1km outside of town on the road to Batalha. Tours wind through the musty, warehouse-like museum and gape at giant 1000-liter storage jars. Unfortunately, the museum skips the paramount stage of the wine cycle: imbibing. At the end you can, however, purchase a bottle or two (from 300$). (Tours in Portuguese only. Open Mon.-Fri. 9am-12:30pm and 2-5:30pm. Free.)

The Three Beiras

Encompassing the regions that stretch from just beneath Porto in the north down to Coimbra, and from the Spanish boundary in the east to the Atlantic Ocean, the three Beiras endure the most extreme weather in Portugal. The **Beira Litoral** includes the long, unspoiled Western coastline, called the Costa da Prata ("Silver Coast"), stretching from the resort town of Figueira de Foz upwards through the up-and-coming resort of Aveiro, and all the way to Porto. Coimbra, a bustling university town overlooking the celebrated Rio Mondego—made famous in Portuguese poetry as the Rio das Musas ("River of the Muses")—dominates the region.

In contrast to the progressive, development-minded towns of the Beira Litoral, the **Beira Alta** ("high edge") and **Beira Baixa** ("low edge"), mountainous regions to the east, remain among the least developed areas in Portugal. Just about the only regions in Portugal that shiver under snowfall, these desolate and poor provinces have always been more traditional than most of the country. Recently an agricultural boom has transformed the region into a quirky center of upward mobility.

The transportation system remains downright archaic. Train connections are few and far between, the trains themselves ancient and wheezing (some pull passenger cars that date from the '30s). Except for the route between Figueira da Foz and Coimbra, buses are quicker and more reliable, though more expensive.

Beautiful forests and small hamlets refresh these tourist-free valleys. Farmers terrace the mountainsides for grape cultivation and fill the horizon with the silvery sheen of olive trees.

■■■ COIMBRA

In spite of its reputation as Portugal's quintessential university town, Coimbra is known more for its conservativeness than for its liberal bent. Capital of Portugal from 1139-1290, Coimbra developed into the country's premier center of learning and founded a university in 1290. After ping-ponging between here and Lisboa, the university was established permanently in Coimbra in 1537, and remained the country's only one until the beginning of the 20th century. Toward the end of the 16th century, Coimbra gained attention as a center of the Inquisition. Centuries later, Salazar (Portugal's longtime Fascist dictator) attended the university as a poor scholarship student and earned one of the highest GPAs in its history. Coimbra's self-assured international elegance militates against its urban woes of grime, filth, and noise. The old town—an amalgamation of medieval churches and monumental Fascist architecture—presides over the rest of the city.

ORIENTATION AND PRACTICAL INFORMATION

The steep streets of Coimbra rise in tiers above the Rio Mondego. Coimbra's center, a tangle of narrow streets, is roughly split into two areas. The lower town lies between the triangle formed by the river, **Largo da Portagem,** and **Praça 8 de Maio.** The upper town spreads on the adjoining hill, accessible through the **Arco de Almedina.** Coimbra has two train stations: Coimbra-A, near the town center by the bridge, and Coimbra-B, 3km northwest of the center. Resign yourself to getting lost at least twice.

Tourist Office: Largo Portagem (tel. 238 86), an olive-green building 2 bl. east of Coimbra-A off Av. Emídio Navarro. Turismo headquarters for central Portugal. Good maps. Accommodation and daytrip info. English and French spoken. Open Mon.-Fri. 9am-7pm, Sat.-Sun. 9am-12:30pm and 2-5:30pm; Oct.-April Mon.-Fri. 9am-6pm, Sat.-Sun. 9am-12:30pm and 2-5:30pm. **Branch office:** Pr. Don Dinis (tel. 325 91), just up the large flight of steps as you enter the university. Postcards and info galore. Same hours as central office. Also a fledgling **branch** (tel. 332 02) located in Pr. República. Open Mon.-Fri. 10am-1pm and 2:30-6pm.

Currency Exchange: Hotel Astória, across *largo* from Turismo. 800$ charge per transaction. Open 24hrs. Bank rates are better for transactions less than 10,000$; try **Montepio Geral,** C. Estrela, around and up from Turismo. 1000$ charge per transaction above 10,000$; otherwise no charge. Open Mon.-Fri. 8:30am-3pm.

Post Office: R. Olímpio Nicolau Rui Fernandes (tel. 243 56), just past the Manga rotunda. **Central office** is in the pink powder puff on Av. Fernão de Magalhães. Both open Mon.-Fri. 8:30am-6:30pm, Sat. 9am-12:30pm, the former for Posta Restante. Several branch offices at Pr. República for basic services. Open Mon.-Fri. 9am-12:30pm and 2:30-6:30pm. **Postal Code:** 3000.

Telephones: In post offices. **Telephone Code:** 039.

Trains: Estação Coimbra-A, Largo das Ameias (tel. 349 98). From the front entrance follow Av. Emídio Navarro along the river all the way to Turismo. **Estação Coimbra-B** (tel. 341 27). Trains from cities outside the region stop only in Coimbra-B, while regional trains stop at both stations. Frequent shuttles connect the two (5min., 100$). To: Aveiro (14 per day, 40min., 420$); Figueira da Foz (1 per hr., 1hr., 255$); Viseu (5 per day, 2½hr., 640$); Porto (14 per day, 3hr., 800$); Lisboa (14 per day, 3hr., 1145$); Paris (1 per day, 22hr., 18,640$).

Buses: Av. Fernão Magalhães (tel. 270 81). To reach the tourist office, turn right from the station and follow the avenue to Coimbra-A and then Largo da Portagem (15min.). To: Lisboa (16 per day, 3hr., 1150$); Porto (5 per day, 6hr., 1000$); Evora (5 per day, 6hr., 1400$); Faro (4 per day, 12hr., 2400$).

Public Transportation: Buses and street cars. Fares: 175$ (single ticket bought on board); 515$ (book of 10). Special tourist passes also available. Ticket books and passes sold in kiosks at Largo da Portagem and Pr. República, among other places. Main lines are #1 (Portagem-Universidade-Estádio); #2 (Pr. República-Fornos); #3 (Portagem-Pr. República-Santo António dos Olivais); #5 (Portagem-Pr. República-São José); #7T (Palácio da Justiça-Estádio-Tovim); #29 (Portagem-near Pousada de Juventude-Hospital); #46 (Cruz de Celas-Pr. da República-Portagem-Santa Clara).

Taxis: Táxis de Coimbra (tel. 48 40 45). Many loiter outside Coimbra-A.

Car Rental: Avis (tel. 347 86). In Coimbra-A, right outside the platform door. Cars start at 4800$ per day, plus 48$ per km, 2100$ for insurance, and 17% tax. Open Mon.-Fri. 8:30am-12:30pm and 2:30-7pm.

Bookstore: Many good ones line R. Ferreira Borges. **Livraria Bertrand,** Largo da Portagem, 9 (tel. 230 14), 1 bl. from Turismo. Good selection of English and French classics. Soft rock music in the background. Open Mon.-Fri. 9am-7pm.

Swimming Pool: Piscina Municipal (tel. 71 29 95). Take bus #5 São José or #1 Estádio from Largo Portagem outside the tourist office. Terrific but often packed 3-pool complex near the stadium. Open 10am-1pm and 2-7pm; June and Sept. Mon.-Sat. 10am-1pm and 2-7pm, Sun. 2-7pm; Oct.-May Mon.-Sat. 12:30-3pm. Admission 150$, under 6 or over 60 free.

Hospital: Hospital da Universidade de Coimbra (tel. 40 04 00). Near the Cruz de Celas stop on lines #3, 7, 7T, and 29.

Emergency: tel. 115.

Police: R. Olímpio Nicolau Rui Fernandes (tel. 220 22), facing the market and post office.

ACCOMMODATIONS AND CAMPING

Notoriously seedy *pensões* line **Rua da Sota** and surrounding streets across from Coimbra-A. Anything decent starts at 3500$ for doubles; pay less and pay the consequences. Fortunately, an excellent HI youth hostel has flung open its doors.

Pousada de Juventude (HI), R. António Henriques Seco, 14 (tel. 229 55). From either Coimbra-A or Largo Portagem, take bus #7, 8, 29, or 46, then walk from Pr. República up R. Lourenço A. Azevedo, left of the Santa Cruz park, and take the second right. If you ask nicely, the bus driver will probably bring you closer and direct you. Great neighborhood. Enormous sunlit rooms (84 beds), large patio, TV room with VCR, bar, kitchen, and gray parrot (Jacó). Reception open 9am-noon and 6pm-midnight. Bag drop-off all day. Curfew midnight. Lockout noon-6pm. 1300$ per person. Doubles 3000$, with bath 3500$. Breakfast included.

Pensão Rivoli, Pr. Comércio, 27 (tel. 255 50), in a mercifully quiet pedestrian plaza off busy R. Ferreira Borges. Neat, well-furnished rooms. Lockout 1am, but you can borrow a key. Singles 2000$. Doubles 4000$.

Residencial Internacional de Coimbra, Av. Emídio Navarro, 4 (tel. 255 03), in front of Coimbra-A. Fluorescent lighting and lumpy pillows may annoy, but rooms are decent-sized and pleasant. Choice of river view or full-sized bathroom. Singles and doubles 3200$. Doubles with bath 4500$. Winter: 2500$; 4000$.

Residência Lusa Atenas (Residencial Eurolusatenas), Av. Fernão de Magalhães, 68 (tel. 264 12), on the main avenue between Coimbra-A and the bus station, 3 bl. north of the former and 10min. south of the latter. Rooms with full bath are comfortable; rooms with showers are somewhat cramped. Beware of pungent mildew. Singles 2500$, with bath 3500$. Doubles 4500$, with bath 5000$. Triples 6000$, with bath 6500$. Breakfast included.

Pensão Aviz, Av. Fernão Magalhães, 64 (tel. 237 18), next to Lusa Atenas. Well-worn rooms are a reasonable budget fall-back. Tiny private baths are more appealing than their common counterparts. Singles 1800-3500$. Doubles 3500-4250$. Triples 4000-5000$.

Camping: Municipal Campground (tel. 70 14 97), corralled in recreation complex with stadium and swimming pool, ringed by noisy avenues. The entrance is at the arch off Pr. 25 de Abril; take same buses as for the pool. Small market open only in summer. Reception 9am-10pm; Oct.-March 9am-6pm. 220$ per person, 165-320$ per tent, 280$ per car. 5% IVA not included. Showers free.

FOOD

Scout out **Rua Direita,** running west off Pr. 8 de Maio; side streets to the west of Pr. Comércio and Largo da Portagem; and the university district around **Praça da República.** University *cantinas* (cafeterias)—at several locations, including one in the old college courtyard—serve students with ID or student-posers without for a mere 250$. (Posing is easy in late June through July when the university hosts foreign programs.) Beware of long lines and bargains in dark neighborhoods where no one should walk alone at night.

Restaurante Esplendoroso, R. da Sota, 29 (tel. 357 11), across from Coimbra-A, up R. da Sota. Excellent Chinese food, prompt service, and a relaxing atmosphere. After dinner, indulge in a flaming *gelado frita con rum* (fried ice cream in rum, 390$). Your tummy will thank you for it. Open daily noon-3pm and 7-11pm.

Churrasqueria do Mondego, R. Sargento Mór, 25 (tel. 233 55), off R. Sota, 1 bl. west of Largo Portagem. Frequented by truck drivers, students, and tourists. Unceremonious service, all at the counter. Their *frango no churrasco* (barbecued ½-chicken, 330$) leaves Colonel Sanders on the other side of the road—watch them cook it over the huge flaming grill. The plucky ask for a brushing of *piri-piri* sauce (it's *hot*). *Menú* 630$. Open noon-3pm and 6-10:30pm.

Café Santa Cruz, Pr. 8 de Maio (tel. 336 17), in what used to be part of the cathedral (still has vaulted ceiling and stained-glass windows). The most famous café in Coimbra. Filled with professors and students. Coffee 60$. Open 7am-2am.

Restaurante Adega Funchal, R. Azeiteiras, 18 (tel. 241 37), on a tiny side street off Pr. Comércio. A notch up from the others; unimpressive decor, but a good variety of well-cooked Portuguese fare, such as *chanfana carne de cabra regional* (goat broiled in red wine, 1000$). Entrees 850-1600$. ½-portions available. Open Sun.-Fri. 7am-2am.

Casino da Urca, R. Baixo (tel. 81 30 59), a teeny square in front of the old Santa Clara convent. Low beamed ceiling and antique farm implements. Rustic scenes painted on the walls. *Espetada da casa* (house kebab, 820$) is mighty savory. Variety of entrees 650-1100$. Open noon-3pm and 7pm-midnight.

Restaurante Democrática, Trav. Rua Nova, 5-7 (tel. 237 84), on a tiny lane off R. Sofia (1st full left after city hall). Quite popular. Strands of garlic dangle overhead. For something different try *espetadas de porco á Africana* (pork kebabs African-style, 890$). Entrees 690-1200$. Open Mon.-Sat. noon-3pm and 7-10pm.

C O I M B R A

SIGHTS

To reach the old center of town, pass through the **Arco de Almedina,** the remnant of a Muslim town wall, next to the Banco Pinto e Sotto Mayor on R. Ferreira Borges. The gate leads to a stepped street named R. Quebra-Costas (Back-Breaker Street). Up a narrow stone stairway looms the hulking 12th-century Romanesque **Sé Velha** (Old Cathedral). Around noon a guide leads visitors interminably around the principal tombs and friezes as Gregorian chants are heard in the background. (Open 9:30am-12:30pm and 2-5:30pm. Admission to cloisters 40$.)

From Pr. Sé Velha, R. Borges Carneiro (behind the cathedral) leads to the **Museu Machado de Castro** (tel. 237 27), famous for its Gothic and Renaissance sculptures. Creepy lighting illuminates ancient sculptures in the underground passageways of the old Roman forum. (Open Tues.-Sun. 10am-5pm. Admission to church only 200$, full museum $500; seniors and Sun. morning free.)

The **Sé Nova** (New Cathedral), across from the museum in Largo da Feira, was built for the Jesuits in the late 16th century by a succession of builders, each of whom tried to outdo the last with elaborateness. The interior, by contrast, is austere. (Open 9am-12:30pm and 2-5pm. Free.)

R. São Pedro paves the way to the **Porta Férrea** (Iron Gate) entrance to the old courtyard of the **universidade.** Now the Law School, these buildings housed Portugal's royal palace when Coimbra was the capital. The staircase at the right leads up to the **Sala dos Capelos,** where portraits of Portugal's kings (six of whom were born in Coimbra) hang below a beautifully decorated 17th-century ceiling. (Open 9am-noon and 2-6pm.) Past the Baroque clock tower are the **capela da universidade** (university chapel) and the 18th-century **biblioteca da universidade** (university library). Press the buzzer to the left of the door to enter three lofty halls with 143,000 books. (Open 9am-12:30pm and 2-5pm. Admission 250$, students and professors free.) From the university, walk downhill alongside the **Aqueducto de São Sebastião** to the **Jardim Botânico's** sculpture and fountains.

The **Mosteiro de Santa Cruz** (Monastery of the Holy Cross) on Pr. 8 de Maio, at the far end of R. Ferreira Borges in the lower city, is a 12th-century monastery with all the usual fixins: a splendid barrel-vaulted **sacristía** (sacristy), ornate **tumulos reals** (where the first two kings of Portugal lie buried), and a 16th-century **claustro.** (Open 9am-noon and 2-6pm. Admission to sacristy, tombs, and cloister 150$.)

In the 14th century, holy Queen Isabel ordered the construction of the great **Convento de Santa Clara-a-Velha,** smack on top of a swamp. The convent sinks a little deeper each year; today it's more than half underground. As soon as the citizens of Coimbra realized what was going down, they rushed to build as a replacement the **Convento de Santa Clara-a-Nova** (1649-1677), where the queen's 14th-century Gothic tomb and a new silver one now rest. (Both convents open 9am-12:30pm and 2-5:30pm.)

Just past Santa Clara-a-Velha, a toy castle gateway leads to **Portugal dos Pequenitos,** a nationalistic little park. Models reproduce Portugal's most famous historical monuments; a miniature house characterizes each region of the country; and a mini-museum is devoted to each former Portuguese colony. (Open 9am-7pm. Admission 350$, children under 10 100$.)

ENTERTAINMENT

Caffeine-happy crowds congregate in outdoor cafés along Pr. da República. To hear the most unrestrained and heartfelt *fado* singers, go after dinner to **Diligência Bar,** R. Nova, 30 (tel. 276 67), off R. Sofia. (*Fado* singing around 10pm-2am.) You may find free-form *fado* in the wee hours at **Bar 1910,** above a gymnasium on R. Simões Castro. (Open until 4am. Beer about 200$.)

Hot **Via Latina** disco, R. Almeida Garret, 1 (tel. 321 98), near the Santa Cruz garden, attracts a young crowd. Hotter **Scotch** (tel. 81 31 36), titters across the river near Convento Santa Clara-a-Nova. Both peak between midnight and 2am. (Sometimes cover charge. Beers about 300$, mixed drinks about 500$.)

Students rampage through the streets during Coimbra's famous week-long festival, the **Queima das Fitas** (Burning of the Ribbons) in the first or second week of May. The festivities begin when graduating students burn the narrow ribbons they received as first-years and receive wide, ornamental ones in return. The continuing carousing features midnight *serenatas* (groups of black-clad serenading youth), wandering musical ensembles, parades, concerts, and folk dancing. Another good time to come to Coimbra is during the **Festas da Rainha Santa,** held the first week of July in even-numbered years, when live choral music echoes through the festooned streets. The **Feira Popular** in the 2nd week of July sports carnival-type rides and games across the river from Turismo and traditional Portuguese dancing exhibitions in Pr. Comércio.

■ NEAR COIMBRA

CONÍMBRIGA

10km south of Coimbra, Conímbriga boasts the largest Roman settlement yet to be excavated in Portugal. Exciting ongoing excavations reveal more of the site each year. Outside the 4th-century town wall, a luxurious villa on the right, several smaller shops and houses, and the baths (complete with sauna and furnace room) on the far left are easily discernible. Some of the mosaics are remarkably elaborate and well preserved; most of the ruins are not. (Ruins open 9am-1pm and 2-8pm; winter 9am-1pm and 2-6pm. Admission Tues.-Sun. includes museum 300$; Mon. ruins only 150$; Sun. morning free.) The nearby **Museu Monográfico de Conímbriga** displays artifacts unearthed in the area. (Museum open Tues.-Sun. 10am-1pm and 2-6pm. Admission Tues.-Sun. includes ruins 300$; Sun. morning free.)

No **buses** run direct to Conímbriga from Coimbra. Rodoviária has the most frequent service (Mon.-Fri. every hr., Sat.-Sun. 3 per day, ½hr., 190$) from Coimbra to **Condeixa,** a town 2km from the ruins. Condeixa is a stop en route to Leiria or Figueira da Foz. The last bus returns to Coimbra at 7:55pm. Since the bus stop in Condeixa is near the highway, some people hitch back to Coimbra, which, as you know, *Let's Go* does not recommend.

BUÇACO FOREST

Portugal's most revered forest has for centuries drawn wanderers in search of a pristine escape from the city. In the 6th century, Benedictine monks settled in the Buçaco Forest, established a monastery, and remained in control until the 1834 abolition of all religious orders. The forest owes its fame, however, to the Carmelite monks who arrived nearly 400 years ago. Selecting the forest for their *desertos* (isolated dwellings for penitence), the Carmelites gradually planted trees and plants from around the world. Today, several hundred species of trees blend together in a botanical fantasy.

Dom Manuel II built the exuberant **Palaçio de Buçaco** that adjoins the old Carmelite **convent** in a flamboyant display of neo-Manueline architecture. The overwrought excess of the palace, now a luxury hotel, is the perfect stone counterpart to the forest's natural abundance. The *azulejos* that adorn the outer walls depict scenes from *Os Lusíadas,* the great Portuguese epic about the Age of Discovery.

The hotel/palace has maps of the forest. Landmarks are the **Fonte Fria** (Cold Fountain), whose waters ripple down entrance steps, the **Vale dos Fetos** (Fern Valley) below, and the **Porta de Reina** (Queen's Gate). The most robust walkers trek one hour along the Via Sacra to a sweeping panorama of the countryside from the **Cruz Alta** viewpoint. The little 17th-century chapels represent stations of the cross.

Bus service from Coimbra to Buçaco continues to Viseu (5 per day, Sat.-Sun. 3 per day, 1hr., 375$) beginning at 7:45am (Sat.-Sun. 9am). Buses leave from Buçaco's station on Av. Fernão de Magalhães, a 15-min. walk from downtown (last bus back to Coimbra leaves Buçaco at 6pm (Sat.-Sun. 5pm).

LUSO

A 4km walk downhill from Buçaco leads to Luso, site of the **Fonte de São João,** the source of all that bottled water you've been drinking while in Portugal (be sure to get directions or a map from the hotel/palace in Buçaco before leaving). A scintillating cold **spring** spouts water for free public consumption. An Olympic-size **swimming pool** lies behind the Grande Hotel das Termas, across from the tourist office. (Admission Mon.-Fri. 750$, Sat.-Sun. 1000$.) The **Balneários Spa** offers massages and thermal baths; service is targeted mainly at those in need of therapeutic treatment. Sauna and bath 1200$, general massage 1500$. (Open 8am-noon and 4-7pm.) Luso's **tourist office** (tel. (031) 93 91 33), on R. Emídio Navarro in the center of town, stocks a list of *pensões* and a map of the area. (Open Mon.-Fri. 9:30am-1pm and 2-6:30pm, Sat.-Sun. 10am-12:30pm and 2:30-5pm.) **Buses** back to Coimbra stop on the same street, a couple bl. above the tourist office and across from the natural springs (Mon.-Fri. 5 per day, Sat.-Sun. 3 per day; last bus back at 6:55pm).

■■■ LEIRIA

Capital of the surrounding district and an important transportation center, Leiria (pop. 103,000) is an agreeable suburban town spread out in a fertile valley 22km from the coast. Leiria's proximity to the seashore and the historic towns of Batalha, Fátima, and Alcobaça make it an excellent base—buses from Leiria run frequently enough to satisfy both culture vultures and beach leeches.

The city's oldest and most magnificent historic pile is the **castelo,** a granite fortification built by Dom Afonso Henriques (the first king) after he snatched the city from the Muslims. The castle teeters dramatically atop the crest of a volcanic hill overlooking the northern edge of town. Left to ruin for hundreds of years, now only the **torre de menagem** (homage tower) and the **sala dos namorados** (lovers' hall) remain. The main attractions are the terrace with a panoramic view of town and the Rio Lis, and the roofless shell of the 14th-century **Igreja da Nossa Senhora da Penha.** (Castle open 9am-6:30pm. Admission 120$.) Down a winding road from the castle (off Largo Cónego Maia, two bl. away and visible from the bus station), the medieval **sé** is simple but elegant—restful for eyes tired by Manueline excesses.

The **Santuário de Nossa Senhora de Encarnação** sits upon a wooded hill on the southern edge of town. Outside, the sanctuary looks fairly ordinary, but inside colorful murals painted above the choir illustrate three local miracles attributed to Mary. To get in, try the unbolted door on the southern wall; the church seems to have no official hours.

Practical Information The **tourist office** (tel. 81 47 48) is across the Jardim Camões in the modern building that looks out on the fountain. Maps and schedules for buses to the beaches of Vieira and Pedrógão. English-speaking staff allows backpackers to store packs temporarily in the spacious office. (Open Mon.-Fri. 9am-7pm, Sat.-Sun. 10am-1pm and 3-7pm; Oct.-April Mon.-Fri. 9am-6pm, Sat.-Sun. 10am-1pm and 3-6pm.) The **post office** (tel. 323 55) is on Av. Combatentes da Grande Guerra, three bl. from the youth hostel. (Open Mon.-Fri. 8:30am-6:30pm, Sat. 9am-12:30pm.) The **postal code** is 2400 and the **telephone code** 044. For medical assistance, call the **hospital** (tel. 81 22 55), on R. Tomar. **Police** (tel. 81 24 47) have a little nook on Largo São Pedro, just below the entrance to the castle.

Buses (tel. 81 15 07) leave from just off Pr. Paulo VI in the new part of town. To: Batalha (6 per day, 15min., 165$); Fátima (5 per day, ½hr., 330$, also 6 *expressos* per day, 500$); Nazaré (5 *expressos* per day, 45min., 650$); Coimbra (7 per day, 1hr., 730$); Lisboa (4 *expressos* per day, 2hr., 1100$); Porto (10 per day, 3½hr., 1200$). Leiria is on the Lisboa-Figueira da Foz **train** line (tel. 88 20 27). To Lisboa (4 per day, 3½hr., 915$) and Figueira (9 per day, 1¼hr., 335$). The train station is 3km outside town in a dismal suburb. Buses for the station leave across the street from Turismo (approximately every hr. 7:15am-11:45pm, every 20min. summer weekdays, 10min., 90$). **24-hr. taxis** (tel. 88 11 47) zip from the bus station to the train station for 450$. They congregate near the bus station.

Accommodations and Food The clean and *confortável* **Pousada de Juventude (HI),** Largo Cândido dos Reis, 7D (tel. 318 68), offers members the cheapest beds in town. Kitchen and laundry facilities available. From the bus station walk to the cathedral. Then exit Largo da Sé (next to Largo Cónego Maia) on R. Barão de Viamonte, a narrow street lined with shops. Largo Cândido dos Reis is about 6 bl. away on the right. (Reception open 9-11am and 6pm-midnight. Lockout noon-6pm, but flexible. 1300$ per person; Oct.-April 1100$.) **Residencial Dom Dinis,** Travessa de Tomar, 2 (tel. 81 53 42), has comfortable, modern rooms with baths, telephones, and satellite TV (MTV!!). Hot water short-lived. Exiting Turismo, make a left and cross the bridge over Rio Lis. Walk up 2 bl., the *travessa* is on the left. (Singles 2800-3000$. Doubles 4500-5000$. Triples 5000$. Breakfast included.) **Pensão Residencial Leirense,** R. Afonso de Albuquerque, 6 (tel. 320 61; fax 320 81), 2 bl. to the right of the *praça,* offers pleasant rooms with unusually narrow beds, full baths, telephones, and your favorite—A/C. (Singles 3500$. Doubles 5500$.) For fruit and vegetables, shop at the **market** (Tues. and Sat. 9am-1pm) in Largo da Feira opposite the gymnasium, located on the far side of the castle from the bus station. **Restaurante O Aquário,** R. Cap. Mouzinho de Albuquerque, 17 (tel. 247 20), is on the main street into town, 2 bl. from the bus station. Affordable prices don't reflect superior quality of the delicious regional specialties. Try their *arroz valenciana* (rice with seafood and other meats, 1200$). Entrees 800-1300$. (Open Fri.-Wed. noon-3:30pm and 7-10pm.) **Restaurante Min Yuan,** R. Sacadura Cabral, 14, off R. Barão de Viamonte, is authentically Chinese. Popular with locals and tourists. Entrees 700-1400$, but the "little things" like appetizers and tea add a hefty sum. (Open noon-3pm and 7-11pm.) **Café-Restaurante Casa Nova,** R. Barão de Viamonte, 53 (tel. 252 63), serves up hulking portions. From the bus station, follow directions for the youth hostel to reach this street. Delicious Portuguese standards such as *bife á cortador* (grilled steak, 1000$) and *bacalhau* (cod, 850$) come with heaps of rice, salad, and fries. Entrees 750-1300$. (Open Sun.-Fri. noon-3pm and 7-10:30pm.)

■■■ BATALHA

A town of 14,000, Batalha is another name for the **Mosteiro de Santa Maria da Vitória,** which rises from the fertile Vale de Lena. Massive and elaborate in gold-hued stone, the *mosteiro* was built by Dom João I in 1385 to commemorate his victory against the Spanish. The complex of cloisters and chapels remains one of Portugal's greatest national monuments.

The church **facade** soars upward in a high but heavy Gothic and Manueline style, opulently decorated right up to the dozens of bell-like spires. Napoleon's uncouth troops used the stained glass windows for target practice and turned the nave into a latrine and a brothel. The **Capela do Fundador,** immediately to the right of the church's entrance, shelters the elaborate sarcophagi of Dom João I and his English-born queen, Philippa of Lancaster. Life-size marble effigies lie on top, their heads resting under intricately carved Gothic *baldechins* (canopies). Above looms a star-shaped vaulted ceiling. In the recesses of the chapel's south side are the tombs of their children, notably that of the Infante Dom Henrique—Henry the Navigator.

The rest of the monastery complex is accessible via a door in the north wall of the church. Dense Manueline tracery covers the broad Gothic arches of the **Claustro de Dom João I.** Sculpted by Afonso Domingues, the delicate columns mark the very beginning of the Manueline style. The **sala do capítulo,** just off the cloister, is a large square room daringly designed to avoid all central supports. Its construction was so dangerous—the roof fell in twice—that only prisoners condemned to death were employed to build it. Here two live Portuguese soldiers stand stonily at the tomb of two unknown Portuguese soldiers. On the wall hangs a mutilated crucifix from a World War I battlefield in Flanders where Portuguese soldiers fought. A gripping sculpture by Antonio Goncalves and Lourenço de Almeida—three Portuguese soldiers representing three eras of Portuguese exploits—is prominently displayed.

To the north of the royal cloister, past the barrel-vaulted granary (now used as an exhibition hall), is the sober **Claustro de Dom Afonso V.** From here you can go outside to visit the chapels behind the chancel of the church. The impressive **Capelas Imperfeitas** (Unfinished Chapels) surround a central octagon of massive buttresses designed to support a large dome. The project was dropped like hotcakes when Manuel I ordered his workers to build a monastery in Belém instead. The chapel in the 2 o'clock position flaunts the most flamboyant stonework in the entire complex and gives some idea of how the finished structure would have looked. (Tel. 964 97; monastery complex open 9am-5:30pm; Oct.-May Mon.-Fri. 9am-5pm. Admission 400$, Oct.-May 250$; students and seniors free.)

Practical Information The **tourist office** (tel. 961 80) has moved to R. Nossa Senhora do Caminho, across from the unfinished chapels of the *mosteiro*. Maps, regional info, and some serious bus information. (Open Mon.-Fri. 10am-1pm and 3-7pm, Sat.-Sun. 10am-1pm and 3-6pm; Oct.-April closes one hr. earlier in afternoon.) The **post office** (tel. 961 11) is on Largo Papa Paulo VI, near the freeway entrance. (Open Mon.-Fri. 9am-12:30pm and 2:30-6pm.) The **postal code** is 2440 and **telephone code** 044. For a **hospital,** call tel. 962 46. In an **emergency,** dial tel. 115. For **police,** call tel. 961 34.

The **bus stop** (tel. 965 05) is across from Pensão Vitória on Largo da Misericórdia. For information, inquire at Café Frazão, diagonally left across the street from Pensão Vitória. Batalha's central location makes for convenient connections to: Leiria (11 per day, 15min., 160$); Fátima (4 per day, 40min., 210$); Alcobaça (13 per day, 45min., 300$); Nazaré, change at Alcobaça (7 per day, 1hr., 410$); Tomar (4 per day, 1½hr., 450$); Lisboa (6 *expressos* per day, 2hr., 900$).

Accommodations and Food Batalha is devoid of cheap beds or even a campground. If marooned here, sleep at **Pensão Vitória** (tel. 966 78), on Largo de Misericórdia in front of the bus stop. The three simple, dark rooms are suitably bare and monastic. (3000$ per room.) The **restaurant** below does wonders with *pudim* (pudding) and is a handy place to wait for the bus.

■ NEAR BATALHA

Witness nature at its most psychedelic in a spectacular series of underground *grutas* (caves) in Estremadura's natural park just south of Batalha. A vast labyrinth of teeny stalagmite and stalactite formations are just a hike away and reachable by bus between **Porto de Mós** (11km) and **Mira de Aire** (15km); the most accessible site is in the latter. A tour guide accompanies you on the descent. About 15km from Porto de Mós, the **Grutas de Santo Antonio** and **Alvados** are a bit more difficult to reach, but equally impressive. Most of the caves have been "enhanced" by background music and strategically placed colored spotlights. The Turismo in Batalha has maps of the region. From the bus stop across from Pensão Vitória, 5 buses per day leave for various caves.

■■■ FÁTIMA

Only Lourdes rivals this holy site in popularity among Christian pilgrims each year. The miracles believed to have occurred here are modern-day phenomena, well-documented and witnessed by thousands of people. On May 13, 1917, Mary appeared before three shepherd children—Lucía, Francisco, and Jacinta—to issue a call for peace and to warn the world of the tragic events that would stem from Russia's godless communism. The incident aroused heated controversy, but the children remained steadfast in their belief despite skepticism from the clergy and attacks from the press. Word of the vision spread throughout Portugal. Bigger and bigger crowds flocked to the site as Our Lady of Fátima returned to speak to the children on the 13th of each month, promising a miracle for her final appearance in October. On that morning, 70,000 people gathered under a torrential rain storm; at noon, the sun spun around in a furious light spectacle and appeared to sink toward the earth. When the light returned to normal, everything was dry and no evidence remained of the morning's rain. The townspeople were convinced by the "fiery signature of God" and built a chapel at the site to honor Mary. Francisco and Jacinta died before reaching adolescence, but Lucía became a nun. There is a movement to have all three canonized. An astounding religious complex now dominates the town, accompanied by a menagerie of cheap religious paraphernalia. Unlike Santiago de Compostela, its Spanish competitor, Fátima has fallen prey to kitsch.

ORIENTATION AND PRACTICAL INFORMATION

Most of Fátima's activity is in and around the basilica complex smack in the center of town. **Avenida Dr. José Alves Correia da Silva,** a long, shady road running just south of the hub-bub, is home to both the bus station and Turismo. A right turn and a 10-min. walk from the bus station leads to Turismo.

Tourist Office: Av. Dr. José Alves Correia da Silva, s/n (tel. 53 11 39). In a modern building with a multilingual touch-screen computer out front. Info on Fátima and surrounding area. English spoken. Open Mon.-Fri. 9am-7pm, Sat.-Sun. 10am-1pm and 3-7pm; Oct.-April Mon.-Fri. 9am-6pm, Sat.-Sun. 10am-1pm and 3-6pm.

Currency Exchange: Uniaõ de Bancos Portugueses, R. Francisco Marto, 139 (tel. 53 39 68). Commission 1000$ for cash; 1000$ plus 9$ for every 1000$ cashed for traveler's checks. Open 8:30am-3pm.

Post Office: R. Cónego Formigão (tel. 53 18 10), on the left before Turismo. Open Mon.-Fri. 8:30am-6pm, Sat. 3-8pm, Sun. 9am-noon; winter Mon.-Fri. 8:30am-6pm. **Postal Code:** 2495.

Telephones: At the post office. **Telephone Code:** 049.

Trains: Listed as "Fátima" (est.) (tel. 461 22) is 20km out of town on Chão de Maçãs. 6 buses per day run there from the bus station (45min., 340$).

Buses: Av. Dr. José Alves Correia da Silva (tel. 53 16 11). Listed as "Cova da Iria." To: Fátima (est.) (6 per day, 45min., 340$); Leiria (11 per day, 45min., 300-450$); Batalha (4 per day, 40min., 230$); Tomar (4 per day, 1hr., 410$); Lisboa (8 per day, 2½hr., 1050$); Porto (7 per day, 3½hr., 1200$).

Taxis: tel. 53 21 92 or 53 12 16.

Hospital: A "health center" in Fátima is on R. Jacinta Marto (tel. 53 18 36), but for a hospital proper you must go to Ourém (tel. 421 30).

Emergency: tel. 115.

Police: R. Francisco Marto (tel. 53 11 05), near Rotunda de Sta. Teresa de Ourém.

ACCOMMODATIONS AND FOOD

Rooms are scarce only during the grand celebrations on the 13th of May and October, the first and last appearances of Mary. Some people discreetly **camp** in the parks around the sanctuary as a last resort. Fátima has a whopping number of *pensões-restaurantes* and *hoteles;* all cluster around the sanctuary, a right turn out of the bus station. Inexpensive restaurants abound on small streets near the center.

Pensão Santo Amaro, R. Francisco Marto, 59 (tel. 53 14 55), near the rotunda de Santa Teresa on the edge of town. Worth the walk and every red *escudo.* All rooms carpeted, and have phone, full bath, TV, and winter heating. Pleasant sitting area, lavish reception, and upscale shopping area. Singles 5500$. Doubles 6000$. Triples 7500$.

Pensão a Paragem (tel. 53 15 58). The cheapest beds in town, upstairs in the bus station. Rooms are clean and pleasant. You'll be serenaded and suffocated by diesel engines, but at least you'll have a private bath to cough in peace and a telephone to call the doctor. Singles 2000$. Doubles 3500$. Triples 5000$.

Pensão Dona Maria, R. Av. Dr. José Alves da Silva, 122 (tel. 53 12 12), between the bus station and Turismo. Laura Ashley ambience, cheery dining room. Pricey for what you get. Singles 4000$. Doubles 7000$. Triples available. 10-20% discount for students with ID. Breakfast included for students.

Adega Funda, R. Francisco Marto (tel. 53 13 72), near the bank. Large wood dining room with black and white photos of Fátima from the '20s. Big portions. Grilled cod 1150$. Entrees 800-1150$. Open 9am-3pm and 6-10pm.

O Portal, R. Santa Isabela (tel. 53 16 89), off R. Francisco Marto. Ordinary café decor. American dramas unfold on the TV, as viewers eat *feijoadas* (pork and beans, 850$). Open 9am-midnight, Sun. 9am-7pm, closed Thurs.

SIGHTS AND ENTERTAINMENT

The sanctuary is set in vibrant parks enclosed by tall leafy trees, blocking out the surrounding commercial areas. At the end of its sunken asphalt football-field-sized plaza rises the awe-inspiring **Basílica do Rosário** (1928). A crystal cruciform nightlight perches atop the tower's seven-ton bronze crown. Many devout approach the Basilica on their knees for the entire length of the plaza. Inside, the off-white stone hall with its tall cylindrical ceiling leads to the blinding high altar. The centerpiece of this striking edifice is a painting of Mary appearing before the three shepherds. A dress code is enforced—no shorts, bathing suits, or other "inappropriate" clothing. (Open 7am-8pm.)

Sheltered beneath a metal and glass canopy, the original **Capelinha das Aparições** (Little Chapel of the Apparitions) was built in 1919. Masses are given here all morning in six languages. The information booth on the left as you face the chapel has the schedule of foreign-language confessions. (Open 9am-7pm.)

The **Museu de Cera de Fátima** (wax museum) tells Fátima's story quite realistically in 29 scenes; there's no proper exit without its "Vision of Hell." To get here from the bus station, turn right at the exit and take the first left uphill; make a right on R. Jacinta Marto. Adjacent gift shop sells plaster saints and postcards bearing the caption "*Rezei por ti em Fátima*" ("I prayed for you in Fátima"). (Open 9:30am-6:30pm; Nov.-March Mon.-Fri. 9:30am-5pm., Sat.-Sun. 9:30am-6pm. Admission 600$.)

The **Museu-Vivo Aparições** uses light, sound, and special effects to recreate that famous apparition. As you face the Basilica the museum lies on your left. Walk through the belt of trees to Hotel Fátima. The museum is in the basement of the shopping complex on the left. (Open 9am-8pm; Nov.-April 9am-6pm. Soundtracks in English, French, German, Italian, or Spanish. Admission 400$.)

Aljustrel, the small village where the famous young trio lived, is 1km away. The entire town has been turned into a museum exhibit. To reach Aljustrel, walk past Turismo along Av. D. José Alves Correia da Silva.

■■■ FIGUEIRA DA FOZ

Wellington landed here in 1808 en route to attack Napoleon's bases in Portugal and Spain. These days the closest you'll come to history and culture are the food and drinks named after them. At the mouth of the Mondego, half-way between Lisboa and Porto, and only an hour or so from Coimbra, Figueira is one of the biggest "party" towns in Portugal, where pleasure-seekers celebrate both the sun and nightfall. At 1km by 3km, the beach is nearly as wide as it is long, and even when packed seems to boast empty sand. At night, tanned folk crowd the bars (12 at last count), the ten discos, and the outdoor cafés, or press their luck at the casino. Although playful and sometimes pricey, Figueira retains a certain down-to-earth atmosphere, and has a lot to offer the budget traveler.

ORIENTATION AND PRACTICAL INFORMATION

Packed with hotels and "aparthotels," **Avenida 25 de Abril** is the busy lifeline that separates town from beach. Four blocks inland and parallel to the avenue, **Rua Bernardo Lopes** harbors semi-affordable *pensões* and restaurants. Much of the action in Figueira happens in the casino-cinema-disco complex on this street.

Tourist Office: Av. 25 de Abril (tel. 226 10), next to Aparthotel Atlântico at the very end of the airport terminal-like complex. Useful map. English spoken. Open 9am-midnight; Oct.-May Mon.-Fri. 9am-12:30pm and 2-5:30pm.

Currency Exchange: Banco Crédito Predial Portugués, R. Joáo de Lemos, a small street between R. Dr. António Dinis and R. Cândido dos Reis. 750$ commission for cash exchange; free for traveler's checks. Open 8:30am-3pm. **Aparthotel Atlântico** or **Grande Hotel da Figueira,** Av. 25 de Abril (tel. 221 46), near Turismo, may change money after hours.

Post Office: Main office at Pr. Infante Dom Henrique, 41 (tel. 227 51), off R. 5 de Outubro. Open for Posta Restante and telephones Mon.-Fri. 8:30am-6:30pm, Sat. 9am-12:30pm. More convenient **branch office** at R. Miguel Bombarda, 76 (tel. 220 56). Open for stamps and telephones Mon.-Fri. 9am-12:30pm and 2:30-6pm. **Postal Code:** 3080.

Telephones: In the post office and in a Telecom trailer above Turismo. Trailer open 2-7pm. English spoken. **Telephone Code:** 033.

Trains: Largo Estação (tel. 284 83), near the bridge. An easy 25-min. walk to Turismo and the beach. Keeping the river to the left, Av. Saraiva de Carvalho becomes R. 5 de Outubro at the fountain, then curves into Av. 25 de Abril. To Coimbra (13 per day, 40min., 300$) and Lisboa (8 per day, 3hr., 1200$).

Buses: Terminal Rodoviário (tel. 230 95). A 15-min. walk to Turismo. Facing the church, turn right onto R. Dr. Santos Rocha. Walk about 10min. toward the waterfront; make a right onto R. 5 de Outubro, which curves into Av. 25 de Abril after a few minutes. Turismo is on the water-level, next to Aparthotel Atlântico. To: Leiria (9 per day, 1¼hr., 570$); Coimbra (6 per day, 2hr., 505$); Faro (1 per day, 12hr., 2400$); Lisboa (4 per day, 3½hr., 1150$); Aveiro (5 per day, 2hr., 630$). **AFGA,** R. Miguel Bombarda, 79 (tel. 277 77), near the post office. To: Porto (Mon.-Fri. 1 per day, 2hr., 900$); Lisboa (3 per day, 3½hr., 1150$); Evora (1 per day, 7hr., 1600$); Faro (1 per day, 10hr., 2800$).

Taxis: tel. 235 00, 237 88, or 232 18. 24-hr. service. At bus or train station.

Bike Rental: AFGA, R. Miguel Bombarda, 79 (tel. 289 89). Pink bikes 750$ per ½-day, 1500$ per day, 5000$ per week. 1000$ deposit. Special group rates. Open Mon.-Fri. 9:30am-1pm and 3-7pm.

English Bookstore: Casa Havanesa, R. Cândido dos Reis, 85 (tel. 229 41), near the casino. Lots of magazines, journals, and mysteries. Open 9am-1pm and 3-7pm.

Laundromat: Lavandaria Agueirense, R. Cândido dos Reis (tel. 223 82), near the municipal garden. Wash and dry 500$ per kg. Dry cleaning: pants 450$, shirts 350$. Open Mon.-Fri. 9am-1pm and 3-7pm, Sat. 3-7pm.

Hospital: Nearest is in Gala, across the Rio Mondego (tel. 310 27 or 316 33). **Emergency:** tel. 115.

Police: R. Joaquim Carvalho (tel. 220 22), near the bus station and park.

ACCOMMODATIONS AND CAMPING

Most expensive July-Aug., also expensive in June. Arrive early to check on vacancies; many managers won't reserve a room by phone in high-season.

Pensão Central, R. Bernardo Lopes, 36 (tel. 223 08), next to Supermarket Ovo, down the street from casino complex and all the action. Spacious, well-furnished, sunlit rooms with newly-built baths. Singles 3000$. Doubles 5000$. Triples 6000$. Winter discount. Breakfast included.

Pensão Residencial Rio-Mar, R. Dr. António Dinis, 90 (tel. 230 53), perpendicular to R. Bernardo Lopes. Spacious and comfortable (albeit old and dark) rooms. Lounge, TV, and a grand breakfast room. Doubles with bidet 3000$, with shower 5000$, with bath 6000$. Discount 40-50% in winter. Breakfast included.

Pensão Residencial Bela Figueira, R. Miguel Bombarda, 13 (tel. 227 28), 2 bl. from the beach. Simply-furnished, plain but comfortable rooms. All with telephones, some with TV. Central heating. Singles 1850-3850$. Doubles 2850-6750$, with bath 3850-7850$. Breakfast included.

Camping: Parque Municipal de Campismo (tel. 327 42 or 231 16). With the beach to your left, walk up Av. 25 de Abril and turn right at the roundabout on R. Alexándre Herculano. Turn left at Parque Santa Catarina going up R. Joaquim

Sotto-Mayor past Palácio Sotto-Mayor. Or take taxi from bus or train station (500$). An excellent site complete with Olympic-size pool, tennis courts, kennel, market, pharmacy, and currency exchange. Reception open 8am-8pm; Oct.-May 8am-7pm. Silence reigns 11pm-7am. June-Sept. each party must have a minimum of 2 people. 350$ per person, 250$ per tent, 350$ per car. Showers 110$.

FOOD

Restaurants are more expensive than the Portuguese norm. Hope lies around **Rua Bernardo Lopes.** A local **market** sells food beside the municipal garden on R. 5 de Outubro. (Open Mon.-Sat. 7am-7pm; winter Sun.-Fri. 8am-5pm, Sat. 8am-1pm.)

Groceries: Supermercado Ovo, on the corner of R. A. Dinis and R. B. Lopes. Imported foods aimed at tourists (yes, you) a bit pricey. Open Mon.-Fri. 9am-1pm and 3-7pm.

Restaurante Rancho, R. Miguel Bombardo, 40-44 (tel. 220 19), 2 bl. up from Turismo. Packed with locals at lunchtime. Hefty, delicious entrees (350-900$) such as *chocos grechados* (grilled squid, 500$). Open Mon.-Sat. 8am-10pm.

Restaurante O Escondidinho, R. Dr. António Dinis, 62 (tel. 224 94), hidden inside the gate. Portuguese and Goanese Indian cuisine. Curry and *piri-piri* (hot sauce) dishes 750-1400$. Open Tues.-Sun. 12:30-2pm and 7:30-11pm.

Restaurante Astória, R. Bernardo Lopes, 57 (tel. 227 28). Limited menu, but filling meals. Manager uses an intercom or yells orders to the cook through the wall. *Frango assado* (grilled chicken, 600$) or mixed salad (450$); cheaper at the bar. Open 9am-midnight.

SIGHTS AND ENTERTAINMENT

The under-rated **Museu Municipal do Doutor Santos Rocha** houses everything from ancient coins to decadent fashions of Portuguese nobility. The building, in Parque Abadias, smack in the middle of the residential district, coddles a collection of ceramic vases excavated in Figueira da Foz and Caldas da Rainha. The museum entrance faces R. Calouste Gulbenkian. (Tel. 245 09; open Tues.-Sun. 9am-12:30pm and 2-5:30pm. Free.) **Casa do Paço,** Largo Prof. Vitar Guerra, 4 (tel. 221 59), is decorated with 6888 Delft tiles that fortuitously washed ashore after a shipwreck. (Open Mon.-Fri. 9:30am-12:30pm and 2-5pm. Free.) The modest exterior of the **Palácio Sotto-Mayor,** on R. Joaquim Sotto Mayor (tel. 221 21), belies the shameless extravagance inside. Lavish green marble columns line the main hallway, and the opulent ceiling is slathered with paintings and decorative panels trimmed in gold-leaf. (Open Tues.-Sun. 2-6pm. Admission 100$.)

The **casino** complex on R. Bernardo Lopes (tel. 220 41) also contains a **nightclub** (300$ cover charge), a **cinema** (admission 350$), and an **arcade.** It costs 172$ for the slot machine and 20$ for bingo. To gamble you must be over 18 and show proper ID. There's also a show, usually live music, at night. (Open 3pm-3am.)

Figueira's standard party mode shifts from high gear to warp speed during the **Festa de São João** (June 19-24). At 5am, a huge rowdy procession heads for nearby Buarcos, where all involved take a so-called *banho santo* (holy bath) in this town's large beach. For 10 days in September, the **Festival de Cinema de Figueira da Foz** screens international flicks.

The forested region north of Figueira in **Serra da Boa Viagem** (4km) has several vantage points with spectacular panoramas of the shoreline below.

■■■ AVEIRO

If you like salt, you'll love Aveiro. An important seaport in the 16th century, the town lost two-thirds of its population after a 1575 storm caused fever-filled marshlands to form. To make matters worse, salt marsh (silt) sealed off its inlet. The phenomena, however, created the vast *ria* (inlet) that extends 45km up the coast, protected by a long sand bar. Islands, salt marshes, sand dunes, and an occasional pine forest now speck the water.

Aveiro proper is graced with a few charming canals, along which streamlined *barcos moliceiros* drift laden with salty seaweed (residents make their living collecting it for fertilizer), their brightly painted bows rising high and curling into fearsome horns. Smaller *barcos saleiros* whisk through the canals past the glistening white salt beds. *Marnotos* (people who work the salt pans) gather salt into baskets and transport it to warehouses along the Canal de São Roque.

These traditional ways of life successfully coexist with the town's current impulse toward resort status. Beautiful beaches to the west of Aveiro are drawing more and more tourists.

ORIENTATION AND PRACTICAL INFORMATION

Salt country is 200km north of Lisboa and 60km south of Porto. Trains are most convenient for travel in and out of Aveiro and the Rota da Luz region. Aveiro is split by the *canal central* and Av. Dr. Lourenço Peixinho, which runs from the train station to **Praça Humberto Delgado** (actually a bridge). North of the *canal central* lies the fishermen's quarter, **Beira Mar.** The town's southern port is the "new" residential district, which actually contains all the historical monuments.

To find **Turismo** (1km), walk up Av. Dr. Lourenço Peixinho (the leftmost street) until the bridge, then veer right. R. João Mendonça runs parallel to the canal. Also, buses run from the train station to the bridge into the rest of town.

Tourist Office: R. João Mendonça, 8 (tel. 236 80 or 207 60). Distributes glossy brochures and sells tickets for day-long boat trips from Aveiro north to Torreira on the *ria* (2000$). Maps and lodging information. English-speaking staff. Open daily 9am-9pm; Sept. 15-June 15 Mon.-Fri. 9am-9pm, Sat. 9am-1pm and 2:30-5:30pm.

Currency Exchange: Hotel Pomba Branca, R. Luís Gomes de Carvalho, 23 (tel. 225 29), not far from the train station. 24-hr. service at bank rates.

Post Office: Pr. Marquês de Pombal (tel. 231 51). Cross the main bridge and walk up R. Coimbra past the town hall. Open for Posta Restante and **telephones** Mon.-Fri. 8:30am-6:30pm, Sat. 9am-12:30pm. Branch office on Av. Dr. Lourenço Peixinho (tel. 201 95). Open for **telephones** same hours as main office. **Postal Code:** 3800.

Telephones: In the **post office. Telephone Code:** 034.

Trains: Largo Estação (tel. 244 85), at the end of Av. Dr. Lourenço Peixinho. To: Agueda (7 per day, 175$); Coimbra (22 per day, 1hr., 420$); Porto (20 per day, ½hr., 320$; express train, 3 per day, 750$); Viseu (5 per day, 4hr., 690$); Lisboa (18 per day, 5hr., 1400$).

Buses: Nearest Rodoviária station is in Agueda, 19km away. Eight buses and trains per day go from the train station to Agueda (200$). **AVIC-Mondego,** R. Comandante Rocha Cunha, 55 (tel. 237 47), runs from the train station to the Agueda station to Figueira da Foz (5 per day, 2¼hr., 600$) and Praia da Mira (5 per day, 45min., 455$).

Ferries: From Forte da Barra to São Jacinto (about 1 per hr., last one back at 7:30pm, 200$). Despite their tantalizing proximity, there is no service between São Jacinto and Barra—only from Forte da Barra.

Taxis: Train station (tel. 229 43); main ave. (tel. 237 66). Taxis congregate around the train station and at the end of R. João Mendonça.

Laundromat: Lavandaria União, Av. Dr. Lourenço Peixinho, 292 (tel. 235 56), near the train station. Wash and dry 450$ per kg. Open Mon.-Fri. 9am-12:30pm and 2:30-7pm.

Hospital: Av. Dr. Artur Ravara (tel. 221 83 or 286 60), near the park across the canal.

Emergency: tel. 115.

Police: Pr. Marquês de Pombal (tel. 220 22).

ACCOMMODATIONS AND CAMPING

Pensões are generally expensive but uncrowded. Reservations are only necessary during festivals and in the dead of summer. Many have discounts in winter.

Residencial Estrêla, R. José Estêvão, 4 (tel. 238 18), on the *praça*. Grand stairway with oval skylight. First-floor rooms are spacious and well-furnished; top-floor ones are cramped but cheaper. Friendly, English-speaking owner. Singles 2000$, with bath 3000$. Doubles 3000-4000$, with bath 5500-6000$. Triples 7000$.

Pensão Palmeira, R. Palmeira, 7-11 (tel. 225 21). From R. Morais (perpendicular to R. José Estevão, parallel to R. João Mendonça), turn left 1 bl. before the church; *pensão* is covered in blue and yellow *azulejos*. Cheerful, well-furnished rooms (some reminiscent of a Barbie Dream House), almost all with bath and TV. Singles 4500$, with bath 6500$. Doubles 5000$, with bath 7000$. Triples 8000$.

Residencial Santa Joana, Av. Lourenço Peixinho, 227 (tel. 286 04), 1 bl. from the train station. Staff may require an interpreter, but rooms are reasonable. Many with phone and TV. Singles 3500$. Doubles 5000$.

Camping: São Jacinto (tel. 482 84; fax 481 22), on the beach northwest of Aveiro. Sometimes crowded. 420$ per person, 355$ per tent, 360$ per car.

FOOD

Seafood restaurants are common but can be expensive. Scrounge for cheaper gruel around **Avenida Dr. Lourenço Peixinho** and **Rua José Estêvão.** Aveiro is known for its *ovos moles* (sweetened egg yolks), available at all cafés in town.

Restaurante Zico, R. José Estêvão, 52 (tel. 296 49). The "in" place according to families and young folk. Pork on *prego de porco* (pork steak with fries, 630$) or try *omelete de camarão* (shrimp omelette, 950$). Entrees 950-1350$. Save room for the caloric desserts. Open Mon.-Sat. 8am-2am.

Restaurante Snack-Bar Amazonas, R. Capitão Sousa Pizarro, 15, Store #2 (tel. 276 60), on a street leading to the park. Prodigious portions—one entree satisfies 2 diners. ½-portions available. Entrees 800-1300$. Open Mon.-Sat. 8am-midnight.

Restaurante Salimar, R. Combatentes da Grande Guerra, 6 (tel. 251 08), 1 bl. from Turismo. Nautical decor. Fragrant *bacalhau no churrasco* (barbecued cod, 900$). Specialty is a bubbling orange-red broth swimming with rice and seafood called *arroz de marisco* 1200$ (for 2 people 2000$). Open 8am-midnight.

SIGHTS AND ENTERTAINMENT

Across from Turismo in Pr. República, the regal **Paço do Concelho** (town hall) radiates a somber elegance with its French windows and bell tower. **Igreja da Misericórdia** vies for attention with its simple yet striking blue facade. 17th-century Lisboeta tiles cover the walls and complement the white window frames.

The real thriller is the **Museu de Aveiro,** in the old Convento de Jesus. Exuberant, flamboyant gilt Baroque woodwork covers the church interior. In 1472, King Afonso and the Infanta Joana, who wished to become a nun against his will, had a royal battle here. She won. Beneath *azulejo* panels depicting the story, Sta. Joana's Renaissance tomb—supported by the heads of four angels—is one of the most famous works of art in the country. (Open Tues.-Sun. 10am-12:30pm and 2-5pm. Admission 200$, seniors and students free.)

The nearby **Igreja das Carmelitas** displays 18th-century *azulejos* in a remarkably symmetrical interior. The ceiling of the nave and the chancel is decorated with paintings depicting the life of Sta. Teresa.

For four weeks beginning in mid-July, the salty city shakes with the **Festa da Ria** (river festival). Dancers groove on a floating stage in the middle of the *canal central.*

Neighboring **beach** towns and the national park, **Dunas de São Jacinto** (sand dunes, approx. 10km away), merit daytrips. **Buses** leave for the beaches from a stop by the canal near the tourist office (17 per day in summer, 7:10am-8:45pm). The bus stops at Forte da Barra (free), where **ferries** run to the town of **São Jacinto** (8 per day, no cars in summer). Two ferries per day also run directly from Aveiro to São Jacinto.

Douro and Minho

Although their landscapes and shared Celtic past invite comparison with neighboring Galicia in Spain, Douro and Minho are more populated, wealthier, and faster developing than much of Galicia. The Kingdom of Portugal came into being here when Afonso Henriques defeated the Moors in 1143 in Guimarães and declared himself ruler.

Hundreds of trellised vineyards in these fertile rolling hills grow grapes for the famous *porto* and *vinho verde* wines. Houses covered in brilliant tiles (*azulejos*) dot town streets. The traditional female costume—including layer upon layer of gold necklaces encrusted with charms—attests to the region's mineral wealth. The mild climate is too cool to attract the beach crowd until July, and only a few ambitious travelers ever make it past Porto to the beautiful towns of the interior: Vila Nova de Cerveira, Braga, Viana do Castelo, and Guimarães.

■■■ PORTO

Magnificently situated on a dramatic gorge cut by the Rio Douro, 6km from the sea, Portugal's second city is an attractive harbor town and the industrial and commercial focal point of the north. Porto glows at night with the artistic lighting of its historic buildings. Granite church towers pierce the skyline, closely packed orange-tiled houses tumble down to the river, and three of Europe's most graceful bridges span the gorge above. Gérard Eiffel supplied the soaring lines of the oldest one, the Ponte de Dona Maria Pia, completed in 1877.

Porto's history is the stuff of which Nationalism is made. Henry the Navigator was born here, and orchestrated the 1415 invasion of Ceuta, which was to become the most important Christian base in Africa. As preparation, residents slaughtered all their cattle, gave all the meat to the Portuguese fleet, and kept only the entrails for themselves. The tasty and ever-popular dish *tripas à moda do Porto* commemorates the culinary self-sacrifice; to this day the people of Porto are known as "*tripeiros*" (tripe-eaters). In the 19th century, residents of Porto fought four times against oppressive regimes.

Porto's greatest fame, however, springs from the taste of its *vinho* rather than the toughness of its citizens. Developed by English merchants in the early 18th century, the Port wine industry across the River Douro in Vila Nova de Gaia drives the city's economy.

ORIENTATION AND PRACTICAL INFORMATION

Constant traffic and a chaotic maze of one-way streets fluster even the most easily oriented of travelers; arm yourself with a map ASAP. At the heart of Porto, **Avenida dos Aliados** forms a long rectangle bordered on the north by **Praça General Humberto Delgado** and on the south by **Praça da Liberdade.** The **Estação São Bento** lies smack in the middle of town, just off Pr. Liberdade. The **Ribeira,** or Esplanade, district is a few blocks to the south, directly across the bridge from **Vila Nova de Gaia,** the *adega* area of wine houses.

Tourist Office: R. Clube dos Fenianos, 25 (tel. 31 27 40), on west side of city hall. Staff doles out detailed map and accommodations advice. Questions are not always answered accurately. English spoken. Open Mon.-Fri. 9am-7pm, Sat. 9am-4pm, Sun. 10am-1pm; Oct.-June Mon.-Fri. 9am-12:30pm and 2-5:30pm, Sat. 9am-4pm. Baby **branch** office on Pr. Don João I, 25 (tel. 31 75 14), on the corner with R. do Bonjardim. Open Mon.-Fri. 9am-7pm, Sat. 9am-2pm, Sun. 10am-2pm.

American Express: Top Tours, R. Alferes Malheiro, 96 (tel. 208 27 85), up R. do Almada from Turismo. It's the second street on the left. Open Mon.-Fri. 9am-12:30pm and 2:30-6:30pm.

Currency Exchange: An office at the **airport** provides service Mon. 9am-8pm, Sat. 9am-4pm. Also, there's a 24-hr. **ATM** on Pr. Liberdade, outside Banco Espírito Santo e Commercial de Lisboa.

Consulates: See Portugal Essentials: Embassies and Consulates.

Post Office: Pr. General H. Delgado (tel. 208 02 51), across from Turismo. Posta Restante 55$ per item. A fascinating collection of postal uniforms on display. Open for stamps Mon.-Fri. 8am-9pm, Sat.-Sun. 9am-6pm. **Postal Code:** 4000.

Telephones: Pr. Liberdade, 62. Open 8am-11:30pm. Also at the post office. **Telephone Code:** 02.

Flights: Aeroporto Francisco de Sá Carneiro (tel. 948 21 41), accessible by bus #44 and 56 from Pr. Lisboa (buses about every 20min.). **TAP Air Portugal,** Pr. Mouzinho de Albuquerque, 105 (tel. 948 22 91). To Lisboa (13,400$) and Madrid (35,200$).

Trains: Estação de São Bento (tel. 200 27 22), centrally located 1 bl. off Pr. Liberdade. Receives some trains, mostly locals and nearby regional routes. All trains pass through **Estação de Campanhã** (tel. 56 41 41), Porto's main station west of the center. Frequent connections to Estação São Bento (5min., 100$). To: Aveiro (22 per day, 1½hr., 320$); Viana do Castelo (12 per day, 2hr., 550$); Braga, via Nine (10 per day, 2hr., 390$); Coimbra (13 per day, 2½hr., 800$); Lisboa (5 per day, 4½hr., 1615$; 8 ALFA per day, 3¼hr., 2950$); Madrid, via Entroncamento (2 per day, 12hr., 7500$); Paris (1 per day, 27hr., 19,000$).

Buses: Garagem Atlântico, R. Alexandre Herculano, 366 (tel. 200 69 54). To: Coimbra (11 per day, 1½hr., 950$); Viseu (2 per day, 2hr., 850$); Lisboa (5 per day, 5hr., 1600$). **Estação de Camionagem** (tel. 200 61 21), 1 bl. from Av. Aliados. To Braga (every ½hr., 1½hr., 550$) and Viana do Castelo (13 per day, 2hr., 610$). **Rodoviária Nacional,** Pr. Filipa de Lencastre (tel. 200 31 52) also runs to Braga and Viana do Castelo. **Rodonarte,** R. Atenou Comercial do Porto—a.k.a. Travessa P. Manuel (tel. 200 43 98), 1 bl. from R. Sá da Bandeira. To Vila Real (7 per day, 4hr., 800$).

Public Transportation: *Passe Turístico* discount pass is available for the Porto transportation system (trolleys, buses, etc.). 3 days 1500$. 7 days 2000$.

Taxis: tel. 48 80 61. 24-hr. service. Taxi stand on Av. Aliados. Fare to youth hostel 500-600$.

English Bookstore: Livraria Diário de Notícias, R. Sá de Bandeira, 5, across from Estação São Bento. Good selection of travel books (including *Let's Go* guides), maps, and paperbacks. Open Mon.-Fri. 9am-12:30pm and 2:30-7pm; winter Mon.-Fri. 9am-12:30pm, Sat. 9am-1pm. **Livraria Britânico (The English Bookshop),** R. José Falcão, 184. Vast choice of paperbacks, plus hardcovers and mags. Open Mon.-Fri. 9am-7pm, Sat. 9am-1pm.

Laundromat: Penguin, Av. Boavista (tel. 69 50 32), in shopping center Brasília. Follow route to youth hostel, but walk uphill 1 bl. further to roundabout. Only self-service place in town. 1300$ per 5.5kg load. Open Mon.-Sat. 10am-11pm.

Public Showers and Toilets: Pr. Liberdade (in the middle of the garden in the traffic island), Pr. Batalha, and Largo do Viriato. Open 24hrs.

Swimming Pool: Piscina Municipal, R. Almirante Leute do Rêgo (tel. 49 33 27). Admission 190$, Sat.-Sun. 230$. Open 10am-12:30pm and 2-6:30pm.

24-hr. Pharmacy: tel. 118 for info on which pharmacy is "on call."

Medical Services: Hospital de Santo António, R. Prof. Vicente José de Carvalho (tel. 200 52 41). **Hospital de São João,** Al Prof. Hernâni Monteiro (tel. 48 71 51). **Ambulance** (tel. 115).

Emergency: tel. 115.

Police: R. Alexandre Herculano (tel. 200 68 21).

ACCOMMODATIONS AND CAMPING

Summer is a challenge. Most of the city's *pensões* lie west of Av. Aliados. Rates for singles are absolutely criminal, and the city's only youth hostel is on the small side.

Pousada de Juventude do Porto (HI), R. Rodrigues Lobo, 98 (tel. 606 55 35), about 2km from the center of town. Take bus #3, 20, or 52 (10min., 140$) from the stop on the lower west end of Pr. Liberdade and hop off at R. Júlio Dinis

PORTO

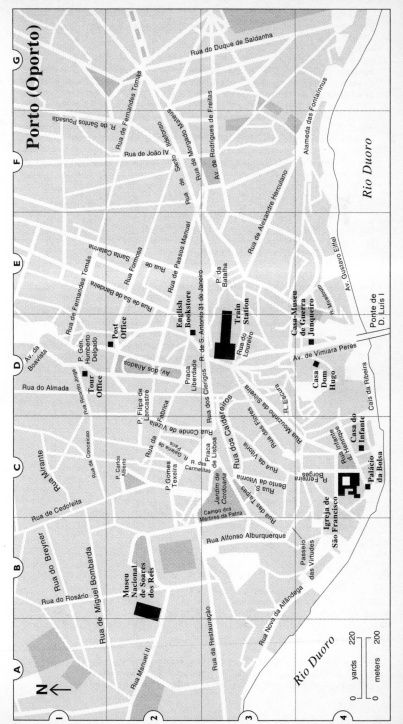

Porto (Oporto)

(driver knows the hostel stop). Game room, library, fine kitchen facilities, and a great stained-glass window for a plush touch. Cramped rooms. They sell discount bus tickets at the reception desk (round-trip 180$). Inevitably full after 10pm. 3-day max. stay. Reception open 9-11am and 6pm-midnight. Curfew midnight. 1300$ per person. Doubles with bath 3500$. Your reservation may be unexpectedly cancelled if a large group arrives.

Pensão São Marino, Pr. Carlos Alberto, 59 (tel. 32 54 99), 1 bl. up from main Turismo. Head up R. Dr. Ricardo Jorge, which turns into R. Conceição; turn left onto R. das Oliveiras, and a quick right onto Pr. Carlos Alberto. Some of the bright, carpeted rooms look onto the dignified *praça*. All have bath or shower, phone, and winter heating. Fills quickly. Singles 3000-4000$. Doubles with shower 4000$, with bath 6000$. Breakfast included.

Residencial Paris, R. da Fábrica, 29 (tel. 32 13 96). Across Pr. Liberdade from the train station, make a left onto R. do Dr. Artur de Magalhães Basto, which quickly turns into R. Fábrica. Room sizes vary from adequate to gigantic. Breakfast room looks onto a garden. Singles 2300$, with bath 3850$. Doubles with shower 3700$, with bath 5100$.

Pensão Estoril, R. Cedofeita, 193 (tel. 200 51 52 or 200 27 51), on a major shopping street radiating from Pr. Carlos Alberto. Colossal, bright rooms in an elegant building with sea-green carpeting. All rooms have radios and winter heating. Lounge with satellite TV. Singles with shower 2500-3000$, with bath 3200$. Doubles with shower 3000-3500$, with bath 4000$. Triples with shower 4800$, with bath 5000$. Quads with shower 6000$, with bath 6400$. Breakfast 360$.

Pensão dos Aliados, R. Elísio de Melo, 27 (tel. 200 48 53; fax 200 27 10), on the left as you walk up Av. Aliados. On a noisy street. Living room with TV. Sumptuous rooms with telephones, wall-to-wall carpeting, and unusually-shaped baths. Singles 4000$, with bath 5500$. Doubles 4700$, with bath 6500$. Triples 6000$, with bath 8450$. Breakfast included. Reserve several days ahead in summer.

Pensão Brasil, R. Formosa, 178 (tel. 31 05 16). From the main tourist office, cross Av. Aliados to R. Formosa—Brasil is about 3½ bl. up. Some of the cheapest rooms in Porto, but not the worst. Doubles are cleaner and brighter than singles. Winter heating. Singles 2500$, with bath 3500$. Doubles with bath 4500$. Triples 4500$.

Residencial Porto Rico, R. Almada, 237 (tel. 31 87 85). From Av. Aliados, go up R. Elísio de Melo; after 2 left-hand bl. turn right on R. Almada. Small but clean rooms with dark wood furniture, phones, and radios. Rooms with baths have TVs and are more appealing. Singles 2500$, with bath 4500$. Doubles 3500$, with bath 5000$. Winter discount. Breakfast included.

Camping: Prelada, Parque de Prelada (tel. 81 26 16), 5km from the beach. Take bus #6 from Pr. Liberdade. 430$ per person, 350$ per tent, 360$ per car. **Salgueiros** (tel. 781 05 00), near Praia de Salgueiros in Vila Nova de Gaia, is less accessible and less equipped, but closer to the surf. 130$ per person and per tent, 100$ per car. Open May-Sept.

FOOD

Atmospheric restaurants border the river in the Ribeira district, particularly on **Cais de Ribeira, Rua Reboleira,** and **Rua de Cima do Muro.** You'll find budget fare in much rowdier and seedier surroundings near Pr. Batalha on **Rua do Cimo de Vila** and **Rua do Cativo.** Cheaper eateries surround the **Hospital de Santo António** and **Praça de Gomes Teixeira,** a few blocks west of Pr. Liberdade. Adventurous gourmands savor the city's specialty, *tripas à moda do Porto* (tripe and beans).

An outdoor food and handicrafts **market** lines Cais de Ribeira daily (8am-8pm). Replete with flowers, fruit, and fish, the **Mercado de Bolhão** bustles on the corner of R. Formosa and R. Sá de Bandeira. (See Accommodations: Pensão Brasil for directions; open Mon.-Fri. 7am-5pm, Sat. 7am-1pm.)

Máximo Restaurante-Café, R. José Falcão, 115 (tel. 208 04 02). From bus station continue up the hill and turn right on R. José Falcão. A SoHo look—white walls, black designer lamps and chairs, and green-gray marble tables—but a local clientele. The food is American: hamburgers 470-710$, salads 330-790$, daily specials 700-1200$. Open Mon.-Sat. 8am-10:30pm.

Churrasqueira Moura, R. Almada, 219-223 (tel. 200 56 36). Toothsome meals among locals include *frango no churrasco* (barbecued chicken with fries, 990$) served with a mongo jar of *piri-piri* (hot sauce). ½-portions available; full portions less than 1300$. Open Mon.-Sat. 9am-10pm.

Taberna Típica, R. Reboleira, 12 (tel. 32 03 73). Stone walls and nautical decor fit the riverside location. The specialty is *arroz de polvo* (octopus rice, 820$). Satisfying *pratos do dia* 750-1400$. Open Thurs.-Tues. 11am-midnight.

Restaurante Abadia, R. Atenou Comercial do Porto (a.k.a. Passos Manuel), 22 (tel. 200 87 57). From Turismo walk down Av. Aliados; after Pr. D. João I, take a left onto Passos Manuel. Waiters, *azulejos,* white tablecloths, and the *menú* win. Seafood specials. Open noon-3pm and 7-10pm. (Under renovation in 1994.)

Taberna do Bebobos, Cais da Ribeira, 21-25 (tel. 31 35 65). Stone walls, round tables, and candlelight. *Sardinhas* (grilled sardines, 920$). Entrees 900-1470$. Open Mon.-Sat. noon-2:30pm and 7-9:30pm.

Restaurante Boa Nova, Muro dos Bacalhoeiros, 115 (tel. 200 60 86), across the square from Típica. Wine served from huge, wooden barrels. *Carapaus fritos* (fried whitefish, 650$). Open Mon.-Sat. 9am-midnight.

Brasa Churrasqueira, Pr. Batalha, 117 (tel. 200 67 85), east of Estação São Bento at the end of R. 31 de Janeiro. Barbecue smoke marks the spot. A roaster's paradise: whole roasted chicken 600$, ½-chicken 450$. Open Wed.-Mon. 9am-10pm.

SIGHTS AND ENTERTAINMENT

In the town center, monumental commercial buildings dwarf the bustle below. Domes, towers, and mansard roofs proclaim a late 19th-century verve, although the avenue was actually developed in the 1920s. The neo-Renaissance **prefeitura** tops off this *belle-époque* time capsule.

South past the alluring blue and yellow *azulejo* facade of **Igreja dos Congregados** is one of Porto's oldest residential districts. Ponderous and fortified, Porto's Romanesque **sé** glowers on a hill above the Ribeira. The Capela do Santíssimo Sacramento to the left of the high altar shines with solid silver and plated gold. During the Napoleonic invasion, crafty townspeople whitewashed the altar to protect it from vandalism. The late 14th-century cloister is wrapped in *azulejo* panels. Climb the staircase to the Renaissance chapter house overlooking the old quarter for a splendid view. (Open 9am-noon and 2-5:30pm. Admission to cloister 100$.)

Narrow R. Dom Hugo runs behind the cathedral through the old city and past the **Casa-Museu de Guerra Junqueiro,** which showcases unexceptional 17th- to 19th-century furniture, pottery, and tapestries. (Open Tues.-Sat. 9am-noon and 2-5pm. Admission 100$.) Out-of-town exhibits visit the museum space at the **Casa Dom Hugo** across the street. (Open Tues.-Sun. 9am-12:30pm and 2:30-5pm. Free.)

The narrow street in front of Igreja dos Grilos leads to R. Mouzinho da Silveira. From here follow signs to the **Palácio da Bolsa** (Stock Exchange), the epitome of 19th-century elegance. The exchange was built in 1834 over the ruins of the old convent of Igreja de São Francisco. A zealous artisan carved the exquisite wooden table in the portrait room with a pocket-knife over a three year period. The ornate **Sala Arabe** (Arabic Room) took 18 years to decorate. Modeled after the Alhambra in Granada, its gold and silver walls are covered with plaques bearing the inscriptions "Glory to Allah" and "Glory to Queen Maria II." The multilingual tour visits the Pátio das Nações, the former trading floor, but the action is closed to visitors. (Open Mon.-Fri. 9am-6pm, Sat.-Sun. 10am-noon and 2-5pm; Oct.-May Mon.-Fri. 9am-noon and 2-5pm. Admission 400$, students 200$; main courtyard free.)

Next door to the Bolsa stands **Igreja de São Francisco.** This Gothic church glitters with one of the most elaborate gilded wood interiors in Portugal. There's a small museum next door. Under the floor, thousands of human bones have been cleaned and stored in the *osseria* to await Judgement Day. (Open Mon.-Sat. 9am-5pm. Admission 250$.)

Home of the municipal archives and a tiny museum, the much-restored **Casa do Infante** (birthplace of Prince Henry the Navigator) stands south of Igreja de São Francisco past Pr. Infante Dom Henrique on R. Alfandega. (Open Mon.-Fri. 9am-noon and 2-5pm.) A few feet away, a marvelous quay filled with shops and restaurants skirts the **Ribeira** (Esplanade). To see more of the Ribeira, take trolley #1 from the nearby Igreja de São Francisco. The cars run along the river to the Foz do Douro, Porto's beach community.

Just up R. Taipas from the museum and church rises the 82m **Torre dos Clérigos** (Tower of Clerics). Built in the middle of the 18th century and long the city's most prominent landmark, its granite tower glimmers like a splendid processional candle. Mount the 200 steps for a vista of the city and the Rio Douro valley. (Open Mon.-Sat. 10:30am-noon and 3-6pm, Sun. 10:30am-1pm and 8-10pm. Free.)

On R. D. Manuel II, past the churches and a forested park, the **Museu Nacional de Soares dos Reis,** built in the 18th century as a royal residence, houses an exhaustive collection of 19th-century Portuguese paintings and sculptures, highlighting those of Soares dos Reis, sometimes called Portugal's Michelangelo. His best-loved piece is of a boy frozen in marble; his most innovative is *O desterrado* (The Exiled). Henrique Pousão's early-late period is also noteworthy. (Closed for renovation in 1994.)

The Portuguese art scene is blessed with a rare modern splash in the **Casa de Serralves (Museu de Arte Moderna),** a recently opened contemporary museum west of the town center. Its elegant marble walls house artist-specific exhibitions of painting, sculpture, architecture, photography, and even video. Ask to see an English video on their life and methods, as all descriptions in the museum are Portuguese. The building crowns an impressive 44 acres of sculptured gardens, fountains, and even old farmlands which tumble toward the Douro River. You are greeted (literally) in one grove by dozens of scarecrows outfitted in the most stylish couture, including hats and handbags. Sip delicately at the nouveau pink tearoom, to the left of the massive central garden. Better yet, savor the beautiful residential area and saunter down Av. Marechal Gomes da Costa until you reach the surprisingly untouched coast. (Museum open Tues.-Fri. 2-8pm, Sat.-Sun. 10am-8pm; park and tearoom have the same hours but close at sundown.) Bus #78 leaves for the museum from Pr. D. João I—ask the driver for the museum stop (about ½-hr. ride to R. Serralves; 140$ one way; return buses function until midnight).

Most of Porto's *caves* or *adegas* (wine lodges) lead free tours (including tasting) of the wineries, where both red and white Port are aged and blended in huge oak barrels. Only human feet crush the grapes. Most of the 80-odd Port lodges ferment across the river, in **Vila Nova de Gaia.** (Walk across the lower level of the Dom Luís I bridge and take a sharp right.) The listings below only scratch the surface. For more information, let your fingers do the walking, particularly if you're interested in a more intimate view of the process.

Sandeman, Largo Miguel Bombarda (tel. 30 40 81), off Diogo Leite. Stocks the best Port and runs almost too organized tours. Amusing museum recounts Sandeman's history. Grape-crushing music video for those who pine daily for MTV. Reservations necessary for large groups. Open 9:30am-1pm and 2-5:30pm. Free.

Cálem, Av. Diogo Leite (tel. 39 40 41), the first warehouse on the street. Multilingual guides. Tours 9:30am-5:30pm. Free.

Ferreira, Av. Diogo Leite, 70 (tel. 370 00 10, ext. 315 Turismo). The crowds are smaller here than at Sandeman's and the Port is nearly as good. Open Mon.-Fri. 9:30am-12:30pm and 2-5pm, Sat. 9:30am-noon. Free.

The tourist office expounds in detail Porto's international film and jazz **festivals.**

■■■ BRAGA

As a Portuguese proverb says, "Coimbra sings, Braga prays, Lisboa shows off, and Porto works." Braga's university is the country's center of theology, and this city is

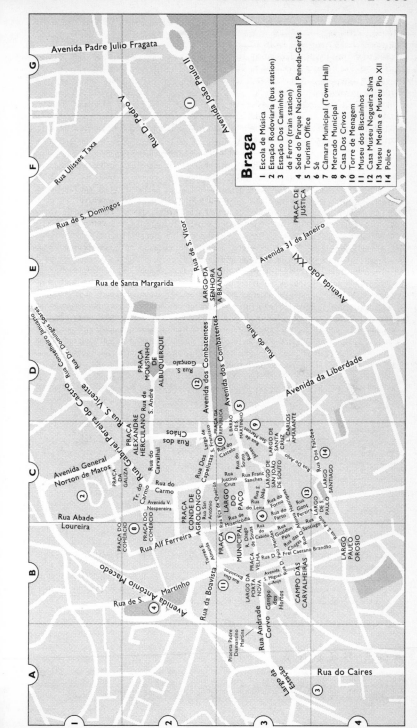

Braga

1 Escola de Música
2 Estação Rodoviaria (bus station)
3 Estação Dos Caminhos de Ferro (train station)
4 Sede do Parque Nacional Peneda-Gerês
5 Tourism Office
6 Sé
7 Câmara Municipal (Town Hall)
8 Mercado Municipal
9 Casa Dos Crivos
10 Torre de Menagem
11 Museu dos Biscainhos
12 Casa Museu Nogueira Silva
13 Museu Medina e Museu Pio XII
14 Police

the seat of the Primate of Portugal. Braga's people are considered by some the most pious, by others the most fanatic, and by all the most politically conservative in the country.

The 1926 coup that ushered Salazar into power was launched from here. Yet in spite of the politics and the immense number of (primarily Gothic) churches in Braga, hedonism marches cheerfully forward in the form of modern bars and discos that keep cropping up. So don't be scared—Braga is an attractive and architecturally rich city.

ORIENTATION AND PRACTICAL INFORMATION

Praça da República lies in the heart of the city. Wide **Avenida da Liberdade** runs north to south from the *praça* to the hills of Pinheiro da Gregória. Perpendicular to Av. Liberdade, Av. Central runs along a tapering park leading into **Largo da Senhora-a-Branca.** If you follow **Rua do Souto,** a pedestrian thoroughfare lined with luxe stores, it becomes **Rua Dom Diogo de Sousa** and then **Rua Andrade de Corvo,** leading straight to the **train station** (15min.). To reach the **bus station,** take R. Chãos from Pr. República until you reach a small square; pick up Av. General Norton de Matos (on your right) and continue to the bus station.

Tourist Office: Av. Central, 1 (tel. 225 50), at the corner of Av. Liberdade. Adequate maps. English spoken. Open Mon.-Fri. 9am-7pm, Sat.-Sun. 9am-12:30pm and 2-5:30pm; winter Mon.-Fri. 9am-7pm, Sat. 9am-5pm.

Currency Exchange: Hotel Carandá, Av. Liberdade, 96 (tel. 61 45 00), a 10-min. walk from the *praça.* No commission. Open 8am-10pm. **Banco Borges and Irmao,** Pr. República, across from Turismo. Open Mon.-Fri. 8:30am-2:30pm.

Post Office: Av. Liberdade (tel. 225 66), 2 bl. south of Turismo. Open Mon.-Fri. 8:30am-6:30pm, Sat. 9am-12:30pm. Open for **telephones** Mon.-Fri. 9am-noon and 2-5pm. Annoyingly distant main office on Ferreiros for Posta Restante. Take bus #27 from Av. Central. Open same hrs. as branch office. **Postal Code:** 4700.

Telephones: In the post office building, and in a kiosk under the Arcada on the *praça.* **Telephone Code:** 053.

Trains: on Largo Estaçao (tel. 736 65). Virtually everything requires a change of train at Nine, ½hr. to the west. To: Barcelos (16 per day, 1hr., 200$); Porto (13 per day, 1½hr., 580$); Viana do Castelo (11 per day, 2hr., 390$); Vila Nova de Cerveira (8 per day, 3hr., 580$); Valença (8 per day, 3hr., 635$, with 2 daily connections to Vigo, Spain); Coimbra (12 per day, 4hr., 905$). At 7:45am and 5:20pm there's an **Inter-Cidades** train that goes with few stops to Porto and then to Lisboa.

Buses: Central de Camionagem (tel. 61 60 80), a few bl. north of the center. A host of bus companies provide service. **Rodoviária** runs to: Porto (10 per day, 1½hr., 580$); Guimarães (6 per day, 1hr., 320$); Campo do Gerês, a.k.a. São João do Campo (6 per day, 1½hr., 500$); Coimbra (4 per day, 3hr., 1100$); Lisboa (8 per day, 8hr., 1800$); Faro (2 per day, 13hr., 2800$). **Hoteleira do Gerês,** a private company, sends blue and white buses to Gerês (10 per day, 1½hr., 505$).

Taxis: tel. 67 23 61. To the youth hostel from the train station 400$.

English Bookstore: best-sellers in **Feira Nova** supermarket (see Food listings).

Hospital: Hospital São Marcos, Largo Carlos Amarante (tel. 61 33 30).

Emergency: tel. 115. .

Police: Campo de Santiago (tel. 61 32 50).

ACCOMMODATIONS AND CAMPING

Braga resounds with *pensões.* The cheapest are concentrated around the **Hospital de São Marcos,** the more expensive around Av. Central.

Pousada de Juventude (HI), R. Santa Margarida, 6 (tel. 61 61 63). From Turismo, walk down Av. Central until the tapering park peters out, then turn left on Largo Senhora-a-Branca. A clean, relaxing stop *en route* to Peneda-Gerês National Park. Reception open 9am-noon and 6pm-midnight. 1200$ per person; Oct.-May 900$ per person. Breakfast included. Reservations recommended July-Aug.

Residencial Inácio Filho, R. Francisco Sanches, 42 (tel. 238 49). From the *praça,* walk down R. Souto 1 bl.; R. Francisco Sanches is the 1st perpendicular pedestrian street. Small, well-kept establishment where you'll get your fill o' Braga's old-fashioned feel. Doubles 4500$, with bath 5000$.

Residência Grande Avenida, Av. Liberdade, 738 (tel. 229 55), around the corner from Turismo. Reception on 3rd floor. Rooms with elegant mirrors and furniture. Victorianesque sitting room. Singles 3000$, with bath 4200$. Doubles 5500$, with bath 6500$. Breakfast included. Reserve 2 weeks ahead in summer.

Residencial dos Terceiros, R. Capelistas, 85 (tel. 704 66 or 704 78), across the street from the Terceiros church and diagonally across the *praça* from Turismo. Simple, new, and neat, with radios, telephones, and free breakfast. All rooms have full bath, some with TV. Laundry machines for guests. Singles 6000$. Doubles 8000$. Triples 9000$. Quads 9900$. Lower in winter.

Camping: Parque da Ponte (tel. 733 55), 2km down Av. Liberdade from the center, next to the stadium and the municipal pool. Buses to and from station stop 20m from the entrance every ½hr. Market and laundry facilities. 300$ per person, 215$ per tent, 250$ per car. Electricity 180$.

FOOD

Braga has many cafés, several superb restaurants, and little in between. Old city, here you come. A municipal **market** invades Pr. Comércio, two blocks from the bus station. (Open Mon.-Sat. 7am-3pm.) This *praça* has a number of restaurants which serve typically heavy Minhoto dishes.

Groceries: Feira Nova, Av. Padre Júlio Fragata (tel. 61 68 13). From Pr. Comércio walk 20min. down Av. Central and continue straight as it becomes R. S. Vitor and R. D. Pedro V. Take a left onto Av. Padre Júlio Fragata. Open Mon.-Fri. 10am-10pm, Sat. 9am-11pm, Sun. 9am-9pm.

Café Vianna, Pr. República, under the arcade across the *praça* from Turismo, look for an offensive statue in front. A snappy café with pink marble and mirrors. Real breakfasts (300-750$), lunches, and dinners (entrees 400-1000$). At night it turns into a popular bar/disco, sometimes with live music. Open Mon.-Sat. 8am-2am.

Restaurante Tia Rosalina, R. Chãos, 25-31 (tel. 225 41). A half bl. up on the left as you go from Turismo up the steep hill toward the bus station. New restaurant with old stone walls, but the rustic atmosphere doesn't slow the waiters down. Entrees 600-1400$. Open Mon.-Sat. 7am-11pm.

Café-Pizzaria Neptuno, in the C.C. do Rechicho shopping complex, store #61 on R. Raio (tel. 61 78 91). Overflowing salads. Tasty thin brick-oven pizza with every imaginable topping. The owner speaks a little English in case you don't know your *cogumelos* from your *cebolas*. Pizzas 600-980$. Open 10am-midnight. (Incidentally, those are mushrooms and onions.)

A Brasileira, Largo Barão de São Martinho, in the square before R. Souto. Romantic café studded with intellectuals. Open Mon.-Sat. 7am-midnight.

Churrasqueira da Sé, D. Paio Mendes, 25. The cathedral barbecue. Quiet, airy eating room serves pork chops, veal, and excellent omelettes. Half-portions (450-750$) are plenty for one person. Open 9am-11pm, closed Wed.

SIGHTS

When Braga isn't ablaze with religious fervor or rollicking students, the city lolls in an affluent lull. Braga's **sé** (Portugal's oldest cathedral) is a heavy granite structure modified many times since its construction in the 11th and 12th centuries. There are guided tours in Portuguese to its **tesouro, coro alto,** and **capelas.** The tour begins in the **sala forte** (strong room), which contains the archdiocese's most precious paintings and relics. Foremost among these is the *Cruzeiro do Brazil,* the plain iron cross of Pedro Alvares Cabral's ship when he discovered Brazil in 1500; it was used in the first Portuguese mass in the New World. The treasury's real treats are the *cofres cranianos* (brain boxes), one of which contains the 6th-century cortex of São Martinho Dume, the first bishop of Braga. The *coro alto* (upper choir) has a pipe organ with 2424 fully functional pipes still used at Mass.

Adjacent to the church, off a Renaissance cloister, molder two historic *capelas tumulares* (tomb chapels). The **Capela dos Reis** (Kings' Chapel) guards the 12th-century stone sarcophagi of Dom Afonso Henriques' parents. More arresting are the mummified remains of a 14th-century archbishop. The 14th-century **Capela de Nossa Senhora da Glória** next door protects the carved tomb of an archbishop, in spite of its Moorish pattern. (Treasury and chapels open 8:30am-6:30pm; Oct.-June 8:30am-12:30pm and 1:30-6:30pm. Admission 200$.)

The street behind the chapel leads to a square flanked by the 17th-century **Capela de Nossa Senhora da Conceição** and the picturesque **Casa dos Coimbras.** The chapel has an interior faced with *azulejos* depicting the story of Adam and Eve and a finely carved *Entombment of Christ.* (Open Mon.-Fri. 9:30am-1pm and 2:30-7pm. Free.)

The Rococo facade of **Igreja de Santa Cruz** gleams across from the monumental **Hospital de São Marcos** on Largo Carlos Amarante. Statues of the Twelve Apostles crown the latter's Baroque facade. Of a completely different spirit is the **Casa dos Crivos** (Screens) on R. São Marcos, with its Moorish latticed screen window covers.

Curvaceous and colorful, the **Jardim de Santa Bárbara** prefaces an archaic set of free-standing arches. Around the corner in the spacious **Praça do Município,** the **Câmara Municipal** (City Hall) and **Biblioteca Municipal** eye each other from either side of a graceful fountain.

A block and a half down R. Souto on the right stands the **Largo do Paço,** an arch-bishop's palace turned university administration building. Heavy black iron chandeliers hang from ornate ceilings of the stone-walled **Salão Medieval.** (Open Mon.-Fri. 9am-noon and 2-8pm. Free.)

ENTERTAINMENT

Braga's nightlife belies the city's conservative reputation. Nothing gets started before 10pm. Discos, pubs, and cafés clutter **Avenida da Liberdade;** try **Trigo-nometria** for the sine of your life. Farther down is the disco **Club '84.**

Braga's Holy Week, at once solemn and festive, features a great religious procession and a busy schedule of parades and concerts all week long. The streets are decorated entirely in purple and black. (Ask at Turismo for a detailed program.) During the **Festival de São João** (June 23-24), the entire main avenue becomes a makeshift disco carnival, with a quacky rubber-duck melee on the last night.

EXCURSIONS

Igreja do Bom Jesús: Braga's most famous landmark is actually 5km out of town on a hillside carpeted in greenery. The 18th-century Igreja's purpose was to recreate a Jerusalem in Braga so that Christians unable to voyage to Palestine could make a pilgrimage here. The **chapel** itself demonstrates scenes from the Passion of Christ, and the famous **Stairway of Five Senses** illustrates tree-like wonders. Reaching the stairway is part of the fun. Take the long, slow walk up the granite-paved pathway that forks into two zig-zagging stairways, or the water-powered funicular ferry (100$). From Braga, buses labeled "#02 Bom Jesús" depart (at 10 and 40min. past the hr; tickets 155$) from the stop in Largo Carlos Amarante, in front of Hospital de São Marcos, and stop at the bottom of the stairway and the funicular.

Citânia de Briteiros: 9km from Bom Jesus, stone house foundations and huts jut out of the hills in the best preserved collection of Celtic ruins in Portugal. Site open 9am-sundown. Admission 200$. Four buses per day leave from in front of the tourist office. Hail bus #12—Pedraiva—and get off at "Lageosa." The site is a 2km walk up the road.

Mosteiro de Tibães: In an unspoiled forest, this 11th-century Benedictine monastery reflects centuries of neglect. Stone tombs rattle eerily underfoot the weathered **claustro.** Adjoining the cloister is a magnificently preserved **igreja,** with a narrow, cylindrical ceiling and ornate high altar. Through the kitchen and the back woods is another chapel. (Open Tues.-Sun. 9am-noon and 2-7pm. Guided tour free.) A city bus rides 6km from Braga to the monastery. Buses labeled "Sarrido" leave from Pr. Conde de Agrolongo, 1 bl. west up R. Capelistas from Pr. República. The stop itself is in front of the "Arca-Lar" store, with the schedule posted (roughly every 2hr., 195$).

Parque Nacional Peneda Gerês: An unspoiled expanse of mountains, lakes, vegetation, and wildlife, Parque Nacional de Peneda Gerês occupies the Vale do Alto just south of the Spanish border at Portela do Homem, 43km north of Braga. Hiking routes between the main village of Gerês and the *miradouro* (lookout point) of Pedra Bela twist past glistening waterfalls and natural pools. On summer weekends, a bus connects several of the villages that inhabit the huge park. 16km east of the main village in São Jão do Campo (a.ka. Campo do Gerês) an **HI Youth Hostel** (tel. 353 39), called Vilardinho das Furnas, borders the park. (1200$ per person. Breakfast included. Call ahead.) Rodoviária Nacional buses (5 per day, 1½hr., 465$) connect São Jão do Campo with Braga, but no direct link to Gerês exists. From there, take a blue-and-white Braga-bound bus, get off at the Rio Caldo stop, and catch Rodoviária's bus coming from Braga to São Jão do Campo.

■ NEAR BRAGA: GUIMARÃES

Known as the "cradle of the nation," Guimarães is now a monumental mid-sized country town roughly 1hr. southwest of Braga by bus or car. In 1143 Dom Afonso Henriques proclaimed himself the first King of Portugal here after defeating the Moors (and consequently eschewing the enlightened aspects of their rule).

Guimarães predates the kingdom of Portugal by a couple of centuries. The Galician countess Mumadona founded a Benedictine monastery here in the 10th century and supervised the construction of the **castelo** (castle), the keep of which remains intact. This impressive granite structure perches on a rocky hill near the center of town. It's viewed as Portugal's foremost historical monument because Dom Afonso Henriques emerged from the womb within its walls. (Open Tues.-Sun. 10am-12:30pm and 2:30-5:30pm. Free.)

While the castle protected its inhabitants from the Normans and the Moors, it provided few creature comforts. So the Dukes of Bragança, the local noble family of a less bellicose age, built a palatial manor house next door, the **Paço dos Duques de Bragança.** The elegant 15th-century *paço*, modeled after the late Gothic palaces of Northern Europe, was toasted as one of the finest noble houses in Portugal. In 1880, the government declared the *paço* a historic monument and began restoration. Inside, there's a museum of 15th-century Portuguese aristocratic life including furniture, silverware, crockery, tapestries, and weapons. In the banquet hall, tables that once seated 15th-century nobles now serve the presidents of Portugal at their conventions. During dinnertime, at least a quarter of the 39 fireplaces burn in order to heat the chilly building. (Open 9am-5:30pm. Admission 300$; Oct.-May 200$, students, seniors, and Thurs. free. Mandatory tour is available in various languages.)

The **Museu de Alberto Sampaio,** located in the Renaissance cloister of the **Igreja Colegiada de Nossa Senhora da Oliveira,** is back in the center of town. The church entrance fronts an arched Medieval square and outdoor temple. Like the castle, the church was commissioned by Mumadona. (Open Tues.-Sun. 9am-noon and 3-6pm. Free.) Next door, the museum collects late Gothic and Renaissance art. The 15th-century Gothic chapel of São Braz holds the granite tomb of Dona Constança de Noronha, first duchess of Bragrança. The courtyard *oliveira* (olive tree) symbolizes the patron saint of Guimarães. (Open Tues.-Sun. 10am-12:30pm and 2-5pm. Admission 200$. Students, seniors, and Sun. morning free.)

Guimarães offers few budget accommodations or restaurants. A bunch of church *padres* run the boarding house-like **Casa de Retiros,** R. Francisco Agra, 163 (tel. 51 15 15). From Turismo, head through Pr. Toural and straight up R. de Santo Antônio; R. Francisco Agra is narrow and curves left when you reach the traffic circle. Don't be scared off by the video camera at the door. The tidy bedrooms come with full bath, radio, phone, heating, and crucifix. The 11:30pm curfew isn't negotiable, and unmarried couples might not be permitted to share quarters. (Singles 3000$. Doubles 5000$. Breakfast included.) For a refreshment and sandwich in summer try the outdoor **café** (open 10am-midnight) under a canopy of trees in the Jardim de Alameda, in front of the Turismo.

The **tourist office** (tel. 41 24 50), hidden by signs pointing to various cities, is on Alameda de São Dámaso, facing Pr. Toural. The maps, unlike the regional guide, are free. (Open 9am-7pm.) The **post office** is at Rua de Santo António, 89 (tel. 41 50 32; open Mon.-Fri. 8:30am-6:30pm, Sat. 9am-12:30pm). The **postal code** is 4800 and the **telephone code** is 053. Call the **hospital,** on Rua dos Cutileiros, near Matadouros, at tel. 51 50 40, **emergencies** at tel. 115, and the **police** (Polícia de Segurança Pública) at Rua Capitão Alfredo Pimenta, next to the fire station (tel. 51 33 34).

To get to the tourist office from the **bus station** (tel. 41 26 46), follow the long street on the bank, Av. de Londres, then turn right at the intersection with a small garden in the traffic island. **Rodoviária** dispatches buses every half hour (last one at 8:25pm) for Braga (45min., 330$), and once a day to Porto (at 9:30 am, 1hr., 580$). Several private companies go everywhere else. **AMI** (tel. 41 26 46), goes locally to São Trocato and Madre de Deus (20 per day, 10-20min., 55$). A **taxi** (tel. 52 25 22) from the center of town up to Penha the shrine on the hill goes for around 1000$. The train station, a 10-minute walk south of Turismo down Av. Afonso Henriques (tel. 41 23 51), has service to Porto (every hr., 17 per day, 1¾hr., 450$).

■■■ VIANA DO CASTELO

Viana sustains the social scene of a beach town without the rampant commercialism of a seaside resort. In addition to the city beach, less crowded sand stretches north and south of town. July and August are a scene—but you can catch the heat and just miss the crowds in June and September. This port town is elegant and immaculate.

ORIENTATION AND PRACTICAL INFORMATION

Avenida dos Combatentes da Grande Guerra, the main avenue, glitters from the **train station** south to the **port,** on the Rio Lima. The **old town** spreads east of the avenue; to the west, the fortress and sea. Most restaurants and accommodations lie on side streets off Av. Combatentes.

Tourist Office: Pr. Erva (tel. 82 26 20), 1 bl. east of Av. Combatentes. From the train station, take the fourth left, then a sudden right. Maps and lists of lodgings in English and French. English spoken. Open Mon.-Sat. 9:30am-12:30pm and 2:30-6pm, Sun. 9:30am-12:30pm. **Branch** for basic info in the train station.

Currency Exchange: Automatic exchange machine outside Caixa Geral de Depósitos on the main boulevard. **Banco Nacional Ultramarino,** Pr. República, 44, on the main square. Open Mon.-Fri. 8:30am-3pm.

Post Office: Av. Combatentes (tel. 82 27 11), across from the train station. Open Mon.-Fri. 8:30am-6:30pm, Sat. 9am-12:30pm. **Postal Code:** 4900.

Telephones: In the post office. **Telephone Code:** 058.

Trains: (tel. 82 22 96), at the northern end of Av. Combatentes, directly under Santa Luzia hill. To: Vila Nova de Cerveira (6 per day, 1hr., 270$); Barcelos (15 per day, 1hr., 235$); Caminha (7 per day, 30min., 170$); Porto (8 per day, 2½hr., 550$); Vigo, Spain, via Valença (2 per day, 2hr., 1200$).

Buses: Rodoviária (tel. 250 47). Except for *expressos* (which leave from Av. Combatentes), all buses leave from **Central de Camionagem,** on the eastern edge of town, a 15-min. walk to the train station. From the bus station walk left, passing through a pedestrian underpass, or take the bus (110$). To Braga (8 per day, 1½hr., 540$). **AVIC** (tel. 82 97 05) and **Auto-Viaçáo do Minho** (tel. 82 88 34) face off on Av. Combatentes. To: Lisboa (2 per day, 6hr., 2000$); Porto (5 per day, 1½hr., 660$).

English Bookstore: Livraria Bertrand, R. Sacadura Cabral, 21 (tel. 82 28 38), off Pr. Erva. Best-sellers and maps. Open Mon.-Fri. 9am-7pm, Sat. 9am-1pm.

Hospital: Av. Abril, 25 (tel. 82 90 81).

Emergency: tel. 115.

Police: R. Aveiro (tel. 82 20 22).

ACCOMMODATIONS AND CAMPING

Except during the week of the Romaria de Nossa Senhora da Agonia in mid-August, accommodations in Viana are easy to find—but not particularly cheap. A good option is a room in a private home. Small, informal *pensões* (usually a few rooms above the family restaurant) are slightly cheaper but far worse in quality. The tourist office has clear, up-to-date lists of local accommodations.

Pensão Guerreiro, R. Grande, 14 (tel. 82 20 99), corner of Av. Combatentes and R. Grande. High ceilings, old-fashioned wallpaper, and big windows. Fight for a view of the port. Singles 1800$. Doubles 3500$. Sept.-June: 1500$; 2500$.

Pensão Vianense, Av. Conde da Carreira, 79 (tel. 82 31 18), the first right out of the train station. Small, plain rooms with fresh paint and pale wood furniture. Singles 2500$. Doubles 3500$. Oct.-May: 2000$; 3000$. Breakfast included.

Pensão Residencial Magalhães, R. Manuel Espregueira, 62 (tel. 82 32 93), 3 bl. from train station. English-speaking management provide spacious rooms and a clean common bath. Singles 2800-3800$, with bath 3800-4800$. Doubles 3500-4500$, with bath 4000-5000$. Triples 4500-5500$, with bath 6000-7000$.

Residência Viana Mar, Av. Combatentes, 215 (tel. 82 89 62). Large, clean, and efficient. Some noise from the avenue may permeate the rooms. Telephone, TV, and winter heating. Singles 3000$. Doubles 3000-5500$. Triples 6500$.

Camping: Two campsites wash up near the Praia do Cabedelo, Viana's ocean beach across the Rio Lima. Take the ferry (70$) and hike the 1km from the terminal, or hop a "Cabedelo" bus (90$) from the bus station or behind the train station near the funicular stop. **INATEL** (tel. 32 20 42), is off Av. Trabalhadores. 230$ per tent, 380$ per trailer. June and Sept.: 200$; 320$. Oct.-May: 150$; 290$. Showers 70$. Tents available for rent. Open Jan. 16-Dec. 15. **Orbitur** (tel. 32 21 67), is closer to the beach, better equipped, and more expensive. 480$ per person, 380$ per tent, 410$ per car. Hot showers 60$. Open Jan. 16-Dec. 15.

FOOD

Bloodthirsty diners drool over local specialty *arroz de sarabulho* (rice cooked in blood and served with sausages and potatoes). The less sanguine substitue *arroz de marisco,* rice cooked with different kinds of shellfish. The large municipal **market** sets up in Pr. Dona Maria II, several blocks east of Av. Combatentes. (Open Mon.-Sat. 8am-3pm.) Friday's market is a more extensive affair; look for it just west of Pr. General Barbosa. (Open 8am-5pm.) Most budget restaurants can be found on the small streets off Av. Combatentes.

Groceries: Brito's-Auto-Serviço, R. Manjovos, 31 (tel. 231 51). From the train station walk down Av. Combatentes; take the fifth side street on the right. Open 8am-12:30pm and 2:30-8pm.

Restaurante "O Vasco," R. Grande, 21 (tel. 246 65), on the side street across from Pensão Guerreiro. A clinically white interior with cheap, good specialties such as *polvo cozido* (boiled octopus) and *rojoes à moda do Minho* (mixed roast meat). Entrees 600-1100$. Open 11am-11pm.

Dolce Vita, R. Poço, 44 (tel. 248 60), across the *praça* from Turismo. Surprisingly wonderful Italian cuisine. Pizza and spaghetti 550-1100$. Portuguese dishes 900-1200$. Open noon-11pm; off-season noon-3pm and 8-11pm.

SIGHTS

Even in a country famous for charming squares, Viana's **Praça da República** is exceptional. In the center of the recently repaved square spouts a 16th-century fountain encrusted with sculpture and crowned by a sphere bearing a Cross of the Order of Christ. The small **Paço do Concelho** (1502), formerly the town hall, seals the square to the east, while diagonally across the playful, flowery facade of the **Igreja da Misericórdia** (1598, rebuilt in 1714) is supported by granite caryatids.

The **Museu Municipal,** west of Av. Combatentes on Largo São Domingos, occupies the former 18th-century palace of Dr. Barbosa Maciel. Amid the small museum's array of 18th-century furnishings and artwork, the prized and coveted possession is the collection of famous *cerâmica de Viana*. The illustrious doctor seems to have had a fascination with blood and gore. (Tel. 242 23; open Tues.-Sun. 9:30am-12:30pm and 2-5pm. Admission 120$; tour in Portuguese included.)

The cliff-like **colina de Santa Luzia** rises north of the city, crowned by an early 20th-century neo-Byzantine church and magnificent Celtic ruins. Take the stairs which link some of the switchbacks in the road. To reach the hilltop, take either the long stairway or the funicular, next to each other 200m behind the train station (walk through the station, over the tracks, and up a set of stone steps). Two cars inch their way up and down (every hr. in the morning, 2 per hr. in the afternoon, 9am-6pm, 70$).

For a better view of the harbor and ocean visit **Castelo de S. Tiago da Barra.** From the train station take the second right off Av. Combatentes (R. Gen. Luis do Rego) and follow this street five blocks and across the dusty parking lot. Built in 1589 by Spanish Felipe II, the walls of the *castelo* rise to the left.

Avoid the beach on Rio Lima, where hungry insects prowl, and head directly for **Praia do Cabedelo.** Take the **ferry** behind the parking lot at the end of Av. Combatentes. (Ferries every ½hr.; May-June and Oct.-Dec. 8:45am-10pm, July-Sept. until midnight, Jan.-April until 5pm; 70$ per ride.)

True beach connoisseurs abandon Viana altogether for those to the north. **Vila Praia de Ancora, Moledo,** and **Caminha,** some of the cleanest and least crowded beaches on the Costa Verde, are nearby. The coastal rail line has frequent stops as far north as Vila Nova de Cerveira and Valença. Vila Praia de Ancora, 16km from Viana, is the largest and most popular. It has two rail stops, the main "Ancora" station and the "Ancora-Praia" *apeadeiro* (only a platform, not a full station) just a few blocks from the beach. Moledo and Caminha, two and four local stops north of Ancora, are equally gorgeous (the train lets you off 1-2km from the sand). *Suburbano* (local) **trains** serve all three beach towns; regional trains do not stop at Moledo (7 per day, 140$ to Ancora-Praia, 160$ to Moledo, 170$ to Caminha).

■■■ NEAR THE RIO MINHO

VILA NOVA DE CERVEIRA

Named for a *cervo* (deer), tranquil Vila Nova de Cerveira gazes gently up at Spain, twitches its tail with apprehension (does this proximity mean tourism?), realizes it's in no danger, and goes about its business on the south bank of the Rio Minho. While the once-strategic town offers little more than lush scenery, its youth hostel makes Vila Nova an excellent base for trips to the handsome beaches of Ancora, Moledo, and Caminha, and to the even smaller towns of Valença do Minho and Ponte de Lima in the Alto Minho interior.

Two of Vila Nova's landmarks stand on the steep hills above the town: a whimsical sculpture that looks inevitably like Bambi, and the ruins of the **Monte Picoto monastery** and chapel. Both are the brainchildren of noted Portuguese architect and sculptor José Rodrigues. Trekkers with *chutzpah* can reach both via hiking trails. The Pr. Liberdade in the town center guards a charming runt of a **castelo,** originally designed in the 14th century as a look-out over Spain.

Vila Nova's **tourist office** (tel. 79 57 87) is at R. Antônio Douro, kitty-corner from Igreja de São Roque. From the train station, turn left and then left again at the first and only major intersection. Maps for Vila Nova and most of Northern Portugal. (Open Mon.-Sat. 9:30am-12:30pm and 2:30-6pm.) The **post office** (tel. 79 51 11) is next door to the bank on Pr. Alto Minho. (Open 9am-12:30pm and 2-5:30pm.) The **postal code** is 4920; the **telephone code** is 051. The **hospital** (tel. 79 53 51) is on the main highway past the edge of town. The **police** (tel. 79 51 13) preside over Largo 16 de Fevreiro. Take the last street on the left as you skip out of town.

The pristine, modern **HI youth hostel** (tel. 79 61 13), is at Largo 16 de Fevreiro, 21. From the train station turn left, then left again at the Fonseca Porto minimarket opposite the TURILIS office (15min.). Guests enjoy large rooms, a grassy patio, TV with VCR, and kitchen. The warden is the town sage. Some English spoken; reservations recommended. (Reception open 9am-noon and 6pm-midnight. 1300$ per person; breakfast included.) The nearest **campground** (tel. (058) 92 24 72) digs in 4km southwest in Vilar de Mouros, an out-of-the-way village called the "Woodstock" of Portugal. (400$ per person, 350$ per tent and per car.) The most popular alimentary scene is the **Café-Restaurante A Forja** on R. 25 de Abril. (Entrees 750-1050$. Open Tues.-Sun. 8am-11pm.) An equally scrumptious option is **Restaurante Abrigo das Andorinhas,** R. Queiroz Ribeiro (tel. 79 53 35), with stone walls and an extensive wine list. (Half-doses 550-850$. Open 8am-2am.)

The **train station** (tel. 79 62 65), is off the highway ½km east of town. To: Valença (9 per day, 25min., 130$, with 2 daily connections to Vigo, Spain); Vila Praia de Ancora (9 per day, 40min., 160$); Viana do Castelo (9 per day, 1hr., 270$); Porto (9 per day, 2½hr., 680$). Three private **bus** companies serve the same route as the train—up river to Valença and down the coast to Porto. **Turilis** buses leave from the Turilis travel agency (tel. 79 58 50) across the highway from the youth hostel. **AVIC** and **A. V. Minho** depart from Café A Forja, Av. 25 de Abril (tel. 79 53 11), between the hostel and the town center. All to: Valença (6 per day, 15min., 285$); Porto (4 per day, 2hr., 825$); Lisboa (3 per day, 7hr., 1950$). A **ferry** (½hr., 60$ per person, 280$ per car) shuttles between Vila Nova de Cerveira and the Galician town of Goyan, with bus connections to Vigo and La Guardia (in Spain).

CAMINHA

Jesus and St. Peter were passing through this town:
St. P: My Lord, what is this place called?
J: Caminha, caminha (walk on, walk on) we're in a hurry!

According to legend, this is how Caminha got its name. Today a steady dribble of unprodded tourists enjoys the hypnotically green hills, wide, luscious beaches, and the whitewashed medieval square.

Caminha dotes on the 15th-century Gothic **Igreja Matriz,** still guarded by an ancient rampart by the river, built during its heyday as a trading port. The masterfully carved wooden ceiling is an incredible contrast to the stark, stone altar. *Azulejos* scale the walls up to the narrow stained-glass windows. (During most of the year, the church is open only for mass (about 6:30pm), though a woman often wandering the grounds has a key. August open 2-5pm. Free.)

If enclosed spaces are getting you down, bask at the town **beach;** take a left on the riverside road, Av. Dantas Carneiro, and keep going for about 1.5km. The zealous will hop on the bus (10min.) or skip the 3km to the wide, unfettered **Moledo beach,** where the swift Rio Minho meets the Atlantic.

The **tourist office** is on R. Ricardo Joaquim Sousa (tel. 92 19 52), near the *igreja.* From the train station, walk straight ahead down Av. Manuel Xavier to a small square, then go down Tr. São João; take the second left and it will be a few baby steps away on the right. (Open Mon.-Sat. 9:30am-12:30pm and 2:30-6pm.) The **post office** (tel. 72 13 02) is in Pr. Pontault-Combault. From the main square, take R. 6 de Setembro. (Open for stamps and phones 9am-12:30pm and 2-5:30pm.) The **postal code** is 4910; the **telephone code** 058. The **Largo do Hospital** (tel. 72 13 06) is behind the town hall. The **police** (tel. 92 11 68) stake out on Av. Sairaiva near the train station.

While most budget travelers daytrip from Viana do Castelo, those who stay in Caminha often sleep in private houses; Turismo can call around on your behalf. Otherwise look around on Largo Sidonio Pais. **Pensão Rio Coura,** Largo Sidonio Pais (tel. 92 11 42), is simple and modest, but the restaurant downstairs enchanting. (Doubles 3500$, with shower 5000$. Winter: 2000$; 3000$.) The **Orbitur** campsite (tel. 92 12 95) is 1.5km south of Caminha on the river. (Open 8am-10pm. 455$ per person, 380$ per tent, and 390$ per car.) Grab the bus headed toward Viana do Castelo (13 per day, 250$). The **Vilar de Mouros** campsite (tel. 92 24 72), is between the Rio Minho and the Rio Coura, 7km east of Caminha (see also: Vila Nova de Cerveira). It's accessible by one morning local bus or by train to Lanhelas with a 2km walk (5 per day). **Restaurante Pero de Caminha,** in the main square, offers pizza and other Italian specialties. Most entrees 650-950$. Try the *Especiale do Chefe* (cheese, mushrooms, ham, asparagus, artichoke hearts, and olives, 950$). (Open noon-3:30pm and 7-10:30pm.)

The **train** station (tel. 92 29 25) is on Av. Saraira de Carvalho. To: Vila Nova de Cerveira (6 per day, 10min., 100$); Lanhelas (6 per day, 10min.); Porto (8 per day, 2-3hr., 710$). AVIC **buses** leave from just off the main *praça.* To: Porto (2hr., 760$); Lisboa (3 expresses per day, 6hr., 2050$). **Taxis** answer at 92 14 01.

VALENÇA DO MINHO

Within easy reach of Vila Nova de Cerveira, **Valença do Minho** marks the entrance to Northern Portugal from Túy, Spain. A 17th-century fortress encloses the city's historic section, offering stunning views of rolling hills and the Rio Minho through its stone arches and cannon portals. Unfortunately, the historic atmosphere is challenged by the presence of Spaniards buying pastel face-towels from every store front (towels are a major industry here). From the town, a winding road rises to the breath-taking summit of **Monte do Faro,** which overlooks the coastline, the Vale do Minho, and the Galician mountains. Valença has earned some notoriety as a smuggling center, chiefly for Spanish cigarettes and Portuguese wine.

The **turismo,** Av. Espanha (tel. 233 74), in hiding behind some trees, offers xeroxed maps of the fort. (Open 9:30am-6pm.) **Pensão Rio Minho** (tel. 223 31) has spacious, tidy rooms next to the train station. (Singles 3000-3500$. Doubles 4000-4500$.) For an affordable meal, dine outside the fortress in the new town. **Restaurante Cristina,** in the *centro comercial* next to the Lara Hotel, serves a hearty *cabrito assado no forno* (oven-roasted kid, 950$). *Prato do dia* 500$. (Open 8am-midnight.)

Valença is a stop on the Porto-Vigo **train** line (7 trains per day from Viana to Valença, 2 of which continue to Vigo, 330$).

PONTE DE LIMA

For an unforgettable daytrip, hop on a bus to **Ponte de Lima.** This highly picturesque town straddles the Rio Lima in the middle of the *vinho verde* (green wine) region. A 15-arch Roman bridge spans the river, which is nearly ½km wide here. **Igreja de São Francisco,** now a museum for temporary exhibits, has carved wood altarpieces and two unusual wooden pulpits. The **tourist office** (tel. 94 23 35) in Pr. República stocks information on accommodations and will arrange for a private home rental if you decide to move in. (Open Mon.-Sat. 9:30am-12:30pm and 2:30-6pm.) Inquire at **Restaurante Catrina** (tel. 94 12 67), near the bridge facing the river, if you plan to spend the night; the owner keeps rooms in his hotel (doubles 4000$). **Restaurante Encanada** (tel. 94 11 89), near the park, next to the market, serves enormous portions (about 900-1300$). The *sarrabulho* (rice and sausage) and the *bacalhau* (cod) are particularly good.

Trás-Os-Montes

The country's most desolate, rough, rainy, and isolated region, Trás-Os-Montes ("behind the mountains") is light-years off the beaten path. A local saying describes the extreme climate as "nine months of winter, three months of hell." Dom Sancho I had to practically beg people to settle here after he incorporated it into Portugal in the 11th century. Jews hid here during the Inquisition because it was so remote.

Getting to Trás-Os-Montes is half the fun; train service is slow and rickety (where it exists at all), and roads are twisty and treacherous. Few tourists pass by, although the region is mobbed with returning emigrants in August. Nonetheless, the area's isolation is much of its appeal, offering hikers splendid, unspoiled natural reserves in the Parque Natural de Alvão (accessible from Vila Real) and the Serra de Montesinho (north of Bragança).

Even the gastronomic specialities hint at Trás-Os-Montes's severity: *cozido à Portuguesa* is made from different kinds of sausages (including blood sausages), weird pig parts, carrots, and turnips. People consume lots of bread and *feijoada à Transmontana* (bean stew).

■■■ BRAGANÇA

Amid the rough terrain of the Serra da Nogueira, Bragança, the capital of Trás-Os-Montes, is dominated by the impeccably preserved medieval village of Cidadela. Within the Cidadela walls, the 13th-century *castelo* presides next to the council chamber, *Domus Municipalis*, attesting to the town's importance in the Middle Ages. Bragança is named for the royal dynasty (House of Bragança) that ruled Portugal for three centuries, until the abolition of the monarchy in 1910. It is an excellent base for exploring the starkly beautiful terrain of the **Parque Natural de Montesinho**, which extends northward into Spain.

ORIENTATION AND PRACTICAL INFORMATION

The **Praça da Sé** is the heart of town. **Avenida Cidade de Zamora** lies a couple blocks north of Pr. Sé. To the west is the **new quarter,** up R. Almirante Reis on Av. João da Cruz. To reach the **castle complex,** on a hill west of Pr. Sé, take **Rua Combatantes da Grande Guerra** and R. T. Coelho.

Tourist Office: Av. Cidade de Zamora (tel. 38 12 73), northeast of the center. From Pr. Sé take R. Abilio Beça, turn left on R. Marqués de Pômbal (2nd street), which leads to Av. Cidade de Zamora; Turismo is on the left side on the corner, built into a stone wall. Maps and pamphlets on surrounding area and help with accommodations. English and French spoken. Open Mon.-Fri. 9am-12:30pm and 2-5:30pm, Sat. 10am-12:30pm; Oct.-May Mon.-Fri. 9am-12:30pm and 2-5pm, Sat. 10am-12:30pm.

Currency Exchange: Many banks line Av. João da Cruz. Open Mon.-Fri. 8:30am-3pm. **Hotel Bragança,** Av. Francisco Sá Carneiro, might oblige after-hours. Try **Montepio Geral,** next door to Hotel Bragança: 1000$ commission plus 90$ tax for traveler's checks.

Post Office: R. 5 de Outubro, s/n (tel. 227 23), on the corner with Av. João da Cruz and R. Almirante Reis. Open for Posta Restante, express mail, and **telephones** Mon.-Fri. 9am-6pm. **Postal Code:** 5300

Telephones: At the **post office. Telephone Code:** 073.

Trains: Largo da Estação, Av. João da Cruz (tel. 223 97), the opposite end of the street from the post office. No trains dare come here, however. The nearest station is in Mirandela. Buses run from here to Mirandela (3 per day, 2½hr., 750$). From Mirandela there are trains to Porto (4 per day, 8hr., 1370$).

Buses: San-Vitur Travel Agency, Av. João da Cruz (tel. 33 18 26) sells tickets and has schedules. Buses leave further up the street, 300m beyond the train station, from the Rodonarte (tel. 33 18 70) stop. To: Vila Real (3 *expressos* per day, 2½hr., 1100$); Porto (3 *expressos* per day, 4½hr., 1250$); Coimbra (4 *expressos* per day, 5¾hr., 1600$); Lisboa (4 *expressos* per day, 7¼hr., 2200$); Zamora, Spain (1 per day, 2½hr., 1925$). For bus to Mirandela, see Trains above.

Public Transportation: Line #7 on the yellow and blue S.T.U.B. buses forges 4km northward to the camp ground. They leave across from Banco de Fomento on the corner of Av. João da Cruz (2 afternoon buses per day, 10min., 140$).

Taxis: (tel. 221 38). Congregate across from the post office; to camp ground 650$.

Hospital: Hospital Distrital de Bragança, Av. Abade de Baçal (tel. 33 12 33), before the stadium on the road to Chaves.

Emergency: tel. 115.

Police: Governo Civil building, R. José Beça (tel. 33 13 54).

ACCOMMODATIONS, CAMPING, AND FOOD

Plenty of cheap *pensões* cluster about **Praça da Sé** and up **Rua Almirante Reis.** Traditional Portuguese fare prowls the Pr. Sé. More modern, expensive cafés and restaurants line **Avenida João da Cruz.** The region is celebrated for *presunto* (cured ham), *salpicão* (sausages), and *cozido* (a stew of boiled meats and vegetables).

Pensão Rucha, R. Almirante Reis, 42 (tel. 33 16 72), on the street connecting Pr. Sé to Av. João da Cruz. The sign is *inside* the doors—look carefully. Clean, old-style lodgings run by an old-style couple. Singles 1800$. Doubles 3500$.

Residencial Nordeste Shalom, Av. Abade de Baçal (tel. 33 16 67), on the road to Chaves across from the stadium and before the train bridge (1½km). As welcoming and peaceful as the name suggests, with satellite TV, modern baths, parking, and lounge. Singles 5100$. Doubles 6600$. Winter discount. Breakfast included.

Camping: Parque de Campismo do Sabor (tel. 268 20), 4km from town on the edge of the Montesinho park (see Public Transportation above). 175$ per person, 140-270$ per tent, 180$ per car. Electricity 70$. Open May-Sept. **Campo Verde** (tel. 993 71), on the road to Vinhais, 8km from town. A new private park. 750$ per person with swimming pool use, 500$ without. 350$ per tent and per car. Electricity 300$.

Restaurante Lá Em Casa, R. Marquês de Pombal, 7 (tel. 221 11). Rustic decor and user-friendly food. *Bacalhau cozido* (boiled codfish, 950$). Entrees 900-1800$, entire meal about 2500$. Open noon-4pm and 6pm-midnight.

Restaurante Poças, R. Combatentes da Grande Guerra, 200 (tel. 33 14 28), off Pr. Sé to the east. Classic grub in a no-frills setting. Often crowded, but lively. *Costeleta de vitela grelhada* (grilled steak, 850$). Most entrees 750-1200$. Open noon-3pm and 7-10pm.

SIGHTS AND ENTERTAINMENT

High above the rest of town, the handsome, brooding **castelo** (10-min. walk down R. Combatentes and R. T. Coelho) houses a **Museu Militar** (military museum). Museum displays range from medieval battle swords to a World War I machine gun nest. (Tel. 223 78; open Fri.-Wed. 9am-noon and 2-5pm. Admission 100$, students with ID 60$.)

The Medieval **pelourinho** (pillory) outside the **torre** bears the coat of arms of the House of Bragança. Impaled atop the whipping post is a prehistoric granite pig. In the Iron Age people were bound to the pig as a punishment.

The **Domus Municipalis,** behind the church opposite the *torre*, contained cisterns in the 13th century, but later became the municipal meeting house. The pentagonal building is actually just one bench-filled room above the cisterns. (If it's closed, the *senhora* across the street at #40 has the key; be sure to tip her.)

Four blocks from the gates of the castle on R. Serpa Pinto, the **Museu Abade de Baçal,** set up in the house of a 17th-century bishop, highlights granite pigs, beds, Portuguese art, and mannequins in regional dress. (Closed for renovation in 1994.)

■■■ VILA REAL

Vila Real teeters over the edge of the gorges of the Corgo and Cabril Rivers in the foothills of the Serra do Marão. This modest community, made affluent by a recent agricultural surge, serves as the principal commercial center for the southern farms of Trás-Os-Montes. The old town center is ringed by new boroughs reaching into the hills; the main street swoons with the heady scent of rosebuds, and its few cafés brim with youth. Vila Real is famed throughout Portugal for its black pottery with a leaden sheen. The town makes a good point of departure for excursions into the fertile fields and rocky slopes of the Serras do Alvão and Marão.

ORIENTATION AND PRACTICAL INFORMATION

100km east of Porto, Vila Real's old town centers on **Avenida Carvalho Araújo,** a broad tree-lined avenue that streams from the post office (off the corner of a small rotunda with fountain) downhill to the Câmara Municipal.

Tourist Office: Av. Carvalho Araújo, 94 (tel. 32 28 19; fax 32 17 12). Good town map and information about Parque Natural do Alvão. English and French spoken. Open 9:30am-7pm; Oct.-March 9:30am-12:30pm and 2-5pm; April-May 9:30am-12:30pm and 2-7pm.

Currency Exchange: Realvitur, Largo do Pioledo, 2 (tel. 32 18 00), 4 bl. uphill from Turismo and to the right. Same rates as the banks but longer hours. Open Mon.-Fri. 9am-7pm, Sat. 9am-1pm.

Post Office: Av. Carvalho Araújo (tel. 32 22 01), up the street and across from the tourist office. Open for Posta Restante and **telephones** Mon.-Fri. 9am-6:30pm. **Postal Code:** 5000.

Telephones: At the **post office. Telephone Code:** 059.

Trains: Av. 5 de Outubro (tel. 32 21 93). To get to the town center, walk straight up Av. 5 de Outubro over the iron bridge onto R. Miguel Bombarda, and turn left on R. Roque da Silveira. With the river on the left, continue to bear left until Av. Primeiro de Maio. Trains crawl; almost everything requires a change at Régua. To: Porto, via Régua (5 per day, 3hr., 820$); Bragança, with changes in Régua, Tua, and from Mirandela by bus (3 per day, 8hr., 850$).

Buses: Rodonorte, R. D. Pedro de Castro (tel. 32 22 47), on a square directly uphill from Turismo. To: Guimarães (3 per day via Amarante, 720$); Porto (3 per day, 2hr., 800$); Lisboa (5 per day, 7hr., 2050$, lunch included). **Rodoviária,** out of Ruicar Travel Agency, R. Gonçalo Cristovão, 16 (tel. 37 12 34), near Rodo Norte uphill on the right. To: Viseu (2 per day, 2½hr., 950$); Coimbra (2 per day, 4½hr., 1150$); Lisboa (2 per day, 8hr., 800$); Bragança (3 per day, 2½hr., 1070$).

Taxis: (tel. 32 12 96). Queue along R. Carvalho Araújo. To Mateus (500$).

Hospital: Hospital Distrital de Vila Real (tel. 34 10 41) in Lordelo, north of the town center.

Emergency: tel. 115.

Police: Largo Comandante Amarante (tel. 32 20 22).

ACCOMMODATIONS, CAMPING, AND FOOD

All accommodations lie close together in the town center. Several cafés along **Avenida Carvalho Araújo** advertise rooms upstairs, and three *pensões* line **Travessa São Domingos,** the side street next to the cathedral. Restaurants around **Avenida António de Azevedo** and **Primeiro de Maio** cook for little in exchange. Across the street from the bus station on R. D. Pedro de Castro, the huge **market** is open Tues.-Fri. 9am-noon.

Residencial Encontro, Av. Carvalho Araújo, 78 (tel. 32 23 25), a few doors down from Turismo. Cozy rooms and immaculate common baths are a good deal if you can stand the noise and sweltering summer heat. Try bargaining down prices if they're not full. Singles 3000$. Doubles with bath 5500$. Breakfast included.

Pensão Mondego, Trav. São Domingos, 11 (tel. 32 30 97), off Av. Carvalho Araújo across from the cathedral. Morning bells substitute for an alarm clock—they're early; they're loud. Bright, carpeted rooms with full baths are a bit worse for wear. Singles 2500$. Doubles with bath 3000$. Quads with bath 6000$.

Camping: Municipal Campground (tel. 247 24), just northeast of town on a bluff above the Corgo River. Get on Av. Marginal and follow the signs. Free swims in the river or the new pool complex. 400$ per person, 250$ per tent and per car.

Restaurante Nova Pompeia, R. Carvalho Araújo, 82 (tel. 728 76), next to tourist office above popular Café Nova Pompeia. Low prices, middling environs, high A/C. *Lulas grelhadas* (grilled squid, 740$). *Prato do día* about 650$. Excellent combination meals 400-850$. Entrees 650-1000$. Open Mon.-Sat. 8am-midnight.

Restaurante 22, Pr. Luís de Camões, 14 (tel. 32 12 96), uphill from tourist office. A classic: small dining room with stone walls, wooden tables, and wine bottles on an overhead shelf. Calming stereo instead of blaring TV. *Bacalhau à "22"* (1100$) makes the chef grin. Entrees 900-1400$. Open Mon.-Sat. 7am-midnight.

SIGHTS AND ENTERTAINMENT

At the lower end of Av. Carvalho Araújo looms the 15th-century **sé,** with its simple interior divided by thick, arched columns. Two blocks east of the cathedral stands the **Capela Nova** (New Chapel), with its floral facade. At the end of R. Combatentes da Grande Guerra loiters **Igreja de São Pedro,** full of 17th-century *azulejos.*

While a superflux of cafés provide the town's main entertainment. Locals meet at at **Copos e Rezas,** Largo do Pioledo, Bloco E, Cave A, or at **Pimms II,** R. de Santa Iria, 40 (tel. 722 99). Kick up your heels at **In Loco,** Calcada (tel. 34 69 24) or **Ritmin,** Largo do Pioledo, C. Comerc. D. Dinis Inja, 22 (tel. 717 89). Vila Real also hosts the wild and crazy (for this area at least) **festivals** of Santo António (June 13) and São Pedro (June 20). Book ahead.

■ NEAR VILA REAL

The village of **Mateus,** 3km east of Vila Real, is world-renowned for its rosé wine. The **Sogrape Winery,** on the main road from Vila Real, 200m from the turn-off for the Palácio Mateus, has a terrific free tour of the wine-processing center (with unlimited free tasting of the strong stuff). (Open 9-11am and 2-4pm; Oct.-May 9am-noon and 2-5pm, though hours are flexible.)

Up the road from the Sogrape Winery, and surrounded by its vineyards, glitters the Baroque **Palácio Mateus** (tel. 32 31 21; fax 32 65 53) featured on the label of every bottle of Mateus rosé wine. Inside hangs an original 1817 edition of Luís de Camões's *Os lusiadas,* Portugal's famous literary epic. In the 18th-century chapel, the 250-year-old remains of a certain São Marco, a Spanish soldier, recline fully dressed in a glass case. (Open 9am-1pm and 2-7pm; winter 9am-12:30pm and 2-6pm. Last of the tedious mandatory tours begin an hour before closing times. Admission to mansion and gardens 850$, to gardens alone 650$.)

Rodonorte (tel. 232 34) operates seven **buses** per day from Vila Real (10min., one-way 125$), departing from the Câmara Municipal in the morning, from Cabanelas bus station in the afternoon. Ask the driver to let you off at Mateus, as the closest proper stop is further down at Abambres. Walk to Abambres to catch the return bus to Vila Real. Many people **walk** from Vila Real to Mateus; the road loops, so follow signs south from Vila Real's train station or north from the main highway out of town. A **taxi** costs 500$.

Using Vila Real as a base, hardy souls explore the **Parque Natural do Alvão,** a protected area spreading to the heights of the Serra do Alvão and Serra do Marão. The hill town of **Lamas de Olo,** teetering 1000m above sea level (a four-hour trudge straight up) is near mysterious granite dwellings and the spectacular **Rio Olo gorge.** No buses serve this region.

Ribatejo and Alentejo

Fertile Ribatejo (named *riba do Tejo*—bank of the Tagus—by its first settlers) fills most of the basin of the Tejo and its main tributary, the Zêzere. Although farmed intensely, the area is best known in Portugal as a pastureland and breeding ground for Arabian horses and great black bulls.

Huge Alentejo *(além do Tejo* means beyond the Tagus) covers almost one-third of the Portuguese land mass, but with a population barely over half a million it remains the least populous region. Aside from the mountainous west, the region is a vast granary, though severe droughts, resistance to contour farming, and overplanting of soil-drying eucalyptus trees have severely affected its agricultural capacity. Ambitious plans to irrigate large tracts of land with water from the Tejo and the Guadiana have been stalled by Lisboa's refusal to cooperate with local governments. Several medieval towns grace the Alentejo Baixo, while Beja is the only major town on the seemingly endless Alentejo Alto plain.

■■■ SANTARÉM

Capital of the Ribatejo province and its major town, Santarém sits on a rocky mound overlooking the Rio Tejo. Santarém's name is derived from Santa Iria, a nun who was accused of lapsed virtue and cast into the river; when she washed up in Santarém her body was autopsied and pronounced innocent. Santarém, Beja, and Braga were the three ruling cities of the ancient Roman province Lusitania. Taken from the Moors by Portuguese King Afonso Henriques in 1147, Santarém was home to several kings. A flourishing medieval center—the town boasted 15 convents—it is known today as the capital of Portugal's Gothic style.

ORIENTATION AND PRACTICAL INFORMATION

The core of this swiftly growing town is formed by the densely packed streets between **Praça Sá da Bandeira** and the park **Portas do Sol,** below which flows the Rio Tejo. **Rua Capelo Ivêns,** which begins at the *praça,* contains the tourist office and many *pensões.*

> **Tourist Office:** R. Capelo Ivêns, 63 (tel. 39 15 12). Helpful staff dispenses maps and information on festivals and accommodations. Helps find bus and train schedules and private rooms for visitors. English spoken. Open Mon.-Fri. 9:30am-12:30pm and 2-6pm, Sat.-Sun. 9:30am-12:30pm and 2-5pm.
>
> **Currency Exchange: Banco Nacional Ultramarino,** on corner of Dr. Texeira Guedes and R. Capelo Ivêns. Open Mon.-Fri. 8:30am-3pm.
>
> **Post Office:** On the corner of Largo Candido do Reis and R. Dr. Texeira Guedes (tel. 280 11). Turn right from the front door of the tourist office, take another right at the next intersection, and walk 2 bl. Open for all services, **telegrams,** and **telephones** Mon.-Fri. 8:30am-6:30pm, Sat. 9am-12:30pm. **Postal Code:** 2000. **Telephone Code:** 043.
>
> **Trains:** (tel. 231 80), 2km outside town with connecting bus service from the bus station (every 30min., 10min., 150$). Otherwise take a taxi (350-400$); it's a steep 20-min. walk up dangerous roads. To: Lisboa (almost every hr., 1hr., 500$); Tomar (every 2hr., 1hr., 360$); Portalegre (4 per day via Entroncamento, 3hr., 885$); Faro (7 per day via Lisboa, 4hr., 1700$); Porto (7 per day, 4hr., 1250$).
>
> **Buses: Rodoviária Tejo,** Av. Brasil (tel. 220 01). Convenient location. To reach the tourist office, walk through the park and cross busy Av. Marquês Sá da Bandeira. Turn right and then left, taking R. Pedro Canavarro uphill, and make a right on R. Capelo Ivêns. To: Lisboa (5 *expressos* per day, 1hr., 850$; others every hr., 1½hr., 700$); Tomar (1 per day, 1½hr., 800$); Caldas de Rainha (2 per day, 1½hr., 590$); Faro (3 per day, 7hr., 2000$).

Taxis: Scaltaxis (tel. 33 29 19) congregate across from the bus station.

Luggage Storage: On the bus station platform (90$ per day). At the train station, on the right as you exit (250$ per day).

Laundromat: Tinturaria Americana, R. João Alfonso, 15 (tel. 235 02). Near the post office; walk down R. Elias Garcia, then take second left. Dry cleaning only. Shirts 250$, pants 400$. Open Mon.-Fri. 9am-1pm and 2:30-7pm, Sat. 9am-3pm.

Hospital: Av. Bernardo Santareno (tel. 37 05 78). From Pr. Sá da Bandeira, walk up R. Cidade da Covilhã which becomes R. Alexandre Herculano. English spoken.

Emergency: tel. 115.

Police: Pr. Sá da Bandeira (tel. 220 22). Follow the signs from the bus station about 100m. English spoken.

ACCOMMODATIONS AND CAMPING

Staying here can be expensive. During the Ribatejo Fair (10 days starting the first Friday in June) prices for rooms increase 10-40%; the tourist office can help find a double in a private house for about 3000-3500$ (2000$ during the rest of the year). True budget *pensões* leave plenty to be desired; those with amenities are often worth the extra money.

Pensão do José (a.k.a. **Pensão da Dona Arminda),** Trav. Froes, 14 and 18 (tel. 230 88), make a left as you exit the Turismo and then take the first right; under sign that reads "rooms." Clean and cozy, on a quiet street. Singles 1500$. Doubles 3000$, with shower 3500$. Higher during fairs, lower in off-season.

Residencial Muralha, R. Pedro Canavarro, 12 (tel. 223 99), between Av. Marquês Sá da Bandeira and R. Capelo Ivêns. Garish colors reminiscent of the 1970s, but a good deal for the price. Singles 2500$, with shower 3200$, with bath 3250$. Doubles with shower 3200-3900$, with bath 4000-4500$. Breakfast included.

Residencial Beirante, R. Alexandre Herculano, 5 (tel. 255 47). Turn left exiting the bus station, bear right at the end of the block onto R. Mercado, then left onto R. Herculano. All rooms with TV, phone, sparkling bathroom, and blessed wall fan. Singles 3750$. Doubles with double bed 5000$, with two beds 6000$. Triples 7000$. Breakfast included.

Residencial Abidis, R. Guilherme de Azevedo, 4 (tel. 220 17), around corner from tourist office. Room quality varies from luxurious to adequate, though prices do not vary accordingly. Soothing, 19th-century-ish decorations, but quite noisy outside. Singles 2500$, with bath 4500$. Doubles 4500$, with bath 6000-7000$. Breakfast included.

Camping: Parque do Campismo Municipal, Largo do Municípo (call Town Hall tel. 33 30 71 for info). From the bus station turn left on Av. Brasil, and take the first right on an unmarked street that leads past the park to R. Cidade da Covilhã. Turn left, then right after the Jardim da República. The campground is small, primitive, and rarely full. Free. Hot showers 60$.

FOOD

Eateries cluster in and around **Rua Capelo Ivêns. The municipal market,** in the colorful pagoda-thing on Largo Infante Santo near the Jardim da República, supplies fresh produce and vegetables. (Open Mon.-Sat. 8am-2pm.)

Groceries: Minipreço Supermarket, R. Pedro Canavarro, 31. The street leading from the bus station to R. Capelo Ivêns. Open Mon.-Sat. 9am-8pm.

Restaurante Pigalle, R. Capelo Ivêns, 15 (tel. 242 05). Always bustling with locals. The bar dominates the scene. Specializes in chicken, *frango batata e salada* (½-chicken with fries and salad, 700$). Entrees (750-1300$) are 100$ less at the *balçao* (bar) than at the table. Open Mon.-Sat. 8am-midnight.

Pastelaria Venezia, R. Capelo Ivêns, 99 (tel. 223 12). Delicious pastries and croissants—an excellent stop for a snack or light lunch. Open Mon.-Sat. 8am-7pm.

Restaurante Caravana, Trav. Froes, 24 (tel. 225 68), a side street off R. Capelo Ivêns; another entrance in the square around the corner. Next to Pensão do José.

Good food in a clean, modest restaurant frequented by locals. Entrees 650-800$.
Open Sun.-Fri. 8am-10:30pm.

Restaurante Solar, Largo Emilio Infante de Câmara, 9-10 (tel. 222 39). Heading
towards the post office on R. Texeira Guedes, make a left onto R. Elias Garcia; the
largo is on the left side of the street. Fresh, high-quality food at a stand-up counter
or in padded chairs. *Truta grelhada* (grilled trout, 950$), *bife de perú* (turkey,
870$). Entrees 700-1200$. Open Sun.-Fri. 9am-midnight.

Restaurante Cascata, R. António Batista, 3 (tel. 241 43), left out of the bus station
and left again. A neighborhood restaurant with an attached *quiosque*. Informal,
family-style dining. A/C. *Prato do dia* 700-850$. Open Sun.-Fri. 8-10:30pm.

SIGHTS AND ENTERTAINMENT

The austere facade of the **Igreja do Seminário dos Jesuitas** dominates Praça Sá da
Bandeira, Santarém's main square. Stone friezes carved like ropes separate each of
its three stories, and Latin mottos from the Bible embellish every lintel and doorway.
To the left of the church, the former Colégio dos Jesuitas conceals two enormous,
overgrown palm trees crammed into a tiny **cloister.** (Church usually open 9am-
5pm; cloister 2-5pm. If either is closed, enter the door to the right of the main
entrance and ask Sr. Domingos to unlock it.)

A statue of the Marquês da Bandeira embellishes the center of the *praça.* If you
stand back-to-back with him (as before a duel), the street to the left, R. Serpa Pinto,
leads to the wonderful **Praça Visconde de Serra Pilar,** formerly Pr. Velha. Centuries
ago in this commercial area, Christians, Moors, and Jews mixed for social and business affairs. The 12th-century **Igreja de Marvilha** has a 16th-century Manueline portal and a 17th-century *azulejo* interior. (Closed for restoration in 1994.) The early
Gothic severity of nearby **Igreja da Graça** contrasts with Marvila's exuberance. In
the chapel to the right of the chancel is the tomb of Pedro Alvares Cabral, the
explorer who discovered Brazil and one of the few *conquistadores* who stayed
alive long enough to be buried in his homeland.

Off R. São Martinho stands the medieval **Torre das Cabaças** (Tower of the
Gourds), so-called because of the eight earthen bowls installed in the 16th century
to amplify the bell's ring. Across the street, the **Museu Arqueológico de São João do
Alporão,** in a former 13th-century church, exhibits the elaborate Gothic "tomb" of
Dom Duarte de Meneses, who was hacked apart while fighting the Muslims.
Entombed in a glass case are what little of his dismembered remains his comrades
could salvage from the battlefield: one tooth. (Open Mon.-Sat. 10am-12:30pm and 2-
6pm; Oct.-May Mon.-Sat. 9am-12:30pm and 2-5:30pm. Free.)

Av. 5 de Outubro ends at the **Portas Do Sol,** a lush paradise of gardens and fountains surrounded by old Moorish walls. Climb up the remaining steps of the citadel
for an awe-inspiring view of the winding Tagus River and the expansive agricultural
fields of the Ribatejo plain.

Santarém shimmies with festivals. Feed your sweet tooth (which consequently
may not age as well as Dom Duarte's) at the **sweets fair** (from the last Wed. to Sun.
in April), featuring calories from all over Portugal. At the same time, **Lusoflora** displays flowers from all over the world. The largest festival is the **Feira Nacional de
Agricultura** (a.k.a. **Feira do Ribatejo),** a national agricultural exhibition. People
come for the 10-day bullfighting and horseracing orgy (starting the first Fri. in June).
Smack your lips at the **Festival e Seminário Nacional de Gastronomia** (the last 10
days of Oct.), in which each region of Portugal has a day to prepare a typical feast
and entertainment.

■■■ TOMAR

For centuries the mysterious Knights Templar plotted from their lair in this small
town straddling the Rio Nabão. Most of Tomar's monuments reflect its former status
as the den of that secretive religious order. The warrior-monks first settled here in
the 12th century, after helping the first king of Portugal, Dom Afonso Henriques,

TOMAR

oust the Moors. It was not until the 14th century, however, when the Templars were fervently persecuted throughout the rest of Europe, that they made Tomar their headquarters. Their celebrated 12th-century convent-castle, perched high above the old town, is one of the great masterpieces of Portuguese architecture.

In 1314, the Knights Templar fell into disfavor with the monarchy, and were ordered to disband. In 1320, they regrouped under the tamer guise of the Order of Christ, but the decline continued. The Napoleonic army ruthlessly trashed the Knights' priceless paintings and sculptures when it seized the castle, and the Order of Christ, the last militant religious order of Christian Europe, was officially disbanded in 1834. Today the only vestiges of centuries of intrigue are the main streets tiled with the Cross of Christ (the Knights' symbol and Portugal's banner during the Age of Exploration).

ORIENTATION AND PRACTICAL INFORMATION

The **Rio Nabão** divides Tomar. The train and bus stations and most accommodations and sights lie on the west bank. **Rua Serpa Pinto** connects the Ponte Velha (old bridge) to the main square, **Praça da República.** Several blocks south of and parallel to Serpa Pinto, **Avenida Dr. Cândido Madureira** runs from the central roundabout to the entrance of the **Mata Nacional** (National Forest), which is crowned by the convent-castle.

Tourist Office: Av. Dr. Cândido Madureira (tel. 32 24 27), facing Parque Mata Nacional. Offers perhaps the most comprehensive map on the Portuguese mainland. Open Mon.-Fri. 9:30am-12:30pm and 2-6pm, Sat.-Sun. 10am-1pm and 3-6pm; Oct.-May Mon.-Fri. 9:30am-12:30pm and 2-6pm, Sat. 10am-1pm.

Currency Exchange: Hotel dos Templários (tel. 32 17 30), next to Parque Mouchão. Look for banks on R. Serpa Pinto.

Post Office: Av. Marquês de Tomar (tel. 31 23 24), across from Parque Mouchão. Open Mon.-Fri. 9am-noon and 2-5pm. **Postal Code:** 2300.

Telephones: At the **post office. Telephone Code:** 049.

Trains: Av. Combatentes da Grande Guerra (tel. 31 28 15), at the southern edge of town. To reach the tourist office, turn right at the door, left on R. Torres Pinheiro, and continue until Av. Dr. Cândido Madureira; it's 2 bl. on the right. Tomar is the northern terminus of a minor line, so most destinations require a transfer at Entrocamento; you can buy the ticket for both legs here. To: Lisboa (12 per day, 2hr., 800$); Coimbra (9 per day, 2hr., 750$); Porto (5 per day, 4½hr., 1235$); Faro, via Lisboa (9hr., 1925$).

Buses: Av. Combatentes da Grande Guerra (tel. 31 27 38), next to the train station. To: Fátima (3 per day, ½hr., 410$); Leiria (2 *expressos* per day, 45min., 505$); Lisboa (6 per day, 2hr., 1050$); Coimbra (2 per day, 2hr., 1000$); Porto (1 per day, 4hr., 1300$); Lagos (1 per day, 8hr., 2100$).

Taxis: tel. 31 30 71, 31 51 48, or 31 28 86. Taxi stand at R. Arcos.

Hitchhiking: As Mickey Rourke said in *Body Heat,* "Don't do it." For Lisboa, Av. D. Nuno Alvares Perreira (which becomes E.N. 110) near the garage at the south end of town. For Porto, R. Coimbra, near Pr. Santo André. For Leiria, Av. Marquês de Tomar, near the public garden at the north end of town.

Hospital: Av. Cândido Madureira (tel. 32 11 00).

Emergency: tel. 115.

Police: R. Dr. Sousa (tel. 31 34 44), behind the *câmara municipal.*

ACCOMMODATIONS AND CAMPING

Finding a place to stay is only a problem during the Festival dos Tabuleiros. Usually Tomar is a buyer's market, so try bargaining prices down.

Pensão Tomarense, R. Torres Pinheiro, 15 (tel. 31 29 48), 1 bl. from Nuno Alvares. Moderately large and noisy rooms facing the street. Moderately large and quiet rooms in back, some with a splendid view of the castle on the hill and the old town. One common bath with hot water; private teeny tub. Singles 1900$, with shower 2400$. Doubles 2500$, with bath 3000$. Breakfast included.

Residencial União, R. Serpa Pinto, 94 (tel. 32 31 61; fax 32 12 99), near Pr. República. Simple wood furniture in bright rooms and white-tiled, immaculate baths. Plush lounge with well-stocked bar. All rooms with bath, telephone, satellite TV, and central heating. Singles 3500$. Doubles 4500-5500$. Triples 6000$. Breakfast included. Reserve several days ahead July-Aug.

Pensão Nuno Alvares, Av. Nuno Alvares, 3 (tel. 31 28 73), 1 bl. from bus and train stations; noise in rooms facing avenue. Slightly run-down but quite clean. Large rooms. Singles 1800$. Doubles 3000$, one double with bath 4000$. Breakfast included.

Residencial Luz, R. Serpa Pinto, 144 (tel. 31 23 17), an excellent location down the street from União. Greenish rooms are somewhat dim and cramped. All rooms with phone. Singles with shower 3000$, with bath 3500$. Doubles with shower 4500$, with bath 5000$. Gargantuan 4- and 6-person rooms with bath 1700-2000$ per person. Oct.-May 20-25% discount.

Pensão Luanda, Av. Marquês de Tomar, 15 (tel. 32 32 00). Quiet location across from the park and river. Modern interior with marble steps. Windows are double-glazed to ensure quiet. All rooms have pristine bath, phone, TV, and central heating. Singles 3500-4500$. Doubles 6000$. 3-person suites 10,000-10,500$. Also a 6-room annex with comparable prices. Oct.-May 10% discount. Breakfast included.

Camping: Parque Municipal de Campismo (tel. 32 26 07), conveniently located across Ponte Velha near the stadium and swimming pool, on the river. Exit off E.N. 110 on the east end of the Nabão bridge. Thickly forested campground with a pool. Reception open 8am-11pm. Hot water 7am-11pm. 220$ per person, per tent, and per car. Showers free. 14km south of Tomar alongside a 1030m dam, **Castelo do Bode** (tel. (041) 99 24 44) enjoys a fine view of the Zêzere valley. River swimming. 450$ per person, 200$ per tent, 200$ per car.

FOOD

Tomar is the picnic capital of Portugal. The **market** (Mon.-Sat. 8am-2pm), on the corner of Av. Norton de Matos and R. Santa Iria on the other side of the river, provides all the fixings. Friday is the big market day (8am-5pm). A section of the lush Parque Mouchão is set aside just for picnickers.

Restaurante Estrela do Céu, Pr. República, 21 (tel. 32 31 38). Possibly the most original menu in the entire region. Creative ex-Sheraton cook invents varied delight. Rustic decor. *Lonbinhos à corredora* (veal with orange, red pepper, and carrot) is one of the specialties. Hefty portions. Entrees 990-1600$. Open Tues.-Sun. 11am-midnight.

Estroia de Tomar, R. Serpa Pinto, 14, near the bridge. Sunlight streams in through the large picture window overlooking the river. Coffee, sandwiches, and home-made pastries including *beija-me depressa* (kiss me quickly). Ice cream 100$ per scoop, 110$ per "American" scoop (i.e., in a sugar cone). Open 8am-midnight.

Restaurante A Bela Vista, Fonte Choupo, 6 (tel. 31 28 70), across Ponte Velha on your left. Dine on the riverside patio under a grape arbor with a handsome view of the castle. Appealing chicken curry (1050$). Diverse entrees 800-1700$. Open Wed.-Mon. noon-3pm and 7-9:30pm.

Snack-Bar Tabuleiro, R. Serpa Pinto, 140 (tel. 31 27 71), near Pr. República. Book is better than the seedy-looking cover. Mouth-watering *bitoque de porco* (625$) comes in an earthen-ware bowl topped with an egg and buried in a heap of fries. Other dishes 550-850$. Open Mon.-Sat. 9:30am-10pm.

Restaurante Piri-Piri, R. Moinhos, 54 (tel. 31 34 94), off R. Serpa Pinto. Simple but calming decor with long, flowing drapes and blue and white *azulejo* pictures. Great *truta grelhada* (grilled trout, 750$) sure to be fresh. Entrees 600-1300$. Open Wed.-Mon. noon-3pm and 7-10pm.

SIGHTS AND ENTERTAINMENT

It's worth trekking in from the far corners of the earth to see the mysterious **Convento de Cristo** grounds, established in 1320 as a refuge for the disbanded Knights Templar. Modeled after the Holy Sepulchre in Jerusalem, the **Templo dos Tem-**

plares contains an ornate octagonal canopy that protects the high altar. Just as Genghis Khan's soldiers slept on horseback, the Knights supposedly attended Mass in the saddle, each under one of the arches. (Temple under renovation in 1994.)

A 16th-century **coro** divulges all the rich seafaring symbolism of the Manueline style: seaweed, coral, anchors, rope, and even artichokes (eaten by mariners to prevent scurvy). The design culminates in two great stained-glass windows on the west wall. Below stands the **Janela do Capítulo** (chapter window), an elaborate, exuberant tribute to the Golden Age of Discoveries.

The **Claustro dos Felipes** honors King Felipe II of Castille, who was crowned here as Felipe I of Portugal during Iberia's unification (1580-1640). It is considered one of Europe's masterpieces of Renaissance architecture. Tucked behind the Palladian main cloister and the nave is **Claustro Santa Barbara,** where grotesque gargoyle rainspouts writhe in pain as they cough up a fountain of water. On the northeast side of the church is the Gothic **Claustro de Cemetério,** the only part of the complex that dates from the time of Henry the Navigator. (Convent tel. 31 34 81; open 9:15am-12:30pm and 2-5:30pm. Admission 300$; Oct.-May 200$. Students, teachers, and seniors free.)

The **Capela de Nossa Senhora da Conceição** (1540-50), on the way back into town, is an excellent example of early Renaissance architecture. (Open 11:15am-12:15pm and 3:30-4:30pm.)

Tomar's **Museu Luso-Hebraico,** in the 15th-century Sinagoga do Arco at R. Dr. Joaquim Jaquinto (a.k.a. R. Judiaria), 73, is Portugal's only significant reminder of what was once a great European Jewish community. Jews worshipped only for a few decades before the ultimatum of 1496: convert or leave. Since then the building has served as a prison, a Christian chapel, a hayloft, and a grocery warehouse until its classification as a national monument in 1921. Two years later, a man named Samuel Schwartz purchased the synagogue, devoted most of his life to its restoration, and donated it to the state in 1939. Timely gift: the government awarded Schwartz and his wife Portuguese citizenship, assuring them sanctuary during World War II. The museum now keeps an unexceptional collection of old tombstones, inscriptions, and donated pieces from around the world. A recent excavation of the adjacent building unearthed a sacred purification bath and accompanying water well and furnace, used by the Jews for ritual purposes and then buried beneath centuries of sidewalks. (Tel. 32 26 96; museum and site open Thurs.-Tues. 9:30am-12:30pm and 2-6pm. At other times, ring at #104.)

Pyromaniacs light up over the **Museu dos Fósforos,** an exhibition of the world's largest matchbox collection. It's in the Convento de São Francisco, just across from the train and bus stations. (Open Sun.-Fri. 2-5pm. Free.)

For a week in either June or July, handicrafts, folklore, *fado,* and theater storm the city during the **Feira Nacional de Artesanato.**

■■■ EVORA

From the rolling plain of cork and olive trees, Evora (pop. 45,000) rises like a megalith on a hill. Considered Portugal's foremost showpiece of medieval architecture, the town also contains the Roman Temple to Diana, labyrinthine streets winding past Moorish arches, and a 16th-century university. Haunting the otherwise cheerful city is the macabre Capela de Ossos (Chapel of Bones), with the remains of over 4000 people. Kings held court here in the 14th century, and three centuries later this city ushered in the revolts against the Spanish. The UN has given Evora "world heritage status" for its cultural history. Today, there are no worries short of a worsening drug problem. Elegant marble-floored shops flash their wares in the windows, university students chat on the streets, and a steady trickle of tourists visit from Lisboa, about 140km to the west.

ORIENTATION AND PRACTICAL INFORMATION

Evora is easily accessible from Lisboa. Several trains per day ply the routes from Lisboa and Faro, and the town is linked by rail with Estremoz, Porto, Portalegre, and Elvas to the north.

No direct bus connects the train station to the center of town. To avoid hiking 700m up R. Dr. Baronha, hail a taxi (400$) or flag down bus #6, which fords the tracks two blocks over (100$, book of 10 tickets 400$, Sat.-Sun. and holidays 420$). Near the edge of town, R. Dr. Baronha turns into R. República, which leads to the main square, **Praça do Giraldo,** home to most monuments and lodgings. From the bus station, simply proceed uphill to the *praça*.

Tourist Office: Pr. Giraldo, 73 (tel. 226 71). Helpful staff compensates for the illegible map by calling around until you have a room. French, German, and English spoken. Open Mon.-Fri. 9am-7pm, Sat.-Sun. 9am-12:30pm and 2-5:30pm; Oct.-May Mon.-Fri. 9am-12:30pm and 2-6pm, Sat.-Sun. 9am-12:30pm and 2-5:30pm.

Currency Exchange: Automatic 24-hr. exchange machine outside the tourist office. **Banco Fonsecas e Burnay,** Pr. Giraldo, 52. Open Mon.-Fri. 8:30am-3pm.

Post Office: R. Olivença (tel. 233 11), 2 bl. north of Pr. Giraldo. Exit the *praça* and walk up R. João de Deus, keeping to the right. Pass under the aqueduct and make an immediate right uphill. Open for mail, Posta Restante, telephone, and **telegrams** Mon.-Fri. 8:30am-6:30pm. (Under renovation in 1994.) Also try office on R. Salvador (tel. 261 03). Same hours and services. **Postal Code:** 7000.

Telephones: At the **post office. Telephone Code:** 066.

Trains: (tel. 221 25), from the main *praça,* walk down R. República until it turns into R. Dr. Baronha. Station at end of road, 1½km from town center. To: Lisboa (5 per day, 3hr., 770$); Faro (1 per day, 6hr., 1380$); Beja (4 per day, 1½hr., 585$); Estremoz (3 per day, 1½hr., 390$).

Buses: R. República (tel. 221 21), opposite Igreja de São Francisco. To: Lisboa (3 per day, 3hr., 1050$); Faro (3 per day, 5hr., 1380$); Vila Real de Santo António (2 per day, 6½hr., 1600$); Beja (3 per day, 1½hr., 850$); Elvas (2 per day, 1½hr., 900$); Porto (7 per day, 7hr., 2100$).

Taxis: tel. 73 47 34. Taxis congregate around the *praça.*

Bicycle Rental: Evora Rent-a-Bike (tel. 76 14 53). Bikes delivered to you. Half-day 1000$. Full-day 1500$.

Luggage Storage: In the **bus station** basement (90$ per day).

English Bookstore: Nazareth, Pr. Giraldo, 46 (tel. 222 21). Small English and French sections upstairs. A superflux of guidebooks, mysteries, and some well-chosen stationery, too. Open Mon.-Fri. 9am-1pm and 3-5pm, Sat. 9am-1pm.

Laundromat: Lavévora, Largo D'Alvaro Velho, 6 (tel. 238 83), off R. Miguel Bombardo. 350$ per kg. Open Mon.-Fri. 9am-1pm and 3-7pm.

Swimming Pool: (tel. 323 24). A splendid complex of 5 pools on the outskirts of town. Admission 500$, under 13 free. Open June-Sept. 10am-8pm, Sun. and holidays 9am-8pm. Swimming until 7pm, closed Mon. mornings. Frequent summer bus service (100$, book of 10 400$).

Hospital: R. Velasco (tel. 250 01, 221 32, or 221 33), close to city wall and intersection with R. D. Augusto Eduardo Nunes.

Emergency: tel. 115.

Police: R. Francisco Soares Lusitánia (tel. 220 22), near the Temple of Diana.

ACCOMMODATIONS AND CAMPING

Most *pensões* reside on side streets around the **Praça do Giraldo.** They're crowded by June, so it's wise to reserve several days ahead. Prices drop about 20% in winter. Ask the tourist office to call around to find you a room. *Quartos* (rooms in private houses) cost 2500-5000$, and are often reasonably pleasant alternatives to crowded *pensões* in the summer.

Residencial Diana, R. Diogo Cão, 2 (tel. 220 08; fax 74 31 01). Follow R. 5 de Outubro from Pr. Giraldo toward the cathedral; take the third right. This *residencial* combines *fin de siècle* charm with modern amenities. Lofty ceilings and pristine baths. The owner also runs the *salão de chá* (tearoom) across the street. Singles 6500$. Doubles 8000$. Oct.-May: 5750$; 6800$.

Pensão Os Manueis, R. Raimundo, 35 (tel. 228 61), around the corner from tourist office. TV in sitting room. Main building with rooms and baths is clean and sunny. The annex across the back street is less so, but rooms are still spacious. Singles 3000-3500$, with bath 4000-4500$. Doubles 3500-4000$, with bath 5500-6000$.

Pensão Giraldo, R. Mercadores, 27 (tel. 258 33), 2 bl. from tourist office. Spacious, tidy rooms just off the *praça*. Singles 2400$, with shower 3500$, with bath 4000$. Doubles 3500$, with shower 4800$, with bath 5500$. Prices higher in summer, depending on demand.

Pensão Residencial O Eborense, Largo da Misericórdia, 1 (tel. 220 31; fax 74 23 67), first right as R. República hooks a left into the center of town, uphill on the left side of the street. Ducal mansion *cum* renovated *pensão*. Rooms seem taller than they are wide. All rooms with telephone, TV, bath, and heating. Singles 7500$. Doubles 9000$. Breakfast included.

Camping Orbitur (tel. 251 90), a two-star park on Estrada das Alcáçovas, which branches off the bottom of R. Raimundo. 40-min. walk to town; only 1 bus daily. Washing machines. Small market. Reception open 8am-10pm. 480$ per person, 400$ per tent, 410$ per car. Shower 50$.

FOOD

Many budget restaurants cook in and around the **Praça do Giraldo.** Food is salty in Evora—bring your diuretics. The **public market** sets up in the small square in front of Igreja de São Francisco and the public gardens, to sell produce, flowers, and a wild assortment of local cheeses (including *queijo de cabra,* goat cheese).

Restaurante A Choupana, R. Mercadores, 16-20 (tel. 244 27), off Pr. Giraldo. Snack-bar on the left (20) and proper *restaurante* on the right (16). Both tastefully decorated. Elegantly prepared Portuguese *nouvelle cuisine. Trutas do Minho* (Minhoesque trout with bacon, 680$). Avoid the astronomical cover charge (it may reach 800$) by rejecting the bread and small salad. Entres mostly 900-1300$. ½-portions 600$. Open 10am-2pm and 7-10pm.

Café-Restaurante A Gruta, Av. General Humberto Delgado, 2 (tel. 281 86), outside the city wall on the way to Pr. Touros. Follow R. República toward the train station and turn right at the end of the park. It's in a cave! Inhale the thick aroma of roasting fowl as you pass by the monstrous grill. Lip-smacking *frango no churrasco* (barbecued chicken) buried under a heap of fries. ½-chicken 500$. Open Sun.-Fri. 11am-3pm and 5-10pm.

Restaurante O Garfo, R. Santa Catarina, 13-15 (tel. 292 56). Leave the square via R. Serpa Pinto and take the first right onto R. Caldeireiros, which turns into R. Santa Catarina after 1 bl. Giant fork on the wall for those who need to consume the yummy entrees (950-1200$) in one bite. *Gaspacho à Aleutejana com peixe frito* (gazpacho with fried fish, 950$). Open 11am-midnight.

SIGHTS

Evora earns the title "museum city" from streets brimming with monuments and architectural riches. Wooden tombstones cover the floor of **Igreja Santo Antão** at the northern end of **Praça do Giraldo.** Its fortress-like outer bulk conceals a serene, vaulted interior space.

Off the east side of the *praça,* R. 5 de Outubro leads to the colossal 12th-century **sé.** The Twelve Apostles that adorn the porch are masterpieces of medieval Portuguese sculpture. The **claustro** of the cathedral (accessible by a small door to the right of the entrance) is in a ponderous 14th-century Romanesque style. Dark staircases spiral to the cloister's roof. The **Museu de Arte Sacra,** in a gallery above the nave, houses the cathedral's treasury and astonishing 13th-century ivory *Virgem do paraíso.* (Cloister and museum open Tues.-Sun. 9am-noon and 2-5pm. Sé free, cloister and museum 250$.)

Adjacent to the north side of the cathedral lounges the 16th-century Episcopal palace, now the **Museu d'Evora,** with a collection ranging from Roman artifacts to

16th- and 17th-century European paintings. The prize of the painting collection is a series of 13 canvases illustrating the life of Mary. (Open Tues.-Sun. 10am-12:30pm and 2-5pm. Admission 200$.)

Evora's most famous monument, the 2nd-century **Templo de Diana,** is across from the museum. The temple of the goddess of the moon, purity, and the hunt was used as a slaughterhouse for centuries. All that remains now is a platform and 13 Corinthian columns.

Facing the temple is the town's best-kept secret, **Igreja de São João Evangelista** (1485). The church is the private property of the Cadaval family, who live in their ancestors' ducal palace next door. (Open 9am-noon and 2-6pm. Admission 200$.) The interior is covered with dazzling *azulejos* that depict the life of St. Lawrence Giustiniani, patriarch of Venice. Ask to see the church's assorted hidden chambers. (Exhaustive tour includes small museum next door. Ring bell of house to get in.)

On the west side of the *largo,* down a flight of steps, is the **Convento de Nossa Senhora do Carmo** (1665), decorated with a Baroque version of Manueline motifs that look like ribbons on a Christmas package.

The *pièce de resistance* of a visit to Evora is, of course, the **Igreja Real de São Francisco,** whose austere bulk represents the finest example of Manueline Gothic architecture in southern Portugal. Its massive portals house endlessly ornate depictions of Christ, including a life-size wooden figure in a glass case. Yet few dilly-dally admiring art, since the church encoffins the rapturously perverse **Capela de Ossos** (Chapel of Bones). Above the door an inscription affirms the sad truth of the human condition: *"Nós ossos que aqui estamos, pelos vossos esperamos"* ("We bones here lie awaiting yours"). Three tireless Franciscan monks ransacked assorted local cemeteries for the remains of 4000 people in order to construct it. Enormous femurs and baby tibias neatly panel every inch of wall space, while rows of skulls and an occasional pelvis line the capitals and ceiling vaults. The decayed and shriveled corpses of an adult and an infant dangle ghoulishly on one wall. The three innovative founders grimace at skeptics from the stone sarcophagus to the right of the altar. (Church and chapel open Mon.-Sat. 8:30am-1pm and 2:30-6pm, Sun. 10-11:30am and 2:30-6pm. Admission to chapel 50$, 50$ to take pictures.)

Just south of the church sprawls the **Jardim Público.** At the northeast end of the park, an exit leads to R. Raimundo, past the 17th-century **Igreja Conventual de Nossa Senhora das Mercês.** The multicolored tile interior is now a museum of decorative arts. (Open Thurs. and Sat.-Sun. 10am-12:30pm and 2-5pm. Free.) From here either continue onto Pr. Giraldo or explore the neighboring side streets, where the stone pavements, whitewashed houses, and connecting arches have changed little since the 13th century, when this was the Jewish quarter of town.

ENTERTAINMENT

Although most of Evora tucks itself in with the sun, **Xeque-Mate,** R. Valdevinos, 21 (second right off R. 5 de Outubro from the *praça),* and **Discoteca Slide,** R. Serpa Pinto, 135, keep the music blaring until 2am. Only couples and single women need apply. Cover charges 1000$ and 500$ respectively; both charges include two beers. Evora's most popular café-bar hangout is **Portugal,** R. João de Deus, 55.

Evora's festival, the **Feira de São João** (last week of June), celebrates the arrival of summer with rides, regional dances, labor organization tents, pungent Portuguese meats, a bullfight, and a circus! (Circus shows twice daily. Admission 1500-2000$.)

■ NEAR EVORA

On a prominent hill 35km northeast of Evora, the tiny village of **Evoramonte** clings to its massive **castelo.** Originally Roman, the castle was remodeled in the 14th and 16th centuries, and now has three lovely vaulted Gothic halls. Evoramonte is famous in Portuguese history as the place where liberal Dom Pedro IV secured the throne for his niece after forcing his reactionary brother to abdicate in 1834. This lovely hamlet makes an excellent day trip.

Evora's most cosmopolitan neighbor, **Monsaraz,** overlooks the Guadiana Valley from a hilltop on the border between Portugal and Spain. The road enters the town through a pointed gateway and leads to the main square. On the south side lies the **Municipio** with an arched veranda, a splendid coat of arms, and the large 16th-century **Igreja Paroquial.** It contains the late-13th-century marble tomb of Gomes Martin, decorated with carved figures in a funeral procession. On R. Direita, a virtually intact 16th-century street, the former **Tribunal** houses a recently discovered allegorical 13th-century fresco. The 18th-century **Hospital da Misericórdia,** opposite the parish church, has a beautiful meeting hall and a chapel of very fine gilded Baroque woodwork.

■■■ ELVAS

Elvas has a history of relationships with Spain, many of which ended in bitterness. Recaptured from the Moors in the 13th century, Elvas became one of Portugal's strongest posts on the border with Spain. After repeated attempts, Spanish troops finally succeeded in capturing the town in 1580, when a Portuguese garrison sold out and accepted a bribe. The greedy garrison made amends, however, and in 1658—decimated to only a thousand by an epidemic—the Portuguese troops managed to defeat a Spanish army of 15,000. During the Peninsular War—when Napoleon tried unsuccessfully to force Portuguese compliance in his Continental System with the help of the Spanish ruler (his own brother)—Elvas was an operational center. Today, relations with Spain are quite balanced—Spaniards invade the border to buy sheets and towels at low Portuguese prices.

Elvas looks over the region from the crown of a steep hill, baking under the Alentejo sun. Arid heat forces people into the shade of canopied sidewalks and cafés and restricts business to the cooler morning and early evening hours. In addition to the fascinating 17th- and 18th-century reinforced battlements, the town retains the character of its Moorish past and has a number of extraordinary churches.

ORIENTATION AND PRACTICAL INFORMATION

Conveniently situated 15km west of the border, Elvas is often a necessary stopover on the voyage to or from nearby Badajoz, Spain. Infrequent buses (80$) connect Elvas' train station to the town center. The bus station is on **Praça da República** (the main square), no more than a five-minute walk from the *pensões* and restaurants. Many stores and restaurants line the busy **Rua da Cadeia** and the two streets perpendicular to it, **Rua da Carreira** and **Rua do Alcamim,** just south of the *praça.*

Tourist Office: Pr. República (tel. (068) 62 22 36). Maps and pamphlets about the rest of Portugal. Open Mon.-Fri. 9am-7pm, Sat. 10am-12:30pm and 2-5:30pm, Sun. 10am-12:30pm and 2:30-5:30pm; winter Mon.-Fri. 9am-12:30pm and 2-5:30pm, Sat.-Sun. 10am-12:30pm and 2-5:30pm.

Currency Exchange: Hotel Dom Luis, Av. Badajoz (tel. 62 27 56), near the aqueduct. Open 24hrs. Look for banks in the main *praça.*

Post Office: R. Cadeia (tel. 62 21 11), at the end of the street across from the hospital. Open for mail and Posta Restante Mon.-Fri. 8:30am-6:30pm, Sat. 9am-12:30pm. **Postal Code:** 7350.

Telephones: At the **post office. Telephone Code:** 069 and 068.

Trains: Fontainhas (tel. 62 28 16), 3km north of city down Campo Maiar road. Connected to Pr. República by bus (Mon.-Fri. 6 per day, Sat. 3 per day, Sun. 2 per day, 80$). To: Badajoz, Spain (3 per day, 15min., 495$); Evora (1 /day, 3hr., 960$).

Buses: Pr. República (tel. 628 75), next to the tourist office. To: the Spanish border at Caia (4 per day, 20min., 180$); Evora (2 per day, 2hr., 900$); Lisboa (4 per day, 4hr., 1300$); constant connections to Badajoz via Caia—change to a Spanish bus at the border.

Hospital: R. Feira (tel. 62 21 77), through the arch from the *praça,* then right.

Emergency: tel. 115.

Police: R. Andrés Gonçalves (tel. 62 26 13).

ACCOMMODATIONS AND CAMPING

Inexpensive accommodations are often full. The few *pensões* are boarding houses for semi-permanent residents, with owners utterly unaccustomed to one-night stands. Renting a room in a private home (try **Carlota Pinto** or **Olga Banha,** both at tel. 62 25 40) may be the only recourse. Bargain the price of a single down to 2500$ maximum, and pay no more than 3500$ for a double. Also, be extremely cautious when accepting a room from people who solicit at the bus station. Be sure to confirm the price and available amenities—especially hot water—in advance.

Maria Garcia (quartos), R. Aires Varela, 5 (tel. 62 21 26), first left below the bus station, off R. João d'Olivença, across the street from Lucinda's. Simply furnished, clean rooms, most with large, cheerful bathrooms. Some rooms with TV and/or fan. Singles 2000$. Doubles 4000-5000$. Oct.-May: 1500$; 3000-4000$.

Lucinda da Conceição Travancas (quartos), R. Aires Vareza, Páteo 2 (tel. 62 08 03), across from Maria's. Two clean rooms in a private home with ornate wood furniture. Singles 2000$. Doubles 3500$, with bath 4500$.

Joaquina T. Dias (quartos), R. João d'Olivença, 5 (tel. 62 21 26), first left below the bus station. Pink beds, haphazard religious iconography, cramped baths, poor lighting, no hot water, and fake television sets. A desperate last resort. Singles 2000$. Doubles 4000$. Oct.-May: 1500$; 3000$.

Camping: Parque da Piedade (tel. 62 37 72), a few km southwest of town. Less-than-clean facilities. 300$ per person, 300-400$ per tent, 300$ per car. Cold showers and water free. Open May-Sept.

Varche (tel. 62 54 02 or 62 47 77), a beautiful secluded orchard 4km from Elvas. Markets, potteries, vineyards. 400$ per person. Hot showers 250$. Electricity 300$. Laundry 600$. 5-person apartment 37,500. Take the Rodoviária bus to Elvas, which stops in Varche, and ask at **Café/Restaurante Pepé** for directions to **Quinta de Torre das Arcas;** or take the road behind **Casa dos Frangos,** a chicken-coop/restaurant on the highway, and bear right where the smooth road ends. Inquiries can be made through RJ and ME Cornwell, Apt. 180, Elvas 7350, Portugal.

FOOD

Perhaps to tempt the Spanish even more, food is inexpensive in Elvas. Every Monday fresh produce is sold at an outdoor **market,** immediately outside town behind the aqueduct.

Groceries: Supermarkets line R. Cadeia. Most open 8am-8pm.

Canal 7, R. Sapateiros, 16 (tel. 62 35 93), on a street just east of Pr. República (follow sign from the *praça*). Good warm food in a small neighborhood joint. Whole chicken to go 550$, ½-chicken with fries (sitting down) 425$. Entrees 450-700$. Open daily noon-3pm and 7-9pm.

Estalagem Dom Sancho, Pr. República, 20 (tel. 62 26 86), across the narrow corner of the *praça* from Turismo. Plush old Portuguese inn with an interior courtyard. Often booked on summer evenings when Spaniards hop over to spray some *pesetas* around. Entrees 900-1500$. Open noon-3pm and 7-10pm.

Bar Os Elvenses, R. Evora, 2 (tel. 62 28 93). Follow R. Carreira (west of R. Alcamin) and bear left at the fork in the street. Filling meals in a sun-drenched interior patio. *Febras de porco* (grilled pork, 800$). Entrees 800-1000$; ½-portions 500$. Open Tues.-Sun. 10am-10pm.

O Vinho Verde, R. Tabolado, 4 (tel. 62 91 69), around the corner from Os Elvenses. You'll need the green wine to quiet your nerves—loud TV reverberates throughout this local bar. *Bitoque* 500$. Entrees 500-800$. Open Fri.-Wed. 10am-3pm and 5-11pm.

Cafeteria-Gelateria Kudissama, R. João d'Olivença, 2 (tel. 62 18 34), first left below the bus station. Popular ice cream parlor and burger joint. Hamburger and fries 350$. Sundaes to die for 350-550$. Open 9am-11pm.

SIGHTS

Elvas' primary spectacle is the **Aqueduto da Amoreira** which, at 8km by 31km, is the largest aqueduct in Europe. The colossal, four-tiered structure emerges from a hill at the entrance to the city and took almost a century (starting in 1529) to construct. Lisboa's largest shopping center, Amoreiras, is styled after it.

Igreja de Nossa Senhora da Assunção dominates the main square, which is itself covered with mosaics. Reconstructed in the 16th century in Manueline style, the church interior is decorated with abstract *azulejos* and covered by a beautifully ribbed and vaulted ceiling. Behind the cathedral and uphill to the right is **Igreja de Nossa Senhora da Consolação,** also known as **Freiras.** Ostensibly Renaissance, the octagonal interior actually explodes, mosque-like, in multicolored geometric tiles. In the three-sided *praça* in front of the church stands another of the city's unique monuments: built in the 16th century, the **pelourinho** is an octagonal pillory that culminates in a pyramid. From here, narrow streets cluttered with colorful houses lead uphill to the **castelo.** Enlarged in the 15th century, the castle was originally constructed by the Moors on the site of a Roman fortress. To the right of the entrance, hidden behind some plants, is a stairwell leading up to the castle walls where you can walk around the periphery.

Walking to the left as you leave the castle, follow the alleys skirting the city walls and pass under the Arco do Miradeiro. Downhill, just below the **Cemetério dos Ingleses** (Graveyard of the Englishmen, so-named for the Protestant Peninsular War soldiers buried there), is the **Ordem Terceira de São Francisco,** also known as **Igreja dos Terceiros.** Ask the sacristan to unlock the cemetery gate. From here there is an amazing view of **Forte da Graça,** high on a hill north of the city. The church itself, built in 1741, has a flashy interior including a richly gilded Baroque high altar. The sacristan likes to show off the small garden in the back with its *azulejo* altar. (All churches and the *castelo* open 9:30am-12:30pm and 2:30-7pm; Oct.-May 9:30am-12:30pm and 2:30-5:30pm.) Entrance to the fort requires signing up at the tourist office the day before; someone from the office accompanies guests in a city vehicle. Is that service or what?

The **Museu Arqueológico e Etnológico** is around the corner from Pensão Central on Largo do Colégio (enter between the library and a large church). Life-size paintings of saints haunt the ex-convent's wide corridors. The museum rooms display, among other items, Roman mosaics and artifacts from Africa and the Portuguese Far East. (Open Tues.-Fri. 9am-1pm and 3-6pm, Sat. 10am-1pm. Admission 150$.)

Elvas' **Casa de Cultura,** in the same white and yellow building complex as the tourist office, features paintings, sculptures, photographs, and music by Portuguese artists. Possible cultural exchange with Spain in the works. (Open 9am-1pm and 2-5pm; winter 9am-12:30pm and 2-5:30pm. Free.)

ENTERTAINMENT

Elvas dies at night (though he's sometimes still spotted buying towels in the supermarket), but the devoutly nocturnal can boogie with the Elvas youth at **Eric's Pub and Discoteca** (tel. 62 20 99), on the outskirts of the city near the public gardens. **Ritmo Da Noite** (tel. 62 34 88) in El Xadai Parque features live music of all varieties and languages. Follow Av. Badajoz (and signs for Lisboa) in the southwest end of the city to reach the park. Another option is the nearby town of Badajoz, Spain—a magnet for Elvas' club-starved youth. The town's annual fair is the week-long **Festa de São Mateus** in late-September—food, folks, and fun.

■■■ BEJA

Tucked in the midst of the vast, monotonous wheat fields of the southern Alentejo, Beja is famous in Portugal as much for its agriculture as for its history of sex and intrigue. In the town's Convento de Nossa Senhora da Conceição, a 17th-century nun allegedly had an affair with a French cavalry officer. The nun's steamy, tell-all account, *Five Love Letters of a Portuguese Nun,* was published in Paris in 1669 and vaulted the town into the annals of sexual impropriety.

In more recent years, Beja has also become known for its communist leanings. Bitter disputes erupted here between landlords and farmers after the 1974 revolution, when the exploited farmers occupied and confiscated many of the large estates. Twenty-one years later, political graffiti still covers the buildings. Perhaps to ensure the town's recent pacification, a German Air Force base lies on the town's outskirts, courtesy of the NATO exchange program. Old homes and modern shops sit in amity on narrow, winding streets.

ORIENTATION AND PRACTICAL INFORMATION

Beja is connected by direct highways to Lisboa (193km to the northwest), Evora (78km to the north), and to the Spanish border at Ficalho (65km due east). Transportation to the Algarve is easier by bus than by train.

Rua de Mértola and **Rua de Capitão João Francisco de Sousa** mark the center of town. The streets are unmarked and confusing, especially in the town center. The **train station** is in the eastern corner of town; those with heavy bags might want to taxi it to the town center (400$) rather than walk for half an hour uphill. The **bus station** is at the southern edge of town. To reach the center from the bus station, walk past the statue and turn left onto Av. Brasil. After one block, turn right at the new white building and go past the post office on the left; continue up the curving street. At the intersection, take a left on R. Capitão J.F. de Sousa (with a small pedestrian square); keep to your right and watch for the tourist office.

> **Tourist Office:** R. Capitão João Francisco de Sousa, 25 (tel. 236 93). Scanty map with mostly unmarked streets, but friendly staff helps find accommodations. Open Mon.-Fri. 9am-8pm, Sat. 10am-6pm; Oct.-May Mon.-Fri. 10am-6pm, Sat. 10am-12:30pm and 2:30-6pm.
>
> **Travel Agent: Agência de Viagens Páx-Júlia,** R. Capitão João Francisco de Sousa (tel. 224 54). **Currency exchange** and car rental (must be 23 and have had license for 1 yr.), and bookings. Limited English. Open Mon.-Fri. 9am-12:30pm and 2-6:30pm, Sat. 9am-noon.
>
> **Post Office:** Largo do Correio (tel. 32 21 11), down the street from Pensão Rocha. Open for Posta Restante and **telephones** Mon.-Fri. 8:30am-6:30pm. **Postal Code:** 7800.
>
> **Telephone Code:** 084.
>
> **Trains:** (tel. 32 50 56), on the eastern edge of town. To: Lisboa (3 per day, 4hr., 915-1000$); Evora (6 per day, 1hr., 585$); Faro (2 per day, 5½hr., 1005$).
>
> **Buses:** R. Cidade de São Paulo (tel. 32 40 44 or 32 26 01), at the roundabout on the corner of Av. Brasil. To: Lisboa (4 *expressos* per day, 3hr., 1100$); Evora (3 per day, 2hr., 850$); Faro (4 per day, 3½hr., 1200$); Real de la Frontera, Spain (1 per day, 1½hr., 800$). Connections to Spain and France.
>
> **Taxis:** tel. 224 74, about 400$ from train station to town center.
>
> **Luggage Storage:** At the **bus station** on the platform, 180$ per day.
>
> **Swimming Pool:** Av. Brasil (tel. 236 26), near bus station and camping. In a fine complex with park and restaurant. Admission to park 50$, for park and swimming 200$. Open Sat.-Thurs. 10am-9pm.
>
> **Hospital:** R. Dr. António F.C. Lima (tel. 32 21 33, midnight-8am tel. 32 28 24). Signs point the way from the bus and train stations.
>
> **Emergency:** tel. 115.
>
> **Police:** R. D. Nuno Alvares Pereira (tel. 32 20 22), 1 bl. downhill from the tourist office and a couple of meters to the left.

ACCOMMODATIONS AND CAMPING

Almost all rooms are within a few blocks of the tourist office and the central pedestrian street. Various *pensões* cluster around **Praça República.** Best to reserve several days in advance, but the tourist office keeps an up-to-date list of accommodations and prices, and can call around on your behalf.

Residencial Coelho, Pr. República, 15 (tel. 240 31; fax 32 89 39). Clean, shady rooms; phone and private baths. Some with view of noisy *praça*. Singles 3700$. Doubles 5000-6000$. Triples 7500$. Quads 8800$. Breakfast included Mon.-Sat.

Casa de Hóspedes Rocha, Largo D. Nuno Alvares Pereira, 12 (tel. 242 71), up the curving street from the post office. Spacious rooms with oak furniture and wood floors. A little worse for wear, but still a good value. Two showers for 20 rooms—wake up early! Plans for expansion may relieve this congestion. Singles 2000$. Doubles 3500$. Triples 4500$.

Residência Bejense, R. Capitão João Francisco de Sousa, 57 (tel. 32 50 01), down the street from the tourist office. Comfortable rooms with white tiled floors—some with TV and phone, most with private bath. Pleasant breakfast room, too. Singles 3500$. Doubles 6500$. Winter: 2500$; 5500$. Under renovation in 1994.

Camping: on the southwest side of town at the end of Av. Vasco da Gama (tel. 243 28), past the stadium. Small, shady, and clean. 315$ per person, 210$ per tent and per car.

FOOD

Most restaurants keep limited hours (noon-2pm and 7-10pm). The local specialty is *migas de pão*, a sausage and bacon dish cooked with bread. The municipal **market** sets up in a building 1 bl. up from the bus station and 1 bl. to the right. (Open 6am-1:30pm.)

Groceries: Urbeja, SA, Largo de São João, 15 (tel. 243 41), one block away from the museum, just beyond the Cine-Teatro. Open Mon.-Sat. 8am-8pm.

Restaurante Tomás, R. Alexandre Herculano, 7 (tel. 32 46 13), beneath the *pensão*. A stylish, award-winning restaurant offering fish and meat dishes (900-1200$). Excellent *carne de porca à alentejano* (1200$). Wide variety of desserts. Open noon-4pm and 7-11pm.

Restaurante Alentejano, Largo dos Duques de Beja (tel. 238 49), across from the museum as you walk down the steps. Simple restaurant with reasonable prices (around 800$) and authentic fare. Open Sat.-Thurs. noon-3pm and 7-10pm.

Café Saiote, R. Biscayinha, 45 (tel. 258 87), off the intersection of Sousa and Mértola. Small, family-run restaurant. Hefty pig steak and cholesterol-rich fries 500$. Entrees 350-700$. Open noon-3pm and 6-11pm.

SIGHTS

The outstanding **Museu Rainha D. Leonor,** in the former Convento da Nossa Senhora da Conceição, is the site of Sister Mariana Alcoforado's famous indiscretion with the French officer. The museum has rebuilt the cell window through which the lovers exchanged secret vows of passion.

Inside, the gilded church's 18th-century *azulejo* panels depict the lives of Mary and St. John the Baptist. Nearby are fine intaglio marble altars and panels of *talha dourada*. Moorish *azulejos* and a Persian-style ceiling make the chapter house look like a mini mosque. The 19th-century costumes on the second floor (closed in 1994) are worn by mannequins that bear a striking resemblance to the young Bette Davis. (Open Tues.-Sun. 9:45am-1pm and 2-5:15pm. 100$, Sun. free, students with ISIC free. Ticket also good for the **Museu Visigótico** behind the *castelo*.)

One block northeast of the convent is the adobe-like **Igreja de Santa María** (13th-century, rebuilt in 15th century). Its corner column is emblazoned with a miniature bull, the city's symbol. From here, R. D. Aresta Branco leads past handsome old houses to the city's massive **castelo,** built around 1300 on the remains of a Roman fortress. It still flaunts an enormous crenellated marble keep, vaulted chambers, and stones covered with cryptic symbols (probably some sort of code). The interior walls are covered with ivy. You can climb its tower, **Torre de Menagem,** for 100$. (Open Tues.-Sun. 10am-1pm and 2-6pm; Oct.-March 9am-noon and 1-4pm.)

Back in the center of town, a Manueline column enhances the long **Praça da República.** On one side stands **Igreja da Misericórdia,** built in 1550 as a market hall.

■ Algarve

This southern coast has sold its soul to commercial capitalism, and it shows. After the Moors were driven from Portugal, the Algarve remained a quiet fisher's backwater; but overdevelopment and foreign tourism are destroying its trademark fishing villages. At least nature has yet to retaliate: sunny, arid weather, ocean winds, and clear skies endure and prevail. The Algarve boasts nearly 3000 hours of sunshine per year; that's an average of 8¼ hours per day.

Aside from the mobbed resorts, plenty of villages welcome budget travelers, particularly between Lagos and Sagres (for instance, Salema and Burgau). Other inexpensive spots include Sagres itself (with ravishing isolated beaches and sheer cliffs) and the relatively underdeveloped region between Olhão and the Spanish border.

Reaching more remote beaches is a snap, as EVA has extensive bus services with convenient schedules and low fares. The train costs less than the bus but only connects major coastal cities, and in some towns the station is a hike from the center.

Hotels and *pensões* usually fill during the peak months of July and August; try the reasonably priced *quarto*. Ask at tourist offices or bars, keep your eyes peeled for signs, or take your chances with the room-pushers who accost incoming travelers at bus and train stations. If you're staying for a month or more with two or three friends, renting an apartment may be affordable (a 4-room apartment rents for up to 200,000$).

Algarve's cuisine relies on the sea. Ubiquitous *sardinha assada* (grilled sardines) often accompany *caldeirada,* a chowder of fish and shellfish, potatoes, and tomatoes perked up with onion and garlic. Sausage is often mixed with shellfish. To gulp it down, try *amêndoa amarga* (almond liqueur) or *medronho* ("firewater" made from miniature strawberries of arbutus trees). Keep an eye on official prices to avoid paying an extra "tourist tax."

The Algarve News (105$) runs articles on trendy clubs, local festivals, special events, and nude beaches. Topless bathing is the fashion here, but bottomless (especially for women) is illegal, offensive to locals, and punishable with a jail term.

■■■ FARO

The golf-club bags aren't as revealing as they seem. Although zillions of northern Europeans begin their holiday in Faro, the Algarve's capital and largest city, few bother to stay longer than it takes for a package tour to ship them to Albufeira or Lagos. Unlike the rest of the Algarve, Faro remains a provincial city.

Faro has a multicultural heritage. It began as a prehistoric fishing village and grew as both a Phoenician and Greek trading post. The Romans turned Faro into a port and administrative center. The city changed hands once again in the 8th century after being conquered by the Arabs, who ultimately lost it to King Alfonso III of Portugal in the 13th century. From the 13th to the 16th centuries Faro grew in importance. Making off with valuable books from the bishop's library—the books that would become some of the first holdings of Oxford's Bodleian library—the English burnt Faro to the ground in 1596. Built afresh, the city crumbled again in an 18th-century earthquake.

ORIENTATION AND PRACTICAL INFORMATION

Faro's commercial center surrounds **Doca de Recreio,** the small dock of empty fishing boats. The main road into town, **Avenida da República,** runs past the train station and bus depot, spilling into a delta of smaller streets at the **Praça D. Francisco Gomes** (a pedestrian mall). **Rua D. Francisco Gomes** and **Rua de Santo António** are the major pedestrian thoroughfares. The tourist office is on **Jardim Manuel Bivar,** the town's small park.

Tourist Office: R. Misericórdia, 8 (tel. 80 36 04), at the far end of Jardim Manuel Bivar. The staff speaks English and can help with accommodations. Open daily 9:30am-7pm.

American Express: Top Tours, Int. Sagres, 73 (tel. 30 27 26). In the nearby village of Quarteira (unfortunately, no office in Faro itself). Open Mon.-Fri. 9:30am-12:30pm and 2-6pm.

Post Office: Largo do Carmo (tel. 82 41 26), across from Igreja de Nossa Senhora do Carmo. Open for Posta Restante and telephones Mon.-Fri. 9am-12:30pm and 2-6pm, Sat. 9am-12:30pm. **Postal Code:** 8000.

Telephones: R. Misericórdia, 1 (tel. 82 06 38), opposite the tourist office. Open Mon.-Fri. 9am-12:30pm and 2-6pm. **Telephone Code:** 089.

Flights: Airport (tel. 80 02 00), 7km west of city. Buses #14 and 16 run from the street opposite the bus station to the airport (every 20min. 7:10am-7:56pm, 20min., 175$). From airport to the bus station, similar frequency and schedule. **TAP Air Portugal** (tel. 80 02 00), on R. D. Francisco Gomes. Open Mon.-Fri. 9am-12:15pm and 2-5:30pm. To: London (1 per day, round-trip 100,000$); Lisboa (one-way 12,400$); Madrid (1 per day via Lisboa, one-way 39,800$). Discounts for youths under 25.

Trains: Largo da Estação (tel. 82 26 53). To get to the tourist office, turn right and walk along the harbor. To: Lisboa (6 per day, 7hr., 1550$); Albufeira (6 per day, 45min.-1hr., 255$); Vila Real de Santo António (13 per day, 1½hr., 390$); Lagos (8 per day, 2½hr., 580$). In spite of number of trains per day, be sure to check schedule, as they are often clustered with long gaps in between departure times.

Buses: EVA, Av. República (tel. 80 33 25). To get to the tourist office, turn right and walk along the harbor. To: Lisboa (7 per day, 7hr., 1800$); Beja (2 *expressos* per day, 3hr., 1200$); Albufeira (16 per day, 1hr., 550$); Olhão (15 per day, 20min., 165$ at booth, 240$ on bus); Vila Real de Santo António (8 per day, 1hr., 550-650$). Their rival, **Caima** (tel. 81 29 80), is across the street and 1 door over. To: Lisboa (every hr., 4½hr., 2100$); Porto (every hr., 8½hr., 2900$); Braga (every hr., 10hr., 2950$).

Taxis: Rotaxi (tel. 82 22 89). From bus station to airport about 1000$. Taxis congregate near Jardim Manuel Bivar (by the tourist office), and at the bus and train stations. Also in front of Hotel Faro on Pr. Francisco Gomes, 2.

Laundromat: Sólimpa, R. Letes, 43 (tel. 82 29 81). Up R. Primeiro de Maio, straight through the *praça*. 1200$ per machine load (wash and dry). Open Mon.-Fri. 9am-1pm and 3-7pm, Sat. 9am-1pm.

Hospital: R. Leão Pinedo (tel. 80 34 11), north of town. **Ambulance,** tel. 81 74 61. **Emergency:** tel. 115.

Police: R. Bernardo de Passos (tel. 82 20 22), off R. 5 de Outubro.

ACCOMMODATIONS AND CAMPING

Rooms vanish in high season. The tourist office's top-20 list of *pensões* helps. Lodgings are concentrated near the bus and train stations.

Pensão Oceano, Trav. Ivens, 21 (tel. 82 33 49), off R. 1 de Maio. Wood Scandinavian furniture, but Hamlet's Denmark was never this cheerful. Attractive Portuguese tilework in the halls and baths. All rooms have bath and telephone. Singles 3000-3500$. Doubles 4000-4500$. Triples 6000$. Breakfast included.

Residencial Madalena, R. Conselheiro Bivar, 109 (tel. 80 58 06). Centrally-located with pleasant, neat rooms. Almost all rooms with full bath, telephone, fan, and heater. Friendly, English-speaking reception. TV room and small bar. Singles 4500$. Doubles 6500$. Winter: 3500$; 5000$. Optional breakfast 300$.

Residencia Pinto, R. 1 de Maio, 27 (tel. 82 28 20), off Pr. D. Francisco Gomes. Thirteen simple, cramped rooms with aging ceilings and multiple common baths. An inexpensive value, especially in the summer. Singles 2000$. Doubles 3000$. Triples 3500$. Oct.-May: 1500$; 2500$; 3000$.

Pensão Nautilus, R. Conselheiro Bivar, 38 (tel. 82 25 57), off Pr. D. Francisco Gomes. Eight basic rooms share one less-than-appealing common bath. English-speaking owner. Singles 1500$. Doubles 2000-3000$.

Camping (tel. 81 78 76) sprawls on the beach, Praia de Faro. Reception open 9am-8:30pm. 300$ per person, 40$ per child, 400$ per tent, 50$ per car. Showers free.

FOOD

Almonds and figs grow on trees in the Algarve, and bakeries whip up incredibly delicious marzipan and fig desserts. Faro has some of the Algarve's chattiest cafés, especially along **Praça D. Francisco Gomes.** At the **market** in Pr. Dr. Francisco Sa Carneiro, locals buy and sell all sorts of fresh seafood. (Open Mon.-Fri. 9am-1pm.)

Restaurante Fim do Mundo, R. Vasco da Gama, 53 (tel. 262 99), off Pr. Ferreira de Almeida. End of the world as we know it, and you'll feel fine with chicken and fries (1100$). Take-out too. Fish omelet 800$. Open Mon. noon-3pm, Wed.-Sun. noon-3pm and 5-10pm.

Pastelària Chantilly, R. Vasco da Gama, 63A (tel. 270 80). Next to Fim do Mundo, this place is the glorious afterlife, where you can indulge in delicious marzipan sweets (110$ each), pastries, and other delectable regional specialties (50-350$). Open Mon.-Sat. 8am-midnight.

Restaurante Dois Irmãos, Largo Terreiro do Bispo, 14, r/c (tel. 82 33 37), across from Centenário. Fish entrees 860-1480$. *Arroz de polvo* (octopus rice, 860$). Open 11am-4pm and 6-11pm.

Restaurante Snack-Bar Centenário, Largo Teneiro Bispo, 4-6 (tel. 82 33 43), on R. Lethes. Classical Portuguese decor: dimly lit but homey. Simple food. Wide assortment of fish and meat dishes 700-1300$. *Pasteis de bacalhau* (cod patties) are a specialty. Open noon-11pm.

Restaurante Chelsea, R. D. Francisco Gomes, 28 (tel. 82 84 95). Not named for the President's daughter, but food a 14-yr.-old would love anyway: pizza (starting at 800$). Elegant sidewalk café downstairs, blue and white Art Deco restaurant upstairs. *Pratos do dia* (700-800$), *menu* (1500$). Open 11am-3pm and 6:30-11pm. (Under renovation in 1995.)

SIGHTS AND ENTERTAINMENT

Near the small harbor and public garden, the 18th-century Arco da Vila pierces the old wall. A narrow road leads through an Arab portico to the Renaissance **sé,** which sits forlornly in a deserted square. The simplicity of the Renaissance interior is relieved by the Capela do Rosório (right), decorated with 17th-century *azulejos,* a red Chinoiserie organ, and sculptures of two Nubians bearing lamps.

One day, not long ago, archeologists unearthed traces of Neolithic civilization under the cathedral—a site also sacred to Romans, Visigoths, and Moors. The **Museu Arqueológico e Lapidar** (behind the church) reflects this hodge-podge of civilizations. The prize piece, a 30- by 20-foot Roman mosaic, has a room all to itself. (Open Mon.-Fri. 9am-noon and 2-5pm. Admission 125$.)

Across from the old city and facing the huge and dusty Largo de São Francisco stands the mighty **Igreja de São Francisco,** whose hulking facade belies a delicate interior. (Open Mon.-Sat. 10am-1pm.) The **Capela dos Ossos** in **Igreja de Nossa Senhora do Carmo** is a wall-to-wall macabre bonanza of crusty bones and fleshless monk skulls borrowed from the adjacent cemetery. (Open 10am-1pm and 3-5pm. Free.) Nearby, **Igreja de São Pedro** displays *azulejos* of St. Peter and twin pulpits atop curving stairs.

The city's **Museu de Etnografia Regional,** occupying an entire wing of the District Assembly Building, introduces guests to the folk life of the Algarve. (Open Mon.-Fri. 9:30am-12:30pm and 2-5:30pm. Admission 100$, students with ID and seniors free.) The **Museu da Marinha** crowns the Departamento Marítimo do Sul (next to Hotel Eva) with the history of Portuguese boats. Here wallow models of the boats that bore Vasco da Gama on his route to India in 1497, the boat that bore imperialists up the Congo River in 1492, the mightiest galleon of the 16th century, and the single vessel that outclassed the Turkish navy in 1717, highlighting a time when the Algarve was on the cutting edge of technology. (Tel. 80 36 01; open Mon.-Fri. 9:30am-12:30pm and 2-5:30pm. Admission 100$, students free.)

Numerous sidewalk **cafés** line the pedestrian walkways off the garden in the center of town. For dancing, try the boisterous (and somewhat expensive) **Scheherazade,** in Hotel Eva on Av. República (tel. 82 34 76). Dancing every Wed., Fri., and Sat. Thurs. night is folklore and *fado* night. The rock-free **beach** hides on an islet off the coast. Take bus #16 from the stop in front of the tourist office (every hr. until 8pm, 150$).

■ NEAR FARO: ALBUFEIRA

To this, the largest seaside resort in the Algarve, tourists come hell-bent on relaxation. The occasional Portuguese fisher seems unfortunately out of place. As the prevalence of English signs, menus, and even breakfast food attests, the hilly city streets emanating from the beach—especially **Rua 5 de Outubro,** the main concourse—are constructed wholly for the benefit of English-speaking visitors. A bit more authentic culture can be found in the winding streets of the **old town,** which come together at **Praça da República,** another touristy area of restaurants and nightclubs.

Like many towns in the Algarve, Albufeira has changed hands several times over the years. It was controlled by the Romans, Visigoths, and Arabs, before the Portuguese took the city in the 13th century. The last holdout of the Moors in southern Portugal, Albufeira tries desperately to preserve graceful Moorish architecture in the old quarters of town. Tiny minarets pierce the small Byzantine dome of **Santana;** an exquisite filigree doorway heralds the **São Sebastão;** an ancient Gothic one fronts the **Misericórdia;** and a barrel-vaulted interior receives worshippers into the **Matiz.**

Albufeira's spectacular beach, **Praia dos Barcos,** is edged with rocky coves. Nearby beaches include Baleira, Oura, and Inatel. Local artisans sell their wares in the **tropical park** at Largo Engenheiro Duarte-Pacheco. Palm-leaf, wrought iron, and stone pieces are specialties of the region.

The hottest clubs in town, **Disco Silvia's** and **Club Disco 7½,** face off on R. São Gonçalo de Lagos, near the east side of the beach. A dandy mingling spot is the **Fastnet Bar** on R. Cândido dos Reis (tel. 58 99 16; open 10am-3am). It nets tourists with Tequila Sunrises, Blue Hawaiians, and *karaoke.* Bands perform almost nightly on the outdoor stage in the *largo.* The tourist office sells **bullfight** tickets (May-Sept. Sat. 5:30pm; tickets 2500-3500$).

Practical Information The **tourist office,** R. 5 de Octubro, 5 (tel. 51 21 44), has maps, brochures, and a list of *quartos* (about 3000-5000$). English spoken. (Open 9:30am-7pm.) The **post office** (tel. 58 66 01) ships packages from next door. (Open Mon.-Fri. 8:30am-6pm.) The **postal code** is 8200; the **telephone code** is 089. The magic number for **taxis** is tel. 58 73 00. The **hospital** patches people up on R. Henrique Calado, off R. Bernardino de Sousa (tel. 51 21 33; for **ambulance** tel. 58 63 33). In an **emergency** dial 115. The **police** (tel. 51 54 20) are near the Mercado Municipal (look for "G.N.R." sign).

The **train station,** 6km inland, is accessible from the center by bus (every 30min., 140$). Albufeira is on the Lagos-Vila Real de Santo António line. Frequent departures to Faro (45min., 250$) and Lagos (1½hr., 380$). The **bus station** (tel. 51 43 01) is at the entrance to town, up Av. Liberdade; walk downhill to reach the center. EVA buses head to Faro (every hr., 1hr., 550$); Portimão (7 per day, 1hr., 500$); and Lagos (7 per day, 1½hr., 750$).

Accommodations and Food Many places are booked solid through travel agents from the last week in June through mid-September. The modern **Pensão Albufeirense,** R. Liberdade, 18 (tel. 51 20 79), 1 bl. from the *largo* through Trav. 5 de Outubro, has a garish interior, comfortable rooms, and a TV lounge. (Singles 3500$. Doubles 5000$. Triples 6500$. Oct.-May: 2000$; 3000$; 4000$.) **Pensão**

Silva, R. Joaquim M. De Mendoça Gouveia (tel. 51 26 69), off R. 5 de Outubro (if you're facing the ocean, it's a small street on the right), is in older building with wood floors and chandeliers. (Singles 3500$. Doubles 4500$. Oct.-May: 2000$; 3500$.) **Camping Albufeira** (tel. 58 95 05; fax 58 93 93) is a few km outside town on the road to Ferreiras. More like a crowded shopping mall than a peaceful retreat, the place boasts four swimming pools, three restaurants, three tennis courts, a supermarket, and a hefty price tag. (700$ per person, per car, and per tent.) The new campground effectively prohibits unofficial camping on nearby beaches.

Budget restaurants spill across the old fishing harbor east of the main beach. **Cantinho Algarvio,** Trav. Cais Herculano (tel. 547 97), serves up a nifty *salade de atum* (tuna) and other entrees for 1500-2500$. (Open 9am-midnight.) Chicken-n-chips buffs patronize the small family-run **Caravela** (tel. 51 56 94), on the corner of R. 5 de Outubro and R. Padre Semedo Azevedo, three blocks from the tourist office. Entrees 650-1250$. (Open Mon.-Sat. noon-midnight.)

■■■ LAGOS

For many, many moons, swarms of Europeans and Australians have sojourned here to worship the almighty Sun, god of Lagos (pop.15,000). Although half-buried under pilgrims, Lagos is less touristed than Albufeira and closer to the beach than Faro. The port and old town pickle a measure of local color; along the narrow pedestrian streets, cosmopolitan bars burble to English pop and sway to jazz. To the west, rock tunnels through the sheer cliffs connect secluded sandy coves, while 4km of uninterrupted beach lounges to the east.

Founded by the Romans, Lagos thrived under the Moors as the largest port between Portugal and North Africa. During the Age of Discovery, the city's shipyards built caravels that came close to falling off the earth. Capital of the Algarve for two centuries, the city was a key port in the slave trade until it was destroyed by the 1755 earthquake.

ORIENTATION AND PRACTICAL INFORMATION

Running the length of the river, **Avenida dos Descobrimentos** carries traffic in and out. **Rua das Portas de Portugal** marks the gateway leading into **Praça Gil Eanes** and the town's glitzy tourist center. Most restaurants, accommodations, and services hover about the *praça* and **Rua 25 de Abril;** they are usually mobbed.

Tourist Office: Largo Marquês de Pombal (tel. 76 30 31), take the side street R. Lina Lectão (off Pr. Gil Eanes) which leads to the Largo. A 20-min. walk from the train station, a 15-min. walk from the bus station. Brochures, maps, and transport information about Lagos and the Algarve. List of *quartos.* English spoken. Open daily 9:30am-12:30pm and 2-7pm; July-Sept. open through lunch hours.

Budget Travel: Club Algarve, R. Marreiros Neto, 25 (tel. 76 23 37), uphill from the tourist office. English spoken. Standard discounts on TAP and British Airways for youths under 25. Open Mon.-Fri. 9am-12:30pm and 2:30-6:30pm; winter Mon.-Fri. 9am-noon and 3-6pm.

Currency Exchange: Caixa Geral de Depósitos, Pr. Gil Eanes. Cash advances. 700$ commission on cash, 1500$ commission on traveler's checks. Open Mon.-Fri. 8:30am-3pm. Also check rates at the numerous banks which line Pr. Gil Eanes and R. Portas de Portugal.

Post Office: R. Portas de Portugal (tel. 76 31 11), between Pr. Gil Eanes and Av. Descobrimentos. Open Mon.-Fri. 9am-6pm; for Posta Restante 9am-noon. **Postal Code:** 8600.

Telephones: Across from post office. Open 8:30am-6pm. **Telephone Code:** 082.

Trains: tel. 76 29 87. On the eastern edge of town across the river from the bus station. To: Lisboa (3 per day, 6½hr., 1700$); Vila Real de Santo António, via Faro (4 per day, 3hr., 1000$); Evora (3 per day, 4½hr., 1380$); Beja (3 per day, 3½hr., 1050$).

Buses: The national bus company, **Rodoviária,** has been privatized in Lagos. **EVA** (tel. 76 29 44) now runs buses in the region. Bus station is on the eastern edge of town, off Av. Descobrimentos. To: Lisboa (8 per day, 5hr., 1900$; also 4 deluxe buses per day, 5hr., 2300$); Sagres (4 per day, 1hr., 415$); Faro (4 per day, 2½hr., 850$); Portimão (17 per day, ½hr., 310$; also 10 express buses per day, 450$).

Taxis: tel. 76 24 69 or 76 30 48. Cabs congregate in front of Pr. Gil Eanes and along R. Portas de Portugal.

Car Rental: Hertz-Portuguesa, Rossio de S. João Ed. Panorama, 3 (tel. 76 00 08), behind the bus station. Must be 21 to rent. Cars start at 6300$ per day in summer, 5500$ per day in winter. Useful for the western tip of the Algarve.

Bike/Moped Rental: Motolagos, R. S. José d'Armas, 17 (tel. 76 03 65), and a booth on R. 25 de Abril. Must be 16 to rent. Mountain bikes 1700$ per day. Motorbikes 2000$ per day. Rates are lower the more days you rent.

English Bookstore: Loja do Livro, R. Dr. Joaquim Tello, 3 (tel. 76 73 47). Best sellers and good mysteries. Open Mon.-Fri. 9am-1pm and 3-5pm.

Laundromat: Lavandaria Luso-Britânica, R. Urbaniz Lapinha (tel. 76 02 50), a small street near Pr. João de Devs. Wash and dry 1300$ per 4kg load. Dry cleaning: pants 1500$, shirt 320$. Open Mon.-Fri. 9am-1pm and 3-7pm, Sat. 9am-1pm.

Medical Services: Hospital, R. Castelo dos Governadores (tel. 76 30 34), next to Igreja Santa María. **Ambulance** (tel. 76 01 15).

Police: General Alberto Silva (tel. 76 29 30), near Pr. República.

ACCOMMODATIONS AND CAMPING

In the summertime, *pensões* fill up and cost a bundle, but the newly opened Youth Hostel is an excellent alternative. Rooms in *casas particulares,* at around 1000$ per person in high-season, can be the greatest values in town. Haggle with owners who wait at train and bus stations and at the tourist office for the best deals. Rooms are often in private homes and sometimes include kitchen access. Be sure to verify that there's hot water and that the location is close to downtown.

Pousada de Juventude de Lagos (HI), R. Lançarote de Freitas, 50 (tel. 76 19 70). From the tourist office, walk up R. Garrett, then hang a left onto R. Cândido dos Reis. The street is on your right. Central courtyard with tables encourages social butterflies. Excellent showers. Fully-equipped kitchen available for use. All-day reception; curfew 2am. HI card mandatory. Multiples 1600$. Doubles with bath 4000$. Oct.-June 16: 1300$; 3500$. Breakfast included. Lockers for luggage storage 200$. Summer reservations recommended; make them through Movijoven, Av. Duque D'Avila, 137, Lisboa 1000.

Residencial Rubi Mar, R. Barroca, 70 (tel. 76 31 65), down R. 25 de Abril and then left on Trav. Senora da Graça. Run by two friendly expatriots from London. Centrally located and comfortable—a good deal if you get here in time to grab one of their eight rooms. Doubles 5000$, with bath 6000$. Quads 7000-8500$. April-July 10: 4000$; 5000$; 6000-8000$. Oct.-March 3000$; 4000$; 5000-7000$. Breakfast included.

Caravela Residencial, R. 25 de Abril, 8 (tel. 76 63 61). Small rooms around a paved courtyard. Singles 3000$, with bath 5000$. Doubles 4000-4750$, with bath 5250$. Prices lower in winter. Breakfast included.

Residência Marazul, R. 25 de Abril, 13 (tel. 76 97 49). Wood-paneled and immaculate quarters. Access to hedonistic, wicker-chaired lounge with a bar and TV/VCR combo. Singles 6000-8200$. Doubles 7500-8500$. Oct.-May: 2750-5200$; 3000-5500$.

Residencial Solar, R. António Crisógono dos Santos, 60 (tel. 76 24 77 or 76 39 17). From the bus station, exit through the back and take a left. After a block the street forks; follow the sign on the right. Bask in the spacious sitting/breakfast room. All rooms with full bath. Prices vary depending on demand; a reasonable deal in any months except July and August. Singles 7000-8000$. Doubles 6000-10,000$. Oct.-May: 4000$; 7000-8000$. Breakfast included.

Camping: Camping is *the* way to experience the Algarve for many Europeans; as a result, sites are crowded and expensive. Jam-packed **Parque de Campismo do Imulagos** (tel. 76 00 31) is annoyingly far away but linked to Lagos by a free shuttle bus. Reception 8am-10pm. 525-850$ per person, 280-470$ per tent and per car, depending on the season. Nearer town on the beautiful Praia Dona Ana is **Camping da Trinidade** (tel. 76 38 93). 347$ per person, 367$ per tent, 215$ per car. Free showers. On a beach 1½km west of Praia da Luz, peaceful **Camping Valverde** (tel. 78 92 11) costs 590$ per person, 495$ per tent, 490$ per car. Guarded, free showers. **Quinta dos Carriços** (tel. 652 01; fax 651 22), 18km west of Lagos, is less crowded and near a terrific beach (550$ per person, per tent, and per car). This few-frills, protected plot of land has a small market. The bus from Lagos to Sagres stops on the road nearby in Salema.

FOOD

Overpriced eateries in and around Praça Gil Eanes and Rua 25 de Abril cater to foreign tourists and have menus in several languages. The search for an inexpensive Portuguese meal may take you far and wide.

Mullin's, R. Cândido dos Reis, 86 (tel. 76 12 81). A Lagos hot spot. Servers dance to the tables with huge portions of spicy food. The crowd quivers with a carnal pulse (or perhaps in reaction to burned mouths). Chicken *piri-piri* (smothered in hot sauce) 1125$. Entrees 900-1950$. Open noon-2am.

Santa Fe Restaurante, R. Silva Lopes, 29 (tel. 76 48 03). A Tex-Mex *restaurante* true to its name: tacos, steaks, and burritos in a Southwestern mood. Former Bostonian owner promises "nothing over 1000$" on the menu. Open noon-2am.

Restaurante Escondidinho, hidden in a dead-end alley in front of the GNR (tel. 76 03 86). From the *praça* walk down Av. Descobrimentos (upstream) and turn left up R. Capelinha; on the left. Toothsome grilled fish. All-you-can-eat sardines at lunch 500$. Fish entrees 800-1200$.

Restaurante A Capoeira, R. 25 de Abril, 76 (tel. 76 34 70). East End of London meets Portuguese fisherman. Steak and kidney pie 1300$, *caldo verde* 390$. Entrees 1200-1600$. Open 11am-11pm.

Pizzaria O Pic Nic, Pr. Gil Eanes, 24 (tel. 76 12 85). O Those Anglicizations. Tiny interior with a large, standard outdoor patio. Frenzied staff. Individual pizzas from 600-900$. Open 9am-2am.

Restaurante O João, R. Silva Lopes, 15 (tel. 76 10 67). Small, simple interior with oak tables and tile floors. Be daring—hamburgers *à casa* (850$). Entrees 850-1200$. Open 10am-4pm and 6pm-midnight.

SIGHTS AND ENTERTAINMENT

The statue marking the entrance to Lagos at **Praça Gil Eanes** is King Dom Sebastião, who inherited the throne as a young tyke in 1557. His precarious reign ended when he set out to conquer Morocco and never returned. Sebastião's death marked the beginning of 60 years of Spanish rule.

Only the altar of **Igreja de Santo António**, off R. São Gonçalo on the west end of the town center, survived the 1755 earthquake; workers painstakingly rebuilt everything else exactly as before. Extraordinary gilded woodwork embellishes the interior. Adjoining the church, the **Museu Municipal** exhibits costumes and weapons. (Open Tues.-Sun. 9:30am-12:30pm and 2-5pm. Admission 200$, free Sun.; students and seniors free.) On either side of Pr. República, near Igreja de Santa María da Misericórdia, molder the evil remains of the 16th-century **Antigo Mercado de Escravos,** modern Europe's first slave market.

Ancient weathered cliffs surround the **beaches.** Follow Av. Descobrimentos (the main waterside avenue) west until the sign for **Praia de Pinhão.** Follow this to the shore and continue on the paths until you discover a suitable cove. The rocks afford tremendous views of the inlets. **Praia Dona Ana's** sculpted cliffs and grottoes appear on at least half of all Algarvian postcards.

More good beaches await at **Salema** and **Burgau,** small towns on the way to Sagres. Several convenient **buses** per day roll between Lagos and Sagres. The trip takes about an hour and costs 415$. There's no schedule at the bus stop in Sagres;

go to the Tourinfo office there to plan the return trip (the bus schedule is on the office wall and a pick-up spot is just in front).

The streets of Lagos pick up late into the evening; the area between Pr. Gil Eanes and Pr. Luís de Camões bursts with cafés. **Café Gil Eanes,** Pr. Gil Eanes, 20, baits especially large crowds. Stop by **Shots in the Dark,** R. 1 de Maio, 16, parallel to and behind R. Cândido dos Reis, to hang out with the international backpacking crowd. The area around R. Marreiros Netto, north of Pr. Gil Eanes, is the newest center of nightlife; bars and clubs here runneth over until well past 3am. Check out **LA Woman,** a Southwestern-theme bar, café, and dance club at R. Marreiro Netto, 54 (tel. 76 41 56). A wooden Indian welcomes you at the door, and the dance floor is 70's-chic. (Open noon-5am.) Every Saturday in summer, posters all over the Algarve announce **bullfights** (5:30pm, admission 2500$), at Largo da Teira, a 15-minute walk or taxi ride (600$) from the town center.

■ NEAR LAGOS

SAGRES

Marooned atop a bleak, scrub-desert promontory on the barren southwest corner of Europe, Sagres's dramatic, desolate location discourages tour groups and upscale travelers—all the better for the charming small town, which remains one of the most unspoiled, beautiful destinations in the Algarve. The area caters mainly to young people, who come to enjoy gorgeous beaches, rugged scenery, and an active social scene at cafés, bars, and two nearby discos.

Prince Henry the Navigator's polygonal stone **fortaleza** dominates the town like a big vulture. From this cliff-top outpost, Prince Hal stroked his beard and formulated his plan to map the world. Vasco da Gama, Magellan, Diaz, and Cabral apprenticed in the school of navigation he founded here. The 15th-century fortress is always open, and the surrounding area yields incredible views of the cliffs and sea—be careful not to fall over the edge.

Uncrowded beaches fringe the peninsula. **Mareta** is at the bottom of the road from Kiosk do Papa; rock formations jut far out into the ocean on both sides of this sandy crescent. The less popular **Tonel** is along the road to the cape.

Tourinfo (see below) offers mountain **bike tours** from the Cape of St. Vincent up the coast to the sublime beach at Vila de Bispo (Tues., Fri., Sun. 10am; make reservations in advance at office). By day, the young set invades **Café Conchinha** (tel. 641 31) in Pr. República, with a café downstairs and restaurant upstairs. (Entrees 650-950$. Open daily 8am-midnight; winter Tues.-Sun. 8am-10pm.) At night the crowd moves across the street to the lively restaurant-bar **Rosa dos Ventos** (tel. 644 80; entrees 800-1200$). Another popular nightspot is **The Last Chance Saloon,** a hunting ground that blasts English dance tunes and overlooks the beach. The small bar hops by 11pm.

Practical Information Since the government tourist office mysteriously closed in 1993, the privately-run **Tourinfo** (tel. 645 20), on Pr. República in the main square, serves as a profit-driven substitute. Recommends accommodations and town events; runs bike tours to St. Vincent (mentioned above, 500$ per person) and guided tours of Sagres (900$ per person); rents bicycles (1900$ per day, 1200$ per ½-day). (Open daily 10am-7pm.) The GALP station at the roundabout and the Kiosk do Papa across from O Dromedário rent bicycles and mopeds. (Bicycles 1500$ and mopeds 2000$ per day; must be 16 to rent.) The **post office** is a left turn at R. Correio, which is down the street from O Dromedário (see below). (Open Mon.-Fri. 9am-12:30pm and 2:30-6pm.) **Postal code:** 8650. The **telephone code** is 082. **Taxis** are at tel. 645 01.

Rodoviária **buses** (tel. 76 29 44) run from Lagos (10 per day, 1hr., 415$).

Accommodations and Food Windows everywhere display signs for rooms in three or four languages. Many are in boarding houses with guest kitchens; prices range from 2500-3500$ for singles and doubles, 3000-4000$ for triples. Experienced hagglers can talk prices down 2000$. If you aren't accosted at the bus stop, look for the signs or ask at the Tourinfo office. **Casa da Lidia** offers singles and doubles for only 1200$ and triples for 2200$. Owner Fransisco Casimir will trundle you and your bag over to his little boarding house in the back of his famed motor tricycle. **Atalaia Apartamentos,** Belceira (tel. 646 81), 2 bl. from the bus stop by the main hotel, is an exceptional value for those who seek a few more amenities. Beautifully furnished apartments with sitting rooms, TV, kitchen, and bath in modern building. Apartments for two 7000$. Doubles with fridges 6000$. April-June: 6000$; 5000$. Nov.-March: 5000$; 4000$. **Camping** unofficially is tricky, as police hassle illegal campers who set up on the main beaches or in the fields. Sleep peacefully instead at the guarded ground near town, close to the beach, just off E.N. 268. (Tel. 643 51; fax 644 45. July-Aug. 420$ per person, 600$ per tent, 350$ per car. June, Sept.-Oct.: 350$; 400$; 270$. Nov.-May: 230$; 270$; 200$. Showers $100.)

The **market** (open Mon.-Sat. 10am-8pm) is off R. Comandante Matoso; turn left at R. do Correio. **Restaurante-Bar Atlántico** (tel. 76 42 36) serves heaping portions of *amêijoas ao natural* (plain clams, 950$). **O Dromedário,** R. Comandante Matoso (tel. 76 42 19), whips out thick fruit shakes (250-450$), sandwiches, original wholemeal pizzas (540-900$), and American-style breakfasts (580-900$). The pizza proved such a hit that the English-speaking owner opened **Bossa Nova** (tel. 645 66) on the patio in back, with pizza, pasta, and more (700-1400$). (Open daily noon-midnight; closed Thurs. in winter.)

Near Sagres: Cabo de São Vicente, Carrapateira, and Odeceixe

Powerful Atlantic winds bring cooler temperatures and large rolling waves to the dazzling coastline west of Sagres. Red rock cliffs tower 70m above the pounding surf, and fields are covered with cacti and desert flowers.

On the way down to the cape from Sagres, **Beliche,** a 17th-century fortress with a tiny chapel, offers a prime view of the coastline. To the right of the entrance, stone stairs tumble down a rocky cliff to Beliche's beach in a perfect horseshoe cove.

Crowning the southwestern tip of continental Europe, **Cabo de São Vicente** was once thought to be *o fim do mundo* (the end of the world). At the far end of the cape, the second most powerful lighthouse in Europe throws its beam 60 miles out to sea beckoning sailors home. (No fixed hours. Get permission to climb to the top from keeper at the gate, who disappears noon-2pm but is usually there in the daytime.) No buses connect the cape with Sagres. The scenic 6-km hike along the paved road from Sagres takes only about an hour.

Don't tell anybody (as we're about to) about undiscovered **Carrapateira,** 24km north of Sagres on the western coast, where you can camp in the summer. To get there, take the road (turn-off at Vila do Bispo) or the bus (7:40am from in front of the Tourinfo office) for Aljezur to the small village of Carrapateira, and proceed 1km down a small dirt road to the coast. At the top of the road, **Restaurante O Cabrita** (tel. 971 28) marks the turn-off and a munchy break. Freshly caught fish grilled on an open-air barbecue. *Robalo* (bass), *anchova* (anchovy), and roast goat (for which this place is named) are specialties. (Entrees 675-950$. Open Tues.-Sun. noon-9:30pm.)

Odeceixe, 20km north of Carrapateira, is the northernmost beach in the Algarve. You can **camp** (tel. 942 45) on the beach where the river meets the sea. Take the 4km road by the edge of town at the bridge marked "camping" (470$ per person and per tent, 330$ per car; free showers). Infrequent **buses** pass through town (1 per day to Lagos with connection to Sagres, 8am) and stop at the station across from the **post office** (R. Estrada Nacional, 19). Room renters plaster the town center, **Largo Primero do Maio,** with advertisements. (Doubles about 1000$.)

OLHÃO

During the Napoleonic War, Olhão (8km east of Faro) profited from Napoleon's blockades by generating a lucrative smuggling trade. Today Olhão is the largest fishing port and fish canning center in the Algarve. Believe it or not, dauntless fishers of Olhão go from the shores of their heavenly beaches all the way to Newfoundland to catch cod. These days, they use navigational tools.

Olhão's handsome **Igreja de Nossa Senhora do Rosário** (1681-1698), at the mouth of the main street, **Avenida da República,** is smack in the middle of the Muslim quarter. Check out the flat roofs and whitewashed facades of the Ria Formosa.

At dusk mosquitoes from the water, drug dealers, and prostitutes feast on the unwary. Ferries at the pier leave for the gorgeous beaches spread across nearby islands. **Ilha da Armona,** the easternmost island, hosts a lively summer community that crowds around the ferry dock but leaves miles of oceanfront almost deserted. You can easily rent bungalows and rooms in private homes here. Ferries run regularly year round (10 per day in summer, 3 per day rest of the year, 15min., 260$ round-trip). **Ilha da Culatra** boasts two beach communities accessible by the same ferry: **Culatra,** an island fishing community and the larger of the two, is known for its hospitality and fine bars; **Farol,** the second stop, offers less crowded beaches. Unfortunately, camping is discouraged on the island. (Ferries every 2hr. in summer, 3-4 per day rest of the year, 35min. to Culatra, 45min. to Farol, 200$ round-trip. In summer, Farol can also be reached from Faro.)

Practical Information The **tourist office** (tel. 71 39 36) is on Largo Sebastão Martins Mestre, an offshoot of R. Comércio. English-speaking staff has maps and ferry schedules. (Open Mon.-Fri. 9:30am-12:30pm and 2-5:30pm, Sat. 9:30am-noon.) The **post office** (tel. 71 20 13) is at Av. República, 17 (open Mon.-Fri. 9am-6pm). The **postal code** is 8700 and the **telephone code** 089.

The **bus station** is on R. General Humberto Delgado, one block west of Av. República. For the tourist office, turn right leaving the station and right again on Av. República, whose left fork is R. Comércio. To Faro (every ½hr., 20min., 165$ in advance, 240$ on bus); Tavira (every hr., 1hr., 300$). The **train station** is one block north of the bus station on Av. Combatentes da Grande Guerra; a left takes you to Av. República, and a right deposits you downtown.

Accommodations and Food Pensão Bela Vista, R. Dr. Teófilo Braga, 65-67 (tel. 70 25 38), offers cheerful tiled rooms with baths emanating from a plant-filled tiled courtyard. Exiting the tourist office, make a left and take the first left; R. Teófilo Braga is the first right. (Singles 4000$. Doubles 5000$. Winter: 3000$; 3500$.) **Residencial Bicuar,** R. Vasco da Gama, 5 (tel. 71 48 16), pampers with oriental rugs, dark burnished furniture, and a small rooftop terrace with a view of the town and sea. From the front door of the tourist office, turn right onto R. Comércio and walk back toward the church, taking your first right on R. São Pedro; it's the first block on your left. (Singles and doubles, some with bath, 4000$; winter 3000$. Reservations advisable July-Aug.) Campers bed at **Parque dos Bancários,** outside of town off E.N. 125. Nine buses per day; schedule in tourist office. These highly recommended, guarded sites have access to the ocean. (Tel. 70 54 02; fax 70 54 05. 520$ per person, 350$ per tent, 380$ per car. Oct.-May: 260$; 175$; 190$. Showers included.) Also has a pool (175$ per person) and tennis courts (175$ per person).

Tasca o Bote on Av. 5 de Outubro, 122, near the market buildings, serves grilled fish and chicken entrees (800-1100$) in a simple atmosphere spruced up with festive paper decoration. Very authentic. (Open Mon.-Sat. 10am-3pm and 7-11pm.) Between the city gardens along the river, two robust red brick buildings house the **market:** half produce and meats, and half a rather smelly fish market. (Open Mon.-Sat. 7am-1pm.) Tourists and locals frequent cafés lining R. Comércio. **Pastelaria Olhão Doce** on R. Comércio (tel. 71 27 15), a local favorite, serves up scrumptious pastries (70-150$), milkshakes (250-260$), hamburgers, sandwiches, and salads (100-450$). (Open Mon.-Sat. 8am-midnight.)

TAVIRA

Farmers on motor scooters reputedly tease police by riding over the Roman pedestrian bridge: that's about as raucous as Tavira gets. The town's serenity is matched by its beauty. Perhaps the loveliest community in the Algarve, Tavira lies on both sides of the slow Gilão river. White houses and palm trees fringe the river banks, and festively Baroque churches speckle the hills above. The easy-going fishing port doesn't sweat it over the recent influx of backpackers. In mid-afternoon, fishers sit in small riverfront warehouses repairing nets alongside their beached craft. Side streets trace the skeleton of the Moorish fortress from which the town sprang.

The seven-arched **Ponte Romana** leads from the center of town around Pr. República across the river to fragrant Pr. 5 de Outubro. Up the stairs at the opposite end of the square is the imposing **Igreja do Carmo.** Its elaborately decorated chancel resembles a 19th-century opera set where false perspectives give the illusion of windows and niches supported by columns. (Open only for mass.) On the other side of the river, steps opposite the tourist office lead to **Igreja da Misericórdia,** whose superb Renaissance doorway glowers with heads sprouting from twisting vines and candelabra. (Open 9am-noon and 2-5:30pm.) Just beyond, the remains of the city's **Castelo Mouro** now enclose a handsome garden (open 9am-5pm).

Local beaches, including **Pedras do Rei,** are nearby and can be reached year-round. To reach Tavira's excellent beach on **Ilha da Tavira,** an island 2km away, take the "Tavira-Quatro Aguas" bus from Pr. República. The ferry between Quatro Aguas and Ilha da Tavira runs between May and mid-Oct., daily until 8pm (10 per day, 5min., 100$ round-trip; keep ticket stub for the return).

Practical Information Turismo (tel. 225 11) will move in 1995 to R. Galeria, 9, just across the street and up the steps to old town from its former location on Pr. República. The English-speaking staff gives out maps and recommends accommodations. (Open 9:30am-7pm; winter 9:30am-12:30pm and 2-5:30pm.) **Taxis** congregate in front of the tourist office (minimum fare 370$), or call tel. 815 44 or 223 54.

Buses leave from the *praça* for Faro (10 per day, 1hr., 390$). One of the nicest, cleanest bus stations in Portugal (tel. 225 46)—but be forewarned, no English is spoken there. **Trains** leave every hour for Vila Real de Santo António (1hr., 240$) and Faro (25min., 255$). To get to the Turismo from the station, walk down Av. Dr. Teixeira and then R. Liberdade.

Accommodations and Food Tavira has one of the choicest *pensões* in the Algarve, **Pensão Residencial Lagôas Bica,** R. Almirante Cândido dos Reis, 24 (tel. 222 52), on the far side of the river. It has nicely furnished, quaint rooms; an outdoor patio; a sitting room; washing facilities; and a fridge for guest use. To reach the *pensão* from Pr. República, cross the bridge and continue straight down R. A. Cabreira; turn right and go down two blocks. (Singles 2200-2500$. Doubles 3500$, with bath 4500$. About 500$ less in winter.) If it is full, cast your gaze across the street to the **Pensão Residencia Almirante** at 51-53 (tel. 221 63). It has four rooms, each with a distinctive personality and a bath. (Singles 2000$. Doubles 3000$. Triples 4000$. Winter discount.) **Pensão Residencial Castelo,** R. Liberdade, 4 (tel. 239 42), is across from the tourist office. You'll sleep in a clean room with a bath, and you might even get a view of the *castelo. Azulejos* (bright Portuguese tiles) line the hallways. (Plans for renovation and expansion may continue through the summer of 1995.) (Singles 4000$. Doubles 5500$. Winter: 2500$; 3000$. Breakfast included.) The city's **campground** (tel. 235 05), with its entourage of snack bars and restaurants, sprawls on the beach of the island 2km from the *praça.* (Open May-Oct. 300$ per person, 500$ per tent.)

Restaurante Bica, underneath the Pensão Lagôas (tel. 23 84 43), serves excellent regional entrees in a simple atmosphere. Munch on pork with mushrooms (800$). Entrees are 650-1000$. (Open 9:30am-midnight.) Seek and ye shall find equally reasonable cafés and restaurants on Pr. República and opposite the garden on R. José Pires Padinha. For a more elegant night on the town, **Restaurante Patio,** R. Antonio

Cabreira, 30 (tel. 230 08), offers pricey shellfish entrees as well as more reasonable fish and meat options. (Fish and meat dishes 850-1300$; shellfish, sell your jewelry.) Accepts many credit cards and traveler's checks.

VILA REAL DE SANTO ANTÓNIO

Vila Real's location at the eastern end of the Algarve and the mouth of the Rio Guardiana on the Spanish border makes it a transfer point to other destinations; you may find yourself passing through this otherwise fairly non-descript town.

The **post office** is on R. Teófilo de Braga, past the intersection with R. Cándido dos Reis (open 8:30am-6pm). The **postal code** is 8900, the **telephone code** 081.

The **Pousada de Juventude (HI),** R. D. Sousa Martins, 40 (tel. 445 65), is a white building on the fifth street into the grid from the river (two bl. to the left of R. Teófilo Braga, the main pedestrian street which borders the *praça*). Living room, bar, and washing facilities. Decent quarters. (Reception open 8am-10pm; lockout noon-6pm. 1300$; low-season 1100$. Breakfast included.) **Residência Baixa Mar,** R. Teófilo Braga, 3 (tel. 435 11), rents simple, small rooms. Common baths. (Singles 3000$. Doubles 5500$. Winter: 2000$; 3000-4000$.) There is a shortage of *residências* in Vila Real. **Restaurante-Snack Bar "O Coração da Cidade,"** R. Teófilo Braga, 19-21 (tel. 433 03), serves up hearty Portuguese fare as well as pizzas. Snack-bar downstairs; cheery pink-and-white *restaurante* with A/C upstairs. (Entrees 850-1500$. Open noon-midnight.) **Restaurante Monumental** on Pr. Marquês de Pombal stays open late. (Entrees 700-1300$. Open 9am-1am.)

Trains service Lagos (4 per day, 4½hr., 860$) and Faro (11 per day, 2½hr., 450$). For trains to Spain, first cross the river by **ferry** to Ayamonte, a delightful fishing town and art colony. (In summer, ferries run 8am-8:30am; 130$ per person, 650$ per car.) From Ayamonte, you can take a **bus** in the main square direct to Sevilla, or to Huelva (every hr., 500ptas) with connections to Sevilla (summer 8 per day, 1200ptas). Pesetas are sold in banks along the port in Ayamonte.

Buses from Vila Real to the rest of the Algarve are more expensive, more reliable, and faster than trains. They zip to Faro (5 *expressos* per day, 1hr., 650$; via Tavira, 2hr., 380$); Lagos (8 per day, 4hr., 950$); and Lisboa (4 per day, 7½hr., 2000$). The last bus leaves at 6:30pm for Faro. Buses leave from the esplanade to the right of the former tourist office.

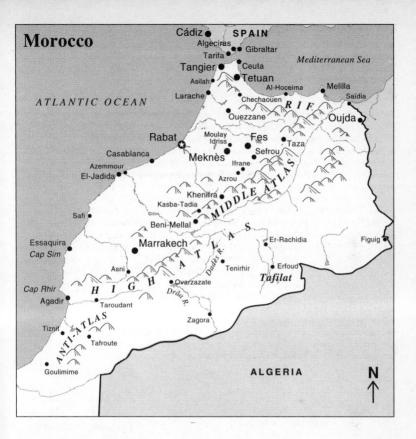

MOROCCO (MAROC) المغرب

US $1 = 9.09 dirhams (dh)
CDN $1 = 6.65dh
UK £1 = 14.04dh
AUS $1 = 6.74dh
NZ $1 = 5.51dh
SA R1 = 2.55dh

1dh = US $0.11
1dh = CDN $0.15
1dh = UK £0.07
1dh = AUS $0.15
1dh = NZ $0.18
1dh = SA R0.39

Essentials

■■■ TOURIST OFFICES

Most cities have a centrally located **Office Nationale Marocaine de Tourisme (ONMT).** They may give you a free map and offer info on sights and markets, accommodations, and official guides. They may also change money when banks are closed. Many towns also have a **Syndicat d'Initiative,** a city tourist office, with the same services. Do not expect well-stocked, well-informed offices of either type.

■■■ EMBASSIES AND CONSULATES

If you're seriously ill or in trouble, contact your consulate if possible, not your embassy (whose function is mainly diplomatic). Consulates can provide legal advice and medical referrals and can contact relatives back home. In extreme cases, they may offer emergency financial assistance. Embassies are in Morocco's capital Rabat; consulates (subdivisions of a country's embassy) are in other major cities. Embassies and consulates keep regular business hours: open from Monday to Friday, out to lunch from 1:30 to 3pm, and closed by 5:30 or 6pm.

> **U.S. Embassy:** 2 av. Marrakech, Rabat (tel. (07) 76 22 65). **Consulate:** 8 blvd. Moulay Youssef, Casablanca (tel. (02) 22 41 49 or (02) 26 45 50). Open Mon.-Fri. 8am-noon and 1:30-5:30pm.
> **Canadian Embassy:** 13 rue Jaafar Es-sadik, Agdal, BP 709, Rabat (tel. (07) 67 28 80; fax (07) 67 21 87).
> **British Embassy:** 17 blvd. de la Tour Hassan, BP 45, Rabat (tel. (07) 72 09 05; fax (07) 70 45 31). **Consulate:** 43 blvd. D'Anfa, BP 13 762, Casablanca (tel. (02) 22 16 53; fax (02) 26 57 79). **Tangier Office of British Embassy,** Flat 14, 7th fl., 41 rue Mohamed V, Tangier (tel. (09) 94 15 57; fax (09) 94 22 84).
> **Australian Embassy:** Refer to Canadian Embassy (above).
> **New Zealand Embassy:** Refer to British Embassy (above).

■■■ ORIENTATION

Large cities break up into a number of separate quarters. Years of French imperialism left behind a **ville nouvelle** (new city) in every town, a district that contains the snazzier hotels and tourist centers. The **medina** (old city) is likely to be labyrinthine, and contain sights such as *mederas,* medieval Qur'anic schools (the major tourist attraction for non-Muslims, who are always forbidden to enter mosques). Adjoining the medina is the **mellah** (the old Jewish quarter; now that most of the Moroccan Jews have moved to Israel, working-class Moroccans have moved in). The **kasbah** is the area surrounding the old fortress. In addition to handicraft **souks** (markets), nearly every city has a weekly *souk* where residents and those from outlying villages meet to transact business.

Directions can be a source of confusion. Many streets, especially those in European colonist tongues, are currently being renamed. *Rue* and *calle* may be called *zankat, derb,* or *sharia.* Also, many stores or restaurants may have no street number; these are only identifed by their street corner or square.

Stores in all cities and most towns sell **toiletries** such as toothpaste, shampoo, and shaving cream. **Toilet paper** *(papier hygenique)* is sold in all grocery stores as well as many newsstands and tobacco shops (2-3dh per roll).

■■■ GETTING AROUND

BY PLANE
Royal Air Maroc (tel. (02) 31 41 41), the national carrier, has a domestic network of flights radiating from posh Mohammed V Airport outside Casablanca. Flights are frequent to Marrakech, Agadir (a resort on the south coast), and less frequent to Tangier, Fès, and Ouarzazate. Students and those under 26 get 25% discounts: Fès or Marrakech to Casablanca for 200dh one-way. Tangier to Marrakech is maybe worth the 700dh, since you'll avoid the overnight train.

BY TRAIN

Trains are far and away the swiftest and comfiest way to travel; service is fairly reliable and surprisingly prompt throughout Morocco. Second-class fares are only a bit more expensive than the corresponding CTM bus fare. In first- and second-class cars, there are non-smoking compartments. Couchettes cost 35dh extra. Make sure that the train you're taking is air-conditioned (*climatisé*). Trains without A/C are not only hot, they're old and uncomfortable. Tickets bought on the train, instead of at the ticket counter, carry a 10% surcharge. Alas, the national rail company, **Office National de Chemin de Fer (ONCF),** has a somewhat limited network. One line runs from the port of Tangier to Rabat, and continues on to Casablanca and Marrakech (the "Marrakech Express"); a second line leaves Rabat for Fès, Algiers, and Tunis. (For Algerian visa information, see Rabat: Practical Information, page 630.)

A **Eurailpass,** good for discounted train travel in Europe, is not valid for train travel in Morocco. **InterRail** *is* valid in Morocco, though the train fares are so low you won't be getting your money's worth.

BY BUS

Buses have more frequent, more extensive service than trains, but you sacrifice comfort for convenience. Before you get on any bus, check on return service and connections from your destination to avoid being stranded: many routes run only once or twice per day. Try to take a bus that originates at your point of departure so it won't be full by the time it gets to you.

Most buses make at least one 20-minute stop. If you wish to explore or stretch your legs, tell the driver you're continuing on the bus—or else you'll be left blubbering in a dust cloud as the vehicle speeds off. Remember that each bus company has its own information window, as in Spain, so you'll have to window-hop for destinations and schedules. Police have been known to stop buses and search all passengers (or only tourists) and their baggage for drugs.

Compagnie de Transports du Maroc (CTM): Morocco's national bus company. The fastest, most luxurious, and most expensive. Generally no reservations necessary, but always inquire ahead of time; on certain busy routes you may want to purchase a ticket a day early.

SATAS: The second largest company. Operates primarily in southwest Morocco. Equal to CTM in speed and reliability, but slightly less comfortable.

Cars publiques: The term for countless other private bus companies. They run both from city to city and from big city to nearby towns and villages. Aside from CTM and SATAS, most companies offer 5 cramped seats per row and terrible ventilation. Buses often average under 50km per hour, since they stop wherever anyone wants to get on or off. Ludicrously cheap (about 10dh per 100km).

BY CAR

When exploring remote areas (especially the Atlas Mountains and desert areas), groups of four or more should consider renting a car. Most rentals are manual transmission; automatics are rare or nonexistent. **Gas** costs about 6.15dh per liter.

The **police** often pull vehicles over for security checks; this is routine throughout Morocco, especially in and around major northern cities. All police officers speak French. You may be interrogated about your travel plans and even searched. A good way to dissolve the tension is to ask directions to your destination immediately after you're stopped. *Always drive with your passport and car papers.* If you're stopped for a traffic violation, you may have to pay the fine on the spot; make sure you get a receipt. By law, **seatbelts** are required outside major towns.

Routes goudronées (principal roads), designated with a "P," are paved and connect most cities. **Pistes** (secondary roads), designated with an "S," are less smooth. You may have to contend with tortuous mountain roads made even more hazardous by loose gravel. In spring, in such regions as the Sahara, frequent flash floods can make roads impassable. Only swimmers or those with water wings should drive in this area at these times.

Buy a detailed **map,** and ask people if the routes you intend to take are passable. Sometimes roads marked on maps have a way of turning into riverbeds and mule tracks. On the other hand, many roads marked as impassable on old maps have been recently cleared and paved. The Michelin map of Morocco is widely available.

In the desert, bring along at least 10 liters of bottled water per person and per radiator, a spare tire, and extra fuel (remember to allow for the expansion of gasoline in the heat). Move rapidly over sand; if you start to bog down, put the car in low gear and put the pedal to the metal. If you come to a stop in soft sand, it's better to get out and push than to sink into tire trenches. Don't drive or park on beaches.

Renting a car is not too difficult. **Afric Car, Moroloc,** and **Locoto** are the large Moroccan companies; also explore the cut-rate rental agencies or the international companies (Avis or Hertz). **Europcar,** whose U.S. affiliate is National Car Rental, **Avis,** and **Hertz** all rent a Renault IV, the most common budget car, at about 250dh per day plus 2.50dh per km. If not included in the price, mandatory insurance costs about 70dh per day. Reserve a few days in advance and bargain. It's cheaper to reserve rental cars from the Americas or the European continent, but many companies are reluctant to insure driving in Morocco. Most companies require renters to be at least 21, but as with most Moroccan rules, rental policies are seldom set in stone. Frequently one year of driving experience is all you'll need.

North Americans should try **Europe By Car,** which allows you to purchase the car from the company for a prearranged period, after which the company buys the vehicle back. The rates are low and the insurance terms good, but you must pay at home and pick up the car before you get to Morocco. (For phone numbers of rental companies, see Spain or Portugal Essentials sections.)

BY TAXI

Petits taxis: For travel within a city. Screamingly inexpensive. Drivers are required by law to turn on the meter. If drivers try to fix a price instead, they may overcharge. Fares are usually 5-7dh, rarely over 10dh; about 50% surcharge on night fares. All *petits* say "Petit Taxi" on their roof racks. They are small tan Renaults that seat at most four passengers.

Grands taxis: For travel anywhere. Mindbogglingly cheap. These are typically beige Mercedes sedans that hold five passengers comfortably. They don't usually cruise for fares like *petits.* Instead, they congregate at a central area in town. Drivers charge by the trip, so prices per passenger decrease according to how full the car is. Often you'll have to wait for a full load (unless you're willing to pay for the empty seats). Make sure you're paying what the locals are.

Trucks (camions): For rural transport. Gaspingly affordable. In the desert, Atlas Mountains, and other rural areas, dubious four-wheeled vehicles such as pickup trucks and farm equipment take over the transportation scene. These often run set routes, but any Moroccan with a car key and an entrepreneurial spirit may offer a ride for payment.

HITCHHIKING

Almost no Moroccans and absolutely no foreigners hitch. Don't even think about being a trend-setter; other forms of transportation are dirt cheap by European and North American standards. If Moroccans do pick up a foreigner, they will most likely expect payment for the ride, just as if the hitcher had climbed into an impromtu *grand taxi* or rural taxi (see Trucks, above).

■■■ ACCOMMODATIONS

Most lodgings that *Let's Go* lists in Morocco are passably clean—not spotless. Sheets may be threadbare, but we've done our best to recommend places where they'll at least be clean. Toilets, especially in medina hotels, may be no more than holes in the ground. Don't count on toilet paper, either. Bugs are sometimes unavoidable, due to the climate, and are not necessarily representative of an establishment's cleanliness. A room's quality may inspire you to bargain despite already-low rates; acting less than eager often helps.

Sometimes a proprietor will let you sleep on the roof for a fraction of the price of a room, an especially attractive option in hot inland cities. Do some comparison shopping; hotels are rarely full to capacity.

YOUTH HOSTELS

The **Fédération Royale Marocaine des Auberges de Jeunesse (FRMAJ)** is the Moroccan Hostelling International (HI) affiliate. A bargain bed costs 15-25dh per night, a few dirhams more for non-members. Moroccan hostels vary widely in quality and are often far from the town center. Reception is only open for limited hours, so call ahead. Curfews and lockouts are rare. To reserve beds in swamped high season (July and August), obtain an **International Booking Voucher** from FRMAJ (or your home country's HI affiliate) and send it to the desired hostel four to eight weeks in advance of your stay. There are hostels in Casablanca, Fès, Marrakech, Rabat, Meknès, and some smaller cities and towns. With hotels as cheap as they are in most Moroccan cities, the chief draw of youth hostels for many is the opportunity to meet other travelers.

Whether officially or unofficially, non-members can stay in Morocco's youth hostels. Some hostels sell **HI membership cards** (75dh) on the spot; otherwise, buy one at FRMAJ's main offices (see addresses below). A **sleepsack** is mandatory; but since linens are rented by hostels less commonly than in Europe, you'll have to bring your own. (To make a cheap sleepsack, see Planning Your Trip: Packing.) For **information** such as hostel addresses, contact FRMAJ, blvd. Oqba Ben Nafii, Meknès (tel. (05) 46 46 98); or at the Casablanca hostel, 6 pl. Amiral Philibert (tel. (02) 22 05 51). (See also Planning Your Trip: Documents: HI Membership.)

HOTELS

As a rule, the cheapest hotels are in the medina. Owners sometimes charge per room rather than per person, hence it's economical to find roommates. An acceptable rate for a budget room is 40dh. Often rooms are rented by the week at 50% of the per-night price. There are two categories of hotels.

Classé: Government regulated and rated on a scale of 1-5 stars. Within each rating there's an additional A-B rating. *Classé* hotels are not necessarily better than their *non-classé* counterparts. In fact, some of the worst hotels in the country are decaying 3- and 4-star hotels, whose government-regulated prices are too high to attract guests, and consequently cannot afford their own upkeep. One-star and some 2-star hotels can, however, be excellent choices for the budget traveler. The listing with prices of all *classé* hotels *(Royaume du Maroc: Guide des Hotels)* is free at tourist offices.

Non-classé: Not regulated, rated, nor price-fixed by the government, so they don't need to meet uniform standards. Much less expensive than *classé*. A high standard *non-classé* hotel should cost 40-70dh per night for a single.

Showers, when available, can cost a few dirham extra; in cheaper places hot water is available only during certain hours, or not at all. **Hammam** (public Turkish baths) or **bains-douches** (individual public showers) run 3-4dh and are a handy source of hot water. There are laundromats in the largest cities, but often a worker in your hotel will do **laundry** for a few dirham a piece. Agree on the price beforehand.

CAMPING

Campgrounds are the cheapest lodging (10dh per person and per tent). Besides the usual site for tents, "camping" often refers to a place where you can rent a small hut or bungalow. The ritzier campgrounds boast a superflux of amenities like pools and nightclubs. Be ready to share your space with scads of Northern European teens. Avoid off-the-road camping even where it's legal; too many tourists have returned from a quick skinny-dip to find their clothes, passport, or airplane ticket absent. If camping unofficially, try to pick a spot where there are other campers nearby.

■■■ FOOD AND DRINK

Moroccan chefs lavish aromatic and colorful spices (pepper, ginger, cumin, saffron), honey, and sugar on their concoctions. The climate and cuisine may upset sensitive digestive tracts. Although the water is said to be safe in the north, unpurified water anywhere is likely to wreak havoc on your stomach. A policy of peeling all fruit and cooking all vegetables will probably stand your stomach in good stead. Avoid salads and raw vegetables on *kefta* sandwiches—these greens will have you shopping for a new roll of toilet paper in no time.

TYPICAL FARE

Couscous—a dish praised by diners around the world—is named for the covered ceramic bowl in which it's cooked and served. Made of semolina grain, onions, beans, fruit, and nuts, here it's served with a sprinkling of saffron-flavored chicken, beef, lamb, or fish. Another lovable specialty is any meat and poultry mixture blanketed in **tajine,** the scrumptious fruit and vegetable stew of olives, prunes, or artichokes. *Tajine* beats *couscous* hands down at a restaurant—the latter is better when made in a private home.

Rich **kefta** (balls of delicately seasoned ground meat, sometimes in a stew) draw mouthfuls of saliva for just 8-10dh. A steaming bowl of **harira,** a savory soup of chicken and chickpeas, can cost as little as 2dh in outdoor stands. **Poulet** (chicken), whether *rôti* (roasted on a spit with olives) or *limon* (lemoned), rules the roost. Gobble **mechoui,** a whole lamb spitted and roasted over an open fire, or **pastilla,** a pastiche of squab, almonds, eggs, butter, cinnamon, and sugar under a pastry shell.

For a lighter repast, slurp sweet natural yogurt with mounds of peaches, nectarines, or strawberries (4dh or more per glass), or try a finely minced, liberally spiced Moroccan salad. Snackers choose among gross briny olives (about 1dh per scoopful), roasted almonds, and cactus-buds (sold on the streets for 1dh per bud). For a righteous low-calorie dessert, munch on fresh fruit such as grapes, honeydew melon, watermelon, plums, apricots, figs, and dates (remember to peel).

MEALS AND RESTAURANTS

A complete meal includes your choice of entree *(tajine, couscous,* or perhaps a third option), salad or *harira,* a side of vegetables, and yogurt or *eine* orange for dessert. If a service charge isn't automatically included, a 10% tip will suffice. Every medina has one-table cubbyholes perfect for the consumption of **brochettes** (grilled lamb, beef, or brain shish kebab in a pita) for 15dh. Dingy-looking medina eateries often hide rapturous meals.

Although Moroccan cuisine emphasizes meat, **vegetarians** make do (and make good) with fresh fruit and packaged yogurt from markets. Restaurants serve a variety of omelettes and lentil dishes.

DRINKS

Drink plenty of purified water. *Sidi Ali* and *Sidi Harazem,* heavily chlorinated mineral waters sold for about 4dh per bottle, are widely available and refreshing. If the bottle isn't completely sealed, it doesn't take Harriet the Spy to realize that it's probably full of tap water. Water-sellers, with their red costumes and cymbals, earn more money posing for tourists' pictures than from dispensing water.

Although Islam forbids alcohol, French, Spanish, and local wines *may* be sold, along with local and imported beers, in many northern towns or tourist centers.

Alcohol is quite scarce, except in swish restaurants. One of the few liquor stores in the country is off the blvd. Muhammad V in Fès.

Introduced by the English in the 18th century, the ritual of preparing **tea** with sprigs of fresh mint and great quantities of sugar figures prominently in daily Moroccan life (4-5dh per pot). In hot weather, gulp tureens of water (bottled, *bien sûr*). Freshly squeezed orange juice (2-4dh per glass) is also ubiquitous.

■■■ COMMUNICATIONS

MAIL AND TELEGRAMS

The most reliable way to send a message is via telegram *(telegramme);* the least is by surface mail, which may take over two months. Telegraph offices are inside **post offices** *(le poste)*. Post offices and shops that sell postcards sell **stamps**. Mail service to Israel is likely to be permitted by Morocco by 1996.

Air mail: *Par avion.* Takes 7-14 days to reach the U.S. and Canada. Postage for a slim letter is about 10dh.

Surface mail: *Par terre.* Takes up to 2 months.

Postcards: *Cartes postales.* Often as swift as air mail. Postage 4-6dh.

Registered or express mail: *Recommande* or *exprès postaux.* The most reliable way to send a letter or parcel. Slightly faster than regular air mail.

General Delivery mail: *Poste Restante.* Letters or packages held for pick-up. Letters should be addressed as follows: LAST NAME, First Name; Poste Restante; Post Office Address; City Name; MOROCCO; AIR MAIL. Mail is frequently misfiled. Ask for mail under both your first and last name; also try "M" for "Mr." or "Ms." You can have mail forwarded to another Poste Restante address if you must leave town while expecting mail. Takes 2 weeks. Fee: 1½dh per item picked up.

American Express: Mail (no packages) held for cardholders at some AmEx offices. See this section in Once There: Communications for Spain or Portugal.

TELEPHONE

Country Code: 212.

Directory Assistance: Contact the local operator. Generally, only Arabic spoken.

Emergency (Police): 19.

International Access Code: 00.

AT&T USA Direct: 00 (wait for second tone) 211 0011.

British Telecom Direct: 00 (wait for second tone) 211 0044.

Canada Direct: 00 (wait for second tone) 211 0010.

Pay phones accept either coins (2dh will cover most local calls) or Moroccan phone cards. Card-operated models are more common. Large-denomination phone cards can be purchased at any **post office.** Entrepreneurial types hang around phone banks (found near all post offices), and will allow you to use their phone cards and pay only for the units used—typically at 2dh per unit, a rate not much worse than the coin-operated rate.

Make international calls—**direct-dial** (an *appel* call) or **collect calls**—from the local telephone office, which is always found in the post office. Either option costs about the same. There are sometimes long lines; allow plenty of time (up to 1 or 2 hours), or just keep coming back until you get speedy service. Talk is not cheap: collect calls to the United States can cost up to $55 for 20 minutes. To make a collect call, ask the desk attendant at the office to place a call **en P.C.V.** ("ahn pay-say-vay"). Write down the country, state, city, and telephone number you're calling, and your name; then take a seat and wait to be called. International calling cards are generally useless from post offices; hotel desks may, however, be able to connect you to an international operator who will process credit or calling card calls. Disturbingly, the Rabat post office will no longer place *P.C.V.* calls; ask your hotel to do it instead.

You may also use **payphones** to place an international call. Insert a high-denomination phonecard into a cardphone and dial 00. The dial tone will turn into a catchy tune: whistle along while dialing the country code and the number you're calling. You may also access an operator in the U.S., Britain, or Canada by dialing one of the numbers above from any payphone; this connection is free

■■■ MONEY

Don't try the black market for currency exchange—you'll be ripped off or robbed. Exchange money at **banks,** where rates are uniform and they don't charge commission. Banking hours are Monday through Friday 8:30-11:30am and 2:15-4pm, Ramadan 9:30am-2pm. It's illegal to import or export *dirhams;* keep receipts and you can re-exchange *dirhams* at the border (but only up to half the amount for which you have receipts). Many banks do not take American Express traveler's cheques but will accept other brands. **Bank BMCE** *does* take AmEx traveler's cheques. Many **ATMs,** such as those of **Wafabank,** accept bank cards that are on the Plus system, as well as Visa credit cards. Obtain a PIN from Visa before you go.

TIPPING

You should tip in Morocco, but it's hard to know when. You *don't* have to tip when someone demands 5dh for showing you to a cab 10 ft. away. You don't owe guardians of monuments anything unless they give you a tour—unlike official guides, they're paid by the government. However, a 2-3dh tip is always appreciated (if, for example, a bus-station employee has dragged you through crowds to a bus that's about to leave), and many times a few *dirhams* open locked gates. Pens, cigarettes, nuts, and aspirin, especially in rural areas, also work wonders. Bathroom guardians frequently demand large tips; ½dh is more than enough.

There is no need to tip taxi drivers in Morocco. In restaurants, 10% is considered sufficient—often it will be included (and itemized) in your bill.

BARGAINING AND SHOPPING

Haggling takes time. Sometimes pretending to head to another shop quickens the process. Bartering is *very* effective in both cities and rural areas. American cigarettes, crappy digital watches, jeans, and t-shirts with English printing are particularly coveted—consider bringing cheap Western stuff to trade. Never go shopping with an official or unofficial guide, who will collect at least 30% in commission. If you decide to take your chances and later find you've been grossly overcharged while accompanied by an official guide, report this promptly to the tourist office and demand a refund. Don't purchase anything if you see loiterers whom a shopkeeper might think are your guides; local boys stand unobtrusively around shops and later claim commissions without ever speaking to the buyer.

■■■ ADDITIONAL CONCERNS

HASHISH

The most famous hashish fields in the world lie north of Fès in the Rif (which rhymes with *kif,* the Arabic word for marijuana). Although *kif* and hash (sometimes called "chocolate" or the Arabic word for hash, *shit)* are often openly smoked, drugs are *not* legal for foreigners or locals. Moroccan law forbids the transport of drugs, and foreigners are officially always in transport. Dealers surround all foreigners and try to peer-pressure them into smoking. No matter how tempting, say you don't smoke, and never admit to having drugs on you: many dealers are narcs.

Police and military personnel make frequent road checks throughout the country. Sometimes entire buses are stopped and searched. Police are far more stringent with tourists than they are with locals, and possession of just a few grams, even a pot seed, is a serious offense—punished by up to six years in jail. You can also get thrown in jail if you are in the company of someone who gets busted. If arrested, you'll find American diplomatic officials remarkably unsympathetic and legally unable to help. Moreover, the U.S. embassy refuses to contact a detainee's family unless s/he personally requests this, an opportunity you may not get. Count on an uncomfortably thorough search by Spanish customs agents upon your return.

HUSTLERS AND GUIDES

Tourists are continually approached by hustlers and guides. Although "guides" are particularly prevalent in Tangier, Fès, and Marrakech, you can't expect to go hassle-free anywhere. As a rule, anyone who approaches you on the street with any sort of offer, question (including the time of day), or request is likely to be hustling you. Moroccan hustlers are famed the world over for their talents, and have developed ingenious schemes to play upon the interests, fears, and guilt of tourists—the best speak flawless French, competent English, and a few words of every other European tongue. Many visitors find this the most trying aspect of Moroccan travel.

Facing the extreme poverty in Morocco, you might have difficulty distinguishing the genuine beggar from the slick grifter. Beware of people who are too insistent, who claim they're students (or Club Med employees or art teachers) wanting to practice English, or whom you meet on a train (and offer to show you around town on arrival). Don't fall for the old line, "if you buy a *djellabah,* you'll look less like a tourist and be hassled less." Other hoaxes include invitations to authentic Moroccan suppers (departure fee charged), introductions to bargain rug stores (overpriced), or requests to read/write a letter in English.

Travelers with large backpacks or bags are more likely to be bothered than those with small daypacks; store your pack immediately after arrival. Travelers who look lost, scared, or overwhelmed are easier prey than those who look confident. If you really are lost, ask directions from someone who won't try to be your guide—a shopkeeper, a police officer, a waiter, etc. Never allow yourself to be led to faraway neighborhoods on any pretense; your companion may refuse to lead you back unless you pay through your nose. Don't leave a car or valuables in any spot you can't find again by yourself. Never, ever, accept an offer of hashish or other drugs.

There are almost no situations for which a guide is required and few for which a guide is helpful—you're almost always better off with *Let's Go* and a map. Unofficial guides are illegal, often ill-informed, and sometimes dangerous. Some travelers simply do not make eye contact with anyone who approaches them on the street; others politely say "no thanks" in their language of choice. Firmly explain that you know where you're going and don't need help. If someone proffers something you don't want, make your refusal absolutely clear from the start. An iffy answer will be taken as a yes. Some hustlers answer dismissals with threatening retorts or questions like, "What's your damage?" or "What are you, a racist?" Despite the guilt they will make you feel ("you're paranoid"), it's easier to cut hustlers off before they've started talking. Never be rude or patronizing, and don't lose your temper. Don't be frightened or too adamant in your refusals unless it's called for.

If you do ever want a guide (for instance, for an off-road trip or a climb up Mt. Toubkal), go to the local tourist office for a competent and honest **official guide.** Always go to the tourist bureau; don't be taken in by bureaucratic-looking name tags and papers. As always, agree on the price before starting out—the tourist office fixes rates at 30dh per half-day, 50dh per day. Official guides may make a commission on anything you buy or eat, so additional purchases will cost you more.

WOMEN TRAVELERS

Morocco can be a psychologically trying country for anyone; given the extra (unasked for) attention that women receive, it can be especially difficult. Women traveling alone or with other women may experience a more threatening form of hustling. Female travelers will be stared at, commented upon, frequently approached by hustlers, and have their butts and breasts squeezed while in a crowd. Moroccan women may hiss at female travelers whom they consider indecently clad. Exercise extreme caution, and don't walk in deserted areas. Always wear a bra; both genders should take care to cover bare knees and shoulders. Take any offer seriously and refuse it firmly. If harassment persists, protest loudly, especially in the presence of onlookers. Memorize the **emergency phone number** for Morocco: 19. (For more tips, see Planning Your Trip: Specific Concerns: Women Travelers in the Essentials section.)

CLOTHES & PACKING

While you can certainly get away with wearing shorts and a tank top in Morocco, you will stick out as a tourist and a target for hustlers. Tourists attempting to blend in wear long pants and a long-sleeve shirt or a long dress. Especially in Tangier, a long-sleeve shirt and long pants can be your passport to freedom from hassles. Don't think that a *djellabah* will make you look even less like a tourist; you'll look more like a sucker. In extreme heat, a hat, shades, and long-sleeved, loose-fitting, light-colored clothing will keep you cooler than a pair of Daisy Dukes and a half-shirt. Moroccan hustlers target their victims by scanning for expensive shoes: buy an inexpensive pair of sandals in a souk, and leave those Ferragamo pumps at home. Sunscreen above SPF 5 is hard to find in Morocco; import from Spain.

■■■ FESTIVALS AND HOLIDAYS

Ramadan is the holy month of Islam. Muslims fast from sun-up to sun-down (roughly 4:30am to 8:30pm) to cultivate spiritual well-being, compassion, and charity. Eating, drinking, smoking, and sex are forbidden until the sun sinks. Ramadan after dark is another story: a siren prompts every adherent to swill a bowl of *harira*, and the feasting, along with religious services, begins. City streets explode with pedestrians, music, and wild festivities. The **Night of Power,** on the 27th day of Ramadan, honors the transmission of the Qur'an from God to Muhammad. When the new moon comes out the king proclaims the end of the holy month, and the public holiday **Aid el-Saghir** marks the end of the daylight fast. Families celebrate with enormous breakfasts and gifts to children.

Nearly all Muslims fast to observe Ramadan. City services continue to operate for the most part, but restaurants and cafés that cater to locals close down during the day. Ramadan falls slightly earlier each year (it's calculated using the Islamic *(hijri)* lunar calendar) so that over the course of three decades it will make a full cycle. In 1995, Ramadan falls between February 1 and March 1.

Non-Muslim travelers should be extremely sensitive to their host country during Ramadan; eat, drink, and smoke as unobtrusively as possible. In rural areas, where locals are not accustomed to tourists, a lack of sensitivity can provoke outright hostility. In large cities such as Tangier and Rabat, many restaurants stay open all day during Ramadan. Elsewhere in the country, all but the fancier tourist establishments close from dawn to dusk.

Local Islamic holidays akin to Catholic patron saint days are called **moussems.** *Moussems* last several days and feature group pilgrimages to local shrines, street bazaars, and agricultural fairs. The rowdier *moussems* treat observers to music-and-dance events that may include charging cavalcades of costumed, armed equestrians. Most *moussems* fall in summer; exact dates vary with the Islamic calendar and the decisions of local governments. The **Meknès festival** (actually held in an outskirt called Tissan around August 18 in 1995), is the grandest of Moroccan *moussems.* During **Aïd el-K'bir** (The Big Feast; May 10, 1995), each family slaughters a sheep to commemorate Abraham's biblical sacrifice. Also catch the **Marrakech Folklore Festival** in September.

Moroccan political festivals include the **Fête du Trône** (Feast of the Throne; March 3) commemorating Muhammad V's return to Morocco after a long exile, and July 9, the **Royal Birthday.** On November 6, swing by the **Fête de la Marche Verte,** which commemorates Morocco's 1975 military acquisition of the southwestern Sahara; and on November 18, give a hurrah in honor of **Independence Day.**

Friday is the Muslim day of rest, but the *ville nouvelle* generally takes Sunday as its day of rest. The medina slows down on Fridays, but never really shuts. Office hours are usually from 8am to 2pm in summer and from 8am to noon and 4 to 6pm in off-season and during Ramadan.

Conversion calendars from Muslim to Gregorian and back ($3 by mail, $2 in person) are available from the Islamic Center of New York, 1711 3rd Ave., New York, NY 10029-7303 (tel. (212) 722- 5234). The booklet *Leisure in Morocco,* free at most Moroccan tourist offices, contains helpful information on dates and places of annual *moussems,* as well as weekly *souks.* Also check local French-language newspapers.

■■■ LIFE AND TIMES

LANGUAGE AND RELIGION

Arabic is the official language, and the government tries to encourage its exclusive use. However, almost all signs, forms, and documents are printed in French as well as Arabic, and virtually all government employees speak French as a second language. In certain northern towns, Spanish fills the linguistic role of the French. Many Moroccans speak English and German as well, but visitors with a facility in French will find interactions much easier.

In this book, city and country names appear first in English, followed by French in parentheses, and third in Arabic. Street names, however, all appear in French.

Moroccan Arabic is not identical to Classical Arabic in spoken form, and local dialects complicate matters even more. Further, Arabic is the native tongue of only 65% of the population (the others speak Berber dialects) and bi- and trilingualism is common (especially in the north). The Berbers are the indigenous peoples of North Africa who today are largely concentrated in Morocco's mountainous areas.

There is much more uniformity of religion than language. Islam is the state religion (the king is also "commander of the faithful"), and less than 1% of the population is non-Muslim. The Islamic calendar began in 622, the year when Muhammad started to rule the Islamic polity. Muslims believe that Muhammad was the last Prophet in a line which includes Noah, Abraham, Moses, and Jesus. He received God's (Allah's) words from the angel Gabriel; these words are recited to the people in the Qur'an. Islam rests on five pillars: the profession of monotheistic faith, prayer, almsgiving, the pilgrimage to Mecca, and fasting during the Holy Month of Ramadan (see Festivals and Holidays). Muhammad led the polity until his death in 632, during which time his words and deeds were recorded in *hadiths* (reports) which comprise the *Sunna,* or exemplary practice of Muhammad. Since the Prophet failed to plan ahead, his death provoked a "who rules?" crisis that lead to the Sunni and Shia division; the former believed that his successor should be chosen among a community of men, the latter insisted that a line of pure spiritual leaders (Imams) were the authentic successors. Most Moroccans are Sunni Muslims.

HISTORY AND POLITICS

Gold, spices, aphrodisiac rhinoceros horn, salt, ebony, ivory, and, of course, camels made Morocco a wealthy pitstop in the trade route between Africa and Europe. Berbers native to the mountains and plateaus met up with Phoenician and Carthaginian colonists on the North African coast by 500 BC. The Romans who followed left behind economic prosperity and a ruin or two. After Titus sacked the Temple in Jerusalem in the 3rd century BC, Jews trickled into the Moroccan cities.

Vandals and Byzantines controlled the area until 683, when the Arabs swept in under Uqua Ibn Nabir. Nabir and his cohorts converted the native Berbers to Islam, founded Qur'anic schools, and made Arabic the dominant language. Berber princess and prophetess Kahina killed herself at the news of the Arab conquest in 702. The many southern Africans in the country share a common history: Arab slave traders kidnapped their ancestors from Mali, Guinea, the Sudan, and Senegal.

Idris (I) Ibn Abdallah, a distant relation to Muhammad the Prophet, fled from the Abbasid rulers (one Islamic dynasty) of Baghdad to found his own Idrissan dynasty and the Kingdom of Fès (789). The Moors later displaced the dynasty from their control room in Spain. By the 11th century Almoravids from the Western Sahara had quashed Spanish-Muslim control and founded their own kingdom in Marrakech. In 1163, High Atlas Berbers or Almohads established the greatest of the western Islamic empires, ruling from Tripoli to Castilla, well into the 13th century. A golden age of Berber Merinid and Wattasid rule (1244-1554) ignited a cultural and intellectual boom and strengthened the link between Morocco and Spain.

As the Christian Reconquista overtook Iberia, a second wave of (Sephardic) Jewish immigrants arrived in Morocco. The Wattasids recruited an army of refugees and mercenary (or converted) Christians to battle the imperialistic Spanish. By the early 1500s, however, the Hapsburgs had established control over Morocco's ports and a number of inland territories.

The Saadis drove out some foreign influence and reunited the country. Under Ahmed el Mansour—a.k.a. Ahmed the Gilded—Morocco expanded its trade in slaves and gold in Timbuktu and parts of the Sudan. When the Alawite dynasty (which has origins in present-day Syria) overthrew the Saadis in 1659, they took over Marrakech and the area around Fès, controlled by religious mystics or marabouts. The Alawite dynasty rules to this day, in spite of European rulers' hopes to dissolve Moroccan unity. England nicked Tangier in 1662 as part of a settlement with weakening Spain. France gradually imposed itself on northern Africa, winning a major battle at Isly in 1844. After the death of Sultan Hassan of Rabat in 1893, his 13-year-old son Abd el-Aziz, an expert at bicycle polo, rose to the throne. The French took advantage of the poor pre-teen, snarfed up Moroccan territories right and left, and eventually occupied Casablanca. By 1912 they had exiled the ruling vizier, Abd el-Hafid, and secured an official Protectorate in the Treaty of Fès. The equivalent Treaty of Algeciras gave the Spanish the same rights. The European powers lacked the energy and resources to rule as directly as they had in the 19th century but persisted in the Colonialist mentality.

In 1921, Abd el Krim, now considered the founder of modern Morocco, organized a rebel army in the Rif Country. Although Krim's rebels claimed nearly 30,000 Spanish lives, the troops of Major Francisco Franco (future Fascist dictator of Spain) aligned with Marshall Pétain's French army and forced the rebels into submission (1926). Moroccan nationalism brewed under increasingly chaotic European rule. Sultan Muhammad V founded the Independence Party in 1944 and ignited the nationalist movement, but the French deported the nationalist leaders and exiled Muhammad in 1952. The ensuing popular unrest (combined with revolt in Algeria) forced the French to abandon their hard line. Muhammad returned to the throne on November 18, 1955 and signed a treaty of independence for French Morocco on March 2, 1956. The independence of most of Spanish Morocco followed one month later, ending Morocco's short (by North African standards) colonial experience.

Muhammad V's successor, King Hassan II, tried to introduce a democratic constitution in the '60s, but two abortive military coups and divisions within the government delayed the first parliamentary elections until 1977. Although today the king theoretically rules with the assistance of a parliament and a Chamber of Representatives, he can dissolve parliament and has played parties off one another as they vied for royal patronage. Morocco's human rights abuses, alleviated only in part during a 1991 initiative, do little to foster a climate of political freedom. However, the king has promised to "improve the balance between legislative and executive powers." After sluggish industrial growth, riots, and the drain of national resources by the civil war in Western Sahara, Morocco has started to boom in the '90s.

WESTERN SAHARA

Morocco has been embroiled in a conflict for years over its claims to territory in the phosphate-rich Western Sahara, maintaining that this area comprised part of the pre-Colonialist Alawite empire. Formerly part of the Spanish Sahara, this area considers itself independent (as do the 71 countries who recognize its Polariso Front as the legitimate government). The Moroccan army built a 1500-mile concrete and barbed-wire wall to fence off the rebel army, and the "Green March" in 1975, led by Hassan

II, staked Morocco's claim to the area. In the escalating conflict, Morocco broke off diplomatic relations with Algeria, who supported the Polisario Front. A United Nations committee interceded on behalf of the rebels, and Algeria and Morocco reinstated uneasy relations in 1988. Western Sahara is now de facto a part of Morocco, though negotiations for a referendum continue.

ART AND ARCHITECTURE

Beautiful buildings glorify Allah; Islam's opposition to idolatry led to an incredible ingenuity in geometric and calligraphic decoration. Colorful geometric patterns swirl across tiles, woodwork, stone, and ceramic. In less doctrinaire times, Almoravid artists slipped in designs that vaguely resemble leaves and flowers.

Calligraphy, particularly elegant renderings and illuminations of Qur'anic verse, became another outlet for creativity as well as for religious devotion. The more puritanical 12th-century Almohads introduced an interlocking almond-and-hexagon pattern to which all calligraphy was to conform. The Merinids who followed relaxed the formalism to include both floral and geometric strains, as manifest in the curved and straight-edged zallij (mosaic tiles).

The spirit of compromise also influenced architecture, which combines the decorative simplicity of Islam with the airiness of Berber spaces. Led by the caliphs of Damascus, most rulers of the Moorish empire embarked upon the construction of full-blown *djemma* or mosques by the 8th century. Two hundred years later, Fès residents built the first Moroccan mosques, el-Andalus and the Kairaouine.

Any place where Muslims pray is a mosque, or *masjid*. The word is best translated as "place of prostration." The direction facing Mecca, in which all prayer is spoken, is called the *qibla*. It is marked by a niche, the *mihrab*. The *imam* (leader of prayer) gives a sermon on Friday from the *minbar* (pulpit). There are two basic designs for mosques: the Arab style, based on Muhammad's house, which has a pillared cloister around a courtyard (hypostyle); and the Persian style, which has a vaulted arch (an *iwan*) on each side. Non-Muslims may not enter Moroccan mosques; tourists are permitted to gawk through the doorways of famous mosques. Out of respect, visitors should stay away during times of worship.

Attached to most mosques are the Qur'anic schools known as *madares* (singular, *madrasa*). To promote Sunni Orthodoxy and religious scholarship, Merinid sultans built these tiny residential colleges in the 14th century. Classrooms, libraries, and the prayer hall surround a central courtyard and fountain. Most Merinid *madares* display the same devotional artistry as the rest of the mosque complex; the Saadien *madrasa* in Marrakech displays a range of wood and marble carving.

Sultans reserved their most dazzling designs for palaces, typically a long, symmetrical series of reception and dwelling rooms studded with decorative gates, hidden gardens, and tiny pools and fountains. Royals built each palace as a testament to the owner's individuality, and the diversity of palatial styles is amazing. More functional than a palace but still highly ornamental, a *bab* is a gate in a Moroccan city's walls.

READING MATTER

Because our map of Morocco doesn't include the Western Sahara, *Let's Go* is banned from Moroccan bookstores. If worse comes to worst, you can check out some of the practical guidebooks of our competitors. Christopher Kininmonth's *Morocco: The Traveller's Guide* introduces Moroccan culture in laconic English. Fatima Mernissi's *Beyond the Veil* describes male-female dynamics in modern Morocco, and Gilles Perrault caused a stir with his tell-all *Our Friend, The King*.

Writing Moroccan guidebooks was popular among European and North American literati. Edith Wharton's *In Morocco* (1925) is a collection of episodic descriptions of Rabat, Salé, Fès, and Meknès. Walter Harris's *Morocco That Was,* a turn-of-the-century journalist's diary, features a wry account of a Brit's kidnapping by the international bandit Raissouli. *The Voices of Marrakech* by Bulgarian Nobel Prize recipient Elias Canetti eloquently records a European Jew's encounter with Moroccan Jews. *The House of Si Abd Allah,* edited by noted scholar Henry Munson, is an oral history of a Moroccan family which provides insight into the country's social history. Paul Bowles, an American who lives in Tangier, sets much of his fiction in Morocco. He has translated several Moroccan works as well.

Albert Camus' classics *The Stranger* and *The Plague,* both set in neighboring Algeria, offer a vision of expatriate life under the Maghreb's sun. Another interesting Western describer of the Maghreb is Isabelle Eberhardt, an early 20th-century traveler who was drowned in a flood in the Algerian Sahara. Her diaries are collected as the *Passionate Nomad.* The beat writers of the 1950s soaked in Moroccan culture (and sampled the Rif's famous crops, by all accounts); William Burrough's *The Naked Lunch* was reportedly written in Tangier.

Among the few Moroccan works available in English, *Love With a Few Hairs,* *M'hashish,* and *The Lemon* are Mohammed Mrabet's snatches of contemporary Moroccan life. Historian Youssef Necrouf's *The Battle of Three Kings* is an entertaining account of medieval violence and intrigue.

If all this sounds like too heavy a form of cultural enrichment, check out modern-day poets Mick Jagger and Tom Waits. Both have houses in Morocco.

Tangier (Tanger) طنجة

Few foreigners are prepared for the shock of landing in Tangier. You will be immediately, consistently, and energetically accosted by locals who wish to be your "guide" (which you don't need), to sell you drugs (don't let it cross your mind), or to point you to brothels. Keep in mind that Tangier, as Morocco's entrance point from the north, has the highest concentration of foreigners and thus the highest concentration of those who want to make their living off them. (See Hustlers and Guides for more information and advice.)

Tangier is not Morocco in microcosm. In fact, it wasn't even a part of Morocco until 1956. Before that, Romans, Vandals, Berbers, and others all had a go at the city. With the marriage of English King Charles II to Portugal's Princess of Braga, Tangier became a British possession. Although by 1912 the Brits, the French, and the Spanish had established themselves in Morocco, Tangier miraculously preserved a neutral status. A 1923 statute recognized the city as an international zone, although the French dominated the scene. A smuggling nucleus in the '40s and '50s, the city's image of illicit activities gives thrill-seekers a delicious *frisson*. Nearly 100 brothels thrived in the '50s until they were forcibly shut down, and hashish flowed (and flows) freely from the Rif mountains. Tangier's foreign community began to dissolve after Morocco gained independence in 1956, although aging expatriates still congregate at the Anglican Church.

Tangier's black market is profitable, but many people in the city remain impoverished. In 1990, street demonstrators clashed with the police following a one-day general strike. All running water in the city is shut off at 6pm.

■■■ ORIENTATION AND PRACTICAL INFORMATION

An hour by hydrofoil and two and a half hours by ferry from Spain, Tangier's main virtue is its train and bus service to southern points. When leaving town, allow plenty of time (1-1½hr. in summer). Obtain a boarding pass from the ferry company representative at the port. Beware of hustlers trying to sell customs departure cards: they're free from customs agents and ferry company representatives. The easiest way to get to the center of town is to hop into one of the blue *petits taxis* in front of the port; don't use "guides" or "students." Negotiate the fare in advance (about 4dh). The **port** is directly below the **medina.** The **Grand Socco,** a busy square, is the medina's commercial center. The sprawling **ville nouvelle** extends from the port area in all directions, particularly to the east along the beaches of the bay. The **train station** is the large, white building about two blocks to the left of the port as you exit; the **bus station** is on av. Louis Van Beethoven, about 2km from the port and medina. To get to the bus station from the port, walk along the beach on av. d'Espagne and turn right on av. Beethoven.

Buses serve the entire city, but it's safer to use the abundant *petits taxis* as long as you have a general idea of where you're going. All roads to Tangier have an old European name and a new Moroccan name. Nearly all street signs give the old name, while most good maps record the new.

Tourist Office: 29 blvd. Pasteur (tel. 93 29 96), 20min. from the port. Walk straight ahead along the beach on av. d'Espagne from the port's exit. Take the 1st right after Hôtel Biarritz onto rue Magellan; at the end turn left and blvd. Pasteur is ahead. Barely helpful; very sketchy map. Open Mon.-Fri. 9am-3pm; Sept.-June Mon.-Fri. 8:30am-noon and 2:30-6:30pm; Ramadan Mon.-Fri. 9am-3pm. **Librairie des Colonnes** (see English Bookstore below) across the street sells decent maps.

Consulates: U.K., 9 rue Amerique du Sud (tel. 93 58 95), near Grand Socco. Money sent from Britain takes 2 days. Open Mon.-Fri. 9am-noon and 1-3:30pm.

Currency Exchange: There's a branch of **BMCE** on most ferries. Many hotels change money, some at a hefty commission. Travel agencies near the port are required to change money at official rates. If you suspect overcharging, demand a receipt. Beware of hustlers who offer to change money.

American Express: Voyages Schwartz, 54 blvd. Pasteur (tel. 93 34 59). Open for mail pickup Mon.-Fri. 9am-12:30pm and 3-7pm, Sat. 9am-12:30pm; during Ramadan Mon.-Fri. 9am-12:30pm and 3-6pm, Sat. 9am-12:30pm. Like all Moroccan AmEx offices, this is a branch office and can't receive wired money. Cardholders may buy traveler's checks with personal checks.

Post Office: 33 blvd. Muhammad V (tel. 93 56 57), the downhill continuation of blvd. Pasteur. Open Mon.-Fri. 8:30am-12:15pm and 2:30-5:45pm.

Telephones: 33 blvd. Muhammad V, to the right and around the corner from the post office. Open 24 hrs. **Telephone Code:** 09.

Airport: A taxi to the airport, 10 mi. from Tangier, costs 70dh for up to 6 people. **Royal Air Maroc,** Place de France (tel. 93 47 22). 700dh to Marrakech.

Trains: av. d'Espagne (tel. 93 45 70), to the left exiting the port. 2nd-class to: Rabat (4 per day, 5-8hr., 79dh); Casablanca (4 per day, 6-9hr., 81.5dh); Marrakech (4 per day, 9-12hr., 134dh); Meknès (3 per day, 5hr., 56dh); Fès (3 per day, 6hr., 67dh).

Buses: rue Louis Van Beethoven at pl. de la Ligue Arabe, 2km from the port. For bus information, ask only policemen or the blue-coated personnel. Give baggage directly to the ticket taker and tip 1-3dh per bag. **CTM** buses to: Rabat (5 per day, 5hr., 67dh); Casablanca (5 per day, 6hr., 89dh); Fès (2 per day, 5½hr., 67dh). CTM and private company buses leave every hr. for Tetuan and Ceuta (1hr., 18dh). **CTM office,** av. d'Espagne (tel. 93 24 15 or 93 11 72), near the train station next to the entrance of the port. Info and tickets. Open 5am-midnight.

Ferries: Voyages Hispamaroc (or any other travel agency) sells tickets. Hispamaroc is on blvd. Pasteur (tel. 93 59 07, 93 27 18 or 93 31 13; fax 94 40 31), below Hôtel Rembrandt. English spoken. Open Mon.-Thurs. 7am-7pm, Fri. 7am-noon, Sat. 7am-2pm. To: Algeciras (7 per day, 2½hr., Class B 2790ptas or 196dh); Tarifa (Mon.-Thurs. at 3:30pm, 1hr., 196dh); Gibraltar (Fri. at 9am, Sat.-Sun. at 4:30pm, 2½hr., 220dh). To reach the ferry companies directly call **Transméditerranea,** 31 av. de la Résistance (tel. 93 48 83); **Limadet Ferry,** av. Prince Moulay Abdellah (tel. 93 39 14); **Comanau,** 43 rue Abou Ala El Maari (tel. 93 26 49); or **Transtour,** 4 rue El Jabha Ouatania (tel. 93 40 04).

Taxis: Fast transport to nearby destinations (Tetuan, Ceuta, Asilah). About 100dh, which can be shared by 5-6 people. Be prepared to haggle. Pick-up points along blvd. Pasteur, Grand Socco, at the port, and by the bus station.

Car Rental: Avis, 54 blvd. Pasteur (tel. 93 30 31). **Hertz,** 36 av. Muhammad V (tel. 93 33 22). Both charge 250dh per day plus 2.50dh per km; 4714dh per week with unlimited mileage. Insurance 75dh per day.

Luggage Storage: At the **bus station** (3dh per bag). Open 4am-midnight.

English Bookstore: Librairie des Colonnes, 54 blvd. Pasteur (tel. 93 69 55). See directions under Tourist Office above. A superb collection of maps and guidebooks, mostly in French. Novels and books on Moroccan culture. Open Mon.-Fri. 9:30am-1pm and 4-7pm, Sat. 10am-1pm.

Late-Night Pharmacy: 22 rue de Fès (tel. 93 26 19), through tiny windows in the green wall on the left side of the entrance. Open Mon.-Fri. 1-4pm and 8pm-9am, Sat.-Sun. 8pm-9am.

Medical Services: Hôpital Al-Kortobi, rue Garibaldi (tel. 93 10 73 or 93 42 42). **Ambulance:** tel. 15. **Red Cross:** 6 rue El Monsoui Dahbi (tel. 93 11 99). **Police:** tel. 19.

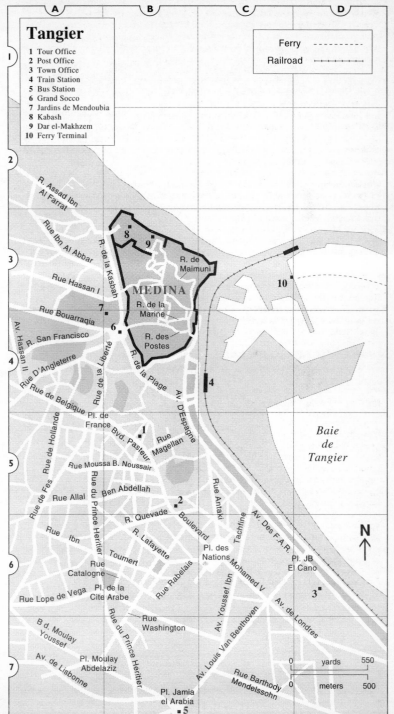

Tangier

1 Tour Office
2 Post Office
3 Town Office
4 Train Station
5 Bus Station
6 Grand Socco
7 Jardins de Mendoubia
8 Kabash
9 Dar el-Makhzem
10 Ferry Terminal

Ferry — — — —
Railroad +—+—+—+

R. Assad Ibn Al Farrat
Rue Ibn Al Abbar
Rue Hassan I
Rue Bouarraqia
R. de la Kasbah
8
9
R. de Maimuni
MEDINA
R. de la Marine
7
6
R. des Postes
Av. Hassan II
R. San Francisco
Rue D'Angleterre
Rue de Belgique
Rue de la Liberté
R. de la Plage
Av. D'Espagne
10
4
Pl. de France
Bvd. Pasteur
1
Rue Magellan
Rue de Hollande
Rue de Fes
Rue Moussa B. Noussair
Rue Allal
Rue du Prince Heritier
Ben Abdellah
2
R. Quevade
Boulevard
Rue Antaki
Tachfine
Av. Des F.A.R.
Baie de Tangier
Rue Ibn
Toumert
R. Lafayette
Pl. des Nations
Rue Rabelais
Av. Youssef Ibn
Mohamed V
Pl. JB El Cano
3
Rue Catalogne
Pl. de la Cite Arabe
Rue Lope de Vega
Rue Washington
Av. de Londres
B.d. Moulay Youssef
Rue du Prince Heritier
Av. Louis Van Beethoven
Av. de Lisbonne
Pl. Moulay Abdelaziz
Rue Barthody Mendelssohn
Pl. Jamia el Arabia
5

N

0   yards   550
0   meters   500

■■■ ACCOMMODATIONS AND CAMPING

IN AND NEAR THE MEDINA

The medina's accommodations are cheaper, dirtier, and closer to the port than the more appealing options in the *ville nouvelle*. The most convenient hotels cluster near **rue Mokhtar Ahardan,** formerly **rue des Postes,** off the Petit Socco. At night the medina can be unsafe.

To enter the medina from the port area, walk down **avenue d'Espagne** to the train station. Take rue Salah Eddine el-Ayoubi, the street straight ahead of the train station and slightly to the left. Follow this uphill to the Grand Socco. Take the first right down rue Semmarine to the Petit Socco. Rue des Postes begins at the end of the Petit Socco closest to the port.

Pension Palace (tel. 93 61 28), downhill, on the alley exiting the Petit Socco to the right. We love it! Sizeable, spotless rooms. Although tiles are the color of grime, they are actually scrubbed fanatically. Inexplicably high beds. Attractive courtyard. Singles 40dh. Doubles 80dh.

Pension Miami, 126 rue Salah Eddine el-Ayoubi (tel. 93 29 00), outside the medina, off rue d'Espagne. Turquoise and magenta rooms, handsomely carved ceilings, and a balconied cloister on each floor. Primitive bathroom. Doubles 60dh. Hot showers 5dh.

Hôtel Continental, 36 rue Dar el Baroud (tel. 93 10 24). From the Petit Socco, take rue de la Marine downhill toward the port to the Continental's blue gate. Veer to the left at the raised overlook. All the romance of a grand hotel going to seed. Large Art Deco rooms with views of the Mediterranean. Full of permanent expatriates. Often swamped by tour groups, so call ahead. Singles 150dh. Doubles 200dh.

IN THE VILLE NOUVELLE

Avenue D'Espagne (straight ahead from port and across from train station) has decent rooms, decent prices. The best values lie far up in the heart of the new city.

Hôtel El Muniria, rue Magellan (tel. 93 53 37), take the first right after Hôtel Biarritz on av. d'Espagne, and follow as it winds uphill. John Sutcliffe, the owner, was a Beat writer. He dismisses Jack Kerouac, Allen Ginsberg, and William S. Burroughs (all of whom slept here) as "a terribly boring lot." Prodigious beds and rooms with terraces overlooking the bay. Cushy lambswool mattresses. Singles 100dh. Doubles 120dh. Hot showers included.

Hôtel de Paris, 42 blvd. Pasteur (tel. 93 81 26), across from the tourist office. Spacious and clean, with large windows and firm beds. Light sleepers will curse the noisiness. Singles 133dh, with shower 169dh. Doubles with shower 211dh. Breakfast included.

Hôtel Valencia, 72 av. d'Espagne (tel. 93 07 70). Located near the port, train station, and medina. Small rooms; clean baths with natty miniature soaps. TV room. Singles with shower 134dh. Doubles with shower 164dh.

Hôtel Magellan, 16 rue Magellan (tel. 93 87 26), just below Muniria. Rooms are clean and some have nice views of the sea. Friendly reception. Singles 50dh. Doubles 100dh. Triples 150dh.

Camping: Camping Miramonte (tel. 93 71 38), set in a lovely green site 1km from the town center (the route is well-marked with signs). Take bus #1, 2, or 21 from the Grand Socco. Bar, grocery store, and restaurant. Reception open 8am-noon and 3-8pm. 10dh per person, 6dh per tent, 5dh per car.

■■■ FOOD

IN AND NEAR THE MEDINA

For the greatest variety and lowest prices, make like a kangaroo and hop from one stall to the next along the **Grand Socco.** Standard Moroccan fare is also served in passable budget restaurants along **rue Mokhtar Ahardan** and just outside the medina on **rue Salah Eddine el-Ayoubi,** which begins across from the train station and runs uphill to the Grand Socco.

Restaurante Africa, 83 rue Salah Eddine el-Ayoubi (tel. 93 54 36), near Pension Miami. Popular. Hassled waiters. Lip-smacking soup precedes delicious lamb *couscous.* Beer and wine. Whopping 4-course *menu du jour* 45dh. Open 9am-12:30am.

Restaurant Ahlen, 8 rue Mokhtar Ahardan (tel. 93 19 54), near the Petit Socco just past Pension Palace. Immense salads (3.50dh), lamb *couscous* (20dh), and chicken (20dh). Open 9am-10pm.

Restaurant Andalus, rue du Commerce. Make a 90° left at downhill end of Petit Socco and go through yellow arch. Small dining grotto buzzing with feverish brouhahas. Hefty sizzling brochettes 18dh. Full meal (entree, bread, olives, peas, and fries, 28dh).

Restaurant Hammadi, 2 rue de la Kasbah (tel. 93 45 14), the continuation of rue d'Italie just past the walls of the medina. Extravagant interior: luxe Moroccan carpeting, plush cushions, low tables, elegant candlelight. Arabic background music. Impeccable service, exalted food. Avoid lunch, when tour groups fill every seat. Specialties are *tajine* (35dh) and *couscous* (30-35dh). Beer and wine. Service 19%. Open Mon.-Sat. (sometimes Sun.) noon-3pm and 8pm-1am.

IN THE VILLE NOUVELLE

Tangier's former status as an international zone shows in *ville nouvelle* cuisine. For hot sandwiches, try the storefronts off **boulevard Pasteur.**

La Grenouille, 3 rue el-Jabba el-Quatania (tel. 93 62 42), just off blvd. Pasteur. The green frog warns of imminent French food. Moroccan and English dishes, too. Popular with expatriates. Delicious *coq au vin* 40dh. Satisfactory *menu* (50dh). Open Tues.-Sun. noon-2:30pm and 7-11pm.

Restaurant No. 1, 1 blvd. Muhammad V (tel. 94 16 74). The flashing neon sign belies a pleasant interior. English-speaking staff is hip to discuss politics and culture. Bar. Entrees around 45dh.

L'Marsa, 92 av. d'Espagne (tel. 93 19 28). Popular restaurant and café. Outdoor dining on the front patio and overhead terrace. Moroccan delicacies shove their way into an otherwise Italian menu. Pizzas (23-42dh), spaghetti (28-45dh), and 10 flavors of Italian ice cream treats (8-20dh). Open 11am-11pm.

■■■ SIGHTS

IN AND NEAR THE MEDINA

Although you don't need a guide to show you around, it's dangerous to wander through the medina or on the beaches at night. Restrict any nighttime exploration to the *ville nouvelle.*

The medina's commercial center is the **Grand Socco,** a busy square and traffic circle cluttered with fruit vendors, parsley stands, and *kebab* and fish stalls. In the colorful **Fès Market**—uphill on rue de la Liberté, across pl. de France, onto rue de Fès, and two bl. down on the right—local merchants cater to Tangier's European community. Rifian Berbers ride into the Dradeb district (west of the Grand Socco along rue Bou Arrakia and northwest on rue de la Montagne) on Thursday and Sunday to vend pottery, parsley, olives, mountain mint, and fresh fruit.

To the northwest, where rue Bou Arrakia joins the Grand Socco (through the door marked #50), a cache of 17th- and 18th-century bronze cannons hide in the shady **Jardins de la Mendoubia. Rue Bou Arrakia,** the junk-dealer's alley, is lined with a motley collection of motorcycle parts, used batteries, brass bedposts, etc.

To reach the **Kasbah,** enter the next large gate to the right of the #50 gate. Veer to the left, then follow rue d'Italie north from the Grand Socco all the way through **Bab Fahs,** the Moorish gateway, and up the steep incline of rue de la Kasbah. This street ends at the horseshoe-shaped **porte de la Kasbah,** which is guarded by particularly industrious hustlers. Rue Riad Sultan runs from the main portal alongside the **Jardins du Soltane,** where artisans weave carpets (open Mon.-Sat. 8am-2pm; off-season 8:30am-noon and 2:30-6pm; admission 5dh). Rue Riad Sultan continues to **place de la Kasbah,** a sunny courtyard and adjacent promontory with a view of the Atlantic all the way to Spain. With your back to the water, walk straight ahead and right toward the far corner of the plaza. Just around the corner to the right, the perky **Mosque de la Kasbah's** octagonal minaret pokes up.

Near the mosque is the main entrance to the **Dar el-Makhzen,** an opulent palace with handwoven tapestries, inlaid ceilings, and foliated archways, where the ruling pasha of Tangier once resided. The palace's **Museum of Moroccan Art** has a first-rate collection of ceramics, carpets, copper, and silver jewelry, as well as Andalusian musical instruments. Its **Museum of Antiquities** houses a collection of ancient tools documenting the archeological history of Tangier. (Palace open Wed.-Mon. 9am-1pm and 3-6pm. Free.)

The **Old American Legation,** 8 rue America, lies south of pl. de la Kasbah in the far corner of the medina. Enter the medina from the archway off rue du Portugal, and look for the yellow archway emblazoned with the U.S. seal. A stately cross between the White House and a Moroccan palace, the United States' first ambassadorial residence (1777) displays a wonderful collection of antique maps and works by 20th-century American artists who lived in Morocco. Downstairs is the correspondence between Sultan Moulay ben Abdellah and George Washington that led the former to be the first to have his country recognize America's independence. The curator explains everything in English. (Open 9am-1pm and 4-6:30pm. 5dh tip is expected.)

The **Forbes** (as in late tycoon Malcolm) **Museum of Military Miniatures** contains the world's largest collection of toy soldiers. Sundry historic battles are meticulously represented in miniature. Gardens behind the museum offer a spectacular view of the ocean and were once the setting of the classic James Bond movie *Never Say Never Again.* To get here from the Kasbah, at the top of rue de la Kasbah turn left onto rue de la Corse. Bear right at the fork onto H. Assad Ibn Farrat and continue straight ahead past a hospital on the right until you reach the white mansion. (Open Fri.-Wed. 10am-5pm. Free.)

IN THE VILLE NOUVELLE

British expatriates frequent **St. Andrew's Church,** an Anglican house of worship designed by British imperialists to look like a mosque (1 bl. southwest of the Grand Socco on rue d'Angleterre). The Lord's Prayer is carved on the chancel arch in decorative Arabic. The gardens and benches offer a chance for recovery from the medina. (Tours by caretaker 9:30am-12:30pm and 2:30-6pm. Tips appreciated.)

The city's most recent monumental construction is the towering **New Mosque,** an ochre and white structure on **place el-Koweit,** southwest of the Grand Socco along rue Sidi Bouabib. It was a gift from the king of Kuwait.

■■■ ENTERTAINMENT

Av. d'Espagne runs along Tangier's expansive **beach.** Stick to the main portions frequented by tourists—the deserted areas are prime locations for muggings.

The most popular evening activity is to sip mint tea and people-watch in a **café** on **boulevard Pasteur.** Pay twice as much for a pot of tea (5-6dh), and you can enjoy the atmosphere where Tangier's intelligentsia come to sip and quip: **Café de Paris,** 1 pl. de France (open until 1am), and **Madame Porte,** on av. Prince Moulay Abdellah at rue el-Mou Hanabi (open until midnight).

Folk music and dance performances are at the **Morocco Palace,** av. du Prince Moulay Abdellah, just off blvd. Pasteur. Belly-dancers, beanie-twirlers, and Berber singers perform to the rhythms of lute, violin, tambourine, and bongo drums. (Open nightly from 10pm. Best on Sat. Cover 45dh, includes 1 drink.)

If thirsty for alcohol or just tired of the noise, try the **Negresco,** 20 rue Mexique (tel. 93 80 97), a relaxed atmosphere with quiet folk music and free hors d'oeuvres. (Beer 18dh, mixed drinks 30-35dh. Open 10am-1am.) The **Tangerinn,** the city's longest running bar, is connected to the Hôtel Muniria on rue Magellan, and also owned bybeat writer/*hôtel* owner John Sutcliffe. You can't avoid mingling with the varied crowd in this relaxed, hassle-free environment. (Open 9pm-2am.)

The Middle Atlas

■■■ MEKNÈS مكناس

Meknès sprawls across a gray-green agricultural checkerboard. The old-city mosques and *madares* peer severely over the valley at new-city concrete. The medieval medina is a smaller, tamer version of its eastern cousin Fès.

Sultan Moulay Ismail transformed the unremarkable provincial capital when he chose it as his seat of power in 1672. The ambitious and ruthless Sultan vowed to subdue the local tribes so severely that even "a Jew or a woman might travel unmolested" across the desert. He sent envoys to Louis XIV and courted conflict with the Spanish. One result of Moulay Ismail's high-intensity rule was the **Dar el-Kebira**, the largest palace in the world, which now lies largely in shambles. Today, the city has the largest Berber population in Morocco; its name, in fact, comes from the Berber tribe Meknassa. In few Moroccan cities is the contrast between rich and poor more pronounced than it is between the Meknès medina and *ville nouvelle.*

ORIENTATION AND PRACTICAL INFORMATION

The old town and monuments of the *ville impériale* are separated from the modern **ville nouvelle** by the **Oued Boufrekane,** a long valley about ½km wide. You can cross it on foot along av. Mouley Ismail or catch local bus #5, 7, or 9. These shuttle between the CTM bus station in the *ville nouvelle* and the colossal **Bab Mansour,** the entrance to the imperial complex that walls in the medina's main attractions. All major services in the *ville nouvelle* center around **pl. Administrative** (a.k.a. pl. de la Grande Poste).

Tourist Office: 27 pl. Administrative (tel. 52 44 26). From the Abdelader train station, walk straight ahead 2 bl., turn left onto Muhammad V, and then immediately right. Cross rue Allal-ben Abdalleh and continue for 2 bl. until you reach the Hôtel de Ville. Skirt to the right and it will be on the right after the post office. Friendly staff; adequate maps. Official guides 50dh per ½day (3 times the price of unofficial guides). Neither is necessary. Open Mon.-Fri. 8am-noon and 4-7pm; mid-Sept. to mid-June Mon.-Fri. 8:30am-noon and 2:30-6:30pm; Ramadan Mon.-Fri. 9am-3pm. **Syndicat d'Initiative:** Esplande de la Foire (tel. 52 01 91), just off av. Moulay Ismail inside the big yellow gate. Less informative than the tourist office. Open same hours.

Currency Exchange: Traveler's checks cannot be changed in the medina banks. Try **Hôtel Rif,** Zenkat Accra, around the corner from the tourist office. Regular bank currency rates. Open 9am-noon and 3-9pm. **B.M.C.E.,** 98 av. des F.A.R. (tel. 52 03 52), has an exchange window. 3dh commission per check. Open 10am-2pm and 4-8pm.

Post Office: pl. Administrative. Open Mon.-Sat. 8:30am-12:15pm and 2:30-6:45pm. **Telephones** available 8am-9pm. Use the side entrance when the post office is closed. **Branch office** on rue Dar Smen, near the medina. Open same hours. **Telephone Code:** 05.

Trains: av. de la Bassa, more than 1km east of the center of the *ville nouvelle.* To get to the center of town, walk out to av. des F.A.R., turn left and then right onto av. Muhammad V. Better still, get off at the smaller, more centrally located **Meknès el-Amir Abdelkader station,** rue d'Alger, 2 bl. from av. Muhammad V. Eight trains per day to: Rabat (2½hr., 47.50dh); Casablanca (3¾hr., 72dh); Fès (50min., 15dh); Oujda (7hr., 101dh).

Buses: CTM, 47 blvd. Muhammad V (tel. 52 25 85), near av. des Forces Armées Royales. To: Rabat (5 per day, 3hr., 32dh); Casablanca (5 per day, 4hr., 55dh); Fès (5 per day, 1½hr., 14.50dh); Tangier (1 per day, 63dh); Ifrane (1 per day, 27dh); Azrou (1 per day, 21.50dh). The bus to Fès often arrives full, so board early in the morning. **Private companies** stop at the pink terminal at the foot of the hill just below Bab Mansour. More frequent service to the Middle Atlas and Fès from here.

Laundromat: Most charge by the piece (7-8dh). Request a per kg price instead. Try **Pressing de la Poste,** 14 rue Dar Smen (tel. 53 09 03), in the *ville nouvelle* across from the post office. Open Mon.-Sat. 9am-1pm and 3-8pm.

Swimming Pool: Municipal Pool, av. Moulay Ismail at av. les Forces Armées Royales, by Oued Boufrekane. Open May-Sept. 10am-4pm. Admission 4dh. A few steps farther down the driveway is a cleaner, less crowded **private pool** with a lawn. Admission 10dh.

Late-Night Pharmacy: Croissant Rouge Pharmacie d' Urgence, pl. Administrative (tel. 52 33 75). Side entrance to the Hôtel de Ville. Open 8:30am-8:30pm.

Hospital: Moulay Ismail, rue des Forces Armées Royales (tel. 52 28 05 or 52 28 06), near av. Moulay Youssef. **Muhammad V** (tel. 52 11 34).

Ambulance: tel. 15.

Police: tel. 19.

ACCOMMODATIONS AND CAMPING

In the Ville Nouvelle

Staying in the *ville nouvelle* means greater comfort, higher cost, and the inconvenience of shuffling across the Oued Boufrekane or retiring early. Nearly everything in the *ville nouvelle* closes after 11pm. Check around **avenue Muhammad V** and **avenue Allal ben Abdallah** for some of the least expensive hotels.

Auberge de Jeunesse (HI), av. Okba Ibn Nafi (tel. 52 46 98), near the stadium. Follow the arrows toward Hôtel Trans Atlantique. Spartan rooms around a garden with outdoor café tables. Laundry sinks, kitchen, and TV lounge. Clean toilets. Reception open Mon.-Sat. 7-10am, noon-4pm, and 7-11pm, Sun. 7-10am and 6-11pm; Oct.-late April Mon.-Sat. 8-10am, noon-3pm, and 6-10:30pm, Sun. 8-10am and 6-10:30pm. 15dh per person. Breakfast 3.50dh. Members only. Cards issued on the spot (75dh and 2 photos).

Hôtel Touring, 34 av. Allal Ben Abdallah (tel. 52 23 51). A good deal. Some rooms are red. Singles with shower 79dh. Doubles with shower 91dh.

Hôtel Majestic, 19 av. Muhammad V (tel. 52 20 35). Astone's throw from train station. Large, tidy rooms. Delightful bathroom and management. Singles 76-157dh, depending on bathroom options. Doubles 97-187dh.

Camping: Municipal Camping Agdal (tel. 53 89 14), on the ramparts of the medina, outdoes any option on the hotel scene. Crowds gather in the beautiful, wooded park to use excellent amenities, including hot showers (5dh extra) and cooking facilities. The restaurant serves a 3-course *menu* for 45dh. Reception open 8am-1pm and 4-8pm. 12dh per adult. 8dh per child, tent, and car.

In the Medina

As always, lodgings in the medina are cheaper and grungier than in the *ville nouvelle.* Budget hotels line **avenue Roumazine,** a spirited street bombarded by music from sideline shops and paced by loping blind dogs. From the bus terminal below Bab Mansour, climb the hill to the *bab* and follow the street as it hooks left to become Dar Smen, which leads into pl. el-Hedine; from there, turn right onto av. Roumazine. No hotel in the medina has modern toilets.

Hôtel Maroc, 7 rue Roumazine (tel. 53 07 05). Bed, table, chair, hanging light bulb. You supply the spice. Ask for a room with a window on the central courtyard. Singles 35dh. Doubles 70dh.

Hôtel Regina, 19 rue Dar Smen (tel. 53 02 80). Turn left at the end of av. Roumazine, where rue Dar Smen runs to pl. el-Hedine. Toasty, musty, well-furnished rooms. Ask to see a room before signing the night away; quality definitely varies. Better sheets here than at the Hôtel Maroc. Singles 30dh. Doubles 40dh.

MEKNÈS

FOOD

The best belly-filling bargains come sizzling off the one-person stalls along the **rue Dar Smen** in the medina between av. Roumazine and pl. el-Hedine. Here whole lambs hang on hooks and well-done brochettes cost 3dh each. On **place el-Hedine,** try a bowl of piping hot *harira* for 2dh. Few restaurants in the medina have menus, so dining here can be a gastronomic (or gastrointestinal) adventure.

In the Medina

Oumnia, Restaurant Marocaine, 8 rue Roumazine (tel. 53 07 64), across from the Apollo Cinema. Knock on locked blue door next to pinball arcade to be let in. Groovy interior, decent food. Drink tea and sit on pillows before a low table in a Berber house. 55dh *menu* includes tea, choice of salad, entree, and dessert.

Cassecroute Ismalia, Zankat Hajj Muhammad Baharee, in the middle of the Souk en Nejjarin (carpenter's *souk*). Difficult to find, but the fresh brochettes are basted in a "special sauce" that draws prominent crowds. Soft drinks and seating upstairs. Two brochette patties, special sauce, on a Berber-seed bun 8dh.

In the Ville Nouvelle

Rotisserie Karam, 2 av. Ghannah (tel. 52 24 75), right off av. Hassan II. For those who assert, "I'm sick of *tajine.* Where can I get a nice bland piece of white-meat chicken?" 24dh *menu* also features "sheese-burger *garni."* Open 11am-11pm.

Restaurant Marhabee, 23 av. Muhammad V (tel. 52 16 32). Cheap, decent food. Good location. *Tajine* 23dh. Brochettes 15dh. Omelettes 6dh. Open 11am-11pm.

SIGHTS AND ENTERTAINMENT

Attenuated by war, weathering, and the Lisbon earthquake of 1755, the ramparts of the **Dar el-Kebira** (Imperial City) testify to Meknès's former preeminence as a capital city. Strolling about the site with a pickax and whip in hand, the vile Moulay Ismail personally supervised the city's construction, encouraging, criticizing, and disfiguring at will. Plundering priceless materials from other parts of the kingdom (notably the Badi Palace in Marrakech and Roman marble from Volubilis), the sultan raised a radiant city for himself. Now only the heavy walls and several large monuments remain. One of Morocco's most awesome portals is **Bab Mansour,** flanked by marble Corinthian columns and filled with green and black tilework.

Passing through the Bab, shake off the amiable guides and hug the wall to your right; after the second gate, keep to the right and you'll see the emerald green roof of the little **Salle des Ambassadeurs.** Now rebuilt, this is where Moulay Ismail conducted diplomatic meetings. Ask the guard to unlock the door leading to the underground **Christian Dungeon,** where the sultans kept 60,000 Christian slaves. (Open Sat.-Thurs. 8:30am-noon and 2:30-6pm, Fri. 8am-noon and 3-6pm.)

As you leave the dungeon, walk through the arch marked by a blue arrow to the mosque and **Tomb of Moulay Ismail.** 1082, the year he began his 57-year reign according to the Islamic calendar, is emblazoned on the front door. This is the only Moroccan shrine open to non-Muslims. Modest dress (i.e. clothes that cover your limbs) is appropriate. The rug-covered area around the tombs is off-limits, but you're welcome on the straw mats of the prayer area. (Open Mon.-Sat. 9am-noon and 3-6pm. Tip the custodian-guide.)

As you exit Bab Mansour, walk straight across busy pl. el-Hedime to the huge multi-colored mosaic on the outer wall of the 19th-century **Dar Jamai Palace,** the courtly mansion built by Jamai, Mouley Hassan's powerful vizier. Now the **Museum of Moroccan Art** (tel. 53 08 63), the palace flaunts the usual assortment of Qu'ranic parchments, traditional garb, tools, and trinkets. The interior is assembled from fragments of earlier 17th- and 18th-century mosques and *madares.* The master bedroom is stuffed with embroidered divans and topped with a magnificent cupola. (Open Wed.-Mon. 9am-noon and 2-7pm.)

As you leave the palace, immediately turn left onto rue Sidi Amar to enter the medina. Follow the alley left, and then fork right to the splendid green, glazed tile minaret of the **Mosquée Kebira** (Great Mosque). Directly across from the mosque is the breathtaking 14th-century **Madrasa Bou Inania,** an outstanding example of Merinid architecture. Get a close-up view of the well-preserved carved inscriptions surrounding the court from the top-floor dormitories, and look at the mosque from the rooftop terrace. (Open 9am-noon and 4-7pm; off-season 8am-noon and 2:30-6pm. Admission 10dh.)

Meknès's **medina** offers spacious, well-worn streets roofed with scalloped sheets of tin. Start just west of the Dar Jamai; as you face the museum, take the alley to the left of the entrance. Push straight ahead to **Souk en Nejjarin,** a major east-west thoroughfare. Bear east (right) past the Medersa of Bou Inania, then south onto the alleyway hugging the eastern wall of the Great Mosque. Watch for a tiny opening on the left, signaled by a set of crumbling, painted cedar doors. This is the crowded **Berber Market,** where you can watch metalworkers hammer silver into tiny chests, cups, and plates. Nearby, sporadic and sometimes feisty auctions follow afternoon prayer. To cover the medina from bottom to top, return by **rue Karmouni.** Back at pl. el-Hedime, beside Bab Mansour, sprouts the daily **vegetable market.**

The **Agdal Basin** was supposed to be a private pool for Moulay Ismail's wives and a reservoir in case of siege. The lake now irrigates the city's numerous gardens, and local kids use it as a swimming hole. Follow the signs for the municipal campground and continue down the road for another 100m. Tiny **Café Agdal** serves cold drinks here for 4dh. Back beside the staircase, a doorway opens into the **Héri** (storehouse), a refreshingly cool granary with enormous cisterns and endless arcaded staples that once held 12,000 horses. (Open daily 9am-noon and 3-6pm. Admission 5dh.) A long but invigorating hike from here northeast along the walls will bring you to **Bab el-Khemis,** the magnificent western gateway to the city. Northeast of the Agdal reservoir, just beside the campgrounds on the far side of the fortifications, stretch the **Agricultural Grounds,** the perfect spot for a shady picnic or stroll.

Just about the only live evening entertainment is in the *ville nouvelle* at the Hôtel Rif, on rue Accra (tel. 52 25 91), near the post office on pl. Administrative. Belly-dancing nightly (8-10pm) and disco music. (Admission 80dh, includes 1 drink.)

■ NEAR MEKNÈS

VOLUBILIS

Thirty km from Meknès are the ruins of the Roman outpost Volubilis; the large complex is filled with beautiful 2nd- and 3rd-century mosaics. The site was once the Roman Empire's most remote outpost; the imperial roads stopped here. You may remember Volubilis if you made it through Martin Scorsese's *The Last Temptation of Christ.* The site closes at dusk. (Entrance fee 20dh.) To get here, hire a *grand taxi* from their breeding grounds on the rue Dar Smen, several hundred meters above Hôtel Regina. The ride should cost about 30dh per person.

MOULAY IDRISS مولاى ادريس

Between Meknès and Volubilis is Moulay Idriss, a pilgrimage town named after the man who brought Islam to Morocco for good, a third-generation descendant of Muhammad. Because the town is holy to Muslims, dress very conservatively here. Non-Muslims cannot visit the mosques or shrines or spend the night in Moulay Idriss, but it's a convenient stop on the taxi ride to Volubilis, and worth a look.

■ ■ ■ FÈS فاس

The medina in Fès is why you came to Morocco. Artisans bang out sheets of brass, donkeys strain under crates of Coca-Cola, *muezzins* wail, and children balance trays of dough on their heads. Your nose will suffer sensory overload as the scent of brochettes on open grills combines with acrid whiffs of hash, the stench of tanning lye, the sweet aroma of cedar shavings, and the fetor of the open sewer (also known as the Oued Fès). Unlike the medinas in other Moroccan cities (most notably Tangier and Casablanca), the Fès medina is not dominated by tourists. UNESCO has designated Fès el-Bali a World Heritage site. The walls of the city are now being restored, and fresh cobblestones and plaster give parts of the medina a super-real, Disney feel.

ORIENTATION AND PRACTICAL INFORMATION

Fès is an extreme case of the modern Moroccan dichotomy: the French-built **ville nouvelle** is broad and orderly, and far from the huge, knotty **medina.** The CTM bus station is in the heart of the *ville nouvelle* (near the budget hotels); the other bus station lies near **Bab Boujeloud,** the main entrance to the medina. The train station is on the outskirts of the *ville nouvelle.*

The old city is divided into two walled-off sections: Fès el-Bali and Fès el-Jdid. Two parallel roads penetrate the medina from Bab Boujeloud to the Kairaouine Mosque in the center of **Fès el-Bali** (Old Fès). The main route is **rue Talaa Kebira;** to reach it, turn left after passing under Bab Boujeloud and immediately entering a small plaza, then turn right to reach the center of Fès el-Bali; the road is filled with butchers and grocers here. It's a half-hour downhill walk to the Kairaouine Mosque. Use the Talaa Kebira to keep your bearings: Fès el-Bali is confusing, but you'll always find *some* way out if you keep walking uphill on progressively wider streets. **Avenue des Français,** just outside Bab Boujeloud, leads to Bab Semmarin, the entrance to the **Fès el-Jdid** (New Fès). Fès el-Jdid is quite easy to navigate on foot.

You can reach Bab Boujeloud from the **ville nouvelle** either by *petit taxi* (12dh) or by bus #2 or 9 (1.60dh) from the stop on **avenue Hassan II,** near **place de la Résistance** (the hub for most city buses). Bus #18 runs from pl. de la Résistance to Bab Ftouh at the opposite end of the medina, near the Andalous Quarter. Bus #3 roars to pl. des Alaouites.

Tourist Office: ONMT, pl. de la Résistance (tel. 62 34 60), at av. Hassan II, in an office building across from the fountain. It's not well marked. From the CTM bus station, turn left onto blvd. Muhammad V and right past the post office onto palm-lined av. Hassan II. From the train station, head straight ahead on rue Chenguit, bear left at pl. Kennedy along av. France, and turn left on av. Hassan II. From Bab Boujeloud Gare Routière, pass under the Bab, continue straight, and turn right at the cinema to reach pl. de l'Istiqlal and catch bus #2 or 9. A *petit taxi* is 8dh. English-speaking staff. Newsstands in the *ville nouvelle* sell better ones. Open Mon.-Fri. 8am-3pm; mid-Sept. to June Mon.-Fri. 8:30am-noon and 2:30-6pm; Ramadan Mon.-Fri. 9am-3pm. **Syndicat d'Initiative,** blvd. Muhammad V, across from BMCE building at av. Slaoui (tel. 247 69). Not well stocked. Official guides found here (40dh per ½-day). Open Mon.-Fri. 8am-3pm; mid-Sept. to June Mon.-Fri. 8:30am-noon and 2:30-6pm.

Currency Exchange: BMCE, pl. Muhammad V, across from the Syndicat d'Initiative, to the right of the main entrance. Handles VISA/MC transactions and traveler's checks. Open Mon.-Thurs. 8:15-11:30am and 2:15-4pm, Fri. 8:15-11:30am and 2:45-4:15pm; off-season Mon.-Fri. 8:30am-noon and 3-5pm. **Les Merinides** (tel. 64 52 25), in the Borj Nord. Open 5-10pm.

Post Office: At the corner of av. Hassan II and blvd. Muhammad V in the *ville nouvelle.* Open for stamps and Poste Restante Mon.-Fri. 8am-3pm; Sept. 16-June Mon.-Fri. 8:30am-6:45pm. Open for **telegrams** Mon.-Fri. 8:30am-9pm. **Branch offices** at pl. d'Atlas and in the medina at pl. Batha. Open same hours.

Telephones: In the **main post office;** enter from blvd. Muhammad V. There's a long line for telephone calls, and an even longer wait for a connection. Open 8:30am-9pm. The **branch post office** in the medina also has international phones, and waits may be shorter. Same hours. **Telephone Code: 06.**

Flights: Aérodrome de Fès-Saïs (tel. 62 47 12 or 62 47 99), 12km out of town along the road to Immouzzèr. Bus #16 leaves from pl. Muhammad V (3dh). Collective taxi (7dh per person). **Royal Air Maroc** (tel. 62 55 16 or 62 55 17), av. Hassan II. To Casa daily, 200dh.

Trains: av. des Almohades (tel. 62 50 01), at rue Chenguit. 2nd-class trains are more expensive than buses, but more comfortable. To: Casablanca (11 per day,

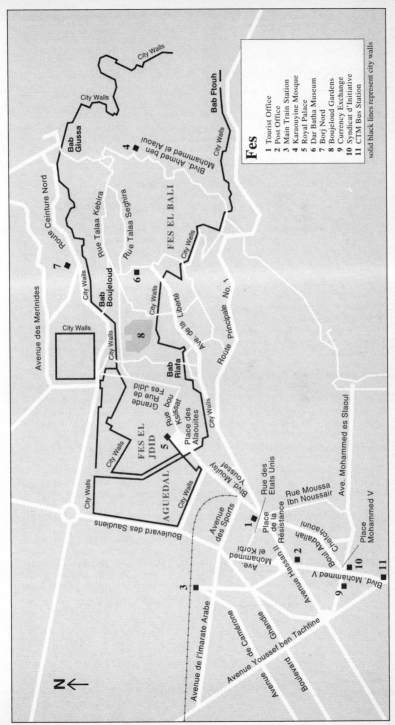

Fes

1 Tourist Office
2 Post Office
3 Main Train Station
4 Karaouyine Mosque
5 Royal Palace
6 Dar Batha Museum
7 Borj Nord
8 Boujeloud Gardens
9 Currency Exchange
10 Syndicat d'Initiative
11 CTM Bus Station

solid black lines represent city walls

4½-5½hr., 87dh); Rabat (12 per day, 3½hr., 62.50dh); Meknès (12 per day, 1hr., 15dh); Oujda (7 per day, 6hr., 83.50dh); Tangier (5 per day, 5½hr., 84dh).

Buses: CTM (tel. 62 20 41 or 62 20 42) and private bus companies have stops at blvd. Muhammad V in the *ville nouvelle* and also just outside Bab Boujeloud. To: Rabat (7 per day, 3hr., 47.50dh); Casablanca (8 per day, 5hr., 69dh); Marrakech (2 per day, 8hr., 110dh); Meknès (8 per day, 1hr., 19.50dh); Tangier (2 per day, 6hr., 77.50dh); Oujda (1 per day, 6½hr., 62dh).

Public Transportation: Numerous buses (1.60dh; fares double after 8:30pm, mid-Sept.-June after 8pm). Pl. de la Résistance is the hub. #2 or 9 from av. Hassan II near the plaza to Bab Boujeloud. #18 from the plaza to Bab Ftouh at the opposite end of the medina, near the Andalous Quarter. #3 from the plaza to pl. des Alaouites. #4 or 9 from *ville nouvelle* (in front of Grand Hôtel) to Fès el-Jdid (Bab Semmarin). #16 from pl. Muhammad V to the airport (3dh).

Taxis: Major stands at the post office, the Syndicat d'Initiative, Bab Boujeloud, and Bab Guissa. Fares double after 8:30pm, Sept. 16-June after 8pm.

Car Rental: Hertz, Hôtel de Fès, av. des Forces Armées Royales (tel. 62 28 12), off the southwestern end of av. Hassan II. Renault IV is 250dh per day plus mileage.

Luggage Storage: At the **train station,** av. des Almohades in the *ville nouvelle*. 2dh per bag for 24hr. Open 6am-11pm.

English Bookstore: 68 av. Hassan II (tel. 208 42), near pl. de la Résistance. All genres: novels, poetry, plays, guidebooks, and phrase books. English-speaking staff. Open Mon.-Fri. 8:30am-12:30pm and 4-7pm. For English-language newspapers and magazines try the newsstand on rue Muhammad V closest to the post office, or the store 1 block away from Muhammad V behind the central market.

Swimming Pool: Municipal Pool, av. Sports, next to the stadium and near the train station in the *ville nouvelle*. Crowded. Open July-Sept. 15 8:30-11:30am and 2:30-5:30pm. Admission 5dh. **Camping Moulay Slimane** (tel. 62 47 12). Call ahead to see if there's water today.

Late-Night Pharmacy: Municipalité de Fès, blvd. Moulay Youssef (tel. 233 80), just uphill from the Royal Palace. Open 8pm-8am.

Police: tel. 19.

ACCOMMODATIONS AND CAMPING

Ville Nouvelle

The new city is a long haul from the medina, but appealing during the old city's tourist season. In August rooms here fill up entirely. Cheap lodgings clump conveniently on or just off the west side of **boulevard Muhammad V,** between av. Muhammad es-Slaoui near the bus station, and av. Hassan II near the post office.

Auberge de Jeunesse (HI), 18 rue Abdeslam Serghini (tel. 62 40 85), in the *ville nouvelle*. From the ONMT tourist office cross the street, turn left onto blvd. Abdallah Chefchaouni, walk 4 bl., turn left, and look for the sign. English-speaking proprietors. Reasonably clean rooms. Shower dribbles hot water in winter only. Reception open 8-10am, noon-3pm, and 6-10pm. HI card with 2 photos (75dh) sold on the spot. 15dh per person. Non-members 17.50dh.

Hôtel Excelsior, 107 rue Larbi el Kaghat (tel. 62 56 02), 6 bl. up blvd. Muhammad V from bus station toward the post office. Clean rooms with stucco walls. Acceptable toilets and showers. Singles with shower 77dh. Doubles with shower 100dh.

Hôtel Central, 50 rue Nador (tel. 62 23 33), en route Hôtel Excelsior (above). Plain rooms, soufflé-style mattresses with slinky satiny bedspreads. Strong, lukewarm showers. A bit noisy. Singles 59dh, with shower 76dh. Doubles 83dh, with shower 94dh, with bath 106dh.

Hôtel CTM, rue Ksarelkbir (tel. 62 28 11). On intimate terms with the buses. Dark hallways belie the wide-open rooms. Shabby Scandinavian-style furniture. Expect street noise. Singles 53dh, with shower 76dh. Doubles 73dh, with shower 96dh.

Hôtel Olympic, just off blvd. Muhammad V (tel. 62 24 03 or 62 45 29), 1 bl. toward av. Hassan II from pl. Muhammad V. Modern rooms with excellent bathrooms, brass beds, phones, and winter heating. The most expensive of the lot, but also the nicest. Singles with bath 150dh. Doubles with bath 179dh.

Fès el-Bali

Step right up to **Bab Boujeloud** for budget rooms—they're cheaper, noisier, and dirtier than rooms in the *ville nouvelle,* but they're oh-so-near the medina.

> **Hôtel du Jardin Public,** 153 Kasbah Boujeloud (tel. 63 30 86), a small alley across from the Bab Boujeloud bus station. A prehistoric hotel with relatively sanitary rooms, some with good views. Moroccan showers (a flight down from most rooms) and toilets. The best of the Boujeloud hotels. Singles 35dh. Doubles 60dh.
>
> **Hôtel Erraha** (tel. 63 32 26), 1 bl. farther from the *bab,* on the right as you approach. Attention ascetics. Passable rooms, but small, bare, and stuffy. Tiny, rock-hard beds. Singles 40dh. Doubles 70dh.

Fès el-Jdid

Escape the Bab Boujeloud hustlers here. The lively main street, **grande rue de Fès Jdid,** runs from Bab Smarine to Bab de Kakene, near the Boujeloud gardens.

> **Hôtel du Commerce,** pl. des Alaouites (tel. 62 22 31), near the Royal Palace. Excitingly clean and pleasant. Paintings of weeping Pierrots in the hall, mauve stucco, and clean tiled showers. Some rooms have terraces overlooking the Royal Palace. Singles 38dh, with terrace 50dh. Doubles 60dh. Showers 4dh.
>
> **Hôtel le Croissant,** 285 grande rue de Fès Jdid (tel. 62 56 37), just 30m from Bab Smarine. Hot and cheap. The better rooms are off a renovated court in back. Pastel green rooms are bare-bones basic. Singles 30dh. Doubles 50dh.

FOOD

Ville Nouvelle

Cheap food huts skulk on the little streets to either side of **boulevard Muhammad V.** See also **rue Kaid Ahmed,** on the left a few bl. down blvd. Muhammad V from the main post office. **Boulangerie Pâtisserie Epi D'or** at 81 blvd. Muhammad V offers a marvelous breakfast. Forty minutes downhill, cleverly-named **Café Zanzi Bar** on rue Abdelkrim el-Khattabi, brews coffee and tea.

The busy, aromatic **municipal market** is where city households stock up on fresh fruit, veggies, fish, meat, and spices. It's opposite Café Zanzi Bar, just off blvd. Muhammad V.

> **Restaurant CTM,** rue Ksar El Kbir under Hôtel CTM. Substantial food at super prices. Fill your stomach with something other than butterflies after the bus ride. *Tajine,* salad, and bread from 30dh. Open 9am-10pm.
>
> **Rotisserie La Rotonde,** rue Nador (tel. 62 05 89), up the street from Hôtel Central. Skewered chicken torsos pirouette in this hole-in-the-wall. Fast food munchies. Succulent bubbling ¼-chicken, sauce, bread, and rice 13dh. Prices lower for take-out. Open 9am-10pm.
>
> **Restaurant Es Saada,** 42 av. Slaoui, a couple bl. off blvd. Muhammad V on the right. Eat outside to escape the boring interior. Lip-smacking, plentiful *menu* 60dh. Open 6:30am-11pm.
>
> **Restaurant Oued de la Bière,** 59 blvd. Muhammad V (tel. 62 53 24). Evocative name. Cooler than the adjoining café on the corner. Wood-panelled walls, Art Deco *élan.* Entrees 48-60dh. *Menu* 80dh. Open noon-3pm and 7pm-midnight.
>
> **Chez Vittoria,** 21 rue Nador (tel. 62 47 30). Off rue Muhammad V, near Hôtel Central. Hokey Italian decor, Moroccan wine, and Italian dishes: that's *amore!*

Fès el-Bali and Fès el-Jdid

Food stalls line the beginning of **Talaa Kebira** and **Talaa Seghira,** the two streets that split off the plaza at the mouth of the *bab.* Choose from *couscous, harira,* brochettes, *kefta-burgers,* and a jumble of oily, diced tomatoes and cucumbers known as *salade.* Look for budget fare just inside **Bab Boujeloud.** If no prices are posted, ask for them before you order. The quiet cafés around the **Place des Alaouites** specialize in almond juice and milk (3.50dh), a most nutritious beverage.

Restaurant des Jeunes, 16 rue Serrajine (tel. 63 49 75), on the right as you enter the *bab*. Stellar reviews. *Tajine* 25dh. Other entrees 20-25dh. *Pastilla* (when available) 30dh. Open 6am-midnight.

Restaurant Bouayad, 26 rue Serrajine (tel. 63 62 78), right next door to the above. Competition keeps prices down, quality up. Good *tajine* or *couscous* 25dh. Salad 2dh. Locals loiter around the clock. Open 24hrs.

SIGHTS

The medina is the most difficult to navigate in Morocco. Scorn the guides who may (or may not) accost you at the gates—this huge, vibrant neighborhood is a joy to be lost in. Keep in mind that walking uphill leads out of the medina; downhill to its center at the *oued*—and wander. If you're short on time or patience, consider hiring an **official guide** at the ONMT tourist office or the Syndicat d' Initiative. A morning tour costs 40dh and ends at noon. To see the medina at its liveliest, visit in the morning or after 5pm. To see the medina when the hustlers have retreated from the mid-afternoon heat, go around 3pm. Don't acknowledge the hustlers, would-be guides, and small children at the gates.

To get there from the *nouvelle ville,* take a *petit taxi* to Bab Boujeloud and work your way to the Kairaouine Mosque (see Orientation, above). Or take bus #2 or 9 to pl. de L'Istiqlal and head to the top of the square. Bear left, then immediately right down a skinny, spindly street. Cross the first busy thoroughfare and pass the Mosque of Sidi Lezzaz. The next big street is **Talaa Kebira,** the main artery that begins at Bab Boujeloud and runs the full length of the medina.

Fès el-Bali

The Dar Batha

A 19th-century palace conceals a well-kept and beautiful museum, the **Dar Batha.** The spacious Moorish mansion was headquarters for Sultan Hassan I and his playboy son Moulay Abd el-Aziz during the final years of decadence before the French occupation. In September, the museum hosts Moroccan music concerts. To reach the Dar Batha from the *ville nouvelle,* take bus #9 in front of the Grand Hôtel or a *petit taxi* to pl. l'Istiqlal outside the medina near Bab Boujeloud. Look for the green tile roofs of the palace. Turn left at the corner from the bus stop, enter the square, and head up the hill on the first left. Red flags mark the entrance on the right. (Open Wed.-Sat. 9am-noon and 3-6pm. Admission 10dh.)

Bab Boujeloud

Begin a tour of the medina at Talaa Kebira, just inside Bab Boujeloud and to the left. The **medieval water clock** here dates from 1357. Farther downhill on the right is the **Madrasa of Bou Inania,** the best-preserved Qu'ranic school in Morocco. Built under the Merinid Dynasty in the mid-14th century, its beautifully carved white plastered walls and *mihrab* remain in remarkably fine condition. A tiny canal separates the school from an adjoining mosque. (Open Sat.-Thurs. 9am-6pm, Fri. 8:30am-10am and 1:30-6pm. Admission 10dh.)

Farther down on Talaa Kebira, past the **Tijania Zaouia** on the left, is the trim **Mosque of Sidi Ahmed Tijani,** an elegant turquoise-tiled minaret. A bit farther down the main route is the small, whitewashed minaret of the **Mzara of Moulay Idriss,** an ancient house of worship. Next door is the lively **drum-makers' fondouk.** Diagonally across the street in the **sheepskin fondouk,** untanned woolly hides are bartered by the dozen. From here, rue Talaa Kebira bows slightly to the right and changes its identity to **rue ech Cherabliyyan.** A traditional **hammam** (bath) bubbles around the corner. Up ahead ex-animal skins convalesce in the **leather souk.** From the *souk,* a right then a left leads to the **place Nejarine,** a small triangular plaza ruled by its dazzling tiled fountain. Just below, an arched doorway leads into the **Nejarine Fondouk,** a fabulous 18th-century shopping area of delicate *mashrabiyya* and handsome balconies. Across the way, camera-shy woodsmiths chisel in the lively **carpenters' fondouk.**

FÈS

Around the Kairaouine Mosque

At the opposite end of the plaza from the fountain is one corner of the great **Zaouia of Moulay Idriss II,** honoring the saint, sultan, and son of the founder of Fès. Inside the *zaouia,* the Mosque of Chorfa houses the saint's tomb. The faithful arrive each morning to worship under the intricate stalactite ceiling. A tiny brass star with a gold slot is set in the wall nearby. Through the slot, they touch the back of the tomb—a practice believed to bring *baraka* (good luck). Non-Muslims are not permitted inside. The **henna souk,** a steep side street up the western wall of the shrine, is a fragrant, spice-filled alley.

The **Madrasa el-Attarin,** left from the corner of Zaouia and downhill, is Fès's finest Merinid monument. (Open 9am-6pm. Admission 10dh.) Turn right then left from the Medrassa to reach the splendid **Kairaouine Mosque.** Every Friday, 2000 flock here to pray—though the mosque can hold up to 20,000 men and 2000 women (who worship around and behind the men). The Kairaouine nurtured many great minds, including that of Pope Sylvester II, who introduced algebra and the number system to Europe. Today the mosque is home to Kairaouine University, where a few hundred students debate Qu'ranic law; founded in 859, the mosque is one of the oldest universities in the world. Worshipers wade through the tiled canal to the right of the entrance to clean their feet before praying. Non-Muslims can gawk and take pictures, but may not enter.

South, past the walls of the mosque, the **place Seffarine** is famous for deafening innocent travelers. **Madrasa Seffarine,** on the left of pl. Seffarine, is the oldest Merinid Qu'ranic school in Morocco (1280). Around the Madrasa Seffarine to the left and through the slender cobbled sidestreet is the smell. A microscopic alley on the right leads from here straight down into the mammoth outdoor **leather tannery.** The skins are soaked in green liquid, rinsed in a washing machine/cement mixer hybrid, dunked in diluted pigeon excrement or waterlogged wheat husks (for suppleness), and saturated in dye.

To get to the smoky **wool-** and **silk-dyers' row** from the pl. Seffarine, take the road leading south from beside the Madrasa Seffarine, head left at the fork, and make a sharp right at the river. Here, dyes boil over wood fires that blaze in old garbage cans. The finished skeins of brilliantly colored wool are so shiny that they appear wet even when dry.

Andalous Quarter

The Andalous Quarter is across the Oued Fès (river) from the heart of Fès el-Bali. Many of the Moors who fled from Muslim Spain (Andalusia) to Morocco during the 15th-century Reconquista settled around the great Almohad house of worship in Fès, the **Andalous Mosque.** Its main attraction is the grandiose 13th-century doorway. To find the mosque, head northwest from Bab Ftouh on the east end of the medina and take the first major left. From Fès el-Bali, cross the river at Port Bein el-Moudoun near the tanneries and head straight down rue Seffrah. The portal on the left side of the mosque offers the best view of the interior.

Fès el-Jdid

Christians, Jews, and Muslims once co-existed in the Fès el-Jdid (New Fès), built by the Merinids in the 13th century. The ancient neighborhood still has narrow side-streets, covered *souks,* and ornamental *mashrabiyya* balconies.

To the north, the arrow-straight **grande rue de Fès el-Jdid** traverses the area. To the south, the grande rue des Merinides cuts the adjacent *mellah.* **Bab Semmarin,** a chunky 20th-century gate, squats between the two areas. To reach Bab Semmarin from the *ville nouvelle,* take bus #4 or 9 from in front of the Grand Hôtel and tell the driver where to let you off. To walk from the *ville nouvelle* to the *mellah* (15min.), take av. Hassan II north past the PTT, veer left at the fork 2 blocks later on blvd. Moulay Hassan, and head straight for the grand place des Alaouites, where the *mellah* and grande rue des Merinides begin. To get here from Fès el-Bali, take bus #9 which returns by way of Bab Semmarin.

King Hassan II's sprawling modern palace, the **Dar el-Makhzen,** borders the **place des Alaouites.** Diagonally off the plaza, **grande rue des Merinides** runs up to Bab Semmarin on the other end of the *mellah.* Off this boulevard, the meter-wide side streets open into miniature underground tailors' shops, half-timbered houses, and sneaky alleyways. At the top of grande rue des Merinides glitters the **jewelers' souk.** Cackling chickens, salty fish, dried okra, and shiny eggplants vie for attention in the animated covered **market,** inside Bab Semmarin at the entrance to Fès el-Jdid proper. Toward the top of the avenue, the *souks* are covered, shading rainbows of *kaftans* and gold-stitched *babouches.*

Bear left at the end of rue des Merinides into the **Petit Mechouar;** on the left is **Bab Dekaken,** the back entrance to the Dar el-Makhzen. Through **Bab es Seba,** an imperial gate opens onto the **Grand Méchouar,** a roomy plaza lined with street-lamps. From here it's an easy walk to Bab Boujeloud—turn through the opening to the right of **Bab el-Seba,** continue straight for ¼km, and veer to the right after passing through a large arch at the end of road. The entrance to the refreshing **Boujeloud Gardens** (closed Mon.) is on the right. The Café La Noria, which borders the gardens, is similarly quite lovely. If you exit the gardens via the archway at the far side, take a left, then a right, and walk downhill to reach Bab Boujeloud.

Outside the Medina Walls

Borj Nord and Borj Sud, the surrounding hills, are an easy bus or *petit taxi* drive away. If driving, bear east from blvd. Moulay Hassan in the *ville nouvelle* toward Taza and Oujda; the highway winds along the city fortifications. After 4km, turn right toward **Borj Sud,** a 16th-century hilltop fortress guarding the southern end of Fès el-Bali. The castle, built by Christian slaves, is largely in ruins but commands an excellent view of the city.

The main highway continues east to **Bab Ftouh,** which arches in a **medieval cemetery.** Farther east, close to the ramparts, is **Bab Khoukha.** From here the walls curve wildly to **Bab Sidi Boujida.** A kink in the highway then leads to the **Jamai Palace,** an exquisite 19th-century dream house raised by Sultan Moulay Hassan's powerful vizier. A luxury hotel, the palace tarries within **Bab Guissa,** where a **pigeon and parakeet market** squawks every Friday morning.

To continue the circuit, keep to the outer road and follow the signs for Hôtel des Merinides, which overlooks the ruins of the **Merinid Tombs.** The tombs once formed the second-largest Merinid necropolis (after the Chellah in Rabat). The domiciles burrowed out of the base of the hill were the **lepers' quarters** in medieval times. The view of the medina is stunning at sunset.

Borj Nord, a short walk down the road from Hôtel des Merinides, looks like a crumbling hilltop fortress over the northern end of the city. It houses the **Museum of Arms,** a cache of weapons which have killed thousands of people. The guided tour lasts over an hour. (Open Wed.-Mon. 9am-noon and 3-6pm. Admission 10dh.)

Ville Nouvelle

The main attraction of the *ville nouvelle* is the superb **Ensemble Artisanal** on blvd. Allah ben Abdallah at the southwestern end of av. Hassan II. Sumptuous Arab carpets, Berber blankets, and other handicrafts fill the garden of the courtyard, where you can watch the artisans at work. In the weaving rooms, hundreds of young girls poke, thread, knot, snip, and pack spools of many-hued wool to create lavish works of art. (Open 8:30am-6:30pm.) Or follow local crowds into the busy, aromatic **municipal market,** just off blvd. Muhammad V (see Food: *Ville Nouvelle*).

ENTERTAINMENT

Catch live Moroccan music and belly dancing in the palatial **Restaurant Firadous's** *salon marocain,* in the Palais Jamai complex, on the right inside the medina's Bab Guissa. An entire evening, beginning with dinner at 8:30pm, costs a cool 140dh. To dance, sashay to **Night Club Oriental** (tel. 62 55 11), in the Grand Hôtel in the center of the *ville nouvelle,* and pay a 60dh cover, which includes one drink.

The Atlantic Coast

■■■ ASILAH أصيلا

The first tourism here was for punishment: in a fit of demographic engineering, the Romans rounded up the residents of Asilah, moved them to a town in Spain, and brought the Spaniards here. Asilah has seen enough tourists since then to learn how to hustle. Indeed staying in Asilah, with swarms of tourists and perhaps the most hustlers per capita of any town in Morocco, can still feel like punishment. Undeterred European visitors continue to make the short trip down from Tangier (50km) to enjoy Asilah's whitewashed buildings, medina, and beautiful beaches.

ORIENTATION AND PRACTICAL INFORMATION

The main street into town is **boulevard Muhammad V,** which ends at the town's center, **place Muhammad V,** a traffic circle. The road to the right leads to a fork in front of the medina. To the right is **rue Zallakah,** which leads to the port. To the left is **avenue Hassan II,** tracing the walls of the medina.

Post Office: Walking on blvd. Muhammad V away from pl. Muhammad V, go 1 bl. past the police station and turn right. Post office is 50m up this road on the left. Open Mon.-Thurs. 8am-3pm, Fri. 8am-12:30pm. **Telephone Code:** 09.

Currency Exchange: BMCE, pl. Muhammad V. Open Mon.-Fri. 8:15am-2:15pm.

Trains: The station is a 20-min. walk from town on the Asilah-Tangier highway, near a strip of campgrounds. To get to town, follow the road by the beach, keeping the sea to your right. A taxi from town costs about 10dh. A bus (3dh) connects the station to town; it leaves from in front of the station immediately after the train arrives. To Tangier (5 per day, 1hr., 1st-class 17.50dh, 2nd-class 12.50dh) and Casablanca, Rabat, and Marrakech (5 per day).

Buses: CTM, off av. Liberté on the way out of town to the highway. CTM and private buses to Tangier (every ½hr. starting at 12:30pm, 10dh) leave from in front of the office. To Casablanca (14 per day, 4½-5½hr., 57dh). Buses depart with surprising promptness and sometimes leave early at the driver's whim.

Taxis: pl. Muhammad V, across from the bus station. *Grands taxis* only. To Tangier about 100dh. To train station 10dh.

Pharmacy: Pharmacie Loukili, av. Liberté (tel. 91 72 78), 1 block from pl. Muhammad V across from the police. Open Mon.-Fri. 9am-1pm and 4-9pm.

Police: Service de Police, av. Liberté at blvd. Muhammad V (tel. 19), 1 block from pl. Muhammad V. Helpful if you arrive at night.

ACCOMMODATIONS AND CAMPING

To rent rooms in a small pension or private home (30-35dh per person), ask around the waterfront or along **rue Zallakah** by the walls of the medina; you can usually get homemade meals for a little extra. Although you're in a home, be careful with your valuables. Otherwise, a variety of reasonably priced (though not cheap by Moroccan standards) hotels lie within walking distance of the beach. Asilah is bursting with campgrounds, some of which rent small, inexpensive "bungalows" to those without tents or sleeping bags. Most campgrounds are near or on the shore toward the train station; others are along the road to Cape Spartel.

Hôtel Sahara, 9 rue Tarfaya (tel. 91 71 85). Take blvd. Muhammad V from pl. Muhammad V, turn away from beach at av. Liberté and left at the next bl. Smallish rooms. Baths are modern, newly-tiled, and squeaky, squeaky clean. TV room with plump pillows. Singles 82dh. Doubles 118dh. Hot showers 5dh.

Hôtel Marhaba, 9 rue Zallakah (tel. 91 71 44), on the right as you approach the medina from pl. Muhammad V. The most popular place with travelers: prime location, low rates, adequate rooms, and perfectly clean bathroom. Travelers report success haggling over room rates. Singles 80dh. Doubles 100dh.

Hôtel Asilah, 79 av. Hassan II (tel. 91 72 86). From rue Zallakah, turn left and follow the walls of the medina along av. Hassan II. Enter on a side street. Small, spartan rooms. Pink Moroccan-style lounge with puffy cushions to sink in. View of medina walls. Singles 60dh. Doubles 80dh. Sept.-May: 40dh; 60dh.

Hôtel Belle Vue, rue Alkansaa (tel 91 77 47). From av. Hassan II, take first immediate left. Higher in quality and prices than others. Singles 120dh. Doubles 200dh.

Camping Echrigui (tel. 91 71 82), 700m from the train station toward town, where the new port finally ends. On a glorious beach, and the walk to town isn't too bad. Office has cushiony salon/lounge. 8dh per person, 9dh per tent and per car. Bungalows with bath and hot shower 70dh, with electricity 100dh.

FOOD

The cheapest and most authentic restaurants clutter **avenue Hassan II,** along the walls of the medina. Famished souls eat their hearts out in one of the tiny stalls with green doors for 20dh. A fruit and vegetable **market** lurks further down av. Hassan II.

Restaurant Café Rabie, 9 av. Hassan II, near the beginning of the medina walls. The chicken, beef, and fish dinners are hypercheap (16-25dh). Spicy *harira* 5dh. Sidewalk patio across the street. Open 9:30am-11:30pm.

Restaurant Najoum, directly below the Marhaba hotel (tel. 91 74 59). Savory swordfish 35dh. English spoken. Open 7am-11pm.

La Alcazabah Restaurant (tel. 91 70 12), at beginning of rue Zallakah by the medina and port. Reputedly the best restaurant in town. Sit inside or upstairs on a terrace overlooking the street and the port. Wine served. English spoken. Entrees 35-70dh. Service charge 10%. Open 8:30am-3:30pm and 6:30pm-2am.

Restaurant Lixus, pl. Muhammad V (tel. 91 73 79). Bland atmosphere, sizable portions (20-30dh). Equally sizable dining room. Open 8am-10pm.

SIGHTS

Asilah has but two attractions: its nearby **beaches** and its shining medina. The beaches just north of town are smooth, sandy, sprawling delights. The beach company is generally congenial, but don't bring a passport or valuables along—there are sometimes muggers, and it's safer to have your hotel management lock things in their safe. Men tend to leer at and harass any women who swim. Five km south of Asilah, an enclosed cove called **Paradise Beach** has fine sand and clear water. The walk down the coast takes one hour; horsecarts from town are faster (50dh).

The **medina,** bounded by heavily fortified stone walls, is easy to navigate. Enter through **Bab Hamar** at the intersection of av. Hassan II and rue Zallakah. Intricately painted stalactite arches and bright tiled burial markers decorate the Portuguese **Palais de Raissouli** on the coastal side of the medina across from the *bab.* (Open only Sundays in off-season 9am-2pm.)

Apart from the regular town market, a Sunday morning Berber market at **souk el-Had el-Gharbia** opens 9km inland from Asilah. Berbers from as far away as the Rif mountains converge on an enclosed area by the tiny village to peddle their wares. Scanty vestiges of the once-sizable Roman metropolis **Admercuri** dot a dusty road 2km farther inland. Ask local children to point the way. There's no public transport to the market.

In August, artists from all over the world flock here for the famous **International Festival.** Painters cover the white walls with murals, and jazz and folk musicians sprinkle sound along the beach.

■■■ RABAT الرباط

Many of those 17th-century pirate expeditions you read about were 1) true, and 2) based in Rabat. The Mediterranean and the Atlantic were the pirates' oysters until the Alaouites roundly subdued them around 1700. Now, however, Rabat is singular

RABAT

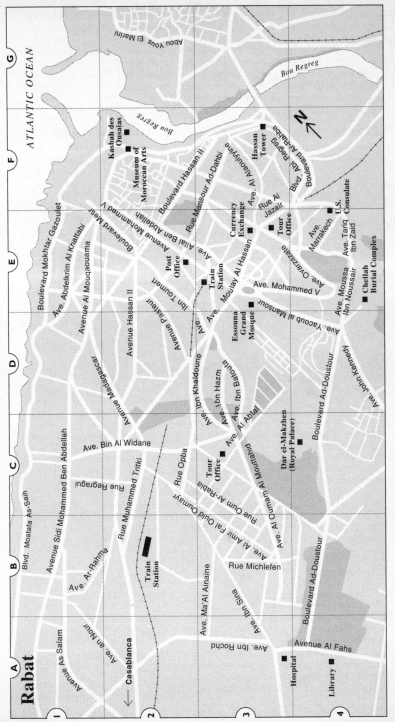

Rabat

ATLANTIC OCEAN

Abou Yous El Marini

Bou Regreg

Bou Regreg

Kasbah des Ousaias

Museum of Moroccan Arts

Boulevard Hassan II

Ave. Mansour Ad-Dahbi

Hassan Tower

Boulevard Abi Regreg

Blvd. Abderrahmania Al-Ravbia

Boulevard Mokhtar Gazoulet

Ave. Abdelkrim Al Khattabi

Ave. Al Mouqaouama

Boulevard Mesr

Avenue Mohammed V

Ave. Allal Ben Abdellah

Ave. Al Alaouiyyine

Rue Al Jazaïr

Currency Exchange

Tour Office

U.S. Consulate

Ave. Marrakech

Ave. Tariq Ibn Zaid

Avenue Hassan II

Ibn Toumert

Post Office

Train Station

Ave. Moulay Al Hassan

Ave. Ouarzazate

Ave. Moussa Ibn Noussair

Chellah Burial Complex

Avenue Pasteur

Ave. Mohammed V

Ave. Yacoub al Mansour

Essouna Grand Mosque

Avenue Madagascar

Ave. Ibn Khaldoune

Ave. Ibn Hazm

Ave. Ibn Batouta

Ave. Al Abtal

Dar el-Makzhen (Royal Palace)

Boulevard Ad-Doustour

Ave. John Kennedy

Ave. Bin Al Widane

Rue Regragui

Rue Muhammed Tritki

Rue Opba

Tour Office

Rue Oum Ar-Rabia

Ave. Al Amir Fal Ould Oumayr

Ave. Al Ouman Al Mouttahib

Blvd. Mostafa As-Salh

Avenue Sidi Mohammed Ben Abdellah

Ave. Ar-Rahma

Train Station

Ave. Ma'Al Ainaine

Ave. Ibn Sina

Rue Michlefen

Boulevard Ad-Doustour

Avenue As Salam

Ave. an Nour

Casablanca

Ave. Ibn Rochd

Avenue Al Fahs

Hospital

Library

in Morocco for the very absence of hustlers. The King lives here and his unflagging interest in his own backyard leads him to deploy discreetly ubiquitous soldiers around the city. Rabat's citizens, moreover, do not rely on tourism for revenue. Since the King co-opts (by creating bureaucratic positions) rather than confronts political opposition, the public sector is large and many are employed in administrative positions. Rabat is also a business capital. Restaurants aren't particularly elegant, the gardens aren't especially fair, and the merchants aren't strikingly cordial. In short, Rabat is a modern city frequented for its facilities, not its charm. It's also the city in Morocco where Western women travelers may feel most comfortable.

ORIENTATION AND PRACTICAL INFORMATION

The town is easy to navigate. **Avenue Muhammad V** parades north-south from the Grand Essouna Mosque, past the train station and the post office, and right through the **medina**. From the train station, turn left down this avenue to reach most budget hotels. **Avenue Allal ben Abdellah** runs parallel to av. Muhammad V, 1 block away (to your right when walking downhill from the train station). Perpendicular to av. Muhammad V is **avenue Hassan II,** which runs east-west along the medina's southern walls. To the east is Rabat's sibling city **Salé;** to the west is the **route de Casablanca,** home of the inconvenient "central" bus station.

Tourist Office: Municipal, 22 rue al-Jazair (tel. 73 05 62). Distant but helpful. Turn right out of the train station, walk up av. Muhammad V to the Grand Essouna Mosque, turn left on av. Moulay Hassan, and bear right onto rue al-Jazair. English-speaking staff. Sketchy maps of Rabat and other large cities. Open Mon.-Fri. 8am-noon; mid-Sept. to June 15 Mon.-Fri. 8am-noon and 12:30-5:30pm; Ramadan Mon.-Fri. 9am-3pm. **Syndicat d'Initiative,** rue Patrice Lumumba (tel. 72 32 72). From the post office, cross av. Muhammad V and head right along rue el-Qahira, which intersects rue Patrice Lumumba a few blocks down. Centrally located. Bare-bones office whose purpose is to arrange official tours. Open 8am-6pm.

Embassies and Consulates: U.S., 2 av. Marrakech (tel. 76 22 65). Look for the flag waving over blvd. Tarik Ibn Ziyad, which runs beside the fortifications on the southeastern edge of town along the river. Consulate open Mon.-Fri. 8:30-11:30am (8:30am-5:30pm for U.S. citizens). 24-hr. emergency phone. **Canadian,** 13 Joafar Essadik, Agday (tel. 77 13 76 or 77 13 77). Open Mon.-Tues. and Thurs.-Fri. 8-11am. **Australian** citizens should go here as well. **U.K.,** 17 blvd. de la Tour Hassan (tel. 72 09 05). Open Mon.-Fri. 8-11:30am. Also handles citizens of **New Zealand. Algerian Visas: Algerian Consulate,** 10 rue d'Azrou off av. Fès (tel. 76 78 58). US and Canadian citizens must go to their own embassies first, then come with forms, 4 photos, and 100dh (US) or 400dh (Canada). U.K. citizens can obtain visas here or at home, but there's a 7-10 day wait in either case. Open Mon.-Fri. 9:30am-2:30pm.

Currency Exchange: Hôtel de la Tour Hassan, 22 av. Chellah (tel. 72 14 01). From the train station, hop across pl. des Alaouites onto el-Forat, cross pl. du Golan (pl. de la Cathédrale) onto Laghouat, walk to the next block, and turn left onto av. Chellah. Official bank rates. Open 8am-noon and 2-6pm.

Post Office: av. Muhammad V (tel. 72 07 31), left from the train station at rue Soekarno. Open Mon.-Fri. 8am-3:30pm; mid-Sept. to June Mon.-Fri. 8:30am-noon and 2-6:45pm.

Telephones: rue Soekarno, facing post office. Open 24hrs. Lines are shortest noon-3pm. You cannot place international collect calls here. Hotels should be able to place your call for you at no charge, however. Also receives Poste Restante (1.70dh per piece). **Telephone Code:** 07.

Flights: International Airport Mohammed V (tel. (02) 33 90 40), in Casablanca. Buses leave for the airport from corner of av. Muhammad V and av. Moulay Youssef, across from the train station (7 per day, 1½hr., 50dh). Very slick trains also run to the airport via Casa. **Royal Air Maroc,** 35 rue Abou Faris Amarini (tel. 70 97 00). Open Mon.-Fri. 8:30am-noon and 2:30-7pm, Sat. 8:30am-noon and 3-6pm. **Air France,** 281 av. Muhammad V (tel. 70 70 66). Open Mon.-Fri. 8:30am-

12:15pm and 2:30-6:30pm, Sat. 9am-12:15pm. Also open for information Sat. 3-6pm. There's also a mini-airport in Rabat (tel. 73 03 16 or 78 92 92).

Trains: Rabat Ville Station, av. Muhammad V at av. Moulay Youssef (tel. 70 14 69). 2nd-class to: Tangier (6 per day, 5½hr., 79dh); Fès (7 per day, 4hr., 62.50dh); Oujda (4 per day, 7hr., 158.50dh); Casablanca (13 per day, 1hr., 24.50dh). The **Trans-Maghreb Express** departs Rabat at 9:50pm, stops at Oujda, Morocco at 8:30am the next day, arrives in Algiers at 8:25pm that night (264dh), and Tunis at 7:30pm the day after that (430dh).

Buses: (tel. 77 51 24) route de Casablanca at pl. Muhammad Zerktouni. Shockingly far from the town center: take *petit taxi* (10dh) or bus #30 from av. Hassan near rue Muhammad V (2.40dh). All the bus companies operate from here. CTM tickets sold at windows #14 and 15; the other windows belong to private companies.
CTM to: Casablanca (6 per day, 1hr., 22dh); Fès (6 per day, 3½hr., 46.50dh) via Meknès (2½hr., 33dh); Tangier (5 per day, 5hr., 67dh); Tetuan (3 per day, 70dh).

Taxis: Stands at the train station, in front of the bus station along av. Hassan II across from Bab Oudaias, and at the entrance to the medina by the corner of av. Hassan II and av. Muhammad V.

Car Rental: Hertz, 467 av. Muhammad V (tel. 76 92 27). Renault IV 250dh per day plus mileage. **Avis,** 7 Zankat (tel. 76 97 59), above Faris El Marin. Another office at the Rabat airport (tel. 76 75 03).

Luggage Storage: At the **train station** (2dh per locked bag). At the **bus station** (3dh per day). Open 6am-9pm.

English Bookstore: American Bookstore, 4 rue Tanja (tel. 76 10 16). Superb shelf on Morocco and Islam, plus an inexplicable predominance of Henry James and Stephen King (5-25dh). Open Mon.-Fri. 9:30am-12:30pm and 2:30-6:30pm, Sat. 10am-1pm. The **newsstand** at the train station carriers an excellent selection of English-language newspapers and magazines.

Library: Dar America, 35 av. al Fahs (tel. 75 07 88), in Souissi near Hôpital Avicenne. Current newspapers and periodicals. Open 10am-noon and 4-6pm.

Laundromat: Rabat Pressing, 67 av. Hassan II (tel. 72 63 61), at Allal ben Abdallah. Pants 12dh, jackets 16-20dh. Hotels usually offer cheaper service. Open Mon.-Sat. 8am-12:30pm and 2:30-7:30pm.

Late-Night Pharmacy: Pharmacie de Préfecture, av. Moulay Slimane (tel. 70 70 72). Take rue Abou Inane, which runs straight ahead from the train station; take a left downhill behind the big church. Hanging red crescent moon outside. Open 8:30pm-8am.

Medical Services: Hôpital Avicenne, av. Ibn Sina (tel. 77 44 11), at the southern end of blvd. d'Argonne; in Souissi just south of Agdal. Free emergency medical care for all. U.S. citizens can also go to the U.S. Embassy for medical care. **Ambulance:** tel. 15.

Police: rue Soekarno (tel. 19), 2 blocks from the post office off av. Muhammad V.

ACCOMMODATIONS AND CAMPING

In the Medina

While most of the town's action is the new city, the medina has cheaper beds. A secret: the Rolex watches peddled here aren't genuine.

Hôtel Maghrib El-Jadid, 2 rue Sebbahi (tel. 73 22 07), at av. Muhammad V, right past entrance to the medina. New bright pink paint and modeling. Clean floors, cot-like beds. Rooftop terrace. English spoken. Singles 45dh. Doubles 50dh. Hot showers 5dh.

Hôtel Marrakech, 10 rue Sebbahi (tel. 277 03), just past the above. Tiles insulate from external heat. Rooms verge on the miniature, but there's a fresh towel every day. Rustic toilets. Singles 50dh. Doubles 80dh. Hot showers 5dh, cold ones 2dh.

Ville Nouvelle

Oh-so-many plush hotels line **avenue Muhammad V, avenue Allal ben Abdellah,** and sidestreets. From the train station's main entrance, turn left onto av. Muhammad V and walk toward the medina. Av. Allal ben Abdellah is one block to the right as you walk downhill.

Auberge de Jeunesse (HI), 43 rue Marassa (tel. 72 57 69), on the road perpendicular to av. Hassan II in the *ville nouvelle,* just outside the medina walls. Drab, cramped rooms around a groovy garden. Shopworn but clean. The staff speaks English and will guard your valuables. No linen available. Reception open 7-9:30am, noon-3pm, and 7pm-midnight; Sept.-June 8-10am, noon-3pm, and 6-10:30pm. HI cards sold on the spot (when they have them). 20dh per person with card, 22.50dh without. Breakfast included (8-9am).

Hôtel Majestic, 121 av. Hassan II (tel. 72 29 97), 2 blocks left of av. Muhammad V. Hardly majestic but not so bad. Rambling beds, clean rooms, and good location near the medina. Lovely, huge bathrooms. Singles 64dh, with shower 76dh. Doubles 88dh, with shower 98dh.

Hôtel Capitol, 34 av. Allal ben Abdellah (tel. 73 12 36). Spacious rooms with beds to melt in. Fresh towels daily, laundry service available, and delectable continental breakfast in the restaurant. There are no shared showers available here, so either take a room with one or make use of the spacious sinks. Singles 64dh, with shower 74dh, with shower and toilet 95dh. Doubles 74dh, with shower 95dh, with shower and toilet 110dh.

Hôtel Central, 2 rue el-Basra (tel. 70 73 56). From the train station, cross av. Muhammad V and walk 2 blocks toward the medina; take the 2nd right immediately after Hôtel Balima. Rooms decorated in white and sizzling hot pink. Sprawling beds and antique-seeming furniture. Frequented by the few other foreigners in Rabat. Singles 70dh, with shower 120dh. Doubles 110dh, with shower 130dh.

Hôtel Velleda, 106 av. Allal ben Abdellah, 4th fl. (tel. 76 95 31 or 76 95 32). Barren but big rooms painted a yellow that makes you yearn for the pink elsewhere. Unidentifiable plants hulk in the sitting area. Sizable breakfast and TV rooms; gloomy halls. Singles 86dh, with shower 127dh. Doubles 107dh, with shower 158dh.

Camping de la Plage (tel. 78 23 68), on the beach across from the Bou Regreg River in Salé. Taxi to the site 10-15dh. Running water, toilets, and a grocery store-*cum*-restaurant. The facilities are primitive and a bit shabby, but the prices rule. Reception open 24hrs. 10.50dh per person, 5dh per tent and per car, slightly more for vans or larger vehicles. Cold showers and electricity included.

FOOD

A meal in the **medina** entails eating alongside entrails. Several inexpensive places stud **avenue Muhammad V.** At the nearby stalls, 18dh brings a plateful of tripe or a veal cutlet, salad, and bread. Budgeteers eat in two areas of the new city: around av. Muhammad V and **avenue Allal ben Abdellah,** a block or two from the medina, and around the train station, just off **avenue Moulay Youssef.** The covered **market** is between the entrance of the medina and pl. du Marché.

Restaurant el-Bahia, av. Hassan II (tel. 73 45 04), to the right going toward the medina on av. Muhammad V. Built into the walls of the medina. Interior court and fountain with goldfish. *Salon marocain* upstairs. Appetizing food at bargain prices. Crowded at lunch. Popular dishes may run out by dinner time. Entrees around 25dh. Open 11am-11pm.

Restaurant Ghazzah, 3 rue Ghazza (tel. 72 45 53), across the street from Hôtel Splendide. Utilitarian decor and Moroccan clientele. Dining cubbyhole upstairs for short customers. Lamb *tajine* 30dh. *Filet du merlan* 25dh. Open 9am-11pm.

Restaurant le Fouquet's, 285 av. Muhammad V (tel. 76 80 07), across the street and downhill from the train station. Cozy and tableclothed: please, look and be French. Specialty fish dishes (65-80dh). *Menu du jour* 60dh. Open 10:30am-3:30pm and 6:30pm-midnight.

Café-Restaurant La Clef (tel. 70 19 72), near the train station. Exiting the station, make a hairpin right onto av. Moulay Youssef, then down the 1st alley on the left. The *salon marocain* has low-slung couches. Yummy *tajine pigeon* (tender pigeon stewed with prunes, almonds, and onions, 38dh) will have you singing high notes. Open noon-4pm and 7-11pm.

Le Broodjest, 78 av. Allal Ben Abdallah. The super-cheap choice. Succulent falafel for 6dh. Hummos plates for 13dh that pack a wallop and can be accompanied with fries for 3dh. Open 11am-midnight.

SIGHTS

The city's landmark, the **Essouna Grand Mosque** at av. Muhammad V and av. Moulay Hassan is bedecked with gold-trimmed windows and sandy-hued arches. A tan and green minaret, pierced by arched windows on five levels, towers over the shingled roof. Intricately carved walls and arches are inside. (Entrance forbidden to non-Muslims.) Av. Moulay Hassan saunters over to the salmon-pink Almohad **Bab el-Rouah** (Gate of the Winds), which sports Kufic inscriptions and arabesques on the arches. Inside the gate to the right is a gallery of contemporary, vaguely Gauguinesque Moroccan paintings. Exhibits change every few weeks, and you can occasionally glimpse the artists *en flagrante*. (Open 8:30am-noon and 2:30-8pm.)

Back through Bab er Rouah and through the wall to the right is the **Dar el-Makhzen** (Royal Palace). Although it was begun in the 18th century, most of the present palace postdates the French occupation. Visitors aren't permitted inside, and those who come too close will be chased away. Photography is permitted.

Beyond the southern extremity of the palace grounds at the end of av. Yacoub el-Mansour loom the decrepit but still impressive remains of the **Chellah burial complex,** a fortified royal necropolis revered since the time of the Almohads. To get here from the palace, walk out the gate adjacent to the palace (**Bab Zaers,** not the entrance gate), and turn left. The views over the Bou Regreg River are terrific. Down the path from the Chellah Gate is Hassan's **mausoleum;** his tombstone is the white prism in the back. The psychedelic-tiled minaret is the highlight of the ruined **mosque.** The mosque is open to non-Muslims since it's no longer in use. There's also a public **park** where narrow footpaths wind through carefully tended gardens.

Across town along av. Abi Regreg (near the Moulay Hassan bridge to Salé) hulks the somber, elegant **Mausoleum of Mohammed V.** Surrounding the white-marble tomb, a wreath of flowers and polished black marble honor the king who led the country to independence. Turquoise and sapphire stained-glass windows ring the gold-leaf dome. (Open 8am-last prayer: around 10pm, winter 8pm. Free.)

The imposing **Hassan Tower** is an unfinished minaret from the 12th century's largest Western mosque. Ambitious Sultan Yacoub el-Mansour wanted to construct the three greatest towers in the world; he set up the Giralda minaret of Sevilla and the Koutoubia of Marrakech before aspiring to this lofty spire, but died before he finished it. Still, at 55m the incomplete turret towers above both its famous siblings. (Interior closed to the public.)

In the northern corner of the medina along Tarik el-Marsa are the walls of the famed **Kasbah des Oudaias,** the *ribat* where, in the 10th century, a garrison of the Oudaia tribe watched the city. Andalusian refugees settled here in the 17th century. **Bab Oudaia,** at the top of the hill, is the more curious of the gates. The **Oudaias Gardens** inside are flower-strewn and serene. Also inside is the **Museum of Moroccan Arts,** parked in two separate parts of the 17th-century palace of Moulay Ismail. Museum contains an intriguing assemblage of musical instruments, traditional Moroccan dress, ceramics, and jewelry. (Museum and garden open 10am-5pm; winter Wed.-Mon. 8:30am-noon and 3-6:30pm. Admission to museum 3dh.)

Rabat's **medina** is entered via av. Muhammad V. To the left lies the **fruit and vegetable market.** Animal parts hang cheek by jowl with sneakers and videotapes on **rue Souiqa,** the first right off Muhammad V. Rue Souiqa eventually turns into **Souk es Sebat,** a narrow alley covered with straw mats as protection from the blazing sun. Renovated in 1887 by Moulay Hassan, the **Grand Mosque** adjoins the *souk*.

South of pl. de la Grande Mosquée, the **archaeological museum** houses a collection of Volubilis bronze works all cast before 25 BC, as well as exhibits on the Roman necropolis of Salé, Phoenician and Carthaginian relics, and the standard room of animal bones. To get here, walk down av. Muhammad V and turn left onto Abd Al Aziz at the Grand Mosque. The museum is on the next street off Abd Al Aziz.

(Open Wed.-Mon. 8:30am-5pm; winter Wed.-Mon. 8:30am-noon and 2-6:30pm. Admission 10dh.)

ENTERTAINMENT

Rabat nightlife entails cinemas and pricey, pseudo-Euro discos, such as **Amnesia,** on rue Monastir near the Cinema Royale. There's a New York checkered cab out front and an airplane and school bus inside. The music is so loud, you'll forget... For something spicier, call the palatial **Tour Hassan Hôtel,** 22 av. Chellah (tel. 72 14 91), to find out if there will be a modern music performance that evening. **Café Balima** (in front of Hôtel Balima on av. Muhammad V near the train station), reported to be the best café in Rabat, is a relaxing spot to sip mint tea.

■■■ CASABLANCA الدار البيضاء

There's no Rick's Café Américain, no one looking at you, kid (except maybe the hustlers who prowl the medina and major boulevards), and not as much to do or see in this modern city of 3.5 million as you might hope. While its romance may disappoint, as a commercial and transportation center, the city is first-rate indeed. The relatively small medina is surrounded by 20th-century, five-to-ten story concrete buildings. Restaurants, cafés, and decent hotels abound. Visitors to "Casa" will experience all the stresses of modernity—but also many of its benefits.

ORIENTATION AND PRACTICAL INFORMATION

Almost 100km directly south of Rabat, Casablanca is easily accessible by plane, bus, and train. Casa's two train stations confuse everyone. **Casa Port** is close to the youth hostel and the city center. **Casa Voyageurs** is close to nothing, and is a 50-minute walk from Casa Port or a 15dh *petit taxi* ride to the city center. To get from Casa Port to the **CTM bus station,** cross the street, follow blvd. Muhammad El Hansali to the end (1km), turn left on av. de l'Armée Royale, and look out for the Hôtel Safir. The station is behind it and to the right.

The city's two main squares, place des Nations Unies and place Muhammad V, also puzzle travelers. **Place Nations Unies** spreads out in front of the Hyatt Regency at the intersection of blvd. Houphouët-Boigny (this blvd. adjoins the Casa Port train station 2 bl. to the north) and, among other streets, av. Hassan II. **Place Muhammad V** is surrounded by government buildings near the main post office (PTT) on av. Hassan II. Head for the area around these squares for most of the action (and mild hustling) in Casa. If worst comes to worst, take a taxi—they're cheap.

Tourist Office: 55 rue Omar Slaoui (tel. 27 95 33 or 27 11 77). From place Muhammad V, walk south along av. Hassan II, turn left onto rue Reitzer, then right onto rue Omar Slaoui. They have maps of the city and southern deserts. Open Mon.-Fri. 8am-noon and 4-7pm; Sept.-May Mon.-Fri. 8:30am-noon and 2:30-6:30pm; Ramadan Mon.-Fri. 9am-3pm. **Syndicat d'Initiative,** 98 blvd. Muhammad V (tel. 22 15 24). Facing the CTM station, walk 1 bl. right on av. des Forces Armées Royales, then left up rue Colbert. Stocked with decent maps and lists of cinemas, health clubs, and discos. Open Mon.-Sat. 8:30am-noon and 3-6:30pm, Sun. 9am-noon; Ramadan 9am-4pm. French is the preferred language here.

Consulates: U.S., 8 blvd. Moulay Youssef (tel. 26 45 50 or 22 41 49). Open Mon.-Fri. 8am-4:30pm. **U.K.,** 60 blvd. d'Anfa (tel. 22 16 53; emergency tel. 11 45 88). Open Mon.-Fri. 8:30am-12:30pm and 2-5:30pm.

Currency Exchange: The airport and larger hotels change money at official rates when banks are closed. Try the Hyatt Regency, Hôtel Suisse, or Hôtel Safir near the bus station. The International Seaman's Center (see Accommodations and Food below) changes money at slightly better than bank rates.

American Express: Voyages Schwartz, 112 av. du Prince Moulay Abdallah (tel. 22 29 47 or 27 80 54; fax 27 31 33; telex 216 40). Standard services, except they don't receive wired money. French spoken. Open Mon.-Fri. 8:30am-noon and 2:30-6:30pm, Sat. 8:30am-noon. Cash transactions only in the morning.

Post Office: Av. de Paris at av. Hassan II, near the neo-Islamic buildings. Send Poste Restante here. Open Mon.-Fri. 8am-noon and 4-7pm; Sept.-May 8:30am-noon and 2:30-6:30pm.

Telephones: Make collect or international calls from phones at the post office (open 8am-11pm). Pay phones on blvd. d'Anfa, just south of blvd. de Paris. **Telephone Code:** 02.

Flights: Aéroport Muhammad V (tel. 33 90 40). Shuttle buses (20dh) run between here and the CTM bus station. Pleasant trains (20dh) run frequently to the Casa Port train station and to Rabat. (Some of the airport shuttle trains stop only at Casa Voyageurs—beware.) Handles all international and most domestic flights. **Aéroport de Casablanca, ANFA** (tel. 91 20 00). Accessible by taxi only (about 150dh). Other domestic flights. **Royal Air Maroc Ticket Office,** 44 av. des Forces Armées Royales (tel. 31 41 41).

Trains: 2 stations. **Casa Port,** Port de Casablanca (tel. 22 30 11), 10min. from the youth hostel. Mainly northbound service. To Rabat (24 per day, 24.50dh). Also Tangier, Meknes, Fès. **Casa Voyageurs,** blvd. Ba Hammed (tel. 24 58 01), way the hell out there. Mainly southbound service. To: Marrakech (4 per day, 5hr., 34dh) and El-Jadida (2 per day, 1½hr., 24dh).

Buses: CTM, 23 rue Léon L'Africain (tel. 26 80 61), off rue Colbert. To: Rabat (20 per day, 1½hr., 24dh); Essaouira, via El-Jadida (2 per day, 5½hr., 76dh); Marrakech (5 per day, 58dh). Shuttle bus to the international airport (every hr. 7am-11pm, 45min., 20dh). Other bus companies leave from pl. Benjdia to Marrakech and points south.

Car Rental: Europcar, 44 av. des Force Armées Royales (tel. 31 37 37). Renault IV for 3 days with unlimited mileage 2600dh. Another office at the airport. **Hertz,** 25 rue de Foucauld (tel. 31 22 23) and at the airport. Same rates as Europcar. **Budget** (tel. 30 14 80) has slightly lower rates and will rent to relative youngsters with at least 1 yr. driving experience.

English Bookstore: American Language Center Bookstore, blvd. Moulay Youssef (tel. 27 95 59), under the American Language Center at pl. de la Fraternité. Vast array of novels and reference books. Open Mon.-Fri. 9:30am-12:30pm and 3:30-7:30pm, Sat. 10am-1pm.

Late-Night Pharmacy: Pharmacie de Nuit, pl. des Nations Unies (tel. 26 94 91). Open 8pm-8am.

Medical Services: Croissant Rouge Marocain, blvd. El Massira El Khadia (tel. 25 25 21). **Permanence,** blvd. d'Anfa, just south of blvd. de Paris. Open 8:30pm-8am. **Ambulance:** tel. 30 30 30.

Police: Bd. Brahim Roudani (tel. 19).

ACCOMMODATIONS

The tourist office and Syndicat d'Initiative keep an exhaustive, graded list of hotels to help standardize price and quality. Many linger about **rue Colbert** and **av. des Forces Armées Royales,** near the bus station, medina, and cheap restaurants.

Auberge de Jeunesse (HI), 6 pl. Amiral Philibert (tel. 22 05 51), 6min. from Casa Port. Cross blvd. Almohades, turn right, walk along the walls for 500m, then turn left up a small ramp-like street. French-speaking staff, but the sitting area's newspapers are in English. Pleasant atmosphere. Several bunk beds to a room. Clean sheets provided. Reception open 8-10am and noon-11pm. 30dh per person; nonmembers 32.50dh. Cold shower and breakfast included.

Hôtel du Centre, av. des Forces Armées Royales (tel. 31 24 48), across from the Royal Mansour Hôtel, which you can't miss (or afford). Clean, white, modern rooms with free towels and bars of soap. A few rough edges: hard beds, tepid water, lame TV room. Singles with shower 126dh. Doubles with shower 159dh. Breakfast 17dh.

Hôtel de Foucauld, 52 rue de Foucauld, also known as rue Araïbi Jilali (tel. 22 26 66), off av. des Forces Armées Royales. Bug free (but not sparkling) beds in dreary green rooms. Mattresses firm as a hero's spine. Some rooms have balconies overlooking the street. Relax in the *salon marocain*. Singles 75dh, with shower 110dh. Doubles 90dh, with shower 130dh.

Hôtel Terminus, 184 blvd. d'Oujda (tel. 24 00 25), diagonally left across pl. Sempard from Gare des Voyageurs. Huge clean rooms, many with lovely balconies. Great for early starts or late endings involving trains. Doubles 85dh.

FOOD

In the *ville nouvelle,* budget eateries concentrate on **rue Colbert.** In the medina, restaurants and food stands sprinkle the vicinity of **rue de Fès.** Shop for staples at the clean and sprawling **Central Market Halls,** 7 rue de Colbert.

Restaurant Widad, 9 rue de Fès. Enter the medina near the Hyatt Regency by blvd. Muhammad el-Hansali. Attentive service and truckloads of food for few *dirhams.* Salad, fruit, and mounds of *couscous* topped with ¼-chicken stewed with vegetables 26dh. Open 11am-10pm.

International Seaman's Center, 118 blvd. Moulay Abderhamane (tel. 30 99 50). In an industrial wasteland 800m east of Casa Port, but worth the walk. Once for sailors only, this sprawling, inviting, casual bar now welcomes foreigners. Friendly American management, outdoor patio, pool table, phones for international calls, and rock blaring all day long.

SIGHTS

Tourist attractions are few. The two main sights are the Hassan II Mosque and the medina. The **medina** is a disappointment after the sprawling, vibrant medinas of Marrakech or Fès, but it's worth a whirl. Haggle over prices.

The biggest sight in Casa, quite literally, is the tremendously large **Hassan II Mosque.** It's very easy to find: from anywhere in Casa, look toward the sea. You will see a shiny new minaret. It will appear large, and you will think that it is nearby. Walk towards it: after a mile or two, you will begin to appreciate its immense scale. (200m-high: that beats the Washington Monument hands-down, bub.) Designed to be the world's largest mosque, it was allegedly built entirely by public subcription. Many Moroccan cafés and homes display their postcard of the mosque, sent to them as thank-you for their contribution. The place is huge and lavish: every inch of it is constructed from Moroccan materials by Moroccans. It is rumored that it will someday be Hassan II's mausoleum. There are also rumors of a scheme to shoot laser beams towards Mecca from the top of its minaret. An **elevator** will take anyone up the side of the world's tallest minaret (5dh), but non-Muslims are not allowed inside the mosque. Do try to get a peek at the cavernous interior, and at the elaborate support structure that allows waves to crash underneath the mosque's glass floor. (The glass was installed to illustrated the Qu'ranic verse "Allah has his throne on the water.") A madrasa is also part of the mosque complex. Traipse through the medina to reach the mosque, or hire a *petit taxi* (10dh) to take you there.

■■■ EL-JADIDA الجديدة

El-Jadida, a 2-hour bus ride from Casablanca, is one of Morocco's Atlantic resorts. With a charming medina, crenellated Portuguese battlements, palmy boulevards, and a first-rate beach, it's the ideal antidote to the hustle of nearby Casa.

El-Jadida has been wealthy by Moroccan standards. The area became agriculturally successful once people figured out that barley was a crop relatively immune to drought. El-Jadida aroused European interest as a port city: Portugal started invading Morocco here in 1513. When Sultan Muhammad bin Abdallah reconquered Morocco in 1769, this was the last Portuguese citadel in the country to fall. After independence, the city became both El-Jadida ("The New One") and a summer retreat for Marrakech's affluent families. European interest, this time by merchants not invaders, resurged in the mid-19th century. Today, El-Jadida is a favorite destination of independent European and North American tourists, as well as Moroccans escaping from more hectic locales.

ORIENTATION AND PRACTICAL INFORMATION

The main centers are **place Muhammad V,** which adjoins blvd. Muhammad V at the post office, and **place el-Hansali,** a pleasant pedestrian square which connects pl. Muhammad V to the old Portuguese medina.

Tourist Office: rue Ibn Khaldoun (tel. 34 27 04), down the street from Hôtel de Bruxelles and Hôtel de Provence. Follow signs from blvd. Muhammad V and the post office. No maps for you, but the map on the wall is useful. Open Mon.-Fri. 8am-noon and 3-6:30pm; mid-Sept. to mid-June Mon.-Fri. 8am-noon.

Post Office: pl. Muhammad V. Open for Poste Restante, **telephones,** and **telegrams** Mon.-Fri. 8am-noon and 4-7pm, Sat. 8am-noon; winter Mon.-Fri. 8am-noon and 2:30-6:30pm, Sat. 8am-noon. **Telephone code:** 03

Trains: The new station is 6km south of town. Free bus in front of the Portuguese ramparts (7:45am) runs to the station. A similar free bus shuttles arrivals into El-Jadida immediately after a train pulls in. To Casablanca and continuing to Rabat (8:15am daily; 32dh and 58dh respectively).

Buses: blvd. Muhammad V. To reach the city center from here, exit to the left on blvd. Muhammad V and continue to pl. Muhammad V (10min.). To: Casablanca (private buses: 5am-7pm every 20min., 3hr., 17dh; CTM: 7am, 9am, 11am, 2:30pm, and 4pm, 2hr., 17dh or 23.50dh); Essaouira (7:30am, 5hr., 40.50dh). Buses south to Essaouira begin in Casablanca and thus have very few seats left by the time they arrive in El-Jadida. Buy ticket as far in advance as possible to be assured of a seat.

Late-Night Pharmacy: av. Ligue Arabe off pl. Muhammad V. Look for the plaque next door to the Croissant Rouge Marocain (Red Cross). Open 10pm-9am.

Hospital: rue Sidi Bouzi (tel. 34 20 04 or 34 20 05), near rue Boucharette at the southern edge of town. **Emergency:** tel. 19.

Police: At bus station, around the corner from the all-night pharmacy, and at the beach (tel. 19).

ACCOMMODATIONS AND CAMPING

For a quiet coastal town, El-Jadida has a surprising number of budget hotels. They drift around **place Muhammad V,** a few blocks from the sea. Ask to see a room before you commit: bugs abound. You may need reservations in July and August.

Hôtel de Provence, 42 rue Fquih Muhammad Errafi (tel. 34 23 47 or 34 41 12; fax 35 21 15). From the post office, head 1 bl. away from the beach. A real gem. Expatriates occupy a good number of the regal rooms. English spoken. Singles 104dh, with shower 126dh. Doubles 141-164dh, with shower 159-186dh. Continental breakfast 17dh.

Hôtel Royal, 108 blvd. Muhammad V (tel. 34 11 00), between the post office and the bus station, across the street from the Shell gas station. Bright rooms with low, comfy beds. Tiled lobby. TV room. Sitting area with nautical-Gothic decor. Singles 50dh, with shower 65dh. Doubles 68dh, with shower 78dh.

Hôtel de Maghreb/Hôtel de France, rue Lescould (tel. 34 21 81), off pl. Hansali. Basically sanitary. This super-cheap, cavernous hotel has incredibly capacious rooms. Singles 25dh. Doubles 36dh.

Camping: Camping International (tel. 34 27 55), on av. des Nations Unies. A large site with standard facilities. 10dh per person, per tent, and per car.

FOOD

Several good restaurants near **place Muhammad V** whip up affordable, savory Moroccan dishes. The listings below are excellent and affordable choices.

Restaurant-Bar-Grill Royal, in the eponymous hotel. Charming patio and garden. Quiet and relaxing. Try *poulet roti* (roasted chicken, 16dh) or *tajine* (16dh). Excellent fresh fish fried at the bar (24dh). Beer 7dh. Open 9am-11pm.

Restaurant la Broche, 46 pl. el-Hansali (tel. 34 22 99), next to the Paris Cinema. Intimate dining rooms. Fresh fruit decor and speedy service. *Tajine* 25-30dh. Fish dishes 20-35dh. Spaghetti 25-35dh. Fresh banana juice 7dh. Open 7am-11pm.

SIGHTS

Completed in 1502, the Portuguese-built **medina** was the first and last Portuguese stronghold in North Africa. Just before retreating, the Portuguese sprinkled the entire city with gunpowder and detonated it. When Sultan Moulay Abderrahman got around to renovating in the 19th century, a *mellah* (Jewish quarter) emerged in one area. Iron balconies, garlanded cornices, and pillared doorways fill all the nooks and crannies here.

Today nearly 5000 people live in the medina, among sundry armaments which attest to its military significance from the 16th century through WWII. Enter through the sturdy, fortified gate that opens off pl. Sidi Muhammad bin Abdallah, at the top of blvd. de Suez. Immediately to the left off rue de Carreira kneels **l'Eglise Portuguese.** This 17th-century church has Spanish walls and a misfit of a French wooden roof. Up rue de Carreira on the left, a yellow plaque marks the entrance to the **Portuguese Cisterns,** one of the few buildings that survived the Portuguese blow-up. Orson Welles used this haunting place as a backdrop for *Othello.* Ask the custodian to unlock the passage to a 16th-century fortress on the roof. (Cisterns open 8am-noon and 4-7pm; winter Mon.-Fri. 8am-noon and 2:30-6:30pm. Admission 10dh plus a tip for the guide who gives the mandatory tour. Free Fri.)

Porta do Mar, the great archway at the end of rue de Carreira, leads to the harbor. The trusty guide from the Cisterns will unlock the entrance to the ramparts, to the right of Porta do Mar. Slightly north, at the top of the incline, the **Bastion de l'Ange** commands a view or the harbor. From here, walk along the walls to the **Bastion of St. Sebastian,** flanked by a Portuguese chapel, or stroll along the jetty to see the entire town.

In the center of the city at pl. Moussa, the Gothic **Church of the Assumption** is now an assembly hall. Nearby is the abandoned Portuguese **Tribunal,** converted into a synagogue after the resettlement of Jews here in 1815. Five km south of the city center is **Sidi Bouzid**—a less crowded and more scenic spot to join the chic soaking up sun. A *grand taxi* there will cost 10dh per person. Alternatively, take the orange #2 bus, which leaves from near the medina, to its final stop.

If you're hankering for some veggies, or fruit, or ram heads, or cow lungs, or bull genitalia, head to the **souk,** held on Wed. near the lighthouse. Local farmers bring their horses to the racetrack on Wed. afternoons. Admission minimal, if collected at all. To get there, walk out of town with the beach on your left (about 2km). You should pass the Royal Stables on the way.

The High Atlas

■■■ ESSAOUIRA الصويرة

Lovely Essaouira flaunts whitewashed walls and brilliant blue shutters. Jimi Hendrix came here in 1968 and triggered a mass hippie migration in his wake. Now that most of the hash smoke has cleared, windsurfers whoop it up (while swimmers flounder) in the rough water and gusty winds off Essaouira's long beach.

To defend his band of pirates, powerful Sultan Muhammad bin Abdallah annihilated Mogador, Portugal, then fled to Essaouira and erected mighty ramparts in the 1760s. Théodore Cornut, a French prisoner forced into service as an architect, designed the ingenious town fortifications. Essaouira had some bad luck in 1844, when the French bombarded it during a conflict with Morocco over its seizure of Algeria. The Essaouirans and the French seem to have reconciled since, however, judging by the crowds of French tourists in town during the summer and the generally friendly treatment they receive.

ORIENTATION AND PRACTICAL INFORMATION

Buses arrive at the new **bus station**, a 10-min. walk from the walls of the medina. To reach the medina entrance, exit the rear of the bus station (the side where the buses park) and walk to the right, past one souk (or deserted wasteland, depending on the time of day) and through another to the gates of the medina. To reach **place Moulay Hassan** from here, continue on this street until just before the second-to-last tier of arches and make a right (if you pass the Hôtel Sahara you've gone too far). Take the next left; when that street dead ends make a right to the city center. Essaouira lacks a tourist office, but the **Hôtel Beau Rivage** (see Accommodations) provides photocopies of a bad map as consolation.

Currency Exchange: Banks cluster around the pl. Prince. **Hôtel Beau Rivage,** pl. Moulay Hassan, cashes traveler's checks (charge 5dh).

Post Office: av. el-Moqaquamah at Lalla Aicha, the 1st left after Hôtel les Isles when walking away from the medina. Near the big red and white radio tower. Open for Poste Restante, **telegrams,** and **telephones** Mon.-Fri. 8am-12:15pm and 2-7:15pm; Oct.-May 8:30am-12:15pm and 2:30-6:45pm.

Telephones: At the **post office.** International calls and **faxes** also at Jack's (see English-Language Periodicals below). **Telephone Code:** 04.

Buses: The most comfy buses are run by the train company, **ONCF,** to connect with trains in Marrakech; they leave from the Hôtel des Iles, where tickets can be purchased. **CTM** (tel. 47 24 68). To: Casablanca (2 per day, 6hr., 79.56dh) and Marrakech (1 per day, 7am, 4hr., 31dh).

Luggage Storage: At the **bus station** (3dh per bag). Open 24hrs.

English-Language Periodicals: Jack's, pl. Moulay Hassan. Also has a small selection of used English paperbacks. Open 10am-2pm and 4-10pm.

Public Showers: Bain-Douche, about 100 yards down the beach from the harbor. Cold showers 1.50dh.

Hospital: av. el-Moqaquamah (tel. 47 27 16), adjacent to the post office.

Police: tel. 19.

ACCOMMODATIONS AND CAMPING

Hôtel Beau Rivage, pl. Moulay Hassan (tel. 47 29 25), in the center of things, directly opposite Jack's Bumper-Sticker Emporium. Pink rooms at penny-pinching prices. The atmosphere is young and hip, the location perfect. Owner cashes traveler's checks at all hours like an ATM. Singles 40dh. Doubles 70dh.

Hôtel des Remparts, 18 rue Ibn Rochdi (tel. 47 31 66), just off pl. Moulay Hassan. Stand facing Sam's Fast Food and take the left-most alley 100m. A vast interior atrium with swooping swallows at dusk. Great view from Essaouira's highest terrace. Budgeters flock to this bargain like vultures. English spoken. More pink rooms. Singles 40dh, with shower 60dh. Doubles 60dh, with shower 80dh.

Hôtel Trafrout, 7 rue de Marrakech. Exit pl. Moulay Hassan to right of Sam's Fast Food and continue on rue Muhammad ben Abdallah until you see a sign on the right; hotel entrance is on this alley. No telephone. Clean but dull. New sheets. Singles 58dh. Doubles 58dh, with shower 75dh.

Camping: Municipal campground (tel. 47 38 17), off av. Muhammad V at the far end of the beach. Essentially a gravel parking lot. 7dh per person.

FOOD

Restaurants congregate in the medina, at the port, and on the waterfront at **avenue Muhammad V.** The so-called **Berber cafés** near Porte Portugaise, off av. de l'Istiqlal, have low tables, straw mats, and fresh fish *tajine* or *couscous* (about 18dh). After the second archway beyond the Porte Portugaise to the right, a handful of Berber cafés sell *kefta* and meatballs for 3dh apiece. Sit at the communal table and point to what you want, but establish prices before chewing.

During the day, crispy fried sardines are peddled at the **port** (6-8 fish, bread, lemon, and tomatoes 6dh).

Café Restaurant Essalem, pl. Moulay Hassan (tel. 47 25 48). Decor promotes bonhomie. Popular hangout since the '60s. Rapturous dishes at fairly low prices. Owner gladly discusses the town's history and gestures at the table where Cat Stevens always sat studying Islam. *Menus* 25, 35, and 45dh. Open 8am-3:30pm and 5:30-11pm.

El Minzah, av. de l'Istiqlal near Porte Portugaise (tel. 47 23 08). Seafood and Moroccan specialties served in an appealing garden. Bargain 58dh *menu* is a cheap feast. Open 9am-3pm and 6-11pm. Visa, MC, AmEx accepted.

Chez Sam, at the end of the harbor overlooking the sea. Warped wood ceilings and Groton's Fish Sticks decor. Steaming pyramid of mussels 25dh. *Menu* 60dh. Fish dishes 40-60dh. Beer and wine. Open noon-2pm and 7pm-midnight. Visa, MC, AmEx accepted.

SIGHTS

Off pl. Moulay Hassan, rue Sidi Muhammad ben Abdallah leads to the heart of the medina. Some alleyways—originally used by escape artists and crafty smugglers—burrow beneath the massive vaults of the city's fortifications. The most dramatic portion of the medina is the sea-sprayed **kasbah** (Skala de la Ville), down the narrow alley across the street from the bus station. A stone ramp leads up to a lookout post, where a battery of Catalan cannon, gun turrets, and fortress ramparts withstand the pounding surf. Watch out for amorous stray dogs.

Below the kasbah rests the delightful **carpenter's district.** In the ramparts' cell-like caverns, skilled woodworkers lay ebony, silver, and lemonwood into the surfaces of fragrant thuya wood boxes. Carpenters sell their woodcrafts directly, although the selection and quality are better at the woodwork emporia on **rue Abdul Aziz el-Fechtaly** (off rue Sidi ben Abdallah in the medina).

Just inside the medina and next to the Centre Artisanal, the town **museum** hoards an eclectic collection of farm implements, manuscripts (including a 13th-century Qur'an), Andalusian musical instruments, and an exhibit on the musicology of the Hamadcha.

■ NEAR ESSAOUIRA

ISLE OF MOGADOR

Like a mythological land from the tales of Tolkien, Mogador, a falcon preserve and the largest of the Isles Purpuraires, bears an ancient and tumultuous history. The Berber king of Mauritania, Juba II, set up dye factories on the islands around 100 BC. In 1506, under King Manuel, the Portuguese contributed a fortress and Moulay Hassan added a prison. The islands are now fishily deserted. Visitors need special permission from *le bureau de province,* av. Muhammad V (by the parking lot outside medina walls), for 20dh. Charter a fishing **boat** to get there (200dh per day).

DIABAT

Jimi Hendrix unsuccessfully attempted to purchase the **beach** of Diabat from the Moroccan government. The police closed down all the accommodations in Diabat—at least officially—after several tourists sleeping on the beach were killed (no connection with Jimi). Recently, however, a campground and one hotel appeared near the beach, about 4km away. To walk to Diabat, sweep along Essaouira's beach to a cape 2km away. Audacious travelers attempt the rocky access road off the coastal route to Agadir. Beware of the perilous crossing on a dilapidated bridge.

Diabat's only remotely nearby hotel, **Auberge Tangaro,** is a ramshackle but cheery outfit with an adjacent restaurant, both run by a hospitable French proprietor. The meager **Camping Tangaro,** in the adjacent enclosure, is a good spot. Both the hotel and campground (6½km from Essaouira) are on the access road between the highway to Agadir and the Diabat beach—just follow the signs from the road.

CAP SIM

Ten km south of Essaouira along the road to Agadir, Rte. 6604 curves to a **beach** marked by a lone whitewashed *marabout* tomb. No buses come from Essaouira. Some travelers take taxis. Some drive (follow the highway to Agadir south until the paved turn-off "Marabout Tomb of Sidi Kaouki;" turn onto it and continue another 11km to the coast). Some walk (4hr.). Halfway between the cape and Diabat beach, a washed-out dirt road (not for cars) winds here from Diabat.

SIDI KAOUKI

Twenty-five km south of Essaouira, Sidi Kaouki is known to Europeans as the best **windsurfing** beach in the world. A blue and white sign points the way from the main road to the beach, where vans with "wind city" bumper stickers crowd the big parking lot near the sand's edge. A constant north-south wind blows waves of stinging sand down a shore filled only with windsurfers. Unfortunately, there are no lifeguards. No public transportation connects to Sidi Kaouki, although **grand taxis** make the round trip from Essaouira for about 150dh.

JEBEL AMSITTENE

The summit of Jebel Amsittene houses a solitary ancient watchtower which provides shade from the intense sun as well as an excellent view of the Haha region. The beekeeper, who occasionally can be found near the summit, escorts visitors to the watchtower. Aside from this hermit, the mountain is uninhabited.

Local **buses** from Essaouira go as far as the turn-off from the highway. From here it's a lonely, grueling nine-km trek to the top. To drive from Essaouira, take the highway toward Agadir until the village of **Smimou** (سميو). Continue another seven km along the highway, staying on the main dirt road (bear right at the first fork and left at the second); it will zip you right to the summit's watchtower. The track is stony and crumbling, but passable.

■■■ MARRAKECH مراكش

Marrakech (pop. 1 million) has enjoyed the role of Moroccan capital on numerous occasions, and although Rabat has served as Morocco's administrative center since the country's colonization by the French, Marrakech remains one of the most fascinating stops for travelers anywhere in the world. The city's medina is huge, labyrinthine, and definitely worth a visit. The Djemâa el-Fna, a large square in the medina, is filled with a cacophonous crowd of snake charmers, musicians, dancers, performance dentists (sorry, you'll just have to see this yourself), acrobats, beggars, peddlers, hash vendors, and, of course, hustlers. Marrakech is also the gateway to the

Sahara for many travelers. In the intense summer heat, early morning and early evening are the best times for activity.

ORIENTATION AND PRACTICAL INFORMATION

All excitement, budget food, and cheap accommodations center on the **Djemâa el-Fna** and surrounding **medina**.

The **Guéliz** or **ville nouvelle** is down av. Muhammad V, past the towering **Koutoubia minaret.** A night or two spent in the relatively hassle-free *Guéliz* may be the perfect antidote to medina life. The bus and train stations, administrative buildings, and luxury hotels are here. Also in the *ville nouvelle* are most of the car rentals, newsstands, banks, and travel agencies. Bus #1 runs between the minaret and the heart of the *ville nouvelle* (1½dh). You can also take one of the many *petits taxis* (bargain down to 5dh per person) or horse-drawn carriages (again bargain fiercely to the posted price of 40dh per hr.).

Tourist Office: Office National Marocain du Tourisme (ONMT), av. Muhammad V (tel. 44 88 99), at pl. Abdel Moumen ben Ali. English spoken. The free brochures have good outlines of the medina *souks.* Multilingual maps. Official guides: ½-day 50dh, full day 100dh. Open 8am-3pm; Sept.-June 8:30am-noon and 2:30-6:30pm; Ramadan 9am-3pm. **Syndicat d'Initiative,** 176 av. Muhammad V (tel. 43 30 97), between the post office and ONMT. Open Mon.-Sat. 8am-3pm; mid-Sept.-June Mon.-Fri. 8am-noon and 3-7pm, Sat. 8am-noon.

Currency Exchange: Banks are seemingly ubiquitous in the *Guéliz.* In the medina they cluster around the post office on the Djemâa el-Fna. Most luxury hotels will change money at late hours.

American Express: Voyages Schwartz, rue Mauritania, 2nd fl. (tel. 43 66 00), off av. Muhammad V, 2nd left after post office. Office open 6am-11pm; bank open Mon.-Fri. 8:30-11:30am and 2:30-4:30pm.

Post Office: pl. XVI Novembre, off av. Muhammad V. Poste Restante here is slow, and Saturdays are a madhouse. Open Mon.-Fri. 8am-noon and 4-7pm, Sat. 8:30-11:30am; winter Mon.-Fri. 8:30am-noon and 2:30-6:30pm, Sat. 8:30-11:30am. **Branch office** in the Djemâa. Open Mon.-Fri. 8:30am-noon and 2:30-6:45pm.

Telephones: In the main **post office.** Open Mon.-Fri. 8am-6:30pm. Also at the less crowded branch post office. Open Mon.-Fri. 8am-3:30pm. **Telephone Code:** 04.

Flights: Aéroport de Marrakech Menara (tel. 44 78 65, 44 79 10, or 44 85 06), 5km south of town. Taxi service about 20dh; no bus. Domestic and international flights on Royal Air Maroc and Royal Air Inter.

Trains: av. Hassan II (tel. 44 77 68 or 44 77 63), 5min. west on av. Hassan II from av. Muhammad V and pl. XVI Novembre. The best way to head north. To: Casablanca (4 per day, 3hr., 52.50dh); Tangier (5 per day, 11hr., 135dh); Meknès (4 per day, 9hr., 109-190.50dh); Fès (6 per day, 10hr., 121.50-153.50dh).

Buses: Outside the medina walls by Bab Doukkala (tel. 43 39 33). The **CTM** window is next to #8. To: Agadir (2 per day, 4hr., 60.50dh); Asni (8 per day, 1½hr., 15dh); Casablanca (4 per day, 4hr., 57.50dh); Fès (2 per day, 10hr., 110dh); Ouarzazate (2 per day, 4hr., 45dh); Zagora (4 per day, 79dh); Essaouira (6 per day, 3hr., 31dh). The **SATAS** window is #14. To Taroudannt at 5am and 4:30pm. One is direct (70dh) and the other is a mountain route that goes through the Tizi-n-Test Pass (55dh). Other windows represent private companies with lower prices, sometimes lower standards, and far more frequent service to certain destinations. Most private buses also stop outside the Bab er Rob, just south of Djemâa el-Fna, but seats are usually gone by then. Start from here to Setti-Fatma in the High Atlas (every ½hr., 11dh).

Taxis: *Grands taxis* leave from Bab er Rob and Djemâa el-Fna for nearby destinations, such as Asni (15dh) and Setti-Fatma (15dh).

Car Rental: Avis, 137 blvd. Muhammad V (tel. 43 37 27), and **Hertz,** 154 blvd. Muhammad V (tel. 43 46 80 or 43 13 94). Both rent Renault IVs for 250dh per day plus mileage. Weekly rates are much lower.

Horse-and-Buggies: Across from Banque du Maroc on the edge of the Djemâa el-Fna, along av. Muhammad V. Bargain to about 40dh per hr. per carriage.

MARRAKECH

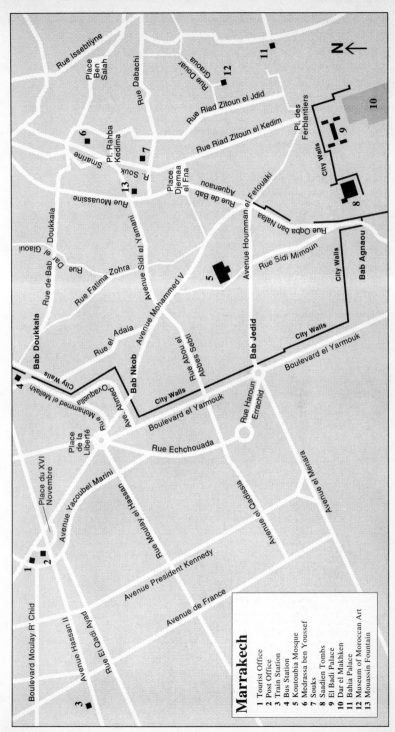

Marrakech

1 Tourist Office
2 Post Office
3 Train Station
4 Bus Station
5 Koutoubia Mosque
6 Medrassa ben Youssef
7 Souks
8 Saadien Tombs
9 El Badi Palace
10 Dar el Makhken
11 Bahia Palace
12 Museum of Moroccan Art
13 Mouassin Fountain

Swimming Pool: Piscine Koutoubia, in the medina off av. Muhammad V, the next left heading toward the new city from the Koutoubia. Now officially coed, although women may be outnumbered by a thousand to one. Open late June-early Sept. Wed.-Mon. 9:30am-noon and 2:30-6pm. Admission about 4dh. For a ritzier swim, try the pool at the **Grand Hotel du Tazi,** near the Hotel Foucauld (40dh). They have a poolside bar, too.

Late-Night Pharmacy: In the fire station complex (tel. at fire station 43 04 15), corner of rue Kahlid Ben El Oualid and av. Nations Unies, 1 bl. north of Hôtel Marrakech. Open Tues.-Sun. 10:30pm-8am.

Medical Emergency: Doctor on call until 10pm at the above late-night pharmacy. It's best to avoid the government-run polyclinique; have a pharmacist recommend a private physician.

Police: tel. 19.

ACCOMMODATIONS AND CAMPING

Apart from the youth hostel and campgrounds, which are far from the medina but close to the train station, all cheap accommodations are within a stone's throw of the Djemâa el-Fna. Many places, including Hôtel Ali, will allow you to sleep on the roof for a fraction of the cost of a room.

Djemâa el-Fna

Hôtel Ali, rue Moulay Ismael, s/n (tel. 44 49 79; fax 43 36 09). Clean, sufficient rooms a few doors from the Djemâa el-Fna. Sunbathing on the terrace. Arranges expeditions for guests to the Atlas Mountains and the Sahara. Great food (see below) All rooms have A/C. Doubles much superior to singles. Singles with shower 90dh. Doubles with shower 120dh. Breakfast included; if you don't eat it, ask for 15dh per person off your room bill.

Hôtel Essaouira, 3 Derb Sidi Bouloukat (tel. 44 38 05). In pl. Djemâa el-Fna, face the Post Office (PTT) and Banque du Maroc. Head down the road in the left corner of the Djemâa, underneath an archway. Take a right onto the street across from a cassette shop, at the pile of garbage; there are also some faded signs. The attractive courtyard imitates the town of Essaouira's cool white and blue color scheme. 35dh per person. Cold showers 5dh.

Hôtel Medina, 1 Derb Sidi Bouloukat (tel. 44 29 97). Next door to Hôtel Essaouira; together they make a good pair to try. Free hot showers. 35dh per person.

Hôtel Gallia, 30 rue de la Recette (tel. 44 59 13). From the Djemâa, take the street to the left of the Banque du Maroc, and the first left after the cinema. Gorgeous Arab-style tiles and carvings ornament the interior. Two airy, leafy patios. Clean bedrooms, each with a different Moroccan blanket for a bedspread. TV room. Cute pet tortoise. Laundry service 5dh per piece. Singles 74dh, with shower 135dh. Doubles 105dh, with shower 156dh.

Hôtel Chella, 14 rue Riad Zitoune Kedim Derb Skaya (tel. 44 19 77). Follow directions for Hôtel Essaouira (above), but take the next right after the garbage pile. Chella is on the right. Courtyard with slender shady orange trees, Saharan murals, and bedrooms with green walls and cushy beds. Singles 30dh. Doubles 60dh. Hot showers 10dh.

Hôtel CTM (tel. 44 43 49 or 44 23 25), facing Djemâa el-Fna left of the Café du Grand Balcon. The courtyard and large terrace have a fabulous view of the Djemâa. Bright pink bedrooms are shabby and beds are very saggy. The rooms in the back are quiet, but those facing the Djemâa are bigger. The former bus station beneath the hotel makes for fabulous parking. Singles 64dh, with shower 74.50dh. Doubles 72.50dh, with shower 92dh. Breakfast on the terrace 16dh.

Hôtel de Foucauld, rue el-Mouahdine (tel. 44 54 99; fax 44 13 44). From Djemâa el-Fna, take the road to the right of the Post Office (PTT) alongside the park, and turn right at the end of the park. Clean, painted rooms with marbled baths and balconies. Capacious rooftop terrace with view of minaret. Closest bar to the Djemâa. Working A/C. Costs a little (OK, a lot) more, but aren't you worth it? Singles with bath 121dh. Doubles with bath 140dh.

Hôtel El At Lal, 48 rue de la Recette (tel. 45 51 29), down the street from the Gallia (above). A treasure trove of Arabic patterned tiles and arabesques on walls, floors, ceilings, toilet paper, etc. The entire place is scrubbed at least three times daily. When their rag and broom befall your room, expect your possessions to be put in perfect order. Single beds are TI-ny. Mostly Arabic spoken. Singles 35dh. Doubles 70dh. Hot showers 10dh.

Ville Nouvelle

Auberge de Jeunesse (HI), rue el-Jahed (tel. 44 77 13), handily 5min. from the train station in the *ville nouvelle*. Exit the train station and turn left down Hassan II. Take the first right at the traffic circle onto av. de France. Take the second right, pass Camping-Caravaning, and continue for 2 long blocks. Take a left and then a right, and the hostel is at the end of the street. It's clean, spartan, and tiled, with a courtyard and terrace. Cold showers only. Open 8-9am, noon-2pm, and 6-10pm. Officially members only. 20dh per person.

Hôtel des Voyageurs, 40 blvd. Muhammad Zerktouni (tel. 44 72 18), off blvd. Muhammad V, about 100m from ONMT tourist office. Ironically, this place is everything that traveling is not: old, dull, and convenient. Central courtyard and beds spread with bright Moroccan blankets. Singles 60dh, with shower 100dh. Doubles 100dh, with shower 120dh.

Camping: Camping-Caravaning Municipal (tel. 44 60 85 or 44 75 43), in a partially wooded park near the train station. From the train station, walk east (left as you exit) to pl. Haile Selassie, make a right onto rue de France, and take the 2nd right. Humongous. Electricity 220V, shop, cold showers, and pool. The premises crawl with opportunists; be careful with your stuff. 10dh per person, 11dh per tent, 8dh per car.

FOOD

Along the fortifications surrounding the city, two **markets** peddle fresh produce. These are a long walk by foot. A closer daily fruit and vegetable market is just outside **Bab Aghmat,** and **Bab el-Kemis** hosts a lively Thursday market. For often delicious bargains, devour the wares from **food stalls** in the Djemâa. The number of options increases three-fold in the evening, when vendors set up their benches. Settle prices first. If unsure of the correct price, hang around and see how much the locals pay. Sample the succulent pulp of prickly cactus buds (not hallucinogenic); the vendor will pinch off the ends and peel back the skin (1dh).

Hôtel Ali (see above). The restaurant serves a swell all-you-can-eat dinner buffet (50dh) on the ground floor all year, and on the rooftop patio on summer nights.

Café-Restaurant-Hôtel de France, pl. Djemâa el-Fna. Typical mediocre *menu* (50dh) in attractive surroundings. The *salon marocain* is the coolest place to eat, while the rooftop is the tallest in the old town and has the best view by night. Open 6am-11pm; winter 5am-10pm.

Café-Patisserie Toubkal, pl. Djemâa el-Fna. No sign, but across from the Hôtel CTM. Refresh your aching body on the shady outdoor patio. Mmm, shish kebab done with fried onions and peppers (18dh). Steaks or brochettes with salad, bread, and fries 22dh. Open 7am-11pm.

Restaurant Etoile de Marrakech, rue Bab Agnaou, a stone's throw from the Djemâa. Pleasing upstairs dining and a starry night panorama high above the bedlam. One of the only places in the area where you can order à la carte without hassle. *Clientèle touristique.* Daily *menu* 25dh. *Tajine* and *couscous* 25dh. Open 11am-11pm.

Chez Chegrouni, 4-6 pl. Djemâa el-Fna, just to the right Café Montréal. Unlabeled and unassuming. Look for the brown and gold awning or follow your nose to 2dh *soupe marocaine*, a meal in itself for the budgeter. Open 5am-noon and 4-11pm.

SIGHTS

Djemâa el-Fna

Welcome to Djemâa el-Fna, the Assembly of the Dead, a hectic, nocturnal outdoor circus. This sideshow was once the spot where sultans had criminals beheaded. As

MARRAKECH

a warning to troublemakers, executioners impaled the dried heads on spikes for public viewing. Today's audiences, often numbering in the thousands, cluster tightly around frenzied street performers. Storytellers, snake charmers, and dentists are merely a few of the entertainers. The snake-charmers are the most notorious extortionists. Don't let one drape a pit viper around your neck; they'll charge you to remove it. After sunset the odder sorts clear out and the vendors take over. By 8pm the square is carpeted with eager merchants plugging ceramics, weavings, carpets, clothing, and souvenirs. The crowds jostle on until midnight.

Almost every tour of Marrakech begins at the 12th-century **Koutoubia Mosque,** whose magnificent **minaret** presides over Djemâa el-Fna. Crowned by a lantern of three golden spheres, the minaret is the oldest and best surviving example of the art of the Almohads, who made Marrakech their capital (1130-1213) and at one time ruled the region from Spain to present-day Tunisia. In 1157, Abd el-Mumin acquired one of four editions of the Qu'ran authorized by the caliph Uthman, and used it as a talisman in battle and inspiration for the design of the second Koutoubia Mosque. Possession of this holy book turned Marrakech into a seat of religious learning. In fact, the name Koutoubia comes from the Arabic *kutubiyyin,* which means "of the books." As with most Moroccan mosques, entrance is forbidden to non-Muslims.

More than 2km of pink-tinged **fortifications** encircle the city on all sides. Thousands of Christian slave laborers lost their lives while building the walls; as they died, their corpses were (allegedly) plastered into the mud-brick.

Bab Agnaou, the most dazzling gate (3 bl. south of the Koutoubia minaret), was formerly portal to the Kasbah of Yacoub el-Mansour. Highly decorative, this 12th-century gate was where mutilated corpses and heads of slain enemies were often displayed as trophies of war.

Bab el-Rob, next to it, was the southern doorway to the city.

Marjorelle Gardens shelter birds and spiny cacti north of the Bab el-Rob, above pl. Mourabite off av. d'el-Jadida. Exquisite landscaping by French artist Louis Marjorelle.

Bab el-Khemis, site of a lively Thursday market, is in the northeast corner of Marrakech, a long swing around town. The bastion was reputedly designed and built by Andalusian architects and artisans.

Bab Aylen, farther south, marks the spot where the Almohads suffered a crushing defeat in 1130 in their first attack on the Almoravid city.

Bab Aghmat, the next gateway along the walls, watches over an extensive daily fruit and vegetable market.

Bab Ahmar, an Alawite gate, opens onto the grounds of the royal palace.

Yves St. Laurent. Watch for him. He is often spotted on a moped whizzing around the Djemâa.

The Medina

The Marrakech medina exists on an imperial scale. The salmon-colored houses are brighter, the streets and *souks* larger, and the smells more invigorating than in other medinas. Enter the medina to the left of Café el Fati. This is the medina's main thoroughfare, the enormous **Souk Smarine,** which takes a turn at the **potters' souk.** Berber blankets, woven by families spinning wool in a tangle of dowels, string, and cards of yarn, pile the alleyways of the **fabric souk.**

Through the first major orange gateway, the first opening on the right leads to the **Zahba Kedima,** a small plaza flanked by the **spice souk** on one side and the **carpet souk** on the other. Choose your spice cure—goat hoof for hair treatment, ground-up ferrets for depression, and live chameleons for sexual frustration.

Continue through the bolts of silks and satins on the Souk Smarine until the road forks. The left road, the **Souk Attarine,** meanders past a few copper and silver merchants. The left path of the second fork leads to the center of the **woodworkers' souk,** where skilled artisans carve tiny chess pieces at an astonishing speed. The second street on the left passes through a section of **basket weavers.** Past the baskets, bubbling cauldrons of color cram the **dyers' souk** stalls. At the end of the street, northeast of the 16th-century Mosque of Mouassin, dust and grime camouflage the **Mouassin Fountain's** gilded cedar corbels and colorful carvings.

The residential area west of the fountain is more domestic. Small doorways open into two-story mini-*souks* in rectangular courtyards. These offshoots are the **fondouks,** neighborhood markets once surrounded on three sides by arcades of shops.

On the road that goes to the right where Souk Attarine forks, an endless selection of Moroccan slippers preens at the **babouche souk.** The right fork at the end of the street leads to the **cherratine souk,** which connects the *babouche souk* to the Souk el-Kbir (the right fork off Souk Smarine as you enter the medina). This street is the **leather souk.** In 1565, Sultan Moulay Abdallah el-Ghalib raised the **Madrasa of ben Youssef** in the center of the medina (backtrack to Souk Smarine, bear right at the fork onto Souk el-Kbir, and follow this to its end); it reigned as the largest Qu'ranic school in the Maghreb until it closed in 1956. Students used the central court's fountain and the corridor's basin for ablutions. Youths attended *madrasa* free of charge, and after finishing their studies often continued at the Karaouiyue University in Fès. (*Madrasa* open Tues.-Sun. 8am-noon and 3-7pm; winter Tues.-Sun. 8am-noon and 2-6pm. Admission 10dh.)

Around the corner, beside the Ben-Youssef mosque, juts the squat, unpainted cupola of 12th-century **Koubba el-Ba'adiyn,** the oldest monument in town. The underside of the fanciful tower is carved in an excessive floral arabesque pattern. The guard can open an ancient wooden door to the subterranean cisterns. (Open 8:30am-noon and 2:30-6pm. Bang on the door to get in if it's closed. Free, but the custodian may charge 10dh plus tip.)

Turn right on the **Souk el-Kbir** to return to the **Djemâa el-Fna.** On the right on the descent toward the Djemâa are the **Anciennes Kissarias,** parallel rows of spindly streets that connect the Souk Attarine and the *babouche souk* to the Souk el-Kmir. Here is the **clothing souk** and the **jewelers' souk.**

If you can stomach it, visit the bubbling cauldrons of the **tannery,** just inside Bab el-Debbagh (gate) in the northeast corner of the medina. Each vat holds a different chemical for each stage of leather production; children dive in to recover the skins and emerge covered with olive-purple slime.

Palaces

The **Saadien Tombs,** modeled after the interior of the Alhambra in Granada, constitute Morocco's most lavish mausoleum. The tombs served as the royal Saadien necropolis during the 16th and 17th centuries, until Moulay Ismail walled them off to efface the memory of his predecessors. In 1912 the burial complex was rediscovered. One **mausoleum** opulently brims with tiles and marble columns, crowned by a gleaming *mihrab.* Batches of brilliant green tile lather the less splendid second mausoleum. In the neighboring **Hall of the Twelve Columns,** trapezoidal tombs rise from a pool of polished marble. The Saadien sultan made his fortune trading salt and sugar for equal weights of Sudanese gold and Italian marble. His four wives, 23 concubines, and the most favored of his hundreds of children are buried close by. The unmarked tombs belong to the women. (Open 8:30am-noon and 2:30-6pm. Admission 10dh. Multilingual tours.) To reach the Saadien Tombs, follow the signs from Bab el-Rob. The turquoise minaret of the **Mosque of the Kasbah,** Sultan Yacoub el-Mansour's own personal mosque, flags the way; veer right into the alley adjoining the mosque.

The **Bahia Palace** was constructed in the late 19th century by Sidi Moussa and his son Ba Ahmed. More powerful than the king himself, these two wallowed in the wealth of the kingdom despite the ugly colonial domination that impoverished the nation. On the eve of the European takeover of Morocco, they constructed the magnificent palace, whose name means "The Riches." Ample traces of their avarice remain: dazzling tilework, crimson curtains, and mahogany furniture fill a seemingly endless procession of reception halls, tea rooms, courtyards, and patios. Sultan Hassan II currently owns Bahia, Morocco's only royal palace open to the public. The **Court of Honor,** a 50m marble-paved corridor, is the roomiest chamber. In the

Moorish Garden, jasmine, mint, orange, grapefruit, and banana trees bloom. (Open 8:30-11:45am and 3-7pm; winter 8:30-11:45am and 2:30-5:45pm. Free. Mandatory official museum tour; 5dh is a respectable contribution.) Facing the Hôtel CTM in the Djemâa, head left through an archway onto rue Riad Zitoun el-Kedim on the right; follow the main thoroughfare to the end, and bear left through pl. des Ferblantiers, curving around 180°. On the right, a reddish-brown archway opens into a long, tree-lined avenue leading to the palace door.

Dar Si Said, a 19th-century palace built by Si Said, brother of Grand Vizier Ba Ahmed and chamberlain of Sultan Moulay el-Hassan, houses the **Museum of Moroccan Art.** The collection features splendid Berber carpets, pottery, jewelry, Essaouiran ebony, and Saadien woodcarving. (Open Wed.-Mon. 8:30am-noon and 2:30-5:45pm. Admission 10dh.) The gleaming Dar Si Said is located on a tiny alley off rue Riad Zitoun el-Jadid, the 2nd right heading north toward the Djemâa el-Fna from the Bahia Palace.

Dar el-Makhzen puts Sultan Hassan II up for the night when he's in town. This sprawling ochre palace is roofed with rounded green tiles. The interior is closed to the public. Swing through the Bab Ahmar to glimpse the **Grand Méchouar.** It's a walled court where European diplomats and heads of state were once received. The **Agdal Gardens** are accessible via a roofed portal overlooking the Grand Méchouar. The 3km enclosure is filled with scrubby olive and fruit trees.

The **Menara Gardens,** a vast enclave of olive groves around an enormous pond, are most beautiful at sunset, when the mauve and tangerine light glints off the artificial lake. The cold green reservoir, 800m by 1200m, dates from the Almohad era. To reach the Gardens, head west through Bab el-Jedid and straight down av. Menara, the wide boulevard that resembles an airport landing strip. To the south (left) lies the expanse of the **Olive Grove of Bab Jedid,** a continuation of the Gardens.

ENTERTAINMENT

El-Bedi Palace is now the site of the annual **Folklore Festival,** which begins the second week of September and lasts for ten days. The extravaganza involves hundreds of performers—mostly acrobats, former Berber soldiers, and saber, rifle, and Ghedra dancers (toned down for the tourist audiences). The ONMT tourist office has performance schedules and sells tickets (40dh). In the evenings, 3-hr. sound and light shows light and sound up the palace pools (every night at 9pm, 40dh).

For less seasonal entertainments, visit the several European-style discos attached to the luxury hotels in town. **Diamond Noir,** at Hôtel Marrakech, pl. de la Liberté (tel. 43 43 51), has no dress code and no cover charge (50dh per drink). Or dress to kill and head over to the truly otherworldly casino at **La Mamounia,** av. Bab Jdid.

■ NEAR MARRAKECH: MT. TOUBKAL

From Marrakech, buses and taxis race across the desert to **Asni,** the start of a lovely sojourn in the **Atlas Mountains.** Mt. Toublal, Morocco's highest peak, is truly unspoilt: please don't ruin it by bringing a large group. *Grands taxis* leave from Bab er Rob and Djemâa el-Fna for Asni (15dh); buses cost the same and are horribly crowded. Asni itself offers some mild hiking opportunities, and some mild opportunities to be huckstered. The **Auberge de Jeunesse** (for the tel.: get the Marrakech operator and ask for "Asni 1") is in a stone hut near the river; it has no cooking facilities, and you must bring a sleeping bag (open all year; 20dh).

Imlil, up the road from Asni, makes the best base for exploring the mountains. From Asni, jump in the back of one of the pickup trucks that shuttle along the route; they are particularly frequent on Saturdays, when Asni has a *souk* (15dh per person, 1hr.). Imlil is a healthy, happy town: the air is cool here (and damn cold at night), and the sound of running water is everywhere. There is no electricity, hot water, or phone lines in Imlil. Stay at the **CAF Refuge,** which has bunks, a kitchen, and luggage storage in a refurbished cottage in the center of town. (Dorm 25dh, with HI card 20dh.) Across the street, **Hôtel Aksoual** charges 40dh per person for a bed.

Café Soleil, by the river, cooks a mean *tajine* (30dh). The **CAF Refuge** and the **"Shopping Center"** in Imlil are both good sources for qualified guides, maps, and hiking equipment. In summer months, sturdy shoes, warm clothes, sunscreen, a sleeping bag, and adequate food and water should take you through the two days you'll likely be away from Imlil while traipsing around Toubkal.

Leave in the morning from Imlil to make it to Toubkal. Take the road up out of town, following the river: you will have a choice of a steep mule track, or an easy, graded road. Choose the road. You'll pass the hilltop village of Aroumd, on the other side of the valley, then descend into a broad valley before beginning to zigzag up the east side. After 1½hr. of spectacular scenery, hikers reach **Sidi Chamarouch,** home to a fiercely-guarded *marabout* shrine. The trail turns right and upwards immediately upon entering the village; the trail past this point is not clear of snow until late April. Next comes the **Toubkal Refuge** (30dh, with HI card 25dh), a welcoming end to a day's pleasant hiking. Ask here for the best ascent of Toubkal (another 2½hr. upwards from here); Toubkal clouds over late in the day; get to the refuge before noon, or plan to ascend Toubkal early the next morning.

■■■ OUARZAZATE ورزازات

The ride to Ouarzazate, on the cusp between the northern cities and southern desert, is so stunning that you will be reduced to monosyllabic "wows" and "gees," and so precarious that—depending on your driver and constitution—you may throw a few gulps and wretches into the mix. The administrative seat of the Moroccan Sahara, Ouarzazate operates a trade in artisanry produced by nomadic and sedentary groups to the east.

Most administrative buildings, cafés, and restaurants are located along **avenue Muhammad V.** Inexpensive lodging can be found either here or on the streets parallel and to the north. The **Kasbah of Taourirt,** 1½km east of town, rises from a sandy riverbed and cradles a neighboring *ksour* within its ramparts. A small portion of the palace interior is open to the public. Step onto the bamboo floors through the doorway just to the left of the Kasbah as you face it from the street. To get to the **frescoes,** walk down av. Muhammad V, away from Marrakech, and bear left at the tourist office. (Open daily 8:30am-noon and 2:30-7:30pm. Admission to palace 5dh.) Head down the alley just to the left as you face the palace entrance. Within, a fabulously preserved medieval labyrinth awaits. Across the highway, a tiny **Centre Artisanale** displays local crafts. From the southern end of Taourirt you can make out the dashing profile of the **Kasbah de la Cigogne** (Kasbah of the Stork), a 2km walk through the desert from Taourirt.

Practical Information The **tourist office** is on av. Muhammad V (tel. 88 24 85), where the road forks to follow the Oued Drâa and the Oued Dadès. Very helpful, English-speaking staff. Ask here for bus information and a directory of hotels and prices in the Drâa and Dadès Valleys. (Open Mon.-Fri. 8am-noon and 4-7pm; Sept.-June Mon.-Fri. 8am-noon and 2:30-6:30pm.) The **Post Office** grooves on av. Muhammad V, to the right of the bus station and next to the tourist office. **International telephones** are in the same building. (Both open Mon.-Sat. 8am-noon and 4-7pm; Sept. 14-June Mon.-Sat. 8am-noon and 2:30-6pm.) The **telephone code** is 04.

CTM Buses are next to the post office. To: Marrakech (4 per day, 4½hr., 49dh); Tinghir, via the Oued Dadès and Boumahe (1 per day, 10:30am, 4hr., 24.50dh); M'hamid, via Oued Drâa and Zagora (1 per day, noon, 6hr., 52.50dh). **Private buses** travel the area around Ouarzazate more frequently. They leave from a station 100m west of CTM in pl. Mouhadine. They have the same prices, can leave at any time, and are much faster. To: Marrakech (5 per day, 3½hr., 70dh) and Zagora (6 per day, 3hr., 35dh).

Accommodations and Camping Bargain hotels are conveniently located near the bus station. **Hôtel Royal,** 24 av. Muhammad V (tel. 88 22 58), next to Chez

Dimitri, has big windows. Some rooms are cramped, and others are spacious. Some rooms have showers, some lack them. (Singles 31-46dh. Doubles 61-81dh.) **Hôtel Es Salaam,** av. Muhammad V, across the street as you emerge from the taxi stand, has simple rooms overlooking an oblong courtyard with indigo-tiled fountains. The showers above the first floor require infinite patience. (Singles with shower 60dh. Doubles 62dh, with shower 82dh.) **Camping Ouarzazate** (tel. 88 25 78), 2km east of town, has adequate facilities, including toilets and cold showers. Walk past the Kasbah and follow the signs for Hôtel Le Zat. (10dh per person, 5dh per tent and per car. 3-course menu at the restaurant is 40dh; breakfast is 15dh.)

Food The **supermarket** on av. Muhammad V, across the street from Hôtel Royal, has an unrivaled selection of cured meats, canned goods, chocolate, wine, and cold beer. **Restaurante-Café Royal,** on av. Muhammad V (tel. 88 24 75), in the hotel of the same name, offers the best seats for neighborhood chess matches and a good meat *tajine* or *couscous* (30dh). Breakfast 10dh. (Open 7am-11pm.) The finest (well, only) Italian cuisine in Ouarzazate is to be had at **Chez Dimitri** on av. Muhammad V. Spaghetti carbonara 47dh. Beer and wine served. (Open 9am-11pm.)

■■■ OUT FROM OUARZAZATE: SAHARAN EXPEDITIONS

The area to the north of Ouarzazate is a hot and dusty palette of desert browns and greens. Small Berber *Kasbahs* (governmental complexes in forts) periodically interrupt the descent to Ouarzazate. Two km past the Kasbah of El Mdént, the turn-off for Tamdaght leads 9km to the ancient *ksour* of **Ait Benhaddou.** (*Ksour* are walled Saharan villages built of mud and broken stones.) Though seemingly abandoned, a handful of Berber families has not yet left the building. The forest of tapered turrets climbs steeply to the ruined Kasbah at the crest of the desert hilltop. You can hire a collective taxi from Ouarzazate all the way here (about 250dh round-trip; the driver waits) or you can get off at Oued El Malleh (10dh per person) and walk the 6km to Ait Benhaddou. Ask at the Ouarzazate tourist office for directions. Once upon a time, the **Kasbah of Tiffletout** aspired to glory despite its name, and housed the standing army of the caliph of the Aluoui. The castle maintains a strong fortified facade, and the central courtyard within is strewn with modern vestiges of the former four-star hotel that shone here. Take a *grand taxi* round-trip from Ouarzazate for 40-50dh.

Most tourists who travel through Ouarzazate are on their way to **Zagora** (زاكورة), the final oasis town before the Sahara begins in earnest. Desert tours by dromedary (two-humped Egyptian camels) begin from Zagora. Call **Caravanes des Nomades** (tel. (04) 84 74 51) before you arrive to haggle over the price. Shrewd negotiators should be able to bargain down to about 200dh per person, per day; this rate will unfortunately increase rather than decrease with larger group size and longer trip length. If you're hoping to see an endless sea of sand dunes, plan on a 7-10 day trip. For the less ambitious, even an overnight trip, on which you and your Berber guides make bread and dinner and sleep in the desert, is unforgettable. For comfort's sake, bring at least twice as much water as they recommend. Trips can also be arranged through hotels in Marrakech (including the Hôtel Ali) and travel agents in Ouarzazate (Palmiers Voyages; tel. (04) 88 26 17). These include chauffeured rental car to Zagora, but are more expensive than negotiating directly with trip providers.

APPENDICES

■■■ GLOSSARY

Terms that recur frequently throughout this book are listed below in alphabetical order. The parentheses after a word indicate its abbreviation (if any) and its language. We abbreviate *castellano* (Castilian) as Cast.; *català* (Catalan) as Cat.; *galego* (Galician) as G; and *portugues* (Portuguese) as P.

GENERAL TERMS

abadía (Cast.)	abbey
acueducto (Cast.)	aqueduct
ajuntament (Cat.)	city hall
albergue (juvenil) (Cast.)	youth hostel
alcazaba (Cast.)	Muslim citadel
alcázar (Cast.)	Muslim fortress-palace
anfiteatro (Cast.)	amphitheater
aqueduto (P.)	aqueduct
arco (P.)	arch
avenida (Av.; Cast., P.)	avenue
avinguda (Av.; Cat.)	avenue
ayuntamiento (Cast.)	city hall
azulejo (P.)	glazed tile
bahía (Cast.)	bay
barrio viejo (Cast.)	old city
baños (Cast.)	baths
biblioteca municipal (P.)	public library
cabo (P.)	cape (land, not clothing)
calle (C.; Cast.)	street
cámara municipal (P.)	town hall
capela (P.)	chapel
capilla mayor (Cast.)	chapel containing high altar
carrer (Cat.)	street
carrera (Cast.)	road
carretera (Ctra.; Cast.)	highway
casa do concello (G.)	city hall
casa particular (Cast. and P.)	lodging in a private home
casco antiguo (Cast.)	old city
castell (Cat.)	castle
castelo (P.)	castle
castillo (Cast.)	castle
catedral (Cast.)	cathedral
(el) centro (Cast.)	city center
ciudad nueva (Cast.)	new city
ciudad vieja (Cast.)	old city
ciutat vella (Cat.)	old city
claustre (Cat.)	cloister
claustro (Cast., P.)	cloister
colegiata (Cast.)	collegiate church
colegio (Cast.)	school
colexiata (G.)	collegiate church

colexio (G.)	school
convento (P.)	convent
coro (Cast, P.)	choir in a church
coro alto (P.)	upper choir
cripta (Cast.)	crypt
cruz (Cast.)	cross
cuevas (Cast.)	caves
ermida (Cat.)	hermitage
ermita (Cast.)	hermitage
església (Cat.)	church
estacão (P.)	station (train or bus)
estación (Cast.)	station (train or bus)
estany (Cat.)	lake
fachada (Cast.)	facade
feira (P.)	outdoor market or fair
feria (Cast.)	outdoor market or fair, carnival
ferrocarriles (FFCC; Cast.)	trains
floresta (P.)	forest
fonte (P.)	fountain
fortaleza (P.)	fortress
fuente (Cast.)	fountain
glorieta (Cast.)	rotary
grutas (P.)	caves
habitaciones (Cast.)	rooms
iglesia (Cast.)	church
igreja (P.)	church
igreja do seminário (P.)	seminary church
igrexa (G.)	church!
illes (Cat.)	islands
jardim botanico (P.)	botanical garden
jardim público (P.)	public garden
jardín público (Cast.)	public gardens
Judería (Cast.)	Jewish quarter
lavandería (Cast.)	laundromat
llotja (Cat.)	stock exchange
lonja (Cast.)	stock exchange
mercado (Cast., P.)	market (usually grocery market)
mercado municipal (Cast., P.)	local farmers' market
mercat (Cat.)	market
mesquita (P.)	mosque
mezquita (Cast.)	mosque
monestir (Cat.)	monastery
monte (Cast.)	mountain
mosteiro (G. and P.)	monastery
Mozarab (Cast.)	style of art developed by Christian artisans under Muslim rule
Mudéjar (Cast.)	style of architecture developed by Muslims under Christian rule
museo (Cast.)	museum
museu (Cat. and P.)	museum
muralla (Cast.)	wall
palacio (Cast.)	palace
palau (Cat.)	palace
parador (nacional) (Cast.)	state-run hotel in a former fortress or palace

parc (Cat.)	park
parque (Cast. and P.)	park
paseo (Po.; Cast.)	promenade
passeig (Pg.; Cat.)	promenade
patio (Cast.)	courtyard
plaça (Pl.; Cat.)	square
plaia (G.)	beach
platja (Cat.)	beach
playa (Cast.)	beach
plaza (Pl.; Cast.)	square
polideportivo (Cast.)	sports center
ponta (P.)	bridge
porta (P.)	gate
portal (Cast.)	entrance hall
pousada (P.)	a state-run hotel
pousada juventude (P.)	youth hostel
praça (Pr.; P.)	square
praia (P.)	beach
praza (Pr.; G.)	square
puente (Cast.)	bridge
quarto (P.)	lodging in a private house
real (Cast.)	royal
red (Cast.)	company
reina/rey (Cast.)	queen/king
ría (G.)	inlet or firth at mouth of a river; estuary
río (Cast.)	river
rio (P.)	river
riu (Cat.)	river
retablo (Cast.)	altarpiece, retable
ronda (Cast.)	rotary
rossio (P.)	rotary
rua (R.; P.)	street
rúa (R.; Cast., G.)	street
sala (Cast.)	room or hall
sardanas (Cast.)	folk dance
Semana Santa (Cast.)	Holy Week (week before Easter Sunday)
serra (Cat.)	mountain range
seu (Cat.)	cathedral
sillería (Cast.)	choir stalls
s/n (sin número) (Cast.)	unnumbered (in addresses)
tesoro (Cast.)	treasury of a church
tesouro (P.)	treasury of a church
torre (Cast., P.)	tower
torre de menagem (P.)	castle keep
universidade (P.)	university
valle (Cast.)	valley

FOOD, DRINK, AND RESTAURANT TERMS

See Essentials sections of Spain and Portugal for fuller explanations.

ajillo (Cast.)	garlic
arroz (Cast.; P.)	rice
asado/a (Cast.)	anything grilled
atún (Cast.)	tuna
bica (Cast.)	generic word for a mixed drink

bocadillo (Cast.)	tapa sandwiched between a hunk of bread
boquerones (Cast.)	smelts
cabrito (P.)	kid goat
caña (Cast.)	normal-sized beer
cerveza (Cast.)	beer (general term)
champiñones (Cast.)	mushrooms
chocos (Cast.)	squid
chorizo (Cast.)	yummy sausage
churrasco (Cast.)	barbecued meat
churros (Cast.)	¡lightly fried breakfast fritters!
cocido (Cast.)	stew with chickpeas
comedor (Cast.)	dining room
comida (Cast.)	lunchtime
copa (Cast.)	generic word for a mixed drink or cup
empanada (Cast.)	meat or vegetable turnover
ensalada (Cast.)	salad
fabada (Cast.)	bean stew
frango no churrasco (P.)	barbecued chicken
gambas (Cast.)	shrimp
gazpacho (Cast.)	cold tomato-based soup with vegetables
horchata (Cast.)	a sweet almond drink
jamón (Cast.)	mountain-cured ham
jerez (Cast.)	sherry
lulas (G.)	squid
menú (Cast., Cat., and P.)	lunch special with bread, drink, and side dish
mercado (Cast. and P.)	market (usually grocery market)
mercat (Cat.)	market
merluza (Cast.)	hake (a white-fleshed fish)
paella (Cast.)	saffron rice with shellfish, meat, and vegetables
para llevar (Cast.)	to go (take-away)
pescado (Cast.)	fish
pincho (Cast.)	tapa on a toothpick, like an hors d'oeuvre
planca (Cast.)	grilled
plato del día (Cast.)	special of the day
platos combinados (Cast.)	entrée and side order
pollo (Cast.)	chicken
prato do dia (P.)	special of the day
pratos combinados (P.)	entrée and side order
queso (Cast.)	cheese
ración, pl. raciones (Cast.)	large size of tapa
serrano (Cast.)	anything smoked or cured
sidra (Cast.)	alcoholic cider
sopa (Cast.)	soup
taberna (Cast.)	tapas bar
tapa, pl. tapas (Cast.)	see Spain: Essentials: Food
tasca (Cast.)	tapas bar
tubo (Cast.)	large-sized beer
zarzuela (Cat.)	seafood and tomato bouillabaisse

■■■ CALENDAR OF FESTIVALS AND HOLIDAYS

SPAIN

Spring

late March:	*Cuenca.*	Week of Religious Music.
March 27-April 3:	*National.*	Semana Santa (Holy Week).
April 23:	*Barcelona.*	St. George's Day and Cervantes Day.
end of April-beginning of May:	*Sevilla.*	Feria de Abril.
May 1:	*National.*	May Day.
first week in May:	*Jerez de la Frontera.*	Horse Fair.
second week in May:	*Córdoba.*	Patio Festival.
mid-May:	*Madrid.*	San Isidro Festival.
May 18-20:	*Almonte (near Huelva).*	Rocío Pilgrimage.
June 1:	*National, with special celebrations in Toledo, La Laguna (near Tenerife), and Granada.*	Corpus Christi.
early June:	*Almonte (Huelva).*	The Rocío Pilgrimage.
June 15-July 15:	*Granada.*	International Music and Dance Festival.

Summer

June 21-29:	*Alicante.*	Festival de Sant Joan.
July 6-14:	*Pamplona/Iruña.*	Fiestas de San Fermín (Running of the Bulls).
July 20-30:	*San Sebastián/ Donostia.*	International Jazz Festival.
July 25:	*National.*	Feast of Santiago.
July 25:	*Villajoyosa (near Alicante).*	Festival of Christians and Moors in Honor of Santa María begins.
Aug. 15:	*National.*	Feast of the Assumption.

Autumn

first week in Sept.:	*Almagro (near Ciudad Real).*	Festival of Classical Drama and Comedy.
first week in Sept.:	*Jerez de la Frontera (near Cádiz).*	Grape Harvest Festival.
early Sept.:	*Villena (near Alacant).*	Festival of Christians and Moors in Honor of Our Lady of Virtue.
late Sept.:	*San Sebastián/ Donostia.*	International Film Festival.
early Oct.:	*Sitges (near Barcelona).*	Festival Internacional de Cine Fantástico.
Oct. 12:		Spain's National Day.

late Oct.:	*Consuegra (near Toledo).*	The Saffron Rose Festival.
late Oct.:	*Valladolid.*	International Film Festival.
Nov. 1:	*National.*	All Saints' Day.

Winter

Dec. 6:	*National.*	Constitution Day.
Dec. 8:	*National.*	Feast of the Immaculate Conception.
Dec. 25:	*National.*	Christmas Day.
Jan. 6:	*National.*	The Epiphany.
Feb. (week before Lent):	*Santa Cruz de Tenerife and Cadiz.*	Carnival.
end of February:	*Villanueva de la Vera (near Cáceres).*	Pero Palo Festival.
second week in March:	*Valencia.*	Fallas de San José.

PORTUGAL

Spring

March 31:	*National, with special celebrations in Braga, Ovar, and Povoa de Varzim.*	Semana Santa (Holy Week) begins.
March 25-April 25:	*Aveiro.*	Feira de Artesanato.
April 14:		Good Friday.
April 25:		Liberty Day.
May:	*Santarém.*	International Film Festival.
May 1:	*National.*	Labor Day.
May 1-3:	*Barcelos.*	Festa das Cruzes (Festival of the Crosses).
May 4-6:	*Ponta Delgada, S. Miguel Island, and Azores.*	Festivals for Senhor Santo Cristo.
May 12-13:	*Fátima.*	Pilgrimage.
May-June (usually every weekend):	*Algarve.*	Music Festival.
May 15-June 16:	*Lisboa.*	Book Fair.

Summer

June 2:	*National.*	Corpus Christi.
June 4-12:	*Santarém.*	National Fair of Agriculture.
June 10:	*National.*	Portugal's and Camões Day.
June 13:	*Lisboa.*	Festival of St. Anthony begins.
June-July:	*Sintra.*	Music Festival.
June 23-24:	*Porto, Figueira, and Braga.*	Festa de São João.
June 24-29:	*Évora.*	Feira de São João.

June 27-29:	Montijo, Ribeira Brava, Sintra, and Évora.	Festa de São Pedro.
early July:	Tomar.	Festa dos Tabuleiros.
early July:	Caldas da Rainha.	Bienal de Escultura.
July:	Santarém.	Feira do Ribatejo.
July:	Silves.	Festa da Cerveja.
July:	Cascais.	Sea Fair.
July 4-Aug. 25:	Estoril.	Handicrafts Fair.
July 5-7:	Vila Franca de Xira (near Ribatejo).	Colete Encarnado (Red Waistcoast Festival).
July 12-21:	Lisboa.	International Handicraft Fair.
July 13-14:	Figueira.	Gala dos Pequenos Cantores.
July 14-Aug. 12:	Aveiro.	Festa da Ria.
July 20:	Marvão.	Festival de Danças Folclóricas Luso-Espanhol.
Aug. 3-5:	National.	Gualterianas Festival (St. Walter's).
Aug. 14-15:	Funchal, Madeira.	Our Lady of the Monte.
Aug. 15:	National.	Feast of the Assumption.
Aug. 17-20:	Viana do Castelo.	Our Lady of Agony Festival.
Aug. 22-Sept. 22:	Viseu.	St. Matthew's Fair.
Aug. 31-Sept. 3:	Palmela.	Wine Harvest Festival.

Autumn

Sept.:	Figueira.	Cinema Festival.
Sept.:	Marvão.	Nossa Senhora da Estrela.
Sept. 6-8:	Algarve.	Folk Music Festival.
Sept. 10:	Madeira, Câmara de Lobos.	Wine Harvest Festival.
Sept. 8-15:	Nazaré.	Our Lady of Nazaré.
Oct. 5:	National.	Republic Day.
Oct. 5-13:	Vila Franca de Xira.	October Fair.
Oct. 6:	Ribeira Brava, Madeira Island.	Band Festival.
Oct. 12-13:	Fátima.	Pilgrimage.
Oct. 24-Nov. 3:	Santarém.	National Festival of Gastronomy.
Nov. 1:	National.	All Saints' Day.

Winter

Dec. 1:	National.	Restorations of Independence.
Dec. 8:	National.	Feast of the Immaculate Conception.
Dec. 25:	National.	Christmas Day.
Dec. 31:	Funchal, Madeira.	Festival of St. Sylvester.
Feb. 9-13:	Loulé, Nazaré, and Ovar.	Carnival.

■■■ CLIMATE

The following information is drawn from the International Association for Medical Assistance to Travelers (IAMAT)'s *World Climate Charts.* In each monthly listing, the first two numbers represent the average daily maximum and minimum temperatures in degrees **Celsius,** while the numbers in parentheses represent the same temperatures in degrees **Fahrenheit.** The remaining numbers indicate the mean rel-

CLIMATE

ative **humidity percentage,** and the average number of days with a measurable amount of **precipitation.** To convert from °C to °F, multiply by 1.8 and add 32. To convert from °F to °C, subtract 32 and multiply by 5/9.

°C	35	30	25	20	15	10	5	0	-5	-10
°F	95	86	75	68	59	50	41	32	23	14

SPAIN

	Jan.		April		July		Oct.	
Avila	7/-2	(45/28)	14/3	(57-37)	28/13	(82/55)	16/6	(61/43)
	78%	6	63%	8	45%	2	70%	7
Barcelona	13/6	(55/43)	18/11	(64/52)	28/21	(82/70)	21/15	(70/59)
	68%	5	66%	9	65%	4	71%	9
Burgos	6/-1	(43/30)	15/4	(59/39)	26/12	(79/54)	16/7	(61/45)
	88%	10	69%	11	63%	5	79%	11
Cáceres	11/4	(52/39)	19/9	(66/48)	34/19	(93/66)	22/12	(72/54)
	79%	9	62%	8	38%	1	62%	7
Cádiz	15/9	(59/48)	20/13	(68/55)	27/20	(81/68)	23/17	(73/63)
	78%	9	71%	6	72%	0	76%	7
Cuenca	8/-2	(46/28)	16/3	(61/37)	30/14	(86/57)	18/6	(64/43)
	80%	7	68%	9	51%	3	71%	7
Granada	12/2	(54/36)	20/7	(68/45)	34/17	(93/63)	23/10	(73/50)
	78%	8	68%	10	48%	1	69%	7
Madrid	9/2	(48/36)	18/7	(64/45)	31/17	(88/63)	19/10	(66/50)
	79%	8	62%	9	46%	2	70%	8
Málaga	17/8	(63/46)	21/13	(70/55)	29/21	(84/70)	23/16	(73/61)
	70%	7	67%	6	66%	0	72%	6
Palma	14/6	(57/43)	19/10	(66/50)	29/20	(84/68)	18/10	(64/50)
	78%	8	72%	6	68%	1	77%	9
Santander	12/7	(53/45)	15/10	(59/50)	22/16	(72/61)	18/12	(64/54)
	74%	16	77%	13	80%	11	78%	14
Santiago de Compa.	10/5	(50/41)	18/8	(64/46)	24/13	(75/55)	21/11	(70/52)
	84%	21	70%	7	65%	1	77%	10
Sevilla	15/6	(59/43)	24/11	(75/52)	36/20	(97/68)	26/14	(79/57)
	81%	8	71%	7	55%	0	74%	6
Valencia	15/6	(59/43)	20/10	(68/50)	29/20	(84/68)	23/13	(73/55)
	67%	5	64%	7	69%	2	70%	7
Zaragoza	10/2	(50/36)	19/8	(66/46)	31/18	(88/64)	14/6	(57/43)
	74%	6	59%	8	54%	3	68%	6

PORTUGAL

	Jan.		April		July		Oct.	
Bragança	8/0	(46/32)	16/5	(61/41)	28/13	(82/55)	18/7	(64/45)
	85%	15	71%	10	62%	3	77%	10
Coimbra	14/5	(57/41)	21/9	(70/48)	29/15	(84/59)	23/12	(73/54)
	75%	15	60%	13	57%	4	65%	13
Evora	12/6	(54/43)	19/10	(66/50)	30/16	(86/61)	22/13	(72/56)
	76%	14	58%	10	39%	1	60%	9
Faro	15/9	(59/48)	20/13	(68/55)	28/20	(82/68)	22/16	(72/61)
	76%	9	68%	6	63%	0	69%	6
Lisboa	14/8	(57/46)	20/12	(68/54)	27/17	(81/63)	22/14	(72/57)
	78%	15	63%	10	55%	2	67%	9
Porto	13/5	(55/41)	18/9	(64/48)	25/15	(77/59)	21/11	(70/52)
	78%	18	69%	13	67%	5	73%	15

MOROCCO

	Jan.		April		July		Oct.	
Essaouira	17/11	(63/51)	19/14	(66/57)	22/17	(71/63)	22/16	(71/61)
	77%	6	81%	5	92%	0	83%	3
Fès	16/4	(60/39)	23/9	(73/49)	36/18	(97/64)	26/13	(78/55)
	79%	8	73%	9	58%	1	64%	7
Marrakech	18/4	(65/40)	26/11	(79/52)	38/19	(101/67)	28/14	(83/57)
	77%	7	65%	6	53%	1	61%	4
Rabat	17/8	(63/46)	22/11	(71/52)	28/17	(82/63)	25/14	(77/58)
	81%	9	75%	7	74%	0	77%	6
Tangier	16/8	(60/47)	18/11	(65/51)	27/18	(80/64)	22/15	(72/59)
	76%	10	73%	8	67%	0	75%	8

■ ■ ■ DETAILS

ADDRESSES

Spain and Portugal: "Av.", "C.", "R.", and "Trav." are abbreviations for street. "Po." and "Pg." are abbreviations for a promenade, "Pl." is a square, and "Glorieta" is a rotary. "Ctra." is the abbreviation for highway. The number of a building follows the street name, unlike in English. The letters "s/n" means the building has no number. Note that the 4th floor to Europeans is the 5th floor to Americans, as Europeans don't count street level as the 1st floor. **Morocco:** Because things are named in French, "av.", "blvd.", "rue", and "calle" mean street; "pl." is a plaza. The number of a building comes before the street name, as in English. When hunting for an address, keep in mind that many streets are being renamed in Arabic; "rue" and "calle" may be replaced by "zankat", "derb", or "sharia."

CLOTHING SIZES AND CONVERSION

Men's Shirts (Collar Sizes)
U.S./U.K.:	14½	15	15½	16	16½
Continent:	37	38	39	40	41

Men's Suits and Coats
U.S./U.K.:	38	40	42	44	46
Continent:	48	50	52	54	56

Women's Blouses and Sweaters
U.S.:	6	8	10	12	14
U.K.:	28	30	32	34	36
Continent:	34	36	38	40	42

Women's Dresses, Coats, and Skirts
U.S.:	4	6	8	10	12	14
U.K.:	6	8	10	12	14	16
Continent:	34	36	38	40	42	44

Men's Shoes
U.S.:	8	9	10	11	12
U.K.	7	8	9	10	11
Continent:	41	42	43	44½	46

Women's Shoes
U.S.:	6	7	8	9	10
U.K.:	4½	5½	6½	7½	8½
Continent:	37	38	39	40	41

LUGGAGE STORAGE

Train and bus station lockers are usually operated by a token (*ficha* in Spanish) for which you pay. Less secure baggage checkrooms may also be found in stations.

Spain: *Consigna Automática* (lockers). *Consigna* (baggage check). The word for luggage is *equipaje,* for backpack *mochila.*

Portugal: *Depósito de Volumes* (baggage checkroom). Usually adjacent to the *chefe da estação* (station chief's office) on the platform. Pay when you reclaim your bag.

Morocco: The baggage check at CTM bus depots is usually safe. If you don't have padlocks on the zippers, however, your bags may not be accepted. Private bus companies also have baggage checkrooms. They're generally trustworthy and accept any kind of bag.

NUDE SUNBATHING

Most towns on the Spanish and Portuguese coast have at least a few nude beaches; some beaches have a separate section for nude sunbathers. Nude sunbathing is most common in resort areas. In **Spain** look for *playa natural* or *playa de nudistas* signs. In **Morocco,** nude sunbathing is unacceptable.

PHARMACIES

Listings of late-night or 24-hour pharmacies are included for every town under the Orientation and Practical Information listings. In Spain, pharmacies are identified by their standard signs bearing a green cross. At least one pharmacy will be open all night in a Spanish town, on a rotating system. To find out which one will be open, look for a notice posted in the windows and doors of any pharmacy, or check the *Farmacia de Guardia* listing on the second or third page of the local paper.

TELEPHONES

Country and City Codes

Spain: 34. Madrid: 1. Barcelona: 3. Sevilla: 5. Toledo: 25. Córdoba: 57. Granada: 58. Valencia: 6. Pamplona: 48. San Sebastián: 43. Santiago de Compostela: 81.

Portugal: 351. Lisbon: 1. Porto: 2. Coimbra: 39.

Morocco: 212. Rabat: 7. Casablanca: 7. Tangier: 9. Marrakech: 4. Fès: 6.

U.S. and Canada: 1. **U.K.:** 44. London: 71. **Ireland:** 353. Dublin: 1. **Australia:** 61. Sydney: 2. Canberra: 6. **New Zealand:** 64.

Emergency Numbers

Spain: 091.

Portugal: 115.

Morocco: 19.

TIME DIFFERENCES

Spain: 6 hours after EST; 1 hour after GMT.

Portugal: 5 hours after EST; same as GMT. Daylight savings is on last Sun. in March (clocks are set 1 hour faster) and the last Sun. in Sept. (clocks are set 1 hour slower); i.e., spring ahead/fall back.

Morocco: Same as Spain.

WEIGHTS AND MEASURES

1 millimeter (mm) = 0.04 inch	1 inch = 25mm
1 meter (m) = 1.09 yards	1 yard = 0.92m
1 kilometer (km) = 0.62 mile	1 mile = 1.61km
1 gram (g) = 0.04 ounce	1 ounce = 25g
1 liter = 1.06 quarts	1 quart = 0.94 liter

INDEX

★ FREE T-SHIRT ★

JUST ANSWER THE QUESTIONS ON THE FOLLOWING PAGES AND MAIL TO:

Let's Go Survey
Macmillan Ltd.
18-21 Cavaye Place
London SW10 9PG

WE'LL SEND THE FIRST 1,500 RESPONDENTS A LET'S GO T-SHIRT!

(Make sure we can read your address.)

■ LET'S GO 1995 READER ■ QUESTIONNAIRE

1) Name _____

2) Address _____

3) Are you: female   male

4) How old are you?   under 17   17-23   24-30   31-40   41-55   over 55

5) Are you (circle all that apply):   at school   at college or university
employed   unemployed   retired

6) What is your annual income?
£10,000-£15,000   £15,000 - £25,000   £25,000 - £40,000   Over £40,000

7) Have you used *Let's Go* before?

   Yes   No

8) How did you hear about *Let's Go* guides?

   Friend or fellow traveller
   Recommended by bookshop
   Display in bookstore
   Advertising in newspaper/magazine
   Review or article in newspaper/
      magazine

9) Why did you choose *Let's Go*?

   Updated every year
   Reputation
   Prominent in-store display
   Price
   Content and approach of books
   Reliability

10) Is *Let's Go* the best guidebook?

   Yes
   No (which is?) _____
   Haven't used other guides

11) When did you buy this book?

   Jan   Feb   Mar   Apr   May   Jun
   Jul   Aug   Sep   Oct   Nov   Dec

12) When did you travel with this book? (Circle all that apply)

   Jan   Feb   Mar   Apr   May   Jun
   Jul   Aug   Sep   Oct   Nov   Dec

13) Roughly how much did you spend per day on the road?

   Under £10   £45-£75
   £10-£25   £75-£100
   £25-£40   Over £100

14) What were the main attractions of your trip?
(Circle top three)

   Sightseeing
   New culture
   Learning language
   Sports/Recreation
   Nightlife/Entertainment
   Local cuisine
   Shopping
   Meeting other travellers
   Adventure/Getting off the beaten
      path

15) How reliable/useful are the following features of *Let's Go*?

   v = very, u = usually, s = sometimes
   n = never, ? = didn't use

Accommodations	v u s n ?
Camping	v u s n ?
Food	v u s n ?
Entertainment	v u s n ?
Sights	v u s n ?
Maps	v u s n ?
Practical Info	v u s n ?
Directions	v u s n ?
"Essentials"	v u s n ?
Cultural Intros	v u s n ?

16) Would you use *Let's Go* again?

Yes
No (why not?) _____

_____

_____

17) Which of the following destinations are you planning to visit as a tourist in the next five years?
(Circle all that apply)

Australasia
Australia
New Zealand
Indonesia
Japan
China
Hong Kong
Vietnam
Malaysia
Singapore
India
Nepal

Europe And Middle East
Middle East
Israel
Egypt
Africa
Turkey
Greece
Scandinavia
Portugal
Spain
Switzerland
Austria
Berlin
Russia
Poland
Czech/Slovak Republic
Hungary
Baltic States

The Americas
Caribbean
Central America
Costa Rica
South America
Ecuador
Brazil
Venezuela
Colombia
Canada
British Columbia
Montreal/Quebec
MaritimeProvinces

18) What **major** destinations (countries, regions, etc.) covered in this book did you visit on your trip?

_____

_____

_____

_____

_____

_____

_____

_____

_____

_____

_____

_____

_____

19) What other countries did you visit on your trip?

_____

_____

_____

_____

_____

20) How did you get around on your trip?

Car	Train	Plane
Bus	Ferry	Hitching
Bicycle	Motorcycle	

Mail this to:

Let's Go Survey

Macmillan Ltd.
18-21 Cavaye Place
London SW10 9PG

Many Thanks For Your Help!

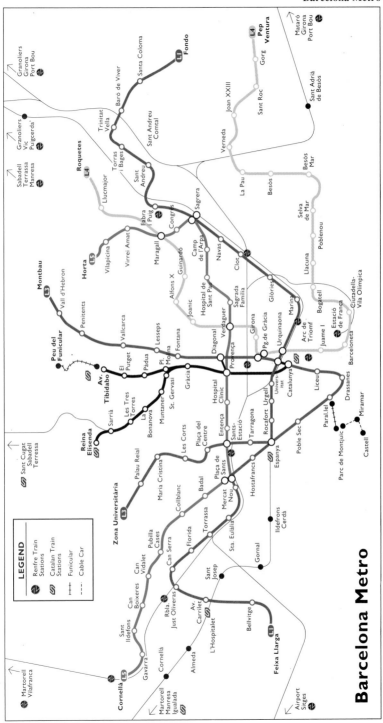

Barcelona Metro

Madrid Metro

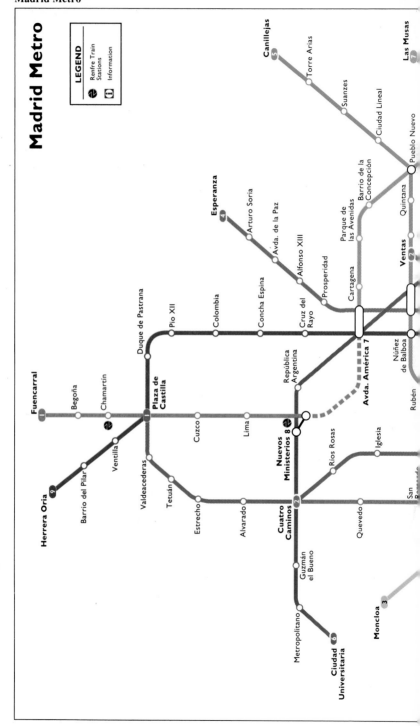

Lisbon Metro

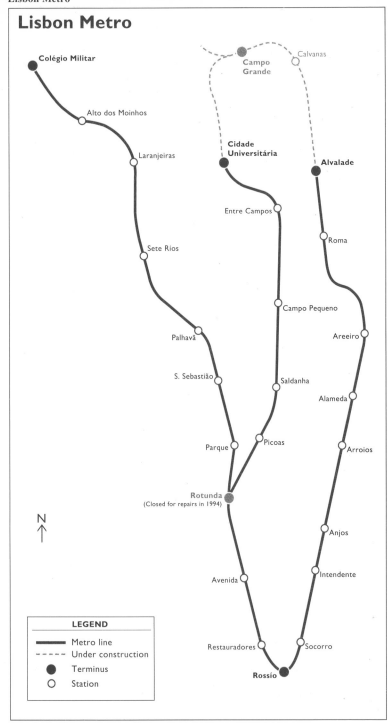

Colégio Militar

Alto dos Moinhos

Laranjeiras

Calvanas

Campo Grande

Cidade Universitária

Alvalade

Entre Campos

Roma

Sete Rios

Campo Pequeno

Areeiro

Palhavã

S. Sebastião

Saldanha

Alameda

Parque

Picoas

Arroios

Rotunda
(Closed for repairs in 1994)

N

Anjos

Intendente

Avenida

Restauradores

Socorro

Rossío

LEGEND

———— Metro line
- - - - Under construction
● Terminus
○ Station